Lecture Notes in Computer Science 12627

More information about this subseries at http://www.springer.com/series/7412

Preface

The Asian Conference on Computer Vision (ACCV) 2020, originally planned to take place in Kyoto, Japan, was held online during November 30 – December 4, 2020. The conference featured novel research contributions from almost all sub-areas of computer vision.

We received 836 main-conference submissions. After removing the desk rejects, 768 valid, complete manuscripts were submitted for review. A pool of 48 area chairs and 738 reviewers was recruited to conduct paper reviews. As in previous editions of ACCV, we adopted a double-blind review process to determine which of these papers to accept. Identities of authors were not visible to reviewers and area chairs; nor were the identities of the assigned reviewers and area chairs known to authors. The program chairs did not submit papers to the conference.

Each paper was reviewed by at least three reviewers. Authors were permitted to respond to the initial reviews during a rebuttal period. After this, the area chairs led discussions among reviewers. Finally, an interactive area chair meeting was held, during which panels of three area chairs deliberated to decide on acceptance decisions for each paper, and then four larger panels were convened to make final decisions. At the end of this process, 254 papers were accepted for publication in the ACCV 2020 conference proceedings.

In addition to the main conference, ACCV 2020 featured four workshops and two tutorials. This is also the first ACCV for which the proceedings are open access at the Computer Vision Foundation website, by courtesy of Springer.

We would like to thank all the organizers, sponsors, area chairs, reviewers, and authors. We acknowledge the support of Microsoft's Conference Management Toolkit (CMT) team for providing the software used to manage the review process.

We greatly appreciate the efforts of all those who contributed to making the conference a success, despite the difficult and fluid situation.

December 2020

Hiroshi Ishikawa
Cheng-Lin Liu
Tomas Pajdla
Jianbo Shi

Organization

General Chairs

Ko Nishino	Kyoto University, Japan
Akihiro Sugimoto	National Institute of Informatics, Japan
Hiromi Tanaka	Ritsumeikan University, Japan

Program Chairs

Hiroshi Ishikawa	Waseda University, Japan
Cheng-Lin Liu	Institute of Automation of Chinese Academy of Sciences, China
Tomas Pajdla	Czech Technical University, Czech Republic
Jianbo Shi	University of Pennsylvania, USA

Publication Chairs

Ichiro Ide	Nagoya University, Japan
Wei-Ta Chu	National Chung Cheng University, Taiwan
Marc A. Kastner	National Institute of Informatics, Japan

Local Arrangements Chairs

Shohei Nobuhara	Kyoto University, Japan
Yasushi Makihara	Osaka University, Japan

Web Chairs

Ikuhisa Mitsugami	Hiroshima City University, Japan
Chika Inoshita	Canon Inc., Japan

AC Meeting Chair

Yusuke Sugano	University of Tokyo, Japan

Area Chairs

Mathieu Aubry	École des Ponts ParisTech, France
Xiang Bai	Huazhong University of Science and Technology, China
Alex Berg	Facebook, USA
Michael S. Brown	York University, Canada

Additional Reviewers

Sathyanarayanan
  N. Aakur
Mahmoud Afifi
Amit Aides
Noam Aigerman
Kenan Emir Ak
Mohammad
  Sadegh Aliakbarian
Keivan Alizadeh-Vahid
Dario Allegra
Alexander Andreopoulos
Nikita Araslanov
Anil Armagan
Alexey Artemov
Aditya Arun
Yuki M. Asano
Hossein Azizpour
Seung-Hwan Baek
Seungryul Baek
Max Bain
Abhishek Bajpayee
Sandipan Banerjee
Wenbo Bao
Daniel Barath
Chaim Baskin
Anil S. Baslamisli
Ardhendu Behera
Jens Behley
Florian Bernard
Bharat Lal Bhatnagar
Uttaran Bhattacharya
Binod Bhattarai
Ayan Kumar Bhunia
Jia-Wang Bian
Simion-Vlad Bogolin
Amine Bourki
Biagio Brattoli
Anders G. Buch
Evgeny Burnaev
Benjamin Busam
Holger Caesar
Jianrui Cai
Jinzheng Cai

Fanta Camara
Necati Cihan Camgöz
Shaun Canavan
Jiajiong Cao
Jiale Cao
Hakan Çevikalp
Ayan Chakrabarti
Tat-Jen Cham
Lyndon Chan
Hyung Jin Chang
Xiaobin Chang
Rama Chellappa
Chang Chen
Chen Chen
Ding-Jie Chen
Jianhui Chen
Jun-Cheng Chen
Long Chen
Songcan Chen
Tianshui Chen
Weifeng Chen
Weikai Chen
Xiaohan Chen
Xinlei Chen
Yanbei Chen
Yingcong Chen
Yiran Chen
Yi-Ting Chen
Yun Chen
Yun-Chun Chen
Yunlu Chen
Zhixiang Chen
Ziliang Chen
Guangliang Cheng
Li Cheng
Qiang Cheng
Zhongwei Cheng
Anoop Cherian
Ngai-Man Cheung
Wei-Chen Chiu
Shin-Fang Ch'ng
Nam Ik Cho
Junsuk Choe

Chiho Choi
Jaehoon Choi
Jinsoo Choi
Yukyung Choi
Anustup Choudhury
Hang Chu
Peng Chu
Wei-Ta Chu
Sanghyuk Chun
Ronald Clark
Maxwell D. Collins
Ciprian Corneanu
Luca Cosmo
Ioana Croitoru
Steve Cruz
Naresh Cuntoor
Zachary A. Daniels
Mohamed Daoudi
François Darmon
Adrian K. Davison
Rodrigo de Bem
Shalini De Mello
Lucas Deecke
Bailin Deng
Jiankang Deng
Zhongying Deng
Somdip Dey
Ferran Diego
Mingyu Ding
Dzung Anh Doan
Xingping Dong
Xuanyi Dong
Hazel Doughty
Dawei Du
Chi Nhan Duong
Aritra Dutta
Marc C. Eder
Ismail Elezi
Mohamed Elgharib
Sergio Escalera
Deng-Ping Fan
Shaojing Fan
Sean Fanello

Moshiur R. Farazi
Azade Farshad
István Fehérvári
Junyi Feng
Wei Feng
Yang Feng
Zeyu Feng
Robert B. Fisher
Alexander Fix
Corneliu O. Florea
Wolfgang Förstner
Jun Fu
Xueyang Fu
Yanwei Fu
Hiroshi Fukui
Antonino Furnari
Ryo Furukawa
Raghudeep Gadde
Vandit J. Gajjar
Chuang Gan
Bin-Bin Gao
Boyan Gao
Chen Gao
Junbin Gao
Junyu Gao
Lin Gao
Mingfei Gao
Peng Gao
Ruohan Gao
Nuno C. Garcia
Georgios Georgakis
Ke Gong
Jiayuan Gu
Jie Gui
Manuel Günther
Kaiwen Guo
Minghao Guo
Ping Guo
Sheng Guo
Yulan Guo
Saurabh Gupta
Jung-Woo Ha
Emanuela Haller
Cusuh Ham
Kai Han
Liang Han

Tengda Han
Ronny Hänsch
Josh Harguess
Atsushi Hashimoto
Monica Haurilet
Jamie Hayes
Fengxiang He
Pan He
Xiangyu He
Xinwei He
Yang He
Paul Henderson
Chih-Hui Ho
Tuan N.A. Hoang
Sascha A. Hornauer
Yedid Hoshen
Kuang-Jui Hsu
Di Hu
Ping Hu
Ronghang Hu
Tao Hu
Yang Hua
Bingyao Huang
Haibin Huang
Huaibo Huang
Rui Huang
Sheng Huang
Xiaohua Huang
Yifei Huang
Zeng Huang
Zilong Huang
Jing Huo
Junhwa Hur
Wonjun Hwang
José Pedro Iglesias
Atul N. Ingle
Yani A. Ioannou
Go Irie
Daisuke Iwai
Krishna Murthy
  Jatavallabhula
Seong-Gyun Jeong
Koteswar Rao Jerripothula
Jingwei Ji
Haiyang Jiang
Huajie Jiang

Wei Jiang
Xiaoyi Jiang
Jianbo Jiao
Licheng Jiao
Kyong Hwan Jin
Xin Jin
Shantanu Joshi
Frédéric Jurie
Abhishek Kadian
Olaf Kaehler
Meina Kan
Dimosthenis Karatzas
Isay Katsman
Muhammad Haris Khan
Vijeta Khare
Rawal Khirodkar
Hadi Kiapour
Changick Kim
Dong-Jin Kim
Gunhee Kim
Heewon Kim
Hyunwoo J. Kim
Junsik Kim
Junyeong Kim
Yonghyun Kim
Akisato Kimura
A. Sophia Koepke
Dimitrios Kollias
Nikos Kolotouros
Yoshinori Konishi
Adam Kortylewski
Dmitry Kravchenko
Sven Kreiss
Gurunandan Krishnan
Andrey Kuehlkamp
Jason Kuen
Arjan Kuijper
Shiro Kumano
Avinash Kumar
B. V. K. Vijaya Kumar
Ratnesh Kumar
Vijay Kumar
Yusuke Kurose
Alina Kuznetsova
Junseok Kwon
Loic Landrieu

Dong Lao
Viktor Larsson
Yasir Latif
Hei Law
Hieu Le
Hoang-An Le
Huu Minh Le
Gim Hee Lee
Hyungtae Lee
Jae-Han Lee
Jangho Lee
Jungbeom Lee
Kibok Lee
Kuan-Hui Lee
Seokju Lee
Sungho Lee
Sungmin Lee
Bin Li
Jie Li
Ruilong Li
Ruoteng Li
Site Li
Xianzhi Li
Xiaomeng Li
Xiaoming Li
Xin Li
Xiu Li
Xueting Li
Yawei Li
Yijun Li
Yimeng Li
Yin Li
Yong Li
Yu-Jhe Li
Zekun Li
Dongze Lian
Zhouhui Lian
Haoyi Liang
Yue Liao
Jun Hao Liew
Chia-Wen Lin
Guangfeng Lin
Kevin Lin
Xudong Lin
Xue Lin
Chang Liu

Feng Liu
Hao Liu
Hong Liu
Jing Liu
Jingtuo Liu
Jun Liu
Miaomiao Liu
Ming Liu
Ping Liu
Siqi Liu
Wentao Liu
Wu Liu
Xing Liu
Xingyu Liu
Yongcheng Liu
Yu Liu
Yu-Lun Liu
Yun Liu
Zhihua Liu
Zichuan Liu
Chengjiang Long
Manuel López Antequera
Hao Lu
Hongtao Lu
Le Lu
Shijian Lu
Weixin Lu
Yao Lu
Yongxi Lu
Chenxu Luo
Weixin Luo
Wenhan Luo
Diogo C. Luvizon
Jiancheng Lyu
Chao Ma
Long Ma
Shugao Ma
Xiaojian Ma
Yongrui Ma
Ludovic Magerand
Behrooz Mahasseni
Mohammed Mahmoud
Utkarsh Mall
Massimiliano Mancini
Xudong Mao
Alina E. Marcu

Niki Martinel
Jonathan Masci
Tetsu Matsukawa
Bruce A. Maxwell
Amir Mazaheri
Prakhar Mehrotra
Heydi Méndez-Vázquez
Zibo Meng
Kourosh Meshgi
Shun Miao
Zhongqi Miao
Micael Carvalho
Pedro Miraldo
Ashish Mishra
Ikuhisa Mitsugami
Daisuke Miyazaki
Kaichun Mo
Liliane Momeni
Gyeongsik Moon
Alexandre Morgand
Yasuhiro Mukaigawa
Anirban Mukhopadhyay
Erickson R. Nascimento
Lakshmanan Nataraj
K. L. Navaneet
Lukáš Neumann
Shohei Nobuhara
Nicoletta Noceti
Mehdi Noroozi
Michael Oechsle
Ferda Ofli
Seoung Wug Oh
Takeshi Oishi
Takahiro Okabe
Fumio Okura
Kyle B. Olszewski
José Oramas
Tribhuvanesh Orekondy
Martin R. Oswald
Mayu Otani
Umapada Pal
Yingwei Pan
Rameswar Panda
Rohit Pandey
Jiangmiao Pang
João P. Papa

Toufiq Parag
Jinsun Park
Min-Gyu Park
Despoina Paschalidou
Nikolaos Passalis
Yash Patel
Georgios Pavlakos
Baoyun Peng
Houwen Peng
Wen-Hsiao Peng
Roland Perko
Vitali Petsiuk
Quang-Hieu Pham
Yongri Piao
Marco Piccirilli
Matteo Poggi
Mantini Pranav
Dilip K. Prasad
Véronique Prinet
Victor Adrian Prisacariu
Thomas Probst
Jan Prokaj
Qi Qian
Xuelin Qian
Xiaotian Qiao
Yvain Queau
Mohammad Saeed Rad
Filip Radenovic
Petia Radeva
Bogdan Raducanu
François Rameau
Aakanksha Rana
Yongming Rao
Sathya Ravi
Edoardo Remelli
Dongwei Ren
Wenqi Ren
Md Alimoor Reza
Farzaneh Rezaianaran
Andrés Romero
Kaushik Roy
Soumava Kumar Roy
Nataniel Ruiz
Javier Ruiz-del-Solar
Jongbin Ryu
Mohammad Sabokrou

Ryusuke Sagawa
Pritish Sahu
Hideo Saito
Kuniaki Saito
Shunsuke Saito
Ken Sakurada
Joaquin Salas
Enrique Sánchez-Lozano
Aswin Sankaranarayanan
Hiroaki Santo
Soubhik Sanyal
Vishwanath Saragadam1
Yoichi Sato
William R. Schwartz
Jesse Scott
Siniša Šegvić
Lorenzo Seidenari
Keshav T. Seshadri
Francesco Setti
Meet Shah
Shital Shah
Ming Shao
Yash Sharma
Dongyu She
Falong Shen
Jie Shen
Xi Shen
Yuming Shen
Hailin Shi
Yichun Shi
Yifei Shi
Yujiao Shi
Zenglin Shi
Atsushi Shimada
Daeyun Shin
Young Min Shin
Kirill Sidorov
Krishna Kumar Singh
Maneesh K. Singh
Gregory Slabaugh
Chunfeng Song
Dongjin Song
Ran Song
Xibin Song
Ramprakash Srinivasan
Erik Stenborg

Stefan Stojanov
Yu-Chuan Su
Zhuo Su
Yusuke Sugano
Masanori Suganuma
Yumin Suh
Yao Sui
Jiaming Sun
Jin Sun
Xingyuan Sun
Zhun Sun
Minhyuk Sung
Keita Takahashi
Kosuke Takahashi
Jun Takamatsu
Robby T. Tan
Kenichiro Tanaka
Masayuki Tanaka
Chang Tang
Peng Tang
Wei Tang
Xu Tang
Makarand Tapaswi
Amara Tariq
Mohammad Tavakolian
Antonio Tejero-de-Pablos
Ilias Theodorakopoulos
Thomas E. Bishop
Diego Thomas
Kai Tian
Xinmei Tian
Yapeng Tian
Chetan J. Tonde
Lei Tong
Alessio Tonioni
Carlos Torres
Anh T. Tran
Subarna Tripathi
Emanuele Trucco
Hung-Yu Tseng
Tony Tung
Radim Tylecek
Seiichi Uchida
Md. Zasim Uddin
Norimichi Ukita
Ernest Valveny

Nanne van Noord
Subeesh Vasu
Javier Vazquez-Corral
Andreas Velten
Constantin Vertan
Rosaura G. VidalMata
Valentin Vielzeuf
Sirion Vittayakorn
Konstantinos Vougioukas
Fang Wan
Guowei Wan
Renjie Wan
Bo Wang
Chien-Yi Wang
Di Wang
Dong Wang
Guangrun Wang
Hao Wang
Hongxing Wang
Hua Wang
Jialiang Wang
Jiayun Wang
Jingbo Wang
Jinjun Wang
Lizhi Wang
Pichao Wang
Qian Wang
Qiaosong Wang
Qilong Wang
Qingzhong Wang
Shangfei Wang
Shengjin Wang
Tiancai Wang
Wenguan Wang
Wenhai Wang
Xiang Wang
Xiao Wang
Xiaoyang Wang
Xinchao Wang
Xinggang Wang
Yang Wang
Yaxing Wang
Yisen Wang
Yu-Chiang Frank Wang
Zheng Wang
Scott Wehrwein

Wei Wei
Xing Wei
Xiu-Shen Wei
Yi Wei
Martin Weinmann
Michael Weinmann
Jun Wen
Xinshuo Weng
Thomas Whelan
Kimberly Wilber
Williem Williem
Kwan-Yee K. Wong
Yongkang Wong
Sanghyun Woo
Michael Wray
Chenyun Wu
Chongruo Wu
Jialian Wu
Xiaohe Wu
Xiaoping Wu
Yihong Wu
Zhenyao Wu
Changqun Xia
Xide Xia
Yin Xia
Lei Xiang
Di Xie
Guo-Sen Xie
Jin Xie
Yifan Xing
Yuwen Xiong
Jingwei Xu
Jun Xu
Ke Xu
Mingze Xu
Yanyu Xu
Yi Xu
Yichao Xu
Yongchao Xu
Yuanlu Xu
Jia Xue
Nan Xue
Yasushi Yagi
Toshihiko Yamasaki
Zhaoyi Yan
Zike Yan

Keiji Yanai
Dong Yang
Fan Yang
Hao Yang
Jiancheng Yang
Linlin Yang
Mingkun Yang
Ren Yang
Sibei Yang
Wenhan Yang
Ze Yang
Zhaohui Yang
Zhengyuan Yang
Anbang Yao
Angela Yao
Rajeev Yasarla
Jinwei Ye
Qi Ye
Xinchen Ye
Zili Yi
Ming Yin
Zhichao Yin
Ryo Yonetani
Ju Hong Yoon
Haichao Yu
Jiahui Yu
Lequan Yu
Lu Yu
Qian Yu
Ruichi Yu
Li Yuan
Sangdoo Yun
Sergey Zakharov
Huayi Zeng
Jiabei Zeng
Yu Zeng
Fangneng Zhan
Kun Zhan
Bowen Zhang
Hongguang Zhang
Jason Y. Zhang
Jiawei Zhang
Jie Zhang
Jing Zhang
Kaihao Zhang
Kaipeng Zhang

Lei Zhang
Mingda Zhang
Pingping Zhang
Qian Zhang
Qilin Zhang
Qing Zhang
Runze Zhang
Shanshan Zhang
Shu Zhang
Wayne Zhang
Xiaolin Zhang
Xiaoyun Zhang
Xucong Zhang
Yan Zhang
Zhao Zhang
Zhishuai Zhang
Feng Zhao
Jian Zhao
Liang Zhao
Qian Zhao
Qibin Zhao

Ruiqi Zhao
Sicheng Zhao
Tianyi Zhao
Xiangyun Zhao
Xin Zhao
Yifan Zhao
Yinan Zhao
Shuai Zheng
Yalin Zheng
Bineng Zhong
Fangwei Zhong
Guangyu Zhong
Yaoyao Zhong
Yiran Zhong
Jun Zhou
Mo Zhou
Pan Zhou
Ruofan Zhou
S. Kevin Zhou
Yao Zhou
Yipin Zhou

Yu Zhou
Yuqian Zhou
Yuyin Zhou
Guangming Zhu
Ligeng Zhu
Linchao Zhu
Rui Zhu
Xinge Zhu
Yizhe Zhu
Zhe Zhu
Zhen Zhu
Zheng Zhu
Bingbing Zhuang
Jiacheng Zhuo
Mohammadreza
    Zolfaghari
Chuhang Zou
Yuliang Zou
Zhengxia Zou

Contents – Part VI

Datasets and Performance Analysis

Applications of Computer Vision, Vision for X

Query by Strings and Return Ranking Word Regions with Only One Look

Peng Zhao⬥, Wenyuan Xue⬥, Qingyong Li$^{(\boxtimes)}$⬥, and Siqi Cai⬥

Beijing Key Lab of Transportation Data Analysis and Mining,
Beijing Jiaotong University, Beijing, China
{18120456,wyxue17,liqy,18120339}@bjtu.edu.cn

Abstract. Word spotting helps people like archaeologists, historian and internet censors to retrieve regions of interest from document images according to the queries defined by them. However, words in handwritten historical document images are generally densely distributed and have many overlapping strokes, which make it challenging to apply word spotting in such scenarios. Recently, deep learning based methods have achieved significant performance improvement, which usually adopt two-stage object detectors to produce word segmentation results and then embed cropped word regions into a word embedding space. Different from these multi-stage methods, this paper presents an effective end-to-end trainable method for segmentation-free query-by-string word spotting. To the best of our knowledge, this is the first work that uses a single network to simultaneously predict word bounding box and word embedding in only one stage by adopting feature sharing and multi-task learning strategy. Experiments on several benchmarks demonstrate that the proposed method surpasses the previous state-of-the-art segmentation-free methods. (The code is available at https://github.com/zhaopeng0103/WordRetrievalNet.)

Keywords: Word spotting · Query-by-String · Segmentation-free · Multi-task learning

1 Introduction

Word spotting [1] is an image retrieval task, which provides a fast way to find regions of interest from document images for people like archaeologists, historian and internet censors. Intuitively, given a set of document images and a query (usually a word image or a word string), the purpose of this task is to find word areas related to the query in document images, and then to return all the retrieved word areas ranked by a certain criterion. For such a task, one possible retrieval method that can be easily come up with is the full-page text detection and recognition. However, word spotting is more efficient, which directly locates keyword regions from document images without extra text recognition and post-processing.

© Springer Nature Switzerland AG 2021
H. Ishikawa et al. (Eds.): ACCV 2020, LNCS 12627, pp. 3–18, 2021.
https://doi.org/10.1007/978-3-030-69544-6_1

When using machines to automatically process handwritten historical documents, we face more challenges than modern printed documents due to various writing style, changeable visual appearance, and uneven background. Moreover, there have special characteristics in handwritten historical documents, such as dense words distribution and overlapping strokes, which make word segmentation difficult.

There are two ways for the word spotting task classification. Firstly, according to whether the query is a cropped word area or a word string, the word spotting task can be classified as Query-by-Example (QbE) [2–6] and Query-by-String (QbS) [2–9]. Generally, QbS is closer to the requirements in real scenes because you do not have to find a real word area and crop it from document images every time. Secondly, word spotting methods can be divided into segmentation-based [2–4,7] and segmentation-free [5,6,8,9] methods by whether it needs to segment word areas in advance of the matching process. The method proposed in Sudholt et al. [2] is the first work to use a deep convolutional neural network for segmentation-based word spotting. Wilkinson et al. [5] proposed a segmentation-free word spotting method, which produces word segmentation results based on Faster R-CNN [10] and then embeds cropped word regions into a word embedding space in which word retrieval is performed. For the reason that segmented word areas are not always available during training, recent works focus more on segmentation-free QbS word spotting.

In this paper we propose a simple and effective end-to-end trainable method for segmentation-free QbS word spotting, which is scale-insensitive and does not need redundant post-processing. To start with, the method extracts and fuses multi-scale features through a deep convolutional neural network [11] embedded with a feature pyramid network (FPN) [12]. After that, based on feature sharing mechanism, the fused features are passed on to three subtasks for multi-task learning. In detail, the first task performs pixel classification by predicting the probability of each pixel belonging to a positive word area. The second task regresses word bounding box by predicting the offsets of a word pixel to its word bounding box boundaries. The third task learns the mapping from the word area to the word embedding. The queries defined by users are retrieved based on the outputs of the three tasks. To the best of our knowledge, this is the first work that utilizes a single network to simultaneously predict word bounding box and word embedding in segmentation-free word spotting. The proposed method achieves state-of-the-art performance on several benchmarks. And the experimental results prove that it is effective to perform word segmentation by directly regressing word bounding box in handwritten historical document images with special characteristics such as dense words distribution and overlapping strokes.

The main contributions of this paper are summarized as follows:

- We propose a novel end-to-end trainable deep model for segmentation-free QbS word spotting in handwritten historical document images, which simultaneously predicts word bounding box and word embedding by adopting feature sharing and multi-task learning strategy in only one stage;

- The proposed method achieves state-of-the-art results in terms of word retrieval performance on public datasets, which demonstrate the effectiveness of segmenting words by directly regressing word bounding box in handwritten historical document images with dense words distribution and overlapping strokes.

The rest of this paper is organized as follows. Section 2 describes some recent approaches in word spotting. Section 3 presents the proposed end-to-end trainable methodology for segmentation-free QbS word spotting. Section 4 demonstrates the effectiveness of the proposed method on several public benchmarks using standard evaluation measures. And conclusions are drawn in Sect. 5.

2 Related Work

2.1 Traditional Word Spotting Methods

In document analysis and recognition literature, most traditional methods for handwritten word spotting are based on Hidden Markov Model (HMM) [13,14], Dynamic Time Warping (DTW) [15,16], RNN [17], Bidirectional long short-term memory (BLSTM) [18]. These methods mainly consist of three steps. The first step is the preprocessing of document images, including image binarization, segmentation and normalization. Afterwards features such as SIFT [19] and HoG [20] extracted from segmented word or line images are embedded into a common representation space. Lastly, word image retrieval lists are acquired by distance measurement criteria such as cosine distance, Euclidean distance and edit distance. Rath et al. [15] presented an algorithm for matching handwritten word images in historical document images, which extracts feature representations from segmented word images and uses DTW for comparison. Rath et al. [16] extended the above work and used DTW to compare variable-length feature sequences for word matching. Frinken et al. [17] proposed to locate words based on the combination of BLSTM and CTC token passing algorithm.

However, these traditional methods generally use hand-crafted features, which typically have poor robustness. The method proposed in this paper utilizes deep learning and convolutional neural network to extract and concatenate low-level texture features with high-level semantic features of images, which can improve accuracy of locating word targets with variable sizes and help to achieve excellent performance.

2.2 Deep Learning Based Word Spotting Methods

In recent years, deep learning based methods have achieved significant performance improvement in handwritten word spotting, which are crucial for promoting the research of word spotting. They are typically classified into segmentation-based and segmentation-free methods.

Segmentation-based word spotting approaches [2–4, 7] have witnessed major advancements with further research on word embedding and extensive application of deep learning. The method proposed in Sudholt et al. [2] is the first work to use a deep CNN architecture for word spotting, which can handle word images with arbitrary size and predict Pyramidal Histogram of Characters (PHOC) [21] representation. Wilkinson et al. [3] employed a triplet CNN to extract word image representation and subsequently embedded it into a novel word embedding, called Discrete Cosine Transform of Words (DCToW). Gomez et al. [7] learned a string embedding space in which distances between projected points are correlated with the Levenshtein edit distance between the original strings based on a siamese network. Finally, Serdouk et al. [4] learned similarities vs differences between word images, then used Euclidean distance for word matching. However, these methods require lots of segmented word areas. Because segmented word areas are not always available during training, this limits the application of handwritten word spotting. Therefore, this paper proposes a segmentation-free word spotting method, which can be applied in any unconstrained scenarios.

Most of the previous segmentation-free word spotting methods [5, 6, 8, 9] are based on sliding windows or connected components or combination of both, depending on how to generate the word image retrieval regions. In the method proposed by Rothacker et al. [8], regions are generated based on sliding windows and queries are modeled by BoF-HMM, where the size of the region for a given query string has to be estimated. Wilkinson et al. [5] predicted word candidate regions based on Faster R-CNN [10], and then embedded clipped candidate regions into a word embedding space in which word retrieval is performed according to the cosine distance from the query. Three different word detectors are adopted to generate word hypotheses in the method proposed by Rothacker et al. [6]. Then the authors used convolution neural network to predict word embedding and performed word spotting through nearest neighbor search. Vats et al. [9] presented a training-free and segmentation-free word spotting method based on document query word expansion and relaxed feature matching algorithm. These methods generate a large number of candidate regions during word segmentation process, resulting in slow processing speed and too many false positives. Our method directly predicts word bounding boxes based on pixel-level segmentation without redundant post-processing processes.

2.3   Scene Text Detection and Recognition Methods

In the last few years, scene text detection methods [22, 23] have attracted extensive attention. EAST [22] adopts fully convolutional network (FCN) [24] to directly produce text regions without unnecessary intermediate steps. PSENet [23] proposes to merge text instances through progressive scale expansion algorithm, which can precisely detect texts with arbitrary shapes. Scene text recognition methods [25] predict character sequences from extracted features. CRNN [25] is the first approach to treat text recognition as a sequence-to-sequence task by combining CNN and RNN in an end-to-end network.

Uniformly, one possible method that can be easily come up with is the full-page text retrieval method, which combines the above text detection and recognition methods into a pipeline and then performs word searching. This method can also achieve word spotting task in historical document images. However, it needs to compare the query with recognition results one-by-one according to whether the content is exactly the same. Different from the above framework, word spotting only needs to label coordinates of query words without recognizing word contents, and then outputs word area retrieval lists ranked by similarity, which is more efficient and more like a tool specifically designed for keyword search tasks. Inspired by scene text detection methods [22,23], the method proposed in this paper combines deep convolutional neural network [11] with feature pyramid network (FPN) [12] to extract image features, and then directly regresses word bounding box and predicts word embedding without complicated post-processing.

3 Method

The proposed method is illustrated in Fig. 1. The input image is first fed into the backbone network to extract multi-scale features and fuse them. Then the fusion features are passed on to three subtasks that predict pixel categories, word bounding boxes and word embeddings, respectively. We present the details of each part in the following subsections.

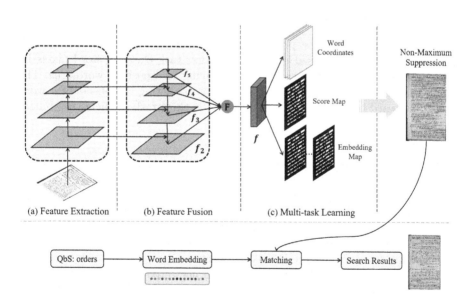

Fig. 1. The pipeline of the proposed method.

3.1   Feature Extraction and Fusion

Words in handwritten historical document images are usually densely distributed and have many overlapping strokes, so it is important to extract appropriate and powerful features. In the proposed method, the ResNet50 [11] pre-trained on ImageNet [26] is adopted as the backbone for feature extraction. Inspired by FPN [12], merging feature maps of different layers may help improve the performance of detecting word areas with various sizes. Therefore, four feature maps are extracted from the ResNet50: the last layer of block1, block2, block3 and block4, whose sizes are $\frac{1}{4}$, $\frac{1}{8}$, $\frac{1}{16}$ and $\frac{1}{32}$ of the input image, respectively. Afterwards we concatenate low-level texture features with high-level semantic features to get four feature maps (f_2, f_3, f_4, f_5), whose dimensions are $\left(N, 256, \frac{H}{4}, \frac{W}{4}\right)$, $\left(N, 256, \frac{H}{8}, \frac{W}{8}\right)$, $\left(N, 256, \frac{H}{16}, \frac{W}{16}\right)$ and $\left(N, 256, \frac{H}{32}, \frac{W}{32}\right)$, respectively. N is the batch size. H and W are the height and width of the input image. In order to encode information with various receptive fields, based on the feature fusion part in [23], these four feature maps are further fused to obtain fusion feature map f with dimension $\left(N, 1024, \frac{H}{4}, \frac{W}{4}\right)$. The above fusion process is defined by function $\mathbb{F}(\cdot)$ as follows:

$$f = \mathbb{F}(f_2, f_3, f_4, f_5) = f_2 \| Up_{\times 2}(f_3) \| Up_{\times 4}(f_4) \| Up_{\times 8}(f_5), \qquad (1)$$

where "$\|$" represents the fusion operation and $Up_{\times 2}(\cdot)$, $Up_{\times 4}(\cdot)$, $Up_{\times 8}(\cdot)$ represent 2, 4, 8 times upsampling, respectively.

3.2   Multi-task Learning

After feature extraction, the proposed method conducts three subtasks simultaneously for joint supervised learning. The first task classifies word pixels by computing the probability of each pixel belonging to a positive word area. The second task regresses word bounding boxes by predicting the offsets of a word pixel to its word bounding box boundaries. The third task predicts the embeddings of word areas.

Word Pixel Classification. For the first task, we feed f into a series of stacked convolutional layers and a Sigmoid layer to produce a single-channel word pixel classification score map with dimension $\left(N, 1, \frac{H}{4}, \frac{W}{4}\right)$, which predicts the probability of each pixel belonging to a positive word area on the resized input image. When building the classification ground truth, we shrink the initial word regions by 0.2 times along the short side of the word boundaries. During training, only the shrinking word regions are treated as positive areas. The areas between the shrinking regions and the bounding boxes are neglected and do not contribute to the classification loss.

There is a strong imbalance between the number of pixels in the foreground and background, because word instances generally occupy only a small region in word areas. In order to prevent predictions of the network biasing to background pixels, we adopt dice coefficient loss [23,27]. The dice coefficient $D\left(\hat{y}_{cls}, y_{cls}\right)$ between word classification predictions $\hat{y}_{cls}$ and ground truth y_{cls} is formulated as:

$$D\left(\hat{y}_{cls}, y_{cls}\right) = \frac{2\sum_{i,j}\hat{y}_{cls}^{i,j} \times y_{cls}^{i,j}}{\sum_{i,j}\left(\hat{y}_{cls}^{i,j}\right)^2 + \sum_{i,j}\left(y_{cls}^{i,j}\right)^2}, \tag{2}$$

where $\hat{y}_{cls}^{i,j}$ and $y_{cls}^{i,j}$ refer to the values of pixel (i,j) in $\hat{y}_{cls}$ and y_{cls}. Thus the word pixel classification loss is defined as:

$$\mathcal{L}_{cls} = 1 - D(\hat{y}_{cls}, y_{cls}). \tag{3}$$

Word Bounding Box Regression. The second task is to obtain the word coordinate map with dimension $\left(N, 4, \frac{H}{4}, \frac{W}{4}\right)$ by feeding f into stacked convolutional layers and a Sigmoid layer. The four channels predict the offsets of a word pixel to the top, bottom, left and right sides of the corresponding word bounding box.

GIoU loss [28] can accurately represent the coincidence degree of two bounding boxes. However, when the target box completely covers the predicted box, it can not distinguish their relative positional relationship. To solve the above shortcomings, DIoU loss [29] tries to predict more accurate word bounding box by adding center point normalized distance. Considering the situation of dense words distribution and overlapping strokes in handwritten historical document images, we adopt the DIoU loss as word regression loss, which can be written as:

$$\mathcal{L}_{bbox} = \frac{1}{|C|}\sum_{i \in C} DIoU\left(\hat{y}_{bbox}, y_{bbox}\right), \tag{4}$$

where C denotes the set of positive elements in the word pixel classification score map, $DIoU\left(\hat{y}_{bbox}, y_{bbox}\right)$ refers to the DIoU loss between the predicted bounding box $\hat{y}_{bbox}$ and the ground truth y_{bbox}.

Word Embedding Prediction. The third task aims to learn the mapping from the word area to the word embedding. We train and evaluate our model using Discrete Cosine Transform of Words (DCToW) introduced in [3], which is a distributed representation of a word and has achieved state-of-the-art results in segmentation-based and segmentation-free word spotting methods [2,5]. The calculation process from a word string to the corresponding word embedding is shown in Fig. 2. Given a word of length l and an alphabet of length k[1], each character in the word is first transformed to a one-hot encoding vector. These vectors are concatenated into a matrix $M \in R^{k \times l}$ for the whole word. Secondly,

---

[1] We use the digits $0-9$ and the lowercase letters $a-z$ in our experiments, that is $k = 36$.

a matrix $N \in R^{k \times l}$ is obtained by applying a Discrete Cosine Transform along the dimension l. Thirdly, the matrix N is cropped and keeps only r first low-frequency components, which denotes as $P \in R^{k \times r}$. Finally, the matrix P is flattened into a vector R with dimension $k \times r$. Specifically, r is set to 3 in our experiments, so the dimension of the word embedding is 108. For words with less than r characters, we pad zeros to get vectors of the same dimension.

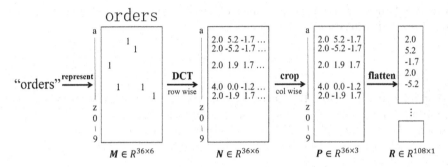

Fig. 2. Word embedding with DCToW. The word string is first represented as matrix M by one-hot encoding. Secondly M is transformed into matrix N through DCT. Thirdly, N is cropped to matrix P. Finally, P is flattened into a 108 dimensional vector R.

The embedding map with dimension $\left(N, E, \frac{H}{4}, \frac{W}{4}\right)$ is obtained by feeding f into stacked convolutional layers and a Sigmoid layer, where E corresponds to the dimension of the word embedding, namely 108. For the generation of the word embedding ground truth, all pixels in the positive word area defined by the first task are assigned to the corresponding word embedding values.

To minimize the error between the predicted word embedding $\hat{y}_{embed}$ and the ground truth y_{embed}, we use the cosine loss introduced in [30], which can be formulated as follows:

$$\mathcal{L}_{embed} = 1 - \cos\left(\hat{y}_{embed}, y_{embed}\right). \tag{5}$$

Overall, the whole loss function can be written as:

$$\mathcal{L}_{all} = \mathcal{L}_{bbox} + \lambda_{cls}\mathcal{L}_{cls} + \lambda_{embed}\mathcal{L}_{embed}, \tag{6}$$

where $\mathcal{L}_{bbox}$, $\mathcal{L}_{cls}$ and $\mathcal{L}_{embed}$ represent the losses for word bounding box regression loss, word pixel classification loss and word embedding loss respectively. λ_{cls} and λ_{embed} balance the importance among these losses, and we set $\lambda_{cls} = 1.0$, $\lambda_{embed} = 1.0$ in our experiments.

Inference Stage. At the stage of inference, the dense predictions are filtered by Non-Maximum Suppression (NMS) to yield final word bounding boxes, as shown in Fig. 1. Then, for each predicted word bounding box, we locate the corresponding area on the multi-dimensional word embedding map and calculate the mean of this area to get the word embedding. Furthermore, the given query string is embedded into the same word embedding space to calculate the cosine distance with predicted word embeddings. The smaller the cosine distance, the greater the similarity. The top N query results with the largest similarity are considered as retrieval results.

3.3   Offline Data Augmentation

Facing the fact that training data is insufficient, we adopt the two offline data augmentation strategies introduced in [5], i.e. the in-place and the full-page augmentation. They help the model to improve the ability of learning word embedding and the accuracy of predicting word bounding box. A comparison of the two strategies is shown in Fig. 3. Given the bounding box for each word in document images, the word area is augmented as follows: random affine transformation, and random morphological dilation or erosion to fatten or thin the ink. The in-place augmentation directly iterates through each word bounding box and augments each word region in-place using the above augmentation, as shown in the left of Fig. 3. The full-page augmentation firstly crops all word areas in document images for the same basic word-level augmentation, then places them row-by-row on a background image without words, as shown in the right of Fig. 3.

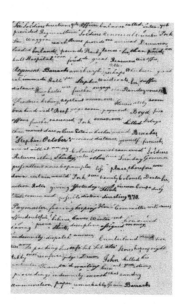

Fig. 3. A visual comparison of the in-place (left) and the full-page (right) augmentation.

4   Experiments

In this section, the datasets used in our experiments and the experimental details are first described. Next, we evaluate the proposed method on the three public benchmarks, and compare it with state-of-the-art methods. Finally, the ablation studies are presented for the proposed method.

4.1   Datasets and Experimental Setup

The proposed method is evaluated on three public benchmarks:

- George Washington Dataset (GW): The George Washington dataset [31] is written by George Washington and his secretaries in the middle of the 18th century. It comprises of 20 pages and 4860 annotated words. Due to the lack of an official partitioning into training and test pages, the 20 pages are split into a training set of 15 pages and a test set of 5 pages according to the common evaluation procedure used in [8], and take the average of four cross validations as the final results.
- Konzilsprotokolle Dataset: The Konzilsprotokolle dataset contains approximately 18000 pages in good preservation state, which includes equal copies of handwritten minutes from formal meeting held by the central administration of Greifswald University between 1794–1797. This dataset is a part of the ICFHR 2016 Handwritten Keyword Spotting Competition (H-KWS2016) [32], which contains 85 document images for training and 25 document images for testing.
- Barcelona Historical Handwritten Marriages Dataset (BH2M): The BH2M dataset [33] consists of 550,000 marriage records stored in 244 books, with marriages held between the 15th and 19th century. A subset of the dataset is used as the IEHHR2017 [34] competition dataset, where 100 images are annotated for training and 25 images for testing.

The proposed method is implemented in PyTorch framework [35], and run on a server with 2.40 GHz CPU, Tesla P100 GPU, Ubuntu 64-bit OS. For the three datasets used in our experiments, we adopt the two data augmentation techniques introduced in Sect. 3.3 to create 1000 augmented document images respectively, resulting in a total of 2000 document images. Our models are initialized with ResNet50 [11] pre-trained on ImageNet [26]. The whole network is trained end-to-end by using ADAM [36] optimizer and the learning rate is initially set to 1e−3. We train each model for 50 epochs with batch size 4, and evaluate the performance on validation dataset every 10 epochs. The model with the highest validation MAP is used for testing.

The online data augmentation for training data is listed as follows: 1) The long sides of the input images are scaled to 2048 pixels, and the short sides are scaled proportionally. 2) 512 × 512 random samples are cropped from the transformed images.

For the three datasets used in the experiments, the models are evaluated by adopting the standard metric used for segmentation-free word spotting, Mean

Average Precision (MAP) [5]. For the GW and BH2M datasets, the QbS evaluations use all unique transcriptions from the test set as queries. For Konzilsprotokolle we use the list of queries for QbS which are defined by the competition [32]. And we use a word classification score threshold of 0.9, a word bounding box nms overlap threshold of 0.4 and a query nms overlap threshold of 0.9.

4.2   Comparisons with State-of-the-Art Methods

As in previous work, we compare the performance of our proposed method with the state-of-the-art methods with the 25% and 50% overlap thresholds, respectively. Table 1 shows the evaluation results on the three datasets, which use the same evaluation protocol of MAP. Different from the previous two-stage method [5], the proposed method combines multi-task learning strategy with end-to-end optimization mechanism, which is the first work to utilize a single network to do segmentation-free QbS word spotting in only one stage. On GW dataset, when the overlap threshold is 50%, our method achieves a MAP of 94.06%, surpassing the state-of-the-art result (91.00%) by more than 3%. Notably, on Konzilsprotokolle dataset, the MAP (73.67%) achieved by our method is lower than [6] with a 50% overlap thresholds. The reason may be that the method in [6] adopts statistical prior knowledge to quantify the heights of word hypotheses while we do not apply this dataset-dependency strategy. The special characteristics of the dataset, such as excessive stroke overlap, also lead to performance degradation. However, when using a 25% overlap thresholds, our method achieves 98.77%, outperforming [6] over 2.77%, which clearly demonstrates that our method can detect more word regions. Figure 4 shows the visualization results of several queries for the proposed method on the GW dataset, which proves that the proposed method can obtain precise word segmentation results.

Table 1. MAP comparison in % with state-of-the-art segmentation-free QbS methods on the GW, Konzilsprotokolle and BH2M datasets. "GW 15–5" means using the 15–5 page train/test split on GW. "25%" and "50%" are the word bounding box overlap thresholds.

Method	GW 15–5		Konzilsprotokolle		BH2M	
	25%	50%	25%	50%	25%	50%
BoF HMMs [8]	80.10	76.50	–	–	–	–
Ctrl-F-Net DCToW [5]	95.20	91.00	–	–	–	–
Rothacker et al. [6]	90.60	84.60	96.00	**89.90**	–	–
Vats et al. [9]	–	–	–	50.91	–	85.72
Resnet50 + FPN (ours)	**96.46**	**94.06**	**98.77**	73.67	**95.30**	**95.09**

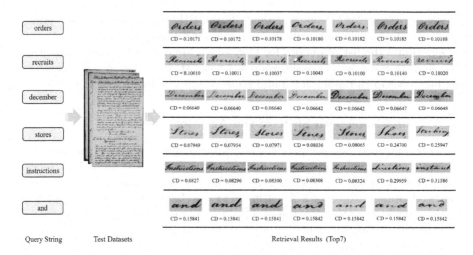

Fig. 4. The visualization results of several queries for the proposed method on GW. The figure shows the top 7 results starting from the left. The correct search results are highlighted in green. "CD" means the cosine distance between the predicted word embedding of the word area and the ground truth. The smaller the cosine distance, the greater the similarity. (Color figure online)

4.3 Ablation Study

Influence of Feature Fusion. The effect of the feature fusion is studied by extracting a single feature map at different layers and exploiting features of f_2, f_3, f_4 and f_5. The models are evaluated on GW and Konzilsprotokolle datasets. Table 2. shows that the MAP on the test datasets drops when only a single feature map is extracted. When only the low-level texture feature f_2 is extracted, the network can not learn deep information due to the lack of high-level semantic features, resulting in poor retrieval performance. When only extracting the high-level semantic feature f_5, the training can not converge very well because of the lack of low-level texture features. Considering various sizes of words in historical document images, fusing feature maps of different layers helps the network to handle word targets with different scales, which further improves the performance of word segmentation and retrieval.

Influence of the Backbone. To further analyze the performance of our method, we investigate the effect of the backbone on the experimental results. Specifically, the following two network architectures are compared with the backbone used in the proposed method, Vgg16 [37] + FPN [12] and Resnet50 [11] + FCN [24]. The models are evaluated on GW and Konzilsprotokolle datasets. Table 3 shows the experimental results, from which we can find that the model with Resnet50 + FPN achieves the best performance than other backbones. This demonstrates the importance of a better backbone network for feature extraction and representation.

Table 2. MAP (%) performance evaluation of feature fusion on GW and Konzilsprotokolle. "GW 15-5" means using the 15–5 page train/test split on GW. "25%" and "50%" are the word bounding box overlap thresholds.

Method	Feature map	GW 15–5		Konzilsprotokolle	
		25%	50%	25%	50%
Resnet50 + FPN	f_5	92.47	75.59	97.54	54.43
Resnet50 + FPN	f_4	92.77	89.82	97.88	65.83
Resnet50 + FPN	f_3	91.35	87.96	97.92	66.48
Resnet50 + FPN	f_2	92.21	89.18	97.10	67.85
Resnet50 + FPN	**fusion**	**96.46**	**94.06**	**98.77**	**73.67**

Table 3. MAP (%) performance evaluation of different backbones on GW and Konzilsprotokolle. "GW 15-5" means using the 15–5 page train/test split on GW. "25%" and "50%" are the word bounding box overlap thresholds.

Backbone	GW 15–5		Konzilsprotokolle	
	25%	50%	25%	50%
Vgg16 + FPN	93.02	86.65	97.77	68.25
Resnet50 + FCN	93.00	90.19	98.38	70.78
Resnet50 + FPN (ours)	**96.46**	**94.06**	**98.77**	**73.67**

4.4 Robustness Analyze

Previous methods evaluate the experimental results only with the queries entirely from unique words in the original test set. In order to explore the robustness of the proposed method, we conduct experiments with another two query test sets, in which only the queries that appear in the training set or not in the training set are preserved. Because the queries used on the Konzilsprotokolle dataset almost totally appear in the corresponding training set, the robustness of the model is analyzed only on GW and BH2M datasets. As shown in Table 4, it can be seen

Table 4. Robustness analyze of the proposed method on GW and BH2M. "all" means using the queries totally from unique words in the test set. "only in train" means using the queries only appear in the training set. "not in train" means using the queries not appear in the training set.

Query set	GW 15–5		BH2M	
	25%	50%	25%	50%
All	96.46	94.06	95.30	95.09
Only in train	97.70	94.98	96.56	96.40
Not in train	93.57	91.71	92.73	92.43

from the results in the last row that the model still achieves high MAP when query words never appear in the training set, which proves the generalization and robustness of our method.

5   Conclusion and Future Work

In this paper, we present an efficient end-to-end trainable model for segmentation-free query-by-string word spotting. Based on feature sharing and multi-task learning strategy, for the first time, our method simultaneously predicts word bounding box and word embedding through a single network. Experiments on word spotting benchmarks demonstrate the superior performance of the proposed method, and prove the effectiveness of segmenting words by directly regressing word bounding box in handwritten historical document images with dense words distribution and overlapping strokes.

Since labeling of training data is time-consuming, in the future, we will consider using weak supervised learning to perform word spotting task on handwritten historical document images, and applying this method to other scenarios such as natural scene images.

References

1. Giotis, A.P., Sfikas, G., Gatos, B., Nikou, C.: A survey of document image word spotting techniques. Pattern Recogn. **68**, 310–332 (2017)
2. Sudholt, S., Fink, G.A.: Phocnet: a deep convolutional neural network for word spotting in handwritten documents. In: Proceedings of the 15th International Conference on Frontiers in Handwriting Recognition (ICFHR), pp. 277–282. IEEE (2016)
3. Wilkinson, T., Brun, A.: Semantic and verbatim word spotting using deep neural networks. In: Proceedings of the 15th International Conference on Frontiers in Handwriting Recognition (ICFHR), pp. 307–312. IEEE (2016)
4. Serdouk, Y., Eglin, V., Bres, S., Pardoen, M.: KeyWord spotting using siamese triplet deep neural networks. In: Proceedings of the 15th International Conference on Document Analysis and Recognition (ICDAR), pp. 1157–1162. IEEE (2019)
5. Wilkinson, T., Lindstrom, J., Brun, A.: Neural Ctrl-F: segmentation-free query-by-string word spotting in handwritten manuscript collections. In: Proceedings of the International Conference on Computer Vision (ICCV), pp. 4433–4442 (2017)
6. Rothacker, L., Sudholt, S., Rusakov, E., Kasperidus, M., Fink, G.A.: Word hypotheses for segmentation-free word spotting in historic document images. In: Proceedings of the 14th International Conference on Document Analysis and Recognition (ICDAR), vol. 1, pp. 1174–1179. IEEE (2017)
7. Gómez, L., Rusinol, M., Karatzas, D.: Lsde: levenshtein space deep embedding for query-by-string word spotting. In: Proceedings of the 14th International Conference on Document Analysis and Recognition (ICDAR), vol. 1, pp. 499–504. IEEE (2017)
8. Rothacker, L., Fink, G.A.: Segmentation-free query-by-string word spotting with bag-of-features HMMs. In: Proceedings of the 13th International Conference on Document Analysis and Recognition (ICDAR), pp. 661–665. IEEE (2015)

9. Vats, E., Hast, A., Fornés, A.: Training-free and segmentation-free word spotting using feature matching and query expansion. In: Proceedings of the 15th International Conference on Document Analysis and Recognition (ICDAR), pp. 1294–1299. IEEE (2019)
10. Ren, S., He, K., Girshick, R., Sun, J.: Faster R-CNN: towards real-time object detection with region proposal networks. In: Advances in Neural Information Processing Systems, pp. 91–99 (2015)
11. He, K., Zhang, X., Ren, S., Sun, J.: Deep residual learning for image recognition. In: Proceedings of the International Conference on Computer Vision and Pattern Recognition (CVPR), pp. 770–778 (2016)
12. Lin, T.Y., Dollár, P., Girshick, R., He, K., Hariharan, B., Belongie, S.: Feature pyramid networks for object detection. In: Proceedings of the International Conference on Computer Vision and Pattern Recognition (CVPR), pp. 2117–2125 (2017)
13. Rodríguez-Serrano, J.A., Perronnin, F.: Handwritten word-spotting using hidden Markov models and universal vocabularies. Pattern Recogn. **42**, 2106–2116 (2009)
14. Rodríguez-Serrano, J.A., Perronnin, F.: A model-based sequence similarity with application to handwritten word spotting. IEEE Trans. Pattern Anal. Mach. Intell. **34**, 2108–2120 (2012)
15. Rath, T.M., Manmatha, R.: Word image matching using dynamic time warping. In: Proceedings of the International Conference on Computer Vision and Pattern Recognition (CVPR), vol. 2, p. II. IEEE (2003)
16. Rath, T.M., Manmatha, R.: Word spotting for historical documents. Int. J. Doc. Anal. Recogn. (IJDAR) **9**, 139–152 (2007)
17. Frinken, V., Fischer, A., Manmatha, R., Bunke, H.: A novel word spotting method based on recurrent neural networks. IEEE Trans. Pattern Anal. Mach. Intell. **34**, 211–224 (2011)
18. Graves, A., Liwicki, M., Fernández, S., Bertolami, R., Bunke, H., Schmidhuber, J.: A novel connectionist system for unconstrained handwriting recognition. IEEE Trans. Pattern Anal. Mach. Intell. **31**, 855–868 (2008)
19. Lowe, D.G.: Distinctive image features from scale-invariant keypoints. Int. J. Comput. Vis. **60**, 91–110 (2004)
20. Dalal, N., Triggs, B.: Histograms of oriented gradients for human detection. In: Proceedings of the International Conference on Computer Vision and Pattern Recognition (CVPR), vol. 1, pp. 886–893. IEEE (2005)
21. Almazán, J., Gordo, A., Fornés, A., Valveny, E.: Word spotting and recognition with embedded attributes. IEEE Trans. Pattern Anal. Mach. Intell. **36**, 2552–2566 (2014)
22. Zhou, X., et al.: East: an efficient and accurate scene text detector. In: Proceedings of the International Conference on Computer Vision and Pattern Recognition (CVPR), pp. 5551–5560 (2017)
23. Wang, W., et al.: Shape robust text detection with progressive scale expansion network. In: Proceedings of the International Conference on Computer Vision and Pattern Recognition (CVPR), pp. 9336–9345 (2019)
24. Long, J., Shelhamer, E., Darrell, T.: Fully convolutional networks for semantic segmentation. In: Proceedings of the International Conference on Computer Vision and Pattern Recognition (CVPR), pp. 3431–3440 (2015)
25. Shi, B., Bai, X., Yao, C.: An end-to-end trainable neural network for image-based sequence recognition and its application to scene text recognition. IEEE Trans. Pattern Anal. Mach. Intell. **39**, 2298–2304 (2016)

26. Krizhevsky, A., Sutskever, I., Hinton, G.E.: Imagenet classification with deep convolutional neural networks. In: Advances in Neural Information Processing Systems, pp. 1097–1105 (2012)
27. Milletari, F., Navab, N., Ahmadi, S.A.: V-net: fully convolutional neural networks for volumetric medical image segmentation. In: Proceedings of the 4th International Conference on 3D Vision (3DV), pp. 565–571. IEEE (2016)
28. Rezatofighi, H., Tsoi, N., Gwak, J., Sadeghian, A., Reid, I., Savarese, S.: Generalized intersection over union: a metric and a loss for bounding box regression. In: Proceedings of the International Conference on Computer Vision and Pattern Recognition (CVPR), pp. 658–666 (2019)
29. Zheng, Z., Wang, P., Liu, W., Li, J., Ye, R., Ren, D.: Distance-IoU loss: faster and better learning for bounding box regression. In: Proceedings of the 34th AAAI Conference on Artificial Intelligence, pp. 12993–13000 (2020)
30. Krishnan, P., Dutta, K., Jawahar, C.V.: Word spotting and recognition using deep embedding. In: Proceedings of the 13th International Workshop on Document Analysis Systems (DASW), pp. 1–6. IEEE (2018)
31. Lavrenko, V., Rath, T.M., Manmatha, R.: Holistic word recognition for handwritten historical documents. In: Proceedings of the 1st International Workshop on Document Image Analysis for Libraries, pp. 278–287. IEEE (2004)
32. Pratikakis, I., Zagoris, K., Gatos, B., Puigcerver, J., Toselli, A.H., Vidal, E.: ICFHR2016 handwritten keyword spotting competition (H-KWS 2016). In: Proceedings of the 15th International Conference on Frontiers in Handwriting Recognition (ICFHR), pp. 613–618. IEEE (2016)
33. Fernández-Mota, D., Almazán, J., Cirera, N., Fornés, A., Lladós, J.: Bh2m: the barcelona historical, handwritten marriages database. In: Proceedings of the 22nd International Conference on Pattern Recognition (ICPR), pp. 256–261. IEEE (2014)
34. Fornés, A., et al.: ICDAR2017 competition on information extraction in historical handwritten records. In: Proceedings of the 14th International Conference on Document Analysis and Recognition (ICDAR), vol. 1, pp. 1389–1394. IEEE (2017)
35. Paszke, A., et al.: Pytorch: an imperative style, high-performance deep learning library. In: Advances in Neural Information Processing Systems, pp. 8026–8037 (2019)
36. Kingma, D.P., Ba, J.: Adam: a method for stochastic optimization. arXiv preprint arXiv:1412.6980 (2014)
37. Simonyan, K., Zisserman, A.: Very deep convolutional networks for large-scale image recognition. arXiv preprint arXiv:1409.1556 (2014)

Single-Image Camera Response Function Using Prediction Consistency and Gradual Refinement

Aashish Sharma[1]($\boxtimes$)(ID), Robby T. Tan[1,2](ID), and Loong-Fah Cheong[1](ID)

[1] National University of Singapore, Singapore, Singapore
aashish.sharma@u.nus.edu, {robby.tan,eleclf}@nus.edu.sg
[2] Yale-NUS College, Singapore, Singapore

Abstract. A few methods have been proposed to estimate the CRF from a single image, however most of them tend to fail in handling general real images. For instance, EdgeCRF based on patches extracted from colour edges works effectively only when the presence of noise is insignificant, which is not the case for many real images; and, CRFNet, a recent method based on fully supervised deep learning works only for the CRFs that are in the training data, and hence fail to deal with other possible CRFs beyond the training data. To address these problems, we introduce a non-deep-learning method using prediction consistency and gradual refinement. First, we rely more on the patches of the input image that provide more consistent predictions. If the predictions from a patch are more consistent, it means that the patch is likely to be less affected by noise or any inferior colour combinations, and hence, it can be more reliable for CRF estimation. Second, we employ a gradual refinement scheme in which we start from a simple CRF model to generate a result which is more robust to noise but less accurate, and then we gradually increase the model's complexity to improve the estimation. This is because a simple model, while being less accurate, overfits less to noise than a complex model does. Our experiments confirm that our method outperforms the existing single-image methods for both daytime and nighttime real images.

Keywords: Camera response function (CRF) · Radiometric calibration

1 Introduction

In most cameras, the camera irradiance has a non-linear correlation to the image intensities. This is caused by the non-linearity of the camera response function (CRF), which is one of the components of the camera imaging pipeline and is intentionally designed to be non-linear to create more aesthetic effects and perform dynamic range compression [1]. Linearising the image intensities through estimating the CRF is critical for many computer vision algorithms, such as

This work is supported by MOE2019-T2-1-130.

H. Ishikawa et al. (Eds.): ACCV 2020, LNCS 12627, pp. 19–35, 2021.
https://doi.org/10.1007/978-3-030-69544-6_2

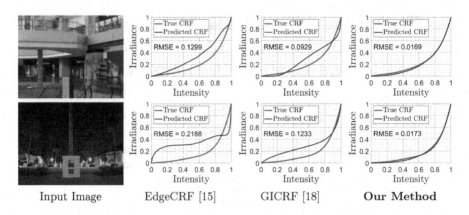

Fig. 1. Results of our single-image CRF estimation method in comparison with those of two existing methods, EdgeCRF [15] and GICRF [18], for both daytime and nighttime image. RMSE is the Root Mean Squares Error between the predicted and true CRF.

shape from shading [2,3], colour constancy [4,5], photometric stereo [6,7], specular removal [8], shadow removal [9], low-light image enhancement [10], etc.

Some CRF methods use multiple images of a static scene taken with different exposures [7,11–13]. To improve the practicality, a few methods utilise a single image, which is considerably more challenging than using multiple images. To accomplish this, the methods require additional constraints, such as: the symmetric nature of the irradiance noise profile [14], or the non-linear distributions of the pixel intensities in the RGB space for pixels around edges [15,16]. The former constraint is applicable only to images that have a considerable large range of intensity values, which is not the case for many real images. The latter constraint is more applicable to many real images, since it only implies RGB images to have non-uniform coloured patches. Unfortunately, the existing methods that use this constraint are erroneous when noise is present in the input image. Recently, a deep-learning based method [17] using a single image is introduced. This method can work robustly on real images; however, it suffers from the generalization problem. It works effectively only for CRFs represented in the training data.

To address the problem of single-image CRF estimation, we introduce a non-deep-learning method based on the ideas of prediction consistency and gradual refinement. First, unlike the existing methods, our method relies more on patches that provide more consistent CRF predictions. This is based on the idea that if a patch provides more consistent CRF predictions, it is likely to be less affected by noise or any inferior colour combinations, and hence, can be more reliable to estimate the CRF. We put more weight on more reliable patches, which renders more robust and accurate CRF estimation.

Second, unlike the existing methods, our method employs a gradual refinement scheme to improve our CRF result. CRF estimation is generally carried out by optimising a CRF model that can linearise the non-linear pixel distributions with minimum error [15]. There are various models that can be employed to represent CRFs (e.g., [6,18–20]). Each model is defined by a set of coefficients, hence the problem of finding the CRF is equivalent to optimizing the coefficients of the CRF model. A model with more coefficients is more accurate, but is also more prone to overfit to noise. Therefore, to gain robustness to noise, our method optimises a simple model first (i.e., one coefficient), and then optimises a more complex model. During the refinement, the CRF result in the current stage is constrained to remain near the CRF result obtained in the previous stage. Figure 1 shows our estimations for both daytime and nighttime real images.

To summarise, in this paper, our main contributions are as follows:

- Unlike existing methods, our method is designed to deal with noise, making it more applicable to general real images. For achieving this, first, we found that different patches are unequal in terms of noise and how much they carry the CRF information (or degree of non-linearity). For instance, in one input image, patches taken from darker regions are more affected by noise compared to patches taken from well-lit regions; on top of this, in a patch, certain colour combinations carry more CRF information compared to other colour combinations. Second, unlike [15], we found non-edge patches can be used to estimate a CRF. Third, we found noise can significantly alter the degree of non-linearity in a patch, which is critical for a robust method to consider. All these findings are new and important for CRF estimation.
- We propose a new approach to compute the reliability of a patch in estimating CRFs. It is based on the consistency among a patch's CRF predictions. More consistency implies more reliability.
- We introduce a gradual refinement scheme, in which we start from a simple model to obtain results that are robust to noise but less accurate, and then we gradually increase the model's complexity to improve the results. We show that our refinement scheme generates better results than those of one-attempt estimation methods. The idea of gradual refinement is, in various forms, already used in computer vision algorithms, however to our knowledge, it is the first time it is designed specifically for single-image CRF estimation.

To our knowledge, our method is the first method that works robustly in well-lit and dimly-lit scenes. We also show that our method has practical applications such as visibility enhancement under nighttime conditions.

2   Related Work

Several methods have been proposed for CRF estimation. Many previous works rely on a sequence of images of the same scene taken with different exposure times [11–13] or varying illumination [1,6]. In addition to the requirement of multiple images, these methods also assume that the camera position is fixed. Some other methods [21–25] have relaxed the fixed camera condition by performing image alignment. In contrast to these multi-image methods, our method requires a single image, and hence, is more applicable.

Lin et al. [15] are the first to demonstrate that the CRF can be recovered from a single colour image. Their method is based on the property that pixels around color boundaries in the camera irradiance form linear distributions in the RGB space. However, due to the non-linear CRF, the pixel distributions become non-linear for the intensity image in the RGB space. Thus the CRF is recovered by finding a CRF model that can linearise the distributions with minimum error. Later, the method is extended to work on grayscale images [16]. The ideas of these two methods are elegant, yet unfortunately they are prone to suffer from noise that is commonly present in real images. Matsushita and Lin [14] use noise profile for CRF estimation, based on the observation that the profile is symmetric in the irradiance domain but due to the non-linear CRF, it becomes asymmetric in the intensity domain. However, this method does not work well if there is insufficient data available for generating the noise profile. Li et al. [26] propose to use the low-rank structure of skin pixels to recover the CRF from an image that contains a human face. This method, therefore, is limited to work on images that consist of human faces. Recently, Li and Peers [17] propose a network to estimate the CRF from a single image by predicting 11 coefficients of the basis functions model [19], for which they use the 201 CRFs from [19] during training. Kao et al. further propose [27], a stacked version of [17], which shares a similar idea of iterative refinement with our method. Both [17] and [27] are supervised learning-based methods and suffer from the generalization problem. This means they cannot work properly for estimating the CRFs that are not represented in the training set. In contrast, our method is not a learning-based method, and hence, does not suffer from the generalization problem of learning-based methods.

Similar to Lin et al. [15], our method uses the non-linear pixel distributions to estimate the CRF from a single image. However, in contrast to the method, our method uses a consistency based metric to take into account the reliability of the patches (containing the distributions) for estimating the CRF. Additionally, unlike the one-attempt estimation approach of their method, our method uses a gradual refinement scheme that provides more robust and accurate CRF results.

3   Proposed Method

The camera imaging pipeline can be represented by [28]:

$$\mathbf{I} = f(T(\mathbf{E})), \tag{1}$$

where $\mathbf{E}$ is the camera irradiance in the RGB colour channels, T is a linear operator for colour transformations (for e.g., white balance), f is a non-linear function representing the CRF, and $\mathbf{I}$ is the RGB image outputted by the camera. Given an image $\mathbf{I}$ (normalised in $[0, 1]$) as input, our goal is to estimate the inverse CRF $g = f^{-1}$, such that the image $g(\mathbf{I})$ becomes linearly related to the camera irradiance $\mathbf{E}$. Figures 2a and 2d shows an example of $\mathbf{I}$ and $g = f^{-1}$ respectively.

3.1   Non-Linearity of Pixel Distributions

From the input image $\mathbf{I}$, we can obtain a set of non-uniform patches. Let Ω represent that set of the patches, and $|\Omega|$ is the number of the patches in the

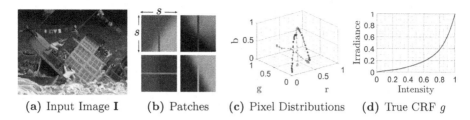

(a) Input Image **I**   **(b)** Patches   **(c)** Pixel Distributions   **(d)** True CRF g

Fig. 2. (a) Input image **I**. (b) Patches around edges in the image **I**. Each patch is of size $s \times s$. The coloured line in a patch shows a pixel distribution scanned horizontally or vertically from that patch. (c) Pixel distributions of the patches plotted in the RGB space. (d) True CRF g. (Color figure online)

set. A patch drawn from this set is represented by $\mathbf{I}^p \in \Omega$, where p is the index of the drawn patch, and $p \in [1, |\Omega|]$. Moreover, let the size of the patch $\mathbf{I}^p$ be $s \times s$; then, $\mathbf{I}^{p,k}$ is a set of pixels in the patch (which we call a pixel distribution) where k is the index of this set of pixels ($k \in [1, s]$). Figure 2a shows an example of an input image **I**. Figure 2b shows an example of some patches, $\mathbf{I}^p$, selected from **I**. Figure 2b also shows the patches with a line in each patch, where the line represents the locations of pixels that form a pixel distribution, $\mathbf{I}^{p,k}$.

Let $\mathbf{E}^{p,k}$ be the corresponding pixel distribution in the camera irradiance, and the three colour channels of $\mathbf{E}^{p,k}$ be represented by $\mathbf{E}_r^{p,k}$, $\mathbf{E}_g^{p,k}$ and $\mathbf{E}_b^{p,k}$. When we transform $\mathbf{E}^{p,k}$ into the RGB space, it will form a straight line; since $\mathbf{E}_r^{p,k}$, $\mathbf{E}_g^{p,k}$ and $\mathbf{E}_b^{p,k}$ are linear to each other. Hence, we can express the linear correlation between two colour channels of the camera irradiance as:

$$\mathbf{E}_g^{p,k} = m_{gr}^{p,k} \, \mathbf{E}_r^{p,k} + b_{gr}^{p,k}, \tag{2}$$

$$\mathbf{E}_b^{p,k} = m_{br}^{p,k} \, \mathbf{E}_r^{p,k} + b_{br}^{p,k}, \tag{3}$$

where $(m_{gr}^{p,k}, b_{gr}^{p,k})$ and $(m_{br}^{p,k}, b_{br}^{p,k})$ are the parameters of the line equations.

Unlike $\mathbf{E}^{p,k}$ that forms a linear distribution, due to the non-linearity of the CRF, $\mathbf{I}^{p,k}$ forms a non-linear distribution in the RGB space, an observation introduced in [15]. Figure 2c shows an example of a few pixel distributions, $\{\mathbf{I}^{p,k}\}_{p=1}^4$, plotted in the RGB space. We can observe the non-linearity in the distributions, which is due to the non-linear CRF shown in Fig. 2d. The reason of the non-linearity of $\mathbf{I}^{p,k}$ in the RGB space can be explained as follows. Since the three colour channels can have the same CRF and the linear operator T can be a linear identity mapping, from Eq. (1), we can obtain: $\mathbf{E}_r^{p,k} = g(\mathbf{I}_r^{p,k})$, $\mathbf{E}_g^{p,k} = g(\mathbf{I}_g^{p,k})$ and $\mathbf{E}_b^{p,k} = g(\mathbf{I}_b^{p,k})$. Substituting these terms in Eqs. (2) and (3), we can obtain the following non-linear equations:

$$\mathbf{I}_g^{p,k} = g^{-1}(m_{gr}^{p,k} \, g(\mathbf{I}_r^{p,k}) + b_{gr}^{p,k}), \tag{4}$$

$$\mathbf{I}_b^{p,k} = g^{-1}(m_{br}^{p,k} \, g(\mathbf{I}_r^{p,k}) + b_{br}^{p,k}). \tag{5}$$

No-Noise Case. Given any pixel distribution $\mathbf{I}^{p,k}$ from a non-uniform patch $\mathbf{I}^p$, where all the pixels are free from any noise and thus follow Eqs. (4) and (5)

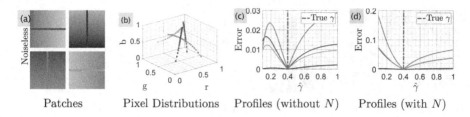

| (a) Patches | (b) Pixel Distributions | (c) Profiles (without N) | (d) Profiles (with N) |

Fig. 3. For the no-noise case, the CRF can be estimated from any non-uniform patch. For the patches shown in (a), the linearisation error profiles without and with the normalization operation are shown in (c) and (d), respectively. We can observe that all the profiles show the correct global minima, and with the normalization operation, we can remove the local minima observed in (c) that occurs due to the scale problem.

strictly, we can estimate the CRF by optimizing a CRF model $\hat{g}$ that can linearise the distribution with minimum error. The subsequent paragraph discusses this idea in more detail.

Figure 3a shows four non-uniform patches taken from a synthetic image with no noise, which is generated using a simple CRF of a gamma function: $\mathbf{I} = f(\mathbf{E}) = \mathbf{E}^{\gamma}$ with $\gamma = 0.4$. Thus, for this case, the CRF model $\hat{g}$, is the gamma model, where we need to find a gamma value $\hat{\gamma}$ to estimate the CRF. One of the simplest ways to find $\hat{\gamma}$ is to try all possible values of $\hat{\gamma}$ in a certain range; and for each of them, we generate the linearised distribution represented by $(\mathbf{I}^{p,k})^{1/\hat{\gamma}}$. Then, we can do a line fitting, and compute the error of each point from the line. This is basically the linearisation or line fitting error for $(\mathbf{I}^{p,k})^{1/\hat{\gamma}}$. Figure 3c shows the linearisation error profiles for the four pixel distributions taken from the four patches shown in Fig. 3a, respectively. The error profile for a pixel distribution is obtained by taking $\hat{\gamma}$ values in the range of $[0, 1]$ with increments of 0.02, and then computing the linearisation error for the distribution for all the $\hat{\gamma}$ values. From the results in Fig. 3c, we can observe that all the error profiles show the correct global minima at $\hat{\gamma} = 0.4$, with zero linearisation error. Note that, in this discussion, for the sake of clarity, we use only one pixel distribution, $\mathbf{I}^{p,k}$, for every patch, $\mathbf{I}^p$. In our actual algorithm, we use all the pixel distributions, $\{\mathbf{I}^{p,k}\}_{k=1}^s$, for every patch, $\mathbf{I}^p$, in the set Ω (see Sect. 3.3).

Scale Problem and the Normalization Operation. From Fig. 3c, we can also observe that all the error profiles show local minima at $\hat{\gamma} = 0.1$. The reason why this occurs is because the line fitting error is affected by the scale of $(\mathbf{I}^{p,k})^{1/\hat{\gamma}}$. As $\hat{\gamma}$ becomes small, the scale of $(\mathbf{I}^{p,k})^{1/\hat{\gamma}}$ also reduces; which in turn reduces the line fitting error. While this is not a significant problem for synthetic images with no noise, for real images where noise is inevitable, these local minima can possibly become global minima (see Fig. 4c). This is one of the reasons that some existing methods [15,16] are erroneous.

To address this problem, we propose to normalise $(\mathbf{I}^{p,k})^{1/\hat{\gamma}}$ in each colour channel before computing the line fitting error. Namely, if N represents the normalization operation, we normalise $(\mathbf{I}^{p,k})^{1/\hat{\gamma}}$ such that $\min(N((\mathbf{I}_c^{p,k})^{1/\hat{\gamma}})) = 0$

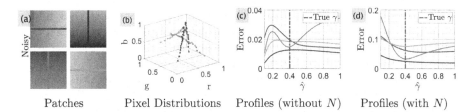

Fig. 4. For the noisy case, the linearisation error gets affected by both noise and non-linearity. For the noisy patches in (a), the profiles without the normalization operation shown in (c) show an incorrect global minima. As shown in (d), the normalization operation can alleviate this problem, but depending upon the noise and non-linearity, some distributions (like the purple and blue) can still provide an inaccurate result. (Color figure online)

and $\max(N((\mathbf{I}_c^{p,k})^{1/\hat{\gamma}})) = 1$ for $c \in \{r, g, b\}$. The normalization operation makes the line fitting error independent of the scale variations caused by $\hat{\gamma}$ (since it is now the same scale for all values of $\hat{\gamma}$). Figure 3d shows the profiles after the normalization operation, which now clearly indicate the correct global minima.

3.2   Effect of Noise on CRF Estimation

For the input image that has no noise, we can recover the CRF from any non-uniform patch, $\mathbf{I}^p$. However, this is not true when the image has noise. To illustrate this, we generate noisy patches (by adding random noise to the noiseless patches in Fig. 3a). Figure 4a shows the generated noisy patches, and Fig. 4b shows the pixel distributions from the noisy patches plotted in the RGB space. Following the same procedure in the no-noise case, we compute the linearisation error profiles for the noisy pixel distributions. Figure 4c and Fig. 4d show the error profiles obtained without and with the normalization operation, respectively.

As shown in Fig. 4c, we can observe that for the noisy patches, most profiles do not show the correct global minima. This is because under the presence of noise, both noise and non-linearity affect the linearisation error. Moreover, we can observe that all the profiles show the global minima at $\hat{\gamma} = 0.1$, which occurs because of the scale problem. Figure 4d shows the profiles after the normalisation operation that removes the scale problem. As a result, some profiles show the correct global minima, and some do not. This depends on the level of noise and the degree of non-linearity in the pixel distribution in the RGB space.

Equations (4) and (5) show that the curviness of a patch (or its distribution $\mathbf{I}^{p,k}$) depends on its colour combination, and thus not all patches carry the CRF information equally. For instance, if the irradiance is achromatic or nearly achromatic, i.e. $\mathbf{E}_r^{p,k} \approx \mathbf{E}_g^{p,k} \approx \mathbf{E}_b^{p,k}$, implying $m_{gr}^{p,k} \approx m_{br}^{p,k} \approx 1$ and $b_{gr}^{p,k} \approx b_{br}^{p,k} \approx 0$, Eqs. (4) and (5) reduce to $\mathbf{I}_r^{p,k} \approx \mathbf{I}_g^{p,k} \approx \mathbf{I}_b^{p,k}$. This means that the line becomes linear for achromatic patches (or achromatic pixel distributions), and they have no information about the CRF. As can be observed in Fig. 3d, the purple coloured profile of the pixel distribution that belongs to a nearly achromatic patch has a considerably shallow minima basin, which means that the distribution is close to being linear. This is what we mean by the degrees of non-linearity of patches (or pixel distributions) are unequal.

Moreover, from Eqs. (4) and (5), we can also observe that due to the presence of both g and g^{-1} in the same equation, there is a "cancellation" effect, which means that in general, the degree of non-linearity in the RGB space is reduced. In other words, the curviness of the pixel distribution in the RGB space is lessened, causing the global minimum to be less obvious. Hence, when the noise comes into the picture, the error profile can be more significantly influenced by the noise, rendering incorrect CRF estimation, which can be observed for the blue and purple coloured distributions in Fig. 4d. Therefore, we need some reliability measure to know the reliability score (which can indicate the degree of genuine non-linearity) of every patch in our set, so that we can rely more on the patches with higher reliability scores to estimate the CRF robustly and accurately. Note that most of the existing methods, particularly [15, 16], assume insignificant noise in the input image and also ignore the patches' varying degrees of non-linearity, and thus treat all the processed patches equally.

3.3 Prediction Consistency for Reliability

To estimate the reliability score of a patch, we propose to use the consistency of the CRF predictions of all the pixel distributions in the patch. In a patch $\mathbf{I}^p$ of resolution $s \times s$, we have s horizontally or vertically scanned pixel distributions, which can provide s estimations of the CRF. If the estimations are more consistent, the reliability score will be higher.

By employing the GGCM model [18] as our CRF model, we can express:

$$\mathbf{I} = f(\mathbf{E}) = (\mathbf{E})^{\gamma_1 + \gamma_2 \mathbf{E} + \ldots + \gamma_c (\mathbf{E})^{c-1}}, \tag{6}$$

where c is the number of coefficients, and $\{\gamma_1, ..., \gamma_c\}$ are the coefficients of the model. Thus by using the estimated coefficients, $\{\hat{\gamma}_1, ..\hat{\gamma}_c\}$, we can obtain the estimated CRF represented by: $\hat{g}(x) = (x)^{\frac{1}{\hat{\gamma}_1 + \hat{\gamma}_2 x + \ldots + \hat{\gamma}_c(x)^{c-1}}}, \forall x \in x$, where x is a set of 100 equidistant values in the range of $[0, 1]$. Let $\hat{g}^{p,k}(x)$ be the estimated CRF from a pixel distribution $\mathbf{I}^{p,k}$ in a patch. Then, we can compute the consistency between the s estimations of the CRF, $\{\hat{g}^{p,k}(x)\}_{k=1}^{s}$, using:

$$\hat{\sigma}^p = \frac{1}{|x|} \sum_{x \in x} \left(\frac{1}{|s|} \sum_{k=1}^{s} \left(\hat{g}^{p,k}(x) - \frac{1}{|s|} \sum_{k=1}^{s} \left(\hat{g}^{p,k}(x) \right) \right)^2 \right). \tag{7}$$

The reliability score of the patch, $\hat{\alpha}^p$, where: $\hat{\alpha}^p = \exp^{\frac{-\hat{\sigma}^p}{0.05}}$. This score will be used in our gradual refinement scheme to weigh the CRF estimate of the corresponding patch (Sect. 3.4).

To compute the CRF estimate of a single patch, $\hat{g}^p(x)$, instead of using the mean of the s predictions, we use the mode of the s predictions. Since, from

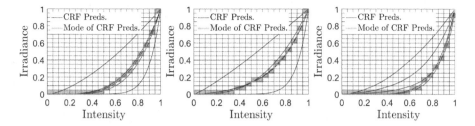

Fig. 5. Examples showing the voting mechanism used for obtaining the mode of the CRF predictions. The mode CRF being discretised looks like a staircase function.

our investigation, in the present of noise, the mean is more influenced by the variations in the predictions than the mode. Here are the details. For every pixel distribution, $\mathbf{I}^{p,k}$ in a patch $\mathbf{I}^p$, we can obtain a CRF estimated curve, $\hat{g}^{p,k}(\mathbf{x})$. If we have s pixel distributions in the patch, then we have s CRF estimated curves, $\{\hat{g}^{p,k}(\mathbf{x})\}_{k=1}^{s}$. We discretise the CRF space (as shown in the examples in Fig. 5) by creating a grid in the space. The grid is a $\Delta \times \Delta$ grid. Meaning, there are Δ columns and Δ rows (where in our implementation $\Delta = 20$, hence our grid has 20×20 cells). Subsequently, we count how many $\{\hat{g}^{p,k}(\mathbf{x})\}_{k=1}^{s}$ that fall into each of the cells. For each column in the grid, we choose the row that has the highest count. If we do this for all columns, we can have our discretised CRF estimate. Mathematically, we express this discretised CRF estimate as:

$$\hat{g}^p(\mathbf{x}) = H\left(\{\hat{g}^{p,1}(\mathbf{x}), \hat{g}^{p,2}(\mathbf{x}), ..., \hat{g}^{p,s}(\mathbf{x})\}, \Delta\right), \forall \mathbf{x} \in \mathbf{x}, \tag{8}$$

where H represents a function that chooses the best CRF for every column or intensity value in the discretised CRF space. In this space, the more correct cells contain higher values (see the examples shown in Fig. 5).

3.4   Gradual Refinement

As we discussed, a CRF model with more coefficients can be more accurate in representing the CRF. However, under the presence of noise, a model with more coefficients is also more prone to overfit to noise. The existing methods [15,16,18] use a one-attempt optimization approach to directly optimise a complex model (model with a high number of coefficients) which under the presence of noise can cause instability. To address this problem, we propose to initialise the CRF estimation using the one-coefficient model (i.e., a model with only one coefficient). The initial result is more robust to noise but less accurate. We then increase the coefficients of the model to estimate more refined CRF result, which we constrain to remain near the previous CRF result. This is the core idea of our gradual refinement scheme. Also, note that while limiting the values of higher-order coefficients can also act as a regularizer, it can suppress the CRF representation capability, since some CRFs can require high values of the coefficients. Our gradual refinement, however, does not have this problem.

At stage t of the refinement process, where $t \in [1, T]$, for a patch $\mathbf{I}^p$, we obtain the CRF prediction $\hat{g}_t^{p,k}(\mathrm{x})$ for its pixel distribution $\mathbf{I}^{p,k}$ by optimising the following objective function:

$$\hat{g}_t^{p,k}(\mathrm{x}) \equiv \{\hat{\gamma}_1^{p,k}, ..\hat{\gamma}_c^{p,k}\} = \underset{\{\hat{\gamma}_1^{p,k}, ..\hat{\gamma}_c^{p,k}\}}{\mathrm{argmin}} \left(\mathcal{L}[N((\mathbf{I}^{p,k})^{\frac{1}{\hat{\gamma}_1^{p,k}+...+\hat{\gamma}_c^{p,k}(\mathbf{I}^{p,k})^{c-1}}})] \right.$$
$$\left. + \lambda((\mathrm{x})^{\frac{1}{\hat{\gamma}_1^{p,k}+...+\hat{\gamma}_c^{p,k}(\mathrm{x})^{c-1}}} - \hat{g}_{t-1}(\mathrm{x}))^2 \right), \forall \mathrm{x} \in \mathrm{x} \quad (9)$$

where c is the number of coefficients at stage t, N is the normalization operation, $\mathcal{L}$ is a function that computes the line fitting error, and λ is a parameter that controls the closeness of the CRF prediction $\hat{g}_t^{p,k}(\mathrm{x})$ to the CRF estimated in the previous stage $\hat{g}_{t-1}(\mathrm{x})$. We keep $\lambda = 0$ at $t = 1$. Having obtained the predictions from the patch's pixel distributions, we compute the reliability score of the patch, $\hat{\alpha}_t^p$, and the CRF estimate from the patch, $\hat{g}_t^p(\mathrm{x})$, (as described in Sect. 3.3).

The CRF estimate at stage t from all the patches, $\hat{g}_t(\mathrm{x})$, is then computed by considering the reliability scores of the patches:

$$\hat{g}_t(\mathrm{x}) = H\left(\{\hat{\alpha}_t^1 \hat{g}_t^1(\mathrm{x}), \hat{\alpha}_t^2 \hat{g}_t^2(\mathrm{x}), ..., \hat{\alpha}_t^{|\Omega|} \hat{g}_t^{|\Omega|}(\mathrm{x})\}, \Delta\right), \forall \mathrm{x} \in \mathrm{x}, \quad (10)$$

where we use the same voting mechanism, except instead of counting the number of predictions for each grid cell, we sum the reliability scores of the predictions for each grid cell. For each column, the row that contains the largest sum is selected.

Practically, to improve the CRF estimation accuracy in the next stage and to keep the runtime of the method small, we remove the patches in Ω whose reliability scores are lower than a certain threshold, τ_{re}. After completion of stage T, i.e. at the end of the refinement process, the estimated CRF $\hat{g}_T(\mathrm{x})$ is a staircase curve. To generate a smooth CRF curve, we fit our c-coefficient CRF model on $\hat{g}_T(\mathrm{x})$:

$$\hat{g}(\mathrm{x}) \equiv \{\hat{\gamma}_1, ..\hat{\gamma}_c\} = \underset{\{\hat{\gamma}_1, ..\hat{\gamma}_c\}}{\mathrm{argmin}} \left((\mathrm{x})^{\frac{1}{\hat{\gamma}_1 + \hat{\gamma}_2 \mathrm{x} + ... + \hat{\gamma}_c(\mathrm{x})^{c-1}}} - \hat{g}_T(\mathrm{x})\right)^2, \forall \mathrm{x} \in \mathrm{x}, \quad (11)$$

where $\hat{g}(\mathrm{x})$ is the final CRF result from our method. See Algorithm 1 for our entire CRF estimation process.

3.5   Selection of Patches

We add a patch into the set Ω if it meets the following criteria:

1. The patch has no under-saturated or over-saturated pixels, i.e. for every pixel in the patch, its magnitude (mean of the three colour channel values) is above τ_{us} and below τ_{os}, where τ_{us} and τ_{os} are the thresholds set for the under-saturated and over-saturated pixels, respectively.
2. The patch is not uniform and contains a mixture of colours, i.e. the variance of all the three colour channel values in the patch is above τ_{un}, where τ_{un} is the threshold set for the uniformity of a patch.

Algorithm 1. Single-Image Camera Response Function using Prediction Consistency and Gradual Refinement

---

1: **Input:** Image **I**.
2: Generate a set of non-uniform patches Ω following the selection process in Sec. 3.5.
3: **for** stage t where $t \in [1, T]$ **do**
4:     **for** patch $\mathbf{I}^p$ of resolution $s \times s$ where $\mathbf{I}^p \in \Omega$ **do**
5:         **for** patch distribution $\mathbf{I}^{p,k}$ where $k \in [1, s]$ **do**
6:             Obtain the CRF estimate for the distribution, $\hat{g}_t^{p,k}(\mathrm{x})$, using Eq. (9).
7:         **end for**
8:         Obtain the CRF estimate for the patch, $\hat{g}_t^p(\mathrm{x})$, using Eq. (8).
9:         Compute the reliability for the patch, $\hat{\alpha}_t^p$, using Eq. (7).
10:     **end for**
11:     Obtain the CRF estimate at stage t, $\hat{g}_t(\mathrm{x})$, using Eq. (10).
12:     Update Ω. Remove the patches whose $\hat{\alpha}_t^p < \tau_{\mathrm{re}}$.
13: **end for**
14: Obtain the final CRF, $\hat{g}(\mathrm{x})$, from $\hat{g}_T(\mathrm{x})$ using Eq. (11).
15: **Output:** Final CRF $\hat{g}(\mathrm{x})$.

---

3. The patch's pixel distributions are not narrow and are well spread in the RGB space, i.e the variance of a colour channel values in the patch is above τ_{na}, where τ_{na} is the threshold set for narrowness of the distributions.

To select the pixel distributions in a patch, we select the distributions by scanning in either horizontal or vertical direction, depending upon which direction the distributions have more variance.

Note that: (1) unlike [15], which uses solely edge patches, our patch selection method also includes patches with any mixture of colours beyond edges. This gives us a more rich set of patches; (2) The selection criteria above are learned empirically, and can be adjusted depending on the conditions of the target images; (3) Our horizontal-vertical scanning technique is not a hard requirement, as any other techniques can also be used. The only reason we opt for the simple scanning technique is to keep our method efficient.

4   Experimental Results

We evaluate our method on general daytime images taken in indoor and outdoor settings. For this, we use the Color-Constancy dataset [29]. We create a test set of 120 images picked randomly from the dataset. The images are taken from three cameras: NikonD40, Canon600D and SonyA57. In the patch selection process, we use the parameters $\{s, \tau_{\mathrm{us}}, \tau_{\mathrm{os}}, \tau_{\mathrm{un}}, \tau_{\mathrm{na}}\} = \{21, 0.15, 0.9, 0.01, 0.065\}$. The parameter for patch resolution, s, is set so that we can have sufficient number of pixels in the pixel distribution to compute the line fitting error. The parameters τ_{un} and τ_{na} are tuned to avoid selecting the uniform patches, and inspecting that the distributions are widely spread in the RGB space. We implement our method in MATLAB and use the function `fmincon` to optimise the coefficients for CRF prediction (Eq. (9)). We set the parameter $\lambda = 0.01$ and $\tau_{re} = 0.3$, that provide the best performance on a separate validation set of 30 images. At stage t, we estimate $c = t$ number of coefficients. Wie set $T = 2$, as it offers a good tradeoff between our method's accuracy and runtime (as shown in our ablation study). Also, as shown in [18], the GGCM model with two coefficients is more accurate than the other models [6, 19, 20] using the same number of coefficients.

For the baseline methods, we use EdgeCRF [15], CRFNet [17] and GICRF [18]. Similar to ours, EdgeCRF and GICRF are not learning based methods, while CRFNet is a learning based method. Since the codes of EdgeCRF and CRFNet are not available, these methods are based on our implementation. To evaluate the accuracy of the CRF result from each method, we compute Root Mean Squares Error (RMSE) between the method's CRF result $\hat{g}(x)$ and the ground-truth CRF $g(x)$ by: RMSE $= \sqrt{\sum_{x \in x}(\hat{g}(x) - g(x))^2}$ (where the ground-truth CRFs are obtained by using images with Macbeth ColorChecker [15, 16, 18, 19] that are provided by the datasets). For each method, we compute the mean, median, standard deviation, minimum and maximum RMSE values obtained on the entire test set. The quantitative results are shown in Table 1 and the qualitative CRF results are shown in Fig. 6. From the results, we can observe that our CRF results are more accurate and stable than the baseline methods.

Table 1. Comparisons with the baseline methods on the daytime test dataset. The numbers represent RMSE. Bold font indicates lowest error

Method	Mean	Median	Std	Min	Max
EdgeCRF [15]	0.1561	0.1596	0.0402	0.0424	0.2522
CRFNet [17]	0.1609	0.1686	0.0538	0.0459	0.2788
GICRF [18]	0.0943	0.0899	0.0340	0.0379	0.2415
Our method	**0.0406**	**0.0301**	**0.0308**	**0.0142**	**0.2077**

Table 2. Comparisons with the baseline methods on the nighttime test dataset. The numbers represent RMSE. Bold font indicates lowest error

Method	Mean	Median	Std	Min	Max
EdgeCRF [15]	0.1738	0.1657	0.0504	0.0593	0.2629
CRFNet [17]	0.2407	0.2549	0.1059	0.0681	0.4428
GICRF [18]	0.1149	0.1078	0.0533	0.0669	0.2819
Our method	**0.0521**	**0.0377**	**0.0350**	**0.0173**	**0.1996**

We evaluate our method on nighttime images taken under varying illumination conditions. For this, we use 20 images taken from our own NikonD80 camera, and 30 images from the SID dataset [30] taken from Sonyα7s camera. For patch selection, the same parameters used in the daytime experiment are used, except for τ_{us} which is relaxed to 0.02 to allow more patches if the images are low-light. We compare our method with the baseline methods, results corresponding to which are shown in Table 2 and Fig. 6 respectively. We can again observe the better performance of our method compared to the baseline methods.

The methods of EdgeCRF and GICRF rely on edges and non-locally planar pixels for their respective algorithms, which can be erroneous under general noisy and nighttime conditions. Especially when the images are near low-light, most of the patches are noisy and nearly achromatic, and they cannot be used for CRF estimation (Sect. 3.2). In contrast, our method estimates the CRF by taking into account the reliability of the patches in generating the CRF estimate. As observed in Sect. 3.2, even if there is a single reliable patch in an image (which can come from the relatively well-illuminated regions in a low-light image), the CRF can be reliably estimated. In addition, contrast to the one-attempt optimisation used by these methods, we use a gradual refinement scheme to gradually improve the CRF results. These factors contribute to our method's better performance for both general daytime and well-to-dim-lit nighttime images.

The results also show the challenges in using a supervised learning based method such as CRFNet for CRF estimation. CRFNet is trained on the 201

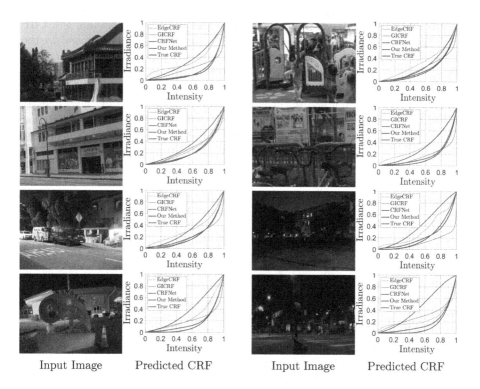

Input Image   Predicted CRF   Input Image   Predicted CRF

Fig. 6. Qualitative comparisons with the baseline methods. As we can observe, compared to the baseline methods, our results are closest to the true CRF, showing our method's robustness in both general daytime and nighttime conditions.

Input Image (11.44)   LIME+BM3D (17.23)   Ours+SID **(24.61)**   Ground Truth

Fig. 7. We show an application of our CRF estimation method for nighttime visibility enhancement. As we can observe, our enhanced image is closest to the ground truth image (highest PSNR), showing that our enhancement is more physically correct.

CRFs from the DoRF dataset [19]. If the testing CRFs are the same as the training CRFs, then CRFNet performs better than our method (in terms of mean RMSE, using the same CRF model, CRFNet's score is 0.0201 while ours is 0.0315). However, if the testing CRFs are different (such as the ones used in our experiments), then our method performs better. Since ours is not a learning based method, it can generalise well to different CRFs and imaging conditions.

Application: Nighttime Enhancement. We show that our CRF estimation method has practical applications, such as visibility enhancement under nighttime conditions. Most existing enhancement methods either assume the CRF to be linear (LIME [31]) or require the RAW image (irradiance image) as the input (SID [30]). The former generates enhancement in a physically incorrect manner, and the latter though being physically correct, is limited in application since RAW images are not available in most practical situations. If we can estimate the CRF, we can linearise the intensity image such that it becomes linearly related to the irradiance image. Therefore, we can combine our CRF estimation method with SID to create an enhancement method that accepts an RGB image as input, and enhances the image in a physically correct manner. The results are shown in Fig. 7. We can observe that the enhanced image from our combined method is closest to the ground truth (highest PSNR), thus showing that the enhancement achieved by our method is more physically correct.

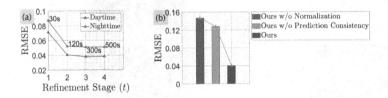

Fig. 8. (a) Effectiveness of our gradual refinement scheme as the results improve gradually with the refinement stage. (b) Using the normalization operation and the prediction consistency are important for the better performance of our method.

5   Ablation Study

Gradual Refinement. Figure 8a shows that our performance improves gradually with the refinement stage t. Since our method's runtime also increases with t, we use $T = 2$ by default as it offers a good tradeoff between our method's runtime and performance. Also, without gradual refinement (i.e. using one-attempt optimisation), our method's performance drops and the mean RMSE increases to 0.0831 from 0.0406 on the daytime test dataset.

Normalization and Prediction Consistency. We compare our method with two variants: (1) ours without using the normalization operation; and (2) ours without using the prediction consistency. The results are shown in Fig. 8b. We can observe that both the normalization operation and prediction consistency are important factors for the better performance of our method.

6   Conclusion

In this paper, we have presented a new method for CRF estimation from a single image using prediction consistency and gradual refinement. We showed that under the presence of noise, not every patch is reliable, and it is important to take into account its reliability in estimating the CRF. To handle this problem, we proposed to use consistency between a patch's CRF predictions as a measure of its reliability. Our method puts more weight on the more reliable patches that provides more accurate results. In addition, we employed a gradual refinement scheme in the CRF estimation that gradually improves the CRF results. Compared to the existing learning and non-learning based methods, our experiments confirmed that our method has good generalization capability, and it provides more accurate results for both general daytime and nighttime real images.

References

1. Kim, S.J., Frahm, J.M., Pollefeys, M.: Radiometric calibration with illumination change for outdoor scene analysis. In: IEEE Conference on Computer Vision and Pattern Recognition (CVPR) (2008)
2. Zhang, R., Tsai, P.S., Cryer, J.E., Shah, M.: Shape-from-shading: a survey. IEEE Trans. Pattern Anal. Mach. Intell. **21**, 690–706 (1999)
3. Nayar, S.K., Ikeuchi, K., Kanade, T.: Shape from interreflections. Int. J. Comput. Vis. **6**, 173–195 (1991). https://doi.org/10.1007/BF00115695
4. Finlayson, G.D., Hordley, S.D., Hubel, P.M.: Color by correlation: a simple, unifying framework for color constancy. IEEE Trans. Pattern Anal. Mach. Intell. **23**, 1209–1221 (2001)
5. Tan, R.T., Nishino, K., Ikeuchi, K.: Color constancy through inverse-intensity chromaticity space. JOSA A **21**, 321–334 (2004)
6. Shi, B., Matsushita, Y., Wei, Y., Xu, C., Tan, P.: Self-calibrating photometric stereo. In: IEEE Conference on Computer Vision and Pattern Recognition (CVPR) (2010)

7. Shi, B., Inose, K., Matsushita, Y., Tan, P., Yeung, S.K., Ikeuchi, K.: Photometric stereo using internet images. In: International Conference on 3D Vision (3DV) (2014)

8. Tan, R.T., Ikeuchi, K.: Separating reflection components of textured surfaces using a single image. IEEE Trans. Pattern Anal. Mach. Intell. **27**, 178–193 (2005)

9. Finlayson, G.D., Drew, M.S., Lu, C.: Entropy minimization for shadow removal. Int. J. Comput. Vis. **85**, 35–57 (2009). https://doi.org/10.1007/s11263-009-0243-z

10. Ying, Z., Li, G., Ren, Y., Wang, R., Wang, W.: A new low-light image enhancement algorithm using camera response model. In: IEEE International Conference on Computer Vision Workshops (ICCVW) (2017)

11. Debevec, P.E., Malik, J.: Recovering high dynamic range radiance maps from photographs. In: Annual Conference on Computer Graphics and Interactive Techniques (SIGGRAPH), SIGGRAPH 1997 (1997)

12. Mitsunaga, T., Nayar, S.K.: Radiometric self calibration. In: IEEE Conference on Computer Vision and Pattern Recognition (CVPR) (1999)

13. Mann, S.: Comparametric equations with practical applications in quantigraphic image processing. IEEE Trans. Image Process. (TIP) **9**, 1389–1406 (2000)

14. Matsushita, Y., Lin, S.: Radiometric calibration from noise distributions. In: IEEE Conference on Computer Vision and Pattern Recognition (CVPR) (2007)

15. Lin, S., Gu, J., Yamazaki, S., Shum, H.Y.: Radiometric calibration from a single image. In: IEEE Conference on Computer Vision and Pattern Recognition (CVPR) (2004)

16. Lin, S., Zhang, L.: Determining the radiometric response function from a single grayscale image. In: IEEE Conference on Computer Vision and Pattern Recognition (CVPR) (2005)

17. Li, H., Peers, P.: CRF-net: single image radiometric calibration using CNNs. In: European Conference on Visual Media Production (CVMP) (2017)

18. Ng, T.T., Chang, S.F., Tsui, M.P.: Using geometry invariants for camera response function estimation. In: IEEE Conference on Computer Vision and Pattern Recognition (CVPR) (2007)

19. Grossberg, M.D., Nayar, S.K.: Modeling the space of camera response functions. IEEE Trans. Pattern Anal. Mach. Intell. (TPAMI) **26**, 1272–1282 (2004)

20. Lee, J.Y., Matsushita, Y., Shi, B., Kweon, I.S., Ikeuchi, K.: Radiometric calibration by rank minimization. IEEE Trans. Pattern Anal. Mach. Intell. (TPAMI) **35**, 144–156 (2012)

21. Kim, S.J., Pollefeys, M.: Robust radiometric calibration and vignetting correction. IEEE Trans. Pattern Anal. Mach. Intell. (TPAMI) **30**, 562–576 (2008)

22. Litvinov, A., Schechner, Y.Y.: Addressing radiometric nonidealities: a unified framework. In: IEEE Conference on Computer Vision and Pattern Recognition (CVPR) (2005)

23. Mann, S., Mann, R.: Quantigraphic imaging: estimating the camera response and exposures from differently exposed images. In: IEEE Conference on Computer Vision and Pattern Recognition (CVPR) (2001)

24. Park, J., Tai, Y.W., Sinha, S.N., So Kweon, I.: Efficient and robust color consistency for community photo collections. In: IEEE Conference on Computer Vision and Pattern Recognition (CVPR) (2016)

25. Díaz, M., Sturm, P.: Radiometric calibration using photo collections. In: IEEE International Conference on Computational Photography (ICCP) (2011)

26. Li, C., Lin, S., Zhou, K., Ikeuchi, K.: Radiometric calibration from faces in images. In: IEEE Conference on Computer Vision and Pattern Recognition (CVPR) (2017)

27. Kao, Y.L., Chen, Y.S., Ouhyoung, M.: Progressive-CRF-net: single image radiometric calibration using stacked CNNs. In: ACM SIGGRAPH 2018 Posters, pp. 1–2 (2018)
28. Kim, S.J., Lin, H.T., Lu, Z., Süsstrunk, S., Lin, S., Brown, M.S.: A new in-camera imaging model for color computer vision and its application. IEEE Trans. Pattern Anal. Mach. Intell. (TPAMI) **34**, 2289–2302 (2012)
29. Cheng, D., Prasad, D.K., Brown, M.S.: Illuminant estimation for color constancy: why spatial-domain methods work and the role of the color distribution. J. Opt. Soc. Am. A: **31**, 1049–1058 (2014)
30. Chen, C., Chen, Q., Xu, J., Koltun, V.: Learning to see in the dark. In: IEEE Conference on Computer Vision and Pattern Recognition (CVPR) (2018)
31. Guo, X., Li, Y., Ling, H.: LIME: low-light image enhancement via illumination map estimation. IEEE Trans. Image Process. **26**, 982–993 (2016)

FootNet: An Efficient Convolutional Network for Multiview 3D Foot Reconstruction

Felix Kok$^{(\boxtimes)}$, James Charles, and Roberto Cipolla

Department of Engineering, University of Cambridge, Cambridge CB2 1PZ, UK
{cyk28,jjc75,rc10001}@cam.ac.uk

Abstract. Automatic biometric analysis of the human body is normally reserved for expensive customisation of clothing items e.g. for sports or medical purposes. These systems are usually built upon photogrammetric techniques currently requiring a rig and well calibrated cameras. Here we propose building on advancements in deep learning as well as utilising technology present in mobile phones for cheaply and accurately determining biometric data of the foot. The system is designed to run efficiently in a mobile phone app where it can be used in uncalibrated environments and without rigs. By scanning the foot with the phone camera, our system recovers both the 3D shape as well as the scale of the foot, opening the door way for automatic shoe size suggestion. Our contributions are (1) an efficient multiview feed forward neural network capable of inferring foot shape and scale, (2) a system for training from completely synthetic data and (3) a dataset of multiview feet images for evaluation. We fully ablate our system and show our design choices to improve performance at every stage. Our final design has a vertex error of only 1 mm (for 25 cm long synthetic feet) and 4 mm error in foot length on real feet.

1 Introduction

Footwear is an essential clothing item for all age groups and genders, serving many practical purposes, such as protection, but also typically worn as a fashion item. It is conventional and often vital for one to physically try on a pair of ready-to-wear shoes prior to deciding upon a purchase. This is cumbersome for in-store shopping but very inefficient and environmentally damaging for online shopping. In this setting, it is standard for many shoes to be transported back and forth between warehouse and customer to accommodate for this try-on process.

Foot length-to-size charts can be easily found on the internet but the conversion tends to vary from brand to brand. Length alone is also often not sufficient to characterise the entire shape of the foot and other measurements such as foot width and instep girth are important for correct fitting. Therefore, a method for easily obtaining a 3D model of the foot would be beneficial as it allows customers to virtually try on shoes to find the best size and shape.

Many products for 2D/3D foot scanning already exist on the market such as those developed by VoxelCare [1] and Vorum [2] but these devices tend to be expensive and are usually not targeted at common shoe customers.

© Springer Nature Switzerland AG 2021
H. Ishikawa et al. (Eds.): ACCV 2020, LNCS 12627, pp. 36–51, 2021.
https://doi.org/10.1007/978-3-030-69544-6_3

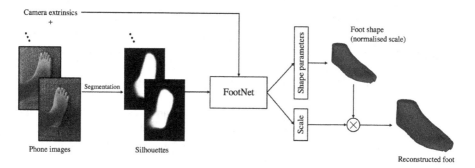

Fig. 1. Overview of the foot reconstruction framework

In this paper, we propose a novel end-to-end framework, which we call Foot-Net, that reconstructs a scale accurate 3D mesh representation of the foot from multiple 2D images. Reconstruction is very quick and can be computed directly on a smart phone.

2   Related Work

Traditional methods take a geometrical approach to tackle the reconstruction problem. Examples of commonly used techniques are passive/active triangulation [1–6] and space carving [7]. Deep learning has been tremendously successful in tackling vision related problems including 3D reconstruction. CNNs for object reconstruction typically have an encoder that maps the input into a latent variable or feature vector, which is then decoded into the desired output depending on how the 3D shape is represented. Common representations include voxel grids, meshes and point clouds.

Voxel Grids. A standard approach is to use up-convolutional layers to directly regress the 3D voxel occupancy probabilities from the latent variables [8–10]. With the availability of inexpensive 2.5D depth sensors (e.g. Microsoft Kinect), methods were proposed to reconstruct objects from depth maps [11–13]. For example, MarrNet [12] uses a two-stage network, where the first stage is an encoder-decoder architecture that predicts the 2.5D sketches (depth, surface normals, and silhouette), and the second stage is another encoder-decoder network that outputs a voxelised shape. These methods have generally been successful in reconstruction tasks but the output resolution is limited due to the high memory requirements, as the memory scales cubically with the voxel resolution. The methods mentioned above produce grids of resolution 32^3 to 64^3, except for MarrNet whose output resolution is 128^3. Approaches such as space partitioning [14,15] and coarse-to-fine refinement [16–18] were able to increase the output voxel size to 256^3 or 512^3.

Meshes. Meshes are less demanding in memory but they are not regularly structured so the network architectures have to be specifically designed.

One approach is to start with a template such as a sphere and deform the template to output the predicted 3D shape [19, 20]. Kato *et al.* [19] proposed a method to approximate the gradient for rendering which enables integration of rendering a mesh into a neural network. Wang *et al.* [20] represents the 3D mesh in a graph-based CNN and predicts the shape by progressively deforming an ellipsoid.

Multiview Networks. The problem of self-occlusion could be overcome by providing more than one viewpoint, especially in reconstructing novel shapes. Several methods were proposed to combine the information from different viewpoints. For example, silhouettes from multiple views can be combined at the input as separate channels and then passed through convolutional layers, or they can be passed into separate convolutional blocks and the outputs are concatenated [21]. The number of viewpoints would be fixed for such models. Choy *et al.* [22] uses a LSTM framework to combine a variable number of views but the output is not consistent if the order of input views is altered. Wiles and Zisserman's [23] uses max-pooling to combine the encoded latent feature vectors from multiple views so that the result is not affected by the order of input images and it could generalise to any number of views.

Foot Reconstruction. Several methods were developed specifically for foot shape reconstruction. For example, Amstutz *et al.* [24] reduces the 3D vertices of feet to only 12 parameters while preserving 92% of the shape variation, using PCA decomposition on a foot dataset. Given multiple images of a foot from different viewpoints, reconstruction is done by optimising the pose parameters, shape parameters and scale. However, their system operates in a very constrained setting, using a camera rig, structured lighting and physical aids for background subtraction. Our solution is for in the wild use, using a mobile phone. Another approach [25] uses deep learning to infer the foot shape from a single depth map by synthesising a new view that contains information of the foot missing from the input. Unfortunately, this method requires a depth sensor such as the Microsoft Kinect to operate.

3   Overview

Our system is illustrated in Fig. 1 and is broken down into three parts:

Acquisition. Our system takes multiple photos of the target from various viewpoints surrounding the foot. Using a smart phone camera we utilise the AR features (ARKit/ARCore) and attach to each image the real world camera extrinsics. The RGB images are preprocessed by passing them through a foot segmentation network.

3D Inference Using FootNet. A deep network ingests the silhouette and camera pose data to infer foot length as well as shape. This regression network (FootNet) takes inspiration from the architecture of SilNet [23] and is able to handle any number of input viewpoints without being affected by the order of inputs. Compared to SilNet which was shown to only handle 1° of freedom in camera pose, FootNet is built to handle all 6. In addition, FootNet regresses to a dense mesh reconstruction rather than a voxel grid and incorporates an efficient encoder based on MobileNet [26] to allow mobile implementation. We also show FootNet works on real data whereas SilNet was only tested on synthetic data.

Foot Shape and Scale. Foot shape is parameterised by a PCA foot model trained from 3D scans of people's feet using a multi-view stereo (MVS) system [27]. We train our deep network to infer these parameters from synthetic data only. Scale of the foot is inferred as a separate output. We next describe our method in detail.

4 Methods

Our network is trained on synthetic foot silhouettes generated using arbitrary foot shapes and camera poses. A PCA based 3D foot mesh is used here and silhouettes are rendered by artificially adjusting camera extrinsics and sampling shape from the PCA model.

4.1 3D Foot Mesh Parameterisation

3D meshes of over 1600 feet are obtained using a MVS system[1] [27]. We apply PCA to this foot dataset, similar to Amstutz *et al.* [24], expressing changes in foot shape based on 10 PCA parameters. The foot mesh is composed of 1602 vertices. Figure 2(a) illustrates the data collection pipeline showing calibration pattern used for multi-view stereo and in Fig. 2(b) the PCA based foot mesh with annotated vertex points representing various anatomical positions on the foot. A comparison of example dense foot meshes and their compact PCA representation is shown in Fig. 3.

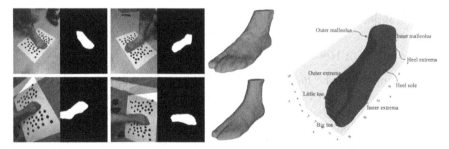

(a) RGB images, segmentation masks and dense meshes   (b) Labelled keypoints

Fig. 2. Constructing the PCA based model. Data collection using MVS is shown in (a) and the final PCA based model with vertex annotations is shown in (b)

---

[1] https://snapfeet.io/en.

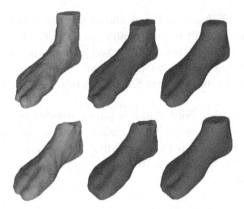

Fig. 3. Comparison of the dense meshes (left column), meshes reconstructed using 1602 PCA coefficients (middle column) and meshes reconstructed using 10 PCA coefficients (right column).

Coef. 1   Coef. 2   Coef. 3   Coef. 4   Coef. 5

Fig. 4. Change in foot shape when one of the PCA coefficients is varied while the others are fixed. Blue: mean foot. Red: coefficient set to largest in dataset. Green: coefficient set to smallest in dataset. (Color figure online)

From Fig. 4, we see that the first coefficient corresponds to the roundness of the toes, the second corresponding to width and thickness, the fourth corresponding to height of the big toe.

4.2 Foot Mesh Reconstruction Model (FootNet)

Having compressed the foot shape to 10 PCA coefficients, our goal is to construct and train a regression model that predicts the coefficients and size given foot silhouettes and the corresponding camera poses. We propose a multi-view framework, inspired by Wiles and Zisserman [23], that can handle any number of viewpoints and is not affected by the order of the inputs. The overall framework is displayed in Fig. 5. To allow more flexibility in the shape prediction, we add two extra output units representing the width deformation, k_w, and height deformation, k_h, which scale the foot vertices in the horizontal (inside to outside) and vertical (sole to ankle) directions respectively:

$$\mathbf{V}_{original} = \begin{bmatrix} \mathbf{v}_x \ \mathbf{v}_y \ \mathbf{v}_z \end{bmatrix} \quad \longrightarrow \quad \mathbf{V}_{deformed} = \begin{bmatrix} \mathbf{v}_x \ k_w\mathbf{v}_y \ k_h\mathbf{v}_z \end{bmatrix} \qquad (1)$$

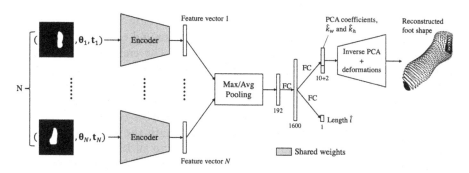

Fig. 5. Foot mesh reconstruction model architecture (FootNet).

At test time, foot segmentation is produced by a separate CNN based on ENet [28] trained on the 1601 collected foot images and silhouettes obtained from reprojection of the dense foot meshes. The main focus of this paper is on inferring the shape and scale of the foot and we are agnostic to the method used for segmentation.

Loss Function. In our framework, we consider shape prediction and length prediction separate tasks each having its own loss function.

Since the ground truth foot shapes are available, an intuitive loss for shape is the 3D vertex error, i.e., mean vertex error on the 1602-vertex point cloud. To compute the shape loss, L_{shape}, the predicted and ground truth shapes are both scaled to 25 cm long and the corresponding vertices ($\mathbf{V}$ and $\hat{\mathbf{V}}$) are compared:

$$L_{vertex}(\mathbf{V}, \hat{\mathbf{V}}) = \frac{1}{m} \sum_{i=1}^{m} d(\mathbf{v}_i, \hat{\mathbf{v}}_i) \tag{2}$$

where $\mathbf{v}_i$ and $\hat{\mathbf{v}}_i$ are the i-th row of $\mathbf{V}$ and $\hat{\mathbf{V}}$ (i.e. 3D coordinates of a vertex) respectively and $d(\mathbf{x}_1, \mathbf{x}_2)$ is the Euclidean distance between $\mathbf{x}_1$ and $\mathbf{x}_2$.

To improve the robustness, the Huber loss [29] is applied to each vertex and the mean is taken.

$$L_{huber}(a; \delta) = \begin{cases} \frac{1}{2}a^2, & |a| \leq \delta, \\ \delta\left(|a| - \frac{1}{2}\delta\right), & otherwise \end{cases} \tag{3}$$

$$L_{shape}(\mathbf{V}, \hat{\mathbf{V}}; \delta) = \frac{1}{m} \sum_{i=1}^{m} L_{Huber}\left(d(\mathbf{v}_i, \hat{\mathbf{v}}_i); \delta_{shape}\right) \tag{4}$$

The scale loss, L_{scale}, is the Huber loss on the foot length and the overall loss function used to train the network is the *weighted loss* between L_{shape} and L_{scale}:

$$L_{scale} = L_{Huber}(l - \hat{l}; \delta_{scale}) \tag{5}$$

$$L = w_{shape} L_{shape} + w_{scale} L_{scale} \tag{6}$$

Architecture. The model has a 3-stage architecture (Fig. 5): *encoding, combining* and *decoding*. The encoder is given a silhouette and camera pose ($\boldsymbol{\theta}$ and $\mathbf{t}$) as inputs and it computes a 1D feature vector. The encoder can be replicated as many times as there are number of views. Since the parameters of all encoders are shared, memory is saved by running the encoder sequentially over input views. The N feature vectors are combined into a single feature vector by a pooling layer. Finally, the decoder regresses the PCA coefficients, the two deformation scaling factors (k_w and k_h) and foot length through two fully connected layers. Linear activation functions are applied to all 13 output units. The reconstructed shape is obtained by applying the inverse PCA to the coefficients, scaling the vertices horizontally and vertically by k_w and k_h respectively (Eq. 1), and finally scaling the overall foot according to the predicted length. A major advantage of this framework is its ability to take into account any number of images and the prediction is not affected by the order of input views since the features are combined by pooling operations.

The encoder (Fig. 6) consists of two branches: the image branch and camera branch. The silhouette is passed through the image branch which is a CNN based on MobileNet. The top fully connected layer and softmax layer of the MobileNet are removed so that it outputs a $7 \times 7 \times 1024$ tensor. The camera branch computes the sin and cos of the three camera angles ($\boldsymbol{\theta}$), combines them with the camera's position vector ($\mathbf{t}$) and passes them through two fully connected layers. The output of the camera branch is broadcast and concatenated to the image branch. Two further convolutional layers are applied to encode the combined output of the two branches to a single 1D feature vector. Dropout at rate 0.5 is applied to the two fully connected layers in the camera branch as well as the output from each encoder before they are combined in the pooling layer. These layers are added to help mitigate noise in camera pose and encourage the network to do well on all views. By incorporating the camera pose, we want the model to learn which specific views of the foot are responsible for specific parts or features of the foot.

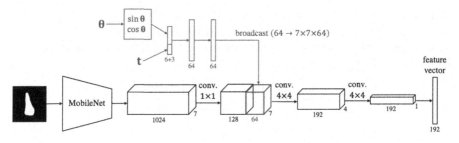

Fig. 6. Encoder architecture.

5   Data

5.1   Synthetic Silhouettes

We generate synthetic foot silhouettes to train the model as it enables us to project the foot with any camera pose desired. We also aim to cover the "foot shape space" more thoroughly by randomly sampling foot shapes in the space, rather than being restricted to those scanned using MVS. A foot silhouette is generated by randomly sampling model parameters, scale and camera pose. The model is then rendered using a perspective projection.

Fig. 7. Examples of randomly sampled foot shapes.

Examples of these randomly generated foot shapes are displayed in Fig. 7. To project the sampled foot mesh, we use a pipeline illustrated in Fig. 8. The camera pose is sampled such that it points approximately at the foot centre. The ranges from which the parameters for silhouette generation are uniformly sampled from are shown in Table 1. For each foot, 7 silhouettes are generated and we ensure that α is roughly uniformly distributed across the 7 views so that different sides of the foot are covered in a set of silhouettes. 12500 silhouette sets are generated and split 75/10/15 into train/val/test. Sample sets are shown in Fig. 9.

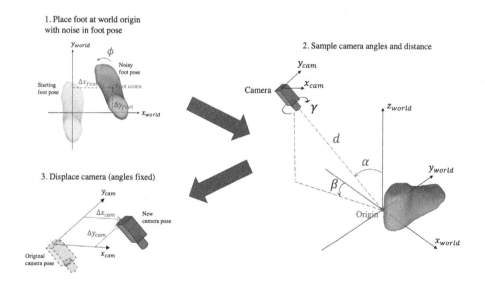

Fig. 8. Pipeline for sampling a foot pose and camera pose. A silhouette is produced by perspective projection of the foot mesh.

Table 1. Ranges of parameters for sampling a foot pose and camera pose using the pipeline in Fig. 8.

Parameter	Range
Foot length	19 to 32 cm
k_w, k_h	0.93 to 1.07
Δx_{foot}, Δy_{foot}	-3 to $+3$ cm
ϕ	$-5°$ to $+5°$
d	45 to 75 cm
α	$-70°$ to $+70°$
β, γ	$-10°$ to $+10°$
Δx_{cam}	-5 to $+5$ cm
Δy_{cam}	-10 to $+10$ cm

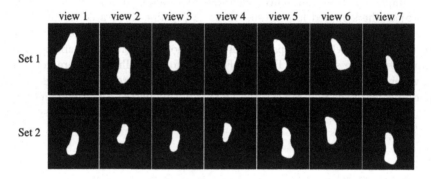

Fig. 9. Sample sets of synthetic silhouettes.

5.2 Real Foot Image Datasets

We collected 2 datasets of real foot images along with camera extrinsics recovered from the smart phone. The 3-view dataset consists of 22 sets of foot images, each containing 3 views (inside, top, outside) of the foot from 11 people. The 20-view dataset consists of 5 sets of foot images, each containing 20 views. For each set of images, the foot is fixed in the same position and the view angles are roughly uniformly distributed from the inside to outside of the foot. The length and width are measured by hand. Camera pose is estimated using the AR features (visual inertial odometry) on current smart phones and foot segmentation is conducted using the pretrained deep neural network described previously.

6   Experiments

Evaluation Metrics. For synthetic silhouettes where the ground truth 3D models of the feet are available, the 3D vertex error (Eq. 2) and width error, after scaling the vertices to a fixed foot length of 25 cm (roughly the length of an average foot), are used for evaluation of the shape performance. The width is defined as the *ball-joint width*, i.e., the 2D distance between the inner and outer extrema (Fig. 2b). For the real image datasets, only the width error is used for shape performance evaluation since we do not have the ground truth 3D vertices. For scale, the results are reported using the l_1-loss between the predicted and ground truth lengths, for both real and synthetic data.

Baseline - Optimisation Method. We compare our model to a traditional 3D optimisation approach of fitting the PCA model to the silhouette data. This approach aims to minimise the overlap of the model projected silhouette with that of the predicted silhouette. We use a differentiable renderer [19] and a silhouette reprojection based on $L2$ distance between the model and predicted silhouettes. This loss function is optimised using Adam [30] jointly across all camera views.

6.1   Shape-Only Model

As an initial experiment, we first test our model for shape reconstruction by removing the scale prediction. This gives us insight into the model's ability to first obtain the correct shape, regardless of scale. The training loss is now only the shape loss L_{shape} (Eq. 4). Since the model is not regressing the foot scale, we centre and scale the foot in the silhouettes such that the foot size relative to the image is fixed. Max-pooling is used for combining the feature vectors from different viewpoints. For each training instance, we sample 3 random views of the same foot. The network is trained using Adam optimiser, batch size of 32, learning rate of 1×10^{-3} and $\delta_{shape} = 3$ mm. The steps per epoch is calculated such that the model on average "sees" every possible combination for every foot.

Table 2. Average vertex error and width error for the shape-only model from different number of views.

Number of views	Vertex error (mm)	Width error (mm)
1	0.9	0.9
2	0.6	0.5
3	0.6	0.4
4	0.5	0.4
5	0.5	0.4
6	0.5	0.4
7	0.5	0.4

On synthetic test data, Table 2 shows that the model achieves very small average errors (<1 mm). For reference, if a model only predicts the mean foot shape, the average errors would be 3.7 mm and 2.6 mm for vertex and width respectively. Even though our model is trained on 3-view inputs, it generalises to other number of viewpoints and the performance generally improves as we increase the number of viewpoints. This is because it is less likely that a part of the foot is hidden when more views are given. As we further increase the number of views, the improvement in vertex accuracy decreases and it eventually converges to a vertex error of 0.5 mm.

The best width error is achieved with only 3 views; further increasing the number of views result in a similar or worse width error. This is because the model is trained to minimise the average vertex error and at any time the model does not know or care about the width error. As more views are given, the model is able to compute a set of PCA coefficients that results in a smaller vertex error, i.e., better overall shape reconstruction, but in return a slight amount of width accuracy is sacrificed.

We can see how the model makes use of different views to predict the foot shape by looking at how the vertex error is distributed across the foot. Figure 10 shows that with just a top-down silhouette, the model tends to produce larger errors around the foot dorsum (top surface of the foot) due to the lack of information of its shape. By incorporating more viewpoints, the overall error is reduced and more evenly distributed across the foot. For both types of input, relatively large error is made on toe and heel regions. This is because the vertices in these areas are more dense and have more variation across different feet.

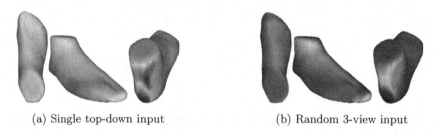

(a) Single top-down input   (b) Random 3-view input

Fig. 10. Vertex error distribution for the model tested on (a) single top-down silhouettes and (b) random 3-view silhouettes. The heatmaps have the same colorscale. (Color figure online)

6.2 Full Model (Shape and Scale)

We now include the length output unit and use the weighted loss (Eq. 6) as training loss. No processing (centering/scaling) is done to the silhouettes. The network is trained on 3-view inputs using Adam optimiser, batch size of 32, $w_{shape} = 1$, $w_{scale} = 0.05$, learning rate $= 1 \times 10^{-3}$, $\delta_{shape} = 3$ mm and $\delta_{scale} = 5$ mm.

Synthetic Test Data. On synthetic test data, our model achieves a vertex error of 1.2 mm, width error of 0.9 mm and length error of 2.1 mm. The length predictions are more accurate than the half-size increments (4.2 mm) in the UK and US shoe sizing systems. Note that there is an increase in the vertex error, from 0.6 mm with the shape-only model. This is mainly due to the fact that the foot is no longer centred in the silhouettes and the size of the foot relative to the image varies, making the task more difficult.

Real Test Data. To optimise the performance on real data, we split the 3-view real foot image dataset into validation and test sets, with 10 and 11 sets of images respectively, and retrained the network using the same set of hyperparameters except that the learning rate is reduced to 5×10^{-4} and early stopping is applied on the *real validation set*. We select the epoch that has the lowest sum of length error and width error on the real validation set as the final model. In addition, we address the domain gap through image augmentation including different degrees and types of blurring for estimating segmentation confidence scores at silhouette periphery, and pixel noise to emulate incorrect segmentation. These augmentations are found to always improve the model performance on real data.

Table 3 shows that there is a large generalisation error going from synthetic to real data for all metrics, which could be due to noise in segmentation and camera pose. The best performance is achieved when the model is trained with max-pooling, and at test time we replace the max-pooling with average-pooling. On synthetic test data, however, doing the same thing would worsen the performance in both the length and shape prediction (length error: from 2.1 to 3.0 mm, vertex error: from 1.2 to 1.5 mm). For the case of synthetic silhouettes, Wiles and Zisserman [23] demonstrated that max-pooling outperforms average-pooling for combining the feature vectors as the former allows the combined features to be jointly recorded by different inputs views and important features from each viewpoint can be passed directly to the decoder so that the model can exploit information from specific views to reconstruct specific parts of the foot. With average-pooling, the important features are averaged out by other views and the model is forced to reconstruct every part of the foot with information from all given views. However for real data, average-pooling outperforms max-pooling because there is a lot more noise in the data (e.g. faulty segmentation/camera calibration). In this case, average-pooling helps reduce the effect of these errors by averaging them out, whereas max-pooling could allow noisy information to flow directly to the decoder.

There is also a big gap between the validation and test performance which is mainly due the small amount of real data available (22 sets of images) and can be overcome by collecting a larger set of data so that the validation results are more reliable.

Table 3. Average length and width errors (mm) on real val/test data.

Trained with	Validation set		Tested with **max-pool**		Tested with **avg-pool**	
	Length error	Width error	Length error	Width error	Length error	Width error
max-pool	5.3	4.4	8.4	4.0	6.5	4.3
avg-pool	5.4	4.2	12.2	3.7	8.3	3.4

6.3 Effect of Silhouette Accuracy

To investigate the error introduced by the imperfect predicted segmentation, we manually segmented 4 sets of foot images from the 3-view real foot image dataset and tested our model (trained with max-pooling) on these ground truth silhouettes. Results are reported in Table 4 and sample reconstructions are displayed in Fig. 11.

In terms of shape, we see from the sample reconstructions that the feet reconstructed using hand-segmented silhouettes are much closer to the actual foot because the shape prediction is heavily influenced by the input silhouettes. For both types of silhouette, the projections of the reconstructed feet fit almost perfectly to the input silhouettes so it is hard for the model to produce an accurate shape prediction when the silhouettes do not represent the actual foot shape due to error by the segmentation network. In terms of length, hand-segmentation in fact worsens the model performance which suggests that there are error sources other than the segmentation network, such as noise in the camera poses and occlusion of the heel by the ankle or leg.

Table 4. Average length and width errors (mm) on 4 sets of test silhouettes for two different segmentation methods (segmentation network in deep network predicted and hand-segmentation), using the model trained with max-pooling.

Pool at test time	Predicted segmentation		Hand segmentation	
	Length error	Width error	Length error	Width error
max-pool	4.5	3.0	5.5	3.8
avg-pool	6.9	5.5	9.1	8.0

6.4 Number of Views

We compare our model with the baseline method on the 20-view real foot image dataset, from 1 to 20 views. For each number of views, the viewpoints are chosen such that the view angles are approximately uniformly distributed. This allows us to analyse the stability of the methods to camera angles. It is found that to achieve good performance consistently, a uniform sample of 3 views is sufficinet for our model whereas the baseline requires at least 6. Table 5 records the mean errors from 6 views onwards which is when both methods have enough views to work at their best. On average, our network outperforms the optimiser in both length and width accuracy.

Table 5. Average length and width errors *from 6 to 20 views* on the 20-view real foot image dataset.

Method	Length error (mm)	Width error (mm)
FootNet (ours)	**4.3 ± 0.4**	**6.9 ± 0.3**
Optimisation	6.4 ± 1.9	7.9 ± 0.5

Prediction Time. For one view, our model and the optimiser take 27 ms and 27000 ms respectively on average to make one reconstruction. For 20 views, our model and the optimiser on average take 435 ms and 98000 ms respectively. The optimiser requires GPUs for its computation whereas our model was tested on

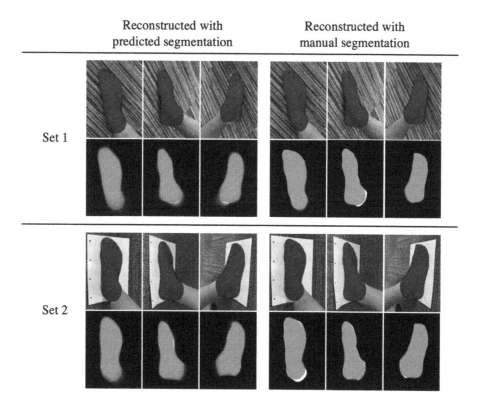

Fig. 11. Sample reconstructions from deep network predicted segmentation (left) and hand segmentation (right). The reconstructed feet are reprojected to the original image and the silhouettes for comparison.

a CPU and is still 2 to 3 orders of magnitude faster as it only requires a single forward pass through the network. This shows that our network is capable of reconstructing the foot using only the computation power of a smart phone in a much quicker time.

7   Conclusion

The aim of this paper is to develop a framework that reconstructs the foot from 2D images on mobile devices. Using PCA, we compress the foot shape to only 10 parameters. We propose a CNN architecture that regresses the shape parameters given multiple foot silhouettes and corresponding camera poses. On synthetic silhouettes, the model achieves very high accuracy (vertex error close to 1 mm and length error of 2 mm) and we demonstrate that it generalises to different number of input views at test time. On real data our model outperforms a classical optimisation-based method both in accuracy and inference speed. Future work will involve improving generalisation of our method to real data.

Acknowledgments. We would like to thank Benjamin Biggs for providing the baseline optimisation code, Stefano Bucciarelli for help with the PCA model construction and TRYA SrL for providing a fraction of their dataset for ground truth 3D images of feet.

References

1. VoxelCare: 3D Laser Foot Scanner. https://www.voxelcare.com/#!/content/3D-Laser-Foot-Scanner. Accessed 24 May 2020
2. Corporation, V.R.: Yeti 3D Scanner. https://vorum.com/yeti-3d-foot-scanner. Accessed 24 May 2020
3. Moons, T., Van Gool, L., Vergauwen, M.: 3D reconstruction from multiple images: part 1 - principles. Found. Trends Comput. Graph. Vis. **4**, 287–404 (2009)
4. Hartley, R., Zisserman, A.: Multiple View Geometry in Computer Vision, 2nd edn. Cambridge University Press, USA (2003)
5. Koyuncu, B., Kullu, K.: Development of an optical 3D scanner based on structured light. In: Proceedings of the 9th WSEAS International Conference on Artificial Intelligence, Knowledge Engineering and Data Bases, pp. 17–22 (2010)
6. Precision3D: Fotoscan 3D Foot Scanner. http://www.precision3d.co.uk/fs.html. Accessed 24 May 2020
7. Kutulakos, K.N., Seitz, S.M.: A theory of shape by space carving. In: ICCV (1999)
8. Tulsiani, S., Zhou, T., Efros, A.A., Malik, J.: Multi-view supervision for single-view reconstruction via differentiable ray consistency. In: CVPR (2017)
9. Tulsiani, S., Efros, A.A., Malik, J.: Multi-view consistency as supervisory signal for learning shape and pose prediction. In: CVPR (2018)
10. Liu, S., Giles, L., Ororbia, A.: Learning a hierarchical latent-variable model of 3D shapes. In: 3DV (2018)
11. Wu, Z., et al.: 3D shapenets: a deep representation for volumetric shapes. In: CVPR (2015)

12. Wu, J., Wang, Y., Xue, T., Sun, X., Freeman, B., Tenenbaum, J.: Marrnet: 3D shape reconstruction via 2.5 d sketches. In: NIPS (2017)
13. Sun, X., et al.: Pix3D: dataset and methods for single-image 3D shape modeling. In: CVPR (2018)
14. Wang, P.S., Liu, Y., Guo, Y.X., Sun, C.Y., Tong, X.: O-CNN: Octree-based convolutional neural networks for 3D shape analysis. ACM Trans. Graph. **36**, 1–11 (2017)
15. Riegler, G., Osman Ulusoy, A., Geiger, A.: Octnet: learning deep 3D representations at high resolutions. In: ICCV (2017)
16. Dai, A., Ruizhongtai Qi, C., Nießner, M.: Shape completion using 3D-encoder-predictor CNNs and shape synthesis. In: CVPR (2017)
17. Cao, Y.P., Liu, Z.N., Kuang, Z.F., Kobbelt, L., Hu, S.M.: Learning to reconstruct high-quality 3D shapes with cascaded fully convolutional networks. In: ECCV (2018)
18. Yang, B., Rosa, S., Markham, A., Trigoni, N., Wen, H.: Dense 3D object reconstruction from a single depth view. IEEE Trans. Pattern Anal. Mach. Intell. **41**, 2820–2834 (2018)
19. Kato, H., Ushiku, Y., Harada, T.: Neural 3D mesh renderer. In: CVPR (2018)
20. Wang, N., Zhang, Y., Li, Z., Fu, Y., Liu, W., Jiang, Y.G.: Pixel2mesh: Generating 3D mesh models from single RGB images. In: ECCV (2018)
21. Dibra, E., Jain, H., Öztireli, C., Ziegler, R., Gross, M.: Hs-nets: estimating human body shape from silhouettes with convolutional neural networks. In: 3DV (2016)
22. Choy, C.B., Xu, D., Gwak, J., Chen, K., Savarese, S.: 3D–r2n2: A unified approach for single and multi-view 3D object reconstruction. In: ECCV (2016)
23. Wiles, O., Zisserman, A.: Silnet : Single-and multi-view reconstruction by learning from silhouettes. In: BMVC (2017)
24. Amstutz, E., Teshima, T., Kimura, M., Mochimaru, M., Saito, H.: PCA based 3D shape reconstruction of human foot using multiple viewpoint cameras. In: ICCV (2008)
25. Lunscher, N., Zelek, J.: Point cloud completion of foot shape from a single depth map for fit matching using deep learning view synthesis. In: ICCV Workshop, pp. 2300–2305 (2017)
26. Howard, A.G., et al.: Mobilenets: efficient convolutional neural networks for mobile vision applications. arXiv preprint arXiv:1704.04861 (2017)
27. Campbell, N.D., Vogiatzis, G., Hernández, C., Cipolla, R.: Using multiple hypotheses to improve depth-maps for multi-view stereo. In: ECCV (2008)
28. Paszke, A., Chaurasia, A., Kim, S., Culurciello, E.: Enet: a deep neural network architecture for real-time semantic segmentation. arXiv preprint arXiv:1606.02147 (2016)
29. Huber, P.J.: Robust estimation of a location parameter. Ann. Math. Statist. **35**, 73–101 (1964)
30. Kingma, D.P., Ba, J.: Adam: a method for stochastic optimization. arXiv preprint arXiv:1412.6980 (2014)

Synthetic-to-Real Domain Adaptation for Lane Detection

Noa Garnett, Roy Uziel, Netalee Efrat, and Dan Levi$^{(\boxtimes)}$

General Motors Technical Center Israel - R&D Labs, Tel Aviv, Israel
{noa.garnett,roy.uziel,netalee.efratsela,dan.levi}@gm.com

Abstract. Accurate lane detection, a crucial enabler for autonomous driving, currently relies on obtaining a large and diverse labeled training dataset. In this work, we explore learning from abundant, randomly generated synthetic data, together with unlabeled or partially labeled target domain data, instead. Randomly generated synthetic data has the advantage of controlled variability in the lane geometry and lighting, but it is limited in terms of photo-realism. This poses the challenge of adapting models learned on the unrealistic synthetic domain to real images. To this end we develop a novel autoencoder-based approach that uses synthetic labels unaligned with particular images for adapting to target domain data. In addition, we explore existing domain adaptation approaches, such as image translation and self-supervision, and adjust them to the lane detection task. We test all approaches in the unsupervised domain adaptation setting in which no target domain labels are available and in the semi-supervised setting in which a small portion of the target images are labeled. In extensive experiments using three different datasets, we demonstrate the possibility to save costly target domain labeling efforts. For example, using our proposed autoencoder approach on the llamas and tuSimple lane datasets, we can almost recover the fully supervised accuracy with only 10% of the labeled data. In addition, our autoencoder approach outperforms all other methods in the semi-supervised domain adaptation scenario.

1 Introduction

Accurate lane detection is a critical enabler for autonomous driving, serving as a primary input for the path planning stage. All current state-of-the-art implementations involve training a single-frame CNN based detector [1–3]. The real-world success of the resulting detector relies on the assumption that the training set reliably represents the operational conditions. This poses the challenge of collecting and labeling images that represent all possible driving scenarios: from highway to urban scenes, in all weather and lighting conditions, covering all lane marking types from all the different geographic regions. Labeling such a

Electronic supplementary material The online version of this chapter (https:// doi.org/10.1007/978-3-030-69544-6_4) contains supplementary material, which is available to authorized users.

© Springer Nature Switzerland AG 2021
H. Ishikawa et al. (Eds.): ACCV 2020, LNCS 12627, pp. 52–67, 2021.
https://doi.org/10.1007/978-3-030-69544-6_4

large and diverse corpus of data is a highly demanding task to say the least. While several highly-diverse on-road datasets were collected and made public, many of them lack lane annotations (e.g. Waymo open dataset [4], nuScenes [5]). Synthetic datasets have also been proposed for training autonomous perception models [6, 7]. Unfortunately, the scene creation is still a manual labor demanding task, but more importantly, lanes are often not inserted as graphical objects but as road texture, and therefore no lane annotation can be automatically extracted.

Recently, [2] introduced a methodology for randomly and efficiently generating synthetic data with lane annotation. This approach has the advantage of generating scenes with high variability in lane topology and 3D geometry, without requiring any manual labor. The caveat lies in the limited variability in the appearance of the lanes and the surrounding scene, and generally in the photo-realism of the resulting images, as can be seen in Fig. 1(a). We propose to leverage this synthetic data generation method, along with unlabeled real-world data, and to perform synthetic-to-real domain adaptation (DA) in order to overcome the appearance gap. This would allow exploiting the variability in lane geometry provided by the synthetic data along with the appearance variability of unlabeled real data.

Although domain adaptation is a well-studied field, it has yet to be applied to lane detection. In this work, we introduce a novel autoencoder-based approach and a new self-supervision objective addressing domain adaptation for the lane detection task. In addition, we explore existing domain adaptation methods by adjusting them to lane detection. We address domain adaptation in two different settings: unsupervised and semi-supervised. In the Unsupervised Domain Adaptation (UDA) setting, training is done with only source domain labeled data and target domain unlabeled data. In the Semi-Supervised Domain Adaptation (SSDA) setting training has additionally access to a small set of labeled examples from the target domain. In both settings, the goal is to learn an accurate model for the target domain, with minimal compromise compared to a fully supervised model.

Our proposed autoencoder-based method, is inspired by a recent study [8], showing that it is feasible to learn human landmark detection from only unlabeled images and unpaired labels. Similarly, we introduce a method that learns to detect lanes using unlabeled images, and a set of ground truth "logical lane images" (Fig. 2(b)), which are not paired with input images. This allows to train a lane detector without even having rendered synthetic data, but with only "logical" top view images of valid lane markings. Based on the assumption that there is a strong correlation between the lanes in a scene and the gradients in the image, we train an autoencoder of the image gradients that passes through a "lane image" bottleneck. Using adversarial training, we force the appearance of the resulting lane image to resemble that of the ground truth lane images.

Self-supervision leverages automatically generated supervision on auxiliary tasks related to the objective task to force the creation of useful intermediate network representations. To this end, we introduce a new self-supervision task, which improves performance on lane detection. We then use target domain self-supervision together with source domain supervised training for domain adaptation. Finally, we implemented three additional approaches that require some adjustment to the lane detection task: image-to-image translation [9], feature distribution alignment using adversarial learning [10] and central moment discrepancy [11]. We evaluate all methods on three datasets: tuSimple [3], llamas [12] and 3DLanes [13]. We show that applying domain adaptation, using several of the tested methods, significantly improves performance on the target domain, as can be observed in Fig. 1(b). We also show that it improves performance in the semi-supervised setting. In particular, our autoencoder approach nearly closes the accuracy gap on two out of the three datasets compared to full supervision with only a tenth of the labels. To summarize, our main contributions are:

- Showing that synthetic-to-real domain adaptation can significantly improve lane detection performance when there is little or no target domain labels
- Introducing a novel autoencoder-based DA approach for lane detection that achieves state-of-the-art performance in the SSDA setting on all tested datasets
- Introducing a new self-supervision objective for lane detection
- Providing a comprehensive comparison and evaluation of proposed and existing methods in both UDA and SSDA settings.

Fig. 1. (a) Examples of images from our source domain, consisting of synthetic images randomly generated using the methodology of [2]. (b) Lane detection results on an example from the 3DLanes dataset [13]. **Top:** result of a model trained with synthetic data without domain adaptation. **Bottom:** After domain adaptation using the self-supervision objective described in Sect. 3. Each result is shown in top-view, as obtained directly from our network, and back-projected to regular view on the right. The result is shown by highlighting in red the detected lane segments for tiles with confidence above a minimum threshold. The brightness of the segment color reflects its confidence score. (Color figure online)

2   Related Work

There has been extensive prior work on unsupervised domain adaptation. The general idea is to align the distributions of the source and target domains at some level of the representation. This can be accomplished by two general strategies. The first strategy attempts to align the two domains at an intermediate feature-level representation. One way to achieve this is to directly minimize the discrepancy between the two distributions using measures such as maximum mean discrepancy (MMD) [14,15] and central moment distance (CMD) [11]. Another approach for bringing representations closer is based on adversarial learning [10,16]. The idea is to train an adversarial discriminator that distinguishes between the two domains, encouraging the generator, in this case, the feature embedding network, to generate indistinguishable feature maps. Feature embedding weights may be shared between the domains [10] or kept separated [16]. Several additional variants of this approach have been proposed: [17] condition the adversarial game not only on the embedding but also on the final output, [18] align the features at multiple levels, and [19] use the discriminator over images generated from the embedding. Our implementation for this approach (**Embedding GAN**) uses a adversarial learning on the feature embedding and shared weights as in [10].

The second strategy uses image-to-image translation to impose alignment at the raw image level. Image translation methods [20,21] learn the mapping between two image domains, and is mainly used for style transfer, object transfiguration, season transfer, and photo enhancement. In the context of domain adaptation, the image translation generates a target domain image from a raw source domain one, allowing to train a model in the supervised setting on a"target-like" dataset [9,22–24]. As shown in [9], the two strategies can be combined to improve performance further. For our task we implement **image translation** using CycleGAN [20].

Self-supervised learning uses an auxiliary task generated automatically from the data itself to train feature representations that would hopefully be useful for the end-goal task. Many auxiliary tasks have been proposed, such as jigsaw puzzle solving [25], image rotation prediction [26], and contrastive predictive coding [27]. Typically, self-supervision is applied to large sets of unlabeled data as a pre-train stage before supervised training [28]. Naturally, as concurrently proposed by [29], self-supervision can be used for unsupervised domain adaptation. The idea is to train the feature embedding on the supervised task using the labeled source dataset, and on the auxiliary task using the unlabeled target images. Assuming the correlation between the tasks, the hope is that the feature embedding will encode the correlated information similarly for both domains. In [29], the feature embedding is further aligned by training the self-supervision task on the source domain.

Compared to the research in domain adaptation for *classification*, much less attention has been paid to domain adaptation for other, more complex, computer vision tasks. Several studies address object detection [30,31], monocular depth estimation [32,33] and semantic segmentation [9,24,34–36]. To our best knowledge, domain adaptation for lane detection has yet to be addressed. While synthetic-to-real adaptation for automotive perception has been previously studied [9,34–37], it was always with manually created synthetic datasets (e.g. vKITTI [7], SYNTHIA [38]) as opposed to the random generation approach we adopt from [2].

3   Methods

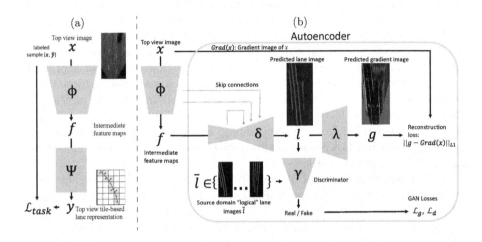

Fig. 2. (a) **Base architecture for lane detection.** $f = \phi(x)$ are intermediate feature maps computed from the top view. $y = \psi(f)$ represents the detected lanes in the tiles representation [13]. This base architecture, used also in inference, is trained end to end in the fully supervised setting. (b) **Our proposed autoencoder architecture for training with unlabeled examples and unpaired top view lane images.** The networks ϕ, δ, λ are trained to minimize the reconstruction loss while $\delta \circ \phi$ and γ are adverserially trained as a generator and discriminator respectively, driving the generated lane image l to resemble ground truth annotations $\bar{l}$. Note that $\delta \circ \phi$ forms an hourglass architecture including skip connections. In g the blue pixels are not considered in the reconstruction loss using the heuristics described in Sect. 3. At inference the network can output $\delta \circ \phi(x)$, which may be additionally transformed to the tile representation using a pretrained transformer network (See Sect. 4 for more details). (Color figure online)

We start by warping the original image I to a virtual top view image $x \in \mathcal{X} = \mathbb{R}^{3 \times H' \times W'}$ using an Inverse Perspective Mapping (IPM), which is a homography defined by the camera's position relative to the local ground plane, its intrinsic parameters and additional parameters embodied by H' and W'. Our lane detection network gets x and outputs a lane representation y describing the lanes in top view. Working in top view has the advantage of translation

invariance, an important property for convolutional networks, and is also beneficial to subsequent modules such as lane clustering and tracking [2,13]. We use
the semi-local tile-based representation, recently proposed in [13], that divides
the top view into $H \times W$ non-overlapping tiles, each roughly corresponding
1.6 by 1.6 m in the real world. For each tile (i, j) the network outputs the
confidence $(b_{(i,j)} \in [0,1])$ that there is a lane passing through the tile, and
regresses using a set of continuous outputs $\mathbf{p}_{(i,j)} \in \mathbb{R}^9$ its position and orientation relative to the rectangle's center, assuming that locally the lane is
linear. We follow the exact representation of [13] except for omitting the elevation offset which is used for detection in 3D. The output is then expressed as:
$y = \{(b_{(i,j)}, \mathbf{p}_{(i,j)}) | i \in [1, \ldots, H], j \in [1, \ldots, W]\} \in \mathcal{Y} = R^{10 \times H \times W}$.

Our base network architecture, used in inference, is illustrated in Fig. 2(a).
It is convenient to present the base network as composed of two stages. First,
an embedding convolutional neural network $\phi : \mathcal{X} \mapsto \mathcal{F} = \mathbb{R}^{C \times H \times W}$ generates
an intermediate feature map representation f, with the same spatial dimensions
as the output, and C channels. Then, an additional convolutional network $\psi :
\mathcal{F} \mapsto \mathcal{Y}$ computes the output y from the intermediate feature maps f. Given
a dataset $\mathcal{D}^l$ consisting of labeled examples $(x, \hat{y}) \in \mathcal{X}, \mathcal{Y}$, the supervised task
function loss is:

$$\mathcal{L}_{task} = \sum_{(x,\hat{y}) \in \mathcal{D}^l} \mathcal{L}_{tiles}(\psi \circ \phi(x), \hat{y})$$

Where $\mathcal{L}_{tiles}(y, \hat{y})$ sums the loss across all tiles for a single output y and ground
truth $\hat{y}$ as described in [13] omitting the elevation component. Note also that
$\hat{y}$ is obtained by projecting *image annotations* to top-view using the same IPM
applied to the image.

In the **fully supervised** setting, we simply have a labeled dataset $\mathcal{D}^l$ and
train the base network with the task loss function $\mathcal{L}_{task}$. In the **unsupervised
domain adaptation** (UDA) setting, we have two datasets, a labeled source
domain dataset $\mathcal{D}_S^l$, and an unlabeled set of images $\mathcal{D}_T^u$ from the target domain.
Finally, in the **semi-supervised domain adaptation** (SSDA) setting we have
in addition, compared to the UDA setting, a small set of labeled target domain
images $\mathcal{D}_T^l$. We next describe our proposed autoencoder (Sect. 3.1) and self-
supervision (Sect. 3.2) approaches followed by a short description of the existing
methods we additionally tested in Sects. 3.3 and 3.4.

3.1   Autoencoder Approach

Our proposed autoencoder approach is inspired by the human landmark detection approach of [8], in which a landmark detector is trained with unlabeled
target domain images, and unpaired ground truth annotations. In our application, this approach is based on the task-specific assumption that in the road
area lane markings correlate with image gradients. Essentially, we train a detector to generate, from an unlabeled input image x, a gray-scale "lane image" that
satisfies two constraints: (1) it looks like a valid ground truth image of lanes
and (2) it holds the information required to reconstruct the original gradients

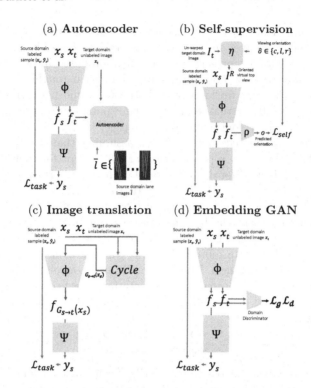

Fig. 3. Architectures for the different domain adaptation approaches in the UDA setting. See Sect. 3 for further details.

in the image. The first constraint is imposed by a discriminator, γ, which tries to distinguish between the generated lane image l and unpaired ground truth lane annotations. The second is imposed by a decoder that tries to reconstruct the original image gradients $Grad(x)$ from l. The entire approach, illustrated in Fig. 2(b), relies on the assumption, that the natural candidate for the encoded image l satisfying both constraints is that of the lanes in the scene.

Formally, our training process gets as input the unlabeled target domain images $\mathcal{D}_T^u$ and a set of source domain ground truth "lane images", $\mathcal{D}_S^{up} = \{\bar{l}\}$, as described next. Given an input image $x \in D_T^u$ and its corresponding feature maps $f = \phi(x)$, an encoder, $\delta : \mathcal{F} \mapsto \mathcal{I}_L = \mathbb{R}^{W/4, H/4}$, generates a gray-scale "lane image" $l = \delta(f) \in \mathcal{I}_L$. The discriminator, γ, is trained to distinguish between the generated lane images and the ground truth lane images. The decoder λ, generates an image g, trained to reconstruct $Grad(x)$ using an L_1 loss:

$$\mathcal{L}_{reconstruct} = \sum_{x \in \mathcal{D}_T^u} \|\lambda \circ \delta \circ \phi(x) - Grad(x)\|_1$$

The GAN loss functions consist of the discriminator loss function $\mathcal{L}_d$, minimized for the discriminator (γ) parameters, and the generator loss function $\mathcal{L}_g$, minimized for the parameters of the generator which in our case is $\delta \circ \phi$. We

left   center   right

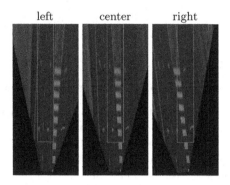

Fig. 4. Self-supervision task for lane detection. Depicted is the same image transformed for the right, center and left viewing directions. The network then gets the central rectangle (outlined in blue) and has to predict the viewing angle it was generated with. (Color figure online)

chose $\mathcal{L}_g, \mathcal{L}_d$ following the Wasserstein GAN with gradient penalty (WGAN-GP) suggested by [39]. Training the network alternates between two objectives: minimizing the discriminator loss $\mathcal{L}_d$ over the parameters of the discriminator, γ, and minimizing a combination of the reconstruction and generator losses $\alpha L_{reconstruct} + L_g$ over the parameters of δ, ϕ and λ.

One hurdle to overcome in this approach is the simple fact that not all gradients in the top-view image $Grad(x)$ can be explained by the lane image, with edges belonging to other road markings, on-road objects, sidewalks and even the lane mark dashing themselves. We implement several heuristics to mitigate the effect of all other factors: we apply a car detector (YOLOv3 [40]) and mark the detected pixels to be ignored in the reconstruction loss. Similarly, we ignore everything outside a dilated convex hull around the lanes detected in l. Finally, as can be seen in Fig. 2(b), the decoder, λ, manages to reconstruct other road markings and lane dash positions, by hiding appearance ques within l, a phenomena observed by [8] as well. This base architecture can be trained in an **unpaired labels** setting, i.e. without having any source domain images, but with only the set of unpaired ground truth lane images from the source domain, $\mathcal{D}_S^{up}$. While in this setting the method converged at times (See result example in the appendix), in general it is highly unstable. This instability was solved by adding direct task supervision using the source dataset in the UDA setting as described next.

In the UDA setting we additionally have source domain images paired with their labels, $\mathcal{D}_S^l$. The data from source domain has, thus, two roles while training - pairs of images and labels are used to minimize $\mathcal{L}_{task}$, and labels are also used to generate lane images $\bar{l}$ for the autoencoder adversarial learning. Figure 3(a) illustrates this UDA architecture. Notice that the feature embedding, ϕ, is shared between the two domains, and hence is the network in which domain adaptation occurs. On the other hand, the high level reasoning network (ψ) producing the final lane result, sees only source domain images, and hence expects the feature maps f to be domain invariant. We follow this decomposition for all our tested domain adaptation methods.

3.2   Self-supervision by Viewing Orientation Prediction

In self-supervision it is important to find an auxiliary task that will train a representation informative for the end-goal task. To this end, we introduce a new self-supervision task illustrated in Fig. 4. The basic idea is to generate one of three viewing angles of the scene and let the network predict which one it is. Since the vehicle orientation is commonly aligned with the lanes, predicting the camera viewing direction is strongly related to the capability to correctly detect the lanes. Formally, each un-warped image I is transformed to a virtual top view according to a selected orientation $\hat{o}$: either the regular central one (c), or one of two additional views in which the camera is virtually panned by 5 degrees to the left (l) or to the right (r). We then crop from the resulting top-view a rectangular image from a fixed area in the center of the view. This orientation dependent transformation, η, is equivalent, up to image sampling differences, to cropping an oriented rectangle from the top-view image x. The self-supervision task is then to predict the orientation o from the cropped rectangle I_r. To this end we train a small classifier network ρ on top of the embedding features: $o = \rho \circ \phi \circ \eta(I, \hat{o})$. The self-supervision objective function $\mathcal{L}_{self}$ is the cross-entropy loss for the three-way classification task. In the UDA setting we train using the self-supervision objective by minimizing $\mathcal{L}_{self}$ for the unlabeled target images and $\mathcal{L}_{task}$ for the labeled source images, as illustrated in Fig. 3.

3.3   Image Translation

As proposed in the Cycada framework for UDA [9], we use CycleGAN [20] for image-to-image translation. Figure 3(c) illustrates the approach. Source images x_s are mapped to target images x_t. We slightly abuse notations for simplicity because here x_s, x_t are the original unwarped images, not in top-view. A discriminator γ_t and generator $G_{s \rightarrow t}$ are trained using the loss:

$$\mathcal{L}_{\text{GAN}}(G_{s \rightarrow t}, \gamma_t) = \min_{G_{s \rightarrow t}} \max_{\gamma_t} \left(\sum_{x_t \in \mathcal{D}_t^u} [\log \gamma_t(x_t)] + \sum_{x_s \in \mathcal{D}_s^l} [\log(1 - \gamma_t(G_{s \rightarrow t}(x_s)))] \right)$$

A discriminator γ_s and generator $G_{t \rightarrow s}$ are trained analogously.

As in CycleGAN [20], cycle-consistency loss is used to ensure image content is preserved while translating the original image. This allows using the source labels y_s with the translated source images, $G_{s \rightarrow t}(x_s)$, to minimize the task loss, $\mathcal{L}_{task}$. We optimize the task loss in a second stage over the translated images (transformed to top-view). Combined single-stage training of the CycleGAN and task loss did not improve performance. We also tried to combine feature-level distribution matching as proposed in the Cycada framework [9], but did not gain any accuracy improvement.

3.4   Feature-Level Distribution Matching

We chose implementing a GAN approach [10] and the Central Moment Discrepancy CMD [11] for feature-level distribution matching. The goal is to push the distribution of the feature map representations for the source domain (f_s) and the target domain (f_t) towards one another. In the **embedding GAN** framework, we train a discriminator to distinguish between the domain of different examples from the feature embedding and a generator, in our case the feature embedding function ϕ, to fool the discriminator. Again, we use the GAN loss functions $\mathcal{L}_g, \mathcal{L}_d$ following the WGAN-GP formulation [39]. In the UDA setting, $\mathcal{L}_{task}$ and $\mathcal{L}_g$ are simultaneously minimized over the source images. Figure 3(d) illustrates this approach. In the **CMD** approach the GAN is replaced by a distance loss on the first two central moments between the two distributions as in [11]. Details for the latter approach are brought in the appendix.

4   Experiments

We test the various approaches for domain adaptation on three different lane detection benchmarks. In each experiment, we set the synthetic dataset as the source domain, and one of the three benchmarks as the target domain. Each training session is run for a fixed number of iterations. In the semi-supervised setting, we choose a **labeled subset** of the training data (roughly 10%), consisting of one or several, separate driving sessions.

4.1   Datasets

Synthetic Dataset. In all our experiments, we follow the methodology proposed in [2] to generate a synthetic dataset as the source domain. Images are generated by randomly drawing the parameters for each scene using the generation method from [2] (See examples in Fig. 1(a)). What is unique about this methodology is its simplicity. As opposed to manually or semi-manually generated synthetic datasets such as [7,38], this methodology uses a very small set of graphical assets and instead achieves scene variability by randomly varying lane topology and geometry. In this sense, it can be viewed as "free data" which can be generated using a simple algorithm and an open-source graphic engine. For each target domain, we generated 50K examples using the same scene parameters, but with camera intrinsic and extrinsic parameters roughly adjusted to the target domain. In our experiments generating more images did not result in accuracy gains. This may be due to the limited variability of the appearance in our synthetic data, or due to the limited variability of the lane geometry in the target domains.

tuSimple. The tuSimple lane dataset [3] consists of 3,626 training and 2,782 test images in mostly highway scenarios. While relatively small and not very diverse, we chose it for being the most studied. We report results on the test set.

llamas. The llamas lane-marker dataset [12] is a newer, much larger dataset, consisting of over 100K labeled images. Created from 14 highway recordings of around 25 km each, together with high accuracy maps in a fully automatic process, it is one of the largest datasets available today. As labels are not available for the test set, we show the evaluation results on a validation set, which consists of a driving session not used during training.

3DLanes. The 3DLanes [13] dataset is the most recent and most diverse dataset among the three. It contains 330000 images labeled in a semi-automated process, in highway and rural environments. Again, we report results on the validation set.

4.2 Evaluation Metrics

Segment-Based Evaluation. In [13], evaluation is preformed only after lane-level clustering. In this study, the goal is to compare the different DA methods directly, and therefore we refrain from applying post-processing methods that can skew the results. For this purpose, we propose a direct tile-representation evaluation formulation. The segment-based evaluation follows the principles of object detection evaluation, where detected lane segments are matched to ground truth ones, and Precision-Recall curves are computed for different matching criteria.

For a single image, the input for the evaluation is an unordered set SEG_{out} comprising of all output lane segments $\mathbf{p}$ (with corresponding detection confidence score b), and the set of all ground truth lane segments obtained using the same representation $SEG_{gt} = \{\hat{\mathbf{p}}\}$. We first compute a symmetric lane segment distance $seg\_dist(\mathbf{p}, \hat{\mathbf{p}})$ for all segment pairs $(\mathbf{p} \in SEG_{out}, \hat{\mathbf{p}} \in SEG_{gt})$, reflecting a geometric distance between the segments in the top view (see appendix for a detailed formulation of seg_dist). We then use the Hungarian algorithm [41] to find a minimum distance matching between the two sets of lane segments. Given a maximum distance seg_dist_{max} (analogous to maximum IoU in object detection), We compute the Recall-Precision (RP) curve, considering all segment matches (in all the test images) with $seg\_dist < seg\_dist_{max}$, by iterating over the confidence values (b) of the detected segments. Each RP curve is summarized as the Average Precision (AP). Our final evaluation metric, the mean Average Precision (mAP), is computed as the average AP for five different maximum matching distances: $seg\_dist_{max} \in \{10\,\mathrm{cm}, 20\,\mathrm{cm}, 30\,\mathrm{cm}, 40\,\mathrm{cm}, 50\,\mathrm{cm}\}$. These distances correspond to real-world distances in the road plane.

Lane-Based Evaluation. For completeness, we also compute the lane-based evaluation metric used in the tuSimple benchmark [3]. This metric requires a single detection per lane, and hence further post-processing, namely clustering of output tiles. To this end, we deploy a simple, heuristic clustering algorithm described in the appendix. In this study, there are several disadvantages to using it. A partial list includes:

- it is indirect by relying on an additional component - the clustering
- it evaluates performance in the image plane and not in top view as our method outputs

– it assumes a known number of lanes in the scene
– we observed that in practice that it is less correlated with performance of the detector

4.3   Implementation Details

All the implemented modules are convolution neural networks. The feature embedding function, ϕ, is based on the VGG architecture [42]. All experiments were run from random initialization for a pre-defined number of iterations. We use the ADAM optimizer [43] without weight decay. For most methods we observed a non-negligible variability in performance between training iterations, even towards the end of each training session. To reduce the effect of this phenomena, all the results we report are averaged over 5 different snapshots 100 iterations apart at the end of the session. The remaining architecture and training protocol details are provided in the appendix.

4.4   Results

Table 1 summarizes our results on each of the three datasets. The first row shows the **fully supervised** result, which serves as the upper bound for all other tested methods. Compared with state-of-the-art (96.6%, [1]) our base supervised method without any bells and whistles reaches 95.1% on the tuSimple benchmark using the tuSimple lane-based evaluation metrics. All the results in Table 1 use our mAP metric. Apparent from the experiments is that the llamas and 3DLanes datasets are indeed more difficult compared to the tuSimple. The **synthetic only** model is trained with the synthetic labeled data without performing any adaptation to the target domain. Of all tested methods, it gives the poorest results due to the noticeable, significant domain gap that can be observed in Fig. 1. This model serves as the baseline for all UDA methods.

Unsupervised Domain Adaptation. In the UDA setting, The baseline-gap (BG) column, specifies the portion of the accuracy gap between the **fully supervised** and the **synthetic only** models, closed by the corresponding method. From the five domain adaptation method tested, three methods, namely **self-supervision (S), image translation (IT)** and **autoencoder (AE)**, gained significant improvements over the non-adapted baseline (**synthetic only**). The remaining two methods, **CMD** and **embedding GAN** gave worse results in most experiments. Among the three leading methods, performance is similar, with slight advantages to one over the other in different experiments. We also tried all combinations of these three methods, with some combinations bringing small additional improvements. Details on the training strategy for combined domain adaptation methods are in the appendix. On the tuSimple and 3DLanes benchmarks the **image-translation** method was the single best performing method while on llamas **self-supervision** performed best. Different combinations of the three leading methods seem to further improve performance, and combining all three (**AE+IT+S**), performed best on two out of the three

Table 1. Results on the tuSimple [3], llamas [12] and 3DLanes [2] datasets using the mean Average Precision (mAP) using the **segment-based** evaluation. Values in the column "**%lbl. data**" correspond to the percent of labeled data *from the respective target domain* used by each method. The "**Syn. data**" column specifies whether synthetic data was used in training. **Unsupervised domain adaptation:** rows in the section marked **UDA** correspond to unsupervised domain adaptation experiments. The BG% (Baseline Gap) for these methods measures the percent of the gap closed between the **synthetic only** and the **fully supervised** mAP: BG(**method**) = (mAP(**method**) − mAP(**synthetic only**))/(mAP(**fully supervised**) − mAP(**synthetic only**)). The best single method and best method combination are marked in bold. **Semi-supervised domain adaptation:** rows in the section marked **SSDA** correspond to semi-supervised domain adaptation experiments. The BG% (Baseline Gap) for these methods measures the percent of the gap closed between the **small+syn. supervision** and the **fully supervised** mAP: BG(**method**) = (mAP(**method**) − mAP(**small+syn. supervision**))/(mAP(**fully supervised**) − mAP(**small+syn. supervision**)). The best single method and best method combination are marked in bold.

		%lbl. data	Syn. data	tuSimple		llamas		3DLanes	
				mAP%	BG%	mAP%	BG%	mAP%	BG%
	fully supervised	100	−	81.1	100	73.2	100	74.5	100
	synthetic only	−	✓	60.5	0	47.8	0	53.8	0
UDA	Autoencoder	−	✓	67.7	35.0	56.0	32.3	57.8	19.1
	Image translation	−	✓	**72.0**	**55.7**	62.3	57.3	**59.3**	**26.5**
	Self supervision	−	✓	66.3	27.9	**63.4**	**61.6**	58.1	20.5
	CMD	−	✓	62.7	10.6	51.9	15.9	55.7	9.0
	Embedding GAN	−	✓	52.1	0	37.8	0	31.9	0
	AE+IT	−	✓	73.4	62.5	65.6	70.0	59.6	27.8
	AE+S	−	✓	70.1	46.3	63.7	62.6	59.7	28.7
	IT+S	−	✓	72.4	57.8	65.3	69.1	60.1	**30.6**
	AE+IT+S	−	✓	**77.1**	**80.5**	**66.0**	**71.6**	59.5	27.5
	small supervision	10	−	74.4	−	60.1	−	56.9	−
	self-sup. w/o syn	10	−	75.2	−	68.6	−	60.1	−
	small+syn. supervision	10	✓	77.5	0	65.5	0	62.0	0
SSDA	Autoencoder	10	✓	**79.3**	**50.0**	**70.5**	**65.6**	**66.9**	**39.0**
	Image translation	10	✓	78.4	25.0	69.1	47.1	64.2	17.5
	Self supervision	10	✓	77.1	0	70.2	61.1	64.0	16.0
	AE+IT	10	✓	78.8	37.7	70.3	63.4	66.2	33.3
	AE+S	10	✓	77.6	4.6	**70.7**	**68.3**	65.2	25.6
	IT+S	10	✓	77.8	8.9	70.1	59.6	65.8	30.4
	AE+IT+S	10	✓	77.7	5.2	70.4	64.5	66.6	36.7

datasets closing more than 70% of the baseline-gap. Notably, in all experiments, training with self-supervision was more stable and reproducible compared with the two competing methods that rely on adversarial training.

Semi-supervised. In this setting we have roughly 10% of the target domain labels. We start with the simplest option, **small supervision**, in which we train a supervised model using this small portion of target domain data. Interestingly, adding labeled synthetic data (**small+syn. supervision**) to the train set, significantly improves performance for all three datasets even without domain adaptation. The latter serves as the baseline for all semi-supervised domain adaptation methods, and used to compute the *BG* measure. In contrast with the other methods, self-supervision does not require source domain data, but can exploit unlabeled target domain images. Our experiments show that this method, **self-sup. w/o syn**, improves accuracy in two out of the three benchmarks.

Semi-supervised Domain Adaptation. As in the UDA setting, we evaluated all domain adaptation methods and combinations, but this time with an extra portion of labeled target domain data. As in the UDA setting we observed inferior performance for the **CMD** and the **embedding GAN** methods, omitted in Table 1 for brevity. As expected the additional labeled data improves the resulting accuracy for each method compared to the UDA setting. Our proposed autoencoder approach outperforms all other single methods on all datasets and all method combinations except for one - **AE+S** on llamas. On tuSimple and llamas the autoencoder approach respectively delivers 1.8% and 2.7% mAP less than the fully supervised model. The practical implication of this result is that using our approach, sacrificing this small loss in accuracy provides a ten fold saving in data annotation. We also note that each experiment we present requires a significant computational effort, and therefore a systematic study of semi-supervision with different amounts of labeling is beyond the scope of this study.

5 Conclusions

We showed that it is possible to improve lane detection when labeled data availability is limited using domain adaptation from random synthetic data. To this end we introduced a new autoencoder approach for domain adaptation and a new task-specific self-supervision objective. We further explored the different existing domain adaptation approaches and their effectiveness for the lane detection task. While these findings have practical implications in autonomous driving research, we suggest further study beyond the scope of this work: experimenting with varying amounts of supervised data in the semi-supervised setting, exploring the effect of the complexity of the synthetic data on the final results, and adapting the detector for lanes in *3D*.

References

1. Hou, Y., Ma, Z., Liu, C., Loy, C.C.: Learning lightweight lane detection CNNs by self attention distillation. In: ICCV, pp. 1013–1021 (2019)
2. Garnett, N., Cohen, R., Pe'er, T., Lahav, R., Levi, D.: 3D-lanenet: end-to-end 3D multiple lane detection. In: ICCV, pp. 2921–2930 (2019)
3. (http://benchmark.tusimple.ai, lane challenge)
4. Sun, P., et al.: Scalability in perception for autonomous driving: Waymo open dataset. CoRR abs/1912.04838 (2019)

5. Caesar, H., et al.: nuscenes: a multimodal dataset for autonomous driving. arXiv preprint arXiv:1903.11027 (2019)
6. Gaidon, A., Wang, Q., Cabon, Y., Vig, E.: Virtual worlds as proxy for multi-object tracking analysis. In: CVPR, pp. 4340–4349 (2016)
7. Gaidon, A., Wang, Q., Cabon, Y., Vig, E.: Virtualworlds as proxy for multi-object tracking analysis. In: CVPR, pp. 4340–4349, IEEE Computer Society (2016)
8. Jakab, T., Gupta, A., Bilen, H., Vedaldi, A.: Learning landmarks from unaligned data using image translation. CoRR abs/1907.02055 (2019)
9. Hoffman, J., et al.: Cycada: cycle consistent adversarial domain adaptation. In: ICML (2018)
10. Ganin, Y., Lempitsky, V.: Unsupervised domain adaptation by backpropagation. In: ICML. Volume 37 of ICML 2015, pp. 1180–1189, JMLR.org (2015)
11. Zellinger, W., Grubinger, T., Lughofer, E., Natschläger, T., Saminger-Platz, S.: Central moment discrepancy (CMD) for domain-invariant representation learning. In: 5th International Conference on Learning Representations, ICLR 2017, Toulon, France, 24–26 April 2017, Conference Track Proceedings, OpenReview.net (2017)
12. Behrendt, K., Soussan, R.: Unsupervised labeled lane markers using maps. In: ICCV (2019)
13. Efrat, N., Bluvstein, M., Garnett, N., Levi, D., Oron, S., Shlomo, B.E.: Semi-local 3D lane detection and uncertainty estimation. CoRR abs/2003.05257 (2020)
14. Bousmalis, K., Trigeorgis, G., Silberman, N., Krishnan, D., Erhan, D.: Domain separation networks. In: NIPS, pp. 343–351, Curran Associates, Inc., (2016)
15. Long, M., Cao, Y., Wang, J., Jordan, M.I.: Learning transferable features with deep adaptation networks. In: ICML. Volume 37 of ICML 2015, pp. 97–105, JMLR.org (2015)
16. Tzeng, E., Hoffman, J., Darrell, T., Saenko, K.: Adversarial discriminative domain adaptation. In: CVPR (2017)
17. Long, M., Cao, Z., Wang, J., Jordan, M.I.: Conditional adversarial domain adaptation. In: Bengio, S., Wallach, H., Larochelle, H., Grauman, K., Cesa-Bianchi, N., Garnett, R. (eds.) NIPS, pp. 1640–1650 (2018)
18. Lahiri, A., Agarwalla, A., Biswas, P.K.: Unsupervised domain adaptation for learning eye gaze from a million synthetic images: an adversarial approach. CoRR abs/1810.07926 (2018)
19. Sankaranarayanan, S., Balaji, Y., Castillo, C.D., Chellappa, R.: Generate to adapt: aligning domains using generative adversarial networks. CoRR abs/1704.01705 (2017)
20. Zhu, J.Y., Park, T., Isola, P., Efros, A.A.: Unpaired image-to-image translation using cycle-consistent adversarial networks. In: ICCV, pp. 2223–2232 (2017)
21. Huang, X., Belongie, S.: Arbitrary style transfer in real-time with adaptive instance normalization. In: ICCV, pp. 1501–1510 (2017)
22. Taigman, Y., Polyak, A., Wolf, L.: Unsupervised cross-domain image generation. In: ICLR, OpenReview.net (2017)
23. Bousmalis, K., Silberman, N., Dohan, D., Erhan, D., Krishnan, D.: Unsupervised pixel-level domain adaptation with generative adversarial networks. In: CVPR, pp. 95–104, IEEE Computer Society (2017)
24. Chen, Y.C., Lin, Y.Y., Yang, M.H., Huang, J.B.: Crdoco: Pixel-level domain transfer with cross-domain consistency (2019)
25. Noroozi, M., Favaro, P.: Unsupervised learning of visual representations by solving jigsaw puzzles. In: Leibe, B., Matas, J., Sebe, N., Welling, M. (eds.) ECCV 2016. LNCS, vol. 9910, pp. 69–84. Springer, Cham (2016). https://doi.org/10.1007/978-3-319-46466-4_5

26. Gidaris, S., Singh, P., Komodakis, N.: Unsupervised representation learning by predicting image rotations. In: ICLR (2018)
27. van den Oord, A., Li, Y., Vinyals, O.: Representation learning with contrastive predictive coding. CoRR abs/1807.03748 (2018)
28. Hénaff, O.J., Razavi, A., Doersch, C., Eslami, S.M.A., van den Oord, A.: Data-efficient image recognition with contrastive predictive coding. CoRR abs/1905.09272 (2019)
29. Sun, Y., Tzeng, E., Darrell, T., Efros, A.A.: Unsupervised domain adaptation through self-supervision. CoRR abs/1909.11825 (2019)
30. Chen, Y., Li, W., Sakaridis, C., Dai, D., Van Gool, L.: Domain adaptive faster R-CNN for object detection in the wild. In: CVPR (2018)
31. Zhu, X., Pang, J., Yang, C., Shi, J., Lin, D.: Adapting object detectors via selective cross-domain alignment. In: CVPR, pp. 687–696 (2019)
32. Abarghouei, A.A., Breckon, T.P.: Real-time monocular depth estimation using synthetic data with domain adaptation via image style transfer. In: CVPR 2018, pp. 2800–2810, IEEE Computer Society (2018)
33. Zheng, C., Cham, T.J., Cai, J.: T2net: synthetic-to-realistic translation for solving single-image depth estimation tasks. In: ECCV, pp. 767–783 (2018)
34. Hong, W., Wang, Z., Yang, M., Yuan, J.: Conditional generative adversarial network for structured domain adaptation. In: CVPR, pp. 1335–1344 (2018)
35. Zhang, Y., Qiu, Z., Yao, T., Liu, D., Mei, T.: Fully convolutional adaptation networks for semantic segmentation. Proceedings of CVPR (2018)
36. Sankaranarayanan, S., Balaji, Y., Jain, A., Lim, S., Chellappa, R.: Learning from synthetic data: addressing domain shift for semantic segmentation. In: CVPR, pp. 3752–3761, IEEE Computer Society (2018)
37. Chen, Y., Li, W., Chen, X., Van Gool, L.: Learning semantic segmentation from synthetic data: a geometrically guided input-output adaptation approach. In: CVPR, pp. 1841–1850 (2019)
38. Ros, G., Sellart, L., Materzynska, J., Vazquez, D., Lopez, A.M.: The synthia dataset: a large collection of synthetic images for semantic segmentation of urban scenes. In: CVPR, pp. 3234–3243 (2016)
39. Gulrajani, I., Ahmed, F., Arjovsky, M., Dumoulin, V., Courville, A.C.: Improved training of wasserstein gans. In: NIPS, pp. 5767–5777 (2017)
40. Redmon, J., Farhadi, A.: Yolov3: An incremental improvement. CoRR abs/1804.02767 (2018)
41. Kuhn, H.W.: The Hungarian method for the assignment problem. Naval Res. Logistics Q. **2**, 83–97 (1955)
42. Simonyan, K., Zisserman, A.: Very deep convolutional networks for large-scale image recognition. CoRR abs/1409.1556 (2014)
43. Kingma, D.P., Ba, J.: Adam: a method for stochastic optimization. arXiv preprint arXiv:1412.6980 (2014)
44. Miyato, T., Kataoka, T., Koyama, M., Yoshida, Y.: Spectral normalization for generative adversarial networks. In: International Conference on Learning Representations (2018)
45. Salimans, T., Goodfellow, I.J., Zaremba, W., Cheung, V., Radford, A., Chen, X.: Improved techniques for training gans. CoRR abs/1606.03498 (2016)

RAF-AU Database: In-the-Wild Facial Expressions with Subjective Emotion Judgement and Objective AU Annotations

Wen-Jing Yan[1], Shan Li[2], Chengtao Que[1], Jiquan Pei[1], and Weihong Deng[2(✉)]

[1] JD Digits, Beijing, China
eagan-ywj@foxmail.com, {quechengtao,peijiquan}@jd.com
[2] Beijing University of Posts and Telecommunications, Beijing, China
{ls1995,whdeng}@bupt.edu.cn

Abstract. Much of the work on automatic facial expression recognition relies on databases containing a certain number of emotion classes and their exaggerated facial configurations (generally six prototypical facial expressions), based on Ekman's Basic Emotion Theory. However, recent studies have revealed that facial expressions in our human life can be blended with multiple basic emotions. And the emotion labels for these in-the-wild facial expressions cannot easily be annotated solely on pre-defined AU patterns. How to analyze the action units for such complex expressions is still an open question. To address this issue, we develop a RAF-AU database that employs a sign-based (i.e., AUs) and judgement-based (i.e., perceived emotion) approach to annotating blended facial expressions in the wild. We first reviewed the annotation methods in existing databases and identified crowdsourcing as a promising strategy for labeling in-the-wild facial expressions. Then, RAF-AU was finely annotated by experienced coders, on which we also conducted a preliminary investigation of which key AUs contribute most to a perceived emotion, and the relationship between AUs and facial expressions. Finally, we provided a baseline for AU recognition in RAF-AU using popular features and multi-label learning methods.

1 Introduction

Of all nonverbal behaviors—body movement, posture, gaze, proxemics and voice—the face is probably the most commanding and complicated, and perhaps the most confusing. The face, and especially facial movement (or expression), is commanding because it is always visible and therefore always providing information such as emotion and intent [1]. Due to their utility for understanding a human being's mental state, the recognition of automatic facial expressions is becoming a popular field in computer vision.

W.-J. Yan and S. Li—Contributed equally to this work.

© Springer Nature Switzerland AG 2021
H. Ishikawa et al. (Eds.): ACCV 2020, LNCS 12627, pp. 68–82, 2021.
https://doi.org/10.1007/978-3-030-69544-6_5

Automatic facial expression recognition relies heavily on training datasets. When training a system to recognize facial expressions, the investigator must assume that the training and test data have been accurately labeled. This assumption may or may not be accurate. Traditionally, researchers have categorized facial expressions as expressing happiness, sadness, surprise, fear, anger and disgust. Each of these prototypical facial expressions can be described via a pattern of action units (AUs), based on the Facial Action Coding System (FACS) developed by Ekman and colleagues [2] and supported by Basic Emotion Theory (BET) [3].

Early in the process, samples of facial expressions are mostly viewed from the front, collected from actors required to pose preset AUs that readily match prototypical facial expressions [4,5]. Thus, recognition of the emotion can be judged against the "correct" expression adopted by the poser. Recently, datasets of spontaneous facial expressions have multiplied [6–10]. This is remarkable progress because the goal of automatic facial expression recognition is to apply to in the real world rather than lab situations (i.e., the ideal world). Facial expressions in real life are "in the wild", meaning that they are not necessarily frontal and direct-gazed, nor demonstrate only a very limited number of AU patterns. There may be various combinations of AUs with different gestures, head poses, gazes, and environments.

Due to the characteristics of in-the-wild facial expressions, applying an emotion label to a certain face can be difficult. AU combinations do not usually fall precisely into the six (or more) prototypical facial expressions [11]. EMFACS [4,12], usually understood as a guide for labeling emotions expressed through AU combinations, has become inappropriate in this content. Though previous research has summarized the relationship between AUs and emotion [13,14], researchers have only provided general or key AUs for certain emotions. Moreover, the coherence problem has long being a topic of debate in the field of facial expression [15–17]. Even for the six universally used and prototypical facial expressions, psychologists have not reached a consensus on the relationship between AU patterns and emotions, let alone facial expressions in the wild. In other words, we cannot simply categorize in-the-wild facial expressions by AU pattern, at least not for the moment.

Generally, psychologists have proposed two approaches to studying nonverbal behavior (including facial expressions), either judgement-based or sign-based [1,13]. In judgement-based approaches, observers make inferences about the meaning of facial actions and assign corresponding labels. When classifying facial expressions into a predefined number of emotions or mental activity categories, the agreement of a group of annotators is taken as ground truth, usually by computing the average of the responses of either experts or non-experts. The rationale that judgement-based approaches can provide "correct" labels can be explained from an evolutionary perspective: the facial expressions broadcast from a sender (i.e., encoding the signal) should be universally understood by a perceiver (i.e., decoding the signal), or they would be useless and therefore removed. Thus, crowdsourced annotation, a practice that employs many perceivers to heuristically label a target, might be a useful way of labeling in-the-wild facial

Fig. 1. Example samples annotated with typical AUs in the RAF-AU dataset.

expressions. As for sign-based approaches, facial motion and deformation are coded into visual classes. Facial actions are then abstracted and described by their location and intensity, such as in FACS. Ideally, a complete description framework would contain all possible perceptible changes that might occur on a face. Most automatic facial expression analysis approaches have attempted to directly categorize facial expressions into basic emotion classes [18] by AUs, a sign-based approach.

The judgement-based approach, with subjective estimation, provides the perceivers' judgement because facial expressions are born to be perceived and understood by conspecifics. From this perspective, conspecifics can provide the correct interpretation of a given facial expression. The sign-based approach, with objective description, can tell the computer where and how the facial movements will occur. Ideally, a qualified mechanism for annotating facial expressions should include both subjective and objective elements.

With such an understanding of facial expressions and their annotation, the present work provides an updated version of the existing RAF-ML database [9], called RAF-AU database[1], which consists of in-the-wild facial expressions with both subjective (i.e., judgement-based) and objective (i.e., sign-based) annotations. The RAF-ML database contains facial images in different occlusions, illuminations and resolutions collected from the social network and provides multiple labels via crowdsourcing annotations for each facial image. To extend this database with objective elements, we conducted AU coding according to strict criteria by two FACS experts. Specially, two experienced coders were requested to independently code each the facial image involving 26 kinds of AUs and

---

[1] http://whdeng.cn/RAF/model3.html.

the inter-coder correlation was 0.6376. To our best knowledge, the RAF-AU database is the first facial expression dataset that includes both subjective emotion judgement and objective AU annotations for multi-label expression analysis in-the-wild. Figure 1 shows example images annotated with typical AUs in the RAF-AU dataset. Using both crowdsourced and AU annotations, we make the first attempt to investigate the relationship between AUs and perceived emotions in the wild. We explored which AUs contributed the most to each facial expression. We then conducted AU detection experiments using popular features and multi-label learning methods. A baseline was provided for AU recognition in the RAF-AU.

2 Related Work

Several surveys have offered overviews of facial expression datasets [19,20]. The present research does not repeat their work, but rather inspects how facial movements were annotated with emotion labels. Many of these databases classified facial expressions into types, based on rules such as those in EMFACS (i.e., mapping AUs to facial expressions). Usually, participants were required to pose "standard" AUs to express so-called prototypical facial expressions, and those that qualified were included in the database.

In the Cohn-Kanade Expression Database [4], emotion labels refer to the expression requested rather than what may actually have been performed. AUs for each facial expression (i.e., the apex frame in a sequence) are converted into emotion-specific expressions (e.g., happiness or anger). BU-3DFE [21] and MMI [22] used a similar technique to assign emotion labels to specific facial movements. Researchers have also used this approach to annotate emotions expressed in spontaneous facial expressions. EmotioNet [6] is a large-scale database with one million facial expression images collected from the Internet. Most samples were annotated by an automatic AU detection algorithm, and the remaining 10% were manually annotated using AUs. EmotioNet contains six basic expressions and one neutral expression. The creators defined unique AU patterns that mapped AUs to specific emotions. Therefore, the emotion labels were inferred from the AUs. For example, if the face showed AU4+AU15, the emotion label attributed was "sadness". Similar mapping rules were used to label compound facial expressions. EmotioNet defined 17 compound expressions, depending on the AU combination. For example, AU4+AU20+AU25 was defined as fearfully angry. Similarly in [14], subjects were required to practice their expressions before each acquisition. They were required to express more than one emotion based on prototypical facial expressions; these were then evaluated by experts for validity. This annotation approach was also based on prototypical facial expression protocol.

The dimension approach was used to annotate facial expressions from valence (unpleasant to pleasant) and arousal (low to high). For example, AffectNet [7] contains more than one million images from the Internet that were obtained by querying different search engines using emotion-related tags. Over 450,000 images include manually annotated labels according to eight basic expressions. Another valence-arousal dataset is Aff-Wild [23,24] which contains 298 videos with spontaneous facial behaviors collected in arbitrary recording conditions. Most recently, the Aff-Wild dataset was extended to the Aff-wild2 [25,26] with more videos and other attribute annotations such as basic expressions and action units. It is by far the largest database providing facial expressions with all three types of behavior states, i.e., valence and arousal (VA), basic expression and facial action unit.

The situation approach derives emotion labels from the situation (with an anticipated emotion) where facial expressions elicited are taken as a cue. The BP4D-Spontaneous database [27] used various tasks in a lab environment to elicit spontaneous facial expressions. For example, smelling an unpleasant odor should be disgusting and thus the facial expression during the task should be one of disgust. The Aff-Wild dataset employed similar elicitation method to record videos containing naturalistic emotional states in arbitrary recording conditions.

The self-report approach is another way of annotating facial expression type. The Belfast Induced Natural Emotion Database [28] is unique. Recordings are accompanied by self-reports of emotion and intensity, serving as continuous trace-style ratings of valence and intensity. Self-reporting may be the most reliable approach to labeling emotion in facial expressions. Facial movements in this database were also annotated with valence and intensity (or arousal) according to the dimension of the emotion. In Belfast, they used many more words to describe each emotion than the popular six prototypical facial expressions. However, self-reported information is not easily collected and may not reflect the inner mind [29] and thus not commonly used.

Crowdsourcing is a judgment-based approach that labels facial expressions based on human perception. The Real-world Affective Face Database (RAF-DB) [8,30] is a real-world database containing 29,672 highly diverse facial images downloaded from the Internet. Images were randomly and equally assigned to each labeler, ensuring that there was no direct correlation among the images labeled by a single annotator. For the manually crowdsourced annotations, seven basic (including neutral) and 11 compound emotion labels were applied to the samples. Each image was ensured to be labeled by approximately 40 independent labelers. Later, RAF-ML [9] was developed. This database contains facial expressions obtained from RAF-DB that offers multiple expressions, and extends the sample collection, 4,908 in total. Another dataset, the Expression in-the-Wild Database (ExpW) [10], contains 91,793 faces downloaded using Google image searches. Each face image was manually annotated and categorized by human beings into one of seven basic expression categories, but the study didn't explain whether this coding was based on heuristic judgement or mapping rules.

In summary, posed facial expressions are uncommon in real life, so many databases collect spontaneous samples. These spontaneous and in-the-wild facial expressions are very difficult to annotate because they do not usually display commonly accepted and pre-defined AU combinations. Mapping rules comprise the most common approach to labeling facial expression type. There are also dimension, situation, self-report, and crowdsourcing approaches. With images of facial expressions downloaded from the Internet, the subject's emotional state and mindset are unknown, and researchers can't simply infer them by the AU combinations displayed. Therefore, a crowdsourcing approach that leverages human perception to apply annotations is the most suitable of those available. In the present work, we provide a dataset of both judgement-based (i.e., subjective) and sign-based (i.e., objective) annotations. Only a combination of subjective and objective annotations will properly disclose the emotional implications of facial expressions. This is what is provided by RAF-AU.

3   RAF-AU

3.1   AU Annotations

Facial images from the Internet vary in quality; this is true not only in terms of image resolution, but also spontaneity, since many are posed and thus not emotion-motivated. There are certain individual differences in facial appearance and habitual movement. Some AUs habitually appear, making emotional perception confusing. For example, a smile with AU9 (i.e., a wrinkled nose) is more likely to appear in women, while people with gag teeth are more likely to display AU10 (a raised upper lip). AU coding of facial expressions requires a baseline (or neutral) image, or it is difficult to judge whether certain expressions were due to the face's original appearance or facial movement. For example, eyebrow AU4 can be a permanent feature or transient movement. If we are forced to imagine a neutral face for each face image, then we have to judge whether the expression is caused by a certain AU, perpetual feature, or the influence of another AU.

In the present research, those with more than two whole faces (305 images in total) were eliminated from the RAF-ML database. There were some images that contained more than two faces. When we checked the voting, we found that participants were not always be voting for the same face. For example, one image contained a smiling face and a sad face, but about 30% of the participants voted happiness while 25% voted sadness. After removing these images, 4,601 were left for further coding.

Two experienced coders independently FACS-coded these face images and arbitrated any disagreement. They usually disagreed on whether a trace of an AU was actually a baseline or emotion-motivated. They also carefully checked and discussed if AUs emerged due to other AUs. The inter-coder correlation (i.e., reliability, see Eq. (1)) was 0.6376. This relatively low reliability was due to the complexity of and lack of clarity in these in-the-wild and blended facial expressions.

$$R = \frac{2 * \#AU(C_1 C_2)}{\#All\_AU}, \tag{1}$$

where $\#AU(C_1 C_2)$ is the number of AUs upon which Coders 1 and 2 agreed and $\#All\_AU$ is the total number of AUs in a facial expression scored by two coders.

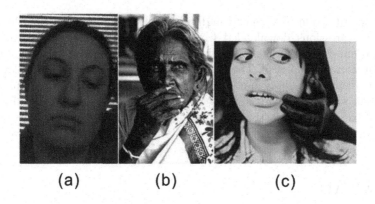

(a)   (b)   (c)

Fig. 2. Examples of "null" images.

There were 253 images annotated as null. Some of these facial images didn't show any AUs. Though there were no AUs for these faces, they were still selected for this database because according to perceivers, they expressed emotions. This is not uncommon because perceived emotion is influenced by gaze, head pose, gesture, and facial appearance. Figure 2 shows some examples labeled as null. In the figure, (a) is null because the faintly discernible AU17 (i.e., Chin raiser) is not sufficiently obvious; without a baseline, we weren't confident we were avoiding a mistake. In (b), the face of this elderly person has many perpetual traces, and therefore was hard to annotate without a baseline. The AU4 marker seemed locally obvious. However, this is an image of an elderly person that did not show a clear vertical grain between the eyebrows. Therefore, we didn't annotate this image with AU4. The forehead in (c) is covered and the mouth may be stretc.hed by an outer force. These AUs are either invisible or involuntary.

3.2   Profile of RAF-AU

This database contains 4,601 images obtained from RAF-ML. We have provided AU annotations for all faces. There were 26 AUs used in the annotations, without action descriptors. We list all used AUs and their frequency in Table 1. It should be noted that the AU distribution was largely imbalanced. For example, only a few AU39 (i.e., compressed nostrils) were found in this dataset. Some representative examples with frequent AUs in the RAF-AU are shown in Fig. 1.

Among these AU annotations, some were one-side AUs. Facial action units are not always the same for left and right halves of faces; they may also vary in intensity. One-sided AUs were labeled as L or R, depending on which half of the face acted. Among the 4,601 faces, we found 219 right-only and 304 left-only AUs. For the unweighted condition (the basic unit was facial expression, and it did not matter if it contained one or more one-sided AUs), we found 163 right-only and 232 left-only AUs. This finding suggests that the left side of the face is more expressive than the right. Psychologists may be interested in these types of characteristics and thus should further investigate this topic. In addition to the

Table 1. Frequency of all used AUs (without action descriptors) coded by manual FACS coders on the RAF-AU dataset. The numbers in parentheses refer to the sample size of one-sided AUs.

AU	Name	Num	AU	Name	Num
1	*Inner Brow Raiser*	1028+(49)	21	*Neck Tightener*	3
2	*Outer Brow Raiser*	701+(95)	22	*Lip Funneler*	196+(148)
4	*Brow Lowerer*	1808+(9)	23	*Lip Tightener*	80+(51)
5	*Upper Lid Raiser*	975+(10)	24	*Lip Pressor*	165+(56)
6	*Cheek Raiser*	404+(46)	25	*Lips part*	2830
7	*Lid Tightener*	347+(14)	26	*Jaw Drop*	1089
9	*Nose Wrinkler*	749+(25)	27	*Mouth Stretc.h*	810
10	*Upper Lip Raiser*	1274+(116)	28	*Lip Suck*	13+(31)
12	*Lip Corner Puller*	1187+(81)	29	*Jaw Thrust*	27
14	*Dimpler*	105+(22)	30	*Jaw Sideways*	9
15	*Lip Corner Depressor*	290+(2)	32	*Lip Bite*	6
16	*Lower Lip Depressor*	720	33	*Cheek Blow*	1
17	*Chin Raiser*	541	34	*Cheek Puff*	9+(1)
18	*Lip Puckerer*	118+(11)	35	*Cheeck Suck*	10+(1)
19	*Tongue Visible*	34	39	*Nostril Compressor*	5
20	*Lip stretcher*	199+(33)	43	*Eyes Closed*	148+(9)

Table 2. AUs that contribute most (variance) for these facial expressions in RAF-AU.

Surprise		Fear		Disgust	
AU25	0.5926	**AU25**	0.5111	**AU10**	0.5964
AU5	0.4665	**AU12**	0.4033	**AU4**	0.5330
AU26	0.3820	**AU27**	0.3729	**AU17**	0.2973
Happiness		Sadness		Anger	
AU12	0.7040	**AU4**	0.6723	**AU25**	0.4659
AU25	0.5143	**AU25**	0.3462	**AU9**	0.4337
AU27	0.2491	**AU1**	0.2979	**AU10**	0.4236

left- and right-only AUs, some AUs only contained top or bottom elements. For example, AU23 indicates tightened lips, and sometimes this is only expressed by half (top or bottom). For these instances, we annotated T for top only and B for bottom only. There were 131 T and 179 B faces in RAF-AU.

By annotating for both AU and perceived emotion, we were able to explore which AUs contributed the most to blended emotions. Through a linear transformation, the AUs and perceived emotions were made equivalent in the same space. That is, the AUs of each image were linearly transformed to obtain the

Table 3. The relationship of the facial expressions based on the AU combination for RAF-AU. Sur = Surprise, Fea = Fear, Dis = Disgust, Hap = Happiness, Sad = Sadness, Ang = Anger, Neu = Neutral.

	Sur	Fea	Dis	Hap	Sad	Ang	Neu
Sur	1.0000	0.6802	0.1733	0.4908	0.3284	0.3688	−0.3784
Fea	0.6802	1.0000	0.3645	0.8168	0.5754	0.7665	−0.8262
Dis	0.1733	0.3645	1.0000	0.2497	0.6997	0.6266	−0.4654
Hap	0.4908	0.8168	0.2497	1.0000	0.5048	0.6207	−0.7539
Sad	0.3284	0.5754	0.6997	0.5048	1.0000	0.6342	−0.4866
Ang	0.3688	0.7665	0.6266	0.6207	0.6342	1.0000	−0.8170
Neu	−0.3784	−0.8262	−0.4654	−0.7539	−0.4866	−0.8170	1.0000

Table 4. The correlation coefficients between the facial expressions for RAF-AU. Sur = Surprise, Fea = Fear, Dis = Disgust, Hap = Happiness, Sad = Sadness, Ang = Anger, Neu = Neutral.

	Sur	Fea	Dis	Hap	Sad	Ang	Neu
Sur	1.0000	0.2706	−0.5585	0.1544	−0.4168	−0.3756	−0.2598
Fea	0.2706	1.0000	−0.4242	−0.2193	−0.1224	−0.1628	−0.3568
Dis	−0.5585	−0.4242	1.0000	−0.2673	0.0686	0.0739	0.1447
Hap	0.1544	−0.2193	−0.2673	1.0000	−0.3023	−0.2986	−0.0387
Sad	−0.4168	−0.1224	0.0686	−0.3023	1.0000	−0.2060	0.0817
Ang	−0.3756	−0.1628	0.0739	−0.2986	−0.2060	1.0000	−0.1858
Neu	−0.2598	−0.3568	0.1447	−0.0387	0.0817	−0.1858	1.0000

expression corresponding to the image. Through matrix transformation, we will be able to get the linear relationship between AUs and perceived emotions. Accordingly, the AUs of each image can be linearly transformed to obtain the expression possibilities corresponding to the image. Table 2 shows the three AUs contributing the most to each facial expression. We explored the inner relationship of the expression itself by using the expression matrix and calculating the relationship of the facial expression based on the AU combination (see Table 3). In addition, we provide the correlation coefficients for the facial expressions in RAF-AU (see Table 4).

4   Baseline Evaluation on RAF-AU

4.1   Pre-processing and Dataset Split

We first filtered out all 253 images annotated with "null" as they may contain irrelevant information which would largely distract the AU detection. Then, we chose 13 kinds of AUs that occur more than 8% base rate in RAF-AU dataset for experiment and analysis. Specifically, each image was annotated +1 or −1 if an AU is present or absent, and 0 for one-sided AUs. During pre-processing, manually annotated five facial landmarks provided in RAF-ML [9] were employed to register all images to a reference face using an affine transformation, resulting 100 * 100 cropped images. Then gray-scale samples were transformed for the following feature extraction. For dataset split, we divided RAF-AU into training part and test part, where the size of the training part is four times larger than the test part.

4.2   Feature Extraction and Classification

For the comparison purpose, we implemented two handcrafted features and three deep learning features. For hand-crafted feature extraction, we have tried histogram of orientated gradients (HOG) [31] and Local binary patterns (LBP) [32]. For HOG, we used this shape-based segmentation dividing the image into 10 * 10 pixel blocks of four 5 * 5 pixel cells with no overlapping. By setting 10 bins for each histogram, we got a 4000-dimensional feature vector per aligned image. For LBP, we selected the 59-bin $LBP_{8,2}^{u2}$ operator, and divided the 100 * 100 pixel images into 100 regions of 10 * 10 grid size, which was empirically found to achieve relatively good performance for expression classification.

For deep learning feature extraction, we first employed the already trained baseDCNN and DBM-CNN provided in [9], then 2000-dimensional deep features learned from raw data can be extracted from the penultimate fully connected layer of these two DCNNs for both training set and test set in RAF-AU. We also tried a multi-label CNN for AU detection. Let us assume that there are k AU categories and n training samples. Given a set of ground truth label $\boldsymbol{y} \in \{-1, +1, 0\}^k$ and the corresponding prediction results $\boldsymbol{p} \in \mathbb{R}^k$ for all k AU labels, the goal is to minimize the following multi-label cross entropy loss:

$$L = \frac{-1}{n} \sum_{i=1}^{n} \sum_{j=1}^{k} \left\{ [y_i^j > 0] \log p_i^j + [y_i^j < 0] \log(1 - p_i^j) \right\}, \tag{2}$$

where $[\cdot]$ is an indicator function that returns 1 if the Boolean expression is true, and 0 otherwise. And y_i^j is the ground truth for the i-th sample of j-th AU, p_i^j is the predicted probability for the i-th sample of j-th AU. We then also extracted the output of the penultimate fully connected layer as the final feature representation, resulting in 2000-dimensional vectors. Table 5 displays detailed network architectures of this AU-CNN trained on the RAF-AU dataset.

During AU detection, support vector machine with linear kernel implemented in LIBSVM [33] was utilized for the one-versus-all binary classification. Given a training set $\{(x_i, y_i), i = 1, \ldots, n\}$, where $x_i \in \mathbb{R}^d$ and $y_i \in \{+1, -1\}$ (samples with one-sided AU has been omitted during this AU detection), then the testing sample can be detected by optimizing:

$$\min_{w} \frac{1}{2} ||w||^2 + C \sum_{i=1}^{n} max(1 - y_i w^T x_i, 0). \tag{3}$$

The penalty parameter C of SVM was fixed to 1 for all different features.

Table 5. The network configuration parameters in the AU-CNN.

Layer type	1	2	3	4	5	6	7	8	9
	Conv	ReLu	MPool	Conv	ReLu	MPool	Conv	ReLu	Conv
Kernel	3	–	2	3	–	2	3	–	3
Output	64	–	–	96	–	–	128	–	128
Stride	1	1	2	1	1	2	1	1	1
Pad	1	0	0	1	0	0	1	0	1
Layer type	10	11	12	13	14	15	16	17	18
	ReLu	MPool	Conv	ReLu	Conv	ReLu	FC	ReLu	FC
Kernel	–	2	3	–	3	–		–	
Output	–	–	256	–	256	–	2000	–	13
Stride	1	2	1	1	1	1		1	
Pad	0	0	1	0	1	0		0	

Table 6. Performances of the AUC-ROC for AU detection on RAF-AU dataset using different features.

AUs	Number	HOG	LBP	BaseDCNN	DBM-CNN	AU-CNN
1	1028	76.83	78.72	72.31	71.74	82.03
2	701	84.67	87.76	83.54	80.67	90.49
4	1808	72.95	74.27	75.67	78.73	86.28
5	975	78.19	76.43	83.25	87.84	88.86
6	404	84.61	80.68	81.98	84.29	87.41
9	749	84.09	88.49	86.79	86.76	90.03
10	1274	78.98	76.63	80.85	81.56	87.89
12	1187	80.51	82.27	86.23	86.17	88.48
16	720	78.47	77.84	77.71	79.67	86.11
17	541	81.81	79.55	80.07	78.29	88.58
25	2830	85.13	86.24	89.87	91.18	95.33
26	1089	66.27	67.72	75.12	78.82	86.31
27	810	91.48	93.11	93.42	93.65	95.77
AVG	–	80.31	80.75	82.06	83.03	**88.73**

4.3 Evaluation Metrics

In terms of evaluating the performance on AU detection, two different metrics were employed: the area underneath the receiver-operator characteristic (ROC) curve (AUC-ROC) and the F1 score. The rank metric ROC curve visualizes the trade-off between sensitivity and specificity by plotting both values as a function of a varying classification threshold. And the threshold metric F1 score is defined as $F1 = \frac{2RP}{R+P}$, where R and P denote recall (the number of correctly

Table 7. Performances of the F1 score for AU detection on RAF-AU dataset using different features.

AUs	Number	HOG	LBP	BaseDCNN	DBM-CNN	AU-CNN
1	1028	33.70	50.00	29.60	35.42	60.47
2	701	45.00	50.23	38.50	32.49	65.59
4	1808	58.86	57.89	62.35	65.47	73.44
5	975	45.43	37.29	51.53	59.52	69.69
6	404	26.09	26.80	17.78	18.18	58.21
9	749	52.94	59.29	52.24	51.48	67.44
10	1274	49.30	49.65	49.52	51.99	68.41
12	1187	54.72	60.29	64.76	62.09	69.62
16	720	21.65	27.03	25.37	31.63	59.38
17	541	7.27	20.74	18.60	16.26	25.64
25	2830	85.07	85.16	87.50	88.87	92.14
26	1089	20.00	17.90	42.11	48.84	64.65
27	810	68.69	72.11	70.99	71.23	82.67
AVG	–	43.75	47.26	46.99	48.73	**65.95**

recognized samples divided by the actual number of all samples with the target AU) and precision (the number of correctly recognized samples divided by the total number of samples detected with the target AU), respectively. We then computed the average over all 13 AUs (AVG) to measure the overall performance.

4.4 AU Detection Results

In Table 6 and Table 7, we show the AUC-ROC and F1 score results for each of the 13 AUs in RAF-AU using four different features, respectively. We also list the statistic regarding the AU occurrence, i.e., the number of positive samples for each AU. It can be seen that the AU distribution in RAF-AU is more imbalanced than those lab-controlled datasets. With regard to individual AU detection, our baselines can yield relatively good performance on frequently occurring AUs (e.g., AUs 25, 27, 5, 4 and 12). However, we also observe a significant drop in the performance on other less common AUs. When comparing different features, the deep learning feature AU-CNN can achieve comparable and better AU detection rates in terms of both average AUC and F1 score. Nevertheless, when compared to the accuracy achieved on other lab-controlled datasets, there is still room for improvement on this challenging realistic dataset which contains various naturalistic illuminations, occlusions, hear poses and obvious imbalanced distribution.

5 Conclusions

In real life, facial expressions occur in the wild, and thus their emotional meaning cannot be absolutely defined. The crowdsourcing approach provides a subjective label based on human perception. Thus, we update the previous RAF-ML database by providing AU coding and removing certain confusing samples. The present database, RAF-AU, provides both AU- and judgement-based annotations from objective and subjective approaches, respectively. Thus, this database provides a fuller picture of given facial expressions. Based on these annotations, we were able to investigate the relationship between objective description and subjective understanding. We also provide a set of baselines for RAF-AU depending on different features. And the deep learning feature obtained using a multi-label AU detection CNN achieve the best detection rate. Further research should be conducted to study this relationship, with more samples and across various cultures.

Acknowledgement. This work was partially supported by the National Natural Science Foundation of China under Grants No. 61871052. We thank Yong Ke, Huaxiu Li for their assistance in AU coding.

References

1. Harrigan, J., Rosenthal, R., Scherer, K.R., Scherer, K.: New Handbook of Methods in Nonverbal Behavior Research. Oxford University Press, Oxford (2008)
2. Ekman, P., Friesen, W.V., Hager, J.C.: Facial Action Coding System: The Manual ON CD ROM, pp. 77–254. A Human Face, Salt Lake City (2002)
3. Russell, J.A., Rosenberg, E.L., Lewis, M.D.: Introduction to a special section on basic emotion theory. Emot. Rev. **3**, 363 (2011)
4. Kanade, T., Cohn, J.F., Tian, Y.: Comprehensive database for facial expression analysis. In: Proceedings Fourth IEEE International Conference on Automatic Face and Gesture Recognition (Cat. No. PR00580), pp. 46–53. IEEE (2000)
5. Lucey, P., Cohn, J.F., Kanade, T., Saragih, J., Ambadar, Z., Matthews, I.: The extended Cohn-Kanade dataset (CK+): a complete dataset for action unit and emotion-specified expression. In: 2010 IEEE Computer Society Conference on Computer Vision and Pattern Recognition Workshops (CVPRW), pp. 94–101. IEEE (2010)
6. Fabian Benitez-Quiroz, C., Srinivasan, R., Martinez, A.M.: EmotioNEt: an accurate, real-time algorithm for the automatic annotation of a million facial expressions in the wild. In: Proceedings of the IEEE Conference on Computer Vision and Pattern Recognition, pp. 5562–5570 (2016)
7. Mollahosseini, A., Hasani, B., Mahoor, M.H.: AffectNet: a database for facial expression, valence, and arousal computing in the wild. IEEE Trans. Affect. Comput. **10**, 18–31 (2017)
8. Li, S., Deng, W.: Reliable crowdsourcing and deep locality-preserving learning for unconstrained facial expression recognition. IEEE Trans. Image Process. **28**, 356–370 (2018)
9. Li, S., Deng, W.: Blended emotion in-the-wild: multi-label facial expression recognition using crowdsourced annotations and deep locality feature learning. Int. J. Comput. Vision **127**, 884–906 (2019)

10. Zhang, Z., Luo, P., Loy, C.C., Tang, X.: From facial expression recognition to interpersonal relation prediction. Int. J. Comput. Vision **126**, 550–569 (2018)
11. Yan, W.J., Wu, Q., Liang, J., Chen, Y.H., Fu, X.: How fast are the leaked facial expressions: the duration of micro-expressions. J. Nonverbal Behav. **37**, 217–230 (2013)
12. Friesen, W.V., Ekman, P., et al.: EMFACS-7: emotional facial action coding system. University of California at San Francisco, vol. 2, p. 1 (1983). Unpublished manuscript
13. Ekman, P., Friesen, W.V.: Nonverbal leakage and clues to deception. Psychiatry **32**, 88–106 (1969)
14. Du, S., Tao, Y., Martinez, A.M.: Compound facial expressions of emotion. Proc. Nat. Acad. Sci. **111**, E1454–E1462 (2014)
15. Ruiz, A., van de Weijer, J., Binefa, X.: From emotions to action units with hidden and semi-hidden-task learning. In: 2015 IEEE International Conference on Computer Vision, ICCV 2015, Santiago, Chile, 7–13 December 2015, pp. 3703–3711. IEEE Computer Society (2015)
16. Durán, J., Reisenzein, R., Fernández-Dols, J.M.: Coherence between emotions and facial expressions. In: The Science of Facial Expression, pp. 107–129 (2017)
17. Kollias, D., Sharmanska, V., Zafeiriou, S.: Face behavior à la carte: expressions, affect and action units in a single network. CoRR abs/1910.11111 (2019)
18. Fasel, B., Luettin, J.: Automatic facial expression analysis: a survey. Pattern Recogn. **36**, 259–275 (2003)
19. Ko, B.: A brief review of facial emotion recognition based on visual information. Sensors **18**, 401 (2018)
20. Li, S., Deng, W.: Deep facial expression recognition: a survey. IEEE Trans. Affect. Comput. 1–1 (2020)
21. Yin, L., Wei, X., Sun, Y., Wang, J., Rosato, M.J.: A 3D facial expression database for facial behavior research. In: 7th International Conference on Automatic Face and Gesture Recognition (FGR06), pp. 211–216. IEEE (2006)
22. Pantic, M., Valstar, M., Rademaker, R., Maat, L.: Web-based database for facial expression analysis. In: 2005 IEEE International Conference on Multimedia and Expo, 5 p. IEEE (2005)
23. Kollias, D., et al.: Deep affect prediction in-the-wild: Aff-Wild database and challenge, deep architectures, and beyond. Int. J. Comput. Vision **127**, 907–929 (2019). https://doi.org/10.1007/s11263-019-01158-4
24. Zafeiriou, S., Kollias, D., Nicolaou, M.A., Papaioannou, A., Zhao, G., Kotsia, I.: Aff-Wild: valence and arousal 'in-the-wild' challenge. In: 2017 IEEE Conference on Computer Vision and Pattern Recognition Workshops, CVPR Workshops 2017, Honolulu, HI, USA, 21–26 July 2017, pp. 1980–1987. IEEE Computer Society (2017)
25. Kollias, D., Zafeiriou, S.: Expression, affect, action unit recognition: Aff-Wild2, multi-task learning and ArcFace. In: 30th British Machine Vision Conference 2019, BMVC 2019, Cardiff, UK, 9–12 September 2019, p. 297. BMVA Press (2019)
26. Kollias, D., Schulc, A., Hajiyev, E., Zafeiriou, S.: Analysing affective behavior in the first ABAW 2020 competition. CoRR abs/2001.11409 (2020)
27. Zhang, X., et al.: BP4D-spontaneous: a high-resolution spontaneous 3D dynamic facial expression database. Image Vis. Comput. **32**, 692–706 (2014)
28. Sneddon, I., McRorie, M., McKeown, G., Hanratty, J.: The Belfast induced natural emotion database. IEEE Trans. Affect. Comput. **3**, 32–41 (2011)
29. Barrett, L.F.: Feelings or words? Understanding the content in self-report ratings of experienced emotion. J. Pers. Soc. Psychol. **87**, 266 (2004)

30. Li, S., Deng, W., Du, J.: Reliable crowdsourcing and deep locality-preserving learning for expression recognition in the wild. In: Proceedings of the IEEE Conference on Computer Vision and Pattern Recognition, pp. 2852–2861 (2017)
31. Dalal, N., Triggs, B.: Histograms of oriented gradients for human detection. In: CVPR, vol. 1, pp. 886–893. IEEE (2005)
32. Ojala, T., Pietikäinen, M., Mäenpää, T.: Multiresolution gray-scale and rotation invariant texture classification with local binary patterns. IEEE Trans. Pattern Anal. Mach. Intell. **24**, 971–987 (2002)
33. Chang, C.C., Lin, C.J.: LIBSVM: a library for support vector machines. ACM Trans. Intell. Syst. Technol. **2**, 27:1–27:27 (2011). Software available at http://www.csie.ntu.edu.tw/~cjlin/libsvm

DoFNet: Depth of Field Difference Learning for Detecting Image Forgery

Yonghyun Jeong[1], Jongwon Choi[2(✉)], Doyeon Kim[1], Sehyeon Park[1], Minki Hong[1], Changhyun Park[1], Seungjai Min[1], and Youngjune Gwon[1]

[1] Samsung SDS, Seoul, Korea
{yhyun.jeong,dy31.kim,singing.park,mkidea.hong,arfken.park,
seungjai.min,gyj.gwon}@samsung.com
[2] Department of Advanced Imaging, Chung-Ang University, Seoul, Korea
choijw@cau.ac.kr

Abstract. Recently, online transactions have had an exponential growth and expanded to various cases, such as opening bank accounts and filing for insurance claims. Despite the effort of many companies requiring their own mobile applications to capture images for online transactions, it is difficult to restrict users from taking a picture of other's images displayed on a screen. To detect such cases, we propose a novel approach using paired images with different depth of field (DoF) for distinguishing the real images and the display images. Also, we introduce a new dataset containing 2,752 pairs of images capturing real and display objects on various types of displays, which is the largest real dataset employing DoF with multi-focus. Furthermore, we develop a new framework to concentrate on the difference of DoF in paired images, while avoiding learning individual display artifacts. Since DoF lies on the optical fundamentals, the framework can be widely utilized with any camera, and its performance shows at least 23% improvement compared to the conventional classification models.

1 Introduction

With rapid growth of vision technologies, online transactions have expanded its influence and even surpassed the proportion of offline transactions. Especially in the financial sector, various time-consuming and cumbersome offline procedures have been transformed into simple online procedures, including processing e-commerce payments, opening bank accounts, and filing for insurance claims.

Taking advantage of a contact-free environment of online transactions, scammers with malicious purposes use manipulated images for online frauds. Various schemes for image forgery are exploited, such as submitting other people's images as one's own for rental listing scams [1], or manipulating images using professional image editing tools, such as Adobe Photoshop, for a compensation fraud of railway delay [2]. As GAN-based synthesized images known as deepfakes have

---

Y. Jeong and J. Choi—Contributed equally.

© Springer Nature Switzerland AG 2021
H. Ishikawa et al. (Eds.): ACCV 2020, LNCS 12627, pp. 83–100, 2021.
https://doi.org/10.1007/978-3-030-69544-6_6

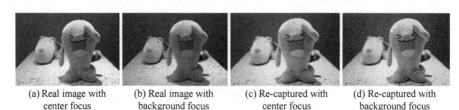

(a) Real image with   (b) Real image with   (c) Re-captured with   (d) Re-captured with
center focus   background focus   center focus   background focus

Fig. 1. Real images and display images with different focus length

achieved highly realistic results, image forgery has become a potential threat in political, economic, and social aspects [3].

Fortunately, due to advancement in deep learning, the manipulating schemes for image forgery can be detected by the recent detection algorithms for deepfake images [4–7] and Photoshopped images [8] with superior performance.

When other people's images are re-captured and submitted as one's own, it is difficult to distinguish such cases by the current detection methods, since the re-captured images are also technically 'real' and not manipulated according to the current standards. To prevent such cases, many companies, especially in the insurance industry [9–11], provide mobile applications specifically developed for secure capturing and submission of images to file claims.

Unfortunately, some forgery methods are still available to fool detection, e.g., taking pictures of printed pictures or displayed objects on the screen. With the advancement of display panels with high resolutions, the display artifacts appear almost invisible when captured in images, which makes it challenging to distinguish between real images (Fig. 1(a)) and display images (Fig. 1(c)). From this point forward, we call the images taken of the real objects as *real images*, and the images taken of the displayed objects on the screen as *display images*. Regarding the current issues in online transactions, a new approach needs to be developed, not only to detect the cases of image forgery but also to prevent the initiation of frauds and scams.

In this paper, we propose a new approach to detect image forgery by analyzing the paired images of real and display, which are supposed to capture the difference in focal lengths as shown in Fig. 1. We begin our study with an intuition that the paired images of real objects contain variance in depth of field due to difference in focal lengths, while pictures of screen panels with displayed objects show consistency in depth. Based on the new dataset with over 2,700 paired images of real or displayed objects, we propose a novel framework for detection of the re-captured images of displayed objects.

The paired images in the dataset can be divided into two categories: the real images and display images. While the real objects are captured for real images, several monitors and a projector with displayed objects are captured for display images. With a detailed analysis of the dataset introduced in this paper, we observe that the appearance of the artifacts varies by the type of displays. Thus, if a classification model concentrates on the presence of the artifacts to distinguish the display images, the model cannot recognize the unknown artifacts outside of training settings. In such cases, failure in detection occurs.

To enhance the generality of the classification model across various types of displays, the proposed framework trains the model to concentrate on the difference in the variance of the depth of the paired images themselves, instead of the artifacts that may diversify based on the display types. With a detailed analysis of our new dataset, we validate the proposed framework through various ablation tests and confirm its superior performance on detecting the display images even with variance in display models across training and test phases.

This paper makes the following contributions:

- Our approach is the first study to detect pictures of display images by exploiting the difference between the paired images with a different focal length.
- We introduce a new dataset of $2,752$ paired images, all of which are labeled as 'real' or 'display.'
- Based on the new network architecture processing the paired images simultaneously, we propose a new mechanism for the classification model to restrain from concentrating on the specific artifacts limited to the display types.
- With a detailed analysis of the new dataset and the superior performance of the proposed framework, we present the results of ablation analysis that validates the effectiveness of our approach.

Our dataset and source code are available online for public access.[1]

2 Related Work

In this section, we discuss the three lines of work most related to this paper: image forgery detection, depth of field, and multi-focus and focusing attention.

2.1 Image Forgery Detection

The rapid technological advancement of computer vision has made possible to produce high-quality forged images. Synthesized images are difficult to distinguish by naked eyes of human and have become almost impossible to detect without an in-depth analysis via trained AI models.

Currently, the most challenging forged images to detect is the GAN-based synthesized images known as deepfakes. With numerous generation models including ProGAN [12], BigGAN [13], CycleGAN [14], StarGAN 1,2 [15,16], StyleGAN 1,2 [17,18], deepfakes have improved to become highly realistic, and the object categories are expanded to include not only human faces but also animals like cats, dogs, and horses, and objects as automobiles, buildings, and paintings. Deepfake detection methods can be divided into two categories: natural characteristic based approach and synthesized artifact based approach. First, natural characteristic based approach focuses on the natural traits such as the

---

[1] https://github.com/SamsungSDS-Team9/DoFNet.

details on head poses and movements [19], the absence of eye-blinking [20], the effect of biological signals as heart rate [21], and variance in lighting conditions and shadows [22–25]. Synthesized artifacts based approach focuses on observing the artifacts generated by GAN and can be categorized into pixel-based and frequency-based methods. The pixel-based method takes image pixels as an input of the classification network [4, 8, 26–32] while the frequency-based method converts the pixel domain (i.e., 2D data) into the frequency domain to take the frequency spectrum as an input of the classification network [5–7, 33–37].

Another image forensic method is to detect the image areas manipulated by Adobe Photoshop. Wang et al. [8] proposes a method for detecting facial warping using the liquifying tool on Adobe Photoshop and reconstructing the original image. Our approach is differentiated that we analyze and prevent image forgery from the initial stage of taking photos, instead of detecting forgeries after being manipulated already.

2.2   Depth of Field

Popularized in photography and cinematography for directing the attention of the viewer, depth of Field (DoF) is an effect when objects within a certain range of distance appear clearly in focus and objects outside of the range, either closer or farther, appear blurry out of focus [38]. As in the work of Wu et al., DoF can be utilized for generating holographic imaging using autofocusing and phase recovery based on deep-learning [39]. Similarly, we also employ the difference of DoF in images to train our model for image forensics.

2.3   Multi-focus and Focusing Attention

Due to limited performance range of DoF of cameras, it can be difficult to take a picture with a clear focus on the entire image. In order to improve this issue, various frameworks have been studied regarding image focusing, including multi-focus and focusing attention mechanisms.

Multi-focus image fusion is fusing multiple images to produce an all-in-focus image. Guo et al. employed conditional generative adversarial network (cGAN) [40] for image-to-image fusion, which is known as FuseGAN [41]. Also, Zhang et al. introduced a large dataset containing realistic multi-focus images paired with their corresponding ground-truth images [42]. As Cheng et al. proposed, when focus is drifted to an unintentional region of the image, focusing attention mechanism can be employed to draw back the attention automatically using Focusing Attention Network (FAN) [43]. Different from the existing methods, we introduce a large dataset containing paired images intentionally focusing in the center and the background of the scene, respectively, and their corresponding display images captured in the same fashion.

To our knowledge, it is the first framework capable of analyzing image forensics from the moment when photos are taken. We achieved superior performance by employing a unique approach to develop our classification model based on the large dataset collected for this study.

3 Depth of Field Dataset

In this section, we introduce our new dataset containing paired images captured with different focal lengths to contain Depth of Field (DoF). DoF shows the variance in depth, especially when the objects located within a specific range of distance called midground appear in focus, while the other objects outside of the range called background appear blurry. The effect of DoF arises due to the physical properties of lenses. As the light passes through the lens of a camera or in our eye, the light source must keep a certain distance away from the lens to converge to a single point on the film or our retina. Based on DoF, we are enabled to not only predict the distances of various objects captured in images but also clearly express the concentrated areas or targeted objects.

3.1 Detecting Display Images Using Paired Images with DoF

Conventionally, the target objects captured for e-commerce transactions are located at the center of the picture and the background is usually more distanced than the objects from the camera lens. Thus, in reality, each and every picture of real objects must contain DoF information. However, DoF captured in a single image is not a crucial factor in detecting image forgery, since both real and display images contain a certain level of DoF in the single image. To distinguish the real images from the display images, we utilize the paired images with variance in focal lengths. The one focusing in the center is called a *center image*, while the other focusing in the background is called *background image*. In the case of display images, the variance in depth would be relatively small between the center and the background images due to similar focal lengths from the camera lens to the display screen. On the contrary, the paired images of real objects contain a wide range of variance in depth between the center and the background regions.

It is beneficial in three aspects to exploit paired images with variance in depth. First, it does not require any additional sensor other than the camera lens itself, which indicates its simplicity in operation and scalability in any type of mobile device with embedded cameras. Second, it is not bound by any type of camera, since DoF is based on the physical properties of the camera lens. Finally, it is not based on the display artifacts, which indicates the generality of our model to accommodate any types of displays, including those unseen during the training phase. Therefore, by training the classification model to concentrate on the difference of DoF between the paired images, our model can distinguish the display images from the real images with superior performance. Unfortunately, the conventional classification model can be easily trained to focus on detecting the artifacts, which leads to limited generality of the classification model for the unknown artifacts in the test phase.

3.2 Data Collection

The DoF dataset is collected by five different models of mobile devices with the mobile application specifically developed to obtain the paired images with

Table 1. Comparison of various multi-focus datasets.

Dataset	Data acquisition method	Size (pair)	Resolution	Realistic	Ground truth
Lytro [44]	Captured by light field camera	20	520 × 520	Yes	No
CNN [45]	Generated based on ImageNet dataset	1,000,000	16 × 16	No	Yes
BAnet [46]	Generated based on Matting dataset	2,268,000	16 × 16	No	Yes
FuseGAN [41]	Generated based on segmentation datasets	5,850	320 × 320	No	Yes
Real-MFF [42]	Captured by light field camera	800	625 × 433	Yes	Yes
Our dataset	Captured by cameras on mobile devices	2,752	720 × 1,280	Yes	Yes

Table 2. Classification performance with a single image and the paired images.

Single image classification						Paired image classification						
Train display	Test displays						Train display	Test displays				
	i-Mac		Samsung		Projector			i-Mac		Samsung		Projector	
	Acc.	A.P.	Acc.	A.P.	Acc	A.P.		Acc.	A.P.	Acc.	A.P.	Acc.	A.P.
5K LCD	99.25	99.26	94.96	85.19	50.00	50.00	5K LCD	100.00	100.00	87.97	87.79	55.97	55.97
WQHD LED	50.38	51.12	100.00	100.00	76.52	76.52	WQHD LED	53.38	52.68	99.25	99.24	85.07	85.07
Projector	49.62	50.38	49.62	50.38	100.00	100.00	Projector	50.8	49.62	50.38	49.62	100.00	100.00

difference in depth. The application allows users to take two pictures at once as a package using the auto-focusing feature of the mobile camera. The paired images focus on the objects located at the center and the background, respectively. Among the various regions other than the center, the top of the center has the largest probability to be the background region. Thus, we set the focus setting to clearly capture the region at the top of the center by auto-focusing.

We construct the dataset into two categories: the paired images of real objects and the paired images of display objects. Since the display images should be similar to the real images, we first collect the paired images of real objects and then gather the paired images of display objects by re-capturing the real images displayed on the screens. To validate the algorithm with various target objects, we employ several object categories including shoes, cosmetics, music albums, DVD, household goods, and beverages. Furthermore, for the robust performance of the classification model in the various capturing environment, we have diversified the background settings, the distance to the target objects, and the capturing angle with the displays. To validate the robustness of the classification model with various unknown artifacts, we employ various models of displays for data collection, including a 5K LCD display of Apple iMac (Retina 5K, 27-in., 2017), a WQHD LED display of Samsung monitor (LS27H850QFKXKR), and a display screen of NEC projector (NP-M311XG). In this way, we collect a large dataset composed of 2,752 pairs of images with 720 × 1,280 resolution for six different object categories. Each object category consists of four pairs of images: a pair of real images, and three pairs of display images obtained from a 5K LCD

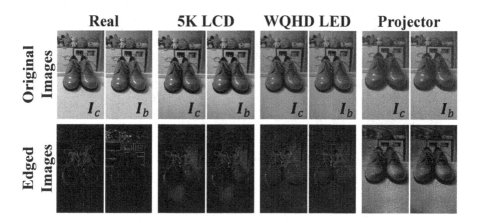

Fig. 2. Various display artifacts in DoF dataset

monitor, a WQHD LED monitor, and a projector screen, respectively. In addition, we compare the DoF dataset with other datasets containing paired images with variance in focal lengths. As indicated in Table 1, our dataset is the largest in size with the highest resolution of paired images among the realistic datasets, which demonstrates the scalability of DoF dataset in various tasks.

3.3 Analysis of Display Artifacts

As illustrated in Fig. 2, some artifacts can be easily discovered in certain parts of the display images. The shapes of the artifacts are various according to the types of displays and the capturing angle with the display panel, so it is impossible to consider all kinds of artifacts in the training phase. Furthermore, it is challenging to train the model to consider every single new artifact whenever a brand-new display is launched.

To show the limited generality of the artifact-based classification, we train a neural network of ResNet-18 [47]. We utilize the center image of the paired images as the input of ResNet-18, which is a binary classification model that determines whether the input is a real image or a display image. This classification model with the single image is noted by *SingleNet-18*, and its detailed settings are given in Sect. 5.1.

As shown in the left side of Table 2, *SingleNet-18* has shown a great performance when the same displaying device is considered in both of the training and test phases, while the performance dramatically drops to almost 50% when new types of displays outside of training phase are employed in the testing phase. This result validates that artifact-based training should be avoided for generalizing the classification model across various displays.

A similar situation happens even when paired images are used as the input of the neural network. We extend the ResNet-18 to accept paired images as inputs. For the input of the paired images, the channel size of the input image of ResNet-

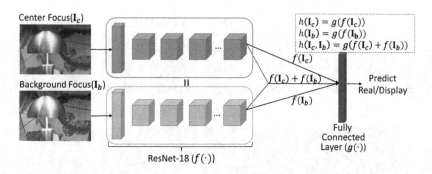

Fig. 3. Overall architecture of the proposed framework

18 has been expanded to 6 channels, and the input is obtained by concatenating the paired images in the channel dimension. This classification model with the paired images is noted by *DualNet-18*, and its settings and hyperparameters are all equivalent to *SingleNet-18*.

The results of *DualNet-18* are given in the right side of Table 2, which are similar to the results of *SingleNet-18*. Even when the paired images are given for the classification model, the wrong direction, cannot be corrected because the artifacts are much easier to be trained than the variance of depth in the paired images. Thus, when we just train the classification model with the conventional training methods, the classification model drives to focus on the artifacts given in the training phase, which reduces the generality of the model dramatically.

4   DoF-Based Detection of Display Images

We propose a new classification model and its training mechanism to concentrate on the variance in depth rather than the display artifacts. When the paired images are given for training, we denote the image with centered focus and the image focused on the background by $\mathbf{I}_c$ and $\mathbf{I}_b$, respectively.

4.1   Network Architecture

The proposed classification model contains two feature extractors and one fully-connected layer, as shown in Fig. 3. Each of the feature extractors is fed by $\mathbf{I}_c$ and $\mathbf{I}_b$, respectively. To let the feature extractors focus on the difference of DoF, the two feature extractors always share their weight parameters. Thus, we use the corresponding notation of $f(\mathbf{I})$ for the two feature generator, which means that the feature vector is the output for the given image of $\mathbf{I}$.

Then, the fully-connected layer determines the classes of the two feature vectors (i.e. $f(\mathbf{I}_c)$ and $f(\mathbf{I}_b)$) given from the feature extractors. By using $f(\mathbf{I}_c)$ and $f(\mathbf{I}_b)$, we consider the three combinations of the features. The first one is the dual combination where the two features are summed before the estimation of the fully-connected layer as $f(\mathbf{I}_c) + f(\mathbf{I}_b)$. The second and third combinations are the single ones where the individual features of $f(\mathbf{I}_c)$ and $f(\mathbf{I}_b)$ are fed into the fully-connected layer. When we denote the operation of the fully-connected layer by the function of $g(\bullet)$, the proposed network gives three outputs for one pair of images as: $g(f(\mathbf{I}_c) + f(\mathbf{I}_b))$, $g(f(\mathbf{I}_c))$, and $g(f(\mathbf{I}_b))$. For the simple representation, we denote the three outputs by $h(\mathbf{I}_c, \mathbf{I}_b)$, $h(\mathbf{I}_c)$, and $h(\mathbf{I}_b)$, respectively. By summing the two features before the fully-connected layer, we can obtain two advantages: first, since the two different features share the weight parameters ofthe fully-connected layer, it results in a more balanced model considering the paired images simultaneously; second, we can avoid overfitting by reducing the size of the fully-connected classifier.

To reduce the computational load and the necessary resources, for the feature extractors, we select the ResNet-18 [47] that is the smallest model among the various ResNet models. Since the network architecture is different from the model with the single image, rather than using the pre-trained network, we initialize the weight parameters according to the He initialization [47].

4.2   Artifact-Free Training Method

The objective of the proposed classification model is to distinguish the display images from the real images by using the difference of DoF in the paired images while ignoring the effect of artifacts. To consider the objective, we build the training loss as follows:

$$\mathcal{L}(\mathbf{I}_c, \mathbf{I}_b) = (1 - \lambda)\mathcal{L}_{dual}(\mathbf{I}_c, \mathbf{I}_b) + \lambda\mathcal{L}_{dof}(\mathbf{I}_c, \mathbf{I}_b) \tag{1}$$

where λ is the scaling factor to control the effect of the two loss terms: $\mathcal{L}_{dual}$ and $\mathcal{L}_{dof}$. We call $\mathcal{L}_{dual}$ and $\mathcal{L}_{dof}$ by the dual classification loss and the DoF loss, respectively. $\mathcal{L}_{dual}$ works as the conventional classification loss to let the neural network classify the given pair of images well. In contrast, $\mathcal{L}_{dof}$ prevents the neural network from being trained by considering the display artifacts. The detailed role and the derivation of $\mathcal{L}_{dual}$ and $\mathcal{L}_{dof}$ are given in the following.

Dual Classification Loss. The dual classification loss is the fundamental loss to classify the real and display images according to their own labels. Thus, the dual classification loss is derived as:

$$\mathcal{L}_{dual}(\mathbf{I}_c^{(i)}, \mathbf{I}_b^{(i)}) = \text{CE}\left(h(\mathbf{I}_c^{(i)}, \mathbf{I}_b^{(i)}), l^{(i)}\right), \tag{2}$$

where $\mathbf{I}_c^{(i)}$ and $\mathbf{I}_b^{(i)}$ are respectively the center and the background images of the i-th pair of images, $l^{(i)} \in \{0, 1\}$ is their ground-truth label, and the $\text{CE}(y, l)$ means the softmax cross-entropy loss letting y go to the one-hot vector of l. In $l^{(i)} \in \{0, 1\}$, 0 represents the label for the real images, while 1 means the label for the display images. Thus, the dual classification loss drives the neural network to predict the correct labels of the given pair of images.

DoF Loss. For the neural network to ignore the effect of the artifacts, the DoF loss utilizes the two outputs from the single inputs, which are $h(\mathbf{I}_c)$ and $h(\mathbf{I}_b)$. Before deriving the single DoF loss, we first describe the difference between the center and background images. When we consider only the center images to detect the display images, the classification model focuses on the display artifacts, since the two images cannot be distinguished from each other without the artifacts. On the contrary, employing the background images of real paired images enables the model to distinguish the display images without the artifacts, since the centered regions of the background images become blurry, in contrast to the display images. Thus, the center and the background images play different roles in the DoF loss, which results in two separated loss terms as follows:

$$\mathcal{L}_{dof}(\mathbf{I}_c, \mathbf{I}_b) = \frac{1}{2}\mathcal{L}_{dof-c}(\mathbf{I}_c) + \frac{1}{2}\mathcal{L}_{dof-b}(\mathbf{I}_b), \tag{3}$$

where $\mathcal{L}_{dof-c}$ is the DoF center loss that considers the center images only and $\mathcal{L}_{dof-b}$ indicates the DoF background loss utilizing only the background images.

Since the classification based on the center images lead the neural network to focus on the artifacts, we adversarially derive the DoF center loss as follows:

$$\mathcal{L}_{dof-c}(\mathbf{I}_c^{(i)}) = \mathrm{CE}\left(h(\mathbf{I}_c^{(i)}), 1\right). \tag{4}$$

According to $\mathcal{L}_{dof-c}$, when only a single center image is given to the network, both of the real and display images are predicted by the same class of 1. Thus, the classification concentrating on the artifacts can be suppressed by the DoF center loss, since the loss drives the neural network to ambiguously detect the display images with only the center images.

In contrast to the center images, the background images are essential for training the difference of DoF. Thus, we derive the DoF background loss by the conventional classification loss as follows:

$$\mathcal{L}_{dof-b}(\mathbf{I}_b^{(i)}) = \mathrm{CE}\left(h(\mathbf{I}_b^{(i)}), l^{(i)}\right). \tag{5}$$

After summing up the entire losses of Eq. 6 for the paired images sampled in the iterative mini-batch, we optimize the neural network by the momentum stochastic gradient descent algorithm [48]. Although the two distinct losses are summed up together, we do not consider any step-by-step training scheme for stable training.

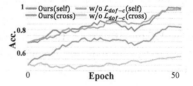

Fig. 4. Analysis for Loss

L_{dual} and L_{dof-c} contradict each other to adversarially train the backbone. To show the effectiveness of the adversarial training, we estimate the test accuracy at every epoch as illustrated in Fig. 4. While the proposed framework improves the cross-display and self-display accuracies, the cross-display accuracy dramatically declines without L_{dof-c}.

4.3 Implementation Details

Before the training phase, all the input images are pre-processed by resizing and random cropping operations. In resizing operation, the original image of 720×1280 pixels is resized into 256×256 pixels, and random cropping operation crops the image into 253×253 pixels from the resized image. Resizing operation is applied to increase the computational efficiency of the neural network, while random cropping operation is necessary to cover the slight movement that can happen essentially during capturing the consecutive paired images. In the test phase, we consider $h(\mathbf{I}_c, \mathbf{I}_b)$ as the prediction of the given pair of images.

The proposed framework is optimized by the Stochastic Gradient Descent method (SGD) with the batch size of 16, executing 50 epochs, and the learning rate begins with 0.1 and later adjusts to 0.01 after 40 epochs. For the stable updates, we utilized the momentom SGD with the momentum of 0.9 and the decay weights of 5×10^{-4}. The λ, that is a scaling factor in Eq. 6, is set to 0.6.

5 Experimental Result

5.1 Setup of Experiments

Dataset Setup and Measurement. Based on the object categories, we split the dataset as follows: 80% as a training set, 10% as a validation set, and the last 10% as a test set. The first experiment trains the model with all of the real images and the display images of a single type of display in the training set. Then, the trained model is evaluated with the display images of two remaining types of displays in the test set. In the second experiment, the display images of two types of displays are utilized in the training phase, while the images of the remaining type of display are used for evaluation in the test phase. To effectively

Table 3. Training of single display

Train displays	Models	WQHD LED		Projector	
		Acc.	A.P.	Acc.	A.P.
5K LCD	SingleNet-18	84.96	85.19	50.00	50.00
	SingleNet-50	89.47	88.23	47.72	50.00
	DualNet-18	87.97	87.79	55.97	55.97
	DualNet-50	88.72	86.87	47.73	50.00
	Ours	**92.48**	**90.55**	**84.85**	**82.84**

Train displays	Models	5K LCD		Projector	
		Acc.	A.P.	Acc.	A.P.
WQHD LED	SingleNet-18	50.38	51.12	76.52	76.52
	SingleNet-50	50.38	51.17	87.12	87.12
	DualNet-18	53.38	52.68	85.07	85.07
	DualNet-50	53.38	54.08	90.91	90.91
	Ours	**90.98**	**90.38**	**98.48**	**98.53**

Train displays	Model	5K LCD		WQHD LED	
		Acc.	A.P.	Acc.	A.P.
Projector	SingleNet-18	49.62	50.38	49.62	50.38
	SingleNet-50	49.62	50.38	61.65	50.38
	DualNet-18	50.38	49.62	50.38	49.62
	DualNet-50	50.38	51.12	58.65	59.26
	Ours	**62.41**	**62.29**	**81.95**	**80.95**

express the performance of our approach, we employ the measurements commonly used in deepfake detection: accuracy (Acc.) and average precision (A.P.) [4–6, 8, 19–21, 30–32, 35, 37]. For experiments, we use GPUs of RTX Titan.

Comparison of Models. For comparison of performance of our model with others, we designed the two simple networks described in Sect. 3.3. *SingleNet-18* exploits only a single image in a classifier, assuming the case of an image forgery by capturing other people's image as one's own. Similar to the backbone of our model, the classification model employs ResNet-18 as the CNN model for distinguishing the real and display images. Moreover, to assess performance with various depth of networks, ResNet-50 is also employed as *SingleNet-50*.

DualNet-18 exploits the paired images with variance in depth; by concatenating the two RGB images, the network considers six channels in total as an input to distinguish between the real images and the display images. We also extend *DualNet-18* by employing ResNet-50, is named as *DualNet-50*. The comparison models including *SingleNet-18*, *SingleNet-50*, *DualNet-18*, and *DualNet-50* are trained by ADAM optimizer [49], with the learning rate of 10^{-4} and the batch size of 16, executing the same number of epochs with the proposed framework. We utilize the ADAM optimizer for the comparison models since the SGD fails to train the neural network with the setting.

5.2 Experiment with Training of Single Display

In the DoF dataset, three types of displays are employed to obtain the display images. To show the robust performance of the framework on the unknown displays, we utilize only the display images captured on a single type of display in the training phase, while the remaining types of displays are employed during the test phase. Thus, we can perform the three experiments respectively utilizing the 5K LCD monitor, the WQHD LED, and the projector in the training phase.

Table 4. Training of multiple displays

Train display	Model	Acc.	A.P.
WQHD LED & Projector	SingleNet-18	54.89	54.20
	SingleNet-50	54.89	55.56
	DualNet-18	55.64	54.97
	DualNet-50	57.14	57.78
	Ours	**81.95**	**77.34**
5K LCD & Projector	SingleNet-18	82.71	82.44
	SingleNet-50	90.23	88.05
	DualNet-18	92.48	92.59
	DualNet-50	88.72	86.87
	Ours	**94.74**	**93.93**
5K LCD & WQHD LED	SingleNet-18	67.91	67.91
	SingleNet-50	66.67	65.97
	DualNet-18	61.19	61.19
	DualNet-50	60.61	58.40
	Ours	**93.28**	**92.56**

As shown in Table 3, the proposed framework has achieved the state-of-the-art performance in all cases. Even though *SingleNet-50* and *DualNet-50* utilize the deeper models than *SingleNet-18* and *DualNet-18*, the performance does not improve at all, which represents the depth of the neural network is not essential to detect DoF in paired images. As the proposed framework, *DualNet-18* and *DualNet-50* also utilize the paired images, their performance declines by 37.12% at most compared to our algorithm. From the result, we can confirm that the proposed framework concentrates on the variance in DoF in the given paired images, while avoiding the supervision affected by the display artifacts. Thus, our algorithm can be trained well by using the DoF properties of the paired images, which indicates that the training dataset with a limited type of display is sufficient for detection.

5.3   Experiment with Training of Multiple Displays

In this experiment, we utilize two types of displays to train the neural network, while the remaining type of display is considered as the test dataset. Thus, we can validate the robustness of the algorithm in the complex environments due to various models of displays. As shown in Table 4, our algorithm achieves the state-of-the-art performance for every combination of the dataset. Interestingly, despite that the display artifacts of the projector are vastly different from the other two types of displays, the proposed framework shows the highest accuracy over 93%, which is superior to other algorithms with accuracy under 68%.

5.4   Ablation Study

To validate the roles of the proposed loss terms in Eq. 6, we conduct several ablation studies. First, we reformulate the entire loss of Eq. 6 to consider the DoF center loss and the DoF background loss separately as follows:

$$\mathcal{L}(\mathbf{I}_c, \mathbf{I}_b) = \lambda_{dual}\mathcal{L}_{dual}(\mathbf{I}_c, \mathbf{I}_b) + \lambda_{dof-c}\mathcal{L}_{dof-c}(\mathbf{I}_c) + \lambda_{dof-b}\mathcal{L}_{dof-b}(\mathbf{I}_b), \qquad (6)$$

where λ_{dof-b} and λ_{dof-c} control the scales of $\mathcal{L}_{dof-c}$ and $\mathcal{L}_{dof-b}$, respectively. With the reformulated equation, we can investigate the individual effect for $\mathcal{L}_{dof-c}$ and $\mathcal{L}_{dof-b}$. When one of the three loss terms is missing, the scale factor corresponding to the missing loss term is set to 0, while the other factors are set to 0.5, respectively. When two loss terms are missing, only the scale factor for the remaining loss term is set to 1, and the other factors become 0.

The first ablation study evaluates the variation of performance when a part of the three loss terms are missing, through the experiments with the training dataset of a single display as in Sect. 5.2.

Table 5 represents the results of the first ablation study. From the results, we can confirm that the proposed framework considering all the loss terms construct the most general model across various types of displays. Interestingly, the model only

Table 5. Ablation study with training of single display

Train display	Objectives			5K LCD		WQHD LED		Projector	
	$\mathcal{L}_{dual}$	$\mathcal{L}_{dof-c}$	$\mathcal{L}_{dof-b}$	Acc.	A.P.	Acc.	A.P.	Acc.	A.P.
5K LCD	✓			95.54	92.96	89.11	86.78	65.28	62.05
		✓		58.93	58.93	55.34	55.34	50.00	50.00
			✓	69.64	66.00	61.39	58.73	22.83	43.96
	✓	✓		82.14	76.74	71.29	66.98	29.35	49.02
	✓		✓	90.18	85.71	83.17	78.70	52.17	51.18
		✓	✓	58.93	58.93	54.46	54.46	45.65	47.73
	✓	✓	✓	**96.99**	**94.37**	**92.48**	**90.55**	**84.85**	**82.84**
WQHD LED	✓			64.27	73.52	98.02	96.49	94.57	92.58
		✓		58.93	58.93	54.46	54.46	50.00	50.00
			✓	58.93	71.37	100.00	100.00	82.61	82.61
	✓	✓		52.68	66.23	99.01	98.21	95.65	94.61
	✓		✓	63.39	74.49	100.00	100.00	92.39	92.39
		✓	✓	68.75	65.35	64.36	60.44	58.70	54.78
	✓	✓	✓	**90.98**	**90.38**	98.48	98.53	**99.25**	**98.53**
Projector	✓			37.50	58.93	64.36	67.31	96.74	93.88
		✓		58.93	58.93	54.46	54.46	50.00	50.00
			✓	41.96	59.55	45.54	54.46	100.00	100.00
	✓	✓		43.75	60.80	81.19	**84.27**	100.00	100.00
	✓		✓	41.07	58.93	45.54	54.46	100.00	100.00
		✓	✓	49.11	60.62	73.26	70.80	88.04	80.70
	✓	✓	✓	**62.41**	**62.29**	**81.95**	80.85	98.48	97.06

with $\mathcal{L}_{dual}$ shows superior performance than the models without $\mathcal{L}_{dof-c}$ or $\mathcal{L}_{dof-b}$, which validates the complementary relationship between the two loss terms in $\mathcal{L}_{dof}$. In addition, the performance declines dramatically when $\mathcal{L}_{dual}$ is missing, which verifies the importance of the paired images to improve the generality of our model.

In the second ablation study, we perform the experiment where all displays are considered for both training and test phases. In this ablation study, we can validate the effect of the three loss terms when the display artifacts in the training dataset also appear in the test phase. As listed in Table 6, interestingly, even when the framework ignores $\mathcal{L}_{dual}$ and $\mathcal{L}_{dof-c}$, the performance does not decrease much from the full framework because the artifacts can be trained only by $\mathcal{L}_{dof-b}$. Although the performance with L_{dof-b} seems stable when trained with all displays, it declines dramatically when tested with unseen displays. The results validate that the three losses are necessary to ignore the display artifacts.

As indicated in the bottom three rows of Table 6, we conduct additional experiments to demonstrate the effectiveness of our framework. *Stacking Feature* concatenates the two features and masks the unused feature by 0, which validates that our scheme of feature summation is superior than the feature concatenation method. *Color Augmentation* considers the additional augmentation method for the color variation, and the consistent results validate that color inconsistency does not affect the classification accuracy. Finally, we validate the effectiveness of our adversarial training scheme with the shared backbone based on the experiments of separating the backbone, which is listed as *Separated Backbone*. Through various ablation studies, we can validate the effectiveness of the proposed framework for DoF-based image forgery detection.

Table 6. Ablation study with every display

$\mathcal{L}_{dual}$	$\mathcal{L}_{dof-c}$	$\mathcal{L}_{dof-b}$	Acc.	A.P.
✓			89.80	84.16
	✓		54.46	54.46
		✓	90.10	84.53
✓	✓		95.05	91.61
✓		✓	89.77	84.13
	✓	✓	54.46	54.46
✓	✓	✓	**96.04**	**93.17**
Stacking Feature			90.70	84.39
Color Augmentation			94.23	89.66
Separated Backbone			89.95	83.33

6   Conclusion

Recently, online transactions have had an exponential growth and expanded to various applications from e-commerce payments to managing financial accounts from mobile phones. Despite the effort of many companies requesting the usage of their own camera applications for submission of images for online transactions, it is difficult to restrict users from taking a picture of a screen displaying objects, instead of real objects. To detect such cases, we introduce a novel approach utilizing paired images with different depth of field (DoF). In contrast to the flat display panel, the target objects in the real environment are located at various focal lengths from the camera lens, creating difference in DoF in captured images. By utilizing this difference, we can distinguish between the real images and the display images. We introduce a new dataset with 2,752 pairs of images capturing real objects or displayed objects on various types of displays. It is the largest real dataset employing DoF with multi-focus. We also propose a new framework for detecting forged images to focus on the difference of DoF in paired images while avoiding learning individual display artifacts. With numerous ablation studies, we validate that our newly proposed framework achieves the state-of-the-art performance using various displays, including those unseen during training.

References

1. Foran, P.: This rental listing scam is on the rise and catching people off guard (2020). https://toronto.ctvnews.ca/this-rental-listing-scam-is-on-the-rise-and-catching-people-off-guard-1.4995168. Accessed 22 June 2020

2. Marcellin, F.: Tackling rail fraud in the UK (2020). https://www.railway-technology.com/features/rail-fraud-in-the-uk/. Accessed 28 Jan 2020
3. Nguyen, T.T., Nguyen, C.M., Nguyen, D.T., Nguyen, D.T., Nahavandi, S.: Deep learning for deepfakes creation and detection. arXiv preprint arXiv:1909.11573 (2019)
4. Cozzolino, D., Thies, J., Rössler, A., Riess, C., Nießner, M., Verdoliva, L.: Forensic-Transfer: weakly-supervised domain adaptation for forgery detection. arXiv (2018)
5. Zhang, X., Karaman, S., Chang, S.: Detecting and simulating artifacts in GAN fake images. In: IEEE International Workshop on Information Forensics and Security, pp. 1–6 (2019)
6. Durall, R., Keuper, M., Keuper, J.: Watch your up-convolution: CNN based generative deep neural networks are failing to reproduce spectral distributions. In: IEEE Conference on Computer Vision and Pattern Recognition, Seattle, WA, United States (2020)
7. Frank, J., Eisenhofer, T., Schönherr, L., Fischer, A., Kolossa, D., Holz, T.: Leveraging frequency analysis for deep fake image recognition. arXiv preprint arXiv:2003.08685 (2020)
8. Wang, S.Y., Wang, O., Zhang, R., Owens, A., Efros, A.A.: CNN-generated images are surprisingly easy to spot...for now. In: IEEE Conference on Computer Vision and Pattern Recognition (2020)
9. Company, S.F.M.A.I.: State farm ® mobile app (2020). https://www.statefarm.com/customer-care/download-mobile-apps/state-farm-mobile-app. Accessed 7 July 2020
10. Metz, J.: How to file a car insurance claim from your couch (2020). https://www.forbes.com/advisor/car-insurance/virtual-claims/. Accessed 8 May 2020
11. Smith, R.: Allstate to move away from physical inspections (2017). https://www.insurancebusinessmag.com/us/news/breaking-news/allstate-to-move-away-from-physical-inspections-66880.aspx/. Accesesed 5 May 2017
12. Karras, T., Aila, T., Laine, S., Lehtinen, J.: Progressive growing of GANs for improved quality, stability, and variation. In: International Conference on Learning Representations (2018)
13. Brock, A., Donahue, J., Simonyan, K.: Large scale GAN training for high fidelity natural image synthesis. In: International Conference on Learning Representations (2019)
14. Zhu, J.Y., Park, T., Isola, P., Efros, A.A.: Unpaired image-to-image translation using cycle-consistent adversarial networks. In: IEEE International Conference on Computer Vision (2017)
15. Choi, Y., Choi, M., Kim, M., Ha, J.W., Kim, S., Choo, J.: StarGAN: unified generative adversarial networks for multi-domain image-to-image translation. In: IEEE Conference on Computer Vision and Pattern Recognition (2018)
16. Choi, Y., Uh, Y., Yoo, J., Ha, J.W.: StarGAN v2: diverse image synthesis for multiple domains. In: IEEE Conference on Computer Vision and Pattern Recognition (2020)
17. Karras, T., Laine, S., Aila, T.: A style-based generator architecture for generative adversarial networks. In: IEEE Conference on Computer Vision and Pattern Recognition, pp. 4401–4410 (2019)
18. Karras, T., Laine, S., Aittala, M., Hellsten, J., Lehtinen, J., Aila, T.: Analyzing and improving the image quality of StyleGAN. CoRR abs/1912.04958 (2019)
19. Yang, X., Li, Y., Lyu, S.: Exposing deep fakes using inconsistent head poses. In: IEEE International Conference on Acoustics, Speech and Signal Processing, pp. 8261–8265 (2019)

20. Li, Y., Chang, M., Lyu, S.: In Ictu Oculi: exposing AI created fake videos by detecting eye blinking. In: 2018 IEEE International Workshop on Information Forensics and Security (WIFS), pp. 1–7 (2018)
21. Ciftci, U.A., Demir, I.: FakeCatcher: detection of synthetic portrait videos using biological signals. arXiv preprint arXiv:1901.02212 (2019)
22. Kee, E., Farid, H.: Exposing digital forgeries from 3-D lighting environments. In: IEEE International Workshop on Information Forensics and Security, pp. 1–6. IEEE (2010)
23. Carvalho, T., Farid, H., Kee, E.R.: Exposing photo manipulation from user-guided 3D lighting analysis. In: Media Watermarking, Security, and Forensics 2015, vol. 9409, p. 940902. International Society for Optics and Photonics (2015)
24. Peng, B., Wang, W., Dong, J., Tan, T.: Improved 3D lighting environment estimation for image forgery detection. In: IEEE International Workshop on Information Forensics and Security (WIFS), 1–6. IEEE (2015)
25. Peng, B., Wang, W., Dong, J., Tan, T.: Optimized 3D lighting environment estimation for image forgery detection. IEEE Trans. Inf. Forensics Secur. **12**, 479–494 (2016)
26. Ye, S., Sun, Q., Chang, E.C.: Detecting digital image forgeries by measuring inconsistencies of blocking artifact. In: IEEE International Conference on Multimedia and Expo, pp. 12–15. IEEE (2007)
27. Tralic, D., Petrovic, J., Grgic, S.: JPEG image tampering detection using blocking artifacts. In: International Conference on Systems, Signals and Image Processing, pp. 5–8. IEEE (2012)
28. Agarwal, S., Farid, H., Gu, Y., He, M., Nagano, K., Li, H.: Protecting world leaders against deep fakes. In: IEEE Conference on Computer Vision and Pattern Recognition Workshops, Long Beach, CA, p. 8. IEEE (2019)
29. Matern, F., Riess, C., Stamminger, M.: Exploiting visual artifacts to expose Deepfakes and face manipulations. In: IEEE Winter Applications of Computer Vision Workshops, pp. 83–92. IEEE (2019)
30. Li, Y., Lyu, S.: Exposing DeepFake videos by detecting face warping artifacts. In: IEEE Conference on Computer Vision and Pattern Recognition Workshops (2019)
31. Montserrat, D.M., et al.: Deepfakes detection with automatic face weighting. arXiv preprint arXiv:2004.12027 (2020)
32. Bayar, B., Stamm, M.C.: A deep learning approach to universal image manipulation detection using a new convolutional layer. In: ACM Workshop on Information Hiding and Multimedia Security, pp. 5–10 (2016)
33. Kirchner, M.: Fast and reliable resampling detection by spectral analysis of fixed linear predictor residue. In: ACM Workshop on Multimedia and Security, pp. 11–20 (2008)
34. Huang, D.Y., Huang, C.N., Hu, W.C., Chou, C.H.: Robustness of copy-move forgery detection under high jpeg compression artifacts. Multimed. Tools Appl. **76**, 1509–1530 (2017)
35. Marra, F., Gragnaniello, D., Verdoliva, L., Poggi, G.: Do GANs leave artificial fingerprints? In: IEEE Conference on Multimedia Information Processing and Retrieval, pp. 506–511. IEEE (2019)
36. Bappy, J.H., Simons, C., Nataraj, L., Manjunath, B., Roy-Chowdhury, A.K.: Hybrid LSTM and encoder-decoder architecture for detection of image forgeries. IEEE Trans. Image Process. **28**, 3286–3300 (2019)
37. Durall, R., Keuper, M., Pfreundt, F.J., Keuper, J.: Unmasking DeepFakes with simple features. arXiv preprint arXiv:1911.00686 (2019)

38. Demers, J.: Depth of field: a survey of techniques. GPU Gems 1, U390 (2004)
39. Wu, Y., et al.: Extended depth-of-field in holographic imaging using deep-learning-based autofocusing and phase recovery. Optica 5, 704–710 (2018)
40. Mirza, M., Osindero, S.: Conditional generative adversarial nets. arXiv preprint arXiv:1411.1784 (2014)
41. Guo, X., Nie, R., Cao, J., Zhou, D., Mei, L., He, K.: FuseGAN: learning to fuse multi-focus image via conditional generative adversarial network. IEEE Trans. Multimedia 21, 1982–1996 (2019)
42. Zhang, J., Liao, Q., Liu, S., Ma, H., Yang, W., Xue, J.h.: Real-MFF dataset: a large realistic multi-focus image dataset with ground truth. arXiv preprint arXiv:2003.12779 (2020)
43. Cheng, Z., Bai, F., Xu, Y., Zheng, G., Pu, S., Zhou, S.: Focusing attention: towards accurate text recognition in natural images. In: Proceedings of the IEEE International Conference on Computer Vision, pp. 5076–5084 (2017)
44. Nejati, M., Samavi, S., Shirani, S.: Multi-focus image fusion using dictionary-based sparse representation. Inf. Fusion 25, 72–84 (2015)
45. Liu, Y., Chen, X., Peng, H., Wang, Z.: Multi-focus image fusion with a deep convolutional neural network. Inf. Fusion 36, 191–207 (2017)
46. Ma, H., Zhang, J., Liu, S., Liao, Q.: Boundary aware multi-focus image fusion using deep neural network. In: 2019 IEEE International Conference on Multimedia and Expo (ICME), pp. 1150–1155. IEEE (2019)
47. He, K., Zhang, X., Ren, S., Sun, J.: Deep residual learning for image recognition. In: Proceedings of the IEEE Conference on Computer Vision and Pattern Recognition, pp. 770–778 (2016)
48. Rumelhart, D.E., Hinton, G.E., Williams, R.J.: Learning representations by back-propagating errors. Nature 323, 533–536 (1986)
49. Kingma, D., Ba, J.: Adam: a method for stochastic optimization. In: International Conference on Learning Representations (2014)

Explaining Image Classifiers by Removing Input Features Using Generative Models

Chirag Agarwal$^{(\boxtimes)}$ and Anh Nguyen

Auburn University, Auburn, AL 36849, USA
chiragagarwall12@gmail.com, anh.ng8@gmail.com

Abstract. Perturbation-based explanation methods often measure the contribution of an input feature to an image classifier's outputs by heuristically removing it via e.g. blurring, adding noise, or graying out, which often produce unrealistic, out-of-samples. Instead, we propose to integrate a generative inpainter into three representative attribution methods to remove an input feature. Our proposed change improved all three methods in (1) generating more plausible counterfactual samples under the true data distribution; (2) being more accurate according to three metrics: object localization, deletion, and saliency metrics; and (3) being more robust to hyperparameter changes. Our findings were consistent across both ImageNet and Places365 datasets and two different pairs of classifiers and inpainters.

1 Introduction

Explaining a classifier's outputs given a certain input is increasingly important, especially for life-critical applications [1,2]. A popular means for visually explaining an image classifier's decisions is an *attribution map* i.e. a heatmap that highlights the input pixels that are the evidence for and against the classification outputs [3]. To construct an attribution map, many methods approximate the attribution value of an input region by the classification probability change when that region is absent i.e. removed from the image. While removing an input feature to measure its attribution is a principle method (i.e. "intervention" in causal reasoning [4]), a key open question is: **How to remove?**

State-of-the-art perturbation-based attribution methods implement the absence of an input feature by replacing it with (a) mean pixels [5,6]; (b) random noise [7,8]; or (c) blurred versions of the original content [9,10]. However, these removal (i.e. perturbation) techniques often produce unrealistic, out-of-distribution images (Fig. 1b,d) on which the classifiers were not trained. Because classifiers are often easily fooled by unusual input patterns [11–13], we hypothesize that such examples might yield heatmaps that are (1) unreliable i.e. sensitive to hyperparameter settings [14]; and (2) not faithful [15].

Electronic supplementary material The online version of this chapter (https://doi.org/10.1007/978-3-030-69544-6_7) contains supplementary material, which is available to authorized users.

© Springer Nature Switzerland AG 2021
H. Ishikawa et al. (Eds.): ACCV 2020, LNCS 12627, pp. 101–118, 2021.
https://doi.org/10.1007/978-3-030-69544-6_7

(a) Real + BB   (b) SP [5]   (c) SP-G   (d) LIME [6] (e) LIME-G   (f) MP2   (g) MP2-G

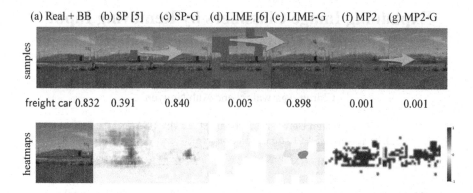

Fig. 1. Three attribution methods, SP [5], LIME [6], and MP2, often produce unrealistic, out-of-distribution perturbation samples. **Top row:** SP slides a 29×29 gray patch across the image (b). LIME grays out a set of random superpixels (d). MP2 blurs out the entire image (f). In contrast, a learned inpainter integrated into these methods produces realistic samples for the same perturbation masks, here, completing the freight car (c), completing the background (e), and removing the car from the scene (g). Note that the freight car class probability is reduced by 53% (i.e. from 0.832 to 0.391) when only a part of the car was occluded (b). However, it is reduced by ~100% down to 0.003 when the car is still present but the background is unnaturally masked out (d). Since the inpainted samples are more realistic, the probability drops are often less (c & e) and substantial only when the object is removed completely (g). **Bottom row:** the inpainted samples yield heatmaps that, in overall, outperform the original methods on the object localization task Sect. 4.3. Here, our heatmaps (SP-G, LIME-G, and MP2-G) are less noisy and more focused on the object.

To combat these two issues, we propose to harness a state-of-the-art generative inpainting model (hereafter, an inpainter) to remove pixels from an input image and fill in with content that is plausible under the true data distribution. We test our approach on three representative attribution methods of Sliding-Patch (SP) [5], LIME [6], and Meaningful-Perturbation (MP) [9] across two large-scale datasets of ImageNet [16] and Places365 [17]. For each dataset, we use a separate pair of pre-trained image classifiers and inpainters. We chose SP, LIME, and MP because they are among the most commonly used and applicable to any classifier. Our main findings include:[1]

1. Inpainting is more effective than common techniques in removing discriminative features. That is, photos with the main object blurred or grayed out are still 3 times more recognizable by classifiers and more similar to the original photo (via MS-SSIM and LPIPS) than photos with objects removed via inpainting (Sect. 4.2).
2. Our results are the first to show that incorporating an inpainter improves perturbation-based attribution methods i.e. producing (1) more plausible perturbation samples; (2) explanations that are similarly or more accurate on three common benchmarks—object localization, deletion, and saliency metrics (Sect. 4.3); and (3) explanations that are more robust to hyperparameter changes i.e. the SAM metric [14] (Sect. 4.4);

---

[1] All our codes are available at https://github.com/anguyen8/generative-attribution-methods.

3. We propose MP2-G (Sect. 3.5), a variant that is substantially more accurate, reliable, and having four hyperparameters fewer than the common MP [9]—a state-of-the-art approach which is the basis for many extensions [18–22].

To the best of our knowledge, this is the first work that shows the effectiveness of generative models in improving the accuracy and reliability of explanation methods.

2 Related Work

Attribution methods can be grouped into two main classes: (1) white- and (2) black-box.

White-Box. Given access to the network architecture and parameters, attribution maps can be constructed analytically from (a) the gradients of the output w.r.t. the input [23], (b) the class activation map in fully-convolutional neural networks [24], (c) both the gradients and activations [25], or (d) the gradient times the input image [26]. However, some gradient-based heatmaps can be too noisy to be human-interpretable [27], and suffer from gradient saturation [28]. To combat these issues, perturbation techniques were also utilized. That is, to make a gradient-based heatmap more robust and smooth, a number of methods essentially average out the resultant heatmaps across a large set of perturbed inputs that are created via (a) adding random noise to the input [9,27], (b) blurring the input [9], or (c) linearly interpolating between the input and a reference "baseline" image [28].

Black-Box. Perturbation-based methods are important for use cases when only a black-box model is given (no network parameters). Black-box methods often remove (i.e. perturb) an input region and take the resultant classification probability change to be the attribution value for that region. While the idea is principle in causal reasoning, the physical interventions—taking an object out of a scene (revealing the content behind it) while keeping other factors unchanged—are impractical in most real-world applications. The absence of an input region is often implemented by replacing it with (a) mean pixels [5,6]; (b) random noise [7,8]; or (c) blurred versions of the original content [9]. However, these removal techniques often produce unrealistic, out-of-samples (Fig. 1), which raises huge concerns on the sensitivity and faithfulness of explanations.

An open question for existing perturbation-based attribution methods is: *Do explanations become more robust and accurate if input features are removed via a strong, natural image prior?* Here, we systematically study this question across three representative attribution methods: two black-box methods that are perturbation-based (i.e. SP and LIME) and one white-box method that relies on both perturbations and gradients (i.e. MP). These representative methods also perturb different types of input features: pixels (i.e. MP), superpixels (i.e. LIME); and square patches (i.e. SP).

The closest to our work is FIDO-CA [29], which extended MP and harnessed an image inpainter to synthesize counterfactual samples to explain classifiers' decisions. However, FIDO-CA [29] underperformed most baselines that do not use inpainters. Inspired by [29], we propose a key change in optimization objectives (see details in Sect. 4) that enabled our approach to improve upon FIDO-CA by a large margin. That is, for the first time, we show that incorporating an inpainter improves the accuracy and robustness of explanation methods.

3 Methods

3.1 Datasets and Networks

Classifiers. Our experiments were conducted using two separate ResNet-50 image classifiers [30] that were pre-trained on the 1000-class ImageNet 2012 [16] and Places365 [17], respectively. The two models were officially released by the PyTorch model zoo [31] and by the authors [32], respectively.

Datasets. We chose these two datasets because they are large, natural-image sets covering a wide range of images from object-centric (i.e. ImageNet) to scenery (i.e. Places365). From the 50,000 ImageNet and 36,500 Places365 validation-set images, we randomly sampled a set of 2000 images correctly classified by their respective ResNet-50 models. We used these two sets of images in all experiments throughout the paper.

Inpainters. For each classifier, pre-trained either on ImageNet or Places365, we used a TensorFlow DeepFill-v1 model pre-trained by [33] on the same respective dataset. DeepFill-v1 takes as input a color image and a binary mask, both at resolution 256×256, and outputs an inpainted image of the same size. In this work, we also tried DeepFill-v2 [34], a free-form inpainting model, but the overall results did not change significantly. Apart from these two, to the best of our knowledge, there are no other publicly available generative inpainters for both ImageNet and Places365 datasets. The DeepFill-v1 inpainter is practically feasible for attribution algorithms as it only takes 0.2s/image on one GPU (and 1.5s/image on CPUs) for inpainting a 512×512 image.

3.2 Problem Formulation

Let $s : \mathbb{R}^{D \times D \times 3} \rightarrow \mathbb{R}$ be an image classifier that maps a square, color image x of spatial dimension $D \times D$ onto a softmax probability of a target class. An attribution map $A \in [-1, 1]^{D \times D}$ associates each input pixel x_i to a scalar $A_i \in [-1, 1]$ which indicates how much x_i contributes for or against the prediction score $s(x)$. We describe below three methods for generating attribution maps together with our respective proposed variants (hereafter, G-methods) which harness a generative inpainter.

3.3 Sliding-Patch (SP)

SP. [5] proposed to slide a gray, occlusion patch across the image and record the probability changes as attribution values in corresponding locations in the heatmap. That is, given a binary occlusion mask $m \in \{0, 1\}^{D \times D}$ (here, 1's inside the patch region and 0's otherwise) and a filler image $f \in \mathbb{R}^{D \times D \times 3}$, a perturbed image $\bar{x} \in \mathbb{R}^{D \times D \times 3}$ (see Fig. 1b) is given by:

$$\bar{x} = x \odot (1 - m) + f \odot m \tag{1}$$

where $\odot$ denotes the Hadamard product and f is a zero image i.e. a gray image[2] before input pre-processing. For every pixel x_i, one can generate a perturbation sample $\bar{x}^i$

---

[2] The ImageNet mean pixel is gray (0.485, 0.456, 0.406).

(i.e. by setting the patch center at x_i) and compute the attribution value $A_i = s(x) - s(\bar{x}^i)$. However, sliding the patch densely across the 224×224 input image is prohibitively slow. Therefore, we chose a 29×29 occlusion patch size with stride 3, which yields a smaller heatmap A' of size 66×66. We bi-linearly upsampled A' to the image size to create the full-res A. See Fig. 1b for an example of SP heatmaps and perturbed images.

We implemented SP by converting a MATLAB implementation [35] into PyTorch. All of our individual experiments in this work were run on a single GTX 1080Ti GPU.

SP-G. Note that the stride, size, and color of a SP sliding patch are three hyperparameters that are often chosen heuristically, and varying them can change the final heatmaps radically [14]. To ameliorate the sensitivity to hyperparameter choices, we propose a variant called SP-G by only replacing the gray filler image of SP with the output image of an inpainter (described in Sect. 3.1) i.e. $f = G(m, x)$ while keeping the rest of SP the same (Fig. 1b vs. c; top row). That is, at every location of the sliding window, SP-G queries the inpainter for content to fill in the window.

3.4 Local Interpretable Model-Agnostic Explanations (LIME)

LIME. While SP occludes one square patch of the image at a time, LIME [6] occludes a random-shaped region. The algorithm first segments the input image into S non-overlapping superpixels [36]. Then, LIME generates a perturbed image $\bar{x}$ by graying out a random set of superpixels among 2^S possible sets. That is, LIME follows Eq. 1 where the pixel-wise mask m is derived from a random superpixel mask $m' \in \{0, 1\}^S$. For each sample $\bar{x}^i$, we measure the output score $s(\bar{x}^i)$ and evenly distribute it among all occluded superpixels in $\bar{x}^i$. Each superpixel's attribution is then inversely weighted by the L_2 distance $\|x - \bar{x}^i\|$ via an exponential kernel and then averaged out across N samples. The resultant attribution a_k of a superpixel k is finally assigned to all pixels in that group in the full-resolution heatmap A. In practice, [6] iteratively optimized for $\{a_k\}_S$ via LASSO for 1000 steps to also maximize the number of zero attributions i.e. encouraging simpler, sparse attribution maps. We used the implementation provided by the authors of LIME [37] and their default hyperparameters of $S = 50$ and $N = 1000$.

LIME-G. While avoiding the bias given by the SP square patch, LIME perturbation samples remain unrealistic. Therefore, we propose LIME-G, a variant of LIME, by only changing the gray image f to a synthesized image $G(m, x)$ as in SP-G while keeping the rest of LIME unchanged.

3.5 Meaningful Perturbation (MP)

MP. As SP and LIME gray out patches and superpixels in the input image, they generate unrealistic counterfactual samples and produce coarse heatmaps. To combat these issues, Fong et al. [9] proposed the MP algorithm i.e. learning a minimal, continuous mask $m \in [0, 1]^{D \times D}$ that blurs out the input image in a way that would minimize the target-class probability. That is, MP attempts to solve the following optimization problem:

$$m^* = \arg\min_m \lambda \|m\|_1 + s(\bar{x}) \tag{2}$$

where $\bar{x}$ is given by Eq. 1 but with $f = B_\sigma(x)$ i.e. the input image blurred by a Gaussian kernel $B_\sigma(.)$ of radius $\sigma = 10$. Note that, in MP, the attribution map A is also the learned mask m. However, solving Eq. 2 directly often yields heatmaps that are noisy and sensitive to hyperparameter changes [14]. Therefore, MP only learned a small 28×28 mask and upsampled it to the image size in every optimization step. In addition, they also encouraged the mask to be smooth and robust to input changes by changing the objective function to the following:

$$m^* = \arg\min_m \lambda_1 \|m\|_1 + \lambda_2 TV(m) + \mathbb{E}_{\tau \sim \mathcal{U}(0,4)} \big[s(\Phi(\bar{x}, \tau)) \big] \qquad (3)$$

where $TV(m) = \sum_i \|\nabla m_i\|_3^3$ i.e. a total-variation norm that acts as a smoothness prior over the mask. The third term is the expectation over a batch of randomly jittered versions of the blurred image $\bar{x}$. That is, $\Phi(.)$ is the jitter operator that translates an image $\bar{x}$ vertically or horizontally by τ pixels where τ is drawn from a discrete uniform distribution $\mathcal{U}(0, 4)$. We randomly initialized the mask from a continuous uniform distribution $\mathcal{U}(0, 1)$ and minimize the objective function in Eq. 3 via gradient descent for 300 steps. Our MP implementation was in PyTorch and followed all the hyperparameters as described in [9].

MP2. In the original formulation, MP is highly sensitive to changes in some of its hyperparameters [14]. In our preliminary experiments (data not shown), we found that integrating an inpainter into the existing unstable MP optimization did not yield more accurate heatmaps. In addition, the L_1 and TV terms (Eq. 3) introduce strong biases that impede the contribution of the content generated by inpainters.

Therefore, we propose MP2, a more reliable and accurate variant by eliminating four hyperparameters from MP: the L_1 norm, TV norm, the jitter operator and the stopping criterion of 300 optimization steps (Sect. 4.3). That is, we still find a minimal mask (Eq. 2) but by initializing it with all zeros and growing the number of 1's (i.e. the blurred region) gradually. Following JSMA [38], in every iteration, we add 1's to two pixels that have the highest gradient norms. We stop the mask optimization when the classification probability reaches random chance, i.e. 0.001 for ImageNet and 0.003 for Places365. As MP, we use the same Gaussian blur radius of 10 and the mask size of 28×28.

MP2-G. We integrate an inpainter G to MP2 by only changing the filler image $f = B_\sigma(x)$ that is used in Eq. 1 to an inpainted image i.e. $f = G(m_b, x)$ where $m_b \in \{0, 1\}^{D \times D}$ is the binary mask learned via MP2 optimization.

4 Experiments and Results

4.1 Inpainter Failed to Synthesize Backgrounds Given only Foreground Objects

Chang et al. [29] proposed to find a minimal set of input pixels that would keep the classification outputs unchanged even when the other pixels in the image are removed (i.e. the "preservation" objective [9]) via an inpainter. Their method, FIDO-CA, uses the same DeepFill-v1 inpainter as in our work; however, their "preservation" objective encourages the inpainter to predict the missing background pixels conditioned on the remaining foreground object—a task that DeepFill-v1 was *not* trained to do and thus produced unrealistic samples as in [29]. In contrast, our MP2-G method harnesses the dual "deletion" objective i.e. finding the smallest set of input pixels which when inpainted would minimize the target-class probability—which intuitively asks the inpainter to replace the main object with some content that is consistent with the background i.e. the training objective of DeepFill-v1.

To compare these two objectives, we randomly chose 50 validation-set images from 52 ImageNet bird classes and computed their segmentation masks via a pre-trained DeepLab model [39]. We found that using the DeepFill-v1 to inpaint the foreground region (i.e. our "deletion" task) yields realistic samples where the object is removed. In contrast, using the inpainter to fill in the missing background area [29] yields unrealistic images whose backgrounds contain features (e.g. bird feathers or beaks) unnaturally pasted from the object (Fig. 2). This result motivated us to integrate DeepFill-v1 into MP2 but with the "deletion" objective.

(a)	(b)	(c)	(d)	(e)	(f)	(g)	(h)
Real	Mask	Preserve [29]	Delete	Real	Mask	Preserve [29]	Delete

Fig. 2. Using the DeepFill-v1 inpainter to fill in the background region (i.e. "preservation" task [29]) yields unrealistic images that contain features unnaturally pasted from the object (c, g). This key difference between the "deletion" (d, h) and "preservation" (c, g) objectives is further reflected in the evaluation results of MP2-G and FIDO-CA [29] where the attribution maps generated using the latter consistently underperforms than MP2-G (Sect. 4.3). See Fig. S3 for more examples of the images.

(a) Real	(b) Blur	(c) Gray	(d) Inpaint	(e) Noise

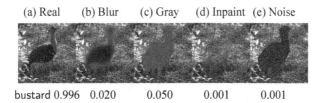

bustard 0.996   0.020   0.050   0.001   0.001

Fig. 3. The results of filling the object mask in a real image (a) via four different filling methods. The shape of the bird is still visible even after blurring (b), graying out (c) or adding random noise (e) to the bird region. The inpainter removes the bird and fills in with some realistic background content (d).

4.2 Inpainter Is Effective in Removing Discriminative Features

While removing objects from an image via DeepFill-v1, qualitatively, yields realistic samples, here, we quantitatively test how effective this strategy is in removing target-class discriminative features in comparison with three existing filling methods: (1) zero pixels; (2) random noise; or (3) blurred versions of the original content. Using the same procedure as described in Sect. 4.1, we randomly sampled 1000 bird images and segmented out the bird in each image. We filled in the object mask in each image via all four methods (Fig. 3) and compared the results (Table 1). Surprisingly, the blurred and grayed-out images are still correctly classified at 26.4% and 13.3% (Table 1), respectively, by a pre-trained Inception-v3 classifier [40], i.e., these perturbed images still contain discriminative features relevant to the target class. In contrast, only 8.9% of the inpainted images were correctly classified suggesting that the inpainter removes the discriminative features more effectively. After the main subject (here, birds) are removed from an image, one would expect the modified image to be perceptually different from the original image (where the bird exists).

Table 1. Evaluation of four different filling methods on 1000 random bird images. The Inception-v3 accuracy scores suggest that inpainting the object mask (d) removes substantially more discriminative features relevant to the removed object compared to blurring (b) or graying out (c). Perceptually, the inpainted images are also more dissimilar to the corresponding real images according two similarity metrics: MS-SSIM (lower is better) and LPIPS (higher is better).

Metrics	Filling methods				
	(a) Real	(b) Blur	(c) Gray	(d) Inpaint	(e) Noise
Inception Acc. (%)	92.30	26.40	13.30	8.90	4.40
MS-SSIM	1.000	0.941	0.731	0.707	0.692
LPIPS	0.000	2.423	3.186	3.208	3.639

Here, we evaluate how each of the four in-filled images $\bar{x}$ (where the bird has been removed) is perceptually dissimilar to the original image x by measuring the MS-SSIM and LPIPS [41] scores between every pair $(x, \bar{x})$. Across both metrics, the inpainted images are consistently more dissimilar from the real images compared to the blurred and grayed-out images. Note that in all three quantitative metrics, the inpainted images are the closest to the noise-filled images (Table 1d–e) despite being substantially more realistic (Fig. 3). Furthermore, the problem with using blurring as a perturbation operation is explicitly seen in cases where attribution maps covers the entire image. This is because for some inputs even blurring out the entire image does not result in a significant probability (Fig. 4). Across the set of 2000 images, the average confidence score on blurring the entire image was 0.3198.

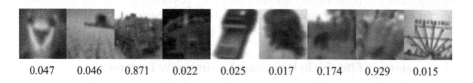

0.047   0.046   0.871   0.022   0.025   0.017   0.174   0.929   0.015

Fig. 4. The target class probability of images do not drop to random guess, i.e. 0.001 for ImageNet, even after perturbing the entire image with a Gaussian blur radius of $\sigma = 10$.

4.3 Are Explanations by G-methods More Accurate?

While there are currently no established ground-truth datasets to evaluate the correctness of an attribution map, prior research often assessed correctness via three common proxy metrics: (1) the object localization task [24]; (2) the deletion task [42]; (3) the saliency metric [7]. Here, we ran 8 algorithms on the ImageNet and Places365 datasets using the default hyperparameters (Sect. 3). The heatmaps are then upsampled to the full image resolution for evaluation on all three measures above.

Table 2. Localization errors (lower is better) for all attribution methods on ImageNet. Naively taking the whole image as a bounding box yields an error of 38.56% (baseline). MP2-G outperformed all methods including MP, MP2 and a related FIDO-CA [29].

Baseline	SP [5]	SP-G	LIME [6]	LIME-G	MP [9]	MP2	MP2-G	FIDO-CA [29]
39.7%	41.9%	**38.95%**	28.05%	**26.55%**	29.35%	24.4%	**24.03%**	27.9%

Object Localization. Zhou et al. [24] proposed to evaluate heatmaps by localizing objects in the ImageNet images, which often contain a single object of a known class. We followed the localization procedure in [9] for the ImageNet dataset. That is, for each algorithm, we derived multiple bounding boxes per heatmap by thresholding it at different values of $t = \alpha\mu_{max}$, where μ_{max} is the maximum intensity in the heatmap and $\alpha \in [0 : 0.05 : 0.95]$. For each α, we computed the Intersection over Union (IoU) score between a derived bounding box and the ImageNet ground-truth. The object localization error was calculated by thresholding each IoU score at 0.5 and averaging them across the number of images. For each method, we chose the best α^* that yielded the lowest error on a held-out set of 1000 ImageNet images (Table 2). **We found that our generative version of the attribution algorithms outperformed their respective counterparts and MP2-G outperformed FIDO-CA**[3] (Table 2). Among the 8 methods, MP2-G obtained the lowest error of 24.03%. Qualitatively, MP2-G generates attribution maps that are more localized to the objects in the image (Fig. 5).

Table 3. Deletion metric (lower is better): SP-G, LIME-G, and MP2-G outperformed their counterparts on both ImageNet and Places365 datasets. G-methods also outperformed a baseline (here, random attribution maps).

Dataset	Baseline	SP [5]	SP-G	LIME [6]	LIME-G	MP [9]	MP2	MP2-G	FIDO-CA [29]
ImageNet	0.2083	0.1996	**0.1769**	0.1355	**0.1171**	0.1654	0.1530	**0.1311**	0.1638
Places365	0.2151	0.2560	**0.1944**	0.1919	**0.1582**	0.2014	0.1980	**0.1871**	0.1987

---

[3] We produced FIDO-CA results using the code provided by the authors [29]. See Sect. A1 for more details.

Deletion Metric. Intuitively, if the attributions in an explanation correctly reflect the importance of input pixels, removing the input pixels of highest attributions should cause a substantial probability drop. The deletion metric [42] measures the area under the curve of the target-class probability as we gradually zero out input pixels of the highest attributions in descending order. The deletion scores are widely used to compare attribution methods [18,43–45] i.e., lower deletion scores are considered more accurate. Here, we evaluated all 8 methods via the code released by [42] where the authors knocked out 224×8 pixels at a time. Similar to object localization results, we observed a consistent trend: **Across both ImageNet and Places365, our G-methods outperformed their counterparts while MP2-G outperformed all algorithms** (Table 3).

Saliency Metric. Dabkowski et al. [7] proposed that if an explanation is accurate then the most salient patch in an image (derived from the attribution map) should have a high prediction score. That is, we took the smallest rectangular patch derived from thresholding the attribution map using an α^* which yielded the least salient metric score on a

(a) Real + BB   (b) MP2-G   (c) SP [5]   (d) LIME [6]   (e) MP [9]   (f) MP2

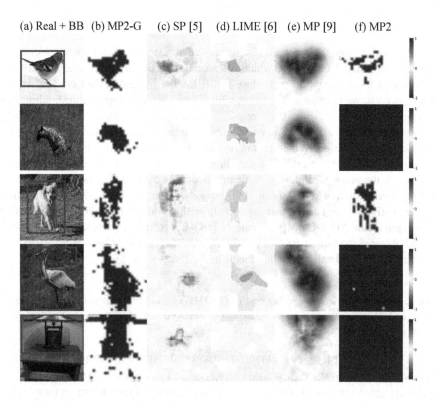

Fig. 5. MP2-G results in attribution maps that localize the objects accurately compared to other perturbation-based methods. From left to right, in each row, we show a real ImageNet image with its ground-truth bounding box (BB) (a), attribution maps from the proposed MP2-G (b) and other existing methods (c–f). Images are randomly chosen. For qualitative evaluation, Figs. S4-S5 show a set of heatmaps and their derived BB's.

held-out dataset of 1000 images (similar to the object localization task). The saliency metric is then defined as $\log\big(\max(a, 0.05)\big) - \log(s(x_p))$ where a is the ratio of the patch size over the image size and $s(x_p)$ is the classification probability for the patch x_p upsampled to the full image size. A lower saliency score indicates a more accurate explanation. **On both ImageNet and Places365, SP-G and MP2-G obtained lower scores than their counterparts while LIME-G was on par with LIME (Table 4). MP2-G outperformed all its baselines, i.e. MP, MP2, and FIDO-CA.** We hypothesize that the difference between LIME vs. LIME-G is small because they operate at the superpixel level and most salient *pixels* might fall in common *superpixels* across their respective explanations. Refer to Fig. S6 for the localization error and saliency metric scores for different α's on the held-out set of 1000 images.

4.4 Are G-methods More Robust to Hyperparameter Changes?

Machine learning methods are highly sensitive to hyperparameters, contributing to the reproducibility crisis [46]. Similarly, perturbation-based attribution methods were recently found to be highly sensitive to common hyperparameters [14]. Such sensitivity poses a huge challenge in (1) evaluating the explanations; and (2) building trust with end users [1]. Our hypothesis is that heuristically-perturbed samples are often far from the true data distribution and thus contribute to the hyperparameter sensitivity of

Table 4. Saliency metric (lower is better): On both ImageNet and Places365, while LIME and LIME-G performed on-par, SP-G and MP2-G consistently outperformed their counterparts (MP2-G outperformed its baselines: FIDO-CA, MP and MP2). The baseline was calculated using a random attribution map.

Dataset	Baseline	SP [5]	SP-G	LIME [6]	LIME-G	MP [9]	MP2	MP2-G	FIDO-CA [29]
ImageNet	0.3294	0.3774	**0.3122**	0.1191	0.1159	0.1182	0.0890	**0.0540**	0.1071
Places365	1.117	1.1311	**1.1148**	0.9597	0.9568	1.0413	0.9331	**0.9156**	0.9263

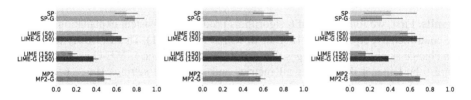

(a) SSIM   (b) Pearson correlation of HOG features (c) Spearman rank correlation

Fig. 6. Error plots for SSIM (a), Pearson correlation of HOG features (b), and Spearman rank correlation (c) scores obtained from 1000 random ImageNet images (higher is better). G-methods are more robust than their counterparts (dark vs light bars). LIME-G, in particular, is robust than LIME on both low and high resolutions i.e. $S \in \{50, 150\}$ (green and blue bars). The same trends were also observed on the Places365 dataset (Fig. S2). The exact numbers are reported in Table S1. (Color figure online)

heatmaps. Here, we test whether our generative methods are more robust to hyperparameter changes than their original counterparts.

Similarity Metrics and Image Sets . Following [14,15], we used three metrics from scikit-image [47] to measure the similarity of heatmaps: the Structural Similarity Index (SSIM), the Pearson correlation of the histograms of oriented gradients (HOGs), and the Spearman rank correlation. We upsampled all heatmaps to the full image size before feeding them into the similarity metrics. We performed the test on a set of 1000 random images from both ImageNet and Places365.

SP Sensitivity Across Patch Sizes. It remains a question how to choose the patch size in the SP algorithm because changing it can change the explanation radically [48]. Therefore, we compare the sensitivity of SP and SP-G when sweeping across 5 patch sizes $p \times p$ with stride 3 where $p \in \{5, 17, 29, 41, 53\}$. We chose this set to cover the common sizes that have been used in the literature. For each input image, we obtained $k = 5$ heatmaps (i.e. each corresponds to a patch size) and then measured the similarity among all $k(k-1)/2 = 10$ possible pairs.

LIME Sensitivity Across Random Batches of Samples. LIME randomly samples N perturbed images $\{\bar{x}^i\}_N$ and uses them to fit a heatmap. Therefore, we compared the sensitivity of LIME and LIME-G across 5 random batches of $N = 500$ perturbation samples. That is, for each input image among the 1000, we generated $k = 5$ heatmaps and computed the similarity among all 10 possible pairs. We ran this experiment for a small and a large heatmap resolution i.e. two numbers of superpixels $S \in \{50, 150\}$ while keeping all other hyperparameters constant.

MP2 Sensitivity Across Mask Sizes. Because optimizing a mask at a high resolution is prohibitively slow, Fong et al. [9] used an MP mask of size 28×28 and upsampled it to the image size when applying the blur operator on the input image. Therefore, the mask size is a hyperparameter of MP2 and MP2-G. Here, we compare the sensitivity by sweeping across the three mask sizes where $D \in \{28, 56, 112\}$. We re-ran each algorithm three times on each input image to yield three heatmaps and computed the average pairwise similarity scores from all possible pairs of heatmaps.

Results. First, we found that all 6 algorithms produce inconsistent explanations across the controlled hyperparameters (Fig. 6; all scores are below 1). That is, LIME heatmaps can change as one simply changes the random seed! However, LIME-G is consistently more robust than LIME across all metrics and superpixel settings (Figs. 6 & S17). Across the patch sizes, SP-G is also consistently more robust than SP (Fig. 6a–b; light vs. dark yellow). SP-G and SP performed on par with high standard deviations under the Spearman rank correlation (Fig. 6c). Across the optimization mask size, MP2-G is consistently more robust than MP2 (Fig. 6; light vs. dark red).

5   The Inner-Workings of Generative Attribution Methods

Here, we further explain why our G-methods are both more (1) accurate in localizing objects (Sect. 4.3) and (2) robust to hyperparameter changes (Sect. 4.4).

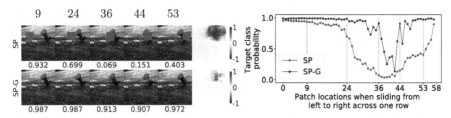

(a) Perturbation samples & heatmaps (rightmost)   (b) GT-class probability over patch locations

Fig. 7. We ran SP and SP-G using a 53×53 patch on a nail class image. Here are the perturbation samples from both methods when the patch is slided horizontally across a row at 5 locations $\{9, 24, 36, 44, 53\}$ (a); and their respective target-class probabilities (b). SP-G samples are more realistic than SP and its heatmap localizes the object accurately (a). That is, the probabilities for SP-G samples are more stable and only substantially drop when the patch covers the object (blue vs. red). See Fig. S7 for more examples. (Color figure online)

5.1   More Accurate Object Localization: A Case Study of SP-G

We found that as the gray patch of SP is slided from left to right across the input image (Fig. 7a; top), the target-class probability gradually decreases and approaches 0 when the patch occludes most of the object (Fig. 7b; red line). Notably, the probability even drops when the patch is far outside the object region (Fig. 7b; red line within $[0, 24]$) due to SP's unrealistic grayish samples. Hence, the probability distributions by SP often yield a large blob of high attributions around the object in the heatmap (Fig. 7a; top-right). In contrast, the inpainted samples of SP-G often keep the probability variance low except when the patch overlaps with the object (Fig. 7b; blue vs. red), yielding heatmaps that are more localized towards the object (Fig. 7a; bottom). Across 1000 random ImageNet images, we found that the average probability change when the SP

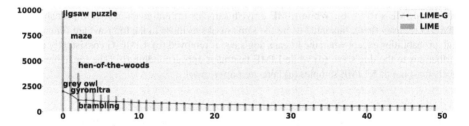

Fig. 8. We ran LIME and LIME-G on 200 images, each run has 500 intermediate perturbation samples. Here, for LIME (light green) and LIME-G (dark green) samples, we show a histogram of the top-1 predicted class labels for all 200 runs× 500 samples = 100,000 images. LIME perturbed samples are highly biased towards few jigsaw puzzle, maze classes (left panel), which is somewhat intuitive given the gray-masked images (see Figs. S8-S13). In contrast, the histogram of LIME-G samples are almost uniform. **x-axis:** For visualization purposes, we sorted the top-1 labels and showed only first 50 labels. See Fig. S16 for an expanded version of the figure. (Color figure online)

53×53 patch is outside the object bounding box is $\sim 2.1 \times$ higher than that of SP-G (i.e. 0.09 vs. 0.04). In sum, our observations here are consistent with the findings that G-methods obtained lower localization errors than the original counterparts.

5.2 More Robust Heatmaps: A Case Study of LIME-G

Here, we provide insights for why LIME-G produced heatmaps that are more consistent than LIME across 5 random batches of samples. We observed that the top-1 predicted labels of $\sim 20.5\%$ of the LIME grayish perturbation samples (e.g. Fig. 9a) were from only three classes {jigsaw puzzle, maze, hen-of-the-wood} whereas the same top-1 label distribution for LIME-G samples was almost uniform (see Fig. 8 for more details). Due to their similar grayish, puzzle-like patterns, many LIME samples across images from different classes (e.g.. dogs or nail) are still classified into the same label! Relatedly, we observed that a LIME perturbation sample is often given a near-zero probability score *regardless of what input feature is being masked out* (Fig. 9a). Therefore, when fitted to N samples, where N is often too small w.r.t. the total 2^S possible samples, the heatmap appears random and changes upon a new set of random masks (Fig. 9b).

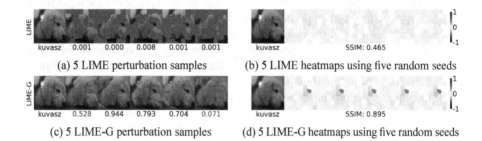

<table>
<tr><td>(a) 5 LIME perturbation samples</td><td>(b) 5 LIME heatmaps using five random seeds</td></tr>
<tr><td>(c) 5 LIME-G perturbation samples</td><td>(d) 5 LIME-G heatmaps using five random seeds</td></tr>
</table>

Fig. 9. In Sect. 4.4, we compared the robustness of LIME vs. LIME-G heatmaps when running using 5 different random seeds. This is an example where LIME-G heatmaps are more consistent than LIME's (d vs. b). While LIME grayish samples (a) are given near-zero probabilities, LIME-G samples (here, inpainted using the same masks as those in the top row) are often given high probabilities except when the kuvasz dog's eye is removed (c). LIME-G consistently assign attributions to the dog's eye (d) while LIME heatmaps appear random (b). The top-1 predicted labels for 4 out of 5 LIME samples (a) here are paper towel.

In contrast, for LIME-G samples, the probabilities consistently drop when some discriminative features (e.g. the kuvasz dog's eye in Fig. 9c) are removed. This phenomenon yields heatmaps that are more consistently localized around the same input features across different random seeds (Fig. 9d). Our explanation also aligns with the finding that when the number of superpixels S increases from 50 to 150 (while the sample size remains at $N = 500$), the sensitivity gap between LIME vs. LIME-G increases by ~ 3 times (Fig. 6a; gap between green bars vs. gap between blue bars). See Figs. S8-S15 for qualitative examples of when LIME-G is more robust than LIME and vice-versa. Quantitatively, we found that the image distribution where LIME-G showed superior robustness over LIME *across all three similarity metrics* mostly contains images of scenes, close-up or tiny objects. In contrast, LIME is more robust than LIME-G on images of mostly birds and medium-sized objects (See Sect. A2 for more details).

6 Discussion and Conclusion

MP2-G outperforming FIDO-CA consistently on all accuracy metrics confirms that the "deletion" objective is more appropriate for MP2 when incorporating generative inpainters. Additionally, discretizing and removing the hyperparameters of the original MP formulation aid in generating attribution maps that achieve better results across localization error, deletion, and saliency metric scores.

Integrating a state-of-the-art inpainter into three representative attribution methods consistently yielded explanations that are (1) more accurate based on three metrics; (2) more robust to hyperparameter changes; and (3) based on more plausible counterfactuals. Our results suggest that harnessing generative models to generate synthetic interventions (here, removal of input features) is a promising direction for future causal explanation methods.

Acknowledgments. We thank Qi Li and Michael Alcorn for helpful feedback. Especially, we thank Naman Bansal for valuable discussions, feedback on the final draft, and an important pointer to a closely related work. AN is supported by the National Science Foundation under Grant No. 1850117, Amazon Research Credits, Auburn University, and donations from Nvidia.

References

1. Doshi-Velez, F., Kim, B.: Towards a rigorous science of interpretable machine learning. arXiv preprint arXiv:1702.08608 (2017)
2. Gunning, D., Aha, D.W.: Darpa's explainable artificial intelligence program. AI Mag. **40**, 44–58 (2019)
3. Montavon, G., Samek, W., Müller, K.R.: Methods for interpreting and understanding deep neural networks. Digit. Sig. Process. **73**, 1–15 (2018)
4. Hagmayer, Y., Sloman, S.A., Lagnado, D.A., Waldmann, M.R.: Causal reasoning through intervention. In: Causal learning: Psychology, philosophy, and computation, pp. 86–100 (2007)
5. Zeiler, M.D., Fergus, R.: Visualizing and understanding convolutional networks. In: Fleet, D., Pajdla, T., Schiele, B., Tuytelaars, T. (eds.) ECCV 2014. LNCS, vol. 8689, pp. 818–833. Springer, Cham (2014). https://doi.org/10.1007/978-3-319-10590-1_53
6. Ribeiro, M.T., Singh, S., Guestrin, C.: Why should i trust you?: explaining the predictions of any classifier. In: Proceedings of the 22nd ACM SIGKDD International Conference on Knowledge Discovery and Data Mining, pp. 1135–1144. ACM (2016)
7. Dabkowski, P., Gal, Y.: Real time image saliency for black box classifiers. In: Advances in Neural Information Processing Systems, pp. 6967–6976 (2017)
8. Lundberg, S.M., Lee, S.I.: A unified approach to interpreting model predictions. In: Advances in Neural Information Processing Systems, pp. 4765–4774 (2017)
9. Fong, R.C., Vedaldi, A.: Interpretable explanations of black boxes by meaningful perturbation. In: Proceedings of the IEEE International Conference on Computer Vision, pp. 3429–3437 (2017)

10. Fong, R., Patrick, M., Vedaldi, A.: Understanding deep networks via extremal perturbations and smooth masks. In: Proceedings of the IEEE International Conference on Computer Vision, pp. 2950–2958 (2019)

11. Alcorn, M.A., Li, Q., Gong, Z., Wang, C., Mai, L., Ku, W.S., Nguyen, A.: Strike (with) a pose: neural networks are easily fooled by strange poses of familiar objects. In: Proceedings of the IEEE Conference on Computer Vision and Pattern Recognition, pp. 4845–4854 (2019)

12. Nguyen, A., Yosinski, J., Clune, J.: Deep neural networks are easily fooled: high confidence predictions for unrecognizable images. In: Proceedings of the IEEE Conference on Computer Vision and Pattern Recognition, pp. 427–436 (2015)

13. Agarwal, C., Nguyen, A., Schonfeld, D.: Improving robustness to adversarial examples by encouraging discriminative features. In: 2019 IEEE International Conference on Image Processing (ICIP), pp. 3801–3505. IEEE (2019)

14. Bansal, N., Agarwal, C., Nguyen, A.: Sam: the sensitivity of attribution methods to hyperparameters. In: Proceedings of the IEEE/CVF Conference on Computer Vision and Pattern Recognition, pp. 8673–8683 (2020)

15. Adebayo, J., Gilmer, J., Muelly, M., Goodfellow, I., Hardt, M., Kim, B.: Sanity checks for saliency maps. In: Advances in Neural Information Processing Systems, pp. 9505–9515 (2018)

16. Russakovsky, O., et al.: ImageNet large scale visual recognition challenge. Int. J. Comput. Vis. **115**, 211–252 (2015)

17. Zhou, B., Lapedriza, A., Khosla, A., Oliva, A., Torralba, A.: Places: a 10 million image database for scene recognition. IEEE Trans. Pattern Anal. Mach. Intell. **40**, 1452–1464 (2017)

18. Wagner, J., Kohler, J.M., Gindele, T., Hetzel, L., Wiedemer, J.T., Behnke, S.: Interpretable and fine-grained visual explanations for convolutional neural networks. In: Proceedings of the IEEE Conference on Computer Vision and Pattern Recognition, pp. 9097–9107 (2019)

19. Qi, Z., Khorram, S., Li, F.: Visualizing deep networks by optimizing with integrated gradients. arXiv preprint arXiv:1905.00954 (2019)

20. Carletti, M., Godi, M., Aghaei, M., Cristani, M.: Understanding deep architectures by visual summaries. arXiv preprint arXiv:1801.09103 (2018)

21. Wang, Y., Hu, X., Su, H.: Learning attributions grounded in existing facts for robust visual explanation. In: XAI, p. 178 (2018)

22. Uzunova, H., Ehrhardt, J., Kepp, T., Handels, H.: Interpretable explanations of black box classifiers applied on medical images by meaningful perturbations using variational autoencoders. In: Medical Imaging 2019: Image Processing, vol. 10949. International Society for Optics and Photonics, p. 1094911 (2019)

23. Simonyan, K., Vedaldi, A., Zisserman, A.: Deep inside convolutional networks: visualising image classification models and saliency maps. arXiv preprint arXiv:1312.6034 (2013)

24. Zhou, B., Khosla, A., Lapedriza, A., Oliva, A., Torralba, A.: Learning deep features for discriminative localization. In: Proceedings of the IEEE Conference on Computer Vision and Pattern Recognition, pp. 2921–2929 (2016)

25. Selvaraju, R.R., Cogswell, M., Das, A., Vedantam, R., Parikh, D., Batra, D.: Grad-CAM: visual explanations from deep networks via gradient-based localization. In: Proceedings of the IEEE International Conference on Computer Vision, pp. 618–626 (2017)

26. Shrikumar, A., Greenside, P., Kundaje, A.: Learning important features through propagating activation differences. In: Precup, D., Teh, Y.W. (eds.) Proceedings of the 34th International Conference on Machine Learning. Proceedings of Machine Learning Research, vol. 70, pp. 3145–3153. International Convention Centre, Sydney . PMLR (2017)

27. Smilkov, D., Thorat, N., Kim, B., Viégas, F., Wattenberg, M.: SmoothGrad: removing noise by adding noise. arXiv preprint arXiv:1706.03825 (2017)

28. Sundararajan, M., Taly, A., Yan, Q.: Axiomatic attribution for deep networks. In: Proceedings of the 34th International Conference on Machine Learning, vol. 70, pp. 3319–3328. JMLR.org (2017)
29. Chang, C.H., Creager, E., Goldenberg, A., Duvenaud, D.: Explaining image classifiers by counterfactual generation. In: International Conference on Learning Representations (2019)
30. He, K., Zhang, X., Ren, S., Sun, J.: Deep residual learning for image recognition. In: Proceedings of the IEEE Conference on Computer Vision and Pattern Recognition, pp. 770–778 (2016)
31. PyTorch: torchvision.models - PyTorch master documentation (2019). https://pytorch.org/docs/stable/torchvision/models.html. Accessed 21 Sept 2019
32. Zhou, B., Lapedriza, A., Khosla, A., Oliva, A., Torralba, A.: CSAILVision/places365: the places365-CNNs for scene classification (2019). https://github.com/CSAILVision/places365. Accessed 21 Sept 2019
33. Yu, J., Lin, Z., Yang, J., Shen, X., Lu, X., Huang, T.S.: Generative image inpainting with contextual attention. In: Proceedings of the IEEE Conference on Computer Vision and Pattern Recognition, pp. 5505–5514 (2018)
34. Yu, J., Lin, Z., Yang, J., Shen, X., Lu, X., Huang, T.S.: Free-form image inpainting with gated convolution. arXiv preprint arXiv:1806.03589 (2018)
35. MathWorks: Network visualization based on occlusion sensitivity (2019). https://blogs.mathworks.com/deep-learning/2017/12/15/network-visualization-based-on-occlusion-sensitivity/. Accessed 17 Sept 2019
36. Achanta, R., Shaji, A., Smith, K., Lucchi, A., Fua, P., Süsstrunk, S.: SLIC superpixels compared to state-of-the-art superpixel methods. IEEE Trans. Pattern Anal. Mach. Intell. **34**, 2274–2282 (2012)
37. Ribeiro, M.: Lime: Explaining the predictions of any machine learning classifier (2019). https://github.com/marcotcr/lime/. Accessed 17 Sept 2019
38. Papernot, N., McDaniel, P., Jha, S., Fredrikson, M., Celik, Z.B., Swami, A.: The limitations of deep learning in adversarial settings. In: IEEE European Symposium on Security and Privacy (EuroS&P), pp. 372–387. IEEE (2016)
39. Chen, L.C., Papandreou, G., Kokkinos, I., Murphy, K., Yuille, A.L.: DeepLab: semantic image segmentation with deep convolutional nets, atrous convolution, and fully connected CRFs. IEEE Trans. Pattern Anal. Mach. Intell. **40**, 834–848 (2017)
40. Szegedy, C., Vanhoucke, V., Ioffe, S., Shlens, J., Wojna, Z.: Rethinking the inception architecture for computer vision. In: Proceedings of the IEEE Conference on Computer Vision and Pattern Recognition, pp. 2818–2826 (2016)
41. Zhang, R., Isola, P., Efros, A.A., Shechtman, E., Wang, O.: The unreasonable effectiveness of deep features as a perceptual metric. In: Proceedings of the IEEE Conference on Computer Vision and Pattern Recognition, pp. 586–595 (2018)
42. Petsiuk, V., Das, A., Saenko, K.: Rise: Randomized input sampling for explanation of black-box models. In: Proceedings of the British Machine Vision Conference (BMVC) (2018)
43. Arras, L., Horn, F., Montavon, G., Müller, K.R., Samek, W.: "What is relevant in a text document?": an interpretable machine learning approach. PloS ONE **12**, e0181142 (2017)
44. Hooker, S., Erhan, D., Kindermans, P.J., Kim, B.: A benchmark for interpretability methods in deep neural networks. In: Advances in Neural Information Processing Systems, pp. 9734–9745 (2019)
45. Samek, W., Binder, A., Montavon, G., Lapuschkin, S., Müller, K.R.: Evaluating the visualization of what a deep neural network has learned. IEEE Trans. Neural Netw. Learn. Syst **28**, 2660–2673 (2016)
46. Hutson, M.: Artificial intelligence faces reproducibility crisis. Science **359**, 725–726 (2018)

47. van der Walt, S.: The scikit-image contributors: scikit-image: image processing in Python. PeerJ **2**, e453 (2014)
48. Zintgraf, L.M., Cohen, T.S., Adel, T., Welling, M.: Visualizing deep neural network decisions: prediction difference analysis. arXiv preprint arXiv:1702.04595 (2017)

Do We Need Sound for Sound Source Localization?

Takashi Oya$^{(\boxtimes)}$, Shohei Iwase$^{(\boxtimes)}$, Ryota Natsume, Takahiro Itazuri,
Shugo Yamaguchi, and Shigeo Morishima

Waseda Research Institute for Science and Engineering, Tokyo, Japan
oya_takashi@ruri.waseda.jp, {sh.iwase,s132800732}@fuji.waseda.jp,
nano.poteto@toki.waseda.jp, wasedayshugo@suou.waseda.jp, shigeo@waseda.jp

Abstract. During the performance of sound source localization which uses both visual and aural information, it presently remains unclear how much either image or sound modalities contribute to the result, i.e. do we need both image and sound for sound source localization? To address this question, we develop an unsupervised learning system that solves sound source localization by decomposing this task into two steps: (i) "potential sound source localization", a step that localizes possible sound sources using only visual information (ii) "object selection", a step that identifies which objects are actually sounding using aural information. Our overall system achieves state-of-the-art performance in sound source localization, and more importantly, we find that despite the constraint on available information, the results of (i) achieve similar performance. From this observation and further experiments, we show that visual information is dominant in "sound" source localization when evaluated with the currently adopted benchmark dataset. Moreover, we show that the majority of sound-producing objects within the samples in this dataset can be inherently identified using only visual information, and thus that the dataset is inadequate to evaluate a system's capability to leverage aural information. As an alternative, we present an evaluation protocol that enforces both visual and aural information to be leveraged, and verify this property through several experiments.

Keywords: Cross-modal learning · Sound source localization · Unsupervised learning

1 Introduction

In many scientific areas, it is common to make a prediction of an objective variable using explanatory variables. Nevertheless, the purpose is not always to generate an accurate prediction, but to investigate which variable is important for a prediction. For example, when using learning methods such as Random Forests [1], or their variants like Gradient Boosted Trees [2–4], quantities such as "variable importance" are widely used to determine the predictive strength

Electronic supplementary material The online version of this chapter (https://doi.org/10.1007/978-3-030-69544-6_8) contains supplementary material, which is available to authorized users.

© Springer Nature Switzerland AG 2021
H. Ishikawa et al. (Eds.): ACCV 2020, LNCS 12627, pp. 119–136, 2021.
https://doi.org/10.1007/978-3-030-69544-6_8

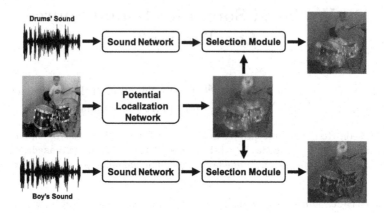

Fig. 1. Overview of our system. The system decomposes sound source localization into two steps, and each step is carried out by a specific module: "potential localization network" and "selection module". More specifically, the potential localization network obtains a heat map of all objects that are capable of producing sound, and given sound features from a sound network, the selection module identifies objects that are actually producing sound. In the example above, as the boy and drums are capable of producing sound, the potential localization network obtains a heat map that responds to their corresponding regions. Then, when human voice is given as input audio, the pixels that correspond to humans are selected by the selection module. On the other hand, when the sound of drums is given, the pixels that correspond to drums are selected.

of specific variables. In a similar manner, linear regression coefficients are known to be very useful to evaluate the contribution of specific variables in a linear regression analysis. However, there are only a few studies that investigate the contributions of each modality in cross-modal perception tasks that leverage both visual and aural information. Our study focuses on the investigation of this issue in sound source localization, which is a cross-modal perception task aiming to determine image pixels that are associated with a given sound source, e.g. selecting the region of trumpet in an image when given sound of trumpet.

In this research, we develop an unsupervised architecture which solves sound source localization by decomposing the problem into two tasks. First, given only an image, our system initially suggests a potential localization map, which is a heat map of all objects that are capable of producing sound. We call this step "potential sound source localization". Then, given a sound, our system identifies which objects within the potential localization map are actually producing sound, and returns a localization map. By comparing the performance of the potential localization map, which is derived only from visual information, and the localization map, which leverages both visual and aural information, we are able to evaluate the contributions of each modality in the benchmark dataset.

As can be seen from Fig. 1, the architecture has 3 components: the potential localization network, the sound network, and the selection module. The potential localization network is an image network that takes an image as an input and returns the potential localization map. Notably, the potential localization network operates independently from the sound network, which returns latent features derived from the sound input. The selection module updates the potential localization map to the localization map using the latent features, by selecting objects from the potential localization map. During the training phase, our model can be trained in an unsupervised manner as we utilize audio-visual correspondence [5], i.e. whether image and sound correspond to each other or not.

As a result, when using both visual and aural information, our system achieves state of the art performance. More significantly, although utilizing only visual information, the potential localization map performs similarly to the localization map, indicating that in the current benchmark dataset, high performance can be achieved without the usage of sound as input. Furthermore, from additional quantitative and qualitative analysis, we have found that for the majority of the samples within the current dataset, the sound-producing object can be inherently identified using only image, as all objects that are capable of producing sound are actually producing sound. This is problematic as this is not the case in the real world, and proper evaluation on a system's capability of leveraging aural information can not be conducted. To overcome this issue, we design an evaluation protocol called *concat-and-localize*, where evaluation is conducted on artificially created samples that enforce the usage of aural information. We verify this property through evaluation of our system using this evaluation protocol.

2   Related Work

Below we provide a list of cross-modal perception tasks that are closely related to the problem of sound source localization. Each task is accompanied with a description of how they are related.

Audio-Visual Correspondence (AVC). Audio and visual events tend to occur concurrently within our daily lives. Additionally, humans learn to localize a sound source without any supervision by experiencing these natural co-occurrences a sufficient number of times since they were born. Like humans, in order for a machine to learn from these natural co-occurrences, Arandjelovic & Zisserman [5] proposed an AVC task that predicts whether a pair of sound clip and an image correspond with one another. The concept of AVC facilitates solutions for other cross-modal perception tasks in an unsupervised fashion, such as audio-visual representation learning [5–7], audio-visual source separation [8–10], and sound source localization [6,9,11–13]. Although our work does not directly map to the AVC task, it indirectly leverages this idea in an unsupervised setting.

Audio-Visual Representation Learning. This task aims to generate representations of image/sound; these representations are useful for image/sound classification, zero-shot detection, cross-modal retrieval and action recognition. Audio-visual representation learning models can be grouped within 3 categories: the use of image features to train a sound network in a supervised manner

[14–17], the use of sound features to train an image network in a supervised manner [5,14,18], and via unsupervised methods [6,7,10,19,20] including networks to classify motion information. Though the aim of representation learning is different from that of sound source localization, some existing works have reported that the internal representation i.e., image features and sound features of the models developed for sound source localization is useful for image/sound classification and action recognition tasks [7,10,20]. Our efforts are different from this task, as we do not focus on internal representations.

Sound Generation from Video. The purpose of this task is sound synthesis based on visual information. Some works in this domain have generated monaural audio from a video [21,22], while other works have converted monaural audio into either binaural audio [23] or spatial audio [24]. Gao and Grauman [23] showed that it is possible to localize sound sources by visualizing regions important in conversion and Morgado et al. [24] showed that it is possible to localize a sound source present in a 360° video. Our work differs from these works as we neither focus on sound synthesis nor do we use binaural audio or spatial audio.

Audio-Visual Source Separation. Audio-visual source separation is a task that utilizes visual information to guide sound source separation, in contrast to blind sound source separation that does not use visual information [25–28]. There are various methods employed for audio-visual source separation: NMF [29–31], subspace methods [32,33], the mix-and-separate method [8–10,12,13,34], and the use of facial information for speech separation [35–38]. Many works have attempted simultaneous sound source separation and sound source localization [8–10,12,13], as it is important to identify which objects are producing sound to perform sound source separation. For example, Zhao et al. [9] proposed a method that assigns sounds to each image pixel and can localize a sound source by visualizing the volume of each image pixel. However, these previous works applied their methods to datasets containing a limited number of categories, such as a music instrument or speech. In contrast, our work does not focus on sound source separation and can be applied to a dataset containing an unconstrained number of categories.

Sound Source Localization. Sound source localization is a classic problem in both science and engineering. In robotics and signal processing research, sound source localization mainly indicates a task that identifies the spatial locations of the sound sources using only aural information from several microphones [39–42]. On the contrary, in computer vision research, sound source localization indicates a task seeking to determine image pixels that are associated with sound sources, usually employing both visual and aural information from a single microphone, i.e., monaural hearing. There exist various studies concerning sound source localization in the computer vision domain, including works that are not based on neural network techniques: mutual information and CCA [43,44], subspace methods [45], and keypoints [46]. After the great success of neural networks in the year 2012 [47], a growing number of works have been conducted that leverage neural network, including the following methods: those that leverage motion information [12,13,19], CAM-based methods [10,20], methods based on attention mechanism [6,11], and methods that can perform concurrent sound source localization and sound source separation [8–10,12,13]. A work that is most similar to the one described in this study is that of Senocak et al. [11], which can be trained in an unsupervised manner and can be applied to a noisy, unlabelled dataset. However, the focus of their work is different from ours, because our study's aim is to investigate the contributions of each modality in sound source localization. Furthermore, our network differs from theirs in that we introduce potential sound source localization network and object selection module.

3   Proposed Framework

3.1   Dataset and Data Preprocessing

As a benchmark, we employ a dataset created by Senocak et al. [11]; this dataset contains 5k random subset selections of Flickr-SoundNet [15], a large unlabelled dataset containing more than 200M matched pairs of images and sounds. In addition, this dataset contains sound source annotations using bounding-boxes, which were assigned by 3 annotators. The image sizes within the dataset are fixed at 256 × 256 pixels, the sampling rate of the sound is fixed at 22.05 kHz, and the length of the sound clips is not fixed.

For image data, we performed a simple preprocessing and augmentation scheme: mean subtraction and random cropping (224 × 224). For audio data, we performed STFT with a window-length of 1022 and a hop-length of 511.

3.2   Potential Localization Network

The overall network architecture is given in Fig. 2. The potential localization network takes image vectors $I_{i,j} \in R^{H \times W}$ with height H and width W as inputs. Then, a VGG-11 network [48] pretrained on ImageNet [49] and two 1×1 convolution layers followed by ReLU [50] were used to extract a positive vector $v_{k,i,j} \in R^{K \times \frac{H}{16} \times \frac{W}{16}}$ that represents image features with K channels. Finally, a potential localization map $P_{i,j} \in R^{\frac{H}{16} \times \frac{W}{16}}$ is computed by applying a 1×1 convolution layer followed by a softmax function, as shown below.

$$P_{i,j} = \frac{\exp[\sum_k (W_k v_{k,i,j}) + b]}{\sum_{i,j} \exp[\sum_k (W_k v_{k,i,j}) + b]}. \tag{1}$$

Here W_k, b are weight and bias term of the 1×1 convolution layer, respectively.

3.3   Sound Network

The sound network takes the amplitudes and phases of a spectrogram as an input. This information is then fed into a VGG-like Network. Here, the sound length is arbitrary, caused by the application of a global average pooling (GAP) layer [51] along the time axis after the VGG-like network has acted on the data. Then, the

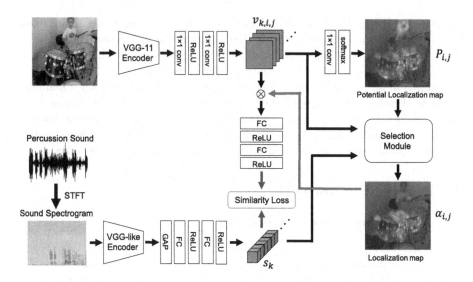

Fig. 2. The detailed network architecture of our unsupervised model. The potential localization map is obtained using image features extracted from the input image. Then from the potential localization map, the image features, and the sound features extracted from the input sound, the selection module produces a localization map. The similarity loss is calculated using sound features and image features of the sound-producing object obtained from the pixel-wise product between the localization map and the image features.

positive vector $s_k \in R^K$ is obtained which represents the sound features after having been fed through two fully-connected (FC) layers followed by a ReLU.

3.4   Selection Module

The selection module takes 3 inputs: image features $v_{k,i,j}$, sound features s_k, and the potential localization map $P_{i,j}$. An attention map $A_{i,j}$ is obtained by calculating the cosine similarity between image features $v_{k,i,j}$, and sound features s_k, as shown below:

$$A_{i,j} = \frac{\sum_k v_{k,i,j} s_k}{\sqrt{\sum_k s_k^2} \sqrt{\sum_k v_{k,i,j}^2}}. \tag{2}$$

It should be noted that $A_{i,j}$ ranges between 0 and 1, as both $v_{k,i,j}$ and s_k are positive. Finally, the localization map $\alpha_{i,j}$ is calculated by L1 normalization along pixels after multiplying $A_{i,j}$ and $P_{i,j}$ together as shown by the following expression:

$$\alpha_{i,j} = \frac{A_{i,j} P_{i,j}}{\sum_{i,j} A_{i,j} P_{i,j}}. \tag{3}$$

3.5   Training Phase

For training, we leverage concepts from an AVC task [5] in which networks are trained to determine whether data pairs (image and sound) correspond to each other. Our loss function which we call "similarity loss" is calculated as follows. We first calculated $\hat{s}_k \in R^K$ by

$$\hat{s}_k = \text{ReLU}(\text{FC}(\text{ReLU}(\text{FC}(\sum_{i,j} v_{k,i,j} \alpha_{i,j}))))). \tag{4}$$

Intuitively, $\hat{s}_k$ indicates image features $v_{k,i,j}$ that were filtered by the localization map $\alpha_{i,j}$.

Then as in a Siamese network [52], the loss function is defined differently for the positive pairs (pairs corresponding to each other) and the negative pairs (pairs not corresponding to each other).

For both positive and negative pairs, the cosine similarity between $\hat{s}_k$ and s_k is used. For the positive pairs, the loss function is given as follows:

$$L = 1 - \frac{\sum_k s_k \hat{s}_k}{\sqrt{\sum_k s_k^2}\sqrt{\sum_k \hat{s}_k^2}}. \tag{5}$$

For the negative pairs, the loss function is given by the following expression:

$$L = \frac{\sum_k s_k \hat{s}_k}{\sqrt{\sum_k s_k^2}\sqrt{\sum_k \hat{s}_k^2}}. \tag{6}$$

The loss function forces $\hat{s}_k$ to be similar to sound features s_k for positive pairs and vice versa for negative pairs. Additional details such as hyperparameters are provided in the supplementary material.

3.6   Inference Phase

As we have shown, the potential localization network does not depend on aural information and works independently from other components. Therefore, a potential localization map $P_{i,j}$ can be obtained using only visual information. On the other hand, aural information is needed to obtain a localization map $\alpha_{i,j}$, since the attention map $A_{i,j}$ necessary to derive $\alpha_{i,j}$ depends on aural information.

4   Experiments

We conducted 3 experiments. First, to verify the claim that potential localization maps respond to objects that potentially produce sound and not to objects that can not produce sound such as tables or chairs, we compared the results of the potential localization map to a saliency map. Then, to investigate the contributions of each modality, we trained our unsupervised method and compared the performance of (i) our potential localization map (ii) our localization map (iii) an existing unsupervised sound source localization method. Finally, we also conducted a similar evaluation in a supervised setting.

4.1   Evaluation Metrics

To evaluate our system, we employ the consensus intersection over union (cIoU) [11], which is similar to intersection over union (IoU), but can be applied when ground truth takes continuous values. The ground truth $G_{i,j}$ is given by

$$G_{i,j} = \sum_{k=1}^{M} \frac{G_{k,i,j}}{M}. \tag{7}$$

Here, M indicates the number of annotators and $G_{k,i,j}$ indicates ground truth by k-th annotator, which takes 1 if the bounding box includes (i, j)-th pixel, and takes 0 otherwise. The definition of cIoU is as follows.

$$cIoU = \frac{\sum_{i,j} G_{i,j} B_{i,j}}{\sum_{i,j} G_{i,j} + \sum_{(i,j) \in \{(i,j)|G_{i,j}=0\}} B_{i,j}}, \tag{8}$$

where $B_{i,j}$ is obtained by binarizing the prediction $P_{i,j}$ using a threshold τ.

$$B_{i,j} = \begin{cases} 1 & (P_{i,j} > \tau) \\ 0 & (otherwise) \end{cases}. \tag{9}$$

Intuitively, the numerator of cIoU indicates the intersection of the ground truth and the prediction, and the denominator indicates the union. Therefore, a higher cIoU score indicates better performance. We also report AUC score, which indicates the area under the curve of cIoU plotted by varying the threshold from 0 to 1. For evaluation, we use the same test set as Senocak et al. [11], which contains 250 pairs of image and sound.

4.2   Configurations

Saliency Map. We obtain the saliency map for the top-1 predicted class and the top-100 predicted classes of the pretrained VGG network using Grad-CAM [53]. We conducted this experiment to address the question: is a potential localization map just a saliency map, thus visualizing the important region for image classification? This experiment allows us to differentiate whether potential localization maps respond only to objects that potentially produce sound or to any given object within the image, including those that can not produce sound. Additional details of this experiment are given in the supplementary material.

Unsupervised Learning. We trained our unsupervised method with various numbers of training samples (1k, 2.5k, 10k, 144k) using pretrained weights for the VGG network. As a means of comparison, both the potential localization map and the localization map were evaluated to investigate the degree to which aural information contributes to the overall performance in the benchmark dataset. We also trained our unsupervised method without pretrained weights, in order to make a fair comparison with results reported in the existing study [11], which

Table 1. Evaluation of localization map and potential localization map in an unsupervised setting. cIoU score with threshold 0.5 and AUC score are calculated for different sized training samples. We also report the results of random prediction. "de novo" indicates training without pretrained weights, and localization map is abbreviated as loc. map. Additional comparison with other methods are listed in the supplementary material.

# of training samples	Loc. map by [11] (reported)		Loc. map (pretrain.)		Potential loc. map (pretrain.)		Loc. map (de novo)		Potential loc. map (de novo)	
	cIoU	AUC	cIoU	AUC	cIoU	AUC	cIoU	AUC	cIoU	AUC
1k	–	–	48.7	46.4	45.9	43.8	36.5	34.1	35.3	33.4
2.5k	–	–	50.3	47.7	48.1	46.0	40.7	37.3	38.5	36.8
10k	43.6	44.9	56.8	50.7	53.9	48.6	48.4	45.3	47.4	44.6
144k	66.0	55.8	68.4	57.0	66.8	56.2	66.7	56.3	65.5	55.5
Random			cIoU		AUC					
			34.1		32.3					

Table 2. Evaluation of potential localization map in a supervised setting, i.e. prediction of U-Net which only uses visual information. We use 2.5k samples for training as in the supervised setting of Senocak et al. [11].

Method	cIoU	AUC
Loc. map by [11] (reported)	80.4	60.3
Potential loc. map	79.3	60.9

does not use pretrained weights. In addition, based on this experiment, we can verify whether our model can be trained without pretrained weights.

Supervised Learning. To also investigate the contribution of visual information in a supervised setting, we trained a U-Net [54] with the ground truth $G_{i,j}$ as a target and use Dice-coefficient as a loss function. Dice-coefficient is defined as

$$DC = \frac{\sum_{i,j} G_{i,j} U_{i,j}}{\sum_{i,j} G_{i,j} + \sum_{i,j} U_{i,j}}, \tag{10}$$

where $U_{i,j}$ indicates the prediction of U-Net. Additional details including hyperparameters are given in the supplementary material.

4.3   Results and Analysis

Table 1 and Table 2 show the results reported by Senocak et al. [11] and the results of our potential localization map and localization map in an unsupervised setting and a supervised setting respectively. Table 3 shows results for the saliency maps. Insights obtained from these results are as follows.

Table 3. Evaluation of saliency maps for the top 1 class and the top 100 classes.

Method	cIoU	AUC
Saliency map for the top1 class	45.7	41.1
Saliency map for the top100 classes	52.7	46.3

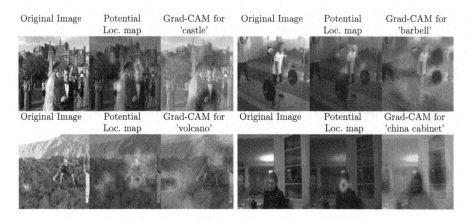

Fig. 3. Visualization results of potential localization map and saliency map (Grad-CAM) for the top 1 class. As the results show, the saliency maps react to objects that can not produce sound like "china cabinet", while our potential localization map does not. For the visualization, we use the model trained with 144k samples and pretrained weights.

Behavioral Analysis of Potential Localization Map. As you can see from Table 1 and Table 3, when more than 10k samples are used to conduct unsupervised training with pretrained weights, and when more than 144k samples are used to conduct training without pretrained weights, our potential localization map outperforms the baselines of saliency maps. This implies our potential localization map technique, trained with a sufficient number of samples can successfully identify objects that potentially produce sound and not just visualize a saliency map. As can be seen in Fig. 3, it can be confirmed that our potential localization map focuses on objects that potentially produce sound, while a saliency map does not.

Assessment of Individual Modalities' Importance When the quantity of training data is within the range 10k to 144k, our localization maps achieve state-of-the-art performance (68.4%, 56.8% in cIoU). More notably, our potential localization map performs comparably to the localization map which uses both visual and aural information (1.6% gap in cIoU for 144k training samples with pretrained weights). The difference in performance is consistent in the supervised setting (1.1% gap in cIoU). This suggests that although sound source localization is a cross-modal task, when evaluated using the current benchmark dataset, visual information is dominant and the combined advantage of having both visual and aural information is not fully assessed.

Original Image	Potential Loc. map	Loc. map	Original Image	Potential Loc. map	Loc. map

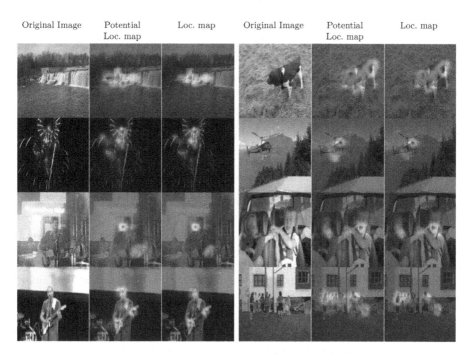

Fig. 4. Visualization results of potential localization maps and localization maps of various objects when all possible objects are producing sound (Type A). Samples in the two top rows only have one object capable of producing sound. Samples in the bottom two rows have multiple objects but the sound of both objects are given. In these cases the results show that the potential localization map and the localization map are very similar. For the visualization, we use the model trained with 144k samples and pretrained weights.

Analysis of the Performance Gap In order to investigate the difference in behavior between the potential localization map and the localization map, we make qualitative observations as shown in Fig. 4 and Fig. 5. As seen from Fig. 4, it can be observed that in an unsupervised setting, when all objects capable of producing sound are actually producing sound, the potential localization map performs similarly to the localization map. We call this type of sample Type A. On the other hand, when only some of the objects capable of producing sound are actually producing sound, such as in Figs. 5, the localization map performs better than the potential localization map. We call this type of sample Type B.

To quantitatively evaluate this difference in behavior between samples that are Type A and Type B, we manually picked out 30 samples for each type from Flickr-SoundNet [15] excluding the samples contained in the current benchmark dataset [11], and then annotated sound sources using bounding-boxes. Further details on the annotation process are given in the supplementary material. IoU and AUC scores for both types were calculated to check which type of samples leads to the difference in performance between potential localization map and

| Original
Image | Potential
Loc. map | Loc. map
when given
human sound | Loc. map
when given
instrument sound | Original
Image | Potential
Loc. map | Loc. map
when given
human sound | Loc. map
when given
machine sound |

Fig. 5. Visualization results of potential localization maps and localization maps of samples with several objects capable of producing sound in the image, but of which only one object is actually producing sound (Type B). The localization map successfully responds to an object that is actually producing sound, while the potential localization map does not. For the visualization, we use the model trained with 144k samples and pretrained weights.

Table 4. IoU score with threshold 0.5 and AUC score for Type A and Type B samples. We use the model trained with 144k samples and pretrained weights.

	Loc. map		Potential loc. map		Perform. gap		Random	
	IoU	AUC	IoU	AUC	IoU	AUC	IoU	AUC
Type A	58.5	49.6	55.7	48.3	2.8	1.3	29.9	28.4
Type B	44.5	38.0	31.9	27.2	12.6	10.8	17.1	16.6

localization map. The results are shown in Table 4. In accordance with our qualitative observation, the results show that the performance gap is smaller in Type A and larger in Type B.

Based on the differences seen between samples of Type A and Type B, it can be implied that the lack of performance gap when evaluated with the current benchmark dataset is caused by the majority of samples within the dataset being Type A. This indicates that, inherently, the majority of sound sources can be inferred based on visual information only, thus confirming that the contribution of aural information is minimal in the current benchmark dataset. This is problematic as a proper evaluation of whether a system is capable of leveraging aural information can not be conducted. It is important to realize that in the real world, there are many examples where objects that are capable of producing sound are silent, and thus the usage of sound would be inevitable. Hence, datasets used for evaluation of sound source localization should necessitate the usage of sound.

5   Alternative Evaluation Protocol

From our observations drawn in Sect. 4.3, it can be deduced that a dataset which consists of abundant samples of Type B is required to properly assess a system's capability of leveraging aural information. However, as the retrieval of such samples in sufficient amounts is implausible, we introduce a *concat-and-localize* method, which is an alternative evaluation protocol that utilizes artificially created samples which structurally have the same properties as Type B.

Table 5. Evaluation of localization map and potential localization map in an unsupervised setting following our evaluation protocol. cIoU score with threshold 0.5 and AUC score are calculated for different sized training samples.

# of training samples	Loc. map (pretrain.)		Potential loc. map (pretrain.)		Perform. gap (pretrain.)		Loc. map (de novo)		Potential loc. map (de novo)		Perform. gap (de novo)	
	cIoU	AUC	cIoU	AUC	cIoU	AUC	cIoU	AUC	cIoU	AUC	cIoU	AUC
1k	24.8	23.5	23.4	21.8	1.4	1.7	21.8	20.4	21.1	20.2	0.7	0.2
2.5k	27.3	24.4	23.5	21.3	3.8	3.1	23.2	21.5	22.9	20.8	0.3	0.7
10k	35.4	29.5	28.2	25.1	7.2	4.4	30.1	26.6	24.0	22.1	6.1	4.5
144k	41.6	35.6	30.2	26.4	11.4	9.2	37.4	31.6	28.9	25.4	8.5	6.2
Random					cIoU	AUC						
					20.0	18.5						

Inspired by the mix-and-separate method used in audio-visual source separation [8–10,12,13,34], the process of artificially creating a sample in our *concat-and-localize* method is as follows. First, two pairs of image and sound are sampled from the test set of the current dataset [11]. The two images are concatenated side-by-side and then rescaled to the size of the original image. Only one of the two sounds is given as input, and the new ground truth is defined as the rescaled original ground truth of the sample corresponding to the input sound as shown in Fig. 6. This process is conducted for both sounds, i.e. two synthetic samples are obtained per process. By design, the newly created sample always consists of multiple objects that are capable of producing sound as each original image contains such objects. In addition, as only one of the sounds is given, we can reproduce a situation where only some of the objects are producing sound, meeting the requirements for the sample to be Type B. Hence, in order to determine whether the sound originates from the objects on the left side of the concatenated image or the ones on the right side, aural information must be leveraged.

We created a new dataset of 1000 samples using the above process and evaluated our system using this dataset. The same metrics (cIoU and AUC) as Sect. 4 were utilized. In Table 5, we show the results of our potential localization map and localization map following the same configuration as Sect. 4. As expected, the results show that the performance gap is significantly greater than the currently adopted evaluation method, especially when training with a large

| Concatenated Image | Potential Loc. map | Ground truth when given left sound | Loc. map when given left sound | Ground truth when given right sound | Loc. map when given right sound |

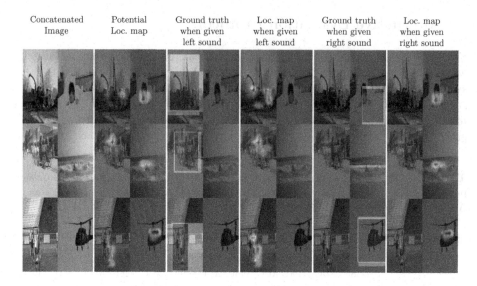

Fig. 6. Visualization results of potential localization maps and localization maps for artificially created samples. When given the concatenated image, the potential localization map shows response to all objects capable of producing sound in both images. Then when given only one of the sounds, the localization map correctly responds to the corresponding object. For the visualization, we use the model trained with 144k samples and pretrained weights.

number of samples (11.4% gap in cIoU with 144k training samples). This can be attributed to the design of our evaluation protocol, where the problem cannot be solved using only visual information. In this respect, our *concat-and-localize* method is more suitable for evaluating cross-modal perception task than simply using the current benchmark dataset.

6   Conclusion

In this paper, we develop an unsupervised architecture that solves sound source localization by decomposing this task into two steps: potential sound source localization and object selection. We provide sufficient evidence to show that our system can localize possible sound sources from only an image, and achieve state-of-the-art in sound source localization when leveraging both image and sound inputs. More importantly, our system, even when using only visual information, performs comparably to our state-of-the-art output which leverages both image and sound, suggesting sound sources can be localized without the usage of sound in the current dataset. From this observation and both qualitative and quantitative analysis, we pointed out the problem of the currently adopted evaluation method, and introduced the *concat-and-localize* method as an alternative. Our evaluation protocol is more suitable for evaluating the cross-modal aspect of sound source localization as the design enforces the usage of both modalities.

For future works, we believe it to be valuable to investigate the importance and contribution of different modalities in other cross-modal perception tasks too, as it may lead to a deeper understanding of the tasks, a dataset with better quality, and a better performance of future models in the real world.

Acknowledgements. This research is supported by the JST ACCEL (JPM-JAC1602), JST-Mirai Program (JPMJMI19B2), JSPS KAKENHI (JP17H06101, JP19H01129 and JP19H04137).

References

1. Breiman, L.: Random forests. Mach. Learn. **45**, 5–32 (2001)
2. Chen, T., Guestrin, C.: XGBoost: a scalable tree boosting system. In: International Conference on Knowledge Discovery and Data Mining (KDD) (2016)
3. Ke, G., et al..: LightGBM: a highly efficient gradient boosting decision tree. In: Neural Information Processing Systems (NIPS) (2017)
4. Prokhorenkova, L., Gusev, G., Vorobev, A., Dorogush, A.V., Gulin, A.: CatBoost: unbiased boosting with categorical features. In: Neural Information Processing Systems (NIPS) (2018)
5. Arandjelovic, R., Zisserman, A.: Look, listen and learn. In: International Conference on Computer Vision (ICCV) (2017)
6. Arandjelović, R., Zisserman, A.: Objects that sound. In: Ferrari, V., Hebert, M., Sminchisescu, C., Weiss, Y. (eds.) ECCV 2018. LNCS, vol. 11205, pp. 451–466. Springer, Cham (2018). https://doi.org/10.1007/978-3-030-01246-5_27
7. Hu, D., Nie, F., Li, X.: Deep multimodal clustering for unsupervised audiovisual learning. In: Computer Vision and Pattern Recognition (CVPR) (2019)
8. Rouditchenko, A., Zhao, H., Gan, C., McDermott, J., Torralba, A.: Self-supervised audio-visual co-segmentation. In: International Conference on Acoustics, Speech and Signal Processing (ICASSP) (2019)
9. Zhao, H., Gan, C., Rouditchenko, A., Vondrick, C., McDermott, J., Torralba, A.: The sound of pixels. In: Ferrari, V., Hebert, M., Sminchisescu, C., Weiss, Y. (eds.) ECCV 2018. LNCS, vol. 11205, pp. 587–604. Springer, Cham (2018). https://doi.org/10.1007/978-3-030-01246-5_35
10. Owens, A., Efros, A.A.: Audio-visual scene analysis with self-supervised multisensory features. In: Ferrari, V., Hebert, M., Sminchisescu, C., Weiss, Y. (eds.) ECCV 2018. LNCS, vol. 11210, pp. 639–658. Springer, Cham (2018). https://doi.org/10.1007/978-3-030-01231-1_39
11. Senocak, A., Oh, T.H., Kim, J., Yang, M.H., So Kweon, I.: Learning to localize sound source in visual scenes. In: Computer Vision and Pattern Recognition (CVPR) (2018)
12. Zhao, H., Gan, C., Ma, W.C., Torralba, A.: The sound of motions. In: International Conference on Computer Vision (ICCV) (2019)
13. Gan, C., Huang, D., Zhao, H., Tenenbaum, J.B., Torralba, A.: Music gesture for visual sound separation. In: Computer Vision and Pattern Recognition (CVPR) (2020)
14. Aytar, Y., Vondrick, C., Torralba, A.: See, hear, and read: deep aligned representations. arXiv preprint arXiv:1706.00932 (2017)
15. Aytar, Y., Vondrick, C., Torralba, A.: SoundNet: learning sound representations from unlabeled video. In: Neural Information Processing Systems (NIPS) (2016)

16. Harwath, D., Glass, J.R.: Learning word-like units from joint audio-visual analysis. In: Association for Computational Linguistics (ACL) (2017)
17. Harwath, D., Torralba, A., Glass, J.: Unsupervised learning of spoken language with visual context. In: Neural Information Processing Systems (NIPS) (2016)
18. Owens, A., Wu, J., McDermott, J.H., Freeman, W.T., Torralba, A.: Ambient sound provides supervision for visual learning. In: Leibe, B., Matas, J., Sebe, N., Welling, M. (eds.) ECCV 2016. LNCS, vol. 9905, pp. 801–816. Springer, Cham (2016). https://doi.org/10.1007/978-3-319-46448-0_48
19. Tian, Y., Shi, J., Li, B., Duan, Z., Xu, C.: Audio-visual event localization in unconstrained videos. In: Ferrari, V., Hebert, M., Sminchisescu, C., Weiss, Y. (eds.) ECCV 2018. LNCS, vol. 11206, pp. 252–268. Springer, Cham (2018). https://doi.org/10.1007/978-3-030-01216-8_16
20. Korbar, B., Tran, D., Torresani, L.: Cooperative learning of audio and video models from self-supervised synchronization. In: Neural Information Processing Systems (NIPS) (2018)
21. Zhou, Y., Wang, Z., Fang, C., Bui, T., Berg, T.L.: Visual to sound: generating natural sound for videos in the wild. In: Computer Vision and Pattern Recognition (CVPR) (2018)
22. Chen, K., Zhang, C., Fang, C., Wang, Z., Bui, T., Nevatia, R.: Visually indicated sound generation by perceptually optimized classification. In: Leal-Taixé, L., Roth, S. (eds.) ECCV 2018. LNCS, vol. 11134, pp. 560–574. Springer, Cham (2019). https://doi.org/10.1007/978-3-030-11024-6_43
23. Gao, R., Grauman, K.: 2.5D visual sound. In: Computer Vision and Pattern Recognition (CVPR) (2019)
24. Morgado, P., Nvasconcelos, N., Langlois, T., Wang., O.: Self-supervised generation of spatial audio for 360° video. In: Neural Information Processing Systems (NIPS) (2018)
25. Lyon, R.F.: A computational model of binaural localization and separation. In: International Conference on Acoustics, Speech and Signal Processing (ICASSP) (1983)
26. Hershey, J.R., Chen, Z., Roux, J.L., Watanabe, S.: Deep clustering: discriminative embeddings for segmentation and separation. In: International Conference on Acoustics, Speech and Signal Processing (ICASSP) (2016)
27. Chen, Z., Luo, Y., Mesgarani, N.: Deep attractor network for single-microphone speaker separation. In: International Conference on Acoustics, Speech and Signal Processing (ICASSP) (2017)
28. Yu, D., Kolbæk, M., Tan, Z.H., Jensen, J.: Permutation invariant training of deep models for speaker-independent multi-talker speech separation. In: International Conference on Acoustics, Speech and Signal Processing (ICASSP) (2017)
29. Parekh, S., Essid, S., Ozerov, A., Duong, N., Pérez, P., Richard, G.: Motion informed audio source separation. In: International Conference on Acoustics, Speech and Signal Processing (ICASSP) (2017)
30. Sedighin, F., Babaie-Zadeh, M., Rivet, B., Jutten, C.: Two multimodal approaches for single microphone source separation. In: European Signal Processing Conference (EUSIPCO) (2016)
31. Gao, R., Feris, R., Grauman, K.: Learning to separate object sounds by watching unlabeled video. In: Ferrari, V., Hebert, M., Sminchisescu, C., Weiss, Y. (eds.) ECCV 2018. LNCS, vol. 11207, pp. 36–54. Springer, Cham (2018). https://doi.org/10.1007/978-3-030-01219-9_3

32. Smaragdis, P., Casey, M.: Audio/visual independent components. In: International Conference on Independent Component Analysis and Signal Separation (ICA) (2003)
33. Pu, J., Panagakis, Y., Petridis, S., Pantic, M.: Audio-visual object localization and separation using low-rank and sparsity. In: International Conference on Acoustics, Speech and Signal Processing (ICASSP) (2017)
34. Gao, R., Grauman, K.: Co-separating sounds of visual objects. In: International Conference on Computer Vision (ICCV) (2019)
35. Ephrat, A., et al.: Looking to listen at the cocktail party: a speaker-independent audio-visual model for speech separation. In: Special Interest Group on Computer GRAPHics and Interactive Techniques (SIGGRAPH) (2018)
36. Gabbay, A., Shamir, A., Peleg, S.: Visual speech enhancement. In: International Speech Communication Association (INTERSPEECH) (2018)
37. Afouras, T., Chung, J.S., Zisserman, A.: The conversation: deep audio-visual speech enhancement. In: International Speech Communication Association (INTERSPEECH) (2018)
38. Llagostera Casanovas, A., Monaci, G., Vandergheynst, P., Gribonval, R.: Blind audiovisual source separation based on sparse redundant representations. Trans. Multimedia **12**, 358–371 (2010)
39. Nakadai, K., Okuno, H.G., Kitano, H.: Real-time sound source localization and separation for robot audition. In: International Conference on Spoken Language Processing (ICSLP) (2002)
40. Argentieri, S., Danès, P., Souères, P.: A survey on sound source localization in robotics: from binaural to array processing methods. Comput. Speech Lang. **34**, 87–112 (2015)
41. Nakamura, K., Nakadai, K., Asano, F., Ince, G.: Intelligent sound source localization and its application to multimodal human tracking. In: International Conference on Intelligent Robots and Systems (IROS) (2011)
42. Strobel, N., Spors, S., Rabenstein, R.: Joint audio-video object localization and tracking. Sig. Process. Mag. **18**, 22–31 (2001)
43. Hershey, J.R., Movellan, J.R.: Audio vision: using audio-visual synchrony to locate sounds. In: Neural Information Processing Systems (NIPS) (1999)
44. Kidron, E., Schechner, Y.Y., Elad, M.: Pixels that sound. In: Computer Vision and Pattern Recognition (CVPR) (2005)
45. Fisher III, J.W., Darrell, T., Freeman, W.T., Viola, P.A.: Learning joint statistical models for audio-visual fusion and segregation. In: Neural Information Processing Systems (NIPS) (2001)
46. Barzelay, Z., Schechner, Y.: Harmony in motion. In: Computer Vision and Pattern Recognition (CVPR) (2007)
47. Krizhevsky, A., Sutskever, I., Hinton, G.E.: ImageNet classification with deep convolutional neural networks. In: Neural Information Processing Systems (NIPS) (2012)
48. Simonyan, K., Zisserman, A.: Very deep convolutional networks for large-scale image recognition. In: International Conference on Learning Representations (ICLR) (2015)
49. Deng, J., Dong, W., Socher, R., Li, L.J., Li, K., Fei-Fei, L.: ImageNet: a large-scale hierarchical image database. In: Computer Vision and Pattern Recognition (CVPR) (2009)
50. Nair, V., Hinton, G.E.: Rectified linear units improve restricted Boltzmann machines. In: International Conference on Machine Learning (ICML) (2010)

51. Lin, M., Chen, Q., Yan, S.: Network in network. In: International Conference on Learning Representations (ICLR) (2014)
52. Bromley, J., Guyon, I., LeCun, Y., Säckinger, E., Shah, R.: Signature verification using a "siamese" time delay neural network. In: Neural Information Processing Systems (NIPS) (1994)
53. Selvaraju, R.R., Cogswell, M., Das, A., Vedantam, R., Parikh, D., Batra, D.: Grad-CAM: visual explanations from deep networks via gradient-based localization. In: International Conference on Computer Vision (ICCV) (2017)
54. Ronneberger, O., Fischer, P., Brox, T.: U-Net: convolutional networks for biomedical image segmentation. In: Navab, N., Hornegger, J., Wells, W.M., Frangi, A.F. (eds.) MICCAI 2015. LNCS, vol. 9351, pp. 234–241. Springer, Cham (2015). https://doi.org/10.1007/978-3-319-24574-4_28

Modular Graph Attention Network for Complex Visual Relational Reasoning

Yihan Zheng[1,2], Zhiquan Wen[1], Mingkui Tan[1], Runhao Zeng[1,2], Qi Chen[1], Yaowei Wang[2(✉)], and Qi Wu[3]

[1] South China University of Technology, Guangzhou, China
yihanzheng7@gmail.com, sewenzhiquan@mail.scut.edu.cn,
mingkuitan@scut.edu.cn
[2] PengCheng Laboratory, Shenzhen, China
wangyw@pcl.ac.cn
[3] The University of Adelaide, Adelaide, Australia
qi.wu01@adelaide.edu.au

Abstract. Visual Relational Reasoning is crucial for many vision-and-language based tasks, such as Visual Question Answering and Vision Language Navigation. In this paper, we consider reasoning on complex referring expression comprehension (c-REF) task that seeks to localise the target objects in an image guided by complex queries. Such queries often contain complex logic and thus impose two key challenges for reasoning: (i) It can be very difficult to comprehend the query since it often refers to multiple objects and describes complex relationships among them. (ii) It is non-trivial to reason among multiple objects guided by the query and localise the target correctly. To address these challenges, we propose a novel Modular Graph Attention Network (MGA-Net). Specifically, to comprehend the long queries, we devise a language attention network to decompose them into four types: basic attributes, absolute location, visual relationship and relative locations, which mimics the human language understanding mechanism. Moreover, to capture the complex logic in a query, we construct a relational graph to represent the visual objects and their relationships, and propose a multi-step reasoning method to progressively understand the complex logic. Extensive experiments on CLEVR-Ref+, GQA and CLEVR-CoGenT datasets demonstrate the superior reasoning performance of our MGA-Net.

1 Introduction

Visual relational reasoning often requires a machine to reason about visual and textual information and the relationships among objects before making a decision. This problem is crucial for many vision-and-language based tasks, such as visual question answering (VQA) [1–3] and vision language navigation (VLN)

Y. Zheng and Z. Wen—Contributed equally.

Electronic supplementary material The online version of this chapter (https://doi.org/10.1007/978-3-030-69544-6_9) contains supplementary material, which is available to authorized users.

© Springer Nature Switzerland AG 2021
H. Ishikawa et al. (Eds.): ACCV 2020, LNCS 12627, pp. 137–153, 2021.
https://doi.org/10.1007/978-3-030-69544-6_9

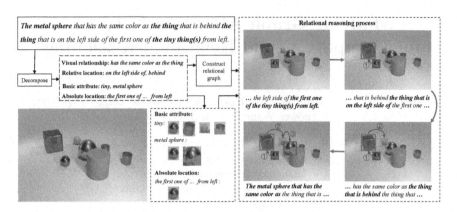

Fig. 1. An example of long-chain visual relational reasoning on CLEVR-Ref+ dataset [7]. The aim is to localise the target "metal sphere" based on the given complex query. To solve this, we propose to model the multi-step relationships via a relational graph step by step, and reason to the target.

[4–6]. However, reasoning can be very difficult because the visual and textual contents are often very complex. How to build a model to perform complex visual relational reasoning and how to validate the reasoning ability of such a model are still unclear.

Fortunately, we find the **complex** referring expression comprehension (c-REF) task [7,8] is a good test bed for visual reasoning methods. Specifically, c-REF requires a machine to reason over multiple objects and localise the target object in the image according to a complex natural language query (see Fig. 1). More critically, the complex visual and textual contents in this task can be a simulation of the complex real-world scenarios.

This task, however, is very challenging due to the following reasons: **a)** The query typically contains multiple types of information, such as the basic attributes, absolute location, visual relationship and relative location (see Fig. 1). It is non-trivial to understand the contents comprehensively in the complex query. **b)** Compared with the general referring expression comprehension (g-REF) task such as ReferCOCO [9,10], the query in c-REF often contains lots of visual relationships for multiple objects. It is very difficult to reason among multiple objects and localise the target correctly.

Recently, Liu *et al.* [7] found that state-of-the-art g-REF models like [11,12] failed to show promising reasoning performance on the c-REF task (*e.g.,* a new CLEVR-Ref+ dataset [7]), where the reasoning chain was long and complex. We find some methods [11,13] perform single-step reasoning to model the relationships between objects. However, the queries in real-world applications often contain complex logic, making them hard to be understood in such a one-step manner. For example, in Fig. 1, relational reasoning is a multi-step process: **Step 1**, select *"the first one of the tiny thing(s) from left"*; **Step 2**, given the object selected in Step 1, find *"the thing that is on the left side of"* them; **Step 3**, find *"the thing that is behind"* the object selected in Step 2; **Step 4**, find *"the metal thing that has the same colour as"* the object selected in Step 3. Although some methods [14,15] attempt to update the object features for more than one step, it performs reasoning with the whole sentence without distinguishing different types of information. In this sense, it cannot handle the complex relationships in the query very well, thus leading to inferior results.

In this paper, we propose a Modular Graph Attention Network (MGA-Net), which considers different information in the query and models object relationships for multi-step visual relational reasoning. First, in order to comprehend the long queries, we propose a **language attention network** to decompose the query into four types, including the basic attributes, the absolute location, the visual relationship and the relative location. Second, based on the language representation of the basic attributes and absolute location, we propose an **object attention network** to find the object that is more relevant to the query. Third, to capture the complex logic in a query, we propose a **relational inference network**. In particular, we build a relational graph to represent the relationships between objects. Based on the graph, we propose a multi-step reasoning method based on Gated Graph Neural Networks (GGNNs) [16] to progressively understand the complex logic and localise the target object. We conduct experiments on CLEVR-Ref+ [7], GQA [8] and CLEVR-CoGenT [7] datasets, which contain multiple types of information in the queries and require relational reasoning to localise the target of interest.

Our main contributions are summarised as follows:

- To comprehend the complex natural language query, we decompose the query into four types and design a functional module for each type of information.
- We construct a relational graph among objects and propose a multi-step reasoning method based on Gated Graph Neural Networks (GGNNs) [16] to progressively understand the complex logic in the query. In this way, our method is able to effectively localise the target object especially when long-chain reasoning is required.
- MGA-Net achieves the best performance on three complex relational reasoning datasets, demonstrating the superiority of our proposed method.

2 Related Work

Visual Relational Reasoning. Many vision-and-language tasks require visual reasoning to focus on the referred object of the query, such as visual question answering (VQA) [3,17,18], visual language navigation (VLN) [4,19,20] and referring expression comprehension (REF) [11,13]. To well complete these high-level tasks, the model requires the ability of complex relational reasoning. Rather than treating the query as a single unit, recent works [21–23] decomposed the query into components and performed the reasoning with each component. Some works [11,24] exploited Neural Module Networks (NMNs) [25] to deal with different types of information. With clearly decomposing the query, the corresponding module networks are appropriately designed to achieve better reasoning ability.

Referring Expression Comprehension (REF). The REF task is to localise the referent in an image with the guidance of a given referring expression. For REF, several datasets such as RefCOCO [9], RefCOCO+ [9] and RefCOCOg [10] were released for research. However, as discussed in [15], the queries in these datasets did not require resolving relations. Moreover, recent research [26] argued that RefCOCO datasets were biased, which meant that we could obtain high accuracy without the queries.[1] To faithfully evaluate the reasoning ability of the models, Liu *et al.* [7] released CLEVR-Ref+ dataset which was approximately unbiased. In this paper, we focus on the complex referring expression comprehension (c-REF) and evaluate our model on CLEVR-Ref+, GQA and CLEVR-CoGenT datasets, which all reduce the statistical biases within the datasets. Different from traditional datasets, the above datasets require long-chain reasoning ability for understanding complex queries.

Graph Neural Networks (GNNs). GNNs [27,28] combine graph and neural networks to enable communication between the linked nodes and build informative representations. Many variants of GNNs, such as Graph Convolution Networks (GCN) [29], Graph Attention Network (GAT) [30] and Gated Graph Neural Networks (GGNNs) [16], were applied to various tasks [15,31,32]. Some recent works [13–15,33–35] performed relational reasoning using graph networks. Li *et al.* [33] constructed three graphs to represent the relations and updated the node features in the graphs with single-step reasoning. Wang *et al.* proposed LGRANs [13], which applied a graph attention network to better aggregate the information from the neighbourhood to perform the reasoning process. However, these methods performed single-step reasoning only, while many queries requiring multi-step reasoning to solve. DGA [34] and CMRIN [35] considered the relation for each pair of objects with a small relative distance, but they both ignored the attribute relation (e.g., two objects have the same colour). Moreover, LCGN [15] took the reasoning process into account and built a graph for multi-step reasoning. However, it encoded the query in a holistic manner without distinguishing different types of information, which was difficult to comprehend the complex query. Different from the above methods, our method distinguishes location relation and attribute relation, which refines the relation representation and contributes to complex relationship modelling. To perform multi-step reasoning, we construct two relational graphs and update the graph representations for multiple times based on the GGNNs [16].

3   Proposed Method

Our aim is to build a model to perform the relational reasoning guided by a complex query and then localise the target in an image. We choose the complex referring expression comprehension (c-REF) task to evaluate our model since

---

[1] Although RefCOCO datasets are biased and do not belong to the c-REF task, we conduct experiments on them and put the results into the supplementary material.

both complex reasoning and localisation are required in this task. Formally, given a natural language query r and its corresponding image I with N objects $\mathcal{O} = \{o_i\}_{i=1}^N$, the goal of c-REF is to identify the target object $o^\star$ by reasoning over the objects $\mathcal{O}$ guided by the query.

Due to the complexity of the queries, how to distinguish different types of information and how to reason among multiple objects guided by the query are very challenging. To deal with these challenges, we decompose the query into different types of information and design a functional module for each type of information. To capture the complex logic in a query, we construct a relational graph to represent the objects and their relationships. Moreover, we propose a multi-step reasoning method based on the relational graph to progressively understand the complex logic and identify the target object.

Our Modular Graph Attention Network (MGA-Net) composes of three components as shown in Fig. 2. First, the **language attention network** decomposes the query r into four types: basic attributes, absolute location, visual relationship and relative location, and obtains the corresponding language representations $\mathbf{s}^{att}$, $\mathbf{s}^{loc}$, $\mathbf{s}^{rel\_vis}$ and $\mathbf{s}^{rel\_loc}$. Second, the **object attention network** represents all candidate objects $\mathcal{O}$ with their visual features and spatial features, and obtains the objects that are relevant to r under the guidance of $\mathbf{s}^{att}$ and $\mathbf{s}^{loc}$. Third, the **relational inference network** constructs a relational graph among objects, and then updates node representations step by step via Gated Graph Neural Networks (GGNNs) guided by $\mathbf{s}^{rel\_vis}$ and $\mathbf{s}^{rel\_loc}$, respectively. Last, we match the updated object representations with the corresponding language representations to obtain the prediction.

3.1 Language Attention Network

A query in c-REF often describes multiple objects with their relationships and contains four types of information, including (1) basic attributes, which contain object category name, size, colour and material; (2) absolute location, which describes the position of the object in the image; (3) visual relationship, which represents the relationships (the same attribute or the inter-action) between objects; (4) relative location, which describes the displacement between objects.

To comprehend the query, some methods [25] adopted off-the-shelf language parser [36] to parse the query. However, as mentioned in [11], the external parser could raise parsing error, which affected the performance of REF. Therefore, instead of relying on the off-the-shelf language parser, we adopt self-attention mechanism to parse the query automatically.

To distinguish different types of information, we design a functional module for each type of information. Specifically, we represent a query with L words $r = \{w_l\}_{l=1}^L$ using the word embeddings $\{\mathbf{e}_l\}_{l=1}^L$, which can be obtained by using a non-linear mapping function or pre-trained word embeddings, such as GloVe [37]. With the word embeddings being the input of a Bi-LSTM model [38], we obtain the hidden state representations $\mathbf{h} = \{\mathbf{h}_l\}_{l=1}^L$, which are the concatenation of the forward and backward hidden vectors of the words. To calculate the attention score of each word in each module, we apply a fully connected layer to the hidden

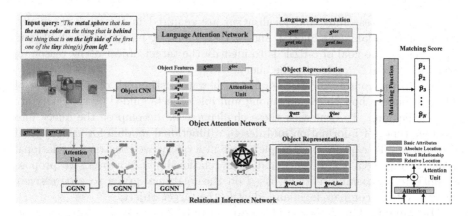

Fig. 2. Overview of Modular Graph Attention Network (MGA-Net) for visual relational reasoning. Our method contains three components. The language attention network decomposes the query into four types with an attention mechanism. The object attention network selects the related objects with their basic attributes and absolute locations. Based on the relational graph, the relational inference network models the complex relationships by a multi-step reasoning method. The final score is obtained by matching four object representations with their corresponding language representations.

state representations $\mathbf{h}$, and normalise the scores with a softmax function. In particular, for each word w_l, we calculate basic attributes attention a_l^{att}, absolute location attention a_l^{loc}, visual relationship attention $a_l^{rel\_vis}$ and relative location attention $a_l^{rel\_loc}$ as follows:

$$a_l^{type} = \frac{\exp\left(\mathbf{w}_a^{type\top}\mathbf{h}_l\right)}{\sum_{k=1}^{L}\exp\left(\mathbf{w}_a^{type\top}\mathbf{h}_k\right)},\tag{1}$$

where $type \in \{att, loc, rel\_vis, rel\_loc\}$ and $\mathbf{w}_a^{type} \in \mathbb{R}^{d_w}$ denotes the parameters of each module and d_w is the dimension of the word embeddings. With the attention scores $\mathbf{a}^{att}$, $\mathbf{a}^{loc}$, $\mathbf{a}^{rel\_vis}$, $\mathbf{a}^{rel\_loc} \in \mathbb{R}^L$ at hand, we obtain the representation for each type of information as follows:

$$\mathbf{s}^{type} = \sum_{l=1}^{L} a_l^{type} \cdot \mathbf{e}_l.\tag{2}$$

With the help of the attention mechanism, we are able to learn the language representations *w.r.t.* the basic attributes, absolute location, relative location and visual relationship.

3.2   Object Attention Network

To localise the object with its properties (*i.e.,* the basic attributes and absolute location), we propose an object attention network. In particular, we represent each object with its attribute feature and location feature. Then, we calculate attention scores for the objects with the guidance of the language representations $\mathbf{s}^{att}$ and $\mathbf{s}^{loc}$. Last, we update the object representations based on their basic attributes and absolute locations.

Basic Attributes Representation. The basic attributes module describes the object category, shape, colour, size and material of the object, which is relative to the visual features. The visual feature $\mathbf{u}_i$ for each object can be obtained by using some certain pre-trained feature extractor (*e.g.*, ResNet101 [39]). Then, we use a multi-layer perception (MLP) f^u with two hidden layers to obtain the basic attributes representation as $\mathbf{x}_i^{att} = f^u(\mathbf{u}_i)$.

Absolute Location Representation. The absolute location module describes the location information of the object. Supposing the width and height of the image are represented as $[W, H]$, and the top-left coordinate, bottom-right coordinate, width and height of object i are represented as $[x_{tl_i}, y_{tl_i}, x_{br_i}, y_{br_i}, w_i, h_i]$, then the spatial feature of object i is represented as a 5-dimensional vector $\mathbf{l}_i = \left[\frac{x_{tl_i}}{W}, \frac{y_{tl_i}}{H}, \frac{x_{br_i}}{W}, \frac{y_{br_i}}{H}, \frac{w_i \cdot h_i}{W \cdot H}\right]$. It denotes the top left and bottom right corner coordinates of the object region (normalised between 0 and 1) and its relative area (*i.e.*, the ratio of the bounding box area to the image area). Since the visual features may also indicate the object location from its background context, we also combine the visual features with the spatial feature, leading to the object location representation of object i as $\mathbf{x}_i^{loc} = \left[f^u(\mathbf{u}_i), f^l(\mathbf{l}_i)\right]$, where f^l is an MLP and $[\cdot, \cdot]$ denotes for concatenation.

Object Attention Module. Under the guidance of language representation $\mathbf{s}^{att}$ and $\mathbf{s}^{loc}$, the object attention module aims at finding the objects that are relevant to the given query. With the object representations $\mathbf{x}_i^{att}$ and $\mathbf{x}_i^{loc}$, the attention weights of object i is calculated as follows,

$$\tilde{a}_i^{o,obj} = \mathbf{w}_o^{obj\top} \tanh\left(\mathbf{W}_{o,s}^{obj}\mathbf{s}^{obj} + \mathbf{W}_{o,x}^{obj}\mathbf{x}_i^{obj}\right),$$

$$a_i^{o,obj} = \frac{\exp\left(\tilde{a}_i^{o,obj}\right)}{\sum_{j=1}^N \exp\left(\tilde{a}_j^{o,obj}\right)}, \tag{3}$$

where $obj \in \{att, loc\}$. $\mathbf{W}_{o,s}^{obj} \in \mathbb{R}^{d_e \times d_w}$ and $\mathbf{W}_{o,x}^{obj} \in \mathbb{R}^{d_e \times d_o}$ are the parameters of two fully connected layers, which transform the language representations $\mathbf{s}^{obj}$ and the object representation $\mathbf{x}_i^{obj}$ into an embedding space, respectively. d_e is the dimension of the embedding space and d_o is the dimension of the object representation. $\mathbf{w}_o^{obj} \in \mathbb{R}^{d_e}$ is the parameters of the object attention module.

With the object attention weights $a_i^{o,att}$ and $a_i^{o,loc}$ at hand, we update the object representations by calculating

$$\hat{\mathbf{x}}_i^{obj} = a_i^{o,obj}\mathbf{x}_i^{obj}, obj \in \{att, loc\}. \tag{4}$$

In this way, the object representations are encoded with the language representations about basic attributes and the absolute location, respectively.

3.3   Relational Inference Network

To capture the complex logic in a query, we represent the input image as a graph, where nodes are objects and edges represent their relationships. Then, we adopt Gated Graph Neural Networks (GGNNs) to update the node representations by aggregating the information from neighbourhoods. However, for each node, a single-step updating cannot guarantee to capture the multi-step relationships between other nodes, making it hard to understand the complex logic in the query for reasoning. In this paper, we propose a multi-step updating method to progressively aggregate relational information for each node guided by the language representations $\mathbf{s}^{rel\_vis}$ and $\mathbf{s}^{rel\_loc}$. This updating method helps to understand the logic in the query and localise the object of interest correctly.

Graph Construction. We build a directed graph $\mathcal{G} = \{\mathcal{V}, \mathcal{E}\}$ over the object set $\mathcal{O}$, where $\mathcal{V} = \{v_i\}_{i=1}^{N}$ is the node set and $\mathcal{E} = \{e_{ij}\}_{i,j=1}^{N}$ is the edge set. Each node v_i corresponds to an object $o_i \in \{\mathcal{O}\}$ and each edge e_{ij} denotes the edge connecting objects o_i and o_j, which represents the relationships between the two objects.

Visual Relationship Representation. The visual relationship module describes the relationships between objects, referring to the attributes of two objects (*e.g.* A and B are in the same colour, size) or the interaction between objects (*e.g.* A holds B). To represent the visual relationship, we obtain the feature of object i by concatenating its visual feature and spatial feature $\mathbf{x}_i^{vis} = [\mathbf{u}_i, \mathbf{l}_i]$. Then, we use an MLP f^{rel_vis} to encode the features of two objects. The edge representation of the visual relationship between object i and object j is calculated as follows,

$$\mathbf{e}_{ij}^{rel\_vis} = f^{rel\_vis}\left(\left[\mathbf{x}_i^{vis}, \mathbf{x}_j^{vis}\right]\right). \tag{5}$$

Relative Location Representation. The relative location module describes the displacement between two objects which reflects the spatial correlation of objects. Here, we represent the spatial relation between two objects v_i and v_j as $\tilde{\mathbf{e}}_{ij} = [\frac{x_{tl_j}-x_{c_i}}{w_i}, \frac{y_{tl_j}-y_{c_i}}{h_i}, \frac{x_{br_j}-x_{c_i}}{w_i}, \frac{y_{br_j}-y_{c_i}}{h_i}, \frac{w_j \cdot h_j}{w_i \cdot h_i}]$, where $[x_{c_i}, y_{c_i}, w_i, h_i]$ is the centre coordinate, width and height of object i, and $[x_{tl_j}, y_{tl_j}, x_{br_j}, y_{br_j}, w_j, h_j]$ is the top-left coordinate, bottom-right coordinate, width and height of the j-th object, respectively. Considering the query like "A is to the left of B", the related object "B" plays an important role in location relationship understanding. We include the visual feature and spatial feature of object j for relative location representations. We obtain the edge representation of the relative location by calculating

$$\mathbf{e}_{ij}^{rel\_loc} = f^{rel\_loc}\left(\left[\tilde{\mathbf{e}}_{ij}, \mathbf{x}_j^{vis}\right]\right), \tag{6}$$

where f^{rel_loc} is an MLP. After learning the edge representation, we obtain the visual relational graph.

Multi-step Reasoning. Based on the constructed graph, we introduce Gated Graph Neural Networks (GGNNs) to iteratively update the node representations by aggregating the relational information and achieve the multi-step reasoning. GGNNs contain a propagation model learned with a gated recurrent update mechanism, which is similar to recurrent neural networks. For each object node in the graph, the propagation process of the t-th step is defined as follows:

$$
\begin{aligned}
\mathbf{z}_i^{rel,(t)} &= \tanh\left(\mathbf{a}_i^{rel\top}\left[\mathbf{h}_1^{rel,(t-1)};\ldots;\mathbf{h}_N^{rel,(t-1)}\right]\right), \\
\mathbf{h}_i^{rel,(t)} &= \text{GRUCell}\left(\mathbf{z}_i^{rel,(t)}, \mathbf{h}_i^{rel,(t-1)}\right),
\end{aligned}
\tag{7}
$$

where $rel \in \{rel\_vis, rel\_loc\}$ and $\mathbf{a}_i^{rel}$ is the i-th row of a propagation matrix $\mathbf{A}^{rel} \in \mathbb{R}^{N \times N}$ that represents the propagation weights. GRUCell is the GRU update mechanism [40]. $\mathbf{h}_i^{rel,(t)}$ is the hidden state of the i-th object at step t.

At each time step, we update the node representations by aggregating the information from the neighbourhoods according to the propagation matrix $\mathbf{A}^{rel}$. However, updating for only one step fails to capture the multi-step relationships between other nodes. Thus, we propose a multi-step updating method, enabling each object to aggregate the relational information in the complex query and progressively understand the complex logic. After T time steps for propagation, the final representation for the i-th node can be obtained by:

$$
\hat{\mathbf{x}}_i^{rel} = \mathbf{h}_i^{rel,(T)}.
\tag{8}
$$

Propagation Matrix. In Eq. (7), we need to compute the propagation matrix $\mathbf{A}^{rel}$ and the initial hidden state $\mathbf{h}_i^{rel,(0)}$ for each node. To this end, we devise an edge attention mechanism. Specifically, with the edge representation $\mathbf{e}_{ij}^{rel\_vis}$ and $\mathbf{e}_{ij}^{rel\_loc}$ in Eqs. (5) and (6), the edge attention for the visual relationship and relative location are calculated as follows,

$$
\begin{aligned}
\tilde{a}_{ij}^{rel} &= \mathbf{w}_e^{rel\top} \tanh\left(\mathbf{W}_{e,s}^{rel}\mathbf{s}^{rel} + \mathbf{W}_{e,x}^{rel}\mathbf{e}_{ij}^{rel}\right), \\
a_{ij}^{rel} &= \frac{\exp\left(\tilde{a}_{ij}^{rel}\right)}{\sum_{k \neq i}\exp\left(\tilde{a}_{ik}^{rel}\right)}, a_{ii}^{rel} = 0,
\end{aligned}
\tag{9}
$$

where $rel \in \{rel\_vis, rel\_loc\}$. $\mathbf{W}_{e,s}^{rel} \in \mathbb{R}^{d_e \times d_w}$ and $\mathbf{W}_{e,x}^{rel} \in \mathbb{R}^{d_e \times d_r}$ are the parameters of two fully connected layers, which transform the expression $\mathbf{s}^{rel}$ and the edge representation $\mathbf{e}_{ij}^{rel}$ into an embedding space, respectively. d_e is the dimension of the embedding space and d_r is the dimension of the edge representation. $\mathbf{w}_e^{rel} \in \mathbb{R}^{d_e}$ are the parameters of the fully connected layers. With the edge attention mechanism, we obtain $a_{ij}^{rel\_vis}$ and $a_{ij}^{rel\_loc}$ to construct the propagation matrices. Then, the initial hidden state of the i-th object can be obtained by calculating $\mathbf{h}_i^{rel,(0)} = \sum_{j=1}^{N} a_{ij}^{rel}\mathbf{e}_{ij}^{rel}$, where $rel \in \{rel\_vis, rel\_loc\}$ and N is the number of nodes.

3.4   Matching Function and Loss Function

Matching Function. To find the target object, we need to compute a matching score for each object. Specifically, we devise a matching function to predict the final scores by matching the language representations and the corresponding object representations, which encode with the properties (in Eq. (4)) and relationships with other objects (in Eq. (8)). The matching score p_i^{type} between the language representation $\mathbf{s}^{type}$ and the object representation $\hat{\mathbf{x}}_i^{type}$ can be calculated as follows:

$$p_i^{type} = \tanh\left(\mathbf{W}_{m,s}^{type}\mathbf{s}^{type}\right)^\top \tanh\left(\mathbf{W}_{m,x}^{type}\hat{\mathbf{x}}_i^{type}\right), \tag{10}$$

where $type \in \{att, loc, rel\_vis, rel\_loc\}$, $\mathbf{W}_{m,s}^{type} \in \mathbb{R}^{d_e \times d_w}$ and $\mathbf{W}_{m,x}^{type} \in \mathbb{R}^{d_e \times d_e}$ are learnable parameters. Similar to the previous studies [11,13], we calculate four weights $[w^{att}, w^{loc}, w^{rel\_vis}, w^{rel\_loc}]$ to represent the contributions of different modules. We apply a fully connected layer to the vector $\mathbf{e} = \sum_{l=1}^{L} \mathbf{e}_l$. The calculation of the weights are as follows,

$$\left[w^{att}, w^{loc}, w^{rel\_vis}, w^{rel\_loc}\right] = \text{softmax}\left(\mathbf{W}_s\mathbf{e}\right), \tag{11}$$

where $\mathbf{W}_s \in \mathbb{R}^{4 \times d_w}$ is the parameter of the fully connected layer, and d_w is the dimension of the word embedding. For object i, the final matching score p_i is calculated by weighted summing up of the p_i^{type} with the four weights:

$$p_i = \sum_{type} w^{type} p_i^{type}. \tag{12}$$

Loss Function. To localise the referent among all objects in the image, we regard it as a multi-class classification task. The probability for object i being the referent is calculated as $\tilde{p}_i = \frac{\exp(p_i)}{\sum_{j=1}^{N}\exp(p_j)}$, where N is the number of object candidates in the image. We choose the cross-entropy loss as the loss function:

$$L = -\sum_{i=1}^{N} y_i \cdot \log\left(\tilde{p}_i\right), \tag{13}$$

where y_i is 1 when object i is the ground truth referent and 0 otherwise. We use the Adam [41] method to minimise the loss.[2]

4   Experiments

In this section, we evaluate the proposed method on a complex referring expression comprehension dataset (*i.e.*, CLEVR-Ref+ [7]). To evaluate the generalisation ability of our method, we further conduct experiments on CLEVR-CoGenT [7]. We also evaluate our method on a question answering dataset (*i.e.*, GQA [8]). Last, we perform ablation studies and visualisation analysis to verify the contributions of each module in our method.[3]

---

[2] We put the training algorithm into the supplementary material.
[3] We put the Implementation Details into the supplementary material.

4.1   Datasets

CLEVR-Ref+ [7] is a synthetic dataset whose images and queries are generated automatically. This dataset is approximately unbiased by employing a uniform sampling strategy. Moreover, it provides complex expressions that require strong visual reasoning ability to be comprehended.

GQA [8] is a real-world VQA dataset with compositional questions over images from Visual Genome data [42]. Like CLEVR-Ref+, GQA mitigates language priors and conditional biases for evaluating the visual reasoning capacity of models. Moreover, the questions in GQA include complex visual relationships among objects. In the GQA dataset, the grounding score is designed to check whether the model focuses on question and answer relevant regions within the images. Since MGA-Net focuses on visual reasoning (such as VQA and REF), the grounding scores of GQA is suitable for evaluating the performance of visual reasoning.

CLEVR-CoGenT [7] is a synthetic dataset, augmented from CLEVR [43] dataset. The queries are also complex, which require resolving relations. Moreover, it has two different conditions, such as Condition A and Condition B, which contain different object attributes.

4.2   Evaluation on CLEVR-Ref+

Comparison with State-of-the-Arts. We compare our MGA-Net with several state-of-the-art methods, including Stack-NMN [44], SLR [12], MAttNet [11], GroundeR [45] and LCGN [15]. From Table 1, our method outperforms all baselines. Specifically, MAttNet decomposes the queries into three parts (visual subject, location and relationship), but it ignores the issue of long-chain reasoning. Thus, MAttNet only achieves the accuracy of 60.9%. Beneficial from the multi-step reasoning based on the graph, LCGN leads to 14% improvement by using the graph network to get the context-aware representation. However, LCGN ignores to distinguish different types of information in the queries and encodes them in a holistic manner. Different from them, our MGA-Net considers the different information in the query and performs multi-step reasoning on the relational graph via GGNNs. With the detected bounding boxes as input, our proposed method achieves the accuracy of 80.1%. Moreover, using ground truth bounding boxes further improves the accuracy to 80.8%.

Effectiveness of Four Modules. MGA-Net decomposes queries into four parts, such as the basic attributes (att), absolute location (loc), relative location (rel_loc) and visual relationship (rel_vis). To evaluate the effect of each module, we conduct the ablation studies on CLEVR-Ref+ dataset. We use the ground truth bounding boxes as input and set the updating step of GGNNs to 3.

Quantitative Results. From Table 2, when only using basic attributes to localise the object (Row 1), the model achieves the accuracy of 62.10%. Row 2 shows the benefits brought by the absolute location module. By combining the visual relationship (Row 3) or the relative location module (Row 4), the accuracy improves

Table 1. Comparisons with state-of-the-arts on CLEVR-Ref+ in Accuracy.

Method	Accuracy (%)
Stack-NMN [44]	56.5
SLR [12]	57.7
MAttNet [11]	60.9
GroundeR [45]	61.7
LCGN [15]	74.8
MGA-Net (with detected bbox)	80.1
MGA-Net (with ground truth bbox)	**80.8**

Table 2. Impact of the four modules on CLEVR-Ref+.

Module	Accuracy (%)
att	62.10
att + loc	65.83
att + loc + rel_vis	72.81
att + loc + rel_loc	76.86
att + loc + rel_vis + rel_loc	**80.87**

Table 3. Comparisons of different models on GQA in terms of Grounding scores.

Method	Grounding score (%)
MAttNet [11]	56.73
LGRANs [13]	84.73
MGA-Net	**87.03**

Table 4. Comparisons with baselines on CLEVR-CoGenT (valA & B) in Accuracy.

Method	valA	valB
SLR [12]	0.63	0.59
MAttNet [11]	0.64	0.63
MGA-Net (with detected bbox)	0.82	0.76
MGA-Net (with ground truth bbox)	**0.83**	**0.78**

significantly, showing the benefit of the relational reasoning modules. Moreover, our MGA-Net with four modules achieves the best performance. These results demonstrate that distinguishing different types of information in the query is important for relational reasoning.

Visualisation. We visualise the four modules in the query in Fig. 3. We highlight the words which are correctly indicated by the corresponding modules according to the weight of each word. These results demonstrate that our proposed four modules have the ability to capture the corresponding phrases.

4.3   Evaluation on GQA

We evaluate MAttNet [11], LGRANs [13] and our MGA-Net on GQA. During training, we regard the mentioned object in the answer as the ground truth and train the models with the balanced training questions. In inference, all balanced validation questions are fed into the model to calculate the grounding scores. Such a score evaluates whether the model focuses on the regions of the image that are relevant to the questions and answers. Since the ground truth bounding boxes of the mentioned objects in the question and answer are not provided on the test-dev and test sets, we evaluate the methods on the validation set.

From Table 3, our MGA-Net outperforms the baselines. For LGRANs [13], it only introduces single-step reasoning, which is unsuitable for long-chain reasoning. Moreover, LGRANs considers the location relation only, and ignores the

Table 5. Impact of the updating step T. We report the accuracy (%) of our method with different values of T on CLEVR-Ref+ and CLEVR-CoGenT (valA & valB). We provide the grounding score (%) of our method with different values of T on GQA.

Dataset	CLEVR-Ref+		CLEVR-CoGenT (valA)		CLEVR-CoGenT (valB)		GQA
Setting	detected bbox	gt bbox	detected bbox	gt bbox	detected bbox	gt bbox	–
$T = 0$	75.81	76.51	76.00	76.24	71.37	72.32	86.01
$T = 1$	79.52	80.25	79.01	79.15	74.26	74.53	86.89
$T = 3$	**80.18**	**80.87**	**82.02**	**82.90**	**76.60**	**78.15**	87.03
$T = 5$	79.05	79.65	79.95	80.36	74.69	76.00	**87.93**

visual relations in the query. In contrast to the LGRANs, we first construct relational graphs among the objects regarding to the location and visual relations. Based on the relational graphs, we are able to conduct multi-step reasoning via GGNNs guided by language representations and thus achieves higher performance than LGRANs. Note that the excellent performance of MAttNet [11] in previous study relies on the attribute features and the phrase-guided "inbox" attention. However, these features cannot be provided by GQA. Besides, MAttNet only decomposes expressions into three modular components that are without multi-step reasoning, which makes it hard to perform the complex compositional reasoning. Thus, the performance of MAttNet degrades significantly on GQA.

4.4 Evaluation on CLEVR-CoGenT

To evaluate the generalisation ability, we train the model on the training set of Condition A and evaluate it on the validation set of Condition A and Condition B (*i.e.,* valA and valB). From Table 4, our MGA-Net outperforms SLR [12] and MAttNet [11] by a large margin. Specifically, in the "detection" setting, our method achieves the accuracy of 0.82 on valA and the accuracy of 0.76 on valB. When using ground truth bounding boxes, the performance of our method is further improved (0.83 on valA and 0.78 on valB). These results further demonstrate the superior generalisation ability of our proposed method.

Note that on the CLEVR-Ref+ and CLEVR-CoGenT datasets, our method achieves comparable performance between using ground truth bounding box and detected bounding box. The reason is that the scene of the image in these datasets is simple, and the objects in the scene are able to be detected accurately and easily.

4.5 Effectiveness of Multi-step Reasoning

Quantitative Results. To evaluate the multi-step reasoning, we verify it on our MGA-Net by setting different updating steps T in GGNNs. From Table 5, on all datasets, the models with GGNNs ($T > 1$) outperform the model without GGNNs ($T = 0$) significantly, which demonstrates the necessity and superiority of the relational reasoning.

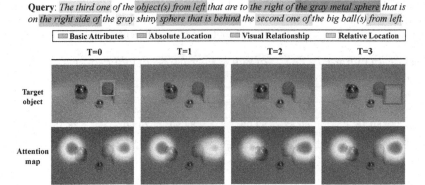

Fig. 3. An example of 3-step reasoning on complex referring expression comprehension. We visualise the attention maps of GGNNs and mark the target object by a bounding box for each step. With the guidance of the expression, the attentive image region changes over updating and the highlighted object corresponds to the ground truth.

Moreover, with the increasing of the updating steps (from $T = 1$ to $T = 3$), the performance of the MGA-Net further improves on all the datasets, which demonstrates the superiority of the multi-step reasoning. But MGA-Net with GGNNs $T = 3$ performs better than that with GGNNs $T = 5$ on CLEVR-Ref+ and CLEVR-CoGenT datasets. This implies that an appropriate number of updating steps helps to obtain the best performance on MGA-Net.

Visualisation. To further illustrate the effectiveness of our method on dealing with long-chain reasoning, we visualise the intermediate results of the model. We set the updating step $T = 3$ in GGNNs, and train the model with the ground truth bounding boxes as inputs on CLEVR-Ref+. Then, we obtain the initial nodes representations ($T = 0$) and the updated node representations in different updating steps ($T = 1, 2, 3$). To predict the score for each node, we match the node representations and the language representations. As shown in the visualisation results in Fig. 3, the attentive image region changes over updating and the highlighted object corresponds to the ground truth.

5   Conclusion

In this paper, we have proposed a new Modular Graph Attention Network (MGA-Net) for complex visual relational reasoning. To cover and represent the textual information, we decompose the complex query into four types and design a module for each type. Meanwhile, we construct the relational graphs among objects. Based on the relational graphs, we devise a graph inference network with GGNNs to update the graph representations step by step. Our method encodes the multi-step relationships among objects and then reasons to the target. Promising results demonstrate the effectiveness and the superior visual relational reasoning ability of our method.

Acknowledgement. This work was partially supported by the Key-Area Research and Development Program of Guangdong Province 2019B010155002, Program for Guangdong Introducing Innovative and Entrepreneurial Teams 2017ZT-07X183, Fundamental Research Funds for the Central Universities D2191240.

References

1. Perez, E., Strub, F., De Vries, H., Dumoulin, V., Courville, A.: FiLM: visual reasoning with a general conditioning layer. In: AAAI Conference on Artificial Intelligence (AAAI) (2018)
2. Hudson, D.A., Manning, C.D.: Compositional attention networks for machine reasoning. In: International Conference on Learning Representations (ICLR) (2018)
3. Mao, J., Gan, C., Kohli, P., Tenenbaum, J.B., Wu, J.: The neuro-symbolic concept learner: interpreting scenes, words, and sentences from natural supervision. In: International Conference on Learning Representations (ICLR) (2019)
4. Anderson, P., et al.: Vision-and-language navigation: interpreting visually-grounded navigation instructions in real environments. In: Proceedings of the IEEE Conference on Computer Vision and Pattern Recognition (CVPR), pp. 3674–3683 (2018)
5. Wang, X., et al.: Reinforced cross-modal matching and self-supervised imitation learning for vision-language navigation. In: Proceedings of the IEEE Conference on Computer Vision and Pattern Recognition (CVPR), pp. 6629–6638 (2019)
6. Nguyen, K., Dey, D., Brockett, C., Dolan, B.: Vision-based navigation with language-based assistance via imitation learning with indirect intervention. In: Proceedings of the of the IEEE Conference on Computer Vision and Pattern Recognition (CVPR), pp. 12527–12537 (2019)
7. Liu, R., Liu, C., Bai, Y., Yuille, A.L.: CLEVR-REF+: diagnosing visual reasoning with referring expressions. In: Proceedings of the of the IEEE Conference on Computer Vision and Pattern Recognition (CVPR), pp. 4185–4194 (2019)
8. Hudson, D.A., Manning, C.D.: GQA: a new dataset for real-world visual reasoning and compositional question answering. In: Proceedings of the of the IEEE Conference on Computer Vision and Pattern Recognition (CVPR), pp. 6700–6709 (2019)
9. Kazemzadeh, S., Ordonez, V., Matten, M., Berg, T.L.: ReferitGame: referring to objects in photographs of natural scenes. In: Proceedings of the Conference on Empirical Methods in Natural Language Processing (EMNLP), pp. 787–798 (2014)
10. Mao, J., Huang, J., Toshev, A., Camburu, O., Yuille, A.L., Murphy, K.: Generation and comprehension of unambiguous object descriptions. In: Proceedings of the IEEE Conference on Computer Vision and Pattern Recognition (CVPR), pp. 11–20 (2016)
11. Yu, L., et al.: MAttNet: modular attention network for referring expression comprehension. In: Proceedings of the IEEE Conference on Computer Vision and Pattern Recognition (CVPR), pp. 1307–1315 (2018)
12. Yu, L., Tan, H., Bansal, M., Berg, T.L.: A joint speaker-listener-reinforcer model for referring expressions. In: Proceedings of the IEEE Conference on Computer Vision and Pattern Recognition (CVPR), pp. 3521–3529 (2017)

13. Wang, P., Wu, Q., Cao, J., Shen, C., Gao, L., Hengel, A.v.d.: Neighbourhood watch: referring expression comprehension via language-guided graph attention networks. In: Proceedings of the IEEE Conference on Computer Vision and Pattern Recognition (CVPR), pp. 1960–1968 (2019)

14. Bajaj, M., Wang, L., Sigal, L.: G3raphGround: graph-based language grounding. In: Proceedings of the IEEE International Conference on Computer Vision (ICCV), pp. 4281–4290 (2019)

15. Hu, R., Rohrbach, A., Darrell, T., Saenko, K.: Language-conditioned graph networks for relational reasoning. In: Proceedings of the IEEE International Conference on Computer Vision (ICCV), pp. 10294–10303 (2019)

16. Li, Y., Tarlow, D., Brockschmidt, M., Zemel, R.S.: Gated graph sequence neural networks. In: International Conference on Learning Representations (ICLR) (2016)

17. Norcliffe-Brown, W., Vafeias, S., Parisot, S.: Learning conditioned graph structures for interpretable visual question answering. In: Advances in Neural Information Processing Systems (NeurIPS), pp. 8334–8343 (2018)

18. Chang, S., Yang, J., Park, S., Kwak, N.: Broadcasting convolutional network for visual relational reasoning. In: Proceedings of the European Conference on Computer Vision (ECCV), pp. 754–769 (2018)

19. Huang, H., Jain, V., Mehta, H., Ku, A., Magalhaes, G., Baldridge, J., Ie, E.: Transferable representation learning in vision-and-language navigation. In: Proceedings of the IEEE International Conference on Computer Vision (ICCV), pp. 7404–7413 (2019)

20. Ke, L., et al.: Tactical rewind: self-correction via backtracking in vision-and-language navigation. In: Proceedings of the IEEE Conference on Computer Vision and Pattern Recognition (CVPR), pp. 6741–6749 (2019)

21. Johnson, J., et al.: Inferring and executing programs for visual reasoning. In: Proceedings of the IEEE International Conference on Computer Vision (ICCV), pp. 2989–2998 (2017)

22. Hu, R., Andreas, J., Rohrbach, M., Darrell, T., Saenko, K.: Learning to reason: end-to-end module networks for visual question answering. In: Proceedings of the IEEE International Conference on Computer Vision (ICCV), pp. 804–813 (2017)

23. Cao, Q., Liang, X., Li, B., Li, G., Lin, L.: Visual question reasoning on general dependency tree. In: Proceedings of the IEEE Conference on Computer Vision and Pattern Recognition (CVPR), pp. 7249–7257 (2018)

24. Hu, R., Rohrbach, M., Andreas, J., Darrell, T., Saenko, K.: Modeling relationships in referential expressions with compositional modular networks. In: Proceedings of the IEEE Conference on Computer Vision and Pattern Recognition (CVPR), pp. 1115–1124 (2017)

25. Andreas, J., Rohrbach, M., Darrell, T., Klein, D.: Neural module networks. In: Proceedings of the IEEE Conference on Computer Vision and Pattern Recognition (CVPR), pp. 39–48 (2016)

26. Cirik, V., Morency, L., Berg-Kirkpatrick, T.: Visual referring expression recognition: what do systems actually learn? In: Proceedings of the Conference of the North American Chapter of the Association for Computational Linguistics: Human Language Technologies (NAACL-HLT), pp. 781–787 (2018)

27. Gori, M., Monfardini, G., Scarselli, F.: A new model for learning in graph domains. In: Proceedings of the IEEE International Joint Conference on Neural Networks (IJCNN), vol. 2, pp. 729–734. IEEE (2005)

28. Scarselli, F., Gori, M., Tsoi, A.C., Hagenbuchner, M., Monfardini, G.: The graph neural network model. IEEE Trans. Neural Networks **20**, 61–80 (2008)

29. Kipf, T.N., Welling, M.: Semi-supervised classification with graph convolutional networks. In: International Conference on Learning Representations (ICLR) (2017)
30. Velickovic, P., Cucurull, G., Casanova, A., Romero, A., Liò, P., Bengio, Y.: Graph attention networks. arXiv preprint arXiv:1710.10903 (2017)
31. Zeng, R., et al.: Graph convolutional networks for temporal action localization. In: Proceedings of the IEEE International Conference on Computer Vision (ICCV), pp. 7094–7103 (2019)
32. Huang, D., Chen, P., Zeng, R., Du, Q., Tan, M., Gan, C.: Location-aware graph convolutional networks for video question answering. In: AAAI Conference on Artificial Intelligence (AAAI), pp. 11021–11028 (2020)
33. Li, L., Gan, Z., Cheng, Y., Liu, J.: Relation-aware graph attention network for visual question answering. In: Proceedings of the IEEE International Conference on Computer Vision (ICCV), pp. 10313–10322 (2019)
34. Yang, S., Li, G., Yu, Y.: Dynamic graph attention for referring expression comprehension. In: Proceedings of the IEEE International Conference on Computer Vision (ICCV), pp. 4644–4653 (2019)
35. Yang, S., Li, G., Yu, Y.: Cross-modal relationship inference for grounding referring expressions. In: Proceedings of the IEEE Conference on Computer Vision and Pattern Recognition (CVPR), pp. 4145–4154 (2019)
36. Zhu, M., Zhang, Y., Chen, W., Zhang, M., Zhu, J.: Fast and accurate shift-reduce constituent parsing. In: ACL, vol. 1, pp. 434–443 (2013)
37. Pennington, J., Socher, R., Manning, C.D.: GloVe: global vectors for word representation. In: Proceedings of the Conference on Empirical Methods in Natural Language Processing (EMNLP), pp. 1532–1543 (2014)
38. Schuster, M., Paliwal, K.K.: Bidirectional recurrent neural networks. IEEE Trans. Signal Process. **45**, 2673–2681 (1997)
39. He, K., Zhang, X., Ren, S., Sun, J.: Deep residual learning for image recognition. In: Proceedings of the IEEE Conference on Computer Vision and Pattern Recognition (CVPR), pp. 770–778 (2016)
40. Cho, K., et al.: Learning phrase representations using RNN encoder-decoder for statistical machine translation. In: Proceedings of the Conference on Empirical Methods in Natural Language Processing (EMNLP), pp. 1724–1734 (2014)
41. Kingma, D.P., Ba, J.: Adam: a method for stochastic optimization. In: International Conference on Learning Representations (ICLR) (2015)
42. Krishna, R., et al.: Visual genome: connecting language and vision using crowd-sourced dense image annotations. Int. J. Comput. Vision **123**, 32–73 (2017)
43. Johnson, J., Hariharan, B., van der Maaten, L., Fei-Fei, L., Zitnick, C.L., Girshick, R.B.: CLEVR: a diagnostic dataset for compositional language and elementary visual reasoning. In: Proceedings of the of the IEEE Conference on Computer Vision and Pattern Recognition (CVPR), pp. 1988–1997 (2017)
44. Hu, R., Andreas, J., Darrell, T., Saenko, K.: Explainable neural computation via stack neural module networks. In: Proceedings of the European Conference on Computer Vision (ECCV), pp. 55–71 (2018)
45. Rohrbach, A., Rohrbach, M., Hu, R., Darrell, T., Schiele, B.: Grounding of textual phrases in images by reconstruction. In: Proceedings of the European Conference on Computer Vision (ECCV), pp. 817–834 (2016)

CloTH-VTON: Clothing Three-Dimensional Reconstruction for Hybrid Image-Based Virtual Try-ON

Matiur Rahman Minar$^{(\boxtimes)}$ and Heejune Ahn

Seoul National University of Science and Technology, Seoul, South Korea
{minar,heejune}@seoultech.ac.kr

Abstract. Virtual clothing try-on, transferring a clothing image onto a target person image, is drawing industrial and research attention. Both 2D image-based and 3D model-based methods proposed recently have their benefits and limitations. Whereas 3D model-based methods provide realistic deformations of the clothing, it needs a difficult 3D model construction process and cannot handle the non-clothing areas well. Image-based deep neural network methods are good at generating disclosed human parts, retaining the unchanged area, and blending image parts, but cannot handle large deformation of clothing. In this paper, we propose CloTH-VTON that utilizes the high-quality image synthesis of 2D image-based methods and the 3D model-based deformation to the target human pose. For this 2D and 3D combination, we propose a novel 3D cloth reconstruction method from a single 2D cloth image, leveraging a 3D human body model, and transfer to the shape and pose of the target person. Our cloth reconstruction method can be easily applied to diverse cloth categories. Our method produces final try-on output with naturally deformed clothing and preserving details in high resolution.

Keywords: Virtual Try-On · 3D cloth reconstruction · Generative model

1 Introduction

Virtual try-on (VTON) technologies can help customers in making their clothing purchase decisions for shopping online. Although 3D model-based VTON approaches could produce realistic 3D VTON results, 3D modeling and scanning for real clothing and human body are time-consuming and expensive [1,2]. Since the emergence of deep learning, 2D image-based approaches have gained more attention, mainly due to the lower costs of 2D data collection and less computational time than 3D [3,4]. However, manipulating the human and clothing shape and texture is an extremely challenging task, due to the huge variety of

Electronic supplementary material The online version of this chapter (https://doi.org/10.1007/978-3-030-69544-6_10) contains supplementary material, which is available to authorized users.

© Springer Nature Switzerland AG 2021
H. Ishikawa et al. (Eds.): ACCV 2020, LNCS 12627, pp. 154–172, 2021.
https://doi.org/10.1007/978-3-030-69544-6_10

Target cloth Target human 3D cloth 3D warped   Try-on

Fig. 1. Results of our CloTH-VTON. From left to right: input clothes, reference humans, reconstructed 3D clothes (shape and pose transferred respectively), and final fusion results. CloTH-VTON produces realistic output with high details.

poses and shapes. Thus, deep neural networks, i.e., image-based and 2D VTON technologies suffer from variations of clothing and human styles. Figure 2 shows a comparison of state-of-the-art (SOTA) methods and their limitations. Especially, 2D image-based methods cannot deform the input clothing to the 3D pose of the target person [5]. From the statistical 3D human model [6] and 3D reconstruction studies, many research works are ongoing on 3D human or clothed-human digitization. Recently, works have been done in 3D garments or clothing reconstruction [1,2,7,8]. However, since the separate reconstruction of clothing and humans is necessary for VTON, prior works on 3D garment reconstruction [1,2,7] methods work only with very limited clothing categories. Also, full 3D reconstruction of human parts like the face with hair for VTON is a more difficult problem [2,7,9,10].

In this paper, our idea is to leverage the advantages from both virtual try-on domains, i.e., 3D model-based and image-based approaches, and make a hybrid pipeline for the image-based virtual try-on task, which is simple and fully-automatic. Hence, we propose *Clothing Three-dimensional reconstruction for Hybrid image-based Virtual Try-ON* (CloTH-VTON). Since 2D non-rigid deformations suffer due to complex 3D poses [5] and 3D model-based techniques are good at realistic deformation of any poses/styles [8], we propose a novel 3D cloth reconstruction method, from a single in-shop cloth image, using 3D SMPL human body mesh model [6]. Using the SMPL model for reconstruction and deformation of clothes can handle any complex human poses. We also exploit the latest deep networks-based VTON techniques for generating the final try-on results. We use a fusion mechanism for blending 3D warped clothes to 2D human images, which generates the photo-realistic outputs with preserving the original pixel quality (Fig. 1).

Our contributions are as follows:

– We propose a hybrid image-based VTON approach, utilizing the benefits of 2D GAN [13] based methods for synthesizing the dis-occluded parts, and 3D model for the 3D posing of the clothing.
– We introduce a novel 3D clothing reconstruction method from a single in-shop cloth image of any style or category, through 2D image matching and 3D depth reconstruction using body depth.

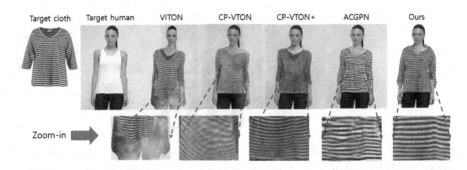

Fig. 2. Limitations from the existing image-based VTON methods. VITON [11] has fusion problems, CP-VTON [4] and CP-VTON+ [5] has texture & blur issue, ACGPN [12] produces the best result among SOTA having texture alteration issue, while CloTH-VTON generates output with the highest possible quality including full details.

– We provide a highly effective fine alignment and fusion mechanism for combining the rendered 3D warped clothing with the generated and original 2D human parts.

2   Related Works

2.1   Image-Based Virtual Try-On (VTON)

(Fixed-Pose) Virtual Try-On. This task is to transfer in-shop cloth to humans, keeping the pose fixed, same as ours. VITON [11] and CP-VTON [4] propose VTON pipelines with two main stages - clothing warping and try-on image synthesis. Sun et al. [14], VTNFP [15], SieveNet [16] proposed an extra stage for full target human segmentation generation including target clothing. ACGPN [12] proposed a two-stage based target segmentation generation for target human body parts and target clothing mask respectively. Some other works are [3,5,8,17–21]. However, challenges remain, such as self-occlusions, heavy misalignment among different poses, and complex clothes shape or textures (Fig. 2).

Multi-pose Guided Virtual Try-On. This task applies a new pose along with the target cloth to the target human, e.g., MG-VTON [22], FIT-ME [23], Zheng et al. [24], FashionOn [25]. They use multi-stage architectures due to the high complexity and large information of features to transfer. Human pose transfer is related to this task except for the target clothing, e.g., ClothFlow [17], Ma et al. [26], Balakrishnan et al. [27] VU-Net [28], and others [29–34].

Person to Person Transfer. Another popular application of image-based VTON is the person to person clothing transfer. SwapNet [35] proposed a garment exchange method between two human images. Outfit-VITON [36] transfers multiple clothing from different human images to another person. Zanfir et al. [37] proposed appearance transfer between human images using 3D SMPL models [6].

However, most works use conditional GANs where results show the limitations in blurring in dis-occluded area and misalignment of transferred clothing to the target human when there is a big difference between two persons' poses and shapes.

2.2   3D Garment/Human Reconstruction and Dressing

3D Pose and Shape Estimation. 3D human pose and shape estimation is one of the most active research areas in 3D human reconstruction. Statistical and parametric human body models, such as SMPL [6] and SMPL-X [38] are accelerating this area rapidly. Frank and Adam [10] models capture markerless motions. To estimate single 3D human pose and shape in an image, SMPLify [39] and SMPLify-X [38] uses optimization techniques, HMR [40] uses learning with 3D supervision, SPIN [41] makes a combination of neural network regression and optimization. OOH [42] estimates 3D humans from object-occluded images, Jiang et al. [43] detect multiple 3D humans from single images, and VIBE [44] estimates multiple 3D humans from videos.

3D Clothed Human Reconstruction. Fully-clothed reconstruction of human texture/depth/geometry from image/video/point-cloud is popular due to AR/ VR potentials, although not for VTON, e.g., PIFuHD [45], PIFusion [46], IF-Nets [47], PIFU [48], Tex2Shape [49], Photo Wake-Up [50], SiClope [51], 360° textures [52], human depth [53].

3D Garment Reconstruction. One major sub-task in our method is to reconstruct 3D cloth models from images. Due to the enormous variety of clothing and fashion, it's highly difficult to reconstruct 3D garment models covering all categories. ClothCap [1] captures cloth models of shirts, pants, jerseys, and skirts from 4D scans of people. Multi-Garment Net [2] makes 3D garment models from 3D scans of people for 3D VTON. They use 3D garment templates for 5 categories: shirt, t-shirt, coat, short-pants, long-pants [2]. Pix2Surf [7] learns to reconstruct 3D clothing from images for 3D VTON, leveraging garment meshes from MGN [2]. Our work is most similar to Minar et al. (2020) [8], where they reconstruct and deform 3D cloth models for image-based VTON. However, they consider 5 clothing categories based on sleeve lengths only, and the final try-on result suffers badly from blurring effects. Some other related works includes Tailornet [54] for predicting realistic 3D clothing wrinkle details, 3D garments from sketches [55], garment animation [56], DeepWrinkles [57].

Despite the high details of 3D clothing models, they mostly require 3D scanning data/templates, fixed categories, and the modeling techniques outside of clothing are still in early stages, which is difficult to apply in VTON task.

3   CloTH-VTON

Figure 3 shows the overall architecture of our proposed CloTH-VTON, which takes a pair of an in-shop cloth image C_{in} and a human image I_{in}, and generates a virtual try-on output I_{out} in the same pose J of I_{in}. First, we generate the target segmentation map S_{body} which guides the following processes for synthesizing the dis-occluded human parts P_{out} and 2D matching mask $M_{out,ref}$ for cloth deformation. Our method reconstructs 3D target cloth model $V_{clothed}$, first through 2D matching between the cloth C_{in} and the matching mask $M_{out,ref}$, then reconstructing $V_{clothed}$ using the standard SMPL [6] model V_{body}. Then, the vertices displacements of $V_{clothed}$ are applied to the estimated 3D target human model $\vec{V}_{body}^{t}$. The non-cloth areas are retained from the original images or synthesized if invisible in the input human image. The final try-on image is blended by a fusion mechanism, retaining the target human properties and high original details of the target cloth. Since the final output is fused by blending masks, not generating using GAN [13] networks, it does not suffer from blurring effects or texture alterations (Fig. 2) which are very common in deep neural network-based image synthesis. Figure 1 shows sample results from our approach.

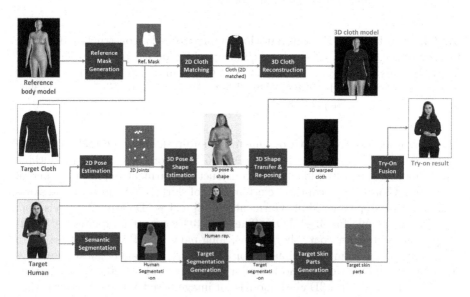

Fig. 3. Overview of our proposed CloTH-VTON. We reconstruct the 3D cloth model of the target cloth by matching silhouettes to the standard body model. Then, we transfer the 3D cloth model to the estimated 3D target human model, to produce the 3D warped cloth. We generate target human skin parts and blend it to the rendered warped cloth along with human representations.

3.1   Segmentation Generation Network (SGN)

The segmentation layout in the try-on output becomes different from the input human image because of the different cloth shape and occluded/dis-occluded parts of the human. Early works like VITON [11] and CP-VTON [4] do not generate an explicit target segmentation. We use an explicit target segmentation generation as ACGPN [12], for utilizing in the cloth matching and parts synthesis. We refer to this stage as the Segmentation Generation Network (SGN), presented in Fig. 4. SGN has U-Net [58] as the generator and the discriminator from Pix2PixHD [59]. SGN learns to generate the target human segmentation, except for the target clothing area.

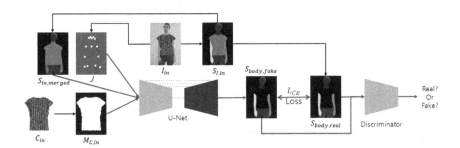

Fig. 4. Segmentation Generation Network (SGN) architecture; to generate the target human body segmentation according to the target cloth.

SGN takes merged human segmentation $S_{in,merged}$, 2D pose as joints J from the input human I_{in}, and cloth mask $M_{C,in}$ from the input cloth C_{in} as inputs. $S_{in,merged}$ comes from the 2D human segmentation $S_{I,in}$ of I_{in}, where clothes on person and affected human body parts, i.e., top-clothes, torso-skin, right and left arms, are merged to a single upper-cloth label. SGN produces $S_{body,fake}$ as output. We calculate Cross-Entropy loss L_{CE} between $S_{body,fake}$ and $S_{body,real}$, along with loss L_{GAN}, which is the sum of GAN losses and GAN feature matching loss from Pix2PixHD [59]. $S_{body,real}$ is parsed from $S_{I,in}$ as the ground-truth for SGN network.

$$L_{SGN} = \lambda_1 L_{CE} + \lambda_2 L_{GAN} \tag{1}$$

3.2   3D Cloth Reconstruction from In-Shop Image

For reconstructing the 3D shape of clothing from in-shop images, we extend the 2D to 3D approach in [8], where they need manual category selection (of 5). We present a fully automatic approach, not restricted to any cloth categories.

Mask Generation Network (MGN). Prior works on 3D garment reconstruction and modeling work with fixed clothing categories [1,2,7,8,54,55] works.

They use reference garment templates [1, 2, 7], trains separate network for predicting 3D models [2, 7], or standard body model silhouette [8]. Since our cloth modeling is similar to Minar et al. [8] without requiring 3D garment templates, we also use silhouette masks of a standard A-posed SMPL [6] body model V_{body}, as the reference for 2D silhouette matching between the target cloth and SMPL [6]. Figure 5 shows 5 reference masks generated for 2D matching of clothes.

Fig. 5. 2D cloth mapping process to the reference SMPL silhouette. From left to right: standard body model and its silhouette, matching masks for long-sleeve, half-sleeve, short-sleeve (half-elbow and quarter elbow respectively), sleeveless clothing categories, and the standard model inputs for generating matching masks with SGN & MGN.

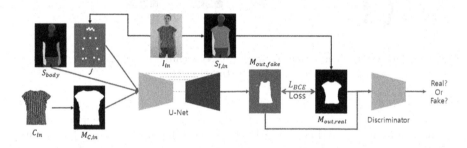

Fig. 6. Mask Generation Network (MGN) architecture; to generate the cloth mask for 2D matching.

To apply cloth matching to other categories, manual matching masks are needed for corresponding clothing categories. While this procedure is easier and generates a tight-fit clothing texture for 3D reconstruction, it is difficult to cover all the clothing categories manually due to diverse clothing styles. Also, making cloth matching masks from SMPL [6] body silhouette does not provide loose-fitting clothing textures. To alleviate this problem and make the process fully-automatic, we use the Mask Generation Network (MGN) for 2D matching, following the semantic generation module of ACGPN [12], since they separated the target cloth mask generation network from segmentation generation. MGN has similar architecture as SGN, as illustrated in Fig. 6.

MGN takes the generated body parts segmentation S_{body} from SGN output, human joints J, and in-shop input cloth mask $M_{C,in}$, as the inputs, and produces target cloth mask on person $M_{out,fake}$ as the output. We calculate binary cross-entropy loss L_{BCE} between $M_{out,fake}$ and real clothes mask on person $M_{out,real}$ from $S_{I,in}$, along with the GAN losses L_{GAN} (Eq. 2).

$$L_{MGN} = \lambda_1 L_{BCE} + \lambda_2 L_{GAN} \tag{2}$$

We made a fused segmentation map of our standard body model, and generated 2D joints as in A-pose (see Fig. 5), to provide input to SGN, which generates the target body segmentation S_{body} in standard pose. MGN takes S_{body} as an input, and infers the matching masks $M_{out,ref}$ for silhouette matching of target cloth to standard SMPL [6] model V_{body}. Figure 7 shows an example of SGN and MGN inference for V_{body}.

Fig. 7. Example of 2D cloth matching for 3D reconstruction. From left to right: Input cloth image, target body segmentation generated by SGN for standard body model, cloth matching mask generated by MGN, cloth texture after 2D matching and overlapped on SMPL silhouette respectively, 3D reconstructed cloth and overlaid on SMPL model respectively.

2D Clothing Matching. We apply Shape-Context Matching (SCM) [60] between the target clothes and their corresponding categorical masks (Fig. 5) or matching masks generated by MGN (Sect. 3.2). Then, we apply Thin-Plate Spline (TPS) [61] transformation on the target clothes, based on the shape correspondences from SCM, to generate the clothing textures to be aligned to the standard SMPL [6] body model V_{body}. Pix2Surf [7] argues that a combination of SCM-TPS may generate holes and artifacts at the clothing boundary. However, since we only use the front images of clothes for image-based VTON, SCM-TPS provides better matching for specific clothes. Figure 7 shows an example of 2D cloth matching and texture extraction for 3D reconstruction.

3D Clothing Model Reconstruction. For 3D reconstruction from the aligned clothing image and projected silhouette, first, vertices of the 3D body mesh V_{body} are projected into 2D image space. When boundary vertices are in 2D space, clothing boundaries are used to find the corresponding points. To make the clothing transfer, i.e., change of its pose and shape easily, a 3D clothing model's vertices are mapped to an SMPL [6] body vertices. We assume that the relation between the clothing and human vertices is isotropic, i.e., the difference in the projection space is also retained in the 3D model. Although this is not strictly true, we make this assumption for practical applications. We define the corresponding points in the clothing boundary as the closest points from the projected vertices. We estimate Thin-Plate Spline (TPS) [61] parameters and apply them to the mesh points. New mesh points are considered as the vertices projected from the 3D mesh of clothing $\mathbf{V_{clothed}}$. From 2D points to 3D points are done with inverse projection with depth obtained from the body with a small constant gap. In reality, the gap between the clothing and body cannot be constant but it works with tight or simple clothes.

$$\mathbf{V_{clothed}} = \mathbf{P}^{-1} \cdot \mathbf{T_{TPS}}(\mathbf{P} \cdot \mathbf{V_{body}}), \mathbf{depth}(\mathbf{V_{body}})), \tag{3}$$

Here, $\mathbf{P}$ is the projection matrix with the camera parameters $\mathbf{K} \cdot [\mathbf{R}|\mathbf{t}]$, $\mathbf{P}^{-1}$ is the inverse projection matrix of the same camera, and $depth(V_{body})$ is the distance from the camera to the vertices. Target clothing images are used as the textures for the 3D clothing mesh. Finally, we obtain the clothing 3D model $V_{clothed}$ by selecting the vertices that are projected onto the clothing image area.

Fig. 8. Sample 3D clothing deformation with 3D human body estimation. From left to right: input cloth, target human, 3D reconstructed cloth model, 3D estimated human body model, 3D deformed cloth model, and the rendered image of 3D warped cloth.

Target Human Model Parameter Estimation. To estimate $\vec{V}_{body}^t$, the SMPL [6] parameters (β, θ) for a human image, we use the SMPLify [39] method. However, any newer and better method can be used since we use estimated parameters only. SMPLify [39] is for full-body images, so we made a few minor optimizations, mainly for our half-body dataset, such as - head pose correction, joints location mapping between the joints of the dataset used in this paper and SMPL's, the SMPLify joints definition, conditional inclusion of invisible joints and initialization step.

3D Clothing Model Deformation. 3D clothing model $V_{clothed}$ and texture information obtained from 3D reconstruction is for the standard shaped and posed person (β_0, θ_0). For the VTON application, we have to apply the shape and pose parameters (β, θ) of the target human image, $\vec{V}_{body}^t$, estimated from the previous step (Sect. 3.2). Instead of applying the shape and pose parameters to the obtained clothed 3D model, we transfer the displacements of clothing vertices to $\vec{V}_{body}^t$, since the application of new parameters to the body model provides much better natural results. Several options can be considered for the transfer, e.g., transferring the physical size of clothing or keep the fit, i.e., keep the displacements from the body to clothing vertices as before. We simply decide the fit-preserving option for showing more natural results for final fitting.

$$\vec{V}^t_{clothed} = \vec{V}^t_{body} + \vec{d}\,in\,(u_x, u_y, u_z | \vec{V}^t_{body}) \tag{4}$$

Hence, we get the 3D deformed model $\vec{V}^t_{clothed}$ of the target cloth. Then, we render $\vec{V}^t_{clothed}$ to get the warped cloth image C_{warped}, to apply to the final try-on, following Minar et al. [8]. Figure 8 shows an example of applying 3D cloth deformation. Additional details are provided in the supplementary material.

3.3   Try-On Generation

To generate the final try-on output image, its common to utilize the generative neural networks [4,12]. However, due to not having enough training data, we chose not to train a network to generate the final results directly. Also, results from the generative networks suffer from blurry output issues due to up-sampling e.g. and texture alterations [4,8]. Therefore, we chose to simply merge the warped clothes into the target human, leveraging the target segmentation from SGN. One problem is getting the accurate target clothing affected human skin parts, i.e., torso-skin, right and left arms/hands. For transition cases like long-sleeve cloth to short-sleeve, hidden skin parts cause artifacts [2]. So, we train a separate network for generating the target skin parts, using the S_{body} output from SGN.

Parts Generation Network (PGN). We refer to this stage as the Parts Generation Network (PGN), which uses similar networks as SGN and MGN. PGN pipeline is drawn in Fig. 9.

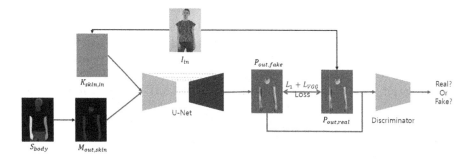

Fig. 9. Parts Generation Network (PGN) architecture; to generate the target skin parts of the input human according to the target cloth.

PGN takes 2 inputs: mask of the target skin parts, $M_{out,skin}$ from the target segmentation S_{body} generated by SGN, and average skin color $K_{skin,in}$ of body skin parts i.e., torso-skin, left-arm and right-arm from the target human image I_{in}. PGN generator produces the target body skin parts, $P_{out,fake}$. We calculate

L_1 loss, VGG loss L_{VGG}, and GAN losses L_{GAN} from Pix2PixHD [59], between the generator output $P_{out,fake}$ and the real human body skin parts $P_{out,real}$ from $S_{I,in}$ (Eq. 5).

$$L_{PGN} = \lambda_1 L_{L1} + \lambda_2 L_{VGG} + \lambda_3 L_{GAN} \tag{5}$$

Try-On Fusion. The final step is to merge all the parts (Eq. 6), i.e., human representation $I_{in,fixed}$ from the target person I_{in}, rendered 3D deformed clothing image C_{warped}, and the generated skin parts P_{out} from PGN, to get the try-on output I_{out}. To make a successful fusion of all these segments, accurate target body segmentation S_{body} and 3D body estimation plays a critical role.

$$I_{out} = I_{in,fixed} + C_{warped} + P_{out} \tag{6}$$

Fig. 10. Sample final fusion for try-on. From left to right: Input cloth image, target human image, rendered 3D warped cloth, human representation from target person, target skin parts generated by PGN, and the final fusion output for virtual try-on.

4   Experiments

4.1   Dataset Preparation

For training and testing, We used the VITON [11] dataset, which contains 14221 training and 2032 testing pairs of in-shop clothes and human images (half-body). VITON resized dataset [4] contains in-shop cloth masks, human poses predicted by OpenPose [62], and human segmentation generated by LIP-SSL [63]. However, as noted by [5], VITON dataset has several problems. LIP [63] segmentation does not have labels for skin in the torso area, i.e., neck, chest, or belly, and labeled those as background. These areas are crucial to estimate the clothing area, so we generated new segmentation with pre-trained CIHP-PGN [64]. Also, many cloth masks are wrong when cloth colors are similar to the background (white). We re-implemented a new mask generator considering the dataset characteristics.

4.2   Implementation Details

Neural Network Training and Testing. All three neural networks in our approach, SGN (Sect. 3.1), MGN (Sect. 3.2) and PGN (Sect. 3.3), shares the common network architecture: U-Net [58] as the generators, and the discriminators from Pix2PixHD [59] network. GAN losses include the generator loss, discriminator losses for real and fake outputs, and the feature-matching loss [59]. All networks are implemented in PyTorch [65], based on the public implementation [66] of ACGPN [12], and each network is trained for 20 epochs with a batch size of 8. It takes 17–20 h of training for each network with 4 TITAN Xp GPUs. For testing, we used two kinds of VITON test input pairs - same-clothes and different-clothes. Same-clothes input pairs are used for evaluating with ground-truth, and different clothes pairs for visual comparison.

Mask Generation for Cloth Matching. We use 5 silhouette masks from the reference SMPL [6] model for 5 clothing categories based on sleeve lengths [8], i.e., long-sleeve, half-sleeve, short-sleeve half-elbow, short-sleeve quarter-elbow, and sleeveless. These categories contains a total of $465 + 130 + 780 + 162 + 252 = 1789$ in-shop clothing images, out of 2032 VITON [11] test dataset clothes (See Fig. 5). For the rest of the clothes, we use the fully-automatic process from Sect. 3.2, to generate a specific matching mask for each cloth. Direct inference with SGN and MGN networks gives several unexpected results when we test with the standard A-posed model input. We assume that, since these networks are trained with the full training set, which is full of various poses and different from A-pose, cause the artifacts. It would be best to train simple networks with fixed A-pose data. However, due to the lack of such data and annotations, we choose to go with a closer path. We collected 1095 human images from the VITON dataset, having very simple poses, e.g., straight hands and standing. These are selected based on the Easy criterion from ACGPN [12]. We train a very simple version of SGN and MGN networks with the easy pose pairs, exclusively for generating reference masks for 2D clothing matching. We follow the same training procedures for these networks as discussed in Sect. 4.2. Then, we generate the cloth-specific silhouette matching mask, using our standard SMPL model inputs, as shown in Figs. 5, 6 and 7.

2D Clothing Matching. We implemented this step in MATLAB, utilizing the original script of SCM [60]. We chose 10 * 10 control points for describing shape contexts between the silhouette masks, and then apply TPS [61] transformation on the input clothes.

3D Clothing Reconstruction and Re-Posing. We use the available public models from SMPL [67] and SMPLify [68], and their python implementations for 3D reconstruction and model transfer. Based on the SMPLify [39] implementation, we also make our implementation for this step using Chumpy [69] and OpenDR [70]. First, the standard SMPL [6] model is reconstructed. Then, we transform the model from 2D space to 3D space, according to the cloth texture from 2D matching, to get the shape information of cloth. Pose and shape parameters are estimated from the human image using SMPLify [39] optimization. Finally, the cloth model is transferred to the 3D body model to get the warped cloth.

Clothing and Human Image Fusion. For final try-on output, we utilize the generated target body segmentation to fuse the human representations, warped clothes, and the generated skin parts into output images.

4.3   Results

We provide both qualitative and quantitative analyses of our results, comparing with existing image-based VTON methods. For qualitative comparisons, we retrained the networks from the available public implementations of the SOTA approaches and reproduced the results.

Qualitative Analysis. We present the qualitative comparisons in Fig. 11 among VITON [11], CP-VTON [4], CP-VTON+ [5], ACGPN [12] and CloTH-VTON, for different clothes input pairs. Newer methods such as CP-VTON+ [5] and ACGPN [12] generates competitive results. However, we can see the clear improvements in our results than the existing methods, especially when the target clothes have detailed textures or the target humans have complex poses. Figure 2 shows the differences in the details of the methods' results. More comparisons & results are provided in the supplementary material.

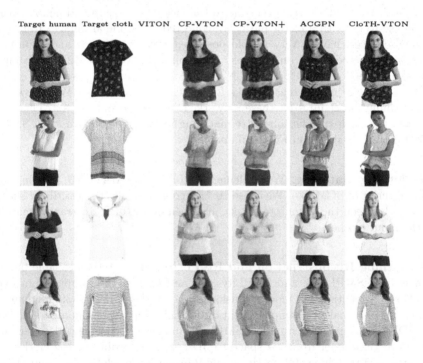

Fig. 11. Visual comparisons between SOTA image-based VTON methods and our CloTH-VTON. For fair comparisons, we present samples from the dataset with complex human poses e.g. cross arms, and target clothes with detailed textures. Our method produces try-on results with the highest details and quality possible.

Quantitative Analysis. We present quantitative comparisons in Table 1. We use the Structural Similarity Index (SSIM) [71] and Inception Score (IS) [72], for comparing with and without ground truths respectively. The values of VTNFP [15] and ACGPN [12] are added from the reported scores in ACGPN [12] paper. The values of CP-VTON+ [5] is added from their paper.

Our SSIM score is slightly lower than CP-VTON+ and ACGPN. SSIM is originally developed for video compression quality measures without geometric distortion, according to a recent study on the limitation of SSIM [73]. We argue that, even though we are comparing with the image-based methods, our method is a hybrid approach from the 3D reconstruction. Therefore, SSIM scores are lower since rendered 3D warped clothes are structurally different from the clothes in images. However, human synthesizing metric like inception score provides the highest score for our results, which proves the capability of our approach.

Table 1. Quantitative comparison with the SOTA image-based VTON methods: VITON [11], CP-VTON [4], VTNFP [15], ACGPN [12], and CP-VTON+ [5].

Metric	VITON	CP-VTON	VTNFP	CP-VTON+	ACGPN	CloTH-VTON
SSIM	0.783	0.745	0.803	0.816	**0.845**	0.813
IS	2.650	2.757	2.784	3.105	2.829	**3.111**

4.4 Discussion

From the results, it is clear that our method is highly competitive against the SOTA image-based VTON approaches. However, there are many rooms for improvement. Such as - target human body segmentation generation, matching mask generation for 2D clothing matching, 3D shape and pose estimation of the human body, realistic clothing deformation, and final fusion. Target human segmentation plays a crucial role in almost all stages, making it one of the most important areas for improvement. The next performance bottleneck is the 2D silhouette matching for transferring the clothing textures to the standard 3D model. Hence, it is important to generate accurate silhouette matching masks for input clothes. 3D body estimation from human images can be done with any SOTA 3D human pose and shape estimation methods, e.g. SPIN [41] or OOH [42]. Also, our current approach is mostly applicable to close-fitting clothes. For reconstruction and deformation of loose-fitting clothes, e.g. dress and skirt, separate clothing deformation techniques like TailorNet [54] can be applied. Final fusion output will be far better based on the improvements in previous stages.

5   Conclusion

We propose a hybrid approach for image-based virtual try-on tasks, combining the benefits of 2D image-based GAN [13] and 3D SMPL [6] model-based cloth manipulation. We present a 2D to 3D cloth model reconstruction method using only a 3D body model, applicable to diverse clothing without requiring 3D garment templates. To integrate from two different domains, we develop target semantic segmentation and clothing-affected body parts generation networks. Our final try-on output provides the photo-realistic results which come with great details, high resolution, and quality.

Acknowledgement. This research was supported by Basic Science Research Program through the National Research Foundation of Korea (NRF) funded by the Ministry of Education (No. 2018R1D1A1B07043879).

References

1. Pons-Moll, G., Pujades, S., Hu, S., Black, M.: Clothcap: seamless 4D clothing capture and retargeting. ACM Trans. Graph. (Proc. SIGGRAPH) **36**, 1–15 (2017)
2. Bhatnagar, B.L., Tiwari, G., Theobalt, C., Pons-Moll, G.: Multi-garment net: learning to dress 3D people from images. In: IEEE International Conference on Computer Vision (ICCV). IEEE (2019)
3. Song, D., Li, T., Mao, Z., Liu, A.A.: Sp-viton: shape-preserving image-based virtual try-on network. Multimedia Tools Appl. **79**, 1–13 (2019)
4. Wang, B., Zheng, H., Liang, X., Chen, Y., Lin, L., Yang, M.: Toward characteristic-preserving image-based virtual try-on network. In: The European Conference on Computer Vision (ECCV) (2018)
5. Minar, M.R., Tuan, T.T., Ahn, H., Rosin, P., Lai, Y.K.: Cp-vton+: Clothing shape and texture preserving image-based virtual try-on. In: The IEEE/CVF Conference on Computer Vision and Pattern Recognition (CVPR) Workshops (2020)
6. Loper, M., Mahmood, N., Romero, J., Pons-Moll, G., Black, M.J.: SMPL: a skinned multi-person linear model. ACM Trans. Graph. (TOG) **34**, 1–16 (2015)
7. Mir, A., Alldieck, T., Pons-Moll, G.: Learning to transfer texture from clothing images to 3D humans. In: IEEE Conference on Computer Vision and Pattern Recognition (CVPR). IEEE (2020)
8. Minar, M.R., Tuan, T.T., Ahn, H., Rosin, P., Lai, Y.K.: 3D reconstruction of clothes using a human body model and its application to image-based virtual try-on. In: The IEEE/CVF Conference on Computer Vision and Pattern Recognition (CVPR) Workshops (2020)
9. Li, T., Bolkart, T., Black, M.J., Li, H., Romero, J.: Learning a model of facial shape and expression from 4D scans. ACM Trans. Graph. (Proc. SIGGRAPH Asia) **36** (2017)
10. Joo, H., Simon, T., Sheikh, Y.: Total capture: a 3D deformation model for tracking faces, hands, and bodies. In: 2018 IEEE/CVF Conference on Computer Vision and Pattern Recognition, pp. 8320–8329 (2018)
11. Han, X., Wu, Z., Wu, Z., Yu, R., Davis, L.S.: Viton: an image-based virtual try-on network. In: The IEEE Conference on Computer Vision and Pattern Recognition (CVPR) (2018)

12. Yang, H., Zhang, R., Guo, X., Liu, W., Zuo, W., Luo, P.: Towards photo-realistic virtual try-on by adaptively generating-preserving image content. In: IEEE/CVF Conference on Computer Vision and Pattern Recognition (CVPR) (2020)
13. Goodfellow, I.J., et al.: Generative adversarial nets. In: NIPS (2014)
14. Sun, F., Guo, J., Su, Z., Gao, C.: Image-based virtual try-on network with structural coherence. In: 2019 IEEE International Conference on Image Processing (ICIP), pp. 519–523 (2019)
15. Yu, R., Wang, X., Xie, X.: Vtnfp: an image-based virtual try-on network with body and clothing feature preservation. In: The IEEE International Conference on Computer Vision (ICCV) (2019)
16. Jandial, S., et al.: Sievenet: a unified framework for robust image-based virtual try-on. In: The IEEE Winter Conference on Applications of Computer Vision (WACV) (2020)
17. Han, X., Hu, X., Huang, W., Scott, M.R.: Clothflow: a flow-based model for clothed person generation. In: The IEEE International Conference on Computer Vision (ICCV) (2019)
18. Jae Lee, H., Lee, R., Kang, M., Cho, M., Park, G.: La-viton: a network for looking-attractive virtual try-on. In: The IEEE International Conference on Computer Vision (ICCV) Workshops (2019)
19. Kubo, S., Iwasawa, Y., Suzuki, M., Matsuo, Y.: Uvton: Uv mapping to consider the 3d structure of a human in image-based virtual try-on network. In: The IEEE International Conference on Computer Vision (ICCV) Workshops (2019)
20. Ayush, K., Jandial, S., Chopra, A., Krishnamurthy, B.: Powering virtual try-on via auxiliary human segmentation learning. In: The IEEE International Conference on Computer Vision (ICCV) Workshops (2019)
21. Yildirim, G., Jetchev, N., Vollgraf, R., Bergmann, U.: Generating high-resolution fashion model images wearing custom outfits. In: The IEEE International Conference on Computer Vision (ICCV) Workshops (2019)
22. Dong, H., et al.: Towards multi-pose guided virtual try-on network. In: The IEEE International Conference on Computer Vision (ICCV) (2019)
23. Hsieh, C.W., Chen, C.Y., Chou, C.L., Shuai, H.H., Cheng, W.H.: Fit-me: Image-based virtual try-on with arbitrary poses. In: 2019 IEEE International Conference on Image Processing (ICIP), pp. 4694–4698. IEEE (2019)
24. Zheng, N., Song, X., Chen, Z., Hu, L., Cao, D., Nie, L.: Virtually trying on new clothing with arbitrary poses. In: Proceedings of the 27th ACM International Conference on Multimedia, pp. 266–274 (2019)
25. Hsieh, C.W., Chen, C.Y., Chou, C.L., Shuai, H.H., Liu, J., Cheng, W.H.: Fashionon: semantic-guided image-based virtual try-on with detailed human and clothing information. In: Proceedings of the 27th ACM International Conference on Multimedia, pp. 275–283 (2019)
26. Ma, L., Jia, X., Sun, Q., Schiele, B., Tuytelaars, T., Van Gool, L.: Pose guided person image generation. In: Advances in Neural Information Processing Systems, pp. 406–416 (2017)
27. Balakrishnan, G., Zhao, A., Dalca, A.V., Durand, F., Guttag, J.: Synthesizing images of humans in unseen poses. In: The IEEE Conference on Computer Vision and Pattern Recognition (CVPR) (2018)
28. Esser, P., Sutter, E., Ommer, B.: A variational U-Net for conditional appearance and shape generation. In: The IEEE Conference on Computer Vision and Pattern Recognition (CVPR) (2018)

29. Ma, L., Sun, Q., Georgoulis, S., Van Gool, L., Schiele, B., Fritz, M.: Disentangled person image generation. In: The IEEE Conference on Computer Vision and Pattern Recognition (CVPR) (2018)
30. Siarohin, A., Sangineto, E., Lathuilière, S., Sebe, N.: Deformable gans for pose-based human image generation. In: The IEEE Conference on Computer Vision and Pattern Recognition (CVPR) (2018)
31. Qian, X., et al.: Pose-normalized image generation for person re-identification. In: The European Conference on Computer Vision (ECCV) (2018)
32. Dong, H., Liang, X., Gong, K., Lai, H., Zhu, J., Yin, J.: Soft-gated warping-gan for pose-guided person image synthesis. In: Advances in Neural Information Processing Systems, vol. 31, pp. 474–484, Curran Associates, Inc., (2018)
33. Zhu, Z., Huang, T., Shi, B., Yu, M., Wang, B., Bai, X.: Progressive pose attention transfer for person image generation. In: The IEEE Conference on Computer Vision and Pattern Recognition (CVPR) (2019)
34. Song, S., Zhang, W., Liu, J., Mei, T.: Unsupervised person image generation with semantic parsing transformation. In: The IEEE Conference on Computer Vision and Pattern Recognition (CVPR) (2019)
35. Raj, A., Sangkloy, P., Chang, H., Lu, J., Ceylan, D., Hays, J.: Swapnet: Garment transfer in single view images. In: The European Conference on Computer Vision (ECCV) (2018)
36. Neuberger, A., Borenstein, E., Hilleli, B., Oks, E., Alpert, S.: Image based virtual try-on network from unpaired data. In: IEEE/CVF Conference on Computer Vision and Pattern Recognition (CVPR) (2020)
37. Zanfir, M., Popa, A.I., Zanfir, A., Sminchisescu, C.: Human appearance transfer. In: Proceedings of the IEEE Conference on Computer Vision and Pattern Recognition, pp. 5391–5399 (2018)
38. Pavlakos, G., et al.: Expressive body capture: 3D hands, face, and body from a single image. In: Proceedings IEEE Conference on Computer Vision and Pattern Recognition (CVPR) (2019)
39. Bogo, F., Kanazawa, A., Lassner, C., Gehler, P., Romero, J., Black, M.J.: Keep it SMPL: automatic estimation of 3D human pose and shape from a single image. In: Leibe, B., Matas, J., Sebe, N., Welling, M. (eds.) ECCV 2016. LNCS, vol. 9909, pp. 561–578. Springer, Cham (2016). https://doi.org/10.1007/978-3-319-46454-1_34
40. Kanazawa, A., Black, M.J., Jacobs, D.W., Malik, J.: End-to-end recovery of human shape and pose. In: Proceedings of the IEEE Conference on Computer Vision and Pattern Recognition, pp. 7122–7131 (2018)
41. Kolotouros, N., Pavlakos, G., Black, M.J., Daniilidis, K.: Learning to reconstruct 3D human pose and shape via model-fitting in the loop. In: Proceedings of the IEEE International Conference on Computer Vision, pp. 2252–2261 (2019)
42. Zhang, T., Huang, B., Wang, Y.: Object-occluded human shape and pose estimation from a single color image. In: The IEEE/CVF Conference on Computer Vision and Pattern Recognition (CVPR) (2020)
43. Jiang, W., Kolotouros, N., Pavlakos, G., Zhou, X., Daniilidis, K.: Coherent reconstruction of multiple humans from a single image. In: Proceedings of the IEEE/CVF Conference on Computer Vision and Pattern Recognition, pp. 5579–5588 (2020)
44. Kocabas, M., Athanasiou, N., Black, M.J.: Vibe: Video inference for human body pose and shape estimation. In: Proceedings of the IEEE/CVF Conference on Computer Vision and Pattern Recognition, pp. 5253–5263 (2020)

45. Saito, S., Simon, T., Saragih, J., Joo, H.: Pifuhd: multi-level pixel-aligned implicit function for high-resolution 3D human digitization. In: Proceedings of the IEEE/CVF Conference on Computer Vision and Pattern Recognition, pp. 84–93 (2020)

46. Li, Z., Yu, T., Pan, C., Zheng, Z., Liu, Y.: Robust 3D self-portraits in seconds. In: Proceedings of the IEEE/CVF Conference on Computer Vision and Pattern Recognition, pp. 1344–1353 (2020)

47. Chibane, J., Alldieck, T., Pons-Moll, G.: Implicit functions in feature space for 3D shape reconstruction and completion. In: Proceedings of the IEEE/CVF Conference on Computer Vision and Pattern Recognition, pp. 6970–6981 (2020)

48. Saito, S., Huang, Z., Natsume, R., Morishima, S., Kanazawa, A., Li, H.: Pifu: pixel-aligned implicit function for high-resolution clothed human digitization. 2019 IEEE/CVF International Conference on Computer Vision (ICCV), pp. 2304–2314 (2019)

49. Alldieck, T., Pons-Moll, G., Theobalt, C., Magnor, M.: Tex2shape: detailed full human body geometry from a single image. In: IEEE International Conference on Computer Vision (ICCV) (2019)

50. Weng, C.Y., Curless, B., Kemelmacher-Shlizerman, I.: Photo wake-up: 3D character animation from a single photo. In: Proceedings of the IEEE Conference on Computer Vision and Pattern Recognition, pp. 5908–5917 (2019)

51. Natsume, R., Saito, S., Huang, Z., Chen, W., Ma, C., Li, H., Morishima, S.: Siclope: silhouette-based clothed people. In: Proceedings of the IEEE Conference on Computer Vision and Pattern Recognition, pp. 4480–4490 (2019)

52. Lazova, V., Insafutdinov, E., Pons-Moll, G.: 360-degree textures of people in clothing from a single image. In: 2019 International Conference on 3D Vision (3DV), pp. 643–653. IEEE (2019)

53. Tang, S., Tan, F., Cheng, K., Li, Z., Zhu, S., Tan, P.: A neural network for detailed human depth estimation from a single image. In: The IEEE International Conference on Computer Vision (ICCV) (2019)

54. Patel, C., Liao, Z., Pons-Moll, G.: Tailornet: predicting clothing in 3D as a function of human pose, shape and garment style. In: IEEE Conference on Computer Vision and Pattern Recognition (CVPR). IEEE (2020)

55. Wang, T.Y., Ceylan, D., Popovic, J., Mitra, N.J.: Learning a shared shape space for multimodal garment design. ACM Trans. Graph. **37**, 1:1–1:14 (2018)

56. Wang, Y., Shao, T., Fu, K., Mitra, N.: Learning an intrinsic garment space for interactive authoring of garment animation. ACM Trans. Graph. **38** (2019)

57. Lahner, Z., Cremers, D., Tung, T.: Deepwrinkles: accurate and realistic clothing modeling. In: The European Conference on Computer Vision (ECCV) (2018)

58. Ronneberger, O., Fischer, P., Brox, T.: U-Net: convolutional networks for biomedical image segmentation. In: Navab, N., Hornegger, J., Wells, W.M., Frangi, A.F. (eds.) MICCAI 2015. LNCS, vol. 9351, pp. 234–241. Springer, Cham (2015). https://doi.org/10.1007/978-3-319-24574-4_28

59. Wang, T.C., Liu, M.Y., Zhu, J.Y., Tao, A., Kautz, J., Catanzaro, B.: High-resolution image synthesis and semantic manipulation with conditional gans. In: Proceedings of the IEEE Conference on Computer Vision and Pattern Recognition (2018)

60. Belongie, S., Malik, J., Puzicha, J.: Shape matching and object recognition using shape contexts. IEEE Trans. Pattern Anal. Mach. Intell. **24**, 509–522 (2002)

61. Bookstein, F.L.: Principal warps: thin-plate splines and the decomposition of deformations. IEEE Trans. Pattern Anal. Mach. Intell. **11**, 567–585 (1989)

62. Cao, Z., Simon, T., Wei, S.E., Sheikh, Y.: Realtime multi-person 2D pose estimation using part affinity fields. In: CVPR (2017)
63. Gong, K., Liang, X., Zhang, D., Shen, X., Lin, L.: Look into person: self-supervised structure-sensitive learning and a new benchmark for human parsing. In: The IEEE Conference on Computer Vision and Pattern Recognition (CVPR) (2017)
64. Gong, K., Liang, X., Li, Y., Chen, Y., Yang, M., Lin, L.: Instance-level human parsing via part grouping network. In: The European Conference on Computer Vision (ECCV) (2018)
65. Paszke, A., et al.: Pytorch: an imperative style, high-performance deep learning library. In: Advances in Neural Information Processing Systems, vol. 32, pp. 8026–8037, Curran Associates, Inc., (2019)
66. Acgpn. (https://github.com/switchablenorms/DeepFashion_Try_On)
67. SMPL. (https://smpl.is.tue.mpg.de/)
68. Smplify. (http://smplify.is.tue.mpg.de/)
69. Chumpy. (https://github.com/mattloper/chumpy)
70. Loper, M.M., Black, M.J.: OpenDR: an approximate differentiable renderer. In: Fleet, D., Pajdla, T., Schiele, B., Tuytelaars, T. (eds.) ECCV 2014. LNCS, vol. 8695, pp. 154–169. Springer, Cham (2014). https://doi.org/10.1007/978-3-319-10584-0_11
71. Wang, Z., Bovik, A.C., Sheikh, H.R., Simoncelli, E.P.: Image quality assessment: from error visibility to structural similarity. IEEE Trans. Image Process. **13**, 600–612 (2004)
72. Salimans, T., et al.: Improved techniques for training gans. In: Advances in Neural Information Processing Systems, vol. 29, pp. 2234–2242, Curran Associates, Inc., (2016)
73. Nilsson, J.A.M.T.: Understanding SSIM. arXiv: 2006.13846 (2020)

Multi-label X-Ray Imagery Classification via Bottom-Up Attention and Meta Fusion

Benyi Hu[1], Chi Zhang[1], Le Wang[1], Qilin Zhang[2], and Yuehu Liu[1(✉)]

[1] College of Artificial Intelligence, Xi'an Jiaotong University, Xi'an, Shaanxi, China
{hby0906,colorzc}@stu.xjtu.edu.cn,{lewang,liuyh}@xjtu.edu.cn
[2] HERE Technology, Chicago, IL, USA
samqzhang@gmail.com

Abstract. Automatic security inspection has received increasing interests in recent years. Due to the fixed top-down perspective of X-ray scanning of often tightly packed luggages, such images typically suffer from penetration-induced occlusions, severe object overlapping and violent changes in appearance. For this particular application, few research efforts have been made. To deal with the overlapping in X-ray images classification, we propose a novel Security X-ray Multi-label Classification Network (SXMNet). Our hypothesis is that different overlapping levels and scale variations are the primary challenges in the multi-label classification problem of prohibited items. To address these challenges, we propose to incorporate 1) **spatial attention** to locate prohibited items despite shape, color and texture variations; and 2) **anisotropic fusion** of per-stage predictions to dynamically fuse hierarchical visual information under violent variations. Motivated by these, our SXMNet is boosted by bottom-up attention and neural-guided Meta Fusion. Raw input image is exploited to generate high-quality attention masks in a bottom-up way for pyramid feature refinement. Subsequently, the per-stage predictions according to the refined features are automatically re-weighted and fused via a soft selection guided by neural knowledge. Comprehensive experiments on the Security Inspection X-ray (SIXray) and Occluded Prohibited Items X-ray (OPIXray) datasets demonstrate the superiority of the proposed method.

1 Introduction

With the increasing traffic in transportation hubs such as airports and high speed rail stations, security inspection procedures are becoming the bottleneck of throughput and causes of delays. However, such measures are indispensable due to security concerns [1,2]. One primary time-consuming security inspection procedure involves X-ray scanning of passenger luggages, which generates pseudo-color images with respect to material properties via a dual energy X-ray scanning process [3]. In this scenario, objects are randomly stacked and heavily overlapped with each other, inducing heavy object occlusions. However, as

© Springer Nature Switzerland AG 2021
H. Ishikawa et al. (Eds.): ACCV 2020, LNCS 12627, pp. 173–190, 2021.
https://doi.org/10.1007/978-3-030-69544-6_11

demonstrated in Fig. 1, the appearance of X-ray imagery is different from regular RGB images in its pseudo colors, textures and its unique partial transparency of materials. With such unique characteristics, dedicated machine learning algorithms and neural networks need to be crafted.

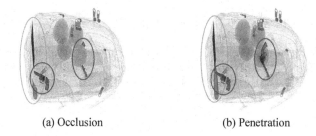

(a) Occlusion   (b) Penetration

Fig. 1. Illustration of exemplar penetration-induced object overlapping. Occluded items in (a), i.e. the gun (red ellipse) in the center and the knife (blue ellipse) in the left appears in (b) via X-ray penetration, with changes in appearance. (Color figure online)

Existing security X-ray scanning requires a trained professional to continuously monitor such images. Such a process is tiresome and difficult to scale up. Therefore, there is an urgent need to improve the automation and accuracy of recognizing prohibited items within X-ray images. Recently, with the prosperity of applying deep learning methods [4], especially the convolutional neural networks, the recognition of prohibited items in X-ray pictures can be regarded as a multi-label classification problem [5].

To recognize prohibited items under penetration-induced overlapping, we assume that low-level information especially colors and edges is the key to distinguish objects in complex and cluttered backgrounds. Moreover, such X-ray images are often consist of objects of dramatically different sizes and existing methods utilize Feature Pyramid Network (FPN) architecture [6] to alleviate scale variation problem, which leverages ConvNet's feature hierarchy to build pyramid features. Afterwards, per-level predictions, i.e. outputs made according to features of each level separately, are combined as final classification output through an average fusion. However, these methods are shown in our paper to be suboptimal, possibly due to their application of static fusion, which we speculate is insufficient to account for the challenging penetration-induced object overlapping [7,8] and violent appearance changes. Since such object overlapping phenomena varies universally and diversely among X-ray images and within the same image, it is reasonable to hypothesize that *features with different spatial attention scores and from different levels contribute unequally in the classification*, which implies the needs for spatial attention and dynamic late fusion.

Based on these assumptions, we propose a framework termed as SXMNet, to solve the challenging penetration-induced overlapping in the X-ray multi-label classification problem. Instead of directly extracting deep features, we construct a bottom-up spatial attention head, which utilizes the hierarchical character of FPN, to select the foreground region from the complex and cluttered backgrounds. Since larger attention masks mean better locating capabilities [9,10], we build bottom-up pathway to expand the resolution of attention masks, concatenating feature maps with the raw input image in several stages to exploit low-level visual information including edges and colors. Furthermore, neural-guided Meta Fusion is proposed to automatically assign soft weights to the pyramid predictions according to the neural knowledge rather than ad-hoc heuristics like scales [11] or gated fusion [12]. Further experiments show that our hypothesis is supported as our method outperforms the baseline by a large margin in the multi-label classification task on X-ray images.

In summary, our major contributions are three-fold:

1) For locating prohibited items in the penetration-induced overlapping scenarios, we present the bottom-up attention mechanism, which utilizes the raw input image in each stage to infuse low-level visual information such as colors, textures and edge information.
2) We propose a plug-in Meta Fusion module to address the scale variation problem, which can learn from other neural networks and re-weight the multi-stage predictions in a dynamic style.
3) To further evaluate the effects and transferability of the proposed Meta Fusion mechanism, we implement it with several architectures and datasets. Comprehensive experiments on the X-ray datasets prove that our approach achieves superior performance over previous ones. Moreover, we validate that neural knowledge is capable of better generalization performance through neural-guided Meta Fusion.

2 Related Work

2.1 Object Recognition Within X-Ray Images

Early work with X-ray security imagery primarily utilizes hand-crafted features like Bag-of-Visual-Words (BoVW) together with Supported Vector Machine (SVM) for classification [13,14]. Recently, object recognition within X-ray images has also witnessed the prominence of powerful features of convolutional neural networks (CNNs) and [15] first introduced the use of CNN to address object classification task by comparing varying CNN architectures to the earlier work extensive BoVW [14]. In the scenario that each image may contain more than one prohibited items, there are two typical types of object recognition methods. The first one worked on the instance level, providing bounding box as well as predicted label for each instance individually [16–19]. The other instead worked on image level which produces a score for each class indicating its presence or absence [20]. [21] augments input images based on generative adversarial networks to improve classification performance. [5] utilizes hierarchical refinement structure to deal with overlapping problem within X-ray images and alleviates data imbalance with a well-designed loss. This paper mainly studies the image-level recognition method.

2.2 Attention Mechanism

Motivated by the human perception process using top information to guide bottom-up feedforward process, attention mechanism has been widely applied to many computer vision tasks such image classification [22,23], scene segmentation [24,25] and visual question answering [26]. Squeeze-and-Excitation Networks (SENet) [27] adaptively re-calibrates channel-wise feature responses by explicitly modeling inter-dependencies between channels. Convolutional Block Attention Module (CBAM) [28] sequentially infers attention maps along both channel-wise and spatial-wise. Recently, attention mechanisms have been introduced to deep neural networks for multi-label image classification. It aims to explicitly or implicitly extract multiple visual representations from a single image character-izing different associated labels [29–32]. In the context of object recognition in X-ray images, researchers realized that these images often contain fewer texture information, yet shape information stands out to be more discriminative [5]. Therefore, we design a bottom-up attention to utilize the low-level visual infor-mation such as color and texture.

2.3 Fusion Mechanism

Fusion strategy includes early fusion (concatenate multiple features) and late fusion (fuse predictions of different models). [33] adopts gated fusion strategy which derives three inputs from an original hazy image to yield the final dehazed image. [34] utilizes a hard constraint on the matrix rank to preserve the consis-tency of predictions by various features. The advantage of combining multi-scale input images for multi-label image classification by employing varying fusion approaches has been proved in [35,36]. In this filed, almost all the methods mentioned above are based on intuition or algebraic knowledge, which may not be the optimal fusion strategy for CNNs. Different from them, our Meta Fusion utilizes neural knowledge to serve as the guidance of the fusion process, super-vising the learning of network in a neural-guided manner.

3   Proposed Approach

3.1 Formulation

For object recognition in X-ray images, the primary characteristic is that the possible number and category of prohibited items appearing in the image is uncertain. Therefore, we formulate it as a multi-label classification problem. Suppose there are C classes of possible items in the dataset. For each given image $\mathbf{x}$, our goal is to obtain a C-dimensional vector $\mathbf{y}$ for each $\mathbf{x}$, each dimension $\mathbf{y}_c$ for $c \in \{0, 1, ..., C\}$, is either 0 or 1, with 1 indicating the specified prohibited item is present in this image and 0 otherwise.

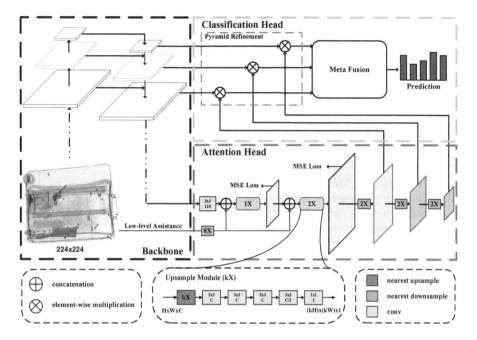

Fig. 2. Overview architecture. Backbone extracts pyramid features shared between attention head and classification head. Attention head effectively outputs attention masks which in return improve the performance of classification head.

3.2   Security X-Ray Multi-label Classification Network

As shown in Fig. 2, our proposed Security X-ray Multi-label Classification Network (SXMNet) consists of three components: backbone, attention head and multi-label classification head. Backbone outputs shared features among two heads, which is implemented using ResNet50 with the Feature Pyramid Network (FPN) architecture [6]. Attention head cooperates both shared features and raw input image to generate attention masks, which serves as a feature selector to distinguish prohibited items during penetration-induced scenarios. Based on the attention masks, multi-label classification head refines pyramid features and computes final predictions with neural-guided Meta Fusion mechanism.

Pyramid Refinement with Bottom-Up Attention. The goal is to predict the category of prohibited items in X-ray security imagery. However, it is difficult to capture distinctive visual features within complex and cluttered imagery due to penetration. To solve this problem, we introduce bottom-up attention guidance to select reliable deep descriptors. Specifically, based on the output pyramid feature $\mathbf{p}^l$, where l indicates the pyramid level, attention head predicts the location of all prohibited items using the predicted heat map. From the last feature maps of the backbone, the attention head is constructed by stacking

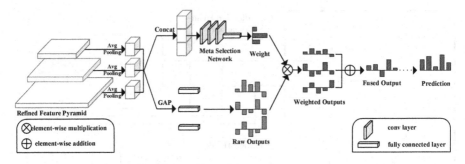

Fig. 3. Pipeline of Meta Fusion. meta fusion consists of two branches: predict-branch outputs predictions corresponding to each pyramid feature, and soft-weight-branch output weights indicating the importance of each pyramid feature. GAP means global average pooling.

Upsample Modules. Similar to [37], each Upsample Module consists of a bilinear upsample layer to expand spatial sizes, several dilated convolutional layers to extract deeper features without losing resolutions and a 1×1 convolutional layer as output layer. Notably, the appearance features from raw input image could provide abundant information to support the localization in penetration-induced overlapping scenes, so we concat the feature and the rescale input image together before each upsampling. Based on the outputs of the attention head, multi-scale feature maps are refined in a pyramid refinement way like [38], where pyramid features are multiplied with its corresponding attention mask simultaneously.

Classification with Meta Fusion. In feature pyramid based classification networks, features of each level, namely $\mathbf{p}^l$, make their own prediction $\mathbf{y}^l$ independently. Traditionally people merge them into the final prediction by simply average them, as denoted in Eq. (1):

$$\mathbf{y} = \frac{1}{n} \sum_{t=l_{min}}^{l_{max}} \mathbf{y}^t, \tag{1}$$

where l_{min} denotes the minimal pyramid level, l_{max} denotes the maximum and $n = l_{max} - l_{min} + 1$.

However, the contributions from different level features should be different [39], weighting the pyramid predictions can produce performance gains. Especially in X-ray images, late fusion of predictions is essential to address penetration problem as we assumed. In addition, CNN model trained on a given X-ray security image dataset will have a higher degree of generalization if applied to other X-ray datasets [40]. Therefore, we propose to insert a meta-selection network [41] into the architecture, which utilizes the neural knowledge to predict weights for soft prediction selection.

As shown in Fig. 3, we pool each pyramid feature so that each having spatial size of 7×7, which is fed to the meta-selection network after concatenation, outputting a vector of the probability distribution as the weights of soft prediction selection. Thus, Eq. (1) is augmented into Eq. (2):

$$y = \sum_{t=l_{min}}^{l_{max}} \mathbf{w}^t \mathbf{y}^t, \tag{2}$$

where $\mathbf{w}^t$ is the output of the meta-selection network.

Details of the meta-selection network is shown in Table 1.

Table 1. The architecture of the meta-selection network used in the proposed method.

Layer	Description	Activation
Input	Refined feature pyramid	None
L-0	Conv, $768 \times 3 \times 3 \rightarrow 256$	ReLU
L-1	Conv, $256 \times 3 \times 3 \rightarrow 256$	ReLU
L-2	Conv, $256 \times 3 \times 3 \rightarrow 256$	ReLU
L-3	Fully connected, $256 \rightarrow 3$	Softmax

Loss Function. The loss function of the proposed network consists of the attention term, meta selection term and multi-label classification term. For attention term, we utilize Mean Squared Error (MSE) to measure the difference between the ground-truth map and the estimated heatmap that the attention head predicted. For the meta selection term, we use the standard Cross-Entropy (CE). In addition, Binary Cross-Entropy (BCE) loss is utilized to optimize the multi-label classification task.

During the stage of training attention head (**stage I**), the loss is:

$$L_I = L_{att}, \tag{3}$$

where L_{att} is the MSE loss of generating attention mask.

During the stage of training classification head (**stage II**), the total classification loss is given as follow:

$$L_{II} = L_{cls} + \lambda L_{meta}, \tag{4}$$

where L_{cls} is the loss of the multi-label classification task, λ is the hyperparameter that controls the contribution of meta-selection loss, L_{meta}.

Ground-Truth Generation. To train the SXMNet, we generate both ground-truth heatmaps and ground-truth meta selection labels. For the heatmaps, we generate an inline ellipse of each annotated bounding box, where pixels inside the ellipse is set to 1 and others are 0. Details of the generated ground-truth are shown in Fig. 5. As for meta selection, first each image is forwarded through all levels of feature pyramid by CHR [5]. The ground-truth is a one-hot vector, with 1 indicating this pyramid level yielding the minimal classification loss and 0 otherwise.

Training Strategy. Different from self attention mechanism, the training scheme of our model consists of two stages. In the **stage I**, we only train the attention task with instance-level annotated data, which provides bounding box for each prohibited item. So only parameters of backbone and the attention head are updated. After **stage I** training is complete, we continue to train it on a large number of image-level annotated data. The predicted attention maps, along with pyramid feature representations of the input image, can be further utilized to improve the multi-label classification performance.

4 Experiments

4.1 Datasets

To evaluate the effectiveness of our proposed methods, we conduct experiments on two benchmark security inspection datasets, *i.e.*, SIXray [5] and OPIXray [42].

SIXray consists of 1,059,231 X-ray images, in which six classes of 8,929 prohibited items. These images are collected using a Nuctech dual-energy X-ray scanner, where the distribution of the general baggage/parcel items corresponds to stream-of-commerce occurrence. In our experiments, we only use the images containing prohibited items and follow the same division protocol as [5], namely 7496 images for training and 1433 images for testing.

Compared with SIXray, OPIXray is more challenging with lower resolution of prohibited items and higher inter-class similarity of them. It contains a total of 8885 X-ray images of 5 categories of cutters (e.g., Folding Knife, Straight Knife, Scissor, Utility Knife, Multi-tool Knife). The dataset is partitioned into a training set and a testing set, with the former containing 80% of the images (7109) and the latter containing 20% (1776). Since these images contain a lot of pure white backgrounds, we crop each image before training.

4.2 Implementation Details

Network Details: In network implementation, $l \in \{3, 4, 5\}$ and $\lambda = 0.1$.

Training Details: We trained our network with SGD optimizer [43]. For **stage I**, total epochs are 350 and the initial learning rate is 1e$-$5, which is divided by 10 after every 100 epochs. For **stage II**, total epochs are 150 and the initial learning rate is 1e$-$1 for fully connected layers and 2e$-$2 for others, which is divided by 10 after every 30 epoch. The batch size is 64 for all training stages.

4.3 Comparison Methods

Baseline Methods: We employ planing training with ResNet [44] and ResNet-FPN [6] as our baselines.

State-of-the-Art Methods: For state-of-the-art methods, we choose the recently proposed CHR [5] which achieves good multi-label classification accuracy on SIXray datasets.

Table 2. Multi-label classification performance (AP, %).

Dataset	Category	ResNet50 [44]	ResNet50-FPN [6]	CHR [5]	Ours
SIXray	Gun	98.70	98.23	98.29	**98.84**
	Knife	92.59	93.45	94.87	**95.22**
	Pliers	96.41	96.66	96.40	**98.33**
	Scissors	91.09	92.30	91.75	**96.11**
	Wrench	86.74	88.66	88.51	**95.38**
	Mean	93.36	93.86	93.96	**96.78**
OPIXray	Folding	92.93	93.92	94.62	**96.11**
	Straight	65.40	64.76	67.42	**75.37**
	Scissor	99.05	99.18	98.93	**99.34**
	Utility	78.25	78.83	80.39	**84.32**
	Multi-tool	96.15	96.20	97.28	**97.69**
	Mean	86.35	86.58	87.73	**90.83**

4.4 Overall Performance

Experimental Results on SIXray. Table 2 shows the results on the SIXray datasets. Since CHR only gives the results on both positive and negative images, we re-train it on the only positive images with the source codes provided by the authors [5]. As shown in the table, we demonstrate that our method achieves the best results across all categories, when comparing the baseline methods and previous state-of-the art. Our method achieves larger performance enhancement, i.e. **2.82%** in terms of mean AP.

Experimental Results on OPIXray. Similar to SIXray, our performance still surpasses other method by a large margin in terms of mAP. We achieve **3.10%** improvements on OPIXray, from Table 2.

4.5 Ablation Studies

Effects of Each Component. To validate the effects of each component, we conduct ablations on the attention mechanism and meta fusion mechanism. As show in Table 3, the attention mechanism brings the largest improvements, i.e. **2.05%** in terms of mean AP, indicating that spatial attention plays an important role in handling heavily clustered in X-ray images. The power of effectively localization in return verifies our assumption: effective spatial attention mechanism could improve recognition performance in penetration-induced over-lapping scenarios. As we assumed, different levels of penetration require anisotropic fusion of predictions and our meta fusion is designed to soft-weight predictions during training. As shown in Table 3, Meta Fusion can result in a slight improvements compared with our attention mechanism, i.e. **0.4%**. With both attention mechanism and meta fusion mechanism, we achieve the best performance on SIXray,

Table 3. Ablation results of each component (AP, %).

	Backbone	FPN	Attention	Meta fusion	mAP
Baseline	ResNet-50				93.36
Ours	ResNet-50	√			93.86
		√	√		95.91
		√		√	94.26
		√	√	√	**96.78**

Table 4. Ablation studies for the effects and transferability of Meta Fusion.

Dataset	SIXray	OPIXray
Gated Fusion [12]	96.15	90.67
Our MF-I	96.33	90.36
Our MF-N	**96.78**	**90.83**

MF-I denotes meta fusion with label provided by intuition. MF-N denotes meta fusion where label is provided by CHR [5].

showing that spatial attention and anisotropic fusion are jointly contributing to the multi-label classification task within X-ray images (Table 4).

Effects and Transferability of Meta Fusion. For better understanding of our proposed Meta Fusion, we conduct experiments on different fusion strategies. We compare three fusion methods including gated fusion, Meta Fusion by Intuition (MF-I) and Meta Fusion by Neural (MF-N). MF-I denotes using intuitive label according to the proportion of the smallest bounding box of prohibited items. Specifically, for proportion under 2%, we set p_3 level as the ground truth, between 2% and 20% are set to p_4 level, and others are p_5 level. MF-N means using the label generated by CHR [5], setting the pyramid level with smallest classification loss as the ground-truth. As shown in Table 3, meta fusion achieves better performance compared with gated fusion. In addition, optimization with label provided by neural knowledge (see +MF-N) allows better utilization of pyramid features than label given by intuition (see +MF-I).

Furthermore, to evaluate the transferability of Meta Fusion, we train our network on OPIXray with label generated by CHR, which is trained only on SIXray. The categories of prohibited items in SIXray is different from those in OPIXray. As shown in the right column of Table 3, Meta Fusion still performs better than naive gated fusion, proving the neural knowledge will be capable of better generalization performance through Meta Fusion. Note that the performances of MF-I on OPIXray is slightly reduced. We speculate that the reason is that prohibited items are much smaller in size than those in SIXray, so the prior knowledge mismatches OPIXray situations.

To facilitate the understanding of our proposed Meta Fusion mechanism, we visualize the distribution of the Meta Fusion label during training and fusion weights during inference, as indicated by the histogram in Fig. 4. The left panel of Fig. 4 shows a histogram of labels provided by prior Knowledge (MF-I) and provided by minimal classification loss according to CHR (MF-N). The figure suggests that the distribution of labels provided by intuition and CHR differs a lot, we conjecture that the proportion of smallest prohibited item always be in a moderate level, so most of the intuitive labels indicate the p_4 as the optimal level, while CHR labels prefer to p_3.

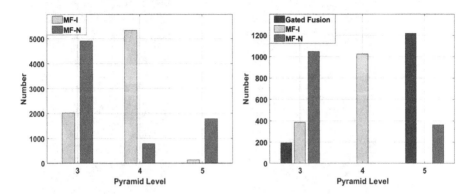

Fig. 4. Histogram of the selected pyramid level on SIXray. (left) shows the histogram of training label provided by prior Knowledge (MF-I) and label provided by minimal classification loss according to CHR (MF-N); (right) shows the histogram of the pyramid level with the max weight predicted by gated fusion, MF-I, and MF-N during inference.

The right panel of the of Fig. 4 shows the distribution of the fusion weights for the test set during inference. We just plot the pyramid layers corresponding to the maximum selection weight for simplicity. As the figure shows, the predicted fusion weights are affected by its training label since the histograms are similar between them. What is more, whether the neural knowledge the network utilizes comes from itself (Gated Fusion) or other networks (MF-N), they perform in a similar manner: both concentrating on the most top (p_5) or most down (p_3) features, neglecting the middle pyramid feature. This phenomenon may suggest that the p_3 and p_5 have the most distinct representations in FPN architecture.

Table 5. Validation of training strategy (AP, %). Our strategy (2nd row) is compared with self attention mechanism (1st row).

Strategy	SIXray (only classification)	SIXray (attention & classification)	Mean
Self	$\checkmark$		94.11
Ours		$\checkmark$	**96.78**

184   B. Hu et al.

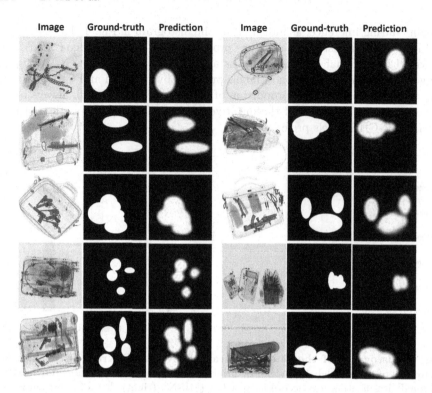

Fig. 5. Qualitative results of attention masks on test set. The results show that
our low-level assistance attention is effective in complex and cluttered background due
to penetration-induced overlapping problem. (Best viewed in color and zoomed in.)
(Color figure online)

Effects of Training Bottom-Up Attention. To determine the cause of the
performance improvement an increase parameters caused by the attention head
or the selection capability of the attention head, we conduct experiments on
different ways of training the attention head. For fair comparison, we keep the
architecture of the network unchanged and only change task used in **stage I**. As
shown in Table 5, Self means self attention, which skips the **stage I** and initial-
izes the network with parameters trained on ImageNet [45], and Ours indicates
our training strategy. Experimental results demonstrate that our training strategy outperforms the self-attention strategy, indicating the capability of locating
prohibited items can be beneficial.

Figure 5 shows some qualitative results of predicted attention masks on the
test set, indicating that our low-level assistance help to discover prohibited items
under complex and cluttered backgrounds.

Table 6. Quantitative results of different output attention resolution.

Resolution	SIXray
28	96.12
56	**96.78**
112	95.47

Table 7. Results of whether concatenating the raw input image while constructing attention head.

	Raw Input Image?	SIXray
Attention		95.72
Attention	$\checkmark$	**96.78**

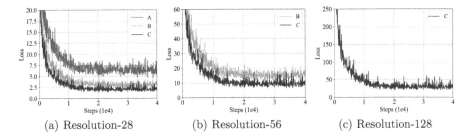

(a) Resolution-28   (b) Resolution-56   (c) Resolution-128

Fig. 6. Attention training loss of each resolution on SIXray. We construct attention head with different outputting resolution masks based on none upsample module (A), 1 upsample modules (B) and 2 upsample modules (C), respectively. It is obviously that network has lower training loss in the former stage with larger masks follows afterwards.

Effects of Resolution of Attention Mask. To demonstrate the impact of the resolution of attention mask, we conduct several experiments with different resolutions of attention masks. As shown in Fig. 6, with more upsampling modules, namely higher outputting attention resolution, the loss of each stage is much smaller, showing large attention mask help precisely locate prohibited items. Based on **stage I** model, we continue training the multi-label classification task. From Table 6, large resolution with better locating ability could further boost the multi-label classification performance. For the case with resolution 112, we observed a significant drop in performance and our preliminary assessment is due to overfitting, possibly due to limited granularity in ground-truth generation.

Effects of Low-Level Assistance. To validate the effects of low-level assistance while building the attention head, we conduct experiments on whether adding the raw input image to construct the attention head. As Table 7 shows, concatenating raw input image as the low-level assistance can bring **1.06%** improvements, indicating that low-level visual information, such as edges and colors, is important in locating objects under heavily cluttered backgrounds.

Table 8. Performance comparison between Meta Fusion-integrated (MF-I, MF-N) network and baselines for two multi-label classification approaches.

Method	SIXray	OPIXray
Res50-FPN [6]	93.86	86.58
Res50-FPN + MF-I	**94.65**	87.33
Res50-FPN + MF-N	94.24	**87.64**
CHR [5]	93.96	87.33
CHR + MF-I	93.87	**88.29**
CHR + MF-N	93.77	87.84

4.6 Comparing with Different Baselines

To further evaluate the effectiveness of Meta Fusion and verify Meta Fusion can be applied to various networks in the prediction fusion stage, we conduct experiments on two approaches with multi-prediction architecture, i.e., Res50-FPN [6] and CHR [5]. The results are shown in Table 8.

As we can see from Table 8, the performance of Meta Fusion-integrated networks are improved by **1.06%** and **0.96%** compared with Res50-FPN, and CHR respectively on OPIXray. Meanwhile, **0.79%** improvement is gained compared with Rer50-FPN on SIXray, which indicates that our module can be inserted as a plug-and-play module into networks with predictions fusion stage and receive a better performance. Note that the performance of MF-integrated CHR on SIXray is sightly below the baseline, and we speculate that the labels are given by CHR trained on SIXray itself, which limits further performance boost.

5 Conclusion

In this paper, we investigate the prohibited items discovery problem in X-ray scanning images. We propose a novel SXMNet to deal with the penetration-induced overlapping with both spatial attention and dynamic fusion. For selecting reliable foregrounds, the raw input image is utilized as low-level assistance to construct attention head in bottom-up pathway. Subsequently, per-stage predictions of refined pyramid features are fused adaptively in a weighted manner, where the weights are dynamically predicted by the proposed neural-guided Meta Fusion scheme. Experimental results demonstrate that presented framework outperforms the baselines and previous state-of-art by a large margin.

Acknowledgement. This work was supported by the National Key R&D Program of China (Grant 2018AAA0102504) and the National Natural Science Foundation of China (Grant 61973245). We thank Xiaojun Lv of Institute of Computing Technologies China Academy of Railway Sciences Corporation Limited for his great contribution to this work.

References

1. Mery, D., Svec, E., Arias, M., Riffo, V., Saavedra, J.M., Banerjee, S.: Modern computer vision techniques for x-ray testing in baggage inspection. IEEE Trans. Syst. Man Cybern. Syst. **47**, 682–692 (2016)
2. Akcay, S., Breckon, T.P.: Towards automatic threat detection: a survey of advances of deep learning within x-ray security imaging. CoRR abs/2001.01293 (2020)
3. Mouton, A., Breckon, T.P.: A review of automated image understanding within 3d baggage computed tomography security screening. J. X Ray Sci. Technol. **23**, 531–555 (2015)
4. LeCun, Y., Bengio, Y., Hinton, G.E.: Deep learning. Nature **521**, 436–444 (2015)
5. Miao, C., et al.: SIXray: a large-scale security inspection x-ray benchmark for prohibited item discovery in overlapping images. In: Proceedings of the IEEE Conference on Computer Vision and Pattern Recognition, pp. 2119–2128 (2019)
6. Lin, T.Y., Dollár, P., Girshick, R., He, K., Hariharan, B., Belongie, S.: Feature pyramid networks for object detection. In: Proceedings of the IEEE Conference on Computer Vision and Pattern Recognition, pp. 2117–2125 (2017)
7. Akcay, S., Breckon, T.P.: An evaluation of region based object detection strategies within x-ray baggage security imagery. In: 2017 IEEE International Conference on Image Processing (ICIP), pp. 1337–1341. IEEE (2017)
8. Mery, D., Arteta, C.: Automatic defect recognition in x-ray testing using computer vision. In: 2017 IEEE Winter Conference on Applications of Computer Vision (WACV), pp. 1026–1035. IEEE (2017)
9. Wei, S.E., Ramakrishna, V., Kanade, T., Sheikh, Y.: Convolutional pose machines. In: Proceedings of the IEEE conference on Computer Vision and Pattern Recognition, pp. 4724–4732 (2016)
10. Sun, K., Xiao, B., Liu, D., Wang, J.: Deep high-resolution representation learning for human pose estimation. In: Proceedings of the IEEE Conference on Computer Vision and Pattern Recognition, pp. 5693–5703 (2019)
11. Wang, J., Chen, K., Yang, S., Loy, C.C., Lin, D.: Region proposal by guided anchoring. In: Proceedings of the IEEE Conference on Computer Vision and Pattern Recognition, pp. 2965–2974 (2019)
12. Cheng, Y., Rui, C., Li, Z., Xin, Z., Huang, K.: Locality-sensitive deconvolution networks with gated fusion for RGB-D indoor semantic segmentation. In: 2017 IEEE Conference on Computer Vision and Pattern Recognition (CVPR) (2017)
13. Mery, D., Svec, E., Arias, M.: Object recognition in baggage inspection using adaptive sparse representations of X-ray images. In: Bräunl, T., McCane, B., Rivera, M., Yu, X. (eds.) PSIVT 2015. LNCS, vol. 9431, pp. 709–720. Springer, Cham (2016). https://doi.org/10.1007/978-3-319-29451-3_56

14. Kundegorski, M.E., Akcay, S., Devereux, M., Mouton, A., Breckon, T.P.: On using feature descriptors as visual words for object detection within x-ray baggage security screening. In: 7th International Conference on Imaging for Crime Detection and Prevention, ICDP 2016, Madrid, Spain, 23–25 November 2016, pp. 1–6. IET/IEEE (2016)

15. Akcay, S., Kundegorski, M.E., Devereux, M., Breckon, T.P.: Transfer learning using convolutional neural networks for object classification within x-ray baggage security imagery. In: 2016 IEEE International Conference on Image Processing, ICIP 2016, Phoenix, AZ, USA, 25–28 September 2016, pp. 1057–1061. IEEE (2016)

16. Steitz, J.-M.O., Saeedan, F., Roth, S.: Multi-view X-Ray R-CNN. In: Brox, T., Bruhn, A., Fritz, M. (eds.) GCPR 2018. LNCS, vol. 11269, pp. 153–168. Springer, Cham (2019). https://doi.org/10.1007/978-3-030-12939-2_12

17. Akcay, S., Kundegorski, M.E., Willcocks, C.G., Breckon, T.P.: Using deep convolutional neural network architectures for object classification and detection within x-ray baggage security imagery. IEEE Trans. Inf. Forensics Secur. **13**, 2203–2215 (2018)

18. Bastan, M.: Multi-view object detection in dual-energy x-ray images. Mach. Vis. Appl. **26**, 1045–1060 (2015)

19. Cao, S., Liu, Y., Song, W., Cui, Z., Lv, X., Wan, J.: Toward human-in-the-loop prohibited item detection in x-ray baggage images. In: 2019 Chinese Automation Congress (CAC), pp. 4360–4364 (2019)

20. Wang, Q., Jia, N., Breckon, T.P.: A baseline for multi-label image classification using an ensemble of deep convolutional neural networks. In: 2019 IEEE International Conference on Image Processing, ICIP 2019, Taipei, Taiwan, 22–25 September 2019, pp. 644–648. IEEE (2019)

21. Yang, J., Zhao, Z., Zhang, H., Shi, Y.: Data augmentation for x-ray prohibited item images using generative adversarial networks. IEEE Access **7**, 28894–28902 (2019)

22. Wang, F., et al.: Residual attention network for image classification. In: 2017 IEEE Conference on Computer Vision and Pattern Recognition, CVPR 2017, Honolulu, HI, USA, 21–26 July 2017, pp. 6450–6458. IEEE Computer Society (2017)

23. Chen, X., et al.: A dual-attention dilated residual network for liver lesion classification and localization on CT images. In: 2019 IEEE International Conference on Image Processing, ICIP 2019, Taipei, Taiwan, 22–25 September 2019, pp. 235–239. IEEE (2019)

24. Fu, J., et al.: Dual attention network for scene segmentation. In: IEEE Conference on Computer Vision and Pattern Recognition, CVPR 2019, Long Beach, CA, USA, 16–20 June 2019, pp. 3146–3154. Computer Vision Foundation/IEEE (2019)

25. Li, K., Wu, Z., Peng, K., Ernst, J., Fu, Y.: Tell me where to look: guided attention inference network. In: 2018 IEEE Conference on Computer Vision and Pattern Recognition, CVPR 2018, Salt Lake City, UT, USA, June 18–22 2018, pp. 9215–9223. IEEE Computer Society (2018)

26. Peng, L., Yang, Y., Wang, Z., Wu, X., Huang, Z.: CRA-Net: composed relation attention network for visual question answering. In: Proceedings of the 27th ACM International Conference on Multimedia, MM 2019, Nice, France, 21–25 October 2019, pp. 1202–1210. ACM (2019)

27. Hu, J., Shen, L., Sun, G.: Squeeze-and-excitation networks. In: 2018 IEEE Conference on Computer Vision and Pattern Recognition, CVPR 2018, Salt Lake City, UT, USA, 18–22 June 2018, pp. 7132–7141. IEEE Computer Society (2018)

28. Woo, S., Park, J., Lee, J.-Y., Kweon, I.S.: CBAM: convolutional block attention module. In: Ferrari, V., Hebert, M., Sminchisescu, C., Weiss, Y. (eds.) ECCV 2018. LNCS, vol. 11211, pp. 3–19. Springer, Cham (2018). https://doi.org/10.1007/978-3-030-01234-2_1
29. Wang, Z., Chen, T., Li, G., Xu, R., Lin, L.: Multi-label image recognition by recurrently discovering attentional regions. In: IEEE International Conference on Computer Vision, ICCV 2017, Venice, Italy, 22–29 October 2017, pp. 464–472. IEEE Computer Society (2017)
30. Zhu, F., Li, H., Ouyang, W., Yu, N., Wang, X.: Learning spatial regularization with image-level supervisions for multi-label image classification. In: 2017 IEEE Conference on Computer Vision and Pattern Recognition, CVPR 2017, Honolulu, HI, USA, 21–26 July 2017, pp. 2027–2036. IEEE Computer Society (2017)
31. You, R., Guo, Z., Cui, L., Long, X., Bao, Y., Wen, S.: Cross-modality attention with semantic graph embedding for multi-label classification. In: The Thirty-Fourth AAAI Conference on Artificial Intelligence, AAAI 2020, The Thirty-Second Innovative Applications of Artificial Intelligence Conference, IAAI 2020, The Tenth AAAI Symposium on Educational Advances in Artificial Intelligence, EAAI 2020, New York, NY, USA, 7–12 February 2020, pp. 12709–12716. AAAI Press (2020)
32. Guo, H., Zheng, K., Fan, X., Yu, H., Wang, S.: Visual attention consistency under image transforms for multi-label image classification. In: IEEE Conference on Computer Vision and Pattern Recognition, CVPR 2019, Long Beach, CA, USA, 16–20 June 2019, pp. 729–739. Computer Vision Foundation/IEEE (2019)
33. Ren, W., et al.: Gated fusion network for single image dehazing. In: 2018 IEEE Conference on Computer Vision and Pattern Recognition, CVPR 2018, Salt Lake City, UT, USA, 18–22 June 2018, pp. 3253–3261. IEEE Computer Society (2018)
34. Dong, X., Yan, Y., Tan, M., Yang, Y., Tsang, I.W.: Late fusion via subspace search with consistency preservation. IEEE Trans. Image Process. **28**, 518–528 (2019)
35. Wang, M., Luo, C., Hong, R., Tang, J., Feng, J.: Beyond object proposals: random crop pooling for multi-label image recognition. IEEE Trans. Image Process. **25**, 5678–5688 (2016)
36. Durand, T., Mordan, T., Thome, N., Cord, M.: WILDCAT: weakly supervised learning of deep convnets for image classification, pointwise localization and segmentation. In: 2017 IEEE Conference on Computer Vision and Pattern Recognition, CVPR 2017, Honolulu, HI, USA, 21–26 July 2017, pp. 5957–5966. IEEE Computer Society (2017)
37. Li, C., et al.: Data priming network for automatic check-out. In: Proceedings of the 27th ACM International Conference on Multimedia, pp. 2152–2160 (2019)
38. Zhong, Z., Zhang, C., Liu, Y., Wu, Y.: VIASEG: visual information assisted lightweight point cloud segmentation. In: 2019 IEEE International Conference on Image Processing (ICIP), pp. 1500–1504. IEEE (2019)
39. Zhu, C., He, Y., Savvides, M.: Feature selective anchor-free module for single-shot object detection. In: Proceedings of the IEEE Conference on Computer Vision and Pattern Recognition, pp. 840–849 (2019)
40. Gaus, Y.F.A., Bhowmik, N., Akcay, S., Breckon, T.P.: Evaluating the transferability and adversarial discrimination of convolutional neural networks for threat object detection and classification within x-ray security imagery. In: Wani, M.A., Khoshgoftaar, T.M., Wang, D., Wang, H., Seliya, N. (eds.) 18th IEEE International Conference on Machine Learning and Applications, ICMLA 2019, Boca Raton, FL, USA, 16–19 December 2019, pp. 420–425. IEEE (2019)
41. Zhu, C., Chen, F., Shen, Z., Savvides, M.: Soft anchor-point object detection. arXiv preprint arXiv:1911.12448 (2019)

42. Wei, Y., Tao, R., Wu, Z., Ma, Y., Zhang, L., Liu, X.: Occluded prohibited items detection: an x-ray security inspection benchmark and de-occlusion attention module. CoRR abs/2004.08656 (2020)
43. Bottou, L.: Large-scale machine learning with stochastic gradient descent. In: Lechevallier, Y., Saporta, G. (eds.) Proceedings of COMPSTAT 2010, pp. 177–186. Springer, Cham (2010). https://doi.org/10.1007/978-3-7908-2604-3_16
44. He, K., Zhang, X., Ren, S., Sun, J.: Deep residual learning for image recognition. In: Proceedings of the IEEE Conference on Computer Vision and Pattern Recognition, pp. 770–778 (2016)
45. Deng, J., Dong, W., Socher, R., Li, L.J., Li, F.F.: ImageNet: a large-scale hierarchical image database. In: 2009 IEEE Computer Society Conference on Computer Vision and Pattern Recognition (CVPR 2009), Miami, Florida, USA, 20–25 June 2009 (2009)

Learning End-to-End Action Interaction by Paired-Embedding Data Augmentation

Ziyang Song[1], Zejian Yuan[1(✉)], Chong Zhang[2], Wanchao Chi[2], Yonggen Ling[2], and Shenghao Zhang[2]

[1] Institute of Artificial Intelligence and Robotics, Xi'an Jiaotong University, Xi'an, China
songzy305@yahoo.com,yuan.ze.jian@xjtu.edu.cn
[2] Tencent Robotics X, Shenzhen, China
aerentzhang@gmail.com, wanchaochi@tencent.com, ylingaa@connect.ust.hk, popshzhang@pku.edu.cn

Abstract. In recognition-based action interaction, robots' responses to human actions are often pre-designed according to recognized categories and thus stiff. In this paper, we specify a new Interactive Action Translation (IAT) task which aims to learn end-to-end action interaction from unlabeled interactive pairs, removing explicit action recognition. To enable learning on small-scale data, we propose a Paired-Embedding (PE) method for effective and reliable data augmentation. Specifically, our method first utilizes paired relationships to cluster individual actions in an embedding space. Then two actions originally paired can be replaced with other actions in their respective neighborhood, assembling into new pairs. An Act2Act network based on conditional GAN follows to learn from augmented data. Besides, IAT-test and IAT-train scores are specifically proposed for evaluating methods on our task. Experimental results on two datasets show impressive effects and broad application prospects of our method.

1 Introduction

Action interaction is an essential part of human-robot interaction (HRI) [1]. For robots, action interaction with human includes two levels: 1) perceiving human actions and understanding intentions behind; 2) performing responsive actions accordingly. Thanks to the development of action recognition methods [2], considerable progress has been made on the first level. As for the second level, robots often perform pre-designed action responses according to recognition results. We call this scheme as recognition-based action interaction. However, colorful appearances of human actions are mapped to a few fixed categories in this way, leading to a few fixed responses. Robots' action responses are thus stiff, lacking in human-like vividity. Moreover, annotating data for training action recognition models consumes manpower.

In this paper, we aim to learn end-to-end interaction from unlabeled action interaction data. Explicit recognition is removed, leaving the interaction implicitly guided by high-level semantic translation relationships. To achieve this goal,

© Springer Nature Switzerland AG 2021
H. Ishikawa et al. (Eds.): ACCV 2020, LNCS 12627, pp. 191–206, 2021.
https://doi.org/10.1007/978-3-030-69544-6_12

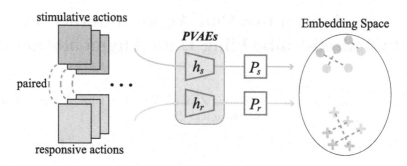

Fig. 1. An overview of our proposed Paired-Embedding (PE) method. Colors distinguish stimulations and responses. Circle and cross denote actions of different semantic categories. Dotted lines describe paired relationships. (Color figure online)

we specify a novel Interactive Action Translation (IAT) task: Given a set of "stimulation-response" action pairs conforming to defined interaction rules and without category labeled, learn a model to generate a response for a given stimulation during inference. The generated results are expected to manifest:

1) reality: indistinguishable from real human actions;
2) precision: conforming to defined interaction rules semantically, conditioned on the stimulation;
3) diversity: be various each time given the same stimulation.

For different interaction scenes and defined rules, paired action data need to be re-collected each time. Thus IAT would be more appealing if learning from a small number of samples. However, the task implicitly seeks for a high-level semantic translation relationship, which is hard to generalize from insufficient data. Moreover, the multimodal distribution of real actions is difficult to approximate without sufficient data. The contradiction between task goals and applications poses the main challenge: to achieve the three generation goals above with small-scale data.

Data augmentation is widely adopted to improve learning on small datasets. Traditional augmentation strategies apply hand-crafted transformations on existing data, thus only bring changes in limited modes. Generative Adversarial Networks (GAN) [3] emerges as a powerful technique to generate realistic samples. Nonetheless, a reliable GAN itself requires large-scale data to train. Some variants of GAN, like ACGAN [4], DAGAN [5], and BAGAN [6], are proposed to augment data for classification tasks. However, all of them need category labels that are not provided in our task. Therefore, a specially designed augmentation method is needed for small-scale unlabeled data in IAT.

We propose a novel Paired-Embedding (PE) method, as Fig. 1 shows. Through encoders in a Paired Variational Auto-Encoders (PVAEs) and PCA-based linear dimension reductions, individual action instances are projected into a low-dimension embedding space. Along with the vanilla VAE objectives [7], we employ a new PE loss utilizing paired relationships between actions to train

PVAEs. Specifically, VAE loss prefers large variance of action embeddings while PE loss pull actions within the same categories together. As a result, action instances are clustered in the embedding space in an unsupervised manner. Subsequently, both two actions in a data pair are allowed to be replaced with other instances in their respective neighborhood, assembling into new pairs conforming to defined interaction rules semantically. Therefore, the diversity of paired data is significantly and reliably enriched. Finally, we train an Act2Act network based on conditional GAN [8] on augmented data to solve our task.

Although IAT is formally an instance-conditional generation task like image translation [9,10], it actually conditions on the semantic category of input action instances. Therefore, evaluation metrics for neither image translation [11,12] nor category-conditional generation [13] is suitable for this task. Considering the three generation goals, we propose two evaluation metrics, IAT-test and IAT-train scores, to compare methods for our task from distinct perspectives. Experiments show that our proposed method gives satisfying generated action responses, both quantitatively and qualitatively.

The major contributions of our work are summarized as follows:

1) We specify a new IAT task, aiming to learn end-to-end action interaction from unlabeled interactive action pairs.
2) We design a PE data augmentation method to resolve the main challenge of our task: learning with a small number of samples.
3) We propose IAT-test and IAT-train scores to evaluate methods on our task, covering three task goals. Experiments prove the satisfying generation effects of our proposed method.

2 Related Work

2.1 Data Augmentation with GAN

It is widely accepted that in deep learning, a larger dataset often leads to a more reliable algorithm. In practical applications, data augmentation by adding synthetic data provides another way to improve performance. The most common data augmentation strategies are applying various hand-designed transformations on existing data. As GAN arises, it is a straightforward idea to use GAN to directly synthesize realistic data for augmentation. However, GAN itself always requires large-scale data for stable training. Otherwise, the quality of synthesized data is not ensured.

Several variants of conditional GAN are proposed for augmenting classification tasks, where category labels are included in GAN training. ACGAN [4] lets the generator and discriminator 'cooperating' on classification in addition to 'competing' on generation. DAGAN [5] aims to learn transformations on existing data for data augmentation. BAGAN [6] restores the dataset balance by generating minority-class samples. Unfortunately, these methods can not be applied to augmenting data without category labels given. Some other GAN-based data augmentation methods are also designed for different tasks, like [14] for emotion classification and [15,16] for person re-identification. They are only suitable for respective tasks but not extensible to our task. Unlike these methods, our proposed method augments IAT data by re-assigning individual actions from existing pairs into new pairs. Data synthesized in this way are undoubtedly natural and realistic. Meanwhile, PE method ensures the same interaction rules on augmented data and existing data, namely the semantic-level reality of augmented data.

2.2 Evaluation Metrics for Generation

Early work often relies on subjective visual evaluation of synthesized samples from generative methods like GAN. Quantitative metrics are proposed in recent years, and the most popular among them are Inception score (IS) [17] and Fréchet Inception distance (FID) [18]. Both of them are based on a pre-trained classification network (for image generation, an Inception network pre-trained on ImageNet). IS predicts category probabilities on generated samples through the classification network and evaluates generated results accordingly. FID directly measures the divergence between distributions of real and synthesized data in feature-level. CSGN [19] has extended IS and FID metrics from image generation to skeleton-based action synthesis. However, they fail to reflect the dependence of generated results upon conditions, thus are unsuitable for conditional generation tasks like ours.

GAN-train and GAN-test scores [13] are proposed for comparing category-conditional GANs. An additional classification network is also introduced. Given category information, the two metrics quantify the correlation between generated samples and conditioned categories besides generating reality and diversity. Nonetheless, category labels are missing in our task and semantic categories are implicitly reflected in paired relationships. Enlightened by GAN-train and GAN-test, we propose IAT-test and IAT-train scores to fit our task. In our metrics, binary classification on data pairs is adopted in the classification network instead of explicit multi-category classification on individual instances.

3   Proposed Method

Our method consists of two parts: a core Paired-Embedding (PE) method for effective and reliable data augmentation, and an Act2Act network following the former. We illustrate the two parts separately in the following.

3.1   Paired-Embedding Data Augmentation

Here we propose a Paired-Embedding (PE) method, which aims to cluster individual action instances in a low-dimension embedding space by utilizing paired relationships between them.

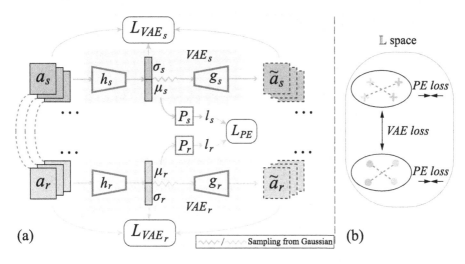

Fig. 2. (a) The structure of Paired Variational Auto-Encoders (PVAEs) and losses for training. (b) Effects of different losses.

Paired Variational Auto-Encoders (PVAEs). PE is based on a Paired Variational Auto-Encoders (PVAEs) consisting of two separate Variational Auto-Encoder (VAE) [7] networks VAE_s and VAE_r with the same architecture, as shown in Fig. 2(a). Following [7], a VAE network is composed of an encoder h and a decoder g. The encoder projects each sample a into (μ, σ), which are parameters of a multivariate Gaussian distribution $N(\mu, \sigma^2 I)$. Then a latent variable is sampled from this distribution to generate $\tilde{a}$ through the decoder. Reconstruction error from $\tilde{a}$ to a and a prior regularization term constitutes VAE loss, i.e.,

$$L_{VAE}(a, \tilde{a}, \mu, \sigma) = ||a - \tilde{a}||^2 + \lambda_{KL} D_{KL}(N(\mu, \sigma^2 I)||N(0, I)) \qquad (1)$$

where D_{KL} is the Kullback-Leibler divergence, with λ_{KL} controlling its relative importance.

We extract individual action instances from original action pairs. The two networks can be respectively trained under VAE loss to model the distribution of stimulative/responsive actions.

Paired-Embedding (PE) Loss. Given an action set, the encoder of VAE projects each action into a μ as the mean of a Gaussian distribution. We collect Gaussian means from all the actions and compute a matrix P for linear dimension reduction, using Principal Component Analysis (PCA) on them. These Gaussian means are further projected by P into an extremely low-dimension embedding space $\mathbb{L}$, namely as $l = P\mu$. Owing to PCA, the variance of Gaussian means is well maintained in the $\mathbb{L}$ space. Both stimulative and responsive actions are projected into the embedding space in this way. For two actions paired in the

---

Algorithm 1. Training of PVAEs

Input: A $= \{\dots, (a_s, a_r), \dots\}$
Output: h_s, g_s, h_r, g_r
1: Initialize h_s, g_s, h_r, g_r
2: **for** *epoch* in $[1, Epochs]$ **do**
3:     # First step under VAE loss
4:     $L_{VAE_s} = 0$, $L_{VAE_r} = 0$
5:     **for** (a_s, a_r) in **A do**
6:         $(\mu_s, \sigma_s) = h_s(a_s)$, $(\mu_r, \sigma_r) = h_r(a_r)$
7:         Sample $z_s \sim N(\mu_s, \sigma_s{}^2 I)$, Sample $z_r \sim N(\mu_r, \sigma_r{}^2 I)$
8:         $\tilde{a}_s = g_s(z_s)$, $\tilde{a}_r = g_r(z_r)$
9:         L_{VAE_s} += $L_{VAE}(a_s, \tilde{a}_s, \mu_s, \sigma_s)$, L_{VAE_r} += $L_{VAE}(a_r, \tilde{a}_r, \mu_r, \sigma_r)$
10:     **end for**
11:     Back-prop L_{VAE_s}, update h_s, g_s; Back-prop L_{VAE_r}, update h_r, g_r
12:     # Second step under PE loss
13:     $\mathbf{M}_s = \{\}$, $\mathbf{M}_r = \{\}$, $\mathbf{M} = \{\}$, $L_P = 0$
14:     **for** (a_s, a_r) in **A do**
15:         $(\mu_s, \sigma_s) = h_s(a_s)$, $(\mu_r, \sigma_r) = h_r(a_r)$
16:         $\mathbf{M}_s.\text{append}(\mu_s)$, $\mathbf{M}_r.\text{append}(\mu_r)$, $\mathbf{M}.\text{append}((\mu_s, \mu_r))$
17:     **end for**
18:     $P_s = \text{PCA}(\mathbf{M}_s)$, $P_r = \text{PCA}(\mathbf{M}_r)$
19:     **for** (μ_s, μ_r) in **M do**
20:         $l_s = P_s \mu_s$, $l_r = P_r \mu_r$
21:         L_P += $L_{PE}(l_s, l_r)$
22:     **end for**
23:     Back-prop L_P, update h_s, h_r
24: **end for**

---

original dataset **A**, we push them towards each other in the embedding space using a Paired-Embedding (PE) loss, i.e.,

$$L_{PE}(l_s, l_r) = ||l_s - l_r||^2, \tag{2}$$

where l_s and l_r are embeddings of an interactive pair of actions in the $\mathbb{L}$ space. Figure 2(a) illustrates such a process.

Training PVAEs. We train VAE_s and VAE_r synchronously and divide each epoch into two steps, as in Algorithm 1. During the first step, the two networks are independently optimized towards minimizing respective VAE loss. In the second step, PE loss serves to guide encoders in two networks.

Such an alternating strategy drives PVAEs from two opposite directions, as Fig. 2(b) shows.

- On the one hand, Gaussian means should scatter for the reconstruction of different action instances. In other words, Gaussian means must maintain a sufficiently large variance, which is transfered almost losslessly to $\mathbb{L}$ space by PCA. Consequently, the first learning step under VAE loss requires a large variance among $\mathbb{L}$ embeddings of stimulative/responsive actions respectively.

– On the other hand, each defined interaction rule is shared among several
action pairs. For these action pairs, semantic category information is unified
while other patterns in action instances are diverse. Since $\mathbb{L}$ space has an
extremely low dimension, embeddings of paired actions can not be close for
all pairs if the space mostly represents patterns apart from semantics. In other
words, PE loss pushes the space towards representing semantic categories of
actions only. Thus, stimulative or responsive actions within the same semantic
category are pulled together in $\mathbb{L}$ space, guided by PE loss.

As a result, actions with similar semantics tend to cluster in the embedding
space. Meanwhile, different clusters are far away from each other to maintain
large variance. Experimental results in Sect. 4.4 further verify this effect.

Data Augmentation with PVAEs. Given a set of individual action instances
(either stimulative or responsive) and the corresponding VAE network from
trained PVAEs, an $N \times N$ matrix C is computed as,

$$C(i,j) = exp(-\frac{||l^{(i)} - l^{(j)}||^2}{2||s \cdot (P\sigma^{(i)})||^2}), \tag{3}$$

where N is the number of action instances, with i and j indexing two samples. A
pre-set scale factor s controls the neighborhood range. After that, we normalize
the sum of each row in C to 1, i.e.,

$$NC(i,j) = \frac{C(i,j)}{\sum_{k=1}^{N} C(i,k)}. \tag{4}$$

The computed NC matrix represents confidence in replacing one action with
another under defined interaction rules. An action is believed to express semantics similar to other actions in its neighborhood, owing to clustering effects in
$\mathbb{L}$ space. We respectively compute two NC matrices for stimulative and responsive action instances and use them to augment action pairs. Two actions from
each action pair in the original dataset are replaced with other samples in their
respective neighborhood, according to NC matrices. Assume that N data pairs
in the original set are evenly distributed in K semantic categories. With replace-
ment, we can optimally attain $\frac{N}{K} \times \frac{N}{K} \times K = \frac{N^2}{K}$ various data pairs conforming
to defined interaction rules. Such an increase in data diversity will significantly
boost the learning effects of IAT task.

3.2 Act2Act: Encoder-Deoder Network Under Conditional GAN

IAT is similar to paired image translation in the task form and goals. Both of
them can be regarded as an instance-conditional generation task. They differ in
that image translation conditions on the structured content of input instance,
while our task implicitly conditions on the higher-level semantics of input
instance. In recent years, GAN-based methods have been successful in image

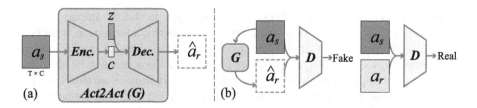

Fig. 3. (a) The Act2Act network and (b) training under conditional GAN.

translation, generating photorealistic results. A similar GAN-based scheme is applied to our task.

Our Act2Act network is stacked with an encoder-decoder architecture, as in Fig. 3(a). It receives a stimulative action a_s as input, and gives an output $\hat{a}_r$ with the same form. Through the encoder, a low-dimension code c is extracted from a_s. A random noise vector z is sampled from zero-mean Gaussian distribution with unit variance, and then combined with c to decode $\hat{a}_r$.

Conditional GAN is applied for training, as Fig. 3(b) shows. The encoder-decoder network is treated as Generator G, with another Discriminator D receives a combination of two action sequences and outputs a score. Given paired training data (a_s, a_r), G is trained to produce $\hat{a}_r$ indistinguishable from a_r. Meanwhile, D is trained to differentiate $(a_s, \hat{a}_r)$ from (a_s, a_r) as well as possible.

Behind the above design lies our understanding of IAT task. We consider the task as an implicit series connection of recognition and category-conditional generation. Therefore, we do not introduce z until input is extracted into c, unlike in [9,10] for image translation. The code c has a very low dimension since we expect it to encode high-level semantics. Correlation between a_s and a_r exists only in semantics, but not low-level appearance. Thus the encoder-decoder network is supervised by conditional GAN only, without reconstruction error from $\hat{a}_r$ to a_r.

4   Experiments

4.1   IAT-Test and IAT-Train

Inspired by [13], we propose IAT-test and IAT-train scores to evaluate methods on our task, as illustrated in Fig. 4. Besides the training set **A** for the task, another set **B** composed of individual actions is introduced. Categories of actions in set **B** are annotated. Based on annotations, we can pair actions in **B** and assign pairs to $\mathbf{B}_{pos}$ or $\mathbf{B}_{neg}$. The former contains action pairs under the same interaction rules as A, while the latter contains the rest, as Fig. 4(a1) shows. Given a model G trained on set **A**, we select stimulative actions from **B** and generate responses for them, resulting in paired action set $\mathbf{B}_g$. Figure 4(a2) illustrates such a process. We evaluate the model G according to $\mathbf{B}_g$ samples in the following ways.

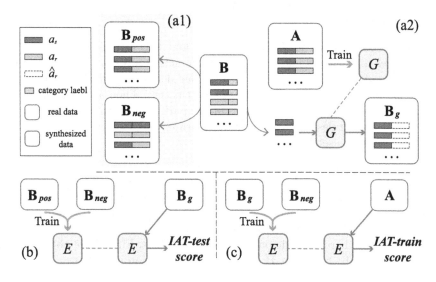

Fig. 4. Illustration of our proposed evaluation metrics.

IAT-Test. With positive samples from $\mathbf{B}_{pos}$ and negative samples from $\mathbf{B}_{neg}$, we train a binary classifier E to judge whether an action pair accords to the defined interaction rules and give a 1/0 score accordingly. K-fold cross-validation is adopted to investigate and ensure the generalization performance of E.

IAT-test is the test score of model E on set $\mathbf{B}_g$, as shown in Fig. 4(b). If $\mathbf{B}_g$ is provided by a perfect model G, IAT-test score should approximate the K-fold validation accuracy of model E during training. Otherwise, a lower score can be attributed to: 1) Generated responses are not realistic enough; 2) Semantic translation relationships captured by G are not precise, especially when generalized to stimulative actions in set $\mathbf{B}$. In other words, IAT-test quantifies how well the generation goals of reality and precision are achieved.

IAT-Train. Here a classifier E similar to the above is trained, with positive samples from $\mathbf{B}_g$ and negative samples from $\mathbf{B}_{neg}$.

IAT-train is the test score of model E on set $\mathbf{A}$, as shown in Fig. 4(c). A low score can appear due to: 1) From unrealistic generation results, E learns features useless for classifying real samples; 2) Incorrect interaction relationships in $\mathbf{B}_g$ misleads the model E. 3) Lack of diversity in $\mathbf{B}_g$ impairs the generalization performance of E. Overall, IAT-train reflects the achievement of all three goals.

Combining the two metrics helps separate diversity from the other generation goals. In other words, when the model G receives a high IAT-test score and a low IAT-train score, the latter can be reasonably attributed to a poor generation diversity.

4.2   Dataset

We evaluate our method on UTD-MHAD [20] and AID [21] datasets, both composed of skeleton-based single-person daily interactive actions. For each dataset, action categories are firstly paired to form our defined interaction rules, such as "tennis serve - tennis swing", "throw - catch", etc. Then action clips in the dataset are divided into two parts: clips in one part are randomly paired according to interaction rules to form set **A** for learning our task; clips in the other part are reserved as set **B** for evaluation.

UTD-MHAD. consists of 861 action clips from 27 categories performed by 8 subjects. Each frame describes a 3D human pose with 20 joints of the whole body. We select 10 of 27 action categories and pair them into 5 meaningful interaction rules. Moreover, we choose to use 9 joints of the upper body only since other joints hardly participate in selected actions. Finally, we obtain a set **A** of 80 action pairs and a set **B** of 160 individual action instances.

AID. consists of 102 long sequences, each containing several short action clips. Each frame describes a 3D human pose with 10 joints of the upper body. After removing 5 corrupted sequences, we have 97 sequences left, performed by 19 subjects and covering 10 action categories. Subsequently, 5 interaction rules are defined on the 10 categories. Finally, we obtain a set **A** of 282 action pairs and a set **B** of 407 individual action instances.

Implementation Details. Similar to [22], action data are represented as normalized limb vectors instead of original joint coordinates. This setting brings two benefits. On the one hand, it eliminates the variance of body sizes of subjects in datasets. On the other hand, it ensures that the lengths of human limbs in each generated sequence are consistent.

Action instances (whether at input or output) in our method are $T \times C$ skeleton action sequences. T indicates the temporal length (unified to 32 frames long on both two datasets) and C is the dimension of a 3D human pose in one frame (normally $C = number\ of\ limbs \times 3$). 1D convolutions are performed in our various networks. All GAN-based models in the following experiments are trained under WGAN-GP [23].

4.3   Comparison with GAN-Based Data Augmentation

As discussed in Sect. 1 and 2.1, GAN-based augmentation methods for classification and other specified tasks can not be applied to our task. Therefore, training an unconditional GAN for directly generating action pairs is left as the only choice for GAN-based data augmentation. We select CSGN [19], which is promising to generate high-quality human action sequences unconditionally. A comparison of data augmentation effects between our PE method and this method is shown in Table 1.

Table 1. Quantitative comparison of data augmentation effects between CSGN and PE.

Data augmentation	UTD-MHAD		AID	
	IAT-test	IAT-train	IAT-test	IAT-train
−	85.32	53.92	87.29	51.17
CSGN [19]	87.86	58.97	89.96	68.82
PE (Ours)	**91.03**	**64.94**	**90.69**	**75.65**

Learning without augmentation gives generation results that are acceptable from reality and precision (a 85.32/87.29 IAT-test score), but extremely disappointing in diversity (a 53.92/51.17 IAT-train score). For augmentation, a CSGN network is first trained to model the distribution of paired action data. Then we mix generated action pairs with existing data to train our Act2Act network. This method benefits the learning of the task followed, especially visible from a significant increase in IAT-train score. However, it still lags behind our method 3.17/0.73 and 5.97/6.83 respectively in two metrics. We examine generated actions from CSGN and find them to be realistic but not diverse enough, thus provide limited modes for augmentation. Such results keep in line with the fact that GAN-based methods need large-scale training data to ensure multimodal generation quality. As a comparison, our PE method is more friendly to this small-scale data. Considerable improvements in diversity of generated action responses reflect similar improvements brought by PE in diversity of paired training data.

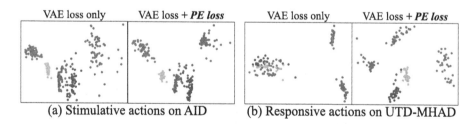

(a) Stimulative actions on AID   (b) Responsive actions on UTD-MHAD

Fig. 5. Action embeddings projected by PVAEs trained with VAE loss only and with PE loss also.

4.4 Ablation Study

Embedding Space. Figure 5 visualizes the distribution of actions in the embedding space, projected by PVAEs trained with/without PE loss. Groundtruth category labels are utilized to color data points for comparison. As can be seen, additional PE loss brings much better clustering effects in both gatherings within categories (especially in Fig. 5(a)) and distances between categories (in Fig. 5(b)).

We analyze two critical hyper-parameters affecting PE data augmentation: the scale factor s and the dimension of $\mathbb{L}$ embedding space $d_{\mathbb{L}}$. Augmentation effects reflected in NC matrices are evaluated from effectiveness F and reliability R. Specifically, F is represented as the probability that each sample is replaced by others to form new pairs, i.e.,

$$F = \frac{1}{N} \sum_{i=1}^{N} \sum_{j=1}^{N} 1(i \neq j) \cdot NC(i,j). \tag{5}$$

Meanwhile, we import groundtruth category labels to calculate the probability of category unchanged after replacement as R, i.e.,

$$R = \frac{1}{N} \sum_{i=1}^{N} \sum_{j=1}^{N} 1(cat^{(i)} = cat^{(j)}) \cdot NC(i,j), \tag{6}$$

where cat is the category of action.

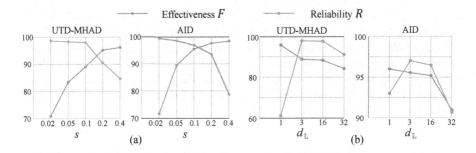

Fig. 6. Data augmentation effects with different (a) scale factors and (b) dimensions of $\mathbb{L}$ space.

As the neighborhood range controlled by s expands, the effectiveness of PE data augmentation increases while the reliability decreases. Figure 6(a) suggests $s = 0.1$ to be the equilibrium point of F and R on both two datasets. Changes brought by different $d_{\mathbb{L}}$ are more complicated. As Fig. 6(b) shows, when $\mathbb{L}$ is a 1-d space, learning PVAEs to cluster actions in it can be difficult. The low reliability reflects relatively weak clustering effects at this time. Then the subtle difference between 3-d and 16-d suggests a very flexible selection range for a reasonable embedding space dimension. When the dimension further increases, augmentation effects start to corrupt, mostly due to the imbalance between PE loss and VAE loss during training PVAEs.

Comparison with Label-Given Methods. Here experiments are conducted in label-given situations to give an upper bound of performance of our method:

1) **Re-assign:** Actions are re-assigned into new pairs according to groundtruth labels. All paired relationships conforming to defined interaction rules are exhausted for the training of Act2Act.

2) **Split:** The network is explicitly split into two parts: a classification part for stimulative actions and a category-conditional generation part for responsive actions. The two parts are independently trained with category labels given and connected in series during inference.

Table 2. Quantitative comparison of generation effects between our proposed method and methods in label-given situations.

Data	Label-given	UTD-MHAD		AID	
		IAT-test	IAT-train	IAT-test	IAT-train
Original	×	85.32	53.92	87.29	51.17
PE aug.	×	91.03	64.94	90.69	75.65
Re-assign	✓	90.97	68.93	93.05	82.15
Split	✓	91.35	71.64	95.04	85.89

As Table 2 shows, methods augmented by PE is very close to label-given methods in performance, compared to the original baseline. With category labels given, we can attain more satisfactory generation results.

4.5   Qualitative Evaluation

Generated responses conditioned on some stimulative actions are shown in Fig. 7. Three samples for random noise vector z in Act2Act are involved in each generation. It is surprising that given the same stimulative action, generated responses from our method are various due to randomness from z. Such variety of actions manifests in several aspects like pose, movement speed and range. In contrast, generation results from the baseline lack such diversity. Take the "knock - push" interaction for instance. Our generated actions tend to "push" towards various directions, while actions from the baseline seem to place hands always at the same height.

Besides, all generated responses from our method belong to respective categories expected by interaction rules. This indicates that within our method, latent code c in Act2Act precisely controls semantic translation. In addition, human-like vividity shown in these generated actions is impressive. Overall, qualitative evaluation further verifies the effectiveness of our method in meeting all three generation goals. There is still distortion in some instances, like the final generated response in "basketball shoot - baseball swing" interaction. We attribute it to the tiny scale of data in UTD-MHAD and the complexity of "baseball swing" action (in such action, hands may overlap each other).

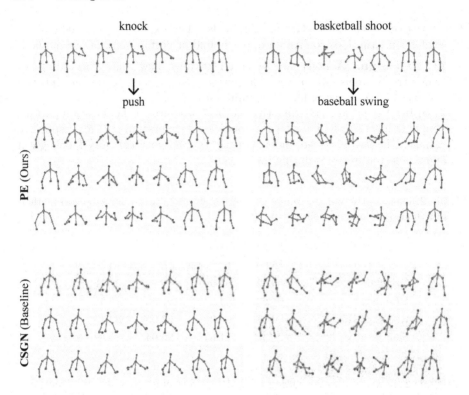

Fig. 7. Examples of generation on UTD-MHAD from our PE method and baseline augmented by CSGN [19]. For each example, the given stimulative action and generated responses corresponding to three random noise vectors are shown. Visualized actions are meanly sampled from 32-frame sequences.

5   Conclusion

In this paper, we specify a novel task to learn end-to-end action interaction and propose a PE data augmentation method to enable learning with small-scale unlabeled data. Another Act2Act network learns from augmented data. Two new metrics are also specially designed to evaluate methods on our task from generation goals of reality, precision and diversity. Our PE method manages to augment paired action data significantly and reliably. Experimental results show its superiority to baseline and other GAN-based augmentation methods, approximating the performance of label-given methods. Given impressively high-quality action responses generated, our work shows broad application prospects in action interaction. We also hope our PE method to enlighten other unsupervised learning tasks with weak information like paired relationships in our task.

Acknowledgement. This work was supported by the National Key R&D Program of China (2016YFB 1001001), the National Natural Science Foundation of China (61976170, 91648121, 61573280), and Tencent Robotics X Lab Rhino-Bird Joint Research Program (201902, 201903).

References

1. Bartneck, C., Belpaeme, T., Eyssel, F., Kanda, T., Keijsers, M., Šabanović, S.: Human-Robot Interaction: An Introduction. Cambridge University Press, Cambridge (2020)
2. Ji, Y., Yang, Y., Shen, F., Shena, H., Li, X.: A survey of human action analysis in HRI applications. IEEE Trans. Circuits Syst. Video Technol. **30**, 2114–2128 (2019)
3. Goodfellow, I.J., et al.: Generative adversarial networks. CoRR abs/1406.2661 (2014)
4. Odena, A., Olah, C., Shlens, J.: Conditional image synthesis with auxiliary classifier GANs. In: ICML (2017)
5. Antoniou, A., Storkey, A.J., Edwards, H.: Data augmentation generative adversarial networks. CoRR abs/1711.04340 (2017)
6. Mariani, G., Scheidegger, F., Istrate, R., Bekas, C., Malossi, A.C.I.: BAGAN: data augmentation with balancing GAN. CoRR abs/1803.09655 (2018)
7. Kingma, D.P., Welling, M.: Auto-encoding variational Bayes. In: ICLR (2014)
8. Mirza, M., Osindero, S.: Conditional generative adversarial nets. CoRR abs/1411.1784 (2014)
9. Isola, P., Zhu, J., Zhou, T., Efros, A.A.: Image-to-image translation with conditional adversarial networks. In: CVPR (2017)
10. Zhu, J., et al.: Toward multimodal image-to-image translation. In: NIPS (2017)
11. Zhang, R., Isola, P., Efros, A.A.: Colorful image colorization. In: Leibe, B., Matas, J., Sebe, N., Welling, M. (eds.) ECCV 2016. LNCS, vol. 9907, pp. 649–666. Springer, Cham (2016). https://doi.org/10.1007/978-3-319-46487-9_40
12. Zhang, R., Isola, P., Efros, A.A., Shechtman, E., Wang, O.: The unreasonable effectiveness of deep features as a perceptual metric. In: CVPR (2018)
13. Shmelkov, K., Schmid, C., Alahari, K.: How good is my GAN? In: Ferrari, V., Hebert, M., Sminchisescu, C., Weiss, Y. (eds.) ECCV 2018. LNCS, vol. 11206, pp. 218–234. Springer, Cham (2018). https://doi.org/10.1007/978-3-030-01216-8_14
14. Zhu, X., Liu, Y., Li, J., Wan, T., Qin, Z.: Emotion classification with data augmentation using generative adversarial networks. In: Phung, D., Tseng, V.S., Webb, G.I., Ho, B., Ganji, M., Rashidi, L. (eds.) PAKDD 2018. LNCS (LNAI), vol. 10939, pp. 349–360. Springer, Cham (2018). https://doi.org/10.1007/978-3-319-93040-4_28
15. Zheng, Z., Zheng, L., Yang, Y.: Unlabeled samples generated by GAN improve the person re-identification baseline in vitro. In: ICCV (2017)
16. Zheng, Z., Yang, X., Yu, Z., Zheng, L., Yang, Y., Kautz, J.: Joint discriminative and generative learning for person re-identification. In: CVPR (2019)
17. Salimans, T., Goodfellow, I.J., Zaremba, W., Cheung, V., Radford, A., Chen, X.: Improved techniques for training GANs. In: NIPS (2016)
18. Heusel, M., Ramsauer, H., Unterthiner, T., Nessler, B., Hochreiter, S.: GANs trained by a two time-scale update rule converge to a local nash equilibrium. In: NIPS (2017)
19. Yan, S., Li, Z., Xiong, Y., Yan, H., Lin, D.: Convolutional sequence generation for skeleton-based action synthesis. In: ICCV (2019)

20. Chen, C., Jafari, R., Kehtarnavaz, N.: UTD-MHAD: a multimodal dataset for human action recognition utilizing a depth camera and a wearable inertial sensor. In: ICIP (2015)
21. Song, Z., et al.: Attention-oriented action recognition for real-time human-robot interaction. CoRR abs/2007.01065 (2020)
22. Ahn, H., Ha, T., Choi, Y., Yoo, H., Oh, S.: Text2Action: generative adversarial synthesis from language to action. In: ICRA (2018)
23. Gulrajani, I., Ahmed, F., Arjovsky, M., Dumoulin, V., Courville, A.C.: Improved training of Wasserstein GANs. In: NIPS (2017)

Sketch-to-Art: Synthesizing Stylized Art Images from Sketches

Bingchen Liu[1,2]($\boxtimes$), Kunpeng Song[1,2], Yizhe Zhu[2], and Ahmed Elgammal[1,2]

[1] Playform - Artrendex Inc., New Brunswick, USA
{bingchen,kunpeng,elgammal}@artrendex.com
[2] Department of Computer Science, Rutgers University, New Brunswick, USA
yizhe.zhu@rutgers.edu
https://www.playform.io/

Abstract. We propose a new approach for synthesizing fully detailed art-stylized images from sketches. Given a sketch, with no semantic tagging, and a reference image of a specific style, the model can synthesize meaningful details with colors and textures. Based on the GAN framework, the model consists of three novel modules designed explicitly for better artistic style capturing and generation. To enforce the content faithfulness, we introduce the dual-masked mechanism which directly shapes the feature maps according to sketch. To capture more artistic style aspects, we design feature-map transformation for a better style consistency to the reference image. Finally, an inverse process of instance-normalization disentangles the style and content information and further improves the synthesis quality. Experiments demonstrate a significant qualitative and quantitative boost over baseline models based on previous state-of-the-art techniques, modified for the proposed task (17% better Frechet Inception distance and 18% better style classification score). Moreover, the lightweight design of the proposed modules enables the high-quality synthesis at 512×512 resolution.

1 Introduction

Synthesizing fully colored images from human-drawn sketches is an important problem, with several real-life applications. For example, colorizing sketches following a specified style can significantly reduce repetitive works in storyboarding. Fruitful results have been achieved in applying deep learning to the art literature [1–3]. Most research works have focused on synthesizing photo-realistic images [4], or cartoonish images [5] from sketches. In this paper, we focus on rendering an image in a specific given artistic style based on a human-drawn sketch as input. The proposed approach is generic, however, what distinguish art images from other types of imagery is the variety of artistic styles that would affect how a sketch should be synthesized into a fully colored and textured image.

Electronic supplementary material The online version of this chapter (https://doi.org/10.1007/978-3-030-69544-6_13) contains supplementary material, which is available to authorized users.

© Springer Nature Switzerland AG 2021
H. Ishikawa et al. (Eds.): ACCV 2020, LNCS 12627, pp. 207–222, 2021.
https://doi.org/10.1007/978-3-030-69544-6_13

Fig. 1. Synthetic images from sketches with different styles. Upper panel: our approach synthesizes from different styles (art movements). The first row shows the reference images from each style, and the second row shows the generated images. Lower panel: our model synthesizes from specific artists' styles by taking paintings from the artists as reference.

In the history of art, style can refer to an art movement (Renaissance style, Baroque style, Impressionism, etc.), or particular artist style (Cezanne style, Monet style, etc.), or a specific artwork style [6]. Style encompasses different formal elements of art, such as the color palette, the rendering of the contours (linear or painterly), the depth of the field (recessional or planer), the style of the brush strokes, the light (diffused or light-dark contrast), etc.

We propose a novel generation task: given an input sketch and a style, defined by a reference image, or an artist name, or a style category, we want to synthesize a fully colored and textured image in that style following the sketch, as shown in Fig. 1. Previous works on synthesizing from sketches do not allow users to specify a style reference [4,7]. We propose a new model to achieve this task, which takes the input sketch and sample reference image(s) from art-historical corpus, defining the desired style, to generate the results.

A sketch contains very sparse information, basically the main composition lines. The model has to guess the semantic composition of the scene and synthesize an image with semantic context implied from the training corpus. E.g., given a corpus of landscape art of different styles, the model needs to learn how different parts of the scene correlate with colors and texture given a choice of style. In the proposed approach, no semantic tagging is required for the sketches nor the style images used at both training and generation phases. The model implicitly infers the scene semantic.

The proposed approach is at the intersection between two different generation tasks: Sketch-to-image synthesis and Style transfer. Sketch-to-image synthesis focuses on rendering a colored image based on a sketch, where recent approaches focused on training deep learning models on a corpus of data, e.g., [7]. However, these approaches do not control the output based on a given style.

More importantly, in our case the reference image should only define the style not the content details. For example, the model should infer that certain plain area of the sketch is sky, trees, mountains, or grass; and infer details of these regions differently given the style image, which might not have the same semantic regions all together (see examples in Fig. 1).

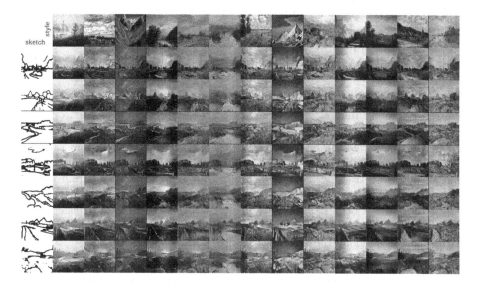

Fig. 2. Synthesized samples in 512×512 resolution. The first column are the input sketches hand-drawn by human, and the first row are the style reference images.

On the other hand, style transfer focuses on capturing the style of an (or many) image and transfer it to a content image [8]. However, we show that such models are not applicable to synthesize stylized images from sketches because of the lack of content in the sketch, i.e., the approach need to both transfer style from the reference image and infer content based on the training corpus.

The proposed model has three novel components, which constitute the technical contributions of this paper, based on a GAN [9] infrastructure:

Dual Mask Injection. A simple trainable layer that directly imposes sketch constraints on the feature maps, to increase content faithfulness.

Feature Map Transfer. An adaptive layer that applies a novel transformation on the style image's feature map, extracting only the style information without the interference of the style images' content.

Instance De-Normalization. A reverse procedure of Instance Norm [10] on the discriminator to effectively disentangle the style and content information.

2   Related Work

Image-to-Image Translation: I2I aims to learn a transformation between two different domains of images. The application scenario is broad, including object transfiguration, season transfer, and photo enhancement. With the generative power of GAN [9], fruitful advances have been achieved in the I2I area. Pix2pix [11] established a common framework to do the one-to-one mapping for paired images using conditional GAN. Then a series of unsupervised methods such as CycleGAN [12–15] were proposed when paired data is not available. Furthermore, multi-modal I2I methods are introduced to simulate the real-world many-to-many mapping between image domains such as MUNIT and Bicycle-GAN [16–21]. However, those I2I methods can not generate satisfying images from the coarse sketch's domain, nor can they adequately reproduce the styles from the reference image, as will be shown in the experiments.

Neural Style Transfer: NST transfers textures and color palette from one image to another. In [8], the problem was formulated by transforming the statistics of multi-level feature maps in CNN layers in the form of a Gram Matrix. The follow-up works of NST have multiple directions, such as accelerating the transfer speed by training feed-forward networks [22,23], and capturing multiple styles simultaneously with adaptive instance normalization [10,24]. However, little attention has been paid on optimizing towards artistic style transfer from a sketch, nor on improving the style transfer quality regarding the fine-grained artistic patterns among the various NST methods [25].

Sketch-to-Image Synthesis: Our task can be viewed from both the I2I and the NST perspectives, while it has its unique challenges. Firstly, unlike datasets such as horse-zebra or map-satellite imagery, the sketch-to-painting dataset is heavily unbalanced and one-to-many. The information in the sketch domain is ambiguous and sparse with only few lines, while in the painting's domain is rich and diverse across all artistic styles. Secondly, "style transfer" approaches focus mainly on color palettes and "oil painting like" textures but pays limited attention to other important artistic attributes such as linear vs. painterly contours, texture boldness, and brush stroke styles. Thirdly, it is much harder for NST methods to be semantically meaningful, as the optimization procedure of NST is only between few images. On the contrary, with a sketch-to-image model trained on a large corpus of images, learning semantics is made possible (the model can find the common coloring on different shapes and different locations across the images) and thus make the synthesized images semantically meaningful.

To our knowledge, there are few prior works close to our task. AutoPainter [26] propose to do sketch-to-image synthesis using conditional GANs, but their model is designed towards cartoon images. ScribblerGAN [7] achieves user-guided sketch colorization but requires the user to provide localized color scribbles. SketchyGAN [4] is the state-of-the-art approach for multi-modal sketch-to-image synthesis, focusing on photo-realistic rendering of images conditioned on object categories. Furthermore, [5,27,28] accomplish the conditioned colorization with a reference image, but they only optimize towards datasets that lack style and content variances. None of those works is specifically geared towards artistic images with the concern of capturing the significant style variances. In contrast, Fig. 1 and Fig. 2 demonstrate the ability of our model to capture the essential style patterns and generate diversely styled images.

3   Methods

In this section, we provide an overview of our model and introduce the detailed training schema. Then three dedicated components will be described.

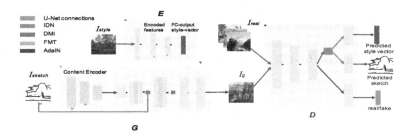

Fig. 3. Overview of the model structure. G adopts a U-Net structure [29]. It takes the features of the reference image I_{style} from E, runs style-conditioned image synthesis on the input sketch image I_{sketch}, and outputs I_g. D takes as input an image (alternatively sampled from real and generated images) and gives three outputs: a predicted style vector, a predicted sketch, and a real/fake signal of the image

As shown in Fig. 3, our model consists of three parts: a generator G, a discriminator D, and a separately pre-trained feature-extractor E. Either an unsupervised Auto-Encoder or a supervised DNN classifier, such as VGG [30] can work as the feature-extractor. During the training of G and D, E is fixed and provides multi-level feature-maps and a style vector of the reference image I_{style}. The feature-maps serve as inputs for G, and the style vector serves as the ground truth for D. We train G and D under the Pix2pix [11] schema. In the synthesis phase, the input style is not limited to one reference image. We can always let E extract style features from multiple images and combine them in various ways (averaging or weighted averaging) before feeding them to G. Apart from the following three modules, our model also includes a newly designed attentional residual block and a patch-level image gradient matching loss, please refer to the appendix for more details.

3.1   Reinforcing Content: Dual Mask Injection

In our case, the content comes in the form of a sketch, which only provides sparse compositional constraints. It is not desirable to transfer composition elements from the style image or training corpus into empty areas of the sketch that should imply textured areas. Typically when training a generator to provide images with diverse style patterns, the model tends to lose faithfulness to the content, which results in missing or excrescent shapes, objects, and ambiguous contours (especially common in NST methods). To strengthen the content faithfulness, we introduce Dual-Mask Injection layer (DMI), which directly imposes the sketch information on the intermediate feature-maps during the forward-pass in G.

Given the features of a style image, in the form of the conv-layer activation $f \in \mathbb{R}^{C \times H \times W}$, we down sample the binary input sketch to the same size of f and use it as a feature mask, denoted as $M_s \in [0,1]^{H \times W}$. The proposed DMI layer will first filter out a *contour-area feature* f_c and a *plain-area feature* f_p by:

$$f_c = M_s \times f, \quad f_p = (1 - M_s) \times f, \tag{1}$$

where $\times$ is element-wise product. For f_c and f_p, the DMI layer has two sets of trainable weights and biases, $w_c, b_c, w_p, b_p \in \mathbb{R}^{C \times 1 \times 1}$, that serve for a **value relocation** purpose, to differentiate the features around edge and plain area:

$$f'_c = w_c \times f_c + b_c, \quad f'_p = w_p \times f_p + b_p \tag{2}$$

Finally, the output feature maps of DMI will be $f' = f'_c + f'_p$.

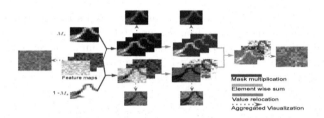

Fig. 4. Forward flow of Dual-Mask Injection layer, we aggregate the first three channels in feature-map as an RGB image for visualization purpose

A real-time forward flow of the DMI layer is shown in Fig. 4. Notice that, when $w = 1$ and $b = 0$, the output feature will be the same as the input, and we set the weights and bias along the channel dimension so that the model can learn to impose the sketch on the feature-maps at different degrees on different channels. By imposing the sketch directly to the feature-maps, DMI layer ensures that the generated images have correct and clear contours and compositions. While DMI serves the same purpose as the masked residual layer (MRU) in SketchyGAN [4], it comes with almost zero extra computing cost, where MRU requires three more convolution layers per unit. In our experiments, our model is two times faster in training compared with SketchyGAN, while yields better results on art dataset. Moreover, the lightweight property of DMI enables our model to achieve great performance on 512×512 resolution, while SketchyGAN was studied only on 128×128 resolution.

3.2 Disentangling Style and Content by Instance De-normalization

To better guide G, D is trained to adequately predict an style latent representation of the input image as well as the content sketch that should match with the input image. Ideally, a well-disentangled discriminator can learn a style representation without the interference of the content information, and retrieve the content sketch regardless of the styles.

Several works have been done in specifically disentangling style and content [31,32], but they only work around the generator side, using AdaIN or Gram-matrix to separate the factors. To train D to effectively disentangle, we propose the Instance De-Normalization (IDN) layer. IDN takes the feature-map of an image as input, then reverses the process of Instance-Normalization [10,24] to produces a style vector and a content feature map. In the training phrase of our model, IDN helps D learn to predict accurate style-vectors and contents of the ground truth images, therefore, helps G to synthesis better.

In AdaIN or IN, a stylized feature-map is calculated by:

$$f_{styled} = \sigma_{style} \times \frac{(f - \mu(f))}{\sigma(f)} + \mu_{style}, \tag{3}$$

where $\sigma(\cdot)$ and $\mu(\cdot)$ calculate the variance and mean of the feature map f respectively. It assumes that while the original feature map $f \in \mathbb{R}^{C \times H \times W}$ contains the content information, some external μ_{style} and σ_{style} can be collaborated with f to produce a stylized feature map. The resulted feature map possesses the style information while also preserves the original content information.

Here, we reverse the process for a stylized feature map f'_{style} by: first predict μ_{style} and σ_{style}, $(\mu_{style}, \sigma_{style}) \in \mathbb{R}^{C \times 1 \times 1}$ from f'_{style}, then separate them out from f'_{style} to get $f_{content}$ which carries the style-invariant content information. Formally, the IDN process is:

$$\mu'_{style} = Conv(f'_{style}), \quad \sigma'_{style} = \sigma(f'_{style} - \mu'_{style}), \tag{4}$$

$$f_{content} = \frac{(f'_{style} - \mu'_{style})}{\sigma'_{style}}, \tag{5}$$

where $Conv(\cdot)$ is 2 conv layers. Note that unlike in AdaIN where μ_{style} can be directly computed from the known style feature f_{style}, in IDN the ground truth style feature is unknown (we don't have f_{style}), thus we should not naively compute the mean of f'_{style}. Therefore, we use conv layers to actively predict the style information, and will reshape the output into a vector as μ'_{style}. Finally, we concatenate μ'_{style} and σ'_{style} to predict the style-vector with MLP, and use conv layers on $f_{content}$ to predict the sketch. The whole IDN process can be trained end-to-end with the target style-vector and target-sketch. Unlike other disentangling methods, we separate the style and content from a structural perspective that is straightforward while maintaining effectiveness.

3.3   Reinforcing Style: Feature Map Transformation

To approach the conditional image generation task, previous methods such as MUNIT [16] and BicycleGAN [17] use a low-dimensional latent vector of I_{style} extracted from some feature extractors E as the conditioning factor. However, we argue that such vector representation carries limited information in terms of style details. Therefore, it is more effective to directly use feature-maps as a conditional factor and information supplier.

214   B. Liu et al.

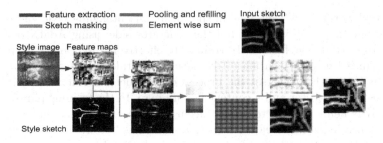

Fig. 5. Process flow of feature-map transformation

Nevertheless, the image feature-maps in CNN usually carry both the style information and strong content information. Such content information can be problematic and is undesired. For instance, if the style image is a house while the input sketch implies a lake, we do not want any shape or illusion of a house within the lake region in the synthesized image. To get rid of the content information, while keeping the richness of the style features, we propose the Feature Map Transformation (FMT). FMT takes the input sketch I_{sketch}, the sketch of the style image $I_{style-sketch}$, and the feature map of the style image f_{style} as inputs, and produces transformed feature-maps f_t. f_t only preserves the desired style features of the style image and discards its content structure. Note that $I_{style-sketch}$ is extracted using simple edge detection methods and f_{style} comes from the feature-extractor E, that are both easy to achieve.

The proposed FMT is a fixed formula without parameter-training. The procedure is illustrated in Fig. 5 with five steps. In step 1, we use $I_{style-sketch}$ as a mask to filter f_{style} and get two sets of features, i.e., f_{style}^c that only have the features around the contours and f_{style}^p with features on plain areas. In step 2, we apply a series of max-pooling and average-pooling to this filtered yet sparse feature values to extract a 4×4 feature-map for each part, namely $f_{style}^{c'}$ and $f_{style}^{p'}$. In step 3, we repeatedly fill the 4×4 $f_{style}^{c'}$ and $f_{style}^{p'}$ into a f_t^c and a f_t^p with the same size of f_{style}. In step 4, we use I_{sketch} as a mask in the same manner to filter these two feature maps, and get $f_t^{c'}$ and $f_t^{p'}$ that have the features of I_{style} but in the shape of I_{sketch}. Finally in step 5, we add the results to get $f_t = f_t^{c'} + f_t^{p'}$ as the output of the FMT layer. We then concatenate f_t to its corresponding feature-maps in G for the synthesis process.

The pooling operation collects the most distinguishable feature values along spatial channel in f_{style}, then the repeat-filling operation expands the collected global statistics, finally the masking operation makes sure the transformed feature-map will not introduce any undesired content information of the style image. FMT provides accurate guidance to the generation of fine-grained style patterns in a straightforward manner, and unlike AdaIN [24] and Gram-matrix [8] which require higher-order statistics. In practice, we apply FMT from the 16×16 to 64×64 feature maps. FMT contains two max-pooling layers and one avg-pooling layer. These layers have 5×5 kernel and stride of 3, which give us a reasonable receptive field to get the highlighted style features. We first use max-pooling to get the most outstanding feature values as the style information, then use the average-pooling to summarize the values into a "mean feature" along the spatial dimensions. The average-pooling can help smooth out some local bias (peak values) and get a more generalized style representation.

3.4   Objective Functions

Besides the original GAN loss, auxiliary losses are adopted in our model. Specifically, when the input is a real image, we train D with a *style loss* and a *content loss*, which minimize the *MSE* of the predicted style vector and sketch with the ground-truth ones respectively. Meanwhile, G aims to deceive D to predict the same style vector as the one extracted from I_{style} and output the same sketch as I_{sketch}. These auxiliary losses strengthen D's ability to understand the input images and let G generate more accurate style patterns while ensuring the content faithfulness. During training, we have two types of input for the model, one is the paired data, where the I_{sketch} and I_{style} are from the same image, and the other is randomly matched data, where I_{sketch} and I_{style} are not paired. We also have a reconstruction *MSE* loss on the paired data.

Formally, D gives three outputs: $S(I)$, $C(I)$, $P(I)$, where $S(I)$ is the predicted style vector of an image I, $C(I)$ is the predicted sketch, and $P(I)$ is the probability of I being a real image. Thus, the loss functions for D and G are:

$$
\begin{aligned}
\mathcal{L}(D) = & \mathbb{E}[\log(P(I_{real}))] + \mathbb{E}[\log(1 - P(G(I_{sketch}, I_{style})))] \\
& + MSE(S(I_{real}), E(I_{real})) + MSE(C(I_{real}), I_{real-sketch}), \qquad (6) \\
\mathcal{L}(G) = & \mathbb{E}[\log(P(G(I_{sketch}, I_{style})))] + MSE(C(G(I_{sketch}, I_{style})), I_{sketch}) \\
& + MSE(S(G(I_{sketch}, I_{style})), E(I_{style})). \qquad (7)
\end{aligned}
$$

and the extra loss for G: $MSE(G(I_{sketch}, I_{style}), I_{style})$ is applied when the inputs are paired. I_{real} is randomly sampled real data and $I_{real-sketch}$ is its corresponding sketch, and I_{sketch} and I_{style} are randomly sampled sketches and referential style images as the input for G.

4   Experiments

We first show comparisons between our model and baseline methods, and then present the ablation studies. The code to reproduce all the experiments with detailed training configurations are included in the supplementary materials, along with a video demonstrating our model in real time. A website powered by the proposed model is available online at: https://www.playform.io, where people can synthesize 512×512 images with their free-hand drawn sketches.

Dataset: Our dataset is collected from Wikiart [33] and consists of 10k images with 55 artistic styles (e.g., impressionism, realism, etc.). We follow the sketch creation method described by [4] to get the paired sketch for each painting.

We split the images into training and testing set with a ratio of 9:1. All the comparisons shown in this section were conducted on the testing set, where both the sketches and the art images were unseen to the models.

Metrics: We use **FID** [34] and a **classification accuracy** for the quantitative comparisons. FID is a popular image generation metric that provides a perceptual similarity between two sets of images. For our task, we generate I_g from all the testing sketches using the same I_{style}, and compute the FID between I_g and the images from the same style. We repeat this process for all style images. We further employ a more direct metric to compute the style classification accuracy of I_g, which leverages a VGG model pre-trained on ImageNet [35] and fine-tuned on art for style classification. Such model is more invariant to compositions, and focuses more on the artistic style patterns. We record how many of I_g are classified correctly as the style of I_{style}, which reflects how well the generator captures the style features and translates them into I_g. The style-classification accuracy for VGG is 95.1%, indicating a trustworthy performance.

4.1 Comparison to Baselines

MUNIT [16] (unsupervised) and BicycleGAN [17] (supervised) are the two state-of-the-art I2I models that are comparable to our model for their ability to do conditional image translation. SketchyGAN [4] is the latest model that is dedicated to the sketch-to-image task. Pix2pix [11] is the fundamental model for the I2I process. In this section, we show comparisons between our model and the aforementioned models. We also include the results from the classical NST method by [8] as a representative of that class of methods. For SketchyGAN (noted as "Pix2pix+MRU" since its main contribution is MRU) and Pix2pix, we adopt their model components but use our training schema to enable them the style-conditioned sketch-to-image synthesis.

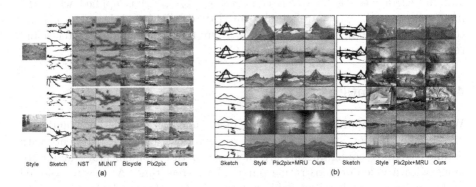

Style Sketch NST MUNIT Bicycle Pix2pix Ours   Sketch Style Pix2pix+MRU Ours   Sketch Style Pix2pix+MRU Ours
(a)   (b)

Fig. 6. Qualitative comparison to baseline models

All the tested models are trained on images with 128×128 resolution due to the compared models' capacity restrictions (our model can easily upscale to

512×512). We make sure all the compared models have a similar generative capacity by having a similar amount of weights in their respective generators. Except for Pix2pix, all the compared models have more total parameters than ours and require a longer time to train. We tested multiple hyper-parameter settings on baseline models and reported the highest figures.

Qualitative results are shown in Fig. 6. Except "Pix2pix+MRU", all the other methods can hardly handle the art dataset and do not produce meaningful results. Due to the limited information in sketches, NST and MUNIT can hardly generate meaningful images, BicycleGAN only generates images with blurry edges and fuzzy colors, and Pix2pix consistently gets undesirable artifacts. Notice that, models like MUNIT and BicycleGAN do work well on datasets with simple sketches, where the images share one standard shape (only cats, shoes) and are well registered with white background, and without any artistic features involved (semantically diversified, different color palettes and texture). In contrast, images in art dataset are much more complicated with multiple objects and different compositions, which result in bad performance for these previous models and show the effectiveness of our proposed components.

Table 1. Quantitative comparison to baseline models

	NST	MUNIT	Pix2pix	BicycleGAN	Pix2pix+MRU	Ours
FID ↓	6.85	7.43 ± 0.08	7.08 ± 0.05	6.39 ± 0.05	5.05 ± 0.13	**4.18 ± 0.11**
Classification score ↑	0.182	0.241 ± 0.012	0.485 ± 0.012	0.321 ± 0.009	0.487 ± 0.002	**0.573 ± 0.011**

The quantitative results, shown in Table 1, concur with the qualitative results. It is worth noticing that, while "Pix2pix+MRU" generates comparably visual-appealing images, our model outperforms it by a large margin especially in terms of style classification score, which indicates the superiority of our model in translating the right style cues from the style image into the generated images.

Comparison to MRU from SketchyGAN: Since SketchyGAN is not proposed for the exemplar-based s2i task, the comparison here is not with Sketchy-GAN as it is, but rather with a modified version with our training schema to suit our problem definition. While the "Pix2pix+MRU" results look good from a sketch colorization perspective, they are not satisfactory from the artistic style transfer perspective compared with the given style images (e.g., texture of flat area, linear vs painterly). As shown in Fig. 6-(b), "Pix2pix+MRU" tends to produce dull colors on all its generations, with an undesired color shift compared to the style images. In contrast, our results provide more accurate color palette and texture restoration. Apart from the quantitative result, "Pix2pix+MRU" is outperformed by our model especially in terms of the fine-grained artistic style features, such as color flatness or fuzziness and edge sharpness.

4.2   Ablation Study

We perform ablation studies to evaluate the three proposed components using a customized Pix2pix+MRU model as the baseline. More experiments can be found in the appendix, including a quantitative evaluation of the content and style disentanglement performance of our model, an effectiveness analysis of an image gradient matching loss for better texture generation, and a more detailed comparison between AdaIN and the proposed FMT for style transfer.

In this section, we show both the cumulative comparisons and individual benefits for each modules. When evaluating FMT, we replace the AdaIN layer on lower level image features with FMT, and show better performance of FMT compared to AdaIN. IDN changes the structure of the discriminator, so when validating the effectiveness of IDN, we add an extra baseline model which has a discriminator naively predicting the sketch and style-vector (noted as "with 2B") from its two separate convolution branches.

In Table 2, the proposed components are cumulatively added to the model. FID and classification scores consistently show that each of the proposed components contributes to the generation performance.

FMT and IDN bring the most significant boost in FID and Classification, respectively. It is worth noticing how the added two branches on the discriminator (with 2B) hurt the performance and how IDN reverses that drawback and further boosts the performance. We hypothesis that naively adding two branches collected conflicting information during training (content and style) and made the models harder to converge. In contrast, IDN neatly eliminates the conflict thanks to its disentangling effect, and takes advantage of both the content and style information for a better generation performance.

Table 2. Ablation study of the proposed components

	Baseline	With DMI	With FMT	With 2B	With IDN
FID ↓	4.77 ± 0.14	4.84 ± 0.09	4.43 ± 0.15	4.73 ± 0.09	**4.18**± 0.11
Classification Score ↑	0.485 ± 0.012	0.507 ± 0.007	0.512 ± 0.009	0.479 ± 0.013	**0.573** ± 0.011

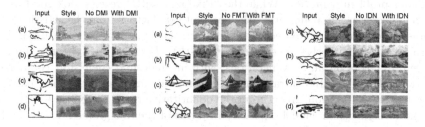

Fig. 7. Qualitative comparisons of DMI, FMT and IDN

Qualitative Comparisons: In Fig. 7, the left panel shows how DMI boosts the content faithfulness to the input sketches. In row (a), the model without DMI misses the sketch lines on the top and right portion, while DMI redeems all the lines in I_{sketch}. In row (b), I_g without DMI is affected by I_{style} which has a flat and empty sky and misses the lines on the top portion of I_{sketch}. In contrast, the model with DMI successfully generates trees, clouds, and mountain views following the lines in I_{sketch}. In row (c), I_g without DMI totally messes up the shapes in the mid area in I_{sketch}, while, in the one with DMI, all the edges are correctly shaped with clear contrast.

The middle panel in Fig. 7 shows how FMT helps translate the style from the input style images. In row (a), FMT helps generate the correct colors and rich textures in the mountain as in I_{style}. In row (b), I_g with FMT inherits the smoothness from I_{style} where the colors are fuzzy and the edges are blurry, while removing FMT leads to sharp edges and flat colors. When I_{style} is flat without texture, FMT is also able to resume the correct style. Row (c) and row (d) demonstrate that when I_{style} is clean and flat without fuzziness, I_g without FMT generates undesired textures while FMT ensures the accurate flat style.

The right panel in Fig. 7 shows how IDN helps maintain a better color palette and generally reduce the artifacts. In row (a) and (b), there are visible artifacts in the sky of the generated images without IDN, while IDN greatly reduces such effects. In row (b) and (c), the images without IDN shows undesired green and purple-brown colors that are not in the given style images, and IDN has better color consistency. In row (c) and (d), there are clear color-shifts in the generated images, which then been corrected in the model with IDN. Please refer to the Appendix for more qualitative comparisons.

4.3   Human Evaluation

We conduct human survey to validate our model's effectiveness compared to the "Pix2pix+MRU" baseline model. The survey is taken by 100 undergraduate students to ensure the quality. In each question, the user is presented with a sketch, a style image and the generated images from baseline (Pix2pix+MRU) and our model (option letters are randomly assigned to reduce bias) and asked: "Which image, a or b, better captures the style in colorizing the sketch?". We collected 1000 results and 63.3% selects our model as the better performer. 13.3% selects "hard to tell". Only 23.4% prefer the baseline model.

4.4   Qualitative Results on Multi Domains

While focused on art, our model is generic to other image domains with superior visual quality than previous models. On more commonly used datasets CelebA and Fashion Apparel, our model also out-performs the baselines and shows the new state-of-the-art performance. Figure 8 shows the results on multiple image domains. In figure (c), the glasses in the sketches are successfully rendered in the generated images even when there is no glasses in the style image. Similarly, the moustache is correctly removed when there is moustache in the style images but

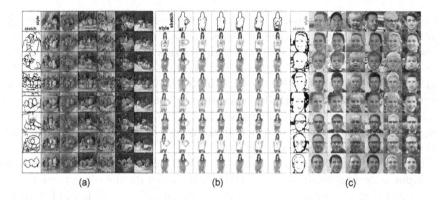

(a)   (b)   (c)

Fig. 8. Synthesize on still-life painting, apparel, and portrait at 512^2 resolution.

is not indicated in the sketches. It's worth noticing that the gender of generated images follows the sketch instead of style. These results show clear evidence that the model learns semantics of input sketch from the training corpus.

5 Discussions

The model yields consistent performance when we try different input settings for the synthesis, including using multiple reference style images rather than one. During the experiments, we also discovered some interesting behaviors and limitations that worth further research. For instance, learning from the corpus can be a good thing for providing extra style cues apart from the style image, however, it may also cause conflicts against it, such as inaccurate coloring and excess shapes. It is worth study on how to balance the representation the model learns from the whole corpus and from the referential style image, and how to take advantage of the knowledge from the corpus for better generation. We sincerely guide the readers to the Appendix for more information.

6 Conclusion

We approached the task of generating artistic images from sketch while conditioned on style images with a novel sketch-to-art model. Unlike photo-realistic datasets, we highlighted and identified the unique properties of artistic images and pointed out the different challenges they possess. Respectively, we proposed methods that can effectively addressed these challenges. Our model synthesizes images with the awareness of more comprehensive artistic style attributes, which goes beyond color palettes, and for the first time, identifies the varied texture, contours, and plain area styles. Overall, our work pushes the boundary of the deep neural networks in capturing and translating various artistic styles, and makes a solid contribution to the sketch-to-image literature.

Acknowledgement. At https://create.playform.io/sketch-to-image, demo of the model in this paper is available. The research was done while Bingchen Liu, Kunpeng Song and Ahmed Elgammal were at Artrendex Inc.

References

1. Elgammal, A., Liu, B., Elhoseiny, M., Mazzone, M.: Can: Creative adversarial networks, generating "art" by learning about styles and deviating from style norms. arXiv preprint arXiv:1706.07068 (2017)
2. Elgammal, A., Mazzone, M., Liu, B., Kim, D., Elhoseiny, M.: The shape of art history in the eyes of the machine. arXiv preprint arXiv:1801.07729 (2018)
3. Kim, D., Liu, B., Elgammal, A., Mazzone, M.: Finding principal semantics of style in art. In: 2018 IEEE 12th International Conference on Semantic Computing (ICSC), pp. 156–163. IEEE (2018)
4. Chen, W., Hays, J.: SketchyGAN: towards diverse and realistic sketch to image synthesis. In: CVPR, pp. 9416–9425 (2018)
5. Zhang, L., Ji, Y., Lin, X., Liu, C.: Style transfer for anime sketches with enhanced residual u-net and auxiliary classifier GAN. In: ACPR, pp. 506–511 (2017)
6. Schapiro, M., Schapiro, M., Schapiro, M., Schapiro, M.: Theory and Philosophy of Art: Style, Artist, and Society, vol. 4. George Braziller, New York (1994)
7. Sangkloy, P., Lu, J., Fang, C., Yu, F., Hays, J.: Scribbler: controlling deep image synthesis with sketch and color. In: CVPR, pp. 5400–5409 (2017)
8. Gatys, L.A., Ecker, A.S., Bethge, M.: Image style transfer using convolutional neural networks. In: CVPR, pp. 2414–2423 (2016)
9. Goodfellow, I., et al.:Generative adversarial nets. In: NIPS, pp. 2672–2680 (2014)
10. Ulyanov, D., Vedaldi, A., Lempitsky, V.: Instance normalization: the missing ingredient for fast stylization. arXiv preprint arXiv:1607.08022 (2016)
11. Isola, P., Zhu, J.Y., Zhou, T., Efros, A.A.: Image-to-image translation with conditional adversarial networks. In: CVPR, pp. 1125–1134 (2017)
12. Zhu, J.Y., Park, T., Isola, P., Efros, A.A.: Unpaired image-to-image translation using cycle-consistent adversarial networks. In: ICCV, pp. 2223–2232 (2017)
13. Liu, M.Y., Breuel, T., Kautz, J.: Unsupervised image-to-image translation networks. In: NIPS, pp. 700–708 (2017)
14. Choi, Y., Choi, M., Kim, M., Ha, J.W., Kim, S., Choo, J.: StarGAN: unified generative adversarial networks for multi-domain image-to-image translation. In: CVPR, pp. 8789–8797 (2018)
15. Yi, Z., Zhang, H., Tan, P., Gong, M.: DualGAN: unsupervised dual learning for image-to-image translation. In: ICCV, pp. 2849–2857 (2017)
16. Huang, X., Liu, M.-Y., Belongie, S., Kautz, J.: Multimodal unsupervised image-to-image translation. In: Ferrari, V., Hebert, M., Sminchisescu, C., Weiss, Y. (eds.) ECCV 2018. LNCS, vol. 11207, pp. 179–196. Springer, Cham (2018). https://doi.org/10.1007/978-3-030-01219-9_11
17. Zhu, J.Y., et al.: Toward multimodal image-to-image translation. In: NIPS, pp. 465–476 (2017)
18. Almahairi, A., Rajeswar, S., Sordoni, A., Bachman, P., Courville, A.: Augmented cycleGAN: learning many-to-many mappings from unpaired data. In: ICML, pp. 195–204 (2018)

19. Lee, H.-Y., Tseng, H.-Y., Huang, J.-B., Singh, M., Yang, M.-H.: Diverse image-to-image translation via disentangled representations. In: Ferrari, V., Hebert, M., Sminchisescu, C., Weiss, Y. (eds.) ECCV 2018. LNCS, vol. 11205, pp. 36–52. Springer, Cham (2018). https://doi.org/10.1007/978-3-030-01246-5_3

20. Liu, B., Song, K., Zhu, Y., de Melo, G., Elgammal, A.: Time: text and image mutual-translation adversarial networks. arXiv preprint arXiv:2005.13192 (2020)

21. Zhu, Y., Min, M.R., Kadav, A., Graf, H.P.: S3vae: Self-supervised sequential VAE for representation disentanglement and data generation. In: Proceedings of the IEEE/CVF Conference on Computer Vision and Pattern Recognition, pp. 6538–6547 (2020)

22. Johnson, J., Alahi, A., Fei-Fei, L.: Perceptual losses for real-time style transfer and super-resolution. In: Leibe, B., Matas, J., Sebe, N., Welling, M. (eds.) ECCV 2016. LNCS, vol. 9906, pp. 694–711. Springer, Cham (2016). https://doi.org/10.1007/978-3-319-46475-6_43

23. Zhang, H., Dana, K.: Multi-style generative network for real-time transfer. In: Leal-Taixé, L., Roth, S. (eds.) ECCV 2018. LNCS, vol. 11132, pp. 349–365. Springer, Cham (2019). https://doi.org/10.1007/978-3-030-11018-5_32

24. Huang, X., Belongie, S.: Arbitrary style transfer in real-time with adaptive instance normalization. In: ICCV, pp. 1501–1510 (2017)

25. Jing, Y., Yang, Y., Feng, Z., Ye, J., Yu, Y., Song, M.: Neural style transfer: a review. arXiv preprint arXiv:1705.04058 (2017)

26. Liu, Y., Qin, Z., Luo, Z., Wang, H.: Auto-painter: cartoon image generation from sketch by using conditional generative adversarial networks. arXiv preprint arXiv:1705.01908 (2017)

27. Zhang, L., Li, C., Wong, T.T., Ji, Y., Liu, C.: Two-stage sketch colorization. In: SIGGRAPH Asia 2018 Technical Papers, p. 261 (2018)

28. Park, T., Liu, M.Y., Wang, T.C., Zhu, J.Y.: Semantic image synthesis with spatially-adaptive normalization. In: CVPR, pp. 2337–2346 (2019)

29. Ronneberger, O., Fischer, P., Brox, T.: U-Net: convolutional networks for biomedical image segmentation. In: Navab, N., Hornegger, J., Wells, W.M., Frangi, A.F. (eds.) MICCAI 2015. LNCS, vol. 9351, pp. 234–241. Springer, Cham (2015). https://doi.org/10.1007/978-3-319-24574-4_28

30. Simonyan, K., Zisserman, A.: Very deep convolutional networks for large-scale image recognition. In: ICLR (2015)

31. Kazemi, H., Iranmanesh, S.M., Nasrabadi, N.: Style and content disentanglement in generative adversarial networks. In: WACV, pp. 848–856 (2019)

32. Karras, T., Laine, S., Aila, T.: A style-based generator architecture for generative adversarial networks. In: CVPR. (2019) 4401–4410

33. Wikiart. (https://www.wikiart.org/)

34. Heusel, M., Ramsauer, H., Unterthiner, T., Nessler, B., Hochreiter, S.: GANs trained by a two time-scale update rule converge to a local nash equilibrium. In: NIPS, pp. 6626–6637 (2017)

35. Russakovsky, O., et al.: ImageNet large scale visual recognition challenge. IJCV **115**, 211–252 (2015)

Road Obstacle Detection Method Based on an Autoencoder with Semantic Segmentation

Toshiaki Ohgushi$^{(\boxtimes)}$, Kenji Horiguchi$^{(\boxtimes)}$, and Masao Yamanaka$^{(\boxtimes)}$

Toyota Motor Corporation, Otemachi, Chiyoda-ku, Tokyo 100-0004, Japan
{toshiaki_ohgushi,kenji_horiguchi,masao_yamanaka}@mail.toyota.co.jp

f

Abstract. Accurate detection of road obstacles is vital for ensuring safe autonomous driving, particularly on highways. However, existing methods tend to perform poorly when analyzing road scenes with complex backgrounds, because supervised approaches cannot detect unknown objects that are not included in the training dataset. Hence, in this study, we propose a road obstacle detection method using an autoencoder with semantic segmentation that was trained with only data from normal road scenes. The proposed method requires only a color image captured by a common in-vehicle camera as input. It then creates a resynthesized image using an autoencoder consisting of a semantic image generator as the encoder and a photographic image generator as the decoder. Extensive experiments demonstrate that the performance of the proposed method is comparable to that of existing methods, even without postprocessing. The proposed method with postprocessing outperformed state-of-the-art methods on the Lost and Found dataset. Further, in evaluations using our Highway Anomaly Dataset, which includes actual and synthetic road obstacles, the proposed method significantly outperformed a supervised method that explicitly learns road obstacles. Thus, the proposed machine-learning-based road obstacle detection method is a practical solution that will advance the development of autonomous driving systems.

1 Introduction

In recent years, advanced driving support systems have been rapidly developed to realize autonomous driving in the future. Human–machine interfaces linked with these systems will be able to support safe, secure, and comfortable driving by informing drivers about changes in the driving environment (e.g., due to traffic congestion, weather, and road obstacles) detected by preceding vehicles and passed on to subsequent vehicles.

According to a report by the Ministry of Land, Infrastructure, Transport, and Tourism in Japan [1], approximately 340,000 road obstacles were identified in 2018 (i.e., almost 1,000 road obstacles per day). Such obstacles regularly cause

Electronic supplementary material The online version of this chapter (https://doi.org/10.1007/978-3-030-69544-6_14) contains supplementary material, which is available to authorized users.

© Springer Nature Switzerland AG 2021
H. Ishikawa et al. (Eds.): ACCV 2020, LNCS 12627, pp. 223–238, 2021.
https://doi.org/10.1007/978-3-030-69544-6_14

224 T. Ohgushi et al.

severe accidents. Therefore, the automation of road obstacle detection as a social system is urgently required because the detection and removing of these road obstacles are performed manually at present.

Several driving environment recognition methods have been proposed based on this background. However, these methods are not suitable for vehicles already on the market because they require special sensors, such as stereo cameras, LIDAR, and radar. Further, special sensors that can be used for autonomous driving are prohibitively expensive and require considerable power. In particular, a machine-learning-based approach is a potential alternative to special-sensor-based approaches. However, collecting a large amount of data required for supervised learning is impractical as the colors, shapes, sizes, and textures of road obstacles can vary substantially, as shown in Fig. 1. Thus, training a classifier to robustly detect road obstacles (i.e., unknown objects) is almost impossible.

In this paper, we propose a road obstacle detection method based on an autoencoder with semantic segmentation. The proposed method requires only a color image captured by a common in-vehicle camera as input. From this image, the method creates a resynthesized image using an autoencoder comprising a semantic image generator [2] as the encoder and a photographic image generator [3] as the decoder. The method then calculates the perceptual loss [3] between the input and resynthesized images and multiplies it by the entropy for the semantic image to generate an anomaly map. Finally, the method localizes road obstacles in the image by applying postprocessing to the anomaly map. Specifically, we sharpen the anomaly map by applying a standard technique for calculating the visual saliency in an image [4,5].

Through extensive experiments, we demonstrate that the performance of the proposed method is comparable with that of existing methods, even without postprocessing. Moreover, the proposed method with postprocessing outperforms state-of-the-art methods on one of the largest publicly available datasets [6]. Additionally, in our tests with the proposed highway dataset, which includes imagery with actual road obstacles, we show that the proposed method provides significant advantages over a supervised method that explicitly learns road obstacles using a semantic segmentation technique.

Fig. 1. Examples of road obstacles [7]. Although some obstacles are more common than others (e.g., burst tire debris, road cones, plywood, square lumber, and scrap iron), predicting exactly what might fall from a truck or a car on the road (e.g., a soccer ball) is impossible.

2   Previous Work

Early studies in the field of road obstacle detection in highway environments strongly relied on stereo vision techniques. For example, Hancock [8] used laser reflectance and stereo vision to detect small road obstacles at long distances. Similarly, William et al. [9] used a multibaseline stereo technique to detect small road obstacles (approximately 14 cm high) at a distance of over 100 m. Even relatively recent research uses stereo cameras or the structure-from-motion technique to detect road obstacles. For instance, Subaru Eyesight [10] is a representative stereo-vision-based system that robustly detects large road obstacles. In addition, Mobileye [11] is a commercially available system that can robustly detect large obstacles at close range using only a monocular camera. Further, Tokudome et al. [12] developed a novel real-time environment recognition system for autonomous driving using a LIDAR sensor.

However, these special-sensor-based approaches require a relatively clean road environment to compute image warping and disparity with high accuracy. In practice, vehicle vibrations render calibrating cameras with long focal lengths highly difficult because two cameras can move independently. Further, it is difficult to obtain high accuracy when using off-the-shelf active sensors over long distances. For example, a LIDAR system (e.g., Velodyne HDL-64E [13]) has a vertical angular resolution of approximately 0.4°. This implies that the maximum distance at which the system can detect only three consecutive points on a small 20-cm-high vertical object is less than 15 m. Although special-sensor-based approaches present several problems as described above, rich features can be extracted in the context of road obstacle detection, particularly when detecting small road obstacles from long distances.

Unlike special-sensor-based approaches, machine-learning-based approaches extract raw images using a common in-vehicle camera and convert the images into rich features by applying advanced machine learning techniques such as autoencoders [14,15], uncertainty-based approaches [16,17], and generative adversarial networks (GANs) [18,19]. In autoencoder-based approaches [14,15], small input patches are compared with the output from a shallow autoencoder trained on road textures only. In principle, road patches from other patches can be distinguished using these approaches. However, other patches include not only road obstacles (i.e., anomaly objects) but also normal objects, such as vehicles, traffic signs, and buildings. Therefore, these approaches yield a significant number of false positives. Uncertainty-based approaches [16,17] rely on the Bayesian SegNet framework and incorporate an uncertainty threshold to detect potentially mislabeled regions, including unknown objects. However, these approaches also yield numerous false positives in irrelevant regions (i.e., boundary regions at semantic labels, such as roads, vehicles, buildings, sky, and nature). In GAN-based approaches [18], an image is passed through an adversarial autoencoder, and then the feature loss between the output and input images is measured. These methods can be used to classify entire images, but not to identify anomalies within the images. Moreover, in GAN-based approaches [19], given a GAN trained to represent an original distribution, an algorithm searches for the latent vector that yields the image that most closely matches the input. However, this is computationally expensive and does not identify anomalies.

A considerably different approach [20] has proven as a promising alternative to the existing techniques previously mentioned. This approach relies on the intuition that a network will yield false labels in regions that contain unexpected objects. Currently, this approach, hereinafter referred to as Resynth, obtains state-of-the-art results when tested on one of the largest publicly available road obstacle detection datasets [6]. Specifically, Resynth uses an existing semantic segmentation algorithm, such as [16] or [21], to generate a semantic map. It then passes this map to a generative network [22] that attempts to resynthesize an input image. If the image contains objects belonging to a class that the segmentation algorithm has not been trained to identify, then the corresponding pixels are mislabeled in the semantic map and, therefore, poorly resynthesized. Finally, Resynth identifies these unexpected objects by detecting significant differences between the original and synthetic images. Specifically, this method introduces a sophisticated neural network (i.e., a discrepancy network). It explicitly trains the discrepancy network to identify meaningful differences in the context of detecting unknown objects by replacing a few object instances with randomly selected labels in the ground-truth semantic map.

However, when trained in a supervised manner, this approach tends to perform poorly on images with complex backgrounds because the network only learns arbitrarily mislabeled semantic maps for normal objects instead of learning mislabeled semantic maps for unknown objects. Moreover, training the discrepancy network is not straightforward because the training process is quite difficult to perform in end-to-end manner.

3   Approach

Our basic idea is the same as that of [20]. However, our implementation is completely different from the existing method and rather reasonable. Specifically, our implementation has three types of components, namely, an autoencoder, an anomaly calculator, and a postprocessor, as shown in Fig. 2. First, the input to the autoencoder consists of only a color image (a) captured by a common in-vehicle camera. Subsequently, the autoencoder generates a semantic map (b) by applying a semantic segmentation technique [2] and creates a resynthesized image (c) using a photographic image synthesis technique [3]. Subsequently, the anomaly calculator generates an anomaly map (f) by multiplying the perceptual loss (d) and entropy (e) for the semantic map. Finally, the postprocessor outputs an obstacle score map (h) by sharpening the anomaly map for each local region (g). The details of these steps are described below.

3.1   Autoencoder

The autoencoder comprises modules for semantic segmentation and resynthesized image generation, as shown in Fig. 2. The autoencoder generates a semantic map and a resynthesized image and outputs them to the anomaly calculator

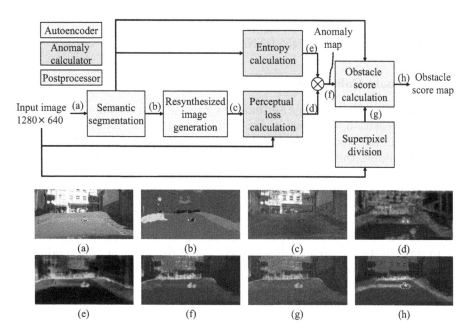

Fig. 2. Schematic overview of our road obstacle detection system. (a) Input image, (b) semantic map, (c) resynthesized image, (d) perceptual loss, (e) entropy map, (f) anomaly map, (g) superpixels, and (h) obstacle score map.

and postprocessor. In particular, we apply a representative semantic segmentation technique (ICNet [2]) to process the input image such that the module segments the input image into 20 types of semantic labels (e.g., road, car, traffic light, and traffic sign). Input images are obtained from Cityscapes, a publicly available dataset of road scenes for assessing and training vision algorithms [23]. Here, we downscale the Cityscapes training dataset to a resolution of $1{,}280 \times 640$ pixels owing to GPU memory constraints. Then, under fixed semantic segmentation model parameters, we concatenate the semantic segmentation module and resynthesized image generation module. Further, we apply an advanced resynthesized image generation technique (cascaded refinement network [3]) to process the semantic map; the module generates an image (i.e., the resynthesized image) that is exactly the same as the input image from the Cityscapes dataset [23]. Among the three types of components, only the autoencoder must learn the model parameters.

In particular, our algorithm can improve the quality of resynthesized images by employing a simple solution: connecting the decoder not to the output of the last layer (i.e., the softmax layer), but to the output of the intermediate layer (i.e., the convolution layer immediately before the softmax layer). Further, this solution performs well without additional functions such as the instance segmentation and instance level feature embedding required in Pix2PixHD [22]. Although Resynth trains the encoder and decoder completely separately owing to heavy memory usage, our algorithm can realize end-to-end learning and rapid inference by concatenating light DNNs.

3.2 Anomaly Calculator

The anomaly calculator comprises modules for entropy calculation and perceptual loss calculation, as shown in Fig. 2. The anomaly calculator generates an anomaly map that comprises an anomaly score at each pixel in the input image and then outputs this anomaly map to the postprocessor. Here, the following assumptions can be made when estimating the semantic labels of an unknown object: The semantic map contains ambiguity around the unknown object, and the resynthesized image yields significant differences in appearance with respect to the input image because of this ambiguity. Therefore, we calculate the entropy for the semantic map to measure the ambiguity and calculate the perceptual loss [3] to measure the differences in appearance. Finally, we define the product of these measures as the anomaly score. Specifically, we define the entropy for the semantic map as follows:

$$ S = U_{bl} \left(- \sum_k p^{(k)} \log(p^{(k)}) \right). \tag{1} $$

Here, $p^{(k)}$ is the probability of the k-th semantic label estimated using the semantic segmentation technique [2] and U_{bl} is a bilinear-interpolation-based upconverter that upconverts the resynthesized image to the same resolution as the input image. Further, we define the perceptual loss between the input and resynthesized images as follows:

$$ \mathcal{L} = \sum_{l=1}^{5} U_{bl} \left(\mathcal{L}^{(l)} \right), \tag{2} $$

$$ \mathcal{L}^{(l)} = ||\Phi^{(l)}(I) - \Phi^{(l)}(R)||_1. \tag{3} $$

Here, I and R are the input and resynthesized images, respectively. In addition, $\Phi^{(l)}$ is the output from the l-th hidden layer of VGG19 [24]. Specifically, $\Phi^{(l)}(l = 1, \ldots, 5)$ are given by the outputs from conv1_2, conv2_2, conv3_2, conv4_2, and conv5_2, as shown in Fig. 3. Thus, we obtain the output from each hidden layer using VGG19 on the input and resynthesized images. Additionally, we define the L1 norm between the output from the l-th hidden layer for the input image and the output from the l-th hidden layer for the resynthesized image as perceptual loss $\mathcal{L}^{(l)}$, as shown in Eq. (3). Further, we calculate the total perceptual loss $\mathcal{L}$ by adding perceptual loss $\mathcal{L}^{(l)}(l = 1, \ldots, 5)$ after adjusting its resolution with upconverter U_{bl}, as shown in Eq. (2). Finally, we generate anomaly map $\mathcal{A}$ by taking the element-wise product of perceptual loss $\mathcal{L}$ and entropy S as follows:

$$ \mathcal{A} = \mathcal{L} \odot S. \tag{4} $$

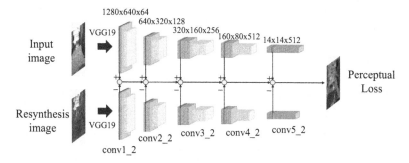

Fig. 3. Schematic overview of our perceptual loss calculation module. We apply VGG19 [24] to the input and resynthesized images. The blue circle comprises two functions. The first function calculates the channel-wise L1 norm for the difference between the output from the i-th hidden layer for the input image and the output from the i-th hidden layer for the resynthesized image. The second function applies upconverter U_{bl} to the map composed of the L1 norm values. (Color figure online)

3.3 Postprocessor

The postprocessor consists of modules for obstacle score calculation and super-pixel division, as shown in Fig. 2. Its aim is to generate an obstacle score map to localize unknown objects in the input image. First, we use simple linear iterative clustering to segment the input image into local regions referred to as super-pixels [25]. We perform this because superpixels are less likely to cross object boundaries, which leads to greater accuracy in segmentation of visually salient regions. Then, we define the obstacle score in the i-th superpixel as follows:

$$L_i = \alpha_i \sum_j n_j p_j \exp\left(-\frac{r_{i,j}^2}{2w^2}\right).$$ (5)

where α_i is the average value of the anomaly score in the i-th superpixel, n_j is the number of pixels in the j-th superpixel, p_j is the average value of the probability for the road label in the j-th superpixel, $r_{i,j}$ is the Euclidean distance between the center position of the i-th superpixel and the center position of the j-th superpixel, and w is the median of the Euclidean distances between the center positions of every pair of superpixels. Finally, the regions in which L_i exceeds a predetermined threshold are identified as those containing an unknown object (i.e., a road obstacle).

4 Experiments

Using two separate datasets, we evaluated the ability of our method to detect road obstacles. We did not use any prior knowledge about road obstacles during training because our focus is on finding unknown anomaly objects.

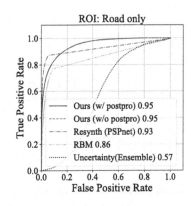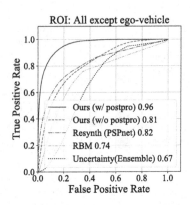

Fig. 4. ROC curves and AUROC scores for the Lost and Found dataset [6]. Resynth (PSPnet) depicts the results of the method reported in [20] using PSPnet [21] as the semantic segmentation technique. Uncertainty (Ensemble) depicts the results of the ensemble-based method reported in [17].

4.1   Lost and Found Dataset

First, we quantitatively evaluated our road obstacle detection method on a publicly available dataset, "Lost and Found" [6]. Instead of using a bounding box to mark the road obstacle region, accurate human-marked labels are provided as the ground truth in this public dataset. We followed a general methodology [20] to evaluate the accuracy of the detected road obstacle region. Specifically, all evaluated methods output a pixel-wise anomaly score. We compared the resulting maps with the ground-truth anomaly annotations using ROC curves and the AUROC (area under the ROC curve) metric. We considered representative existing methods (Resynth [20], a restricted Boltzmann machine [15], and an uncertainty-based method (Uncertainty) [17]) as baselines. Further, we evaluated our approach using obstacle score maps (i.e., with postprocessing) and using only anomaly maps (i.e., without postprocessing).

The ROC curves and AUROC scores obtained using these methods are shown in Fig. 4. The curves on the left were obtained by restricting the evaluation to the road, as defined by the ground-truth annotations. Similarly, the curves on the right were computed over the entire images, excluding the ego-vehicle regions only. The performance of our approach without postprocessing is comparable to that of Resynth [20] and superior to that of the other methods. Moreover, our approach with postprocessing achieves the highest AUROC scores among all methods. In particular, the road obstacle detection performance is substantially improved by applying postprocessing, as shown in Fig. 4.

Figure 5 shows an example of maps generated for an image with a road obstacle, which is captured primarily in the middle of the road (a). The semantic segmentation module outputs false labels in the road obstacle region (b). Then, the resynthesized image generation module obtains an image with significant differences in appearance with respect to the road obstacle region in the input

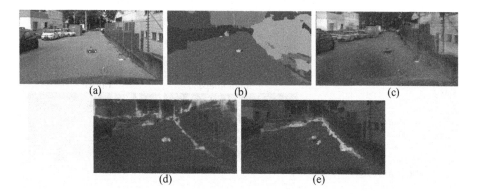

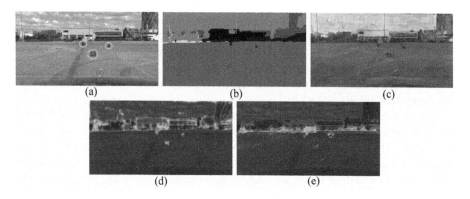

Fig. 5. Example of maps generated for a synthetic image with a road obstacle. (a) Input image, (b) semantic map, (c) resynthesized image, (d) anomaly map, and (e) obstacle score map. (Color figure online)

Fig. 6. Example of maps generated for a synthetic image with multiple road obstacles. (a) Input image, (b) semantic map, (c) resynthesized image, (d) anomaly map, and (e) obstacle score map. (Color figure online)

image (c). Thus, the anomaly calculator generates relatively high anomaly scores around the road obstacle (d). Finally, the road obstacle is highlighted by the postprocessor, which enhances the anomaly score only around the road and suppresses the anomaly score in other regions (e).

The yellow car parked sideways causes a misclassification during semantic segmentation. Such misclassifications decrease the quality of resynthesized images as well, and these may lead to false positives in road obstacle detection.

Figure 6 shows an example of maps generated for an image that contains multiple obstacles (a). Although relatively small obstacles are captured, the anomaly score accounts for them accurately (e). For this case as well as the above, we can observe that misclassifications caused around obstacle regions (b); and it leads to poor quality of resynthesis (c).

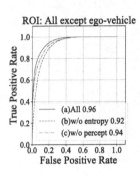

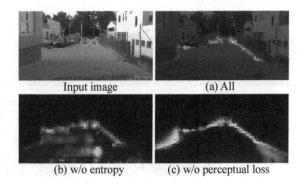

Fig. 7. ROC curves and AUROC scores for ablation experiments.

Fig. 8. Output image examples for ablation experiments.

Ablation Experiment. To investigate how each component contributes to anomaly detection performance, ablation experiments were conducted. Figure 7 shows the ROC curve and AUC scores of model (a), which contains all modules shown in Fig. 2; model (b), from which the entropy calculation module has been removed; and model (c), from which the perceptual loss calculation module has been removed.

The results show that model (c) outperforms model (b). This could result from the fact that perceptual loss tends to produce relatively more false negatives (Fig. 8(b)), as perceptual loss responds to a corrupt portion of the resynthesized image sensitively and produces blurred score maps owing to the lower resolution of the latter layers of VGG (i.e., conv4_2, conv5_2). Meanwhile, the entropy score calculated from semantic segmentation labels can catch the edges of class boundaries. However, the entropy score tends to be high even in well-resynthesized areas, and the perceptual loss score is low (e.g., the corner of the building on the left in Fig. 8(c)).

By multiplying the perceptual loss map and entropy map, an improved anomaly score that reflects the benefits of both maps can be acquired (Fig. 8(a)). Actually, we can verify that the best AUC score is obtained when all components are used.

4.2   Our Highway Anomaly Dataset

We quantitatively evaluated our road obstacle detection method in tests using our highway anomaly dataset, which is shown in Fig. 9. The dataset is composed of (a) a training dataset captured under normal highway driving conditions without road obstacles, (b) a validation dataset, and (c) a test dataset; the latter two datasets include actual and synthetic road obstacles, such as traffic cones and objects falling from other vehicles. The respective datasets include approximately 5000, 300, and 200 photo and segmentation ground truth image pairs. First, we trained our autoencoder with the Cityscapes dataset and fine-tuned

(a) Training   (b) Validation   (c) Test

Fig. 9. Examples from our highway anomaly dataset.

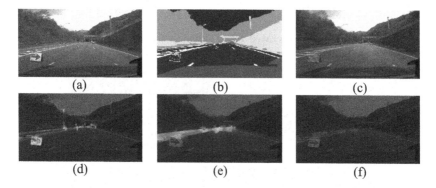

Fig. 10. Example of maps generated for a synthetic image. (a) Input image, (b) semantic map, (c) resynthesized image, (d) anomaly map, (e) obstacle score map, and (f) detection result.

it using our training dataset. The validation dataset was then used for determining the threshold for detecting road obstacle areas. Finally, we evaluated the performance using the test dataset and the threshold described above.

Figure 10 shows an example of maps generated for a synthetic image (a), in which a warning sign can be observed. The semantic segmentation module outputs false labels in the road obstacle region (b). Then, the resynthesized image generation module obtains an image with significant differences in appearance with respect to the road obstacle region in the input image (c). Hence, the anomaly calculator generates relatively high anomaly scores around the road obstacle (d). Further, the postprocessor sharpens the anomaly score around the road and suppresses the anomaly score in other regions, such as the boundaries between the trees and sky in the distance (e). Finally, we identify the region wherein the obstacle score $\mathcal{L}$ exceeds the predetermined threshold $\mathcal{T}$ as the road obstacle (f). We determined the threshold $\mathcal{T}$ using 300 validation images (different from the abovementioned 200 test images) including actual and synthetic road obstacles, such that the F-measure of the detected road obstacle regions was maximized.

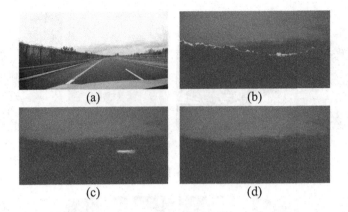

Fig. 11. Example of maps generated for an image without road obstacles. (a) Input image, (b) anomaly map, (c) obstacle score map, and (d) detection result.

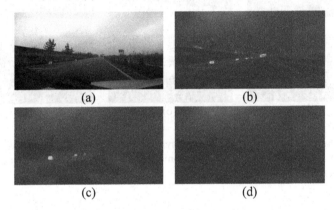

Fig. 12. Example of maps generated for an image containing small road obstacles. (a) Input image, (b) anomaly map, (c) obstacle score map, and (d) detection result.

Fig. 13. Example of maps generated for an image containing large road obstacles. (a) Input image, (b) anomaly map, (c) obstacle score map, and (d) detection result.

Table 1. Performance comparison.

Evaluation metric	W/ explicit learning	W/O explicit learning		
	ICNet	GAN Resynth	Ours	
			W/O post-processing	W/post-processing
Mean F-measure	0.142	0.103	0.231	0.300
Global F-measure	0.197	0.040	0.333	0.452
Mean IoU	0.092	0.063	0.154	0.219
Global IoU	0.109	0.020	0.200	0.292

Figure 11 shows an example of maps generated for an image without road obstacles, which can be observed as a normal driving environment on the highway (a). The anomaly map has relatively high scores around the boundaries between the trees and road in the input image (b). However, the anomaly scores are suppressed by the postprocessing of the anomaly map (c). Consequently, our approach succeeds in obtaining the true negative as an entire image by thresholding the obstacle score map (d). Our approach yields almost no false positives in normal driving environments, such as that shown in (a).

Figure 12 shows an example of maps generated for an image containing road obstacles, which are warning signs that are temporarily arranged at equal intervals on the road (a). The anomaly map can detect extremely small road obstacles in the distance (b). Further, even if the anomaly scores are suppressed by applying postprocessing for the anomaly map (c), our approach succeeds in detecting small road obstacles at a distance (d).

Figure 13 shows an example of maps generated for an image containing large road obstacles; in this case, the obstacles are sections of a large emergency vehicle temporarily parked on the roadside (a). The emergency vehicle in the image consists of a truck, a lift attached to a base, and a warning sign attached to the truck. The truck should be recognized as a normal object, whereas the lift and warning sign should be detected as anomalies (i.e., road obstacles). The anomaly map succeeds in obtaining relatively high scores around the lift and warning sign (b). However, the anomaly scores for the warning sign are suppressed by the postprocessing of the anomaly map (c). Therefore, our approach fails to discriminate the warning sign from the road, although it succeeds in detecting the lift close to the road (d). In principle, it is quite difficult for our approach to detect road obstacles that are not on roads.

Finally, we compared the performance of four different approaches: ICNet [2], Resynth [20], our approach with postprocessing, and our approach without postprocessing. Specifically, we explicitly trained the ICNet to learn road obstacles using the above validation images. Table 1 compares the performance of these four approaches. Our approach outperforms ICNet [2] and Resynth [20], even without postprocessing, as shown in Table 1. Here, the mean F-measure is the average of the F-measures calculated for each test image, the global F-measure indicates the F-measure calculated using all test images, the mean Intersection-over-Union (IoU) indicates the average value of the IoUs calculated for each test image, and the global IoU indicates the IoU calculated using all test images.

The processing time required for creating an obstacle score map composed of 1,280 × 640 pixel images was approximately 1 s when using a Tesla V100 equipped with 16.0 GB RAM. Regarding the processing time for each component in our system, the autoencoder required 72.5 [ms] (13.8 fps), the anomaly calculator required 1,053 ms (0.95 fps), and the postprocessor required 667 ms (1.5 fps). This observation indicates that the computation time should be improved, particularly for the anomaly calculator. This remains an issue for further research.

5   Conclusion

In this study, we proposed a road obstacle detection method based on an autoencoder with semantic segmentation. The proposed method is purely unsupervised; therefore, it does not require any prior knowledge of road obstacles. In particular, the method requires only a color image captured by a common in-vehicle camera as input. The method creates a resynthesized image using an autoencoder composed of a semantic image generator as the encoder and a photographic image generator as the decoder.

Subsequently, the method calculates the perceptual loss between the input and resynthesized images and multiplies the perceptual loss by the entropy for the semantic image to generate an anomaly map. Finally, the method localizes a road obstacle in the image by applying visual-saliency-based postprocessing to the anomaly map.

In particular, the method can improve the quality of resynthesized images by employing a simple solution: connecting the decoder not to the output of the last layer (i.e., the softmax layer) but to the output of the intermediate layer (i.e., the convolution layer immediately before the softmax layer). Moreover, this solution performs well without additional functions, such as instance segmentation or instance level feature embedding. Although the existing method must train the encoder and decoder completely separately owing to heavy memory usage, it can realize end-to-end learning and rapid inference by concatenating light DNNs.

Through extensive experiments, we demonstrated that the performance of the proposed method is comparable to that of existing methods, even without postprocessing. Additionally, the proposed method with postprocessing outperforms state-of-the-art methods on one of the largest publicly available datasets. Further, in evaluations using our Highway Anomaly Dataset containing actual and synthetic road obstacles, the proposed method significantly outperformed a supervised method that explicitly learns road obstacles using a semantic segmentation technique. This unsupervised machine-learning-based road obstacle detection method is a practical solution that will advance the development of autonomous driving systems.

References

1. Ministry of Land, Infrastructure, Transport and Tourism: Number of fallen objects handled by expressway companies in 2018. (https://www.mlit.go.jp/road/sisaku/ijikanri/pdf/h30rakkabutu_nexco.pdf)

2. Zhao, H., Qi, X., Shen, X., Shi, J., Jia, J.: ICNet for real-time semantic segmentation on high-resolution images. In: Ferrari, V., Hebert, M., Sminchisescu, C., Weiss, Y. (eds.) ECCV 2018. LNCS, vol. 11207, pp. 418–434. Springer, Cham (2018). https://doi.org/10.1007/978-3-030-01219-9_25
3. Chen, Q., Koltun, V.: Photographic image synthesis with cascaded refinement networks. In: 2017 IEEE International Conference on Computer Vision (ICCV), pp. 1520–1529 (2017)
4. Goferman, S., Zelnik-Manor, L., Tal, A.: Context-aware saliency detection. In: Proceedings of IEEE Conference on Computer Vision and Pattern Recognition, pp. 2376–2383 (2010)
5. Masao, Y.: Salient region detection by enhancing diversity of multiple priors. IPSJ Trans. Math. Model. Appl. **9**, 13–22 (2016)
6. Pinggera, P., Ramos, S., Gehrig, S., Franke, U., Rother, C., Mester, R.: Lost and found: detecting small road hazards for self-driving vehicles. In: 2016 IEEE/RSJ International Conference on Intelligent Robots and Systems (IROS), pp. 1099–1106 (2016)
7. Shutoko; Metropolitan Expressway Company Limited: Current state of road obstacles. http://www.shutoko.jp/use/safety/emergency
8. Hancock, J.: High-speed obstacle detection for automated highway applications. Technical report, CMU Technical Report (1997)
9. Williamson, T., Thorpe, C.: Detection of small obstacles at long range using multi baseline stereo. In: IEEE International Conference on Intelligent Vehicles (1998)
10. SUBARU: EyeSight. http://www.subaru.com/engineering/eyesight.html
11. Yoffie, D.B.: Mobileye: The Future of Driverless Cars. HBS CASE COLLECTION, Harvard Business School Case (2015)
12. Tokudome, N., Ayukawa, S., Ninomiya, S., Enokida, S., Nishida, T.: Development of real-time environment recognition system using lidar for autonomous driving, pp. 1–4 (2017)
13. Velodyne: HDL-64E. http://velodynelidar.com/lidar/
14. Munawar, A., Vinayavekhin, P., Magistris, G.D.: Limiting the reconstruction capability of generative neural network using negative learning. In: 2017 IEEE 27th International Workshop on Machine Learning for Signal Processing (MLSP), pp. 1–6 (2017)
15. Creusot, C., Munawar, A.: Real-time small obstacle detection on highways using compressive RBM road reconstruction. In: 2015 IEEE Intelligent Vehicles Symposium (IV), pp. 162–167 (2015)
16. Alex Kendall, V.B., Cipolla, R.: Bayesian segnet: Model uncertainty in deep convolutional encoder-decoder architectures for scene understanding. In: Kim, T.-K., Stefanos Zafeiriou, G.B., Mikolajczyk, K. (eds.) Proceedings of the British Machine Vision Conference (BMVC), pp. 57.1–57.12. BMVA Press (2017)
17. Lakshminarayanan, B., Pritzel, A., Blundell, C.: Simple and scalable predictive uncertainty estimation using deep ensembles. In: Guyon, I., Luxburg, U.V., Bengio, S., Wallach, H., Fergus, R., Vishwanathan, S., Garnett, R. (eds.) Advances in Neural Information Processing Systems, vol. 30, pp. 6402–6413. Curran Associates, Inc. (2017)
18. Akcay, S., Atapour-Abarghouei, A., Breckon, T.P.: GANomaly: semi-supervised anomaly detection via adversarial training. In: Jawahar, C.V., Li, H., Mori, G., Schindler, K. (eds.) ACCV 2018. LNCS, vol. 11363, pp. 622–637. Springer, Cham (2019). https://doi.org/10.1007/978-3-030-20893-6_39

19. Schlegl, T., Seeböck, P., Waldstein, S.M., Schmidt-Erfurth, U., Langs, G.: Unsupervised anomaly detection with generative adversarial networks to guide marker discovery. In: Niethammer, M., et al. (eds.) IPMI 2017. LNCS, vol. 10265, pp. 146–157. Springer, Cham (2017). https://doi.org/10.1007/978-3-319-59050-9_12

20. Lis, K., Nakka, K., Fua, P., Salzmann, M.: Detecting the unexpected via image resynthesis. In: The IEEE International Conference on Computer Vision (ICCV) (2019)

21. Zhao, H., Shi, J., Qi, X., Wang, X., Jia, J.: Pyramid scene parsing network. In: CVPR (2017)

22. Wang, T.C., Liu, M.Y., Zhu, J.Y., Tao, A., Kautz, J., Catanzaro, B.: High-resolution image synthesis and semantic manipulation with conditional GANs. In: Proceedings of the IEEE Conference on Computer Vision and Pattern Recognition (2018)

23. Cordts, M., et al.: The cityscapes dataset for semantic urban scene understanding. In: Proceedings of the IEEE Conference on Computer Vision and Pattern Recognition (CVPR) (2016)

24. Simonyan, K., Zisserman, A.: Very deep convolutional networks for large-scale image recognition. In: International Conference on Learning Representations (2015)

25. Achanta, R., Shaji, A., Smith, K., Lucchi, A., Fua, P., Söck, S.: Slic superpixels (2010)

SpotPatch: Parameter-Efficient Transfer Learning for Mobile Object Detection

Keren Ye[1(✉)], Adriana Kovashka[1], Mark Sandler[2], Menglong Zhu[3], Andrew Howard[2], and Marco Fornoni[2]

[1] University of Pittsburgh, Pittsburgh, USA
{yekeren,kovashka}@cs.pitt.edu
[2] Google Research, Pittsburgh, USA
{sandler,howarda,fornoni}@google.com
[3] DJI Technology LLC, Shenzhen, China
mzhu.upenn@gmail.com

Abstract. Deep learning based object detectors are commonly deployed on mobile devices to solve a variety of tasks. For maximum accuracy, each detector is usually trained to solve one single specific task, and comes with a completely independent set of parameters. While this guarantees high performance, it is also highly inefficient, as each model has to be separately downloaded and stored. In this paper we address the question: can task-specific detectors be trained and represented as a shared set of weights, plus a very small set of additional weights for each task? The main contributions of this paper are the following: 1) we perform the first systematic study of parameter-efficient transfer learning techniques for object detection problems; 2) we propose a technique to learn a model patch with a size that is dependent on the difficulty of the task to be learned, and validate our approach on 10 different object detection tasks. Our approach achieves similar accuracy as previously proposed approaches, while being significantly more compact.

1 Introduction

Mobile object detection models are fundamental building blocks for daily-used mobile applications. For example, face detectors are used for locking/unlocking the latest generation phones and for building social apps such as Snapchat. In the early years, most computer vision models were deployed on servers, which meant that images had to be sent from the device to the server and that users had to wait for the server responses. This process was sensitive to network outages, provided on-device latency that was often not tolerable, and burdened the server clusters with high loads of client requests.

With the advance of mobile hardware technology, on-device computation became more and more affordable. Meanwhile, advances in neural network architectures made model inference increasingly more efficient. On the one hand,

---

K. Ye—Work partially done during an internship at Google.
M. Zhu—Work done at Google.

H. Ishikawa et al. (Eds.): ACCV 2020, LNCS 12627, pp. 239–256, 2021.
https://doi.org/10.1007/978-3-030-69544-6_15

Fig. 1. The challenge of updating a mobile object detector. Suppose a general-purpose object detector is already deployed on-device. In a naive setting, adding support for detecting new entities would require downloading a completely separate model, with large network costs. Our goal is to reduce the network costs by *"patching"* the existing model to also support the new entities.

MobileNets [1–3] optimize the network architecture by decomposing convolutions into more efficient operations. Such designs provide general and compact backbones for mobile inference. On the other hand, one-stage detection architectures such as SSD [4] and Yolo [5] provide mobile-friendly detection heads.

Due to the combination of the above advancements, object detection models are now massively being moved from server-side to on-device. While this constitutes great progress, it also brings new challenges (see Fig. 1). Specifically, multiple isolated models are often downloaded to perform related tasks. Suppose that a well-performing mobile model is downloaded for general-purpose object detection, with 10MB data traffic costs. Suppose then that the user requests an additional functionality that requires detecting new entities, like faces or barcodes: this will naively require to download a new model, with an extra 10MB data cost. Each time a new task will need to be supported, the user and the network operator will incur an additional 10 MB data cost. The question is then: can we instead "patch" the previously downloaded general-purpose object detector to solve also the new tasks? If so, how can we minimize the size of the "patch" while maintaining high accuracy on the new task? To answer these questions, we studied two experimental scenarios that mimic two practical use-cases for "patching" mobile detection models:

1. Adapting an object detector to solve a new task.
2. Updating an existing model, whenever additional training data is available.

To learn the model patch, we propose an approach simultaneously optimizing for accuracy and footprint (see Fig. 2 for an overview): 1) for each layer, we minimize the size of the patch by using a 1-bit representation of the weight residuals; 2) we employ a gating mechanism to selectively patch only important layers, while reusing the original weights for the remaining ones. We evaluate our problem on ten different object detection tasks, using an experimental setup similar to [6], which we refer to as "Detection Decathlon". We also showcase our method's ability to efficiently update the model when new data becomes available. To the best of our knowledge, this is the first systematic study of parameter-efficient transfer learning techniques on object detection tasks.

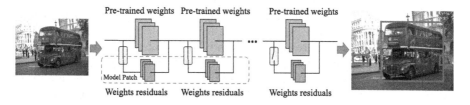

Fig. 2. SpotPatch: demonstrating the gating mechanism. During training, our model optimizes both the detection performance and the number of patched layers by opening, or closing per-layer gates. During deployment, only the *opened routes* constitute the model patch. We use a 1-bit representation for the weights residuals, significantly reducing the patch footprint.

2 Related Work

The most relevant approaches for our work fall into three main categories: (1) Model footprint reduction, aimed at reducing the number of trainable parameters, or the bit-size representation for each parameter. (2) Dynamic routing, adapting the network architecture at training time, based on well-designed cost functions. (3) Transfer learning and domain adaptation, ensuring representation transferability across tasks and domains.

Reducing the Model Footprint works involve various approaches that directly reduce the model size. Instead of fine-tuning the whole network [7] or the last few layers [8–11] proposed to learn a set of parameters dispersed throughout the network. They experimented with updating batch normalization and depthwise convolution kernels, resulting in small model patches providing high classification accuracy. Similar findings were also published in [12].

Quantization is a technique commonly used in on-device models to reduce model size. Post-training quantization [13] can be applied to quantize a pre-trained floating-point precision model, while quantization-aware training [14–17] ensures that the quantization effects are already modeled at training time.

Ideas inspired by the quantization literature are used in transfer and multi-task learning to reduce the footprint of the model for the target tasks. For example, in [18], learned binary masks are element-wise multiplied to the source kernels to obtain the convolutional kernels to be used on the target task. In [19], the binary masks are augmented with floating-point scalars to produce an affine transformation of the kernel. Our method learns similar kernel masks, but we go one step further by automatically selecting the subset of layers to patch.

Dynamic routing works adapt the network structure to optimize a pre-defined objective. [20] trained a gating network selecting a sparse combination of experts based on input examples. [21] created a model allowing selective execution. In their setting, given an input, only a subset of neurons is executed. [22] reduced the number of ResNet [23] layers by bypassing residual blocks using a gating mechanism. [24] built a dynamic routing network to choose between using either the pre-trained frozen blocks, or the re-trained blocks.

Our approach differs from all these studies in that: (1) our dynamic model architecture is conditioned on dataset rather than on input; (2) we optimize (reduce) the number of patched layers; and (3) one of the route types, in our design, is specialized to use binary weights to further reduce footprint.

Transfer learning and domain adaptation works study the ability of models to transfer across tasks, in terms of achieving optimal accuracy in novel situations. In transfer learning, the target label set might differ from the source task. In domain adaptation, the classes may be the same, but have inherently different distributions. Some transfer and adaptation techniques minimize the discrepancy between tasks or domains in terms of the feature representation [25–34]. If the classes are the same, the deviation between classifier weights across domains can be minimized [35,36]. One of the most established recent benchmarks for transfer of classification networks is the Visual Decathlon Challenge [6], in which a decathlon-inspired scoring function is used to evaluate how well a single network can solve 10 different classification tasks. In the object detection literature, [37] proposes to use a source domain to generate boxes of different levels of class-specificity, to transfer to a target domain where only image-level labels are available. *In contrast to optimizing accuracy despite limited data in the target domain,* as is often the objective of domain adaptation, in this work we are concerned with preserving high accuracy while *minimizing the footprint* of the task-specific model patches.

3   Approach

To simplify notation, we assume a deep neural network $\mathcal{M}$ of depth N is composed of a set of layers represented by their weights $\theta = \{\mathbf{W}_1, \ldots, \mathbf{W}_N\}$, plus an activation function Φ. The transformation computed by the network is represented using Eq. 1, where x is the input and z_i denotes the i-th hidden state.

$$\begin{cases} z_i = \Phi(\mathbf{W}_i z_{i-1}), & z_0 = x \\ \mathcal{M}(x) = \mathbf{W}_N z_{N-1} \end{cases} \tag{1}$$

To adapt $\mathcal{M}$ to solve a new task, we seek a task-specific parameter $\theta' = \{\mathbf{W}'_1, \ldots, \mathbf{W}'_N\}$ that optimizes the loss on the target dataset. In addition, since we do not want to fully re-learn θ', we look for a transformation with minimum cost (measured in terms of footprint) to convert the original θ to θ'. Assume the transformation function can be expressed as $\theta' = f(\theta, \gamma)$ where γ is an additional set of parameters for the new task, and f is a function that combines the original parameters θ with the parameter "patch" γ (as a very simple example, through addition). Our goal is to reduce the bit size of γ. In our experiments, we use relative footprint $\frac{\text{bitsize}(\gamma)}{\text{bitsize}(\theta)}$ and patch size bitsize(γ) as footprint metrics.

We propose two approaches to compress the patch γ, namely *task-specific weight transform* and *spot patching*. The former is inspired by the early Adaptive-SVM approaches such as [36,38], their Deep Neural Network counterparts such as [19], as well as quantization methods [15] and the low-rank representations [39].

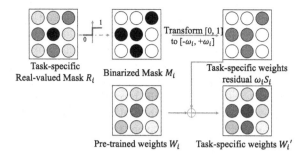

Fig. 3. The weight patching model. The pre-trained weights are augmented using a task-specific scaled sign matrix. For deployment, only the binary masks $\mathbf{M}_i$ and the scaling factors ω_i are stored in the model patch.

The latter is inspired by the dynamic routing approaches such as [24] and channel pruning methods such as [40,41].

3.1 Task-Specific Weight Transform

We denote the pre-trained weights by $\theta = \{\mathbf{W}_1, \ldots, \mathbf{W}_N\}$ and define the task-specific weight trasformation as:

$$\mathbf{W}'_i = \mathbf{W}_i + \omega_i \mathbf{S}_i \tag{2}$$

where $\mathbf{S}_i$ is a 1-bit matrix of the same shape as $\mathbf{W}_i$ containing $\{-1, +1\}$ and ω_i is a scaling factor. For implementation convenience we use $\mathbf{M}_i$ as a 1-bit mask tensor with values in $\{0, 1\}$, and define $\mathbf{S}_i = 1 - 2\mathbf{M}_i$. This formulation is equivalent to Eq. 2 in [19], with k_0 set to 1, and k_2 set to $-2k_1$. The reason we instead chose our formulation is that we empirically found the learned k_2 in [19] to be roughly distributed as $-2k_1$. We thus directly formulated Eq. 2 as learning a properly scaled zero-centered residual.

The incremental footprint of the model in Eq. 2 is $\{\omega_i, \mathbf{M}_i | i \in \{1, \ldots, N\}\}$, or roughly 1-bit per model weight, with a negligible additional cost for the per-layer scalar ω_i. To learn the 1-bit mask $\mathbf{M}_i$, we follow the same approach as [18] and [19]. We define the process in Eq. 3, and illustrate it in Fig. 3. During training, real-valued mask variables are maintained ($\mathbf{R}_i$ in Eq. 3) and differentiable binarization is applied to learn the masks. The binarization function is a hard thresholding function, and its gradient is set to that of the *sigmoid* function σ. After training, only the binarized masks and the per-layer scaling factors are used to deploy the model patch.

$$\mathbf{M}_i = \text{Binarize}(\mathbf{R}_i) \tag{3}$$

3.2 Spot Patching

Assuming a 32-bit float representation, the task-specific weight transform produces patches 1/32 the size of the original network, regardless of the target dataset. However, our intuition is that the difficulty of adapting a model should also depend on the target dataset, so the footprint should vary for different tasks.

We design a gating mechanism to adapt the model complexity to different tasks. The process is defined in Eq. 4, and Fig. 2 shows the idea. Simply speaking, we add a *gate* g_i for each network layer. The layer uses the original pre-trained weights if the gate value is 0; otherwise, the layer uses weight transform to update the parameters. The benefit of using the gating indicator g_i is that it allows to search for a task-specific subset of layers to patch, *rather than patching all layers*. Compared to patching the whole network, it reduces the patch footprint to $\gamma = \{\omega_i, \mathbf{M}_i | \ i \in \{1, \ldots, N\}$ and $g_i = 1\}$.

$$\mathbf{W}'_i = \mathbf{W}_i + \underbrace{g_i}_{\text{gating}} \omega_i(1 - 2\mathbf{M}_i) \tag{4}$$

$$g_i = \text{Binarize}(f_i) \tag{5}$$

To learn g_i, we simply use the same differentiable binarization trick as for learning the $\mathbf{M}_i$. In Eq. 5, f_i is real-valued, and it is only used during training. To force the number of patched layers to be small, we minimize the number of patched layers $\sum_{i=1}^{N} g_i$ in the training loss (see next Sect. 3.3).

SpotPatch gating module design follows the same vein of dynamic routing approaches, especially [24]. The difference with respect to [24] lies in the fact that SpotPatch applies binary quantization to the tuning route (Sect. 3.1), greatly reducing the footprint. On the one hand, SpotPatch gating module can be seen as a simpler version of [24], in that we use the same differentiable binarization trick for both generating the binary masks, and directly optimizing the gating variables. On the other hand, our loss function explicitly minimizes the number of patched layers (see next Sect. 3.3), hence delivering a task-adaptive footprint, rather than a fix-sized one as in [24]. For example, [24] would provide a 300%, or 1000% footprint increase (they provided two models) to solve 10 classification tasks, while our method only requires an extra 35% footprint to solve 9 additional object detection tasks.

3.3   Our Final Task-Adaptive Detector

Our final model on a new task is similar to Eq. 1, with the parameters replaced by Eq. 4. During training, we use floating-point numbers and differentiable binarization (Eq. 3 and Eq. 5). During deployment, bit representations are used to efficiently encode the learned patch. Since the Batch Normalization layers did not constitute much of the footprint, we also trained task-specific Batch Normalization layers in addition to the convolutional weight residuals ([19] also patches BN layers). We use Eq. 6 to optimize the task-specific patch γ:

$$L(\gamma) = L_{det}(\gamma) + \lambda_{sps}L_{sps}(\gamma) + \lambda_{adp}L_{adp}(\gamma) \tag{6}$$

where: $L_{det}(\gamma)$ is the detection loss optimizing both the class confidence scores and the box locations. $L_{sps}(\gamma) = \sum_{i=1}^{N} g_i$ is the sparsity-inducing loss, pushing the number of patched layers to be small. Finally, $L_{adp}(\gamma) = \sum_{i=1}^{N} \|\omega_i\|_2^2$ is the domain-adaptation loss forcing the scaling factors ω_i to be small, and thus θ' to be similar to θ. In this way, the pre-trained general-purpose source model serves as a strong prior for the task-specific target model. A similar loss to L_{adp} has been employed in prior domain adaptation works [36,38], to force the adapted weights to be small and train accurate models with limited data. We provide an ablation study for λ_{sps} in Sect. 4.4, while for λ_{adp} we use the constant value of 2E-5, as selected in preliminary experiments.

4 Experiments

We propose two scenarios for patching a mobile object detector, and design experiments to validate our model for both use-cases.

Adapting an Object Detector to Solve a New Task. For this scenario (Sect. 4.1), assume that we released a mature generic object detector to our users. However, if the user wants to perform a new unsupported detection task, we need to adapt the generic detector to solve the new task. For example, we may transform it into a product detector, or we may turn it into a pet detector. In this scenario, the challenge is to accurately and efficiently solve the new task.

Updating an Existing Detection Model, Whenever Additional Training Data for the Same Task is Available. For this use-case (Sect. 4.2), suppose we released an initial mobile model. We gather more training data after the model is released to the users. We then want to update the users models to improve the accuracy, while keeping the download byte size to be small. In this case, we assume that there is no significant shift in the data distribution, yet the initial model may be inaccurate because of the cold start.

In addition to the above settings, in Sect. 4.3 we consider the more practical 8-bit model quantization scenario. In Sect. 4.4 we study the effect of the sparsity constraint. In Sect. 4.5 we provide visualizations of the learned model patches.

Implementation Details. Our experimental configuration is based on the SSD-FPNLite architecture [42,43], a practical mobile-friendly architecture. Slightly departing from the original configuration, we use the MobileNetV2 [3] architecture with 320×320 inputs.

Baselines. We compare with the following transfer learning baselines:

- FINE-TUNING [44]: This method fine-tunes the whole network. It provides a strong baseline in terms of accuracy, at the expense of a very large footprint.
- TOWER PATCH [44]: This method re-trains only the parameters in the detection head of the model. It is an adaptation and enhancement of the classifier last layer fine-tuning method, for object detection.
- BN PATCH [11], DW PATCH [11], BN+DW PATCH [11,12]: These methods learn task-specific BatchNorm, Depthwise, or BatchNorm + Depthwise layers, respectively. They provide a patch with a tiny footprint.

- PIGGYBACK [18]: Learns task-specific binary masks, and uses element-wise multiplication to apply the masks and obtain the task-specific convolutional kernels. Since the masks are binary, the 1-bit patch has a very low footprint.
- WEIGHTTRANS [19]: This baseline also relies on binary masks. It applies affine transformations on the masks to get the task-specific kernels.

We reproduced all approaches using the SSD-FPNLite architecture for the following reasons: 1) most papers only report results for classification tasks, or for a few detection datasets; 2) implementations based on different network architectures make comparing the footprint challenging. In all our experiments we thus use our implementation of these methods. We did not re-implement and evaluate [24], as this approach creates weight residuals with the same bit-size as the original ones, i.e. full float kernels. It is thus not effective at significantly reducing the patch footprint, requiring as large as 3x or 10x (compared to the original model) additional footprints on the Visual Decathlon Challenge. As explained in next Sect. 4.1, we use finetuning as the baseline for parameter-*inefficient* transfer learning.

Metrics. To evaluate the detection performance, we use the mAP@0.5, which is the mean Average Precision over all classes, considering the generous threshold of IoU ≥ 0.5. For the footprint, we report the ratio $\frac{\text{bitsize}(\gamma)}{\text{bitsize}(\theta)}$ between the size of the additional parameters γ necessary to solve the new tasks, and the size of the original model θ. Section 4.1 and 4.2 consider 32-bit float models, in which the footprint metric is identical to that of Visual Decathlon Challenge [6]. In this case (32-bit float), the 1-bit binary masks (e.g., [18,19]) reduce the representation footprint by 32x. Section 4.3 considers instead the 8-bit representation, as it is more relevant for mobile applications.

4.1   Detection Decathlon

We use the OpenImages V4 [45] as the dataset for training the generic object detection model. This is a large-scale dataset featuring 1.74 million images of common objects from 600 different classes. Our fully-trained mobile model achieves 27.6% mAP@0.5 on the OpenImage V4 validation set. We then consider adapting the OpenImage V4 pre-trained model to nine additional detection tasks (see Table 1), and compare models on the basis of how well they solve all the problems (mAP@0.5), and how small is their footprint.

For the datasets used in the Detection Decathlon, the Caltech-UCSD Birds [47] (Bird), Cars [49] (Car), and Stanford Dogs [53] (Dog) are fine-grained categorization datasets. They provide center-view objects with bounding box annotations. The WiderFace [46] (Face) and Kitti [48] (Kitti) are human-related datasets. The former features human faces in different contexts and scales; the latter features vehicles and pedestrians for self-driving studies. The Oxford-IIIT Pet [50] (Pet) and Retail Product Checkout [52] (RPC) require both the fine-grained classification as well as localization. They involve many categories that appear in different locations and scales. Finally, the Pascal VOC [54] (VOC)

Table 1. Detection Decathlon datasets. Number of samples and classes for each dataset used in our benchmark. Some datasets did not provide testing annotations; we thus evaluate on the held-out validation sets.

Name	#Trainval	#Eval	#Classes	Name	#Trainval	#Eval	#Classes
OID [45]	1,668,276	-	601	Face [46]	12,880	3,226	1
Birds [47]	3,000	3,033	200	Kitti [48]	6,981	500	2
Cars [49]	8,144	8,041	196	Pet [50]	3,180	500	37
COCO [51]	118,287	5,000	80	RPC [52]	5,400	600	200
Dogs [53]	12,000	8,580	120	VOC [54]	16,551	4,952	20

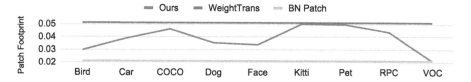

Fig. 4. Per-dataset footprint. SPOTPATCH footprint varies between that of PIGGY-BACK and that of BN PATCH, depending on the complexity of the task.

and COCO [51] (COCO) are common object detection datasets. The class labels defined in them are subsets of those in OpenImage V4.

Different from the Visual Decathlon challenge, we assume the performance and footprint of the model on the original task (OpenImages V4) are unchanged, and only compare the models accuracy and footprint on the remaining nine tasks. We refer to the above problem as the *Detection Decathlon* problem. Similarly to [6] we also provide a decathlon-inspired scoring function to evaluate the performance of each method on the benchmark:

$$Score = 10000\frac{1}{D}\sum_{d=1}^{D}\left(\frac{|s_d - b_d|^+}{1 - b_d}\right)^2 \tag{7}$$

where: the score s_d is the mAP of the considered approach on the d task; b_d is the score of a strong *baseline* on the d task; 10,000 is the maximum achievable score, and D is the total number of tasks to be solved. Similarly to [6], we select b_d to be the mAP of FINE-TUNING on task d, and normalize it so that its total score on the benchmark is 2,500. Specifically we set: $b_d = 2\,\mathrm{mAP}_d(\text{FINE-TUNING}) - 1$.

To compare efficiency and effectiveness of different methods using one single metric, we finally report the *Score/Footprint* ratio [19]. For a given method, this metric practically measures the performance achieved for every Mb of footprint.

Table 2 and Fig. 4 shows our main results. Our first observation is that *patching an object detector is more challenging than patching a classifier*. Notably, none of the tested methods matches the FINE-TUNING Score, or mAP. The enhanced last layer fine-tuning method, TOWER PATCH, only achieves 33% of the FINE-TUNING score. Patching dispersed bottleneck layers provides reason-

Table 2. Detection Decathlon. Footprint, per-dataset mAP, Average mAP, Score and Score/Footprint for each method. Best method (other than fine-tuning) in **bold**, second-best underlined. High score, low footprint, and high score/footprint ratio is good. Ours is the most parameter-efficient method in terms of Score/Footprint. It achieves mAP and Score comparable to the most accurate approach (WEIGHTTRANS 65.2%), with a 24% reduction in footprint.

Method	Footprint	Bird	Car	COCO	Dog	Face	Kitti	Pet	RPC	VOC	Average mAP	Score	Score/Footprint
FINE-TUNING	9.00	40.8	90.4	39.7	68.5	35.6	71.9	90.9	99.5	68.3	67.3	2500	278
TOWER PATCH	0.35	10.0	25.5	31.4	21.2	29.1	49.7	66.1	87.6	70.6	43.5	827	2362
BN PATCH	**0.19**	22.6	71.6	30.2	47.8	26.0	50.7	80.6	92.0	**71.1**	54.7	910	<u>4789</u>
DW PATCH	0.34	22.6	69.2	30.7	43.6	26.4	52.1	80.0	92.6	<u>70.8</u>	54.2	898	2642
BN+DW PATCH	0.50	27.3	80.9	31.0	52.7	28.0	53.1	83.3	95.7	70.6	58.1	1012	2023
PIGGYBACK	<u>0.30</u>	32.2	87.5	32.4	60.8	28.6	57.4	87.7	97.0	66.0	61.1	1353	4509
WEIGHTTRANS	0.46	**36.6**	**90.3**	**37.2**	**66.6**	**30.6**	**65.3**	90.5	<u>98.7</u>	70.7	**65.2**	**1987**	4319
OURS	0.35	<u>35.8</u>	<u>89.8</u>	<u>36.6</u>	<u>63.3</u>	<u>30.1</u>	<u>64.0</u>	<u>90.3</u>	**98.9**	70.6	<u>64.4</u>	<u>1858</u>	**5310**

able improvements. For example in terms of Score, BN PATCH, DW PATCH, and BN+DW PATCH are 10.0%, 8.6%, and 22.4% relatively better than TOWER PATCH, and they all provide less than 0.50 footprints. However, the gap with respect to FINE-TUNING is still large. They only maintain less than 40.5% of the FINE-TUNING Score. The kernel quantization methods PIGGYBACK and WEIGHTTRANS maintain at least 54.1% of the FINE-TUNING Score, while keeping the footprint below 0.46. SPOTPATCH achieves comparable performance to WEIGHTTRANS at only a 0.35 footprint. It also maintains 74.3% of the FINE-TUNING Score.

Our approach provides the best tradeoff by being parameter-efficient and yet accurate, as measured by the Score/Footprint ratio. This is achieved by learning patches with a task-adaptive footprint, resulting on average in a 24% footprint reduction with respect to WEIGHTTRANS, with only minor loss in accuracy.

4.2   Model Updating

For this experiment, we use the COCO dataset [51]. First, we trained detection models (initialized from ImageNet [55] pre-trained model) on 10%, 20%, 40%, and 80% of the COCO training set. These models achieved 20.9%, 24.2%, 31.4%, and 35.7% mAP@0.5 on the COCO17 validation set, respectively. Then, we applied different patching approaches to update these imprecise models, using 100% of the COCO data. We then compared mAP@0.5 of the patched models, as well as the resulting patch footprints.

Table 3 shows the results. Similar to the Detection Decathlon, we observe that none of the tested approaches is able to achieve the same mAP as fine-tuning. Ours is the only method that can adapt the footprint according to the source model quality and the amount of new training data: At 10% training data, we achieve comparable mAP as WEIGHTTRANS (32.0% v.s. 32.7%) at a comparable footprint (5.04% v.s. 5.15%). However, when more data is available,

Table 3. Model updating. Our method achieves comparable mAP and smaller footprint than the strongest baseline. The percentages (e.g. 10%) indicate the amount of data to train the source model. The best method is shown in **bold**, second-best underlined. Only one footprint number is shown for the baseline methods because they generate the same footprint regardless of the task.

Method	Footprint (%)				mAP (%)			
	10%	20%	40%	80%	10%	20%	40%	80%
Fine-Tuning	100.0				37.6	37.6	38.2	38.5
Tower Patch	3.85				24.5	26.7	32.4	35.8
Bn Patch	**2.08**				26.2	28.1	33.0	35.8
Dw Patch	3.76				25.9	27.8	33.1	**36.0**
Bn+Dw Patch	5.59				26.8	28.7	33.4	<u>35.9</u>
Piggyback	3.32				26.4	28.3	32.0	35.3
WeightTrans	5.15				**32.7**	**32.4**	**34.8**	<u>35.9</u>
Ours	5.04	4.98	4.21	**2.08**	<u>32.0</u>	<u>31.4</u>	<u>34.2</u>	35.8

the patch footprint generated by our approach is smaller than WeightTrans (2.08% v.s. 5.15%), while accuracy remains comparable (35.8% v.s. 35.9%).

To summarize, our method can effectively adapt the patch footprint to the amount of new data to be learned by the patch, while maintaining high accuracy.

4.3 Accuracy-Footprint Tradeoff in 8-Bit Models

To compute the footprint, both Sect. 4.1 and 4.2 account for the binary mask size as 1/32 of the float kernel size. This convention is widely accepted by the participants in the Visual Decathlon Challenge. However, in practical mobile applications, quantization-aware training [14–17] is often used to train a model using 8 bits per weight – i.e., reduce the model size by 4x, without losing accuracy. In the 8-bit model scenario, the relative footprint gains achieved by binary masks are thus 4x smaller than in the 32-bit model scenario. We estimate the footprint of 8-bit models in the Detection Decathlon and assume quantization-aware training does not significantly hurt the detection performance [15]. I.e., we did not train the 8-bit models but assume the mAP to be roughly the same as the 32-bit counterpart. To compare with the relative gains in the 32-bit scenarion, we show both of them side-by-side in Fig. 5.

As shown in Fig. 5, in the 8-bit scenario our method becomes more parameter-efficient than Piggyback and WeightTrans. The reason lies in the fact that ours is the only mask-based approach to explicitly minimize the number of masks in each patch. In Table 4, our model is thus as much as 26% and 36% more parameter-efficient than Piggyback and WeightTrans, respectively (0.83 v.s. 1.12, 1.29). Our method would save additional 0.9Mb in network costs compared to WeightTrans *per download*. Please note that while adding more tasks does

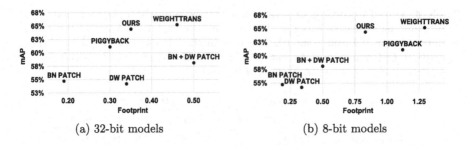

(a) 32-bit models   (b) 8-bit models

Fig. 5. Detection Decathlon: mAP v.s. Footprint. We show the object detection mAP versus footprint, for both 32-bit and 8-bit models. The x-axis denotes the patch footprint for the Detection Decathlon while the y-axis indicates the detection performance measured by mAP@0.5. We expect a good model to have both a high mAP and a low footprint.

Table 4. Detection Decathlon: mAP and patch size. The patch size is measured by the expected download bytes to solve the additional nine tasks. It depends on both the model backbone and the method. Excluding the final layer in the classification head, the size of a single Mobilenet-v2 SSD-FPNLite detector is 7.99 Mb for a 32-bit model, and 2.00 Mb for an 8-bit model.

		TYPE	FINE-TUNING	TOWER PATCH	BN PATCH	DW PATCH	BN+DW PATCH	PIGGY BACK	WEIGHT TRANS	OURS
mAP (%)	-		67.3	43.5	54.7	54.2	58.1	61.1	65.2	64.4
Footprint	32-bit	9.00	0.35	0.19	0.34	0.50	0.30	0.46	0.35
	8-bit						1.12	1.29	0.83
Patch size	32-bit	71.9 Mb	2.77 Mb	1.50 Mb	2.71 Mb	4.02 Mb	2.39 Mb	3.70 Mb	2.79 Mb
	8-bit	18.0 Mb	692 Kb	37 4Kb	677 Kb	1.01 Mb	2.25 Mb	2.58 Mb	1.66 Mb

not directly translate into mAP losses, footprint gains keep cumulating. In practical mobile application this effect would be amplified, as the same patch would need to be downloaded as many times as there are users. We thus argue that in practical mobile applications the 36% footprint reduction achieved by our method over WEIGHTTRANS, with only a 0.8% average mAP loss (64.4% v.s. 65.2%), constitutes a *significant improvement* over WEIGHTTRANS.

To summarize, in practical 8-bit scenarios our method can potentially reduce WEIGHTTRANS *footprint by 36%, with only a negligible loss in performance. It is also the most parameter-efficient mask-based method.*

4.4 Impact of the Sparsity Constraint

Next, we show the tradeoff between footprint and performance can further be selected by tuning λ_{sps}. We perform a study on the Detection Decathlon tasks: we vary λ_{sps} while keeping all other hyper-parameters the same.

Table 5 shows the results. We observed that the λ_{sps} has a direct impact on the percentage of patched layers and the patch footprint. In general, a large λ_{sps} value forces the footprint to be small, while a small λ_{sps} leads to a more accurate

Table 5. Impact of sparsity constraint. We show the percentage of patched layers, relative footprint, and mAP regarding models trained using different λ_{sps}.

	Patched layers (%)			Footprint (%)			mAP (%)		
	1E−03	1E−04	1E−05	1E−03	1E−04	1E−05	1E−03	1E−04	1E−05
Bird	12.7	8.5	7.0	3.93	2.97	2.93	35.8	35.8	34.0
Car	12.7	25.4	29.6	3.39	3.89	3.92	89.3	89.8	89.7
COCO	19.7	42.3	53.5	4.12	4.62	4.76	35.5	36.6	36.8
Dog	22.5	19.7	87.3	4.14	3.54	5.09	64.9	63.3	66.0
Face	29.6	32.4	95.8	3.45	3.39	5.12	28.6	30.1	30.4
Kitti	31.0	69.0	81.7	4.08	5.01	4.77	58.8	64.0	63.3
Pet	22.5	53.5	52.1	4.24	4.97	4.32	90.9	90.3	90.5
RPC	42.3	53.5	67.6	4.67	4.37	4.68	98.3	98.9	98.9
VOC	0.0	0.0	2.8	2.08	2.08	2.54	70.5	70.6	69.9
	Avg Patched layers (%)			Sum Footprint (%)			Avg mAP (%)		
	21.4	33.8	53.1	34.1	34.8	38.1	63.6	64.4	64.4

model. If we only use a small value ($\lambda_{sps} = 1.00\mathrm{E}{-}05$), the method still patches the majority of the model layers (53.1% in average), with a corresponding mAP of 64.4%. However, if we increase λ_{sps} to $1.00\mathrm{E}{-}03$, the proportion of patched layers is significantly reduced (21.4%) and mAP is only slightly reduced to 63.6%. We use $\lambda_{sps} = 1.00\mathrm{E}{-}4$ throughout the paper.

Table 5 also highlights how the patching difficulty on different tasks varies. For example, the VOC target task is the most similar to the OpenImages source task. Our method learned that updating the batch normalization layers is enough. It thus degraded to BN PATCH, as almost none of the layers were patched.

4.5 Visualization of Model Patches

Next, we shed light on the nature of the patches learned by SpotPatch, and the effect of the source/target task similarity. Figure 6 shows the results for all the convolutional layers of the FPNLite model. For the Detection Decathlon problem, our approach patched fewer layers on the target tasks most similar to the source one, while modified more layers on the most dissimilar target tasks. Our model learned that it is okay to leave all of the convolutional layers unchanged, for the VOC dataset. In this case, it degraded to the BN PATCH approach, which tunes only the batch normalization layers. The reason, we argue, is that VOC labels are a subset of the OpenImages V4 labels. In contrast, our model patched 69.0% of the model layers for the Kitti task. Though the Kitti dataset features everyday objects such as vehicles and pedestrians, the appearance of these objects is significantly different from OpenImages V4 because they are captured by cameras mounted on cars for autonomous driving research.

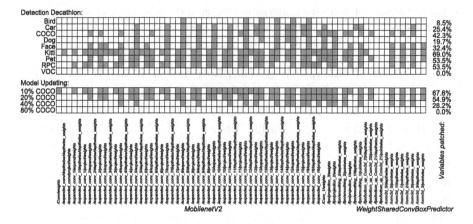

Fig. 6. Patched layers for different tasks. We emphasize our method learned different model patches based on the complexity of the tasks. In the figure, each row denotes a patching policy for a specific dataset, and each column represents the gating indicator of a particular layer. For each row, a red block means that the learned model patch includes the weights residuals of the specific kernel. White blocks indicate that the source kernel is reused as is, with no contribution to the footprint. We show the proportion of patched layers on the right. Best viewed with 200% zoom-in.

Similar observations are made on the model updating. To patch the pre-trained models armed with 40% and 80% COCO information, our method patched 28.2% and 0.0% of the layers. However, for the imprecise and low-quality pre-trained models, for example, the models with 10% and 20% COCO information, our model patched 67.6% and 54.9% of the layers.

The patched models also shared some common patterns. Our method did not patch the first few convolutional layers and the FPN upsampling layers for most tasks. We argue the reason is that these layers are responsible for recognizing fundamental visual features that can be shared across domains.

5   Conclusion

In this paper we drew the foundations for investigating parameter-efficient transfer learning in the context of mobile object detection. We introduced the Detection Decathlon problem, and provided the first systematic study of parameter-efficient transfer learning on this task. We proposed the SpotPatch approach, using task-specific weight transformations and dynamic routing to minimize the footprint of the learned patch. We also demonstrated how to use our technique for updating a pre-trained model. In all the considered benchmarks SpotPatch was shown to provide similar mAP as standard Weight-Transform, while being significantly more parameter-efficient. Additional potential gains were shown in the case of 8-bit quantization. We also noted how differently from classification benchmarks, none of the tested approaches was actually able to beat fine-tuning mAP, which calls for more work on the Detection Decathlon task.

References

1. Howard, A., et al.: Searching for mobilenetv3. In: The IEEE International Conference on Computer Vision (ICCV) (2019)
2. Howard, A.G., et al.: Mobilenets: efficient convolutional neural networks for mobile vision applications. arXiv preprint arXiv:1704.04861 (2017)
3. Sandler, M., Howard, A., Zhu, M., Zhmoginov, A., Chen, L.C.: Mobilenetv 2: inverted residuals and linear bottlenecks. In: The IEEE Conference on Computer Vision and Pattern Recognition (CVPR) (2018)
4. Liu, W., et al.: SSD: single shot MultiBox detectord. In: Leibe, B., Matas, J., Sebe, N., Welling, M. (eds.) ECCV 2016. LNCS, vol. 9905, pp. 21–37. Springer, Cham (2016). https://doi.org/10.1007/978-3-319-46448-0_2
5. Redmon, J., Divvala, S., Girshick, R., Farhadi, A.: You only look once: unified, real-time object detection. In: Proceedings of the IEEE Conference on Computer Vision and Pattern Recognition, pp. 779–788 (2016)
6. Rebuffi, S.A., Bilen, H., Vedaldi, A.: Learning multiple visual domains with residual adapters. In: Advances in Neural Information Processing Systems, pp. 506–516 (2017)
7. Cui, Y., Song, Y., Sun, C., Howard, A., Belongie, S.: Large scale fine-grained categorization and domain-specific transfer learning. In: The IEEE Conference on Computer Vision and Pattern Recognition (CVPR) (2018)
8. Oquab, M., Bottou, L., Laptev, I., Sivic, J.: Learning and transferring mid-level image representations using convolutional neural networks. In: The IEEE Conference on Computer Vision and Pattern Recognition (CVPR) (2014)
9. Thomas, C., Kovashka, A.: Seeing behind the camera: identifying the authorship of a photograph. In: The IEEE Conference on Computer Vision and Pattern Recognition (CVPR).(2016)
10. Yosinski, J., Clune, J., Bengio, Y., Lipson, H.: How transferable are features in deep neural networks? In: Ghahramani, Z., Welling, M., Cortes, C., Lawrence, N.D.,Weinberger, K.Q. (eds.) Advances in Neural Information Processing Systems 27, pp. 3320–3328. Curran Associates, Inc. (2014)
11. Mudrakarta, P.K., Sandler, M., Zhmoginov, A., Howard, A.: K for the price of 1. parameter efficient multi-task and transfer learning. In: International Conference on Learning Representations (2019)
12. Guo, Y., Li, Y., Feris, R.S., Wang, L., Rosing, T.S.: Depthwise convolution is all you need for learning multiple visual domains. In: AAAI (2019)
13. Tensorflow: Post training quantization (2020). https://www.tensorflow.org/lite/performance/post_training_quantization. Accessed 08 Dec 2020
14. Baskin, C., et al.: Uniq: Uniform noise injection for non-uniform quantization of neural networks. arXiv preprint arXiv:1804.10969 (2018)
15. Jacob, B., et al.: Quantization and training of neural networks for efficient integer-arithmetic-only inference. In: The IEEE Conference on Computer Vision and Pattern Recognition (CVPR) (2018)
16. Hubara, I., Courbariaux, M., Soudry, D., El-Yaniv, R., Bengio, Y.: Quantized neural networks: training neural networks with low precision weights and activations. J. Mach. Learn. Res. **18**, 6869–6898 (2017)
17. Tensorflow: Quantization-aware training (2020). https://github.com/tensorflow/tensorflow/tree/r1.15/tensorflow/contrib/quantize. Accessed 08 Dec 2020

18. Mallya, A., Davis, D., Lazebnik, S.: Piggyback: adapting a single network to multiple tasks by learning to mask weights. In: Ferrari, V., Hebert, M., Sminchisescu, C., Weiss, Y. (eds.) ECCV 2018. LNCS, vol. 11208, pp. 72–88. Springer, Cham (2018). https://doi.org/10.1007/978-3-030-01225-0_5

19. Mancini, M., Ricci, E., Caputo, B., Bulò, S.R.: Adding new tasks to a single network with weight transformations using binary masks. In: Leal-Taixé, L., Roth, S. (eds.) ECCV 2018. LNCS, vol. 11130, pp. 180–189. Springer, Cham (2019). https://doi.org/10.1007/978-3-030-11012-3_14

20. Shazeer, N., et al.: Outrageously large neural networks: the sparsely-gated mixture-of-experts layer. arXiv preprint arXiv:1701.06538 (2017)

21. Liu, L., Deng, J.: Dynamic deep neural networks: Optimizing accuracy-efficiency trade-offs by selective execution. In: Thirty-Second AAAI Conference on Artificial Intelligence (2018)

22. Veit, A., Belongie, S.: Convolutional networks with adaptive inference graphs. In: Ferrari, V., Hebert, M., Sminchisescu, C., Weiss, Y. (eds.) ECCV 2018. LNCS, vol. 11205, pp. 3–18. Springer, Cham (2018). https://doi.org/10.1007/978-3-030-01246-5_1

23. He, K., Zhang, X., Ren, S., Sun, J.: Deep residual learning for image recognition. In: The IEEE Conference on Computer Vision and Pattern Recognition (CVPR) (2016)

24. Guo, Y., Shi, H., Kumar, A., Grauman, K., Rosing, T., Feris, R.: Spottune: transfer learning through adaptive fine-tuning. In: The IEEE Conference on Computer Vision and Pattern Recognition (CVPR) (2019)

25. Carlucci, F.M., D'Innocente, A., Bucci, S., Caputo, B., Tommasi, T.: Domain generalization by solving jigsaw puzzles. In: The IEEE Conference on Computer Vision and Pattern Recognition (CVPR) (2019)

26. Chen, Y., Li, W., Sakaridis, C., Dai, D., Van Gool, L.: Domain adaptive faster R-CNN for object detection in the wild. In: The IEEE Conference on Computer Vision and Pattern Recognition (CVPR) (2018)

27. Ganin, Y., et al.: Domain-adversarial training of neural networks. J. Mach. Learn. Res. **17**, 2030–2096 (2016)

28. Herath, S., Harandi, M., Fernando, B., Nock, R.: Min-max statistical alignment for transfer learning. In: Proceedings of the IEEE Conference on Computer Vision and Pattern Recognition, pp. 9288–9297 (2019)

29. Long, M., Zhu, H., Wang, J., Jordan, M.I.: Unsupervised domain adaptation with residual transfer networks. In: Advances in Neural Information Processing Systems (NeurIPS), pp. 136–144 (2016)

30. Sun, Q., Liu, Y., Chua, T.S., Schiele, B.: Meta-transfer learning for few-shot learning. In: Proceedings of the IEEE Conference on Computer Vision and Pattern Recognition, pp. 403–412 (2019)

31. Tzeng, E., Hoffman, J., Saenko, K., Darrell, T.: Adversarial discriminative domain adaptation. In: The IEEE Conference on Computer Vision and Pattern Recognition (CVPR) (2017)

32. Vu, T.H., Jain, H., Bucher, M., Cord, M., Perez, P.: DADA: depth-aware domain adaptation in semantic segmentation. In: The IEEE International Conference on Computer Vision (ICCV) (2019)

33. Wang, T., Zhang, X., Yuan, L., Feng, J.: Few-shot adaptive faster R-CNN. In: Proceedings of the IEEE Conference on Computer Vision and Pattern Recognition, pp. 7173–7182 (2019)

34. Yin, X., Yu, X., Sohn, K., Liu, X., Chandraker, M.: Feature transfer learning for face recognition with under-represented data. In: Proceedings of the IEEE Conference on Computer Vision and Pattern Recognition, pp. 5704–5713 (2019)

35. Kovashka, A., Grauman, K.: Attribute adaptation for personalized image search. In: The IEEE International Conference on Computer Vision (ICCV) (2013)

36. Yang, J., Yan, R., Hauptmann, A.G.: Adapting SVM classifiers to data with shifted distributions. In: Seventh IEEE International Conference on Data Mining Workshops (ICDMW 2007), pp. 69–76. IEEE (2007)

37. Uijlings, J., Popov, S., Ferrari, V.: Revisiting knowledge transfer for training object class detectors. In: The IEEE Conference on Computer Vision and Pattern Recognition (CVPR) (2018)

38. Kovashka, A., Grauman, K.: Attribute adaptation for personalized image search. In: Proceedings of the IEEE International Conference on Computer Vision, pp. 3432–3439 (2013)

39. Li, Y., Gu, S., Gool, L.V., Timofte, R.: Learning filter basis for convolutional neural network compression. In: The IEEE International Conference on Computer Vision (ICCV) (2019)

40. Gordon, A., et al.: MorphNet: fast & simple resource-constrained structure learning of deep networks. In: The IEEE Conference on Computer Vision and Pattern Recognition (CVPR) (2018)

41. Liu, Z., Li, J., Shen, Z., Huang, G., Yan, S., Zhang, C.: Learning efficient convolutional networks through network slimming. In: The IEEE International Conference on Computer Vision (ICCV) (2017)

42. Huang, J., et al.: SSD-FPNLITE architecture for object detection (2020). https://github.com/tensorflow/models/blob/master/research/object_detection/samples/configs/ssd_mobilenet_v1_fpn_shared_box_predictor_640x640_coco14_sync.config. Accessed 08 Dec 2020

43. Lin, T.Y., Goyal, P., Girshick, R., He, K., Dollar, P.: Focal loss for dense object detection. In: The IEEE International Conference on Computer Vision (ICCV) (2017)

44. Huang, J., et al.: Speed/accuracy trade-offs for modern convolutional object detectors. In: The IEEE Conference on Computer Vision and Pattern Recognition (CVPR) (2017)

45. Kuznetsova, A., et al.: The open images dataset v4: Unified image classification, object detection, and visual relationship detection at scale. arXiv preprint arXiv:1811.00982 (2018)

46. Yang, S., Luo, P., Loy, C.C., Tang, X.: Wider face: a face detection benchmark. In: The IEEE Conference on Computer Vision and Pattern Recognition (CVPR) (2016)

47. Welinder, P., et al.: Caltech-UCSD birds 200. In: Technical Report CNS-TR-2010-001, California Institute of Technology (2010)

48. Geiger, A., Lenz, P., Urtasun, R.: Are we ready for autonomous driving? the KITTI vision benchmark suite. In: The IEEE Conference on Computer Vision and Pattern Recognition (CVPR) (2012)

49. Krause, J., Stark, M., Deng, J., Fei-Fei, L.: 3D object representations for fine-grained categorization. In: Proceedings of the IEEE International Conference on Computer Vision Workshops (2013)

50. Parkhi, O.M., Vedaldi, A., Zisserman, A., Jawahar, C.: Cats and dogs. In: The IEEE Conference on Computer Vision and Pattern Recognition (CVPR) (2012)

51. Lin, T.-Y., et al.: Microsoft COCO: common objects in context. In: Fleet, D., Pajdla, T., Schiele, B., Tuytelaars, T. (eds.) ECCV 2014. LNCS, vol. 8693, pp. 740–755. Springer, Cham (2014). https://doi.org/10.1007/978-3-319-10602-1_48

52. Wei, X.S., Cui, Q., Yang, L., Wang, P., Liu, L.: RPC: a large-scale retail product checkout dataset. arXiv preprint arXiv:1901.07249 (2019)

53. Khosla, A., Jayadevaprakash, N., Yao, B., Fei-Fei, L.: Novel dataset for fine-grained image categorization. In: First Workshop on Fine-Grained Visual Categorization, IEEE Conference on Computer Vision and Pattern Recognition, Colorado Springs, CO (2011)

54. Everingham, M., Van Gool, L., Williams, C.K.I., Winn, J., Zisserman, A.: The pascal visual object classes (VOC) challenge. Int. J. Comput. Vis. **88**, 303–338 (2010)

55. Deng, J., Dong, W., Socher, R., Li, L.J., Li, K., Fei-Fei, L.:ImageNet: a large-scale hierarchical image database. In: 2009 IEEE conference on computer vision and pattern recognition, pp. 248–255. IEEE (2009)

Trainable Structure Tensors for Autonomous Baggage Threat Detection Under Extreme Occlusion

Taimur Hassan$^{(\boxtimes)}$ and Naoufel Werghi

Center for Cyber-Physical Systems (C2PS), Khalifa University, Abu Dhabi, UAE
{taimur.hassan,naoufel.werghi}@ku.ac.ae

Abstract. Detecting baggage threats is one of the most difficult tasks, even for expert officers. Many researchers have developed computer-aided screening systems to recognize these threats from the baggage X-ray scans. However, all of these frameworks are limited in identifying the contraband items under extreme occlusion. This paper presents a novel instance segmentation framework that utilizes trainable structure tensors to highlight the contours of the occluded and cluttered contraband items (by scanning multiple predominant orientations), while simultaneously suppressing the irrelevant baggage content. The proposed framework has been extensively tested on four publicly available X-ray datasets where it outperforms the state-of-the-art frameworks in terms of mean average precision scores. Furthermore, to the best of our knowledge, it is the only framework that has been validated on combined grayscale and colored scans obtained from four different types of X-ray scanners.

Keywords: X-ray imagery · Object detection · Instance segmentation · Structure tensors

1 Introduction

Detecting threats concealed within the baggage has gained the utmost attention of aviation staff throughout the world. While X-ray imagery provides a thorough insight into the baggage content, manually screening them is a very cumbersome task, requiring constant attention of the human observer. To cater this, many researchers have developed autonomous frameworks for recognizing baggage threats from the security X-ray scans. At first, these frameworks employed conventional machine learning to identify contraband items. However, due to the subjectiveness in their feature sets, they were confined to small-scale datasets and limited experimental settings. More recently, deep learning has boosted the performance of baggage threat detection frameworks. In this paper, we discuss the pioneer works for detecting baggage threats, and for a detailed survey, we refer the readers to the work of [1].

© Springer Nature Switzerland AG 2021
H. Ishikawa et al. (Eds.): ACCV 2020, LNCS 12627, pp. 257–273, 2021.
https://doi.org/10.1007/978-3-030-69544-6_16

1.1 Conventional Machine Learning Methods

Initial methods developed for screening prohibited items used classification [2], detection [3] and segmentation [4] strategies. The classification schemes are driven through hand-engineered features [5,6] and key-point descriptors such as SURF [7], FAST-SURF [8] and SIFT [5,9] in conjunction with Support Vector Machines (SVM) [2,7,8], Random Forest [6] and K-Nearest Neighbor (K-NN) [10] models for recognizing baggage threats. Contrary to this, researchers have also proposed object detection schemes employing fused SPIN and SIFT descriptors derived from multi-view X-ray imagery [3]. Moreover, 3D feature points driven through the structure from motion have also been utilized in recognizing the potential baggage threats [9]. Apart from this, the segmentation schemes utilizing region-growing and SURF features along with the Neighbor Distance achieved good performance for recognizing prohibited baggage items [4].

1.2 Deep Learning Methods

The initial wave of deep learning methods employed transfer learning [11,12] for recognizing the baggage threats followed by object detection [13–17], and segmentation strategies [18,19]. Recently, researchers used anomaly detection [20,21] as a means to handle data scarcity while recognizing potential baggage threats. Moreover, attention modules [14] and maximum likelihood estimations [22] have also been explored for detecting the contraband items. Apart from this, Miao et al. [15] exploited the imbalanced and extremely cluttered nature of the baggage threats by introducing a large-scale dataset dubbed Security Inspection X-ray (SIXray) [15]. They also proposed a class-balanced hierarchical framework (CHR) to recognize the contraband items from the highly complex scans of the SIXray [15] dataset. Furthermore, Hassan et al. developed a Cascaded Structure Tensor (CST) framework that alleviates contours of the contraband items to generate object proposals which are classified through the ResNet-50 [23] model. CST is validated on publicly available GRIMA X-ray Database (GDXray) [24] and SIXray [15] datasets. Moreover, Wei et al. [25] developed De-occlusion Attention Module (DOAM), a plug and play module that can be paired with object detectors to recognize and localize the occluded contraband items from the baggage X-ray scans. DOAM has been rigorously tested on a publicly available Occluded Prohibited Items X-ray (OPIXray) dataset introduced in [25].

Detecting occluded and extremely cluttered contraband items from the baggage X-ray scans is a very challenging task [11,18]. Towards this end, frameworks such as CHR [15], CST [17], and DOAM [25] possess the capability to identify occluded baggage items. However, these frameworks are either tested on a single dataset [15,25] or cannot be generalized for the multiple scanner specifications due to exhaustive parametric tuning [17]. To cater these limitations, this paper presents a single-staged instance segmentation framework that leverages proposed trainable structure tensors to recognize the contours of the prohibited items while suppressing the irrelevant baggage content as shown in Fig. 1. To summarize, the main features of the paper are:

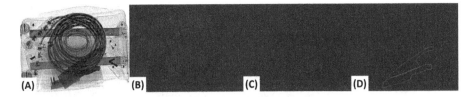

Fig. 1. (A) Baggage X-ray scan from the SIXray [15] dataset, (B) best tensor representation obtained through the modified structure tensor approach [17], (C) suppression of the irrelevant baggage content through proposed trainable structure tensors, (D) predicted boundaries of the contraband items.

- A novel trainable structure tensors scheme to highlight transitional patterns of the desired objects by analyzing predominant orientations of the associated image gradients.
- A single-staged instance segmentation framework capable of recognizing extremely cluttered and occluded contraband items from scans acquired through diverse ranging scanner specifications.
- A rigorous validation of the proposed framework on four publicly available X-ray datasets for recognizing baggage threats under extreme occlusion.

Rest of the paper is organized as follows: Sect. 2 describe the proposed framework in detail, Sect. 3 presents the experimental setup along with the datasets description, the implementation details and the evaluation metrics. Section 4 discuss the experimental results and Sect. 5 concludes the paper.

2   Proposed Framework

The block diagram of the proposed framework is shown in Fig. 2. First of all, we compute the best tensor representation of the input scan through the structure tensor module. Afterward, we pass it through the multi-class encoder-decoder backbone that only retains the transitional patterns of the threatening items while suppressing the rest of the baggage content. The extracted contours are post-processed and then utilized in generating the bounding boxes and masks of the corresponding suspicious items. The detailed description of each module is presented below:

2.1   Structure Tensor Module

When the input X-ray scan is loaded into the proposed system, it is passed through the structure tensor module which highlights the transitions of each object (within the input scan) by summarizing the predominant orientations of its image gradients within the specified neighborhood of each pixel. However, the conventional structure tensor approach only computes the outer product of image gradients oriented at x and y direction, which limits the extraction of

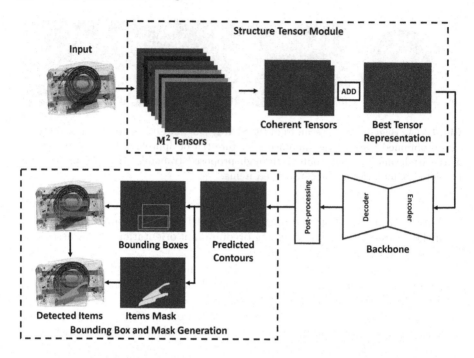

Fig. 2. Block diagram of the proposed framework.

objects that are oriented only at these directions. To cater this, Hassan et al. [17] recently proposed a modified structure tensor approach in which they compute the outer product of image gradients (dubbed tensor) oriented in any direction. Furthermore, instead of finding the strong orientations within the specified neighborhood of any pixel (as done in the conventional structure tensor), the modified structure tensor approach selects the coherent tensors according to their norm, such that they represent maximum transitions of each object within the candidate scan. But the modified structure tensor approach is still limited in differentiating between contours of the contraband items and normal baggage content. To overcome this, we present a novel trainable structure tensor scheme. Before discussing our approach, we first present both the original structure tensor and the modified structure tensor scheme for the sake of completeness.

Structure Tensor: is a 2×2 matrix defined by the outer product of image gradients (oriented at x and y direction) within the specified neighborhood of each pixel. It summarizes the distribution of predominant orientations (for each object transition) within the associated image gradients and tells the degree to which these orientations are coherent. For the ith pixel in the input scan, the structure tensor $S(i)$ is defined as:

$$S(i) = \begin{bmatrix} \sum_j \varphi_{(j)} (\nabla^x_{(i-j)})^2 & \sum_j \varphi_{(j)} (\nabla^x_{(i-j)} . \nabla^y_{(i-j)}) \\ \sum_j \varphi_{(j)} (\nabla^y_{(i-j)} . \nabla^x_{(i-j)}) & \sum_j \varphi_{(j)} (\nabla^y_{(i-j)})^2 \end{bmatrix}, \quad (1)$$

where φ is a Gaussian filter, ∇^x and ∇^y are the gradients oriented at x and y direction, respectively. Afterward, the degree of coherency or anisotropy is measured through:

$$c_d = \left(\frac{\lambda_1 - \lambda_2}{\lambda_1 + \lambda_2} \right)^2, \quad (2)$$

where c_d quantifies the degree of coherency, λ_1 and λ_2 are the eigenvalues of $S(i)$.

Modified Structure Tensor: The modified version of structure tensor can highlight the transitional patterns of the objects oriented in any direction by utilizing its respective image gradients [17]. For the M image gradients oriented at M directions within the candidate scan, the modified structure tensor is defined as a $M \times M$ matrix such that:

$$\begin{bmatrix} \varphi * (\nabla^0 . \nabla^0) & \varphi * (\nabla^1 . \nabla^0) & \cdots & \varphi * (\nabla^{M-1} . \nabla^0) \\ \varphi * (\nabla^0 . \nabla^1) & \varphi * (\nabla^1 . \nabla^1) & \cdots & \varphi * (\nabla^{M-1} . \nabla^1) \\ \vdots & \vdots & \ddots & \vdots \\ \varphi * (\nabla^0 . \nabla^{M-1}) & \varphi * (\nabla^1 . \nabla^{M-1}) & \cdots & \varphi * (\nabla^{M-1} . \nabla^{M-1}) \end{bmatrix}, \quad (3)$$

where each tensor $\varphi * (\nabla^m . \nabla^n)$ is an outer product of image gradients (oriented at m and n direction) and the smoothing filter. Here, the gradient orientations (θ) are computed as: $\vartheta = \frac{2\pi \tau}{M}$ where τ varies from 0 to $M - 1$. Since, the multi-oriented block-structured tensor matrix (in Eq. 3) is symmetrical, only the $\frac{M(M+1)}{2}$ (out of M^2) tensors are unique, and from these unique tensors, the most coherent ones (containing the maximum transitions of the baggage content) are selected according to their norm [17]. Afterward, the selected tensors are added together to generate a single coherent representation of the object transitions as shown in Fig. 1 (B).

Proposed Trainable Structure Tensor: The modified structure tensor approach (proposed in [17]) can identify the transitional patterns of any object within the candidate scan by analyzing the predominant orientations of its image gradients (which leads towards the detection of concealed and cluttered contraband items [17]). However, it cannot differentiate between the transitions of the contraband items and the normal baggage content. Therefore, to remove the noisy and irrelevant proposals it requires extensive screening efforts. Furthermore, CST framework [17] uses an additional classifier to recognize the proposals of each contraband item within the candidate scan. Also, it has to be tuned for each dataset separately due to which it does not generalize well on multi-vendor X-ray scans [17]. To address these limitations, we present a trainable structure tensor approach that employs an encoder-decoder backbone to extract and recognize contours of the highly cluttered, concealed, and overlapping contraband items, while suppressing the rest of the baggage content. The utilization of the encoder-decoder backbone eliminates the need for the additional classification network and it not only localizes each item through the bounding boxes but generates their masks as well. Therefore, unlike the object detection methods proposed in recent works [15,17,25] for baggage threat detection, we propose a single-staged instance segmentation framework which, to the best of our knowledge, is the first framework in its category specifically designed to recognize the cluttered contraband items from the multi-vendor baggage X-ray scans.

2.2   Bounding Box and Mask Generation

After extracting and recognizing the contours of the contraband items, we first perform morphological post-processing to filter the false positives. Then, for each contraband item, we use its boundary to generate its bounding box (through the minimum bounding rectangle technique [26]) and the mask (by filling the inner pixels with one's).

3   Experimental Setup

This section contains the details about the datasets, the implementation of the proposed framework, and the metrics which we used to validate the proposed framework.

3.1   Datasets

The proposed framework has been validated on four publicly available grayscale and colored X-ray datasets. The detailed description of these datasets is presented below:

GDXray (first introduced in 2015 [24]) is the benchmark dataset for the non-destructive testing [24]. It contains 19,407 grayscale X-ray scans from the *welds, casting, baggage, nature,* and *settings* categories. For the baggage threat recognition, the only relevant category is *baggage* which contains 8,150 grayscale baggage X-ray scans containing suspicious items such as *razors, guns, knives* and *shuriken* along with their detailed ground truth markings. Moreover, we used 400 scans for the training purposes and the rest of the scans for the testing purposes as per the dataset standard [24].

SIXray (first introduced in 2019 [15]) is another publicly available dataset containing 1,059,231 highly complex, and challenging colored baggage X-ray scans. Out of these 1,059,231 scans, 1,050,302 are negatives (that contains only the normal baggage content) whereas 8,929 scans are positive (containing the contraband items such as *guns, knives, wrenches, pliers, scissors* and *hammers*). Furthermore, the dataset contains detailed box-level markings of these items. To reflect the imbalanced nature of the positive scans, the dataset is arranged into three subsets namely SIXray10, SIXray100 and SIXray1000 [15]. Moreover, each subset is partitioned into a ratio of 4 to 1 (i.e. 80% of the scans were used for training while 20% of the scans were used for the testing purposes as per the dataset standard [15]).

OPIXray (first introduced in 2020 [25]) is a publicly available colored X-ray imagery dataset for the baggage threat detection [25]. It contains a total of 8,885 X-ray scans from which 7,109 are arranged for the training purposes and the rest of 1,776 are dedicated for testing purposes [25] (with the ratio of about 4 to 1). Furthermore, the datasets contains detailed box-level annotations of the five categories, namely, *folding knives, straight knives, utility knives, multi-tool knives*, and *scissors*. In addition to this, the test scans within the OPIXray are categorized into three levels of occlusion [25].

COMPASS-XP (first introduced in 2019 [27]) is another publicly available dataset designed to validate the autonomous baggage threat recognition frameworks. The dataset contains matched photographic and X-ray imagery representing a single item in each scan. Unlike GDXray [24], SIXray [15], and OPIXray [25], the COMPASS-XP dataset [27] is primarily designed for the image classification tasks where the ground truths are marked scan-wise indicating the presence of a normal or dangerous item within each scan. The total scans within COMPASS-XP dataset [27] are 11,568. From these scans, we used 9,254 for training purposes and the rest of 2,314 for testing purposes maintaining the ratio of 4 to 1.

Combined Dataset: Apart from validating the proposed framework on each of the four datasets separately, we combined them to validate the generalization capacity of the proposed framework against multiple scanner specifications. In a combined dataset, we used a total of 864,147 scans for training and the rest of 223,686 scans for the testing purposes.

3.2   Implementation Details

The proposed framework has been implemented using Python 3.7.4 with TensorFlow 2.2.0 and also the MATLAB R2020a on a machine having Intel Core i7-9750H@2.6 GHz processor and 32 GB RAM with a single NVIDIA RTX 2080 with cuDNN v7.5 and a CUDA Toolkit 10.1.243. The optimizer used during the training was ADADELTA [28] with a default learning and decay rate of 1.0 and 0.95, respectively. The source code is publicly available on GitHub[1].

---

[1] Source Code: https://github.com/taimurhassan/TST.

Table 1. Performance comparison of different encoder-decoder and fully convolutional networks in terms of DC and IoU for recognizing baggage threats. Bold indicates the best performance while the second-best performance is underlined.

Metric	Dataset	SegNet [29]	PSPNet [30]	UNet [31]	FCN-8 [32]
IoU	GDXray [24]	**0.7635**	0.6953	0.7564	0.6736
	SIXray [15]	**0.6071**	0.5341	0.6013	0.4897
	OPIXray [25]	0.6325	0.5689	**0.6478**	0.5018
	COMPASS-XP [27]	**0.5893**	0.5016	0.5743	0.4473
	Combined	**0.5314**	0.4832	0.5241	0.4103
DC	GDXray [24]	**0.8658**	0.8202	0.8613	0.8049
	SIXray [15]	**0.7555**	0.6963	0.7510	0.6574
	OPIXray [25]	0.7748	0.7252	**0.7862**	0.6682
	COMPASS-XP [27]	**0.7415**	0.6680	0.7295	0.6181
	Combined	**0.6940**	0.6515	0.6877	0.5818

3.3 Evaluation Metrics

The proposed framework has been evaluated using a variety of evaluation metrics as presented below:

Dice Coefficient and Intersection-Over-Union: Dice Coefficient (DC) and Intersection-over-Union (IoU) measures the ability of the proposed framework that how accurately it has extracted the contraband items w.r.t the ground truths. DC is computed as $DC = \frac{2T_p}{2T_p + F_p + F_n}$ and IoU is computed as $IoU = \frac{T_p}{T_p + F_p + F_n}$, where T_p denotes the true positives, F_p denotes the false positives and F_n denotes the false negatives. Moreover, we also computed the mean dice coefficient and mean IoU for each dataset by taking the average of DC and IoU scores, respectively for each contraband item category.

Mean Average Precision (mAP) is another metric that we used to validate the performance of the proposed framework for accurately detecting the prohibited items. The mAP scores in the proposed framework are calculated using the IoU threshold of 0.5.

4   Results

This section presents a thorough evaluation of the proposed framework on four publicly available datasets as well as on their combined representation. Furthermore, this section presents a detailed comparison of the proposed system with state-of-the-art frameworks.

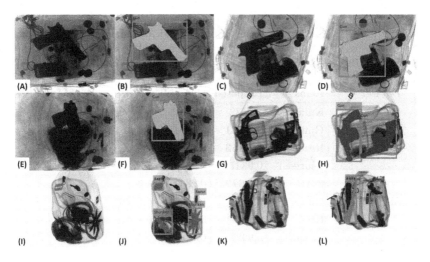

Fig. 3. Visual examples showcasing the performance of the proposed framework on GDXray dataset.

4.1 Ablation Study

We present an ablation study to determine 1) the optimal number of image gradients, their orientations, along with the number of coherent tensors which are to be selected within the structure tensor module to highlight the transitions of the contraband items, and 2) determining the optimal choice of encoder-decoder (or fully convolutional) backbone.

Number of Orientations and Coherent Tensors: Although including more image gradients (with more orientations) further reveals the transitional details of the baggage items within the candidate scan but it also makes the framework more vulnerable to noise and misclassifications. Similarly, considering more tensors (for generating the coherent representation) also affects the overall accuracy of the detection system [17]. Although, the proposed framework is more robust against these issues as compared to the CST framework [17], mainly because of the removal of the irrelevant proposal screening process. But increasing the number of orientations and tensors do affect the ability of the encoder-decoder backbone to correctly recognize the boundaries of the contraband items. Therefore, after rigorous experimentation on each dataset, we selected the number of image gradients (M) to be 4 and the number of coherent tensors (K) to be 2, and these configurations have also been recommended in [17].

Backbone Network: The proposed framework employs an encoder-decoder or a fully convolutional network as a backbone to extract contours of the contraband item while simultaneously suppressing the rest of the baggage content. Here, we evaluated some of the popular architectures such as PSPNet [30], SegNet [29],

Table 2. Performance comparison of the proposed framework on GDXray [24], SIXray [15] and OPIXray [25] dataset in terms of mAP. Bold indicates the best performance while '-' indicates that the metric is not computed. CST and CHR frameworks are driven through ResNet-50 [23].

Dataset	Items	Proposed	CST [17]	CHR [15]	DOAM [25]
GDXray [24]	Knife	0.9632	**0.9945**	–	–
	Gun	**0.9761**	0.9101	–	–
	Razor	**0.9453**	0.8826	–	–
	Shuriken	0.9847	**0.9917**	–	–
	mAP	**0.9672**	0.9343	–	–
SIXray [15]	Gun	0.9734	**0.9911**	0.8640	–
	Knife	**0.9681**	0.9347	0.8536	–
	Wrench	0.9421	**0.9915**	0.6818	–
	Scissor	0.9348	**0.9938**	0.5923	–
	Pliers	**0.9573**	0.9267	0.8261	–
	Hammer	**0.9342**	0.9189	–	–
	mAP	0.9516	**0.9595**	0.7635	–
OPIXray [25]	Folding	0.8024	–	–	**0.8137**
	Straight	**0.5613**	–	–	0.4150
	Scissor	0.8934	–	–	**0.9512**
	Multi-tool	0.7802	–	–	**0.8383**
	Utility	**0.7289**	–	–	0.6821
	mAP	**0.7532**	–	–	0.7401

UNet [31] and FCN [32]. Table 1 shows the comparison of these models on each dataset in terms of DC and IoU. We can observe that for the majority of the datasets, the best performance is achieved by the SegNet model [29], whereas the UNet [31] stood the second-best. Due to this, we prefer the use of SegNet [29] as a backbone within the proposed framework.

4.2 Evaluations on GDXray Dataset

First of all, we evaluated the proposed framework on the GDXray [24] dataset and also compared it with the state-of-the-art solutions as shown in Table 2. Here, we can observe that the proposed framework obtained the mAP score of 0.9672 leading the second-best CST framework by 3.40%. Although the proposed framework achieved the overall best performance in terms of mAP on the GDXray dataset, it lags from the CST framework by 3.14% for extracting *knives* and 0.705% for extracting the *shuriken*. Moreover, Fig. 3 shows the qualitative evaluations of the proposed framework where we can observe how robustly it has extracted the contraband items like *guns, shuriken razors*, and *knives*.

4.3   Evaluations on SIXray Dataset

After evaluating the proposed framework on GDXray [24], we tested it on the SIXray [15]. SIXray, to the best of our knowledge, is one of the largest security inspection datasets containing highly complex baggage X-ray scans. In terms of mAP, the proposed framework stood second-best by achieving a score of 0.9516, lagging from the CST framework [17] by only 0.823% (please see Table 2). However, it achieved a considerable edge over CST framework [17] for extracting *knives*, *pliers* and *hammers* i.e., it leads the CST [17] by 3.45% for detecting *knives*, 3.19% for recognizing *pliers*, and 1.63% for detecting *hammers*. Apart from this, the performance of the proposed framework on each SIXray subset is shown in Table 3. Here, we can observe that although the performance of the proposed framework is lagging behind the CST framework [17] on each subset, it's still outperforming CHR [15] with a large margin. Moreover, on SIXray10, its lagging from CST framework [17] by 0.342% only. This is because the proposed framework possesses the ability to suppress the boundaries of normal baggage content. Even when it's trained on an imbalanced ratio of positive and negative scans, it shows a considerably good performance in recognizing the baggage threats. However, the CST framework [17] stood first on each subset because it has been trained on the balanced set of object proposals in each subset.

Apart from this, the qualitative evaluation of the proposed framework on SIXray [15] dataset is presented in Fig. 4.

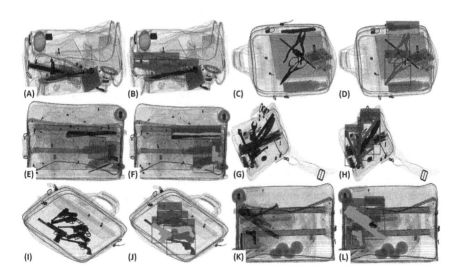

Fig. 4. Visual examples showcasing the performance of the proposed framework on SIXray dataset.

4.4 Evaluations on OPIXray Dataset

The third dataset on which the proposed framework is evaluated is the OPIXray [25]. OPIXray is the recently introduced dataset containing highly occluded color X-ray scans. From Table 2, we can see that the proposed framework achieved the mAP score of 0.7532, outperforming DOAM [25] by 1.73%. From Table 2, we can also observe that although DOAM has a considerable edge over the proposed framework for extracting *folding knives*, *multi-tool knives* and the *scissors*. But since it lags from the proposed framework by 26.06% for extracting *straight knives* and by 6.42% for extracting *utility knives*, it stood the second-best. Apart from this, the qualitative evaluations of the proposed framework on the OPIXray dataset are shown in Fig. 5.

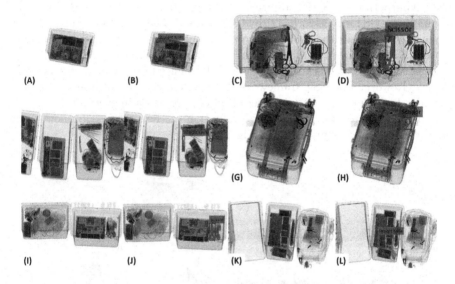

Fig. 5. Visual examples showcasing the performance of the proposed framework on OPIXray dataset.

Table 3. Performance comparison of proposed framework with CST [17] and CHR [15] on each SIXray subset in terms of mAP. Bold indicates the best performance while the second-best performance is underlined. Here, CST [17] and CHR [15] are driven through ResNet-50 [23].

Subset	Proposed	CST [17]	CHR [15]
SIXray10	0.9601	**0.9634**	0.7794
SIXray100	0.8749	**0.9318**	0.5787
SIXray1000	0.7814	**0.8903**	0.3700

4.5   Evaluations on COMPASS-XP Dataset

The last dataset on which we evaluated the proposed framework is the COMPASS-XP dataset [27]. COMPASS-XP [27] is different than GDXray [24], SIXray [15] and OPIXray [25] dataset as it contains the scans showcasing only a single item, and its primarily designed for evaluating the image classification frameworks. Nevertheless, we used this dataset for validating the performance of the proposed framework. The qualitative evaluations on COMPASS-XP [27] are shown in Fig. 6 where we can observe that the proposed framework is quite robust in picking different suspicious items. Apart from this, the proposed framework achieved the overall mAP score of 0.5842 on the COMPASS-XP dataset [27]. Moreover, to the best of our knowledge, there is no literature available to date that utilizes the COMPASS-XP dataset [27] for validating the baggage threat detection framework.

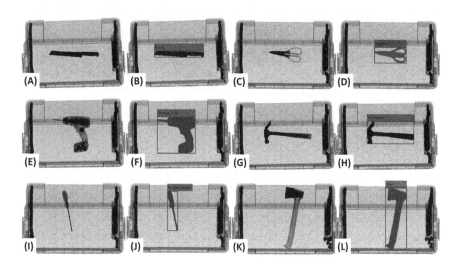

Fig. 6. Visual examples showcasing the performance of the proposed framework on COMPASS-XP dataset.

4.6   Evaluations on Combined Dataset

To evaluate the generalization capacity of the proposed framework on multi-vendor grayscale and colored X-ray scans, we combined all the four datasets and tested the proposed framework on the combined dataset. As observed in Fig. 7 that despite the large differences in the scan properties, the proposed framework has been able to accurately recognize the contraband items while generating good quality masks. Apart from this, the proposed framework achieved an overall mAP score of 0.4657 when evaluated on a diverse ranging 223,686 multi-vendor baggage X-ray scans.

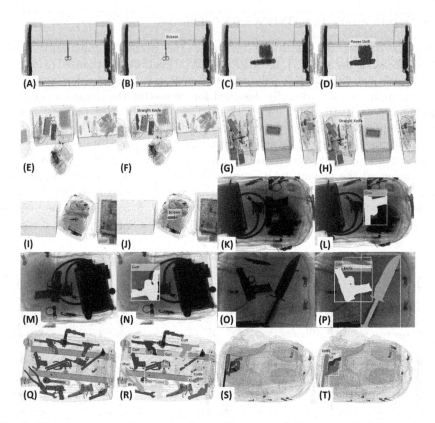

Fig. 7. Visual examples showcasing the performance of the proposed framework on combined dataset.

Here, we would also like to highlight that the proposed framework does get some false negatives (and false positives as well) while suppressing the irrelevant contours. Although, the false positives are handled through morphological post-processing. But, unfortunately, the proposed framework is somewhat limited to false negatives e.g.. see the extracted *scissor* in Fig. 5 (D), *pliers* in Fig. 4 (D), *scissor* in Fig. 7 (B), *gun* in Fig. 7 (N), and *pliers* in Fig. 7 (R). However, since the proposed framework is leveraged through pixel-wise recognition, we believe that this limitation is not drastic. Because even some pixels of the threatening items are classified as false negatives, the proposed framework does recognize the threatening items as a whole.

5   Conclusion

This paper presents a single-staged instance segmentation framework capable of recognizing highly cluttered, concealed, and overlapping contraband items from the multi-vendor baggage X-ray scans. The proposed framework is based on a novel trainable structure tensor scheme that only highlights the transitional patterns of the contraband items, leading to their accurate detection. Furthermore, the proposed framework has been rigorously tested on four publicly available datasets where it outperformed state-of-the-art solutions in terms of mAP scores. In the future, the proposed detection framework can be extended to detect the contours of the 3D printed objects within the baggage X-ray scans. Furthermore, it can also be tested for object detection and instance segmentation on normal photographic imagery.

References

1. Akçay, S., Breckon, T.: Towards automatic threat detection: a survey of advances of deep learning within X-ray security imaging. preprint arXiv:2001.01293 (2020)
2. Turcsany, D., Mouton, A., Breckon, T.P.: Improving feature-based object recognition for X-ray baggage security screening using primed visual words. In: 2013 IEEE International Conference on Industrial Technology (ICIT), pp. 1140–1145. IEEE (2013)
3. Baştan, M.: Multi-view object detection in dual-energy X-ray images. Mach. Vis. Appl. **26**, 1045–1060 (2015)
4. Heitz, G., Chechik, G.: Object separation in x-ray image sets. In: IEEE International Conference on Computer Vision and Pattern Recognition (CVPR), pp. 2093–2100 (2010)
5. Zhang, J., et al.: Joint shape and texture based X-ray cargo image classification. In: IEEE International Conference on Computer Vision and Pattern Recognition (CVPR) Workshops, pp. 266–273 (2014)
6. Jaccard, N., Rogers, T.W., Griffin, L.D.: Automated detection of cars in transmission X-ray images of freight containers. In: AVSS, pp. 387–392 (2014)
7. Baştan, M., Yousefi, M.R., Breuel, T.M.: Visual words on baggage X-ray images. In: Real, P., Diaz-Pernil, D., Molina-Abril, H., Berciano, A., Kropatsch, W. (eds.) CAIP 2011. LNCS, vol. 6854, pp. 360–368. Springer, Heidelberg (2011). https://doi.org/10.1007/978-3-642-23672-3_44
8. Kundegorski, M.E., Akçay, S., Devereux, M., Mouton, A., Breckon, T.P.: On using feature descriptors as visual words for object detection within X-ray baggage security screening. In: IEEE International Conference on Imaging for Crime Detection and Prevention (ICDP) (2016)
9. Mery, D., Svec, E., Arias, M.: Object recognition in baggage inspection using adaptive sparse representations of X-ray images. In: Bräunl, T., McCane, B., Rivera, M., Yu, X. (eds.) PSIVT 2015. LNCS, vol. 9431, pp. 709–720. Springer, Cham (2016). https://doi.org/10.1007/978-3-319-29451-3_56
10. Riffo, V., Mery, D.: Automated detection of threat objects using adapted implicit shape model. IEEE Trans. Syst. Man Cybern.: Syst. **46**, 472–482 (2015)
11. Akçay, S., Kundegorski, M.E., Willcocks, C.G., Breckon, T.P.: Using deep convolutional neural network architectures for object classification and detection within X-ray baggage security imagery. IEEE Trans. Inf. Forensics Secur. **13**, 2203–2215 (2018)
12. Jaccard, N., Rogers, T.W., Morton, E.J., Griffin, L.D.: Detection of concealed cars in complex cargo X-ray imagery using deep learning. J. X-Ray Sci. Technol. **25**, 323–339 (2017)

13. Liu, Z., Li, J., Shu, Y., Zhang, D.: Detection and recognition of security detection object based on YOLO9000. In: 2018 5th International Conference on Systems and Informatics (ICSAI), pp. 278–282. IEEE (2018)

14. Xu, M., Zhang, H., Yang, J.: Prohibited item detection in airport X-ray security images via attention mechanism based CNN. In: Lai, J.-H., et al. (eds.) PRCV 2018. LNCS, vol. 11257, pp. 429–439. Springer, Cham (2018). https://doi.org/10.1007/978-3-030-03335-4_37

15. Miao, C., et al.: SIXray: a large-scale security inspection X-ray benchmark for prohibited item discovery in overlapping images. In: IEEE International Conference on Computer Vision and Pattern Recognition (CVPR), pp. 2119–2128 (2019)

16. Gaus, Y.F.A., Bhowmik, N., Akçay, S., Breckon, T.: Evaluating the transferability and adversarial discrimination of convolutional neural networks for threat object detection and classification within X-ray security imagery. In: 18th IEEE International Conference on Machine Learning and Applications (ICMLA) (2019)

17. Hassan, T., Bettayeb, M., Akçay, S., Khan, S., Bennamoun, M., Werghi, N.: Detecting prohibited items in X-ray images: a contour proposal learning approach. In: 27th IEEE International Conference on Image Processing (ICIP) (2020)

18. Gaus, Y.F.A., Bhowmik, N., Akçay, S., Guillén-Garcia, P.M., Barker, J.W., Breckon, T.P.: Evaluation of a dual convolutional neural network architecture for object-wise anomaly detection in cluttered X-ray security imagery. In: 2019 International Joint Conference on Neural Networks (IJCNN), pp. 1–8 (2019)

19. An, J., Zhang, H., Zhu, Y., Yang, J.: Semantic segmentation for prohibited items in baggage inspection. In: Cui, Z., Pan, J., Zhang, S., Xiao, L., Yang, J. (eds.) IScIDE 2019. LNCS, vol. 11935, pp. 495–505. Springer, Cham (2019). https://doi.org/10.1007/978-3-030-36189-1_41

20. Akcay, S., Atapour-Abarghouei, A., Breckon, T.P.: GANomaly: semi-supervised anomaly detection via adversarial training. In: Jawahar, C.V., Li, H., Mori, G., Schindler, K. (eds.) ACCV 2018. LNCS, vol. 11363, pp. 622–637. Springer, Cham (2019). https://doi.org/10.1007/978-3-030-20893-6_39

21. Bhowmik, N., Gaus, Y.F.A., Akçay, S., Barker, J.W., Breckon, T.P.: On the impact of object and sub-component level segmentation strategies for supervised anomaly detection within X-ray security imagery. In: Proceedings of the International Conference on Machine Learning Applications (ICMLA) (2019)

22. Griffin, L.D., Caldwell, M., Andrews, J.T.A., Bohler, H.: "Unexpected item in the bagging area": anomaly detection in X-ray security images. IEEE Trans. Inf. Forensics Secur. **14**, 1539–1553 (2019)

23. He, K., Zhang, X., Ren, S., Sun, J.: Deep residual learning for image recognition. In: IEEE Conference on Computer Vision and Pattern Recognition (CVPR), pp. 770–778 (2016)

24. Riffo, V., Lobel, H., Mery, D.: GDXray: the database of X-ray images for nondestructive testing. J. Nondestruct. Eval. **34**, 42 (2015)

25. Wei, Y., Tao, R., Wu, Z., Ma, Y., Zhang, L., Liu, X.: Occluded prohibited items detection: an X-ray security inspection benchmark and de-occlusion attention module (2020)

26. Caldwell, D.R.: Unlocking the mysteries of the bounding box. Coord.: Online J. Map Geogr. Round Table Am. Libr. Assoc. **Series A**(2), 1–20 (2005)

27. Griffin, L.D., Caldwell, M., Andrews, J.T.A.: COMPASS-XP dataset. Computational Security Science Group, UCL (2019)

28. Zeiler, M.D.: ADADELTA: an adaptive learning rate method. arXiv:1212.5701 (2012)

29. Badrinarayanan, V., Kendall, A., Cipolla, R.: SegNet: a deep convolutional encoder-decoder architecture for image segmentation. IEEE Trans. Pattern Anal. Mach. Intell. **39**, 2481–2495 (2017)
30. Zhao, H., Shi, J., Qi, X., Wang, X., Jia, J.: Pyramid scene parsing network. In: IEEE International Conference on Computer Vision and Pattern Recognition (CVPR), pp. 2881–2890 (2017)
31. Ronneberger, O., Fischer, P., Brox, T.: U-Net: convolutional networks for biomedical image segmentation. In: Navab, N., Hornegger, J., Wells, W.M., Frangi, A.F. (eds.) MICCAI 2015. LNCS, vol. 9351, pp. 234–241. Springer, Cham (2015). https://doi.org/10.1007/978-3-319-24574-4_28
32. Long, J., Shelhamer, E., Darrell, T.: Fully convolutional networks for semantic segmentation. In: IEEE International Conference on Computer Vision and Pattern Recognition (CVPR), pp. 3431–3440 (2015)

Audiovisual Transformer with Instance Attention for Audio-Visual Event Localization

Yan-Bo Lin[1] and Yu-Chiang Frank Wang[1,2(✉)]

[1] Graduate Institute of Communication Engineering, National Taiwan University,
Taipei, Taiwan
{yblin98,ycwang}@ntu.edu.tw
[2] ASUS Intelligent Cloud Services, Taipei, Taiwan

Abstract. Audio-visual event localization requires one to identify the event label across video frames by jointly observing visual and audio information. To address this task, we propose a deep learning framework of cross-modality co-attention for video event localization. Our proposed audiovisual transformer (AV-transformer) is able to exploit intra and inter-frame visual information, with audio features jointly observed to perform co-attention over the above three modalities. With visual, temporal, and audio information observed across consecutive video frames, our model achieves promising capability in extracting informative spatial/temporal features for improved event localization. Moreover, our model is able to produce instance-level attention, which would identify image regions at the instance level which are associated with the sound/event of interest. Experiments on a benchmark dataset confirm the effectiveness of our proposed framework, with ablation studies performed to verify the design of our propose network model.

1 Introduction

In real-world activities, visual and audio signals are both perceived by humans for perceptual understanding. In other words, both visual and audio data should be jointly exploited for understanding the observed content or semantic information. Recently, audio-visual event localization [1–5] attracts the attention from computer vision and machine learning communities. As depicted in Fig. 1, this task requires one to identify the content information (e.g., categorical labels) for each frame or segment in an video, by observing both visual and audio features across video frames. Audio-visual event localization can be viewed as a cross-modality learning task, which deals with the challenging task that the feature representations and distributions across visual and audio domains are very different. To explore audiovisual representation, joint learning of multi-modal deep

Electronic supplementary material The online version of this chapter (https://doi.org/10.1007/978-3-030-69544-6_17) contains supplementary material, which is available to authorized users.

Co-Attention	Video	Audio	Visual / Audio Label	Ground Truth

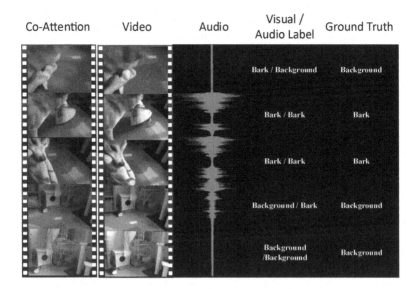

Bark / Background — Background

Bark / Bark — Bark

Bark / Bark — Bark

Background / Bark — Background

Background /Background — Background

Fig. 1. Illustration of audio-visual event localization (recognizing video event with matched visual and audio information). Note that the first column shows our correct localization outputs with cross-modality co-attention, the 2nd and 3rd columns show the video and audio inputs across five consecutive frames, with ground truth visual/audio and event labels depicted in the last two columns.

networks across these two domains have been studied, e.g., classification [6,7], lip reading [8–10] and sound synthesis [11,12]. These works demonstrate that such audio-visual based models can be applied to several downstream tasks. However, these models rely on the simultaneous presence of both visual and audio information. In other words, they cannot deal with scenarios with partial modality information observed. On the other hand, methods for locating sound source models [13–16] have also been proposed via exploiting mutual information between audio and visual data. However, these models cannot easily attend proper regions of instances or distinguish sounding objects from silent ones.

To this end, we propose a novel deep attention model which jointly performs visual, temporal, and audio cross-modality co-attention to better associate audio and visual information for video event localization. This is realized by our proposed audiovisual transformer (AV-transformer) for jointly encoding intra-frame and inter-frame patches, followed by exploitation of encoded intra-frame and inter-frame visual and audio features. As a result, one important features of our proposed attention model is that we not only improve the overall localization (i.e., classification) performances, it further attends proper regions across video frames (e.g., the corresponding object of interest in Fig. 1). More importantly, we will show that our model is not limited to the use of fully supervised video data (i.e., visual and audio labels annotated for each frame). Learning of our model in a weakly supervised setting can be conducted, in which only an overall soft label at the video level is observed during training.

The contributions of this work are highlight below:

- We propose an audiovisual transformer (AV-transformer) for visual, temporal, and audio co-attention, with the goal of solving event localization tasks.
- Without attention supervision during training, our model is able to perform instance-level attention by jointly encoding intra and inter-frame image patches and audio features.
- Experimental results demonstrate that our proposed model performs favorably against state-of-the-art approaches in various settings, while instance-level attention can be additionally achieved by our model.

2   Related Work

Video Classification. Methods based on deep neural networks have shown promising performances on the task of video classification [17–23], which takes visual and temporal information for predicting action or event categories for input videos. To explore the aforementioned spatial-temporal features from videos, 3D convolutional networks are utilized, in which 3D architectures with 3D kernels are considered [24–26]. On the other hand, long short term memory (LSTM) networks [17] has also been employed to observe 2D CNN features over time. Such recurrent neural networks (RNN) [17,27,28] are alternative ways to learn the temporal relation between frames. However, since uses of RNNs might limit the length of the input video to be observed [27,28], some works choose to sample frames from the entire video to learn robust reasoning relational representation [20,21,23,29,30].

Relating Audio and Visual Features. While RNN-based models have been widely applied to extract spatial-temporal features from videos, such methods do not consider audio features when modeling temporal information. To address this issue, cross-modality learning using audio and visual data are proposed [12,31–35]. For example, Aytar et al. [32] learn the joint representation from audio-visual data, with the goal to identifying the content using data in either modality. Arandjelovic and Zisserman [31] also exploit the variety of audio-visual information for learning better representation in audio-visual correspondence tasks. Furthermore, they [15] visualize sound localization in visual scenes, which would serve as the bridge connecting between audio and visual modality. Owens et al. [16] leverage ambient sounds when observing visual contents to learn robust audio-visual representations. The resulting representation is further utilized to perform video tasks of action recognition, visualization of the sound sources, and on/off-screen source separation. These studies [15,16] apparently show that sound source localization can be guided by semantic visual-spatial information, and verify that these cross-modality features would be beneficial in the aforementioned video-based applications.

Aside from learning audio-visual representation, works like [8–10] demonstrate that such audio-visual based models can be applied to synthesize videos with face images (e.g., with lip motion), corresponding to the input free-form spoken audio. Concurrently, some audio-related tasks [13,16,34,36,37] also utilize visual representation to solve speech separation [16,37], musical instruments [13,34,38–40] and objects [36]. Most of these methods maintain a "mix and separate" training scenario where the training videos are first mixed and separated afterward. For instance, MP-Net [39] initially separates sound with large energy from mixtures which is composed of any arbitrary number of sounds. the sound with small magnitude would keep emerging afterwards. Furthermore, by detecting sounding objects to guide the learning process using unlabeled video data, Gao et al. [40] propose a framework to bridge the localized object regions in a video with the corresponding sounds to achieve instance-level audio-visual source separation. Methods like [38,41] utilize visual motions or body gesture to separate sound signals, and thus audio-visual source separation can be performed for different instruments.

Nevertheless, while the aforementioned works show promising results in learning audio-visual representation, it is still challenging to address audio-visual event localization, which requires one to identify the event with both visual and audio modality properly presented, especially in a weakly supervised setting (i.e., no frame-level ground truth annotation).

Audio-Visual Event Localization. Audio visual event localization aims to detect events in videos, which requires both audio and visual activities and events to be identified. Early works [1,3,4,42] are proposed to jointly learn audio-visual information in each local segments of the input video. However, due to potential inconsistency between information observed from audio and visual signals, the data from either modality with insignificant cues may interfere the event prediction. Therefore, works [2,5] tackle with this issue by disregarding information from audio/visual data with irrelevant categorical events. Nevertheless, the aforementioned methods only consider the correlation between audio and visual in a video segment at the same time frame. To address this issue, we further jointly exploit relationship between visual patches and audio signal from video segments within the same or across time interval, which allows our model to learn segment-wise events with the guidance of nearby audio and visual frames. In the next section, we will present and discuss the details of our proposed co-attention model, which jointly exploits visual, temporal, and audio data for improved localization and instance-level visualization.

3 Proposed Method

3.1 Notations and Problem Formulation

In this paper, we design a novel deep neural network model for audio-visual event localization. In order to deal with cross-modality signals observed from audio and video data with the ability to identify the event of interest, our model exploits visual information within and across video frames. Together with the audio tracks, the proposed model not only performs satisfactory localization

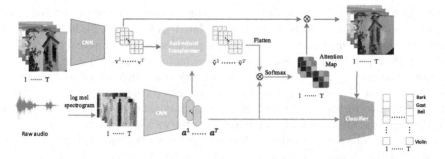

Fig. 2. Overview of our proposed audiovisual transformer (AV-transformer) for instance-attended audio-visual event localization. Note that $\otimes$ denotes matrix multiplication, and the softmax operation is performed on each row in the AV-transfomer module.

performances, it also exhibits promising capability in attending the objects in the input video associated to that event.

For the sake of completeness, we first define the settings and notations which will be used in this paper. Following [1], two training schemes for audio-visual event localization are considered: *supervised* and *weakly-supervised* learning. Given a video sequence with T seconds long, it is split audio a and video v tracks separately into T non-overlapping segments $\{a^t, v^t\}_{t=1}^{T}$, where each segment is 1s long (since the event boundary is labeled at second-level). For the supervised setting, segment-wised labels denote $\mathbf{y}^t = \left\{ y_k^t | y_k^t \in \{0, 1\}, \sum_{k=1}^{C+1} y_k^t = 1, t \in \mathbb{N} \right\}$, $\mathbf{y}^t \in \mathbb{R}^{C+1}$, where t denotes the segment index and C denotes total event categories. We note that, considering the category of background, the total number of event categories becomes $C + 1$. In the supervised setting, every segment-wise labels are observed during the training phase.

As for the scheme of weakly-supervised learning, we only access to the video-level event labels $\mathbf{Y} \in \mathbb{R}^{C+1}$ during the training phase (e.g., event category for a whole video). As for the background event, we take different event categories from audio and visual contents as inputs (e.g., dog image and goat sound). Note that predicted video-level event labels are processed by max pooling through time the segment event labels $\hat{\mathbf{m}} = \max \{\mathbf{m}^t\}_{t=1}^{T}$, where $\mathbf{m}, \hat{\mathbf{m}} \in \mathbb{R}^{C+1}$. $\mathbf{m}^t$ is the prediction from audio-visual event localization network. For this weakly supervised setting, while it is less likely to be affected by noise from either modality at the segment level during training, it also makes the learning of our model more difficult.

Figure 2 depicts our proposed AV-transformer for audio-visual event localization. It is worth noting that, cross-modality instance-level attention can be performed by our proposed framework. We now discuss the details of our model in the following subsections.

3.2   Jointly Learning Intra and Inter-frame Visual Representation

Visual attention has been widely utilized in recent VQA and audio-visual related tasks [1,14,15,43–47]. Although convolution neural networks have been successfully applied in the above works to identify spatial regions of interest with impressive results, such attention is typically performed at the pixel level, based on the information observed for the corresponding tasks (e.g., guidance at the network outputs) [13–16,47].

For the task of audio-visual event localization, one needs to identify the video segments with the event of interest. It would be preferable if one can attend on the object of interest at the instance level during localization, which would further improve the localization accuracy.

Previously, [48] considered local context information by feeding image patches into a LSTM, which can facilitate understanding objects in image scenes for VQA tasks. [49] introduced non local block for video understanding. These blocks are used to learn visual context information from image patches through space, time or spacetime by transformer encoder [50]. Thus, inspired by [48] and [49], we present a unique audiovisual transformer (AV-transformer) as shown in Fig. 3 to encode local context information into proper representation, so that object instances corresponding to event of interest can be attended accordingly. To achieve this goal, we input local image patches of successive video frames and audio segments into our audiovisual transformer, which encodes the image patches of that frame in a sequential yet temporal visual features.

More precisely, we divide a input video frame at time step t into R patches, and extract the CNN feature for each patch. These visual representations of each region are denoted as $\{\mathbf{v}_r^t, r = 1, 2..., R\}$, where $\mathbf{v}_r^t \in \mathbb{R}^{1 \times K}$ represents the visual features of the rth patch. These visual features and audio features $\mathbf{a}^t$ are served as the inputs to the audiovisual transformer, which is described below:

$$\tilde{\mathbf{v}}^t = Trans(\mathbf{v}^{t-1}, \mathbf{v}^t, \mathbf{v}^{t+1}, \mathbf{a}^t), \tag{1}$$

where $Trans(.)$ denotes the audiovisual transformer, the attention block in our unique audiovisual transformer can be further described as follows:

$$\mathbf{Attn}_{r,i}^t = (\theta(\mathbf{v}_r^t) + \mathbf{a}^t) \sum_{k=t-1}^{t+1} \phi(\mathbf{v}_i^k) \;\; \forall i \in R,$$

$$\tilde{\mathbf{v}}_r^t = \sum_{\forall r,i \in R} \text{Softmax}(\mathbf{Attn}_{r,i}^t)(\mathbf{v}_r^t) \tag{2}$$

where $\tilde{\mathbf{v}}_r^t$ indicates intra/inter-frame visual representation of the rth image patch at audio instant t. $\mathbf{Attn}$ shows the relation between patch i and j at time t. $\theta(.)$ and $\phi(.)$ are multilayer perceptrons. We note that the Softmax(.) operation is performed at each row. We gather R patches for co-attention visual representations of video frame at time t, that is, $\tilde{\mathbf{v}}^t = \{\tilde{\mathbf{v}}_1^t, ..., \tilde{\mathbf{v}}_R^t\} \in \mathbb{R}^{R \times K}$.

It can be seen that, by advancing our audiovisual transformer, visual representation encoded would describe local spatial and temporal information within

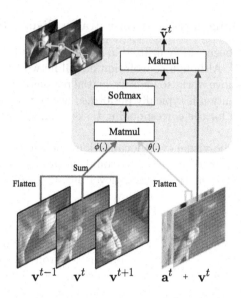

Fig. 3. Audiovisual transformer: visual feature $\tilde{\mathbf{v}}^t$ is encoded by jointly observing audio $\mathbf{a}^t$ and $\mathbf{v}^t$ visual context at time t, followed by visual context over consecutive frames ($\mathbf{v}^{t-1}$, $\mathbf{v}^t$ and $\mathbf{v}^{t+1}$).

successive video frames. By combing local, temporal and audio information in this stages, this audiovisual transformer allows improved attention at the instance-level as later verified.

3.3 Instance Attention for Event Localization

The visual encoders introduced in the previous subsections exploit local spatial and short-term temporal information. As noted above, to perform frame-level audio-visual event localization, it would be necessary to integrate the audio features into consideration.

Some previous works [13–16] have presented to explore the relationship between audio and visual scenes. They show that correlations between these two modalities can be utilized to find image regions that are highly correlated to the audio signal. However, these works only consider single image inputs and its corresponding sound signals, which might result in incorrect association due to overfitting to the visual content. Another concern is that, if more than one instance visually correspond to the event of interest, how to identify the object instance would not be a trivial task. Take an audio-visual event in which a person is playing violin solo in a string quartet for example, it would be challenging to identify which image region is related to the audio signal, if only a single frame input is observed.

To address the above challenge, we propose to perform cross-modality co-attention over visual, temporal, and audio features. By taking temporal infor-

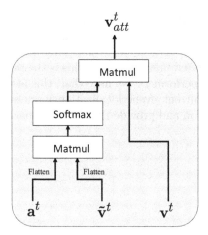

Fig. 4. Instance Attention: Observing locally and temporally visual-attended features $\tilde{\mathbf{v}}^t$ and audio inputs $\mathbf{a}^t$ to output the final co-attention features $\mathbf{v}_{att}^t$ for audiovisual event localization. Note that we remove the subscript r (patch index) of visual features for simplicity.

mation into consideration, our intra and inter-frame visual features would be associated with the audio features, which would make the localization of audio-visual events more applicable. To achieve this goal, we advance the concept of self-attention [50] for computing a soft confidence score map, indicating the correlation between the attended visual and audio features. Different from existing co-attention mechanisms like [1,13–15,48,51], our input visual features jointly take spatial and temporal information via intra and inter-frame encoding, followed by joint attention of audio features. Thus, our co-attention model would be more robust due to the joint consideration of information observed from three distinct yet relevant data modalities.

As depicted in Fig. 4, we obtain the r th local visual feature $\tilde{\mathbf{v}}_r^t$ at time t, where $r = 1, ..., R$, and our co-attention model aims to produce the weight to depict how relevant $\mathbf{v}_r^t$ and $\mathbf{a}^t$ is. The attention score M_r^t can be interpreted as the probability that location r is the right location related to the sound context. Note that M_r^t in our co-attention model is computed by:

$$M_r^t = \text{Softmax}(\tilde{\mathbf{v}}_r^t \cdot (\mathbf{a}^t)'), \tag{3}$$

where $\cdot$ indicates the dot product and $'$ denotes transpose operation. Note that visual and audio representation are in the same dimension, that is, $\tilde{\mathbf{v}}_r^t, \mathbf{a}^t \in \mathbb{R}^{1 \times D}$. With all local visual features are observed, we pool the associated outputs by a weighted sum M to obtain the final visual attention representation of the image at time t, i.e.,

$$\mathbf{v}_{att}^t = \sum_{r=1}^{R} M_r^t \mathbf{v}_r^t. \tag{4}$$

With this cross-modality co-attention mechanism, our visual attention feature $\mathbf{v}_{att}^t$ would exclude local image regions which are irrelevant to the audio signal, and better bridges between the visual content and the audio concept by preserving the audio-related image regions. This is the reason why *instance-level* visual attention can be performed. We note that, this attention feature $\mathbf{v}_{att}^t$ can be easily deployed in current event localization models (e.g., [1,42]). We will detail this implementation and provide thorough comparisons in the experiment section.

4   Experiments

4.1   Dataset

For the audio-visual event localization, we follow [1] and consider the *Audio-Visual Event* (AVE) [1] dataset (a subset of Audioset [52]) for experiments (e.g., Church bell, Dog barking, Truck, Bus, Clock, Violin, etc.). This AVE dataset includes 4143 videos with 28 categories, and audio-visual labels are annotated at every second.

4.2   Implementation Details

In this section, we present the implementation details about the evaluation frameworks. For visual embedding, we utilize the VGG-19 [53] pre-trained on ImageNet [54] to extract 512-dimensional visual feature for each frame. The feature map of whole video frames with T seconds long is $\mathbb{R}^{T \times 7 \times 7 \times 512}$. We obtain 7×7 channels and 512 dimension with each channel. Each channel is processed by multilayer perceptrons (MLP) into 128 dimensions. Then, we reshape 7×7 channels into 49 channels corresponding to aforementioned total image regions R. As for audio embedding, we extract a 128-dimensional audio representation for each 1-second audio segment via VGGish [55], which is pre-trained on YouTube-8M [52]. Thus, we have audio features produced in a total of T seconds, i.e., $\mathbb{R}^{T \times 128}$.

For both fully supervised and weakly-supervised audio-visual event localization, we consider **frame-wise accuracy** as the evaluation metric. That is, we compute the percentage of correct matchings over all test input frames as the prediction accuracy. We note that, for fair comparisons, we apply VGG-19 as the visual backbone and VGGish as audio embedding models.

4.3   Experiment Results

Quantitative Results. We compare the performance of supervised event localization using baseline and recent models. [1] choose to concatenate audio and visual outputs from LSTMs and audio-guided visual attention. [42] apply an additional LSTM to serve as the final prediction classifier. DAM [2] advance state-of-the-art results in this task by jointly exploiting audiovisual relevant

Table 1. Performance comparisons using baseline or state-of-the-art localization methods in **supervised** (i.e., ground truth y_t observed for each frame during training) and **weakly supervised** (i.e., only ground truth Y observed for training). The numbers in bold indicate the best results (i.e., methods with our proposed instance attention mechanism). $*$ indicates the reproduced performance using the same pre-trained VGG-19 feature and the same weakly supervised setting for a fair comparison.

Method	Accuracy (%) fully supervised	Accuracy (%) weakly supervised
Audio only+LSTM	59.5	53.4
Visual only+LSTM	55.3	52.9
AVEL [1]	71.4	63.7
AVSDN [42]	72.6	68.4
AVEL+Att [1]	72.7	66.7
DAM [2]	74.5	–
Xuan et al.* [5]	75.1	67.8
Ramaswamy et al.[4]	74.8	68.9
AVIN [3]	75.2	69.4
AVSDN+Ours	75.8	**70.2**
AVEL+Ours	**76.8**	68.9

events. Note that, DAM requires event labels at each segment for calculating the audiovisual segment relevance. Thus, DAM would not be evaluated in the weakly supervised setting. In this work, we adapt our instance attention visual features in AVEL and AVSDN. Table 1 summarizes the performances of our methods and others in fully supervised on the AVE dataset. As for the weakly supervised setting, we repeat the same experiments and list the performance comparisons also in Table 1.

From tables presented, it is clear that use of our instance attention features would increase the localization accuracy. In other words, either observing frame-level or video-level labels, our proposed audiovisual transformer would properly extract cross-modality features for improved audio-visual event localization.

Qualitative Results. We now present example visualization results in fully supervised settings using the AVEL classifier. The attention output produced by ours and the method of [1] are shown in Fig. 5 and 6, respectively. We note that, the current co-attention method [1] (Fig. 5) only considers the patch-wise relationship between audio notion and visual feature extracted by CNN. Thus, this mechanism only focuses on local regions but ignores relationship between neighboring patches. To address this issue, our AV-transformer jointly exploits intra-frame and inter-frame visual patches and audio information. The encoded visual features derived from our AV-transformer preserve not only local patches information but neighboring patches with the same semantics. Furthermore, the inter-frame representation can facilitate the smoothness of attended regions

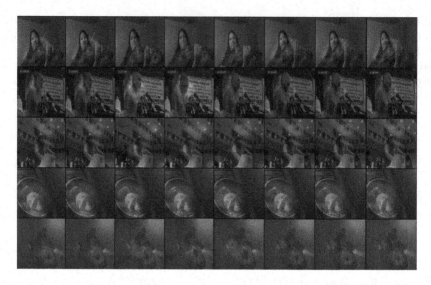

Fig. 5. Example attention results using AVEL [1] with their attention model of AVEL [1]: Each row shows a video input with visually attended regions. Take row 2 and 3 for example, it can be seen that AVEL with their attention model would incorrectly attend the regions of human voice which was not actually associated with the sound of human voice.

across frames. We note that, in the second and third rows, there were several non-interested people in the background. It would distracted the attention. Our method could attend on the proper regions under the similar object in the scene. In the forth and fifth rows, there were people cooking and riding motorcycle. Our model is able to not only attend on sounding objects but precisely preserve edge of objects.

The above quantitative and qualitative result successfully verify the effectiveness and robustness of our proposed cross-modality co-attention model. It not only produces improved audio-visual event localization result; more importantly, it is able to attend visually informative local regions across frames, and performs instance-level visual attention. This is also the reason why improved event localization performances can be expected.

User Studies. To evaluate the quality of qualitative results, we invite 20 people to watch the video with different attention results from audio-guided [1], audio-visual object localization [14,15], and ours. The participants voted the best results of three samples for each instance. We observe 72.2% (Ours), 16.7% [1], and 11.1% [14,15]. These results would also support our quantitative comparisons in Table 1.

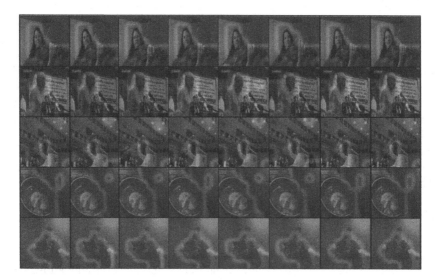

Fig. 6. Example attention results using AVEL [1] **with our instance attention model:** Each row shows a video input with visually attended regions. It can be seen that our model produced satisfactory attention outputs with the corresponding audio-visual events.

Table 2. Comparisons of recent audio-visual co-attention mechanisms [1,14,15] with integrating different visual representation in fully **supervised** setting (i.e., all ground truth y_t observed during training). The numbers in bold indicate the best results (i.e., with our instance attention).

Visual representation	Classifier			
	MLP	LSTM	AVSDN	AVEL
MLP+AG	64.0	69.0	73.1	72.7
MLP+AVOL	65.2	70.1	73.7	74.8
Conv3d+AG	64.9	71.0	73.8	75.2
Conv3d+AVOL	64.5	69.4	73.6	73.6
LSTM+AG	61.2	67.7	72.6	74.3
LSTM+AVOL	66.9	70.5	73.2	75.4
AV-Transformer+AG	65.9	67.2	74.0	74.1
Ours	**67.6**	**71.4**	**75.8**	**76.8**

4.4   Ablation Studies

In this section, we verify the design and contributions of our audiovisual transformer and different visual co-attention mechanisms [1,14,15]. This would support the learning and exploitation of intra and inter-frame visual representation for audio-visual event localization.

Inter-Frame Visual Representation. As to study the effects of learning inter-frame visual representations for instance attention, we consider different methods to model such inter-frame visual features. To model across frames visual representation, we utilize 3D convolutional networks [24] (Conv3D) and LSTM [56] network in our work. We note that, for standard Convolutional Neural Network [57] and the recent I3D Network [26], both based on consecutive video frames and optical flow, are also able to perform such modeling. In this ablation study, for fair comparisons, we only consider Conv3D and LSTM which do not require calculation of optical flow information. As for Conv3D, the inter-frame visual features can be modeled by Conv3D directly. However, LSTM only receives 1D embedding over times. Thus, we use the same location at every video frame as 1D embedding vector sequence, then the LSTM is applied to model temporal feature until every location across frames are processed.

Table 3. Comparisons of audiovisual representation in our AV-transformer. We explore different interactions on across frames, single frames and audio in fully **supervised** setting (i.e., all ground truth y_t observed during training). The numbers in bold indicate the best results (i.e., our full model of instance attention).

Audiovisual representation	Classifier			
	MLP	LSTM	AVSDN	AVEL
Intra	65.8	66.9	72.3	75.0
Intra+inter	66.3	70.4	72.2	75.4
Intra+audio	67.2	69.3	73.9	74.8
Inter+audio	66.1	66.8	72.1	74.3
Ours	**67.6**	**70.7**	**75.8**	**76.8**

We note that, the visual features derived from multilayer perceptron (MLP), Conv3D, LSTM and our AV-transformer are able to be utilized in current co-attention [1,14,15] methods. There are two typical co-attention mechanisms: audio-guided (AG) [1] and audio-visual object localization (AVOL) [14,15] co-attention. To be more specific, AVOL measures the correlation between visual patches and audio data based on cosine similarity, while AG determines the associated correlation via learning a neural net. Note that, we use AVOL in our instance attention. Therefore, we not only present different methods to encode inter-frame visual features but also test them on the two co-attention methods. As shown in Table 2, our instance attention performs favorably against other models with inter-frame visual encoding. In this table, the suffix of visual representation is the co-attention method (e.g., AG and AVOL). It is also worth noting that, our method also performed against different co-attention mechanisms. Another advantage of our approach is that, since our inter-frame visual features are calculated by intra-frames regardless the fixed kernel size, whose computation cost is lower than the models using Conv3D and LSTM. Based on the above results and observations, we can also confirm the jointly learning of intra and inter-frame visual features would be preferable in our cross-modality co-attention model, which would result in satisfactory event localization performances.

Audiovisual Representation of AV-Transformer. As to study the effects of jointly learning intra-frame and inter-frame visual representations in our audio-visual transformer. Besides, we exploit the audio interaction between each visual patch. As shown in Table 3, intra shows the only usage of time t frame in our AV-transformer, which means only $k = t$ in Eq. (2) without audio feature $\mathbf{a}^t$. Inter indicates three successive time step $k = t - 1, t, t + 1$, and audio illustrates audio feature $\mathbf{a}^t$ in Eq. (2). Table 3 verifies the effectiveness of jointly considering spatial, temporal visual information and audio signals for cross-modality co-attention for audio visual event localization to better associate audio and visual information for the task.

5 Conclusion

We presented a deep learning framework of Audiovisual Transformer, with the ability of cross-modality instance-level attention for audio-visual event localization. Our model jointly exploits intra and inter-frame visual representation while observing audio features, with the self-attention mechanism realized in a transformer-like architecture in supervised or weakly-supervised settings. In addition to promising performances on event localization, our model allows instance-level attention, which is able to attend the proper image region (at the instance level) associated with the sound/event of interest. From our experimental results and ablation studies, the use and design of our proposed framework can be successfully verified.

Acknowledgement. This work is supported in part by the Ministry of Science and Technology of Taiwan under grant MOST 109-2634-F-002-037.

References

1. Tian, Y., Shi, J., Li, B., Duan, Z., Xu, C.: Audio-visual event localization in unconstrained videos. In: Ferrari, V., Hebert, M., Sminchisescu, C., Weiss, Y. (eds.) ECCV 2018. LNCS, vol. 11206, pp. 252–268. Springer, Cham (2018). https://doi.org/10.1007/978-3-030-01216-8_16
2. Wu, Y., Zhu, L., Yan, Y., Yang, Y.: Dual attention matching for audio-visual event localization. In: ICCV (2019)
3. Ramaswamy, J.: What makes the sound?: a dual-modality interacting network for audio-visual event localization. In: ICASSP (2020)
4. Ramaswamy, J., Das, S.: See the sound, hear the pixels. In: Proceedings of the IEEE Winter Conference on Applications of Computer Vision (WACV) (2020)

5. Xuan, H., Zhang, Z., Chen, S., Yang, J., Yan, Y.: Cross-modal attention network for temporal inconsistent audio-visual event localization. In: AAAI (2020)
6. Hu, D., Li, X., et al.: Temporal multimodal learning in audiovisual speech recognition. In: CVPR (2016)
7. Kiela, D., Grave, E., Joulin, A., Mikolov, T.: Efficient large-scale multi-modal classification. In: AAAI (2018)
8. Chung, J.S., Senior, A.W., Vinyals, O., Zisserman, A.: Lip reading sentences in the wild. In: CVPR (2017)
9. Wiles, O., Koepke, A.S., Zisserman, A.: X2Face: a network for controlling face generation using images, audio, and pose codes. In: Ferrari, V., Hebert, M., Sminchisescu, C., Weiss, Y. (eds.) ECCV 2018. LNCS, vol. 11217, pp. 690–706. Springer, Cham (2018). https://doi.org/10.1007/978-3-030-01261-8_41
10. Zhou, H., Liu, Y., Liu, Z., Luo, P., Wang, X.: Talking face generation by adversarially disentangled audio-visual representation. In: AAAI (2019)
11. Zhou, H., Liu, Z., Xu, X., Luo, P., Wang, X.: Vision-infused deep audio inpainting. In: ICCV (2019)
12. Owens, A., Isola, P., McDermott, J., Torralba, A., Adelson, E.H., Freeman, W.T.: Visually indicated sounds. In: CVPR (2016)
13. Zhao, H., Gan, C., Rouditchenko, A., Vondrick, C., McDermott, J., Torralba, A.: The sound of pixels. In: Ferrari, V., Hebert, M., Sminchisescu, C., Weiss, Y. (eds.) ECCV 2018. LNCS, vol. 11205, pp. 587–604. Springer, Cham (2018). https://doi.org/10.1007/978-3-030-01246-5_35
14. Senocak, A., Oh, T.H., Kim, J., Yang, M.H., Kweon, I.S.: Learning to localize sound source in visual scenes. In: CVPR (2018)
15. Arandjelović, R., Zisserman, A.: Objects that sound. In: Ferrari, V., Hebert, M., Sminchisescu, C., Weiss, Y. (eds.) ECCV 2018. LNCS, vol. 11205, pp. 451–466. Springer, Cham (2018). https://doi.org/10.1007/978-3-030-01246-5_27
16. Owens, A., Efros, A.A.: Audio-visual scene analysis with self-supervised multisensory features. In: Ferrari, V., Hebert, M., Sminchisescu, C., Weiss, Y. (eds.) ECCV 2018. LNCS, vol. 11210, pp. 639–658. Springer, Cham (2018). https://doi.org/10.1007/978-3-030-01231-1_39
17. Donahue, J., et al.: Long-term recurrent convolutional networks for visual recognition and description. In: TPAMI (2017)
18. Karpathy, A., Toderici, G., Shetty, S., Leung, T., Sukthankar, R., Li, F.: Large-scale video classification with convolutional neural networks. In: CVPR (2014)
19. Zolfaghari, M., Oliveira, G.L., Sedaghat, N., Brox, T.: Chained multi-stream networks exploiting pose, motion, and appearance for action classification and detection. In: ICCV, pp. 2923–2932 3 (2017)
20. Wang, L., et al.: Temporal segment networks: towards good practices for deep action recognition. In: Leibe, B., Matas, J., Sebe, N., Welling, M. (eds.) ECCV 2016. LNCS, vol. 9912, pp. 20–36. Springer, Cham (2016). https://doi.org/10.1007/978-3-319-46484-8_2
21. Zolfaghari, M., Singh, K., Brox, T.: ECO: efficient convolutional network for online video understanding. In: Ferrari, V., Hebert, M., Sminchisescu, C., Weiss, Y. (eds.) ECCV 2018. LNCS, vol. 11206, pp. 713–730. Springer, Cham (2018). https://doi.org/10.1007/978-3-030-01216-8_43
22. Xie, S., Sun, C., Huang, J., Tu, Z., Murphy, K.: Rethinking spatiotemporal feature learning: speed-accuracy trade-offs in video classification. In: Ferrari, V., Hebert, M., Sminchisescu, C., Weiss, Y. (eds.) ECCV 2018. LNCS, vol. 11219, pp. 318–335. Springer, Cham (2018). https://doi.org/10.1007/978-3-030-01267-0_19

23. Zhou, B., Andonian, A., Oliva, A., Torralba, A.: Temporal relational reasoning in videos. In: Ferrari, V., Hebert, M., Sminchisescu, C., Weiss, Y. (eds.) ECCV 2018. LNCS, vol. 11205, pp. 831–846. Springer, Cham (2018). https://doi.org/10.1007/978-3-030-01246-5_49

24. Tran, D., Bourdev, L.D., Fergus, R., Torresani, L., Paluri, M.: C3D: generic features for video analysis. arXiv (2014)

25. Tran, D., Ray, J., Shou, Z., Chang, S., Paluri, M.: Convnet architecture search for spatiotemporal feature learning. CoRR abs/1708.05038 (2017)

26. Carreira, J., Zisserman, A.: Quo vadis, action recognition? A new model and the kinetics dataset. In: CVPR (2017)

27. Lev, G., Sadeh, G., Klein, B., Wolf, L.: RNN Fisher vectors for action recognition and image annotation. In: Leibe, B., Matas, J., Sebe, N., Welling, M. (eds.) ECCV 2016. LNCS, vol. 9910, pp. 833–850. Springer, Cham (2016). https://doi.org/10.1007/978-3-319-46466-4_50

28. Li, Z., Gavrilyuk, K., Gavves, E., Jain, M., Snoek, C.G.M.: VideoLSTM convolves, attends and flows for action recognition. In: CVIU (2016)

29. Bilen, H., Fernando, B., Gavves, E., Vedaldi, A., Gould, S.: Dynamic image networks for action recognition. In: CVPR, pp. 3034–3042 (2016)

30. Bilen, H., Fernando, B., Gavves, E., Vedaldi, A.: Action recognition with dynamic image networks. In: TPAMI (2018)

31. Arandjelovic, R., Zisserman, A.: Look, listen and learn. In: ICCV (2017)

32. Aytar, Y., Vondrick, C., Torralba, A.: SoundNet: learning sound representations from unlabeled video. In: NeurIPS (2016)

33. Owens, A., Wu, J., McDermott, J.H., Freeman, W.T., Torralba, A.: Ambient sound provides supervision for visual learning. In: Leibe, B., Matas, J., Sebe, N., Welling, M. (eds.) ECCV 2016. LNCS, vol. 9905, pp. 801–816. Springer, Cham (2016). https://doi.org/10.1007/978-3-319-46448-0_48

34. Gao, R., Grauman, K.: 2.5d-visual-sound. In: CVPR (2019)

35. Tian, Y., Guan, C., Goodman, J., Moore, M., Xu, C.: An attempt towards interpretable audio-visual video captioning. arXiv (2018)

36. Gao, R., Feris, R., Grauman, K.: Learning to separate object sounds by watching unlabeled video. In: Ferrari, V., Hebert, M., Sminchisescu, C., Weiss, Y. (eds.) ECCV 2018. LNCS, vol. 11207, pp. 36–54. Springer, Cham (2018). https://doi.org/10.1007/978-3-030-01219-9_3

37. Ephrat, A., et al.: Looking to listen at the cocktail party: a speaker-independent audio-visual model for speech separation. ACM TOG (2018)

38. Zhao, H., Gan, C., Ma, W.C., Torralba, A.: The sound of motions. In: ICCV (2019)

39. Xu, X., Dai, B., Lin, D.: Recursive visual sound separation using minus-plus net. In: ICCV (2019)

40. Gao, R., Grauman, K.: Co-separating sounds of visual objects. In: ICCV (2019)

41. Gan, C., Huang, D., Zhao, H., Tenenbaum, J.B., Torralba, A.: Music gesture for visual sound separation. In: CVPR (2020)

42. Lin, Y.B., Li, Y.J., Wang, Y.C.F.: Dual-modality seq2seq network for audio-visual event localization. In: ICASSP (2019)

43. Kim, K.-M., Choi, S.-H., Kim, J.-H., Zhang, B.-T.: Multimodal dual attention memory for video story question answering. In: Ferrari, V., Hebert, M., Sminchisescu, C., Weiss, Y. (eds.) ECCV 2018. LNCS, vol. 11219, pp. 698–713. Springer, Cham (2018). https://doi.org/10.1007/978-3-030-01267-0_41

44. Nguyen, D.K., Okatani, T.: Improved fusion of visual and language representations by dense symmetric co-attention for visual question answering. In: CVPR (2018)

45. Bai, Y., Fu, J., Zhao, T., Mei, T.: Deep attention neural tensor network for visual question answering. In: Ferrari, V., Hebert, M., Sminchisescu, C., Weiss, Y. (eds.) ECCV 2018. LNCS, vol. 11216, pp. 21–37. Springer, Cham (2018). https://doi.org/10.1007/978-3-030-01258-8_2

46. Shi, Y., Furlanello, T., Zha, S., Anandkumar, A.: Question type guided attention in visual question answering. In: Ferrari, V., Hebert, M., Sminchisescu, C., Weiss, Y. (eds.) ECCV 2018. LNCS, vol. 11208, pp. 158–175. Springer, Cham (2018). https://doi.org/10.1007/978-3-030-01225-0_10

47. Das, A., Agrawal, H., Zitnick, C.L., Parikh, D., Batra, D.: Human attention in visual question answering: do humans and deep networks look at the same regions? In: EMNLP (2016)

48. Yu, D., Fu, J., Mei, T., Rui, Y.: Multi-level attention networks for visual question answering. In: CVPR (2017)

49. Wang, X., Girshick, R.B., Gupta, A., He, K.: Non-local neural networks. In: CVPR (2018)

50. Vaswani, A., et al.: Attention is all you need. In: NeurIPS (2017)

51. Kim, J., et al.: Multimodal residual learning for visual QA. In: NeurIPS (2016)

52. Gemmeke, J.F., Ellis, D.P.W., et al.: Audio set: an ontology and human-labeled dataset for audio events. In: ICASSP (2017)

53. Simonyan, K., Zisserman, A.: Very deep convolutional networks for large-scale image recognition. arXiv (2014)

54. Deng, J., Dong, W., Socher, R., Li, L.J., Li, K., Fei-Fei, L.: ImageNet: a large-scale hierarchical image database. In: CVPR (2009)

55. Hershey, S., Chaudhuri, S., et al.: CNN architectures for large-scale audio classification. In: ICASSP (2017)

56. Hochreiter, S., Schmidhuber, J.: Long short-term memory. In: Neural computation (1997)

57. Simonyan, K., Zisserman, A.: Two-stream convolutional networks for action recognition in videos. In: NeurIPS (2014)

Watch, Read and Lookup: Learning to Spot Signs from Multiple Supervisors

Liliane Momeni, Gül Varol$^{(\boxtimes)}$, Samuel Albanie, Triantafyllos Afouras, and Andrew Zisserman

Visual Geometry Group, University of Oxford, Oxford, UK
{liliane,gul,albanie,afourast,az}@robots.ox.ac.uk

Abstract. The focus of this work is *sign spotting*—given a video of an isolated sign, our task is to identify *whether* and *where* it has been signed in a continuous, co-articulated sign language video. To achieve this sign spotting task, we train a model using multiple types of available supervision by: (1) *watching* existing sparsely labelled footage; (2) *reading* associated subtitles (readily available translations of the signed content) which provide additional *weak-supervision*; (3) *looking up* words (for which no co-articulated labelled examples are available) in visual sign language dictionaries to enable novel sign spotting. These three tasks are integrated into a unified learning framework using the principles of Noise Contrastive Estimation and Multiple Instance Learning. We validate the effectiveness of our approach on low-shot sign spotting benchmarks. In addition, we contribute a machine-readable British Sign Language (BSL) dictionary dataset of isolated signs, BSLDICT, to facilitate study of this task. The dataset, models and code are available at our project page (https://www.robots.ox.ac.uk/~vgg/research/bsldict/).

1 Introduction

The objective of this work is to develop a *sign spotting* model that can identify and localise instances of signs within sequences of continuous sign language. Sign languages represent the natural means of communication for deaf communities [1] and sign spotting has a broad range of practical applications. Examples include: indexing videos of signing content by keyword to enable content-based search; gathering diverse dictionaries of sign exemplars from unlabelled footage for linguistic study; automatic feedback for language students via an "auto-correct" tool (e.g. "did you mean this sign?"); making voice activated wake word devices accessible to deaf communities; and building sign language datasets by automatically labelling examples of signs.

The recent marriage of large-scale, labelled datasets with deep neural networks has produced considerable progress in audio [2,3] and visual [4,5] keyword

---

L. Momeni, G. Varol and S. Albanie—Equal contribution.

Electronic supplementary material The online version of this chapter (https://doi.org/10.1007/978-3-030-69544-6_18) contains supplementary material, which is available to authorized users.

© Springer Nature Switzerland AG 2021
H. Ishikawa et al. (Eds.): ACCV 2020, LNCS 12627, pp. 291–308, 2021.
https://doi.org/10.1007/978-3-030-69544-6_18

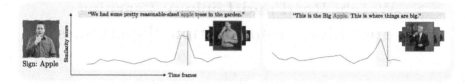

Fig. 1. We consider the task of *sign spotting* in co-articulated, continuous signing. Given a query dictionary video of an isolated sign (e.g. "apple"), we aim to identify *whether* and *where* it appears in videos of continuous signing. The wide domain gap between dictionary examples of *isolated* signs and target sequences of *continuous* signing makes the task extremely challenging.

spotting in *spoken languages*. However, a direct replication of these keyword spotting successes in sign language requires a commensurate quantity of labelled data (note that modern audiovisual spoken keyword spotting datasets contain millions of densely labelled examples [6,7]). Large-scale corpora of continuous, co-articulated[1] signing from TV broadcast data have recently been built [8], but the labels accompanying this data are: (1) sparse, and (2) cover a limited vocabulary.

It might be thought that a sign language dictionary would offer a relatively straightforward solution to the sign spotting task, particularly to the problem of covering only a limited vocabulary in existing large-scale corpora. But, unfortunately, this is not the case due to the severe *domain differences* between dictionaries and continuous signing in the wild. The challenges are that sign language dictionaries typically: (i) consist of *isolated signs* which differ in appearance from the *co-articulated* sequences of continuous signs (for which we ultimately wish to perform spotting); and (ii) differ in speed (are performed more slowly) relative to co-articulated signing. Furthermore, (iii) dictionaries only possess a few examples of each sign (so learning must be *low shot*); and as one more challenge, (iv) there can be multiple signs corresponding to a single keyword, for example due to regional variations of the sign language [9]. We show through experiments in Sect. 4, that directly training a sign spotter for continuous signing on dictionary examples, obtained from an internet-sourced sign language dictionary, does indeed perform poorly.

To address these challenges, we propose a unified framework in which sign spotting embeddings are learned from the dictionary (to provide broad coverage of the lexicon) in combination with two additional sources of supervision. In aggregate, these multiple types of supervision include: (1) *watching* sign language and learning from existing sparse annotations; (2) exploiting weak-supervision by *reading* the subtitles that accompany the footage and extracting candidates for signs that we expect to be present; (3) *looking up* words (for which we do not have labelled examples) in a sign language dictionary (see Fig. 2 for an overview). The recent development of large-scale, subtitled corpora of continuous signing providing sparse annotations [8] allows us to study this problem setting directly. We formulate our approach as a Multiple Instance Learning problem

---

[1] *Co-articulation* refers to changes in the appearance of the current sign due to neighbouring signs.

in which positive samples may arise from any of the three sources and employ Noise Contrastive Estimation [10] to learn a domain-invariant (valid across both isolated and co-articulated signing) representation of signing content.

We make the following six contributions: (1) We provide a machine readable British Sign Language (BSL) dictionary dataset of isolated signs, BSLDICT, to facilitate study of the sign spotting task; (2) We propose a unified Multiple Instance Learning framework for learning sign embeddings suitable for spotting from three supervisory sources; (3) We validate the effectiveness of our approach on a co-articulated sign spotting benchmark for which only a small number (low-shot) of isolated signs are provided as labelled training examples, and (4) achieve state-of-the-art performance on the BSL-1K sign spotting benchmark [8] (closed vocabulary). We show qualitatively that the learned embeddings can be used to (5) automatically mine new signing examples, and (6) discover "faux amis" (false friends) between sign languages.

2   Related Work

Our work relates to several themes in the literature: *sign language recognition* (and more specifically *sign spotting*), *sign language datasets*, *multiple instance learning* and *low-shot action localization*. We discuss each of these themes next.

Sign Language Recognition. The study of automatic sign recognition has a rich history in the computer vision community stretching back over 30 years, with early methods developing carefully engineered features to model trajectories and shape [11–14]. A series of techniques then emerged which made effective use of hand and body pose cues through robust keypoint estimation encodings [15–18]. Sign language recognition also has been considered in the context of sequence prediction, with HMMs [11,13,19,20], LSTMs [21–24], and Transformers [25] proving to be effective mechanisms for this task. Recently, convolutional neural networks have emerged as the dominant approach for appearance modelling [21], and in particular, action recognition models using spatio-temporal convolutions [26] have proven very well-suited for video-based sign recognition [8,27,28]. We adopt the I3D architecture [26] as a foundational building block in our studies.

Sign Language Spotting. The sign language spotting problem—in which the objective is to find performances of a sign (or sign sequence) in a longer sequence of signing—has been studied with Dynamic Time Warping and skin colour histograms [29] and with Hierarchical Sequential Patterns [30]. Different from our work which learns representations from multiple weak supervisory cues, these approaches consider a fully-supervised setting with a single source of supervision and use hand-crafted features to represent signs [31]. Our proposed use of a dictionary is also closely tied to *one-shot/few-shot learning*, in which the learner is assumed to have access to only a handful of annotated examples of the target category. One-shot dictionary learning was studied by [18] – different to their approach, we explicitly account for dialect variations in the dictionary (and validate the improvements brought by doing so in Sect. 4). Textual descriptions from a dictionary of 250 signs were used to study zero-shot learning by [32] – we instead consider the practical setting in which a handful of video examples are available per-sign (and make this dictionary available). The use of dictionaries to locate signs in subtitled video also shares commonalities with *domain adaptation*, since our method must bridge differences between the dictionary and the target continuous signing distribution. A vast number of techniques have been proposed to tackle distribution shift, including several adversarial feature alignment methods that are specialised for the few-shot setting [33,34]. In our work, we explore the domain-specific batch normalization (DSBN) method of [35], finding ultimately that simple batch normalization parameter re-initialization is most effective when jointly training on two domains after pre-training on the bigger domain. The concurrent work of [36] also seeks to align representation of isolated and continuous signs. However, our work differs from theirs in several key aspects: (1) rather than assuming access to a large-scale labelled dataset of isolated signs, we consider the setting in which only a handful of dictionary examples may be used to represent a word; (2) we develop a generalised Multiple Instance Learning framework which allows the learning of representations from weakly aligned subtitles whilst exploiting sparse labels and dictionaries (this integrates cues beyond the learning formulation in [36]); (3) we seek to label and improve performance on co-articulated signing (rather than improving recognition performance on isolated signing). Also related to our work, [18] uses a "reservoir" of weakly labelled sign footage to improve the performance of a sign classifier learned from a small number of examples. Different to [18], we propose a multi-instance learning formulation that explicitly accounts for signing variations that are present in the dictionary.

Sign Language Datasets. A number of sign language datasets have been proposed for studying Finnish [29], German [37,38], American [27,28,39,40] and Chinese [22,41] sign recognition. For British Sign Language (BSL), [42] gathered a corpus labelled with sparse, but fine-grained linguistic annotations, and more recently [8] collected BSL-1K, a large-scale dataset of BSL signs that were obtained using a mouthing-based keyword spotting model. In this work, we contribute BSLDICT, a dictionary-style dataset that is complementary to the datasets of [8,42] – it contains only a handful of instances of each sign, but achieves a comprehensive coverage of the BSL lexicon with a 9K vocabulary (vs a 1K vocabulary in [8]). As we show in the sequel, this dataset enables a number of sign spotting applications.

Multiple Instance Learning. Motivated by the readily available sign language footage that is accompanied by subtitles, a number of methods have been proposed for learning the association between signs and words that occur in the subtitle text [15,18,43,44]. In this work, we adopt the framework of Multiple Instance Learning (MIL) [45] to tackle this problem, previously explored by [15,46]. Our work differs from these works through the incorporation of a dictionary, and a principled mechanism for explicitly handling sign variants, to guide the learning process. Furthermore, we generalise the MIL framework so that it can learn to further exploit sparse labels. We also conduct experiments

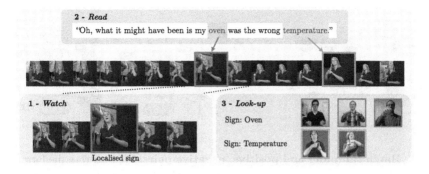

Fig. 2. The proposed *Watch, Read and Lookup* framework trains sign spotting embeddings with three cues: (1) *watching* videos and learning from sparse annotation in the form of localised signs (lower-left); (2) *reading* subtitles to find candidate signs that may appear in the source footage (top); (3) *looking up* corresponding visual examples in a sign language dictionary and aligning the representation against the embedded source segment (lower-right).

at significantly greater scale to make use of the full potential of MIL, considering more than two orders of magnitude more weakly supervised data than [15, 46].

Low-Shot Action Localization. This theme investigates semantic video localization: given one or more query videos the objective is to localize the segment in an untrimmed video that corresponds semantically to the query video [47–49]. Semantic matching is too general for the sign-spotting considered in this paper. However, we build on the temporal ordering ideas explored in this theme.

3   Learning Sign Spotting Embeddings from Multiple Supervisors

In this section, we describe the task of *sign spotting* and the three forms of supervision we assume access to. Let $\mathcal{X}_{\mathfrak{L}}$ denote the space of RGB video segments containing a frontal-facing individual communicating in sign language $\mathfrak{L}$ and denote by $\mathcal{X}_{\mathfrak{L}}^{\text{single}}$ its restriction to the set of segments containing a single sign. Further, let $\mathcal{T}$ denote the space of subtitle sentences and $\mathcal{V}_{\mathfrak{L}} = \{1, \ldots, V\}$ denote the *vocabulary*—an index set corresponding to an enumeration of written words that are equivalent to signs that can be performed in $\mathfrak{L}^2$.

Our objective, illustrated in Fig. 1, is to discover all occurrences of a given keyword in a collection of continuous signing sequences. To do so, we assume access to: (i) a subtitled collection of videos containing continuous signing, $\mathcal{S} = \{(x_i, s_i) : i \in \{1, \ldots, I\}, x_i \in \mathcal{X}_{\mathfrak{L}}, s_i \in \mathcal{T}\}$; (ii) a sparse collection of temporal sub-segments of these videos that have been annotated with their corresponding word, $\mathcal{M} = \{(x_k, v_k) : k \in \{1, \ldots, K\}, v_k \in \mathcal{V}_{\mathfrak{L}}, x_k \in$

---

[2] Sign language dictionaries provide a word-level or phrase-level correspondence (between sign language and spoken language) for many signs but no universally accepted *glossing* scheme exists for transcribing languages such as BSL [1].

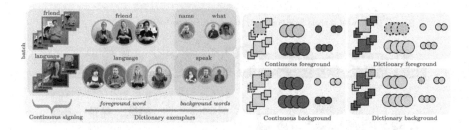

Fig. 3. Batch sampling and positive/negative pairs: We illustrate the formation of a batch when jointly training on continuous signing video (squares) and dictionaries of isolated signing (circles). **Left:** For each continuous video, we sample the dictionaries corresponding to the labeled word (foreground), as well as to the rest of the subtitles (background). **Right:** We construct positive/negative pairs by anchoring at 4 different portions of a batch item: continuous foreground/background and dictionary foreground/background. Positives and negatives (defined across continuous and dictionary domains) are green and red, respectively; anchors have a dashed border (see Appendix C.2 for details). (Color figure online)

$\mathcal{X}_{\mathcal{L}}^{\text{single}}, \exists (x_i, s_i) \in \mathcal{S} \, s.t. \, x_k \subseteq x_i \}$; (iii) a curated *dictionary* of signing instances $\mathcal{D} = \{(x_j, v_j) : j \in \{1, \ldots, J\}, x_j \in \mathcal{X}_{\mathcal{L}}^{\text{single}}, v_j \in \mathcal{V}_{\mathcal{L}}\}$. To address the sign spotting task, we propose to learn a *data representation* $f : \mathcal{X}_{\mathcal{L}} \rightarrow \mathbb{R}^d$ that maps video segments to vectors such that they are *discriminative* for sign spotting and *invariant* to other factors of variation. Formally, for any labelled pair of video segments $(x, v), (x', v')$ with $x, x' \in \mathcal{X}_{\mathcal{L}}$ and $v, v' \in \mathcal{V}_{\mathcal{L}}$, we seek a data representation, f, that satisfies the constraint $\delta_{f(x)f(x')} = \delta_{vv'}$, where δ represents the Kronecker delta.

3.1   Integrating Cues Through Multiple Instance Learning

To learn f, we must address several challenges. First, as noted in Sect. 1, there may be a considerable distribution shift between the dictionary videos of isolated signs in $\mathcal{D}$ and the co-articulated signing videos in $\mathcal{S}$. Second, sign languages often contain multiple sign variants for a single written word (resulting from regional dialects and synonyms). Third, since the subtitles in $\mathcal{S}$ are only weakly aligned with the sign sequence, we must learn to associate signs and words from a noisy signal that lacks temporal localisation. Fourth, the localised annotations provided by $\mathcal{M}$ are sparse, and therefore we must make good use of the remaining segments of subtitled videos in $\mathcal{S}$ if we are to learn an effective representation.

Given full supervision, we could simply adopt a pairwise metric learning approach to align segments from the videos in $\mathcal{S}$ with dictionary videos from $\mathcal{D}$ by requiring that f maps a pair of isolated and co-articulated signing segments to the same point in the embedding space if they correspond to the same sign (*positive* pairs) and apart if they do not (*negative* pairs). As noted above, in practice we do not have access to positive pairs because: (1) for any annotated segment $(x_k, v_k) \in \mathcal{M}$, we have a set of potential sign variations represented in the dictionary (annotated with the common label v_k), rather than a single unique sign; (2) since $\mathcal{S}$ provides only weak supervision, even when a word is mentioned in the subtitles we do not know where it appears in the continuous signing sequence (if it appears at all). These ambiguities motivate a Multiple Instance Learning [45] (MIL) objective. Rather than forming positive and negative pairs, we instead form positive *bags* of pairs, $\mathcal{P}^{\text{bags}}$, in which we expect at least one pairing between a segment from a video in $\mathcal{S}$ and a dictionary video from $\mathcal{D}$ to contain the same sign, and negative bags of pairs, $\mathcal{N}^{\text{bags}}$, in which we expect no (video segment, dictionary video) pair to contain the same sign. To incorporate the available sources of supervision into this formulation, we consider two categories of positive and negative bag formations, described next (due to space constraints, a formal mathematical description of the positive and negative bags described below is deferred to Appendix C.2).

Watch and Lookup: Using Sparse Annotations and Dictionaries. Here, we describe a baseline where we assume no subtitles are available. To learn f from $\mathcal{M}$ and $\mathcal{D}$, we define each positive bag as the set of possible pairs between a *labelled (foreground)* temporal segment of a continuous video from $\mathcal{M}$ and the examples of the corresponding sign in the dictionary (green regions in Fig. A.2). The key assumption here is that each labelled sign segment from $\mathcal{M}$ matches *at least one* sign variation in the dictionary. Negative bags are constructed by (i) anchoring on a continuous foreground segment and selecting dictionary examples corresponding to different words from other batch items; (ii) anchoring on a dictionary foreground set and selecting continuous foreground segments from other batch items (red regions in Fig. A.2). To maximize the number of negatives within one minibatch, we sample a different word per batch item.

Watch, Read and Lookup: Using Sparse Annotations, Subtitles and Dictionaries. Using just the labelled sign segments from $\mathcal{M}$ to construct bags has a significant limitation: f is not encouraged to represent signs beyond the initial vocabulary represented in $\mathcal{M}$. We therefore look at the subtitles (which contain words beyond $\mathcal{M}$) to construct additional bags. We determine more positive bags between the set of *unlabelled (background)* segments in the continuous footage and the set of dictionaries corresponding to the background words in the subtitle (green regions in Fig. 3, right-bottom). Negatives (red regions in Fig. 3) are formed as the complements to these sets by (i) pairing continuous background segments with dictionary samples that can be excluded as matches (through subtitles) and (ii) pairing background dictionary entries with the foreground continuous segment. In both cases, we also define negatives from other batch items by selecting pairs where the word(s) have no overlap, e.g., in Fig. 3, the dictionary examples for the background word 'speak' from the second batch item are negatives for the background continuous segments from the first batch item, corresponding to the unlabelled words 'name' and 'what' in the subtitle.

To assess the similarity of two embedded video segments, we employ a similarity function $\psi : \mathbb{R}^d \times \mathbb{R}^d \to \mathbb{R}$ whose value increases as its arguments become more similar (in this work, we use cosine similarity). For notational convenience below, we write ψ_{ij} as shorthand for $\psi(f(x_i), f(x_j))$. To learn f, we consider a generalization of the InfoNCE loss [50,51] (a non-parametric softmax loss formulation of Noise Contrastive Estimation [10]) recently proposed by [52]:

$$\mathcal{L}_{\text{MIL-NCE}} = -\mathbb{E}_i \left[\log \frac{\sum_{(j,k) \in \mathcal{P}(i)} \exp(\psi_{jk}/\tau)}{\sum_{(j,k) \in \mathcal{P}(i)} \exp(\psi_{jk}/\tau) + \sum_{(l,m) \in \mathcal{N}(i)} \exp(\psi_{lm}/\tau)} \right], \quad (1)$$

where $\mathcal{P}(i) \in \mathcal{P}^{\text{bags}}$, $\mathcal{N}(i) \in \mathcal{N}^{\text{bags}}$, τ, often referred to as the *temperature*, is set as a hyperparameter (we explore the effect of its value in Sect. 4).

3.2   Implementation Details

In this section, we provide details for the learning framework covering the embedding architecture, sampling protocol and optimization procedure.

Embedding Architecture. The architecture comprises an I3D spatio-temporal trunk network [26] to which we attach an MLP consisting of three linear layers separated by leaky ReLU activations (with negative slope 0.2) and a skip connection. The trunk network takes as input 16 frames from a 224×224 resolution video clip and produces 1024-dimensional embeddings which are then projected to 256-dimensional sign spotting embeddings by the MLP. More details about the embedding architecture can be found in Appendix C.1.

Joint Pretraining. The I3D trunk parameters are initialised by pretraining for sign classification jointly over the sparse annotations $\mathcal{M}$ of a continuous signing dataset (BSL-1K [8]) and examples from a sign dictionary dataset (BSLDICT) which fall within their common vocabulary. Since we find that dictionary videos of isolated signs tend to be performed more slowly, we uniformly sample 16 frames from each dictionary video with a random shift and random frame rate n times, where n is proportional to the length of the video, and pass these clips through the I3D trunk then average the resulting vectors before they are processed by the MLP to produce the final dictionary embeddings. We find that this form of random sampling performs better than sampling 16 consecutive frames from the isolated signing videos (see Appendix C.1 for more details). During pretraining, minibatches of size 4 are used; and colour, scale and horizontal flip augmentations are applied to the input video, following the procedure described in [8]. The trunk parameters are then frozen and the MLP outputs are used as embeddings. Both datasets are described in detail in Sect. 4.1.

Minibatch Sampling. To train the MLP given the pretrained I3D features, we sample data by first iterating over the set of labelled segments comprising the sparse annotations, $\mathcal{M}$, that accompany the dataset of continuous, subtitled sampling to form minibatches. For each continuous video, we sample 16 consecutive frames around the annotated timestamp (more precisely a random offset within 20 frames before, 5 frames after, following the timing study in [8]). We randomly sample 10 additional 16-frame clips from this video outside of the labelled window, i.e., continuous background segments. For each subtitled sequence, we sample the dictionary entries for all subtitle words that appear in $\mathcal{V}_\mathcal{L}$ (see Fig. 3 for a sample batch formation).

Table 1. Datasets: We provide (i) the number of individual sign videos, (ii) the vocabulary size of the annotated signs, and (iii) the number of signers for BSL-1K and BSLDICT. BSL-1K is large in the number of annotated signs whereas BSLDICT is large in the vocabulary size. Note that we use a different partition of BSL-1K with longer sequences around the annotations as described in Sect. 4.1.

Dataset	#Videos	Vocab	#Signers
BSL-1K[8]	273K	1,064	40
BSLDICT	14,210	9,283	>28

Our minibatch comprises 128 sequences of continuous signing and their corresponding dictionary entries (we investigate the impact of batch size in Sect. 4.3). The embeddings are then trained by minimising the loss defined in Eq. (1) in conjunction with positive bags, $\mathcal{P}^{\text{bags}}$, and negative bags, $\mathcal{N}^{\text{bags}}$, which are constructed on-the-fly for each minibatch (see Fig. 3).

Optimization. We use a SGD optimizer with an initial learning rate of 10^{-2} to train the embedding architecture. The learning rate is decayed twice by a factor of 10 (at epoch 40 and 45). We train all models, including baselines and ablation studies, for 50 epochs at which point we find that learning has always converged.

Test Time. To perform spotting, we obtain the embeddings learned with the MLP. For the dictionary, we have a single embedding averaged over the video. Continuous video embeddings are obtained with sliding window (stride 1) on the entire sequence. We calculate the cosine similarity score between the continuous signing sequence embeddings and the embedding for a given dictionary video. We determine the location with the maximum similarity as the location of the queried sign. We maintain embedding sets of all variants of dictionary videos for a given word and choose the best match as the one with the highest similarity.

4   Experiments

In this section, we first present the datasets used in this work (including the contributed BSLDICT dataset) in Sect. 4.1, followed by the evaluation protocol in Sect. 4.2. We illustrate the benefits of the *Watch, Read and Lookup* learning framework for sign spotting against several baselines with a comprehensive ablation study that validates our design choices (Sect. 4.3). Finally, we investigate three applications of our method in Sect. 4.4, showing that it can be used to (i) not only spot signs, but also identify the specific sign variant that was used, (ii) label sign instances in continuous signing footage given the associated subtitles, and (iii) discover "faux amis" between different sign languages.

4.1   Datasets

Although our method is conceptually applicable to a number of sign languages, in this work we focus primarily on BSL, the sign language of British deaf communities. We use BSL-1K [8], a large-scale, subtitled and sparsely annotated dataset of more than 1000 h of continuous signing which offers an ideal setting in which to evaluate the effectiveness of the *Watch, Read and Lookup* sign spotting framework. To provide dictionary data for the *lookup* component of our approach, we also contribute BSLDICT, a diverse visual dictionary of signs. These two datasets are summarised in Table 1 and described in more detail below.

BSL-1K. [8] comprises a vocabulary of 1,064 signs which are sparsely annotated over 1,000 h of video of continuous sign language. The videos are accompanied by subtitles. The dataset consists of 273K localised sign annotations, automatically generated from sign-language-interpreted BBC television broadcasts, by leveraging weakly aligned subtitles and applying keyword spotting to signer *mouthings*. Please refer to [8] for more details on the automatic annotation pipeline. In this work, we process this data to extract long videos with subtitles. In particular, we pad $+/-2$ s around the subtitle timestamps and we add the corresponding video to our training set if there is a sparse annotation word falling within this time window, assuming that the signing is reasonably well-aligned with its subtitles in these cases. We further consider only the videos whose subtitle duration is longer than 2 s. For testing, we use the automatic test set (corresponding to mouthing locations with confidences above 0.9). Thus we obtain 78K training and 3K test videos, each of which has a subtitle of 8 words on average and 1 sparse mouthing annotation.

BSLDICT. BSL dictionary videos are collected from a BSL sign aggregation platform signbsl.com [53], giving us a total of 14,210 video clips for a vocabulary of 9,283 signs. Each sign is typically performed several times by different signers, often in different ways. The dictionary consists of at least 28 different signers: the videos are downloaded from 28 known website sources and each source has at least 1 signer. The dictionary videos are of isolated signs (as opposed to co-articulated in BSL-1K): this means (i) the start and end of the video clips usually consist of a still signer pausing, and (ii) the sign is performed at a much slower rate for clarity. We first trim the sign dictionary videos, using body keypoints estimated with OpenPose [54] which indicate the start and end of wrist motion, to discard frames where the signer is still. With this process, the average number of frames per video drops from 78 to 56 (still significantly larger than co-articulated signs). To the best of our knowledge, BSLDICT is the first curated, BSL sign dictionary dataset for computer vision research, which will be made available. For the experiments in which BSLDICT is filtered to the 1,064 vocabulary of BSL-1K (see below), we have a total of 2,992 videos. Within this subset, each sign has between 1 and 10 examples (average of 3).

4.2 Evaluation Protocols

Protocols. We define two settings: (i) training with the entire 1064 vocabulary of annotations in BSL-1K; and (ii) training on a subset with 800 signs. The latter is needed to assess the performance on novel signs, for which we do not have access to co-articulated labels at training. We thus use the remaining 264

Table 2. The effect of the loss formulation: Embeddings learned with the classification loss are suboptimal since they are not trained for matching the two domains. Contrastive-based loss formulations (NCE) significantly improve, particularly when we adopt the multiple-instance variant introduced as our Watch-Read-Lookup framework of multiple supervisory signals.

Embedding arch	Supervision	Train (1064)		Train (800)	
		Seen (264)		Unseen (264)	
		mAP	R@5	mAP	R@5
I3D^{BSLDICT}	Classification	2.68	3.57	1.21	1.29
I3D$^{\text{BSL-1K}}$ [8]	Classification	13.09	17.25	6.74	8.94
I3D$^{\text{BSL-1K,BSLDICT}}$	Classification	19.81	25.57	4.81	6.89
I3D$^{\text{BSL-1K,BSLDICT}}$+MLP	Classification	36.75	40.15	10.28	14.19
I3D$^{\text{BSL-1K,BSLDICT}}$+MLP	InfoNCE	42.52	53.54	10.88	14.23
I3D$^{\text{BSL-1K,BSLDICT}}$+MLP	Watch-Lookup	43.65	53.03	11.05	14.62
I3D$^{\text{BSL-1K,BSLDICT}}$+MLP	Watch-Read-Lookup	**48.11**	**58.71**	**13.69**	**17.79**

words for testing. This test set is therefore common to both training settings, it is either 'seen' or 'unseen' at training. However, we do not limit the vocabulary of the dictionary as a practical assumption, for which we show benefits.

Metrics. The performance is evaluated based on ranking metrics. For every sign s_i in the test vocabulary, we first select the BSL-1K test set clips which have a mouthing annotation of s_i and then record the percentage of dictionary clips of s_i that appear in the first 5 retrieved results, this is the 'Recall at 5' (R@5). This is motivated by the fact that different English words can correspond to the same sign, and vice versa. We also report mean average precision (mAP). For each video pair, the match is considered correct if (i) the dictionary clip corresponds to s_i and the BSL-1K video clip has a mouthing annotation of s_i, and (ii) if the predicted location of the sign in the BSL-1K video clip, i.e. the time frame where the maximum similarity occurs, lies within certain frames around the ground truth mouthing timing. In particular, we determine the correct interval to be defined between 20 frames before and 5 frames after the labeled time (based on the study in [8]). Finally, because BSL-1K test is class-unbalanced, we report performances averaged over the test classes.

4.3   Ablation Study

In this section, we evaluate different components of our approach. We first compare our contrastive learning approach with classification baselines. Then, we investigate the effect of our multiple-instance loss formulation. We provide ablations for the hyperparameters, such as the batch size and the temperature, and report performance on a sign spotting benchmark.

Table 3. Extending the dictionary vocabulary: We show the benefits of sampling dictionary videos outside of the sparse annotations, using subtitles. Extending the lookup to the dictionary from the subtitles to the full vocabulary of BSLDICT brings significant improvements for novel signs (the training uses sparse annotations for the 800 words, and the remaining 264 for test).

Supervision	Dictionary Vocab	mAP	R@5
Watch-Read-Lookup	800 training vocab	13.69	17.79
Watch-Read-Lookup	9k full vocab	**15.39**	**20.87**

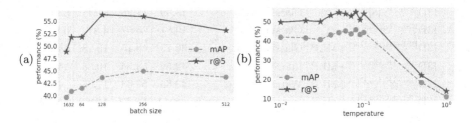

Fig. 4. The effect of (a) the **batch size** that determines the number of negatives across sign classes and (b) the **temperature** hyper-parameter for the MIL-NCE loss in Watch-Lookup against mAP and R@5 (trained on the full 1064 vocab.)

I3D Baselines. We start by evaluating baseline I3D models trained with classification on the task of spotting, using the embeddings before the classification layer. We have three variants in Table 2: (i) I3D^{BSL-1K} provided by [8] which is trained only on the BSL-1K dataset, and we also train (ii) I3D^{BSLDICT} and (iii) I3D$^{BSL-1K,BSLDICT}$. Training only on BSLDICT (I3D^{BSLDICT}) performs significantly worse due to the few examples available per class and the domain gap that must be bridged to spot co-articulated signs, suggesting that dictionary samples alone do not suffice to solve the task. We observe improvements with fine-tuning I3D^{BSL-1K} jointly on the two datasets (I3D$^{BSL-1K,BSLDICT}$), which becomes our base feature extractor for the remaining experiments to train a shallow MLP.

Loss Formulation. We first train the MLP parameters on top of the frozen I3D trunk with classification to establish a baseline in a comparable setup. Note that, this shallow architecture can be trained with larger batches than I3D. Next, we investigate variants of our loss to learn a joint sign embedding between BSL-1K and BSLDICT video domains: (i) standard single-instance InfoNCE [50,51] loss which pairs each BSL-1K video clip with *one* positive BSLDICT clip of the same sign, (ii) Watch-Lookup which considers multiple positive dictionary candidates, but does not consider subtitles (therefore limited to the annotated video clips). Table 2 summarizes the results. Our Watch-Read-Lookup formulation which effectively combines multiple sources of supervision in a multiple-instance framework outperforms the other baselines in both *seen* and *unseen* protocols.

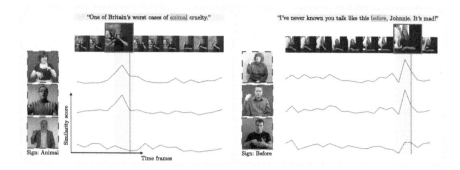

Fig. 5. Sign variant identification: We plot the similarity scores between BSL-1K test clips and BSLDICT variants of the sign "animal" (left) and "before" (right) over time. The labeled mouthing times are shown by red vertical lines and the sign proposal regions are shaded. A high similarity occurs for the first two rows, where the BSLDICT examples match the variant used in BSL-1K. (Color figure online)

Extending the Vocabulary. The results presented so far were using the same vocabulary for both continuous and dictionary datasets. In reality, one can assume access to the entire vocabulary in the dictionary, but obtaining annotations for the continuous videos is prohibitive. Table 3 investigates removing the vocabulary limit on the dictionary side, but keeping the continuous annotations vocabulary at 800 signs. We show that using the full 9k vocabulary from BSLDICT significantly improves the results on the unseen setting.

Batch Size. Next, we investigate the effect of increasing the number of negative pairs by increasing the batch size when training with Watch-Lookup on 1064 categories. We observe in Fig. 4(a) an improvement in performance with greater numbers of negatives before saturating. Our final Watch-Read-Lookup model has high memory requirements, for which we use 128 batch size. Note that the effective size of the batch with our sampling is larger due to sampling extra video clips corresponding to subtitles.

Temperature. Finally, we analyze the impact of the temperature hyperparameter τ on the performance of Watch-Lookup. We observe a major decrease in performance when τ approaches 1. We choose $\tau = 0.07$ used in [51,55] for all other experiments. Additional ablations are provided in Appendix B.

BSL-1K Sign Spotting Benchmark. Although our learning framework primarily targets good performance on unseen continuous signs, it can also be naively applied to the (closed-vocabulary) sign spotting benchmark proposed by [8]. We evaluate the performance of our Watch-Read-Lookup model and achieve a score of 0.170 mAP, outperforming the previous state-of-the-art performance of 0.160 mAP [8].

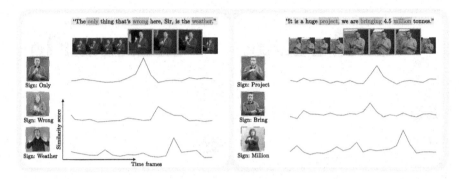

Fig. 6. Densification: We plot the similarity scores between BSL-1K test clips and BSLDICT examples over time, by querying only the words in the subtitle. The predicted locations of the signs correspond to the peak similarity scores.

4.4 Applications

In this section, we investigate three applications of our sign spotting method.

Sign Variant Identification. We show the ability of our model to spot specifically which variant of the sign was used. In Fig. 5, we observe high similarity scores when the variant of the sign matches in both BSL-1K and BSLDICT videos. Identifying such sign variations allows a better understanding of regional differences and can potentially help standardisation efforts of BSL.

Dense Annotations. We demonstrate the potential of our model to obtain dense annotations on continuous sign language video data. Sign spotting through the use of sign dictionaries is not limited to mouthings as in [8] and therefore is of great importance to scale up datasets for learning more robust sign language models. In Fig. 6, we show qualitative examples of localising multiple signs in a given sentence in BSL-1K, where we only query the words that occur in the subtitles, reducing the search space. In fact, if we assume the word to be known, we obtain 83.08% sign localisation accuracy on BSL-1K with our best model. This is defined as the number of times the maximum similarity occurs within $-20/+5$ frames of the end label time provided by [8].

"Faux Amis". There are works investigating lexical similarities between sign languages manually [56,57]. We show qualitatively the potential of our model to discover similarities, as well as "faux-amis" between different sign languages, in particular between British (BSL) and American (ASL) Sign Languages. We retrieve nearest neighbors according to visual embedding similarities between BSLDICT which has a 9K vocabulary and WLASL [28], an ASL isolated sign language dataset, with a 2K vocabulary. We provide some examples in Fig. 7.

Fig. 7. "**Faux amis**" **in BSL/ASL:** Same/similar manual features for different English words (left), as well as for the same English words (right), are identified between BSLDICT and WLASL isolated sign language datasets.

5 Conclusions

We have presented an approach to spot signs in continuous sign language videos using visual sign dictionary videos, and have shown the benefits of leveraging multiple supervisory signals available in a realistic setting: (i) sparse annotations in continuous signing, (ii) accompanied with subtitles, and (iii) a few dictionary samples per word from a large vocabulary. We employ multiple-instance contrastive learning to incorporate these signals into a unified framework. Our analysis suggests the potential of sign spotting in several applications, which we think will help in scaling up the automatic annotation of sign language datasets.

Acknowledgements. This work was supported by EPSRC grant ExTol. The authors would to like thank A. Sophia Koepke, Andrew Brown, Necati Cihan Camgöz, and Bencie Woll for their help. S.A would like to acknowledge the generous support of S. Carlson in enabling his contribution, and his son David, who bravely waited until after the submission deadline to enter this world.

References

1. Sutton-Spence, R., Woll, B.: The Linguistics of British Sign Language: An Introduction. Cambridge University Press, London (1999)
2. Coucke, A., Chlieh, M., Gisselbrecht, T., Leroy, D., Poumeyrol, M., Lavril, T.: Efficient keyword spotting using dilated convolutions and gating. In: ICASSP (2019)
3. Véniat, T., Schwander, O., Denoyer, L.: Stochastic adaptive neural architecture search for keyword spotting. In: ICASSP (2019)
4. Momeni, L., Afouras, T., Stafylakis, T., Albanie, S., Zisserman, A.: Seeing wake words: audio-visual keyword spotting. In: BMVC (2020)
5. Stafylakis, T., Tzimiropoulos, G.: Zero-shot keyword spotting for visual speech recognition in-the-wild. In: Ferrari, V., Hebert, M., Sminchisescu, C., Weiss, Y. (eds.) ECCV 2018. LNCS, vol. 11208, pp. 536–552. Springer, Cham (2018). https://doi.org/10.1007/978-3-030-01225-0_32
6. Chung, J.S., Senior, A., Vinyals, O., Zisserman, A.: Lip reading sentences in the wild. In: CVPR (2017)
7. Afouras, T., Chung, J.S., Zisserman, A.: LRS3-TED: a large-scale dataset for visual speech recognition. arXiv preprint arXiv:1809.00496 (2018)

8. Albanie, S., et al.: BSL-1K: scaling up co-articulated sign language recognition using mouthing cues. In: Vedaldi, A., Bischof, H., Brox, T., Frahm, J.-M. (eds.) ECCV 2020. LNCS, vol. 12356, pp. 35–53. Springer, Cham (2020). https://doi.org/10.1007/978-3-030-58621-8_3

9. Schembri, A., Fenlon, J., Rentelis, R., Cormier, K.: British Sign Language Corpus Project: A corpus of digital video data and annotations of British Sign Language 2008–2017 (Third Edition) (2017)

10. Gutmann, M., Hyvärinen, A.: Noise-contrastive estimation: a new estimation principle for unnormalized statistical models. In: Proceedings of the Thirteenth International Conference on Artificial Intelligence and Statistics, pp. 297–304 (2010)

11. Kadir, T., Bowden, R., Ong, E.J., Zisserman, A.: Minimal training, large lexicon, unconstrained sign language recognition. In: Proceedings of the BMVC (2004)

12. Tamura, S., Kawasaki, S.: Recognition of sign language motion images. Pattern Recogn. **21**, 343–353 (1988)

13. Starner, T.: Visual recognition of American sign language using hidden Markov models. Master's thesis, Massachusetts Institute of Technology (1995)

14. Fillbrandt, H., Akyol, S., Kraiss, K.: Extraction of 3D hand shape and posture from image sequences for sign language recognition. In: IEEE International SOI Conference (2003)

15. Buehler, P., Everingham, M., Zisserman, A.: Learning sign language by watching TV (using weakly aligned subtitles). In: Proceedings of the CVPR (2009)

16. Cooper, H., Pugeault, N., Bowden, R.: Reading the signs: a video based sign dictionary. In: ICCVW (2011)

17. Ong, E., Cooper, H., Pugeault, N., Bowden, R.: Sign language recognition using sequential pattern trees. In: CVPR (2012)

18. Pfister, T., Charles, J., Zisserman, A.: Domain-adaptive discriminative one-shot learning of gestures. In: Fleet, D., Pajdla, T., Schiele, B., Tuytelaars, T. (eds.) ECCV 2014. LNCS, vol. 8694, pp. 814–829. Springer, Cham (2014). https://doi.org/10.1007/978-3-319-10599-4_52

19. Agris, U., Zieren, J., Canzler, U., Bauer, B., Kraiss, K.F.: Recent developments in visual sign language recognition. Univ. Access Inf. Soc. **6**, 323–362 (2008)

20. Forster, J., Oberdörfer, C., Koller, O., Ney, H.: Modality combination techniques for continuous sign language recognition. In: Pattern Recognition and Image Analysis (2013)

21. Camgoz, N.C., Hadfield, S., Koller, O., Bowden, R.: SubUNets: end-to-end hand shape and continuous sign language recognition. In: ICCV (2017)

22. Huang, J., Zhou, W., Zhang, Q., Li, H., Li, W.: Video-based sign language recognition without temporal segmentation. In: AAAI (2018)

23. Ye, Y., Tian, Y., Huenerfauth, M., Liu, J.: Recognizing American sign language gestures from within continuous videos. In: CVPRW (2018)

24. Zhou, H., Zhou, W., Zhou, Y., Li, H.: Spatial-temporal multi-cue network for continuous sign language recognition. CoRR abs/2002.03187 (2020)

25. Camgoz, N.C., Koller, O., Hadfield, S., Bowden, R.: Sign language transformers: joint end-to-end sign language recognition and translation. In: CVPR (2020)

26. Carreira, J., Zisserman, A.: Quo Vadis, action recognition? A new model and the Kinetics dataset. In: CVPR (2017)

27. Joze, H.R.V., Koller, O.: MS-ASL: a large-scale data set and benchmark for understanding American sign language. In: BMVC (2019)

28. Li, D., Opazo, C.R., Yu, X., Li, H.: Word-level deep sign language recognition from video: a new large-scale dataset and methods comparison. In: WACV (2019)

29. Viitaniemi, V., Jantunen, T., Savolainen, L., Karppa, M., Laaksonen, J.: S-pot - a benchmark in spotting signs within continuous signing. In: LREC (2014)
30. Eng-Jon Ong, Koller, O., Pugeault, N., Bowden, R.: Sign spotting using hierarchical sequential patterns with temporal intervals. In: CVPR (2014)
31. Farhadi, A., Forsyth, D.A., White, R.: Transfer learning in sign language. In: CVPR (2007)
32. Bilge, Y.C., Ikizler, N., Cinbis, R.: Zero-shot sign language recognition: can textual data uncover sign languages? In: BMVC (2019)
33. Motiian, S., Jones, Q., Iranmanesh, S.M., Doretto, G.: Few-shot adversarial domain adaptation. In: NeurIPS (2017)
34. Zhang, J., Chen, Z., Huang, J., Lin, L., Zhang, D.: Few-shot structured domain adaptation for virtual-to-real scene parsing. In: ICCVW (2019)
35. Chang, W.G., You, T., Seo, S., Kwak, S., Han, B.: Domain-specific batch normalization for unsupervised domain adaptation. In: CVPR (2019)
36. Li, D., Yu, X., Xu, C., Petersson, L., Li, H.: Transferring cross-domain knowledge for video sign language recognition. In: CVPR (2020)
37. Koller, O., Forster, J., Ney, H.: Continuous sign language recognition: towards large vocabulary statistical recognition systems handling multiple signers. Comput. Vis. Image Underst. **141**, 108–125 (2015)
38. von Agris, U., Knorr, M., Kraiss, K.: The significance of facial features for automatic sign language recognition. In: 2008 8th IEEE International Conference on Automatic Face Gesture Recognition (2008)
39. Athitsos, V., et al.: The American sign language lexicon video dataset. In: CVPRW (2008)
40. Wilbur, R.B., Kak, A.C.: Purdue RVL-SLLL American sign language database. School of Electrical and Computer Engineering Technical report, TR-06-12, Purdue University, W. Lafayette, IN 47906 (2006)
41. Chai, X., Wang, H., Chen, X.: The devisign large vocabulary of Chinese sign language database and baseline evaluations. Technical report VIPL-TR-14-SLR-001. Key Lab of Intelligent Information Processing of Chinese Academy of Sciences (CAS), Institute of Computing Technology, CAS (2014)
42. Schembri, A., Fenlon, J., Rentelis, R., Reynolds, S., Cormier, K.: Building the British sign language corpus. Lang. Document. Conserv. **7**, 136–154 (2013)
43. Cooper, H., Bowden, R.: Learning signs from subtitles: a weakly supervised approach to sign language recognition. In: CVPR (2009)
44. Chung, J.S., Zisserman, A.: Signs in time: encoding human motion as a temporal image. In: Workshop on Brave New Ideas for Motion Representations, ECCV (2016)
45. Dietterich, T.G., Lathrop, R.H., Lozano-Pérez, T.: Solving the multiple instance problem with axis-parallel rectangles. Artif. Intell. **89**, 31–71 (1997)
46. Pfister, T., Charles, J., Zisserman, A.: Large-scale learning of sign language by watching TV (using co-occurrences). In: BMVC (2013)
47. Feng, Y., Ma, L., Liu, W., Zhang, T., Luo, J.: Video re-localization. In: Ferrari, V., Hebert, M., Sminchisescu, C., Weiss, Y. (eds.) Computer Vision – ECCV 2018. LNCS, vol. 11218, pp. 55–70. Springer, Cham (2018). https://doi.org/10.1007/978-3-030-01264-9_4
48. Yang, H., He, X., Porikli, F.: One-shot action localization by learning sequence matching network. In: CVPR (2018)
49. Cao, K., Ji, J., Cao, Z., Chang, C.Y., Niebles, J.C.: Few-shot video classification via temporal alignment. In: CVPR (2020)

50. Oord, A.v.d., Li, Y., Vinyals, O.: Representation learning with contrastive predictive coding. arXiv preprint arXiv:1807.03748 (2018)
51. Wu, Z., Xiong, Y., Yu, S.X., Lin, D.: Unsupervised feature learning via nonparametric instance discrimination. In: CVPR (2018)
52. Miech, A., Alayrac, J.B., Smaira, L., Laptev, I., Sivic, J., Zisserman, A.: End-to-end learning of visual representations from uncurated instructional videos. In: CVPR (2020)
53. https://www.signbsl.com/. (British sign language dictionary)
54. Cao, Z., Hidalgo, G., Simon, T., Wei, S.E., Sheikh, Y.: OpenPose: realtime multi-person 2D pose estimation using Part Affinity Fields. In: arXiv preprint arXiv:1812.08008 (2018)
55. He, K., Fan, H., Wu, Y., Xie, S., Girshick, R.: Momentum contrast for unsupervised visual representation learning. In: CVPR (2020)
56. SignumMcKee, D., Kennedy, G.: Lexical comparison of signs from American, Australian, British and New Zealand sign languages. An anthology to honor Ursula Bellugi and Edward Klima, The signs of language revisited (2000)
57. Aldersson, R., McEntee-Atalianis, L.: A lexical comparison of Icelandic sign language and Danish sign language. Birkbeck Stud. Appl. Ling. **2**, 123–158 (2007)

Domain-Transferred Face Augmentation Network

Hao-Chiang Shao[1], Kang-Yu Liu[2], Chia-Wen Lin[2(✉)], and Jiwen Lu[3]

[1] Department of Statistics and Information Science, Fu Jen Catholic University,
Taipei City, Taiwan
[2] Department of Electrical Engineering, National Tsing Hua University,
Hsinchu, Taiwan
cwlin@ee.nthu.edu.tw
[3] Department of Automation, Tsinghua University, Beijing, China

Abstract. The performance of a convolutional neural network (CNN) based face recognition model largely relies on the richness of labelled training data. However, it is expensive to collect a training set with large variations of a face identity under different poses and illumination changes, so the diversity of within-class face images becomes a critical issue in practice. In this paper, we propose a 3D model-assisted domain-transferred face augmentation network (DotFAN) that can generate a series of variants of an input face based on the knowledge distilled from existing rich face datasets of other domains. Extending from StarGAN's architecture, DotFAN integrates with two additional subnetworks, i.e., face expert model (FEM) and face shape regressor (FSR), for latent facial code control. While FSR aims to extract face attributes, FEM is designed to capture a face identity. With their aid, DotFAN can separately learn facial feature codes and effectively generate face images of various facial attributes while keeping the identity of augmented faces unaltered. Experiments show that DotFAN is beneficial for augmenting small face datasets to improve their within-class diversity so that a better face recognition model can be learned from the augmented dataset.

1 Introduction

Face recognition is one of the most considerable research topics in the field of computer vision. Benefiting from meticulously-designed CNN architectures and loss functions [1–3], the performance of face recognition models have been significantly advanced. The performance of a CNN-based face recognition model largely relies on the richness of labeled training data. However, collecting a training set with large variations of a face identity under different poses and illumination changes is very expensive, making the diversity of within-class face images a critical issue in practice. This is a considerable problem in developing a surveillance system for small to medium sized real-world applications. In such cases, each identity usually has only a few face samples (we call it **Few-Face learning problem**), so what dominates the recognition accuracy is the data processing strategy, rather than the face recognition algorithm.

© Springer Nature Switzerland AG 2021
H. Ishikawa et al. (Eds.): ACCV 2020, LNCS 12627, pp. 309–325, 2021.
https://doi.org/10.1007/978-3-030-69544-6_19

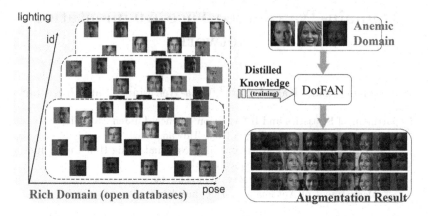

Fig. 1. DotFAN aims to enrich an anemic domain via identity-preserving face generation based on the knowledge, i.e., separated facial representation, distilled from data in a rich domain.

A face recognition model may fail, if the training set is too anemic to support the model. To avoid this circumstance, our idea is to distill the knowledge within a rich data domain and then transfer the distilled knowledge to enrich an incomprehensive set of training samples in a target domain via domain-transferred augmentation. Specifically, we aim to train a composite network, which learns a attribute-decomposed representation of faces from rich face datasets, so that this network can generate face variants—each associating with a different pose angle, a different facial expression, or a shading pattern due to different illumination condition—of each face subject in an anemic dataset for the data augmentation purpose. Hence, we propose in this paper a **Domain-transferred Face Augmentation Network (DotFAN)**, that aims to learn the distributions of the faces of distinct identities in the feature space from rich training data so that it can augment face data, including frontalized neutral faces, during inference by transferring the knowledge it learned, as its design concept illustrated in Fig. 1.

The proposed DotFAN is a face augmentation approach through which any identity class—no matter a minority class or not—can be enriched by synthesizing face samples based on the knowledge learned from rich face datasets of other domains via domain transfer. To this end, DotFAN first learns a facial representation from rich datasets to decompose the face information into essential facial attribute codes that are vital for identity identification and face manipulation. Then, exploiting this attribute-decomposed facial representation, DotFAN can generate synthetic face samples neighboring to the input faces in the sample space so that the diversity of each face-identify class can be significantly enhanced. As a result, the performance of a face recognition model trained on the enriched dataset can be improved as well.

Utilizing two auxiliary subnetworks, namely a data-driven face-expert model (FEM) [4,5] and a model-assisted face shape regressor (FSR), DotFAN operates in a model-assisted data-driven fashion. FEM is a purely data-driven subnetwork pretrained on a domain rich in face identities, whereas FSR is driven by a 3D face model and pretrained on another domain with rich poses and expressions. Hence,

FEM ensures that the synthesized variants of an input face are of the same identity as the input, while FSR collaborating with illumination code enables the model to generate faces with various poses, lighting (shading) conditions, and different expressions. In addition, inspired by FaceID-GAN [6], we use a 3D face model (e.g., 3DMM [7]) to characterize face attributes related to pose and expression with only hundreds of parameters. Thereby, the size of FSR, and its training set of faces with labelled poses and expressions as well, is largely reduced, making it realizable with a light CNN with a much reduced number of parameters. Furthermore, the loss terms related to FEM and FSR act as regularizers during the training stage. This design prevents DotFAN from common issues in data-driven approaches, e.g. overfitting due to small training dataset.

Moreover, DotFAN is distinguishable from FaceID-GAN because of following reasons. First, based on a 3-player game strategy, FaceID-GAN regards its face-expert model as an additional discriminator that needs to be trained jointly with its generator and discriminator in an adversarial training manner. Because its face-expert model assists its discriminator rather than its generator, FaceID-GAN guarantees only the upper-bound of identity-dissimilarity. Also, this design may prevent FaceID-GAN's face expert model from pretraining and impede the whole training speeds. Furthermore, since it cannot be pretrained on a rich-domain data, this makes it difficult to transfer knowledge from a rich dataset to another in an on-line learning manner. On the contrary, DotFAN regards its FEM as a regularizer to guarantee that the identity information is not altered by the generator. Accordingly, FEM can be pretrained on a rich dataset and play a role of an inspector in charge of overseeing identity-preservability. This design not only carries out the identity-preserving face generation task, but also stabilizes and speeds up the training process by not intervening the competition between generator and discriminator. DotFAN has four primary contributions.

- We are the first to propose a domain-transferred face augmentation scheme that can easily transfer the knowledge distilled from a rich domain to an anemic domain, while preserving the identity of augmented faces in the target domain.
- DotFAN provides a learning-based universal solution for the **Few-Face** problem. Specifically, i) when a face recognizer is re-trainable, DotFAN enriches the **Few-Face Set** by data augmentation, and then the recognizer can be re-trained on the enriched set to improve its performance; and, ii) if the face recognizer is pretained on an incomprehensive dataset (e.g., with mainly frontal faces and/or neutral illumination) and is NOT re-trainable, DotFAN can assist the recognizer by frontalizing/neutralizing a to-be-recognized face.
- Through a concatenation of facial attribute codes learned separately from existing face datasets, DotFAN offers a unique unified framework that can incorporate prominent face attributes (pose, illumination, shape, expression) for face recognition and can be easily extended to other face related tasks.
- DotFAN well beats the state-of-the-arts by a significant gain margin in face recognition application with small-size training data available. This makes it a powerful tool for low-shot learning applications.

2   Related Work

Recently, various algorithms have been proposed to address the issue of small sample size with dramatic variations in facial attributes in face recognition [8–11]. This section reviews works on GAN-based image-to-image translation, face generation, and face frontalization/rotation techniques related to face augmentation.

(A) GAN-Based Image-to-Image Translation

GAN and its variants have been widely adopted in a variety of fields, including image super-resolution, image synthesis, image style transfer, and domain adaptation. DCGAN [12] incorporates deep CNNs into GAN for unsupervised representation learning. DCGAN enables arithmetic operations in the feature space so that face synthesis can be controlled by manipulating attribute codes. The concept of generating images with a given condition has been adopted in succeeding works, such as Pix2pix [13] and CycleGAN [14]. Pix2pix requires pair-wise training data to derive the translation relationship between two domains, whereas CycleGAN relaxes such limitation and exploits unpaired training inputs to achieve domain-to-domain translation. After CycleGAN, StarGAN [8] addresses the multi-domain image-to-image translation issue. With the aids of a multi-task learning setting and a design of domain classification loss, StarGAN's discriminator minimizes only the classification error associated to a known label. As a result, the domain classifier in the discriminator can guide the generator to learn the differences among multiple domains. Recently, an attribute-guided face generation method based on a conditional CycleGAN was proposed in [9]. This method synthesizes a high-resolution face based on an low-resolution reference face and an attribute code extracted from another high-resolution face. Consequently, by regarding faces of the same identity as one sub-domain of faces, we deem that face augmentation can be formulated as a multi-domain image-to-image translation problem that can be solved with the aid of attribute-guided face generation strategy.

(B) Face Frontalization and Rotation

We regard the identity-preserving face rotation task as an inverse problem of the face frontalization technique used to synthesize a frontal face from a face image with arbitrary pose variation. Typical face frontalization and rotation methods synthesize a 2D face via 3D surface model manipulation, including pose angle control and facial expression control, such as FFGAN [15] and FaceID-GAN [6]. Still, some designs utilize specialized sub-networks or loss terms to reach the goal. For example, based on TPGAN [16], the pose invariant module (PIM) proposed in [17] contains an identity-preserving frontalization sub-network and a face recognition sub-network; the CNN proposed in [18] establishes a dense correspondence between paired non-frontal and frontal faces; and, the face normalization model (FNM) proposed in [5] involves a face-expert network, a pixel-wise loss, and a face attention discriminators to generate a faces with canonical-view and neutral expression. Finally, some methods approached this issue by means of disentangled representations, such as DR-GAN [19] and CAPG-GAN [20]. The

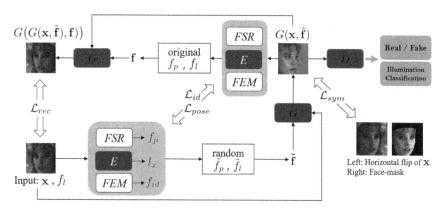

Fig. 2. Data flow of DotFAN's training process. FEM and FSR are independently pre-trained subnetworks, whereas E, G, and D are trained as a whole. $\tilde{f}_p$ and $\tilde{f}_l$ denote respectively a pose code and an illumination code randomly given in the training routine; and, f_l is the ground-truth illumination code provided by the training set. For inference, the data flow begins from $\mathbf{x}$ and ends at $G(\mathbf{x}, \tilde{\mathbf{f}})$. Note that $\tilde{\mathbf{f}} = [l_x, f_{id}, \tilde{f}_p, \tilde{f}_l]$ and $\mathbf{f} = [E(G(\mathbf{x}, \tilde{\mathbf{f}})), \Phi_{fem}(G(\mathbf{x}, \tilde{\mathbf{f}})), f_p, f_l]$.

former utilizes an encoder-decoder structure to learn a disentangled representation for face rotation, whereas the latter adopts a two-discriminator framework to learn simultaneously pose and identity information.

(C) Data Augmentation for Face Recognition

To facilitate face recognition, there are several face normalization and data augmentation methods. Face normalization methods aim to align face images by removing the volatility resulting from illumination variations, changes of facial expressions, and different pose angles [5], whereas the data augmentation method attempts to increase the richness of face images, often in aspects of pose angle and illumination conditions, for the training routine. To deal with illumination variations, conventional approaches utilized either physical models, e.g. Retinex theory [21], or 3D reconstruction strategy to remove/correct the shadow on a 2D image [22,23]. Moreover, to mitigate the influence brought by pose angles, two categories of methods were proposed, namely pose-invariant face recognition methods and face rotation methods. While the former category focuses on learning pose-invariant features from a large-scale dataset [24,25], the latter category, including face frontalization techniques, aims to learn the relationship between rotation angle and resulting face image via a generative model [6,15–17,19,20]. Because face rotation methods are designed to increase the diversity of the viewpoints of face image data, they are also beneficial for augmentation tasks.

Based on these meticulous designs, DotFAN is implemented as an extension of StarGAN, involving an encoder-decoder framework and two sub-networks for learning attribute codes separately, and triggered by several loss terms, including reconstruction loss and domain classification loss, as will be elaborated later.

3   Domain-Transferred Face Augmentation

DotFAN is a framework to synthesize face images of one domain based on the knowledge, i.e., attribute-decomposed facial representation, learned from others. For a given input face $\mathbf{x}$, the generator G of DotFAN is trained to synthesize a face $G(\mathbf{x}, \mathbf{f})$ based on an input attribute code $\mathbf{f}$ comprising i) a general latent code $l_\mathbf{x} = E(x)$ extracted from $\mathbf{x}$ by the general facial encoder, ii) an identity code f_{id} indicating the face identity, iii) an attribute code f_p describing facial attributes including pose angle and facial expressions, and iv) an illumination code f_l. Through this design, a face image can be embedded via a concatenation of several attribute codes, i.e., $\mathbf{f} = [l_\mathbf{x}, f_{id}, f_p, f_l]$. Figure 2 depicts the flow-diagram of DotFAN, and each component will be elaborated in following subsections.

3.1   Attribute-Decomposed Facial Representation

To obtain a decomposed representation, the attribute code $\mathbf{f}$ used by DotFAN for generating face variants is derived collaboratively by a general facial encoder E, a face-expert sub-network FEM, a shape-regression sub-network FSR, and an illumination code f_l. FEM and FSR are two well pre-trained sub-networks. FEM learns to extract identity-aware features from faces (of each identity) with various head poses and facial expressions, whereas FSR aims to learn pose features based on a 3D model. The illumination code is a 14×1 one-hot vector specifying 1 label-free case (corresponding to data from CASIA [26]) and 13 illumination conditions (associated with selected Multi-PIE dataset [27]).

(A) **Face-Expert Model (FEM)** Φ_{fem}: FEM Φ_{fem}, architecturally a ResNet-50, enables DotFAN to extract and to transplant the face identity from an input source to synthesized face images. Though conventionally face identity extraction is considered as a classification problem and optimized by using a cross-entropy loss, recent methods, e.g., CosFace [3] and ArcFace [2], proposed to adopt angular information instead. ArcFace maps face features onto a unit hyper-sphere and adjust between-class distances by using a pre-defined margin value so that a more discriminative feature representation can be obtained. Using ArcFace's loss function, FEM ensures not merely a fast training speed for learning face identity but also the efficiency in optimizing the whole DotFAN network.

(B) **Face Shape Regressor (FSR):** FSR, denoted as Φ_{fsr}, aims to extract face attributes including face shape, pose, and expression. Based on a widely used 3D Morphable Model (3DMM [7]), we designed our FSR as a model-assisted CNN rather than a fully data-driven network, which is complex and must be trained on a large variety of labeled face samples for characterizing face attributes because of the lack in prior knowledge. Because 3DMM can fairly and accurately characterize the face attributes using only hundreds of parameters, the model size of FSR can be significantly reduced. Firstly, we follow HPEN's strategy [28] to prepare ground-truth 3DMM parameters $\Theta_\mathbf{x}$ of an arbitrary face $\mathbf{x}$ from CASIA dataset [7]. Then, we train FSR via Weighted Parameter Distance Cost

(WPDC) [29] defined in Eq. (1), with a modified importance matrix, as shown in Eq. (2).

$$\mathcal{L}_{wpdc} = \left(\varPhi_{fsr}(\mathbf{x}) - \varTheta_{\mathbf{x}}\right)^t \mathbf{W}\left(\varPhi_{fsr}(\mathbf{x}) - \varTheta_{\mathbf{x}}\right) \tag{1}$$

$$\mathbf{W} = (w_R, w_T, w_{shape}, w_{exp}), \tag{2}$$

where w_R, $w_{t_{3d}}$, w_{shape}, and w_{exp} are distance-based weighting coefficients for the $\varTheta_{\mathbf{x}}$ (consisting of a 9×1 vectorized rotation matrix R, a 3×1 translation vector T, a 199×1 vector α_{shape}, and a 29×1 α_{exp}) derived by 3DMM. Note that the facial attribute code $f_p = \varPhi_{fsr}(\mathbf{x})$ extracted by FSR is a 240×1 vector mimicking $\varTheta_{\mathbf{x}}$. While training DotFAN, we keep α_{shape}'s counterpart—representing facial shape—in f_p unchanged, and we replace f_p's other code segments corresponding to translation T, rotation R, and expression α_{exp} by arbitrary values.

(C) General Facial Encoder E and Illumination Code f_l: E is used to capture other features, which cannot be represented by shape and identity codes, on a face. f_l is a one-hot vector specifying the lighting condition, based on which our model synthesizes a face. Note that because CASIA has no shadow labels, for f_l of a face from CASIA, its former 13 entries are set to be 0's and its 14th entry $f_l^{casia} = 1$; this means to skip shading and to generate a face with the same illumination setting and the same shadow as the input.

3.2 Generator

The generator G takes an attribute code $\mathbf{f} = [l_{\mathbf{x}},\ f_{id},\ f_p,\ f_l]$ as its input to synthesize a face $G(\mathbf{x}, \mathbf{f})$. Described below are loss terms composing the loss function of our generator.

(A) Reconstruction Loss
In our design, we exploit a reconstruction loss to retain face contents after performing two transformations dual to each other. That is,

$$\mathcal{L}_{rec} = \|G\big(G(\mathbf{x}, \tilde{\mathbf{f}}), \mathbf{f}\big) - \mathbf{x}\|_2^2 / N, \tag{3}$$

where N is the number of pixels, $G(\mathbf{x}, \tilde{\mathbf{f}})$ is a synthetic face derived according to an input attribute code $\tilde{\mathbf{f}}$. This loss guarantees our generator can learn the transformation relationship between any two dual attribute codes.

(B) Pose-Symmetric Loss
Based on a common assumption that a human face is symmetrical, a face with an x° pose angle and a face with a $-x^\circ$ angle should be symmetric about the 0° axis. Consequently, we design a pose-symmetric loss based on which DotFAN can learn to generate $\pm x^\circ$ faces from either training sample. This pose-symmetric loss is evaluated with the aid of a face-mask $M(\cdot)$, which is defined as a function of 3DMM parameters predicted by FSR and makes this loss term focus on the face region by filtering out the background, as described below:

$$\mathcal{L}_{sym} = \|M(\hat{\mathbf{f}}^-) \cdot \big(G(\mathbf{x}, \hat{\mathbf{f}}^-) - \hat{\mathbf{x}}^-\big)\|_2^2 / N. \tag{4}$$

Here, $\hat{\mathbf{f}}^- = [l_{\mathbf{x}}, f_{id}, \hat{f}_p^-, f_l]$, in which $\hat{f}_p^- = \Phi_{fsr}(\hat{\mathbf{x}}^-)$, and the other three attribute codes are extracted from $\mathbf{x}$. Additionally, $\hat{\mathbf{x}}^-$ is the horizontally-flipped version of $\mathbf{x}$. In sum, this term measures the L_2-norm of the difference between a synthetic face and the horizontally-flipped version of $\mathbf{x}$ within a region-of-interest defined by a mask M.

(C) Identity-Preserving Loss

We adopt the following identity-preserving loss to ensure that the identity code of a synthesized face $G(\mathbf{x}, \tilde{\mathbf{f}})$ is identical to that of input face $\mathbf{x}$. That is,

$$\mathcal{L}_{id} = \|\Phi_{fem}(\mathbf{x}) - \Phi_{fem}(G(\mathbf{x}, \tilde{\mathbf{f}}))\|_2^2 / N_1, \tag{5}$$

where N_1 denotes the length of $\Phi_{fem}(\mathbf{x})$.

(D) Pose-Consistency Loss

This term guarantees that the pose and expression feature extracted from a synthetic face is consistent with $\tilde{f}_p$ used to generate the synthetic face. That is,

$$\mathcal{L}_{pose} = \|\tilde{f}_p - \Phi_{fsr}(G(\mathbf{x}, \tilde{\mathbf{f}}))\|_2^2 / N_2, \tag{6}$$

where N_2 denotes the length of $\tilde{f}_p$.

3.3   Discriminator

By regarding faces of the same identity as one sub-domain of faces, the task of augmenting faces of different identities becomes a multi-domain image-to-image translation problem addressed in StarGAN [8]. Hence, we exploit an adversarial loss to make augmented faces photo-realistic. To this end, we use the domain classification loss to verify if $G(\mathbf{x}, \tilde{\mathbf{f}})$ is properly classified to a target domain label f_l, which we used to specify the illumination condition of $G(\mathbf{x}, \tilde{\mathbf{f}})$. In addition, in order to stabilize the training process, we adopted the loss design used in WGAN-GP [30]. Consequently, these two loss terms can be expressed as follows:

$$\begin{aligned} \mathcal{L}_{adv}^D &= D_{src}(G(\mathbf{x}, \tilde{\mathbf{f}})) - D_{src}(\mathbf{x}) + \lambda_{gp} \cdot \left(\|\nabla_{\hat{x}} D_{src}(\hat{x})\|_2 - 1\right)^2 \\ \mathcal{L}_{adv}^G &= -D_{src}(G(\mathbf{x}, \tilde{\mathbf{f}})), \end{aligned} \tag{7}$$

where λ_{gp} is a trade-off factor for the gradient penalty, $\hat{x}$ is uniformly sampled from the linear interpolation between $\mathbf{x}$ and synthesized $G(\mathbf{x}, \tilde{\mathbf{f}})$, and D_{src} reflects a distribution over sources given by the discriminator; and,

$$\begin{aligned} \mathcal{L}_{cls}^D &= -\log D_{cls}(f_l|\mathbf{x}) \\ \mathcal{L}_{cls}^G &= -\log D_{cls}(\tilde{f}_l|G(\mathbf{x}, \tilde{\mathbf{f}})), \end{aligned} \tag{8}$$

where f_l is the ground-truth illumination code of $\mathbf{x}$, and $\tilde{f}_l$ is the illumination code embedded in $\tilde{\mathbf{f}}$.

In sum, the discriminator aims to produce probability distributions over both source and domain labels, i.e., $D : \mathbf{x} \rightarrow \{D_{src}(\mathbf{x}), D_{cls}(\mathbf{x})\}$. Empirically, $\lambda_{gp} = 10$.

3.4 Full Objective Function

In order to optimize the generator and alleviate the training difficulty, we pre-trained FSR and FEM with corresponding labels. Therefore, while training the generator and the discriminator, no additional label is needed. The full objective functions of DotFAN can be expressed as:

$$\mathcal{L}_G = \mathcal{L}_{adv}^G + \mathcal{L}_{cls}^G + \mathcal{L}_{id} + \mathcal{L}_{pose} + \mathcal{L}_{sym} + \mathcal{L}_{rec}$$
$$\mathcal{L}_D = \mathcal{L}_{adv}^D + \mathcal{L}_{cls}^D. \tag{9}$$

Two loss terms in $\mathcal{L}_D$ are equal-weighted; and, the weighting factors of terms in $\mathcal{L}_G$ in turn are 1, 1, 8, 6, 5, and 5. Note that the alternative training of generator and discriminator was performed with ratio 1 : 1.

4 Experimental Results

4.1 Dataset

DotFAN is trained jointly on **CMU Multi-PIE** [27] and **CASIA** [26]. Multi-PIE contains more than $750,000$ images of 337 identities, each with 20 different sorts of illumination and 15 different poses. We select images of pose angles ranging in between $\pm 45°$ and illumination codes from 0 to 12 to form our first training set, containing totally $84,000$ faces. From this training set, DotFAN learns the representative features for a wide range of pose angles, illumination conditions, and resulting shadows. Our second dataset is the whole CASIA set that contains $494,414$ images of $10,575$ identifies, each having about 50 images of different poses and expressions. Since CASIA contains a rich collection of face identities, it helps DotFAN learn features for representing identities.

To evaluate the performance of DotFAN on face synthesis, four additional datasets are used: **LFW** [31], **IJB-A** [32], **SurveilFace-1**, and **SurveilFace-2**. LFW has $13,233$ images of $5,749$ identities; IJB-A has $25,808$ images of 500 identities; SurveilFace-1 has $1,050$ images of 73 identities; and SurveilFace-2 contains $1,709$ images of 78 identities. We evaluate the performance of DotFAN's face frontalization on LFW and IJB-A. Besides, because faces in two Surveil-Face datasets are taken in uncontrolled real working environments, they are contaminated by strong backlight, motion blurs, extreme shadow conditions, or influences from various viewpoints. Hence, they mimic the real-world conditions and thus are suitable for evaluating the face augmentation performance. The two SurveilFace sets are private data provided by a video surveillance provider. We will make them publicly available after removing personal labels.

We exploit CelebA to simulate the data augmentation process. CelebA contains $202,599$ images of $10,177$ identities with 40 kinds of diverse binary facial attributes. We randomly select a fixed number of images of each face identity from CelebA to form our simulation set, called "**sub-CelebA**" and conducted data augmentation experiments on both CelebA and sub-CelebA by using Dot-FAN.

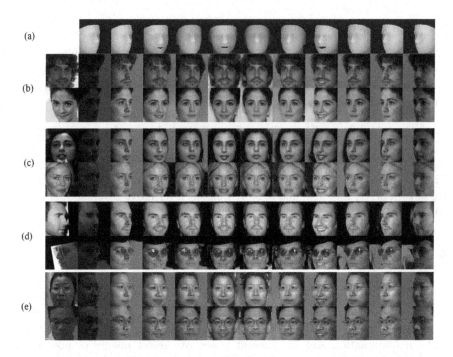

(a)

(b)

(c)

(d)

(e)

Fig. 3. Synthesized faces for face samples from different datasets generated by DotFAN. The left-most column shows the inputs with random attributes (e.g., poses, expressions, and motion blurs). The top-most row illustrates 3D templates with specific poses and expressions. To guarantee the identity information of each synthetic face is observable, columns 3–11 show shadow-free results, and columns 2 and 12 show faces with shadows. (a) 3D templates. (b) CelebA, (c) LFW, (d) CFP, and (e) SurveilFace.

Moreover, we demonstrate all face images in grayscale because of two reasons. First, two **SurveilFace** datasets are all grayscale. Second, DotFAN was trained partially on Multi-PIE in which images have reddish color-drift, so the same color-drift may occur on faces generated by DotFAN. Because such color-drift never degrades the recognition accuracy, we decided not to demonstrate color faces to avoid misunderstanding.

4.2   Implementation Details

Before training, we align the face images in the Multi-PIE and CASIA by MTCNN [33]. Structurally, our FEM is obtained by Resnet-50 pretained on MS-Celeb-1M [34], and FSR is implemented by a MobileNet [35] pretained on CASIA. To train DotFAN, each input face is resized to 112×112. Both generator and discriminator exploit Adam optimizer [36] with $\beta_1 = 0.5$ and $\beta_2 = 0.999$. The total number of training iterations is 420,000 with a batch-size of 28, and the number of training epochs is 12. The learning rate is initially set to be 10^{-4} and begins to decay after the 6-th training epoch.

4.3   Face Synthesis

We verify the efficacy of DotFAN through the visual quality of i) face frontalization and ii) face rotation results.

(A) Face Frontalization: First, we verify if the identity information extracted from a frontalized face, produced by DotFAN, is of the same class as the identity of a given source face. Following [6], we measure the performance by using a face recognition model trained on MS-Celeb-1M. Next, we conduct frontalization experiments on LFW. Table 1 shows the comparison of face verification results of frontalized faces. This experiment set validates that i) compared with other methods, DotFAN achieves comparable visual quality in face frontalization, ii) shadows can be effectively removed by DotFAN, and iii) both DotFAN and casia-DotFAN (i.e., a DotFAN trained only on CASIA dataset) outperform other methods in terms of verification accuracy, especially in the experiment on IJB-A shown in Table 1(b), where DotFAN reports a much better TAR, i.e., 89.3% on FAR@0.001 and 93.7% on FAR@0.01, than existing approaches.

(B) Face Rotation: Figure 3 demonstrates DotFAN's capability in synthesizing faces of given attributes, including pose angles, facial expressions, and shadows, while retaining the associated identities. The source faces presented in the leftmost column in Fig. 3 come from four datasets, i.e., CelebA, LFW, CFP [37], and SurveilFace. CelebA and LFW are two widely-adopted face datasets; CFP contains images with extreme pose angles, e.g., $\pm 90°$; and, SurveilFace contains faces of variant illumination conditions and faces affected by motion-blurs. This experiment shows that DotFAN can stably synthesize visually-pleasing face images based on 3DMM parameters describing 3D templates. Finally, Fig. 4 shows some synthesized faces with shadows assigned with four different illumination codes. Note that all synthesized faces presented in this paper are produced by the same DotFAN model without manually data-dependent modifications.

Table 1. Verification Table. (a) Verification accuracy on LFW. (b) True-Accept-Rate (TAR) of verifications on IJB-A. Note that while DotFAN has an FEM trained on MS-Celeb-1M in our design, the FEM of casia-DotFAN was trained on CASIA dataset.

(a)		(b)		
Method	Verification accuracy	Method	FAR@0.01	FAR@0.001
HPEN [28]	96.25 ± 0.76	PAM [24]	73.3 ± 1.8	55.2 ± 3.2
FF-GAN [15]	96.42 ± 0.89	DCNN [38]	78.7 ± 4.3	–
FaceID-GAN [6]	97.01 ± 0.83	DR-GAN [19]	77.4 ± 2.7	53.9 ± 4.3
		FF-GAN [15]	85.2 ± 1.0	66.3 ± 3.3
		FaceID-GAN [6]	87.6 ± 1.1	69.2 ± 2.7
casia-DotFAN	$\mathbf{98.55 \pm 0.52}$	casia-DotFAN	$\mathbf{90.5 \pm 0.7}$	$\mathbf{82.3 \pm 2.4}$
DotFAN	$\mathbf{99.18 \pm 0.39}$	DotFAN	$\mathbf{93.7 \pm 0.5}$	$\mathbf{89.3 \pm 1.0}$

Fig. 4. Face augmentation examples (CelebA) containing augmented faces with 4 illumination conditions and 7 poses.

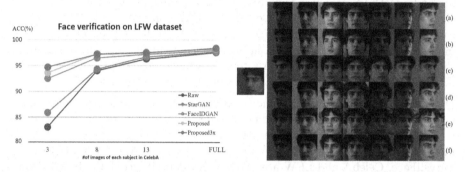

Fig. 5. Comparison of face verification accuracy on LFW trained on different augmented dataset. The horizontal spacing highlights the size of raw training dataset sampled from CelebA.

Fig. 6. Ablation study on loss terms. (a) Full loss. (b) w/o $\mathcal{L}_{id}$, (c) w/o $\mathcal{L}_{cls}$, (d) w/o $\mathcal{L}_{rec}$, (e) w/o $\mathcal{L}_{pose}$, and (f) w/o $\mathcal{L}_{sym}$.

4.4 Face Augmentation

Because DotFAN is a face augmentation network, experiments in this subsection were designed to show how face recognition accuracy can be improved with DotFAN-augmented training data. We adopted MobileFaceNet to be our face recognition network rather than other SOTAs because it's suitable to be deployed on mobile/embedded devices (less than 1M parameters) for small/medium sized real-world applications.

To evaluate the comprehensiveness of domain-transferred augmentation by DotFAN, we perform data augmentation on the same dataset by using DotFAN, FaceID-GAN, and StarGAN first; then, we compare the recognition accuracy of different MobileFaceNet models [39], each trained on an augmented dataset, by testing them on LFW and SurveilFace. StarGAN used in this experiment is trained on Mutli-PIE that is rich in illumination conditions; meanwhile, the FaceID-GAN is trained on CASIA to learn pose and expression representations.

Table 2. Performance comparison of face recognition models trained on different datasets. Here, **Sub-CelebA**(x) denotes a subset formed by randomly selecting x images of each face subject from CelebA

Method	LFW		SurveilFace-1			SurveilFace-2		
	ACC	AUC	@FAR=0.001	@FAR=0.01	AUC	@FAR=0.001	@FAR=0.01	AUC
(a) **Sub-CelebA(3)** (totally 30, 120 images)								
RAW	83.1	90.2	20.5	34.4	83.2	18.0	33.3	84.8
StarGAN	85.9	92.5	25.1	39.6	87.5	27.4	46.7	91.4
FaceID-GAN	92.5	97.6	34.6	53.5	92.8	32.3	54.0	94.3
Proposed 1x	93.6	98.1	35.7	56.2	93.6	34.7	57.8	95.0
Proposed 3x	94.7	98.7	36.8	58.3	94.6	36.5	60.8	95.6
(b) **Sub-CelebA(8)** (totally 75, 796 images)								
RAW	94.0	98.5	37.8	58.7	94.4	38.3	61.0	95.2
StarGAN	94.3	98.5	42.6	60.7	94.9	42.8	65.6	95.8
FaceID-GAN	96.5	99.3	48.1	65.6	96.0	45.7	67.9	96.8
Proposed 1x	97.3	99.5	53.2	71.2	97.0	49.1	72.2	97.2
Proposed 3x	97.2	99.5	53.2	68.9	96.9	47.3	70.0	97.1
(c) **Sub-CelebA(13)** (totally 116, 659 images)								
RAW	96.3	99.1	47.4	67.8	96.2	43.5	67.0	96.5
StarGAN	96.7	99.3	48.3	68.1	96.7	46.3	70.0	96.7
FaceID-GAN	97.2	99.5	53.3	71.3	97.0	50.2	72.3	97.4
Proposed 1x	97.6	99.6	56.2	75.1	97.7	50.4	73.9	97.7
Proposed 3x	97.5	99.7	56.7	75.5	97.7	53.9	72.2	97.8
(d) **CelebA (full CelebA dataset, 202, 599 images)**								
RAW	97.6	99.6	53.5	73.8	97.7	48.7	73.0	97.5
StarGAN	97.7	99.6	55.0	74.2	97.7	53.0	73.8	97.6
FaceID-GAN	98.0	99.7	57.6	76.4	98.1	54.1	76.5	98.0
Proposed 1x	98.3	99.8	62.4	80.9	98.4	57.1	76.7	98.1
Proposed 3x	98.4	99.7	61.4	78.9	98.2	54.7	77.8	98.0

Table 2 summarizes the results of this experiment set. We interpret the results focusing on Sub-experiment(a). In Sub-experiment(a), we randomly select 3 faces of each identity from CelebA to form the **RAW** training set, namely **Sub-CelebA(3)**, leading to about 30, 000 training samples in raw Sub-CelebA(3). The MobileFaceNet trained on raw Sub-CelebA(3) achieves a verification accuracy of 83.1% on LFW, a true accept rate (TAR) of 20.5% at FAR = 0.001 on SurveilFace-1, and a TAR of 18.0% at FAR = 0.001 on SurveilFace-2. After giving each face in raw Sub-CelebA(3) a random facial attribute $\tilde{f}_p$ and a random illumination code $\tilde{f}_l$ to generate a new face and thus to double the size of the training set via DotFAN, the verification accuracy on LFW becomes 93.6%, and the TAR values on SurveilFace datasets are all nearly doubled, as shown in the row named **Proposed 1x**. This shows DotFAN is effective in face data augmentation and outperforms StarGAN and FaceID-GAN significantly. Furthermore, when we augment about 90, 000 additional faces to quadruple the size of training set, i.e., **Proposed 3x**, we have only a minor improvement in verification accuracy compared to **Proposed 1x**. This fact reflects that the marginal benefit a model can extract from the data diminishes as the number of samples increases when there is information overlap among data, as is what reported in [40]. Consequently, Table 2 and Fig. 5 reveal following remarkable points.

- First, by integrating attribute controls on pose angle, illuminating condition, and facial expression with an identity-preserving design, DotFAN outperforms StarGAN and FaceID-GAN in domain-transferred face augmentation tasks.
- Second, DotFAN's results obey *the law of diminishing marginal utility* in Economics[1] [41], as demonstrated in all **(Proposed 1x, Proposed 3x)** data pairs. Take LFW-experiment in Table 2(a) for example. An additional one-unit consumption of training data (1x-augmentation) brings an accuracy improvement, i.e., marginal utility, of 93.6%-83.1%=10.5%; when two more additional units (3x-augmentation) are given, the improvement of accuracy is only 94.7% − 93.6% = 1.1%. Therefore, a **1x** procedure is adequate to enrich a small dataset, and our experiments also show that the **Proposed 3x** procedure seems to reach the upper-bound of data richness.
- Third, although the improvement in verification accuracy decreases as the size of raw training set increases, DotFAN achieves a significant performance gain on augmenting a small-size face training set, as demonstrated in all (RAW, Proposed 1x) data pairs.

4.5 Ablation Study

We then verify the effect brought by each loss term. Figure 6 depicts the faces generated by using different combinations of loss terms. The top-most row shows faces generated with the full generator loss $\mathcal{L}_G$ in Eq. (9), whereas the remaining rows respectively show synthetic results derived without one certain loss term.

As shown in Fig. 6(b), without $\mathcal{L}_{id}$, DotFAN fails to preserve the identity information although other facial attributes can be successfully retained. By contrast, without $\mathcal{L}_{cls}$, DotFAN cannot control the illumination condition, and the resulting faces all share the same shade (see Fig. 6(c)). These two rows evidence that $\mathcal{L}_{cls}$ and $\mathcal{L}_{id}$ are indispensable in DotFAN design. Moreover, Fig. 6(d) shows some unrealistic faces, e.g., a rectangular-shaped ear in the frontalized face; accordingly, $\mathcal{L}_{rec}$ is important for photo-realistic synthesis. Finally, Fig. 6(e)–(f) show that $\mathcal{L}_{pose}$ and $\mathcal{L}_{sym}$ are complementary to each other. As long as either of them functions, DotFAN can generate faces of different face angles. However, because $\mathcal{L}_{sym}$ is designed to learn only the mapping relationship between $+x°$ face and $-x°$ face by ignoring background outside the face region, artifacts may occur in the background region if $\mathcal{L}_{sym}$ works solely (see Fig. 6(e)).

5   Conclusion

We proposed a Domain-transferred Face Augmentation network (DotFAN) for generating a series of variants of an input face image based on the knowledge of

---

[1] This law primarily says that the marginal utility of each homogeneous unit decreases as the supply of units increases, and vice versa.

attribute-decomposed face representation distilled from huge datasets. DotFAN is designed in StarGAN's style with two extra subnetworks to learn separately the facial attribute codes and produce a normalized face so that it can effectively generate face images of various facial attributes while preserving identity of synthetic images. Moreover, we proposed a pose-symmetric loss through which DotFAN can synthesize a pair of pose-symmetric face images directly at once. Extensive experiments demonstrate the effectiveness of DotFAN in augmenting small-sized face datasets and improving their within-subject diversity. As a result, a better face recognition model can be learned from an enriched training set derived by DotFAN.

References

1. He, K., Zhang, X., Ren, S., Sun, J.: Deep residual learning for image recognition. In: Proceedings of the IEEE Conference on Computer Vision and Pattern Recognition, pp. 770–778 (2016)
2. Deng, J., Guo, J., Xue, N., Zafeiriou, S.: ArcFace: additive angular margin loss for deep face recognition. In: Proceedings of the IEEE Conference on Computer Vision and Pattern Recognition, pp. 4690–4699 (2019)
3. Wang, H., et al.: CosFace: large margin cosine loss for deep face recognition. In: Proceedings of the IEEE Conference on Computer Vision and Pattern Recognition, pp. 5265–5274 (2018)
4. Cole, F., Belanger, D., Krishnan, D., Sarna, A., Mosseri, I., Freeman, W.T.: Synthesizing normalized faces from facial identity features. In: Proceedings of the IEEE Conference on Computer Vision and Pattern Recognition, pp. 3703–3712 (2017)
5. Qian, Y., Deng, W., Hu, J.: Unsupervised face normalization with extreme pose and expression in the wild. In: Proceedings of the IEEE Conference on Computer Vision and Pattern Recognition, pp. 9851–9858 (2019)
6. Shen, Y., Luo, P., Yan, J., Wang, X., Tang, X.: FaceID-GAN: learning a symmetry three-player GAN for identity-preserving face synthesis. In: Proceedings of the IEEE Conference on Computer Vision and Pattern Recognition, pp. 821–830 (2018)
7. Blanz, V., Vetter, T., et al.: A morphable model for the synthesis of 3D faces. In: Proceedings of the ACM SIGGRAPH (1999)
8. Choi, Y., Choi, M., Kim, M., Ha, J.W., Kim, S., Choo, J.: StarGAN: unified generative adversarial networks for multi-domain image-to-image translation. In: Proceedings of the IEEE Conference on Computer Vision and Pattern Recognition, pp. 8789–8797 (2018)
9. Lu, Y., Tai, Y.-W., Tang, C.-K.: Attribute-guided face generation using conditional CycleGAN. In: Ferrari, V., Hebert, M., Sminchisescu, C., Weiss, Y. (eds.) ECCV 2018. LNCS, vol. 11216, pp. 293–308. Springer, Cham (2018). https://doi.org/10.1007/978-3-030-01258-8_18
10. Li, T., et al.: BeautyGAN: instance-level facial makeup transfer with deep generative adversarial network. In: Proceedings of the ACM Multimedia, pp. 645–653 (2018)
11. Shen, W., Liu, R.: Learning residual images for face attribute manipulation. In: Proceedings of the IEEE Conference on Computer Vision and Pattern Recognition, pp. 4030–4038 (2017)

12. Radford, A., Metz, L., Chintala, S.: Unsupervised representation learning with deep convolutional generative adversarial networks. arXiv preprint arXiv:1511.06434 (2015)
13. Isola, P., Zhu, J.Y., Zhou, T., Efros, A.A.: Image-to-image translation with conditional adversarial networks. In: Proceedings of the IEEE Conference on Computer Vision and Pattern Recognition, pp. 1125–1134 (2017)
14. Zhu, J.Y., Park, T., Isola, P., Efros, A.A.: Unpaired image-to-image translation using cycle-consistent adversarial networks. In: Proceedings of the IEEE International Conference on Computer Vision, pp. 2223–2232 (2017)
15. Yin, X., Yu, X., Sohn, K., Liu, X., Chandraker, M.: Towards large-pose face frontalization in the wild. In: Proceedings of the IEEE International Conference on Computer Vision, pp. 3990–3999 (2017)
16. Huang, R., Zhang, S., Li, T., He, R.: Beyond face rotation: global and local perception GAN for photorealistic and identity preserving frontal view synthesis. In: Proceedings of the IEEE International Conference on Computer Vision, pp. 2439–2448 (2017)
17. Zhao, J., et al.: Towards pose invariant face recognition in the wild. In: Proceedings of the IEEE Conference on Computer Vision and Pattern Recognition, pp. 2207–2216 (2018)
18. Zhang, Z., Chen, X., Wang, B., Hu, G., Zuo, W., Hancock, E.R.: Face frontalization using an appearance-flow-based convolutional neural network. IEEE Trans. Image Process. **28**, 2187–2199 (2018)
19. Tran, L., Yin, X., Liu, X.: Disentangled representation learning GAN for pose-invariant face recognition. In: Proceedings of the IEEE Conference on Computer Vision and Pattern Recognition, pp. 1415–1424 (2017)
20. Hu, Y., Wu, X., Yu, B., He, R., Sun, Z.: Pose-guided photorealistic face rotation. In: Proceedings of the IEEE Conference on Computer Vision and Pattern Recognition, pp. 8398–8406 (2018)
21. Land, E.H., McCann, J.J.: Lightness and retinex theory Lightness and retinex theory. JOSA **61**, 1–11 (1971)
22. Finlayson, G.D., Hordley, S.D., Drew, M.S.: Removing shadows from images. In: Heyden, A., Sparr, G., Nielsen, M., Johansen, P. (eds.) ECCV 2002. LNCS, vol. 2353, pp. 823–836. Springer, Heidelberg (2002). https://doi.org/10.1007/3-540-47979-1_55
23. Wang, Y., et al.: Face relighting from a single image under arbitrary unknown lighting conditions. IEEE Trans. Pattern Anal. Mach. Intell. **31**, 1968–1984 (2008)
24. Masi, I., Rawls, S., Medioni, G., Natarajan, P.: Pose-aware face recognition in the wild. In: Proceedings of the IEEE Conference on Computer Vision and Pattern Recognition, pp. 4838–4846 (2016)
25. Cao, K., Rong, Y., Li, C., Tang, X., Loy, C.C.: Pose-robust face recognition via deep residual equivariant mapping. In: Proceedings of the IEEE Conference on Computer Vision and Pattern Recognition, pp. 5187–5196 (2018)
26. Yi, D., Lei, Z., Liao, S., Li, S.Z.: Learning face representation from scratch. arXiv preprint arXiv:1411.7923 (2014)
27. Gross, R., Matthews, I., Cohn, J., Kanade, T., Baker, S.: Multi-pie. Image Vis. Comput. **28**, 807–813 (2010)
28. Zhu, X., Lei, Z., Yan, J., Yi, D., Li, S.Z.: High-fidelity pose and expression normalization for face recognition in the wild. In: Proceedings of the IEEE Conference on Computer Vision and Pattern Recognition, pp. 787–796 (2015)

29. Zhu, X., Lei, Z., Liu, X., Shi, H., Li, S.Z.: Face alignment across large poses: a 3D solution. In: Proceedings of the IEEE Conference on Computer Vision and Pattern Recognition, pp. 146–155 (2016)
30. Gulrajani, I., Ahmed, F., Arjovsky, M., Dumoulin, V., Courville, A.C.: Improved training of Wasserstein GANs. In: Proceedings of the Advances in Neural Information Processing Systems, pp. 5767–5777 (2017)
31. Huang, G.B., Mattar, M., Berg, T., Learned-Miller, E.: Labeled faces in the wild: a database for studying face recognition in unconstrained environments (2008)
32. Klare, B.F., et al.: Pushing the frontiers of unconstrained face detection and recognition: IARPA. Janus Benchmark A. In: Proceedings of the IEEE Conference on Computer Vision and Pattern Recognition, pp. 1931–1939 (2015)
33. Dai, J., He, K., Sun, J.: Instance-aware semantic segmentation via multi-task network cascades. In: Proceedings of the IEEE Conference on Computer Vision and Pattern Recognition, pp. 3150–3158 (2016)
34. Guo, Y., Zhang, L., Hu, Y., He, X., Gao, J.: MS-Celeb-1M: a dataset and benchmark for large-scale face recognition. In: Leibe, B., Matas, J., Sebe, N., Welling, M. (eds.) ECCV 2016. LNCS, vol. 9907, pp. 87–102. Springer, Cham (2016). https://doi.org/10.1007/978-3-319-46487-9_6
35. Howard, A.G., et al.: MobileNets: efficient convolutional neural networks for mobile vision applications. arXiv preprint arXiv:1704.04861 (2017)
36. Kinga, D., Adam, J.B.: A method for stochastic optimization. In: Proceedings of the International Conference on Learning Representations, vol. 5 (2015)
37. Sengupta, S., Chen, J.C., Castillo, C., Patel, V.M., Chellappa, R., Jacobs, D.W.: Frontal to profile face verification in the wild. In: Proceedings of the IEEE Winter Conference on Applications of Computer Vision, pp. 1–9 (2016)
38. Chen, J.C., Patel, V.M., Chellappa, R.: Unconstrained face verification using deep CNN features. In: Proceedings of the IEEE Winter Conference on Applications of Computer Vision, pp. 1–9 (2016)
39. Chen, S., Liu, Y., Gao, X., Han, Z.: MobileFaceNets: efficient CNNs for accurate real-time face verification on mobile devices. In: Zhou, J., et al. (eds.) CCBR 2018. LNCS, vol. 10996, pp. 428–438. Springer, Cham (2018). https://doi.org/10.1007/978-3-319-97909-0_46
40. Cui, Y., Jia, M., Lin, T.Y., Song, Y., Belongie, S.: Class-balanced loss based on effective number of samples. In: Proceedings of the IEEE Conference on Computer Vision and Pattern Recognition, pp. 9268–9277 (2019)
41. Mankiw, N.G.: Principles of Economics. Cengage Learning, Boston (2020)

Pose Correction Algorithm for Relative Frames Between Keyframes in SLAM

Youngseok Jang[ID], Hojoon Shin[ID], and H. Jin Kim[✉][ID]

Seoul National University, Seoul 08826, Republic of Korea
duscjs59@gmail.com, asdwer20@gmail.com, hjinkim@snu.ac.kr

Abstract. With the dominance of keyframe-based SLAM in the field of robotics, the relative frame poses between keyframes have typically been sacrificed for a faster algorithm to achieve online applications. However, those approaches can become insufficient for applications that may require refined poses of all frames, not just keyframes which are relatively sparse compared to all input frames. This paper proposes a novel algorithm to correct the relative frames between keyframes after the keyframes have been updated by a back-end optimization process. The correction model is derived using conservation of the measurement constraint between landmarks and the robot pose. The proposed algorithm is designed to be easily integrable to existing keyframe-based SLAM systems while exhibiting robust and accurate performance superior to existing interpolation methods. The algorithm also requires low computational resources and hence has a minimal burden on the whole SLAM pipeline. We provide the evaluation of the proposed pose correction algorithm in comparison to existing interpolation methods in various vector spaces, and our method has demonstrated excellent accuracy in both KITTI and EuRoC datasets.

1 Introduction

Simultaneous localization and mapping (SLAM) has been the focus of numerous research in the field of robotics. SLAM involves estimating the ego-motion of a mobile robot while simultaneously reconstructing the surrounding environment. To this end, visual sensors and laser scanners have been commonly used to perceive the surrounding environment. Vision sensors, in particular, have been most widely adopted due to the wealth of visual information that they can provide at a comparatively low price point. Hence, a vast portion of the SLAM research has been conducted with vision sensors such as monocular, stereo cameras, or RGB-D sensors [1–4].

Operating back-end refinement systems such as pose graph optimization (PGO) or bundle adjustment (BA) on all frames can become taxing especially in large-scale environments. To reduce computation time while preserving performance, most modern visual SLAM algorithms adopt keyframe-based approaches

---

Y. Jang and H. Shin—These authors contributed equally to this manuscript.

© Springer Nature Switzerland AG 2021
H. Ishikawa et al. (Eds.): ACCV 2020, LNCS 12627, pp. 326–340, 2021.
https://doi.org/10.1007/978-3-030-69544-6_20

which refine only keyframes that contain useful information for SLAM. In other words, keyframe-based SLAM approaches effectively filters the input measurements so that only those that contain significant changes are used in the refinement process, resulting in shorter computation time and local minima avoidance. They allow for the robust estimation of poses and reconstruction of the surrounding map in real-time.

While keyframe-based SLAM methods have dominated SLAM research, they refine the keyframe poses and do not propagate the corrections to the relative frames between keyframes. Because such systems can only make use of selected keyframes that are relatively sparse compared to the raw input measurements, they are not suitable for applications that require corrected poses at high frequency. In particular, multi-robot systems that utilize inter-robot relative poses to integrate multiple observations from team robots require a high robot pose density that existing keyframe-based SLAM methods cannot provide. Therefore, an algorithm that can correct poses of relative frames each time the keyframe poses are updated by the back-end of keyframe-based SLAM is required.

Some attempts to correct the relative poses between keyframes have been made in past works using hierarchical PGO. Hierarchical PGO involves dividing the full pose graph into subgraphs that contain representative keyframes called keynodes. The back-end refinement process is conducted only on these selected keynodes and propagated down the hierarchy. The propagation is usually done through either optimization methods or non-optimization methods such as interpolation. Optimization-based correction methods [5–7] exhibit high accuracy but requires long computation time, making them difficult to operate in real-time. Non-optimization methods [8–10], on the other hand, either treat each subgraph as a rigid body or convert the 3D pose into a vector space and interpolates within the given space, allowing for extremely fast operation. However, in such methods, the interpolation factor can become numerically sensitive when the change in a given axis is small. Furthermore, because the method does not consider the measurement constraints between poses, the correction can potentially break these constraints. These two methods will be further discussed in Sect. 2.

This paper proposes a pose correction algorithm for relative frames between keyframes. The algorithm requires just the estimated pose output from a SLAM system to operate, meaning that it can be easily integrated into any existing keyframe-based SLAM methods. The generated pose correction also preserves measurement constraints such as image coordinates of visual features without using optimization, enabling fast computation. The proposed algorithm is compared to existing interpolation-based correction methods in various vector spaces and demonstrates superior accuracy and computation time.

The remainder of this paper is structured as follows. The next section reviews related works regarding pose correction and the problem setup and notation are provided in Sect. 3. Section 4 describes the proposed pose correction algorithm using measurement constraints. The evaluation results using KITTI and EuRoC datasets are presented in Sect. 5, and the conclusion of this paper is provided in Sect. 6.

2   Related Work

This section of the paper discusses the existing work regarding hierarchical PGO and the interpolation in various vector spaces. As mentioned above, distribution of the corrections down to the lower levels of the hierarchy in previous attempts have either used optimization methods or non-optimization methods. This paper will henceforth refer to the former as non-naïve methods and the latter as naïve methods.

The non-naïve approaches to hierarchical PGO involve propagating the refinements of the keyframes to the relative frames through optimization methods. [5,6] proposed separating the full pose graph into sequentially generated and conditionally independent subgraphs. Pose corrections can be conducted by propagating the error from the most recent subgraph. [7] followed a similar approach but optimized each subgraph independently. While optimizing each hierarchical subgraph is guaranteed to yield accurate results, the procedure requires high computation times and is not suitable for large-scale SLAM applications. Furthermore, because the implementation requires fundamental changes in the SLAM algorithm itself, it is very difficult to integrate such methods into existing keyframe-based SLAM algorithms without affecting the functionality of the algorithms.

The naïve methods simplify the constraints between relative frames to propagate the corrections. Interpolation is the most common example of such simplification methods. However, due to the nature of interpolations, if the rate of change between poses are small, the interpolation factor can become numerically sensitive, resulting in extreme values. Furthermore, the accuracy of the methods also suffers, as the interpolation is only concerned with the keyframe poses and does not consider the measurement constraints present in the pose graph. There have been past attempts to develop alternative methods to interpolation. [8] proposed an algorithm that utilized the quaternion spherical linear interpolation (slerp) algorithm developed in [11] to distribute the pose correction to each frame along the traveled path. However, the method requires the covariance of the edges between nodes and also assumes spherical covariances to compute the interpolation factor. Computing the covariance accurately is very difficult and further assumption of spherical covariance that is not guaranteed SLAM applications can further exacerbate the error. [9] proposed a method where the correction was propagated to the subgraph by treating each subgraph as a rigid body. This simplification assumes that each relative frame receives the same correction and also ignores the measurement constraints between relative frames. More recently, [10] proposed a LiDAR-based online mapping algorithm that treats individual scans as subgraphs and propagates the corrections between scan poses using B-spline interpolation. However, this method discards the measurement constraints of relative frames between keyframes and does not hold true if the path generated by the robot does not follow a B-spline trajectory.

The interpolation and linearization of various vector spaces that were used in the naïve methods have also been studied extensively [12–15]. Pose corrections require the frame poses to be expressed in SE(3). While the translation component of the SE(3) matrix can be readily interpolated, interpolating the rotation

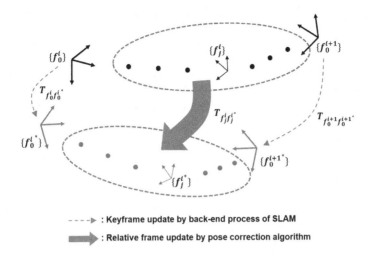

$----\blacktriangleright$: Keyframe update by back-end process of SLAM

$\blacksquare\!\!\!\longrightarrow$: Relative frame update by pose correction algorithm

Fig. 1. The refinement process for keyframes and relative frames. The pose correction algorithm for relative frames is triggered each time keyframes are updated by back-end of SLAM.

matrix may break the SO(3) constraint that defines the rotation matrix. Hence, the rotation matrix must be converted to a vector space in the form of Euler angles, quaternions, so(3), or rotation axis and angle. In this paper, the numerical robustness of these manifolds was tested for their application in the interpolation of robot poses.

3   Problem Statement

As mentioned previously, most high-performance SLAM algorithms only refine the keyframe poses, which may be too sparse for certain applications. Hence, this paper proposes a fast and easily integrable pose correction algorithm for relative frames between keyframes. The previous approaches have typically used interpolation-based correction methods to achieve fast computation for online robot applications. However, such methods are inherently limited by their numerical sensitivity under singular cases involving small changes in a select axis, and may potentially break measurement constraints even under non-singular conditions. The proposed algorithm is not only capable of preserving measurement constraints under most circumstances, but can also robustly correct poses under singular conditions.

Figure 1 depicts the correction of relative frames between keyframes when the keyframes have been updated by a refinement process such as PGO or BA. $\{f_0^i\}$ and $\{f_j^i\}$ are the coordinates of the ith keyframe and the jth relative frame connected to the ith keyframe, respectively. The updated keyframe and the corrected relative frame are denoted as $\{f_0^{i^*}\}$ and $\{f_j^{i^*}\}$. $T_{f_1 f_2}$ is the SE(3) transformation from the $\{f_1\}$ coordinate frame to the $\{f_2\}$ coordinate frame. The aim is to approximate the relative frame correction transformation $T_{f_j^i f_j^{i*}}$ given the keyframe update transformations $T_{f_0^i f_0^{i*}}$ and $T_{f_0^{i+1} f_0^{i+1*}}$.

Interpolation approaches are typically used to correct the relative poses between keyframes. However, element-wise interpolation of a matrix in the SE(3) may break the rotation matrix SO(3) constraints $\left(\det(R) = +1 \text{ and } R^{\mathrm{T}} R = I\right)$. To prevent this, the SE(3) matrix should first be converted into a vector. The general equation for the interpolation of an SE(3) matrix after the conversion to a vector is as follows:

$$x_{f_0^{i*} f_j^{i*}} = x_{f_0^i f_j^i} + \left(x_{f_0^{i*} f_0^{i+1*}} - x_{f_0^i f_0^{i+1}}\right) \frac{x_{f_0^i f_j^i}}{x_{f_0^i f_0^{i+1}}} \tag{1}$$

where $x_{f_1 f_2} = f\left(T_{f_1 f_2}\right)$, $f : \mathrm{SE}(3) \mapsto \mathbb{R}^{n \times 1}$, and n is the dimension of the transformed vector space. The above equation was used to interpolate poses in a variety of vector spaces and the results of the interpolation served as the baseline for comparison with the proposed algorithm. The spaces formed by XYZ and the translation portion of the se(3) were used to represent translation while Euler angle, quaternion, and so(3) spaces were used to express rotations. As mentioned above, if even just one component of $x_{f_0^i f_0^{i+1}}$ is small, the resulting interpolation factor becomes numerically sensitive. In particular, if a front-view camera is mounted on a mobile robot or a vehicle, the motion in the z-axis which is the direction of the camera light rays becomes dominant, meaning that the changes in the x and y-axis will be extremely small. Such conditions have a high possibility of resulting in the aforementioned singular case.

4   Pose Correction Algorithm

In this section, the proposed pose correction algorithm is described in detail. The algorithm can be easily integrated into existing keyframe-based SLAM methods as shown in the Fig. 2. Typical SLAM front-end systems estimate the relative pose between the newly acquired image and the most relevant keyframe. Back-end systems select keyframes from the input images and perform graph-based optimization with the keyframes as nodes to improve the keyframe poses. Measurement constraints have been typically used to formulate the likelihood function in optimization methods, but not used in non-optimization methods for faster computation. The aim of the proposed algorithm was to preserve the measurement constraints for robustness and accuracy similar to that of the optimization methods, but with a fast computation time similar to that of the non-optimization methods.

The algorithm is triggered when the keyframes are updated and corrects the relative frames connected to the updated keyframes. KF_{up} in Fig. 2 represents the index of the keyframe refined by the back-end and RF_i is the relative frame index connected to the ith keyframe. The correction $T_{f_j^i f_j^{i*}}$ of the relative frames $\{f_j^i\}$ positioned between the ith and $i + 1^{\mathrm{th}}$ keyframes can be computed using the keyframe update information $T_{f_0^i f_0^{i*}}$ and $T_{f_0^{i+1} f_0^{i+1*}}$.

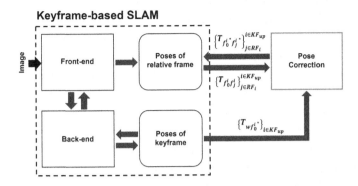

Fig. 2. The overall framework of a keyframe-based SLAM system with the added the pose correction module.

4.1 Measurement Constraints

The correction model will now be derived using the measurement constraints. To simplify the notation, we will omit f from the frame notations $\{f_j^i\}$ and show $\{i_j\}$ when the frame notations are used as subscripts or superscripts. Equations (2) and (3) show the projection equation of $\{f_0^i\}$ and $\{f_0^{i*}\}$ respectively.

$$\{f_0^i\}: \quad {}^{i_0}P_k = {}^{i_0}\lambda_k K^{-1 \, i_0}\bar{u}_k \tag{2}$$

$$\{f_0^{i*}\}: \quad {}^{i_0^*}P_k^* = {}^{i_0^*}\lambda_k^* K^{-1 \, i_0^*}\bar{u}_k \tag{3}$$

$$\text{where} \quad {}^{i_0}P_k = \begin{bmatrix} X \\ Y \\ Z \end{bmatrix}_k^{i_0}, \quad {}^{i_0}\bar{u}_k = \begin{bmatrix} u \\ v \\ 1 \end{bmatrix}_k^{i_0}.$$

Here, ${}^{i_0}P_k$, ${}^{i_0}\bar{u}_k$ and ${}^{i_0}\lambda_k$ are the 3-D position, the homogeneous pixel coordinates, and depth of the kth feature with respect to $\{f_0^i\}$, respectively. K is the intrinsic parameter matrix, and the position of the updated landmark ${}^{i_0^*}P_k$ can be expressed using (2) and (3) as follows:

$$
\begin{aligned}
{}^{i_0^*}P_k^* &= R_{i_0^* i_0}\left({}^{i_0}P_k + {}^{i_0}\delta P_k\right) + t_{i_0^* i_0} \\
&\approx \frac{{}^{i_0^*}\lambda_k^*}{{}^{i_0}\lambda_k}\, {}^{i_0}P_k \quad \left(\because \; {}^{i_0}\bar{u}_k = {}^{i_0^*}\bar{u}_k\right)
\end{aligned}
\tag{4}
$$

where $R_{i_0^* i_0}$ and $t_{i_0^* i_0}$ are the rotation and translation from $\{f_0^{i*}\}$ to $\{f_0^i\}$, respectively. ${}^{i_0}\delta P_k$ is the variation of the kth landmark position by the refinement process of SLAM. (4) was derived using the condition that the measurement of the landmark remains constant regardless of the pose corrections. The projection equation of $\{f_j^i\}$ and $\{f_j^{i*}\}$ with respect to the updated landmark ${}^{i_0^*}P_k^*$ shown in (4) can now be expressed as follows:

$$\{f_j^i\} : \frac{^{io}\lambda_k}{^{io^*}\lambda_k^*} R_{iji_0}{}^{io^*} P_k^* + t_{ij i_0} = {}^{ij}\lambda_k K^{-1}{}^{ij}\bar{u}_k \tag{5}$$

$$\{f_j^{i^*}\} : R_{ij^* i_0^*}{}^{io^*} P_k^* + t_{ij^* i_0^*} = {}^{ij^*}\lambda_k^* K^{-1}{}^{ij^*}\bar{u}_k \tag{6}$$

$$^{io^*} P_k^* = \frac{^{io^*}\lambda_k^*{}^{ij}\lambda_k}{^{io}\lambda_k} R_{i_0 i_j} K^{-1}{}^{ij}\bar{u}_k + \frac{^{io^*}\lambda_k^*}{^{io}\lambda_k} t_{i_0 i_j} \tag{7}$$

$$= {}^{ij^*}\lambda_k^* R_{i_0^* i_j^*} K^{-1}{}^{ij^*}\bar{u}_k + t_{i_0^* i_j^*} . \tag{8}$$

Using the fact that the measurement $^{ij}\bar{u}_k$ observed in each image remains constant regardless of the update, (9) can be derived from (7) and (8).

$$\left(\frac{^{io^*}\lambda_k^*{}^{ij}\lambda_k}{^{ij^*}\lambda_k^*{}^{io}\lambda_k} R_{i_0 i_j} - R_{i_0^* i_j^*} \right) {}^{ij^*}\lambda_k^* K^{-1}{}^{ij^*}\bar{u}_k + \frac{^{io^*}\lambda_k^*}{^{io}\lambda_k} t_{i_0 i_j} - t_{i_0^* i_j^*} = 0 . \tag{9}$$

The depth value of each feature increases as the translational difference between the keyframes in which the features were observed increases. Using this characteristic and assuming that the translation ratio and the depth ratio are equal, the following condition is derived:

$$s_i = \frac{^{io^*}\lambda_k^*}{^{io}\lambda_k} \approx \frac{\left\| t_{i_0^*(i+1)_0^*} \right\|_2^2}{\left\| t_{i_0(i+1)_0} \right\|_2^2}, \quad \frac{^{io^*}\lambda_k^*{}^{ij}\lambda_k}{^{ij^*}\lambda_k^*{}^{io}\lambda_k} \approx 1 . \tag{10}$$

Applying the (10) to (9) yields an identical Eq. (11) for $\left({}^{ij^*}\lambda_k^* K^{-1}{}^{ij^*}\bar{u}_k \right)$. For the identical equation to hold for all measurements, the solution must be expressed as in (12).

$$\left(R_{i_0 i_j} - R_{i_0^* i_j^*} \right) {}^{ij^*}\lambda_k^* K^{-1}{}^{ij^*}\bar{u}_k + s_i t_{i_0 i_j} - t_{i_0^* i_j^*} = 0 \tag{11}$$

$$R_{i_0^* i_j^*} = R_{i_0 i_j}, \quad t_{i_0^* i_j^*} = s_i t_{i_0 i_j} . \tag{12}$$

(12) was derived using the measurement constraint between the ith keyframe and $\{f_j^i\}$. Applying the same procedure to the $i+1^{\text{th}}$ keyframe yields (13).

$$R_{(i+1)_0^* i_j^*} = R_{(i+1)_0 i_j}, \quad t_{(i+1)_0^* i_j^*} = s_i t_{(i+1)_0 i_j} . \tag{13}$$

4.2   Fusion with Two Constraints

By fusing the conditions (12) and (13) derived previously, $T_{i_0 i_j^*}$ can now be computed. The gap between the solutions to the aforementioned conditions can be expressed as follows:

$$\delta R = R_{i_0*i_j*}^{KF_i}{}^T R_{i_0*(i+1)_0*} R_{(i+1)_0*i_j*}^{KF_{i+1}} \tag{14}$$

$$= R_{i_0 i_j}{}^T R_{i_0*(i+1)_0*} R_{(i+1)_0 i_j}$$

$$\delta t = t_{i_0*i_j*}^{KF_i} + R_{i_j*i_0*} t_{i_0*(i+1)_0*} + R_{i_j*(i+1)_0*} t_{(i+1)_0*i_j*}^{KF_{i+1}}$$

$$= R_{i_j*i_0*}\left(t_{i_0*(i+1)_0*} - s_i(t_{i_0 i_j} - R_{i_0*(i+1)_0*} t_{(i+1)_0 i_0}) \right)$$

where $R_{i_0*i_j*}^{KF_i}$ and $t_{i_0*i_j*}^{KF_i}$ are the corrected relative rotation and translation computed from (12), and $R_{i_0*i_j*}^{KF_{i+1}}$ and $t_{i_0*i_j*}^{KF_{i+1}}$ are the correction terms computed from (13). The δR and δt terms in (14) are expressed with respect to $\{f_j^*\}$, which is estimated under the conditions given in (12). To compensate for the gap, fusion as expressed in (16) is performed to estimate the corrected relative frame.

$$R_{i_0*i_j*} = R_{i_0*i_j*}^{KF_i} \cdot \text{SLERP}\left(\delta R, \ \alpha_j^i\right) \tag{15}$$

$$t_{i_0*i_j*} = t_{i_0*i_j*}^{KF_i} + \text{LERP}\left(R_{i_0*i_j*}\delta t, \ \alpha_j^i\right) \tag{16}$$

where SLERP($\cdot$) and LERP($\cdot$) are spherical linear interpolation and linear interpolation functions, respectively. δR is converted to a quaternion space to be utilized in the SLERP function. α_j^i is the interpolation factor which should reflect the reliability of conditions given by (12) and (13). Since the number of reliable edges increases as the distance between frames decreases due to the increase in the number of shared features, the ratio of the distance from $\{f_j^i\}$ to $\{f_0^i\}$ and the distance from $\{f_j^i\}$ to $\{f_0^{i+1}\}$ was used as the interpolation factor in this paper.

5   Experimental Result

This section provides the results of the proposed pose correction algorithm integrated with ORB-SLAM2 [1] which is one of the most popular keyframe-based SLAM. As mentioned above, the existing interpolation-based methods were tested in various vector spaces to function as a baseline for comparison. The interpolations for translation were done in XYZ and the translation component v of the se(3) spaces, while the rotation components were interpolated in Euler angles, quaternion, and so(3) spaces. The stereo images of KITTI [16] and EuRoC [17] benchmarks datasets were used for analysis. ORB-SLAM2 was used to generate the poses of frames, though any appropriate keyframe-based SLAM can be applied.

There are two types of refinements that occur in the back-end of SLAM: local BA and global BA. Local BA occurs when a new keyframe is added and refines only keyframes that have a strong connection to the newly added keyframe. Global BA occurs when a loop is detected and refines all keyframes that are in the map. The proposed pose correction module is triggered whenever local or global BA takes place and uses the updated keyframes and their relative frames as inputs. We analyze the accuracy of the corrected relative frame poses and the computation time required to compute the correction. However, because the keyframe poses computed by the SLAM system inherently contain error, the difference between the corrected relative frames poses and the ground truth (GT) may not purely reflect the correction performance. Therefore, an additional post processing step was introduced to the SLAM system to directly evaluate the correction performance of the algorithm. The poses of keyframes that lie on the estimated trajectory by ORB-SLAM2 with the correction module was additionally updated to their GT poses so that the keyframes now lie on the GT. The proposed algorithm was used to correct the relative frames so that the final output of the SLAM is corrected to the GT. The difference between these final corrected relative frame poses and the GT poses was used as the error metric for correction. Tests were performed on a laptop (Y520-15IKBN, 16 G B RAM with Intel i7-7700HQ @ 2.80 GHz × 4cores).

5.1 KITTI Dataset

The KITTI dataset [16] is generated from a stereo camera mounted on top of a vehicle, where the yaw motion and the camera z-axis movement are dominant with minimal motion along other axis due to the characteristics of a vehicle platform.

The ORB-SLAM2 and correction algorithm results obtained from the sequences (00–10) of the KITTI dataset are summarized in Table 1 and 2 respectively. No-correction in Table 2 refers to the results obtained from the simple concatenation of relative frames and keyframes without correction. The proposed algorithm outperformed all the baseline interpolation methods in all sequences except for sequence 01. As can be seen in Table 1, almost all image frames became keyframes using ORB-SLAM2 in sequence 01, meaning that the correction module had a minimal effect. For translation, the proposed algorithm nearly doubled the mean accuracy of the baseline method in sequences 00, 02, 03, 07 and 08. Furthermore, the algorithm yielded a lower standard deviation when compared to the baseline methods. Since standard deviation indicates the robustness of the system in a variety of situations, it can be concluded that the proposed algorithm is not numerically sensitive compared to the baseline methods. Rotation, on the other hand, does not exhibit significant differences in accuracy between methods. This is because the KITTI dataset was acquired using a ground vehicle, resulting in very little rotation aside from yaw. There are, however, significant differences in the standard deviation for rotation, meaning that singular cases occur in certain areas of the sequences, resulting in significant error. In some sequences, especially for rotations, the baseline methods yielded worse results than the no-correction method. Because rotation has such a small error even prior to correction, the numerical error has a significant effect on the results.

The resultant trajectory from each translation space for the select segments A and B in sequence 00 is shown in Fig. 3. Segment A visualizes the varying performance of the baseline methods, as both the XYZ and v interpolations stray wildly from the GT poses, even more so than the no-correction method. The proposed method, however, was able to remain consistent with the GT poses throughout the entire segment. Segment B shows the singular case in v, resulting in a huge deviation away from the GT. It is worth noting that the singularity occurred only in the v space interpolation and not the XYZ space interpolation. This is a clear depiction of the numerical sensitivity of the existing baseline methods, as such deviations can result in large error that may be even worse than the cases without correction at all. The proposed algorithm, however, performed robustly in both cases, demonstrating the improved accuracy and numerical robustness the algorithm has over the baseline methods.

Table 1. The results of ORB-SLAM2 in KITTI dataset. The number of keyframes and all frames and loop closures are indicated as shown.

KITTI	00	01	02	03	04	05	06	07	08	09	10
# of Keyframes	1355	1047	1742	226	155	717	473	251	1199	588	321
# of All Frames	4541	1101	4661	801	271	2701	1101	1101	4071	1504	1201
Loop	O	X	O	X	X	O	O	O	X	X	X

Table 2. The summary of results for the KITTI dataset. The blue indicates the lowest error while red indicates the highest error. Each cell contains the mean $\pm$ standard deviation, and (median). v represents the translation component of se(3) space.

Seq.	Translation (cm)				Rotation ($\times 10^{-1}$deg)				
	No-Correction	XYZ	v	Proposed	No-Correction	Euler	Quat	so(3)	Proposed
00	2.034±1.76	1.919±3.91	2.949±9.84	0.947±0.79	0.618±0.59	0.891±1.37	0.954±1.60	0.955±1.60	0.473±0.35
	(1.425)	(0.984)	(1.037)	(0.698)	(0.445)	(0.472)	(0.473)	(0.473)	(0.378)
01	1.874±0.52	0.885±0.46	1.083±0.84	0.915±0.46	0.190±0.08	0.190±0.08	0.191±0.09	0.191±0.09	0.188±0.08
	(1.890)	(0.788)	(0.876)	(0.833)	(0.188)	(0.188)	(0.189)	(0.189)	(0.188)
02	1.737±1.13	1.535±1.90	1.786±2.37	0.916±0.61	0.442±0.31	0.561±0.56	0.591±0.67	0.592±0.67	0.392±0.25
	(1.458)	(0.993)	(1.05)	(0.762)	(0.362)	(0.377)	(0.382)	(0.382)	(0.327)
03	1.455±0.87	1.610±2.07	1.692±2.10	0.775±0.47	0.478±0.23	0.594±0.53	0.558±0.40	0.559±0.40	0.456±0.21
	(1.228)	(0.985)	(1.002)	(0.665)	(0.403)	(0.417)	(0.417)	(0.417)	(0.393)
04	1.015±0.50	0.798±0.50	0.818±0.52	0.726±0.42	0.267±0.15	0.346±0.32	0.346±0.32	0.346±0.32	0.254±0.14
	(1.021)	(0.701)	(0.731)	(0.658)	(0.023)	(0.242)	(0.240)	(0.239)	(0.225)
05	1.495±1.32	1.008±0.83	1.166±1.31	0.849±0.63	0.469±0.34	0.672±0.85	0.746±1.14	0.746±1.14	0.405±0.28
	(1.074)	(0.747)	(0.757)	(0.656)	(0.375)	(0.420)	(0.422)	(0.422)	(0.328)
06	1.204±1.06	0.813±0.81	0.814±0.80	0.639±0.43	0.339±0.25	0.711±1.78	0.658±1.47	0.723±1.97	0.283±0.17
	(0.855)	(0.591)	(0.585)	(0.509)	(0.258)	(0.292)	(0.292)	(0.295)	(0.248)
07	2.034±2.17	2.648±4.74	2.784±5.02	1.372±2.12	0.537±0.42	0.717±1.03	0.679±0.84	0.679±0.84	0.418±0.28
	(1.267)	(0.875)	(0.886)	(0.701)	(0.428)	(0.423)	(0.423)	(0.423)	(0.342)
08	2.153±2.01	1.464±1.72	1.571±1.89	0.883±0.62	0.481±0.35	0.658±0.74	0.759±1.13	0.762±1.14	0.394±0.26
	(1.49)	(0.925)	(0.957)	(0.714)	(0.394)	(0.420)	(0.425)	(0.425)	(0.335)
09	1.362±0.82	0.997±0.70	1.179±1.12	0.868±0.52	0.415±0.27	0.499±0.44	0.527±0.53	0.527±0.53	0.381±0.24
	(1.167)	(0.819)	(0.875)	(0.755)	(0.367)	(0.378)	(0.382)	(0.383)	(0.334)
10	1.484±1.22	1.078±0.98	1.443±1.77	0.806±0.62	0.502±0.32	0.719±0.71	0.730±0.76	0.730±0.76	0.438±0.28
	(1.108)	(0.788)	(0.854)	(0.626)	(0.447)	(0.536)	(0.536)	(0.537)	(0.386)

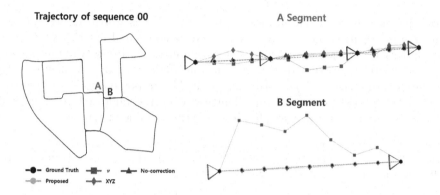

Fig. 3. The translational results of the correction algorithm for two select segments in sequence 00 of KITTI.

5.2   EuRoC Dataset

The EuRoC dataset [17] is generated from a stereo camera mounted on a micro aerial vehicle (MAV) and contains a more diverse range of motion compared to the KITTI data. The MAV was flown in an industrial environment (machine room) and two different rooms with a motion capture system in place. There are a total of 11 sequences, with each sequence classified as easy, medium, and difficult depending on the motion of the MAV and the room environment. Since ORB-SLAM2 does not provide sufficient results for V2_03_difficult due to significant motion blur in some of the frames, the particular sequences were not used in this paper.

The results of the ORB-SLAM2 and correction algorithm obtained from the remaining ten sequences are described in Tables 3 and 4, respectively. The EuRoC dataset is generated in a much smaller environment than the KITTI dataset, resulting in sparser keyframes. Furthermore, because the motion of a MAV is erratic compared to a ground vehicle, the pose error from SLAM is more significant than the KITTI dataset. Hence, the need for a correction algorithm is more apparent. The proposed algorithm demonstrates significantly improved results for both translation and rotation and the improvements are clearer than the KITTI dataset. In sequence V102, for example, the standard deviation of the algorithm was almost four times lower than that of the second best method for translation (no-correction) and five times lower than that of the second best method for rotation (no-correction), demonstrating its robustness. The mean and median values have also been halved, showcasing the accuracy of the algorithm.

The corrected trajectory for select segments of sequence V102 is shown in Fig. 4. Unlike the KITTI dataset, the no-correction method becomes meaningless, as the concatenation of relative frames and keyframes results in discontinuous trajectories as shown in both segments A and B. Furthermore, in both segments, the baseline methods failed to remain consistent with the GT, showing significant deviations in particular around the second keyframe in segment A.

In segment B, the numerical sensitivity of the v space interpolation method causes the corrected poses to deviate significantly from the GT trajectory. The XYZ space interpolation method is also unable to achieve the desired correction and results in significant clustering around the midpoint between the two keyframes. The proposed method, on the other hand, was able to remain close to the GT trajectory with no singularities. Hence, even under erratic motion that causes the baseline methods to fail, the proposed algorithm was still able to generate accurate and robust corrections.

Table 3. The number of keyframes and all frames within the EuRoC dataset. The sequences with loop closures are indicated.

EuRoC	Machine Hall					Vicon Room				
	01	02	03	04	05	101	102	103	201	202
# of Keyframes	483	431	436	302	353	109	151	208	216	271
# of All Frames	3638	2999	2662	1976	2221	2871	1670	2093	2148	2309
Loop	X	X	X	X	O	X	X	O	X	X

Table 4. The summary of results for the EuRoC dataset. The conventions are same as in Table 2.

Seq.	Translation (cm)				Rotation (deg)				
	No-Correction	XYZ	v	Proposed	No-Correction	Euler	Quat	so(3)	Proposed
MH01	8.130±7.53 (4.817)	4.385±9.58 (1.076)	5.026±10.84 (1.219)	1.937±2.28 (1.076)	5.904±7.69 (2.095)	4.014±5.14 (1.453)	3.827±4.68 (1.529)	3.840±4.70 (1.532)	3.214±4.78 (1.110)
MH02	7.592±7.90 (4.783)	3.028±5.03 (0.913)	2.947±4.87 (0.977)	1.974±2.75 (0.766)	2.212±2.70 (1.174)	2.456±4.20 (0.724)	2.632±4.73 (0.706)	2.654±4.79 (0.706)	1.672±2.17 (0.759)
MH03	22.693±24.15 (15.429)	11.755±16.50 (4.596)	15.135±24.25 (5.254)	5.047±6.31 (2.244)	4.455±5.20 (2.852)	3.687±5.12 (1.502)	4.028±6.64 (1.479)	4.247±7.55 (1.496)	3.236±3.79 (1.374)
MH04	15.201±15.92 (10.145)	6.229±10.01 (1.260)	6.427±9.93 (1.468)	2.994±4.88 (0.913)	2.605±2.81 (1.669)	2.301±3.64 (0.747)	2.239±3.53 (0.735)	2.221±3.49 (0.735)	1.260±1.34 (0.772)
MH05	13.922±15.47 (9.113)	5.928±15.00 (1.374)	4.847±9.92 (1.497)	1.753±2.47 (0.686)	2.376±3.08 (1.090)	1.660±2.59 (0.598)	1.885±3.14 (0.595)	1.951±3.34 (0.597)	0.969±1.27 (0.443)
V101	25.256±27.57 (16.314)	23.694±38.42 (8.886)	24.674±32.08 (10.596)	9.682±13.43 (5.475)	17.598±20.90 (9.802)	13.402±19.10 (5.417)	17.400±25.00 (6.230)	17.844±25.86 (6.230)	5.732±9.19 (3.008)
V102	28.821±33.85 (15.540)	24.904±45.06 (4.680)	26.179±39.96 (7.292)	6.548±9.65 (2.651)	22.823±38.48 (9.039)	21.537±43.96 (5.196)	20.791±39.68 (5.332)	20.973±39.66 (5.428)	4.841±5.74 (2.475)
V103	17.162±19.95 (9.932)	15.725±30.72 (3.755)	21.530±52.15 (4.757)	6.410±9.15 (2.027)	13.051±13.45 (8.663)	10.602±14.66 (4.226)	8.516±12.07 (3.584)	8.441±11.94 (3.560)	6.457±9.22 (2.674)
V201	5.090±4.36 (3.877)	2.771±4.57 (1.110)	2.617±3.53 (1.217)	1.488±1.72 (0.747)	3.784±4.22 (2.375)	4.486±7.77 (1.400)	5.421±10.84 (1.401)	5.664±11.64 (1.407)	1.473±1.63 (0.878)
V202	11.916±11.99 (8.187)	11.250±22.75 (2.764)	10.486±20.86 (2.841)	4.308±5.47 (1.890)	8.694±9.44 (5.637)	7.329±10.264 (3.300)	8.677±14.22 (3.062)	8.760±14.42 (3.071)	3.539±4.07 (1.883)

5.3   Computation Time

The proposed correction module triggers whenever keyframe refinement, or in other words BA, occurs in keyframe-based SLAM. Table 5 shows the amount of time required for the algorithm to compute a single correction in a MATLAB environment. Although there were no significant differences between the proposed and baseline algorithms for translation, the proposed algorithm required

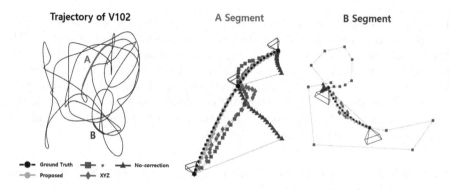

Fig. 4. The results of the corrected translation for two select segments in V102 of EuRoC.

the most time for rotation. This is because the SLERP algorithm used in the proposed algorithm requires more computations than a simple interpolation approach. However, the difference in the median computation time is approximately 1 millisecond and the algorithm only runs when a new keyframe is selected or when a loop is closed, meaning that the computation time required is insignificant when compared to the entire SLAM pipeline. In addition, the standard deviation of the computation time is large compared to the median value. This is due to the presence of loops within certain sequences, which results in a global BA. As discussed previously, global BA updates all keyframes, meaning that all relative frames must be corrected. Hence, typical computation time for a typical local BA is similar to that of the median value.

Table 5. The computation time taken for a single correction operation. The conventions are same as in Table 2.

Translation (msec)			Rotation (msec)			
XYZ	v	Proposed	Euler	Quat	so(3)	Proposed
0.340 ± 0.86 (0.170)	0.698 ± 1.74 (0.313)	0.356 ± 0.89 (0.135)	1.781 ± 4.66 (0.702)	2.205 ± 5.66 (0.944)	0.689 ± 1.69 (0.318)	3.916 ± 9.87 (1.441)

6   Conclusion

In this paper, we have proposed a lightweight pose correction algorithm for relative frames between keyframes that can be easily integrated into existing keyframe-based SLAM systems. The algorithm was derived by preserving the measurement constraints of two updated keyframes and utilizing the notion that the measurement observed in both keyframes remains constant regardless of the update. By doing so, the algorithm avoids singularities and numerical sensitivity that existing interpolation-based methods suffer from. The algorithm was applied to poses generated from the current state-of-the-art ORB-SLAM2 in KITTI and EuRoC datasets. The algorithm demonstrated results superior to the existing interpolation methods in both translation and rotation for all three datasets. The computation time of the proposed algorithm was only a few milliseconds longer than the baseline methods, which is negligible in the overall SLAM process. Applications requiring visual information that may appear in non-keyframes can benefit from the proposed algorithm with negligible cost to computation time. Since the proposed module can be easily attached to existing keyframe-based SLAM systems, the algorithm may be used in a wide range of fields.

References

1. Mur-Artal, R., Tardós, J.D.: Orb-slam2: an open-source slam system for monocular, stereo, and RGB-D cameras. IEEE Trans. Rob. **33**, 1255–1262 (2017)
2. Engel, J., Koltun, V., Cremers, D.: Direct sparse odometry. IEEE Trans. Pattern Anal. Mach. Intell. **40**, 611–625 (2017)
3. Forster, C., Zhang, Z., Gassner, M., Werlberger, M., Scaramuzza, D.: SVO: semidirect visual odometry for monocular and multicamera systems. IEEE Trans. Rob. **33**, 249–265 (2016)
4. Engel, J., Schöps, T., Cremers, D.: LSD-SLAM: large-scale direct monocular SLAM. In: Fleet, D., Pajdla, T., Schiele, B., Tuytelaars, T. (eds.) ECCV 2014. LNCS, vol. 8690, pp. 834–849. Springer, Cham (2014). https://doi.org/10.1007/978-3-319-10605-2_54
5. Piniés, P., Tardós, J.D.: Scalable slam building conditionally independent local maps. In: 2007 IEEE/RSJ International Conference on Intelligent Robots and Systems, pp. 3466–3471. IEEE (2007)
6. Piniés, P., Tardós, J.D.: Large-scale slam building conditionally independent local maps: application to monocular vision. IEEE Trans. Rob. **24**, 1094–1106 (2008)
7. Suger, B., Tipaldi, G.D., Spinello, L., Burgard, W.: An approach to solving large-scale slam problems with a small memory footprint. In: 2014 IEEE International Conference on Robotics and Automation (ICRA), pp. 3632–3637. IEEE (2014)
8. Grisetti, G., Grzonka, S., Stachniss, C., Pfaff, P., Burgard, W.: Efficient estimation of accurate maximum likelihood maps in 3D. In: 2007 IEEE/RSJ International Conference on Intelligent Robots and Systems, pp. 3472–3478. IEEE (2007)
9. Grisetti, G., Kümmerle, R., Stachniss, C., Frese, U., Hertzberg, C.: Hierarchical optimization on manifolds for online 2D and 3D mapping. In: 2010 IEEE International Conference on Robotics and Automation, pp. 273–278. IEEE (2010)
10. Droeschel, D., Behnke, S.: Efficient continuous-time slam for 3D lidar-based online mapping. In: 2018 IEEE International Conference on Robotics and Automation (ICRA), pp. 1–9. IEEE (2018)
11. Shoemake, K.: Animating rotation with quaternion curves. In: Proceedings of the 12th Annual Conference on Computer Graphics and Interactive Techniques, pp. 245–254 (1985)
12. Stuelpnagel, J.: On the parametrization of the three-dimensional rotation group. SIAM Rev. **6**, 422–430 (1964)
13. Shuster, M.D., et al.: A survey of attitude representations. Navigation **8**, 439–517 (1993)
14. Barfoot, T., Forbes, J.R., Furgale, P.T.: Pose estimation using linearized rotations and quaternion algebra. Acta Astronaut. **68**, 101–112 (2011)

15. Blanco, J.L.: A tutorial on se(3) transformation parameterizations and on-manifold optimization. University of Malaga, Technical report 3 (2010)
16. Geiger, A., Lenz, P., Stiller, C., Urtasun, R.: Vision meets robotics: the kitti dataset. Int. J. Robot. Res. **32**, 1231–1237 (2013)
17. Burri, M., et al.: The EUROC micro aerial vehicle datasets. Int. J. Robot. Res. **35**, 1157–1163 (2016)

Dense-Scale Feature Learning in Person Re-identification

Li Wang[1,2,3], Baoyu Fan[1,2(✉)], Zhenhua Guo[1,2], Yaqian Zhao[1,2],
Runze Zhang[1,2], Rengang Li[1,2], and Weifeng Gong[1,2]

[1] Inspur Electronic Information Industry Co., Ltd., Jinan, China
`li.wang.upc@foxmail.com`,
{`fanbaoyu,guozhenhua,zhaoyaqian,zhangrunze,lirg,gongwf`}`@inspur.com`
[2] State Key Laboratory of High-end Server Storage Technology, Jinan, China
[3] College of Control Science and Engineering,
China University of Petroleum (East China), Qingdao, China

Abstract. For mass pedestrians re-identification (Re-ID), models must
be capable of representing extremely complex and diverse multi-scale features. However, existing models only learn limited multi-scale features
in a multi-branches manner, and directly expanding the number of scale
branches for more scales will confuse the discrimination and affect performance. Because for a specific input image, there are a few scale features
that are critical. In order to fulfill vast scale representation for person Re-
ID and solve the contradiction of excessive scale declining performance,
we proposed a novel Dense-Scale Feature Learning Network (DSLNet)
which consist of two core components: Dense Connection Group (DCG)
for providing abundant scale features, and Channel-Wise Scale Selection
(CSS) module for dynamic select the most discriminative scale features
to each input image. DCG is composed of a densely connected convolutional stream. The receptive field gradually increases as the feature
flows along the convolution stream. Dense shortcut connections provide
much more fused multi-scale features than existing methods. CSS is a
novel attention module different from any existing model which calculates attention along the branch direction. By enhancing or suppressing
specific scale branches, truly channel-wised multi-scale selection is realized. To the best of our knowledge, DSLNet is most lightweight and
achieves state-of-the-art performance among lightweight models on four
commonly used Re-ID datasets, surpassing most large-scale models.

1 Introduction

Person re-identification (Re-ID) intends to automatically identify an individual
across non-overlapping camera views deployed at different times and locations.
The pedestrian image varies dramatically between different cameras, due to the
complexity of the realistic environment, such as light modification, posture variability, variety of view, scale change, partial occlusion. So, how to obtain and
select the most beneficial multi-scale features becomes critical to improve the
performance of person re-identification.

© Springer Nature Switzerland AG 2021
H. Ishikawa et al. (Eds.): ACCV 2020, LNCS 12627, pp. 341–357, 2021.
https://doi.org/10.1007/978-3-030-69544-6_21

The pedestrian image contains a plethora of multi-scale information. For example, for the pedestrian in Fig. 1(a), their dressing is very similar (both wear grey top and black shorts), but their somatotype is not identical. So, the large-scale body features become a crucial discriminating factor in this case. For the pedestrians in Fig. 1(b), they are very similar in dress and bodily form, but their shoes and shorts are varied. So, small-scale information has become a vital identification factor.

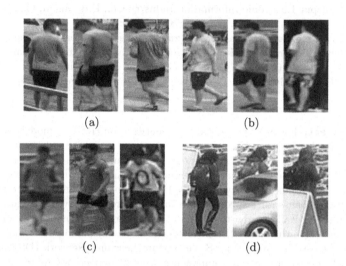

(a)   (b)

(c)   (d)

Fig. 1. The pedestrian image contains a plethora of multi-scale information. Larger-scale features and smaller-scale features can identify pedestrians in subfigure (a) and (b). However, only multiple-scales are not enough, and the fusion of multi-scale information is more discriminative (T-shirt with logo features that are more discriminative in subfigure (c)). Moreover, as multi-scale information becomes more abundant, selecting the discriminative information becomes more important(as shown in sub-figure (d), how key features can be filtered under occluded conditions becomes critical).

Under many circumstances, only multiple-scales are not enough and the person can only be successfully matched through fusion between multi-scale information. For example, for the pedestrian in Fig. 1(c), the impostor needs to be distinguished through the logo on T-shirt, and without T-shirt as context, the logo no longer has discriminating power. Therefore, only by combining a variety of scale information can the most favourable pedestrian features be obtained.

Furthermore, besides the ability to obtain pedestrian features at multi-scale scales, it is also needed to select more discriminative information from an enormous number of scale features and remove redundant features. As shown in Fig. 1(d), the leftmost pedestrian image is not occluded and the pedestrian image in the middle is partially occluded, so the backpacks and tops of pedestrians become crucial identification information. It is of critical importance to filter features and remove redundant features for Re-ID tasks.

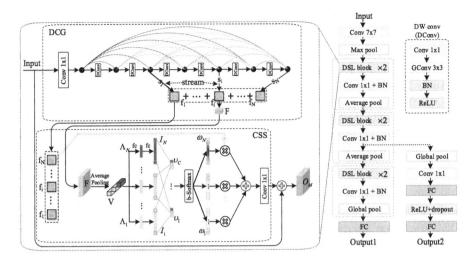

Fig. 2. The structure of dense-scale feature learning network.

To solve the problem of multi-scale acquisition and effective scale selection, many of scholars put forward various solutions. In terms of multi-scale learning, [1,2] that improve the multi-scale ability by using filters with different size, however the capacity will be significantly limited only by changing the convolution kernels size. OSNet [3] has designed a multi-branch block to obtain features with different scales. However, the multi-scale learning ability is greatly affected by the number of branches. A few attempts at learning multi-scale features also exist [1,4]. Yet, none has proposed a good solution to fully learn effective scale information.

In terms of scale selection, SENet [5] adopts the strategy of feature recalibration to suppress or enhance the corresponding channel in the feature map. OSNet designed an attention structure (Aggregation Gate) as same as SENet, which applies it to multiple independent branches. However, the Aggregation Gate is actually trained to identify critical channels under the intra-scale features, and inter-scale features selection among multi-branches is implicitly realised only by sharing aggregation gate weights. However, for person re-identification, intra-scale feature selection would not be enough, and inter-scale feature selection is also critical because integrate multiple key scales features as contextual information can enhance the discrimination.

To this end, we proposed the dense-scale feature learning network (DSLNet), a simple yet efficient multi-scale representation network which can extract more luxurious scale features while obtaining the most favourable scale features, and it is also extremely lightweight.

As shown in Fig. 2, The core of the dense-scale feature learning network is the DSL block which consists of two parts: Dense Connection group (DCG) and the Channel-Wise Scale Selection module (CSS).

In DCG, multi-scale feature mining is realized through the stack of depth-wise separable convolutions, and multi-scale feature fusion is realized through dense connection. Additionally, DCG introduces multiple streams and outputs the corresponding feature maps which provide an enormous number of scale features.

The structure of DCG has the following three advantages: First, provide rich multi-scale fusion features. The small scale feature information can flow to the large scale feature in a dense style, and then fuse information through addition, which provides multi-scale fusion information with the largest capacity. Secondly, output fusion information in a more sophisticated way. Different convolution layers contain various types of fusion features. DCG attaches multiple streams and outputs feature maps in early layers which can provide more abundant multi-scale fusion features in a more advanced way. Thirdly, being lightweight. DCG uses deep separable convolution (DW conv) which reduces the parameters under the premise of preserving the accuracy, and the dense connection style also makes more effective use of the stacked convolution layers.

DCG provides rich multi-scale features also introduces a lot of noise information. Too rich scale features without a selection will confuse the discrimination. So we designed the channel-wise scale selection module (CSS) which dynamically select the inter-scale features in multiple streams. As shown in Fig. 2, CSS learns the weighted attention with fused multi-scale features because the weights of each scale should not be calculated independently. Second, establish independent sub-network for each stream to learn the corresponding channel weights. Third, the truly inter-scale channel selection mechanism. Different from [3,5], CSS changes sigmoid activation for each stream with a unified softmax activation function and calculates the softmax attention among corresponding channels in different streams. This change will lead to a realization of inter-scale feature selection. The benefit of these changes will be further discussed in the experiment section.

Additionally, we go one step further. We proposed an enhanced hard triplet loss (E-TriHard), which reduces the distance gap between intra-class and inter-class while reducing the absolute value of the inter-class. The experimental results (as shown in Table 3) verify that using E-TriHard loss during the fine-tuning phase will further improve the performance of DSLNet.

2   Related Work

2.1   Deep Person Re-ID

In recent years, the person re-identification algorithm based on deep learning has achieved state-of-the-art performance and become a critical research direction. Person re-identification can be divided into two steps: representation learning and metric learning. They are closely related and rely on each other.

In [6–9], feature learning methods based on body parts are proposed to learn salient pedestrian features. However, this kind of approach is restricted due to the limitation of variable body parts spatial distribution and features misalignment problem. The global feature learning methods are developed by [10–12]. However, the global feature tends to overlook detailed information about the image, which restricts the expression ability. In order to obtain more discriminative information, the multi-scale feature representation method is proposed. [3, 13] achieve multi-scale feature mining by designing multiple branching network structures. However, only stacking branches or changing convolution kernels has limited capacity.

For metric learning, the main research direction focuses on optimizing the loss function, including Contrastive Loss [14], Triplet Loss [15], Quadruplet Loss [16], lifted loss [17], and so on. The development of the hard sample mining methods, including hard triplet mining [18], margin sample mining [19], has gained great success in person Re-ID and attracted more attention.

In this paper, we proposed a dense-scale representation network. Compared with the above representation learning methods, DSLNet can learn more rich multi-scale features in a granular way through dense-scale feature fusion and reuse. In addition, we proposed an enhanced hard triplet loss function, which can enlarge the gap between the intra-class and inter-class while keeping the absolute value of the intra-class distance low.

2.2 Attention Mechanisms

With the rise and development of deep learning, attention model is widely used in various fields, such as natural language processing [20], action recognition [21]. The attention-driven approaches to power networks to acquire discriminative human representation are thus received widespread attention.

In [22–25], spatial attention modules are proposed to learn attention regions or to extract features at salient spatial locations. However, spatial attention methods depend on the specific network model structure and have weak generality. Channel-wise attention modules are proposed to enhance the channel-wise feature map representation. Squeeze-and-excitation network [5] compresses feature maps according to the channel-wise dimension to learn the discriminative representation of channels. OSNet [3] takes a similar attention structure to SENet and pushes it into multiple branches. In this paper, we propose a novel channel-wise scale selection module that dynamically weights the discriminative features in multiple streams from the fused dense-scale information.

3   Proposed Algorithm

In this section, we present DSLNet, a novel and efficient multi-scale learning neural network for the person Re-ID task. Firstly, we elaborate on the important components of DSLNet basic block (DSL block). Then we present the detailed architecture of DSLNet.

3.1   Dense Connection Group

In the person Re-ID task, only multiple scales are far from enough, and the feature can be more discriminative through fusion between multi-scale information.

To achieve multi-scale feature fusion, we extend the residual structure by introducing a dense connection group (DCG), The structure of the DCG is shown in Fig. 2.

Given an input x_0, DCG consists of L feature extractors, and each feature extractor implements a nonlinear transformation $H_i(\cdot)$, the output of DCG can be expressed as follows:

$$x_i = H_i(x_0 + x_1 + \cdots\cdots, x_{i-1}) \quad i \in [1, L] \tag{1}$$

where x_i represents the output of DCG on various scales. Each filter will fuse the output of the former, and the receptive field will increase while the multi-scale features are merging. Due to the dense connection, each layer contains the information of all previous layers, which implements feature fusion with rich scales.

Moreover, to better balance the trade-off between scale mining capability and calculation cost, we carefully select the number of filters. Meanwhile, DSL block adopts the DW conv, further reducing the FLOPS and parameters while maintaining the accuracy.

3.2 Channel-Wise Scale Selection Module

The dense connection group provides extremely rich multi-scale fusion features also introduces many redundant features. In fact, only a limited number of scales may be needed for the final authentication. So, how to extract the most discriminative features from the rich scale information is very critical. Therefore, we introduce the attention mechanism to realize the discriminative multi-scale feature selection.

As shown in Fig. 2, the dense-scale channel-wise selection module (CSS) consists of three stages: dense-scale feature fusion, attention learning, channel-wise feature selection.

In the first stage, CSS obtains dense-scale features from the dense connection group (DCG) and then adopts element-wise addition to fuse the features. Next, CSS use the global average pooling layer to compress each channel. The process can be formulated as:

$$F = \sum_{i=1}^{N} s_i, F \in \mathbb{R}^{H \times W \times C} \tag{2}$$

$$V_c = \sum_{w=1}^{W} \sum_{h=1}^{H} F_c(i, j)/(H \times W) \tag{3}$$

where N represents the number of output streams in DCG, s_i represents the feature map of the $i - th$ stream in DCG. F stands for fused features. H and W denotes the width and height of F, c represents the $c - th$ channel of F. V represents the channel weight statistics and $V = [V_1, \cdots, V_c, \cdots V_C]$.

For attention learning, CSS learns the channel weights for each DCG stream from the vector V. First, the vector V is split into N groups, then the CSS module establishes multiple sub-streams that contain two fully connected layers. Λ_n will pass through the corresponding sub-stream to learn the channel weights I_n.

$$I_n = \varphi_n(\Lambda_n) \tag{4}$$

where $\varphi_n(\cdot)$ represents the mapping function formed by two fully connected layers, and n represents the $n-th$ stream in CSS. I represents the set of channel weights for all DCG streams, $I = [I_1, \cdots I_n, \cdots, I_N]$.

For channel-wise feature selection, CSS recombinants and normalizes the corresponding channel weights in I, so as to truly realize inter-scale feature selection. Specifically, CSS traverses I to extract the corresponding elements in the I_n and reconstructs a new vector v (as shown in Fig. 2), $v \in \mathbb{R}^{1 \times N}$, and uses softmax layer to normalize v. Finally, v will replace the corresponding elements in I_n and get the renewed channel weight vector ω_n, $\omega_n \in \mathbb{R}^{1 \times C}$. The process of recombining elements and normalization enables inter-scale feature selection, and all weight expressions are derived from the dense-scale fusion features.

Finally, the reconstruction weight ω_n is multiplied from the features of the corresponding CSS stream, the weighted features of all streams are finally fused, the output of the CSS can be formulated below:

$$D = \sum_{n=1}^{N} \omega_n \odot F_n \tag{5}$$

where $\odot$ denotes the Hadamard product and D denotes the final learned weighted features.

3.3 Loss Function Design

In the process of training, loss function can supervise the learning of network, thus affecting the recognition performance of the model. Therefore, the selection and design of loss function plays an important role in image retrieval [26], face recognition [27] and person re-identification [22,28]. We use two training methods: trained from scratch and fine-tuning from the ImageNet pre-trained models to evaluate the proposed algorithm. Different training processes use different loss functions.

For training from scratch, we use cross entropy loss to optimize the model. For fine-tuning, firstly, we use the cross entropy loss to train the model. Secondly, we optimize the hard triplet loss function and train the network with the improved loss function.

The hard triplet loss function can be expressed as:

$$L_{TriHard} = \frac{1}{N_t} \sum_{a=1}^{N_t} [\max_{y_p=y_a} d(f_a, f_p) - \min_{y_n \neq y_a} d(f_a, f_n) + m]_+ \tag{6}$$

where $[\cdot]_+$ represents $\max(\cdot, 0)$, N_t represents the number of triples in each batch, $d(\cdot, \cdot)$ stands for metric distance function and we adopt the Euclidean distance. m represents the margin of the hard triplet loss. f_p is positive sample features, f_n is negative sample features, f_a represents anchor sample features, $dist^a_{ap} = \max\limits_{y_p = y_a} d(f_a, f_p)$, $dist^a_{ap}$ represents the maximum intra-class distance of anchor samples. $dist^a_{an} = \min\limits_{y_n \neq y_a} d(f_a, f_n)$, $dist^a_{an}$ represents the minimum inter-class distance of anchor samples.

The hard triplet loss is widely used in person re-identification, however, it only considers the distance gap between $d(f_a, f_p)$ and $d(f_a, f_n)$ and ignores their absolute values [29]. To compensate for the drawbacks of the hard triplet loss, we add a regularization term to reduce the distance gap between intra-class and inter-class while reducing the absolute value of the inter-class. The enhanced hard triplet loss function(E-TriHard) is formulated as follows:

$$L_{E\_TriHard} = L_{TriHard} + \beta \frac{1}{N_t} \sum_{a=1}^{N_t} \left(\frac{dist^a_{ap}}{dist^a_{an}} \right) \tag{7}$$

The final loss function used in the training process is formulated as:

$$L_{final} = L_{soft\,max} + \alpha L_{E\_TriHard} \tag{8}$$

where, $\alpha, \beta \in (0, 1]$, two hyper-parameters α and β are fixed in the experiments.

3.4   Network Architecture

Based on the DSLBlock, the structure of DSLNet is meticulously designed. As shown in Table 1, the stem of DSLNet is composed of a 7×7 convolution layer with a stride of 2 and a 3×3 maxpooling layer. Subsequently, we stack the DSLBlock layer-by-layer to construct the DSLNet. DSLNet contains three stages, with each stage including two DSL Blocks. The feature map can be down-sampled with each stage. Additionally, during the training phase, we add an auxiliary branch at the second stage of the network. Auxiliary branch facilitates information flow to the early layers and relieves the gradient vanishing problem. Finally, we add global average pooling and fully-connected layer for training. The network structure and parameters of DSLNet are shown in Table 1.

Table 1. Architecture of DSLNet with input image size 256×128. c: The number of input channels. k: Operation type. s: Stride. n: Number of repetitions of this layer operation

Output	Layer	c	k	s	n
128×64	conv2d	60	7×7	2	1
64×32	max pool	60	3×3	2	1
64×32	DSL block	252	DW conv	1	2
64×32	conv2d	252	1×1	1	1
32×16	average pool	252	2×2	2	1
32×16	DSL block	384	DW conv	1	2
32×16	conv2d	384	1×1	1	1
16×8	average pool	384	2×2	2	1
16×8	DSL block	516	DW conv	1	2
16×8	conv2d	516	1×1	1	1
1×1	global average pool	516	16×8	1	1
1×1	fc	516	fc	1	1
Params	1.9M				
Flops	825.0M				

4   Experimental Results

4.1   Datasets and Evaluation Metrics

Four mainstream challenging Re-ID datasets are used to verify the proposed model, including Market-1501 [Zheng et al. 2015], DukeMTMC-Re-ID [Ristani et al. 2016], MSMT17 [Wei et al. 2018] and CUHK03 [Li et al. 2014]. Among them, Market-1501 includes 32,668 images of 1501 pedestrians, of which, 12,396 images of 751 identities were used for training and the rest for testing. Duke MTMC-Re-ID consists of 36,411 images of 1,812 identities, of them, 1,404 identities were captured by more than two cameras, and the rest only appeared in only one camera. Compared to other datasets, MSMT17 is a larger and more realistic Re-ID dataset which was published in 2018, it contains 126,411 pedestrian images of 4101 identities, 32621 of these images with 1041 identities were selected as the training set, and the rest 93820 images with 3060 other identities were used for testing. The CUHK03 dataset is composed of 14,097 pedestrian images of 1,467 identities, with each person having 9.6 images on average, and the CUHK03 dataset contains two subsets that provide hand-labeled and DPM detected bounding boxes respectively. We evaluate our proposed model on DPM detected subset.

4.2   Implementation Details

In our experiments, we employ two training methods: training from scratch and fine-tuning from the ImageNet pre-trained model.

For training from scratch, we use the stochastic gradient descent algorithm to optimize the model and epoch is set to 350. The learning rate is decayed using the cosine annealing strategy with the initialization value of 0.0015. In the fine-tuning stage, the AMS-Grad optimizer is used. The pre-trained weight is frozen at the first 10 epochs, and only the randomly initialized classifier can be trained. The epoch is set to 250. The learning rate decay strategy adopts the cosine annealing strategy, and the initial learning rate is 0.065. Two loss functions, cross-entropy loss and E-TriHard loss, are used in the fine-tuning stage. For E-TriHard loss, we set the hyperparameters α and β to 0.5 and 0.8, respectively.

In all experiments, the batch size is set to 64, and the weight decay is set to 5e-4. Images are resized to 256×128, and the corresponding data enhancement methods are adopted. In the verification stage, we delete the auxiliary branch and extract the 512-D features from the last fully-connected layer of the main branch and use the cosine distance for measurement. For all experiments, we use single query evaluation and simultaneously adopt both Rank-1 (R1) accuracy and the mean average precision (mAP) to evaluate the performance of DSLNet. All experiments are conducted based on the deep learning framework of PyTorch, and we use NVIDIA V100 GPU to train the model.

4.3   Performance Evaluation

Trained from Scratch. Based on DSL block, we build a lightweight DSLNet which can obtain dense-scale information and realize channel-wise scale feature selection. For each DSL block, we stack six depth-wise separable convolutions in series to obtain various scale receptive fields and simultaneously add dense connections in DSL block for the fuse of multi-scale features at a granular level. We trained the proposed model from scratch and compared it with state-of-the-art models using the same training strategy. The results are shown in Table 2.

From Table 2, we can see that DSLNet outperforms the other methods in all datasets. More concretely, DSLNet achieves the best rank-1 value and mAP accuracy of 94.0% and 83.9% in Market1501 datasets, and 86.9%/74.8% on Duke. While OSNet, the second-best method, arrives at 93.6%/81.0% and 84.7%/68.6%, respectively. The gap is even more significant in the CUHK03 and MSMT17 databases. For R1, DSLNet outperforms OSNet by more than 6% improvement of R1 rate on CUHK03. For mAP, DSLNet beats OSNet by 6.8% on CUHK03 and 9.0% on MSMT17.

Furthermore, DSLNet is the most light-weighted model which only has 1.9M parameters. OSNet has similar parameter amount to MobileNetV2, both of which are 2.2M. DSLNet has created an elegant and effective backbone network, which uses fewer parameters to achieve the best performance.

Fine-tuning from ImageNet. In order to highlight the significance of the proposed DSLNet for person Re-ID task, we compare it with some recent remarkable works. We conduct pre-training of DSLNet on the ImageNet dataset and then use the pre-trained weight to conduct fine-tuning on the Re-ID dataset. All results are summarized in Table 3.

Table 2. Trained from scratch.

Method	Venue	Params(M)	GFLOPs	Duke		Market1501	
				R1	mAP	R1	mAP
MobileNetV2 [30]	CVPR'18	2.2	**0.2**	75.2	55.8	87.0	69.5
BraidNet [31]	CVPR'18	–	–	76.4	59.5	83.7	69.5
HAN [22]	CVPR'18	2.7	1.09	80.5	63.8	91.2	75.7
OSNet [32]	ICCV'19	2.2	0.98	84.7	68.6	93.6	81.0
DSLNet	*ours*	**1.9**	0.82	**86.9**	**74.8**	**94.0**	**83.9**
Method	Venue	Params(M)	GFLOPs	CUHK03		MSMT17	
				R1	mAP	R1	mAP
MobileNetV2 [30]	CVPR'18	2.2	**0.2**	46.5	46.0	50.9	27.0
HAN [22]	CVPR'18	2.7	1.09	41.7	38.6	–	–
OSNet [32]	ICCV'19	2.2	0.98	57.1	54.2	71.0	43.3
DSLNet	*ours*	**1.9**	0.82	**63.8**	**61.0**	**75.0**	**52.3**

From Table 3, it can be seen that DSLNet achieves higher R1/mAP than the other methods on four mainstream datasets. For R1, DSLNet achieves the highest rate of 73.6% on CUHK03 and 89.5% on Duke, while OSNet arrives at the rate of 69.1%/88.6% respectively. For mAP, DSLNet beats OSNet by 3.7% on CUHK03 and 3.6% on Duke. On MSMT17, which is the largest one among the four commonly used Re-ID datasets, DSLNet outperforms OSNet by a significant margin. Concretely, DSLNet achieves the R1/mAP of 80.2%/57.3%, respectively, while OSNet just arrives at 78.7%/52.9%. Adding E-TriHard loss to the training process will further improve the performance of DSLNet. On Market1501 and Duke, DSLNet (E-TriHard) achieves the R1/mAP of 95.1%/87.3% and 90.4%/78.5%. On CUHK03 and MSMT17, DSLNet (E-TriHard) arrives at 76.8%/72.4% and 82.1%/59.4%. The performance on Re-ID benchmarks, especially on Market1501 and Duke, has been saturated lately. Therefore, the improvements obtained are significant.

Furthermore, we can also see that DSLNet achieves the best results with the smallest model. DGNet, IANet, CAMA, st-ReID adopted the backbone based on ResNet50, which involved the parameters amount of more than 23.5M, VA-reID [33] employed the SeResNeXt backbone network with the parameter amount of more than 46M. In comparison, our model is dozens of times smaller than theirs. These experimental results validate the efficiency and robustness of DSLNet, which is due to the multi-scale feature extraction and fusion ability of DSLNet.

4.4 Ablation Study

In order to verify the influence of different components of DSLNet, we conduct related ablation experiment on the CUHK03 dataset. We verify the influence of DCG/CSS components on the performance, respectively.

Table 3. Fine-tuning from ImageNet. †: reproduced by us.

Method	Venue	Backbone	Params (M)	Duke		Market1501	
				R1	mAP	R1	mAP
IANet [34]	CVPR'19	ResNet	>23.5	87.1	73.4	94.4	83.1
DGNet [35]	CVPR'19	ResNet	>23.5	86.6	74.8	94.8	86.0
st-ReID [36]	AAAI'19	ResNet	>23.5	**94.4**	**83.9**	**98.1**	87.6
VA-reID [33]	AAAI'20	SeResNeXt	>46.9	91.6	84.5	96.2	91.7
LUO [29]	TMM'19	ResNext	46.9	90.1	79.1	95.0	88.2
Auto-ReID [37]	ICCV'19	ResNet	13.1	–	–	94.5	85.1
OSNet [32]	ICCV'19	OSNet	2.2	88.6	73.5	94.8	84.9
DSLNet	*ours*	DSLNet	**1.9**	89.5	77.1	94.5	85.1
DSLNet (E-TriHard)	*ours*	DSLNet	**1.9**	90.4	78.5	95.1	87.3
Method	Venue	Backbone	Params(M)	CUHK03		MSMT17	
				R1	mAP	R1	mAP
CAMA [38]	CVPR'19	ResNet	>23.5	66.6	64.2	–	–
IANet [34]	CVPR'19	ResNet	>23.5	–	–	75.5	46.8
DGNet [35]	CVPR'19	ResNet	>23.5	65.6	61.1	77.2	52.3
Auto-ReID [37]	ICCV'19	ResNet	13.1	73.3	69.3	78.2	52.5
OSNet [32]	ICCV'19	OSNet	2.2	69.1†	65.7†	78.7	52.9
DSLNet	*ours*	DSLNet	**1.9**	73.6	69.4	80.2	57.3
DSLNet (E-TriHard)	*ours*	DSLNet	**1.9**	**76.8**	**72.4**	**82.1**	**59.4**

Validity of Dense Connection. The dense connection group obtains different scale receptive fields by convolution layer stacking and realizes contextal information fusion by dense connection. To verify the effectiveness of the dense connection in DCG, we remove all dense connections from DSL blocks in ablation experiment and compare the impact on the final performance. Baseline stands for delete all dense connections in DSLNet. Add DC means adding dense connection to DSL blocks.

As shown in Table 4, by adding dense connections, the performance of the model is improved significantly, which benefits from the reuse of multi-scale features, and the fusion of context information. Add DC outperforms baseline model by more than 2% improvement of R1 rate and 1.8% improvement on mAP accuracy. It proves that the design of dense connection is reasonable and effective.

Validity of CSS. Too rich features without an effective selection mechanism can undermine the classifier's discriminatory ability. Attention mechanism-based approaches can be effective in addressing the problem of feature selection. To verify CSS's validity, we introduce the attention model from [3,5] into DSLNet for comparison experiments. As shown in Table 5, Baseline stands for removing CSS module from DSL blocks. SENet Attention represents adding the SENet attention structure to the baseline model. OSNet Attention means adding independent attention models to the baseline model for all streams, yet the weights of all attention models are shared. CSS is our proposed approach.

Table 4. Validity of dense connection

Model	Architecture	CUHK03	
		R1	mAP
1	Baseline	61.4	59.2
2	Add DC	**63.8**	**61.0**

Table 5. Validity of CSS

Model	Architecture	CUHK03	
		R1	mAP
1	Baseline	56.2	54.2
2	SENet Attention	62.2	60
3	OSNet Attention	62.5	59.9
4	CSS	**63.8**	**61.0**

From the experimental results, we can find that: 1) Adding the attention network will significantly improve the baseline model's performance, validate that the attention mechanism-based feature selection mode is essential for Re-ID tasks. 2) CSS model outperforms all other attention benchmarks by a clear margin. Compared with model 2 and model 3, with the introduction of CSS, R1/mAP can be improved by 1.6%/1.0% and 1.3%/1.1%, respectively. CSS fuses the features from multiple streams to dynamically adjust the weights of all channels in the DCG, truly realizing the role of channel-wise feature selection across streams. The experimental results verify the superiority of the CSS method.

4.5 Visualizations

Visualization of Learned Features. To validate the effectiveness of DSLNet to represent and select multi-scale features, we extract the feature map of the last convolutional layer for visualization and observe whether the DSLNet focuses more on the key regions. We use the visualization method of [39], which summits the feature maps along the channel dimension and then performs a spatial euclidean normalization for a bright feature display. As shown in Fig. 3, the rightmost column represents the DSLNet activation map. The middle column represents the activation map with all dense connections removed from the DSLNet. We can see that DSLNet mines more effective multi-scale information, as shown in the second example on the first line, where the logo on the pedestrian bag is activated, in the second example on the second line, where the pedestrian's shoes and handbag activate a larger and more pronounced area. Other examples in Fig. 3 also show that DSLNet highlights more salient features of the same target. DCG provides the abundant of multi-scale feature combinations, and CSS modules enable efficient discriminating feature selection. These qualitative results confirm the ability of DSLNet for effective feature representation and selection.

4.6 Visual Retrieval Results

To further demonstrate the robustness and effectiveness of DSLNet, we acquire the eight nearest retrieval results of query images for analysis.

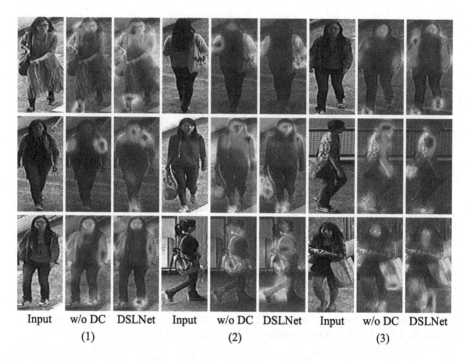

Input   w/o DC   DSLNet   Input   w/o DC   DSLNet   Input   w/o DC   DSLNet

(1)   (2)   (3)

Fig. 3. Visualizations of the activation map. From left to right, each of the three images constitutes a set of comparison experiments, the right column represents the DSLNet activation map. The middle column represents the activation map with all dense connections removed from the DSLNet. We can see that with the addition of dense connections, DSLNet highlights more salient features.

We select the retrieval results of query samples under blur, occlusion, and illumination change. One can see that DSLNet can still get correct retrieval results in an unfavorable environment. The above experiments further prove the robustness and effectiveness of DSLNet, which benefits from the dense-scale feature representation and discriminative feature selection ability.

5   Conclusions

In this paper, we proposed DSLNet, an efficient multi-scale representation network which can extract dense-scale features while selecting discriminative multi-scale information. In the future, we will do further research to investigate the potential of DSLNet in other visual recognition tasks.

Acknowledgments. The paper is funded by the Key Scientific and Technical Innovation Engineer Project of Shandong (No. 2019JZZY011101).

References

1. Qian, X., Fu, Y., Jiang, Y.G., Xiang, T., Xue, X.: Multi-scale deep learning architectures for person re-identification. In: Proceedings of the IEEE International Conference on Computer Vision, pp. 5399–5408 (2017)
2. Chang, X., Hospedales, T.M., Xiang, T.: Multi-level factorisation net for person re-identification. In: Proceedings of the IEEE Conference on Computer Vision and Pattern Recognition, pp. 2109–2118 (2018)
3. Zhou, K., Yang, Y., Cavallaro, A., Xiang, T.: Omni-scale feature learning for person re-identification. In: Proceedings of the IEEE International Conference on Computer Vision, pp. 3702–3712 (2019)
4. Chen, Y., Zhu, X., Gong, S.: Person re-identification by deep learning multi-scale representations. In: Proceedings of the IEEE International Conference on Computer Vision Workshops, pp. 2590–2600 (2017)
5. Hu, J., Shen, L., Sun, G.: Squeeze-and-excitation networks. In: Proceedings of the IEEE conference on computer vision and pattern recognition, pp. 7132–7141 (2018)
6. Sun, Y., Zheng, L., Yang, Y., Tian, Q., Wang, S.: Beyond part models: person retrieval with refined part pooling (and a strong convolutional baseline). In: Ferrari, V., Hebert, M., Sminchisescu, C., Weiss, Y. (eds.) ECCV 2018. LNCS, vol. 11208, pp. 501–518. Springer, Cham (2018). https://doi.org/10.1007/978-3-030-01225-0_30
7. Ustinova, E., Ganin, Y., Lempitsky, V.: Multi-region bilinear convolutional neural networks for person re-identification. In: 2017 14th IEEE International Conference on Advanced Video and Signal Based Surveillance (AVSS), pp. 1–6. IEEE (2017)
8. Wei, L., Zhang, S., Yao, H., Gao, W., Tian, Q.: Glad: Global-local-alignment descriptor for pedestrian retrieval. In: Proceedings of the 25th ACM International Conference on Multimedia, pp. 420–428 (2017)
9. Zhao, H., et al.: Spindle net: person re-identification with human body region guided feature decomposition and fusion. In: Proceedings of the IEEE Conference on Computer Vision and Pattern Recognition, pp. 1077–1085 (2017)
10. Li, D., Chen, X., Zhang, Z., Huang, K.: Learning deep context-aware features over body and latent parts for person re-identification. In: Proceedings of the IEEE Conference on Computer Vision and Pattern Recognition, pp. 384–393 (2017)
11. Zheng, F., et al.: Pyramidal person re-identification via multi-loss dynamic training. In: Proceedings of the IEEE Conference on Computer Vision and Pattern Recognition, pp. 8514–8522 (2019)
12. Dai, Z., Chen, M., Gu, X., Zhu, S., Tan, P.: Batch dropblock network for person re-identification and beyond. In: Proceedings of the IEEE International Conference on Computer Vision, pp. 3691–3701 (2019)
13. Wang, G., Yuan, Y., Chen, X., Li, J., Zhou, X.: Learning discriminative features with multiple granularities for person re-identification. In: 2018 ACM Multimedia Conference on Multimedia Conference, pp. 274–282. ACM (2018)
14. Varior, R.R., Haloi, M., Wang, G.: Gated siamese convolutional neural network architecture for human re-identification. In: Leibe, B., Matas, J., Sebe, N., Welling, M. (eds.) ECCV 2016. LNCS, vol. 9912, pp. 791–808. Springer, Cham (2016). https://doi.org/10.1007/978-3-319-46484-8_48
15. Chechik, G., Sharma, V., Shalit, U., Bengio, S.: Large scale online learning of image similarity through ranking. J. Mach. Learn. Res. **11**, 1109–1135 (2010)
16. Chen, W., Chen, X., Zhang, J., Huang, K.: Beyond triplet loss: a deep quadruplet network for person re-identification. In: Proceedings of the IEEE Conference on Computer Vision and Pattern Recognition, pp. 403–412 (2017)

17. Oh Song, H., Xiang, Y., Jegelka, S., Savarese, S.: Deep metric learning via lifted structured feature embedding. In: Proceedings of the IEEE Conference on Computer Vision and Pattern Recognition, pp. 4004–4012 (2016)
18. Hermans, A., Beyer, L., Leibe, B.: In defense of the triplet loss for person re-identification. arXiv preprint arXiv:1703.07737 (2017)
19. Xiao, Q., Luo, H., Zhang, C.: Margin sample mining loss: a deep learning based method for person re-identification. arXiv preprint arXiv:1710.00478 (2017)
20. Yang, Z., He, X., Gao, J., Deng, L., Smola, A.: Stacked attention networks for image question answering. In: Proceedings of the IEEE Conference on Computer Vision and Pattern Recognition, pp. 21–29 (2016)
21. Sudhakaran, S., Escalera, S., Lanz, O.: Lsta: Long short-term attention for egocentric action recognition. In: Proceedings of the IEEE Conference on Computer Vision and Pattern Recognition, pp. 9954–9963 (2019)
22. Li, W., Zhu, X., Gong, S.: Harmonious attention network for person re-identification. In: Proceedings of the IEEE Conference on Computer Vision and Pattern Recognition, pp. 2285–2294 (2018)
23. Xu, J., Zhao, R., Zhu, F., Wang, H., Ouyang, W.: Attention-aware compositional network for person re-identification. In: Proceedings of the IEEE Conference on Computer Vision and Pattern Recognition, pp. 2119–2128 (2018)
24. Kim, W., Goyal, B., Chawla, K., Lee, J., Kwon, K.: Attention-based ensemble for deep metric learning. In: Ferrari, V., Hebert, M., Sminchisescu, C., Weiss, Y. (eds.) ECCV 2018. LNCS, vol. 11205, pp. 760–777. Springer, Cham (2018). https://doi.org/10.1007/978-3-030-01246-5_45
25. Lan, X., Wang, H., Gong, S., Zhu, X.: Deep reinforcement learning attention selection for person re-identification. arXiv preprint arXiv:1707.02785 (2017)
26. Gordo, A., Almazán, J., Revaud, J., Larlus, D.: Deep image retrieval: learning global representations for image search. In: Leibe, B., Matas, J., Sebe, N., Welling, M. (eds.) ECCV 2016. LNCS, vol. 9910, pp. 241–257. Springer, Cham (2016). https://doi.org/10.1007/978-3-319-46466-4_15
27. Liu, W., Wen, Y., Yu, Z., Li, M., Raj, B., Song, L.: Sphereface: Deep hypersphere embedding for face recognition. In: Proceedings of the IEEE Conference on Computer Vision and Pattern Recognition, pp. 212–220 (2017)
28. Zhong, Z., Zheng, L., Cao, D., Li, S.: Re-ranking person re-identification with k-reciprocal encoding. In: Proceedings of the IEEE Conference on Computer Vision and Pattern Recognition, pp. 1318–1327 (2017)
29. Luo, H., Jiang, W., Gu, Y., Liu, F., Liao, X., Lai, S., Gu, J.: A strong baseline and batch normalization neck for deep person re-identification. arXiv preprint arXiv:1906.08332 (2019)
30. Sandler, M., Howard, A., Zhu, M., Zhmoginov, A., Chen, L.C.: Mobilenetv 2: Inverted residuals and linear bottlenecks. In: Proceedings of the IEEE Conference on Computer Vision and Pattern Recognition, pp. 4510–4520 (2018)
31. Wang, Y., Chen, Z., Wu, F., Wang, G.: Person re-identification with cascaded pairwise convolutions. In: Proceedings of the IEEE Conference on Computer Vision and Pattern Recognition, pp. 1470–1478 (2018)
32. Zhou, K., Yang, Y., Cavallaro, A., Xiang, T.: Omni-scale feature learning for person re-identification. In: The IEEE International Conference on Computer Vision (ICCV) (2019)
33. Zhu, Z., et al.: Aware loss with angular regularization for person re-identification. AAA I, 13114–13121 (2020)

34. Hou, R., Ma, B., Chang, H., Gu, X., Shan, S., Chen, X.: Interaction-and-aggregation network for person re-identification. In: Proceedings of the IEEE Conference on Computer Vision and Pattern Recognition, pp. 9317–9326 (2019)
35. Zheng, Z., Yang, X., Yu, Z., Zheng, L., Yang, Y., Kautz, J.: Joint discriminative and generative learning for person re-identification. In: Proceedings of the IEEE Conference on Computer Vision and Pattern Recognition, pp. 2138–2147 (2019)
36. Wang, G., Lai, J., Huang, P., Xie, X.: Spatial-temporal person re-identification. In: Proceedings of the AAAI Conference on Artificial Intelligence, vol. 33, pp. 8933–8940 (2019)
37. Quan, R., Dong, X., Wu, Y., Zhu, L., Yang, Y.: Auto-reid: searching for a part-aware convnet for person re-identification. In: Proceedings of the IEEE International Conference on Computer Vision, pp. 3750–3759 (2019)
38. Yang, W., Huang, H., Zhang, Z., Chen, X., Huang, K., Zhang, S.: Towards rich feature discovery with class activation maps augmentation for person re-identification. In: Proceedings of the IEEE Conference on Computer Vision and Pattern Recognition, pp. 1389–1398 (2019)
39. Zagoruyko, S., Komodakis, N.: Paying more attention to attention: Improving the performance of convolutional neural networks via attention transfer. arXiv preprint arXiv:1612.03928 (2016)

Class-Incremental Learning with Rectified Feature-Graph Preservation

Cheng-Hsun Lei, Yi-Hsin Chen, Wen-Hsiao Peng, and Wei-Chen Chiu$^{(\boxtimes)}$

National Chiao Tung University, Hsinchu, Taiwan
{raygoah.cs07g,yhchen.iie07g}@nctu.edu.tw, {wpeng,walon}@cs.nctu.edu.tw

Abstract. In this paper, we address the problem of distillation-based class-incremental learning with a single head. A central theme of this task is to learn new classes that arrive in sequential phases over time while keeping the model's capability of recognizing seen classes with only limited memory for preserving seen data samples. Many regularization strategies have been proposed to mitigate the phenomenon of catastrophic forgetting. To understand better the essence of these regularizations, we introduce a feature-graph preservation perspective. Insights into their merits and faults motivate our weighted-Euclidean regularization for old knowledge preservation. We further propose rectified cosine normalization and show how it can work with binary cross-entropy to increase class separation for effective learning of new classes. Experimental results on both CIFAR-100 and ImageNet datasets demonstrate that our method outperforms the state-of-the-art approaches in reducing classification error, easing catastrophic forgetting, and encouraging evenly balanced accuracy over different classes. Our project page is at : https://github.com/yhchen12101/FGP-ICL.

1 Introduction

Class-incremental learning [1] is a difficult yet practical problem for visual recognition models. The task requires the model with a single classification head to learn new classes that arrive sequentially while preserving its knowledge on the old ones. It is worth noting that class-incremental learning is different from task-incremental learning [2–6], which learns to handle multiple tasks (i.e. roups of classes, possibly from different datasets) given sequentially. In particular, task-incremental learning has a unique assumption that the task indices of classes are known during both training and test time. Thus, the model typically aims to learn a shared feature extractor across tasks under the multi-head setup (i.e. each task has its own head). Even though there are some works [3,7,8] addressing class-incremental learning from the perspective of task-incremental learning,

---

C.-H. Lei and Y.-H. Chen—Both authors contributed equally to the paper.

Electronic supplementary material The online version of this chapter (https://doi.org/10.1007/978-3-030-69544-6_22) contains supplementary material, which is available to authorized users.

H. Ishikawa et al. (Eds.): ACCV 2020, LNCS 12627, pp. 358–374, 2021.
https://doi.org/10.1007/978-3-030-69544-6_22

the differences stemmed from the aforementioned assumption clearly distinguish these works from typical class-incremental learning. This paper focuses on the more difficult yet practical setup to learn a single-head classifier without task identification.

Generally, class-incremental learning is faced with two major challenges: (1) the model needs to be updated on-the-fly upon the arrival of training data of new classes, and (2) there is only limited memory space (also known as experience reply buffer) for retaining partially the training data of previously learned classes. It is shown in [1] that naively fine-tuning the model on newly received training data of incoming classes without considering the previously learned classes often suffers from *catastrophic forgetting* [9]; that is, the classification accuracy on old classes may decline dramatically when the model attempts to learn new classes.

Several prior works based on deep learning models have been proposed to deal with catastrophic forgetting. They can roughly be categorized into three types: the parameter-based, distillation-based, and generative-model-based approaches. The parameter-based methods aim to restrict the update on network parameters that are highly sensitive to the recognition accuracy of old classes [2,3,10,11], and to conserve the usage of network parameters in learning new classes [12–14]. Identifying and regularizing those important network parameters can be prohibitively expensive, especially with large learning models. By contrast, the distillation-based methods leverage the idea of knowledge distillation [15], requiring that the model updated with the training data of new classes should produce similar predictions to the old model over the previously learned classes [1,4,16–21]. They typically need a divergence measure to be defined that measures the similarity between the old and new predictions. In particular, this class of methods is often influenced by the amount of data available in the experience reply buffer on which the similarity measurement is conducted. The generative-model-based methods replace the experience replay buffer with deep generative models [22], so that these generative models can later be utilized to generate synthetic training data for old classes while updating the model to learn new classes [23–25]. Obviously, their capacity for learning the distribution of old data crucially affects the quality of generated training data.

This work presents a new geometry-informed attempt at knowledge distillation for class-incremental learning. Instead of devising new divergences for similarity measurement, our work stresses preserving the geometric structure of the feature space. Specifically, we first (1) analyze the objectives used in the existing distillation-based algorithms from a *feature-graph preservation* perspective. By inspection of their merits and faults, we then (2) propose *weighted-Euclidean regularization* to preserve the knowledge of previously learned classes while providing enough flexibility for the model to learn new classes. Lastly, we (3) introduce *rectified cosine normalization* to learn discriminative feature representations, together with the objective of binary cross-entropy.

2   Related Work

Parameter-Based. Parameter-based methods attempt to identify the network parameters that have a profound impact on the classification accuracy of previously learned classes once altered. These important parameters are encouraged to be fixed during the incremental learning in order to resolve the issue of catastrophic forgetting (e.g.. MAS [2], EWC [3], SI [10], and RWalk [11]). Other works such as Rahaf *et al.* [12], Piggy-back [13], and Packnet [14] further advance freeing up the remaining parameters selectively in learning new classes. This is achieved by learning a weighting mask, pruning the network, or adding specifically-designed regularization. Because separate parts of the network can be activated for different tasks, parameter-based methods often find application in task-incremental learning. They however incur heavy computation in identifying and regularizing important network parameters.

Generative-Model-Based. Generative-model-based methods, such as [23–25], turn to generative models as a means of keeping the training data of old classes. Since the experience replay buffer has a limited size, the training data of previously learned classes can only be retrained partially. This leads to an imbalanced distribution of training data between the new and old classes. To overcome this issue, generative-model-based methods employ generative models to generate synthetic training data for old classes in the course of incremental learning. It is worth noting that the use, storage, and training of these generative models can cause a considerable complexity increase.

Distillation-Based. Knowledge distillation [15] is originally proposed to distill the knowledge from a teacher network (which is typically a network with larger capacity) and transfer it to a student network (which is a smaller network than the teacher), by encouraging the student to have a similar posterior distribution to the teacher's. This concept is adapted to preserve the model's knowledge of old classes for class-incremental learning. LwF [4] is the first work to apply knowledge distillation to incremental learning, introducing a modified cross-entropy loss function. **iCaRL** [1] uses binary cross-entropy as a new distillation loss, provides a mechanism for selecting old-class exemplars, and classifies images with the *nearest-mean-of-exemplars* criterion. Castro *et al.* [17] proposes a framework, termed **End-to-End** in this paper, that adopts the ordinary cross-entropy as the distillation loss in learning end-to-end the feature representation and the classifier. In particular, it introduces balanced fine-tuning as an extra training step to deal with the data imbalance between the old and new classes. **BIC** [20] proposes a bias correction method to address the data imbalance, achieving excellent accuracy on large datasets. **Hou19** [18] proposes several designs, including the cosine normalization, the less-forget constraint, and the inter-class separation, to encourage the classifier to treat old and new classes more uniformly. Based on **Hou19**'s training strategies, Liu *et al.* [21], termed **Mnemonics**, further optimize the parameterized exemplars by a bi-level optimization program. Both **Hou19** and **Mnemonics** rely on a well-pretrained feature extractor to obtain superior performance on incremental learning.

3 Proposed Method

This section presents our strategies – namely, weighted-Euclidean regularization and rectified cosine normalization – for dealing with catastrophic forgetting and effective new class learning in the scenario of class-incremental learning.

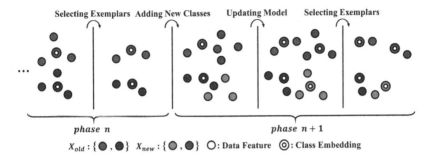

Fig. 1. Illustration of the class-incremental learning process: (1) selecting exemplars, (2) adding the data samples of new classes, and (3) updating the model.

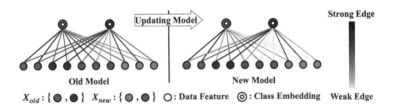

Fig. 2. Knowledge distillation from a bipartite feature-graph preservation perspective, with the bottom row and top row denoting the feature vectors of data samples and the class embeddings respectively. Minimizing the distillation loss is viewed as the structure (i.e. edge strength) preservation of such a bipartite graph during the model update.

Figure 1 illustrates the learning of data features and class embeddings (i.e. the classifier's weight vectors) from one incremental learning phase n to the next $n + 1$. As shown, the data of different classes arrive sequentially in different *phases*. We denote the old data that have arrived before phase $n + 1$ as X_{old} and the new data arriving in phase $n + 1$ as X_{new}. Assuming we already have a model capable of classifying the classes C_{old} in the X_{old}, we now aim to train the model to additionally learn the new classes C_{new} in X_{new}. However, there is limited memory for storing data samples; we can only preserve some exemplars chosen from the seen samples before phase $n + 1$. Thus, the training is based on the dataset $X_{all} = X_{new} \cup X_{exem}$, where X_{exem} is composed of the exemplars of C_{old} (i.e X_{exem} is a tiny subset of X_{old}) and the number of exemplars that can be kept is constrained by the memory size.

3.1   Mitigating Catastrophic Forgetting

To motivate the need for our weighted-Euclidean regularization, we introduce a feature-graph preservation perspective on knowledge distillation. This new perspective reveals the essence of existing distillation-based regularization schemes in how they tackle catastrophic forgetting and highlights the striking feature of our method.

Knowledge Distillation in Class-Incremental Learning. We begin by revisiting the prior works from iCaRL [1] and End-to-End [17]. To prevent class-incremental learning from catastrophic forgetting, both models introduce a distillation loss that requires the model after the gradient update (termed the *new* model) to produce a similar prediction on C_{old} to that made by the model before the update (termed the *old* model), for any data in X_{all}. In symbols, for a data sample $x_k \in X_{all}$, iCaRL [1] computes the distillation loss $\mathcal{L}_{dist\_bce}(x_k)$ to be the sum of the binary cross-entropy between the old prediction $p_{i|k}^*$ and the new prediction $p_{i|k}$ over different classes $i \in C_{old}$:

$$\mathcal{L}_{dist\_bce}(x_k) = \sum_{i \in C_{old}} \left\{ 1 \times \left[-p_{i|k}^* \log p_{i|k} - (1 - p_{i|k}^*) \log(1 - p_{i|k}) \right] \right\}, \quad (1)$$

where $p_{i|k} = \sigma(a_{i|k})$ is the sigmoid output of the activation $a_{i|k} = w_i^T f_k + b_i$ evaluated based on the new model, with w_i, b_i representing the weight vector and bias of the i-th classifier respectively, and f_k denoting the feature vector of x_k; and $p_{i|k}^* = \sigma(a_{i|k}^*)$ is computed similarly yet with the activation $a_{i|k}^* = w_i^{*T} f_k^* + b_i^*$ evaluated with the old model. In contrast, the Eq. (3) in the End-to-End [17] paper minimizes the KL-divergence[1] between $p_{i|k}^*$ and $p_{i|k}$ over $i \in C_{old}$ for preserving knowledge learned in previous phases:

$$\mathcal{L}_{dist\_KL}(x_k) = \sum_{i \in C_{old}} \left\{ p_{i|k}^* \times \left[\log p_{i|k}^* - \log p_{i|k} \right] \right\}, \quad (2)$$

where $p_{i|k} = softmax(a_{i|k})$ (respectively $p_{i|k}^* = softmax(a_{i|k}^*)$) is the softmax output of the activation $a_{i|k}/T$ (respectively, $a_{i|k}^*/T$) attenuated by a temperature parameter T.

Close examination of Eqs. (1) and (2) above suggests a more general distillation loss of the form

$$\mathcal{L}_{dist}(x_k) = \sum_{i \in C_{old}} \left\{ \gamma_{i|k} \times \mathcal{D}(p_{i|k}^*, p_{i|k}) \right\}, \quad (3)$$

with $\mathcal{D}(p_{i|k}^*, p_{i|k})$ measuring the discrepancy between the old and new predictions (i.e. $p_{i|k}^*$ and $p_{i|k}$) for class i, and $\gamma_{i|k}$ weighting the contribution of $\mathcal{D}(p_{i|k}^*, p_{i|k})$ to the resulting loss $\mathcal{L}_{dist}(x_k)$. Note that a non-zero discrepancy value $\mathcal{D}(p_{i|k}^*, p_{i|k})$, be it positive or negative, signals a change in the model's prediction. By Eq. (3),

---

[1] This amounts to minimizing the cross-entropy $\sum_i \{-p_{i|k}^* \times \log p_{i|k}\}$ between $p_{i|k}^*$ and $p_{i|k}$ over $i \in C_{old}$ since $p_{i|k}^*$ is not affected by the model update.

iCaRL [1] is seen to have $\gamma_{i|k} = 1$ and $\mathcal{D}(p_{i|k}^*, p_{i|k})$ the same as the binary cross-entropy between $p_{i|k}^*$ and $p_{i|k}$, while End-to-End [17] sets $\gamma_{i|k}$ and $\mathcal{D}(p_{i|k}^*, p_{i|k})$ to $p_{i|k}^*$ and $(\log p_{i|k}^* - \log p_{i|k})$, respectively.

Knowledge Distillation as Feature-Graph Preservation. A graph interpretation can help us understand better what we are observing from Eq. (3). We first note that Eq. (3) is to be optimized towards zero for all x_k in X_{all} and is concerned with the change in relations between the feature vector f_k of certain $x_k \in X_{all}$ and the class embeddings $w_i, \forall i \in C_{old}$. Their relations are seen to be quantified by $p_{i|k}$; specifically, the higher the value of $p_{i|k}$, the more strongly related the f_k and w_i is. This relationship, as depicted in Fig. 2, can be visualized as a bipartite graph, where the feature vectors f_k of all $x_k \in X_{all}$ form a set of vertices that is disjoint from another set of vertices comprising $w_i, i \in C_{old}$. The graph is bipartite because Eq. (3) does not concern the relations among vertices in each of these sets, and each f_k is connected to all the w_i with edge weights specified by $p_{i|k}$. We then view the optimization of the distillation loss over $x_k \in X_{all}$ towards zero as the structure preservation of such a bipartite graph when the learning progresses from one phase to another. This perspective is motivated by the fact that $\mathcal{D}(p_{i|k}^*, p_{i|k})$ in Eq. (3) reflects how the strength of an edge changes as a result of the model update in a learning phase. In particular, edge-adaptive preservation is achieved when $\gamma_{i|k}$ is assigned non-uniformly.

To shed light on the rationale of our design, we now delve deeper into iCaRL [1] and End-to-End [17] in terms of their edge weighting scheme $\gamma_{i|k}$, edge strength specification $p_{i|k}$, and edge discrepancy measure $\mathcal{D}(p_{i|k}^*, p_{i|k})$. First, iCaRL [1] applies equal weighting to all edges on the bipartite graph by having $\gamma_{i|k} = 1, \forall i, k$, suggesting that the strength of every edge should be preserved equally after the model update. In contrast, End-to-End [17] attaches more importance to stronger edges from the viewpoint of the old model by having $\gamma_{i|k} = p_{i|k}^*$. Second, using sigmoid activation in Eq. (1), iCaRL [1] evaluates the edge strength $p_{i|k}$ as a function of the similarity between f_k and w_i alone, whereas the softmax activation (cp. Eq. (2)) in End-to-End [17] renders $p_{i|k}$ dependent on the relative similarities between f_k and all the $w_i, i \in C_{old}$. As such, End-to-End [17] imposes the additional constraint $\sum_i \gamma_{i|k} = \sum_i p_{i|k}^* = 1$ on edge weighting, implying a dependent weighting scheme across edges connecting f_k and $w_i, i \in C_{old}$. Third, the discrepancy measure $\mathcal{D}(p_{i|k}^*, p_{i|k})$ involves $p_{i|k}^*$ and $p_{i|k}$, which in turn depends on the activations $a_{i|k}^*$ and $a_{i|k}$, respectively. These activations reflect explicitly the similarity, or the geometrical relation, between f_k and w_i in the feature space. When viewed as a function of $a_{i|k}$, the $\mathcal{D}(p_{i|k}^*, p_{i|k})$ in both iCaRL [1] and End-to-End [17] is non-symmetrical with respect to $a_{i|k}^*$; that is, the same deviation of $a_{i|k}$ from $a_{i|k}^*$ yet in different signs causes $\mathcal{D}(p_{i|k}^*, p_{i|k})$ to vary differently. This implies that their distillation losses may favor some non-symmetrical geometry variations in the feature space.

Weighted-Euclidean Regularization. In designing the distillation loss, we deviate from the divergence-based criterion to adopt a feature-graph preservation approach. This is motivated by our use of the nearest-mean-of-exemplars

364 C.-H. Lei et al.

classifier, which stresses the geometric structure of the feature space. From the above observations, we conjecture that good regularization for knowledge distillation in the feature space should possess three desirable properties, including (1) prioritized edge preservation, (2) independent edge strength specification, and (3) $a_{i|k}^*$-symmetric discrepancy measure. The first allows more flexibility in adapting feature learning to new classes while preserving old knowledge, by prioritizing stronger edges. The second dispenses with the constraint that $\sum_i \gamma_{i|k} = \sum_i p_{i|k}^* = 1$, since the sum-to-one constraint is essential to a cross-entropy interpretation in End-to-End [17], but is not necessary when $p_{i|k}^*$ is regarded as an edge weighting $\gamma_{i|k}$ from our feature-graph viewpoint. The third is to penalize equally the positive and negative deviation from $a_{i|k}^*$ for a geometrically-symmetric preservation of the graph in the feature space. To this end, our *weighted-Euclidean regularization* chooses $a_{i|k}, p_{i|k}, \gamma_{i|k}$ and $D(p_{i|k}^*, p_{i|k})$ to be

$$a_{i|k} = -\frac{\|\bar{w}_i - \bar{f}_k\|_2^2}{2}, \qquad p_{i|k} = \frac{1}{Z}\exp\{a_{i|k}\}, \qquad \gamma_{i|k} = p_{i|k}^*$$

$$D(p_{i|k}^*, p_{i|k}) = \left(\log p_{i|k}^* - \log p_{i|k}\right)^2 = \left(a_{i|k}^* - a_{i|k}\right)^2 \tag{4}$$

where $\bar{w}_i, \bar{f}_k$ are the class embedding and feature vector with rectified cosine normalization (in Sect. 3.2), Z is a normalization constant, and $a_{i|k}^*, p_{i|k}^*$ are the activation and edge strength evaluated with the old model. In particular, we choose the activation $a_{i|k} = -\|\bar{w}_i - \bar{f}_k\|_2^2/2$ to match the criterion of the nearest-mean-of-exemplars classification [1] at test time. It then follows from Eq. (3) that our distillation loss has a form of

$$\mathcal{L}_{dist\_wE}(x_k) = \sum_{i \in C_{old}} \left\{\exp(-\frac{\|\bar{w}_i^* - \bar{f}_k^*\|_2^2}{2}) \times \left(\|\bar{w}_i^* - \bar{f}_k^*\|_2^2 - \|\bar{w}_i - \bar{f}_k\|_2^2\right)^2\right\},$$

$$\tag{5}$$

where constant terms have been omitted for brevity. Extensive experiments in Sect. 4.3 validate the deceptively simple design of our distillation loss and confirms its superior performance to the seemingly more principled divergence-based methods (e.g.. End-to-End [17]).

3.2 Learning New Classes

Learning new classes in the context of incremental learning is often faced with data imbalance. Each new class usually has more training data than an old class since only a limited amount of old data can be stored (as exemplars in the memory). To address this issue, we adopt a two-pronged approach: (1) minimizing binary cross-entropy as the classification loss and (2) applying *rectified cosine normalization* to increase class separation in the feature space.

Classification Loss. In the literature [1,17,18], there are two main choices of the classification loss: cross-entropy and binary cross-entropy. The former is mostly used for multi-class classification while the latter is popular for multi-label classification. In the context of class-incremental learning (a kind of multi-class

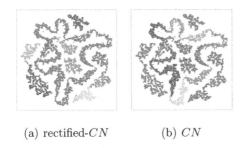

(a) rectified-CN (b) CN

Fig. 3. A toy example based on MNIST for showcasing the benefit of our rectified cosine normalization (denoted as rectified-CN) with respect to the typical cosine normalization (denoted as CN). The colorized dots in (**a**) (respectively (**b**)) are the t-SNE visualization of the feature representations for images of 10 digit classes, which are obtained from the classifier trained with adopting our rectified-CN (respectively CN); while the gray dots are the features from the classifier of using CN (respectively rectified-CN).

classification), the study in [18] shows that the model trained with cross-entropy tends to bias in favor of new classes by increasing their class embeddings w_i and bias terms b_i, to take advantage of the imbalanced data distribution for lower classification errors (i.e. the model would quickly adapt to new classes without being able to maintain well the knowledge of old classes). This is because cross-entropy adopts a softmax activation function, which determines the class prediction based on the *relative* strength of the class activations, thereby creating the aforementioned short cut. With the aim of achieving more evenly distributed classification accuracy, we choose the stricter binary cross-entropy to leverage its property that the activation of each class is weighted *absolutely* rather than *relatively* in determining the class prediction. In symbols, it is evaluated as

$$\mathcal{L}_{bce}(x_k) = - \sum_{i \in C_{all}} \left[\delta_{y_i = y_k} \log(\sigma(a_{i|k})) + \delta_{y_i \neq y_k} \log(1 - \sigma(a_{i|k})) \right], \quad (6)$$

where y_k is the label of the data sample x_k, $C_{all} = C_{old} \cup C_{new}$, and δ is an indicator function.

Rectified Cosine Normalization. In [18], they additionally adopt cosine normalization to address data imbalance by normalizing the class embedding w_i and the feature vector f_k in evaluating the activation $a_{i|k} = \bar{w}_i^T \bar{f}_k$, where $\bar{w}_i, \bar{f}_k$ are the normalized class embedding and feature vector. Here we further develop a *rectified cosine normalization* technique, which is empirically shown to encourage greater separation between incrementally-learned classes in the feature space than the typical cosine normalization. Our rectified cosine normalization is implemented by (1) augmenting, during training with Eq. (6), every class embedding w_i with a learnable bias b_i and every feature vector f_k with a constant 1 for separate normalization; and by (2) involving, at test time, only the feature vector f_k (without augmentation) in the nearest-mean-of-exemplars classification [1].

Step 1 gives rise to an *augmented feature space* of $W_i = (w_i, b_i)$ and $F_k = (f_k, 1)$, with the activation[2] evaluated as $a_{i|k} = \bar{W}_i^T \bar{F}_k$ where the bar indicates normalization.

Here we use MNIST dataset [26], which is composed of images of handwritten digits, to showcase the benefit of our rectified cosine normalization. We construct the classifier by a shallow network (including 2 convolutional layers followed by 3 fully connected layers with an output size of 3, which implies that the feature vector f is three-dimensional), and train it with whole 10 digit classes. Figure 3 shows the t-SNE visualization of the feature representations f learned from both the model variants of using our rectified cosine normalization and the typical cosine normalization. It is clear to see that our proposed normalization scheme better encourages the separation between classes. In Sect. 4.3, we present an ablation study to demonstrate the effectiveness of our rectified cosine normalization in improving incremental accuracy.

3.3   Objective Function

We combine the binary cross-entropy classification loss, rectified cosine normalization, and the weighted-Euclidean regularization to build our overall objective:

$$\mathcal{L}(\mathbf{x}) = \frac{1}{N} \sum_{k=1}^{N} (L_{bce}(x_k) + \lambda \mathcal{L}_{dist\_wE}(x_k)), \tag{7}$$

where $a_{i|k} = \bar{W}_i^T \bar{F}_k$ in $\mathcal{L}_{bce}(x_k)$, $\{x_1, x_2, \ldots, x_N\}$ is a mini-batch drawn from X_{all}, and λ is the hyper-parameter used to balance $\mathcal{L}_{bce}$ against $\mathcal{L}_{dist\_wE}$. Inspired by [27], we choose λ as follows in recognizing that: in the early stages of incremental learning, when the relative size of old classes to new classes is small, the weighted-Euclidean regularization should be de-emphasized as the feature extractor may not be well learned yet. Note that the ratio $|C_{old}|/|C_{all}|$ is updated constantly along the incremental learning process.

$$\lambda = \lambda_{base} \sqrt{\frac{|C_{old}|}{|C_{all}|}}, \tag{8}$$

where $\lambda_{base} = 0.1$ is set empirically.

4   Experimental Results

Datasets and Baselines. We follow the same experiment protocol as prior works. Two datasets, CIFAR-100 [28] and ImageNet [29] with 100 classes selected randomly, are used for experiments. The data samples of these 100 classes comprise a data stream that arrives in a class-incremental manner in 10 phases, each

---

[2] This activation is to be distinguished from the one $a_{i|k} = -\|\bar{w}_i - \bar{f}_k\|_2^2 / 2$ for weighted-Euclidean regularization.

adding 10 new classes to those already received in previous phases. Particularly, we adopt two training scenarios. One is to train the model from scratch, i.e. the model starts with random initialization and learns 100 classes incrementally. The other follows [18] to train the model with the first 50 classes in order to have a reasonably good feature extractor to begin with. Then the remaining 50 classes are split evenly and learned in 5 sequential phases. The baselines include iCaRL [1], End-to-End [17], BIC [20], Hou19 [18], and Mnemonics [21].

Metrics. The evaluation basically adopts the same common metrics used in prior works, including incremental accuracy and average incremental accuracy [1,17,18]. Additionally, we introduce phase accuracy. *Incremental accuracy* [17], also known simply as accuracy in [1], is the accuracy for classifying all the seen classes at the end of each training phase. It is the most commonly used metric but has the limitation of showing only one single accuracy value over the seen classes as a whole without giving any detail of how the model performs on separate groups of classes (learned incrementally in each phase). *Average incremental accuracy* simply takes the average of the incremental accuracy values obtained from the first training phase up to the current phase. The results are given in parentheses for the last phase in Fig. 4. *Phase accuracy* is evaluated at the end of the entire incremental training to present the average classification accuracy on separate groups of classes, where each group includes several classes that are added into the training at the same phase. It provides a breakdown look at whether the model would favor some groups of classes over the others as a consequence of catastrophic forgetting.

Implementation Details. For a fair comparison, we follow the baselines to use a 32-layer (respectively, 18-layer) ResNet [30] as the feature extractor for CIFAR-100 (respectively, ImageNet), and a fully connected layer as the linear classifier. In particular, we remove the last ReLU layer for rectified cosine normalization. The memory size is fixed at 1000 or 2000, and the exemplars of old classes are chosen by the herd selection [31] proposed in iCaRL [1]. At test time, we apply the same *nearest-mean-of-exemplars* classification strategy as iCaRL.

4.1 Incremental Accuracy Comparison

Figure 4 presents incremental accuracy against the number of classes learned over the course of incremental learning, while Table 1 summarizes the results at the end of the entire training. Notice that we use five random orderings of classes to build up class-incremental phases, where the metrics are evaluated and averaged over these five orderings. Please also note that the figures showing the experimental results are better viewed in color and zoomed in for details.

We see that on CIFAR-100, when learning from scratch, our model outperforms all the baselines in almost every training phase, showing a significant boost in incremental accuracy especially with memory size 1000. In comparison, the recent state-of-the-arts from Hou19 [18] and Mnemonics [21] perform significantly worse as they rely heavily on a well-learned feature extractor (which is hard to obtain while being trained from scratch). When starting from 50 classes, ours performs the best with memory size 1000, and comparably to both Hou19 [18] and Mnemonics [21] with memory size 2000. Furthermore, our model shows higher average incremental accuracy than the baselines in nearly every setting, as shown in parentheses in Fig. 4. On ImageNet, our model performs comparably to End-to-End [17] and BIC [20] when learning from scratch with $M = 2K$ and is superior to the competing methods by a large margin when learning from 50 classes. To sum up, our method shows consistently higher incremental accuracy than the other baselines on different datasets with varied characteristics.

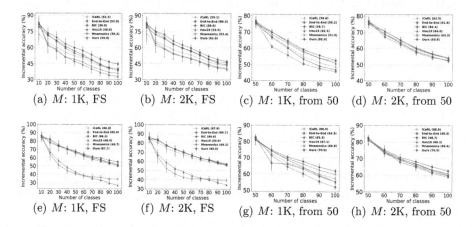

Fig. 4. Incremental accuracy on CIFAR-100 (top row) and ImageNet (bottom row), for memory sizes $M = 1K, 2K$ and training scenarios "FS" and "from 50". Average incremental accuracy of each method is shown in parentheses.

Table 1. Comparison of incremental accuracy at the end of training

Training scenario	from scratch				from 50 classes			
Dataset	CIFAR		ImageNet		CIFAR		ImageNet	
Memory size	1K	2K	1K	2K	1K	2K	1K	2K
iCaRL [1]	38.8	43.1	52.9	55.5	48.5	52.4	57.2	60.7
End-to-End [17]	40.0	46.0	50.4	56.7	45.8	53.0	52.1	58.9
BIC [20]	38.6	44.0	51.5	56.1	46.9	52.4	55.3	59.7
Hou19 [18]	32.7	39.9	27.1	34.4	51.0	**54.5**	55.2	60.1
Mnemonics [21]	35.9	40.9	34.6	39.4	52.0	54.2	59.8	61.0
Ours	**44.7**	**47.2**	**55.1**	**57.0**	**52.8**	54.0	**61.9**	**62.6**

4.2   Phase Accuracy Comparison

Fig. 5 presents the phase accuracy for different methods to compare their effectiveness in preserving knowledge of old classes. Generally, balanced phase accuracy is desirable. It is important to point out that there is a fundamental trade-off between incremental accuracy and phase accuracy. For a fair comparison, we particularly choose the training scenario "from 50", where the baselines perform more closely to our method in terms of incremental accuracy evaluated at the end of the entire training. Shown in parentheses is the mean absolute deviation from the average of each method's phase accuracy. The smaller the deviation, the more balanced the classification accuracy is in different training phases.

Our scheme is shown to achieve the minimum mean absolute deviation in phase accuracy on CIFAR-100 and ImageNet. Remarkably, among all the baselines, Hou19 [18] and Mnemonics [21] have the closest incremental accuracy to ours, yet with considerable variations in phase accuracy.

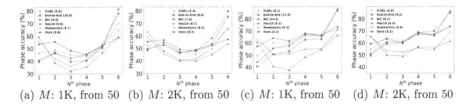

(a) M: 1K, from 50   (b) M: 2K, from 50   (c) M: 1K, from 50   (d) M: 2K, from 50

Fig. 5. Phase accuracy comparison: (a) (b) are results on CIFAR-100 and (c) (d) on ImageNet. M is the memory size, and the model is pre-trained with 50 classes. The mean absolute deviation in phase accuracy is shown in parentheses.

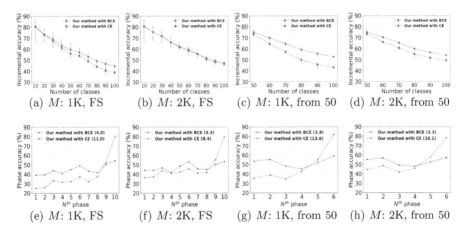

(a) M: 1K, FS   (b) M: 2K, FS   (c) M: 1K, from 50   (d) M: 2K, from 50

(e) M: 1K, FS   (f) M: 2K, FS   (g) M: 1K, from 50   (h) M: 2K, from 50

Fig. 6. Comparison of binary cross-entropy and cross-entropy as the classification loss on CIFAR-100 for memory sizes $M = 1K, 2K$ and training scenarios "FS" and "from 50". The results are evaluated in terms of incremental accuracy. The bars are evaluated by five random orderings of classes.

4.3 Ablation Studies

Binary Cross-entropy (BCE) versus Cross-entropy (CE) as Classification Loss. We observe the performance differences by replacing BCE in our method with CE while keeping the other aspects (including rectified cosine normalization and weighted-Euclidean regularization) untouched. Figure 6 shows that BCE achieves consistently higher incremental accuracy than CE under all the settings. Moreover, BCE presents more evenly balanced phase accuracy whereas CE displays a tendency of biasing towards those new classes in the last phase.

How Effective is Rectified Cosine Normalization in Improving Incremental Accuracy? Fig. 7 presents results comparing rectified cosine normalization against cosine normalization in terms of incremental accuracy. Recall that rectified cosine normalization is proposed as a means to increase class separation and thus classification accuracy. To see the performance differences, we train a variant of our method by replacing solely rectified cosine normalization with cosine normalization (while keeping the other aspects the same). From Fig. 7, our rectified cosine normalization starts with similar incremental accuracy to cosine normalization in early phases and gradually develops higher accuracy along the incremental learning process, which validates our analysis in Sect. 3.2.

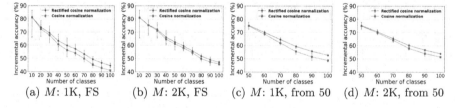

(a) M: 1K, FS   (b) M: 2K, FS   (c) M: 1K, from 50   (d) M: 2K, from 50

Fig. 7. Comparison between rectified cosine normalization and cosine normalization on CIFAR-100 in terms of incremental accuracy, for memory sizes $M = 1K, 2K$ and training scenarios "FS" and "from 50".

Efficacy of Weighted-Euclidean Regularization in Balancing New Class Learning and Old Knowledge Preservation. Fig. 8 compares our weighted-Euclidean regularization $\mathcal{L}_{dist\_wE}$ with various distillation losses (see Sect. 3.1 for $\mathcal{L}_{dist\_bce}$ and $\mathcal{L}_{dist\_KL}$, and Hou19 [18] for L_{dis}^{G}) by examining their trade-offs between incremental and phase accuracy. These variants are tested on the same base model of using BCE and rectified cosine normalization. We see that weighted-Euclidean regularization achieves higher incremental accuracy among the competing methods, and shows lowest or the second-lowest mean absolute deviation (MAD) in phase accuracy in most cases (cf. training all classes together in batch mode leads to 2.5 MAD in phase accuracy). These suggest that our weighted-Euclidean regularization enables the model to strike a better balance between new class learning and old knowledge preservation.

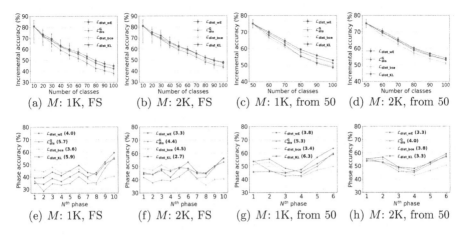

(a) M: 1K, FS   (b) M: 2K, FS   (c) M: 1K, from 50   (d) M: 2K, from 50

(e) M: 1K, FS   (f) M: 2K, FS   (g) M: 1K, from 50   (h) M: 2K, from 50

Fig. 8. Comparison of various distillation losses on CIFAR-100, for memory sizes $M = 1K, 2K$ and training scenarios "FS" and "from 50", with the mean absolute deviation in phase accuracy shown in parentheses.

Uniform vs. Non-uniform $\gamma_{i|k}$ Assignment. This experiment investigates the sole benefits of prioritized edge preservation (i.e. non-uniform assignment of $\gamma_{i|k}$) in our weighted-Euclidean regularization. We construct a variant of our method by setting $\gamma_{i|k}$ in Eq. (4) to 1 and observe the performance differences. As shown in Fig. 9, the non-uniform assignment of $\gamma_{i|k}$ in our scheme leads to higher incremental accuracy and lower mean absolute deviations in phase accuracy.

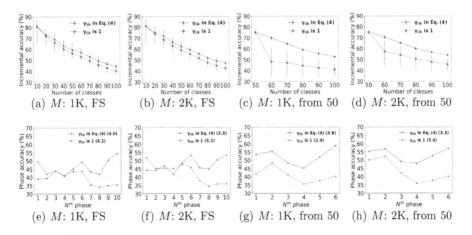

(a) M: 1K, FS   (b) M: 2K, FS   (c) M: 1K, from 50   (d) M: 2K, from 50

(e) M: 1K, FS   (f) M: 2K, FS   (g) M: 1K, from 50   (h) M: 2K, from 50

Fig. 9. Comparison of uniform versus non-uniform $\gamma_{i|k}$ assignment on CIFAR-100 for memory sizes $M = 1K, 2K$ and training scenario "FS" and "from 50," with the mean absolute deviation in phase accuracy (the bottom row) shown in parentheses. The bars in the top row are evaluated by five random orderings of classes.

In addition, the smaller variations in incremental accuracy (cp. the bars in the top row of Fig. 9) suggest that our method with prioritized edge preservation is less sensitive to the learning order of object classes.

5   Conclusion

We introduce a feature-graph preservation perspective to study the essence of various knowledge distillation techniques in how they preserve the structure of the feature graph along the phases of class-incremental learning. Developed based on three desirable properties, our weighted-Euclidean regularization is shown to benefit the balance between new class learning and old knowledge preservation. Furthermore, our rectified cosine normalization effectively improves incremental accuracy due to greater class separation. With all the techniques combined, our model consistently outperforms the state-of-the-art baselines on CIFAR-100 and ImageNet datasets.

References

1. Rebuffi, S.A., Kolesnikov, A., Sperl, G., Lampert, C.H.: ICARL: incremental classifier and representation learning. In: IEEE Conference on Computer Vision and Pattern Recognition (CVPR) (2017)
2. Aljundi, R., Babiloni, F., Elhoseiny, M., Rohrbach, M., Tuytelaars, T.: Memory aware synapses: learning what (not) to forget. In: Ferrari, V., Hebert, M., Sminchisescu, C., Weiss, Y. (eds.) ECCV 2018. LNCS, vol. 11207, pp. 144–161. Springer, Cham (2018). https://doi.org/10.1007/978-3-030-01219-9_9
3. Kirkpatrick, J., et al.: Overcoming catastrophic forgetting in neural networks. In: Proceedings of the National Academy of Sciences (PNAS) (2017)
4. Li, Z., Hoiem, D.: Learning without forgetting. IEEE Trans. Pattern Anal. Mach. Intell. (TPAMI) **40**, 2935–2947 (2017)
5. Hou, S., Pan, X., Loy, C.C., Wang, Z., Lin, D.: Lifelong learning via progressive distillation and retrospection. In: Ferrari, V., Hebert, M., Sminchisescu, C., Weiss, Y. (eds.) ECCV 2018. LNCS, vol. 11207, pp. 452–467. Springer, Cham (2018). https://doi.org/10.1007/978-3-030-01219-9_27
6. Aljundi, R., Chakravarty, P., Tuytelaars, T.: Expert gate: lifelong learning with a network of experts. In: IEEE Conference on Computer Vision and Pattern Recognition (CVPR) (2017)
7. Lopez-Paz, D., Ranzato, M.: Gradient episodic memory for continual learning. In: Advances in Neural Information Processing Systems (NIPS) (2017)
8. Chaudhry, A., Ranzato, M., Rohrbach, M., Elhoseiny, M.: Efficient lifelong learning with a-gem. In: International Conference on Learning Representations (ICLR) (2019)
9. McCloskey, M., Cohen, N.J.: Catastrophic interference in connectionist networks: the sequential learning problem. In: Psychology of Learning and Motivation (1989)
10. Zenke, F., Poole, B., Ganguli, S.: Continual learning through synaptic intelligence. In: International Conference on Machine Learning (ICML) (2017)

11. Chaudhry, A., Dokania, P.K., Ajanthan, T., Torr, P.H.S.: Riemannian walk for incremental learning: understanding forgetting and intransigence. In: Ferrari, V., Hebert, M., Sminchisescu, C., Weiss, Y. (eds.) ECCV 2018. LNCS, vol. 11215, pp. 556–572. Springer, Cham (2018). https://doi.org/10.1007/978-3-030-01252-6_33
12. Aljundi, R., Rohrbach, M., Tuytelaars, T.: Selfless sequential learning. In: International Conference on Learning Representations (ICLR) (2019)
13. Mallya, A., Davis, D., Lazebnik, S.: Piggyback: adapting a single network to multiple tasks by learning to mask weights. In: Ferrari, V., Hebert, M., Sminchisescu, C., Weiss, Y. (eds.) ECCV 2018. LNCS, vol. 11208, pp. 72–88. Springer, Cham (2018). https://doi.org/10.1007/978-3-030-01225-0_5
14. Mallya, A., Lazebnik, S.: Packnet: adding multiple tasks to a single network by iterative pruning. In: IEEE Conference on Computer Vision and Pattern Recognition (CVPR) (2018)
15. Hinton, G., Vinyals, O., Dean, J.: Distilling the knowledge in a neural network. In: NIPS Workshop on Deep Learning and Representation Learning (2014)
16. Belouadah, E., Popescu, A.: DeeSIL: deep-shallow incremental learning. In: Leal-Taixé, L., Roth, S. (eds.) ECCV 2018. LNCS, vol. 11130, pp. 151–157. Springer, Cham (2019). https://doi.org/10.1007/978-3-030-11012-3_11
17. Castro, F.M., Marín-Jiménez, M.J., Guil, N., Schmid, C., Alahari, K.: End-to-end incremental learning. In: Ferrari, V., Hebert, M., Sminchisescu, C., Weiss, Y. (eds.) ECCV 2018. LNCS, vol. 11216, pp. 241–257. Springer, Cham (2018). https://doi.org/10.1007/978-3-030-01258-8_15
18. Hou, S., Pan, X., Loy, C.C., Wang, Z., Lin, D.: Learning a unified classifier incrementally via rebalancing. In: IEEE Conference on Computer Vision and Pattern Recognition (CVPR) (2019)
19. Jung, H., Ju, J., Jung, M., Kim, J.: Less-forgetful learning for domain expansion in deep neural networks. In: AAAI Conference on Artificial Intelligence (AAAI) (2018)
20. Wu, Y., Chen, Y., Wang, L., Ye, Y., Liu, Z., Guo, Y., Fu, Y.: Large scale incremental learning. In: IEEE Conference on Computer Vision and Pattern Recognition (CVPR) (2019)
21. Liu, Y., Su, Y., Liu, A.A., Schiele, B., Sun, Q.: Mnemonics training: multi-class incremental learning without forgetting. In: IEEE Conference on Computer Vision and Pattern Recognition (CVPR) (2020)
22. Goodfellow, I., et al.: Generative adversarial nets. In: Advances in Neural Information Processing Systems (NIPS) (2014)
23. Shin, H., Lee, J.K., Kim, J., Kim, J.: Continual learning with deep generative replay. In: Advances in Neural Information Processing Systems (NIPS) (2017)
24. He, C., Wang, R., Shan, S., Chen, X.: Exemplar-supported generative reproduction for class incremental learning. In: British Machine Vision Conference (BMVC) (2018)
25. Ostapenko, O., Puscas, M., Klein, T., Jahnichen, P., Nabi, M.: Learning to remember: a synaptic plasticity driven framework for continual learning. In: IEEE Conference on Computer Vision and Pattern Recognition (CVPR) (2019)
26. LeCun, Y., Bottou, L., Bengio, Y., Haffner, P.: Gradient-based learning applied to document recognition. Proc. IEEE **86**, 2278–2324 (1998)
27. Taitelbaum, H., Ben-Reuven, E., Goldberger, J.: Adding new classes without access to the original training data with applications to language identification. In: Annual Conference of the International Speech Communication Association (INTERSPEECH) (2018)

28. Krizhevsky, A.: Learning multiple layers of features from tiny images. Technical report (2009)
29. Deng, J., Dong, W., Socher, R., Li, L.J., Li, K., Fei-Fei, L.: Imagenet: a large-scale hierarchical image database. In: IEEE Conference on Computer Vision and Pattern Recognition (CVPR) (2009)
30. He, K., Zhang, X., Ren, S., Sun, J.: Deep residual learning for image recognition. In: IEEE Conference on Computer Vision and Pattern Recognition (CVPR) (2016)
31. Welling, M.: Herding dynamical weights to learn. In: International Conference on Machine Learning (ICML) (2009)

Patch SVDD: Patch-Level SVDD for Anomaly Detection and Segmentation

Jihun Yi🆔 and Sungroh Yoon$^{(\boxtimes)}$🆔

Data Science and Artificial Intelligence Laboratory Electrical and Computer
Engineering, Seoul National University, Seoul, South Korea
{t080205,sryoon}@snu.ac.kr

Abstract. In this paper, we address the problem of image anomaly
detection and segmentation. Anomaly detection involves making a binary
decision as to whether an input image contains an anomaly, and anomaly
segmentation aims to locate the anomaly on the pixel level. Support vector data description (SVDD) is a long-standing algorithm used for an
anomaly detection, and we extend its deep learning variant to the patch-
based method using self-supervised learning. This extension enables
anomaly segmentation and improves detection performance. As a result,
anomaly detection and segmentation performances measured in AUROC
on MVTec AD dataset increased by 9.8% and 7.0%, respectively, compared to the previous state-of-the-art methods. Our results indicate the
efficacy of the proposed method and its potential for industrial application. Detailed analysis of the proposed method offers insights regarding its behavior, and the code is available online (https://github.com/
nuclearboy95/Anomaly-Detection-PatchSVDD-PyTorch).

1 Introduction

Anomaly detection is a binary classification problem to determine whether an
input contains an anomaly. Detecting anomalies is a critical and long-standing
problem faced by the manufacturing industry. Anomaly detection is usually formulated as a one-class classification because abnormal examples are either inac-
cessible or insufficient to model distribution during the training. When concentrating on image data, detected anomalies can also be localized, and anomaly
segmentation problem is to localize the anomalies at the pixel level. In this study,
we tackle the problems of image anomaly detection and segmentation.

One-class support vector machine (OC-SVM) [1] and support vector data
description (SVDD) [2] are classic algorithms used for one-class classification.
Given a kernel function, OC-SVM seeks a max-margin hyperplane from the
origin in the kernel space. Likewise, SVDD searches for a data-enclosing hypersphere in the kernel space. These approaches are closely related, and Vert et al. [3]
showed their equivalence in the case of a Gaussian kernel. Ruff et al. [4] proposed a deep learning variant of SVDD, Deep SVDD, by deploying a deep neural

Electronic supplementary material The online version of this chapter (https://
doi.org/10.1007/978-3-030-69544-6_23) contains supplementary material, which is
available to authorized users.

H. Ishikawa et al. (Eds.): ACCV 2020, LNCS 12627, pp. 375–390, 2021.
https://doi.org/10.1007/978-3-030-69544-6_23

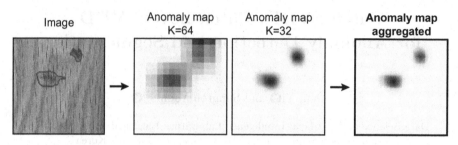

Fig. 1. Proposed method localizes defects in an MVTec AD [8] **image.** Patch SVDD performs multi-scale inspection and combines the results. As a result, the anomaly map pinpoints the defects (contoured with a red line). (Color figure online)

network in the place of the kernel function. The neural network was trained to extract a data-dependent representation, removing the need to choose an appropriate kernel function by hand. Furthermore, Ruff et al. [5] re-interpreted Deep SVDD in an information-theoretic perspective and applied to semi-supervised scenarios.

In this paper, we extend Deep SVDD to a patch-wise detection method, thereby proposing Patch SVDD. This extension is rendered nontrivial by the relatively high level of intra-class variation of the patches and is facilitated by self-supervised learning. The proposed method enables anomaly segmentation and improves anomaly detection performance. Figure 1 shows an example of the localized anomalies using the proposed method. In addition, the results in previous studies [6,7] show that the features of a randomly initialized encoder might be used to distinguish anomalies. We detail the more in-depth behavior of random encoders and investigate the source of separability in the random features.

2   Background

2.1   Anomaly Detection and Segmentation

Problem Formulation. Anomaly detection is a problem to make a binary decision whether an input is an anomaly or not. The definition of *anomaly* ranges from a tiny defect to an out-of-distribution image. We focus here on detecting a defect in an image. A typical detection method involves training a scoring function, $\mathcal{A}_\theta$, which measures the abnormality of an input. At test time, inputs with high $\mathcal{A}_\theta(\mathbf{x})$ values are deemed to be an anomaly. A *de facto* standard metric for evaluating the scoring function is the area under the receiver operating characteristic curve (AUROC), as expressed in Eq. 1 [9].

$$\text{AUROC}\left[\mathcal{A}_\theta\right] = \mathbb{P}\left[\mathcal{A}_\theta(\mathbf{X}_{\text{normal}}) < \mathcal{A}_\theta(\mathbf{X}_{\text{abnormal}})\right]. \tag{1}$$

A good scoring function is, thus, one that assigns a low anomaly score to normal data and a high anomaly score to abnormal data. Anomaly segmentation

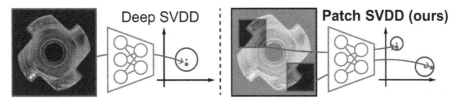

Fig. 2. Comparison of Deep SVDD [4] and the proposed method. Patch SVDD performs inspection on every patch to localize a defect. In addition, the self-supervised learning allows the features to form multi-modal clusters, thereby enhancing anomaly detection capability. The image is from MVTec AD [8] dataset.

problem is similarly formulated; anomaly score is estimated for each pixel (i.e., an anomaly map), and AUROC is measured using the pixels.

Auto Encoder-Based Methods. Early deep learning approaches to anomaly detection used auto encoders [10–12]. These auto encoders were trained with the normal training data and did not provide accurate reconstruction of abnormal images. Therefore, the difference between the reconstruction and the input indicated abnormality. Further variants have been proposed to utilize structural similarity indices [13], adversarial training [11], negative mining [12], and iterative projection [14]. Certain previous works utilized the learned latent feature of the auto encoder for anomaly detection. Akcay et al. [15] defined the reconstruction loss of the latent feature as an anomaly score, and Yarlagadda et al. [16] trained OC-SVM [1] using the latent features. More recently, several methods have made use of factors other than reconstruction loss, such as restoration loss [17] and an attention map [18].

Classifier-Based Methods. After the work of Golan et al. [19], discriminative approaches have been proposed for anomaly detection. These methods exploit an observation that classifiers lose their confidence [20] for the abnormal input images. Given an unlabeled dataset, a classifier is trained to predict synthetic labels. For example, Golan et al. [19] randomly flip, rotate, and translate an image, and the classifier is trained to predict the particular type of transformation performed. If the classifier does not provide a confident and correct prediction, the input image is deemed to be abnormal. Wang et al. [21] proved that such an approach could be extended to an unsupervised scenario, where the training data also contains a few anomalies. Bergman et al. [22] adopted an open-set classification method and generalized the method to include non-image data.

SVDD-based Methods. SVDD [2] is a classic one-class classification algorithm. It maps all the normal training data into a predefined kernel space and seeks the smallest hypersphere that encloses the data in the kernel space. The anomalies are expected to be located outside the learned hypersphere. As a kernel function deter-

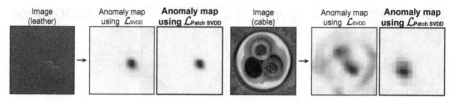

Fig. 3. Comparison of anomaly maps generated using two different losses. For a relatively simple image (leather), the encoders trained with either $\mathcal{L}_{SVDD}$ or $\mathcal{L}_{Patch\ SVDD}$ both localize the defect (contoured with a red line) well. By contrast, when the image has high complexity (cable), $\mathcal{L}_{SVDD}$ fails to localize the defect. The image is from MVTec AD [8] dataset. (Color figure online)

mines the kernel space, the training procedure is merely deciding the radius and center of the hypersphere.

Ruff et al. [4] improved this approach using a deep neural network. They adopted the neural network in place of the kernel function and trained it along with the radius of the hypersphere. This modification allows the encoder to learn a data-dependent transformation, thus enhancing detection performance on high-dimensional and structured data. Ruff et al. [5] further applied this method to a semi-supervised scenario.

2.2   Self-supervised Representation Learning

Learning a representation of an image is a core problem of computer vision. A series of methods have been proposed to learn a representation of an image without annotation. One branch of research suggests training the encoder by learning with a *pretext task*, which is a self-labeled task to provide synthetic learning signals. When a network is trained to solve the pretext task well, the network is expected to be able to extract useful features. The pretext tasks include predicting relative patch location [6], solving a jigsaw puzzle [23], colorizing images [24], counting objects [25], and predicting rotations [26].

3   Methods

3.1   Patch-Wise Deep SVDD

Deep SVDD [4] trains an encoder that maps the entire training data to features lying within a small hypersphere in the feature space. The authors trained the encoder, f_θ, to minimize the Euclidean distances between the features and the center of the hypersphere using the following loss function:

$$\mathcal{L}_{SVDD} = \sum_{i}^{N} \|f_\theta(\mathbf{x}_i) - \mathbf{c}\|_2 , \tag{2}$$

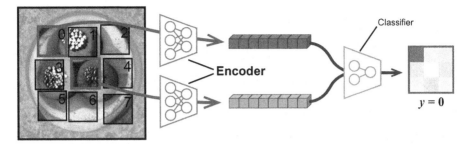

Fig. 4. Self-supervised learning [6]. The encoder is trained to extract informative features so that the following classifier can correctly predict the relative positions of the patches. Once the training is complete, the classifier is discarded. Note that the two encoders share their weights, as in Siamese Network [27]. The image is from MVTec AD [8] dataset.

where $\mathbf{x}$ is an input image, i is a data index, and N denotes the number of the training data. At test time, the distance between the representation of the input and the center is used as an anomaly score. The center $\mathbf{c}$ is calculated in advance of the training, as shown in Eq. 3. Therefore, the training pushes the features around a single center. Note that the authors removed the bias terms in the network to avoid a trivial solution (i.e., the encoder outputs a constant).

$$\mathbf{c} \doteq \frac{1}{N} \sum_{i}^{N} f_{\theta}^{\mathrm{untrained}}(\mathbf{x}_i). \tag{3}$$

In this study, we extend this approach to patches; the encoder encodes each patch, not the entire image, as illustrated in Fig. 2. Accordingly, inspection is performed for each patch. Patch-wise inspection has several advantages. First, the inspection result is available at each position, and hence we can localize the positions of defects. Second, such fine-grained examination improves overall detection performance.

A direct extension of Deep SVDD [4] to a patch-wise inspection is straightforward. A patch encoder, f_{θ}, is trained using $\mathcal{L}_{\mathrm{SVDD}}$ with $\mathbf{x}$ replaced with a patch, $\mathbf{p}$. The anomaly score is defined accordingly, and the examples of the resulting anomaly maps are provided in Fig. 3. Unfortunately, the detection performance is poor for the images with high complexity. This is because patches have high intra-class variation; some patches correspond to the background, while the others may contain the object. As a result, mapping all the features of dissimilar patches to a single center and imposing a uni-modal cluster weaken the connection between the representation and the content. Therefore, using a single center $\mathbf{c}$ is inappropriate, yet deciding on the appropriate number of multiple centers and the allocation of patches to each center are cumbersome.

To bypass the above issues, we do not explicitly define the centers and allocate the patches. Instead, we train the encoder to gather semantically similar patches by itself. The semantically similar patches are obtained by sampling spatially

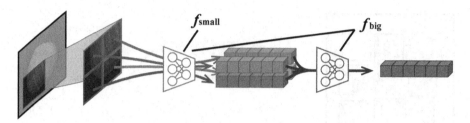

Fig. 5. Hierarchical encoding. An input patch is divided into a 2×2 grid of sub-patches, and the sub-patches are independently encoded using the smaller encoder (f_{small}). The output features are aggregated to produce a single feature. The image is from MVTec AD [8] dataset.

adjacent patches, and the encoder is trained to minimize the distances between their features using the following loss function:

$$\mathcal{L}_{\text{SVDD}'} = \sum_{i,i'} \| f_\theta(\mathbf{p}_i) - f_\theta(\mathbf{p}_{i'}) \|_2 , \tag{4}$$

where $\mathbf{p}_{i'}$ is a spatially jittered $\mathbf{p}_i$. Furthermore, to enforce the representation to capture the semantics of the patch, we add the following self-supervised learning.

3.2 Self-supervised Learning

Doersch et al. [6] trained an encoder and classifier pair to predict the relative positions of two patches, as depicted in Fig. 4. A well-performing pair implies that the trained encoder extracts useful features for location prediction. Aside from this particular task, previous research [23,26,28] reported that the self-supervised encoder functions as a powerful feature extractor for downstream tasks.

For a randomly sampled patch $\mathbf{p}_1$, Doersch et al. [6] sampled another patch $\mathbf{p}_2$ from one of its eight neighborhoods in a 3×3 grid. If we let the true relative position be $y \in \{0, ..., 7\}$, the classifier C_ϕ is trained to predict the position correctly; i.e., $y = C_\phi(f_\theta(\mathbf{p}_1), f_\theta(\mathbf{p}_2))$. The size of the patch is the same as the receptive field of the encoder. To prevent the classifier from exploiting short-cuts [7] (e.g., color aberration), we randomly perturb the RGB channels of the patches. Following the approach by Doersch et al. [6], we add a self-supervised learning signal by adding the following loss term:

$$\mathcal{L}_{\text{SSL}} = \texttt{Cross-entropy}\left(y, C_\phi\left(f_\theta(\mathbf{p}_1), f_\theta(\mathbf{p}_2)\right)\right). \tag{5}$$

As a result, the encoder is trained using a combination of two losses with the scaling hyperparameter λ, as presented in Eq. 6. This optimization is performed using stochastic gradient descent and Adam optimizer [29].

$$\mathcal{L}_{\text{Patch SVDD}} = \lambda \mathcal{L}_{\text{SVDD}'} + \mathcal{L}_{\text{SSL}}. \tag{6}$$

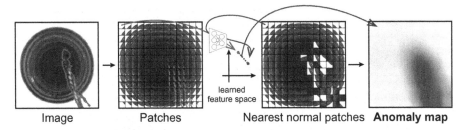

| Image | Patches | Nearest normal patches | **Anomaly map** |

Fig. 6. Overall flow of the proposed method. For a given test image, Patch SVDD divides the image into patches of size K with strides S and extracts their features using the trained encoder. The L2 distance to the nearest normal patch in the feature space becomes the anomaly score of each patch. The resulting anomaly map localizes the defects (contoured with a red line). The image is from MVTec AD [8] dataset. (Color figure online)

3.3 Hierarchical Encoding

As anomalies vary in size, deploying multiple encoders with various receptive fields helps in dealing with variation in size. The experimental results in Sect. 4.2 show that enforcing a hierarchical structure on the encoder boosts anomaly detection performance as well. For this reason, we employ a hierarchical encoder that embodies a smaller encoder; the hierarchical encoder is defined as

$$f_{\text{big}}(\mathbf{p}) = g_{\text{big}}(f_{\text{small}}(\mathbf{p})). \tag{7}$$

An input patch $\mathbf{p}$ is divided into a 2×2 grid, and their features are aggregated to constitute the feature of $\mathbf{p}$, as shown in Fig. 5. Each encoder with receptive field size K is trained with the self-supervised task of patch size K. Throughout the experiment, the receptive field sizes of the large and small encoders are set to 64 and 32, respectively.

3.4 Generating Anomaly Maps

After training the encoders, the representations from the encoder are used to detect the anomalies. First, the representation of every normal train patch, $\{f_\theta(\mathbf{p}_{\text{normal}})|\mathbf{p}_{\text{normal}}\}$, is calculated and stored. Given a query image $\mathbf{x}$, for every patch $\mathbf{p}$ with a stride S within $\mathbf{x}$, the L2 distance to the nearest normal patch in the feature space is then defined to be its anomaly score using Eq. 8. To mitigate the computational cost of the nearest neighbor search, we adopt its approximate algorithm[1]. As a result, the inspection of a single image from MVTec AD [8] dataset for example, requires approximately 0.48 s.

$$\mathcal{A}_\theta^{\text{patch}}(\mathbf{p}) \doteq \min_{\mathbf{p}_{\text{normal}}} \|f_\theta(\mathbf{p}) - f_\theta(\mathbf{p}_{\text{normal}})\|_2. \tag{8}$$

---

[1] https://github.com/yahoojapan/NGT.

| Image | Anomaly map | Image | Anomaly map | Image | Anomaly map |

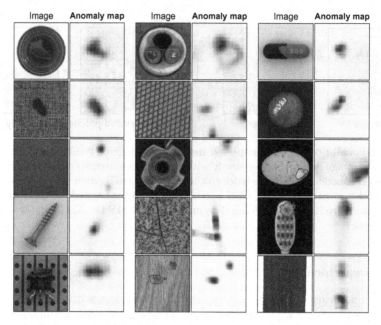

Fig. 7. Anomaly maps generated by the proposed method. Patch SVDD generates anomaly maps of each image in fifteen classes of MVTec AD [8] dataset. The ground truth defect annotations are depicted as red contours in the image, and the darker heatmap indicates higher anomaly scores.

Patch-wise calculated anomaly scores are then distributed to the pixels. As a consequence, pixels receive the average anomaly scores of every patch to which they belong, and we denote the resulting anomaly map as $\mathcal{M}$.

The multiple encoders discussed in Sect. 3.3 constitute multiple feature spaces, thereby yielding multiple anomaly maps. We aggregate the multiple maps using element-wise multiplication, and the resulting anomaly map, $\mathcal{M}_{\text{multi}}$, provides the answer to the problem of anomaly segmentation:

$$\mathcal{M}_{\text{multi}} \doteq \mathcal{M}_{\text{small}} \odot \mathcal{M}_{\text{big}}, \tag{9}$$

where $\mathcal{M}_{\text{small}}$ and $\mathcal{M}_{\text{big}}$ are the generated anomaly maps using f_{small} and f_{big}, respectively. The pixels with high anomaly scores in the map $\mathcal{M}_{\text{multi}}$ are deemed to contain defects.

It is straightforward to address the problem of anomaly detection. The maximum anomaly score of the pixels in an image is its anomaly score, as expressed in Eq. 10. Figure 6 illustrates the overall flow of the proposed method, and its pseudo-code is provided in the supplementary materials.

$$\mathcal{A}_{\theta}^{\text{image}}(\mathbf{x}) \doteq \max_{i,j} \mathcal{M}_{\text{multi}}(\mathbf{x})_{ij}. \tag{10}$$

Table 1. Anomaly detection (left) and segmentation (right) performances on MVTec AD [8] dataset. The proposed method, Patch SVDD, achieves the state-of-the-art performances on both tasks.

Method	AUROC
Task: Anomaly Detection	
Deep SVDD [4] ICML' 18	0.592
GEOM [19] NeurIPS' 18	0.672
GANomaly [15] ACCV' 18	0.762
ITAE [17] arXiv' 19	0.839
Patch SVDD (Ours)	**0.921**

Method	AUROC
Task: Anomaly Segmentation	
L2-AE	0.804
SSIM-AE	0.818
VE VAE CVPR' 20 [18]	0.861
VAE Proj ICLR' 20 [14]	0.893
Patch SVDD (Ours)	**0.957**

4   Results and Discussion

To verify the validity of the proposed method, we applied it to MVTec AD [8] dataset. The dataset consists of 15-class industrial images, each class categorized as either an *object* or *texture*. Ten *object* classes contain regularly positioned objects, whereas the *texture* classes contain repetitive patterns. The implementation details used throughout the study are provided in the supplementary materials, and please refer to [8] for more details on the dataset.

4.1   Anomaly Detection and Segmentation Results

Fig. 7 shows anomaly maps generated using the proposed method, indicating that the defects are properly localized, regardless of their size. Table 1 shows the detection and segmentation performances for MVTec AD [8] dataset compared with state-of-the-art baselines in AUROC. Patch SVDD provides state-of-the-art performance over the powerful baselines including auto encoder-based and classifier-based methods and outperforms Deep SVDD [4] by 55.6% improvement. Detailed numerical results are provided in the supplementary materials.

4.2   Detailed Analysis

t-SNE Visualization. Figure 8 shows t-SNE visualizations [30] of the learned features of multiple train images. Patches located at the points shown in Fig. 8(b) are mapped to the points with the same color and size in Fig. 8(a) and Fig. 8(c). In Fig. 8(a), the points with similar color and size form clusters in the feature space. Since the images in the cable class are regularly positioned, the patches from the same position have similar content, even if they are from different images. Likewise, for the regularly positioned *object* classes, the points with similar color and size in t-SNE visualization (i.e., the patches with similar positions) can be regarded to be semantically similar. By contrast, features of the leather class in Fig. 8(c) show the opposite tendency. This is because the patches in *texture* classes are analogous, regardless of their position in the image; the positions of the patches are not quite related to their semantics for the *texture* images.

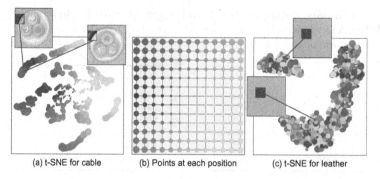

(a) t-SNE for cable   (b) Points at each position   (c) t-SNE for leather

Fig. 8. t-SNE visualizations [30] **of the learned features.** The color and size of each point represent the position (θ and r of the polar coordinates) within an image (b). From its color and size, we can infer the positions of the corresponding patches of the features in (a, c).

Table 2. The effect of the losses. Modifying $\mathcal{L}_{SVDD}$ to $\mathcal{L}_{SVDD'}$ and adopting $\mathcal{L}_{SSL}$ both improve the anomaly detection (Det.) and segmentation (Seg.) performances.

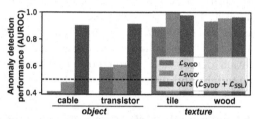

Fig. 9. The effects of the losses vary among classes. $\mathcal{L}_{SSL}$ is particularly beneficiary to the *object* classes.

$\mathcal{L}_{SVDD}$	$\mathcal{L}_{SVDD'}$	$\mathcal{L}_{SSL}$	Det.	Seg.
✓	✗	✗	0.703	0.832
✗	✓	✗	0.739	0.880
✗	✓	✓	0.921	0.957

Effect of Self-supervised Learning. Patch SVDD trains an encoder using two losses: $\mathcal{L}_{SVDD'}$ and $\mathcal{L}_{SSL}$, where $\mathcal{L}_{SVDD'}$ is a variant of $\mathcal{L}_{SVDD}$. To compare the roles of the proposed loss terms, we conduct an ablation study. Table 2 suggests that the modification of $\mathcal{L}_{SVDD}$ to $\mathcal{L}_{SVDD'}$ and the adoption of $\mathcal{L}_{SSL}$ improve the anomaly detection and segmentation performances. Figure 9 shows that the effects of the proposed loss terms vary among classes. Specifically, the *texture* classes (e.g. tile and wood) are less sensitive to the choice of loss, whereas the *object* classes, including cable and transistor, benefit significantly from $\mathcal{L}_{SSL}$.

To investigate the reason behind these observations, we provide (in Fig. 10) t-SNE visualizations of the features of an *object* class (the transistor) for the encoders trained with $\mathcal{L}_{SVDD}$, $\mathcal{L}_{SVDD'}$, and $\mathcal{L}_{SVDD'} + \mathcal{L}_{SSL}$. When training is performed with $\mathcal{L}_{SVDD}$ (Fig. 10(a)) or $\mathcal{L}_{SVDD'}$ (Fig. 10(b)), the features form a uni-modal cluster. In contrast, $\mathcal{L}_{SSL}$ results in multi-modal feature clusters on the basis of their semantics (i.e., color and size), as shown in Fig. 10(c). The multi-modal property of the features is particularly beneficial to the *object* classes, which have high intra-class variation among the patches. Features of the patches with dissimilar semantics are separated, and hence anomaly inspection using those features becomes more deliberate and accurate.

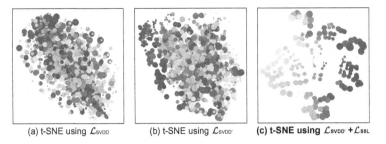

(a) t-SNE using $\mathcal{L}_{\text{SVDD}}$ (b) t-SNE using $\mathcal{L}_{\text{SVDD'}}$ **(c) t-SNE using $\mathcal{L}_{\text{SVDD'}} + \mathcal{L}_{\text{SSL}}$**

Fig. 10. Features of the multiple train images in the transistor class by the encoders trained with different losses. Adopting $\mathcal{L}_{\text{SSL}}$ (c) enables the representations to form clusters on the basis of their semantics.

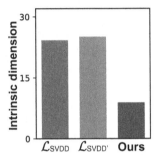

Fig. 11. Intrinsic dimensions of the features under different losses.

Fig. 12. The effect of hierarchical encoding. Aggregating the results from multi-scale inspection boosts the performance, and adopting hierarchical structure to the encoder is helpful as well.

The intrinsic dimensions (ID) [31] of the features also indicate the effectiveness of $\mathcal{L}_{\text{SSL}}$. The ID is the minimal number of coordinates required to describe the points without significant information loss [32]. A larger ID denotes that the points are spreaded in every direction, while a smaller ID indicates that the points lie on low-dimensional manifolds with high separability. In Fig. 11, we show the average IDs of features in each class trained with three different losses. If the encoder is trained with the proposed $\mathcal{L}_{\text{Patch SVDD}}$, features with the lowest ID are yielded, implying that these features are neatly distributed.

Hierarchical Encoding. In Sect. 3.3, we proposed the use of hierarchical encoders. Figure 12 shows that aggregating multi-scale results from multiple encoders improves the inspection performances. In addition, an ablation study with a non-hierarchical encoder shows that the hierarchical structure itself also boosts performance. We postulate that the hierarchical architecture provides regularization for the feature extraction. Note that the non-hierarchical encoder has a number of parameters similar to that of the hierarchical counterpart.

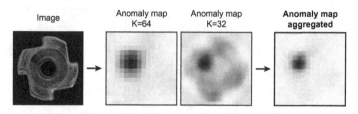

Image   Anomaly map K=64   Anomaly map K=32   **Anomaly map aggregated**

Fig. 13. Multi-scale inspection. Patch SVDD performs multi-scale inspection and aggregates the results. The image is from MVTec AD [8] dataset.

We provide an example of multi-scale inspection results, together with an aggregated anomaly map, in Fig. 13. The anomaly maps from various scales provide complementary inspection results; the encoder with a large receptive field coarsely locates the defect, whereas the one with a smaller receptive field refines the result. Therefore, an element-wise multiplication of the two maps localizes the accurate position of the defect.

Hyperparameters. As shown in Eq. 6, λ balances $\mathcal{L}_{\text{SVDD'}}$ and $\mathcal{L}_{\text{SSL}}$. A large λ emphasizes gathering of the features, while a small λ promotes their informativeness. Interestingly, the most favorable value of λ varies among the classes. Anomalies in the *object* classes are well detected under a smaller λ, while the *texture* classes are well detected with a larger λ. Figure 14 shows an example of this difference; the anomaly detection performance for the cable class (*object*) improves as λ decreases, while the wood class (*texture*) shows the opposite trend. As discussed in the previous sections, this occurs because the self-supervised learning is more helpful when the patches show high intra-class variation, which is the case for the *object* classes. The result coincides with that shown in Fig. 9 because using $\mathcal{L}_{\text{SVDD'}}$ as a loss is equivalent to using $\mathcal{L}_{\text{Patch SVDD}}$ with $\lambda \gg 1$.

The number of feature dimensions, D, is another hyperparameter of the encoder. The anomaly inspection performance for varying D is depicted in Fig. 15(a). A larger D signifies improved performance—a trend that has been discussed in a self-supervised learning venue [28]. Figure 15(b) indicates that the ID of the resulting features increases with increasing D. The black dashed line represents the $y = x$ graph, and it is the upper bound of ID. The average ID of features among the classes saturates as $D = 64$; therefore, we used a value of $D = 64$ throughout our study.

Random Encoder. Doersch et al. [6] showed that randomly initialized encoders perform reasonably well in image retrieval; given an image, the nearest images in the random feature space look similar to humans as well. Inspired by this observation, we examined the anomaly detection performance of the random encoders and provided the results in Table 3. As in Eq. 8, the anomaly score is defined to be the distance to the nearest normal patch, but in the random feature space. In the case of certain classes, the features of the random encoder

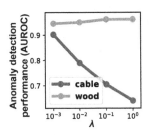
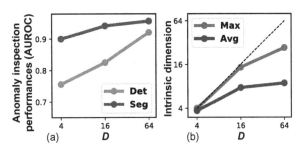

Fig. 14. Anomaly detection performances for the two classes show the opposite trends as λ varies.

Fig. 15. The effect of the embedding dimension, D. Larger D yields better inspection results (a) and larger intrinsic dimensions (b).

are effective in distinguishing between normal and abnormal images. Some results even outperform the trained deep neural network model (L2-AE).

Here, we investigate the reason for the high separability of the random features. For simplicity, let us assume the encoder to be a one-layered convolutional layer parametrized by a weight $W \neq \mathbf{0}$ and a bias b followed by a nonlinearity, σ. Given two patches $\mathbf{p}_1$ and $\mathbf{p}_2$, their features h_1 and h_2 are provided by Eq. 11, where $*$ denotes a convolution operation.

$$
\begin{aligned}
h_1 &= \sigma(W * \mathbf{p}_1 + b) \\
h_2 &= \sigma(W * \mathbf{p}_2 + b).
\end{aligned}
\tag{11}
$$

As Eq. 12 suggests, when the features are close, so are the patches, and vice versa. Therefore, nearest patch in the feature space is likely to be so in the image space.

$$
\begin{aligned}
\|h_1 - h_2\|_2 \approx 0 &\Leftrightarrow (W * \mathbf{p}_1 + b) - (W * \mathbf{p}_2 + b) \approx 0 \\
&\Leftrightarrow W * (\mathbf{p}_1 - \mathbf{p}_2) \approx 0 \\
&\Leftrightarrow \|\mathbf{p}_1 - \mathbf{p}_2\|_2 \approx 0.
\end{aligned}
\tag{12}
$$

In Table 3, we also provide the results for anomaly detection task using the nearest neighbor algorithm using the raw patches (i.e., $f_\theta(\mathbf{p}) = \mathbf{p}$ in Eq. 8). For certain classes, the raw patch nearest neighbor algorithm works surprisingly well. The effectiveness of the raw patches for anomaly detection can be attributed to the high similarity among the normal images.

Furthermore, the well-separated classes provided by the random encoder are well-separated by the raw patch nearest neighbor algorithm, and vice versa. Together with the conclusion of Eq. 12, this observation implies the strong relationship between the raw image patch and its random feature. To summarize, the random features of anomalies are easily separable because they are alike the raw patches, and the raw patches are easily separable.

Table 3. Nearest neighbor algorithm using the random encoders and raw patches for MVTec AD [8] dataset. For certain classes, the nearest neighbor algorithm using the random features shows good anomaly detection performance. For those classes, using the raw patches also yields high performance.

Classes	Random encoder		Raw patch		L2-AE
	Det.	Seg.	Det.	Seg.	Seg.
Bottle	0.89	0.80	**0.92**	0.82	0.91
Cable	0.56	0.70	0.57	0.84	0.73
Capsule	0.67	**0.93**	0.67	**0.94**	0.79
Carpet	0.42	0.66	0.48	0.74	0.54
Grid	0.75	0.61	0.83	0.76	0.96
Hazelnut	0.83	**0.93**	0.83	**0.95**	0.98
Leather	0.69	0.85	0.69	0.88	0.75
Metal_nut	0.37	0.79	0.52	0.89	0.88
Pill	0.72	**0.92**	0.77	**0.92**	0.89
Screw	0.69	**0.93**	0.56	**0.93**	0.98
Tile	0.68	0.54	0.70	0.51	0.48
Toothbrush	0.81	**0.95**	**0.92**	**0.97**	0.97
Transistor	0.53	0.88	0.68	**0.92**	0.91
Wood	**0.90**	0.74	**0.94**	0.78	0.63
Zipper	0.70	0.84	**0.94**	**0.92**	0.68

5   Conclusion

In this paper, we proposed Patch SVDD, a method for image anomaly detection and segmentation. Unlike Deep SVDD [4], we inspect the image at the patch level, and hence we can also localize defects. Moreover, additional self-supervised learning improves detection performance. As a result, the proposed method achieved state-of-the-art performance on MVTec AD [8] dataset.

In previous studies [23, 24], images were featurized prior to the subsequent downstream tasks because of their high-dimensional and structured nature. However, the results in our analysis suggest that a nearest neighbor algorithm with a raw patch often discriminates anomalies surprisingly well. Moreover, since the distances in random feature space are closely related to those in the raw image space, random features can provide distinguishable signals.

Acknowledgement. This work was supported by the National Research Foundation of Korea (NRF) grant funded by the Korea government (Ministry of Science and ICT) [2018R1A2B3001628], the Brain Korea 21 Plus Project in 2020, and Samsung Electronics.

References

1. Schölkopf, B., Platt, J.C., Shawe-Taylor, J., Smola, A.J., Williamson, R.C.: Estimating the support of a high-dimensional distribution. Neural Comput. **13**, 1443–1471 (2001)
2. Tax, D.M., Duin, R.P.: Support vector data description. Mach. Learn. **54**, 45–66 (2004). https://doi.org/10.1023/B:MACH.0000008084.60811.49
3. Vert, R., Vert, J.P.: Consistency and convergence rates of one-class SVMs and related algorithms. J. Mach. Learn. Res. **7**, 817–854 (2006)
4. Ruff, L., et al.: Deep one-class classification. In: ICML (2018)
5. Ruff, L., et al.: Deep semi-supervised anomaly detection. In: ICLR (2020)
6. Doersch, C., Gupta, A., Efros, A.A.: Unsupervised visual representation learning by context prediction. In: ICCV (2015)
7. Minderer, M., Bachem, O., Houlsby, N., Tschannen, M.: Automatic shortcut removal for self-supervised representation learning. In: ICML (2020)
8. Bergmann, P., Fauser, M., Sattlegger, D., Steger, C.: Mvtec AD-A comprehensive real-world dataset for unsupervised anomaly detection. In: CVPR (2019)
9. Calders, T., Jaroszewicz, S.: Efficient AUC optimization for classification. In: Kok, J.N., Koronacki, J., Lopez de Mantaras, R., Matwin, S., Mladenič, D., Skowron, A. (eds.) PKDD 2007. LNCS (LNAI), vol. 4702, pp. 42–53. Springer, Heidelberg (2007). https://doi.org/10.1007/978-3-540-74976-9_8
10. Lu, Y., Xu, P.: Anomaly detection for skin disease images using variational autoencoder. arXiv preprint arXiv:1807.01349 (2018)
11. Sabokrou, M., Khalooei, M., Fathy, M., Adeli, E.: Adversarially learned one-class classifier for novelty detection. In: CVPR (2018)
12. Perera, P., Nallapati, R., Xiang, B.: Ocgan: one-class novelty detection using gans with constrained latent representations. In: CVPR (2019)
13. Bergmann, P., Löwe, S., Fauser, M., Sattlegger, D., Steger, C.: Improving unsupervised defect segmentation by applying structural similarity to autoencoders. arXiv preprint arXiv:1807.02011 (2018)
14. Dehaene, D., Frigo, O., Combrexelle, S., Eline, P.: Iterative energy-based projection on a normal data manifold for anomaly localization. In: ICLR (2020)
15. Akcay, S., Atapour-Abarghouei, A., Breckon, T.P.: GANomaly: semi-supervised anomaly detection via adversarial training. In: Jawahar, C.V., Li, H., Mori, G., Schindler, K. (eds.) ACCV 2018. LNCS, vol. 11363, pp. 622–637. Springer, Cham (2019). https://doi.org/10.1007/978-3-030-20893-6_39
16. Yarlagadda, S.K., Güera, D., Bestagini, P., Maggie Zhu, F., Tubaro, S., Delp, E.J.: Satellite image forgery detection and localization using gan and one-class classifier. Electron. Imaging **2018**, 214 (2018)
17. Huang, C., Cao, J., Ye, F., Li, M., Zhang, Y., Lu, C.: Inverse-transform autoencoder for anomaly detection. arXiv preprint arXiv:1911.10676 (2019)
18. Liu, W., et al.: Towards visually explaining variational autoencoders. In: CVPR (2020)
19. Golan, I., El-Yaniv, R.: Deep anomaly detection using geometric transformations. In: NeurIPS (2018)
20. Hendrycks, D., Gimpel, K.: A baseline for detecting misclassified and out-of-distribution examples in neural networks. In: ICLR (2017)
21. Wang, S., et al.: Effective end-to-end unsupervised outlier detection via inlier priority of discriminative network. In: NeurIPS (2019)

22. Bergman, L., Hoshen, Y.: Classification-based anomaly detection for general data. In: ICLR (2020)
23. Noroozi, M., Favaro, P.: Unsupervised learning of visual representations by solving jigsaw puzzles. In: Leibe, B., Matas, J., Sebe, N., Welling, M. (eds.) ECCV 2016. LNCS, vol. 9910, pp. 69–84. Springer, Cham (2016). https://doi.org/10.1007/978-3-319-46466-4_5
24. Zhang, R., Isola, P., Efros, A.A.: Colorful image colorization. In: Leibe, B., Matas, J., Sebe, N., Welling, M. (eds.) ECCV 2016. LNCS, vol. 9907, pp. 649–666. Springer, Cham (2016). https://doi.org/10.1007/978-3-319-46487-9_40
25. Noroozi, M., Pirsiavash, H., Favaro, P.: Representation learning by learning to count. In: ICCV (2017)
26. Gidaris, S., Singh, P., Komodakis, N.: Unsupervised representation learning by predicting image rotations. In: ICLR (2018)
27. Koch, G., Zemel, R., Salakhutdinov, R.: Siamese neural networks for one-shot image recognition. In: ICML Deep Learning Workshop, vol. 2, Lille (2015)
28. Kolesnikov, A., Zhai, X., Beyer, L.: Revisiting self-supervised visual representation learning. In: CVPR, pp. 1920–1929 (2019)
29. Kingma, D.P., Ba, J.: Adam: a method for stochastic optimization. In: ICLR (2015)
30. Maaten, L.V.D., Hinton, G.: Visualizing data using t-SNE. J. Mach. Learn. Res. **9**, 2579–2605 (2008)
31. Facco, E., d'Errico, M., Rodriguez, A., Laio, A.: Estimating the intrinsic dimension of datasets by a minimal neighborhood information. Sci. Rep. **7**, 1–8 (2017)
32. Ansuini, A., Laio, A., Macke, J.H., Zoccolan, D.: Intrinsic dimension of data representations in deep neural networks. In: NeurIPS (2019)

Towards Robust Fine-Grained Recognition by Maximal Separation of Discriminative Features

Krishna Kanth Nakka[1]([envelope])[ID] and Mathieu Salzmann[1,2][ID]

[1] CVLab, EPFL, Lausanne, Switzerland
{krishna.nakka,mathieu.salzmann}@epfl.ch
[2] ClearSpace, Écublens, Switzerland

Abstract. Adversarial attacks have been widely studied for general classification tasks, but remain unexplored in the context of fine-grained recognition, where the inter-class similarities facilitate the attacker's task. In this paper, we identify the proximity of the latent representations of *local* regions of different classes in fine-grained recognition networks as a key factor to the success of adversarial attacks. We therefore introduce an attention-based regularization mechanism that maximally separates the latent features of discriminative regions of different classes while minimizing the contribution of the non-discriminative regions to the final class prediction. As evidenced by our experiments, this allows us to significantly improve robustness to adversarial attacks, to the point of matching or even surpassing that of adversarial training, but without requiring access to adversarial samples. Further, our formulation also improves detection AUROC of adversarial samples over baselines on adversarially trained models.

Keywords: Fine-grained recognition · Adversarial defense · Network interpretability

1 Introduction

Deep networks yield impressive results in many computer vision tasks [1–4]. Nevertheless, their performance degrades under adversarial attacks, where natural examples are perturbed with human-imperceptible, carefully crafted noise [5]. Adversarial attacks have been extensively studied for the task of general object recognition [5–10], with much effort dedicated to studying and improving the robustness of deep networks to such attacks [11–13]. However, adversarial attacks and defense mechanisms for fine-grained recognition problems, where one can expect the inter-class similarities to facilitate the attacker's task, remain unexplored.

Electronic supplementary material The online version of this chapter (https://doi.org/10.1007/978-3-030-69544-6_24) contains supplementary material, which is available to authorized users.

© Springer Nature Switzerland AG 2021
H. Ishikawa et al. (Eds.): ACCV 2020, LNCS 12627, pp. 391–408, 2021.
https://doi.org/10.1007/978-3-030-69544-6_24

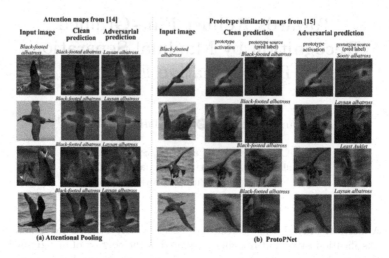

Fig. 1. Interpreting adversarial attacks for fine-grained recognition. We analyze the attention maps, obtained with [14] (a) and [15] (b), of four images from the *Black-footed albatross* class. Under PGD attack, these images are misclassified as closely-related bird species, such as *Layman albatross*, because the classifiers focus on either confusing regions that look similar in these classes, such as the bird's beak, or non-discriminative background regions, such as water.

In this paper, we therefore analyze the reasons for the success of adversarial attacks on fine-grained recognition techniques and introduce a defense mechanism to improve a network's robustness. To this end, we visualize the image regions mostly responsible for the classification results. Specifically, we consider both the attention-based framework of [14], closely related to class activation maps (CAMs) [16], and the recent prototypical part network (ProtoPNet) of [15], designed for fine-grained recognition, which relates local image regions to interpretable prototypes. As shown in Fig. 1, an adversarial example activates either confusing regions that look similar in samples from the true class and from the class activated by the adversarial attack, such as the beak of the bird, or, in the ProtoPNet case, non-discriminative background regions, such as water. This suggests that the latent representations of these confusing regions are close, and that the ProtoPNet classifier exploits class-irrelevant background information. These two phenomena decrease the margin between different classes, thus making the network more vulnerable to attacks.

Motivated this observation, we introduce a defense mechanism based on the intuition that the discriminative regions of each class should be maximally separated from that of the other classes. To this end, we design an attention-aware model that pushes away the discriminative prototypes of the different classes. The effectiveness of our approach is illustrated in Fig. 2, where the prototypes of different classes are nicely separated, except for those corresponding to non-discriminative regions. However, by means of an attention mechanism, we enforce these non-discriminative prototypes to play no role in the final class prediction.

Ultimately, our approach reduces the influence of the non-discriminative regions on the classification while increasing the magnitude of the displacement in the latent space that the attacker must perform to successfully move the network's prediction away from the true label.

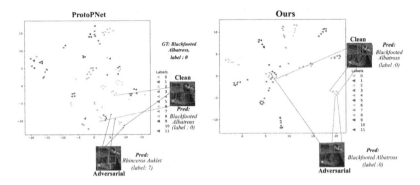

Fig. 2. t-SNE visualization of the prototypes from 12 fine-grained classes of the CUB200 dataset. In ProtoPNet [15], the prototypes of different classes are not well separated, making the network vulnerable to attacks. By contrast, our approach yields well-separated discriminative prototypes, while clustering the background ones, which, by means of an attention mechanism do not participate the prediction. This complicates the attacker's task.

As evidenced by our experiments, our approach significantly outperforms in robustness the baseline ProtoPNet and attentional pooling network, in some cases reaching adversarial accuracies on par with or higher than their adversarially-trained [17, 18] counterparts, but at virtually no additional computational cost.

Our main contributions can be summarized as follows. We analyze and explain the decisions of fine-grained recognition networks by studying the image regions responsible for classification for both clean and adversarial examples. We design an interpretable, attention-aware network for robust fine-grained recognition by constraining the latent space of discriminative regions. Our method improves robustness to a level comparable to that of adversarial training, without requiring access to adversarial samples and without trading off clean accuracy. Further, our approach improves the AUROC score of adversarial example detection by 20% over baselines for adversarial trained networks. We release the source code of our experiments at We release the source code of our experiments at https://github.com/krishnakanthnakka/RobustFineGrained/.

2 Related Work

Adversarial Robustness. DNNs were first shown to be vulnerable to adversarial, human-imperceptible perturbations in the context of general image recognition. Such attacks were initially studied in [19], quickly followed by the simple single-step Fast Gradient Sign Method (FGSM) [5] and its multiple-step BIM variant [7]. In [10], the attacks were stabilized by incorporating momentum in the gradient computation. Other popular attacks include DeepFool [8], which iteratively linearizes the classifier to compute minimal perturbations sufficient for the sample to cross the decision boundary, and other computationally more expensive attacks, such as CW [9], JSMA [6], and others [20–22]. As of today, Projected Gradient Descent (PGD) [11], which utilizes the local first-order network information to compute a maximum loss increment within a specified ℓ_∞ norm-bound, is generally considered as the most effective attack strategy.

Despite a significant research effort in devising defense mechanisms against adversarial attacks [23–26], it was shown in [27] that most such defenses can easily be breached in the white-box setting, where the attacker knows the network architecture. The main exception to this rule is adversarial training [11], where the model is trained jointly with clean images and their adversarial counterparts. Many variants of adversarial training were thus proposed, such as ensemble adversarial training [18] to soften the classifier's decision boundaries, ALP [12] to minimize the difference between the logit activations of real and adversarial images, the use of additional feature denoising blocks [13], of metric learning [28,29], and of regularizers to penalize changes in the model's prediction w.r.t. the input perturbations [30,31]. Nevertheless, PGD-based adversarial training remains the method of choice, thanks to its robustness and generalizability to unseen attacks [5,7–9,32].

Unfortunately, adversarial training is computationally expensive. This was tackled in [33] by recycling the gradients computed to update the model parameters so as to reduce the overhead of generating adversarial examples, albeit not remove this overhead entirely. More recently, [34] showed that combining the single-step FGSM with random initialization is almost as effective as PGD-based training, but at a significantly lower cost. Unlike all of the adversarial training strategies, our approach does not require computing adversarial images, and does not depend on a specific attack scheme. Instead, it aims to ensure a maximal separation between the different classes in high attention regions. This significantly differs from [35,36], which clusters the penultimate layer's global representation, without focusing on discriminative regions and without attempting to separate these features. Furthermore, and more importantly, in contrast to all the above-mentioned methods, our approach is tailored to fine-grained recognition, making use of the representations that have proven effective in this field, such as Bags of Words (BoW) [37,38] and VLAD [39,40], which have the advantage over second-order features [41–43] of providing some degree of interpretability.

Interpretability. Understanding the decisions of a DNN is highly important in real-world applications to build user trust. In the context of general image recognition, the trend of interpreting a DNN's decision was initiated by [44], followed by the popular CAMs [16]. Subsequently, variants of CAMs [45,46] and other visualization strategies [47] were proposed.

Here, in contrast to these works, we focus on the task of fine-grained recognition. In this domain, BoW-inspired representations, such as the one of

[15,48–51], were shown to provide some degree of interpretability. While most methods [48–51] allows one to highlight the image regions important for classification, it does not provide one with visual explanations of the network's decisions. This is addressed by ProtoPNet [15], which extracts class-specific prototypes. However, the feature embedding learnt by ProtoPNet gives equal importance to all image regions, resulting in a large number of prototypes representing non-discriminative background regions, as illustrated by Fig. 1. Here, we overcome this by designing an attention-aware system that learns prototypes which are close to high-attention regions in feature space, while constraining the non-discriminative regions from all classes to be close to each other. Furthermore, we show that this brings about not only interpretability, but also robustness to adversarial attacks, which has never been studied in the context of fine-grained recognition.

3   Interpreting Adversarial Attacks

Before delving into our method, let us study in more detail the experiment depicted by Fig. 1 to understand the decision of a fine-grained recognition CNN under adversarial attack. For this analysis, we experiment with two networks: the second-order attentional pooling network of [14] and the ProtoPNet of [15], both of which inherently encode some notion of interpretability in their architecture, thus not requiring any post-processing. Specifically, [14] uses class attention maps to compute class probabilities, whereas [15] exploits the similarity between image regions and class-specific prototypes. We analyze the reasons for the success of adversarial attacks on four images from the *Black-footed albatross* class.

As shown in Fig. 1(a), under attack, [14] misclassifies all four images to *Layman albatross*. Note that these two classes belong to the same general *Albatross* family, and, for clean samples, the region with the highest attention for these two classes is the bird's beak. Because the discriminative regions for these two classes correspond to the same beak region, which looks similar in both classes, the attack becomes easier as minimal perturbation is needed to change the class label.

In the case of ProtoPNet [15], while the network also consistently misclassifies the attacked images, the resulting label differs across the different images, as shown in Fig. 1(b). In the top row, the situation is similar to that occurring with the method of [14]. By contrast, in the second row, the region activated in the input image corresponds to a different semantic part (wing) than that activated in the prototype (beak). Finally, in the last two rows, the network activates a background prototype that is common across the other categories and thus more vulnerable to attacks.

In essence, the mistakes observed in Fig. 1 come from either the discriminative regions of two different classes being too close in feature space, or the use of non-discriminative regions for classification. This motivates us to encourage the feature representation of discriminative regions from different classes to be maximally separated from each other, while minimizing the influence of background regions by making use of attention and by encouraging the features in these regions to lie close to each other so as *not* to be discriminative. This will complicate the attacker's task, by preventing their ability to leverage non-discriminative regions and forcing them to make larger changes in feature space to affect the prediction.

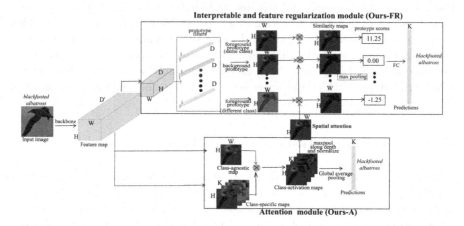

Fig. 3. Overview of our framework. Our approach consists of two modules acting on the features extracted by a backbone network. The attention module extracts attention maps that help the network to focus on the discriminative image regions. The feature regularization module further uses the attention maps to encourage separating the learned prototypes belonging to different classes.

4   Method

In this section, we introduce our approach to increasing the robustness of fine-grained recognition by maximal separation of class-specific discriminative regions. Figure 3 gives an overview our framework, which consists of two modules post feature extraction: (i) An attention module that learns class-specific filters focusing on the discriminative regions; and (ii) a feature regularization module that maximally separates the class-specific features deemed discriminative by the attention module. Through the feature regularization module, we achieve the dual objective of providing interpretability and increasing the robustness of the backbone network to adversarial attacks.

Note that, at inference time, we can either use the entire framework for prediction, or treat the attention module, together with the backbone feature extractor, as an standalone network. As will be demonstrated by our experiments, both strategies yield robustness to adversarial attacks, which evidences that our approach in fact robustifies the final feature map. Below, we first describe the overall architecture of our framework and then discuss the feature regularization module in more detail.

4.1   Architecture

Formally, let $\mathbf{I}_i$ denote an input image, and $\mathbf{X}_i \in \mathbb{R}^{H \times W \times D'}$ represent the corresponding feature map extracted by a fully-convolutional backbone network. Our architecture is inspired by the ProtoPNet of [15], in the sense that we also rely on class-specific prototypes. However, as shown in Sect. 3, ProtoPNet fails to learn discriminative prototypes, because it allows the prototypes to encode non-discriminative background information and to be close in feature space even if they belong to different classes. To address this, we propose to focus on the important regions via an attention mechanism and to regularize the prototypes during training.

Specifically, our attention module consists of two sets of filters: (i) A class-agnostic $1 \times 1 \times D'$ filter yielding a single-channel map of size $H \times W$; and (ii) K class-specific $1 \times 1 \times D'$ filters producing K maps of size $H \times W$ corresponding to the K classes in the dataset. Each of the class-specific map is then multiplied by the class-agnostic one, and the result is spatially averaged to generate a K-dimensional output. As shown in [14], this multiplication of two attention maps is equivalent to a rank-1 approximation of second-order pooling, which has proven to be well-suited to aggregate local features for fine-grained recognition.

The second branch of our network extracts interpretable prototypes and is responsible to increase the robustness of the features extracted by the backbone. To this end, $\mathbf{X}_i$ is first processed by two 1×1 convolutional layers to decrease the channel dimension to D. The resulting representation is then passed through a prototype layer that contains m learnable prototypes of size $1 \times 1 \times D$, resulting in m similarity maps of size $H \times W$. Specifically, the prototype layer computes the residual vector $\mathbf{r}$ between each local feature and each prototype, and passes this distance through an activation function defined as $f(\mathbf{r}) = \log\left((\|\mathbf{r}\|_2^2 + 1)/(\|\mathbf{r}\|_2^2 + \gamma)\right)$, where γ is set to $1e-5$. In contrast to [15], to focus on discriminative regions, we modulate the resulting similarity maps with an attention map $\mathbf{A}_i$, computed by max-pooling the final class-specific maps of the attention module. We then spatially max-pool the resulting attention-aware similarity maps to obtain similarity scores, which are passed through the final classification layer to yield class probabilities. As in [15], we make the prototypes class specific by splitting the m prototypes into K sets of c prototypes and initializing the weights of the classification layer of the prototype branch to $+1$ for positive connections between prototype and class label and -0.5 for negative ones. While exploiting attention encourages the prototypes to focus on the discriminative regions, nothing explicitly prevents prototypes from different classes to remain close in feature space, thus yielding a small margin between different classes and making the classifier vulnerable to attacks. This is what we address below.

4.2   Discriminative Feature Separation

To learn a robust feature representation, we introduce two feature regularization losses that aim to maximally separate the prototypes of different classes. Let $\mathbf{x}_i^t$

represent a local feature vector at location t in feature map $\mathbf{X}_i$ from image $\mathbf{I}_i$ with label y_i. Furthermore, let $N = W \cdot H$ be the total number of feature vectors in $\mathbf{X}_i$, and $\mathbf{P}_{y_i}$ be the set of prototypes belonging to class y_i.

Our regularization consists of two attention-aware losses, a clustering one and a separation one. The attentional-clustering loss pulls the high-attention regions in a sample close to the nearest prototype of its own class. We express this as

$$L_{clst}^{att}(\mathbf{I}_i) = \sum_{t=1}^{N} a_i^t \min_{l:\mathbf{p}_l \in \mathbf{P}_{y_i}} \|\mathbf{x}_i^t - \mathbf{p}_l\|_2^2 , \tag{1}$$

where a_i^t is the attention value at location t in $\mathbf{A}_i$. By contrast, the attentional-separation loss pushes the high-attention regions away from the nearest prototype of any other class. We compute it as

$$L_{sep}^{att}(\mathbf{I}_i) = - \sum_{t=1}^{N} a_i^t \min_{l:\mathbf{p}_l \notin \mathbf{P}_{y_i}} \|\mathbf{x}_i^t - \mathbf{p}_l\|_2^2 . \tag{2}$$

While these two loss functions encourage the prototypes to focus on high-attention, discriminative regions, they leave the low-attention regions free to be close to any prototype, thus increasing the vulnerability of the network to attacks. We therefore further need to push the non-discriminative regions away from such informative prototypes. A seemingly natural way to achieve this would consist of exploiting inverted attention maps, such as $1 - \mathbf{a}_t$ or $1/\mathbf{a}_t$. However, in practice, we observed this to make training unstable. Instead, we therefore propose to make use of the attention maps from *other* samples to compute the loss for sample i. Specifically, we re-write our regularization loss for sample i as

$$L_{reg}(\mathbf{I}_i) = \sum_{j=1}^{B} \sum_{t=1}^{N} \lambda_1 a_j^t \min_{l:\mathbf{p}_l \in \mathbf{P}_{y_i}} \|\mathbf{x}_i^t - \mathbf{p}_l\|_2^2 - \lambda_2 a_j^t \min_{l:\mathbf{p}_l \notin \mathbf{P}_{y_i}} \|\mathbf{x}_i^t - \mathbf{p}_l\|_2^2 , \tag{3}$$

where B is the number of samples in the mini-batch. When $j = i$, we recover the two loss terms defined in Eqs. 1 and 2. By contrast, when $j \neq i$, we exploit the attention map of a different sample. The intuition behind this is that either the attention map of sample j focuses on the same regions as that of sample i, and thus the loss serves the same purpose as when using the attention of sample i, or it focuses on other regions, and the loss then pushes the corresponding feature map, encoding a low-attention region according to the attention map of sample i, to its own prototype in class y_i. In practice, we have observed this procedure to typically yield a single background prototype per class. These background prototypes inherently become irrelevant for classification because they correspond to low-attention regions and have thus a similarity score close to zero, thanks to our attention-modulated similarity maps. As such, we have empirically found that all background prototypes tend to cluster.

Ultimately, we write our total loss function for sample i as

$$L(\mathbf{I}_i) = CE_{att}(\mathbf{I}_i) + CE_{reg}(\mathbf{I}_i) + L_{reg}(\mathbf{I}_i),$$

where CE_{att} and CE_{reg} represent the cross-entropy loss of the attention module and the feature regularization module, respectively.

At inference time, we perform adversarial attacks on the joint system by exploiting the cross-entropy loss of both the attention and feature regularization module. Furthermore, we also attack the attention module on its own, showing that, together with the feature extraction backbone, it can be used as a standalone network and also inherits robustness from our training strategy.

5 Experiments

5.1 Experimental Setting

Datasets. We experiment on two popular fine-grained datasets, Caltech UCSD Birds (CUB) [52] and Stanford Cars-196 [53].

Threat Model. We consider both white-box and black-box attacks under an ℓ_∞-norm budget. We evaluate robustness for two attack tolerances $\epsilon = \{2/255, 8/255\}$. In addition to the popular 10-step PGD attack [11], we test our framework with FGSM [5], BIM [7], and MI [10] attacks. For PGD attacks, we set the step size α to $1/255$ for $\epsilon = 2/255$ and to $2/255$ for $\epsilon = 8/255$. For the other attacks, we set number of iterations to 10 and the step size α to ϵ divided by the number of iterations, as in [28,35]. For black-box attacks, we transfer the adversarial examples generated using 10-step PGD with $\epsilon = 8/255$ and $\alpha = 2/255$ on either a similar VGG16 [54] architecture, or a completely different DenseNet-121 [55] architecture. We denote by BB-V and BB-D the black-box attacks transferred from VGG16 and DenseNet-121, respectively.

Networks. We evaluate our approach using 3 backbone networks: VGG-16 [54], VGG-19 [54] and ResNet-34 [56]. Similarly to [15], we perform all experiments on images cropped according to the bounding boxes provided with the dataset, and resize the resulting images to 224×224. For both VGG-16 and VGG-19, we use the convolutional layers until the 4th block to output 7×7 spatial maps of 512 channels. For ResNet-34, we take the network excluding the final global average pooling layer as backbone. We initialize the backbone networks with weights pretrained on ImageNet [2].

Evaluated Methods. As baselines, we use the attentional pooling network (AP) of [14], and the state-of-the-art ProtoPNet of [15]. We use **Ours-FR** and **Ours-A** to denote the output of our feature regularization module and of our attention module, respectively. In other words, AP and Ours-A share the *same* architecture at inference time, and Ours-FR is an attention-aware variant of ProtoPNet. To further boost the performance of the baselines and of our approach, we perform adversarial training. Specifically, we generate adversarial examples using the recent fast adversarial training strategy of [34], which relies on a single step FGSM with random initialization. During training, we set ϵ to $8/255$ and α to $\{0.5\epsilon, 1.25\epsilon\}$ as suggested in [34]. This was shown in [34] to perform on par with

PGD-based adversarial training, while being computationally much less expensive. For our approach, during fast adversarial training, we use the cross-entropy loss of both modules to generate the adversarial images. We denote by AP* and ProtoPNet* the adversarially-trained AP and ProtoPNet baselines, respectively, and by **Ours-FR*** and **Ours-A*** the adversarially-trained counterparts of our two sub-networks. We also compare with state-of-the-art defense [35] which regularizes the hidden space with additional prototype conformity loss (PCL). Lastly, we also evaluate triplet-loss [57] based feature separation of penultimate layer global features as another baseline. Due to the space limitation, we provide more experimental training details in the supplementary material.

Table 1. Classification accuracy of different networks with ℓ_∞ based attacks on CUB200. The best result of each column and each backbone is shown in bold. The last two columns correspond to black-box attacks with PGD attack.

Base Network	Attacks (Steps, ϵ)	Clean (0,0)	FGSM (1,2)	FGSM (1,8)	BIM (10,2)	BIM (10,8)	PGD (10,2)	PGD (10,8)	MIM (10,2)	MIM (10,8)	BB-V (10,2)	BB-D (10,8)
VGG-16	AP [14]	78.0%	36.5%	31.0%	27.7%	14.6%	23.5%	11.7%	30.2%	16.7%	9.6%	60.4%
	AP+ Triplet [57]	**81.0%**	49.5%	36.6%	33.5%	11.2%	26.5%	8.50%	37.7%	14.3%	8.54%	63.4%
	AP+ PCL [35]	80.0%	41.0%	33.1%	32.9%	13.6%	23.5%	9.6%	35.3%	17.1%	10.6%	65.8%
	Ours-A	80.4%	47.2%	**40.2%**	40.0%	23.2%	35.3%	21.8%	42.2%	26.4%	12.9%	66.9%
	ProtoPNet [15]	69.0%	19.9%	8.10%	3.80%	0.00%	2.20%	0.00%	5.00%	0.10%	**22.9%**	58.5%
	ProtoPNet+Ours	73.2%	49.9%	42.2%	42.5%	35.3%	38.4%	30.1%	42.9%	37.5%	15.4%	59.7%
VGG-19	AP [14]	75.7%	20.4%	14.5%	13.4%	6.9%	10.5%	5.7%	14.8%	6.9%	21.1%	61.3%
	AP+ Triplet [57]	**82.0%**	53.9%	38.2%	35.0%	12.4%	27.7%	9.40%	39.4%	15.3%	17.40%	64.9%
	AP+ PCL [35]	76.9%	20.3%	14.8%	12.1%	5.7%	8.8%	4.2%	13.9%	6.8%	19.8%	60.2%
	Ours-A	79.7%	51.4%	**44.6%**	42.3%	26.5%	36.8%	26.3%	45.0%	42.6%	29.8%	68.2%
	ProtoPNet [15]	73.8%	22.9%	11.1%	3.2%	0.0%	1.2%	0.0%	3.6%	0.0%	21.0%	58.0%
	Ours-FR	75.4%	52.2%	46.3%	46.6%	41.3%	42.4%	31.0%	44.4%	37.6%	30.4%	63.7%
ResNet-34	AP [14]	**79.9%**	30.4%	26.3%	18.0%	7.20%	13.2%	5.8%	22.3%	8.6%	43.0%	59.4%
	AP+ Triplet [57]	78.6%	25.6%	18.7%	11.4%	2.9%	7.1%	1.8%	14.7%	3.8%	42.11%	58.4%
	AP+ PCL [35]	77.9%	30.1%	24.5%	21.4%	13.3%	17.6%	11.6%	23.9%	15.3%	45.7%	61.4%
	Ours-A	79.0%	**32.3%**	**27.0%**	24.8%	20.5%	22.5%	19.8%	26.2%	22.0%	48.6%	63.2%
	ProtoPNet [15]	75.1%	23.2%	12.8%	7.80%	1.80%	4.10%	1.00%	8.90%	2.20%	39.1%	53.0%
	Ours-FR	**76.3%**	30.7%	22.0%	19.3%	13.6%	14.2%	13.0%	19.1%	13.8%	46.0%	60.0%

5.2 Results on CUB 200

Quantitative Analysis. We first compare the accuracy of our method to that of the baselines with the three backbone networks on CUB200. Table 1 and Table 2 provide the results for vanilla and fast adversarial training, respectively. On the clean samples, **Ours-FR** typically surpasses its non-attentional counterpart **ProtoPNet** [15], and **Ours-A** yields the better accuracy than baseline AP and AP+PCL across all backbones. This is true both without (Table 1) and with (Table 2) adversarial training.

Under adversarial attack, our approach, without and with adversarial training, yields better robustness under almost all attacks and backbones. Importantly, the boost in performance is larger for attacks with larger perturbations. Furthermore, our model trained with clean samples sometimes outperform even the adversarially-trained baselines. For example, on VGG-16 with PGD attack with $\epsilon = 8/255$, **AP*** yields an accuracy of 16.9% (Table 2) while **Ours-A** reaches 21.8% accuracy (Table 1). This evidences the ability of our feature regularization module to learn robust features, even without seeing any adversarial examples. This is further supported by the fact that, despite **AP** and **Ours-A** having the same architecture at inference, **Ours-A** is more robust to attacks. Our method outperforms AP+PCL in most cases since PCL do not take into account subtle difference in local regions and regularizes global representation only. Furthermore, in contrast to adversarially-trained models, our vanilla approach does not trade off clean accuracy for robustness. For example, on VGG-16, while adversarial training made the clean accuracy of **AP*** drop to 54.9% (Table 2), that of **Ours-A** is 80.4% (Table 1). In other words, we achieve good robustness *and* clean accuracy.

Table 2. Classification accuracy of different robust networks with ℓ_∞ based attacks on CUB200. The best result of each column and each backbone is shown in bold. The last two columns correspond to black-box attacks with PGD attack.

Base Network	Attacks (Steps, ϵ)	Clean (0,0)	FGSM (1,2)	FGSM (1,8)	BIM (10,2)	BIM (10,8)	PGD (10,2)	PGD (10,8)	MIM (10,2)	MIM (10,8)	BB-V (10,8)	BB-D (10,8)
VGG-16	AP* [14]	54.9%	44.9%	24.2%	41.9%	18.2%	41.2%	16.9%	41.9%	18.7%	54.6%	54.0%
	AP+PCL* [35]	60.7%	50.5%	28.5%	47.1%	22.8%	46.7%	21.6%	47.2%	23.5%	59.5%	59.9%
	Ours-A*	**63.1%**	**56.1%**	**34.8%**	51.7%	**29.6%**	**50.8%**	28.0%	**52.0%**	**32.5%**	**66.3%**	**68.0%**
	ProtoPNet* [15]	60.1%	44.5%	26.9%	**57.1%**	10.9%	35.9%	10.3%	37.6%	13.5%	58.4%	59.1%
	Ours-FR*	63.0%	53.3%	37.3%	49.4%	30.4%	48.1%	**28.6%**	49.7%	31.1%	61.1%	62.0%
VGG-19	AP* [14]	58.0%	47.5%	29.1%	44.3%	25.6%	44.0%	24.34%	44.4%	26.2%	57.0%	57.3%
	AP+PCL* [35]	61.8%	52.1%	30.9%	48.9%	24.7%	48.6%	23.3%	49.1%	25.4%	60.5%	60.9%
	Ours-A*	**68.2%**	**57.1%**	36.5%	**53.2%**	30.4%	**52.6%**	**29.2%**	**53.5%**	31.2%	**66.2%**	**66.9%**
	ProtoPNet* [15]	55.1%	40.0%	28.9%	26.5%	11.3%	29.7%	9.60%	25.6%	10.2%	53.6%	53.9%
	Ours-FR*	64.4%	55.5%	**37.4%**	51.2%	**30.6%**	50.4%	28.7%	52.1%	**32.3%**	62.5%	63.2%
ResNet-34	AP* [14]	55.6%	47.8%	29.2%	44.80%	21.0%	44.5%	19.4%	44.9%	21.9%	55.3%	55.2%
	AP+PCL* [35]	54.5%	45.4%	26.9%	42.3%	18.2%	41.9%	16.4%	42.4%	19.1%	54.0%	54.0%
	Ours-A*	**62.2%**	**54.2%**	**35.7%**	**51.5%**	**25.5%**	**51.0%**	**23.1%**	**51.6%**	**26.6%**	**61.5%**	**61.9%**
	ProtoPNet* [15]	**57.9%**	46.5%	30.3%	41.1%	21.1%	40.3%	18.4%	41.5%	20.9%	56.9%	57.0%
	Ours-FR*	57.6%	49.5%	32.3%	45.8%	23.2%	44.9%	19.9%	46.1%	24.6%	57.1%	57.0%

Transferability Analysis. To evaluate robustness to black-box attacks, we transfer adversarial examples generated from substitute networks to our framework and to the baselines. As substitute models, we use a VGG-16 [54] and DenseNet-121 [55] backbone followed by global average pooling and a classification layer. The corresponding results are reported in the last two columns of Table 1 and Table 2. As in the white-box case, our approach outperforms the baselines in this black-box setting, thus confirming its effectiveness at learning robust features.

Qualitative Analysis. Let us now qualitatively evidence the benefits of our approach. To this end, in Fig. 4, we visualize the 10 class-specific prototypes learned by ProtPNet and by our approach for the *Blackfooted albatross* class.

Table 3. Ablation study. Contribution of each proposed feature regularization module in classification accuracy of undefended VGG-16 network.

Network	Att-clustering loss	Att-separation loss	Clean (0,0)	PGD (10,8)	Network	Att-clustering loss	Att-separation loss	Clean (0,0)	PGD (10,8)
AP [14]	–	–	78.0%	11.7%	ProtoPNet [15]	–	–	69.0%	0.0%
Ours-A	–	–	78.7%	14.07%	Ours-FR	–	–	75.7%	13.76%
	–	✓	79.6%	0.0%		–	✓	69.8%	0.0%
	✓	–	80.0%	19.3%		✓	–	73.7%	18.7%
	✓	✓	80.4%	21.8%		✓	✓	73.2%	30.1%

Specifically, we show the activation heatmaps of these prototypes on the source image that they have been projected to. Note that ProtoPNet learns multiple background prototypes, whereas our approach encodes all the background information in a *single non-discriminative* prototype. Furthermore, ProtoPNet [15] focuses on much larger regions, which can be expected to be less discriminative than the fine-grained regions obtained using our approach. This is due to our use of attention, which helps the prototypes to focus on the areas that are important for classification.

In Fig. 5, we analyze the effect of adversarial attacks on AP, ProtoPNet and our approach (all without adversarial training) by visualizing the attention maps and/or a few top activated prototypes along with their similarity scores for a *Blackfooted albatross* image with and without attack. Without attack, AP activates a larger region than our attention module. Furthermore, ProtoPNet activates a prototype from a different class (*Cape glossay starling*), while our approach focuses on the correct class only. This already shows that the features learned by these baselines are less discriminative, making them more vulnerable to adversarial attacks. As a matter of fact, under attack, AP focuses on a different region that is not discriminative for the *Blackfooted albatross* class. Similarly, ProtoPNet activates prototypes of different classes with high similarity scores, highlighting non-discriminative regions. By contrast, the prototypes activated by our approach remain the same as in the clean case, thus corresponding to the correct class.

Gradient Obfuscation. As suggested in [27], we check the gradient obfuscation to ensure that proposed approach do not give false sense of security. As shown in Fig. 6, VGG-16 trained with our feature regularization performance drops as the perturbation norm increases. Further, from Table 1 and 4, the black-box attacks are less successful than white box attacks. Both these experiments suggest ou formulation do not suffer from gradient obfuscation.

Adversarial Sample Detection. Our formulation also helps in detecting adversarial samples due to well separation of discriminative regions. Following [58], we learn a logistic detector by computing mahalanobis distance to the nearest class-conditional Gaussian distribution as the feature at every layer of the network. As shown in Fig. 7, our proposed feature regularization approach increases the detection AUROC performance over the baselines by around 20%.

Ablation Study. To understand the importance of each module in achieving robustness, we perform ablation study on VGG-16. As shown from Table 3, our attention-aware formulation performs better than baseline even without feature regularization. However by adding attentional cluster and separation cost, we achieve significant improvements over the baselines.

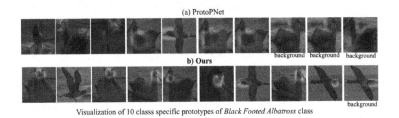

Visualization of 10 class specific prototypes of *Black Footed Albatross* class

Fig. 4. Comparison of the prototypes learned with ProtoPNet [15] and with our approach on CUB. ProtoPNet yields multiple background prototypes and prototypes that focus on large regions. By contrast, our prototypes are finer-grained and thus more representative of the specific class in the images.

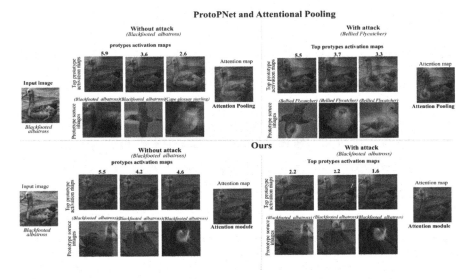

Fig. 5. Comparison of the activated image regions without and with attack. Without attack, the baselines (AP and ProtoPNet) tend to rely on relatively large regions, sometimes corresponding to wrong classes, for prediction. By contrast, our approach focuses more closely on the discriminative regions. Under PGD attack, this phenomenon is further increased, with ProtoPNet and AP activating incorrect prototypes and regions. The activations obtained with our approach remain similar to those obtained without attacks, albeit with a decrease in the similarity scores, indicated above the top prototype activation maps.

Table 4. Classification accuracy of different undefended networks with ℓ_∞ based attacks on Cars196.

Base Network	Attacks (Steps, ϵ)	Clean (0,0)	FGSM (1,2)	FGSM (1,8)	BIM (10,2)	BIM (10,8)	PGD (10,2)	PGD (10,8)	MIM (10,2)	MIM (10,8)	BB-V (10,2)	BB-D (10,8)
VGG-16	AP [14]	**91.2%**	52.6%	40.2%	37.4%	10.5%	28.8%	6.93%	41.7%	12.9%	12.5%	82.5%
	AP+Triplet [57]	91.1%	54.3%	**43.5%**	42.4%	14.9%	34.1%	9.54%	45.5%	19.2%	15.6%	**84.7%**
	AP+PCL [35]	90.2%	51.7%	40.5%	39.3%	14.1%	31.8%	9.44%	42.5%	17.5%	16.7%	83.9%
	Ours-A	88.5%	**58.7%**	40.2%	**48.0%**	**28.6%**	**46.5%**	**21.7%**	**53.2%**	**33.2%**	19.9%	82.2%
	ProtoPNet [15]	**84.5%**	31.2%	9.85%	4.78%	0.01%	2.23%	0.00%	6.5%	0.01%	**27.8%**	**75.5%**
	Ours-FR	83.8%	**60.1%**	**52.0%**	**51.3%**	**41.0%**	**47.8%**	**32.9%**	**51.8%**	**43.9%**	23.4%	75.1%
VGG-19	AP	**91.5%**	50.1%	37.8%	33.4%	10.3%	23.83%	6.93%	37.9%	12.7%	20.7%	82.8%
	AP+Triplet [57]	91.0%	56.2%	45.1%	40.5%	13.0%	30.3%	8.70%	45.3%	16.7%	29.0%	85.0%
	AP+PCL [35]	91.3%	61.3%	49.9%	49.0%	19.7%	40.2%	14.1%	52.4%	23.4%	30.6%	**85.7%**
	Ours-A	88.7%	**64.4%**	**54.8%**	**56.4%**	**36.7%**	**51.7%**	**33.4%**	**58.1%**	**41.0%**	**35.9%**	82.5%
	ProtoPNet [15]	**85.6%**	34.1%	20.8%	11.3%	1.11%	4.40%	0.5%	14.2%	1.39%	26.5%	75.5%
	Ours-FR	85.0%	**62.4%**	**54.7%**	**54.5%**	**45.7%**	**51.2%**	**38.5%**	**54.3%**	**47.6%**	**36.1%**	**76.8%**

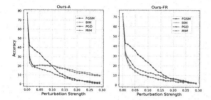

Fig. 6. Performance of VGG-16 with our proposed approach under different perturbation strengths.

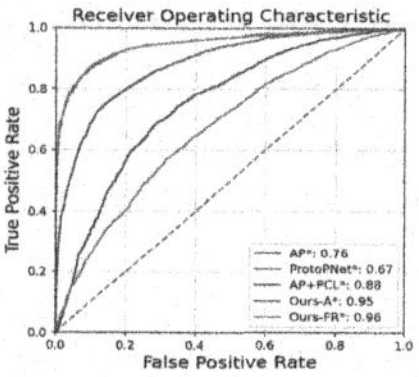

Fig. 7. ROC curves for adversarial sample detection on robust VGG-16 with PGD attack.

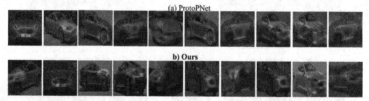

Visualization of 10 class specific prototypes of *Acura TL Sedan 2012* class

Fig. 8. Comparison of the prototypes learned with ProtoPNet [15] and with our approach on Stanford-Cars. ProtoPNet yields prototypes that cover large regions, whereas our prototypes more focused.

5.3   Results on Stanford Cars

We now present on results on Stanford Cars [53]. In Table 4, we report the results obtained using vanilla training. As in the CUB case, our approach yields better robustness than the baselines. We provide a qualitative analysis and the results obtained with adversarial training in the supplementary material.

In Fig. 8, we compare the prototypes learned with ProtoPNet and with our approach for the *Accura TL Sedan* class. As before, while the prototypes learned by ProtoPNet cover large regions, those obtained with our framework are more focused on the discriminative parts of the car.

6   Conclusion

In this paper, we have performed the first study of adversarial attacks for fine-grained recognition. Our analysis has highlighted the key factor for the success of adversarial attacks in this context. This has inspired us to design an attention- and prototype-based framework that explicitly encourages the prototypes to focus on the discriminative image regions. Our experiments have evidenced the benefits of our approach, able to match and sometimes even outperform adversarial training, despite not requiring seeing adversarial examples during training and further improving AUROC score of adversarial sample detection.

Acknowledgments. This work was funded in part by the Swiss National Science Foundation.

References

1. Long, J., Shelhamer, E., Darrell, T.: Fully convolutional networks for semantic segmentation. In: Proceedings of the IEEE Conference on Computer Vision and Pattern Recognition, pp. 3431–3440 (2015)
2. Krizhevsky, A., Sutskever, I., Hinton, G.E.: Imagenet classification with deep convolutional neural networks. In: Advances in Neural Information Processing Systems, pp. 1097–1105 (2012)
3. Karpathy, A., Toderici, G., Shetty, S., Leung, T., Sukthankar, R., Fei-Fei, L.: Large-scale video classification with convolutional neural networks. In: Proceedings of the IEEE conference on Computer Vision and Pattern Recognition, pp. 1725–1732 (2014)
4. Zhang, C., Li, H., Wang, X., Yang, X.: Cross-scene crowd counting via deep convolutional neural networks. In: Proceedings of the IEEE Conference on Computer Vision and Pattern Recognition, pp. 833–841 (2015)
5. Goodfellow, I.J., Shlens, J., Szegedy, C.: Explaining and harnessing adversarial examples. arXiv preprint arXiv:1412.6572 (2014)
6. Papernot, N., McDaniel, P., Jha, S., Fredrikson, M., Celik, Z.B., Swami, A.: The limitations of deep learning in adversarial settings. In: 2016 IEEE European Symposium on Security and Privacy (EuroS&P), pp. 372–387. IEEE (2016)
7. Kurakin, A., Goodfellow, I., Bengio, S.: Adversarial examples in the physical world. arXiv preprint arXiv:1607.02533 (2016)
8. Nguyen, A., Yosinski, J., Clune, J.: Deep neural networks are easily fooled: high confidence predictions for unrecognizable images. In: Proceedings of the IEEE Conference on Computer Vision and Pattern Recognition, pp. 427–436 (2015)
9. Carlini, N., Wagner, D.: Towards evaluating the robustness of neural networks. In: 2017 IEEE Symposium on Security and Privacy (SP), pp. 39–57. IEEE (2017)
10. Dong, Y., et al.: Boosting adversarial attacks with momentum. In: Proceedings of the IEEE Conference on Computer Vision and Pattern Recognition, pp. 9185–9193 (2018)

11. Madry, A., Makelov, A., Schmidt, L., Tsipras, D., Vladu, A.: Towards deep learning models resistant to adversarial attacks. arXiv preprint arXiv:1706.06083 (2017)
12. Kannan, H., Kurakin, A., Goodfellow, I.: Adversarial logit pairing. arXiv preprint arXiv:1803.06373 (2018)
13. Xie, C., Wu, Y., Maaten, L.V.D., Yuille, A.L., He, K.: Feature denoising for improving adversarial robustness. In: Proceedings of the IEEE Conference on Computer Vision and Pattern Recognition, pp. 501–509 (2019)
14. Girdhar, R., Ramanan, D.: Attentional pooling for action recognition. In: Advances in Neural Information Processing Systems, pp. 34–45 (2017)
15. Chen, C., Li, O., Tao, D., Barnett, A., Rudin, C., Su, J.K.: This looks like that: deep learning for interpretable image recognition. In: Advances in Neural Information Processing Systems, pp. 8928–8939 (2019)
16. Zhou, B., Khosla, A., Lapedriza, A., Oliva, A., Torralba, A.: Learning deep features for discriminative localization. In: Proceedings of the IEEE Conference on Computer Vision and Pattern Recognition, pp. 2921–2929 (2016)
17. Tsipras, D., Santurkar, S., Engstrom, L., Turner, A., Madry, A.: Robustness may be at odds with accuracy. arXiv preprint arXiv:1805.12152 (2018)
18. Tramèr, F., Kurakin, A., Papernot, N., Goodfellow, I., Boneh, D., McDaniel, P.: Ensemble adversarial training: Attacks and defenses. arXiv preprint arXiv:1705.07204 (2017)
19. Szegedy, C., et al.: Intriguing properties of neural networks. arXiv preprint arXiv:1312.6199 (2013)
20. Xu, K., et al.: Structured adversarial attack: towards general implementation and better interpretability. arXiv preprint arXiv:1808.01664 (2018)
21. Su, J., Vargas, D.V., Sakurai, K.: One pixel attack for fooling deep neural networks. IEEE Trans. Evol. Comput. 23, 828–841 (2019)
22. Narodytska, N., Kasiviswanathan, S.: Simple black-box adversarial attacks on deep neural networks. In: 2017 IEEE Conference on Computer Vision and Pattern Recognition Workshops (CVPRW), pp. 1310–1318. IEEE (2017)
23. Papernot, N., McDaniel, P., Wu, X., Jha, S., Swami, A.: Distillation as a defense to adversarial perturbations against deep neural networks. In: 2016 IEEE Symposium on Security and Privacy (SP), pp. 582–597. IEEE (2016)
24. Samangouei, P., Kabkab, M., Chellappa, R.: Defense-gan: protecting classifiers against adversarial attacks using generative models. arXiv preprint arXiv:1805.06605 (2018)
25. Xie, C., Wang, J., Zhang, Z., Ren, Z., Yuille, A.: Mitigating adversarial effects through randomization. arXiv preprint arXiv:1711.01991 (2017)
26. Song, Y., Kim, T., Nowozin, S., Ermon, S., Kushman, N.: Pixeldefend: leveraging generative models to understand and defend against adversarial examples. arXiv preprint arXiv:1710.10766 (2017)
27. Athalye, A., Carlini, N., Wagner, D.: Obfuscated gradients give a false sense of security: circumventing defenses to adversarial examples. arXiv preprint arXiv:1802.00420 (2018)
28. Mao, C., Zhong, Z., Yang, J., Vondrick, C., Ray, B.: Metric learning for adversarial robustness. In: Advances in Neural Information Processing Systems, pp. 478–489 (2019)
29. Ding, G.W., Sharma, Y., Lui, K.Y.C., Huang, R.: Mma training: direct input space margin maximization through adversarial training. In: International Conference on Learning Representations (2019)

30. Ross, A.S., Doshi-Velez, F.: Improving the adversarial robustness and interpretability of deep neural networks by regularizing their input gradients. In: Thirty-Second AAAI Conference on Artificial Intelligence (2018)
31. Zhang, H., Yu, Y., Jiao, J., Xing, E.P., Ghaoui, L.E., Jordan, M.I.: Theoretically principled trade-off between robustness and accuracy. arXiv preprint arXiv:1901.08573 (2019)
32. Tramer, F., Carlini, N., Brendel, W., Madry, A.: On adaptive attacks to adversarial example defenses. arXiv preprint arXiv:2002.08347 (2020)
33. Shafahi, A., et al.: Adversarial training for free! In: Advances in Neural Information Processing Systems, pp. 3353–3364 (2019)
34. Wong, E., Rice, L., Kolter, J.Z.: Fast is better than free: revisiting adversarial training. arXiv preprint arXiv:2001.03994 (2020)
35. Mustafa, A., Khan, S., Hayat, M., Goecke, R., Shen, J., Shao, L.: Adversarial defense by restricting the hidden space of deep neural networks. In: Proceedings of the IEEE International Conference on Computer Vision, pp. 3385–3394 (2019)
36. Mustafa, A., Khan, S.H., Hayat, M., Goecke, R., Shen, J., Shao, L.: Deeply supervised discriminative learning for adversarial defense. IEEE Transactions on Pattern Analysis and Machine Intelligence (2020)
37. Jégou, H., Douze, M., Schmid, C., Pérez, P.: Aggregating local descriptors into a compact image representation. In: 2010 IEEE Computer Society Conference on Computer Vision and Pattern Recognition, pp. 3304–3311. IEEE (2010)
38. Wang, Z., Li, H., Ouyang, W., Wang, X.: Learnable histogram: statistical context features for deep neural networks. In: Leibe, B., Matas, J., Sebe, N., Welling, M. (eds.) ECCV 2016. LNCS, vol. 9905, pp. 246–262. Springer, Cham (2016). https://doi.org/10.1007/978-3-319-46448-0_15
39. Arandjelovic, R., Gronat, P., Torii, A., Pajdla, T., Sivic, J.: Netvlad: CNN architecture for weakly supervised place recognition. In: Proceedings of the IEEE Conference on Computer Vision and Pattern Recognition, pp. 5297–5307 (2016)
40. Girdhar, R., Ramanan, D., Gupta, A., Sivic, J., Russell, B.: Actionvlad: learning spatio-temporal aggregation for action classification. In: Proceedings of the IEEE Conference on Computer Vision and Pattern Recognition, pp. 971–980 (2017)
41. Yu, K., Salzmann, M.: Statistically-motivated second-order pooling. In: Proceedings of the European Conference on Computer Vision (ECCV), pp. 600–616 (2018)
42. Kong, S., Fowlkes, C.: Low-rank bilinear pooling for fine-grained classification. In: Proceedings of the IEEE Conference on Computer Vision and Pattern Recognition, pp. 365–374 (2017)
43. Gao, Y., Beijbom, O., Zhang, N., Darrell, T.: Compact bilinear pooling. In: Proceedings of the IEEE Conference on Computer Vision and Pattern Recognition, pp. 317–326 (2016)
44. Zeiler, M.D., Fergus, R.: Visualizing and understanding convolutional networks. In: Fleet, D., Pajdla, T., Schiele, B., Tuytelaars, T. (eds.) ECCV 2014. LNCS, vol. 8689, pp. 818–833. Springer, Cham (2014). https://doi.org/10.1007/978-3-319-10590-1_53
45. Selvaraju, R.R., Cogswell, M., Das, A., Vedantam, R., Parikh, D., Batra, D.: Gradcam: visual explanations from deep networks via gradient-based localization. In: Proceedings of the IEEE International Conference on Computer Vision, pp. 618–626 (2017)
46. Chattopadhay, A., Sarkar, A., Howlader, P., Balasubramanian, V.N.: Gradcam++: generalized gradient-based visual explanations for deep convolutional networks. In: 2018 IEEE Winter Conference on Applications of Computer Vision (WACV), pp. 839–847. IEEE (2018)

47. Nguyen, A., Dosovitskiy, A., Yosinski, J., Brox, T., Clune, J.: Synthesizing the preferred inputs for neurons in neural networks via deep generator networks. In: Advances in Neural Information Processing Systems, pp. 3387–3395 (2016)

48. Nakka, K.K., Salzmann, M.: Deep attentional structured representation learning for visual recognition. arXiv preprint arXiv:1805.05389 (2018)

49. Wei, X.S., Xie, C.W., Wu, J., Shen, C.: Mask-CNN: localizing parts and selecting descriptors for fine-grained bird species categorization. Pattern Recogn. **76**, 704–714 (2018)

50. Fu, J., Zheng, H., Mei, T.: Look closer to see better: recurrent attention convolutional neural network for fine-grained image recognition. In: Proceedings of the IEEE Conference on Computer Vision and Pattern Recognition, pp. 4438–4446 (2017)

51. Wang, Y., Morariu, V.I., Davis, L.S.: Learning a discriminative filter bank within a CNN for fine-grained recognition. In: Proceedings of the IEEE Conference on Computer Vision and Pattern Recognition, pp. 4148–4157 (2018)

52. Wah, C., Branson, S., Welinder, P., Perona, P., Belongie, S.: The caltech-ucsd birds-200-2011 dataset (2011)

53. Krause, J., Stark, M., Deng, J., Fei-Fei, L.: 3D object representations for fine-grained categorization. In: Proceedings of the IEEE International Conference on Computer Vision Workshops, pp. 554–561 (2013)

54. Simonyan, K., Zisserman, A.: Very deep convolutional networks for large-scale image recognition. arXiv preprint arXiv:1409.1556 (2014)

55. Huang, G., Liu, Z., Van Der Maaten, L., Weinberger, K.Q.: Densely connected convolutional networks. In: Proceedings of the IEEE Conference on Computer Vision and Pattern Recognition, pp. 4700–4708 (2017)

56. He, K., Zhang, X., Ren, S., Sun, J.: Deep residual learning for image recognition. In: Proceedings of the IEEE Conference on Computer Vision and Pattern Recognition, pp. 770–778 (2016)

57. Schroff, F., Kalenichenko, D., Philbin, J.: Facenet: a unified embedding for face recognition and clustering. In: Proceedings of the IEEE Conference on Computer Vision and Pattern Recognition, pp. 815–823 (2015)

58. Lee, K., Lee, K., Lee, H., Shin, J.: A simple unified framework for detecting out-of-distribution samples and adversarial attacks. In: Advances in Neural Information Processing Systems, pp. 7167–7177 (2018)

Visually Guided Sound Source Separation Using Cascaded Opponent Filter Network

Lingyu Zhu$^{(\boxtimes)}$ ⓘ and Esa Rahtu$^{(\boxtimes)}$ ⓘ

Tampere University, Tampere, Finland
{lingyu.zhu,esa.rahtu}@tuni.fi

Abstract. The objective of this paper is to recover the original component signals from a mixture audio with the aid of visual cues of the sound sources. Such task is usually referred as visually guided sound source separation. The proposed *Cascaded Opponent Filter* (COF) framework consists of multiple stages, which recursively refine the source separation. A key element in COF is a novel opponent filter module that identifies and relocates residual components between sources. The system is guided by the appearance and motion of the source, and, for this purpose, we study different representations based on video frames, optical flows, dynamic images, and their combinations. Finally, we propose a *Sound Source Location Masking* (SSLM) technique, which, together with COF, produces a pixel level mask of the source location. The entire system is trained in an end-to-end manner using a large set of unlabelled videos. We compare COF with recent baselines and obtain the state-of-the-art performance in three challenging datasets (*MUSIC, A-MUSIC*, and *A-NATURAL*).

1 Introduction

Sound source separation [1–4] is a classical audio processing problem, where the objective is to recover original component signals from a given mixture audio. Well known example of such task is the cocktail party problem, where multiple people are talking simultaneously (e.g. at a cocktail party) and the observer is attempting to follow one of the discussions. The general form of the problem is challenging and highly underdetermined. Fortunately, one is often able to leverage additional constraints from external cues, such as vision. For instance, the cocktail party problem turns more tractable by observing the lip movements of people [5]. Similar visual cues have also been applied in other sound separation tasks [6–12]. This type of problem setup is often referred as visually guided sound source separation (see e.g. Fig. 1).

Besides separating the component signals from the mixture, one is often interested in identifying the source location. Such task would be intractable from a single audio channel, but could be approached using e.g. microphone

---

Electronic supplementary material The online version of this chapter (https://doi.org/10.1007/978-3-030-69544-6_25) contains supplementary material, which is available to authorized users.

© Springer Nature Switzerland AG 2021
H. Ishikawa et al. (Eds.): ACCV 2020, LNCS 12627, pp. 409–426, 2021.
https://doi.org/10.1007/978-3-030-69544-6_25

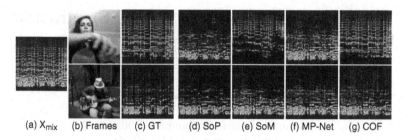

(a) X_{mix} (b) Frames (c) GT (d) SoP (e) SoM (f) MP-Net (g) COF

Fig. 1. Visually guided sound source separation aims at splitting the input mixture (column (a)) into component signals corresponding to the given visual cues (column (b)). The proposed COF approach results in better separation performance over the baseline methods SoP [8], SoM [9], and MP-Net [10] on MUSIC dataset [8].

arrays [13]. Alternatively, the sound source location could be determined from the visual data [14,15], which are more often available.

This paper proposes a new approach for visually guided sound source separation and localisation. Our system (Fig. 2), referred as Cascaded Opponent Filter (COF), consists of an initial separation stage and one or more subsequent cascaded Opponent Filter (OF) modules (Fig. 4). The OF module utilises visual cues from *all* videos to reconstruct each component audio. This is in contrast to most previous works (e.g. [8,9]), where the separation is done only based on the corresponding video. The OF module is very light containing only 17 parameters (in our case) and we show that it can greatly improve the sound separation performance over the recent single stage systems [8,9] and recursive method [10].

Moreover, since motion is strongly correlated to sound formation [9], we build our system on both appearance and motion representations. To this end, we examine multiple options based on video frames, optical flows, dynamic images [16], and their combinations. Finally, we introduce a Sound Source Location Masking (SSLM) network that, in conjunction with COF, is able to pin point pixel level segmentation of the sound source location. Qualitative results indicate sharper and more accurate results compared to the baselines [8–10]. The entire system is trained using a self-supervised setup with a large set of unlabelled videos.

2   Related Work

Cross-modal Learning from Audio and Vision. Aytar *et al.* [17] presented a method for learning joint audio-visual embeddings by minimizing the KL-divergence of their representations. Owens *et al.* [18] proposed a synchronization based cross-modal approach for visual representation learning. Arandjelovic *et al.* [19,20] associated the learnt audio and visual embeddings by asking whether they originate from the same video. Nagrani *et al.* [21] learned to identify face and voice correspondences. More recent works, include transferring mono- to binaural audio using visual features [11], audio-video deep clustering [22], talking face generation [23], audio-driven 3D facial animation prediction [24], vehicle tracking with stereo sound [25], visual-to-auditory [26,27], audio-visual navigation [28,29], and speech embedding disentanglements [30]. Unlike these works, (visually guided) sound source separation aims at splitting the input audio into original components signals.

Video Sequence Representations. Most early works in video representations were largely based on direct extensions of the image based models [31–33]. More recently, these have been replaced by deep learning alternatives operating on stack of consecutive video frames. These works can be roughly divided into following categories: 1) 3D CNN applied on spatio-temporal video volume [34]; 2) two-stream CNNs [35–37] applied on video frames and separately computed optical flow frames; 3) LSTM [38], Graph CNN [39] and attention clusters [40] based techniques; and 4) 2D CNN with the concept of dynamic image [16]. Since most of these methods are proposed for action recognition problem, it is unclear which representation would be best suited for self-supervised sound source separation. Therefore, this paper evaluates multiple options and discusses their pros and cons.

(Visually Guided) Sound Source Separation. The sound source separation task is extensively studied in the audio processing community. Early works were mainly based on probabilistic models [1–4], while recent methods utilise deep learning architectures [41–44]. Despite of the substantial improvements, the pure audio based source separation remains a challenging task. At the same time, visually guided sound source separation has gained increasing attention. Ephrat *et al.* [5] extracted face embeddings to facilitate speech separation. Similarly, Gao *et al.* [6,12] utilised object detection and category information to guide source separation. Gan *et al.* [45] associated body and finger movements with audio signals by learning a keypoint-based structured representation. While impressive, these methods rely on the external knowledge of the video content (e.g. speaking faces, object types, or keypoints).

The works by Zhao *et al.* [8,9] and Xu *et al.* [10] are most related to ours. In [8] the input spectrogram is split into components using U-Net [46] architecture and the separated outputs are constructed as a linear combinations of these. The mixing coefficients are estimated by applying Dilated ResNet to the keyframes representing the sources. The subsequent work [9] introduced motion features and improvements to the output spectrogram prediction. Both of these methods operate in a single stage manner directly predicting the final output. Alternatively, Xu *et al.* [10] proposed to separate sounds by recursively removing large energy components from the sound mixture. Our work explores multiple approaches to utilize the appearance and motion information to refine the sound source separation in multi-stages. The proposed Opponent Filter uses visual features of a sound source to look for incorrectly assigned sound components from opponent sources, resulting in accurate sound separation.

Sound Source Localization. Early work by Hershey *et al.* [47] localised sound sources by modeling the audio-visual synchrony as a non-stationary Gaussian

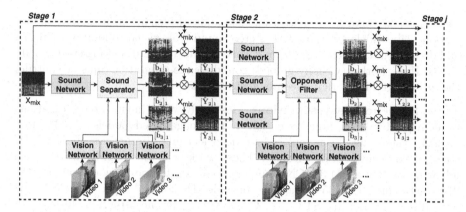

Fig. 2. Architecture of the proposed Cascaded Opponent Filter (COF) network. COF operates in multiple stages: In the first stage, visual representations (vision network) and sound features (sound network) are passed to the sound separator and further produce a binary mask $\hat{b}$ (Eq. (1), (2)) for each output source. Stage two refines the separation result $\hat{Y}$ using the opponent filter (OF) module guided by the visual cues. Later stages are identical to second stage with OF module. The sound networks share parameters only if they are in the same stage. The vision networks share parameters (within and across stages) if they have same architecture.

process. Barzelay *et al.* [48] applied cross-modal association and visual localization by temporal coincidences. Based on canonical correlations, Kidron *et al.* [49] localized visual events associated with sound sources. Recently, Senocak *et al.* [50] learned to localize sound sources in visual scenes by transferring the sound-guided visual concepts to sound context vector. Arandjelovic *et al.* [20] obtained locations by comparing visual and audio embeddings using a coarse grid. Class activation maps were used by [7,51]. Gao *et al.* [12] localised potential sound sources via a separate object detector. Rouditchenko *et al.* [52] segmented visual objects by leveraging a task of sound separation. Zhao *et al.* [8,9] and Xu *et al.* [10] visualise the sound sources by calculating the sound volume at each spatial location. In contrast to these methods, which either produce coarse sound location or rely on the external knowledge, we propose a self-supervised SSLM network to localise sound sources on a pixel level.

3   Method

This section describes the proposed visually guided sound source separation method. We start with a short overview and then continue to detailed describe each component.

3.1   Overview

The inputs to our system consist of a mixture audio (e.g. band playing) and a set of videos, each representing one component of the mixture (e.g. person playing

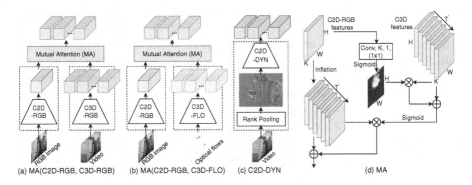

Fig. 3. Architecture of (a) MA(C2D-RGB, C3D-RGB), (b) MA(C2D-RGB, C3D-FLO), (c) C2D-DYN, and (d) MA: Mutual Attention module.

a guitar). The objective of the system is to recover the component sound signals corresponding to each video sequence. Figure 2 illustrates an overview of the approach. Note that the audio signals are represented as spectrograms, which are obtained from the audio stream using Short-term Fourier transform (STFT).

The proposed system consists of multiple cascaded stages. The first stage contains three components: 1) a sound network that splits the input spectrogram into a set of feature maps; 2) a vision network that converts the input video sequences into compact representations; and 3) a sound separator that produces spectrum masks (not shown in Fig. 2) of the component audios (one per video) based on the outputs of the sound and vision networks.

The second stage contains similar sound and vision networks as the first one (internal details may differ). However, instead of the sound separator, the second stage contains a special Opponent Filter (OF) module, which enhances the separation result by transferring sound components between the sources. The output of the filter is passed to the next stage or used as the final output. The following stages are identical to the second one and, for this reason, we refer our method as cascaded opponent filter (COF) network. The final component audios are produced by applying the inverse STFT to the predicted component spectrograms.

In addition, we propose a new Sound Source Location Masking (SSLM) network (not shown in Fig. 2) that indicates the pixels with highest impact on the sound source separation (i.e. source location). The entire network is trained in an end-to-end fashion using artificially generated examples. That is, we take two or more videos and create an artificial mixture by summing the corresponding audio tracks. The created mixture and video frames are provided to the system, which then has to reproduce the original component audios. In the following sections, we will present each component with more details and provide the learning objective used in the training phase.

3.2   Vision Network

The vision network aims at converting the input video sequence (or keyframe) into a compact representation that contains the necessary information of the sound source. Sometimes already a pure appearance of the source (e.g. instrument type) might be sufficient, but, in most cases, the motions are vital cues to facilitate the source separation (e.g. hand motion, mouth motion, etc.). The appropriate representation may have high model/computation complexity and, to seek for a balance between computational complexity and performance, we study several visual representation options. The models are introduced in the following and the detailed network architectures are provided in the supplementary material. In all cases, we assume that the input video sequence is of size $3 \times 16H \times 16W$ and has T frames.

The first option, referred as **C2D-RGB**, is a pure appearance-based representation. This is obtained by applying a dilated ResNet18 [53] to a single keyframe extracted from the sequence. More specifically, given an input RGB image of size $3 \times 16H \times 16W$, the C2D-RGB produces a representation of size $K \times H \times W$. Dynamic image [16] is a compact representation, which summarises the appearance and motion of the entire video sequence into a single RGB image by rank pooling the original pixel data. The second option, referred as **C2D-DYN**, first converts the input video into a dynamic image (size $3 \times 16H \times 16W$) and then applies a dilated ResNet18 [53] to produce a representation of size $K \times H \times W$. Figure 3c illustrates C2D-DYN option.

The third option, referred as **C3D-RGB**, applies 3D CNN to extract the appearance and motion information from the sequence simultaneously. C3D-RGB uses 3D version of ResNet18 and produces a representation of size $T' \times K \times H \times W$. The optical flow [35,54,55] explicitly describes the motion between the video frames. The fourth option, referred as **C3D-FLO**, first estimates the optical flow between the consecutive video frames using LiteFlowNet [55], and then applies 3D ResNet18 to the obtained flow sequence. C3D-FLO produces a representation of size $T' \times K \times H \times W$.

In addition, following the recent work [36] in action recognition, we propose a set of two stream options by combining pairs of C2D-RGB, C3D-RGB, and C3D-FLO representations using Mutual Attention (MA) module. The module is depicted in Fig. 3d. It enhances the sound source relevant motions and eliminates motion irrelevant appearance by giving the mutual attention mechanism. Finally, we receive the mutual attentive features of dimension $T' \times K \times H \times W$ from the two-stream structures, which are referred to as **MA(C2D-RGB, C3D-RGB)** and **MA(C2D-RGB, C3D-FLO)**. Figure 3a and 3b illustrate these options. We omit the model of two 3D streams MA(C3D-RGB, C3D-FLO) due to large size of the resulting model.

3.3   Sound Network

The sound network splits the input audio spectrogram into a set of feature maps. The network is implemented using U-Net [46] architecture and it converts

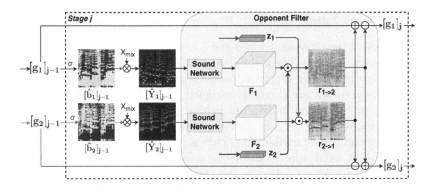

Fig. 4. An illustration of the Opponent Filter (OF) module at stage j in the case of two sound sources. The input consists of the visual representation $\mathbf{z}$ and the previous spectrum mask $[g]_{j-1}$, for both sources. First, we obtain the spectrograms $\hat{Y}$ for both sources from the spectrum masks (Eq. (2)). Second, the spectrograms are turned into feature maps F with the sound network (Sect. 3.3). Third, the visual representation $\mathbf{z}_2$ and the feature map F_1 are used to identify components from the source 1 that should belong to the source 2 ($r_{1->2}$ in figure). The spectrum masks are updated accordingly by subtracting from $[g_1]_{j-1}$ and adding to $[g_2]_{j-1}$. Similar operation is done for the source 2. Finally, the updated spectrum masks $[g_1]_j$ and $[g_2]_j$ are passed to the next stage.

the input spectrogram of size $HS \times WS$ into an output of size $HS \times WS \times K$. Note that the number of created feature maps K is equal to the visual feature dimension K in the previous section. At the first stage, the input to the sound network is the original mixture spectrogram X_{mix}, while in later stages, the sound network operates on the current estimates of the component spectrograms. This allows stages to focus on different details of the spectrogram. In the following, we will denote the kth feature map, produced by the sound network for an input spectrogram X, as $S(X)_k$.

3.4 Sound Separator

The sound separator combines the visual representations with the sound network output and produces an estimate of the component signals. First, we apply global max pooling operation over the spatial dimensions ($H \times W$) of the visual representation. For 3D CNN-based options, we further apply max pooling layer along the temporal dimension (T'). As a result, we obtain a feature vector $\mathbf{z}$ with K elements. We combine $\mathbf{z}$ with sound network output using a linear combination to predict the spectrum masks g as Eq. (1).

$$g(\mathbf{z}, X) = \sum_{k=1}^{K} \alpha_k \, \mathbf{z_k} * S(X)_k + \beta,\qquad(1)$$

where α_k and β are learnable weight parameters, $\mathbf{z}_k$ is the kth element of visual vector $\mathbf{z}$, and $S(X)_k$ is the kth sound network feature map for a spectrogram X.

3.5   Opponent Filter Module

The structure of the Opponent Filter (OF) module is illustrated in Fig. 4 in the case of two sound sources. The main idea in the OF is to use visual representation of the source n to identify spectrum components from the source m that should belong to source n but are currently assigned to m. These are then transferred from source m to n. The motivation behind the construction is to utilise all visual representations $z_1, \ldots, z_N$ to determine each component audio, instead of using only the corresponding one. This is in contrast to the previous works SoP [8], SoM [9] (and approximately for MP-Net [10]), where the output for each source is determined solely by the same visual input. Our approach leads to more efficient use of the visual cues, which is reflected by the performance improvements shown in the experiments (see Sect. 4.2). Moreover, in our case ($K = 16$), the selected architecture requires only 17 parameters (consist of 16 α_k values and one β as shown in Eq. (3)), which makes it very light and efficient to learn. The OF module is used in all but the first stage of the COF.

More specifically, the OF module takes the visual representation $\mathbf{z}$ and the previous spectrum mask $[g]_{j-1}$ for each sound source as an input. Firstly, the spectrum masks are converted to the spectrograms $\hat{Y}$ as

$$\hat{b} = th(\sigma(g)), \quad \hat{Y} = \hat{b} \otimes X_{mix} \tag{2}$$

where σ denotes the sigmoid function, th represents the thresholding operation with value 0.5, and $\otimes$ is the element-wise product. In other words, we first map g into a binary mask $\hat{b}$, and then produce the estimate of the output component spectrogram as an element-wise multiplication between the binary mask $\hat{b}$ and the original mixture spectrogram X_{mix}. g and $\hat{Y}$ are provided for the upcoming stage as inputs (or used as the final output). We denote the outputs corresponding to nth video at stage j as $[g_n]_j$, $[\hat{b}_n]_j$, and $[\hat{Y}_n]_j$. The obtained spectograms are passed to the sound network (see Sect. 3.3), which converts them to feature maps of size $HS \times WS \times K$ denoted by F_n for the source n.

Secondly, the OF module takes one source at a time, referred using index $n \in [1, N]$, and iterates over the remaining sources $m \in \{[1, N] | m \neq n\}$. N is the number of sources in sound mixture. For each pair (n, m) the filter determines a component of source m that should be reassigned to the source n as

$$r_{m->n} = \sum_{k=1}^{K} \alpha_k \mathbf{z_{n,k}} * F_{m,k} + \beta \tag{3}$$

where $\mathbf{z}_{n,k}$ is the kth element of visual representation of sound n. $F_{m,k}$ is the kth sound network feature maps of sound m. The $r_{m->n}$ denotes the residual spectrum components identified from source m that should belong to source n but are currently assigned to m. The obtained component will be subtracted from the spectrum mask $[g_m]_{j-1}$ and added to $[g_n]_{j-1}$ as follows

$$[g_m]_j = [g_m]_{j-1} \ominus r_{m->n} \tag{4}$$

$$[g_n]_j = [g_n]_{j-1} \oplus r_{m->n} \tag{5}$$

where the $[g_n]_j$ is the spectrum mask (Eq. (1)) of nth video in stage j, $r_{m->n}$ is the residual spectrum components from sound m to sound n. $\oplus$ and $\ominus$ denote the element-wise sum and subtraction, respectively.

The overall process can be summarized in the following Algorithm 1,

---

Algorithm 1. Algorithm of Opponent Filter (OF) module

1: **for** n = 1 ... N **do**
2:    **for** m = 1 ... N **do**
3:       **if** $n \neq m$ **then**
4:          $r_{m->n} = \sum_{k=1}^{K} \alpha_k \mathbf{z_{n,k}} * F_{m,k} + \beta$ ▷ obtain $r_{m->n}$
5:          $[g_m]_j \leftarrow [g_m]_{j-1} \ominus r_{m->n}$ ▷ subtract $r_{m->n}$ from $[g_m]_{j-1}$
6:          $[g_n]_j \leftarrow [g_n]_{j-1} \oplus r_{m->n}$ ▷ add $r_{m->n}$ to $[g_n]_{j-1}$
7:       **end if**
8:    **end for**
9: **end for**
10: **return** $[g]_j$ ▷ return $[g]_j$ of all the sound sources

---

3.6   Learning Objective

The model parameters are optimised with respect to the binary cross entropy (BCE) loss that is evaluated between the predicted and ground truth masks over all stages. More specifically,

$$\mathcal{L}_{sep} = \sum_{j=1}^{J} r_j \, BCE([\hat{b}]_j, b_{gt}) \tag{6}$$

where r_j is a weight parameter, $[\hat{b}]_j$ is the predicted binary mask, b_{gt} is the ground truth mask (determined by whether the target sound is the dominant component in the mixture), and J is the total number of stages.

3.7   Sound Source Location Masking Network

The objective of the Sound Source Location Masking (SSLM) network is to identify a minimum set of input pixels, for which the COF network would produce almost identical output as for the entire image. In practice, we follow the ideas presented in [56], and build an auxiliary network to estimate a sound source location mask that is applied to the input RGB frames. The SSLM is trained together with the overall model in a self-supervised manner (please see supplementary material). The input video frames are first passed through the SSLM component which outputs a weighted location mask [0,1] having same spatial size as the input frame. The input video frames are multiplied element-wise with the

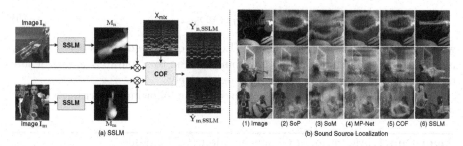

(a) SSLM

(1) Image (2) SoP (3) SoM (4) MP-Net (5) COF (6) SSLM

(b) Sound Source Localization

Fig. 5. (a) The diagram of the Sound Source Location Masking (SSLM) network and (b) Visualizing sound source location of our methods in comparison with baseline models SoP [8], SoM [9], and MP-Net [10] on MUSIC dataset.

mask, and the result is passed to the COF model. We illustrate the overall structure of the SSLM in Fig. 5a. The final optimisation is done by minimising the following loss function,

$$\mathcal{L} = \sum_{j=1}^{J} r_j \, l_{diff}([\hat{b}_{SSLM}]_j, [\hat{b}]_j) + \lambda \frac{1}{q} \parallel SSLM(I) \parallel_1, \tag{7}$$

where l_{diff} denotes the difference between the $[\hat{b}_{SSLM}]_j$ and $[\hat{b}]_j$ by L_1 norm, $[\hat{b}_{SSLM}]_j$ is the output sound separation mask obtained using only selected pixels, $[\hat{b}]_j$ is the output separation mask for the original image. r_j and λ are hyperparameters which control the contribution of each loss factor. The $\lambda \frac{1}{q} \parallel SSLM(I) \parallel_1$ norm produces a location mask with only small number of non-zero values. q is the total number of pixels of the $SSLM(I)$.

4   Experiments

We evaluate the proposed approach using Multimodel Sources of Instrument Combinations (MUSIC) [8] dataset, and two sub-sets of AudioSet [57]: A-MUSIC and A-NATURAL. The proposed model is trained using artificial examples, generated by adding audio signals from two or more training videos. The performance of the final sound source separation is measured in terms of standard metrics: Signal to Distortion Ratio (SDR), Signal to Interference Ratio (SIR), and Signal to Artifact Ratio (SAR). Higher is better for all metrics[1].

4.1   Datasets and Implementation Details

MUSIC. The Multimodel Sources of Instrument Combinations (MUSIC) [8] dataset is a relatively small, but has high quality. Most of the video frames are

---

[1] Note that SDR and SIR scores measure the separation accuracy, SAR captures only the absence of artifacts (and hence can be high even if separation is poor).

well aligned with the audio signals and have little off-screen noise. Part of the original MUSIC dataset is no longer available in YouTube (10% missing at the time of writing). In order to keep dataset size, we replaced the missing entries with similar YouTube videos. Baseline methods (e.g., SoP [8]) in original paper split the dataset into 500 training and 130 validation videos, and report the performances on the validation set (train/test split are not published). Instead, we follow the standard practice of reporting the performance on a separate hold-out test set. For this purpose, we randomly split the dataset into 400 training, 100 validation, and 130 test videos. This leads to 20% less training videos compared to [8]. All tested methods are trained and evaluated with the same data and pre-processing steps (see implementation details).

Table 1. The sound separation results of the proposed COF network, conditioning on appearance cues, on MUSIC test dataset

Models	SDR	SIR	SAR
COF - 1 stage	5.38	11.00	9.77
COF$_{addition}$ - 2 stages	6.29	11.83	10.21
COF$_{subtraction}$ - 2 stages	6.30	12.61	10.13
COF - 2 stages	**8.25**	**14.24**	**12.02**

A-MUSIC and A-NATURAL. AudioSet consists of an expanding ontology of 632 audio event classes and is a collection of over 2 million 10-s sound clips drawn from YouTube videos. Many of the AudioSet videos have limited quality and sometimes the visual content might be uncorrelated to the audio track. A-MUSIC dataset is a trimmed musical instrument dataset from AudioSet. It has around 25k videos spanning ten instrumental categories. A-NATURAL dataset is a trimmed natural sound dataset from AudioSet. It contains around 10k videos which cover 10 categories of natural sounds. We split both the A-MUSIC and A-NATURAL dataset samples to 80%, 10%, and 10% as train, validation and test set. More details of datasets are discussed in the supplementary material.

Implementation Details. We sub-sample each audio signals at 11kHz and randomly crop an audio clip of 6 s for training. A Time-Frequency (T-F) spectrogram of size 512×256 is obtained by applying STFT, with a Hanning window size of 1022 and a hop length of 256, to the input sound clip. We further re-sample this spectrogram to a T-F representation of size 256×256 on a log-frequency scale. We extract video frames at 8fps and give a single RGB image to the C2D-RGB model, $T = 48$ frames to C2D-DYN and all the discussed C3D models. Further implementation details are provided in the supplementary material.

4.2 Opponent Filter

In this section, we assess the performance of the OF module. For simplicity we use only the appearance based features (C2D-RGB) in all stages. The baseline is provided by the basic single stage version denoted as COF - 1 stage, which does not contain the opponent filter module. The results provided in Table 1 indicate a clear improvement from the OF stages.

In addition, we evaluate the impact of the "addition" and "subtraction" branches in the OF module. To this end, we implement two versions $COF_{addition}$ and $COF_{subtraction}$, which include only the "addition" (Eq. (5)) or "subtraction" (Eq. (4)) operation in the OF, respectively. The corresponding results in Table 1 indicate that both versions obtain similar performance which is between the baseline and the full model. We conclude that both operations are essential part of the OF module and contribute equally to the sound separation result.

Table 2. The sound separation results with COF, conditioning on different visual cues, on the MUSIC test dataset. Table contains three blocks: 1) single-stage COF associated with visual cues predicted from MA-RGB, MA-FLO, and C2D-DYN; 2) two-stage extension of the models in the first block; 3) two-stage COF with C2D-RGB at stage 1 and C3D-RGB, C3D-FLO, or C2D-DYN at stage 2

	Models	SDR	SIR	SAR
1	COF(MA-RGB)	6.68	12.24	10.63
	COF(MA-FLO)	5.84	11.39	10.27
	COF(C2D-DYN)	6.37	11.75	10.79
2	COF(MA-RGB, MA-RGB)	8.78	15.07	12.10
	COF(MA-FLO, MA-FLO)	8.71	15.07	11.83
	COF(C2D-DYN, C2D-DYN)	8.95	15.03	12.07
3	COF(C2D-RGB, C3D-RGB)	8.97	15.06	**12.53**
	COF(C2D-RGB, C3D-FLO)	9.04	15.28	12.24
	COF(C2D-RGB, C2D-DYN)	**9.17**	**15.32**	12.37

4.3 Visual Representations

We firstly separate sounds by implementing a single stage network, associating with the appearance and motion cues discussed in Sect. 3.2. We denote the MA(C2D-RGB, C3D-RGB) and MA(C2D-RGB, C3D-FLO) as MA-RGB and MA-FLO in Table 2. As is shown in the block 1 of Table 2, the results with appearance and motion cues clearly surpass the network with only appearance cues from C2D-RGB in Table 1, which proposes that the motion representation is important for the sound separation quality. Block 2 shows the performance of how the visual information separates sounds in a two-stage manner. Explicitly, we replace the vision network at each stage in Fig. 2 with MA-RGB, MA-FLO, and C2D-DYN. Block 1 and 2 report that the three two-stage networks obtain similar performance and outperform their single-stage counterparts from block 1 with a large margin.

Finally, we evaluate an option where the first stage utilises only appearance based option and the second stage applies motion cues. In practice, we combine C2D-RGB with C3D-RGB, C3D-FLO, or C2D-DYN. The results in block 3 of Table 2, indicate that this combination obtains similar or even better performance than the options where motion information was provided for both stages. We conclude that the appearance information is enough to facilitate coarse separation at first stage. The motion information is only needed at the later stages to provide higher separation quality. It is worth noting that the COF(C2D-RGB, C2D-DYN) combination has less computation complexity and better performance compared to the 3D CNN alternatives. **Therefore, we apply C2D-RGB for the 1st stage and C2D-DYN for the later stages for all the remaining experiments**.

Table 3. Sound separation performance with 2 and 3 stages COF models compared with three recent baselines SoP [8], SoM [9], and MP-Net [10], on MUSIC, A-MUSIC, and A-NATURAL datasets. The top 2 results are bolded.

Models\Datasets	MUSIC			A-MUSIC			A-NATURAL		
	SDR	SIR	SAR	SDR	SIR	SAR	SDR	SIR	SAR
SoP	5.38	11.00	9.77	2.05	5.36	10.69	2.83	7.24	8.51
SoM	4.83	11.04	8.67	2.56	5.98	8.80	2.56	7.69	8.02
MP-Net	5.71	11.36	10.45	2.34	5.27	**11.27**	3.20	8.17	8.68
COF - 2 stages	**9.17**	**15.32**	**12.37**	**3.31**	**7.08**	10.74	**4.00**	**8.85**	**8.70**
COF - 3 stages	**10.07**	**16.69**	**13.02**	**5.42**	**9.47**	10.94	**4.10**	8.60	**10.58**

4.4   Comparison with the State-of-the-Art

We compare the 2-stage and 3-stage of the proposed COF model with three recent baseline methods SoP [8], SoM [9], and MP-Net [10]. For SoP we use the publicly available implementation from the original authors. For SoM and MP-Net we use our own implementations since there were no publicly available versions. The corresponding results for MUSIC[2], A-MUSIC, and A-NATURAL datasets are provided in Table 3, Fig. 1, and Fig. 6. The quantitative results indicate that our model outperforms the baselines with a large margin across all three datasets.

Increasing the Number of Stages: We observe that the computational cost increases approximately linearly with respect to the number of stages. The performance generally improves until it reaches a plateau. COF with 2, 3, 4, and 5

---

[2] We note that due to the differences in the dataset and evaluation protocol (see Sect. 4.1.) the absolute results differ from those reported in [8] and [9] for MUSIC.

stages obtain SDRs of 9.17, 10.07, 10.12, and 10.32 on MUSIC dataset, respectively. The corresponding FLOPs (GMACS) are 8.05, 12.06, 16.06, and 20.07. The performance plateaus at 3 stages, which led to a compromise at this point.

Mixture of Three Sources: We assess the COF model using a mixture of three sound sources from the MUSIC dataset. In this case, the two-stage model obtains SDR: 3.33, SIR: 10.32, and SAR: 6.70 which are clearly higher than SDR: 1.30, SIR: 8.66, and SAR: 5.73 obtained with MP-Net [10] that is particularly designed for the multi-source case. As discussed in Sect. 3.5, the computational cost of COF scales approximately linearly with the number of sources. For instance, the FLOPs (GMACS) for 2, 3, 4, 5, 10, and 15 sources are 8.05, 11.09, 14.12, 17.16, 32.36, and 47.62 respectively.

4.5   Visualizing Sound Source Locations

We compare the sound source localizing capability of our best two-stage model with state-of-the-art methods in Fig. 5b. Columns (2)–(5) display the sound energy distributions of spatial location in heatmaps on input frame during inference. COF produces precise associations between visual representation and separated sounds, though columns (5) is just the visualization from the first stage of COF. As we know, the spatial features from ConvNet usually have small resolution (14 × 14 pixels in this work). Thus, the final visualized location is generally coarse after up-sampling the heatmap to the resolution of the input image. Differently, our proposed SSLM learns to predict a pixel-level sound source location

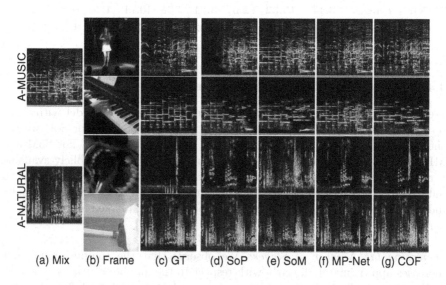

(a) Mix   (b) Frame   (c) GT   (d) SoP   (e) SoM   (f) MP-Net   (g) COF

Fig. 6. Visualizing sound source separation of our 2-stage COF model on A-MUSIC and A-NATURAL datasets, in comparison with baseline methods SoP [8], SoM [9], and MP-Net [10].

mask, as shown in column (6), which precisely localizes sound sources and preserves high quality of sound separation. Further examples are provided in the supplementary material.

5   Conclusions

We proposed an innovative framework of visually guided Cascaded Opponent Filter (COF) network to recursively refine sound separation with visual cues of sound sources. The proposed Opponent Filter (OF) module uses visual features of all sound sources to look for incorrectly assigned sound components from opponent sounds, resulting in accurate sound separation. For this purpose, we studied different visual representations based on video frames, optical flows, dynamic images, and their combinations. Moreover, we introduced a Sound Source Location Making (SSLM) network, together with COF, to precisely localize sound sources.

Acknowledgement. This work is supported by the Academy of Finland (projects 327910 & 324346).

References

1. Ghahramani, Z., Jordan, M.I.: Factorial hidden Markov models. Mach. Learn. **29**, 472–478 (1996). https://doi.org/10.1023/A:1007425814087
2. Roweis, S.T.: One microphone source separation. In: Advances in Neural Information Processing Systems, pp. 793–799 (2001)
3. Cichocki, A., Zdunek, R., Phan, A.H., Amari, S.I.: Nonnegative Matrix and Tensor Factorizations: Applications to Exploratory Multi-way Data Analysis and Blind Source Separation. Wiley, Hoboken (2009)
4. Virtanen, T.: Monaural sound source separation by nonnegative matrix factorization with temporal continuity and sparseness criteria. IEEE Trans. Audio Speech Lang. Process. **15**, 1066–1074 (2007)
5. Ephrat, A., et al.: Looking to listen at the cocktail party: a speaker-independent audio-visual model for speech separation. arXiv preprint arXiv:1804.03619 (2018)
6. Gao, R., Feris, R., Grauman, K.: Learning to separate object sounds by watching unlabeled video. In: Proceedings of the European Conference on Computer Vision (ECCV), pp. 35–53 (2018)
7. Owens, A., Efros, A.A.: Audio-visual scene analysis with self-supervised multisensory features. In: Proceedings of the European Conference on Computer Vision (ECCV), pp. 631–648 (2018)
8. Zhao, H., Gan, C., Rouditchenko, A., Vondrick, C., McDermott, J., Torralba, A.: The sound of pixels. In: Proceedings of the European Conference on Computer Vision (ECCV), pp. 570–586 (2018)
9. Zhao, H., Gan, C., Ma, W.C., Torralba, A.: The sound of motions. In: Proceedings of the IEEE International Conference on Computer Vision, pp. 1735–1744 (2019)
10. Xu, X., Dai, B., Lin, D.: Recursive visual sound separation using minus-plus net. In: Proceedings of the IEEE International Conference on Computer Vision, pp. 882–891 (2019)

11. Gao, R., Grauman, K.: 2.5 D visual sound. In: Proceedings of the IEEE Conference on Computer Vision and Pattern Recognition, pp. 324–333 (2019)
12. Gao, R., Grauman, K.: Co-separating sounds of visual objects. In: Proceedings of the IEEE International Conference on Computer Vision, pp. 3879–3888 (2019)
13. Pertilä, P., Mieskolainen, M., Hämäläinen, M.S.: Closed-form self-localization of asynchronous microphone arrays. In: Joint Workshop on Hands-Free Speech Communication and Microphone Arrays, vol. 2011, pp. 139–144. IEEE (2011)
14. Tian, Y., Shi, J., Li, B., Duan, Z., Xu, C.: Audio-visual event localization in unconstrained videos. In: Proceedings of the European Conference on Computer Vision (ECCV), pp. 247–263 (2018)
15. Hu, D., Nie, F., Li, X.: Deep multimodal clustering for unsupervised audiovisual learning. In: Proceedings of the IEEE Conference on Computer Vision and Pattern Recognition, pp. 9248–9257 (2019)
16. Bilen, H., Fernando, B., Gavves, E., Vedaldi, A., Gould, S.: Dynamic image networks for action recognition. In: Proceedings of the IEEE Conference on Computer Vision and Pattern Recognition, pp. 3034–3042 (2016)
17. Aytar, Y., Vondrick, C., Torralba, A.: Soundnet: learning sound representations from unlabeled video. In: Advances in Neural Information Processing Systems, pp. 892–900 (2016)
18. Owens, A., Wu, J., McDermott, J.H., Freeman, W.T., Torralba, A.: Ambient sound provides supervision for visual learning. In: Leibe, B., Matas, J., Sebe, N., Welling, M. (eds.) ECCV 2016. LNCS, vol. 9905, pp. 801–816. Springer, Cham (2016). https://doi.org/10.1007/978-3-319-46448-0_48
19. Arandjelovic, R., Zisserman, A.: Look, listen and learn. In: Proceedings of the IEEE International Conference on Computer Vision, pp. 609–617 (2017)
20. Arandjelovic, R., Zisserman, A.: Objects that sound. In: Proceedings of the European Conference on Computer Vision (ECCV), pp. 435–451 (2018)
21. Nagrani, A., Albanie, S., Zisserman, A.: Seeing voices and hearing faces: cross-modal biometric matching. In: Proceedings of the IEEE Conference on Computer Vision and Pattern Recognition, pp. 8427–8436 (2018)
22. Alwassel, H., Mahajan, D., Torresani, L., Ghanem, B., Tran, D.: Self-supervised learning by cross-modal audio-video clustering. arXiv preprint arXiv:1911.12667 (2019)
23. Zhou, H., Liu, Y., Liu, Z., Luo, P., Wang, X.: Talking face generation by adversarially disentangled audio-visual representation. In: Proceedings of the AAAI Conference on Artificial Intelligence, vol. 33, pp. 9299–9306 (2019)
24. Cudeiro, D., Bolkart, T., Laidlaw, C., Ranjan, A., Black, M.J.: Capture, learning, and synthesis of 3D speaking styles. In: Proceedings of the IEEE Conference on Computer Vision and Pattern Recognition, pp. 10101–10111 (2019)
25. Gan, C., Zhao, H., Chen, P., Cox, D., Torralba, A.: Self-supervised moving vehicle tracking with stereo sound. In: Proceedings of the IEEE International Conference on Computer Vision, pp. 7053–7062 (2019)
26. Hu, D., Wang, D., Li, X., Nie, F., Wang, Q.: Listen to the image. In: Proceedings of the IEEE Conference on Computer Vision and Pattern Recognition, pp. 7972–7981 (2019)
27. Gan, C., Huang, D., Chen, P., Tenenbaum, J.B., Torralba, A.: Foley music: learning to generate music from videos. arXiv preprint arXiv:2007.10984 (2020)
28. Chen, C., Jain, U., Schissler, C., Gari, S.V.A., Al-Halah, Z., Ithapu, V.K., Robinson, P., Grauman, K.: Audio-visual embodied navigation. arXiv preprint arXiv:1912.11474 (2019)

29. Gan, C., Zhang, Y., Wu, J., Gong, B., Tenenbaum, J.B.: Look, listen, and act: towards audio-visual embodied navigation. In: 2020 IEEE International Conference on Robotics and Automation (ICRA), pp. 9701–9707. IEEE (2020)

30. Nagrani, A., Chung, J.S., Albanie, S., Zisserman, A.: Disentangled speech embeddings using cross-modal self-supervision. arXiv preprint arXiv:2002.08742 (2020)

31. Laptev, I., Marszalek, M., Schmid, C., Rozenfeld, B.: Learning realistic human actions from movies. In: 2008 IEEE Conference on Computer Vision and Pattern Recognition, pp. 1–8. IEEE (2008)

32. Wang, H., Ullah, M.M., Klaser, A., Laptev, I., Schmid, C.: Evaluation of local spatio-temporal features for action recognition (2009)

33. Klaser, A., Marszałek, M., Schmid, C.: A spatio-temporal descriptor based on 3D-gradients (2008)

34. Tran, D., Bourdev, L., Fergus, R., Torresani, L., Paluri, M.: Learning spatiotemporal features with 3d convolutional networks. In: Proceedings of the IEEE International Conference on Computer Vision, pp. 4489–4497 (2015)

35. Simonyan, K., Zisserman, A.: Two-stream convolutional networks for action recognition in videos. In: Advances in Neural Information Processing Systems, pp. 568–576 (2014)

36. Carreira, J., Zisserman, A.: Quo vadis, action recognition? A new model and the kinetics dataset. In: Proceedings of the IEEE Conference on Computer Vision and Pattern Recognition, pp. 6299–6308 (2017)

37. Zhan, X., Pan, X., Liu, Z., Lin, D., Loy, C.C.: Self-supervised learning via conditional motion propagation. In: Proceedings of the IEEE Conference on Computer Vision and Pattern Recognition, pp. 1881–1889 (2019)

38. Donahue, J., et al.: Long-term recurrent convolutional networks for visual recognition and description. In: Proceedings of the IEEE Conference on Computer Vision and Pattern Recognition, pp. 2625–2634 (2015)

39. Wang, X., Gupta, A.: Videos as space-time region graphs. In: Proceedings of the European Conference on Computer Vision (ECCV), pp. 399–417 (2018)

40. Long, X., Gan, C., De Melo, G., Wu, J., Liu, X., Wen, S.: Attention clusters: purely attention based local feature integration for video classification. In: Proceedings of the IEEE Conference on Computer Vision and Pattern Recognition, pp. 7834–7843 (2018)

41. Simpson, A.J.R., Roma, G., Plumbley, M.D.: Deep karaoke: extracting vocals from musical mixtures using a convolutional deep neural network. In: Vincent, E., Yeredor, A., Koldovský, Z., Tichavský, P. (eds.) LVA/ICA 2015. LNCS, vol. 9237, pp. 429–436. Springer, Cham (2015). https://doi.org/10.1007/978-3-319-22482-4_50

42. Chandna, P., Miron, M., Janer, J., Gómez, E.: Monoaural audio source separation using deep convolutional neural networks. In: Tichavský, P., Babaie-Zadeh, M., Michel, O.J.J., Thirion-Moreau, N. (eds.) LVA/ICA 2017. LNCS, vol. 10169, pp. 258–266. Springer, Cham (2017). https://doi.org/10.1007/978-3-319-53547-0_25

43. Hershey, J.R., Chen, Z., Le Roux, J., Watanabe, S.: Deep clustering: discriminative embeddings for segmentation and separation. In: 2016 IEEE International Conference on Acoustics, Speech and Signal Processing (ICASSP), pp. 31–35. IEEE (2016)

44. Grais, E.M., Plumbley, M.D.: Combining fully convolutional and recurrent neural networks for single channel audio source separation. In: Audio Engineering Society Convention 144, Audio Engineering Society (2018)

45. Gan, C., Huang, D., Zhao, H., Tenenbaum, J.B., Torralba, A.: Music gesture for visual sound separation. In: Proceedings of the IEEE/CVF Conference on Computer Vision and Pattern Recognition, pp. 10478–10487 (2020)

46. Ronneberger, O., Fischer, P., Brox, T.: U-Net: convolutional networks for biomedical image segmentation. In: Navab, N., Hornegger, J., Wells, W.M., Frangi, A.F. (eds.) MICCAI 2015. LNCS, vol. 9351, pp. 234–241. Springer, Cham (2015). https://doi.org/10.1007/978-3-319-24574-4_28

47. Hershey, J.R., Movellan, J.R.: Audio vision: using audio-visual synchrony to locate sounds. In: Advances in Neural Information Processing Systems, pp. 813–819 (2000)

48. Barzelay, Z., Schechner, Y.Y.: Harmony in motion. In: 2007 IEEE Conference on Computer Vision and Pattern Recognition, pp. 1–8. IEEE (2007)

49. Kidron, E., Schechner, Y.Y., Elad, M.: Pixels that sound. In: 2005 IEEE Computer Society Conference on Computer Vision and Pattern Recognition (CVPR 2005), vol. 1, pp. 88–95. IEEE (2005)

50. Senocak, A., Oh, T.H., Kim, J., Yang, M.H., So Kweon, I.: Learning to localize sound source in visual scenes. In: Proceedings of the IEEE Conference on Computer Vision and Pattern Recognition, pp. 4358–4366 (2018)

51. Owens, A., Wu, J., McDermott, J.H., Freeman, W.T., Torralba, A.: Learning sight from sound: ambient sound provides supervision for visual learning. Int. J. Comput. Vis. **126**, 1120–1137 (2018). https://doi.org/10.1007/s11263-018-1083-5

52. Rouditchenko, A., Zhao, H., Gan, C., McDermott, J., Torralba, A.: Self-supervised audio-visual co-segmentation. In: ICASSP 2019–2019 IEEE International Conference on Acoustics, Speech and Signal Processing (ICASSP), pp. 2357–2361. IEEE (2019)

53. He, K., Zhang, X., Ren, S., Sun, J.: Deep residual learning for image recognition. In: Proceedings of the IEEE Conference on Computer Vision and Pattern Recognition, pp. 770–778 (2016)

54. Sun, D., Yang, X., Liu, M.Y., Kautz, J.: Pwc-net: CNNs for optical flow using pyramid, warping, and cost volume. In: Proceedings of the IEEE Conference on Computer Vision and Pattern Recognition, pp. 8934–8943 (2018)

55. Hui, T.W., Tang, X., Change Loy, C.: Liteflownet: a lightweight convolutional neural network for optical flow estimation. In: Proceedings of the IEEE Conference on Computer Vision and Pattern Recognition, pp. 8981–8989 (2018)

56. Hu, J., Zhang, Y., Okatani, T.: Visualization of convolutional neural networks for monocular depth estimation. In: Proceedings of the IEEE International Conference on Computer Vision, pp. 3869–3878 (2019)

57. Gemmeke, J.F., et al.: Audio set: an ontology and human-labeled dataset for audio events. In: 2017 IEEE International Conference on Acoustics, Speech and Signal Processing (ICASSP), pp. 776–780. IEEE (2017)

Channel Recurrent Attention Networks for Video Pedestrian Retrieval

Pengfei Fang[1,2(✉)] (ID), Pan Ji[3] (ID), Jieming Zhou[1,2] (ID), Lars Petersson[2] (ID), and Mehrtash Harandi[4] (ID)

[1] The Australian National University, Canberra, Australia
Pengfei.Fang@anu.edu.au
[2] DATA61-CSIRO, Syndey, Australia
[3] OPPO US Research Center, Melbourne, Australia
[4] Monash University, Melbourne, Australia

Abstract. Full attention, which generates an attention value per element of the input feature maps, has been successfully demonstrated to be beneficial in visual tasks. In this work, we propose a fully attentional network, termed *channel recurrent attention network*, for the task of video pedestrian retrieval. The main attention unit, *channel recurrent attention*, identifies attention maps at the frame level by jointly leveraging spatial and channel patterns via a recurrent neural network. This channel recurrent attention is designed to build a global receptive field by recurrently receiving and learning the spatial vectors. Then, a *set aggregation* cell is employed to generate a compact video representation. Empirical experimental results demonstrate the superior performance of the proposed deep network, outperforming current state-of-the-art results across standard video person retrieval benchmarks, and a thorough ablation study shows the effectiveness of the proposed units.

Keywords: Full attention · Pedestrian retrieval · Channel recurrent attention · Global receptive field · Set aggregation

1 Introduction

This work proposes *Channel Recurrent Attention Networks* for the purpose of pedestrian retrieval[1], in challenging video data.

Pedestrian retrieval, or person re-identification (re-ID), a core task when tracking people across camera networks [1], attempts to retrieve all correct

---

[1] For the remainder of this paper, we shall use the terms "pedestrian retrieval" and "person re-identification" interchangeably.

P. Ji—Work done while at NEC Laboratories America.

Electronic supplementary material The online version of this chapter (https://doi.org/10.1007/978-3-030-69544-6_26) contains supplementary material, which is available to authorized users.

© Springer Nature Switzerland AG 2021
H. Ishikawa et al. (Eds.): ACCV 2020, LNCS 12627, pp. 427–443, 2021.
https://doi.org/10.1007/978-3-030-69544-6_26

matches of a person from an existing database, given a target query. There are many challenges to this task, with a majority stemming from a poor quality or large variation of the captured images. This often leads to difficulties in building a discriminative representation, which in turn results in a retrieval system to mismatch its queries. Video-, as opposed to single image-, person re-ID offers the possibility of a richer and more robust representation as temporal cues can be utilized to obtain a compact, discriminative and robust video representation for the re-ID task. In many practical situations, the retrieval performance suffers from spatial misalignment [2–4], caused by the movement of body parts, which affects the retrieval machine negatively. Focusing on this issue, many efforts have been made to develop visual attention mechanisms [3,5–8], which makes the network attend to the discriminative areas within person bounding boxes, relaxing the constraints stemming from spatial nuances.

Attention mechanisms have been demonstrated to be successful in various visual tasks, such as image classification [9,10], object detection [11], scene segmentation [12,13] to name just a few. Generally speaking, attention mechanisms can be grouped into channel attention [9], spatial attention [14], and full attention [5], according to the dimensions of the generated attention maps. The channel attention usually summarizes the global spatial representation of the input feature maps, and learns a channel pattern that re-weights each slice of the feature maps. In contrast, the spatial attention learns the spatial relationships within the input feature maps and re-weights each spatial location of the feature maps. Lastly, full attention not only learns the channel patterns, but also preserves spatial information in the feature maps, which significantly improves the representation learning [15].

Various types of full attention mechanisms have been studied extensively for the task of pedestrian retrieval [5–7]. In [5], the fully attentional block re-calibrates the channel patterns by a non-linear transformation. Thereafter, higher order channel patterns are exploited to attend to the channel features [6,7]. However, the aforementioned attention fails to build *long-range* spatial relationships due to the use of a 1×1 convolution. The work in [3] learns spatial interactions via a convolutional layer with a larger kernel size (3×3), but the attention module therein still only has a small spatial receptive field. In visual attention, we want the network to have the capacity to view the feature maps globally and decide what to focus on for further processing [11]. A global view can be achieved by applying fully connected (FC) layers, which, unfortunately, introduces a huge number of learnable parameters if implemented naively.

In this work, we propose a full attention mechanism, termed *channel recurrent attention*, to boost the video pedestrian retrieval performance. The channel recurrent attention module aims at creating a global view of the input feature maps. Here, the channel recurrent attention module benefits from the recurrent operation and the FC layer in the recurrent neural network. We feed the vectorized spatial map to the Long Short Term Memory (LSTM) sequentially, such that the recurrent operation of the LSTM captures channel patterns while the FC layer in the LSTM has a global receptive field of each spatial slice. To handle video data, we continue to develop a *set aggregation* cell, which aggregates the frame features into a discriminative clip representation. In the set aggregation cell, we re-weight each element of the corresponding frame features, in order to selectively emphasize useful features and suppress less informative features, with the aid of the associated clip features. The **contributions** of this work include:

- The proposal of a novel channel recurrent attention module to jointly learn spatial and channel patterns of each frame feature map, capturing the global view of the feature maps. To the best of the authors' knowledge, this is the first attempt to consider the global spatial and channel information of feature maps in a full attention design for video person re-ID.
- The development of a simple yet effective set aggregation cell, which aggregates a set of frame features into a discriminative clip representation.
- State-of-the-art performance across standard video re-ID benchmarks by the proposed network. The generalization of the attention module is also verified by the competitive performance on the single image re-ID task.

2   Related Work

This section summarizes the related work of pedestrian retrieval and relevant attention mechanisms.

Several approaches have been investigated to improve the state-of-the-art retrieval performance for both single image and video person re-ID [1,16]. Focusing on deep neural networks [17], metric learning and representation learning are the two dominating approaches in modern person re-ID solutions [1]. In [18], the similarity of input pairs is calculated by a siamese architecture [19]. The improved deep siamese network learns an image-difference metric space by computing the cross-input relationships [20].

In representation learning, the pedestrian is represented by the concatenation of multi-level features along the deep network [21] or by combining the person appearance and body part features [3]. Beyond single image-based person re-ID methods, efficient temporal modeling [22] is further required when working with video clips. This is challenging as there is a need to create a compact video representation for each identity. McLaughlin *et al.* proposed average and max temporal pooling for aggregating frame features and each frame feature is the output of a recurrent neural network [23].

Recent work has shown that person re-ID benefits significantly from attention mechanisms highlighting the discriminative areas inside the person bounding boxes when learning an embedding space [3,5–7,24,25]. In [24,25], the spatial attention mask is designed to attend one target feature map or various feature maps along the deep network. In [5], a fully attentional block is developed to re-calibrate the channel features. Second or higher order statistical information is also employed in full attention frameworks [6,7]. The full attention shape map is also generated in the harmonious attention module [3], by integrating channel attention and spatial attention. The aforementioned attention mechanism either fails to build spatial-wise relationships, or receives a limited spatial receptive field. Unlike the above methodology of full attention, we intend to develop an attention mechanism which preserves the advantage of the common full attention, while also perceiving a global spatial receptive field of the feature maps.

3 Method

This section details the proposed deep network in a top-down fashion: starting with the problem formulation of the application, followed by the network architecture and the main attention module in the network, namely, the channel recurrent attention module. Thereafter, we also introduce a set aggregation cell, to encode a compact clip representation.

Notation. We use $\mathbb{R}^n$, $\mathbb{R}^{h \times w}$, $\mathbb{R}^{c \times h \times w}$ and $\mathbb{R}^{t \times c \times h \times w}$ to denote the n-dimensional Euclidean space, the real matrix space (of size $h \times w$), and the image and video spaces, respectively. A matrix or vector transpose is denoted by the superscript $\top$. The symbol $\odot$ and $\oplus$, represent the Hadamard product (*i.e.*, element-wise multiplication) and element-wise summation. $\sigma : \mathbb{R} \to [0, 1]$ is the sigmoid function. BN $: \mathbb{R}^n \to \mathbb{R}^n, \mathrm{BN}(\boldsymbol{x}) := \gamma \frac{\boldsymbol{x} - \mathrm{E}[\boldsymbol{x}]}{\sqrt{\mathrm{Var}[\boldsymbol{x}]}} + \beta$ and ReLU $:$ $\mathbb{R} \to \mathbb{R}_{\geq 0}, \mathrm{ReLU}(x) := \max(0, x)$ refer to batch normalization and rectified linear unit. ϕ, φ, ϖ and ψ are used to represent embedding functions (*e.g.*, linear transformations, or self-gating layer).

3.1 Problem Formulation

Let a fourth-order tensor, $\boldsymbol{T}_i = [T_i^1, T_i^2, \ldots, T_i^N] \in \mathbb{R}^{N \times C \times H \times W}$, denote the i-th video sequence of a pedestrian, where N, C, H, and W are the number of frames, channels, height and width, respectively. Each video sequence $\boldsymbol{T}_i$ is labeled by its identity, denoted by $y_i \in \{1, \ldots, k\}$. The training set with M video sequences is described by $\mathbb{T} = \{\boldsymbol{T}_i, y_i\}_{i=1}^M$. The video person re-ID model, $f_\theta : \mathcal{T} \to \mathcal{F}$, describes a non-linear embedding from the video space, $\mathcal{T}$, to an embedding space, $\mathcal{F}$, in which the intra-class/person distance is minimized and the inter-class/person distance is maximized. The target of training a deep neural network is to learn a set of parameters, $\theta^\star$, with minimum loss value (*e.g.*, $\mathcal{L}$), satisfying: $\theta^\star = \arg\min_\theta \sum_{i=1}^M \mathcal{L}(f_\theta(\boldsymbol{T}_i), y_i)$. In the training stage, we randomly sample batches of video clips, where each video clip has only t frames (randomly chosen). Such frames are order-less and hence, we are interested in set-matching for video re-ID.

3.2 Overview

We begin by providing a sketch of our design first. In video person re-ID, one would ideally like to make use of a deep network to extract the features of the frames and fuse them into a compact and discriminative clip-level representation. In the lower layers of our design, we have five convolutional blocks along with channel recurrent attention modules at positions P_1, P_2 and P_3 (see Fig. 1). Once the deep network extracts a set of frame features (*i.e.*, $[\boldsymbol{f}^1, \ldots, \boldsymbol{f}^t]$ in Fig. 1), a set aggregation cell is utilised to fuse frame features into a compact clip-level feature representation (*i.e.*, $\boldsymbol{g}$). The final clip representation is $\boldsymbol{F} = \mathrm{ReLU}\big(\mathrm{BN}(\boldsymbol{W}_1^\top \boldsymbol{g})\big)$, followed by another FC layer to perform identity prediction (*i.e.*, $p = \boldsymbol{W}_2^\top \boldsymbol{F}$), where $\boldsymbol{W}_1, \boldsymbol{W}_2$ are the learnable parameters in the FC layers. We note that the output of the middle convolutional layers captures rich spatial and channel information [6,11], such that the attention modules can make better use of this available information.

The network training benefits from multi-task learning, which formulates the network training as several sub-tasks. Our work follows [22], and trains the network using a triplet loss and a cross-entropy loss. The details of the loss functions are described in the supplementary material.

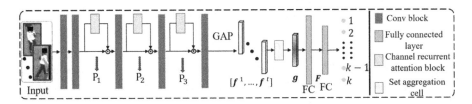

Fig. 1. The proposed deep neural network with channel recurrent attention modules and a set aggregation cell.

3.3 Channel Recurrent Attention

We propose the channel recurrent attention module (see Fig. 2), which learns the spatial and channel patterns globally in a collaborative manner with the assistance of an LSTM, over the feature maps of each frame. To be specific, we model the input feature maps as a sequence of spatial feature vectors, and feed it to an LSTM to capture global channel patterns by its recurrent operation. In our design, the hidden layer (*e.g.*, FC) of the LSTM unit, can be understood as having a global receptive field, acting on each spatial vector while sharing weights with other spatial vectors, addressing the limitation of a small receptive field in CNNs. In Sect. 4, our claim is empirically evaluated in an ablation study.

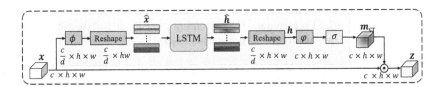

Fig. 2. The architecture of the proposed channel recurrent attention module.

Let $x \in \mathbb{R}^{c \times h \times w}$ be the input of the channel recurrent attention module. In our implementation, we project x to $\phi(x)$, reducing the channel dimension by a ratio of $1/d$, and reshape the embedded tensor $\phi(x)$ to a matrix $\hat{x} = [\hat{x}_1, \ldots, \hat{x}_{\frac{c}{d}}]^\top \in \mathbb{R}^{\frac{c}{d} \times hw}$, where a row of $\hat{x}$ (e.g., $\hat{x}_i \in \mathbb{R}^{hw}, i = 1, \ldots, \frac{c}{d}$) denotes the spatial vector of a slice. The effect of the ratio $1/d$ is studied in Sect. 4.2. A sequence of spatial vectors is then fed to an LSTM unit and the LSTM generates a sequence of hidden states, in matrix form:

$$\hat{h} = \mathrm{LSTM}(\hat{x}) = [\hat{h}_1, \ldots, \hat{h}_{\frac{c}{d}}]^\top, \tag{1}$$

where $\hat{h}_i \in \mathbb{R}^{hw}, i = 1, \ldots, c/d$ is a sequence of hidden states and $\mathrm{LSTM}(\cdot)$ represents the recurrent operation in an LSTM. The insight is illustrated by the unrolled LSTM, shown in Fig. 5(a). $\hat{h}$ is further reshaped to the same size as the input tensor $\phi(x)$ (i.e., $h = \mathrm{Reshape}(\hat{h}), h \in \mathbb{R}^{\frac{c}{d} \times h \times w}$). The final attention value is obtained by normalizing the embedded h, written as:

$$m_{\mathrm{cr}} = \sigma(\varphi(h)). \tag{2}$$

Here, $\varphi(h), m_{\mathrm{cr}} \in \mathbb{R}^{c \times h \times w}$. This normalized tensor acts as a full attention map and re-weighs the elements of the associated frame feature map (see Fig. 2), by element-wise multiplication:

$$z = m_{\mathrm{cr}} \odot x. \tag{3}$$

Remark 1. There are several studies that use LSTMs to aggregate features [26, 27] (see Fig. 3(a) and 3(b)), or generate attention masks [24,28] (see Fig. 3(c)). Our channel recurrent attention module (see Fig. 3(d)) is significantly different from existing works as shown in Fig. 3. The designs in [26] and [27] employ an LSTM to *aggregate* features either from input feature maps [26], or a sequence of frame features in a video [27]. In [24,28], an attention value for each spatial position of the feature maps (i.e., spatial attention) is constructed recursively, while ignoring the relation in the channel dimension. In contrast, our channel recurrent attention generates an attention value per element of the feature maps (i.e., full attention), thereby enabling the ability to learn richer spatial and channel features.

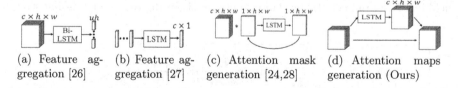

(a) Feature aggregation [26]   (b) Feature aggregation [27]   (c) Attention mask generation [24,28]   (d) Attention maps generation (Ours)

Fig. 3. Schematic comparison of our attention mechanism and existing LSTM-based works. In (c), the notation $*$ denotes a weighted sum operation.

3.4 Set Aggregation

To encode a compact clip representation, we further develop a set aggregation cell to fuse the per frame features (see Fig. 4 for a block diagram). The set aggregation cell highlights the frame feature, with the aid of the clip feature, firstly, and then aggregates them by average pooling.

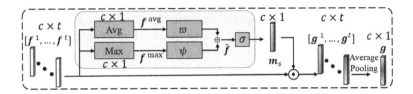

Fig. 4. The architecture of the proposed set aggregation cell.

Let $[\boldsymbol{f}^1, \dots, \boldsymbol{f}^t], \boldsymbol{f}^j \in \mathbb{R}^c$ be a set of frame feature vectors, encoded by a deep network (see Fig. 1). The set aggregation cell first re-weights the frame features. In our implementation, we combine average pooling and max pooling to aggregate frame features. This is due to the fact that both pooling schemes encode different statistical information and their combination is expected to increase the representation capacity. More specifically, each element in $\boldsymbol{f}^{\mathrm{avg}}$ and $\boldsymbol{f}^{\mathrm{max}}$ are defined as $f_i^{\mathrm{avg}} = \mathrm{avg}(f_i^1, \dots, f_i^t) = \frac{1}{t}\sum_{j=1}^{t}(f_i^j)$ and $f_i^{\mathrm{max}} = \max(f_i^1, \dots, f_i^t)$, respectively. Each aggregation is followed by self-gating layers (*i.e.*, ϖ and ψ in Fig. 4) to generate per-element modulation weights, and fused by element-wise summation as:

$$\hat{\boldsymbol{f}} = \varpi(\boldsymbol{f}^{\mathrm{avg}}) \oplus \psi(\boldsymbol{f}^{\mathrm{max}}). \tag{4}$$

This is then followed by normalizing the fused weights to produce the final mask (*e.g.*, $\boldsymbol{m}_{\mathrm{s}} = \sigma(\hat{\boldsymbol{f}})$) which is applied as follows:

$$\boldsymbol{g}^j = \boldsymbol{m}_{\mathrm{s}} \odot \boldsymbol{f}^j, \; j = 1, \dots, t. \tag{5}$$

Finally, we use average pooling to obtain the clip feature, $\boldsymbol{g} = 1/t\sum_{j=1}^{t}\boldsymbol{g}^j$. We note that in our network the parameters in the two self-gating layers are not shared. This is to increase the diversity of features which is beneficial, and we evaluate it in Sect. 4.

Remark 2. The set aggregation cell is inspired by the Squeeze-and-Excitation (SE) block [9], in the sense that frame features will be emphasized under the context of the global clip-level features, but with a number of simple yet important differences: **(i)** The SE receives a feature map as input, while the input of our set aggregation is a set of frame features. **(ii)** The SE only uses global average pooling to encode the global feature of the feature maps, while the set aggregation employs both average and max pooling to encode hybrid clip features, exploiting more diverse information present in the frame features.

3.5   Implementation Details

Network Architecture and Training. We implemented our approach in the PyTorch [29] deep learning framework. We chose ResNet-50 [30] as the backbone network, pre-trained on ImageNet [31]. In a video clip with t frames, each frame-level feature map, produced by the last convolutional layer, is squeezed to a feature vector $f^j \in \mathbb{R}^{2048}, j = 1, \ldots, t$ by global average pooling (GAP). Subsequently, the set aggregation cell fuses the frame features to a compact clip feature vector g. Following g, the final clip-level person representation F is embedded by a fully connected (FC) layer with the dimension 1024. Thereafter, another FC layer is added for the purpose of final classification during training. In the channel recurrent attention module, the ratio d is set to 16 for the PRID-2011 and iLIDS-VID datasets, and 8 for the MARS and DukeMTMC-VideoReID datasets, and the LSTM unit has one hidden layer. In the set aggregation cell, the self-gating layer is a bottleneck network to reduce the number of parameters, the dimension of the hidden vector is $2048/r$, and we choose $r = 16$ as in [9], across all datasets. The ReLU and batch normalization are applied to each embedding layer and self-gating layer. The details of the datasets is described in Sect. 4.1.

We use the Adam [32] optimizer with default momentum. The initial learning rate is set to 3×10^{-4} for PRID-2011 and iLIDS0-VID, and 4×10^{-4} for MARS and DukeMTMC-VideoReID. The mini-batch size is set to 16 for the PRID-2011 and iLIDS-VID datasets and 32 for the MARS and DukeMTMC-VideoReID datasets, respectively. In a mini-batch, both P and K are set to 4 for the PRID-2011 and iLIDS-VID, whereas $P = 8$, $K = 4$ for the MARS and DukeMTMC-VideoReID. The margin in the triplet loss, $i.e.$, ξ, is set to 0.3 for all datasets. The spatial size of the input frame is fixed to 256×128. Following [22], t is chosen as 4 in all experiments and 4 frames are *randomly* sampled in each video clip [22,33]. Our training images are randomly flipped in the horizontal direction, followed by random erasing (RE) [34]. We train the network for 800 epochs. The learning rate decay is set to 0.1, applied at the 200-th, 400-th epoch for the PRID-2011 and iLIDS-VID, and the 100-th, 200-th, 500-th epoch for the MARS and DukeMTMC-VideoReID, respectively. Moreover, it is worth noting that we do not apply re-ranking to boost the ranking result in the testing phase.

4   Experiment on Video Pedestrian Retrieval

4.1   Datasets and Evaluation Protocol

In this section, we perform experiments on four standard video benchmark datasets, *i.e.*, PRID-2011 [35], iLIDS-VID [36], MARS [37] and DukeMTMC-VideoReID [38] to verify the effectiveness of the proposed attentional network. **PRID-2011** has 400 video sequences, showing 200 different people where each person has 2 video sequences, captured by two separate cameras. The person bounding box is manually labeled. **iLIDS-VID** contains 600 image sequences of 300 pedestrians, captured by two non-overlapping cameras in an airport. Each of the training and test sets has 150 person identities. In this dataset, the target person is heavily occluded by other pedestrians or objects (*e.g.*, baggage). **MARS** is one of the largest video person re-ID datasets which contains $1,261$ different identities and $20,715$ video sequences captured by 6 separate cameras. The video sequences are generated by the GMMCP tracker [39], and for each frame, the bounding box is detected by DPM [40]. The dataset is split into training and testing sets that contain 631 and 630 person identities, respectively. **DukeMTMC-VideoReID** is another large video person re-ID dataset. This dataset contains 702 pedestrians for training, 702 pedestrians for testing as well as 408 pedestrians as distractors. The training set and testing set has $2,196$ video sequences and $2,636$ video sequences, respectively. The person bounding boxes are annotated manually.

Following existing works, we use both the cumulative matching characteristic (CMC) curve and mean average precision (mAP) to evaluate the performance of the trained re-ID system.

4.2   Ablation Study

This section demonstrates the effectiveness of the proposed blocks and the selection of appropriate hyper parameters via a thorough battery of experiments.

Effect of Channel Recurrent Attention. Here, we evaluate the effectiveness of the proposed channel recurrent attention, and verify our claim that our channel recurrent attention is able to capture more structure information as we sequentially feed the spatial vector to the LSTM. To show the design is reasonable, we compare our channel recurrent attention with two variations, namely, the spatial recurrent attention and the conv attention.

In the spatial recurrent attention, the LSTM receives a sequence of channel features from feature maps as input, with the recurrent operator along the spatial domain. In more detail, in channel recurrent attention (see Fig. 2), the input is a sequence of spatial vectors, (*e.g.*, $\hat{x} = [\hat{x}_1, \ldots, \hat{x}_{\frac{c}{d}}]^\top \in \mathbb{R}^{\frac{c}{d} \times hw}$). In the spatial recurrent attention, the input is a sequence of channel vectors, (*e.g.*, $\hat{x} = [\hat{x}_1, \ldots, \hat{x}_{hw}]^\top \in \mathbb{R}^{hw \times \frac{c}{d}}$). Though the recurrent operation along the spatial domain is also able to learn the pattern spatially, the spatial recurrent attention lacks explicit modeling in the spatial domain. Figure 5 shows the schematic difference between channel recurrent attention (see Fig. 5(a)) and spatial recurrent attention (see Fig. 5(b)).

In addition, to verify the necessity of a global receptive field in our channel recurrent attention, we further replace the LSTM with a convolutional layer with a similar parameter size, which is called a conv attention. The architecture of the conv attention is shown in Fig. 6. In the Conv block, the kernel size is 3×3 and the sliding step is 1, and it produces a tensor with the shape of $\frac{c}{d} \times h \times w$. The generated attention mask can be formulated as $m_{\text{conv}} = \sigma\big(\varphi\big(\text{Conv}(\phi(x))\big)\big)$, where $\text{Conv}(\cdot)$ indicates the convolutional operation.

Table 1 compares the effectiveness of three attention variations. It is shown that our channel recurrent attention has a superior performance over the other

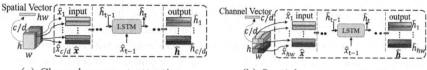

(a) Channel recurrent attention.   (b) Spatial recurrent attention.

Fig. 5. Schematic comparison between channel recurrent attention and spatial recurrent attention.

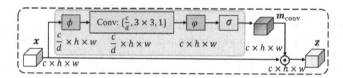

Fig. 6. The architecture of the proposed conv attention module.

Table 1. Comparison of three attention variations across four datasets. CRA: Channel Recurrent Attention; SRA: Spatial Recurrent Attention; CA: Conv Attention.

		PRID-2011		iLIDS-VID		MARS		DukeMTMC-VideoReID	
Method		R-1	mAP	R-1	mAP	R-1	mAP	R-1	mAP
(i)	No Attention	85.4	91.0	80.0	87.1	82.3	76.2	87.5	86.2
(ii)	+ CRA	**92.1**	**94.6**	**87.0**	**90.6**	**86.8**	**81.6**	**94.7**	**94.1**
(iii)	+ SRA	87.9	92.1	83.3	87.4	84.6	78.4	89.4	87.8
(iv)	+ CA	89.6	92.8	84.2	88.2	85.2	79.7	91.2	90.1

two variations. As can be observed, the channel recurrent attention cell improves the accuracy significantly across all four datasets. This observation supports our assumption that the attention receives a performance gain from explicit modeling of the global receptive field in each slice of the feature maps.

Effect of the Position of Channel Recurrent Attention. The position of the channel recurrent attention block affects the information in the spatial or the channel dimensions. We want to explore the rich spatial and channel information; thus, we only consider the feature maps from the middle of the deep network as input to channel recurrent attention (*i.e.*, P_1, P_2, and P_3 in Fig. 1). The comparison is illustrated in Table 2. It shows that the system receives a better gain when adding the channel recurrent attention module at position P_2, which aligns with our motivation that more spatial information is utilized in the feature maps. The works [6,11] also present a similar observation. When applying the attention in P_1, P_2 and P_3, the network performs at its best.

Effect of Reduction Ratio $1/d$ in Channel Recurrent Attention. The ratio $1/d$ in the embedding function $\phi(\cdot)$ (see Fig. 2) is to reduce the channel dimensionality of the input feature maps, consequently, reducing the sequence length input to the LSTM; thus, it is an important hyper-parameter in the channel recurrent attention. Table 3 reveals that the best performance is obtained

Table 2. Effect of the position of channel recurrent attention across four datasets. CRA: Channel Recurrent Attention.

		PRID-2011		iLIDS-VID		MARS		DukeMTMC-VideoReID	
Position		R-1	mAP	R-1	mAP	R-1	mAP	R-1	mAP
(i)	No Attention	85.4	91.0	80.0	87.1	82.3	76.2	87.5	86.2
(ii)	+ CRA in P_1	89.6	92.2	85.3	88.2	85.0	80.6	92.7	92.2
(iii)	+ CRA in P_2	91.0	94.4	86.7	90.2	86.4	81.2	94.2	93.4
(iv)	+ CRA in P_3	90.3	92.6	86.0	88.4	86.1	80.8	93.5	92.7
(v)	+ CRA in P_1&P_2&P_3	**92.1**	**94.6**	**87.0**	**90.6**	**86.8**	**81.6**	**94.7**	**94.1**

when $d = 16$ for small-scale datasets and $d = 8$ for large-scale datasets. This could be due to the fact that training a network with a large amount of training samples is less prone to overfitting. Furthermore, this table also shows the fact that the LSTM has difficulties in modeling very long sequences (*e.g.* smaller d in Table 3). However, when the sequences are too short (*e.g.*, $d = 32$), the channel features are compressed, such that some pattern information is lost.

Table 3. Effect of reduction ratio $1/d$ in channel recurrent attention across four datasets.

		PRID-2011		iLIDS-VID		MARS		DukeMTMC-VideoReID	
Reduction Ratio		R-1	mAP	R-1	mAP	R-1	mAP	R-1	mAP
(i)	No Attention	85.4	91.0	80.0	87.1	82.3	76.2	87.5	86.2
(ii)	$d = 2$	88.7	92.1	84.0	88.7	84.8	80.2	93.4	92.8
(iii)	$d = 4$	89.8	92.6	85.6	89.1	85.2	80.3	93.9	93.4
(iv)	$d = 8$	91.0	93.2	86.3	89.4	**86.8**	**81.6**	**94.7**	94.1
(v)	$d = 16$	**92.1**	**94.6**	**87.0**	**90.6**	85.5	80.7	94.3	**94.3**
(vi)	$d = 32$	91.0	93.8	82.7	88.9	84.3	79.8	93.2	93.4

Why using LSTM in the Channel Recurrent Attention? In our channel recurrent attention, we use the LSTM to perform the recurrent operation for the spatial vector. We observed that once the order of the spatial vectors is fixed, the recurrent operation in the LSTM is able to learn useful information along the channel dimension. We further investigated using Bi-LSTM to replace the LSTM in the attention and evaluate its performance. Compared with LSTM, the Bi-LSTM only brings a marginal/no performance gain across different datasets, whereas it almost doubles the number of parameters and FLOPs in the attention model. Please refer to Sect. 1 of the supplementary material for details of those experiments. These empirical experimental results support the use of a regular LSTM in our attention module.

Effect of Set Aggregation. Table 4 shows the effectiveness of set aggregation and the effectiveness of different pooling schemes in the set aggregation block. It is clear that the individual set aggregation improves the network performance and the combination of attention modules continues to increase the performance gain; showing that two attention modules mine complementary information in the network. Furthermore, all pooling schemes improve the results of the network, showing that the network receives gains from set aggregation. The combination of the average pooling and the max pooling scheme with non-sharing weights further shows its superiority over the individual average or max pooling schemes. This observation can be interpreted as the average and max pooled features have complementary information when encoding clip-level representations.

Table 4. Effect of set aggregation across four datasets. CRA: Channel Recurrent Attention, SA: Set Aggregation, †: Sharing weights, ‡: Non-sharing weights.

Method		PRID-2011		iLIDS-VID		MARS		DukeMTMC-VideoReID	
		R-1	mAP	R-1	mAP	R-1	mAP	R-1	mAP
(i)	No Attention	85.4	91.0	80.0	87.1	82.3	76.2	87.5	86.2
(ii)	+ CRA	92.1	94.6	87.0	90.6	86.8	81.6	94.7	94.1
(iii)	+ SA (Average & Max Pooling)	87.6	92.3	84.7	89.1	85.2	80.5	91.2	88.9
(iv)	+ CRA & SA (Avg Pooling)	94.4	95.2	87.9	91.2	87.2	82.2	95.6	95.0
(v)	+ CRA & SA (Max Pooling)	93.3	94.8	87.3	90.8	86.9	81.2	95.2	94.6
(vi)	+ CRA & SA† (Avg & Max Pooling)	95.5	96.1	88.2	92.4	87.7	82.6	95.9	95.3
(vii)	+ CRA & SA‡ (Avg & Max Pooling)	**96.6**	**96.9**	**88.7**	**93.0**	**87.9**	**83.0**	**96.3**	**95.5**

4.3   Comparison to the State-of-the-Art Methods

To evaluate the superiority of our deep attentional network, we continue to compare our results with the current state-of-the-art approaches, shown in Table 5 and Table 6.

PRID-2011. On the PRID-2011 dataset, our network improves the state-of-the-art accuracy by 1.1% in R-1, compared to GLTR [51]. As for the mAP, our approach outperforms [43] by 2.4%. When compared to SCAN [46], which uses optical flow, our approach outperforms it by 1.3% in R-1.

iLIDS-VID. On the iLIDS-VID dataset, our approach improves the state-of-the-art mAP value by 5.2%, compared to [43]. As for the R-1 accuracy, our approach also achieves a new state-of-the-art, outperforming [33] by a comfortable 2.4%. In addition, our approach continues to outperform SCAN + optical flow [46] by 0.7% in R-1.

MARS. On the MARS dataset, our approach achieves state-of-the-art performances on mAP and competitive performance on the CMC curve. In particular, our approach outperforms VRSTC [50] on mAP, R-5 and R-10. It is worth mentioning that VRSTC uses a generator for data augmentation. Furthermore, when compared to other methods, we observe that our approach outperforms GLTR [51] by 1.3%/4.6% in R-1/mAP.

Table 5. Comparison with the SOTA methods on PRID-2011, iLIDS-VID and MARS datasets.

Method	Publication	PRID-2011					iLIDS-VID					MARS				
		R-1	R-5	R-10	R-20	mAP	R-1	R-5	R-10	R-20	mAP	R-1	R-5	R-10	R-20	mAP
RFA-Net [27]	ECCV'16	58.2	85.8	93.4	97.9	-	49.3	76.8	85.3	90.0	-	-	-	-	-	-
McLaughlin et al. [23]	CVPR'16	70.0	90.0	95.0	97.0	-	58.0	84.0	91.0	96.0	-	-	-	-	-	-
MSCAN [41]	CVPR'17	-	-	-	-	-	-	-	-	-	-	71.8	86.6	-	93.1	56.1
Zhou et al. [42]	CVPR'17	79.4	94.4	-	99.3	-	55.2	86.5	-	97.0	-	70.6	90.0	-	97.6	50.7
Chen et al. [43]	CVPR'18	88.6	99.1	-	-	90.9	79.8	91.8	-	-	82.6	81.2	92.1	-	-	69.4
+ Optical flow		93.0	99.3	100.0	100.0	94.5	85.4	96.7	98.8	99.5	87.8	86.3	94.7	-	98.2	76.1
QAN [44]	CVPR'17	90.3	98.2	99.3	100.0	-	68.0	86.8	-	97.4	-	73.7	84.9	-	91.6	51.7
Li et al. [45]	CVPR'18	93.2	-	-	-	-	80.2	-	-	-	-	82.3	-	-	-	65.8
Gao et al. [22]	BMVC'18	-	-	-	-	-	-	-	-	-	-	83.3	93.8	96.0	97.4	76.7
SCAN [46]	TIP'19	92.0	98.0	100.0	100.0	-	81.3	93.3	96.0	98.0	-	86.6	94.8	-	98.1	76.7
+ Optical flow		95.3	99.0	100.0	100.0	-	88.0	96.7	98.0	100.0	-	87.2	95.2	-	98.1	77.2
STIM-RRU [47]	AAAI'19	92.7	98.8	-	99.8	-	84.3	96.8	-	100.0	-	84.4	93.2	-	96.3	72.7
COSAM [8]	ICCV'19	-	-	-	-	-	79.6	95.3	-	-	-	84.9	95.5	-	97.9	79.9
STAR+Optical flow [48]	BMVC'19	93.4	98.3	100.0	100.0	-	85.9	97.1	98.9	99.7	-	85.4	95.4	96.2	97.3	76.0
STA [49]	AAAI'19	-	-	-	-	-	-	-	-	-	-	86.3	95.7	-	98.1	80.8
VRSTC [50]	CVPR'19	-	-	-	-	-	83.4	95.5	97.7	99.5	-	88.5	96.5	97.4	-	82.3
Zhao et al. [33]	CVPR'19	93.9	99.5	-	100.0	-	86.3	97.4	-	99.7	-	87.0	95.4	-	98.7	78.2
GLTR [51]	ICCV'19	95.5	100.0	-	-	-	86.0	98.0	-	-	-	87.0	95.7	-	98.2	78.4
Baseline	-	85.4	98.9	98.9	98.9	91.0	80.0	95.3	98.7	99.3	87.1	82.3	93.9	95.8	97.2	76.2
Ours	-	96.6	98.9	100.0	100.0	96.9	88.7	97.3	99.3	100.0	93.0	87.9	96.6	97.5	98.8	83.0

440   P. Fang et al.

Table 6. Comparison with the SOTA methods on DukeMTMC-VideoReID dataset.

Method	Publication	DukeMTMC-VideoReID				
		R-1	R-5	R-10	R-20	mAP
ETAP-Net [38]	CVPR'18	83.6	94.6	-	97.6	78.3
STAR+Optical flow [48]	BMVC'19	94.0	99.0	99.3	99.7	93.4
VRSTC [50]	CVPR'19	95.0	99.1	99.4	-	93.5
STA [49]	AAAI'19	96.2	99.3	-	99.7	94.9
GLTR [51]	ICCV'19	**96.3**	99.3	-	99.7	93.7
Baseline	-	87.5	96.5	97.2	98.3	86.2
Ours	-	**96.3**	**99.4**	**99.7**	**99.9**	**95.5**

DukeMTMC-VideoReID. As for this new dataset, our network continues to show its superior performance (see Table 6). Our approach is superior to GLTR by 1.8% on mAP, and outperform the state-of-the-art mAP value of STA by 0.6%, and our network also achieves competitive performance on the CMC metric, outperforming the state-of the-art on R-5, R-10 and R-20.

We visualize the feature maps from the baseline network and our channel recurrent attention network, trained on the MARS dataset. The feature maps are obtained in P_2 (see Fig. 1). In Fig. 7, we observed that compared to the baseline network, our attention network highlights more areas of human bodies, which verifies the effectiveness of our network qualitatively. Please refer to the supplementary material for further visualizations.

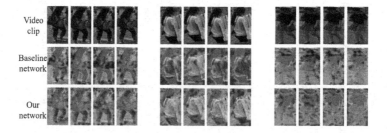

Fig. 7. Visualization of feature maps. We sample three video clips from different pedestrians and visualize the feature maps.

5   Experiments on Single Image Pedestrian Retrieval

To show the generalisation of the proposed channel recurrent attention, we employ it in a single image pedestrian retrieval task. We select a strong baseline network from [6], and insert the channel recurrent attention after each convolutional block. The deep network is fine-tuned from ImageNet pre-training [31] and trained with the same hyper-parameter setting as in [6]. We use **CUHK01** [52] and **DukeMTMC-reID** [53] to evaluate the performance of the network. Please refer to the supplementary material for the details of the datasets. We use mAP and the CMC curve to evaluate the performance. Table 7 and Table 8 illustrate that our approach achieves competitive results to existing state-of-the-art approaches, showing the effectiveness and generalization of our channel recurrent attention module.

Table 7. Comparison with the SOTA on CUHK01 dataset.

Method	Publication	CUHK01			
		R-1	R-5	R-10	R-20
Zhao *et al.* [54]	ICCV'17	75.0	93.5	95.7	97.7
Spindle Net [55]	CVPR'17	79.9	94.4	97.1	98.6
PBR [2]	ECCV'18	80.7	94.4	97.3	98.6
Baseline	-	79.3	92.7	95.8	98.2
Ours	-	**83.3**	**96.3**	**98.4**	**98.9**

Table 8. Comparison with the SOTA on DukeMTMC-reID dataset.

Method	Publication	DukeMTMC-reID			
		R-1	R-5	R-10	mAP
OS-Net [56]	ICCV'19	88.6	-	-	73.5
BAT-net [6]	ICCV'19	87.7	94.7	96.3	77.3
ABD-Net [57]	ICCV'19	89.0	-	-	**78.6**
Baseline	-	85.4	93.8	95.5	75.0
Ours	-	**89.2**	**95.6**	**96.9**	78.3

6 Conclusion

This work proposes a novel deep attentional network for task of video pedestrian retrieval. This network benefits from the developed channel recurrent attention and set aggregation modules. The channel recurrent attention module is employed for a global view to feature maps, to learn the channel and spatial pattern jointly, given a frame feature maps as input. Then the set aggregation cell continues to re-weight each frame feature and fuses them to get a compact clip representation. Thorough evaluation shows that the proposed deep network achieves state-of-the-art results across four standard video-based person re-ID datasets, and the effectiveness of each attention is further evaluated by extensive ablation studies.

References

1. Zheng, L., Yang, Y., Hauptmann, A.G.: Person re-identification: Past, present and future (2016) arXiv:1610.02984 [cs.CV]
2. Suh, Y., Wang, J., Tang, S., Mei, T., Mu Lee, K.: Part-aligned bilinear representations for person re-identification. In: ECCV (2018)
3. Li, W., Zhu, X., Gong, S.: Harmonious attention network for person re-identification. In: CVPR (2018)
4. Zhou, J., Roy, S.K., Fang, P., Harandi, M., Petersson, L.: Cross-correlated attention networks for person re-identification. In: Image and Vision Computing (2020)
5. Wang, C., Zhang, Q., Huang, C., Liu, W., Wang, X.: Mancs: a multi-task attentional network with curriculum sampling for person re-identification. In: ECCV (2018)
6. Fang, P., Zhou, J., Roy, S.K., Petersson, L., Harandi, M.: Bilinear attention networks for person retrieval. In: ICCV (2019)
7. Chen, B., Deng, W., Hu, J.: Mixed high-order attention network for person re-identification. In: ICCV (2019)

8. Subramaniam, A., Nambiar, A., Mittal, A.: Co-segmentation inspired attention networks for video-based person re-identification. In: ICCV (2019)
9. Hu, J., Shen, L., Sun, G.: Squeeze-and-excitation networks. In: CVPR (2018)
10. Woo, S., Park, J., Lee, J.Y., So Kweon, I.: Cbam: convolutional block attention module. In: ECCV (2018)
11. Wang, X., Girshick, Gupta, A., He, K.: Non-local neural networks. In: CVPR (2017)
12. Fu, J., et al.: Dual attention network for scene segmentation. In: CVPR (2019)
13. Li, W., Jafari, O.H., Rother, C.: Deep object co-segmentation. In: ACCV (2018)
14. Wang, F., et al.: Residual attention network for image classification. In: CVPR (2017)
15. Hjelm, R.D., et al.: Learning deep representations by mutual information estimation and maximization. In: ICLR (2019)
16. Gong, Shaogang., Cristani, Marco., Yan, Shuicheng, Loy, Chen Change (eds.): Person Re-Identification. ACVPR. Springer, London (2014). https://doi.org/10.1007/978-1-4471-6296-4
17. LeCun, Y., Bengio, Y., Hinton, G.: Deep learning. Nature (2015)
18. Yi, D., Lei, Z., Li, S.Z.: Deep metric learning for person re-identification. In: ICPR (2014)
19. Bromley, J., Guyon, I., LeCun, Y., Säckinger, E., Shah, R.: Signature verification using a "siamese" time delay neural network. In: NeurIPS (1993)
20. Ahmed, E., Jones, M., Marks, T.K.: An improved deep learning architecture for person re-identification. In: CVPR (2015)
21. Wu, S., Chen, Y.C., Li, X., Wu, A.C., You, J.J., Zheng, W.S.: An enhanced deep feature representation for person re-identification. In: WACV (2016)
22. Gao, J., Nevatia, R.: Revisiting temporal modeling for video-based person ReID. arXiv:1805.02104 (2018)
23. McLaughlin, N., Martinez del Rincon, J., Miller, P.: Recurrent convolutional network for video-based person re-identification. In: CVPR (2016)
24. Liu, H., Feng, J., Jiang, J., Yan, S.: End-to-end comparative attention networks for person re-identification (2016) arXiv:1606.04404 [cs.CV]
25. Liu, X., et al.: Hydraplus-net: attentive deep features for pedestrian analysis. In: ICCV (2017)
26. Bai, X., Yang, M., Huang, T., Dou, Z., Yu, R., Xu, Y.: Deep-Person: learing discriminative deep features for person re-identification. Pattern Recognition (2020)
27. Yan, Y., Ni, B., Song, Z., Ma, C., Yan, Y., Yang, X.: Person re-identification via recurrent feature aggregation. In: ECCV (2016)
28. Zhao, B., Wu, X., Feng, J., Peng, Q., Yan, S.: Diversified visual attention networks for fine-grained object classification. In: TMM (2017)
29. Paszke, A., et al.: Automatic differentiation in pytorch. In: NeurIPS (2017)
30. He, K., Zhang, X., Ren, S., Sun, J.: Deep residual learning for image recognition. In: CVPR (2016)
31. Russakovsky, O., et al.: Imagenet large scale visual recognition challenge. In: IJCV (2015)
32. Kingma, D.P., Ba, J.: Adam: A Method for Stochastic Optimization. arXiv:1412.6980 (2014)
33. Zhao, Y., Shen, X., Jin, Z., Lu, H., Hua, X.S.: Attribute-driven feature disentangling and temporal aggregation for video person re-identification. In: CVPR (2019)
34. Zhong, Z., Zheng, L., Kang, G., Li, S., Yang, Y.: Random erasing data augmentation. arXiv:1708.04896 (2017)

35. Hirzer, M., Beleznai, C., Roth, P.M., Bischof, H.: Person re-identification by descriptive and discriminative classification. In: Image Analysis (2011)
36. Wang, T., Gong, S., Zhu, X., Wang, S.: Person re-identification by discriminative selection in video ranking. In: TPAMI (2016)
37. Zheng, L., Bie, Z., Sun, Y., Wang, J., Su, C., Wang, S., Tian, Q.: Mars: A video benchmark for large-scale person re-identification. In: ECCV (2016)
38. Wu, Y., Lin, Y., Dong, X., Yan, Y., Ouyang, W., Yang, Y.: Exploit the unknown gradually: One-shot video-based person re-identification by stepwise learning. In: CVPR (2018)
39. Dehghan, A., Assari, S.M., Shah, M.: Gmmcp tracker: globally optimal generalized maximum multi clique problem for multiple object tracking. In: CVPR (2015)
40. Felzenszwalb, P.F., Girshick, R.B., McAllester, D., Ramanan, D.: Object detection with discriminatively trained part-based models. In: TPAMI (2010)
41. Li, D., Chen, X., Zhang, Z., Huang, K.: Learning deep context-aware features over body and latent parts for person re-identification. In: CVPR (2017)
42. Zhou, Z., Huang, Y., Wang, W., Wang, L., Tan, T.: See the forest for the trees: joint spatial and temporal recurrent neural networks for video-based person re-identification. In: CVPR (2017)
43. Chen, D., Li, H., Xiao, T., Yi, S., Wang, X.: Video person re-identification with competitive snippet-similarity aggregation and co-attentive snippet embedding. In: CVPR (2018)
44. Liu, Y., Junjie, Y., Ouyang, W.: Quality aware network for set to set recognition. In: CVPR (2017)
45. Li, S., Bak, S., Carr, P., Wang, X.: Diversity regularized spatiotemporal attention for video-based person re-identification. In: CVPR (2018)
46. Zhang, R., et al.: Scan: self-and-collaborative attention network for video person re-identification (2018) arXiv:1807.05688 [cs.CV]
47. Liu, Y., Yuan, Z., Zhou, W., Li, H.: Spatial and temporal mutual promotion for video-based person re-identification. In: AAAI (2019)
48. Wu, G., Zhu, X., Gong, S.: Spatio-temporal associative representation for video person re-identification. In: BMVC (2019)
49. Fu, Y., Wang, X., Wei, Y., Huang, T.: STA: spatial-temporal attention for large-scale video-based person re-identification. In: AAAI (2019)
50. Hou, R., Ma, B., Chang, H., Gu, X., Shan, S., Chen, X.: VRSTC: occlusion-free video person re-identification. In: CVPR (2019)
51. Li, J., Wang, J., Tian, Q., Gao, W., Zhang, S.: Global-local temporal representation for video person re-identification. In: ICCV (2019)
52. Li, W., Zhao, R., Wang, X.: Human reidentification with transferred metric learning. In: ACCV (2012)
53. Ristani, E., Solera, F., Zou, R., Cucchiara, R., Tomasi, C.: Performance measures and a data set for multi-target, multi-camera tracking. In: ECCVworkshop on Benchmarking Multi-Target Tracking (2016)
54. Zhao, L., Li, X., Zhuang, Y., Wang, J.: Deeply-learned part-aligned representations for person re-identification. In: ICCV (2017)
55. Zhao, H., et al.: Spindle net: person re-identification with human body region guided feature decomposition and fusion. In: CVPR (2017)
56. Zhou, K., Yang, Y., Cavallaro, A., Xiang, T.: Learning generalisable omni-scale representations for person re-identification. arXiv:1910.06827v2 (2019)
57. Chen, T., et al.: Abd-net: attentive but diverse person re-identification. In: ICCV (2019)

In Defense of LSTMs for Addressing Multiple Instance Learning Problems

Kaili Wang[1](✉), Jose Oramas[2], and Tinne Tuytelaars[1]

[1] KU Leuven, ESAT-PSI, Leuven, Belgium
{kaili.wang,tinne.tuytelaars}@esat.kuleuven.be
[2] University of Antwerp, imec-IDLab, Antwerp, Belgium
jose.oramas@uantwerpen.be

Abstract. LSTMs have a proven track record in analyzing sequential data. But what about unordered instance bags, as found under a Multiple Instance Learning (MIL) setting? While not often used for this, we show LSTMs excell under this setting too. In addition, we show that LSTMs are capable of indirectly capturing instance-level information using only bag-level annotations. Thus, they can be used to learn instance-level models in a weakly supervised manner. Our empirical evaluation on both simplified (MNIST) and realistic (Lookbook and Histopathology) datasets shows that LSTMs are competitive with or even surpass state-of-the-art methods specially designed for handling specific MIL problems. Moreover, we show that their performance on instance-level prediction is close to that of fully-supervised methods.

1 Introduction

Traditional single-instance classification methods focus on learning a mapping between a feature vector (extracted from a single instance) w.r.t. a specific class label. In a complementary fashion, Multiple Instance Learning (MIL) [1] algorithms are tasked with learning how to associate a set of elements, usually referred to as a "bag", with a specific label. In comparison, MIL methods usually require weaker supervision in the form of bag-level labels. The MIL problem has a long history, and various solutions have been proposed over time. Here, we advocate the use of standard LSTM networks in this context, as a strong baseline, yielding competitive results under a wide range of MIL settings.

Long short-term memory (LSTM) networks [2] have been proposed as an extension over standard recurrent neural networks, to store information over long time intervals in sequential data. They have been used extensively and very successfully for modeling sentences (sequences of words) in text documents [3], e.g. for machine translation [4] or sentiment analysis [5]. Later, they have been employed in several other fields including computer vision [6–10] and speech processing [3,11]. LSTMs provide great flexibility for handling data sequences. There

Electronic supplementary material The online version of this chapter (https://doi.org/10.1007/978-3-030-69544-6_27) contains supplementary material, which is available to authorized users.

is no need to know the length of the sequence beforehand, and they can operate on sequences of variable size. In addition, they are capable of accumulating information by using a memory mechanism with add/forget [12] functionality.

As they need the input to be provided as a sequence, LSTMs do not seem an appropriate choice for analyzing unordered bags at first - but is that so ? Obviously, the capability to remember the temporal (order) information can be attributed to the *memory* ability of LSTMs. This memory ability is capable of capturing other types of information beyond order as well. Take the LSTMs used for action recognition as an example. For some finegrained actions (e.g.. opening or closing a door), the order of the events is key and this is picked up by the LSTM. However, for other actions the context information provides the most important cue (e.g.. playing tennis or cooking). This does not depend on the temporal order, but can still be learned using LSTM.

Starting from an unordered bag, we can always transform it into a sequence by imposing a random order on the instances, making it suitable for LSTMs. The order is not relevant, but that does not matter: the LSTM can still process the data and extract useful information from it. In fact, this is also how humans often deal with unordered bags: e.g., if one is asked to count the number of rotten apples in a basket, most of us would just pick the apples one by one, in random order, inspect them and keep track of the count. The order does not matter, but nevertheless, treating them in a sequential order comes very naturally.

The observations above clearly hint to a promising capability of LSTMs for addressing MIL problems. Yet, LSTMs are not often used in this way (see our related work section for a few notable exceptions). Therefore, we present a systematic analysis on the performance of LSTMs when addressing MIL problems. More specifically, we conduct a series of experiments considering different factors that may affect the performance of LSTMs. First, we consider the standard MIL problem [13–15], with bags of instances without sequential order. Second, we study the effect of the order in which the instances of each bag are fed to the LSTM network. Likewise, in a third test, we investigate the influence of the cardinality (size) of the bag on performance. Fourth, we assess the effect that the complexity of the data has on the previous observations. Toward this goal we conduct experiments considering bags derived from the MNIST dataset [16], clothing-item images from the Lookbook dataset [17] and Histopathology images [18]. Fifth, we inspect how the internal state of the LSTM changes when observing each of the instances of the bag. Moreover, we propose an LSTM-based framework that can predict the instance-level labels by only using bag-level labels, in a weakly supervised manner.

Our contributions are three-fold: i) We advocate the application of LSTM networks on general MIL problems, as a means for encoding more general underlying structures (i.e. not limited to ordered data) within bags of instances. ii) We conduct an extensive systematic evaluation showing that LSTMs are capable of capturing information within bags that go beyond ordered sequences. Moreover, we show that their performance is, surprisingly, comparable or even superior to that of methods especially designed to handle MIL problems. iii) We propose a framework for weakly supervised learning based on LSTM, capable of modeling distributions at the instance-level, using only bag-level annotations.

2   Related Work

Efforts based on LSTMs/RNNs aiming at modelling unordered bags are quite rare. [19,20] propose a memory-based recurrent architecture and apply it on sorting [19] and traversal of graphs [20], where the input data can be regarded as unordered bags. [21] considers a fashion outfit to be a sequence (from top to bottom) and each item in the outfit as an instance. Then, a LSTM model is trained to sequentially predict the next item conditioned on previous ones to learn their compatibility relationships. Later, [22] used a CNN-RNN model to perform multiple label predictions, where LSTMs were used to decode the labels in an unordered manner. Different from this work which focused on the decoding part, we investigate the encoding of the unordered bags. [23] proposed to learn permutation-invariant bag representations by summing features across instances and applying non-linear transformations. This can be regarded as a specific case of [18] where the weight of the instances are uniform. [24] uses LSTMs to capture the function over the sets, which is different from ours, whereas we use LSTM to model the set representation and learn instance-level distributions from the set label. These works either use LSTMs to handle unordered data on some specific settings [21,23] or use them just as side experiments [19,20]. Here, we propose the use of LSTMs to address more *general* MIL problems.

On the task of modeling general bag representations, we position our approach w.r.t. efforts based on neural networks, specifically those with deep architectures since our work is based on LSTMs. Please refer to [13–15] for detailed surveys covering non-deep methods. [25] proposed a multiple instance neural network to estimate instance probabilities. This idea is further extended in [26] which uses a neural network to learn a bag representation and directly carry out bag classification without estimating instance-level probabilities or labels. In parallel, [18] proposed an attention mechanism to learn a pooling operation over instances. The weights learned for the attention mechanism on instances can serve as indicators of the contribution of each instance to the final decision – thus, producing explainable predictions. [27] proposed a similar idea, using the computed bag representations, to measure distances between image bags. [28] proposed to update the contributions of the instances by observing all the instances of the bag a predefined number of iterations. Along a different direction, [29] proposed a hierarchical bag representation in which each bag is internally divided into subbags until reaching the instance level. Very recently, [30] proposed to consider the instances in the bags to be non-i.i.d. and used graph neural networks to learn a bag embedding.

Similar to [18,26] we embed the instance features from each bag into a common space and the bag representation is used to make direct bag predictions. Similar to [28,30] we aim at learning the underlying structure within the bags. Different from [30], our method does not rely on hand-tuned parameters, e.g.. manual graph construction. Moreover, the improvement in performance displayed by our method is not sensitive to the possible lack of structure within each bag. Compared to [28], our method only requires *a single pass* through all the instances. Moreover, our method is able to go beyond binary classification tasks and handle more complex classification and regression tasks. Finally, most of the works mentioned above operate under the standard Multiple Instance (MI) assumption. In contrast, the proposed approach is able to learn the underlying structure of bags of instances, thus, being robust to several MI assumptions/problems [15].

3   Methodology

We begin our analysis by defining the different parts that compose it. First, we formally define MIL problems and draw pointers towards different MI assumptions that they commonly consider. Then, we introduce the LSTM-based pipeline that will be considered to model bags of instances throughout our analysis.

3.1   Underlying Structures Within Bags of Instances

As was said earlier, underlying sequential structures between the instances within a bag is a cue that LSTMs are capable of encoding quite effectively. In fact, this capability have made them effective at handling problems defined by these sequences, e.g.. actions, speech, text. However, this sequential order is just one of many possible underlying structures that could be present between the instances within the bags processed by a LSTM. Encoding these underlying structures and making predictions about bags of instances is the main objective of Multiple Instance Learning (MIL) [13–15]. We will conduct our analysis from the perspective of MIL, where LSTMs will play an active role in modeling the underlying bag structure.

Given the bag $X_j = \{x_1, x_2, ..., x_m\}$ of instances x_i with latent instance-level labels $C_j = \{c_1, c_2, ..., c_m\}$, traditional MIL problems aim at the prediction of bag-level labels y_j for each bag X_j. The MIL literature covers several underlying bag structures, referred to as *assumptions*, that have been commonly considered in order to define bag-level labels. We refer the reader to [13–15] for different surveys that have grouped these assumptions based on different criteria.

3.2   Proposed Pipeline

The proposed pipeline consists of three main components. Given a bag X of m instances x_i, each of the instances x_i is encoded into a feature representation f_i through the *Instance Description Unit*. Then, each element is fed to the *Iterative bag Pooling Unit*, producing the aggregated bag representation S. Finally, a prediction $\hat{y}$ is obtained by evaluating the bag representation via the *Prediction Unit* (Fig. 1).

Instance Description Unit. This component receives the bag of instances in raw form, i.e. each of the instances $x_i \in \mathbb{R}^{[d]}$ that compose it, in its original format. It is tasked with encoding the input bag data into a format that can be

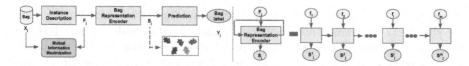

Fig. 1. Left: Proposed approach pipeline. Right: Iterative bag pooling unit. The bag representation S_j^i is updated each time the representation f_i of an element is observed.

processed by the rest of the pipeline. As such, it provides the proposed method with robustness to different data formats/modalities. More formally, given a dataset $\{X_j, y_j\}$ of bags X_j paired with their corresponding bag-level labels y_j, each of the bags X_j is encoded into a feature $F_j = \{f_1, f_2, ..., f_m\}$. This is achieved by pushing each of the instances x_i that compose it, through a feature encoder $\tau(.)$ producing the instance-level representation $f_i = \tau(x_i), f_i \in \mathbb{R}^{[n]}$. Selection of this component depends on the modality of the data to be processed, e.g.. VGG [31] or ResNet [32] features for still images, Word2Vec [33] or BERT [34] for text data, or rank-pooled features [35] or dynamic images [36] for video data.

Maximizing Mutual Information from Instances. Mutual information can be used to measure the (possibly non-linear) dependency between two variables, noted as $I(A; B)$. Maximizing mutual information between input instance and its representation helps the model learn a better representation [37,38]. It is useful as a regularizer especially when learning a model from scratch. In our method, we follow [37] where the total objective function is:

$$L = \alpha \cdot max(MI_{global}) + \beta \cdot max(MI_{local}) + \gamma \cdot PriorMatching \tag{1}$$

MI_{global} and MI_{local} are the global and local Mutual information where the latter one is calculated between intermediate feature map and final representation. $PriorMatching$ is used to match the output of the IDU to a prior: combined with the maximization of mutual information, Eq. 1 can constrain representations according to desired statistical properties. For the sake of space, please refer to [37] and the supplementary material for more details regarding the derivation.

Bag Representation Encoder. The main goal of this component is to derive a bag-level representation $S_j \in \mathbb{R}^{[n]}$ that is able to encode all the instances x_i, and any possible underlying structure between them. As mentioned earlier, LSTM is utilized to model the underlying [unordered] structure in the bag.

We aim at learning a bag representation that is independent of both the cardinality m of the bag and the nature of the underlying structure. Starting from the element-level representations F_j computed in the previous step, this is achieved by iteratively looking at the representations f_i, from each of the instances x_i, one at a time. In each iteration i an updated bag-level representation S_j^i is computed. In parallel, following the LSTM formulation, a feedback loop provides information regarding the stateof the bag representation that will be considered at the next iteration $i+1$. Finally, after observing all the m instances x_i in the bag, the final bag representation $S_j^m|_{i=m}$ is taken as the output S_j of this component.

The notion behind this iterative bag pooling idea is that instances observed at specific iterations can be used to compute a more-informed bag-level representation at later iterations. Thus, allowing to encode underlying relationships or structures among the instances of the bag. While this iterative assumption may hint at a sequence structure requirement within each bag, our empirical evaluation strongly suggests this not to be the case. (see Sect. 4.2)

In practice, we use Bi-directional LSTMs which observe the instances in a bag from the left-to-right and right-to-left directions. This will further ensure that the context in which the instances of the bag occur is properly modelled.

Prediction Unit. Having a bag-level representation S_j for bag X_j, this component is tasked with making a bag-level prediction $\hat{y}_j = g(S_j)$ that will serve as final output for the pipeline. The selection of the prediction function $g(.)$ is related to the task of interest. This unit provides our method with flexibility to address both classification and regression tasks.

4   Analysis

4.1   What Kind of Information Can Be Captured by LSTMs?

This experiment focuses on performing multiple instance predictions based on visual data. Following the protocol from [18] we use images from the MNIST dataset [16] to construct image bags to define four scenarios, each following a different assumption: *Single digit occurrence, Multiple digit occurrence, Single digit counting* and *Outlier detection.*

For this series of experiments, we use a LeNet as Instance Descriptor unit (IDU) and an LSTM with an input and cell state with 500 dimensions as Bag Representation Encoder (BRE), respectively. Both the IDU and BRE components are trained jointly from scratch. We compare the obtained performance w.r.t. the attention-based model from [18] and the dynamic pooling method from [28]. Mean error rate in the binary classification task is adopted as performance metric in these experiments. Please note, we *do not* traverse all the possible permutations in the following experiments. On the contrary, only a small proportion of them are seen by the model.

The main objective of this experiment is to answer the following questions: i) whether other underlying bag structures, outside of sequential order, can be encoded properly by LSTMs?, and ii) *how competitive are LTSMs when compared with methods from the MIL literature specifically designed for modeling the underlying bag structures?*

Single Digit Occurrence. In this scenario we follow the standard MI assumption and label a bag as positive if at least one digit '9' occurs in the bag. The digit '9' is selected since it can be easily mistaken with digit '4' and '7' [18], thus, introducing some instance-level ambiguity. We define bags with mean cardinality $m = 10$, and verify the effect that m has on performance by testing two standard deviation values, $\sigma = 2$ and $\sigma = 8$. We repeat this experiment five times generating different bags and weight initializations. We report mean performance in Table 1 (col. II and III).

Discussion: The results indicate that, in this task, our performance is comparable with the state-of-the-art for lower values of σ and superior as σ increases. This is to some extent expected, since at lower σ the cardinality (i.e. the number of instances) of each bag is almost fixed. This setting is favorable for the attention-based method since it operates in a feed-forward fashion. Yet, note the high standard deviation in performance produced by this baseline. On the contrary, at higher σ values there is a higher variation of cardinality across bags. Under this setting, feed-forward approaches start to produce higher errors. Here our method produces superior performance, $\sim$1.4% points (pp) w.r.t. to the state-of-the-art.

Table 1. Mean error rate (in percentage points) of experiments considering digits from the MNIST dataset. (*) refers to baselines which include the Mutual Information loss.

Method	single digit($\sigma = 2$)	single digit($\sigma = 8$)	multiple digits	digit counting	outlier detection
Atten. Based	**2.8 ± 4.8**	4.5 ± 0.4	28.5 ± 0.7	33.4 ± 19.3	37.0*
Gated Atten. Based	4.0 ± 0.9	4.6 ± 0.5	27.4 ± 0.9	11.9 ± 3.6	37.4*
Dyn. Pool	5.6 ±1.1	6.1 ± 1.2	28.5 ± 6.6	25.4 ± 1.8	40.9*
Ours w/o Mut. Info.	3.5 ± 1.1	**3.1 ± 0.5**	6.4± 1.4	9.0 ± 2.7	50.0
Ours	4.0± 0.4	4.1 ± 1.4	**3.5 ± 1.3**	**7.4 ± 1.2**	**2.07**

Multiple Digit Occurrence. This is an extension of the previous scenario in which instead of focusing on the occurrence of a single digit class, the model should recognize the occurrence of instances of two digit classes (presence-based MI assumption [15]). More specifically, a bag is labeled positive if both digits '3' and '6' occur in it, without considering the order of occurrence. For this scenario 1,000 bags are sampled for training. Results are reported in Table 1 (col. IV).

Discussion: It is remarkable that when making this simple extension of considering the occurrence of multiple digits, i.e. '3' and '6', the state-of-the-art methods suffer a significant drop in performance. This drop put the state-of-the-art methods $\sim$27 pp below, on average, w.r.t. the performance of our method. Please note that in this experiment the order (or location) of the two digits does *not* matter. This supports previous observations that LSTMs can indeed handle multiple instances of interest, independent of the ordering in which they occur within the bags. In this scenario, where observing multiple instances is of interest, the model needs to "remember" the information that it has seen in order to asses whether instances of the classes of interest have been encountered. The feed-forward models lack information persistence mechanisms; which translates to a poor ability to remember and to handle multiple instances of interest. Surprisingly, in spite of its iterative nature, the Dynamic pooling method is not able to preserve the information it has observed across iterations, resulting in similar performance as the other baselines.

Digit Counting. Previous scenarios addressed the classification task of predicting positive/negative bag-level labels. In contrast, in this scenario, we focus on the regression task of counting the number of instances of a specific digit class of interest within the bag (presence-based MI assumption). In order to make our approach suitable to address a regression problem, instead of using a classifier as prediction unit we use a regressor whose continuous output is rounded in order to provide a discrete count value as output. In this experiment the digit '9' is selected as the class to be counted. The mean cardinality of each bag is fixed to $m = 15$. Performance is reported in Table 1 (col. V).

Discussion: From Table 1 (col. V) the same trend can be observed: our method has superior performance and higher stability than the attention-based model and other baselines. When conducting this counting task, our method obtains a performance that is superior by 24 pp w.r.t. the attention-based model and by 16 pp w.r.t. the dynamic pooling. These results further confirm the capability of LSTMs to handle this type of unordered regression problems [39].

Digit Outlier Detection. This task is concerned with identifying whether a bag contains a digit which is different from the majority (outlier). Different from *Single digit occurrence*, this task is more difficult since the model has to understand: i) the two digit classes that might be present in the bag, and ii) the proportion condition that makes the bag an outlier. This is different from *Single digit occurrence* where it only needed to identify the "witness" digit '9'. Besides, there is no restriction on the outlier and majority digits, they can be any digit class from MNIST dataset. This constitutes a collective MI assumption since all the instances determine the underlying structure of the bag. Therefore, given the complexity of this task, in this experiment we apply the mutual information loss on every baseline method in order to assist their training. We use 10,000 bags to train the model and 2,000 bags to test. The bag cardinality is 6 with 1 standard deviation. Table 1 (col. VI) shows quantitative results of this experiment.

Discussion: It is remarkable that, even after applying the mutual information loss on the other baselines, they still have a low performance on this task. We notice that the Attention and Gated Attention methods work slightly better than Dynamic Pooling. More importantly, our method, based on LSTMs, outperforms the baselines by a large margin ($\sim$36 pp). This suggests that LSTMs are quite capable at modeling this type of bag structure, even to the point of outperforming MIL methods tailored to model bag-based structures.

4.2   Does the Result Depend on the Order Chosen?

The short answer is no. The reason is that in the training phase we push the bags with different orders (as a form of data augmentation) to the model while the bag labels are the same. By following this procedure the loss function will not penalize differences in the order in which the instances are observed. To further verify this, we repeated the test phase of our experiments 100 times with the contents of each bag (cardinality = m, in total m! combinations) shuffled thus producing bags with 100 different orders. Then, similar to Sect. 4.1, we measure the error rate and report the mean performance. The obtained error rate is $(4.2 \pm 0.6)\%$, $(3.5 \pm 0.4)\%$, $(7.8 \pm 0.7)\%$ for the Single-digit, Multiple-digit and Digit counting experiments, respectively ($m = 10, 12, 15$ respectively). They are very close to the numbers reported in Table 1. The results verify that the LSTM is able to learn, to a good extent, that the underlying MIL assumptions were permutation invariant - changing the order of instances of a bag has a relatively low effect on the prediction in most of the cases.

4.3   Does the Result Depend on the Cardinality of the Bag?

No, modeling bag representations via LSTMs seems robust enough to bags with different cardinalitiy (sizes). We verify this by conducting an extended experiment based on the *multiple instance occurrence* scenario. Firstly, we consider bags with higher cardinality but keep *only one relevant instance pair ('3', '6') present* using one of our trained models (mean bag cardinality $m = 12$). We obtained error rates of 7%, 14.5%, 42%, and 44% for bag cardinality 20, 50, 100 and 200, respectively. This result is not surprising since during training the bag cardinality was much lower. To have a fair experiment, we use bags with higher cardinality to finetune our model, using 1/5 amount of the original number of training bags (i.e. now we use 200 bags). Similarly, the larger bags still contain only one pair of relevant digits. This results in error rates of $(2.38 \pm 0.41)\%$, $(3.13 \pm 0.89)\%$, $(4.25 \pm 1.3)\%$ for mean bag cardinality of 50, 100 and 200, respectively. This shows that LSTMs are still capable of modeling unordered bags even when bags with significantly higher cardinality are considered, although, unsurprisingly, training and testing conditions should match.

4.4   Effect of the Complexity of the Data

In this section, we shift our analysis to real-world data. Summarizing, the results show that our method still works comparable and even better than the baselines.

Fig. 2. Examples of instances for the original (left), occluded (middle) and database images (right) in our cross-domain clothing retrieval experiment.

Cross-Domain Clothing Retrieval. For this experiment, we divide images from the Lookbook dataset into two domains: catalog clothing images and their corresponding human model images where a person is wearing the clothing product, see Fig. 2. Each clothing product has one catalog image and several human model images. We only consider the products with five or more human model images, resulting in 6616 unique products (latent classes c_i) with around 63k images in total. Every product image has 5–55 human model images. The training bag contains 4000 classes while the validation and test bags have 616 and 2000 classes, respectively. We run two experiments on this dataset as described in the following sections. Given the higher complexity of images in this dataset, we use a pre-trained VGG16 [31] as IDU. Since this unit is pretrained, the mutual information loss is not applied for this unit in this experiment. Moreover, we set the dimensionality of the input and cell state of our LSTM to $n = 2048$.

For this experiment, human model images are used as queries while catalog images serve as database, thus, defining a many-to-one retrieval setting. The cardinality of each bag is the same as the number of human model images of each product (class). We conduct two variants of this experiment. On the first variant we use the complete image, as it is originally provided. The second is an occluded variant where every human model image in a bag is divided into a 4×4 grid of 16 blocks. 12 of these blocks are occluded by setting all the pixels therein to black. By doing so, every single image in a bag can only show part of the information while their combination (i.e. the whole bag) represents the complete clothing item. Catalog images in the database are not occluded in this experiment. This experiment can be regarded as an extreme case of standard MI assumption, where all the instances in each bag is positive.

As baselines, in addition to the attention-based model we follow DeepFashion [40], and train a model to perform retrieval by computing the distances by considering single image representations instead of bag-based representations. Following the multiple queries approach from [41], we report performance of three variants of this method: *Single-AVE*, where the distance of each bag is computed as the average of the distances from every image in the bag w.r.t. an item in the database; *Single-MIN*, where the distance of the bag is defined as the minimum distance of an image in the bag w.r.t. an item in the database; and *Single Fea. AVE*, where the distance of the bag is calculated as the distance of a prototype element w.r.t. an item in the database. As prototype element we use

Table 2. Retrieval on the original Lookbook dataset.

Method	rec.@1	rec.@10	rec.@20	rec.@50
Atten.	13.75	39.25	49.70	63.60
Dyn. Pool	16.75	47.65	59.45	73.60
Single AVE	20.55	57.05	68.25	81.90
Single MIN	22.60	58.15	**69.20**	82.50
Single Fea. AVE	20.15	56.25	67.85	81.50
Ours w/o mut. info.	**22.95**	**58.65**	68.70	**83.00**

Table 3. Retrieval on the occluded Lookbook dataset.

Method	rec.@1	rec.@10	rec.@20	rec.@50
Atten.	3.55	20.6	32.95	53.65
Dyn. Pool	1.95	11.95	29.35	32.55
Single AVE	3.65	23.85	35.06	56.10
Single MIN	5.25	26.05	37.35	55.00
Single Fea. AVE	5.10	25.60	36.95	54.65
Ours w/o mut. info.	**9.25**	**34.75**	**45.00**	**61.80**

the average feature representation $\overline{f_i}$ from the representation f_i of every element in the bag. We refer to these baselines as *Single-image models*.

Discussion: Table 2 shows that in the original setting our method tends to obtain superior recall values in the majority of the cases, with the exception of the case when the closest 20 items (recall@20) are considered. When looking at the occluded variant of the experiment, a quick glance at Table 3 shows that, compared to the original setting, absolute performance values on this setting are much lower. This is to be expected since this is a more challenging scenario where the model needs to learn the information cumulatively by aggregating information from parts of different images. In this occluded setting, our method clearly outperforms all the baselines. This could be attributed to the information persistence component from the LSTMs. This component allows our method to select what to remember and what to ignore from each of the instances that it observes when updating the bag representation used to compute distances. The difference w.r.t. to the *Single-AVE* and *Single-MIN* baselines is quite remarkable given that they require a significant larger number of element-wise distance computations w.r.t. items in the database. This may lead to scalability issues when the dataset size increases, as the computation cost will grow exponentially.

Moreover, in both occluded and non-occluded datasets, we notice that the *Single-image model* baselines have a superior performance w.r.t. the attention-based model and dynamic pooling model. We hypothesize that is because the single-image models can better exploit important features, e.g. discriminative visual patches, since they compute distances directly in an instance-wise fashion. In contrast, it is likely that some of these nuances might get averaged out by the feature aggregation step that is present in the attention-based model.

Colon Cancer Prediction. This task consists of predicting the occurrence of Colon cancer from histopathology images. The used Colon cancer dataset contains $100\ 500 \times 500$ H&E images with a total of 22k annotated nuclei. There are four types of nuclei: *epithelial, inflammatory, fibroblast*, and *miscellaneous*. This experiment focuses on identifying whether colon cancer histopathology images contain a specific type of nuclei. We follow the protocol from [18] and treat every H&E image as a bag composed by instances (patches) of 27×27 pixels centered on detected nuclei. The bag cardinality varies from 6 to 796 depending on the number of nuclei present in the image. Following a standard MI assumption, a bag is considered positive if it contains *epithelial* nuclei since Colon cancer originates from epithelial cells [18,42] This produces a dataset with 51 and 48 positive and negative bag examples, respectively. We extend this dataset via data augmentation as in [18].

We adapt an architecture which is similar to [43] to define the IDU and a 512 dimension input and cell state to define the LSTM (BRE). The whole model is trained from scratch. Following the protocol, only bag-level binary labels are used for training. We conduct experiments considering the same baselines as in previous experiments. We apply five-fold cross validation and report the mean performance and standard deviation. For reference, we also provide the results presented in [18] for the baselines Atten.* and Gated Atten.*. Table 4 shows quantitative results in terms of Accuracy and F1-Score.

Discussion: This experiment, where a bag can have up to 796 instances, serves a good test-bed to assess the performance of the proposed method on bags with high cardinality. From the results in Table 4, we can notice that our method still outperforms all the considered baselines.

Table 4. Colon cancer experiment results.

Metric	Atten.*	Gated Atten.*	Atten.	Gated Atten.	Dyn. Pool	Ours w/o mut. info.	Ours
Accuracy	90.40 ± 1.10	89.80 ± 2.00	88.79 ± 6.16	86.89 ± 3.93	87.89 ± 2.37	90.89 ± 2.06	**92.74 ± 2.41**
F1-Score	90.10 ± 1.10	89.30 ± 2.20	88.85 ± 6.35	86.87 ± 6.67	88.18 ± 2.11	90.66 ± 2.80	**93.08 ± 1.36**

5   From Internal States to Instance-Level Representations

Previous efforts [2,7,44] based on ordered bags have shown that the internal state of the representation within the LSTMs can be used to predict future instances. Here, we have shown that LSTMs can also encode other types of bag-based information internally. This begs the question - *what else can the internal representation in LSTMs reveal in the unordered setting?*. Here we conduct an analysis aiming to answer this question.

5.1   Weakly Supervised Learning of Instance-Level Distributions

We have presented using LSTM to make predictions from a bag-level representation S_j through the use of a prediction function $g(\cdot)$. There is a connection between the MIL task and the distribution of the instance representation. Based on this observation we put forward the following hypotheses:

- *Hypothesis 1: A model trained for a MIL task can learn the underlying distribution over the instances.*
- *Hypothesis 2: A prediction function $g(\cdot)$ trained on the bag representation S can be used to make instance-level predictions if the distribution from S, influenced by the underlying MI assumption, is close to that of F.*

We propose the following approach to recover the underlying instance-level representation and make instance-level predictions. We break down the instance bag $X = \{x_1, x_2, ..., x_m\}$ into m singleton bags $X_1 = \{x_1\}$, $X_2 = \{x_2\}$, ..., $X_m = \{x_m\}$. The singleton bag $X_j = \{x_j\}$ is sent to the model, passing the IDU and the LSTM. Afterwards, the output S_j of the LSTM from every singleton is collected into a feature matrix $\mathbb{S}, \mathbb{S} \in \mathbb{R}^{[m \times n]}$. Then, k-means clustering algorithm is applied on $\mathbb{S}$ with the number of clusters determined by the corresponding MIL task. We use a similar metric to clustering purity, where we calculate the purity of each cluster first and average them instead of calculating the purity of all samples. By doing this we avoid problems caused by imbalanced data. The clustering performance reflects the ability of modeling the distribution of instances for the model.

5.2   Weakly Supervised Instance-Level Learning

In Sect. 5.1 we presented two hypotheses related to the weakly supervised instance-level learning. We will address them in this section.

Modelling Instance-level Representations. In Sect. 4.1 and 4.4, we trained both IDU and LSTM from scratch by considering the bag-level labels only. This can be regarded as weakly supervised learning if the goal is to make instance-level predictions. For attention-based methods, we collect the output of IDU and multiply with weight 1, since it is a singleton bag and there is no LSTM. Following this procedure, both methods use the features after their respective units handling the MIL task. We evaluate instances from both testing/training bag for the baseline and our model, respectively. We choose the Gated-Attention model as a baseline since it works best among the attention-based methods in Sect. 4.1. Table 5 reports the clustering performance metric described in Sect. 5.1.

Table 5. Instance clustering accuracy from MNIST-bag task models.

Task	Gated Atten. (test/train)	Ours (test/train)
single digit (2 classes)	98.69/98.92	97.59/97.42
multiple digits (3 classes)	85.92/87.47	**97.94/97.06**
digit counting (2 classes)	99.22/99.31	99.15/99.23
outlier detection (10 classes)	59.33/57.02	**97.96/97.52**

Table 6. Instance label accuracy for Colon cancer dataset.

Method	TP (test/train)	TN (test/train)	mean Acc (test/train)
Atten	32.42/21.25	**98.45/99.22**	65.43/63.60
Ours	**73.47/70.73**	92.39/92.28	**82.93/81.51**
Supervised	*78.92/92.09*	*91.14/98.22*	*85.03/95.16*

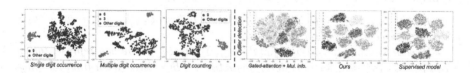

Fig. 3. t-SNE visualization of features extracted from **our** MIL model in three MNIST bag tasks (left) and with baseline models in *Outlier detection* (right).

Discussion: Table 5 indicates that for simple tasks, such as *single digit occurrence* and *digit counting*, both attention-based and our methods can distinguish the background digits and witness digits. To handle the MIL task, the model just needs to differentiate between the witness digit ("9") from other digits. Therefore, there should only be two clusters/classes. Three clusters/classes are assigned to *multiple digits* because the model needs to distinguish the two witness digits from the others.

For the case of *outlier detection*, in order to detect the outlier(s) from a bag, the model needs to distinguish every digit. For this reason, once capable of handling this MIL task, the models should also have the ability to cluster/classify the 10 digits. It is clear that our model trained for this task has learned very good discriminative features for all 10-class digits, while the attention-based method fails, even when the mutual information loss is still applied on top of it. The clustering accuracy is close to the known performance of ~98% accuracy of the supervised LeNet model [16]. This is strong evidence showing that our method is able to learn an instance-level representation in a weakly supervised manner. In addition, Fig. 3 shows the t-SNE visualizations for features extracted by our method in the testing bag of the four tasks. The figure shows how discriminative the singleton features are. These results prove that our *Hypothesis 1* is correct.

Instance-Level Prediction: The colon cancer dataset contains 7,722 epithelial nuclei and 14,721 other nuclei. We select one of the models we trained earlier and treat the patches as singleton bags (i.e. bags only contain one patch). The singleton bags are sent to the model to make instance-level predictions: epithelial or not. In the meantime we also use the same training-test split to train a fully supervised model. We report the instance-level accuracy in Table 6. In addition, Fig. 4 shows the patches that are classified as epithelial nuclei.

Discussion. This task meets the requirement of *Hypothesis 2*: the bag representation S contains the information whether the epithelial nuclei exist in a bag, which is close to what would be expected from instance-level feature F. Our model achieves the best performance for bag-level prediction. It also has a good performance on the instance-level prediction. The mean accuracy is close to the supervised model and significantly better (~18 pp) than that of the Attention-based model. It clearly shows that our MIL model can be used to predict the instance labels. In addition, Fig. 4 shows that our model has a better ability to identify the nuclei of interest, which can be useful for pathologists.

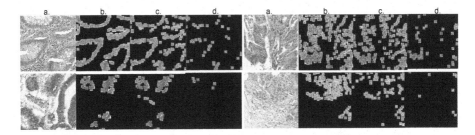

Fig. 4. a) The original H&E image. b) The epithelial nuclei patches (Ground-Truth). c) The epithelial nuclei patches detected by our MIL model. d) The epithelial nuclei patches detected by attention-based MIL model

6 Conclusion

We investigate the potential of LSTMs at solving MIL problems. Through an extensive analysis we have shown that LSTMs can indeed capture additional information of the underlying structure within the bags. Our results suggest that its performance at modeling more general bag structures is comparable and even better than that from methods tailored for MIL problems. Our method can also model the instance-level distribution in a weakly supervised manner.

Acknowledgement. This work was partially supported by the KU Leuven AI impuls, FWO G.0A47.20N, and a NVIDIA Academic Hardware Grant.

References

1. Sammut, C., Webb, G.I.: Multi-instance learning. Encyclopedia of Machine Learning (2011)
2. Hochreiter, S., Schmidhuber, J.: Long short-term memory. Neural Comput. **9**, 1735–1780 (1997)
3. Sundermeyer, M., Schlüter, R., Ney, H.: LSTM neural networks for language modeling (2012)
4. Sutskever, I., Vinyals, O., Le, Q.V.: Sequence to sequence learning with neural networks. In: Ghahramani, Z., Welling, M., Cortes, C., Lawrence, N.D., Weinberger, K.Q. (eds.) Advances in Neural Information Processing Systems **27**, pp. 3104–3112. Curran Associates, Inc. (2014)
5. Le, Q.V., Mikolov, T.: Distributed representations of sentences and documents. In: ICML. JMLR Workshop and Conference Proceedings, JMLR.org (2014)
6. Liu, J., Shahroudy, A., Xu, D., Wang, G.: Spatio-temporal LSTM with trust gates for 3d human action recognition. In: Leibe, B., Matas, J., Sebe, N., Welling, M. (eds.) ECCV (2016)
7. Shi, X., Chen, Z., Wang, H., Yeung, D.Y., Wong, W.K., WOO, W.C.: Convolutional LSTM network: a machine learning approach for precipitation nowcasting. In: Cortes, C., Lawrence, N.D., Lee, D.D., Sugiyama, M., Garnett, R. (eds.) Advances in Neural Information Processing Systems 28, pp. 802–210. Curran Associates, Inc. (2015)
8. Alahi, A., Goel, K., Ramanathan, V., Robicquet, A., Fei-Fei, L., Savarese, S.: Social LSTM: human trajectory prediction in crowded spaces. In: The IEEE Conference on Computer Vision and Pattern Recognition (CVPR) (2016)
9. Zhu, W., Lan, C., Xing, J., Zeng, W., Li, Y., Shen, L., Xie, X.: Co-occurrence feature learning for skeleton based action recognition using regularized deep LSTM networks. In: Thirtieth AAAI Conference on Artificial Intelligence (2016)
10. Singh, B., Marks, T.K., Jones, M., Tuzel, O., Shao, M.: A multi-stream bidirectional recurrent neural network for fine-grained action detection. In: The IEEE Conference on Computer Vision and Pattern Recognition (CVPR) (2016)
11. Graves, A., Schmidhuber, J.: Framewise phoneme classification with bidirectional lstm and other neural network architectures. Neural Networks, pp. 5–6 (2005)
12. Gers, F.A., Schmidhuber, J., Cummins, F.: Learning to forget: continual prediction with LSTM. Neural Comput. **12**, 2451–2471 (1999)
13. Amores, J.: Multiple instance classification: review, taxonomy and comparative study. Artif. Intell. **201**, 81–105 (2013)

14. Carbonneau, M.A., Cheplygina, V., Granger, E., Gagnon, G.: Multiple instance learning: a survey of problem characteristics and applications. ArXiv abs/1612.03365 (2018)
15. Foulds, J., Frank, E.: A review of multi-instance learning assumptions. Knowledge Eng. Rev. **25**, 1–25 (2010)
16. LeCun, Y., Cortes, C.: MNIST handwritten digit database (2010)
17. Yoo, D., Kim, N., Park, S., Paek, A.S., Kweon, I.: Pixel-level domain transfer. In: ECCV (2016)
18. Ilse, M., Tomczak, J.M., Welling, M.: Attention-based deep multiple instance learning. arXiv preprint arXiv:1802.04712 (2018)
19. Graves, A., Wayne, G., Danihelka, I.: Neural turing machines. CoRR abs/1410.5401 (2014)
20. Graves, A., et al.: Hybrid computing using a neural network with dynamic external memory. Nature (2016)
21. Han, X., Wu, Z., Jiang, Y.G., Davis, L.S.: Learning fashion compatibility with bidirectional LSTMS. In: ACM MM. MM 2017 (2017)
22. Yazici, V.O., Gonzalez-Garcia, A., Ramisa, A., Twardowski, B., van de Weijer, J.: Orderless recurrent models for multi-label classification (2019)
23. Zaheer, M., Kottur, S., Ravanbakhsh, S., Poczos, B., Salakhutdinov, R.R., Smola, A.J.: Deep sets. In: Guyon, I., Luxburg, U.V., Bengio, S., Wallach, H., Fergus, R., Vishwanathan, S., Garnett, R. (eds.) Advances in Neural Information Processing Systems 30, pp. 3391–3401. Curran Associates, Inc. (2017)
24. Pabbaraju, C., Jain, P.: Learning functions over sets via permutation adversarial networks. CoRR abs/1907.05638 (2019)
25. Ramon, J., De Raedt, L.: Multiple instance neural networks. In: ICML Workshop on Attribute-value and Relational Learning (2000)
26. Wang, X., Yan, Y., Tang, P., Bai, X., Liu, W.: Revisiting multiple instance neural networks. Pattern Recognition **74**, 15–24 (2018)
27. Liu, Y., Yan, J., Ouyang, W.: Quality aware network for set to set recognition (2017)
28. Yan, Y., Wang, X., Guo, X., Fang, J., Liu, W., Huang, J.: Deep multi-instance learning with dynamic pooling. In: Asian Conference on Machine Learning (2018)
29. Tibo, A., Jaeger, M., Frasconi, P.: Learning and interpreting multi-multi-instance learning networks. arXiv:1810.11514 (2018)
30. Tu, M., Huang, J., He, X., Zhou, B.: Multiple instance learning with graph neural networks. In: ICML Workshop on Learning and Reasoning with Graph-Structured Representations (2019)
31. Simonyan, K., Zisserman, A.: Very deep convolutional networks for large-scale image recognition. arXiv:1409.1556 (2014)
32. He, K., Zhang, X., Ren, S., Sun, J.: Deep residual learning for image recognition. In: CVPR (2015)
33. Mikolov, T., Sutskever, I., Chen, K., Corrado, G.S., Dean, J.: Distributed representations of words and phrases and their compositionality. In: Burges, C.J.C., Bottou, L., Welling, M., Ghahramani, Z., Weinberger, K.Q. (eds.) Advances in Neural Information Processing Systems 26, pp. 3111–3119. Curran Associates, Inc. (2013)
34. Devlin, J., Chang, M., Lee, K., Toutanova, K.: BERT: pre-training of deep bidirectional transformers for language understanding. In: arXiv:1810.04805 (2018)
35. Fernando, B., Gavves, E., Oramas M., J., Ghodrati, A., Tuytelaars, T.: Rank pooling for action recognition. In: TPAMI (2016)
36. Bilen, H., Fernando, B., Gavves, E., Vedaldi, A.: Action recognition with dynamic image networks. TPAMI **40**, 2799–2813 (2018)

37. Hjelm, R.D., et al.: Learning deep representations by mutual information estima-
    tion and maximization. In: International Conference on Learning Representations
    (2019)
38. Yang, X., Deng, C., Zheng, F., Yan, J., Liu, W.: Deep spectral clustering using
    dual autoencoder network. In: CVPR (2019)
39. Suzgun, M., Gehrmann, S., Belinkov, Y., Shieber, S.M.: LSTM networks can per-
    form dynamic counting. ACL 2019 Workshop on Deep Learning and Formal Lan-
    guages (2019)
40. Liu, Z., Luo, P., Qiu, S., Wang, X., Tang, X.: Deepfashion: Powering robust clothes
    recognition and retrieval with rich annotations. In: Proceedings of IEEE Conference
    on Computer Vision and Pattern Recognition (CVPR) (2016)
41. Arandjelović, R., Zisserman, A.: Multiple queries for large scale specific object
    retrieval. In: BMVC (2012)
42. Ricci-Vitiani, L., Lombardi, D.G., Pilozzi, E., Biffoni, M., Todaro, M., Peschle, C.,
    De Maria, R.: Identification and expansion of human colon-cancer-initiating cells.
    Nature **445**, 111–115 (2007)
43. Sirinukunwattana, K., Raza, S.E.A., Tsang, Y., Snead, D.R.J., Cree, I.A., Rajpoot,
    N.M.: Locality sensitive deep learning for detection and classification of nuclei in
    routine colon cancer histology images. In: IEEE Transactions on Medical Imaging
    (2016)
44. Liang, X., Lee, L., Dai, W., Xing, E.P.: Dual motion gan for future-flow embed-
    ded video prediction. In: International Conference on Computer Vision. Volume
    abs/1708.00284. pp. 1762–1770 (2017)

Addressing Class Imbalance in Scene Graph Parsing by Learning to Contrast and Score

He Huang[1]([✉]), Shunta Saito[2], Yuta Kikuchi[2], Eiichi Matsumoto[2], Wei Tang[1], and Philip S. Yu[1]

[1] University of Illinois at Chicago, Chicago, USA
{hehuang,tangw,psyu}@uic.edu
[2] Preferred Networks Inc., Tokyo, Japan
{shunta,kikuchi,matsumoto}@preferred.jp

Abstract. Scene graph parsing aims to detect objects in an image scene and recognize their relations. Recent approaches have achieved high *average* scores on some popular benchmarks, but fail in detecting rare relations, as the highly long-tailed distribution of data biases the learning towards frequent labels. Motivated by the fact that detecting these rare relations can be critical in real-world applications, this paper introduces a novel integrated framework of classification and ranking to resolve the class imbalance problem in scene graph parsing. Specifically, we design a new Contrasting Cross-Entropy loss, which promotes the detection of rare relations by suppressing incorrect frequent ones. Furthermore, we propose a novel scoring module, termed as Scorer, which learns to rank the relations based on the image features and relation features to improve the recall of predictions. Our framework is simple and effective, and can be incorporated into current scene graph models. Experimental results show that the proposed approach improves the current state-of-the-art methods, with a clear advantage of detecting rare relations.

1 Introduction

As an extension to object detection [4], scene graph parsing [5,6] aims to detect not only objects, *e.g.*, *persons* and *bikes*, in an image scene but also recognize their relationships (also called *predicates*), *e.g.*, *ride* and *push*. It is a fundamental tool for several applications such as image captioning [7], image retrieval [8] and image generation [9]. Due to the combinatorially large space of valid relation triplets <subject, predicate, object> and the polysemy of a predicate in different contexts, the task of scene graph parsing is challenging.

Recent scene graph parsing systems [2,3,5,10–12] are built on deep neural networks due to their ability to learn robust feature representations for both images and relational contexts directly from data. Xu *et al.* [5] use GRU [13] to approximate a conditional random field to jointly infer objects and predicates. Zellers *et al.* [3] propose to utilize the statistical distribution of relation triplets

© Springer Nature Switzerland AG 2021
H. Ishikawa et al. (Eds.): ACCV 2020, LNCS 12627, pp. 461–477, 2021.
https://doi.org/10.1007/978-3-030-69544-6_28

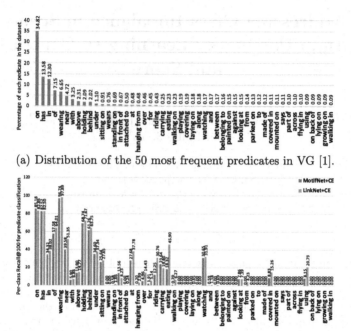

(a) Distribution of the 50 most frequent predicates in VG [1].

(b) Per-class Recall@100 of LinkNet [2] and MotifNet [3] evaluated on the predicate classification task.

Fig. 1. Motivation of this work: (a) the predicate distribution is highly long-tailed, and (b) two current state-of-the-art models [2,3] perform poorly on rare relations.

as external prior knowledge. Yang *et al.* [11] propose to incorporate a GCN [14] for predicting the predicates.

While these approaches can achieve high *average* scores on some popular benchmarks, their effectiveness is largely jeopardized in case of rare relationships. For example, Fig. 1(a) and Fig. 1(b) respectively show the distribution of predicates in the Visual Genome dataset (VG) [1] and the performances of two state-of-the-art methods, *i.e.*, LinkNet [2] and MotifNet [3]. Both approaches perform quite well on frequent relations, *e.g.*, on and has, but their performances degrade significantly on less common predicates, *e.g.*, lying on and flying in. The recalls of several rare relations are even zero. Actually, the average recalls of each class (*i.e.*, *macro-averaged Recall@100*) are only 15.3% and 16.9% for MotifNet [3] and LinkNet [2] respectively. By contrast, they can achieve around 67% *micro-averaged Recall@100*, which is calculated in a class-agnostic way. In other words, a high micro-averaged recall is achieved at the cost of sacrificing the performance on rare classes.

This is because the distribution of the predicates is highly long-tailed, and learning therefore tends to bias towards frequent relations so as to boost the overall performance. However, we argue that detecting those rare or *abnormal* relations is critical in practice. For example, consider a common predicate on and a rare one `lying on` in the VG dataset. Although these two terms are closely related, it is crucial for a surveillance camera to distinguish between `<person, on, street>` and `<person, lying on, street>`, since the latter may imply an emergency that requires immediate reactions.

Another limitation of previous approaches is that they model the task as a pure classification problem, by training with two cross-entropy loss functions for `subjects/objects` and `predicates` respectively. This approach is problematic as the evaluation metric is recall@K, which not only depends on classification accuracy but also is sensitive to the ranks of predicted relation triplets. While an object may either exist or not in an image, there is always at least one relationship between any two existing objects, e.g., `left` or `right`. When people annotate the VG [1] dataset, they only label the most important or nontrivial relations but ignore the others. As a result, the detection of an existing but trivial relation will be counted as a *false positive* because it is unlabeled in the dataset. To achieve a high recall for a given number of predictions, we need to not only classify the relations correctly but also rank the nontrivial relations higher than the trivial ones.

To overcome these challenging issues, this paper introduces a novel method which solves predicate classification and relation ranking in a unified framework. We first introduce a loss function, termed as the Contrasting Cross-Entropy (CCE) loss, to handle the class imbalance problem. This is achieved by simultaneously maximizing the predicted probability of the correct class and minimizing that of the hardest negative class. By suppressing incorrect frequent relations, the CCE loss promotes the recall of rare predicates. Furthermore, we propose a novel network module, called Scorer, to tackle the ranking problem. It scores a predicted relation triplet by comparing it with all other triplets as well as exploiting the global context information. Ablation study indicates that (1) the CCE loss significantly improves the detection of rare relationships and (2) the Scorer network helps boost the recall by learning to rank. Experimental results show that the proposed CCE loss and Scorer network can improve the state-of-the-art methods on three tasks. The contributions of this paper are:

- We provide a brand-new perspective on Scene Graph Parsing (SGP). To our knowledge, this is the first attempt to formulate it as a joint task of classification and ranking.
- We propose a simple but effective Contrasting Cross-Entropy (CCE) loss to alleviate the class imbalance problem. By contrasting for each relation the predicted probabilities of the correct label and the hardest incorrect one, it suppresses the incorrect frequent relations and significantly improves the detection performance on rare classes.
- We introduce a novel Scorer network to tackle the ranking problem and improve the recall of baselines by a large margin. It innovatively bridges the point-wise and list-wise ranking approaches to take advantages of both. Specifically, our Scorer exploits a self-attention layer to compare one relation triplet with all the others in a listwise fashion, from which learning to

rank is achieved via a point-wise cross-entropy loss. To our knowledge, this unification is unique and novel.

– Our novel framework is general and light-weighted. It can be easily applied to any scene graph models trained with cross-entropy. We conduct extensive experiments and show that our combined CCE-Scorer framework with LinkNet [2] as the base scene graph model achieves new state-of-the-art results on three scene graph detection tasks.

2 Related Work

Scene Graph Parsing. There have been several lines of research on scene graph parsing [5,15,16] and visual relationship detection [6,17] over the past few years. IMP [5] uses GRUs [13] to approximate a CRF and proposes an iterative message passing mechanism. Zellers *et al.* [3] propose a powerful baseline that infers the relation between two objects by simply taking the most frequent relation between the object pair in training set. By incorporating the frequency baseline, MotifNet [3] uses bi-directional LSTMs[18] to decode objects and relations sequentially. Recently, Gu *et al.* [19] propose to extract commonsense knowledge of predicted objects from knowledge bases. Another line of work try to design more sophisticated message passing methods to fine-tune object and predicate features [16,20,21]. LinkNet [2] exploits a new Relation Embedding module based on the self-attention to refine object features, which are then used to construct and refine predicate features. Graph RCNN [11] performs reasoning over the scene graph via a Relation Proposal Network, and then applies a graph convolutional network [14] to refine features.

KERN [10] tries to solve the class imbalance problem and uses *mean recall@K* as evaluation metric that can better represent the model's performance. However, KERN [10] tackles this problem by designing a complex network structure, while our proposed framework does not rely on particular network structure and is general and can be easily applied to any scene graph models that train with a cross-entropy loss, such as KERN [10] itself. Experiments show that our framework can improve the performance of KERN [10] by around 1% to 2%.

Zhan *et al.* [22] propose a module that classifies each predicted predicate as either determined or not, which is related to our proposed Scorer network. However, their module is simply a stack of fully-connected layers applied to each prediction individually and does not care about ranking, while ours utilizes information from both image-level and different relations. More importantly, Zhan *et al.* [22] do not consider ranking and only use their module in training, while our Scorer module is used also during inference to generate the ranks of predicted relation triplets.

Class Imbalance. This problem has been widely studied in both image classification [23,24] and object detection [25]. The most basic approaches are over-sampling minor classes and under-sampling major classes, both of which are prone to overfit. Another common approach is to multiply the loss of each class by its inverse frequency in the dataset. Sampling hard negatives is also widely studied in object detection to address the imbalance problem [26,27]. Recently, more advanced loss functions have been proposed to address this problem [28–30]. However, the class imbalance problem in scene graph parsing is rarely studied [10]. To the best of our knowledge, we are among the first to study this problem in depth and propose a general attentive solution that significantly mitigates the problem.

Contrasting Learning. The contrasting mechanism has been widely used for various applications, by pushing the scores of positive samples or matched sample pairs higher than those of negative ones [31–34]. Different from these previous approaches, we contrast for each relation the predicted probabilities of the correct and incorrect classes to suppress the incorrect frequent relations. In other words, they contrast data samples while we contrast classes, and the goals are different. While [35,36] also contrast classes, our design is different from theirs. They push down all negative classes to maximize the overall discriminativeness while we deliberately inhibit only the hardest negative class, which is critical to suppress the incorrect frequent relations. Besides, the contrasting loss in [35] includes a very complex normalization term while our CCE loss is much simpler and computationally efficient. [36] uses Gaussian as the distance metric while we use cross-entropy. Zhang *et al.* [37] propose a graphical contrastive loss that discriminate positive <subject, object> pairs from negative ones, which is different from us since our CCE loss contrast the classes of predicted relations. While all these work focus on one task, to the best of our knowledge, we are the first to apply a contrasting max-margin based loss together with a ranking objective in scene graph parsing.

Learning to Rank. Our work is also related to the field of *learning to rank* [38], which aims to predict the ranks of a set of samples in a non-decreasing order. There are three popular approaches to address this problem, *i.e.*, *point-wise* [39], *pair-wise* [39–41] and *list-wise* [41,42]. Different from prior work, our proposed Scorer network innovatively bridges the point-wise and list-wise ranking approaches by exploiting a self-attention module to compare one relation triplet with all the others in a list-wise fashion, from which learning to rank is achieved via a point-wise cross-entropy loss.

3   Proposed Approach

3.1   Problem Definition

The task of scene graph parsing [3,5] requires a model to take an image as input and then output an ordered set of relation triplets $\mathcal{T} = \{\mathcal{T}_i | i = 1, ..., M\}$, where $\mathcal{T}_i = $ <subject, predicate, object> and M is the number of relation triplets in the given image, each subject/object is from a set of object classes $\mathcal{C}$, and each predicate is from a set of predicate classes $\mathcal{R}$. The triplets in set $\mathcal{T}$ are ranked according to their confidence predicted by the model.

Current scene graph models rely on pretrained object detectors, *e.g.*, Faster R-CNN [4], to obtain the bounding boxes of objects and their features. Given N object proposals from the object detector, the scene graph model predicts their object labels. For each pair of predicted objects, the model generates a relation feature for this <subject, object> pair, which is then classified among the $|\mathcal{R}|$ predicate classes. Note that there are $N(N-1)$ relation features in total, excluding self-relations. The classification of objects and predicates are trained using separate cross-entropy loss functions in most existing scene graph models [2,3,5,10]. In practice, to handle un-annotated relations, an **unknown** class is introduced so that classification is performed among $|\mathcal{R}|+1$ classes. During inference, the predicate's label is found by ignoring the Softmax score of the **unknown** class and taking the label with the largest probability among the rest $|\mathcal{R}|$ classes.

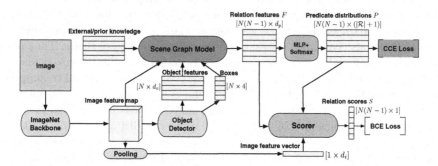

Fig. 2. An overview of the proposed framework. Here N is the number of detected objects in the input image, and (d_o, d_i, d_p) are the feature dimensions of (object, image, predicate). The core components are the Contrasting Cross-Entropy (CCE) loss for predicate classification and the Scorer network for relation ranking. Since these two components do not require modifying the chosen scene graph model, any existing scene graph model that trains with cross-entropy can be easily plugged into our framework. The external/prior knowledge is specific to the chosen base scene graph model. For example, MotifNet [3] and many other models [2,37] use the probability distribution of predicates given the subjects and objects.

After obtaining the predicted triplets $\mathcal{T}$ and a given set of ground-truth triplets $\mathcal{T}^*$, the result is evaluated by calculating *macro-averaged recall@K*, also known as $mR@K$ [10]:

$$mR@K = \frac{1}{|\mathcal{R}|} \sum_{r \in \mathcal{R}} \frac{\text{\# of correctly predicted } r \text{ in } \mathcal{T}[:K]}{\text{\# of } r \text{ in } \mathcal{T}^*}, \qquad (1)$$

where $\mathcal{T}[:K]$ represents the top-K triplets in the predicted $\mathcal{T}$. This metric is calculated per test image, and then the average $mR@K$ is used as the metric.

3.2   Overview of Framework

The overall framework of our proposed method is illustrated in Fig. 2. The main pipeline is general among most scene graph models: an image is first fed into a backbone image classifier pretrained on ImageNet [43], and then the output image feature tensor is fed into an object detector pretrained on the Visual Genome dataset [1] to obtain a set of N object proposals. By using any existing scene graph models as the base scene graph model, we obtain $N(N-1)$ relation features $F \in \mathbb{R}^{N(N-1) \times d_p}$ and their probability distributions $P \in \mathbb{R}^{N(N-1) \times (|\mathcal{R}|+1)}$ among the $|\mathcal{R}|+1$ predicate classes. These predicate distributions are used in our novel CCE loss for predicate classification, while the Scorer network takes the relation features, predicate distributions as well as the global image feature to generate the significance scores for each of the $N(N-1)$ relations. The scores are then used to rank the relations during inference.

3.3 Contrasting Cross Entropy Loss

As widely studied, classification models trained with a cross-entropy (CE) loss can be highly biased towards frequent classes and thus perform badly on rare ones. Methods such as Focal Loss (FL) [28] have been proposed to address this problem in object detection, but the class imbalance problem in scene graph parsing is less explored. In this section, we propose a simple but effective Contrasting Cross-Entropy (CCE) loss that can significantly improve mean recall@K and can be applied to any existing scene graph model using cross-entropy loss. Recall that the cross-entropy (CE) loss for one relation is defined as:

$$\mathcal{L}_{\mathrm{CE}}(\mathbf{p}, \mathbf{y}) = - \sum_{i=1}^{|\mathcal{R}|+1} \mathbf{y}_i \log \mathbf{p}_i, \tag{2}$$

where $\mathbf{p}$ is the probability distribution over the $|\mathcal{R}|+1$ predicate classes including the unknown class, and $\mathbf{y}$ is the one-hot encoded ground-truth label vector.

As minimizing cross-entropy loss is equivalent to maximizing the log probability of the correct class, in order to handle the class imbalance problem, we also force the model to minimize the log probability of the hardest negative class, and design our Contrasting Cross-Entropy (CCE) loss as:

$$\mathcal{L}_{\mathrm{CCE}}(\mathbf{p}, \mathbf{y}) = \max(\mathcal{L}_{\mathrm{CE}}(\mathbf{p}, \mathbf{y}) - \mathcal{L}_{\mathrm{CE}}(\mathbf{p}, \hat{\mathbf{y}}) + \alpha, 0), \tag{3}$$

where $\hat{\mathbf{y}}$ is the sampled hardest negative label, and α is a hyper-parameter to control the margin. Our intuition is that the hardest negative classes usually correspond to frequent relations. By suppressing the Softmax scores of incorrect frequent classes, this loss function can help the model perform better on rare classes. Here we choose the hardest negative label by first ignoring the unknown class (*i.e.* $\mathbf{p}_1$) and taking the incorrect class with the highest probability, *i.e.*, $c = \arg\max_{j>1, \mathbf{y}_j = 0} \mathbf{p}_j$, and $\hat{\mathbf{y}} = \{\hat{\mathbf{y}}_i | i \in [1, |\mathcal{R}|+1]\}$, where:

$$\hat{\mathbf{y}}_i = \begin{cases} 1, & \text{if } i = c \\ 0, & \text{otherwise.} \end{cases} \tag{4}$$

3.4 Learning to Score Relations

In this section, we introduce how we design our Scorer network, which produces a score of each predicted relation triplet by utilizing the relation feature and the predicate distribution produced by a base scene graph model. By exploiting a self-attention module to compare each relation triplet with all the others, it learns to rank the nontrivial relations higher than the trivial ones and thus reduces *false positives*.

As illustrated in Fig. 3, the relation features and predicate probability distributions from the base scene graph model are fed into two different multi-layer perceptron (MLP) networks, where the two MLPs serve as non-linear transformation functions. The output of two MLPs are added along the feature dimension, and then the input image feature extracted by the ImageNet backbone is concatenated to each relation feature to let the relation feature maintain global information of the image.

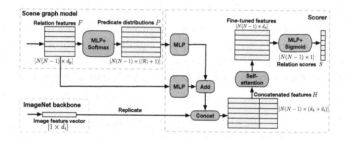

Fig. 3. The proposed Scorer network that learns to score each predicted relation triplet.

As the significance of a relation is also dependent on the existence of other relations, it is necessary to compare all detected relations before assigning their significance scores. In order to perform such reasoning, the combined relation features are fed into a dot-product self-attention (SA) module [44] to pass information among different relations:

$$\text{SA}(H) = \text{Softmax}(f_{\text{query}}(H)f_{\text{key}}(H)^{\intercal})f_{\text{value}}(H), \tag{5}$$

where $H \in \mathbb{R}^{N(N-1)\times(d_h+d_i)}$ is a matrix containing relation features concatenated with image features, while $f_{\text{query}}(\cdot)$, $f_{\text{key}}(\cdot)$ and $f_{\text{value}}(\cdot)$ are non-linear transformation functions applied to H. Then a final MLP with Sigmoid as its last activation function is applied to obtain the scores $S \in \mathbb{R}^{N(N-1)\times1}$ which contains the significance score s for each predicted relation triplet.

Although the goal of Scorer is to predict the significance scores of relations, we do not have ground-truth scores. Remember that we only need to rank the annotated relations higher than the un-annotated ones (whose predicate labels are given as `unknown`), so we treat all annotated relations equally and assign 1 as their significance scores, while all un-annotated relations are assigned with 0

Table 1. Quantitative comparison of different methods. *Note that we directly used the KERN [10] checkpoint trained on SGCls and test on all three tasks without fine-tuning for SGGen, while the KERN paper [10] finetunes for SGGen. We do not finetune for SGGen since we treat scene graph parsing as an extension of object detection, thus the bounding box regression should be solved by the object detector.

Task	SGGen			SGCls			PredCls		
Macro-averaged Recall@K	K=20	K=50	K=100	K=20	K=50	K=100	K=20	K=50	K=100
MotifNet [3]	2.09	3.37	4.52	6.22	7.62	8.06	10.87	14.18	15.31
LinkNet [2]	2.58	4.03	5.43	6.64	8.11	8.69	12.02	15.64	16.98
MotifNet+Focal [28]	1.68	3.16	4.50	5.79	7.56	8.41	10.13	14.11	16.12
LinkNet+Focal [28]	1.51	2.99	4.62	6.1	8.41	9.52	11.02	15.85	18.35
KERN [10] w/o fine-tuning*	2.24	3.96	5.39	7.68	9.36	10.00	13.83	17.72	19.17
KERN+CCE+Scorer	**2.95**	**4.85**	**6.06**	**9.39**	**11.28**	**11.94**	**16.61**	**20.57**	**22.14**
MotifNet+CCE+Scorer	**3.06**	**4.72**	**6.11**	**7.89**	**9.91**	**10.61**	**15.03**	**19.62**	**21.49**
LinkNet+CCE+Scorer	**3.14**	**4.96**	**6.23**	**9.32**	**11.53**	**12.48**	**17.53**	**22.23**	**24.22**
KERN [10] paper (fine-tuned)	N/A	6.4	7.3	N/A	9.4	10.0	N/A	17.7	19.2

scores. In this case, the Scorer module can be trained with a binary cross-entropy (BCE) loss for each predicted relation triplet:

$$\mathcal{L}_{\text{BCE}}(s, q) = -q \log(s) - (1 - q) \log(1 - s), \qquad (6)$$

where s is an output score of Scorer and $q = 0$ indicates the ground-truth label of this predicate belongs to the **unknown** class, otherwise $q = 1$. We have also tried other loss functions for regression, such as mean-square error and hinge loss, but we found that BCE works best.

During inference, the output scores of the Scorer network are used to determine the ranks of predicted relation triplets (the higher the score, the higher the rank), which are then used for calculating $mR@K$.

The whole framework is trained by combining $\mathcal{L}_{\text{CCE}}$ and $\mathcal{L}_{\text{BCE}}$ and other loss functions $\mathcal{L}_{\text{other}}$ specific to the chosen base scene graph model:

$$\mathcal{L} = \lambda_1 \mathcal{L}_{\text{CCE}} + \lambda_2 \mathcal{L}_{\text{BCE}} + \mathcal{L}_{\text{other}}, \qquad (7)$$

where λ_1 and λ_2 are two hyper-parameters to balance the two loss terms.

4 Experiments

4.1 Experiment Settings

Dataset. Visual Genome [1] (VG) is the largest scene graph dataset containing 108,077 images with an average of 38 objects and 22 relation triplets per image. As there exist different splits for the VG dataset, we adopt the most widely used one [5], which contains 75,651 images for training (including 5,000 for validation) and 32,422 images for testing. There are numerous objects and predicates in the original VG dataset, but many of them have very low frequencies and quality.

We follow Xu *et al.* [5] and only use the most frequent 150 object classes and 50 most frequent predicate classes in VG.

Tasks. We adopt the most widely studied tasks [2,3,5,22] for evaluation: (1) **Scene Graph Generation** (SGGen) aims to simultaneously localize and classify objects in an image, and predict the potential predicate between each pair of detected objects. An object is considered to be correctly detected if its intersection over union (IoU) with a ground-truth object is over 0.5. (2) **Scene Graph Classification** (SGCls) provides the model with a set of bounding boxes of objects, and requires the model to predict the object labels as well as the pairwise relations between the objects. (3) **Predicate Classification** (PredCls) requires the model to predict the potential predicates between each pair of objects, where the object locations and labels are given as groundtruth.

Metric. As discussed in previous sections, the widely used *micro-averaged Recall@K (R@K)* can be highly biased towards frequent classes and cannot tell whether a model is performing well on both frequent and rare classes. Instead, we use the *macro-averaged Recall@K (mR@K)* (Eq. 1), *i.e.*, "mean recall@K" [10], as our evaluation metric, which treats major and minor classes alike. We adopt the widely used protocol for determining whether a predicted relation triplet matches groundtruth as in [3,5].

4.2   Baselines

We use three of the current state-of-the-art methods **MotifNet** [3], **LinkNet** [2] and **KERN** [10] as the base scene graph models in our framework and study how our proposed method can help them improve their performance on rare predicate classes. KERN [10] is a recent approach that also tries to solve the class imbalance problem in scene graph parsing by designing a more complex network structure, and also uses the same evaluation metric as we do. As **Focal Loss** [28] is a popular method that addresses the class imbalance problem in object detection, we also try applying it to LinkNet [2] and MotifNet [3] in the scene graph parsing setting to see if it helps alleviate class imbalance in scene graph parsing.

4.3   Implementation Details

We use pretrained VGG16 [45] as our ImageNet backbone and Faster R-CNN [4] pretrained on VG [1] as the object detector. For MotifNet [3] and KERN [10], we use the official code provided by the authors[1,2], and use the same set of hyperparameters for the models as they are provided in their code base. Although there is no official implementation for LinkNet [2], we found an unofficial one[3] that produces results close to those in the original paper. We apply our proposed CCE loss and Scorer to KERN [10], LinkNet [2] and MotifNet [3] without

---

[1] https://github.com/rowanz/neural-motifs.
[2] https://github.com/HCPLab-SYSU/KERN.
[3] https://github.com/jiayan97/linknet-pytorch.

modifying their original model architectures, and only take the relation features before and after their final MLPs together with the global-average pooled image feature extracted from VGG16 pretrained on ImageNet [43] as input to our Scorer module. The two MLPs in our Scorer are both implemented as one fully connected layer of 512 units and a ReLU activation. The non-linear transformation functions $f_{\text{query}}(\cdot)$, $f_{\text{key}}(\cdot)$ and $f_{\text{value}}(\cdot)$ in Eq. 5 are implemented as a fully connected layer with 256 units, and the last MLP in Scorer compresses the 256-dim features to scalars followed by a Sigmoid function. *We only tune λ_1 and λ_2 for loss weights in Eq. 7 and keep other hyper-parameters fixed, while we found that setting $\alpha = 0$ generally works well for all models.* For fair comparison, we train all models on the SGCls tasks, and then directly evaluate on all three tasks without fine-tuning for each task. The random seed is fixed as 42 for all experiments. Our code is available online[4].

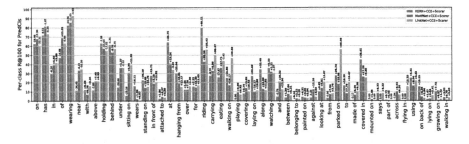

Fig. 4. Per-class Recall@100 for KERN [10], LinkNet [2] and MotifNet [3] with CCE loss and Scorer, evaluated on the PredCls task. The number above each bar indicates the absolute increase (+) or decrease (−) in each predicate compared with the corresponding base scene graph model trained with cross-entropy. Predicates are sorted according to their frequencies in Fig. 1(a).

4.4   Results

We present the quantitative results for our methods together with those of baselines in Table 1. As can be seen from the table, although MotifNet [3] and LinkNet [2] are among the current state-of-the-art methods that have high *micro-averaged Recall@K* (R@K) of around 67%, they have relatively low *macro-averaged Recall@K* (mR@K), where their mR@100 are 15.31% and 16.98% for the easiest PredCls task. As the tasks become more challenging, their performance for SGCls and SGGen are much worse, which shows that they work badly on detecting rare predicate classes. Among all methods without fine-tuning for SGGen, our proposed framework with LinkNet [2] as the base scene graph model achieves the highest mR@K in all three tasks and all Ks. In the PredCls task, the

---

[4] https://github.com/stevehuanghe/scene_graph.

LinkNet+CCE+Scorer method outperforms KERN [10] by a significant margin
of around 4% to 5%. For the other two more challenging tasks SGCls and SGGen,
LinkNet+CCE+Scorer method still outperforms KERN w/o fine-tuning by 2%
and 1% respectively, which show the effectiveness of our proposed framework.
Our method with MotifNet [3] and KERN [10] as the base scene graph models also outperform all other methods without our proposed framework, which
demonstrates that our framework is not specifically designed for a single model
but can help improve the performance of different existing scene graph models
trained with cross-entropy loss. It can also be noticed that, our framework with
LinkNet [2] performs better than the one with MotifNet [3], which is reasonable
as LinkNet [2] itself outperforms MotifNet [3] when they are both trained with
cross-entropy loss. Our framework with KERN [10] achieves a performance that
lies between the other two base models trained with our framework. The reason
may be that the architecture of KERN [10] is more complex and requires extra
hyper-parameter search and more delicate training techniques.

As for Focal Loss [28], we can see that it helps both LinkNet [2] and
MotifNet [3] improve the results when $K = 100$ for all three tasks, but it does
not work well with a smaller K such as $K = 20$. This result is not surprising,
since the Focal Loss does not have an explicit mechanism to rank the predicted
relations, and we have discussed in previous sections that the scene graph parsing task requires the model to not only classify predicates correctly but also
know how to discriminate more important relations from trivial ones to achieve
higher (mean) recall@K. The KERN model fine-tuned for SGGen achieves the
highest scores on the hardest task SGGen, while the KERN without fine-tuning
performs much worse than the fine-tuned version, which shows that fine-tuning
is really important for this task. However, for fair comparison, we only compare
the no-fine-tuned version with others.

Table 2. Ablation study for CCE loss and Scorer.

Task	SGGen			SGCls			PredCls		
Macro-averaged Recall@K	K=20	K=50	K=all	K=20	K=50	K=all	K=20	K=50	K=all
MotifNet	2.09	3.37	6.81	6.22	7.62	8.31	10.87	14.18	16.19
MotifNet+CCE	1.43	2.97	**7.94**	4.63	6.68	**9.17**	7.87	12.91	**18.93**
MotifNet+Scorer	**2.37**	**3.56**	7.23	**6.36**	**7.65**	8.34	11.79	14.78	16.71
MotifNet+CCE+Scorer	3.06	4.72	9.21	7.89	9.91	10.93	15.03	19.62	22.57
LinkNet	2.58	4.03	7.87	6.64	8.11	9.02	12.02	15.64	17.86
LinkNet+CCE	1.32	2.73	**8.63**	5.38	8.04	**11.28**	9.07	14.30	**22.06**
LinkNet+Scorer	**2.71**	**4.17**	7.65	**6.79**	8.18	8.94	**12.41**	**15.62**	17.77
LinkNet+CCE+Scorer	3.14	4.96	10.32	9.32	11.53	12.94	17.53	22.23	25.30
LinkNet+Ours w/o SA	2.68	4.21	8.99	7.86	10.07	11.57	14.96	19.79	23.15

We also investigate the changes in each predicate's recall@100 on the Pred-
Cls task, as illustrated in Fig. 4. We can see that our framework can generally
improve the performance of base scene graph model in many rare classes starting from standing on, which occupies only 1.1% of all training samples. More

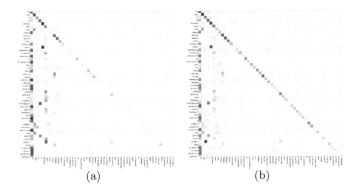

(a)   (b)

Fig. 5. Confusion matrix evaluated on VG's training set: (a) LinkNet [2] with cross-entropy (CE) loss and (b) LinkNet with our proposed contrasting cross-entropy (CCE) loss. The darker the color on diagonal line the better the model. The x-axis shows predicted labels, while the y-axis indicates true labels. Predicates are sorted according to their frequencies in Fig. 1(a).

remarkably, our framework with LinkNet as the base model increases the recall for a very rare predicate **parked on** (0.13% coverage in the whole dataset) from 0% to 56.08%. Among the top-5 most frequent predicates (**on, has, in, of,** and **wearing**) covering 74.5% of all relations in the dataset, our methods sacrifice some performance in **on, has** and **wearing**, which is reasonable and acceptable as we try to focus more on fine-grained predicates instead of these coarse-grained ones. Nonetheless, we also have an increase in a highly frequent class **in**. Among all 50 predicates, our framework helps increase the per-class recall@100 of 29, 37, and 42 classes when trained with KERN [10], MotifNet [3] and LinkNet [2] respectively, which again demonstrates that our framework can help increase the per-class recall of most predicates, whether they are frequent or not. More importantly, our framework helps improve the per-class recall of 18 of the rarest 20 predicates with MotifNet [3] and LinkNet [2], while the performance of 14 of the rarest 20 classes is also improved for KERN [10] trained with our framework. Since KERN [10] is already designed to address the class imbalance problem, it makes sense that our framework does not improve KERN's performance as much as it does with MotifNet [3] and LinkNet [2].

4.5   Ablation Study

CCE loss aims to improve the model's ability to classify rare classes, but it is not designed for ranking the predicted relations. In order to study the model's classification ability without being affected by the ranks of predictions, we study the mR@all for three tasks, as shown in Table 2. As we can see, our CCE loss increases the mR@all for three tasks with two different base scene graph models [2,3]. The CCE loss works well when K is large, but not when K is small like 20 and 50, since a smaller K will cause the metric mR@K to be more limited by the ranking performance of the model. As CCE is only designed for classification, it is not surprising that it does not work well when the metric is more dependent on ranking performance.

We also plot the confusion matrices calculated on the training set to see how well trained models can fit the training data. As shown in Fig. 5(a), LinkNet [2] trained with cross-entropy loss is highly biased towards the largest class "on", and many points on the diagonal line has shallow color which shows that the model has poor performance in classifying these classes correctly. On the other hand, Fig. 5(b) shows that LinkNet trained with CCE loss achieves better performance on many classes, as the color on diagonal line is much darker than the left one, which shows that the CCE loss can significantly alleviate the class imbalance problem in scene graph parsing.

The **Scorer**, on the other hand, aims to improve the model's performance in ranking its output relations to achieve higher mR@K when K is small. As shown in Table 2, our Scorer can help improve mR@20 and mR@50 in all cases. For K=all, MotifNet+Scorer has small improvements over MotifNet itself, while LinkNet+Scorer has a small decrease of average 0.13% compared with LinkNet [2] without Scorer, which is reasonable since mR@all is more dependent on the model's classification ability than ranking. Although the base models trained with Scorer alone does not have significant improvement over the ones without, it is worth noting that, together with our CCE loss, the whole proposed framework can significantly improve the mean recall@K of both LinkNet [28] and MotifNet [3] in all three tasks, as shown in Table 2.

Self-attention. In the last row of Table 2, we show the results of LinkNet [2] with our CCE+Scorer framework but without self-attention, where we simply replace the self-attention module by a fully-connected network applied on each relation triplet individually (pure point-wise ranking). From the results we can see that although the proposed framework without self-attention still outperforms the LinkNet [2] baseline, its performance is worse than the one with self-attention (point-wise and list-wise combined ranking). This observation proves that it is important to compare each predicted relation with others by passing information among them, and justifies our design of the Scorer module that unifies both list-wise and point-wise ranking methods in a novel way.

5   Conclusion

In this paper, we show that although current scene graph models achieve high *micro-averaged recall@K* (R@K), they suffer from not being able to detect rare classes, and that *macro-averaged recall@K* (mR@K) is a more suitable metric as it treats both frequent and rare classes the same. To tackle the class imbalance problem, we first formulate the task as a combination of classification and ranking, and then we design a framework which consists of a Contrasting Cross-Entropy (CCE) loss and a Scorer module respectively for these two sub-tasks. Our proposed framework is general and can be applied to any existing scene graph models trained with cross-entropy. Extensive experiments demonstrate the effectiveness of our framework with KERN [10], LinkNet [2] and MotifNet [3].

Acknowledgement. This work is supported in part by NSF under grants III-1763325, III-1909323, and SaTC-1930941.

References

1. Krishna, R., Zhu, Y., Groth, O., Johnson, J., Hata, K., Kravitz, J., Chen, S., Kalantidis, Y., Li, L.J., Shamma, D.A., et al.: Visual genome: Connecting language and vision using crowdsourced dense image annotations. Int. J. Comput. Vision **123**, 32–73 (2017)
2. Woo, S., Kim, D., Cho, D., Kweon, I.S.: Linknet: Relational embedding for scene graph. In: Advances in Neural Information Processing Systems, pp. 560–570 (2018)
3. Zellers, R., Yatskar, M., Thomson, S., Choi, Y.: Neural motifs: scene graph parsing with global context. In: Proceedings of the IEEE Conference on Computer Vision and Pattern Recognition, pp. 5831–5840 (2018)
4. Ren, S., He, K., Girshick, R., Sun, J.: Faster R-CNN: towards real-time object detection with region proposal networks. In: Advances in Neural Information Processing Systems, pp. 91–99 (2015)
5. Xu, D., Zhu, Y., Choy, C.B., Fei-Fei, L.: Scene graph generation by iterative message passing. In: Proceedings of the IEEE Conference on Computer Vision and Pattern Recognition, pp. 5410–5419 (2017)
6. Lu, C., Krishna, R., Bernstein, M., Fei-Fei, L.: Visual relationship detection with language priors, pp. 852–869 (2016)
7. Yang, X., Tang, K., Zhang, H., Cai, J.: Auto-encoding scene graphs for image captioning. In: Proceedings of the IEEE Conference on Computer Vision and Pattern Recognition, pp. 10685–10694 (2019)
8. Johnson, J., et al.: Image retrieval using scene graphs. In: Proceedings of the IEEE Conference on Computer Vision and Pattern Recognition, pp. 3668–3678 (2015)
9. Johnson, J., Gupta, A., Fei-Fei, L.: Image generation from scene graphs. In: Proceedings of the IEEE Conference on Computer Vision and Pattern Recognition, pp. 1219–1228 (2018)
10. Chen, T., Yu, W., Chen, R., Lin, L.: Knowledge-embedded routing network for scene graph generation. In: Proceedings of the IEEE Conference on Computer Vision and Pattern Recognition, pp. 6163–6171 (2019)
11. Yang, J., Lu, J., Lee, S., Batra, D., Parikh, D.: Graph R-CNN for scene graph generation. In: Proceedings of the European Conference on Computer Vision (ECCV), pp. 670–685 (2018)
12. Dai, B., Zhang, Y., Lin, D.: Detecting visual relationships with deep relational networks. In: Proceedings of the IEEE Conference on Computer Vision and Pattern Recognition, pp. 3076–3086 (2017)
13. Cho, K., Van Merriënboer, B., Gulcehre, C., Bahdanau, D., Bougares, F., Schwenk, H., Bengio, Y.: Learning phrase representations using RNN encoder-decoder for statistical machine translation. arXiv preprint arXiv:1406.1078 (2014)
14. Kipf, T.N., Welling, M.: Semi-supervised classification with graph convolutional networks. In: ICLR (2017)
15. Herzig, R., Raboh, M., Chechik, G., Berant, J., Globerson, A.: Mapping images to scene graphs with permutation-invariant structured prediction. In: Advances in Neural Information Processing Systems, pp. 7211–7221 (2018)

16. Li, Y., Ouyang, W., Zhou, B., Shi, J., Zhang, C., Wang, X.: Factorizable net: an efficient subgraph-based framework for scene graph generation. In: Proceedings of the European Conference on Computer Vision (ECCV), pp. 335–351 (2018)
17. Yu, R., Li, A., Morariu, V.I., Davis, L.S.: Visual relationship detection with internal and external linguistic knowledge distillation. In: Proceedings of the IEEE International Conference on Computer Vision, pp. 1974–1982 (2017)
18. Hochreiter, S., Schmidhuber, J.: Long short-term memory. Neural Comput. **9**, 1735–1780 (1997)
19. Gu, J., Zhao, H., Lin, Z., Li, S., Cai, J., Ling, M.: Scene graph generation with external knowledge and image reconstruction. In: Proceedings of the IEEE Conference on Computer Vision and Pattern Recognition, pp. 1969–1978 (2019)
20. Qi, M., Li, W., Yang, Z., Wang, Y., Luo, J.: Attentive relational networks for mapping images to scene graphs. In: Proceedings of the IEEE Conference on Computer Vision and Pattern Recognition, pp. 3957–3966 (2019)
21. Wang, W., Wang, R., Shan, S., Chen, X.: Exploring context and visual pattern of relationship for scene graph generation. In: Proceedings of the IEEE Conference on Computer Vision and Pattern Recognition, pp. 8188–8197 (2019)
22. Zhan, Y., Yu, J., Yu, T., Tao, D.: On exploring undetermined relationships for visual relationship detection. In: Proceedings of the IEEE Conference on Computer Vision and Pattern Recognition (2019)
23. Buda, M., Maki, A., Mazurowski, M.A.: A systematic study of the class imbalance problem in convolutional neural networks. CoRR abs/1710.05381 (2017)
24. Japkowicz, N., Stephen, S.: The class imbalance problem: a systematic study. Intell. Data Anal. **6**, 429–449 (2002)
25. Oksuz, K., Cam, B.C., Kalkan, S., Akbas, E.: Imbalance problems in object detection: a review. arXiv preprint arXiv:1909.00169 (2019)
26. Rota Bulo, S., Neuhold, G., Kontschieder, P.: Loss max-pooling for semantic image segmentation. In: Proceedings of the IEEE Conference on Computer Vision and Pattern Recognition, pp. 2126–2135 (2017)
27. Shrivastava, A., Gupta, A., Girshick, R.: Training region-based object detectors with online hard example mining. In: Proceedings of the IEEE Conference on Computer Vision and Pattern Recognition, pp. 761–769 (2016)
28. Lin, T.Y., Goyal, P., Girshick, R., He, K., Dollár, P.: Focal loss for dense object detection. In: Proceedings of the IEEE International Conference on Computer Vision, pp. 2980–2988 (2017)
29. Qian, Q., Chen, L., Li, H., Jin, R.: Dr loss: improving object detection by distributional ranking. arXiv preprint arXiv:1907.10156 (2019)
30. Chen, K., Li, J., Lin, W., See, J., Wang, J., Duan, L., Chen, Z., He, C., Zou, J.: Towards accurate one-stage object detection with AP-loss. In: Proceedings of the IEEE Conference on Computer Vision and Pattern Recognition, pp. 5119–5127 (2019)
31. Chopra, S., Hadsell, R., LeCun, Y.: Learning a similarity metric discriminatively, with application to face verification. In: 2005 IEEE Computer Society Conference on Computer Vision and Pattern Recognition (CVPR'05), vol. 1, pp. 539–546. IEEE (2005)
32. Kim, M., Sahu, P., Gholami, B., Pavlovic, V.: Unsupervised visual domain adaptation: A deep max-margin gaussian process approach. In: Proceedings of the IEEE Conference on Computer Vision and Pattern Recognition, pp. 4380–4390 (2019)
33. Wang, X., Gupta, A.: Unsupervised learning of visual representations using videos. In: Proceedings of the IEEE International Conference on Computer Vision, pp. 2794–2802 (2015)

34. Zhang, C., Jia, B., Gao, F., Zhu, Y., Lu, H., Zhu, S.C.: Learning perceptual inference by contrasting. In: Advances in Neural Information Processing Systems, pp. 1073–1085 (2019)
35. Elsayed, G., Krishnan, D., Mobahi, H., Regan, K., Bengio, S.: Large margin deep networks for classification. In: Advances in neural information processing systems, pp. 842–852 (2018)
36. Hayat, M., Khan, S., Zamir, S.W., Shen, J., Shao, L.: Gaussian affinity for max-margin class imbalanced learning. In: Proceedings of the IEEE International Conference on Computer Vision, pp. 6469–6479 (2019)
37. Zhang, J., Shih, K.J., Elgammal, A., Tao, A., Catanzaro, B.: Graphical contrastive losses for scene graph generation. arXiv preprint arXiv:1903.02728 (2019)
38. Liu, T.Y., et al.: Learning to rank for information retrieval. Found. Trends® Inf. Retrieval **3**, 225–331 (2009)
39. Sculley, D.: Combined regression and ranking. In: Proceedings of the 16th ACM SIGKDD International Conference on Knowledge Discovery and Data Mining, ACM, pp. 979–988 (2010)
40. Ibrahim, O.A.S., Landa-Silva, D.: ES-rank: evolution strategy learning to rank approach. In: Proceedings of the Symposium on Applied Computing, ACM, pp. 944–950 (2017)
41. Moon, T., Smola, A., Chang, Y., Zheng, Z.: Intervalrank: isotonic regression with listwise and pairwise constraints. In: Proceedings of the third ACM International Conference on Web Search and Data Mining, ACM, pp. 151–160 (2010)
42. Wang, X., Hua, Y., Kodirov, E., Hu, G., Garnier, R., Robertson, N.M.: Ranked list loss for deep metric learning. In: Proceedings of the IEEE Conference on Computer Vision and Pattern Recognition (2019)
43. Deng, J., Dong, W., Socher, R., Li, L.J., Li, K., Fei-Fei, L.: Imagenet: a large-scale hierarchical image database. In: IEEE Conference on Computer Vision and Pattern Recognition. IEEE 2009, pp. 248–255 (2009)
44. Vaswani, A., et al.: Attention is all you need. In: Advances in Neural Information Processing Systems, pp. 5998–6008 (2017)
45. Simonyan, K., Zisserman, A.: Very deep convolutional networks for large-scale image recognition. arXiv preprint arXiv:1409.1556 (2014)

Show, Conceive and Tell: Image Captioning with Prospective Linguistic Information

Yiqing Huang⬤ and Jiansheng Chen$^{(\boxtimes)}$⬤

Department of Electronic Engineering, Tsinghua University, Beijing, China
huang-yq17@mails.tsinghua.edu.cn, jschenthu@mail.tsinghua.edu.cn

Abstract. Attention based encoder-decoder models have achieved competitive performances in image captioning. However, these models usually follow the auto-regressive way during inference, meaning that only the previously generated words, namely the explored linguistic information, can be utilized for caption generation. Intuitively, enabling the model to conceive the prospective linguistic information contained in the words to be generated can be beneficial for further improving the captioning results. Consequently, we devise a novel Prospective information guided LSTM (Pro-LSTM) model, to exploit both prospective and explored information to boost captioning. For each image, we first draft a coarse caption which roughly describes the whole image contents. At each time step, we mine the prospective and explored information from the coarse caption. These two kinds of information are further utilized by a Prospective information guided Attention (ProA) module to guide our model to comprehensively utilize the visual feature from a semantically global perspective. We also propose an Attentive Attribute Detector (AAD) which refines the object features to predict the image attributes more precisely. This further improves the semantic quality of the generated caption. Thanks to the prospective information and more accurate attributes, the Pro-LSTM model achieves near state-of-the-art performances on the MSCOCO dataset with a 129.5 CIDEr-D.

1 Introduction

Image captioning aims at automatically generating the descriptions for images in natural language. This task can facilitate lots of practical applications such as human-machine interaction and content based image retrieval. To date, the encoder-decoder framework [1] equipped with attention modules [2–11] has become prevalent in image captioning. Generally, these models utilize CNN as the encoder to extract visual features from the image, and leverage language decoders such as RNN or the Transformer [12] to generate the captions.

Electronic supplementary material The online version of this chapter (https://doi.org/10.1007/978-3-030-69544-6_29) contains supplementary material, which is available to authorized users.

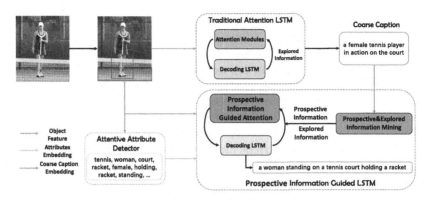

Fig. 1. While most image captioning models can only utilize the explored information, our model additionally incorporates prospective linguistic information to boost captioning. Object features extracted by the Faster-RCNN [13] are both exploited to generate a coarse caption and refined to predict the image attributes via Attentive Attribute Detector (AAD). The proposed Prospective information guided LSTM (Pro-LSTM) finally leverages the prospective information to guide the attention modules to better attend to the visual features, leading to image captions of higher quality.

These decoders usually infer the caption in an auto-regressive manner. Specifically, when generating the current word, only the linguistic information contained in the previously generated words are utilized. For convenience, we call such linguistic information as the *explored information* in this work. Oppositely, the linguistic information contained in the words to be generated, namely the *prospective information*, is seldom considered. This is logical considering that in an auto-regressive process, exact prospective information keeps unknown. However, suppose there is a way to get the prospective information in advance, even roughly, it is possible for the decoder to synthesize more refined and accurate image descriptions under the guidance of a 'conceived' global linguistic context.

Actually, when human beings compose a sentence, they usually draft a coarse version first; and then polish it with both prospective and explored linguistic information to obtain a more descriptive and accurate sentence. In image captioning, such a strategy can be imitated by firstly generating a coarse caption using a pre-trained auto-regressive captioning model. Although the coarse caption may not be perfect, roughly it is still a semantically correct description of the overall content of the image, as shown in the blue circle in Fig. 1. Thus, the coarse caption can be regarded as a reasonable representation of the global linguistic information from which the prospective information can be effectively extracted. Specifically in our proposal, at each time step, the prospective&explored information mining module adaptively renews the prospective information and the explored information. It should be noticed that the prospective information may not necessarily be related to the succeeded words in the coarse caption. It denotes the information contained in words that have not yet been generated by the current time step. In our method, we extract the prospective information from coarse caption words of which the semantic information is less correlated to that contained in the previously generated words. Such words are closely related to the input image and contain additional linguistic information that is complementary to the explored information.

Both prospective information and explored information are further exploited by the Prospective information guided Attention (ProA) module in the green circle of Fig. 1. Considering that the explored information is deterministic and relatively more reliable, we utilize it to augment the visual features directly as linguistic feature. The prospective information, however, contains additional semantic information upon current linguistic context. Thus, we do not directly utilize it as a feature but combine it with the current linguistic context to guide the attention modules semantically from a global perspective. By jointly using the prospective and explored information, our model attends to more appropriate visual features based on a better grasp of the complete linguistic context.

Besides exploiting the image features and the coarse caption, we also leverage the image attributes, the most salient concepts contained in the image, in our model, as shown in the orange circle in Fig. 1. While most works [14,15] directly adopt the image features in attribute detection, we propose to refine these features for better detection performance to further strengthen the captioning model. Our proposed Attentive Attribute Detector (AAD) leverages the Graph Convolutional Network (GCN) to model the similarity between the image features and the attribute embedding in the refinement process. We notice that with proper selections of similarity formulation and activation function, the GCN can actually be transformed to a multi-head attention [12] module.

Benefiting from both prospective information contained in the coarse caption and the explicit semantic information brought about by the image attributes, the proposed Pro-LSTM model can generate precise and detailed image captions. The main contributions of our work are as follows: **1)** We introduce Pro-LSTM which additionally utilizes prospective information to facilitate better usage of visual and language information to boost image captioning. **2)** We introduce an AAD which refines the image features in order to predict the image attributes more precisely. **3)** The Pro-LSTM model achieves state-of-the-art image captioning performance of 129.5 CIDEr-D score on the MSCOCO benchmark dataset [16]. We notice that captions generated by Pro-LSTM are sometimes even more descriptive than the human-labeled ground truth captions, indicating the effectiveness of introducing the prospective information.

2   Related Work

Neural Image Captioning. The neural network based encoder-decoder framework was first proved to be effective in image captioning in [1]. Later on, the attention mechanism has been introduced to boost the vanilla encoder-decoder framework. For example, spatial attention [5], semantic attention [6], adaptive attention [4], bottom-up and top-down attention [2] were introduced to exploit the visual information in different ways for generating better descriptions. Recently, Huang et al. [17] modified the attention module by adopting another attention over it to obtain more appropriate attention results. While these auto-regressive methods focus on better exploiting the explored information at each time step, we explore how to additionally utilize the prospective information to utilize both the visual information and the language information. We will also show that our method is compatible with the state-of-the-art AoA [17] method.

Exploitation of Prospective Information. Realizing that only leveraging the explored information is not sufficient for captioning, researchers began to study the possibility of exploiting the complementarity between the explored information and the prospective information. Wang *et al.* [18] adopted the bidirectional LSTMs to generate two sentences in both forward-pass and backward-pass independently. Nevertheless, as they merely integrated the two generated sentences by selecting the one with larger probability, their method was essentially exploiting the explored and inversely-explored information but not the prospective information. Look&modify [19] was devised to modify the coarse captions with the residual information. However, they roughly integrate the word embedding of the words in the coarse caption without explicit model the relationships between the words. Recently, Ge *et al.* [20] proposed to attend to both the coarse caption and the visual features respectively to generate a better description. However, they treat the coarse caption just like the attributes and fail to model the interaction between prospective information and visual information. In our proposal, both the prospective and explored information are thoroughly exploited to guide the model towards more appropriate visual attention.

3   Preliminary

Before introducing our framework, we briefly introduce the Multi-Head Attention (MHA) [12]. The multi-head attention was first introduced in the Transformer model [12]. The *scaled dot-product attention* is the core component of multi-head attention. Given a query $\mathbf{q}_i$, a set of keys $\mathbf{K} = (\mathbf{k}_1, \ldots, \mathbf{k}_n)$ and a set of values $\mathbf{V} = (\mathbf{v}_1, \ldots, \mathbf{v}_n)$ where $\mathbf{q}_i, \mathbf{k}_i, \mathbf{v}_i \in \mathbb{R}^d$, the output of the scaled dot-product attention is the weighted sum of $\mathbf{v}_i$. The weights are determined by the dot-product of $\mathbf{q}_i$ and $\mathbf{k}_j$. Additionally, the dot-products are divided by the square root of dimension d. In practice, the queries are packed together as a matrix $\mathbf{Q} = (\mathbf{q}_1, \ldots, \mathbf{q}_m)$ to compute the above process in parallel as in (1).

$$Attention(\mathbf{Q}, \mathbf{K}, \mathbf{V}) = Softmax(\frac{\mathbf{Q}\mathbf{K}^\top}{\sqrt{d}})\mathbf{V} \tag{1}$$

Multi-head attention (MHA) is an extension of the above attention mechanism. The queries, keys and values are firstly linearly projected to h subspaces. Then the scaled dot-product attention is applied to the h heads separately in (2), where $i \in \{1, \ldots, h\}$. The h outputs are finally concatenated to form the output of MHA as in (3), where $\mathbf{W}_i^Q, \mathbf{W}_i^K, \mathbf{W}_i^V \in \mathbb{R}^{d \times \frac{d}{h}}$ and $\mathbf{W}^{MHA} \in \mathbb{R}^{d \times d}$ are trainable parameters.

$$\mathbf{H}_i = Attention(\mathbf{Q}\mathbf{W}_i^Q, \mathbf{K}\mathbf{W}_i^K, \mathbf{V}\mathbf{W}_i^V) \tag{2}$$

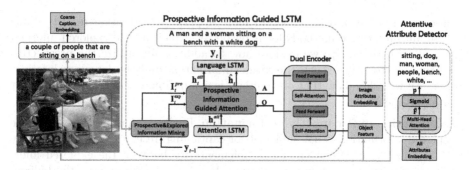

Fig. 2. The overall framework of our proposal. The framework is composed of an Attentive Attribute Detector (AAD), and a Prospective information guided LSTM (Pro-LSTM) caption generator. The object features (shown in red lines) are firstly extracted to generates a coarse caption with a pre-trained captioning model. Concurrently, AAD refines the object features with attribute embedding and predicts the probabilities **p** of the image attributes with the refined feature $\tilde{\mathbf{F}}$. The Pro-LSTM dynamically mines the prospective and explored information inside the coarse caption embedding (shown in blue line) and guide our model to more properly attend to the visual features through the Prospective information guided Attention (ProA) module. (Color figure online)

$$\hat{\mathbf{V}} = MHA(\mathbf{Q}, \ \mathbf{K}, \ \mathbf{V}) = Concat(\mathbf{H}_1, \ ..., \ \mathbf{H}_h)\mathbf{W}^{MHA} \qquad (3)$$

4   Methodology

As shown in Fig. 2, the overall framework of our model follows the encoder-decoder paradigm. Firstly, we introduce the Pro-LSTM model, which is equipped with a Prospective information guided Attention (ProA) module to generate improved image captions with the guidance of prospective information. We then describe the Attentive Attribute Detector (AAD) which refines the object features with multi-head attention to better predict image attributes.

4.1   Prospective Information Guided LSTM

As shown in the middle green circle in Fig. 2, the Pro-LSTM model is composed of a *Dual Encoder* and an *LSTM decoder*. The MHA [12] based dual encoder consists of two separate components that encode the object features and the image attributes respectively. The LSTM decoder is a two-layer LSTM, where the first LSTM layer and the second LSTM layer are called the attention LSTM and language LSTM respectively. The implementations of these two LSTM layers are similar to that proposed in [2] except for the attention module and some inputs. It additionally takes in a coarse caption and leverages the ProA module to decode these features in order to obtain plausible and detailed image descriptions.

Dual Encoder. Generally, the components of the dual encoder are implemented similarly using the structure defined in Eq. 4, where $\mathbf{Z}$ denotes the object feature or the attribute feature to be encoded, *FFN* and *MHA* are short for Feed-Forward Network and Multi-Head Attention in [12]. The selected top-L attributes are ranked by the predicted confidence p. We stack the attention blocks for 6 times. The outputs of the 6th attention block of the object encoder and the attribute encoder are denoted as $\mathbf{O} \in \mathbb{R}^{M \times d}$ and $\mathbf{A} \in \mathbb{R}^{L \times d}$ respectively.

$$Encoder(\mathbf{Z}) = Stack(FFN(MHA(\mathbf{Z}, \mathbf{Z}, \mathbf{Z}))) \times 6 \qquad (4)$$

Prospective&Explored Information Mining. The structure of this module is shown in the left of Fig. 3. The idea of information mining is inspired by the phenomenon that the semantically similar words are close in the word embedding space [21,22]. We notice that such a phenomenon also exists in the word embedding trained along with the image captioning network. Thus, we compute the cosine similarity between the current input word $\boldsymbol{y}_{t-1}$ and the words in the coarse caption $\hat{\mathbf{W}} = [\hat{\boldsymbol{w}}_1, ..., \hat{\boldsymbol{w}}_{T'}], \hat{\boldsymbol{w}}_i \in \mathbb{R}^{1 \times d}$ at each time step to select the prospective words and the explored words.

$$cosine_t^i = \frac{\hat{\boldsymbol{w}}_i * \boldsymbol{y}_{t-1}}{\|\hat{\boldsymbol{w}}_i\| \|\boldsymbol{y}_{t-1}\|} \qquad (5)$$

At the first time step, there is no word in the explored word set $\mathbf{W}_t^{exp}$ and all the words in the coarse caption are in the prospective word set $\mathbf{W}_t^{pro}$. Then, at each time step, the words in the coarse caption that are similar to ($cosine_t^i > 0.9$) current input words are recognized as previously generated words. These words are added to the explored word set and are removed from the prospective word set simultaneously. As such, the prospective word set $\mathbf{W}_t^{pro}$ always consists of words that contain unrevealed semantic information at the current time step. We then adopt self-attention to the two word sets as in Eq. 6, which transforms these sets of word embedding to a high-level representation of prospective information and explored information respectively.

$$\mathbf{I}_t^{pro} = MHA(\mathbf{W}_t^{pro}, \mathbf{W}_t^{pro}, \mathbf{W}_t^{pro}), \ \mathbf{I}_t^{exp} = MHA(\mathbf{W}_t^{exp}, \mathbf{W}_t^{exp}, \mathbf{W}_t^{exp}) \qquad (6)$$

Prospective Information Guided Attention. While most previous works focused on how to exploit the explored information, we additionally explore the effectiveness of using the prospective information to guide the attention mechanism in order to better utilize the visual information and the semantic information jointly. The right side of Fig. 3 shows the detailed architecture of the Prospective information guided Attention (ProA) module, which is composed of four attention sub-layers, an augmentation sub-layer, and a fusion sub-layer.

Suppose we are generating the tth word $\boldsymbol{y}_t$ at the current time step. The attention LSTM takes in the concatenation of current input word $\boldsymbol{y}_{t-1}$, the

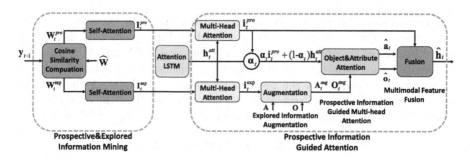

Fig. 3. The architecture of the proposed prospective&explored information mining module and the ProA module. The prospective and explored information are leveraged to guide visual attention to attend to more appropriate visual features in different ways. The object attention and attribute attention are implemented separately, they are combined in this figure since they share similar structure.

averaged object feature $\bar{\mathbf{O}}$, and the output of the language LSTM in the last time step h_{t-1}^{lan} to generates the current attention query h_t^{att} as in Eq. 7.

$$h_t^{att} = LSTM_{att}(h_{t-1}^{att}, \ [h_{t-1}^{lan}; \ \bar{\mathbf{O}}; \ y_{t-1}]) \tag{7}$$

Multi-head attention is then applied to the prospective information $\mathbf{I}_t^{pro}$ and explored information $\mathbf{I}_t^{exp}$ respectively to obtain the corresponding features, namely the prospective feature i_t^{pro} and the explored feature i_t^{exp} in Eq. 8.

$$i_t^{pro} = MHA(h_t^{att}, \ \mathbf{I}_t^{pro}, \ \mathbf{I}_t^{pro}), \ i_t^{exp} = MHA(h_t^{att}, \ \mathbf{I}_t^{exp}, \ \mathbf{I}_t^{exp}) \tag{8}$$

After grasping the prospective and explored features, we leverage them for guiding the model to attend to the encoded object features $\mathbf{O}$ and image attributes $\mathbf{A}$ more properly. Considering that the explored feature is basically the integration of the information of previously generated words, it is appropriate to let the model attend to it when generating the none visual words like articles and prepositions at the current time step. Thus, we directly augment the encoded visual feature with the explored feature as in Eq. 9.

$$\mathbf{O}_t^{aug} = [\mathbf{O}; \ i_t^{exp}], \ \mathbf{A}_t^{aug} = [\mathbf{A}; \ i_t^{exp}] \tag{9}$$

Such an augmentation can be viewed as a modification of the Transformer [12] or the adaptive attention module [4]. While the encoded features in the Transformer are fixed in the whole captioning generation process, our model dynamically augments the explored feature to the encoded feature for facilitating the inclusion of new information at each time step. Comparing with the adaptive attention which directly attends to the visual features and the language features, we additionally leverage multi-head attention to make these features more informative.

The prospective feature i_t^{pro}, however, can be viewed as the future information 'conceived' by the captioning model. Although this information may not be precise as the coarse caption may not always be satisfying, it is probably a useful supplement to the current linguistic context h_t^{att}. Thus, we integrate the prospective feature i_t^{pro} with h_t^{att} to form a new guide and implement the visual attention mechanism from a global perspective. We modify the vanilla scaled dot-product attention in Eq. 1 in the multi-head attention module to Eq. 10 and Eq. 11, so that the prospective information is leveraged as part of the query to attend to the augmented object features. In these equations, $\mathbf{W}^{attn} \in \mathbb{R}^{2d \times d}$ are trainable parameters and $\boldsymbol{\alpha}_t \in \mathbb{R}^d$ is the fusion weight vector. Similar modification is also applied to the augmented attribute features $\mathbf{A}_t^{aug}$ to generate the attribute context $\hat{a}_t$. The corresponding equations are very similar to Eq. 10 and Eq. 11 and are omitted for conciseness.

$$Attention^{pro}(\boldsymbol{h}_t^{att}, \boldsymbol{i}_t^{pro}, \mathbf{O}_t^{aug}) = Softmax(\frac{(\boldsymbol{\alpha}_t \boldsymbol{i}_t^{pro} + (1 - \boldsymbol{\alpha}_t)\boldsymbol{h}_t^{att})\mathbf{O}_t^{aug\top}}{\sqrt{d}})\mathbf{O}_t^{aug} \quad (10)$$

$$\hat{o}_t = MHA^{pro}(\boldsymbol{h}_t^{att}, \boldsymbol{i}_t^{pro}, \mathbf{O}_t^{aug}), \quad \boldsymbol{\alpha}_t = Sigmoid(Concat(\boldsymbol{h}_t^{att}, \boldsymbol{i}_t^{pro})\mathbf{W}^{attn}) \quad (11)$$

After the generation of the object context $\hat{o}_t$ and the attribute context $\hat{a}_t$, we integrate them with the prospective feature to form the attended feature. We concatenate the output of the attention LSTM and the prospective feature to form the fusion weights as in Eq. 12. The concatenation is then fed to a linear layer, the weight of which is $\mathbf{W}^{fuse} \in \mathbb{R}^{2d \times 3d}$. The output of the linear layer, which is of size $3d$, is reshaped to $3 \times d$ and further input to the Softmax layer to compute the fusion weights. The fused attended feature is obtained as in Eq. 13.

$$\boldsymbol{\beta}_t = Softmax(Reshape(Concat(\boldsymbol{h}_t^{att}, \boldsymbol{i}_t^{pro})\mathbf{W}^{fuse})) \quad (12)$$

$$\hat{h}_t = \boldsymbol{\beta}_t^1 * \hat{o}_t + \boldsymbol{\beta}_t^2 * \hat{a}_t + \boldsymbol{\beta}_t^3 * \boldsymbol{i}_t^{pro} \quad (13)$$

Thanks to the global linguistic information brought about by the coarse caption, the model can exploit the visual information and language information more thoroughly by utilizing the complementarity between prospective and explored information contained in $\hat{h}_t$. As such, image descriptions that are not only reasonable in general but also accurate in details can be possibly generated. Finally, the concatenation of the attended feature $\hat{h}_t$ and the output of attention LSTM h_t^{att} is fed to the language LSTM to generate h_t^{lan} as in Eq. 14.

$$h_t^{lan} = LSTM_{lan}(h_{t-1}^{lan}, [\boldsymbol{h}_t^{att}; \hat{h}_t]) \quad (14)$$

The output of the language LSTM if firstly sent to a fully connected layer to generate the logits and then sent to a softmax layer to generate the probability for each word in the vocabulary as is in Eq. 15, where $\mathbf{W}^p \in \mathbb{R}^{d \times k}$ and $\boldsymbol{b}^p \in \mathbb{R}^k$ are trainable parameters and k is the vocabulary size.

$$p_t^w = Softmax(h_t^{lan}\mathbf{W}^p + \boldsymbol{b}^p) \quad (15)$$

4.2   Attentive Attribute Detector

While previous attribute detectors [14,15] directly utilize the image features extracted from CNN for attribute detection without further polishing, we alternatively explore the effectiveness of refining the visual features in advance. Suppose that we need to predict the probability of P attributes with M object features, we can view the object features as M nodes in a graph and the embedding of all the attributes as P exterior nodes. We model the relationship between these two kinds of nodes and refine the object features via a special kind of one-layer Graph Convolutional Network (GCN). We follow [23] to construct the GCN layer, of which the mathematical formulation is shown in Eq. 16, where $\mathbf{W} \in \mathbb{R}^{d \times d}$ is the parameter of the linear layer and f is the activation function; function $A(\mathbf{F}, \mathbf{E})$ models the similarity between the object features $\mathbf{F} \in \mathbb{R}^{M \times d}$ and the attribute embedding $\mathbf{E} \in \mathbb{R}^{P \times d}$.

$$\tilde{\mathbf{F}} = f(A(\mathbf{F}, \mathbf{E})\mathbf{F}\mathbf{W}) \tag{16}$$

In our work, we take the recently proposed scaled dot-product formulation [12] to model such similarity. In this formulation, the attribute embedding $\mathbf{E}$ can be viewed as queries ($\mathbf{Q}$), while the object features $\mathbf{F}$ can be viewed as keys ($\mathbf{K}$) and values ($\mathbf{V}$) as in Eq. 17. Thus, the M object features are refined to P compound features $\tilde{\mathbf{F}} \in \mathbb{R}^{P \times d}$ that are more appropriate for predicting the probability of each image attribute.

$$\tilde{\mathbf{F}} = f(Softmax(\frac{\mathbf{E}\mathbf{F}^{\top}}{\sqrt{d}})\mathbf{F}\mathbf{W}) \tag{17}$$

In practice, the scaled dot-product formulation can be extended to the aforementioned MHA to further increase the model capacity. Actually, when the relationship is modeled by the scaled dot-product and f is set to identity mapping, GCN is transformed to MHA. Note that, when the number of interior nodes and exterior nodes is unequal ($M \neq P$), this kind of GCN cannot be stacked as usual GCN layers. That's why we call MHA a special kind of one-layer GCN with additional exterior nodes. The output of MHA is sent to a linear layer and then activated by the sigmoid function to predict the probability distribution $p \in \mathbb{R}^{P \times 1}$ of image attributes as in Eq. 18, where $\mathbf{W}^{Attr} \in \mathbb{R}^{d \times 1}$ are trainable parameters.

$$p = Sigmoid(MHA(\mathbf{E}, \mathbf{F}, \mathbf{F})\mathbf{W}^{Attr}) \tag{18}$$

The structure of AAD is shown in the right orange circle in Fig. 2. We model the task of attribute detection as P binary classification task and leverage the focal loss [24] in training. For each image, we send the embedding of top L attributes $\mathbf{G} \in \mathbb{R}^{L \times d}$ that are predicted with the highest confidences to the Pro-LSTM model to exert the attribute information.

4.3   Loss Functions

Our image captioning model is trained in two phases. In the first phase, we use the traditional cross-entropy (XE) loss. In the second phase, we modify the Self-Critical Sequence Training (SCST) [25] to directly optimize the CIDEr-D metric.

Table 1. *F1* scores of two attribute detectors with top-*L* attributes. We reproduce the MIL based detector with Up-down feature for fair comparison.

L	5	10	15	20	25
MIL* [14]	0.286	0.420	0.435	0.422	0.395
AAD (ours)	0.352	0.442	**0.459**	0.454	0.437

The gradient of $loss_{RL}^{w}$ can be approximated as Eq. 19, where $r(w_{1:T}^{s})$, $r(\tilde{w}_{1:T})$ and $r(\hat{w}_{1:T})$ are the CIDEr-D rewards for the randomly sampled caption, greedy decoded caption, and the input coarse caption respectively. We also impose the random caption to outperform the coarse caption in the SCST phase.

$$\nabla_{\theta} loss_{RL}^{w} = -(r(\boldsymbol{w}_{1:T}^{s}) - 0.5 * r(\tilde{w}_{1:T}) - 0.5 * r(\hat{\boldsymbol{w}}_{1:T})) \nabla_{\theta} log(\boldsymbol{p}^{w}(w_{1:T}^{s})) \quad (19)$$

5   Experiments

5.1   Experimental Settings

We evaluate our model on the MSCOCO captioning dataset [16]. Words that appear in the training set for over 4 times are selected to form a $k = 10369$ size vocabulary. Similar to [14,15], the top-ranked 1000 words are selected to form the attribute vocabulary. We follow the widely adopted Karpathy's data split [26] in offline evaluation. We utilize the 36×2048 object feature released in Up-down [2] for both attribute detection and image captioning and set the hidden size $d = 1024$. Our models are trained 15 epochs under XE loss and another 10 epochs under SCST [25] with a mini-batch size of 40. We use the following metrics in evaluation: Bleu [27], Meteor [28], Rouge-L [29], CIDEr-D [30] and SPICE [31].

5.2   Performance Evaluation and Analysis

Attribute Detection. We first evaluate the attribute detection performance of our proposed AAD using the average *F1* score on the MSCOCO test split. Table 1 compares the detection performance of AAD with the MIL based [14] attribute detector. The MIL detector firstly utilizes one feature to predict the probabilities for all attributes, which may not be accurate; and then integrates the probabilities of all proposals with MIL. The proposed AAD, however, predicts the confidence of each attribute with the integrated and refined features of all the object features. It can be seen that AAD outperforms the MIL detector for different values of L, suggesting the effectiveness of our proposal.

MSCOCO Offline Evaluation. Table 2 shows the single-model performance of the proposed Pro-LSTM model and recent state-of-the-art methods. The Up-Down [2] method extracts image features with bottom-up attention and generates image captions with top-down attention. The proposed two-layer LSTM

Table 2. Single-model image captioning performance (%) on the COCO 'Karpathy' test split, where B@N, M, R, C and S are short for Bleu@N, Meteor, Rouge-L, CIDEr-D and SPICE scores. * indicates the results obtained from the publicly available code. Top-2 scores in each column are marked in **boldface** and <u>underline</u> respectively.

Methods	Cross-entropy loss						CIDEr-D optimization					
Metric	B@1	B@4	M	R	C	S	B@1	B@4	M	R	C	S
Up-Down [2]	77.2	36.2	27.0	56.4	113.5	20.3	79.8	36.3	27.7	56.9	120.1	21.4
SGAE [32]	–	–	–	–	–	–	<u>80.8</u>	38.4	28.4	58.6	127.8	22.1
Look&Modify [19]	76.9	36.1	–	56.4	112.3	20.3	–	–	–	–	–	–
MaBi-LSTM [20]	**79.3**	36.8	28.1	56.9	116.6	–	–	–	–	–	–	–
AoA [17]	77.4	**37.2**	**28.4**	**57.5**	119.8	21.3	80.2	38.9	**29.2**	**58.8**	**129.8**	22.4
AoA* [17]	77.4	37.0	28.2	<u>57.3</u>	118.4	<u>21.5</u>	80.4	<u>39.0</u>	28.9	58.7	128.8	22.5
Pro-LSTM (Ours)	<u>77.8</u>	<u>37.1</u>	28.2	<u>57.3</u>	<u>120.2</u>	<u>21.5</u>	**81.0**	**39.2**	<u>29.0</u>	**58.8**	<u>129.5</u>	<u>22.6</u>
Pro-LSTM+AoA*	77.7	<u>37.1</u>	<u>28.3</u>	57.2	**120.5**	**21.6**	<u>80.8</u>	<u>39.0</u>	<u>29.0</u>	**58.9**	**129.8**	**22.7**

Table 3. Performance (%) on the online MSCOCO evaluation server, where Σ denotes model ensemble. Top-2 rankings are indicated by superscript for each metric

Methods	Bleu-1		Bleu-4		Meteor		Rouge-L		CIDEr-D	
	c5	c40	c5	c40	c5	c40	c5	c40	c5	c40
SCST$^\Sigma$ [25]	–	–	35.2	64.5	27.0	35.5	56.3	70.7	114.7	116.7
Up-Down$^\Sigma$ [2]	80.2^2	95.2^1	36.9	68.5	27.6	36.7	57.1	72.4	117.9	120.5
SGAE$^\Sigma$ [32]	–	–	38.5^1	69.7^1	28.2	37.2	58.6^1	73.6^2	123.8^2	126.5^1
AoA* [17]	79.9	94.4	38.0^2	69.1^2	28.6^2	37.7^2	58.2	73.4	123.2	125.8^2
Pro-LSTM (ours)	80.3^1	94.8^2	38.5^1	69.7^1	28.7^1	38.0^1	58.4^2	73.7^1	124.1^1	126.5^1

is leveraged as our backbone model. Our proposed Pro-LSTM outperforms the SGAE [32] shows that incorporating coarse caption is more beneficial than utilizing the scene graph features. Although Snammani [19] and Ge et al. [20] also use the coarse caption, they fail to let it guide their model but treat it as semantic feature. Our method outperforms MaBi-LSTM in most metrics indicates the effectiveness of leveraging prospective information as appropriate guidance for the attention modules in the image captioning model. The AoA [17] model modifies the attention modules to achieve state-of-the-art performance. However, they fail to leverage the prospective information. We re-train the AoA* model with the released publicly available code to generate the coarse caption in our experiments. The experimental results show that our method extensively exploits the global information from the coarse caption and enhances the CIDEr-D for 1.8 and 0.7 respectively in XE and SCST. Our method is compatible with the AoA method as the combination of Pro-LSTM and AoA* yields the best performance.

MSCOCO Online Evaluation. We submit the single-model captioning results of both the AoA* model and our proposed Pro-LSTM to the online testing

Table 4. The performance of utilizing different modules in XE training.

Method	Bleu-1	Bleu-4	Meteor	Rouge-L	CIDEr-D	SPICE
Baseline	76.8	36.5	28.0	56.9	116.7	21.1
Baseline+AAD	77.2	36.7	28.2	57.0	118.3	21.3
Baseline+ProA	77.7	36.9	28.3	57.1	119.1	21.5
Pro-LSTM	77.8	37.1	28.2	57.3	120.2	21.5

Table 5. The performance of using prospective information and explored information in XE training.

Methods	Bleu-1	Bleu-4	Meteor	Rouge-L	CIDEr-D	SPICE
Pro-LSTM - augmentation	77.8	37.0	28.2	57.2	119.7	21.5
Pro-LSTM - guidance	77.4	36.7	28.1	57.0	118.9	21.3
Pro-LSTM - fusion	77.5	36.8	28.2	57.2	119.3	21.4
Pro-LSTM	77.8	37.1	28.2	57.3	120.2	21.5

server[1]. Table 3 shows the online performance of officially published state-of-the-art works. Our proposed Pro-LSTM achieves performance improvements over the AoA* model. The performance of Pro-LSTM is among the top-2 in all the compared methods across all the metrics. Specifically, a single Pro-LSTM model even outperforms the ensemble of SGAE models.

6   Ablation Study

6.1   Effectiveness of Modules

In Table 4, we assess the contribution of each module in our proposed method. We firstly form a baseline model similar to that proposed in Up-Down [2] except that we leverage multi-head attention to encode the object feature and generate the object context. We then add the attentive attribute detector to the baseline model to exploit the attribute information. Concurrently, we also replace the vanilla multi-head attention module with our proposed prospective information guided attention module as is shown in the third row. It can be noticed that leveraging the global information to guide the attention module is more beneficial than utilizing the image attributes only. Naturally, comprehensively using these two modules in our proposed Pro-LSTM leads to the most favorable performance.

6.2   Effectiveness of ProA

The effectiveness of our proposed ProA module mainly comes from the joint utilization of both prospective and explored information. More specifically, we

---

[1] https://competitions.codalab.org/competitions/3221.

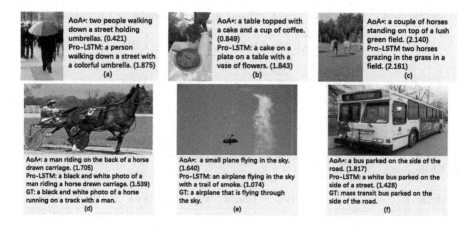

Fig. 4. Qualitative results of the generated captions and corresponding CIDEr-D scores in MSCOCO test split. One ground truth caption is shown for (d), (e), and (f) respectively. Pro-LSTM effectively utilizes the prospective information in the AoA* generated coarse captions to narrate more precise and detailed captions. In some cases, the captions generated by Pro-LSTM can more informative even when their CIDEr-D scores are lower than that of AoA* captions.

leverage the explored information to augment the visual features and utilize the prospective information to guide the attention module. And we finally fuse the multimodal features to further enhance the performance. Thus, we test the effectiveness of each sub-module in Fig. 3 by eliminating it from the Pro-LSTM model. The corresponding results are shown in Table 5. The performance only decreases a little without using the explored information for feature augmentation. This is understandable since such information has already been embedded to the LSTM hidden states. Additionally leverage it in the attention module leads to incremental improvements only. In contrast, eliminating the guidance of prospective information results in a significant performance drop. This further verifies that grasping the global linguistic context in attention modules through utilizing the prospective information is essentially beneficial for image captioning. Fusing the prospective information with visual information is also beneficial for captioning since this enables the model to better conceive future semantics. To conclude, we observe that effectively utilizing the prospective information in the ProA module leads to better captioning performance as we expect.

7   Qualitative Results

Figure 4 compares the captions generated by the AoA* model and that by the Pro-LSTM model. Generally, AoA* sometimes generates grammatically correct but semantically flawed sentences. However, these sentences still contain useful descriptions that can help Pro-LSTM to correctly attend to corresponding visual features, such as 'walking' and 'cake' in Fig. 4(a)(b). In Fig. 4(c), AoA* only infers that the horses are *'standing'* in the field. With the help of prospective information, the Pro-LSTM model grasps the semantic that the horses are in a field via the language information, and further induces that they are *'grazing'* as it is a common behavior under this circumstance. For Fig. 4(d), Pro-LSTM describes the color scheme while AoA* fails to do so. This is probably because that *'black'* and *'white'* are successfully detected by AAD. Thus, Pro-LSTM can leverage these attributes via ProA. Interestingly, we notice that the CIDEr-D scores may even drop when the Pro-LSTM predicted captions are more accurate and detailed as in Fig. 4(e), (f). This is due to the fact that some of the image details successfully revealed by Pro-LSTM are actually missing in the human-labeled ground truth, such as *'smoke'* in Fig. 4(e) and *'white'* in Fig. 4(f). Under the commonly used token-based metrics which compute exact word matching instead of considering semantic accuracy, this may lead to a performance drop.

Fig. 5. Qualitative result illustrating how AAD and ProA affect the caption generation process. $\mathbf{W}_t^{pro}$ is the prospective word set, $\bar{\alpha}_t$ is the average weight of prospective information in Eq. 10, $\bar{\beta}_t^2$ and $\bar{\beta}_t^3$ are average weights of attribute information and prospective information in Eq. 13 respectively.

We further demonstrate how AAD and ProA affect the captioning model in Fig. 5 by showing the weight of corresponding information when the model generates *'laying'* and *'teddy'*. Our model generates *'laying'* rather than *'sitting'* mainly due to prospective information in the word *'bed'*. The average weight $\bar{\alpha}_t$ of the prospective information is large enough to guide our model to choose the visual features that are more correlated to *'bed'*. Moreover, as the word *'laying'* is detected as one of the image attributes, the prospective information therefore tends to assign relatively larger weights to attribute information in the fusion sub-module in Eq. 12. Consequently, *'sitting'* in the coarse caption is replaced by the more appropriate *'laying'*. When the generation of the whole sentence is about to terminate, e.g. when the Pro-LSTM generates *'teddy'*, the prospective information is not rich enough in helping to generate new words. Nevertheless, thanks to the accurate AAD, *'teddy'* and *'bear'* are successfully detected as image attributes to aid Pro-LSTM in generating a more detailed sentence by replacing *'stuffed animal'* with *'teddy bear'*.

8   Conclusions

We propose a Prospective information guided LSTM (Pro-LSTM) model which comprehensively exploits both prospective and explored linguistic information to boost image captioning. Generally, thorough utilization of the prospective information from the coarse caption makes it possible for the model to attend to proper information from a global perspective. Specifically, with the help of the proposed AAD and ProA module, the Pro-LSTM model can appropriately attend to the object features and image attributes, and adaptively decide when to utilize visual information and when to make use of the language information. As such, sentences with richer and more accurate semantics can be generated. Our method achieves state-of-the-art performances on the benchmark MSCOCO dataset. Comprehensive ablation studies further demonstrate the effectiveness of our method. For future work, we are going to streamline our model to achieve end-to-end training of Pro-LSTM and AAD. This work was supported by the National Natural Science Foundation of China under Grant 61673234.

References

1. Vinyals, O., Toshev, A., Bengio, S., Erhan, D.: Show and tell: a neural image caption generator. In: Proceedings of the IEEE Conference on Computer Vision and Pattern Recognition, pp. 3156–3164 (2015)
2. Anderson, P., et al.: Bottom-up and top-down attention for image captioning and visual question answering. In: Proceedings of the IEEE Conference on Computer Vision and Pattern Recognition, vol. 3, p. 6 (2018)
3. Chen, L., et al.: SCA-CNN: spatial and channel-wise attention in convolutional networks for image captioning. In: Proceedings of the IEEE Conference on Computer Vision and Pattern Recognition, pp. 6298–6306. IEEE (2017)
4. Lu, J., Xiong, C., Parikh, D., Socher, R.: Knowing when to look: adaptive attention via a visual sentinel for image captioning. In: Proceedings of the IEEE Conference on Computer Vision and Pattern Recognition, pp. 3242–3250. IEEE (2017)
5. Xu, K., et al.: Show, attend and tell: neural image caption generation with visual attention. In: Proceedings of International Conference on Machine Learning, pp. 2048–2057 (2015)
6. You, Q., Jin, H., Wang, Z., Fang, C., Luo, J.: Image captioning with semantic attention. In: Proceedings of the IEEE Conference on Computer Vision and Pattern Recognition, pp. 4651–4659 (2016)
7. Yao, T., Pan, Y., Li, Y., Qiu, Z., Mei, T.: Boosting image captioning with attributes. In: Proceedings of the IEEE International Conference on Computer Vision, pp. 22–29 (2017)
8. Yao, T., Pan, Y., Li, Y., Mei, T.: Exploring visual relationship for image captioning. In: Ferrari, V., Hebert, M., Sminchisescu, C., Weiss, Y. (eds.) Computer Vision – ECCV 2018. LNCS, vol. 11218, pp. 711–727. Springer, Cham (2018). https://doi.org/10.1007/978-3-030-01264-9_42
9. Ke, L., Pei, W., Li, R., Shen, X., Tai, Y.W.: Reflective decoding network for image captioning. arXiv preprint arXiv:1908.11824 (2019)
10. Huang, Y., Chen, J., Ouyang, W., Wan, W., Xue, Y.: Image captioning with end-to-end attribute detection and subsequent attributes prediction. IEEE Trans. Image Process. **29**, 4013–4026 (2020)
11. Pan, Y., Yao, T., Li, Y., Mei, T.: X-linear attention networks for image captioning. In: Proceedings of the IEEE/CVF Conference on Computer Vision and Pattern Recognition, pp. 10971–10980 (2020)

12. Vaswani, A., et al.: Attention is all you need. In: Advances in Neural Information Processing Systems, pp. 5998–6008 (2017)
13. Ren, S., He, K., Girshick, R., Sun, J.: Faster R-CNN: towards real-time object detection with region proposal networks. In: Advances in Neural Information Processing Systems (2015)
14. Fang, H., et al.: From captions to visual concepts and back. In: Proceedings of the IEEE Conference on Computer Vision and Pattern Recognition, pp. 1473–1482 (2015)
15. Gan, Z., et al.: Semantic compositional networks for visual captioning. In: Proceedings of the IEEE Conference on Computer Vision and Pattern Recognition, vol. 2 (2017)
16. Chen, X., et al.: Microsoft coco captions: data collection and evaluation server. arXiv preprint arXiv:1504.00325 (2015)
17. Huang, L., Wang, W., Chen, J., Wei, X.Y.: Attention on attention for image captioning. In: Proceedings of the IEEE International Conference on Computer Vision, pp. 4634–4643 (2019)
18. Wang, C., Yang, H., Bartz, C., Meinel, C.: Image captioning with deep bidirectional LSTMs. In: Proceedings of the 24th ACM International Conference on Multimedia, pp. 988–997. ACM (2016)
19. Sammani, F., Elsayed, M.: Look and modify: modification networks for image captioning. arXiv preprint arXiv:1909.03169 (2019)
20. Ge, H., Yan, Z., Zhang, K., Zhao, M., Sun, L.: Exploring overall contextual information for image captioning in human-like cognitive style. arXiv preprint arXiv:1910.06475 (2019)
21. Mikolov, T., Chen, K., Corrado, G., Dean, J.: Efficient estimation of word representations in vector space. arXiv preprint arXiv:1301.3781 (2013)
22. Pennington, J., Socher, R., Manning, C.: Glove: global vectors for word representation. In: Proceedings of the 2014 Conference on Empirical Methods in Natural Language Processing, pp. 1532–1543 (2014)
23. Chen, Z.M., Wei, X.S., Wang, P., Guo, Y.: Multi-label image recognition with graph convolutional networks. In: Proceedings of the IEEE Conference on Computer Vision and Pattern Recognition, pp. 5177–5186 (2019)
24. Lin, T.Y., Goyal, P., Girshick, R., He, K., Dollár, P.: Focal loss for dense object detection. IEEE Trans. Pattern Anal. Mach. Intell. 42(2), 318–327 (2018)
25. Rennie, S.J., Marcheret, E., Mroueh, Y., Ross, J., Goel, V.: Self-critical sequence training for image captioning. In: Proceedings of the IEEE Conference on Computer Vision and Pattern Recognition, pp. 1179–1195 (2017)
26. Karpathy, A., Fei-Fei, L.: Deep visual-semantic alignments for generating image descriptions. In: Proceedings of the IEEE Conference on Computer Vision and Pattern Recognition, pp. 3128–3137 (2015)
27. Papineni, K., Roukos, S., Ward, T., Zhu, W.J.: BLEU: a method for automatic evaluation of machine translation. In: Proceedings of the 40th Annual Meeting on Association for Computational Linguistics, pp. 311–318 (2002)
28. Denkowski, M.J., Lavie, A.: Meteor universal: language specific translation evaluation for any target language. In: Proceedings of the 9th Workshop on Statistical Machine Translation, pp. 376–380 (2014)
29. Lin, C.Y.: Rouge: A package for automatic evaluation of summaries. In: Proceedings of Text Summarization Branches Out, pp. 1–8 (2004)
30. Vedantam, R., Lawrence Zitnick, C., Parikh, D.: Cider: consensus-based image description evaluation. In: Proceedings of the IEEE Conference on Computer Vision and Pattern Recognition, pp. 4566–4575 (2015)

31. Anderson, P., Fernando, B., Johnson, M., Gould, S.: SPICE: semantic propositional image caption evaluation. In: Leibe, B., Matas, J., Sebe, N., Welling, M. (eds.) ECCV 2016. LNCS, vol. 9909, pp. 382–398. Springer, Cham (2016). https://doi.org/10.1007/978-3-319-46454-1_24

32. Yang, X., Tang, K., Zhang, H., Cai, J.: Auto-encoding scene graphs for image captioning. In: Proceedings of the IEEE Conference on Computer Vision and Pattern Recognition, pp. 10685–10694 (2019)

Datasets and Performance Analysis

RGB-T Crowd Counting from Drone: A Benchmark and MMCCN Network

Tao Peng, Qing Li, and Pengfei Zhu[(✉)]

College of Intelligence and Computing, Tianjin University, Tianjin 300072, China
{wspt,liqing,zhupengfei}@tju.edu.cn

Abstract. Crowd counting aims to identify the number of objects and plays an important role in intelligent transportation, city management and security monitoring. The task of crowd counting is much challenging because of scale variations, illumination changes, occlusions and poor imaging conditions, especially in the nighttime and haze conditions. In this paper, we present a drone based RGB-Thermal crowd counting dataset (DroneRGBT) that consists of 3600 pairs of images and covers different attributes, including height, illumination and density. To exploit the complementary information in both visible and thermal infrared modalities, we propose a multi-modal crowd counting network (MMCCN) with a multi-scale feature learning module, a modal alignment module and an adaptive fusion module. Experiments on DroneRGBT demonstrate the effectiveness of the proposed approach.

Keywords: Crowd counting · RGB-T

1 Introduction

Crowd analysis is of great importance because of a great practical demands such as assembly controlling and other security services. However, it is slow and unreliable to count people using any crowd monitoring system that relies on humans. There is a need for an automatic computer vision algorithm that can accurately count the number of people in crowded scenes based on images and videos of the crowds. Therefore, crowd counting has been widely studied and a growing number of network models have been developed to deliver promising solutions for this mission. These methods usually generate the density map according to the input image, and obtain the crowd counting by integrating the predicted density map.

Previous work [1–4] for scene analysis are mostly based on visible data. However, visible data may have drawbacks of illumination changes and poor imaging conditions in the nighttime. The thermal infrared data has been proven to be effective in boosting image analysis [5–8], and allows scene perception in day and night. However, the research of RGB-T crowd-counting is limited by the lack of

---

T. Peng and Q. Li–These authors contributed equally to this paper as co-first authors.

© Springer Nature Switzerland AG 2021
H. Ishikawa et al. (Eds.): ACCV 2020, LNCS 12627, pp. 497–513, 2021.
https://doi.org/10.1007/978-3-030-69544-6_30

a comprehensive image benchmark. Therefore, we construct a drone based RGB-Thermal crowd counting dataset, named as DroneRGBT, which consists of 3600 pairs of images and covers different attributes, including height, illumination and density. Compared with the existing crowd-counting datasets, the proposed DroneRGBT has the following main characteristics: 1) Different from most of the existing datasets, it is a drone-view datasets with multi-modalities. 2) Its alignment across modalities is highly accurate, and does not require any pre- or post-processing. 3) It is a large-scale dataset and collected in many different scenes, with 175,698 annotated instances.

With the created benchmark, we propose a novel approach for RGB-T crowd-counting. The main goals of our framework are: 1) The pipeline can predict density map according to a single modality only so that it can still work well when any modality data is missing. 2) Two modalities reuse the model as much as possible to reduce the amount of model parameters. 3) The fusion results are better than the results based on single modality. Hence, our pipeline, named Multi-Modal Crowd Counting Network (MMCCN), is based on ResNet-50 with three specific modules, i.e., multi-scale feature learning module, modal alignment module, adaptive fusion module. All the modules are optimized jointly and trained in an end-to-end manner. The pipeline can effectively extract low-level modality-specific feature and high-level modality-aligned semantic feature, and adaptively combine the prediction results to acquire a good fusion estimation. We design some experiments to demonstrate that our proposed pipeline can effectively utilize two modalities, RGB-Thermal, to estimate more accurate density map, resulting in more precise counting. Compared with other baselines in different aspects, we conclude that our model is more efficient than two-stream baseline and more precise than simple average baseline. Additionally, we also propose a special modal transfer method for our MMCCN framework to solve the problem of modal missing or the case of having single modality only. To be specific, we present a DM-CycleGAN, which can effectively generate thermal infrared data through visible data. During the training process of DM-CycleGAN, we introduce a density-map (DM) loss. It can make the generated image and the real image as similar as possible in the space which is used to count the instances. Extensive experiments prove that the transfer performance of DM-CycleGAN is better than that of original CycleGAN in field of crowd-counting. Figure 1 demonstrates the flowchart of the proposed method.

This paper makes three major contributions for RGB-T crowd-counting.

* We create a new benchmark dataset containing 3600 registered RGB and thermal image pairs with ground truth annotations for evaluating RGB-T crowd counting methods.
* We propose a novel end-to-end pipeline, MMCCN, for RGB-T crowd-counting. Extensive experiments on our benchmark dataset demonstrate the effectiveness of the proposed approach and the importance of each component of the pipeline.
* We prove a useful way to use massive pairs of registered multi-modal images to train a modal transfer model. The proposed model, DM-CycleGAN, can

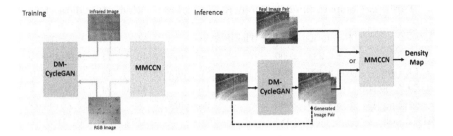

Fig. 1. MMCCN and DM-CycleGAN can be trained by using DroneRGBT benchmark. In the inference process, a pair of registered RGB-T data or data generated by DM-CycleGAN can be used as the input of MMCCN to estimate the density map.

effectively generate thermal infrared data though visible data and improve the counting performance in multi-modal tasks.

2 Related Work

2.1 Crowd Counting Datasets

According to image acquisition methods, the existing crowd counting datasets can be divided into three parts: surveillance-view datasets, free-view datasets and drone-view datasets. **Surveillance-view datasets** are collected by surveillance camera, which usually contain crowd images in specific indoor scenes or small-area outdoor locations. UCSD [9], Mall [10], WorldExpo'10 [11] and ShanghaiTech Part B [12] are typical surveillance-view datasets. **Free-view datasets** contain images collected from the Internet. The attributes of these type datasets vary significantly. There are also many free-view datasets for evaluation criteria, such as UCF_CC_50 [13], UCF-QNRF [14] and ShanghaiTech Part A [12]. Our dataset is a **drone-view based dataset** which is collected by UAV.

2.2 Crowd Counting Methods

In recent years, there are more and more researches on crowd counting and more recent methods used CNNs to tackle crowd counting [1–3,12,15]. Zhang et al. [12] propose a classical and lightweight counting model called Multi-Column Convolutional Neural Network (MCNN), which can estimate density map by learning the features for different head sizes by each column CNN. A spatial FCN (SFCN) [3] is designed by Wang et al. to produce the density map. After the spatial encoder, a regression layer is added in SFCN. In this work, we propose a baseline network which is used to predict crowd number on RGB-T datasets.

Table 1. Comparison of the DroneRGBT dataset with existing datasets.

Dataset	Resolution	Frames	Thermal	View	Max	Min	Ave	Total
UCSD [9]	158 × 238	2000	–	Surveillance	46	11	24.9	49,885
MALL [10]	640 × 480	2000	–	Surveillance	53	13	31.2	62,316
UCF_CC_50 [13]	–	50	–	Free	4543	94	1279	63,974
WorldExpo [11]	576 × 720	3980	–	Surveillance	253	1	50.2	199,923
SHT A [12]	–	482	–	Free	3139	33	501	241,677
SHT B [12]	768 × 1024	716	–	Surveillance	578	9	123	88,488
UCF-QNRF [14]	–	1535	–	Free	12,865	49	815	1,251,642
DroneRGBT	512×640	3600	√	Drone	403	1	48.8	175,698

Dark   Dusk   Light   Low   Medium   High
(a)   (b)

Fig. 2. Some example image pairs in the DroneRGBT dataset.

2.3 Multi-modal Learning

Multi-Modal learning has drawn more attentions in the computer vision community. In this paper, we focus on integrating RGB and thermal infrared data [16–19]. The typical problems that use these two modalities are as follows. (1) **RGB-T Saliency Detection.** Li et al. [16] propose a novel approach, multitask manifold ranking with cross-modality consistency, for RGB-T saliency detection. (2) **RGB-T tracking.** Li et al. [18] provided a graph-based cross-modal ranking model for RGB-T tracking, in which the soft cross-modality consistency between modalities and the optimal query learning are introduced to improve the robustness. Different from these typical works, our work focus on crowd-counting and it is the first benchmark and baseline for RGB-T crowd-counting.

3 DroneRGBT Benchmark

3.1 Data Collection and Annotation

Our DroneRGBT dataset is captured by drone-mounted cameras (DJI Phantom 4, Phantom 4 Pro and Mavic), covering a wide range of scenarios, e.g., campus, street, park, parking lot, playground and plaza. After cleaning the unavailable data, we use the Homography method to register RGB images with infrared

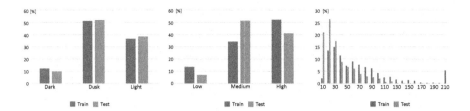

Fig. 3. The distribution of illumination, height, and density attributes in the training set and the testing set from left to right. Bars represent the percentage of this property in the training and testing sets.

image. We label the number of people based on the head count of infrared images. The ground truth annotation file is saved as xml format.

And then, we divide the training set and the test set according to the illumination. We first divide the dataset into three categories: dark, dusk, and light, and then divide each category into two parts, one part for training and the other for testing, while ensuring that the training set and testing set have different scenes to reduce the chances of overfitting to particular scenes.

3.2 Data Characteristic

The DroneRGBT dataset is the first drone-view crowd counting dataset with both RGB and thermal infrared data and it contains images pairs taken at different locations with large variations in scale, viewpoint and background clutters. Table 1 compares the basic information of DroneRGBT and existing datasets. In addition to the above properties, DroneRGBT is more diverse than other datasets. Specifically, the following main aspects are considered in creating the DroneRGBT dataset.

* *Illumination.* The image pairs are captured under different light conditions, such as *dark*, *dusk* and *light*. Under different conditions, the difference in illumination is obvious, which can be distinguished by experience.
* *Scale.* Like most of surveillance-view and free-view based benchmarks which usually include instances with different scales, different object scales are also taken into account for our dataset. So our dataset are collected in different altitudes which significantly affects the scales of object. We delineate 30–50 m as low altitude, 50–80 m as medium, and 80–100 m as high.
* *Density.* Density means the number of objects in each image pair. In our dataset, the density varies from 1 to 403. The distribution of our dataset based on these attributes is shown in Fig. 3.

Some typical sample image pairs in different attributes from our DroneRGBT dataset are shown in Fig. 2. It shows the diversity of our datasets.

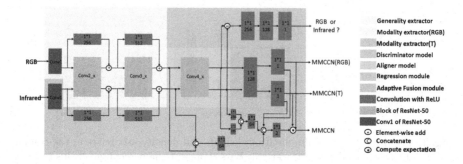

Fig. 4. The architecture of our multi-modal crowd counting network. The pipeline is color-filled to represent the different modules as shown in the color legend on the right side of the figure. Numbers in blue rectangles stand for the kernel size of convolution and numbers of kernel. The block is corresponding to the Table 1 in the paper [20]. (Color figure online)

3.3 Evaluation Metrics

Following previous works for crowd counting, we use the Mean Absolute Error (MAE) and Root Mean Squared Error (RMSE) to evaluate the performance of our proposed method. The MAE and RMSE can be computed as:

$$MAE = \frac{1}{n} \sum_{i=1}^{n} \left| C_i - \hat{C}_i \right|, \quad RMSE = \sqrt{\frac{1}{n} \sum_{i=1}^{n} \left(C_i - \hat{C}_i \right)^2} \tag{1}$$

where n is the number of images, C_i is the counting label of people and $\hat{C}_i$ is the estimated value for the i-th test image.

4 Proposed Approach

4.1 Multi-Modal Crowd Counting Network

The pipeline of Multi-Modal Crowd Counting Network (MMCCN) is shown in Fig. 4. Our network is based on ResNet-50 [20] with three specific modules, i.e., multi-scale feature learning module, modal alignment module, adaptive fusion module. The feature learning module is used to extract both generality feature and modality-special feature of the input data. The pair of extracted features are separately fed into the modal alignment module to further extract the high-level semantic feature and each pair of semantic feature are aligned to same feature space at the same time. After using the high-level semantic feature to regress the crowd number, the pipeline fuse the prediction output based on visible spectrum and thermal infrared data by adaptive fusion module to obtain the final result.

Multi-scale Feature Learning Module. Due to different principles of imaging physics, the distributions between visible spectrum and thermal infrared data are different. One intuitive thought will be to extract their discriminative features respectively. However, it will increase the parameters of network and might degrade efficiency. Besides, two-stream also ignore modality-shared feature learning. To reduce computational burden, we use generality extractor to obtain the common information and modality extractor to extract modality-special feature. The generality extractor is the first two blocks of ResNet-50. Modality extractor, where consists of a convolution layer, is used to extract modality-special feature representations with a little computational burden.

In multi-scale feature learning module, each block has a modality extractor. The outputs of each generality extractor and modality extractor is element-wise added together. For example, the feature of thermal infrared data f^T is computed by Eq. 2.

$$f^T = F_g(T; \sigma_g) + F_m^T(T; \sigma_m^T) \tag{2}$$

where F_g and F_m^T stand for generality extractor and modality extractor of thermal modality, respectively. And σ_g and σ_m^T are the parameters of the corresponding extractors. So, the feature of thermal infrared data depends on both σ_g and σ_m^T. Although the modality extractor only has less parameters, the module also can effectively extract discriminative feature of visible spectrum and thermal infrared data respectively. The reason is as follows. Firstly, Eq. 2 can be simplified when we denote the transfer function as a convolution operation. And then we can merge the matrix as follows.

$$f^T = W_g * T + W_m^T * T = (W_g + W_m^T) * T = M^T * T \tag{3}$$

where W_g represents the parameter of generality extractor and W_m^T stands for that of modality extractor. Convolution operation is denoted as $*$. As a result, we can find a new weight matrix M^T which can focus on modality-specific feature.

Modal Alignment Module. Our hypothesis is that the distribution changes between bi-modality are low-level characteristics rather than high-level. The high-level semantic information between visible spectrum and thermal infrared data is similar, because these pairs of images are shot in the same place with registration. Therefore, we try to reuse the latter network and attend to map the RGB input to features which are aligned with thermal feature space. In the spirit of adversarial training in GAN [21,22], the modal alignment module is trained by a minimax game. It consists of a aligner model and a discriminator model. The aligner learn to align the feature maps between RGB and thermal infrared data, and the discriminator differentiate the feature distributions. These two models are alternatively optimized and compete with each other. Specifically, the backbone of aligner, which aims to align feature, is the *Conv4_x* of ResNet-50 with 1 stride for all convolution. In order to avoid gradient unstable, we explore the least squares loss rather than the sigmoid cross entropy loss function to optimize the our model, where the least squares loss function can relieves the problem of vanishing gradients. Therefore, the loss for learning the aligner is:

$$\min_{A} J(A) = \min_{A} \frac{1}{2} E_{f^V \sim P_{f^V}} [D(A(f^V)) - c]^2 \qquad (4)$$

where A stands for the aligner and D means the discriminator. The low-level modality-special feature of visible spectrum data extracted by multi-scale feature learning module is denoted as f^V. The discriminator would differentiate the complicated feature space, which has 3 convolution layers with 1×1 kernel size. And it is optimized via:

$$\min_{D} J(D) = \min_{D} \frac{1}{2} E_{f^T \sim P_{f^T}} [D(A(f^T)) - a]^2 + \frac{1}{2} E_{f^V \sim P_{f^V}} [D(A(f^V)) - b]^2 \quad (5)$$

The definitions of symbols are same as the earlier ones. To make A align the modal features as close as possible, we set $c = b$. So, by using the 0–1 binary coding scheme, the parameters is set by $a = c = 1$ and $b = 0$ in this model. By alternative updating of D and A, decision boundary of the least squares loss function can force the aligner to generate feature of both modality toward decision boundary. Note that the discriminator model is only used in training processing to provide the supervised signal for the align model. During the inference process, only the align model is used to obtain aligned high-level features.

Adaptive Fusion Module. By using a regression module, we can obtain the density map predicted through visible spectrum and thermal infrared input, respectively. M^T denote the density map predicted by our pipeline when the input is thermal infrared data. M^V is density map when the input is visible spectrum data. In ensemble learning, the result of multiple-model fusion usually can achieve better than the direct result of single model. Therefore, the prediction result of our model is a expectation, which combines M^T and M^V.

$$E(M) = M^T \times p(M^T) + M^V \times p(M^V) \qquad (6)$$

where $p(M^T)$ is the probability of M^T. Similarly, the probability of M^V is denoted as $p(M^V)$. The probability here means the confidence of corresponding output. Given that the confidence depends on the pair of input, we use a additional network to regress the probability based on multi-scale feature. The details of this module are shown in Fig. 4. Therefore, $p(M) = \tilde{p}(M) \times \hat{p}(M)$, where $\tilde{p}$ is the prior confidence and $\hat{p}$ is the confidence predicted by network. Using Eq. 6, each modality density map multiplies corresponding confidence map to get the final result. All the parameters of the pipeline are learned by minimizing the loss function $J(M)$.

$$
\begin{aligned}
J(M) = \frac{1}{MN} \sum_{j=1}^{M} \sum_{k=1}^{N} [(E(M)_{i,j} - M_{i,j}^{GT})^2 \\
+ \lambda_T (M_{i,j}^T - M_{i,j}^{GT})^2 + \lambda_V (M_{i,j}^V - M_{i,j}^{GT})^2]
\end{aligned}
\qquad (7)
$$

where M^{GT} is the ground-truth of the density map. λ_T and λ_V are weighting factors of loss.

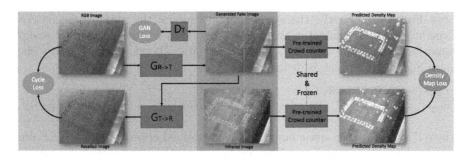

Fig. 5. The framework of the DM-CycleGAN. The pipeline in blue color area is the original CycleGAN, and the extra branch of our DM-CycleGAN are shown in red color area. Pre-trained model is shared and frozen. (Color figure online)

Loss Function. Our final objective for network becomes

$$J = J(M) + \lambda_a(J(D) + J(A)) \tag{8}$$

where λ_a is the weight for the align loss. $J(D)$ is just used to optimize the discriminator model.

4.2 DM-CycleGAN

In some cases, due to lack of the infrared acquisition equipment, the thermal infrared data is not acquired. So, we consider whether we can utilize the visible data to generate infrared data and use generated infrared data and visible data as the input of our MMCCN network for crowd-counting. The original idea was to use CycleGAN [23] to handle this modality transfer problem, which translates visible data into infrared data. However, given that the loss function of CycleGAN do not constrain local details, original CycleGAN can not focus on local patterns and texture features. So, we propose a modality translator, called DM-CycleGAN, to generate meaningful infrared image.

Framework. For making generated image meaningful, we assume that the distance between the generated image and the real image in the space which is used to count the instances needs to as close as possible. In this pipeline, a pre-trained crowd counter is viewed as the spatial mapping converter, which can transfer the image from image space into density-map space. Therefore, the fake image generated by the original CycleGAN and real infrared image are transferred into density-map space by this converter, respectively. And a Density Map Mean Square Loss is introduced to force generated image to become close to real image in density-map space. This extra loss can force GAN to focus on person in the image. The specific description of the DM-CycleGAN framework is shown in Fig. 5.

Loss Function. Firstly, the symbol definitions are the same as CycleGAN. Generator and discriminator are defined as G and D, respectively. $\mathcal{R}$ and $\mathcal{T}$ stand for visible data and thermal infrared data. Therefore, the Density Map Mean Square (DM) Loss is defined as:

$$
\begin{aligned}
&\mathcal{L}_{DM}\left(G_{\mathcal{R}\to\mathcal{T}}, G_{\mathcal{T}\to\mathcal{R}}, \mathcal{R}, \mathcal{T}\right) = \\
&\mathbb{E}_{(i_{\mathcal{T}}, i_{\mathcal{R}})\sim I_{\mathcal{T},\mathcal{R}}}\left[MSE(\mathcal{C}(G_{\mathcal{R}\to\mathcal{T}}(i_{\mathcal{R}})), \mathcal{C}(i_{\mathcal{T}})) + MSE(\mathcal{C}(G_{\mathcal{R}\to\mathcal{T}}(G_{\mathcal{T}\to\mathcal{R}}(i_{\mathcal{T}})), \mathcal{C}(i_{\mathcal{T}})))\right]
\end{aligned}
\tag{9}
$$

where $\mathcal{C}$ stands for the space mapping by pre-trained crowd-counter, MSE represents the mean square error between the generated image and real image in density-map space. Finally, the final objective of DM-CycleGAN is defined as:

$$
\begin{aligned}
&\mathcal{L}_{\text{final}}\left(G_{\mathcal{R}\to\mathcal{T}}, G_{\mathcal{T}\to\mathcal{R}}, D_{\mathcal{R}}, D_{\mathcal{T}}, \mathcal{R}, \mathcal{T}\right) \\
&= \mathcal{L}_{GAN}\left(G_{\mathcal{R}\to\mathcal{T}}, D_{\mathcal{T}}, \mathcal{R}, \mathcal{T}\right) \\
&+ \mathcal{L}_{GAN}\left(G_{\mathcal{T}\to\mathcal{R}}, D_{\mathcal{R}}, \mathcal{T}, \mathcal{R}\right) \\
&+ \lambda\mathcal{L}_{\text{cycle}}\left(G_{\mathcal{R}\to\mathcal{T}}, G_{\mathcal{T}\to\mathcal{R}}, \mathcal{R}, \mathcal{T}\right) \\
&+ \mu\mathcal{L}_{DM}\left(G_{\mathcal{R}\to\mathcal{T}}, G_{\mathcal{T}\to\mathcal{R}}, \mathcal{R}, \mathcal{T}\right)
\end{aligned}
\tag{10}
$$

where the definition of $\mathcal{L}_{GAN}$ and $\mathcal{L}_{\text{cycle}}$ are the same as original CycleGAN,

$$
\begin{aligned}
&\mathcal{L}_{GAN}\left(G_{\mathcal{R}\to\mathcal{T}}, D_{\mathcal{T}}, \mathcal{R}, \mathcal{T}\right) \\
&= \mathbb{E}_{i_{\mathcal{T}}\sim I_{\mathcal{T}}}\left[\log\left(D_{\mathcal{T}}\left(i_{\mathcal{T}}\right)\right)\right] + \mathbb{E}_{i_{\mathcal{R}}\sim I_{\mathcal{R}}}\left[\log\left(1 - D_{\mathcal{T}}\left(G_{\mathcal{R}\to\mathcal{T}}\left(i_{\mathcal{R}}\right)\right)\right)\right]
\end{aligned}
\tag{11}
$$

$$
\begin{aligned}
&\mathcal{L}_{\text{cycle}}\left(G_{\mathcal{R}\to\mathcal{T}}, G_{\mathcal{T}\to\mathcal{R}}, \mathcal{R}, \mathcal{T}\right) \\
&= \mathbb{E}_{i_{\mathcal{R}}\sim I_{\mathcal{R}}}\left[\|G_{\mathcal{T}\to\mathcal{R}}\left(G_{\mathcal{R}\to\mathcal{T}}\left(i_{\mathcal{R}}\right)\right) - i_{\mathcal{R}}\|_1\right] + \mathbb{E}_{i_{\mathcal{T}}\sim I_{\mathcal{T}}}\left[\|G_{\mathcal{R}\to\mathcal{T}}\left(G_{\mathcal{T}\to\mathcal{R}}\left(i_{\mathcal{T}}\right)\right) - i_{\mathcal{T}}\|_1\right]
\end{aligned}
\tag{12}
$$

And the λ and μ are the weights of cycle-consistent loss and density-map loss, respectively.

5   Experiments

5.1   Experiments on DroneRGBT Dataset

Training Details. The training dataset of DroneRGBT consists of 1800 pairs of registered images and corresponding ground truth annotation files. The annotation is converted into a binary map with a Gaussian filter of standard deviation 5. In addition, data augmentations like rotation, random crop are used to avoid overfitting. The optimizer we use is Adam [24] with the following hyper parameters: learning rate 10^{-5} with stepped decay rate 0.995, $\beta_1 = 0.9$, $\beta_2 = 0.999$, batch size $= 8$. And λ_T, λ_V, λ_a are set by 1, 1 and 0.005. We alternatively optimized the aligner model and discriminator model of modal alignment module with the adversarial loss for aligning two domain. In adversarial learning, we utilized the Adam optimizer with a learning rate of 10^{-5} and a stepped decay rate of 0.98 every 100 joint updates, with weight clipping for the discriminator being 0.03. Prior confidence $\tilde{p}(M^T)$ and $\tilde{p}(M^V)$ are set as 1 and 0, respectively.

The backbone of our network is ResNet-50. What we should pay special attention to is that there are several Batch-Normalization layers in the ResNet. However, the calculation procedure of Batch-Normalization layer is different between

Table 2. The performance of state-of-art methods with different modalities on DroneRGBT. MAE and RMSE are shown.

Method	Journal/Venue & Year	Thermal		RGB	
		MAE	RMSE	MAE	RMSE
MCNN [12]	CVPR 2016	13.64	19.77	31.13	40.87
CMTL [26]	AVSS 2017	19.35	27.05	19.14	28.46
MSCNN [27]	ICIP 2017	14.89	20.41	23.38	28.40
ACSCP [28]	CVPR 2018	13.06	20.29	18.87	28.31
SANET [29]	ECCV 2018	12.13	17.52	14.91	21.66
StackPooling [30]	CoRR 2018	9.45	14.63	14.72	20.90
DA-NET [31]	Access 2018	9.41	14.10	13.92	20.31
CSRNet [15]	CVPR 2018	8.91	13.80	13.06	19.06
SCAR [32]	NeuCom 2019	8.21	13.12	11.72	18.60
CANNET [33]	CVPR 2019	7.78	12.31	10.87	17.58
BL [34]	CVPR 2019	7.41	11.56	10.90	16.80

training process and inference process [25]. In the training process, 'mean' and 'variance' are computed by the samples in the mini-batch. 'mean' and 'variance' used in the inference process are the 'moving average mean' and 'moving average variance' counted by training data. In this pipeline, two domains (visible data and thermal infrared data) are share the backbone network. So, 'moving average mean' and 'moving average variance' may be computed by both visible data and thermal infrared data so that the distribution between train data and test data becomes more and more different, and as a result it leads to a bad inference result. In our experiment, when the Batch-Normalization layers is frozen during training, the network is easier to overfitting. So, we use different routes to calculate statistics of dataset, respectively.

Compared with Baseline. Firsly, we try to prove that multi-modal fusion can achieve better results than single mode. Therefore, we test the performance of state-of-art models on the single modality of our benchmark dataset. We select several advanced RGB crowd counter for evaluations, including MCNN [12], CMTL [26], MSCNN [27], ACSCP [28], SANET [29], StackPooling [30], DA-NET [31], CSRNet [15], SCAR [32], CANNET [33], BL [34]. Specifically, these models are trained by a single modal data and tested in corresponding modal test dataset, respectively. The experiment results is shown in Table 2.

In addition, in order to evaluate that our proposed model can more effectively and efficiently integrate the two modal features, we compare our method with other baseline models. Baseline #1 This pipeline is a two-stream network which each stream is the first three blocks of ResNet-50 and is used to extract modal-specific feature. And then the output of each stream are concatenated in channel dimension. After reducing the dimension by a convolution layer with 1 * 1 kernel

Table 3. Comparison of our approach with other proposed baseline on DroneRGBT dataset.

Method	Precision		Model size (M)	Speed (fps)	GFLOPs
	MAE	RMSE			
Baseline #1	7.18	11.43	20.72	22	16.54
Baseline #2	11.07	17.15	9.39	24	15.00
MMCCN	7.27	11.45	10.47	17	16.55

Table 4. The performance of three heads on several break-down subsets.

Method	Overall		Dark		Dusky		Light	
	MAE	RMSE	MAE	RMSE	MAE	RMSE	MAE	RMSE
MMCCN (RGB)	11.53	16.75	19.76	24.52	11.14	16.07	10.03	15.23
MMCCN (T)	7.49	11.91	**11.35**	**15.95**	7.09	11.19	7.16	11.69
MMCCN	**7.27**	**11.45**	12.02	15.96	**6.92**	**11.00**	**6.83**	**10.69**

size, the high-level fusion feature is learned by the backend network. The regression module of this pipeline is same as our proposed pipeline. Baseline #2 Apart from the first convolution layer which is used to extract modal-specific feature, the whole pipeline is share the same weight like siamese network [35]. The final prediction result is the average of the prediction by each branch. Comparison results are shown in Table 3.

It can be seen that our MMCCN performs favorably against the state-of-the-art methods. Our MMCCN obtains 7.27 MAE score and 11.45 RMSE score, but the most competitor BL [34] gets 7.41 MAE score and 11.56 RMSE score. The result shows that modality fusion can further improve the counting result. Compared with other two baselines, although the accuracy of our model is slightly lower than that of the baseline #1, our model has less parameters, and each modality is decoupled in MMCCN so that it can work well even if the input is only a single modality. Because there is no module coupling between MMCCN(T) and MMCCN(RGB), they can work independently and still achieve competitive prediction results. Further more, the performance of three heads on several break-down subsets is shown in Table 4.

Ablation Study. To analyse the importance of each component of our proposed MMCCN model, we additionally construct some variants and evaluate them on the Drone-RGBT dataset. MMCCN (sBN) means that the Batch-Normalization layer of model only has one route as the original ResNet. MMCCN (fBN) stands for the Batch-Normalization of the pipeline is frozen when training the network. MMCCN (w/o mam) indicates the model that removes discriminator model of Modal Alignment Module. And the network is only trained by loss $J(M)$.

Table 5. Comparison of our approach with its variants to prove the importance of each component.

Method	Overall	
	MAE	RMSE
MMCCN (sBN)	17.56 (↓ 10.29)	22.34 (↓ 10.89)
MMCCN (fBN)	11.46 (↓ 4.19)	16.41 (↓ 4.96)
MMCCN (w/o me)	7.34 (↓ 0.07)	11.74 (↓ 0.29)
MMCCN (w/o mam)	7.28 (↓ 0.01)	11.76 (↓ 0.31)
MMCCN	7.27	11.45

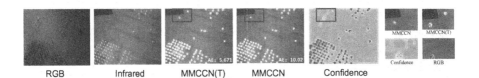

RGB   Infrared   MMCCN(T)   MMCCN   Confidence

Fig. 6. Qualitative results of MMCCN.

MMCCN (w/o me) denotes the method that further remove two modality extractors of Multi-scale Feature Learning Module.

All variants are trained on the training set and tested on the testing set. The training steps and other parameters are identical, and meanwhile the evaluation protocol in different experiments are same too. From Table 5, it shows that our MMCCN achieves better results than its variants.

Qualitative Results. From the quantitative results, we find that fusion based on confidence can improve the prediction results. To test the difference between the density map predicted by MMCCN and MMCCN(T), we visualize the density map respectively shown in Fig. 6. In addition, we also visualize the confidence map predicted by our Adaptive Fusion Module. From the qualitative results, we find that due to the noise of infrared data, result of MMCCN(T) may contain some false positives. By utilizing both RGB and Infrared feature, model will reduce the confidence of false positive. As the result, the prediction results improved.

5.2 Experiments on Single Modality

Training Details. DM-CycleGAN is trained on the training set of DroneRGBT. During the training phase, the λ and μ are set as 10 and 100, respectively. We use the Adam solver with a batch size of 1. All networks were trained from scratch with a learning rate of 0.0002. Data augmentations like rotation, random crop are used to avoid overfitting.

Table 6. The performance of generated image on pre-trained MMCCN.

Method	MMCCN		SSIM
	MAE	RMSE	
MMCCN (RGB)	11.53	16.75	–
CycleGAN*	13.45	18.99	0.44
DM-CycleGAN*	10.92	16.19	0.49

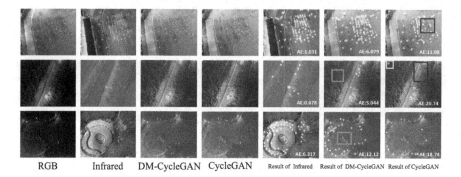

RGB   Infrared   DM-CycleGAN CycleGAN   Result of Infrared   Result of DM-CycleGAN Result of CycleGAN

Fig. 7. Qualitative results of CycleGAN and DM-CycleGAN. (Color figure online)

Results on MMCCN Without Re-Trained. We generate fake infrared images by using the visible data in our testing set of DroneRGBT. To test the meaningful of the generated image, we take the generated images as the input of the MMCCN to test whether it can improve the prediction results compared with the single modality. The MMCCN(RGB) method corresponds to the MMCCN method only accepting RGB image. The DM-CycleGAN* and CycleGAN* method receive both RGB image and infrared image. But the infrared image in DM-CycleGAN* is generated from DM-CycleGAN, and CycleGAN* method generates infrared image through CycleGAN. Results in Table 6 shows that DM-CycleGAN* performs inferior than MMCCN(RGB) (*i.e.*, 10.92 MAE score vs. 11.53 MAE score). It proves that multi-modality can improve the results though the information content of fake infrared image is based on visible image. At the same time, the Structural Similarity Index (SSIM) between the generated image and real image are also shown in this table. This experiment proves DM-CycleGAN and MMCCN can be used together to boost the result when we only have one modal data.

Qualitative Results. Some generated images and corresponding real thermal infrared images are shown in Fig. 7. Besides, we visualize the density map predicted by thermal infrared head of our model–MMCCN(T). From the results, we find that the infrared images generated by CycleGAN will miss some local information so that the MMCCN can not detect the person (red rectangle). At the same time, without the constraint of DM loss, false positive will appear (yellow rectangle). Our DM-CycleGAN can focus on the local details of people so that it will be predicted by MMCCN. However, it will also miss some information compared with real data due to poor visibility of visible data (green rectangle).

6 Conclusions

In this paper, we presented a benchmark for RGB-T crowd counting. This is a drone-view dataset with different attributes. With the benchmark, we proposed a Multi-Modal Crowd Counting Network for RGBT crowd-counting. DM-CycleGAN is proposed for generating the infrared data for MMCCN when we only have visible data. Through analyzing the quantitative and qualitative results, we demonstrated the effectiveness of the proposed approach.

Acknowledgments. This work was supported in part by the National Natural Science Foundation of China under Grant 61876127 and Grant 61732011, Natural Science Foundation of Tianjin under Grant 17JCZDJC30800 and The Applied Basic Research Program of Qinghai under Grants 2019-ZJ-7017.

References

1. Laradji, I.H., Rostamzadeh, N., Pinheiro, P.O., Vazquez, D., Schmidt, M.: Where are the blobs: counting by localization with point supervision. In: Ferrari, V., Hebert, M., Sminchisescu, C., Weiss, Y. (eds.) ECCV 2018. LNCS, vol. 11206, pp. 560–576. Springer, Cham (2018). https://doi.org/10.1007/978-3-030-01216-8_34
2. Sam, D.B., Surya, S., Babu, R.V.: Switching convolutional neural network for crowd counting. In: 2017 IEEE Conference on Computer Vision and Pattern Recognition (CVPR), pp. 4031–4039. IEEE (2017)
3. Wang, Q., Gao, J., Lin, W., Yuan, Y.: Learning from synthetic data for crowd counting in the wild. In: Proceedings of the IEEE Conference on Computer Vision and Pattern Recognition, pp. 8198–8207 (2019)
4. Ranjan, V., Le, H., Hoai, M.: Iterative crowd counting. In: Ferrari, V., Hebert, M., Sminchisescu, C., Weiss, Y. (eds.) ECCV 2018. LNCS, vol. 11211, pp. 278–293. Springer, Cham (2018). https://doi.org/10.1007/978-3-030-01234-2_17
5. Li, C., Wu, X., Zhao, N., Cao, X., Tang, J.: Fusing two-stream convolutional neural networks for RGB-T object tracking. Neurocomputing **281**, 78–85 (2018)
6. López-Fernández, L., Lagüela, S., Fernández, J., González-Aguilera, D.: Automatic evaluation of photovoltaic power stations from high-density RGB-T 3D point clouds. Remote Sens. **9**, 631 (2017)
7. Zhai, S., Shao, P., Liang, X., Wang, X.: Fast RGB-T tracking via cross-modal correlation filters. Neurocomputing **334**, 172–181 (2019)
8. Zhang, X., Ye, P., Peng, S., Liu, J., Xiao, G.: DSiamMFT: an RGB-T fusion tracking method via dynamic Siamese networks using multi-layer feature fusion. Signal Process. Image Commun. **84**, 15756 (2020)
9. Chan, A.B., Liang, Z.S.J., Vasconcelos, N.: Privacy preserving crowd monitoring: Counting people without people models or tracking. In: 2008 IEEE Conference on Computer Vision and Pattern Recognition, pp. 1–7. IEEE (2008)

10. Chen, K., Loy, C.C., Gong, S., Xiang, T.: Feature mining for localised crowd counting. In: BMVC, vol. 1, p. 3 (2012)
11. Zhang, C., Kang, K., Li, H., Wang, X., Xie, R., Yang, X.: Data-driven crowd understanding: a baseline for a large-scale crowd dataset. IEEE Trans. Multimedia **18**, 1048–1061 (2016)
12. Zhang, Y., Zhou, D., Chen, S., Gao, S., Ma, Y.: Single-image crowd counting via multi-column convolutional neural network. In: Proceedings of the IEEE Conference on Computer Vision and Pattern Recognition, pp. 589–597 (2016)
13. Idrees, H., Saleemi, I., Seibert, C., Shah, M.: Multi-source multi-scale counting in extremely dense crowd images. In: Proceedings of the IEEE Conference on Computer Vision and Pattern Recognition, pp. 2547–2554 (2013)
14. Idrees, H., et al.: Composition loss for counting, density map estimation and localization in dense crowds. In: Ferrari, V., Hebert, M., Sminchisescu, C., Weiss, Y. (eds.) ECCV 2018. LNCS, vol. 11206, pp. 544–559. Springer, Cham (2018). https://doi.org/10.1007/978-3-030-01216-8_33
15. Li, Y., Zhang, X., Chen, D.: CSRNET: dilated convolutional neural networks for understanding the highly congested scenes. In: Proceedings of the IEEE Conference on Computer Vision and Pattern Recognition, pp. 1091–1100 (2018)
16. Li, C., Wang, G., Ma, Y., Zheng, A., Luo, B., Tang, J.: A unified RGB-T saliency detection benchmark: dataset, baselines, analysis and a novel approach. arXiv preprint arXiv:1701.02829 (2017)
17. Tu, Z., Xia, T., Li, C., Wang, X., Ma, Y., Tang, J.: RGB-T image saliency detection via collaborative graph learning. IEEE Trans. Multimedia **22**, 160–173 (2019)
18. Li, C., Liang, X., Lu, Y., Zhao, N., Tang, J.: RGB-T object tracking: benchmark and baseline. Pattern Recogn. **96**, 106977 (2019)
19. Li, C., Cheng, H., Hu, S., Liu, X., Tang, J., Lin, L.: Learning collaborative sparse representation for grayscale-thermal tracking. IEEE Trans. Image Process. **25**, 5743–5756 (2016)
20. He, K., Zhang, X., Ren, S., Sun, J.: Deep residual learning for image recognition. In: Proceedings of the IEEE Conference on Computer Vision and Pattern Recognition, pp. 770–778 (2016)
21. Radford, A., Metz, L., Chintala, S.: Unsupervised representation learning with deep convolutional generative adversarial networks. arXiv preprint arXiv:1511.06434 (2015)
22. Mao, X., Li, Q., Xie, H., Lau, R.Y., Wang, Z., Paul Smolley, S.: Least squares generative adversarial networks. In: Proceedings of the IEEE International Conference on Computer Vision, pp. 2794–2802 (2017)
23. Zhu, J.Y., Park, T., Isola, P., Efros, A.A.: Unpaired image-to-image translation using cycle-consistent adversarial networks. In: Proceedings of the IEEE International Conference on Computer Vision, pp. 2223–2232 (2017)
24. Kingma, D.P., Ba, J.: Adam: a method for stochastic optimization. arXiv preprint arXiv:1412.6980 (2014)
25. Ioffe, S., Szegedy, C.: Batch normalization: accelerating deep network training by reducing internal covariate shift. arXiv preprint arXiv:1502.03167 (2015)
26. Sindagi, V.A., Patel, V.M.: CNN-based cascaded multi-task learning of high-level prior and density estimation for crowd counting. In: 2017 14th IEEE International Conference on Advanced Video and Signal Based Surveillance (AVSS), pp. 1–6. IEEE (2017)
27. Zeng, L., Xu, X., Cai, B., Qiu, S., Zhang, T.: Multi-scale convolutional neural networks for crowd counting. In: 2017 IEEE International Conference on Image Processing (ICIP), pp. 465–469. IEEE (2017)

28. Shen, Z., Xu, Y., Ni, B., Wang, M., Hu, J., Yang, X.: Crowd counting via adversarial cross-scale consistency pursuit. In: Proceedings of the IEEE Conference on Computer Vision and Pattern Recognition, pp. 5245–5254 (2018)
29. Cao, X., Wang, Z., Zhao, Y., Su, F.: Scale aggregation network for accurate and efficient crowd counting. In: Ferrari, V., Hebert, M., Sminchisescu, C., Weiss, Y. (eds.) ECCV 2018. LNCS, vol. 11209, pp. 757–773. Springer, Cham (2018). https://doi.org/10.1007/978-3-030-01228-1_45
30. Huang, S., Li, X., Cheng, Z.Q., Zhang, Z., Hauptmann, A.: Stacked pooling: improving crowd counting by boosting scale invariance. arXiv preprint arXiv:1808.07456 (2018)
31. Zou, Z., Su, X., Qu, X., Zhou, P.: DA-NET: learning the fine-grained density distribution with deformation aggregation network. IEEE Access **6**, 60745–60756 (2018)
32. Gao, J., Wang, Q., Yuan, Y.: Scar: spatial-/channel-wise attention regression networks for crowd counting. Neurocomputing **363**, 1–8 (2019)
33. Liu, W., Salzmann, M., Fua, P.: Context-aware crowd counting. In: Proceedings of the IEEE Conference on Computer Vision and Pattern Recognition, pp. 5099–5108 (2019)
34. Ma, Z., Wei, X., Hong, X., Gong, Y.: Bayesian loss for crowd count estimation with point supervision. In: Proceedings of the IEEE International Conference on Computer Vision, pp. 6142–6151 (2019)
35. Chopra, S., Hadsell, R., LeCun, Y.: Learning a similarity metric discriminatively, with application to face verification. In: 2005 IEEE Computer Society Conference on Computer Vision and Pattern Recognition (CVPR 2005), vol. 1, pp. 539–546. IEEE (2005)

Webly Supervised Semantic Embeddings
for Large Scale Zero-Shot Learning

Yannick Le Cacheux[✉], Adrian Popescu, and Hervé Le Borgne

Université Paris-Saclay, CEA, List, 91120 Palaiseau, France
yannicklecacheux@gmail.com

Abstract. Zero-shot learning (ZSL) makes object recognition in images possible in absence of visual training data for a part of the classes from a dataset. When the number of classes is large, classes are usually represented by semantic class prototypes learned automatically from unannotated text collections. This typically leads to much lower performances than with manually designed semantic prototypes such as attributes. While most ZSL works focus on the visual aspect and reuse standard semantic prototypes learned from generic text collections, we focus on the problem of semantic class prototype design for large scale ZSL. More specifically, we investigate the use of noisy textual metadata associated to photos as text collections, as we hypothesize they are likely to provide more plausible semantic embeddings for visual classes if exploited appropriately. We thus make use of a source-based filtering strategy to improve the robustness of semantic prototypes. Evaluation on the large scale ImageNet dataset shows a significant improvement in ZSL performances over two strong baselines, and over usual semantic embeddings used in previous works. We show that this improvement is obtained for several embedding methods, leading to state of the art results when one uses automatically created visual and text features.

1 Introduction

Zero-shot learning (ZSL) is useful when an artificial agent needs to recognize classes which have no associated visual data but can be represented by semantic knowledge [1]. The agent is first trained with a set of seen classes, which have visual samples. Then, it needs to recognize instances from either only unseen classes (classical zero-shot learning scenario) or both seen and unseen classes (generalized zero-shot learning). To do so, it has access to visual features and to semantic class prototypes. Most (generalized) zero-shot learning works focus on the proposal of adapted loss functions [2–7] or on the induction of visual features for unseen classes via generative approaches [8–11]. Here, we use standard components for the visual part of the ZSL pipeline and instead study the influence

---

Electronic supplementary material The online version of this chapter (https://doi.org/10.1007/978-3-030-69544-6_31) contains supplementary material, which is available to authorized users.

© Springer Nature Switzerland AG 2021
H. Ishikawa et al. (Eds.): ACCV 2020, LNCS 12627, pp. 514–531, 2021.
https://doi.org/10.1007/978-3-030-69544-6_31

of semantic class prototypes. Early works exploit manually created attributes [12–14] to define these prototypes. While efficient, it requires a very costly annotation effort and is difficult to scale to large datasets. Different strategies were proposed to automate the creation of prototypes in order to tackle large scale ZSL. An early attempt [15] exploited WordNet to extract part attributes. This method nevertheless assumes that tested datasets can be mapped to WordNet, which is often impossible. The current trend, which leverages advances in natural language processing [16–18], is to exploit standard word embeddings as semantic prototypes. These embeddings are extracted from generic large scale text collections such as Wikipedia [16,17] or Common Crawl [19,20]. The advantage of such methods is that prototype creation is based solely on webly supervised or unsupervised collections. However, following [21,22], only standard embeddings extracted from generic collections were tested in ZSL.

We tackle the creation of semantic class prototypes for large scale ZSL via a method enabling to suitably leverage more adapted text collections for word embedding creation. The standard generic texts are replaced by metadata associated with photo corpora because the latter are more likely to capture relevant visual relations between words. Our method includes processing of the textual content to improve the semantic plausibility of prototypes [20] and exploits a source-based voting strategy to improve robustness of word co-occurrences [23,24]. We evaluate the proposed approach for automatic building of semantic prototypes using different text collections. We also perform an ablation study to test the robustness with respect to collection size and provide a detailed error analysis. Results for a large scale collection show our approach enables consistent performance improvement compared to existing automatic prototypes. Interesting performance is also obtained for smaller datasets, where the proposed prototypes reduce the gap with manual prototypes. Our contributions can be summarized as follows:

- We focus on the understudied problem of semantic prototype design for ZSL, and propose a method to create better embeddings from noisy tags datasets.
- We conduct extensive experiments and ablation studies to (1) demonstrate the effectiveness of the proposed method; (2) provide a variety of results with different embeddings which can be used for future fair comparison; (3) provide insight on the remaining challenges to close the gap between manual and unsupervised semantic prototypes.
- We collect new corpora and produce state-of-the-art semantic class prototypes for large-scale ZSL which will be released to the community. The code is released at https://github.com/yannick-lc/semantic-embeddings-zsl.

2   Related Work

Zero-Shot Learning. Zero-shot learning [25–28] attempts to classify samples belonging to *unseen classes*, for which no training samples are available. Visual samples are available during training for *seen classes* and both seen classes and unseen classes have "semantic" prototypes associated to them.

The first ZSL approaches were introduced a decade ago [26–28] and a strong research effort has been devoted to the topic ever since [1,3,29–33]. Several of these works relied on a triplet loss to group relevant visual sample close to the prototype in the joint space while discarding irrelevant ones [2,4–7,34]. In the generalized zero-shot learning (GZSL) setting, performance is evaluated both on seen and unseen classes [35]. Then, a strong bias towards recognizing seen classes appears [36]. It is nevertheless possible to tune the hyper-parameters of a ZSL method to boost its performance in a GZSL setting [37]. Recent generative approaches propose to learn discriminative models on unseen classes from artificial samples resulting from a generative model previously learned on seen classes [8–11]. The transductive ZSL setting assumes that the unlabelled visual testing samples can be used during training [38–41]. This usually boosts the performance, but we consider such a hypothesis too restrictive in practice, and this setting is out of the scope here.

Semantic Representation. Semantic prototypes can be created either manually or automatically. Since the former are difficult to scale, we focus on automatically created ones, that usually rely on large-scale datasets collected on the Web. The extraction of word representations from the contexts in which they appear is a longstanding topic in natural language processing (NLP). Explicit Semantic Analysis (ESA) [42] is an early attempt to exploit topically structured collections to derive vectorial representations of words. It proposes to represent each word by its tf-idf weights with regard to a large collection of Wikipedia entries (articles). ESA was later improved by adding a temporal aspect to it [43] or by the detection and use of concepts instead of unigrams [44]. ESA and its derivates have good performance in word relatedness and text classification tasks. However, they are relatively difficult to scale because they live in the vectorial space defined by Wikipedia concepts which typically includes millions of entries.

The most influential word representation models in the past years are based on the exploitation of the local context. Compared to ESA, they have the advantage of being orders of magnitude more compact, with typical sizes in the range of hundreds of dimensions. word2vec embeddings [45] are learned from co-occurrences in local context window which are modeled using continuous bag-of-words and skip grams. This model usually outperforms bag-of-words [19,20,45]. Some preprocessing steps such as removal of duplicate sentences, phrase detection to replace unigrams, use of subword information or frequent word subsampling is beneficial to the performances [20]. One shortcoming of word embeddings as proposed in [45] is that they only take into account the local context of words. GloVe [18] was introduced as an alternative method which also includes a global component obtained via matrix factorization. The model trains efficiently only on non-zero word-word co-occurrence matrix instead of a sparse matrix or on local windows. It provides superior performance compared to continuous bag-of-words and skip gram models on a series of NLP tasks, including word analogy and similarity. The FastText model [19] derives from that proposed by Mikolov but considers a set of n-grams that can compose the words, compute some embeddings then represent a word as the sum of the vector representation of its n-grams. It thus models the internal structure of the words and allows to compute out of vocabulary word representations. The state of the art in a large array of natural language processing task was recently improved by the introduction of contextual models such as ELMo [46], GPT [47] or BERT [48]. These approaches make use of deep networks and model language at sentence level instead of word level as was the case for skip grams and GloVe. While very interesting for tasks in which words are contextualized, they are not directly applicable to our ZSL scenario which requires the representation of individual words/class names.

Multimodal Representations. The word representation approaches presented above exploit only textual resources and there are also attempts to create multimodal word embeddings. Early works projected the vocabulary on a bag-of-visual-words space for image retrieval [49]. More recently, vis-w2v [50] exploits synthetic scenes to learn visual relations between classes. The main challenge here is to model the diversity of natural scenes via synthetic scenes. ViCo [51] exploit word co-occurrences in natural images in order to improve purely textual GloVe embeddings. Visual and textual components complement each other and thus improve performance in tasks such as visual question answering, image retrieval or image captioning. However, an inherent drawback of all these multimodal representations requires representative images of any word to consider and is thus not usable in ZSL for unseen classes. Regarding visual features only, [52,53] showed that one can train convolutional networks on a dataset of unannotated images collected on the Web, and that these networks perform well in a transfer learning context. Previous works in ZSL used embeddings to represent the semantic prototype, either at a small scale on CUB [54] or at a larger scale on ImageNet, using word2vec [2,35,55] (possibly trained on wikipedia [6,21]), GloVe [22,34], FastText or ELMo [56]. However, they only use publicly available pre-trained models, while we propose a method to design prototypes that perform better in a ZSL context.

3   Semantic Class Prototypes for Large Scale ZSL

Problem Formulation. The zero-shot learning (ZSL) task considers a set $\mathscr{C}_s$ of *seen* classes used during training and a set $\mathscr{C}_u$ of *unseen* classes that are available for the test only. In generalized zero-shot learning (GZSL), additional samples from the seen classes are used for testing as well. However, in both cases, $\mathscr{C}_s \cap \mathscr{C}_u = \emptyset$. Each class has a semantic *class prototype* $\mathbf{s}_c \in \mathbb{R}^K$ that characterizes it. We consider a training set $\{(\mathbf{x}_i, y_i), i = 1 \ldots N\}$ with labels $y_i \in \mathscr{C}_s$ and visual features $\mathbf{x}_i \in \mathbb{R}^D$. The task is to learn a compatibility function $f : \mathbb{R}^D \times \mathbb{R}^K \rightarrow \mathbb{R}$ assigning a similarity score to a visual sample $\mathbf{x}$ and a class prototype $\mathbf{s}$. f is usually obtained by minimizing a regularized loss function:

$$\frac{1}{N}\sum_{i=1}^{N}\sum_{c=1}^{|\mathscr{C}_s|}\mathscr{L}(f(\mathbf{x}_i, \mathbf{s}_c), y_i) + \lambda\Omega[f] \qquad (1)$$

where Ω is a regularization term weighted by λ which constrains the parameters of f, and $\mathscr{L}$ is a loss function. Once a function f is learned, the testing phase consists in determining the label $\hat{y} \in \mathscr{C}_u$ (or $\hat{y} \in \mathscr{C}_s \cup \mathscr{C}_u$ for GZSL) corresponding to a visual sample $\mathbf{x}$ such that $\hat{y} = \arg\max_{c \in \mathscr{C}_u} f(\mathbf{x}, \mathbf{s}_c)$.

We propose to automatically derive semantic class prototypes $\mathbf{s}_c$ with a method able to adequately leverage noisy corpora which are adapted for visual tasks instead of standard text corpora previously used in ZSL [16,18,19]. More specifically, a corpus must contain enough visual information to enable to learn discriminative embeddings. We therefore create two corpora, $\mathbf{fl_{wiki}}$ and $\mathbf{fl_{cust}}$, with this goal in mind.

Corpus Collection. $\mathbf{fl_{wiki}}$ is constituted based on Wikipedia. We select salient concepts by ranking English Wikipedia entries by their number of incoming links and keeping the top $120,000$ of the list. The default Flickr ranking algorithm is then used to collect up to 5000 photo metadata for each concept. Metadata fields which are exploited here include: (1) *title* – a free text description of the photo (2) *tags* – a list of tags attributed to the photo and (3) the unique identifier of the user. Note that there is no guarantee as to the relevance of textual metadata for the content of each photo since the users are free to upload any text they wish. Also, photo annotations can be made in any language. We illustrate title and tags from Flickr with the following examples: *"Ísmáfur Pagophila eburnea Ivory Gull"* and *"minnesota flying inflight gull arctic juvenile duluth rare lakesuperior canalpark ivorygull saintlouiscounty"*. The title includes the Icelandic, Latin and English variants of the name while the tags give indications about the location and activity of the ivory gull. Importantly, tags can be single words (*"gull"*) or concatenated ones (*"ivorygull"*, *"lakesuperior"*). This first collection is made of 62.7 million image metadata pieces and 1.11 billion words.

The fl_{wiki} collection allows to learn generic embeddings that can be used to address large scale ZSL. However, these embeddings are still quite "generic" since they are representative of the Wikipedia concepts. For a given ZSL problem, the visual samples of unseen classes are unknown during training, but the name of these classes can be known before the actual production (testing) phase. Such a hypothesis is implicitly made by most generative ZSL approaches, which synthesize faked visual samples from the prototype only [8–11]. Following a similar hypothesis, we build $\mathbf{fl_{cust}}$, a custom subset of FlickR, which is built using the class names from the three ZSL used in evaluation datasets (ImageNet-ZSL, CUB and AWA). The collection process is similar to that deployed for fl_{wiki}. The only difference is that we use specific class names, which may each have several variants. This collection includes 61.9 million metadata pieces and 995 million unique words.

Each collection therefore consists in a list of $C \leq 120,000$ concepts. For each class c, we have a metadata set $\mathcal{M}_c = \{m_1, \ldots, m_{N_c}\}$ made of $N_c \leq 5,000$ metadata pieces. Each metadata piece m_n consists in a user ID id_n and a list of T_n words $\mathcal{W}_n = \{w_1, \ldots, w_{T_n}\}$, where the words are extracted from titles and tags. T_n is typically in the range of one to two dozens. Note that stop words were discarded during preprocessing.

Creation of Embeddings. To create text representations, a vocabulary $\mathcal{V} = \{v_1, \ldots, v_V\}$ is constituted to include all V distinct words in the corpus. We similarly create a set $\mathcal{U} = \{u_1, \ldots, u_U\}$ of all distinct users IDs. The usual skip-gram task [16] aims to find word representations which contain predictive information regarding the words surrounding a given word. Given a sequence $\{w_1, \ldots, w_T\}$ of T training words such that $w_t \in \mathcal{V}$ and a context of size S, the objective is to maximize

$$\sum_{t=1}^{T} \sum_{\substack{-S \leq i \leq S \\ i \neq 0}} \log p(w_{t+i}|w_t) \tag{2}$$

Writing $v_{w_t} \in \mathcal{V}$ the unique word associated with the tth training word w_t and $\mathbf{v}_{w_t}$ and $\mathbf{v}'_{w_t}$ the corresponding "input" and "output" vector representations, $p(w_i|w_t)$ can be computed such that

$$p(w_i|w_t) = \frac{\exp(\mathbf{v}'^{\top}_{w_i} \mathbf{v}_{w_t})}{\sum_{j=1}^{V} \exp(\mathbf{v}'^{\top}_{j} \mathbf{v}_{w_t})} \tag{3}$$

Unlike in standard text collections, such as Wikipedia, the order of words in each metadata collection $\mathcal{M}_n$ is arbitrary. Consequently, using a fixed size window to capture the context of a word is not suitable. We tested the use of fixed size windows in preliminary experiments and results were suboptimal.

Instead, we consider that two words v_i and v_j appear in the same context if both of them appear in the same list of words $\mathcal{W}_n$ of metadata result m_n. The skip-gram objective in Eq. 2 can therefore be rewritten as

$$\sum_{c=1}^{C} \sum_{n=1}^{N_c} \sum_{\substack{(v_i, v_j) \\ v_i, v_j \in \mathcal{W}_n, \ i \neq j}} \log p(v_i|v_j) \tag{4}$$

This is equivalent to extracting all pairs of words (v_i, v_j) such that v_i, v_j belong to the same $\mathcal{W}_n$ in a training file, and feeding this resulting corpus to a word embedding model. This has the advantage of enabling the use of available implementations such as word2vec [16] to learn the word embeddings.

Addressing Repetitive Tags. It is noteworthy that many users perform bulk tagging [24] which consists in attributing the same textual description to a whole set of photos. Users also do semi-bulk, i.e. they attribute a part of tags to an entire photo set and then complete these annotations with photo-specific tags. Bulk is known to bias language models obtained from Flickr [23,24]. To account for this problem, we add an additional processing step for the two collections. The authors of [23] and [24] suggested to replace simple tag co-occurrences by the number of distinct Flickr users who associated the two words and reported interesting gains in image retrieval and automatic geotagging respectively.

In our case, this translates into adding a pair (v_i, v_j) in the training file only once for each user and thus avoiding the effect of bulk tagging. A positive side effect of filtering pairs with unique users is that the size of the training file is reduced and embeddings are learned faster. A comparison of performance obtained with raw co-occurrence and with user filtering is provided in the supplementary material.

The same ideas can easily be applied to other word embedding approaches. In the next section, we provide experimental results with three such approaches: word2vec [16], GloVe [18] and FastText [19].

4   Experiments

4.1   Evaluation Protocol

Baseline Methods. To the best of our knowledge, our work is the first to explicitly address the problem of semantic class prototype design for large scale ZSL. We compare to the pre-trained embeddings (noted **pt**), as they are usually used in previous ZSL works [2,22,55]. word2vec is trained on Google News with 100 billion words, GloVe is trained on Common Crawl with 840 billion words and the same collection with 600 billion words is used for FastText.

We also propose two baseline methods, (**wiki**) and (**clue**), to which ours can be fairly compared. They consist in learning the embeddings from two different text collections. Wikipedia (**wiki**) is classically exploited to create embeddings because it covers a wide array of topics [42]. *wiki* content is made of entries which describe unambiguous concepts with well formed sentences such as *"The ivory gull is found in the Arctic, in the northernmost parts of Europe and North America."*. The encyclopedia provides good baseline models for a wide variety of tasks [16,18,20]. Here we exploit a dump from January 2019 which includes 20.84 billion words. It is the same data as that from which were extracted the 120,000 concepts for our method. While useful to create transferable embeddings, Wikipedia text does nevertheless not specifically describe visual relations between words. The second baseline is based on visually oriented textual content similar to the one used in our method. The ClueWeb12 [57] collection (**clue**) consists of over 700 million Web pages which were collected so as to cover a wide variety of topics and to avoid spam. We extracted visual metadata from the *title* and *alt* HTML attributes associated to *clue* images. The title content is quite similar to that we extracted from FlickR in our method. *clue* content is often made of short texts such as *"ivory gull flying"* which does not encode a lot of context. After sentence deduplication [20], the resulting collection includes 628 million unique metadata pieces and 3.69 billion words.

Evaluation Datasets. The generic object recognition in ZSL requires to be evaluated at a large scale and is thus usually conducted on ImageNet [58]. Frome et al. [2] proposed to use the $1,000$ classes of ILSVRC for training and different subsets of the remaining $20,841$ classes to test. However, it has been recently showed that a structural bias appears in this setting which allows a "trivial model" to outperform most existing ZSL models [22]. For this reason, we adopt the evaluation protocol proposed by Hascoet *et al.* that considers the same training classes as Frome *et al.* but uses 500 classes with a minimal structural bias for testing [22].

To get insight into the gap existing between manual attributes and unsupervised embeddings, we also conduct experiments on two smaller benchmarks on which the ZSL task is usually conducted with manual attributes specific to each dataset: Caltech UCSD Birds 200-2011 (CUB) [13] and Animals with Attributes 2 (AwA2) [21]. CUB is a fine-grained dataset of 11788 pictures representing 200 bird species and AWA2 a coarse-grained dataset of 37322 pictures depicting 50 animal species. The manual attributes of CUB and AwA2 are respectively 312 and 85-dimensional. In our setting, we are only concerned with semantic prototypes which can be obtained automatically; our results therefore cannot be directly compared to the state-of-the-art algorithms which exploit manual attributes. For CUB and AWA2, we adopt the experimental protocol of Xian *et al.* [21] which relies on *proposed splits* that avoid any overlap between the (unseen) test classes and the ImageNet classes used to pretrain visual features on ILSVRC. For ImageNet, we use the same visual features as [22] while for CUB and AwA2 we adopt those of [21].

ZSL Methods. Experiments are conducted with different existing ZSL methods: we provide results for DeViSE [2], ESZSL [3] and ConSE [32] as they are the three standard methods used in [22], and therefore the only methods for which comparable results are currently available. Although results for other models – namely GCN-6 [59], GCN-2 and ADGPM [60] – are also reported in [22], these models are based on graph-convolutional networks [61] which make use of additional intermediate nodes in the WordNet hierarchy. Such methods are outside the scope of this study. We additionally provide results for SynC [6] as well as two linear methods, consisting in a linear projection from the visual to the visual space ($\text{Linear}_{V \to S}$), and a linear projection from the semantic to the visual space ($\text{Linear}_{S \to V}$) inspired by [30], who proposed to compute similarities in the visual space to avoid the hubness problem [62].

We train the models with the usual protocol for ZSL: hyperparameters are determined using a subset of training classes as validation. We sample respectively 200 and 50 such classes at random among the 1000 and 150 training classes of ImageNet and CUB, and use the 8 classes not in ILSVRC among the

Table 1. ZSL accuracy at large scale (ImageNet dataset), for three embedding models. Each time, the three baselines (*pt*, *wiki* and *clue*) are compared to our method $\text{fl}_{\textbf{wiki}}$ and its variation $\text{fl}_{\textbf{cust}}$. Results marked with "*" correspond to a setting close to Table 2 from Hascoet *et al.* [22], and are consistent with reported results.

Model	word2vec					GloVe					FastText				
Source	*pt*	wiki	clue	$\text{fl}_{\textbf{wiki}}$	$\text{fl}_{\textbf{cust}}$	*pt*	wiki	clue	$\text{fl}_{\textbf{wiki}}$	$\text{fl}_{\textbf{cust}}$	*pt*	wiki	clue	$\text{fl}_{\textbf{wiki}}$	$\text{fl}_{\textbf{cust}}$
$\text{Linear}_{V \to S}$	*6.8*	9.8	9.6	10.5	12.6	*10.2*	6.2	4.2	9.6	9.2	*6.0*	8.9	2.8	11.6	**14.2**
$\text{Linear}_{S \to V}$	*11.6*	11.8	12.2	12.8	17.1	*14.1*	7.9	8.0	9.2	11.4	*14.4*	12.1	8.0	13.3	**17.2**
ESZSL	*10.5*	10.0	10.7	9.5	15.3	*14.1**	8.0	10.3	11.1	12.0	*14.2*	10.1	1.1	11.9	**15.8**
ConSE	*9.9*	10.5	11.3	11.9	13.5	*11.3**	8.1	7.8	11.3	11.9	*11.0*	10.5	5.4	12.6	**14.5**
Devise	*9.0*	9.8	9.9	9.6	13.3	*11.0**	5.9	5.4	3.8	3.4	*12.3*	10.1	5.6	10.3	**13.8**
SynC_{o-vs-o}	*12.2*	12.4	12.6	12.5	16.3	*15.0*	10.9	11.2	12.4	13.3	*14.6*	12.6	7.0	13.2	**16.5**

40 training classes of AwA2. Since ConSE and DeViSE results depend on a random initialization of the models' parameters, we report results averaged over 5 runs for these two models.

Implementation Details. Word embeddings are computed using the original implementations of word2vec [16], GloVe [18] and FastText[19], with the same hyperparameters (see supplementary materials). In particular, we follow the usual text processing steps they propose. Semantic prototypes for all classes are computed using the same protocol as [22] for fair comparison. For the same reason, we use the implementation from [22] to run DeViSE, ESZSL, ConSE. We use the implementation from [6] for SynC, and use a custom straightforward implementation for $\text{Linear}_{V \to S}$ and $\text{Linear}_{S \to V}$. All semantic prototypes are $\ell 2$-normalized except with ESZSL to have a setting similar to [22] when applicable. We report results without such a normalization in the supplementary materials, even though the trend is mostly the same.

4.2   Comparison to Other Approaches

The main results of the evaluation are reported in Table 1 for ImageNet. They confirm the relevance of our method and text collections to learn semantic prototypes for ZSL, as the best results are consistently obtained with our prototypes. Specifically, for ImageNet, the best result reported on the unbiased split in [22] is 14.1 with ADGPM, and 13.5 with a "traditional" ZSL model (not making use of additional nodes in the class hierarchy), which used GloVe embeddings pretrained on Common Crawl. By contrast, our best result is 17.2 with FastText, obtained with embeddings trained on a much smaller dataset.

We also provide results for CUB and AwA2 in Table 2. These results are less relevant since manual attributes exist for these smaller scale datasets, but still provide interesting insights. Importantly, these results are obtained using *unsupervised* prototypes and should not be directly compared to results obtained with manual attributes. On CUB, the best results are obtained with the embeddings

Table 2. ZSL accuracy at smaller scale with unsupervised semantic class prototypes. Results are reported on the CUB and Awa2 datasets, for three embedding models.

Model	word2vec					GloVe					FastText				
Source	pt	wiki	clue	fl_{wiki}	fl_{cust}	pt	wiki	clue	fl_{wiki}	fl_{cust}	pt	wiki	clue	fl_{wiki}	fl_{cust}
CUB dataset															
Linear$_{V \to S}$	7.5	14.0	13.9	12.2	16.3	8.0	11.6	9.8	12.7	14.2	7.2	13.8	12.2	11.6	**17.5**
Linear$_{S \to V}$	11.3	18.0	17.2	21.5	23.0	18.2	16.0	13.4	14.6	19.0	16.1	16.2	16.0	19.9	**24.4**
ESZSL	15.8	20.4	17.9	23.0	25.2	19.9	17.5	16.9	19.0	20.8	21.1	18.7	1.7	23.5	**26.5**
ConSE	8.3	19.5	21.6	18.0	21.1	14.1	15.1	14.9	16.8	18.4	14.0	17.7	19.9	17.6	**23.4**
Devise	12.6	17.0	15.8	19.0	19.2	14.6	16.3	9.9	18.4	14.8	16.0	13.2	13.7	17.4	**22.5**
SynC$_{o-vs-o}$	15.3	19.8	17.3	20.3	21.3	17.6	17.2	17.6	21.6	20.5	17.0	15.0	15.7	20.2	**24.0**
Awa2 dataset															
Linear$_{V \to S}$	31.1	40.2	38.5	**43.6**	37.9	40.4	26.9	34.6	40.5	43.3	42.1	39.9	28.1	38.5	41.6
Linear$_{S \to V}$	38.1	44.1	49.7	53.9	55.0	56.6	42.4	48.1	41.2	**57.7**	54.7	49.3	14.4	50.4	46.5
ESZSL	40.9	42.2	55.8	53.1	57.1	**61.4**	37.7	49.0	48.2	44.3	48.2	37.6	7.9	49.7	54.6
ConSE	27.4	31.3	34.3	**43.3**	39.2	31.3	27.4	29.8	38.4	41.4	34.7	31.3	16.7	42.3	42.1
Devise	37.2	34.1	46.6	33.7	43.4	43.2	42.6	44.9	30.6	36.4	52.0	40.7	13.5	32.7	37.6
SynC$_{o-vs-o}$	43.9	41.1	45.8	47.1	47.5	46.9	46.6	47.4	50.0	52.1	53.3	40.0	15.2	45.5	48.1

learned on the fl_{cust} collection for the three configurations and significantly outperform previous embeddings. Interestingly, there does not seem to be a clear tendancy on AwA2. It turns out that performance obtainable with unsupervised prototypes on AwA2 is already quite close to performance with manual attributes – see Sect. 4.4. Our method is therefore unable to provide a significant improvement, unlike on the other two datasets.

Within each embeddings methods for all three datasets, the best results are usually obtained with fl_{cust} and fl_{wiki} usually performs better than baseline methods. The gain is especially large when compared to the largest available pretrained models for word2vec and FastText. This result is obtained although the largest collections used to create pretrained embeddings are 2 to 3 orders of magnitude larger than the collections we use. For GloVe on ImageNet, the model pretrained on Common Crawl has the best performance. This embedding has poor behavior for all smaller scale datasets, indicating that the combination of local and global contexts at its core is able to capture interesting information at large scale. While its performance on the smaller pretrained dataset is significantly lower than that of FastText, the two models are nearly equivalent when trained on Common Crawl. A similar finding was reported for text classification tasks [20]. The strong performance of fl_{cust} follows intuition since the collection was specifically built to cover the concepts which appear in the three test dataset. This finding confirms the usefulness of smaller but adapted collections for NLP applications such as medical entity recognition [63] or sentiment analysis [64]. Note that we also combined fl_{wiki} and fl_{cust} to obtain a more generic Flickr model. The obtained results were only marginally better compared to the single use of fl_{cust} and are reported in the supplementary material.

Overall, the best performance is usually obtained with fl_{cust} and FastText embeddings.

Table 3. ZSL performance with 0%, 50%, 75% and 90% data removed from wiki and fl_{cust} collections, on the ImageNet dataset. With FastText embeddings.

Collection	Data removed	0%	50%	75%	90%
wiki	Linear$_{S \to V}$	12.1	11.6	11.3	10.2
	ESZSL	10.1	9.8	9.9	9.6
	ConSE	10.5	11.0	10.5	9.9
	Devise	10.1	8.3	8.7	8.0
fl_{cust}	Linear$_{S \to V}$	17.2	16.8	16.3	15.6
	ESZSL	15.8	15.1	15.3	14.3
	ConSE	14.5	14.1	14.1	14.3
	Devise	13.8	13.4	13.2	12.5

4.3   Influence of Text Collection Size

The quality of semantic embeddings is influenced by the size of the text collections used to learn them. Existing comparisons are usually done among different collections [16, 18, 19]. While interesting, these comparisons do not provide direct information about the robustness of each collection. To test robustness, we ablate 50%, 75% and 90% of fl_{cust} and wiki collections and report results for ImageNet using FastText embeddings in Table 3. As expected, performance is correlated to the collection size, with the best results being obtained for full text collections and the worst when 90% of them is removed. Interestingly, the performance drop is not drastic for either of the collection. For instance, with only 10% of the initial collections, accuracy drops from 12.1 to 10.2 for *wiki* (15.7% relative drop) and from 17.2 to 15.6 for fl_{cust} (9.3% relative drop). Indeed, according to the Zipf's law, the sorted frequency of words in a language is a decreasing power law. Hence, small corpus contain most of frequent words and increasing their size is useful only to address rare cases. The relative drop is smaller for fl_{cust} compared to wiki, showing that a collection which is adapted for the task is more robust to changes in the quantity of available data.

4.4   Comparison to Manual Attributes

Although our webly semantic prototypes enable to achieve much better results than with previously available prototypes extracted from text corpora, it is still interesting to compare them to what can be achieved with hand-crafted attributes. Such attributes do not exist for very large scale datasets such as ImageNet, but they are provided with smaller scale datasets such as CUB and AwA2.

   To quantify how much better hand-crafted prototypes perform when compared to webly supervised prototypes, we conducted an ablation study on CUB attributes similar to Sect. 4.3. We started with the full list of attributes, initially comprising 312 attributes for each bird species, and randomly removed

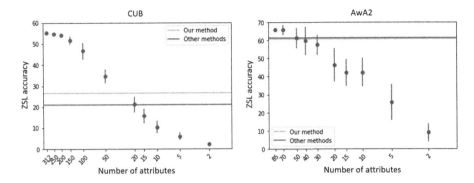

Fig. 1. Ablation of manual attributes on CUB and AwA2. Measured with the linear model, averaged over 10 runs (points and bars are mean ± std) with different attributes removed each time. Best results for prototypes based on word embeddings are also reported (horizontal lines).

attributes while measuring the resulting ZSL score. The scores where obtained with the Linear$_{S \to V}$ model due to its good results, robustness and simplicity. To account for the noise caused by the randomness of the removed attributes, each reported score is the average of 10 measurements, each with different random attributes removed. The remaining attributes are $\ell 2$-normalized, and the hyper-parameter is re-selected by cross-validation for each run. Figure 1 provides a visualization of the result; a table with the exact scores is available in the supplementary materials.

On CUB, there is still a substantial margin for improvement; even though our method enables a significant increase over other methods, it is still barely above results achievable by selecting only 20 attributes among the 312 initial attributes. Interestingly, the difference between webly supervised and hand-crafted prototypes is not so pronounced on the AwA2 dataset; the ZSL accuracy between the two settings is even surprisingly close. This may be explained by the fact that AwA2 only contains 10 test classes; class prototypes need not enable a ZSL model to subtly distinguish very similar classes. Consequently, our best result is comparable to the best result enabled by previous methods.

4.5 Error Analysis

We analyze how far incorrect predictions are from the correct class by computing the distance between the predicted class and the correct class. We define the distance between two classes as the shortest path between them in the WordNet hierarchy. For a given distance d, we measure the number of predictions that are exactly d nodes away from the correct class – a distance of 0 being a correct prediction. Results for $wiki$ and fl_{cust} are presented in Fig. 2(a); the general tendency seems to be that classes farther away from the correct class are less likely to be predicted. Note that no two test classes are a distance of one from

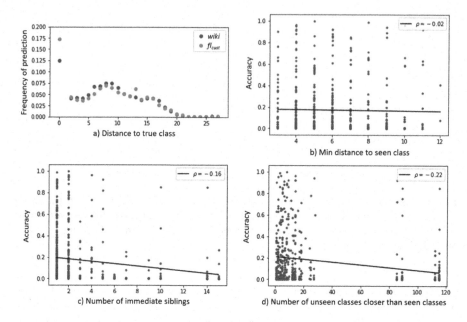

Fig. 2. (a) Distance from predicted class to correct class in the WordNet hierarchy. Correlation ρ between ZSL accuracy and (b) distance to the closest seen class (c) the number of immediate unseen test class siblings (d) the number of unseen classes closer than the closest seen class, for all 500 unseen ImageNet classes.

each other, since it is not possible for a test class to be a direct parent or child of another test class.

We further analyze the main factors behind classification errors. Experiments below are conducted on ImageNet, with the $\text{Linear}_{S \to V}$ model trained using the FastText fl_{cust} embeddings. Our first hypothesis was that the distance between unseen and seen classes influences classification accuracy: the less an unseen class resembles any seen class, the harder it is to identify. To test this hypothesis, we consider for each unseen class c_u the minimal distance to a seen class $\min_{c \in \mathscr{C}_s} d(c_u, c)$, and analyze its relation to the prediction accuracy. The resulting plot is displayed in Fig. 2(b). Surprisingly, the distance to the closest seen class seems to have little to no effect on the accuracy (correlation $\rho = -0.02$).

Another hypothesis was that unseen classes close to other unseen classes are harder to classify than isolated unseen classes, as more confusions are possible. For each unseen class, we therefore compute the number of immediate siblings, a sibling being defined as an unseen class having the same parent in the WordNet hierarchy as the reference (unseen) class. The link between this metric and class accuracy is slightly stronger, with a correlation $\rho = -0.16$ as illustrated in Fig. 2(c), but still weak overall.

We combine these two hypotheses by considering the number of unseen classes closer than the closest seen class for each unseen class. The link with class accuracy is more pronounced than by simply considering the number of siblings, with a correlation $\rho = -0.22$ as illustrated in Fig. 2(d). Examples of classes at both ends of the spectrum are visible in Fig. 3: unseen class *morel* (on the left) is close to seen class *agaric* and has no unseen siblings; its class accuracy is 0.63. On the other hand, classes *holly*, *teak* and *grevillea* (on the right) have many unseen siblings and are far from any seen class; their respective accuracy are 0.01, 0.00 and 0.03. More generally, classes which are descendant of the intermediate node *woody plant* have an average accuracy of 0.053. The full graph visualization of the 1000 training classes, 500 testing classes and intermediate nodes of the ImageNet ZSL dataset is provided in the supplementary materials.

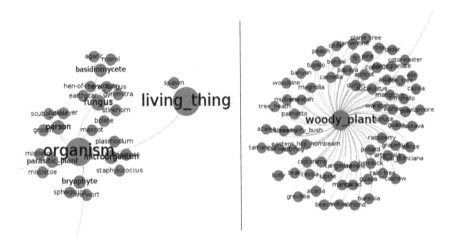

Fig. 3. Graph visualization of parts of the WordNet hierarchy. Green and pink leaves are resp. seen and unseen classes. Intermediate nodes are orange if there is no seen class among their children, and blue otherwise. Full graph is available in the supp. materials. (Color figure online)

5 Conclusion

We proposed a new method to build semantic class prototypes automatically, thus enabling to better address large scale ZSL. Our results indicate that appropriately learning embeddings on specialized collections made of photo metadata is better than exploiting generic embeddings as it was done previously in ZSL. This still stands when generic embeddings are learned with collections which are two to three orders of magnitude larger than specialized collections. Among photo metadata based collection, the use of Flickr seems preferable to that of metadata associated to photos from Web pages. This is notably an effect of a better semantic coverage of classes in Flickr compared to ClueWeb12.

References

1. Socher, R., Ganjoo, M., Manning, C.D., Ng, A.: Zero-shot learning through cross-modal transfer. In: Advances in Neural Information Processing Systems, pp. 935–943 (2013)
2. Frome, A., Corrado, G.S., Shlens, J., Bengio, S., Dean, J., Mikolov, T., et al.: Devise: a deep visual-semantic embedding model. In: Advances in Neural Information Processing Systems, pp. 2121–2129 (2013)
3. Romera-Paredes, B., Torr, P.: An embarrassingly simple approach to zero-shot learning. In: International Conference on Machine Learning, pp. 2152–2161 (2015)
4. Akata, Z., Reed, S., Walter, D., Lee, H., Schiele, B.: Evaluation of output embeddings for fine-grained image classification. In: Computer Vision and Pattern Recognition, pp. 2927–2936. IEEE (2015)
5. Akata, Z., Perronnin, F., Harchaoui, Z., Schmid, C.: Label-embedding for image classification. Pattern Anal. Mach. Intell. **38**, 1425–1438 (2016)
6. Changpinyo, S., Chao, W.L., Gong, B., Sha, F.: Synthesized classifiers for zero-shot learning. In: Computer Vision and Pattern Recognition, pp. 5327–5336. IEEE (2016)
7. Annadani, Y., Biswas, S.: Preserving semantic relations for zero-shot learning. In: Computer Vision and Pattern Recognition, pp. 7603–7612 (2018)
8. Verma, V.K., Rai, P.: A simple exponential family framework for zero-shot learning. In: Ceci, M., Hollmén, J., Todorovski, L., Vens, C., Džeroski, S. (eds.) ECML PKDD 2017. LNCS (LNAI), vol. 10535, pp. 792–808. Springer, Cham (2017). https://doi.org/10.1007/978-3-319-71246-8_48
9. Bucher, M., Herbin, S., Jurie, F.: Zero-shot classification by generating artificial visual features. In: RFIAP (2018)
10. Verma, V.K., Arora, G., Mishra, A., Rai, P.: Generalized zero-shot learning via synthesized examples. In: Computer Vision and Pattern Recognition (2018)
11. Xian, Y., Lorenz, T., Schiele, B., Akata, Z.: Feature generating networks for zero-shot learning. In: Computer Vision and Pattern Recognition (2018)
12. Patterson, G., Hays, J.: Sun attribute database: discovering, annotating, and recognizing scene attributes. In: Computer Vision and Pattern Recognition, pp. 2751–2758. IEEE (2012)
13. Wah, C., Branson, S., Welinder, P., Perona, P., Belongie, S.: The Caltech-UCSD Birds-200-2011 dataset. Technical report CNS-TR-2011-001, California Institute of Technology (2011)
14. Lampert, C.H., Nickisch, H., Harmeling, S.: Attribute-based classification for zero-shot visual object categorization. Pattern Anal. Mach. Intell. **36**, 453–465 (2014)
15. Rohrbach, M., Stark, M., Schiele, B.: Evaluating knowledge transfer and zero-shot learning in a large-scale setting. In: Computer Vision and Pattern Recognition, pp. 1641–1648 (2011)
16. Mikolov, T., Sutskever, I., Chen, K., Corrado, G.S., Dean, J.: Distributed representations of words and phrases and their compositionality. In: Advances in Neural Information Processing Systems, pp. 3111–3119 (2013)
17. Huang, E., Socher, R., Manning, C., Ng, A.: Improving word representations via global context and multiple word prototypes. In: Proceedings of the 50th Annual Meeting of the Association for Computational Linguistics (Volume 1: Long Papers), Jeju Island, Korea, pp. 873–882. Association for Computational Linguistics (2012)

18. Pennington, J., Socher, R., Manning, C.: Glove: global vectors for word representation. In: Proceedings of the 2014 Conference on Empirical Methods in Natural Language Processing (EMNLP), Doha, Qatar, pp. 1532–1543. Association for Computational Linguistics (2014)
19. Bojanowski, P., Grave, E., Joulin, A., Mikolov, T.: Enriching word vectors with subword information. Trans. Assoc. Comput. Linguist. **5**, 135–146 (2017)
20. Mikolov, T., Grave, E., Bojanowski, P., Puhrsch, C., Joulin, A.: Advances in pre-training distributed word representations. In: Proceedings of the Eleventh International Conference on Language Resources and Evaluation (LREC 2018), Miyazaki, Japan, European Languages Resources Association (ELRA) (2018)
21. Xian, Y., Lampert, C.H., Schiele, B., Akata, Z.: Zero-shot learning-a comprehensive evaluation of the good, the bad and the ugly. Pattern Anal. Mach. Intell. **41**, 2251–2265 (2018)
22. Hascoet, T., Ariki, Y., Takiguchi, T.: On zero-shot recognition of generic objects. In: Computer Vision and Pattern Recognition (2019)
23. Popescu, A., Grefenstette, G.: Social media driven image retrieval. In: Proceedings of the 1st ACM International Conference on Multimedia Retrieval, ICMR 2011, New York, NY, USA, pp. 33:1–33:8. ACM (2011)
24. O'Hare, N., Murdock, V.: Modeling locations with social media. Inf. Retr. **16**, 30–62 (2013)
25. Akata, Z., Perronnin, F., Harchaoui, Z., Schmid, C.: Label-embedding for attribute-based classification. In: Computer Vision and Pattern Recognition, pp. 819–826 (2013)
26. Lampert, C.H., Nickisch, H., Harmeling, S.: Learning to detect unseen object classes by between-class attribute transfer. In: Computer Vision and Pattern Recognition, pp. 951–958. IEEE (2009)
27. Larochelle, H., Erhan, D., Bengio, Y.: Zero-data learning of new tasks. In: AAAI Conference on Artificial Intelligence (2008)
28. Palatucci, M., Pomerleau, D., Hinton, G.E., Mitchell, T.M.: Zero-shot learning with semantic output codes. In: Advances in Neural Information Processing Systems, pp. 1410–1418 (2009)
29. Zhang, Z., Saligrama, V.: Zero-shot learning via semantic similarity embedding. In: International Conference on Computer Vision, pp. 4166–4174 (2015)
30. Shigeto, Y., Suzuki, I., Hara, K., Shimbo, M., Matsumoto, Y.: Ridge regression, hubness, and zero-shot learning. In: Appice, A., Rodrigues, P.P., Santos Costa, V., Soares, C., Gama, J., Jorge, A. (eds.) ECML PKDD 2015. LNCS (LNAI), vol. 9284, pp. 135–151. Springer, Cham (2015). https://doi.org/10.1007/978-3-319-23528-8_9
31. Rahman, S., Khan, S., Porikli, F.: A unified approach for conventional zero-shot, generalized zero-shot, and few-shot learning. IEEE Trans. Image Process. **27**, 5652–5667 (2018)
32. Norouzi, M., et al.: Zero-shot learning by convex combination of semantic embeddings. In: International Conference on Learning Representations (2014)
33. Xian, Y., Akata, Z., Sharma, G., Nguyen, Q., Hein, M., Schiele, B.: Latent embeddings for zero-shot classification. In: Computer Vision and Pattern Recognition, pp. 69–77 (2016)
34. Changpinyo, S., Chao, W.L., Gong, B., Sha, F.: Classifier and exemplar synthesis for zero-shot learning. arXiv preprint arXiv:1812.06423 (2018)
35. Chao, W.-L., Changpinyo, S., Gong, B., Sha, F.: An empirical study and analysis of generalized zero-shot learning for object recognition in the wild. In: Leibe, B., Matas, J., Sebe, N., Welling, M. (eds.) ECCV 2016. LNCS, vol. 9906, pp. 52–68. Springer, Cham (2016). https://doi.org/10.1007/978-3-319-46475-6_4

36. Xian, Y., Schiele, B., Akata, Z.: Zero-shot learning - the good, the bad and the ugly. In: Computer Vision and Pattern Recognition, pp. 3077–3086. IEEE (2017)
37. Le Cacheux, Y., Le Borgne, H., Crucianu, M.: From classical to generalized zero-shot learning: a simple adaptation process. In: Kompatsiaris, I., Huet, B., Mezaris, V., Gurrin, C., Cheng, W.-H., Vrochidis, S. (eds.) MMM 2019. LNCS, vol. 11296, pp. 465–477. Springer, Cham (2019). https://doi.org/10.1007/978-3-030-05716-9_38
38. Fu, Y., Hospedales, T.M., Xiang, T., Gong, S.: Transductive multi-view zero-shot learning. Pattern Anal. Mach. Intell. **37**, 2332–2345 (2015)
39. Kodirov, E., Xiang, T., Fu, Z., Gong, S.: Unsupervised domain adaptation for zero-shot learning. In: International Conference on Computer Vision, pp. 2452–2460 (2015)
40. Rohrbach, M., Ebert, S., Schiele, B.: Transfer learning in a transductive setting. In: Advances in Neural Information Processing Systems, pp. 46–54 (2013)
41. Song, J., Shen, C., Yang, Y., Liu, Y., Song, M.: Transductive unbiased embedding for zero-shot learning. In: Computer Vision and Pattern Recognition, pp. 1024–1033 (2018)
42. Gabrilovich, E., Markovitch, S.: Computing semantic relatedness using wikipedia-based explicit semantic analysis. In: Proceedings of the 20th International Joint Conference on Artificial Intelligence, IJCAI 2007, San Francisco, CA, USA, pp. 1606–1611. Morgan Kaufmann Publishers Inc. (2007)
43. Radinsky, K., Agichtein, E., Gabrilovich, E., Markovitch, S.: A word at a time: computing word relatedness using temporal semantic analysis. In: Proceedings of the 20th International Conference on World Wide Web, WWW 2011, New York, NY, USA, pp. 337–346. ACM (2011)
44. Hassan, S., Mihalcea, R.: Semantic relatedness using salient semantic analysis. In: Proceedings of the Twenty-Fifth AAAI Conference on Artificial Intelligence, AAAI 2011, pp. 884–889. AAAI Press (2011)
45. Mikolov, T., Sutskever, I., Chen, K., Corrado, G.S., Dean, J.: Distributed representations of words and phrases and their compositionality. In: Burges, C.J.C., Bottou, L., Welling, M., Ghahramani, Z., Weinberger, K.Q. (eds.) Advances in Neural Information Processing Systems, vol. 26, pp. 3111–3119. Curran Associates, Inc. (2013)
46. Peters, M., et al.: Deep contextualized word representations. In: Proceedings of the 2018 Conference of the North American Chapter of the Association for Computational Linguistics: Human Language Technologies, Volume 1 (Long Papers), New Orleans, Louisiana, pp. 2227–2237. Association for Computational Linguistics (2018)
47. Radford, A., Narasimhan, K., Salimans, T., Sutskever, I.: Improving language understandingby generative pre-training (2018)
48. Devlin, J., Chang, M.W., Lee, K., Toutanova, K.: BERT: Pre-training of deep bidirectional transformers for language understanding. In: Proceedings of the 2019 Conference of the North American Chapter of the Association for Computational Linguistics: Human Language Technologies, Volume 1 (Long and Short Papers), Minneapolis, Minnesota, pp. 4171–4186. Association for Computational Linguistics (2019)
49. Znaidia, A., Shabou, A., Le Borgne, H., Hudelot, C., Paragios, N.: Bag-of-multimedia-words for image classification. In: 2012 21st International Conference on Pattern Recognition (ICPR), pp. 1509–1512. IEEE (2012)

50. Kottur, S., Vedantam, R., Moura, J.M.F., Parikh, D.: Visual word2vec (vis-w2v): learning visually grounded word embeddings using abstract scenes. In: Computer Vision and Pattern Recognition. (2016)
51. Gupta, T., Schwing, A., Hoiem, D.: Vico: word embeddings from visual co-occurrences. In: International Conference on Computer Vision (2019)
52. Joulin, A., van der Maaten, L., Jabri, A., Vasilache, N.: Learning visual features from large weakly supervised data. In: Leibe, B., Matas, J., Sebe, N., Welling, M. (eds.) ECCV 2016. LNCS, vol. 9911, pp. 67–84. Springer, Cham (2016). https://doi.org/10.1007/978-3-319-46478-7_5
53. Vo, P., Ginsca, A.L., Le Borgne, H., Popescu, A.: Harnessing noisy web images for deep representation. In: Computer Vision and Image Understanding (2017). Online Jan 2017
54. Akata, Z., Malinowski, M., Fritz, M., Schiele, B.: Multi-cue zero-shot learning with strong supervision. In: Computer Vision and Pattern Recognition (2016)
55. Le Cacheux, Y., Le Borgne, H., Crucianu, M.: Modeling inter and intra-class relations in the triplet loss for zero-shot learning. In: International Conference on Computer Vision, Seoul, Korea (2019)
56. Le Cacheux, Y., Le Borgne, H., Crucianu, M.: Using sentences as semantic representations in large scale zero-shot learning. In: Bartoli, A., Fusiello, A. (eds.) Computer Vision – ECCV 2020 Workshops, ECCV 2020. Lecture Notes in Computer Science, vol. 12535. Springer, Cham (2020). https://doi.org/10.1007/978-3-030-66415-2_42
57. Callan, J.: The lemur projectand its clueweb12 dataset (2012)
58. Deng, J., Dong, W., Socher, R., Li, L.J., Li, K., Fei-Fei, L.: ImageNet: a large-scale hierarchical image database. In: Computer Vision and Pattern Recognition, pp. 248–255. IEEE (2009)
59. Wang, X., Ye, Y., Gupta, A.: Zero-shot recognition via semantic embeddings and knowledge graphs. In: Proceedings of the IEEE Conference on Computer Vision and Pattern Recognition, pp. 6857–6866 (2018)
60. Kampffmeyer, M., Chen, Y., Liang, X., Wang, H., Zhang, Y., Xing, E.P.: Rethinking knowledge graph propagation for zero-shot learning. In: Proceedings of the IEEE Conference on Computer Vision and Pattern Recognition, pp. 11487–11496 (2019)
61. Kipf, T.N., Welling, M.: Semi-supervised classification with graph convolutional networks. arXiv preprint arXiv:1609.02907 (2016)
62. Radovanović, M., Nanopoulos, A., Ivanović, M.: Hubs in space: popular nearest neighbors in high-dimensional data. J. Mach. Learn. Res. **11**, 2487–2531 (2010)
63. El Boukkouri, H., Ferret, O., Lavergne, T., Zweigenbaum, P.: Embedding strategies for specialized domains: application to clinical entity recognition. In: Proceedings of the 57th Annual Meeting of the Association for Computational Linguistics: Student Research Workshop, Florence, Italy, pp. 295–30. Association for Computational Linguistics (2019)
64. Kameswara Sarma, P., Liang, Y., Sethares, B.: Domain adapted word embeddings for improved sentiment classification. In: Proceedings of the Workshop on Deep Learning Approaches for Low-Resource NLP, Melbourne, pp. 51–59. Association for Computational Linguistics (2018)

Compensating for the Lack of Extra Training Data by Learning Extra Representation

Hyeonseong Jeon[1], Siho Han[2], Sangwon Lee[2], and Simon S. Woo[2]([✉])

[1] Department of Artificial Intelligence, Sungkyunkwan University,
Suwon, South Korea
cutz@g.skku.edu
[2] Department of Applied Data Science, Sungkyunkwan University,
Suwon, South Korea
{siho.han,lee1465,swoo}@g.skku.edu

Abstract. Outperforming the previous state of the art, numerous deep learning models have been proposed for image classification using the ImageNet database. In most cases, significant improvement has been made through novel data augmentation techniques and learning or hyper-parameter tuning strategies, leading to the advent of approaches such as FixNet, NoisyStudent, and Big Transfer. However, the latter examples, while achieving the state-of-the-art performance on ImageNet, required a significant amount of *extra training data*, namely the JFT-300M dataset. Containing 300 million images, this dataset is 250 times larger in size than ImageNet, but is publicly unavailable, while the model pre-trained on it is. In this paper, we introduce a novel framework, Extra Representation (ExRep), to surmount the problem of not having access to the JFT-300M data by instead using ImageNet and the publicly available model that has been pre-trained on JFT-300M. We take a *knowledge distillation* approach, treating the model pre-trained on JFT-300M as well as on ImageNet as the teacher network and that pre-trained only on ImageNet as the student network. Our proposed method is capable of learning additional representation effects of the teacher model, bolstering the student model's performance to a similar level to that of the teacher model, achieving high classification performance even without extra training data.

1 Introduction

The success of deep learning has been prominent in the image classification domain [1–4], partly, yet most importantly, since the ImageNet Large Scale Visual Recognition Challenge (ILSVRC) 2012 with the development of the ImageNet database. Even after ILSVRC 2012, ImageNet has been the de facto standard benchmark dataset for image classification. A sizeable body of research [5,6]

Electronic supplementary material The online version of this chapter (https://doi.org/10.1007/978-3-030-69544-6_32) contains supplementary material, which is available to authorized users.

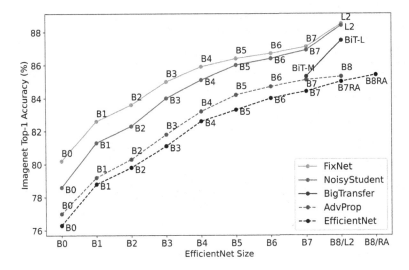

Fig. 1. Top-1 accuracy on ImageNet. Dotted lines represent the performance without extra training data, whereas solid lines represent that with extra training data. RA denotes RandAugment. (Color figure online)

involved the ImageNet data for the evaluation of their methods in terms of classification accuracy. However, the proposed methods typically relied on convolutional neural networks (CNNs), facing inevitable limitations due to their lack of generalization ability to the ImageNet validation set.

Only a few approaches managed to overcome these limitations by self-training with a noisy student (NoisyStudent) [7], fixing the train-test resolution (FixNet) [8], or scaling up pre-training (Big Transfer or BiT) [9]. From Fig. 1, we can observe that the latter (solid red, yellow, and blue lines in Fig. 1) approaches achieve higher top-1 accuracy than the state-of-the-art architecture, EfficientNet (black dotted line in Fig. 1), using extra training data. NoisyStudent introduced a novel training strategy, that is, self-training with a noisy student; FixNet proposed an effective training method, using the train-test image resolution discrepancy; BiT took a transfer learning approach similar to that used for language modeling, whereby a model pre-trained on a large task is fine-tuned for use in a smaller task. The achievement of high top-1 accuracy of these three methods is attributed to multiple factors, such as a massive number of parameters (NoisyStudent and FixNet each has about 480 million parameters), high resolution images by 800×800 interpolations, AutoAugment [10] by policy gradient agents, and optimized architectures by neural architecture search [11]. Most importantly, however, all three methods exploit vast amounts of extra training data, which, as shown in many cases, such as for CIFAR10 and CIFAR100 [12], and SVHN [13], generally leads to higher classification performance.

Developed by Google for internal use, the JFT-300M dataset [14] consists of 300 million images labeled with 18,291 categories. While offering an impressive

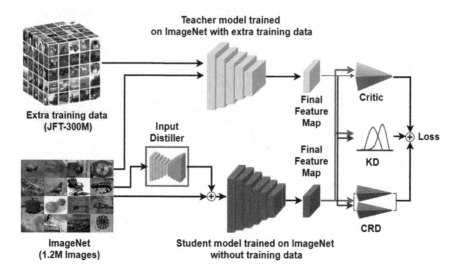

Fig. 2. Overview of our ExRep framework. The input distiller (red box) learns the discrepancy between ImageNet and JFT-300M and the output is fed to the student model. From the final feature maps of the teacher and student models are computed three loss functions—the critic loss, the knowledge distillation (KD) loss, and the contrastive representation distillation (CRD) loss. (Color figure online)

amount of 1.2 million images, ImageNet pales in comparison to the JFT-300M dataset, solely considering the number of samples. Nonetheless, the JFT-300M dataset is not publicly available, making it nearly impossible to reproduce the results yielded by approaches using this data. In this work, we aim at achieving a classification performance that is on par with those of the aforementioned models, which used the JFT-300M dataset as extra training data. In particular, based on the hypothesis that the model pre-trained on both ImageNet and JFT-300M (the "teacher model") contains significantly more representational information than that pre-trained only on ImageNet (the "student model"), as demonstrated by the high classification performance of NoisyStudent [7], FixNet [8], and BiT [9], we leverage the discrepancy (the "extra representation") between the teacher and student models; if the student model learns to replicate the representational behavior of the teacher model, then the student model would be able to achieve equally high classification performance on ImageNet as the teacher model.

As shown in Fig. 2, we apply knowledge distillation [14] to achieve our learning objective, which is to transfer the knowledge acquired by the teacher model during pre-training to the student model. We introduce an autoencoder-based *input distiller* (red box in Fig. 2) to replicate the effect of training on JFT-300M by feeding the reconstructed output of the input distiller to the student model, which differs from many prior works that directly train the weights of the student model. We also propose a novel adversarial training [15] technique to effectively train our input distiller, which acts as the generator in Generative Adversarial Networks (GANs). We place the discriminator at the final feature layer of the pre-trained models to distinguish whether the output is from the teacher model or the student model. Finally, we compute the loss function by aggregating the critic loss, the knowledge distillation (KD) loss [14], and the contrastive representation distillation (CRD) [16] loss obtained by comparing the final feature maps of the teacher and student models, as shown in Fig. 2. Consequently, we can effectively represent the additional representation that would have been available had we had direct access to the JFT-300M dataset itself. This training procedure thus renders the model representation more informative, enabling us to achieve high classification performance as if our training set also consisted of JFT-300M; we refer to the integrated, end-to-end framework comprised of these components as ExRep. We also demonstrate that ExRep can be used to train a randomly initialized model without any extra training data and that ExRep is reproducible even if models are trained using randomly initialized weights.

2 Related Work

Image classification. Since the advent of Xception [5], CNN architectures have been deeper and broader: combining ResNet [4] and Xception, ResNeXt [17] achieved high classification performance on ImageNet. Also, the use of optimal CNN blocks, enabled by neural architecture search [11], led to popular models, such as EfficientNet (B0 through B7 or L2, depending on the compound scaling) [6]. Since most approaches exploiting extra training data use EfficientNet as their backbone network, we also use EfficientNet to prepare our teacher and student models for knowledge distillation. However, previous methods also incorporate other methods, such as novel learning strategies or data augmentation techniques, to further improve the ImageNet classification performance beyond the one that can be achieved by the sole use of EfficientNet as the backbone.

Image Classification with Extra Training Data. Many prior works utilize large datasets for model representations by weakly supervised learning [9,18,19]. Joulin et al. [19] used the Flickr-100M dataset [20], although the performance was lower than that of approaches using JFT-300M [14] or Instagram-1B [21], which is an internal dataset for Facebook generated from Instagram images. NoisyStudent [7], FixNet [8], and BiT [9] used the JFT-300M dataset, based on weakly supervised learning. NoisyStudent applied self-training, where the teacher model and a bigger and noisy student model guide each other by exchanging feedback. FixNet employed different train-test resolutions, demonstrating that a low train resolution with a fine-tuning of the model at the test resolution improves the test classification accuracy. BiT combined well-organized components and simple heuristic methods from prior works on image classification, using upstream pre-training and downstream fine-tuning (a huge pre-trained model and a tiny fine-tuned model), Group Normalization [22], and Weight Standardization [23]. BiT has BiT-S, BiT-M, and BiT-L as the model size grows. As of now, these methods constitute state of the art for image classification on ImageNet (see Fig. 1), but are not reproducible using a randomly initialized training model due to the limited access to the JFT-300M dataset; that is, only the model pre-trained on JFT-300M is publicly available instead of the dataset itself.

Image Classification Without Extra Training Data. Leveraging policy gradient agents for parameter search for image augmentation, AutoAugment (AA) [10] achieved high classification accuracy on ImageNet without extra training data. RandAugment (RA) [24], of which the performance is shown in Fig. 1, reduced the search space of AA, achieving the highest accuracy with the EfficientNet-B8 backbone; however, RA is computationally expensive. Unlike other methods using adversarial examples [25,26], which only focus on model robustness against adversarial attacks, AdvProp [27] aims at improving model generalization as well. They apply Auxiliary Batch Normalization (ABN) [28] for the training of a novel classifier. Based on these prior work, we attempt to further improve the classification performance without using any extra training data.

Knowledge Distillation. Applied for the computation of our loss function as well, knowledge distillation [14] (KD) has been proposed to alleviate the computational cost resulting from training a large model or an ensemble of models by transferring the acquired knowledge to a smaller model. The latter student model is trained under the guidance of the large pre-trained teacher model, such that the student model replicates the soft targets of the teacher model. Yim et al. [29] proposed a weight-based knowledge distillation method, where the flow of solution procedure (FSP) matrix, defined by the Gramian matrix of adjacent layers in the same model, is learned during the training phase. This approach is similar to ours in that an additional layer is added, but ours, which is the input distiller, is added to the input images and not to the intermediate layers [29].

Zagoruyko and Komodakis [30] proposed to transfer the neuron responses during the process by which the student model learns to classify images; this work additionally suggests an attention transfer method whereby the activation-based and gradient-based spatial attention maps are matched. The attention-based method has been further generalized by Huang and Wang [31], who proposed to minimize the Maximum Mean Discrepancy (MMD) metric of the distributions of neuron selectivity patterns between the teacher and student models. Heo et al. [32] proposed an activation transfer loss that is minimized when the activation boundaries formed by hidden neurons in the student model coincide with those in the teacher model.

However, most prior works, attempting to minimize the Kullback–Leibler (KL) divergence between the probabilistic outputs of the teacher and student models, tend to overlook important structural knowledge of the teacher model. Motivated by InfoNCE loss [33], Tian et al. [16] thus proposed CRD, which formulates a contrastive learning objective by which the student model is trained to capture additional information in the teacher model's data representation, achieving superior performance to those of previous approaches using attention-based KD [30,31] and initialization-based KD [32,34]. Therefore, in our work, we

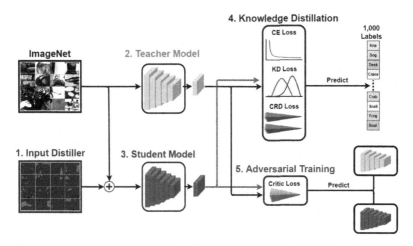

Fig. 3. Illustration of our training pipeline. CE, KD, and CRD denote Cross Entropy, Knowledge Distillation, and Contrastive Representation Distribution, respectively. Models in the two black boxes at the lower right corner represent the teacher model (top) and the student model (bottom). The CE, KD, and CRD losses are used to predict 1,000 labels, whereas the critic loss is used to predict whether the final feature map is from the teacher model or the student model. Inside a blue box is a model with trainable weights, while inside a black box is a model with frozen weights. (Color figure online)

use an autoencoder-based input distiller, which learns the discrepancy between the teacher and student models by accounting for the loss computed by the aggregation of the critic loss, the KD loss [14], and the CRD loss [16].

3   Our Method

As shown in Fig. 3, depicting the details of our proposed method ExRep, the first step is to distill the knowledge of the teacher model for the student model. Here, the input distiller is trained using the pre-trained models.

EfficientNet. We implemented EfficientNet-B1 NoisyStudent, our teacher model, and EfficientNet-B1, our student model. Our choice of EfficientNet-B1 as the backbone is attributed to its relatively small number of parameters (7.8M), which enables efficient computation. The weights of the model pre-trained on JFT-300M in PyTorch are available here[1].

3.1   Input Distiller

Our input distiller, shown in Supp. Section C, is a ResNet-based autoencoder comprised of simple residual blocks, each of which consists of convolution (Conv),

---

[1] https://github.com/rwightman/pytorch-image-models

Instance Normalization (IN), and LeakyReLU layers. In ExRep, the input distiller learns the representational discrepancy between the teacher and student models through knowledge distillation. More specifically, let x_i denote the ith input image and θ_g denote the weights of the input distiller f; then, the output $\tilde{x}_i$ of f with the same dimension as x_i is defined as

$$\tilde{x}_i = f_{\theta_g}(x_i) + x_i, \tag{1}$$

which is then fed into the student model. The output of the input distiller $\tilde{x}_i$ acts as a weight-based noisy sample equivalent to augmented data or adversarial examples.

Role of the Input Distiller. Our proposed pipeline comprises three stages: 1) knowledge distillation using the input distiller (Table 1), 2) application of the input distiller to the training of a classifier lacking extra training data (Section A in Supp.), and 3) inference without using the input distiller (Table 1). Note that in the first stage, we distill the knowledge acquired during training into the KD and CRD losses for the input distiller to learn the representation effect of the extra training data. Hence the role of the input distiller is not to enhance the effect of knowledge distillation itself, but to capture and later reuse the extra representation to assist the training of another classifier lacking extra training data. Removing the input distiller, we would fail to effectively capture the extra representation due to the insufficient number of trainable parameters.

3.2   Knowledge Distillation Loss

Using the KD function, proposed by Hinton et al. [14], the student model is trained such that its output is similar to that of the teacher model by minimizing the KL divergence. However, our approach differs in that we aim to imitate the teacher model's representation and produce the effect of using extra training data without actually using it by adding trainable weights to the input images.

Let y_i, $\hat{y}_i^T$, and $\hat{y}_i^S$ denote the ith label, the label predicted by the teacher model, and that predicted by the student model, respectively. Then, the respective outputs z^T and z^S of the teacher and student models following activation by a softmax function σ are defined as

$$z^T = \sigma\left(\frac{\hat{y}_i^T}{\tau}\right), \quad z^S = \sigma\left(\frac{\hat{y}_i^S}{\tau}\right), \quad \sigma = \frac{\exp(\hat{y}_i)}{\Sigma_j \exp(\hat{y}_j)}, \tag{2}$$

where τ is the temperature. Using the softmax outputs z^T and z^S in Eq. 2, we first compute the KL divergence loss as follows:

$$\mathcal{L}_{KL} = \tau^2 KL(z^T, z^S). \tag{3}$$

We also compute the CE loss using $\hat{y}_i^S$ and y_i as follows:

$$\mathcal{L}_{CE} = J(\hat{y}_i^S, y_i),$$
$$J(\hat{y}_i, y_i) = -y_i log(\hat{y}_i). \tag{4}$$

We then compute the final KD loss, which ought to be minimized during training, as the sum of the KL divergence loss and the CE loss, each weighted by λ_{KL} and λ_{CE}, respectively, as follows:

$$\underset{\theta_T}{\text{argmin}}\, \mathcal{L}_{KD} = \lambda_{KL}\mathcal{L}_{KL} + \lambda_{CE}\mathcal{L}_{CE}. \tag{5}$$

3.3   Contrastive Representation Distillation Loss

The CRD loss [16] applies contrastive learning, whereby the model learns a closer representation for the pairs of the same class (positive sample pairs) than for those of different classes (negative sample pairs) in ImageNet.

Feature Embedding. Let o^T and o^S denote the respective final feature maps of f_{θ_T} (the teacher model) and f_{θ_S} (the student model) before the logit layer. The embeddings of o^T and o^S through the linear transformation functions l_{θ_S} and l_{θ_T}, e^T and e^S are normalized using the $L2$ norm as follows:

$$
\begin{aligned}
e^T &= l_{\theta_T}(o_i^T)/\Sigma_i\|l_{\theta_T}(o_i^T)\|_2^2, \\
e^S &= l_{\theta_S}(o_i^S)/\Sigma_i\|l_{\theta_S}(o_i^S)\|_2^2, \\
o_i^T &= f_{\theta_T}(\tilde{x}_i), \quad o_i^S = f_{\theta_S}(\tilde{x}_i).
\end{aligned}
\tag{6}
$$

The linear transformation functions l_{θ_T} and l_{θ_S} in Eq. 6 are updated by iterative gradient descent.

Negative Sampling. Since the negative sample space is significantly larger than the positive sample space (999 classes v. 1 class), negative sampling is used for an efficient computation of negative sample pairs. A negative sample x_j is defined such that $y_i \neq y_j$. Tian et al. [16] demonstrated that negative sampling leads to higher classification performance than when using intra-class sampling. We define the score function s, the range of which falls within 0 and 1, based on negative sampling for the discriminator, which estimates the class probability as follows:

$$s(e^T, e^S) = \frac{\exp(e^T e^S/\tau)}{\exp(e^T e^S/\tau) + (N/M)}, \tag{7}$$

where N is the number of negative sample pairs and M is the dataset cardinality.

Contrastive Loss. Let C denote a random variable equal to 0 when the input pairs are positive samples and 1 when they are negative samples. Since s is a score function, we treat the contrastive loss as a binary CE term, where the number of negative samples N is multiplied by the positive sample variable $(C = 0)$ to offset the effect of larger samples among negative ones:

$$f_{CRD} = \mathbb{E}_{s(e^T,e^S|c=1)}[\log s(e^T, e^S)] + N\mathbb{E}_{s(e^T,e^S|c=0)}[\log(1 - s(e^T, e^S)], \tag{8}$$

where f_{CRD} denotes the CRD function. The CRD loss is then defined as:

$$\underset{\theta_T}{\text{argmin}}\, \underset{o}{\min}\, \mathcal{L}_{CRD} = -\lambda_{CRD} f_{CRD}, \tag{9}$$

where λ_{CRD} is a balancing parameter. Our final CRD loss term accounting for feature embedding and negative sampling in Eq. 9 is denoted by $\mathcal{L}_{CRD}$.

Algorithm 1. Adversarial training algorithm, where m is the minibatch size.

1: **Require:** a target data $\{(x_1, y_1), (x_2, y_2), ..., (x_n, y_n)\}$.
2: **for** each epoch **do**
3:     Sample minibatch $X_m, Y_m = \{(x_i, y_i), ..., (x_m, y_m)\}$
4:     Input distiller $\tilde{X}_m = f_{\theta_g}(X_m)$
5:     $o_m^T, o_m^S = f_{\theta_T}^T(X_m), f_{\theta_S}^S(\tilde{X}_m)$
6:     Update the critic by ascending the stochastic gradient:
            $\nabla_{\theta_d} \frac{1}{m} \Sigma_{i=1}^m [\log D(o_m^T) + \log(1 - D(o_m^S))]$.
7:     Update the input distiller by descending the stochastic gradient:
            $\nabla_{\theta_g} \frac{1}{m} \Sigma_{i=1}^m \log(1 - D(G(o_m^T)))$.
8: **end for**

3.4   Adversarial Training Loss

Adversarial training was first introduced in GANs [15]. In our work, we use adversarial training to provide extra representation to the student model. Similarly to a discriminator, we introduce a critic that decides whether the final feature map is from the teacher model or the student model, while the input distiller plays the role of a generator. Let f_{θ_g} and f_{θ_d}, referred to as G and D, denote the input distiller and the critic model, respectively. From Eq. 1 and Eq. 6, we obtain the final feature map o^S of the student model as follows:

$$V(D, G) = \mathbb{E}_{x \sim P(x)}[\log D(o^T)] + \mathbb{E}_{\tilde{x} \sim P(\tilde{x})}[\log(1 - D(o^S))],$$
$$o^S = f_{\theta_s}(G(x) + x). \tag{10}$$

Then, the critic loss $\mathcal{L}_{Critic}$ is defined as follows:

$$\min_G \max_D \mathcal{L}_{Critic} = \lambda_{Critic} V(D, G), \tag{11}$$

where λ_{Critic} is a balancing parameter. The critic loss $\mathcal{L}_{Critic}$ in Eq. 11 enables the input distiller to generate a representation much closer to that of the teacher model from that of the student model. Although our critic objective is similar to the projected gradient descent (PGD) [26], where examples generated by G attempt to deceive D through imitation of the teacher model's representation, ours differs in that our perturbation has trainable weights obtained from the input distiller.

Final Loss Function. Our final loss function $\mathcal{L}_{Final}$ is computed as the sum of $\mathcal{L}_{KD}$, $\mathcal{L}_{CRD}$, and $\mathcal{L}_{Critic}$ as follows:

$$\mathcal{L}_{Final} = \mathcal{L}_{KD} + \mathcal{L}_{CRD} + \mathcal{L}_{Critic}. \tag{12}$$

Practical Implementation of Critic Loss. The implementation of $\mathcal{L}_{Critic}$ is presented in Algorithm 1. Note that in practice, we update D and G sequentially: D is updated first and then G is updated to deceive D. To perform this, we split $\mathcal{L}_{Final}$ into $\mathcal{L}_{Critic}$ and the remaining terms; D is updated separately, while G is updated based on $\mathcal{L}_{KD}$ and $\mathcal{L}_{CRD}$, while fixing the critic loss. Algorithm 2 shows the entire pipeline of ExRep, where stages 1 to 5 represent the procedures depicted in Fig. 3.

Algorithm 2. Pseudo code of ExRep, where n is the ImageNet size and (x_i, y_i) is the ith input image and label.

Require: ImageNet data $\{(x_1, y_1), (x_2, y_2), ..., (x_n, y_n)\}$, the input distiller f_{θ_g}, the teacher model f_{θ_T}, the student model f_{θ_S}, the critic model $f_{\theta_{Critic}}$ and the weights θ_{CRD} of $\mathcal{L}_{CRD}$.

1: Input Distiller: $\{(x_1, y_1), (x_2, y_2), ..., (x_n, y_n)\}$ is fed to f_{θ_g}, and generates $\{\tilde{x}_1, \tilde{x}_2, ..., \tilde{x}_m\}$.

    Input: Data (x_i, y_i)

    Output: Data $(\tilde{x}_i, y_i)$

    Objective: $\tilde{x}_i = f_{\theta_g}(x_i) + x_i$.

2: Teacher Model: The input images are fed to f_{θ_T}.

    Input: Data (x_i, y_i)

    Output: Final feature map o^T and prediction $\hat{y}_i^T$

3: Teacher Model: $\{(x_1, y_1), (x_2, y_2), ..., (x_n, y_n)\}$ added to the output of f_{θ_g} is fed to f_{θ_S}.

    Input: Data $(\tilde{x}_i, y_i)$

    Output: Final feature map o^S and prediction $\hat{y}_i^S$

4: Knowledge Distillation: Using o^T, o^S, $\hat{y}_i^T$, and $\hat{y}_i^S$, compute $\mathcal{L}_{CE}$ and $\mathcal{L}_{KL}$.

    Input: Final feature maps o^T, o^S, and predictions $\hat{y}_i^T$, $\hat{y}_i^S$

    Output: $\mathcal{L}_{KD}$

    Objective: $\text{argmin}_{\theta_T} \mathcal{L}_{KD} = \lambda_{KL}\mathcal{L}_{KL} + \lambda_{CE}\mathcal{L}_{CE}$.

5: Adversarial Training: The critic model decides whether the final feature map is from the teacher model or the the student model.

    Input: Final features o^T, o^S

    Output: $\mathcal{L}_{Critic}$

    Objective: $\min_G \max_D \mathcal{L}_{Critic} = \lambda_{Critic}V(D, G)$.

3.5   Inference and Application

During training, the input distiller is also trained based on the CE, KD, CRD, and Adv losses. During inference, the input distiller is not used; only the student model is evaluated on the validation set of ImageNet. We can also apply ExRep to other datasets, such as CIFAR10, to train a novel classifier in that dataset, using the input distiller pre-trained during training. We refer to this phase as the application stage, which is explained in Supp. Section A.

4   Experimental Results

In this section, we provide the details of our experiments, including the datasets, the baseline and pre-trained models, and the results. Our training process is presented in detail in Supp. Section D.

4.1   Datasets

ImageNet 2012. ImageNet [35] contains around 1.2 million images labeled with 1,000 categories. To standardize all images with different sizes, we resize them to 224×224 and 240×240 using bicubic interpolation in EfficientNet-B0 and EfficientNet-B1, respectively. For efficient negative sampling, we use a memory buffer as in [16]. The classification performance is evaluated on the ImageNet validation set.

4.2 Baselines

EfficientNet. We conduct experiments on ImageNet with EfficientNet-B0 and B1 as the backbone networks. With a small number of parameters, EfficientNet achieved a performance comparable to those of ResNext [17] and NASNet [11]. We decide to use a small sized EfficientNet (B0 and B1) for efficient computation.

NoisyStudent. NoisyStudent used JFT-300M as extra training data for self-training. We implement NoisyStudent (EfficientNet-B1 and B0) to evaluate the performance on ImageNet, using the pre-trained models in PyTorch. The input image size is 240×240 (B1) and 224×224 (B0), and random crops are applied during the pre-training phase of NoisyStudent. We set the percentage of the center crop to be 88.2% for B1 and 87.5% for B0.

FixNet. FixNet also used JFT-300M as extra training data. However, their pre-trained weights in EfficientNet-B0 and B1 are not released. Therefore, we refer to the performance results presented by Touvron et al. [8] for comparison.

AdvProp. AdvProp achieved high performance without using extra training data by using adversarial examples to improve the classification performance through self-supervised training. We set the input size and the percentage of the center crop to be the same as those for NoisyStudent. Similarly, we use the $L2$ norm as in the original AdvProp [27] for our evaluation.

4.3 Pre-trained Models

We use NoisyStudent (EfficientNet-B0 and B1) as the teacher model, and EffcientNet-B0 and B1 pre-trained only on ImageNet as the student model. NoisyStudent is trained on samples of the extra training data through self-training, using additional data augmentation. On the contrary, FixNet's training process is more complicated: the model is pre-trained on a smaller size of inputs and fine-tuned on a larger size of inputs. Since our goal is to produce the effect of using extra training data without actually using it, we chose NoisyStudent as our teacher model.

4.4 Performance Evaluation

Top-1 Accuracy and Top-5 Accuracy. We used top-1 and top-5 accuracy for the evaluation of the classification performance. Top-1 accuracy measures how the model correctly predicts the target label. Top-5 accuracy checks if the target label is included in one of the top 5 predictions. We chose these two metrics to

Table 1. Performance results. EfficientNet PyTorch represents the original Efficient-Net model pre-trained on ImageNet without extra training data. All methods use EfficientNet-B0 and EfficientNet-B1 as the backbone networks. Note that both NoisyStudent and FixNet use extra training data (JFT-300M) during training on ImageNet, whereas AdvProp, EfficientNet PyTorch, and ExRep only use the ImageNet training data. The best results are highlighted in bold.

Method	Extra training data	Size	Top-1 ACC	Top-5 ACC
EfficientNet-B1 NoisyStudent	JFT-300M	240	81.3%	95.7%
EfficientNet-B0 NoisyStudent	JFT-300M	224	78.6%	94.3%
EfficientNet-B1 FixNet	JFT-300M	240	82.6%	96.5%
EfficientNet-B0 FixNet	JFT-300M	224	80.2%	95.4%
EfficientNet-B1 AdvProp	–	240	79.2%	94.3%
EfficientNet-B0 AdvProp	–	224	77.0%	93.2%
EfficientNet-B1 PyTorch	–	240	78.8%	94.1%
EfficientNet-B0 PyTorch	–	224	77.6%	93.5%
EfficientNet-B1 ExRep	–	240	**79.8%**	**94.5%**
EfficientNet-B0 ExRep	–	224	**77.9%**	**93.6%**

examine how our model accurately selects the correct label, as well as how often the model includes the correct label within the top 5 predictions.

ExRep Performance. We present our performance results in Table 1, where the same test dataset (ImageNet 2012 benchmark) is used. Note that we use NoisyStudnet as the teacher model and EfficientNet PyTorch as the student model. We also use EfficientNet-B0 and EfficientNet-B1 as the backbone networks with input sizes 224×224 and 240×240, respectively. ExRep achieves 79.8% top-1 accuracy and 94.5% top-5 accuracy for EfficientNet-B1, and 77.9% top-1 accuracy and 93.6% top-5 accuracy for EfficientNet-B0 without extra training data, outperforming AdvProp.

EfficientNet PyTorch vs. ExRep. EfficientNet PyTorch is trained on ImageNet with the model in the work of Tan and Le [6], which is pre-trained on ImageNet without extra training data. We used EfficientNet PyTorch as the student model of ExRep. As shown in Table 1, ExRep achieves 1.0% higher top-1 accuracy and 0.4% higher top-5 accuracy for EfficientNet-B1 and 0.3% higher top-1 accuracy and 0.1% higher top-5 accuracy for EfficientNet-B0 compared to those of EfficientNet PyTorch for both EfficientNet-B1 and B0. EfficientNet-B1 shows a higher performance increase compared to that of EfficientNet-B0, because the teacher model (NoisyStudent) in EfficientNet-B0 NoisyStudent has lower incremental performance than that of EfficientNet-B1 NoisyStudent.

AdvProp vs. ExRep. AdvProp achieves 0.4% higher top-1 accuracy and 0.2% higher top-5 accuracy than those of EfficientNet PyTorch for EfficientNet-B1 but

Table 2. Ablation study for the input distiller and adversarial training. Adv-training denotes adversarial training. In this experiment, we use EfficientNet-B0 and EfficientNet-B1 as the backbone network.

Method	Base model	Top-1 ACC	Top-5 ACC	Reusable
w/o input distiller (KD+CRD)	EfficientNet-B0	78.0%	93.8%	X
w/o input distiller (KD+CRD)	EfficientNet-B1	80.1%	95.1%	X
w input distiller (KD+CRD+Adv)	EfficientNet-B0	77.9%	93.6%	O
w input distiller (KD+CRD+MSE)	EfficientNet-B0	77.6%	93.5%	O
w input distiller (KD+CRD+Adv)	EfficientNet-B1	79.9%	95.1%	O
w input distiller (KD+CRD+MSE)	EfficientNet-B1	79.7%	95.1%	O

achieves lower performance for EfficientNet-B0. However, ExRep achieves 0.7% higher top-1 accuracy and 0.1% higher top-5 accuracy for EfficientNet-B1, and 0.9% higher top-1 accuracy and 0.4% higher top-5 accuracy for EfficientNet-B0. Therefore, ExRep exhibits greater generalization ability on ImageNet regardless of the model size (B1 and B0).

EfficientNet-B0 vs. EfficientNet-B1. ExRep with EfficientNet-B1 achieves the highest top-1 and top-5 accuracy compared to ExRep with EfficientNet-B0. While EfficientNet-B1 achieves 1.2% higher top-1 accuracy and 0.6% higher top-5 accuracy compared to those of EfficientNet-B0, ExRep with EfficientNet-B1 achieves 1.9% higher top-1 accuracy and 0.9% higher top-5 accuracy.

NoisyStudent vs. FixNet. FixNet shows higher top-1 accuracy and top-5 accuracy for both EfficientNet-B1 and EfficientNet-B0 in general. As the teacher model has more informative representation, the student model learns useful representation as well. Therefore, we expect that FixNet will have higher distillation performance using our framework, although not experimented in this work, since the FixNet weights are currently unavailable.

5   Ablation Study

In this section, we present an ablation study to demonstrate the effectiveness of the input distiller and adversarial training (Sect. 3.1, Sect. 3.4, and Eq. 11) used in our ExRep: 1) the KD and CRD losses without the input distiller, 2) the KD, CRD, and adversarial losses with the input distiller, and 3) the KD, CRD, and Mean Squared Error (MSE) losses with the input distiller.

Input Distiller Effect. As shown in Table 2, we experiment with ExRep, which is trained on ImageNet. The input distiller may harm the performance of the original knowledge distillation, but only to a minimal degree, and most importantly, it renders the extra representation reusable for the training of a novel classifier without any available extra training data. In the ablation study presented in Table 2, the performance was compared for the exclusion of the

Table 3. Performance results on ResNeXt. ResNeXt SWSL represents semi-weakly supervised ResNeXT.

Method	Extra training data	Size	Top-1 ACC	Top-5 ACC
ResNeXt SWSL [36]	Billion-scale	224	82.1%	96.2%
ResNeXt	–	224	79.7%	94.6%
ResNeXt ExRep	–	224	81.1%	95.1%

adversarial and MSE losses using the input distiller to demonstrate the effects of those terms.

ResNeXt and Billion-Scale Dataset. We also carried out an experiment to validate the generalization of our method. Semi-weakly supervised ResNeXt (ResNeXt SWSL) is trained on the Billion-scale dataset [36], which is an internal dataset of Facebook. This ResNeXt SWSL achieves 82.1% top-1 accuracy on 224×224 size of ImageNet. On the other hands, The vanilla ResNeXt achieves 79.7% top-1 accuracy. Our ExRep achieves 81.1% top-1 accuracy. It represents that ExRep can adjust to different CNN architecture (EfficientNet and ResNeXt) and other extra training dataset (JFT-300M and Billion-scale) (Table 3).

6 Conclusion

In this paper, we introduce ExRep, a novel ImageNet image classification framework. Our proposed method does not require direct access to extra training data to achieve high classification performance, unlike the previous state-of-the-art approaches that exploited the JFT-300M dataset, which is not publicly available. We instead use a teacher model pre-trained on ImageNet as well as on JFT-300M to distill its knowledge acquired during training for the student model pre-trained only on ImageNet. ExRep outperforms AdvProp, the state-of-the-art, which does not use extra training data as in our case, and achieves a performance comparable to those of NoisyStudent and FixNet, which use JFT-300M data for training in addition to ImageNet. We show that ExRep can be applied to other datasets as well, demonstrating the effectiveness of our proposed method. While ExRep achieves a performance comparable to those of previous state-of-the-art approaches, there is still room for improvement. For instance, we plan to integrate BiT, NoisyStudent, and FixNet based on more complex backbone architectures, such as EfficientNet-B7, EfficientNet-L2, and BiT-L, which are more computationally expensive and time-consuming. We expect that the use of more complex teacher models will improve the classification performance; we also aim to further optimize ExRep. Our ExRep implementation is available here[2].

---

[2] https://github.com/cutz-j/ExRep.

Acknowledgements. This work was partly supported by Institute of Information & communications Technology Planning & Evaluation (IITP) grant funded by the Korea government (MSIT) (No. 2019-0-00421, AI Graduate School Support Program (Sungkyunkwan University)), and the National Research Foundation of Korea (NRF) grant funded by the Korea government (MSIT) (2019M3F2A1072217 and 2020R1C1C1006004). Also, this research was results of a study on the "HPC Support" Project, supported by the 'Ministry of Science and ICT' and NIPA.

References

1. Krizhevsky, A., Sutskever, I., Hinton, G.E.: ImageNet classification with deep convolutional neural networks. In: Advances in Neural Information Processing Systems, pp. 1097–1105 (2012)
2. Simonyan, K., Zisserman, A.: Very deep convolutional networks for large-scale image recognition. arXiv preprint arXiv:1409.1556 (2014)
3. Szegedy, C., et al.: Going deeper with convolutions. In: Proceedings of the IEEE Conference on Computer Vision and Pattern Recognition, pp. 1–9 (2015)
4. He, K., Zhang, X., Ren, S., Sun, J.: Deep residual learning for image recognition. In: Proceedings of the IEEE Conference on Computer Vision and Pattern Recognition, pp. 770–778 (2016)
5. Chollet, F.: Xception: deep learning with depthwise separable convolutions. In: Proceedings of the IEEE Conference on Computer Vision and Pattern Recognition, pp. 1251–1258 (2017)
6. Tan, M., Le, Q.V.: EfficientNet: rethinking model scaling for convolutional neural networks. arXiv preprint arXiv:1905.11946 (2019)
7. Xie, Q., Luong, M.T., Hovy, E., Le, Q.V.: Self-training with noisy student improves ImageNet classification. In: Proceedings of the IEEE/CVF Conference on Computer Vision and Pattern Recognition, pp. 10687–10698 (2020)
8. Touvron, H., Vedaldi, A., Douze, M., Jégou, H.: Fixing the train-test resolution discrepancy. In: Advances in Neural Information Processing Systems, pp. 8252–8262 (2019)
9. Kolesnikov, A., et al.: Big transfer (BiT): general visual representation learning. arXiv preprint arXiv:1912.11370 (2019)
10. Cubuk, E.D., Zoph, B., Mane, D., Vasudevan, V., Le, Q.V.: Autoaugment: learning augmentation policies from data. arXiv preprint arXiv:1805.09501 (2018)
11. Zoph, B., Vasudevan, V., Shlens, J., Le, Q.V.: Learning transferable architectures for scalable image recognition. In: Proceedings of the IEEE Conference on Computer Vision and Pattern Recognition, pp. 8697–8710 (2018)
12. Krizhevsky, A., Hinton, G., et al.: Learning multiple layers of features from tiny images (2009)
13. Netzer, Y., Wang, T., Coates, A., Bissacco, A., Wu, B., Ng, A.Y.: Reading digits in natural images with unsupervised feature learning (2011)
14. Hinton, G., Vinyals, O., Dean, J.: Distilling the knowledge in a neural network. arXiv preprint arXiv:1503.02531 (2015)
15. Goodfellow, I., et al.: Generative adversarial nets. In: Advances in Neural Information Processing Systems, pp. 2672–2680 (2014)
16. Tian, Y., Krishnan, D., Isola, P.: Contrastive representation distillation. arXiv preprint arXiv:1910.10699 (2019)

17. Xie, S., Girshick, R., Dollár, P., Tu, Z., He, K.: Aggregated residual transformations for deep neural networks. In: Proceedings of the IEEE Conference on Computer Vision and Pattern Recognition, pp. 1492–1500 (2017)
18. Mahajan, D., et al.: Exploring the limits of weakly supervised pretraining. In: Ferrari, V., Hebert, M., Sminchisescu, C., Weiss, Y. (eds.) ECCV 2018. LNCS, vol. 11206, pp. 185–201. Springer, Cham (2018). https://doi.org/10.1007/978-3-030-01216-8_12
19. Joulin, A., van der Maaten, L., Jabri, A., Vasilache, N.: Learning visual features from large weakly supervised data. In: Leibe, B., Matas, J., Sebe, N., Welling, M. (eds.) ECCV 2016. LNCS, vol. 9911, pp. 67–84. Springer, Cham (2016). https://doi.org/10.1007/978-3-319-46478-7_5
20. Thomee, B., et al.: YFCC100M: the new data in multimedia research. Commun. ACM **59**, 64–73 (2016)
21. Zhai, X., et al.: A large-scale study of representation learning with the visual task adaptation benchmark. arXiv preprint arXiv:1910.04867 (2019)
22. Wu, Y., He, K.: Group normalization. In: Ferrari, V., Hebert, M., Sminchisescu, C., Weiss, Y. (eds.) ECCV 2018. LNCS, vol. 11217, pp. 3–19. Springer, Cham (2018). https://doi.org/10.1007/978-3-030-01261-8_1
23. Qiao, S., Wang, H., Liu, C., Shen, W., Yuille, A.: Weight standardization. arXiv preprint arXiv:1903.10520 (2019)
24. Cubuk, E.D., Zoph, B., Shlens, J., Le, Q.V.: Randaugment: practical automated data augmentation with a reduced search space. In: Proceedings of the IEEE/CVF Conference on Computer Vision and Pattern Recognition Workshops, pp. 702–703 (2020)
25. Goodfellow, I.J., Shlens, J., Szegedy, C.: Explaining and harnessing adversarial examples. arXiv preprint arXiv:1412.6572 (2014)
26. Madry, A., Makelov, A., Schmidt, L., Tsipras, D., Vladu, A.: Towards deep learning models resistant to adversarial attacks. arXiv preprint arXiv:1706.06083 (2017)
27. Xie, C., Tan, M., Gong, B., Wang, J., Yuille, A.L., Le, Q.V.: Adversarial examples improve image recognition. In: Proceedings of the IEEE/CVF Conference on Computer Vision and Pattern Recognition, pp. 819–828 (2020)
28. Ioffe, S., Szegedy, C.: Batch normalization: accelerating deep network training by reducing internal covariate shift. arXiv preprint arXiv:1502.03167 (2015)
29. Yim, J., Joo, D., Bae, J., Kim, J.: A gift from knowledge distillation: fast optimization, network minimization and transfer learning. In: Proceedings of the IEEE Conference on Computer Vision and Pattern Recognition, pp. 4133–4141 (2017)
30. Zagoruyko, S., Komodakis, N.: Paying more attention to attention: improving the performance of convolutional neural networks via attention transfer. arXiv preprint arXiv:1612.03928 (2016)
31. Huang, Z., Wang, N.: Like what you like: knowledge distill via neuron selectivity transfer. arXiv preprint arXiv:1707.01219 (2017)
32. Heo, B., Lee, M., Yun, S., Choi, J.Y.: Knowledge transfer via distillation of activation boundaries formed by hidden neurons. Proc. AAAI Conf. Artif. Intell. **33**, 3779–3787 (2019)
33. van den Oord, A., Li, Y., Vinyals, O.: Representation learning with contrastive predictive coding. arXiv preprint arXiv:1807.03748 (2018)

34. Romero, A., Ballas, N., Kahou, S.E., Chassang, A., Gatta, C., Bengio, Y.: FitNets: hints for thin deep nets. arXiv preprint arXiv:1412.6550 (2014)
35. Russakovsky, O., et al.: ImageNet large scale visual recognition challenge. Int. J. Comput. Vision **115**, 211–252 (2015)
36. Yalniz, I.Z., Jégou, H., Chen, K., Paluri, M., Mahajan, D.: Billion-scale semi-supervised learning for image classification. arXiv preprint arXiv:1905.00546 (2019)

Class-Wise Difficulty-Balanced Loss
for Solving Class-Imbalance

Saptarshi Sinha$^{(\boxtimes)}$ ⓘ, Hiroki Ohashi, and Katsuyuki Nakamura ⓘ

Hitachi, Ltd. Research and Development Group, Tokyo 185-8601, Japan
{saptarshi.sinha.hx,hiroki.ohashi.uo,katsuyuki.nakamura.xv}@hitachi.com

Abstract. Class-imbalance is one of the major challenges in real world datasets, where a few classes (called majority classes) constitute much more data samples than the rest (called minority classes). Learning deep neural networks using such datasets leads to performances that are typically biased towards the majority classes. Most of the prior works try to solve class-imbalance by assigning more weights to the minority classes in various manners (e.g., data re-sampling, cost-sensitive learning). However, we argue that the number of available training data may not be always a good clue to determine the weighting strategy because some of the minority classes might be sufficiently represented even by a small number of training data. Overweighting samples of such classes can lead to drop in the model's overall performance. We claim that the 'difficulty' of a class as perceived by the model is more important to determine the weighting. In this light, we propose a novel loss function named Class-wise Difficulty-Balanced loss, or CDB loss, which dynamically distributes weights to each sample according to the difficulty of the class that the sample belongs to. Note that the assigned weights dynamically change as the 'difficulty' for the model may change with the learning progress. Extensive experiments are conducted on both image (artificially induced class-imbalanced MNIST, long-tailed CIFAR and ImageNet-LT) and video (EGTEA) datasets. The results show that CDB loss consistently outperforms the recently proposed loss functions on class-imbalanced datasets irrespective of the data type (i.e., video or image).

1 Introduction

Since the advent of Deep Neural Networks (DNNs), we have seen significant advancement in computer vision research. One of the reasons behind this success is the wide availability of large-scale annotated image (e.g., MNIST [1], CIFAR [2], ImageNet [3]) and video (e.g., Kinetics [4], Something-Something [5], UCF [6]) datasets. But unfortunately, most of the commonly used datasets do not resemble the real world data in a number of ways. As a result, performance of state-of-the-art DNNs drop significantly in real-world use-cases. One of the major challenges in most real-world datasets is the class-imbalanced data distribution with significantly long tails, i.e., a few classes (also known as 'majority classes') have much higher number of data samples compared to the other classes (also

© Springer Nature Switzerland AG 2021
H. Ishikawa et al. (Eds.): ACCV 2020, LNCS 12627, pp. 549–565, 2021.
https://doi.org/10.1007/978-3-030-69544-6_33

known as 'minority classes'). When DNNs are trained using such real-world datasets, their performance gets biased towards the majority classes, i.e., they perform highly for the majority classes and poorly for the minority classes.

Several recent works have tried to solve the problem of class-imbalanced training data. Most of the prior solutions can be fairly classified under 3 categories :- (1) Data re-sampling techniques [7–9] (2) Metric learning and knowledge transfer [10–13] (3) Cost-sensitive learning methods [14–17]. Data re-sampling techniques try to balance the number of data samples between the majority and minority classes by either over-sampling from the minority classes or under-sampling from the majority classes or using both. Generating synthetic data samples for minority classes [7,18,19] from given data is another re-sampling technique that tries to increase the number of minority class samples. Since the performance of a DNN depends entirely on it's ability to learn to extract useful features from data, "what training data is seen by the DNN" is a very important concern. In that context, data re-sampling strategies introduce the risks of losing important training data samples by under-sampling from majority classes and network overfitting due to over-sampling minority classes. Metric-learning [10,11], on the other hand, aims to learn an appropriate representation function that embeds data to a feature space, where the mutual relationships among the data (e.g., similarity/dissimilarity) are preserved. It has the risk of learning a biased representation function that has learned more from the majority classes. Hence some works [12] tend to use sampling techniques with metric learning, which still faces the problems of sampling, as discussed above. Few recent researches have also tried to transfer knowledge from the majority classes to the minority classes by adding an external memory [20], which is non-trivial and expensive. Due to these concerns, the work in this paper focuses on cost-sensitive learning approaches. Cost-sensitive learning methods penalize the DNN higher for making errors on certain samples compared to others. They achieve this by assigning weights to different samples using various strategies. Typically, most prior cost-sensitive learning strategies [13,15,21] assume that the minority classes are always weakly represented. They ensure that the samples of the minority class get higher weights so that the DNN can be penalized more for making mistakes on the minority class samples. One such popular strategy is to distribute weights in inverse proportion to the class frequencies [13,22]. However, certain minority classes might be fairly represented by a small amount of samples.

Figure 1 gives an example of a class-imbalanced dataset where certain classes such as 'clean' and 'spread' are sparsely populated but can easily be learned to generalize by the classifier. Overweighting samples of such classes might lead to biasing the DNN's performance. In such situations, number of available training data per class might not be a good clue to determine sample weights.

Instead, we claim that the 'difficulty' of a class as perceived by the DNN might be a more important and helpful clue for weight assignment. The concept of 'difficulty' has been previously used by some sample-level weight assigning techniques such as focal loss [14] and GHM [17]. They reweight each sample

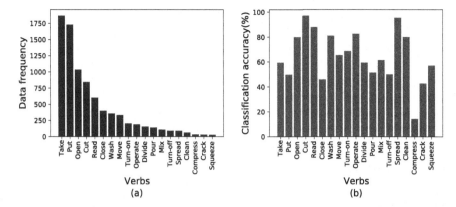

Fig. 1. (a) Class-imbalanced data distribution of EGTEA dataset. (b) Class-wise classification accuracies of a 3D-ResNeXt101 trained on the imbalanced EGTEA dataset using unweighted softmax cross-entropy loss function. It is interesting to notice that even though classes like 'Clean' and 'Spread' have very small number of data samples, the classifier finds it relatively easier to learn such classes compared to certain densely populated classes such as 'Take' and 'Put'. Therefore it is not obvious to assume that the sparsely populated classes will always be the most weakly represented.

individually by increasing weights for hard samples and reducing weights for easy samples. The increasing popularity of focal loss [14] in class-imbalanced classification tasks is based on the assumption that minority classes should have more hard samples compared to majority classes. The assumption does stand true if we compare the proportion of hard samples for the minority and majority classes. But, in terms of absolute number of hard samples, the majority classes still might surpass the minority classes simply because they have much more data samples than the minority classes. In such cases, giving high weights to all hard samples irrespective of their classes might overweight the majority classes and therefore still bias the performance of the DNN. We believe that the above drawback can be solved by considering class-level difficulty rather than sample-level. To the best of our knowledge, ours is the first work to introduce the concept of class-level difficulty for solving class-imbalance. Based on the analysis, we develop a novel weighting strategy that dynamically re-balances the loss for each sample based on the instantaneous difficulty of it's class as perceived by a DNN.

Such a strategy measures the instantaneous difficulty of each class without relying on any prior assumptions and then dynamically assigns weights to the samples of the class in proportion to the difficulty of the class. Extensive experiments on multiple datasets indicate that our class-difficulty based dynamic weighting strategy can provide a significant improvement in the performance of the commonly used loss functions under class-imbalanced situations.

The key contributions of this paper can be summarized as follows: (1) We propose a way to measure the dynamic difficulty of each class during training and use the class-wise difficulty scores to re-balance the loss for each sample, thereby giving a class-wise difficulty-balanced (CDB) loss. (2) We show that using our weighting strategy can give commonly used loss functions (e.g., cross-entropy) a significant boost in performance on multiple class-imbalanced datasets. We conduct experiments on both image and video datasets and find that our weighting strategy works well irrespective of the data type. Our research on quantifying the dynamic difficulty of the classes and using it for weight distribution might prove useful for researchers focusing on class-imbalanced datasets.

2   Related Works

As discussed in Sect. 1, most prior works that try to solve class-imbalance can be categorized into 3 domains: (1) Data re-sampling techniques, (2) Metric learning and knowledge transfer and (3) Cost-sensitive learning methods.

2.1   Data Re-sampling

Data re-sampling techniques try to balance the number of samples among the classes by using various sampling techniques during the data pre-processing. The sampling techniques, used for the purpose, either randomly over-sample data from the minority classes or randomly under-sample data from the majority classes or both. Over-sampling from the minority classes [8,23] replicates the available data samples in order to increase the number of samples. But such a practice introduces the risk of overfitting. Synthetic Minority Over-sampling Technique (SMOTE) [7], proposed by Chawla et al., increases the number of data samples for the minority classes by creating synthetic data using interpolation among the original data points. Though SMOTE only used the minority class samples while generating data samples, later variants of SMOTE (e.g., Border-line SMOTE [18] and Safe-level SMOTE [19]) take the majority class samples into consideration as well. But such data generation techniques do not guarantee that the synthesized data points will always follow the actual data distribution of the minority classes. On the other hand, under-sampling techniques [9,24] reduce data from the majority classes and might result in cutting out some important data samples.

2.2   Metric Learning and Knowledge Transfer

Metric learning aims to learn an embedding function that can embed data to a feature space where the inter-data relationships are preserved. Contrastive embedding [25] is learned using paired data samples to minimize the distance between the features of same class samples while maximizing the distance between different class samples. Song et al. [10] proposed a structured feature embedding based on positive and negative samples pairs in the dataset. Triplet loss [26], on the other hand, uses triplets instead of pairs, where one sample is considered the anchor. Metric learning still faces the risk of learning embedding functions biased towards the majority classes. Some recent works (e.g., OLTR [20]) have also tried to transfer knowledge from the majority classes to the minority classes either by meta learning [13] or by adding an external memory module [20]. Even though OLTR [20] performs well for long-tailed classification, as pointed out by [27], their design of external memory modules might be a non-trivial and expensive task.

2.3   Cost-Sensitive Learning

Cost-sensitive learning techniques try to penalize the DNN higher for making prediction mistakes on certain data samples than on the others. To achieve that, different weights are assigned to different samples and the penalty incurred on each data sample is scaled up/down using the corresponding weight. Research in this domain mainly target to find an effective way to assign these weights to the samples. To solve class-imbalance, majority of the works propose techniques that assign higher weights to the minority class samples. Such techniques ensure that the DNN gets higher penalty for making mistakes on the minority class samples. One such simple and commonly used weight distribution technique is to use the inverse class-frequencies as the weights for the samples each class [13,22]. Later variants of this technique [21] use a smoothed version of the square root of class-frequencies for the weight distribution. Class-balanced loss [15] proposed by Lin et al. calculates the effective number of samples of each class and uses it to assign weights to the samples. All of the above mentioned works assume that the minority classes are always the most weakly represented classes and therefore needs high weights. But that assumption might not always be true because certain minority class might be sufficiently represented by a small number of samples. Giving high weights to the samples of such classes might cause drop in overall performance. Therefore, Tsung-Yi et al. proposed a sample-based weighting technique called "Focal loss" [14], where each sample is assigned a weight based on it's difficulty. The difficulty of each sample is quantified in terms of the loss incurred by the DNN on that sample, where more lossy samples imply more difficult samples. Though focal loss [14] was originally proposed for dense object detection tasks, it has also become popular in class-imbalanced classification tasks [15]. The minority classes are expected to have more difficult samples compared to the majority classes and therefore get high weights by focal loss. Indeed the proportion of difficult samples in a minority class is more than that in the majority class. However, in terms of absolute number of difficult samples, the majority class surpasses the minority class, as it is much more populated than the minority class. Therefore, giving high weights to all difficult samples irrespective of their classes still biases the DNN's performance.

Our work also lies in the regime of cost-sensitive learning. We propose a dynamic weighting system that dynamically assigns weights to each sample of each class based on the instantaneous difficulty of the class, rather than that of each sample, as perceived by the DNN. Our weighting system helps to boost the performance of commonly used loss functions (e.g., cross-entropy loss) in class-imbalanced situations.

3 Proposed Method

3.1 Measuring Class Difficulty

Human beings use the metric 'difficulty' majorly to give a qualitative description of things, for example "this task is very difficult" or "this game is so easy". Similar behavior can also be seen in neural networks where they find some parts of a task much more difficult to perform compared to the others. For example, while training on a multi-class classification task, the classifier will find some classes easier to learn than the others. We propose to measure the difficulty of each class as perceived by the DNN and use it as clue to determine the weights for the samples. But, as difficulty is a qualitative metric, there is no direct way to add a quantitative value to it. Humans tend to classify a task as difficult, if they can not perform well in it. We use a similar approach to use the neural network's performance to measure the difficulty of classes. During training, the neural network's performance for each class is measured on a validation data set, which is then used to calculate the class-wise difficulty. The neural network's performance for any class c is measured as its classification accuracy on class c, $A_c = n_c/N_c$, where N_c denotes the total number of samples of class c in validation data and n_c denotes the number of class c samples in validation data that the model classifies correctly. Then the difficulty of class c, d_c, is measured as $d_c = 1 - A_c$. A neural network's perception of "how much a class is difficult to learn" changes as the training process of the network progresses. With time, the network's performance for each class improves and as a result, the perceived difficulty of each class also reduces. Therefore, we calculate the class-difficulties as a function of time as well. The difficulty of class c after training time (i.e., time during training) t can be calculated as

$$d_{c,t} = 1 - A_{c,t} , \tag{1}$$

where $A_{c,t}$ is the neural network's classification accuracy for class c on the validation data after training time t.

3.2 Difficulty-Based Weight Distribution

Once the class-wise difficulty is quantified, then it can be used to assign weights to the classes during training. It is fairly obvious that the classes, that are difficult to learn should be given higher weights compared to the easier classes. Therefore the weight for class c after training time t can be calculated as

$$w_{c,t} = (d_{c,t})^\tau = (1 - A_{c,t})^\tau , \tag{2}$$

where $d_{c,t}$ is the difficulty of class c after time t and τ is a hyper-parameter. The weight distribution $w_t = \{w_{1,t}, w_{2,t}, \ldots, w_{C,t}\}$ over all C classes can be computed by repeating Eq. 2 for all classes.

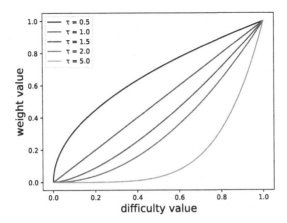

Fig. 2. Effect of changing τ on the difficulty-based weight distribution. Increasing value of τ puts heavier weights on the samples of the classes with higher difficulty, while lowering weights for the easier classes.

The hyper-parameter τ is introduced to control how much we down-weight the samples of the easy classes. Increasing value of τ relatively increases the classifier's focus on the difficult classes.

Figure 2 shows how change in the value of τ changes the weight values for classes of different difficulties. Its effect is almost similar to that of the focusing parameter γ in focal loss [14]. The performance of our proposed method varies significantly with change in value of τ and the best value for τ differs from dataset to dataset. Unfortunately, the only way to search for the best value of τ is by trial and error. To avoid that, we propose a way to dynamically update the value of τ. For dynamically updating τ, the value of τ after training time t is calculated as

$$\tau_t = \frac{2}{1 + \exp(-b_t)} \, , \tag{3}$$

where b_t measures the bias in the performance of the classifier over C classes as

$$b_t = \frac{\max_{c=1,2,...,C} A_{c,t}}{\min_{c'=1,2,...,C} A_{c',t} + \epsilon} - 1 \, . \tag{4}$$

In Eq. 4, ϵ is a small positive value ($= +0.0001$) introduced to handle situations where $\min_{c'=1,2,...,C} A_{c',t} = 0$. Equation 3 increases the value of τ when the classification performance of the classifier is highly biased (i.e., high b_t) and decreases it in case of low bias (i.e., less b_t).

3.3 Class-Wise Difficulty-Balanced Softmax Cross-Entropy Loss

Suppose when an input data is fed to the classifier after training time t during training, the predicted output of the classifier for all C classes are

$z_t = \{z_{1,t}, z_{2,t}, \ldots, z_{C,t}\}$. The probability distribution $p_t = \{p_{1,t}, p_{2,t}, \ldots, p_{C,t}\}$ over all the classes is computed using the softmax function, which is

$$p_{j,t} = \frac{\exp z_{j,t}}{\sum_{i=1}^{C} \exp z_{i,t}} \ \forall j \in 1, 2, \ldots, C \ . \tag{5}$$

For an input data sample of class k, cross-entropy (CE) loss function computes the loss after training time t as

$$\mathrm{CE}(p_t, k) = -\log p_{k,t} \ . \tag{6}$$

For the same input data sample, our class-wise difficulty-balanced softmax cross-entropy (CDB-CE) loss function computes the loss after training time t as

$$\mathrm{CDB\text{-}CE}(w_t, p_t, k) = -w_{k,t} \log p_{k,t} \ . \tag{7}$$

To make the weights time-dependent, we calculate them after each epoch using the model's class-wise validation accuracy.

4   Experiments

To demonstrate our proposed solution's ability to generalize to any data-type or dataset, we evaluate the effectiveness of our solution on 4 different datasets namely MNIST, long-tailed CIFAR, ImageNet-LT and EGTEA. MNIST, long-tailed CIFAR and ImageNet-LT are image datasets while EGTEA is a video dataset.

4.1   Datasets

MNIST. From the standard MNIST handwritten digit recognition dataset [1], we generate a class-imbalanced binary classification task using a subset of the dataset. The experimental setup is exactly same as given in [28]. We select a total of 5000 training images of class '4' and '9' where '9' is chosen as the majority class. We calculate the 'majority class ratio' as

$$\text{majority class ratio} = \frac{\text{no. of training samples in majority class}}{\text{no. of training samples}} \ . \tag{8}$$

Increasing the majority class ratio increases the imbalance in the training dataset. We also use a validation set which is created by selecting 500 images for each of the two classes from the original dataset but these images are different from the 5000 images selected for training. A test set was also created by randomly selecting 800 images for each of the classes from the original MNIST test set.

Long-Tailed CIFAR. We conduct experiments on long-tailed CIFAR-100 [2]. First a validation set was created from the original training set by randomly selecting 50 images per class. After the separation of the validation set, the remaining images in the training set were used to create a long-tailed version of the dataset using the exact same procedure as stated in [15]. The number of training images per class are reduced following an exponential function $n = n_c \mu^c$, where c is the 0-based index of the class and n_c is the remaining number of training images of class c after separation of the validation set and $\mu \in (0,1)$. Similar to [15], the 'imbalance' factor of a dataset is defined as the number of training samples in the largest class divided by that of the smallest class. The test set used for experiment is exactly same as the original CIFAR test set available and is a balanced set.

ImageNet-LT. We also conduct experiments on the long-tailed version of the original ImageNet-2012 [3], as constructed in [20]. It comprises of 115,800 images from 1000 categories, where the most frequent class has 1280 image samples and the least frequent class has only 5 images. The test set is balanced. The split constructed by [20] also provides a validation set that is separate from the test set and training set.

EGTEA. We also conduct experiments on the EGTEA Gaze+ dataset [29]. This is an egocentric dataset that contains trimmed video clips of many kitchen-related actions. These video clips are extracted segments from longer videos that were collected by 32 different subjects. Each video clip is assigned a single action label and the challenge is to train a classifier to classify the actions from the provided video clips. Each action label is made up of a verb and a set of nouns (e.g., the action 'Wash Plate' is made up of the verb 'Wash' and noun 'Plate'). The noun classification task is very similar to the image classification task. So, for our experiments, we focus on the verb classification in order to test our proposed method on diverse tasks. This dataset has 19 different verb classes (e.g., 'Open', 'Wash' etc.). EGTEA Gaze+ [29] is inherently class-imbalanced. Figure 1(a) shows the data distribution of the EGTEA dataset. For our experiments, we use the split1 of the EGTEA dataset (8299 training video clips and 2022 testing video clips). We create our validation set by using the training video clips from subjects P20 to P26, resulting in 1927 validation video clips and 6372 training clips.

4.2   Implementation Details

We use a LeNet-5 [30] model for MNIST unbalanced binary classification experiments following [28]. The model is trained for 4000 epochs on a single NVIDIA GeForce GTX 1080 GPU with a batch size of 100. As optimizer, we use Stochastic Gradient Descent (SGD) with momentum of 0.9, weight decay of 0.0005 and an initial learning rate of 0.001, which is decayed by 0.1 after 3000 epochs. The trained model is tested on the balanced test set.

For experiments on long-tailed CIFAR, we follow the exact same implementation strategy as provided in [15]. We train a ResNet-32 [31] model for 200 epochs using a batch size of 128 on 4 NVIDIA Titan X GPUs. We use SGD optimizer with momentum 0.9 and weight decay of 0.0005. An initial learning rate of 0.1 is used, which is decayed by 0.01 after 160 and 180 epochs.

For experiments on ImageNet-LT, we use the same setup as in [20]. We use ResNet-10 [31] model for the purpose. The trained model is tested on the balanced test data. For EGTEA dataset, we use a 3D-ResNeXt101 [32,33] model and train it for 100 epochs on 8 NVIDIA Titan X GPUs using a batch size of 32. SGD with momentum 0.9 is used with a weight decay of 0.0005 and an initial learning rate of 0.001, which is decayed by 0.1 after 60 epochs. During training, we sample 10 RGB frames from each video clip by dividing the clip into 10 equal segments followed by randomly selecting one RGB frame from each segment. We use random-cropping, random-rotating and horizontal-flipping as data augmentation. Training input size is $10 \times 3 \times 224 \times 224$. During testing and validation, we sample 10 RGB frames at equal intervals from each video clip.

We use PyTorch [34] framework for all our implementations. For all datasets, our CDB-CE loss implementation calculates the class-wise weights after every epoch using the model's class-wise validation accuracy.

4.3 Results on Unbalanced MNIST Binary Classification

Similar to [28], we increase the majority class ratio defined in Eq. 8 from 0.9 to 0.995 by increasing the number of training samples of majority class, while keeping the total number of training samples constant at 5000. Following implementation details of [28], we retrain LeNet-5 [30] for each majority class ratio using different loss functions and compare the error rate of the trained model on the test set. Table 1 compares the effect of increasing majority class ratio on the test error rates of LeNet-5, trained using various weighted and unweighted loss functions. For comparison, we use the mean and standard deviation of the classification error rates achieved over 10 runs using random splits. The compared loss functions include (1) Unweighted Cross-Entropy (CE), which uses an unweighted softmax cross-entropy loss function to train the model; (2) inverse class-frequency weighting (IFW) [22], which uses a weighted softmax cross-entropy loss function where the weight for each class is calculated using the inverse of it's frequency; (3) Focal loss [14], ClassBalanced (CB) loss [15], Equalization loss (EQL) [16] and L2RW [28] are state-of-the-art loss functions.

As can be seen from Table 1, our class-wise difficulty-balanced cross-entropy (CDB-CE) loss function performs better than the others. But to ensure a good performance, it is important to select an appropriate value of τ. Hence we conduct another experiment to investigate the effect of changing τ on the performance of our method. For that, we compare the performance of our CDB-CE loss function for different values of τ and different majority class ratios. The results of the experiment are listed in Table 2.

As can be seen from Table 2, increasing value of τ initially helps in improving the performance of our method but after a certain point, it leads to a drop in the performance. We believe that the drop comes due to the excessive down-weighting of the samples of the easy classes. In Table 2, our method works well over a wide range of τ values. The best value for τ varies even with the majority class ratio. But one interesting thing to notice is that even though dynamically updating τ does not always give the best performance, it's performance is never

Table 1. Mean and standard deviation of classification error rates (%) of LeNet-5 [30] trained for MNIST [1] imbalanced binary classification using different loss functions for different majority class ratios. Here we show the best results obtained by each of the loss functions in our implementation. For class-wise difficulty-balanced softmax cross-entropy (CDB-CE) loss (Ours), we report the results with dynamically updated τ.

Maj. class ratio	0.9	0.95	0.98	0.99	0.995
Unweighted CE	1.50 ± 0.51	2.36 ± 0.46	5.09 ± 0.41	8.59 ± 0.41	14.35 ± 1.10
IFW [22]	1.16 ± 0.40	1.74 ± 0.31	3.13 ± 0.74	6.01 ± 0.56	8.94 ± 0.70
Focal loss [14]	1.74 ± 0.26	2.78 ± 0.29	6.67 ± 0.63	11.11 ± 1.20	17.17 ± 0.86
CB loss [15]	1.07 ± 0.23	1.79 ± 0.39	3.58 ± 0.71	5.88 ± 1.20	8.61 ± 1.11
EQL [16]	1.49 ± 0.34	2.26 ± 0.41	2.43 ± 0.14	2.60 ± 0.33	3.71 ± 0.41
L2RW [28]	1.24 ± 0.69	1.76 ± 1.12	2.06 ± 0.85	2.63 ± 0.65	3.94 ± 1.23
CDB-CE (Ours)	$\mathbf{0.74 \pm 0.14}$	$\mathbf{1.27 \pm 0.33}$	$\mathbf{1.65 \pm 0.26}$	$\mathbf{2.39 \pm 0.41}$	$\mathbf{3.71 \pm 0.27}$

Table 2. Mean and standard deviation of classification error rates (%) of LeNet-5 [30] trained for MNIST imbalanced binary classification using our CDB-CE loss with different values of τ For dynamically updating τ (last row), we update the value of τ after every epoch as given in Eq. 3.

Maj. class ratio	0.9	0.95	0.98	0.99	0.995
$\tau = 0.5$	1.06 ± 0.34	1.43 ± 0.24	1.93 ± 0.27	2.59 ± 0.44	4.03 ± 0.41
$\tau = 1.0$	0.90 ± 0.27	1.38 ± 0.20	1.86 ± 0.30	2.49 ± 0.57	3.94 ± 0.36
$\tau = 1.5$	0.85 ± 0.19	1.35 ± 0.31	1.71 ± 0.28	2.31 ± 0.38	$\mathbf{3.54 \pm 0.25}$
$\tau = 2.0$	0.75 ± 0.15	1.21 ± 0.32	1.75 ± 0.36	$\mathbf{2.23 \pm 0.34}$	3.65 ± 0.41
$\tau = 5.0$	0.88 ± 0.25	$\mathbf{1.19 \pm 0.36}$	2.00 ± 0.32	2.51 ± 0.41	3.78 ± 0.43
$\tau = 7.0$	0.96 ± 0.20	1.20 ± 0.20	2.04 ± 0.30	2.64 ± 0.40	4.13 ± 0.37
dyn. updated τ	$\mathbf{0.74 \pm 0.14}$	1.27 ± 0.33	$\mathbf{1.65 \pm 0.26}$	2.39 ± 0.41	3.71 ± 0.27

too far from the best and it consistently outperforms all the existing methods listed in Table 1. Therefore, dynamically updating τ can be a default choice to select the value of τ in case one wants to avoid trial and error searching for the best τ.

4.4 Results on Long-Tailed CIFAR-100

We conduct extensive experiments on long-tailed CIFAR-100 dataset [2,15] as well. ResNet-32 [31] is retrained for different imbalance factors in the training dataset, using different loss functions. Table 3 reports the classification accuracy (%) of each such trained model on the CIFAR-100 test set. We compare the results of our method with that of Focal loss [14], Class-Balanced loss [15], L2RW [28], Meta-Weight Net [35] and Equalization loss [16].

As can be seen from Table 3, our CDB-CE loss with dynamically updated τ provides better performance than the others in most cases. But as stated in Sect. 4.3, the results of our method depend highly on the value of τ. Hence, we conduct a further study of how the performance of our method varies on the

Table 3. Top-1 classification accuracy (%) of ResNet-32 trained on long-tailed CIFAR-100 training data. † means that the result has been copied from the origin paper [15,35,36]. For CDB-CE loss (Ours), we report the results with dynamically updated τ.

Imbalance	200	100	50	20	10
Focal loss † [14]	35.62	38.41	44.32	51.95	55.78
Class-Balanced † [15]	36.23	39.60	45.32	52.99	57.99
L2RW † [28]	33.38	40.23	44.44	51.64	53.73
Meta-Weight Net † [35]	**37.91**	42.09	46.74	**54.37**	58.46
Equalization loss[a] † [16]	37.34	40.54	44.70	54.12	58.32
LDAM-DRW † [36]	–	42.04	–	–	58.71
CDB-CE (Ours)	37.40	**42.57**	**46.78**	54.22	**58.74**

[a]The equalization loss results reported in [16] use more augmentation techniques (e.g., Cutout [37], autoAugment [38]) compared to [15,35]. Hence for fair comparison, we report the results that we achieved without using the additional augmentation.

Table 4. Top-1 classification accuracy (%) of ResNet-32 trained using class-wise difficulty-balanced cross-entropy (ours) loss function for different values of τ. $\tau = 0$ means the original unweighted softmax cross-entropy loss function.

Imbalance	200	100	50	20	10
$\tau = 0$	34.95	38.21	43.89	51.34	55.65
$\tau = 0.5$	37.21	41.26	46.13	**54.60**	58.29
$\tau = 1.0$	**37.99**	41.67	46.45	53.48	**59.47**
$\tau = 1.5$	37.63	**42.70**	**47.09**	52.74	58.68
$\tau = 2.0$	37.03	42.44	46.94	53.00	58.65
$\tau = 5.0$	36.81	40.62	45.45	51.67	54.48
Dynamically updated τ	37.40	42.57	46.78	54.22	58.74

long-tailed CIFAR-100 dataset with the change in τ. The results are shown in Table 4.

Using $\tau = 0$ makes our CDB-CE loss drop back to the original unweighted softmax cross-entropy loss function. From Table 4, almost a wide range of values for τ helps our weighted loss to get better results than the baseline of $\tau = 0$. Again the interesting thing is even though dynamically updating τ does not give the best results, it's performance is not far from the best and it outperforms existing methods of Table 3 in majority of the cases.

Table 5. Top-1 classification accuracy (%) of ResNet-10 on ImageNet-LT for different methods. † means that the result has been copied from the origin paper [16, 20, 27].

Method	Top-1 accuracy (%)
Focal loss † [14]	30.50
OLTR † [20]	35.60
Joint training † [27]	34.80
Equalization loss † [16]	36.44
OLTR [20] + CDB-CE (Ours)	36.70
Joint training [27] + CDB-CE (Ours)	37.10
CDB-CE (Ours)	**38.49**

4.5 Results on ImageNet-LT

We compare the performance of our method on ImageNet-LT with other state-of-the-art methods. For comparison, we use the top-1 classification accuracy as our evaluation metric. The results are listed in the Table 5.

For OLTR [20] + CDB-CE and Joint training [27] + CDB-CE, we implemented our method in the original implementations of [20, 27] available on github. From Table 5, it can be seen that our CDB-CE loss not only achieves the best result but it also helps to boost the performance of OLTR and Joint training.

4.6 Results on EGTEA

We also conduct extensive experiments on EGTEA [29] dataset. As shown in Fig. 1, EGTEA dataset is inherently class-imbalanced. The average amount of training samples per class is 1216.0 for the five most frequent classes while for the rest of the 14 classes, the average is only 158.5. That is why we define the five most frequent classes (i.e., 'Take', 'Put', 'Open', 'Cut' and 'Read') together as our 'majority classes' and the rest of the classes as our 'minority classes'. Table 6 reports the results on the test split of a 3D-ResNeXt101, trained on EGTEA dataset using various loss functions. For comparison, we use four different metrics (1) 'Acc@Top1' is the micro-average of the top-1 accuracies of all the classes (2) 'Acc@Top5' is the micro-average of the top-5 accuracies of all the classes (3) 'Recall' is the macro-average of the recall values of all the classes (4) 'Precision' is the macro-average of the precision values of all the classes.

From Table 6, our proposed method achieves significant performance gains in all the metrics compared to other loss functions. In order to ensure that these gains are not entirely because of the majority classes, we conduct a further study, where we compare the performance of different loss functions on the 'majority classes' and 'minority classes' separately. The results are tabulated in Table 7.

Table 7 confirms that our proposed method helps to improve the macro-averaged recall and precision on the 'minority classes'. Though we see a drop in

Table 6. 3D-ResNeXt101 results on EGTEA test set. For class-wise difficulty-balanced cross entropy (ours), we use dynamically updated τ.

	Acc@Top1	Acc@Top5	Recall	Precision
Unweighted CE	67.41	95.40	64.77	61.73
Focal loss [14]	64.34	94.36	59.17	59.09
Class-Balanced loss [15]	66.86	95.69	63.26	63.39
CDB-CE (Ours)	**69.14**	**96.84**	**66.24**	**63.86**

Table 7. 3D-ResNeXt101 results on the 'majority classes' and 'minority classes' for different training loss functions. As explained before, the five most frequent classes together constitute the 'majority classes' while the rest of them are the 'minority classes'. We use 'Recall' and 'Precision' for comparison.

	Majority classes		Minority classes	
	Recall	Precision	Recall	Precision
Unweighted CE	74.91	**75.62**	61.14	56.75
Focal loss [14]	70.27	75.00	55.21	53.40
Class-Balanced loss [15]	**75.95**	73.75	58.72	59.68
CDB-CE (Ours)	74.42	73.51	**63.31**	**60.42**

average recall and precision for the 'majority classes' using our method, Table 6 shows that we achieve an overall performance gain for both precision and recall. Therefore, improvement on the 'minority classes' accounts for the overall gain.

5   Conclusion

In this paper, we have proposed a new weighted-loss method for solving class-imbalance. The key idea of our method is to take the difficulty of each class into consideration, rather than the number of training samples of the class, for assigning weights to samples. Based on this idea, we define a quantification for the dynamic difficulty of each class. Further we propose a difficulty-based weighting system that dynamically assigns weights to the samples based on the difficulty of their classes. We also conduct extensive experiments on artificially induced class-imbalanced MNIST, CIFAR and ImageNet datasets and inherently class-imbalanced EGTEA dataset. The experimental results show that using our weighting strategy with cross-entropy loss function helps to boost its performance and achieve best results on imbalanced datasets. Moreover, achieving good results on both image and video datasets show that the benefit of our method is not limited to any particular type of data.

References

1. Deng, L.: The MNIST database of handwritten digit images for machine learning research [best of the web]. IEEE Signal Process. Mag. **29**, 141–142 (2012)
2. Krizhevsky, A.: Learning multiple layers of features from tiny images. University of Toronto (2012)
3. Deng, J., Dong, W., Socher, R., Li, L., Kai, L, Li, F.-F.: ImageNet: a large-scale hierarchical image database. In: 2009 IEEE Conference on Computer Vision and Pattern Recognition, pp. 248–255 (2009)
4. Carreira, J., Zisserman, A.: Quo Vadis, action recognition? A new model and the kinetics dataset. In: The IEEE Conference on Computer Vision and Pattern Recognition (CVPR) (2017)
5. Goyal, R., et al.: The "something something" video database for learning and evaluating visual common sense. In: The IEEE International Conference on Computer Vision (ICCV) (2017)
6. Soomro, K., Zamir, A.R., Shah, M.: UCF101: a dataset of 101 human actions classes from videos in the wild. CoRR abs/1212.0402 (2012)
7. Chawla, N.V., Bowyer, K.W., Hall, L.O., Kegelmeyer, W.P.: SMOTE: synthetic minority over-sampling technique. J. Artif. Intell. Res. **16**, 321–357 (2002)
8. Bennin, K.E., Keung, J., Phannachitta, P., Monden, A., Mensah, S.: MAHAKIL: diversity based oversampling approach to alleviate the class imbalance issue in software defect prediction. IEEE Trans. Software Eng. **44**, 534–550 (2018)
9. Liu, X., Wu, J., Zhou, Z.: Exploratory undersampling for class-imbalance learning. IEEE Trans. Syst. Man Cybern. Part B (Cybernetics) **39**, 539–550 (2009)
10. Oh Song, H., Xiang, Y., Jegelka, S., Savarese, S.: Deep metric learning via lifted structured feature embedding. In: Proceedings of the IEEE Conference on Computer Vision and Pattern Recognition (CVPR) (2016)
11. Sohn, K.: Improved deep metric learning with multi-class n-pair loss objective. In: Lee, D.D., Sugiyama, M., Luxburg, U.V., Guyon, I., Garnett, R. (eds.) Advances in Neural Information Processing Systems, vol. 29, pp. 1857–1865. Curran Associates, Inc. (2016)
12. Huang, C., Li, Y., Loy, C.C., Tang, X.: Learning deep representation for imbalanced classification. In: Proceedings of the IEEE Conference on Computer Vision and Pattern Recognition (CVPR) (2016)
13. Wang, Y.X., Ramanan, D., Hebert, M.: Learning to model the tail. In: Guyon, I., et al. (eds.) Advances in Neural Information Processing Systems, vol. 30, pp. 7029–7039. Curran Associates, Inc. (2017)
14. Lin, T.Y., Goyal, P., Girshick, R., He, K., Dollar, P.: Focal loss for dense object detection. In: The IEEE International Conference on Computer Vision (ICCV) (2017)
15. Cui, Y., Jia, M., Lin, T.Y., Song, Y., Belongie, S.: Class-balanced loss based on effective number of samples. In: The IEEE Conference on Computer Vision and Pattern Recognition (CVPR) (2019)
16. Tan, J., et al.: Equalization loss for long-tailed object recognition. In: The IEEE/CVF Conference on Computer Vision and Pattern Recognition (CVPR) (2020)
17. Li, B., Liu, Y., Wang, X.: Gradient harmonized single-stage detector. CoRR abs/1811.05181 (2018)

18. Han, H., Wang, W.-Y., Mao, B.-H.: Borderline-SMOTE: a new over-sampling method in imbalanced data sets learning. In: Huang, D.-S., Zhang, X.-P., Huang, G.-B. (eds.) ICIC 2005. LNCS, vol. 3644, pp. 878–887. Springer, Heidelberg (2005). https://doi.org/10.1007/11538059_91

19. Bunkhumpornpat, C., Sinapiromsaran, K., Lursinsap, C.: Safe-Level-SMOTE: safe-level-synthetic minority over-sampling TEchnique for handling the class imbalanced problem. In: Theeramunkong, T., Kijsirikul, B., Cercone, N., Ho, T.-B. (eds.) PAKDD 2009. LNCS (LNAI), vol. 5476, pp. 475–482. Springer, Heidelberg (2009). https://doi.org/10.1007/978-3-642-01307-2_43

20. Liu, Z., Miao, Z., Zhan, X., Wang, J., Gong, B., Yu, S.X.: Large-scale long-tailed recognition in an open world. In: Proceedings of the IEEE/CVF Conference on Computer Vision and Pattern Recognition (CVPR) (2019)

21. Mikolov, T., Sutskever, I., Chen, K., Corrado, G., Dean, J.: Distributed representations of words and phrases and their compositionality. CoRR abs/1310.4546 (2013)

22. Huang, C., Li, Y., Loy, C.C., Tang, X.: Learning deep representation for imbalanced classification. In: 2016 IEEE Conference on Computer Vision and Pattern Recognition (CVPR), pp. 5375–5384 (2016)

23. Amin, A.: Comparing oversampling techniques to handle the class imbalance problem: a customer churn prediction case study. IEEE Access **4**, 7940–7957 (2016)

24. Tsai, C.F., Lin, W.C., Hu, Y.H., Yao, G.T.: Under-sampling class imbalanced datasets by combining clustering analysis and instance selection. Inf. Sci. **477**, 47–54 (2018)

25. Hadsell, R., Chopra, S., LeCun, Y.: Dimensionality reduction by learning an invariant mapping. In: 2006 IEEE Computer Society Conference on Computer Vision and Pattern Recognition (CVPR 2006), vol. 2, pp. 1735–1742 (2006)

26. Ge, W., Huang, W., Dong, D., Scott, M.R.: Deep metric learning with hierarchical triplet loss. In: Ferrari, V., Hebert, M., Sminchisescu, C., Weiss, Y. (eds.) ECCV 2018. LNCS, vol. 11210, pp. 272–288. Springer, Cham (2018). https://doi.org/10.1007/978-3-030-01231-1_17

27. Kang, B., et al.: Decoupling representation and classifier for long-tailed recognition. In: Eighth International Conference on Learning Representations (ICLR) (2020)

28. Ren, M., Zeng, W., Yang, B., Urtasun, R.: Learning to reweight examples for robust deep learning. CoRR abs/1803.09050 (2018)

29. Li, Y., Liu, M., Rehg, J.M.: In the eye of beholder: joint learning of gaze and actions in first person video. In: Ferrari, V., Hebert, M., Sminchisescu, C., Weiss, Y. (eds.) ECCV 2018. LNCS, vol. 11209, pp. 639–655. Springer, Cham (2018). https://doi.org/10.1007/978-3-030-01228-1_38

30. Lecun, Y., Bottou, L., Bengio, Y., Haffner, P.: Gradient-based learning applied to document recognition. Proc. IEEE **86**, 2278–2324 (1998)

31. He, K., Zhang, X., Ren, S., Sun, J.: Deep residual learning for image recognition. CoRR abs/1512.03385 (2015)

32. Xie, S., Girshick, R.B., Dollár, P., Tu, Z., He, K.: Aggregated residual transformations for deep neural networks. CoRR abs/1611.05431 (2016)

33. Hara, K., Kataoka, H., Satoh, Y.: Can spatiotemporal 3D CNNs retrace the history of 2D CNNs and ImageNet? In: The IEEE Conference on Computer Vision and Pattern Recognition (CVPR) (2018)

34. Ketkar, N.: In: Introduction to PyTorch, pp. 195–208. Apress, Berkeley (2017)

35. Shu, J., et al.: Meta-weight-net: Learning an explicit mapping for sample weighting. In: Wallach, H., Larochelle, H., Beygelzimer, A., d'Alché-Buc, F., Fox, E., Garnett, R. (eds.) Advances in Neural Information Processing Systems, vol. 32, pp. 1919–1930. Curran Associates, Inc. (2019)
36. Cao, K., Wei, C., Gaidon, A., Arechiga, N., Ma, T.: Learning imbalanced datasets with label-distribution-aware margin loss. In: Wallach, H., Larochelle, H., Beygelzimer, A., d'Alché-Buc, F., Fox, E., Garnett, R. (eds.) Advances in Neural Information Processing Systems, vol. 32, pp. 1567–1578. Curran Associates, Inc. (2019)
37. Devries, T., Taylor, G.W.: Improved regularization of convolutional neural networks with cutout. CoRR abs/1708.04552 (2017)
38. Cubuk, E.D., Zoph, B., Mane, D., Vasudevan, V., Le, Q.V.: Autoaugment: learning augmentation strategies from data. In: The IEEE Conference on Computer Vision and Pattern Recognition (CVPR) (2019)

OpenTraj: Assessing Prediction Complexity in Human Trajectories Datasets

Javad Amirian[1]([✉]), Bingqing Zhang[2], Francisco Valente Castro[3],
Juan José Baldelomar[3], Jean-Bernard Hayet[3], and Julien Pettré[1]

[1] Univ Rennes, Inria, CNRS, IRISA, Rennes, France
{javad.amirian,julien.pettre}@inria.fr
[2] University College London, London, UK
bingqing.zhang.18@ucl.ac.uk
[3] CIMAT, A.C., Guanajuato, Mexico
{francisco.valente,juan.baldelomar,jbhayet}@cimat.mx

Abstract. Human Trajectory Prediction (HTP) has gained much momentum in the last years and many solutions have been proposed to solve it. Proper benchmarking being a key issue for comparing methods, this paper addresses the question of evaluating how complex is a given dataset with respect to the prediction problem. For assessing a dataset complexity, we define a series of indicators around three concepts: Trajectory predictability; Trajectory regularity; Context complexity. We compare the most common datasets used in HTP in the light of these indicators and discuss what this may imply on benchmarking of HTP algorithms. Our source code is released on Github (https://github.com/crowdbotp/OpenTraj).

Keywords: Human trajectory prediction · Trajectory dataset · Motion prediction · Trajectory forecasting · Dataset assessment · Benchmarking

1 Introduction

Human trajectory prediction (HTP) is a crucial task for many applications, ranging from self-driving cars to social robots, etc. The communities of computer vision, mobile robotics, and crowd dynamics have been noticeably active on this topic. Many outstanding prediction algorithms have been proposed, from physics-based social force models [1–3] to data-driven models [4–6].

In parallel, efforts have been made towards a proper benchmarking of the existing techniques. This has led to the creation of pedestrians trajectories datasets for this purpose, or to the re-use of datasets initially designed for other purposes, such as benchmarking Multiple Object Tracking algorithms. Most HTP works [3–5,7] report performance on the sequences of two well-known HTP datasets: the ETH dataset [2] and the UCY dataset [8]. The metrics for comparing prediction performance involve the Average Displacement Error (ADE) and the Final Displacement

© Springer Nature Switzerland AG 2021
H. Ishikawa et al. (Eds.): ACCV 2020, LNCS 12627, pp. 566–582, 2021.
https://doi.org/10.1007/978-3-030-69544-6_34

Fig. 1. Taxonomy of trajectories datasets for Human Trajectory Prediction. (Color figure online)

Error (FDE) on standardized prediction tasks. Other datasets have been used in the same way, but performance comparisons are sometimes subject to controversy, and it remains hard to highlight how significant good performance on a particular sequence or dataset means about a prediction algorithm.

In this paper, we address the following questions: (1) How to measure the complexity or difficulty of a particular dataset for the prediction task? (2) How do the currently used HTP datasets compare to each other? Can we draw conclusions about the strengths/weaknesses of state of the art algorithms?

Our contributions are two-fold: (1) We propose a series of meaningful and interpretable indicators to assess the complexity behind an HTP dataset, and (2) we analyze some of the most common datasets through these indicators.

In Sect. 3, we categorize datasets complexity along three axes, trajectories predictability, trajectories regularity, and context complexity. In Sect. 4, we define indicators quantifying the complexity factors. In Sect. 5, we apply these indicators on common HTP datasets and we discuss the results in Sect. 6.

2   Related Work: HTP Datasets

Due to the non-rigidness nature of the human body or occlusions, people tracking is a difficult problem and has attracted notable attention. Many video datasets have been designed as benchmarking tools for this purpose and used intensively in HTP. Following the recent progress in autonomous driving, other datasets have emerged, involving more complex scenarios. In this section, we propose a taxonomy of HTP datasets and review some of the most representative ones.

2.1   The Zoo of HTP Datasets: A Brief Taxonomy

Many intertwined factors explain how some trajectories or datasets are harder to predict than others for HTP algorithms. In Fig. 1, we summarize essential factors behind prediction complexity, as circles; we separate hidden (blue) and controlled (green) factors. Among hidden factors, we emphasize those related to

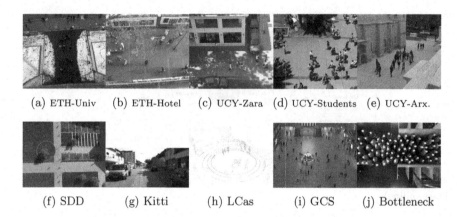

(a) ETH-Univ   (b) ETH-Hotel   (c) UCY-Zara   (d) UCY-Students   (e) UCY-Arx.

(f) SDD   (g) Kitti   (h) LCas   (i) GCS   (j) Bottleneck

Fig. 2. Sample snapshots from a few common HTP datasets.

the acquisition (noisy data), to the environment (multi-modality), or to crowd-related factors (interactions complexity). Some factors can be controlled, such as the recording platform or the choice of the location. To illustrate the variety of setups, snapshots from common HTP datasets are given in Fig. 2.

Raw data may be recorded by a single [2] or multiple [9] sensors, ranging from monocular cameras [10–12] to stereo-cameras, RGB-D cameras, LiDAR, RADARs, or a mix [9,13]. Sensors may provide 3D annotations, but most HTP algorithms run on 2D data (the ground plane), and we focus here on 2D analysis.

Annotation is either manual [2,8,14], semi-automatic [15], or fully automatic, using detection algorithms [10]. In most datasets, the annotations provide the agents' positions in the image. Annotated positions can be projected from image coordinates to world coordinates, given homographies or camera projection matrices. For moving sensors (robots [16] or cars [9,13,14]), the data are sensor-centered, but odometry data are provided to get all positions in a common frame.

2.2   A Short Review of Common HTP Datasets

HTP Datasets from Static Cameras and Drones. The Performance Evaluation of Tracking and Surveillance (PETS) workshops have released several datasets for benchmarking Multiple Object Tracking [17] systems. In particular, the 11 sequences of the PETS'2009 dataset [18], recorded through 8 monocular cameras, include data from *acting* pedestrians, with different levels of density, and have been used in HTP benchmarking [19]. The Town-Centre dataset [12] was also released for visual tracking purposes, with annotations of video footage monitoring a busy town center. It involves around two thousand walking pedestrians with well structured (motion along a street), natural behaviors. The Wild Track dataset [20] was designed for testing person detection in harsh situations (dense crowds) and provides 312 pedestrian trajectories in 400-frame sequences (from 7 views) at 2 fps. The EIF dataset [21] gives ~90k trajectories of persons in a university courtyard, from an overhead camera. The BIWI pedestrian dataset [2] is composed of 2 scenes with hundreds of trajectories of pedestrians engaged in walking activities. The ATC [22] dataset contains annotations for 92 days of pedestrian trajectories in a shopping mall, acquired from 49 3D sensors.

The UCY dataset [8] provides three scenes with walking/standing activities. Developed for crowd simulation, it exhibits different crowd density levels and a clear flow structure. The Bottleneck dataset [23] also arose from crowd simulation and involved crowd controlled experiments (e.g., through bottlenecks).

VIRAT [24] has been designed for activity recognition. It contains annotated trajectories on 11 distinct scenes, in diverse contexts (parking lot, university campus) and mostly natural behaviors. It generally involves one or two agents and objects. A particular case of activity recognition is the one of sports activities [25], for which many data are available through players tracking technology.

The Stanford Drone Dataset (SDD) [11] is a large scale dataset with 60 sequences in eight scenes, filmed from a still drone. It provides trajectories of ~19k moving agents in a university campus, with interactions between pedestrians, cyclists, skateboarders, cars, buses. DUT and CITR [15] datasets have also been acquired from hovering drones for evaluating inter-personal and car-pedestrian interactions. They include, respectively, 1793 and 340 pedestrian trajectories. The inD dataset [10], acquired with a static drone, contains more than 11K trajectories of road users, mostly motorized agents. The scenarios are oriented to urban mobility, with scenes at roundabouts or road intersections. Ko-PER [26] pursues a similar motivation of monitoring spaces shared between cars and non-motorized users. It provides trajectories of pedestrians and vehicles at one road intersection, acquired through laser scans and videos. Similarly, the VRU dataset [27] features around 80 cyclists trajectories, recorded at an urban intersection using cameras and LiDARs. The Forking Paths Dataset [28] was created under the Carla 3D simulator, but it uses real trajectories, which are extrapolated by human annotators to simulate multi-modality with different latent goals.

AV Datasets. Some datasets offer data collected for training/benchmarking algorithms for autonomous vehicles (AV). They may be more difficult because of the mobile data acquisition and because the trajectories are often shorter. LCAS [29] was acquired from a LiDAR sensor on a mobile robot. KITTI [14] has been a popular benchmarking source in computer vision and robotics. Its tracking sub-dataset provides 3D annotations (cars/pedestrians) for ~20 LiDAR and video sequences in urban contexts. AV companies have recently released their datasets, as Waymo [13], with hours of high-resolution sensor data or Argo AI with its Argoverse [30] dataset, featuring 3D tracking annotations for 11k tracked objects over 113 small sequences. Nutonomy disclosed its nuScenes dataset [9] with 85 annotated scenes in the streets of Miami and Pittsburgh.

Benchmarking Through Meta-datasets. Meta-datasets have been designed for augmenting the variety of environments and testing the generalization capacities of HTP systems. TrajNet [19] includes ETH, UCY, SDD and PETS; in [31],

Becker et al. proposed a comprehensive study over the TrajNet training set, giving tips for designing a good predictor and comparing traditional regression baselines vs. neural-network schemes. Trajnet++ [32] proposes a hierarchy of categorization among trajectories to better understand trajectory distributions within datasets. By mid-2020, over 45 solutions have been submitted on Trajnet, with advanced prediction techniques [4,5,31,33,34], but also Social-Force-based models [1], and variants of linear predictors, that give accuracy levels of 94% of the best model [34]. In this work, we give tools to get a deeper understanding of the intrinsic complexities behind these datasets.

3   Problem Description and Formulation of Needs in HTP

3.1   Notations and Problem Formulation

A trajectory dataset is referred to as $\mathbb{X}$. We assume that it is made of N_a trajectories of distinct agents. To be as fair as possible in our comparisons, we mainly reason in terms of absolute time-stamps, even though the acquisition frequency may vary. Within $\mathbb{X}$, the full trajectory of the i-th agent ($i \in [1, N_a]$) is denoted by $\mathbf{T}^i$, its starting time as τ^i, its duration as δ^i. For $t \in [\tau^i, \tau^i + \delta^i]$, we refer to the state of agent i at t as $\mathbf{x}_t^i$. We observe $\mathbf{x}_t^i$ only for a finite subset of timestamps (at camera acquisition times). The *frames* are defined as the set of observations at those times and are denoted by $\mathbf{F}_t$. Each frame contains K_t agents samples.

The state $\mathbf{x}_t^i$ includes the 2D position $\mathbf{p}_t^i$ in a Cartesian system in *meter*. It is often obtained from images and mapped to a world frame; the velocity $\mathbf{v}_t^i$, in m/s, can be estimated by finite differences or filtering.

To compare trajectories, following a common practice in HTP, we split all the original trajectories into N_t trajlets with a common duration $\Delta = 4.8$ s. HTP uses trajlets of Δ_{obs} seconds as observations and the next Δ_{pred} seconds as the prediction targets. Hereafter, the set of distinct trajectories of duration Δ obtained this way are referred to as $\mathbf{X}^k$ where $k \in [1, N_t]$ covers the trajlets (with potentially repetitions of the same agent). Typically, $N_t \gg N_a$. Each trajlet may be seen as an observed part and its corresponding target is referred to as $\mathbf{X}_+^k$.

In the following, we use functions operating at different levels, with different writing conventions. *Trajectory-level functions* $F(\mathbf{X})$, with capital letters, act on trajlets $\mathbf{X}$. Sometimes, we consider the values of F at specific time values t, at we denote the functions as $F_t(\mathbf{X})$. *Frame-level functions* $\mathcal{F}(\mathbf{F})$ act on frames $\mathbf{F}$.

3.2   Datasets Complexity

We define three families of indicators over trajectory datasets that allow us to compare them and identify what makes them more "difficult" than other.

Predictability. A dataset can be analyzed through how easily individual trajectories can be predicted given the rest of the dataset, independently from the predictor. Low predictability on the trajlet distribution $p(\mathbf{X})$ makes forecasting systems struggle with multi-modal predictive distributions, e.g., at crossroads.

In that case, stochastic forecasting methods may be better than deterministic ones, as the latter typically average over the outputs seen in the training data.

Trajectory (ir)regularity. Another dataset characterization is through geometrical and physical properties of the trajectories, to reflect irregularities or deviations to "simple" models. We will use speeds, accelerations for that purpose.

Context Complexity. Some indicators evaluate the complexity of the context, i.e., external factors that influence the course of individual trajectories. Typically, crowd density has a strong impact on the difficulty of HTP.

These indicators operate at different levels and may be correlated. For example, complex scenes or high crowdedness levels may lead to geometric irregularities in the trajectories and to lower predictability levels. Finally, even though it is common to *combine* datasets, our analysis is focused on individual datasets.

4   Numerical Assessment of a HTP Dataset Complexity

Based on the elements from Sect. 3, we propose several indicators for assessing a dataset difficulty, most of the kind $F(\mathbf{X}^k)$, defined at the level of trajlets $\mathbf{X}^k$.

4.1   Overall Description of the Set of Trajlets

To explore the distribution $p(\mathbf{T})$ in a dataset, we first consider the distributions of pedestrian positions at a timestep t. We parametrize each trajlet by fitting a cubic spline $\mathbf{p}_k(t)$ with $t \in [0, 4.8]$. For $t \in [0, 4.8]$, we get 50 time samples $\mathcal{S}(t) = \{\mathbf{p}_k(t), \ 1 \leq k \leq N_t\}$ and analyze $\mathcal{S}(t)$ through clustering and entropy:

- **Number of Clusters** $M_t(\mathbb{X})$: We fit a Gaussian Mixture Model (GMM) to our sample set using Expectation Maximization and select the number of clusters with the Bayesian Information Criterion [35].
- **Entropy** $H_t(\mathbb{X})$: We get a kernel density estimation of $\mathcal{S}(t)$ (see below in Sect. 4.2) and use the obtained probabilities to estimate the entropy.

High entropy means that many data points do not occur frequently, while low entropy means that most data points are "predictable". Similarly, a large number of clusters would require a more complex predictive model. Both indicators give us an understanding of how homogeneous through time are all the trajectories in the dataset.

4.2   Evaluating Datasets Trajlet-Wise Predictability

To quantify the trajectory predictability, we use the conditional entropy of the predicted part of the trajectory, given its observed part. Some authors [36] have used alternatively the maximum of the corresponding density. For a trajectory $\mathbf{X}^k \cup \mathbf{X}_+^k$, we define the conditional entropy conditioned to the observed $\mathbf{X}^k$ as

$$H(\mathbf{X}^k) = -E_{\mathbf{X}_+}[\log p(\mathbf{X}_+ | \mathbf{X}^k)]. \tag{1}$$

We use kernel density estimation with the whole dataset $\mathbb{X}$ (N_t trajectories) to estimate it. We have N_{obs} observed points during the first Δ_{obs} seconds (trajlet $\mathbf{X}_k$) and N_{pred} points to predict during the last Δ_{pred} seconds (trajlet $\mathbf{X}_k^+$). We define a Gaussian kernel K_h over the sum of Euclidean distances between the consecutive points along two trajectories $\mathbf{X}$ and $\mathbf{X}'$ with N points each (in $\mathbb{R}^{2N}$):

$$K_{h,N}(\mathbf{X}, \mathbf{X}') = \frac{1}{(2\pi h^2)^N} \exp(-\frac{1}{2h^2}\|\mathbf{X} - \mathbf{X}'\|^2), \tag{2}$$

where h is a common bandwidth factor for all the dimensions. We get an approximate conditional density as the ratio of the two kernel density estimates

$$p(\mathbf{X}_+|\mathbf{X}^k) \approx \frac{\frac{1}{N_t}\sum_{l=1}^{N_t} K_{h,N_{obs}+N_{pred}}(\mathbf{X}^k \cup \mathbf{X}_+, \mathbf{X}^l \cup \mathbf{X}_+^l)}{\frac{1}{N_t}\sum_{l=1}^{N_t} K_{h,N_{obs}}(\mathbf{X}^k, \mathbf{X}^l)}. \tag{3}$$

Since $K_{h,N_{obs}+N_{pred}}(\mathbf{X}^k \cup \mathbf{X}_+, \mathbf{X}^l \cup \mathbf{X}_+^l) = K_{h,N_{obs}}(\mathbf{X}^k, \mathbf{X}^l)K_{h,N_{pred}}(\mathbf{X}_+, \mathbf{X}_+^l)$, we can express the distribution of Eq. 3 as the following mixture of Gaussian:

$$p(\mathbf{X}_+|\mathbf{X}^k) \approx \sum_{l=1}^{N_t} \omega_l(\mathbf{X}^k)K_{h,N_{pred}}(\mathbf{X}_+, \mathbf{X}_+^l) \text{ with } \omega_l(\mathbf{X}^k) = \frac{K_{h,N_{obs}}(\mathbf{X}^k, \mathbf{X}^l)}{\sum_{l=1}^{N_t} K_{h,N_{obs}}(\mathbf{X}^k, \mathbf{X}^l)}. \tag{4}$$

For a trajlet $\mathbf{X}^k$, we estimate $H(\mathbf{X}^k)$ by sampling M samples $\mathbf{X}_+^{(m)}$ from Eq. 4:

$$H(\mathbf{X}^k) \approx -\frac{1}{M} \sum_{m=1}^{M} \log(\sum_{l=1}^{N_t} \omega_l(\mathbf{X}^k)K(\mathbf{X}_+^{(m)}, \mathbf{X}_+^l)). \tag{5}$$

4.3 Evaluating Trajectories Regularity

In this section, we define geometric and statistical indicators evaluating how *regular* individual trajectories $\mathbf{X}^k$ in a dataset may be.

Motion Properties. A first series of indicators are obtained through *speed distributions*, where speed is defined as: $s(\mathbf{x}_t) = \|\mathbf{v}_t\|$. At the level of a trajectory $\mathbf{X}^k$, we evaluate the mean and the largest deviation of speeds along the trajectory

$$S^{avg}(\mathbf{X}^k) = \underset{t\in[\tau^k,\tau^k+\delta^k]}{\text{average}} (s(\mathbf{x}_t)) \tag{6}$$

$$S^{rg}(\mathbf{X}^k) = \max_{t\in[\tau^k,\tau^k+\delta^k]} (s(\mathbf{x}_t)) - \min_{t\in[\tau^k,\tau^k+\delta^k]} (s(\mathbf{x}_t)). \tag{7}$$

The higher the speed, the larger the displacements and the more uncertain the target whereabouts. Also, speed variations can reflect on high-level properties such as people activity in the environment or the complexity of this environment.

Regularity is evaluated through accelerations $a(\mathbf{x}_t) \approx \frac{1}{dt}[s(\mathbf{x}_{t+dt}) - s(\mathbf{x}_t)]$. It can reflect the interactions of an agent with its environment according to social-force model [1]: agents typically keep their preferred speed while there is no reason to change it. High accelerations appear when an agent avoids collision or joins a group. We consider the average and maximal accelerations along $\mathbf{X}^k$:

$$A^{avg}(\mathbf{X}^k) = \underset{t\in[\tau^k,\tau^k+\delta^k]}{\text{average}} (|a(\mathbf{x}_t)|); \quad A^{max}(\mathbf{X}^k) = \underset{t\in[\tau^k,\tau^k+\delta^k]}{\max}(|a(\mathbf{x}_t)|). \quad (8)$$

Non-linearity of Trajectories. *Path efficiency* is defined as the ratio of the distance between the trajectory endpoints over the trajectory length:

$$F(\mathbf{X}^k) = \frac{\|p_{\tau^k+\delta^k} - p_{\tau^k}\|}{\int_{t=\tau^k}^{\tau^k+\delta^k} dl}. \quad (9)$$

The higher its value, the closer the path is to a straight line, so we would expect that the prediction task will be "easier" for high values of $F(\mathbf{X}^k)$.

Another indicator is the average angular deviation from a linear motion. To estimate it, we align all trajlets by translating them to the origin of coordinate system and rotating them such that the first velocity is aligned with the x axis:

$$\hat{\mathbf{X}}^k = \left[\mathbf{R}(-\angle \mathbf{v}_0^k) \ -\mathbf{p}_0^k\right] \begin{bmatrix} \mathbf{X}^k \\ 1 \end{bmatrix}^T. \quad (10)$$

Then the deviation of a trajectory $\mathbf{X}^k$ at t and its average value are defined as:

$$D_t(\mathbf{X}^k) = \angle \hat{\mathbf{X}}_t^k \text{ and } D(\mathbf{X}^k) = \underset{t\in[\tau^k,\tau^k+\delta^k]}{\text{average}} (D_t(\mathbf{X}^k)). \quad (11)$$

4.4 Evaluating the Context Complexity

The data acquisition context may impact HTP in different ways. It may ease the prediction by introducing correlations: With groups, it can be easier to predict one's motion from the other group members. In general, social interactions result into adjustments that may be generate non-linearities (and lower predictability).

Collision Avoidance is the most basic type of interaction. Higher density resulting into more interactions, this aspect is also evaluated by the density metrics below. However, high-density crowds may ease the prediction (e.g., laminar flow of people). To reflect the intensity of collision avoidance-based interactions, we use the *distance of closest approach* (DCA) [37] at t, for a pair of agents (i,j):

$$\text{dca}(t,i,j) = \sqrt{\|\mathbf{x}_t^i - \mathbf{x}_t^j\|^2 - (\max(0, \frac{(\mathbf{v}_t^i - \mathbf{v}_t^j)^T(\mathbf{x}_t^i - \mathbf{x}_t^j)}{\|\mathbf{v}_t^i - \mathbf{v}_t^j\|}))^2}, \quad (12)$$

and for a trajlet $\mathbf{X}^k$ (relative to an agent i_k), we consider the overall minimum

$$C(\mathbf{X}^k) = \underset{t\in[\tau^k,\tau^k+\delta^k]}{\min} \underset{j}{\min} \text{dca}(t,i_k,j). \quad (13)$$

In [38], the authors suggest that time-to-collision (TTC) is strongly correlated with trajectory adjustments. The TTC for a pair of agents i, j, modeled as disks of radius R, for which a collision will occur when keeping their velocity, is

$$\tau(t, i, j) = \frac{1}{\|\mathbf{v}_t^i - \mathbf{v}_t^j\|^2} [\delta_t^{ij} - \sqrt{(\delta_t^{ij})^2 - \|\mathbf{v}_t^i - \mathbf{v}_t^j\|^2 (\|\mathbf{x}_t^i - \mathbf{x}_t^j\|^2 - 4R^2)}] \quad (14)$$

where $\delta_t^{ij} = (\mathbf{v}_t^i - \mathbf{v}_t^j)^T (\mathbf{x}_t^i - \mathbf{x}_t^j)$. In [38], the authors also proposed quantifying the interaction strength between pedestrians as an energy function of τ:

$$E(\tau) = \frac{k}{\tau^2} e^{-\frac{\tau}{\tau^+}}, \quad (15)$$

with k a scaling factor and τ^+ an upper bound for TTC. Like [38], we estimate the actual TTC probability density between pedestrians (from Eq. 14) over the probability density that would arise without interaction (using the time-scrambling approach of [38]). Then we estimate $E(\tau)$ with Eq. 15. As the range of well-defined values for τ may be small, we group the data into 0.2 s intervals and use t-tests to find out the lower bound τ^- when two consecutive bins are significantly different ($p < 0.05$). The upper bound τ^+ is fixed as 3 s. TTC and energy interaction are extended for trajlets (only if there exists future collision):

$$T(\mathbf{X}^k) = \min_{t \in [\tau^k, \tau^k + \delta^k]} \min_j \tau(t, i_k, j) \text{ and } E(\mathbf{X}^k) = E(T(\mathbf{X}^k)). \quad (16)$$

Density and Distance Measures. For a frame $\mathbf{F}_t$, the *Global Density* is defined as the number of agents per unit area $\mathcal{D}(\mathbf{F}_t) = \frac{K_t}{\mathbf{A}(\mathbb{X})}$, with K_t the number of agents present at t and $\mathbf{A}(\mathbb{X})$ the spatial extent of $\mathbb{X}$, evaluated from the extreme x, y values. The *Local Density* measures the density in a neighborhood. Plaue et al. [39] infer it with a nearest-neighbour kernel estimator. For a point $\mathbf{x}_t$,

$$\rho(\mathbf{x}_t) = \frac{1}{2\pi} \sum_{i=1}^{K_t} \frac{1}{(\lambda d_t^i)^2} \exp\left(-\frac{\|\mathbf{x}_t^i - \mathbf{x}_t\|^2}{2(\lambda d_t^i)^2}\right), \quad (17)$$

with $d_t^i = \min_{j \neq i} \|\mathbf{x}_t^i - \mathbf{x}_t^j\|$ the distance from i to its nearest neighbor and $\lambda > 0$ a smoothing parameter. ρ is used to evaluate a trajlet-wise local density indicator

$$L(\mathbf{X}^k) = \max_{t \in [\tau^k, \tau^k + \delta^k]} \rho(\mathbf{x}_t^{i_k}). \quad (18)$$

5   Experiments

In this section, we analyze some common HTP datasets in the light of the indicators presented in the previous section. In Table 1, we give statistics (location, number of agents, duration. . .) for the datasets we have chosen to evaluate. We

Table 1. General statistics of assessed datasets. The columns present the type of location where the data is collected, the acquisition means, number of annotated pedestrians, the -rounded- duration (in minute or hour), the total duration of all trajectories, number of trajlets, and percent of non-static trajlets, respectively.

Dataset	Location	Acquisition	#peds	duration	total dur.	#trajlets	non-static
ETH Univ	univ entrance	top-view cam	360	13m	1h	823	93%
Hotel	urban street	top-view cam	390	12m	0.7h	484	66%
UCY Zara	urban street	top-view cam	489	18m	2.1h	2130	75%
Students	univ campus	top-view cam	967	11.5m	4.5h	4702	96%
SDD Coupa		drone cam	297	26m	4.5h	5,394	41%
Bookstore	univ campus	drone cam	896	56m	9.5h	11,239	54%
DeathCircle			917	22.3m	4.2h	8,288	62%
inD inD-Loc(1)	urban intersection	drone cam	800	180m	7.1h	8302	94%
inD-Loc(2)			2.1k	240m	18h	21234	95%
Bottleneck 1D Flow(w=180)	simulated corridor	top-view cam	170	1.3m	1h	940	99%
2D Flow(w=160)			309	1.3m	1.5h	1552	100%
Edinburgh Sep{1,2,4,5,6,10}	univ forum	top-view cam	1.2k	9h	3h	2124	83%
GC Station	train station	surveillance cam	17k	1.1h	79h	76866	99%
Wild-Track	univ campus	multi-cam	312	3.3m	1.3h	1215	57%
KITTI	urban streets	lidar& multi-cam	142	5.8m	0.3h	253	93%
LCas-Minerva	univ-indoor	lidar	878	11m	4.8h	3553	83%

gather the most commonly used in HTP evaluation (ETH, UCY, SDD in particular) and datasets coming from a variety of modalities (static cameras, drones, autonomous vehicles. . .), to include different species from the zoo of Sect. 2.1.

For those including very distinct sub-sequences, e.g., ETH, UCY, SDD, inD, and Bottleneck (also denoted by BN in the figures), we split them into their constituting sequences. Also, note that we have focused only on pedestrians (no cyclist nor cars). We also ruled out any dataset containing less than 100 trajectories (e.g., UCY Arxiepiskopi or PETS).

To analyze a dataset $\mathbb{X}$, we apply systematically the following preprocessing

1. Projection to world coordinates, when necessary;
2. Down-sampling the annotations to a 2–3 fps framerate;
3. Application of a Kalman smoothing with a constant acceleration model;
4. Splitting of the resulting trajectories into trajlets $\mathbf{X}^k$ of length $\Delta = 4.8\,\mathrm{s}$ and filtering out trajlets shorter than $1\,\mathrm{m}$.

We finally recall the trajlet-wise indicators we have previously introduced:

Overall description	Entropy $H_t(\mathbb{X}^k)$ and clusters $M_t(\mathbb{X})$ (Sect. 4.1).
Predictability	Cond. entropy $H(\mathbf{X}^k)$ (Eq. 5).
Regularity	Speed $S^{avg}(\mathbf{X}^k), S^{rg}(\mathbf{X}^k)$ (Eq. 7).
	Acceleration $A^{avg}(\mathbf{X}^k), A^{max}(\mathbf{X}^k)$ (Eq. 8).
	Efficiency $F(\mathbf{X}^k)$ (Eq. 9).
	Angular deviation $D(\mathbf{X}^k)$ (Eq. 11).
Context	Closest approach $C(\mathbf{X}^k)$ (Eq. 13).
	Time-to-collision $T(\mathbf{X}^k)$, energy $E(\mathbf{X}^k)$ (Eq. 16).
	Local density $L(\mathbf{X}^k)$ (Eq. 18)

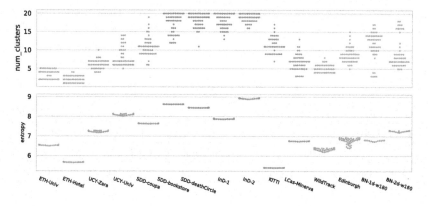

Fig. 3. Entropy $H_t(\mathbb{X})$ and number of clusters $M_t(\mathbb{X})$, as described in Sect. 4.1, at different progression rates t, for a dataset $\mathbb{X}$. Each dot corresponds to one t.

Overall Description of the Set of Trajlets. For the indicators of Sect. 4.2, we have chosen $h = 0.5\,\mathrm{m}$ for the Gaussian in the kernel-based density estimation; the number of samples used to evaluate the entropy is $M = 30$; the maximal number of clusters when clustering unconditional or conditional trajectories distributions is 21. In Fig. 3, we plot the distributions of the overall entropy and number of clusters, at different progression rates along the dataset trajectories. Without surprise, higher entropy values are observed for the less structured datasets (without main directed flows) such as SDD or inD. The number of clusters follows a similar trend, indicating possible multi-modality.

Predictability Indicators. In Fig. 4, we depict the values of $H(\mathbf{X}^k)$, with one dot per trajlet $\mathbf{X}^k$. Interestingly, excepting the Bottleneck sequences, where high density generates randomness, the support for the entropy distributions are similar among datasets. What probably makes the difference are the tails in these distributions: large lower tails indicate high proportions of easy-to-predict trajlets, while large upper tails indicate high proportions of hard-to-predict trajlets.

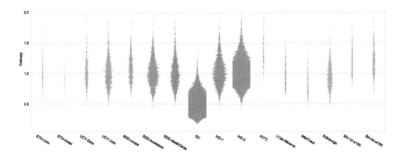

Fig. 4. Conditional entropies $H(\mathbf{X}^k)$.

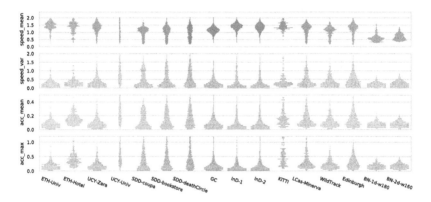

Fig. 5. Speed and acceleration indicators $S^{avg}(\mathbf{X}^k), S^{rg}(\mathbf{X}^k), A^{avg}(\mathbf{X}^k), A^{max}(\mathbf{X}^k)$. From top to bottom: speed means and variations, mean and max. accelerations.

Regularity Indicators. In Fig. 5, we depict the distributions of the regularity indicators $S^{avg}(\mathbf{X}^k), S^{rg}(\mathbf{X}^k), A^{avg}(\mathbf{X}^k), A^{max}(\mathbf{X}^k)$ from Eqs. 7 and 8. Speed averages are generally centered around 1 and 1.5 m/s. Disparities among datasets appear with speed variations and average accelerations: ETH or UCY Zara sequences do not exhibit large speed variations, e.g. compared to Wild Track. In Fig. 6a, we depict the path efficiency $F(\mathbf{X}^k)$ fro Eq. 9, and we observe that ETH, UCY paths tend to be straighter. More complex paths appear in Bottleneck, due to the interactions within the crowd, or in SDD-deathCircle, EIF, due to the environment complexity. In Fig. 6b, deviations $D_t(\mathbf{X}^k)$ are displayed for different progression rates along the trajectories, and reflect similar trends.

Context Complexity Indicators. For estimating the TTC in Eq. 14, we set $R = 0.3$ m, and for the interaction energy of Eq. 15, we set $k = 1$. The local density of Eq. 18 uses $\lambda = 1$. In Fig. 7, we display the collision avoidance-related indicators (TTC, DCA and interaction energy) described in Sect. 4.4, while in Fig. 8, we depict the density-related indicators. Most samples have low interaction energy, but interesting interaction levels are visible Zara, InD. The global density for most

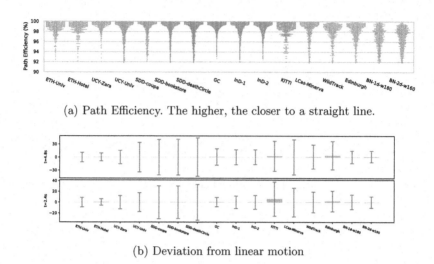

(a) Path Efficiency. The higher, the closer to a straight line.

(b) Deviation from linear motion

Fig. 6. Regularity indicators: Path efficiency and deviation from linear motion.

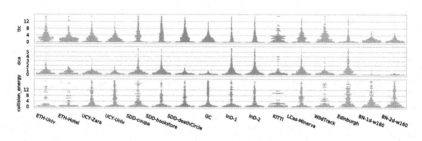

Fig. 7. Collision avoidance-related indicators: From top to bottom, time-to-collision, Distance of closest approach and Interaction energy.

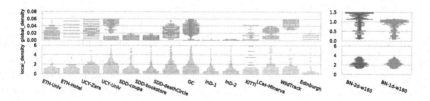

Fig. 8. Density indicators: On the top, global density (one data point for each frame); on the bottom, local density (one data point for each trajlet).

datasets stays less than $0.1\ p/m^2$ while in InD(1&2), Edinburgh and SDD (Coupa & Bookstore), it is even less than 0.02. Bottleneck (1d & 2d) are significantly high density scenarios. For this reason why we depict them separately. Most natural trajectory datasets have a local density about 0–$4\,\mathrm{p/m^2}$ while such number is higher (2–$4\,\mathrm{p/m^2}$) in Bottleneck. With both density indicators, a dataset such as

WildTrack has a high global density and low local density, indicating a relatively sparse occupation. Conversely, low global density and high local density in Ind suggests the pedestrians are more clustered. This observation is also reflected in the interaction and entropy indicators as well.

6   Discussion

Among the findings from the previous Section, Fig. 4 shows that the predictability among most datasets varies in mostly the same ranges. Regarding the motion properties of the datasets (see Fig. 5), another finding is pedestrians' average speed, which, in most cases, varies from 1.0 to 1.5 m/s. However, this is not the case for *Bottleneck* dataset, because the high density of the crowd does not allow the pedestrians to move with a 'normal' speed. In the SDD dataset, we observe multiple pedestrians strolling the campus. As shown in Fig. 6b these low-speed motions are usually associated with high deviation from linear motion, though part of this effect is related to the complexity of the scene layout.

Also, for most of the datasets, the speed variation of trajlets remains almost below 0.5. This is not a true hypothesis for *LCas* and *WildTrack*. As one would expect, the distribution of mean/max acceleration of trajlets is highly correlated with speed variations. In Fig. 6a we see that almost all values are bigger than 90%. For *Bottleneck* we see this phenomenon, where by increasing the crowd density and decreasing crowd speed, the paths become less efficient.

7   Conclusions and Future Work

We have presented in this work a series of indicators for gaining insight into the intrinsic complexity of Human Trajectory Prediction datasets. These indicators cover concepts such as trajectory predictability and regularity, and complexity in the level of inter-pedestrian interactions. In light of these indicators, datasets commonly used in HTP exhibit very different characteristics. In particular, it may explain why predictions techniques that do not use explicit modeling of social interactions, and consider trajectories as independent processes, may be rather successful on datasets where e.g., most trajectories have low collision energy; it may also indicate that some of the more recent datasets with higher levels of density and interaction between agents could provide more reliable information on the quality of the prediction algorithm. Finally, the trajlet-wise analysis presented here opens the door to some evolution in benchmarking processes, as we could evaluate scores by re-weighting the target trajlets in the function of the presented indicators.

Acknowledgements. This research is supported by the CrowdBot H2020 EU Project http://crowdbot.eu and by the Intel Probabilistic Computing initiative. The work done by Francisco Valente Castro was sponsored using an MSc Scholarship given by CONA-CYT with the following scholar registry number 1000188.

References

1. Helbing, D., Molnar, P.: Social force model for pedestrian dynamics. Phys. Rev. E **51**, 4282–4286 (1995)
2. Pellegrini, S., Ess, A., Schindler, K., van Gool, L.: You'll never walk alone: modeling social behavior for multi-target tracking. In: Proceedings of the IEEE International Conference on Computer Vision (ICCV), pp. 261–268 (2009)
3. Yamaguchi, K., Berg, A.C., Ortiz, L.E., Berg, T.L.: Who are you with and where are you going? In: Proceedings of the IEEE Conference on Computer Vision and Pattern Recognition (CVPR), pp. 1345–1352 (2011)
4. Alahi, A., Goel, K., Ramanathan, V., Robicquet, A., Fei-Fei, L., Savarese, S.: Social LSTM: human trajectory prediction in crowded spaces. In: Proceedings of the Conference on Computer Vision and Pattern Recognition (CVPR), pp. 961–971 (2016)
5. Gupta, A., Johnson, J., Fei-Fei, L., Savarese, S., Alahi, A.: Social GAN: socially acceptable trajectories with generative adversarial networks. In: Proceedings of the Conference on Computer Vision and Pattern Recognition (CVPR), pp. 2255–2264 (2018)
6. Salzmann, T., Ivanovic, B., Chakravarty, P., Pavone, M.: Trajectron++: dynamically-feasible trajectory forecasting with heterogeneous data. arXiv preprint abs/2001.03093 (2020)
7. Amirian, J., Hayet, J.B., Pettré, J.: Social ways: learning multi-modal distributions of pedestrian trajectories with GANs. In: Proceedings of the International Conference on Computer Vision and Pattern Recognition Workshops (CVPRW), pp. 2964–2972 (2019)
8. Lerner, A., Chrysanthou, Y., Lischinski, D.: Crowds by example. Comput. Graph. Forum **26**, 655–664 (2007)
9. Caesar, H., et al.: nuScenes: a multimodal dataset for autonomous driving. In: Proceedings of the International Conference on Computer Vision and Pattern Recognition (CVPR), pp. 11621–11631 (2020)
10. Bock, J., Krajewski, R., Moers, T., Runde, S., Vater, L., Eckstein, L.: The inD dataset: a drone dataset of naturalistic road user trajectories at German intersections. arXiv preprint abs/1911.07692 (2019)
11. Robicquet, A., Sadeghian, A., Alahi, A., Savarese, S.: Learning social etiquette: human trajectory understanding in crowded scenes. In: Leibe, B., Matas, J., Sebe, N., Welling, M. (eds.) ECCV 2016. LNCS, vol. 9912, pp. 549–565. Springer, Cham (2016). https://doi.org/10.1007/978-3-319-46484-8_33
12. Benfold, B., Reid, I.: Guiding visual surveillance by tracking human attention. In: Proceedings of the British Machine Vision Conference (BMVC) (2009)
13. Sun, P., et al.: Scalability in perception for autonomous driving: Waymo open dataset. arXiv preprint abs/1912.04838 (2019)
14. Geiger, A., Lenz, P., Stiller, C., Urtasun, R.: Vision meets robotics: the KITTI dataset. Int. J. Robot. Res. **32**, 1231–1237 (2013)
15. Yang, D., Li, L., Redmill, K., Ozguner, U.: Top-view trajectories: a pedestrian dataset of vehicle-crowd interaction from controlled experiments and crowded campus. In: Proceedings of the IEEE Intelligent Vehicles Symposium (IV), pp. 899–904 (2019)
16. Ess, A., Leibe, B., Van Gool, L.: Depth and appearance for mobile scene analysis. In: Proceedings of the IEEE International Conference on Computer Vision (ICCV), pp. 1–8 (2007)

17. Leal-Taixé, L., Milan, A., Reid, I., Roth, S., Schindler, K.: MOTChallenge 2015: towards a benchmark for multi-target tracking. arXiv preprint abs/1504.01942 (2015)
18. Ferryman, J., Shahrokni, A.: PETS 2009: dataset and challenge. In: Proceedings of the IEEE International Workshop on Performance Evaluation of Tracking and Surveillance (PETS), pp. 1–6 (2009)
19. Sadeghian, A., Kosaraju, V., Gupta, A., Savarese, S., Alahi, A.: TrajNet: towards a benchmark for human trajectory prediction. arXiv preprint abs/1805.07663 (2018)
20. Chavdarova, T., et al.: WILDTRACK: a multi-camera HD dataset for dense unscripted pedestrian detection. In: Proceedings of the International Conference on Computer Vision and Pattern Recognition (CVPR), pp. 5030–5039 (2018)
21. Majecka, B.: Statistical models of pedestrian behaviour in the forum. Master's thesis, School of Informatics, University of Edinburgh (2009)
22. Brscic, D., Kanda, T., Ikeda, T., Miyashita, T.: Person position and body direction tracking in large public spaces using 3D range sensors. IEEE Trans. Hum.-Mach. Syst. **43**, 522–534 (2013)
23. Seyfried, A., Passon, O., Steffen, B., Boltes, M., Rupprecht, T., Klingsch, W.: New insights into pedestrian flow through bottlenecks. Transp. Sci. **43**, 395–406 (2009)
24. Oh, S., et al.: A large-scale benchmark dataset for event recognition in surveillance video. In: Proceedings of the International Conference on Computer Vision and Pattern Recognition (CVPR), pp. 3153–3160 (2011)
25. Harmon, M., Lucey, P., Klabjan, D.: Predicting shot making in basketball learnt from adversarial multiagent trajectories. arXiv preprint abs/1609.04849 (2016)
26. Strigel, E., Meissner, D., Seeliger, F., Wilking, B., Dietmayer, K.: The Ko-PER intersection laser scanner and video dataset. In: Proceedings of the IEEE International Conference on Intelligent Transportation Systems (ITSC), pp. 1900–1901 (2014)
27. Bieshaar, M., Zernetsch, S., Hubert, A., Sick, B., Doll, K.: Cooperative starting movement detection of cyclists using convolutional neural networks and a boosted stacking ensemble. arXiv preprint abs/1803.03487 (2018)
28. Liang, J., Jiang, L., Murphy, K., Yu, T., Hauptmann, A.: The garden of forking paths: towards multi-future trajectory prediction. In: Proceedings of the International Conference on Computer Vision and Pattern Recognition, pp. 10508–10518 (2020)
29. Yan, Z., Duckett, T., Bellotto, N.: Online learning for human classification in 3D lidar-based tracking. In: Proceedings of the IEEE/RSJ International Conference on Intelligent Robots and Systems (IROS), pp. 864–871 (2017)
30. Chang, M.F., et al.: Argoverse: 3D tracking and forecasting with rich maps. In: Proceedings of the International Conference on Computer Vision and Pattern Recognition (CVPR), pp. 8748–8757 (2019)
31. Becker, S., Hug, R., Hübner, W., Arens, M.: An evaluation of trajectory prediction approaches and notes on the TrajNet benchmark. arXiv preprint abs/1805.07663 (2018)
32. Kothari, P., Kreiss, S., Alahi, A.: Human trajectory forecasting in crowds: a deep learning perspective (2020)
33. Ellis, D., Sommerlade, E., Reid, I.: Modelling pedestrian trajectory patterns with gaussian processes. In: Proceedings of the IEEE International Conference on Computer Vision Workshops (ICCVW), pp. 1229–1234 (2009)
34. Giuliari, F., Hasan, I., Cristani, M., Galasso, F.: Transformer networks for trajectory forecasting. arXiv preprint abs/2003.08111 (2020)

35. Claeskens, G., Hjort, N.L.: Cambridge series in statistical and probabilistic mathematics. In: The Bayesian Information Criterion, pp. 70–98. Cambridge University Press, Cambridge (2008)
36. Li, M., Westerholt, R., Fan, H., Zipf, A.: Assessing spatiotemporal predictability of LBSN: a case study of three foursquare datasets. GeoInformatica **22**, 541–561 (2016)
37. Olivier, A.H., Marin, A., Crétual, A., Berthoz, A., Pettré, J.: Collision avoidance between two walkers: role-dependent strategies. Gait Posture **38**, 751–756 (2013)
38. Karamouzas, I., Skinner, B., Guy, S.J.: Universal power law governing pedestrian interactions. Phys. Rev. Lett. **113**, 238701 (2014)
39. Plaue, M., Chen, M., Bärwolff, G., Schwandt, H.: Trajectory extraction and density analysis of intersecting pedestrian flows from video recordings. In: Proceedings of the ISPRS Conference on Photogrammetric Image Analysis, pp. 285–296 (2011)

Pre-training Without Natural Images

Hirokatsu Kataoka[1]([✉]), Kazushige Okayasu[1,2], Asato Matsumoto[1,3],
Eisuke Yamagata[4], Ryosuke Yamada[1,2], Nakamasa Inoue[4], Akio Nakamura[2],
and Yutaka Satoh[1,3]

[1] National Institute of Advanced Industrial Science and Technology (AIST),
Tokyo, Japan
hirokatsu.kataoka@aist.go.jp
[2] Tokyo Denki University, Tokyo, Japan
[3] University of Tsukuba, Tsukuba, Japan
[4] Tokyo Institute of Technology, Tokyo, Japan

Abstract. Is it possible to use convolutional neural networks pre-trained without any natural images to assist natural image understanding? The paper proposes a novel concept, Formula-driven Supervised Learning. We automatically generate image patterns and their category labels by assigning fractals, which are based on a natural law existing in the background knowledge of the real world. Theoretically, the use of automatically generated images instead of natural images in the pre-training phase allows us to generate an infinite scale dataset of labeled images. Although the models pre-trained with the proposed Fractal DataBase (FractalDB), a database without natural images, does not necessarily outperform models pre-trained with human annotated datasets at all settings, we are able to partially surpass the accuracy of ImageNet/Places pre-trained models. The image representation with the proposed FractalDB captures a unique feature in the visualization of convolutional layers and attentions.

1 Introduction

The introduction of sophisticated pre-training image representation has lead to a great expansion of the potential of image recognition. Image representations with e.g., the ImageNet/Places pre-trained convolutional neural networks (CNN), has without doubt become the most important breakthrough in recent years [1,2]. We had lots to learn from the ImageNet project, such as huge amount of annotations done by crowdsourcing and well-organized categorization based on WordNet [3]. However, due to the fact that the annotation was done by a large number of unspecified people, most of whom are unknowledgeable and not experts in image classification and the corresponding areas, the dataset contains mistaken, privacy-violated, and ethics-related labels [4,5]. This limits the ImageNet to only non-commercial usage because the images included in the dataset does not clear the right related issues. We believe that this aspect of pre-trained models significantly narrows down the prospects of vision-based recognition.

Electronic supplementary material The online version of this chapter (https://doi.org/10.1007/978-3-030-69544-6_35) contains supplementary material, which is available to authorized users.

H. Ishikawa et al. (Eds.): ACCV 2020, LNCS 12627, pp. 583–600, 2021.
https://doi.org/10.1007/978-3-030-69544-6_35

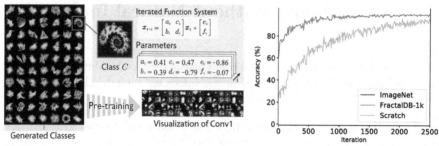

(a) The pre-training framework with Fractal geometry for feature representation learning. We can enhance natural image recognition by pre-training without natural images.

(b) Accuracy transition among ImageNet-1k, FractalDB-1k and training from scratch.

Fig. 1. Proposed *pre-training without natural images* based on fractals, which is a natural formula existing in the real world (Formula-driven Supervised Learning). We automatically generate a large-scale labeled image dataset based on an iterated function system (IFS).

We begin by considering what a pre-trained CNN model with a million natural images is. In most cases, representative image datasets consist of natural images taken by a camera that express a projection of the real world. Although the space of image representation is enormous, a CNN model has been shown to be capable of recognition of natural images from among around one million natural images from the ImageNet dataset. We believe that labeled images on the order of millions have a great potential to improve image representation as a pre-trained model. However, at the moment, a curious question occurs: *Can we accomplish pre-training without any natural images for parameter fine-tuning on a dataset including natural images?* To the best of our knowledge, the ImageNet/Places pre-trained models have not been replaced by a model trained without natural images. Here, we deeply consider pre-training without natural images. In order to replace the models pre-trained with natural images, we attempt to find a method for automatically generating images. Automatically generating a large-scale labeled image dataset is challenging, however, a model pre-trained without natural images makes it possible to solve problems related to privacy, copyright, and ethics, as well as issues related to the cost of image collection and labeling.

Unlike a synthetic image dataset, could we automatically make image patterns and their labels with image projection from a mathematical formula? Regarding synthetic datasets, the SURREAL dataset [6] has successfully made training samples of estimating human poses with human-based motion capture (mocap) and background. In contrast, our Formula-driven Supervised Learning and the generated formula-driven image dataset has a great potential to automatically generate an image pattern and a label. For example, we consider using *fractals*, a sophisticated natural formula [7]. Generated fractals can differ drastically with a slight change in the parameters, and can often be distinguished in the real-world. Most natural objects appear to be composed of complex patterns, but fractals allow us to understand and reproduce these patterns.

We believe that the concept of pre-training without natural images can simplify large-scale DB construction with formula-driven image projection in order to efficiently use a pre-trained model. Therefore, the formula-driven image dataset that includes automatically generated image patterns and labels helps to efficiently solve some of the current issues involved in using a CNN, namely, large-scale image database construction without human annotation and image downloading. Basically, the dataset construction does not rely on any natural images (e.g. ImageNet [1] or Places [2]) or closely resembling synthetic images (e.g., SURREAL [6]). The present paper makes the following contributions.

The concept of pre-training without natural images provides a method by which to automatically generate a large-scale image dataset complete with image patterns and their labels. In order to construct such a database, through exploration research, we experimentally disclose ways to automatically generate categories using fractals. The present paper proposes two sets of randomly searched fractal databases generated in such a manner: FractalDB-1k/10k, which consists of 1,000/10,000 categories (see the supplementary material for all FractalDB-1k categories). See Fig. 1(a) for Formula-driven Supervised Learning from categories of FractalDB-1k. Regarding the proposed database, the FractalDB pre-trained model outperforms some models pre-trained by human annotated datasets (see Table 6 for details). Furthermore, Fig. 1(b) shows that FractalDB pre-training accelerated the convergence speed, which was much better than training from scratch and similar to ImageNet pre-training.

2   Related Work

Pre-training on Large-Scale Datasets. A number of large-scale datasets have been released for exploring how to extract an image representation, e.g., image classification [1,2], object detection [8–10], and video classification [11,12]. These datasets have contributed to improving the accuracy of DNNs when used as (pre-)training. Historically, in multiple aspects of evaluation, the ImageNet pre-trained model has been proved to be strong in transfer learning [13–15]. Moreover, several larger-scale datasets have been proposed, e.g., JFT-300M [16] and IG-3.5B [17], for further improving the pre-training performance.

We are simply motivated to find a method to automatically generate a pre-training dataset without any natural images for acquiring a learning representation on image datasets. We believe that the proposed concept of pre-training without natural images will surpass the methods mentioned above in terms of fairness, privacy-violated, and ethics-related labels, in addition to the burdens of human annotation and image download.

Learning Frameworks. Supervised learning with well-studied architectures is currently the most promising framework for obtaining strong image representations [18–25]. Recently, the research community has been considering how to decrease the volume of labeled data with {un, weak, self}-supervised learning in order to avoid human labeling. In particular, self-supervised learning can be used to create a pre-trained model in a cost-efficient manner by using *obvious* labels. The idea is to make a simple but suitable task, called a pre-text task [26–31]. Though the early approaches (e.g., jigsaw puzzle [27], image rotation [31],

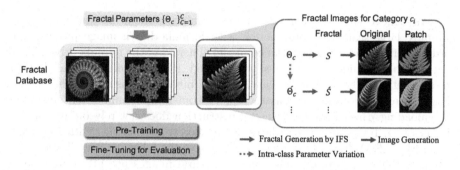

Fig. 2. Overview of the proposed framework. Generating FractalDB: Pairs of an image I_j and its fractal category c_j are generated without human labeling and image downloading. Application to transfer learning: A FractalDB pre-trained convolutional network is assigned to conduct transfer learning for other datasets.

and colorization [29]) were far from an alternative to human annotation, the more recent approaches (e.g., DeepCluster [32], MoCo [33], and SimCLR [34]) are becoming closer to a human-based supervision like ImageNet.

The proposed framework is complementary to these studies because the above learning frameworks focus on how to represent a natural image based on an existing dataset. Unlike these studies, the proposed framework enables the generation of new image patterns based on a mathematical formula in addition to training labels. The SSL framework can replace the manual labeling supervised by human knowledge, however, there still exists the burdens of image downloading, privacy violations and unfair outputs.

Mathematical Formula for Image Projection. One of the best-known formula-driven image projections is fractals. Fractal theory has been discussed in a long period (e.g., [7,35,36]). Fractal theory has been applied to rendering a graphical pattern in a simple equation [37–39] and constructing visual recognition models [40–43]. Although a rendered fractal pattern loses its infinite potential for representation by projection to a 2D-surface, a human can recognize the rendered fractal patterns as natural objects.

Since the success of these studies relies on the fractal geometry of naturally occurring phenomena [7,44], our assumption that fractals can assist learning image representations for recognizing natural scenes and objects is supported. Other methods, namely, the Bezier curve [45] and Perlin noise [46], have also been discussed in terms of computational rendering. We also implement and compare these methods in the experimental section (see Table 9).

3 Automatically Generated Large-Scale Dataset

Figure 2 presents an overview of the Fractal DataBase (FractalDB), which consists of an infinite number of pairs of fractal images I and their fractal categories c with iterated function system (IFS) [37]. We chose fractal geometry because the function enables to render complex patterns with a simple equation that are closely related to natural objects. All fractal categories are randomly searched (see Fig. 1(a)), and the intra-category instances are expansively generated by considering category configurations such as rotation and patch. (The augmentation is shown as $\theta \to \theta'$ in Fig. 2.)

In order to make a pre-trained CNN model, the FractalDB is applied to each training of the parameter optimization as follows. (i) Fractal images with paired labels are randomly sampled by a mini batch $B = \{(I_j, c_j)\}_{j=1}^{b}$. (ii) Calculate the gradient of B to reduce the loss. (iii) Update the parameters. Note that we replace the pre-training step, such as the ImageNet pre-trained model. We also conduct the fine-tuning step as well as plain transfer learning (e.g., ImageNet pre-training and CIFAR-10 fine-tuning).

3.1   Fractal Image Generation

In order to construct fractals, we use IFS [37]. In fractal analysis, an IFS is defined on a complete metric space $\mathcal{X}$ by

$$\text{IFS} = \{\mathcal{X}; w_1, w_2, \cdots, w_N; p_1, p_2, \cdots, p_N\}, \tag{1}$$

where $w_i : \mathcal{X} \to \mathcal{X}$ are transformation functions, p_i are probabilities having the sum of 1, and N is the number of transformations.

Using the IFS, a fractal $S = \{x_t\}_{t=0}^{\infty} \in \mathcal{X}$ is constructed by the random iteration algorithm [37], which repeats the following two steps for $t = 0, 1, 2, \cdots$ from an initial point x_0. (i) Select a transformation w^* from $\{w_1, \cdots, w_N\}$ with pre-defined probabilities $p_i = p(w^* = w_i)$ to determine the i-th transformation. (ii) Produce a new point $x_{t+1} = w^*(x_t)$.

Since the focus herein is on representation learning for image recognition, we construct fractals in the 2D Euclidean space $\mathcal{X} = \mathbb{R}^2$. In this case, each transformation is assumed in practice to be an affine transformation [37], which has a set of six parameters $\theta_i = (a_i, b_i, c_i, d_i, e_i, f_i)$ for rotation and shifting:

$$w_i(x; \theta_i) = \begin{bmatrix} a_i & b_i \\ c_i & d_i \end{bmatrix} x + \begin{bmatrix} e_i \\ f_i \end{bmatrix}. \tag{2}$$

An image representation of the fractal S is obtained by drawing dots on a black background. The details of this step with its adaptable parameters is explained in Sect. 3.3.

3.2   Fractal Categories

Undoubtedly, automatically generating categories for pre-training of image classification is a challenging task. Here, we associate the categories with fractal parameters a–f. As shown in the experimental section, we successfully generate a number of pre-trained categories on FractalDB (see Fig. 5) through formula-driven image projection by an IFS.

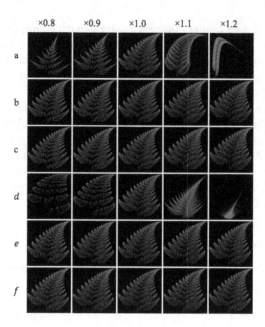

Fig. 3. Intra-category augmentation of a *leaf* fractal. Here, a_i, b_i, c_i, and d_i are for rotation, and e_i and f_i are for shifting.

Since an IFS is characterized by a set of parameters and their corresponding probabilities, i.e., $\Theta = \{(\theta_i, p_i)\}_{i=1}^{N}$, we assume that a fractal category has a fixed Θ and propose 1,000 or 10,000 randomly searched fractal categories (FractalDB-1k/10k). The reason for 1,000 categories is closely related to the experimental result for various #categories in Fig. 4.

FractalDB-1k/10k consists of 1,000/10,000 different fractals (examples shown in Fig. 1(a)), the parameters of which are automatically generated by repeating the following procedure. First, N is sampled from a discrete uniform distribution, $\mathbb{N} = \{2, 3, 4, 5, 6, 7, 8\}$. Second, the parameter θ_i for the affine transformation is sampled from the uniform distribution on $[-1, 1]^6$ for $i = 1, 2, \cdots, N$. Third, p_i is set to $p_i = (\det A_i)/(\sum_{i=1}^{N} \det A_i)$ where $A_i = (a_i, b_i; c_i, d_i)$ is a rotation matrix of the affine transformation. Finally, $\Theta_i = \{(\theta_i, p_i)\}_{i=1}^{N}$ is accepted as a new category if the filling rate r of the representative image of its fractal S is investigated in the experiment (see Table 2). The filling rate r is calculated as the number of pixels of the fractal with respect to the total number of pixels of the image.

3.3 Adaptable Parameters for FractalDB

As described in the experimental section, we investigated the several parameters related to fractal parameters and image rendering. The types of parameters are listed as follows.

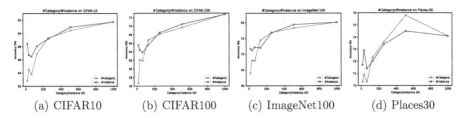

(a) CIFAR10   (b) CIFAR100   (c) ImageNet100   (d) Places30

Fig. 4. Effects of #category and #instance on the CIFAR-10/100, ImageNet100 and Places30 datasets. The other parameter is fixed at 1,000, e.g. #Category is fixed at 1,000 when #Instance changed by {16, 32, 64, 128, 256, 512, 1,000}.

#Category and #Instance. We believe that the effects of #instance on intra-category are the most effective in the pre-training task. First, we change the two parameters from 16 to 1,000 as {16, 32, 64, 128, 256, 512, 1,000}.

Patch vs. Point. We apply a 3×3 patch filter to generate fractal images in addition to the rendering at each 1×1 point. The patch filter makes variation in the pre-training phase. We repeat the following process t times. We set a pixel (u, v), and then a random dot(s) with a 3×3 patch is inserted in the sampled area.

Filling Rate r. We set the filling rate from 0.05 (5%) to 0.25 (25% at 5% intervals, namely, {0.05, 0.10, 0.15, 0.20, 0.25}. Note that we could not get any randomized category at a filling rate of over 30%.

Weight of Intra-category Fractals (w). In order to generate an intra-category image, the parameters for an image representation are varied. Intra-category images are generated by changing one of the parameters a_i, b_i, c_i, d_i, and e_i, f_i with weighting parameter w. The basic parameter is from $\times 0.8$ to $\times 1.2$ at intervals of 0.1, i.e., {0.8, 0.9, 1.0, 1.1, 1.2}). Figure 3 shows an example of the intra-category variation in fractal images. We believe that various intra-category images help to improve the representation for image recognition.

#Dot (t) and Image Size (W, H). We vary the parameters t as {100K, 200K, 400K, 800K} and (W and H) as {256, 362, 512, 764, 1024}. The averaged parameter fixed as the grayscale means that the pixel value is $(r, g, b) = (127, 127, 127)$ (in the case in which the pixel values are 0 to 255).

4   Experiments

In a set of experiments, we investigated the effectiveness of FractalDB and how to construct categories with the effects of configuration, as mentioned in Sect. 3.3. We then quantitatively evaluated and compared the proposed framework with Supervised Learning (ImageNet-1k and Places365, namely ImageNet [1] and Places [2] pre-trained models) and Self-supervised Learning (DeepCluster-10k [32]) on several datasets [1,2,8,47,48].

In order to confirm the properties of FractalDB and compare our pre-trained feature with previous studies, we used the ResNet-50. We simply replaced the pre-trained phase with our FractalDB (e.g., FractalDB-1k/10k), without changing the fine-tuning step. Moreover, in the usage of fine-tuning datasets, we conducted a standard training/validation. Through pre-training and fine-tuning, we assigned the momentum stochastic gradient descent (SGD) [49] with a value 0.9, a basic batch size of 256, and initial values of the learning rate of 0.01. The learning rate was multiplied by 0.1 when the learning epoch reached 30 and 60. Training was performed up to epoch 90. Moreover, the input image size was cropped by 224×224 [pixel] from a 256×256 [pixel] input image.

4.1 Exploration Study

In this subsection, we explored the configuration of formula-driven image datasets regarding Fractal generation by using CIFAR-10/100 (C10, C100), ImageNet-100 (IN100), and Places-30 datasets (P30) datasets (see the supplementary material for category lists in ImageNet-100 and Places-30). The parameters corresponding to those mentioned in Sect. 3.3.

#Category and #instance (see Figs. 4(a), 4(b), 4(c) and 4(d))→ Here, the larger values tend to be better. Figure 4 indicates the effects of category and instance. We investigated the parameters with {16, 32, 64, 128, 256, 512, 1,000} on both properties. At the beginning, a larger parameter in pre-training tends to improve the accuracy in fine-tuning on all the datasets. With C10/100, we can see +7.9/+16.0 increases on the performance rate from 16 to 1,000 in #category. The improvement can be confirmed, but is relatively small for the #instance per category. The rates are +5.2/+8.9 on C10/100.

Hereafter, we assigned 1,000 [category] × 1,000 [instance] as a basic dataset size and tried to train 10k categories since the #category parameter is more effective in improving the performance rates.

Patch vs. point (see Table 1)→ Patch with 3×3 [pixel] is better. Table 1 shows the difference between 3×3 patch rendering and 1×1 point rendering. We can confirm that the 3×3 patch rendering is better for pre-training with 92.1 vs. 87.4 (+4.7) on C10 and 72.0 vs. 66.1 (+5.9) on C100. Moreover, when comparing random patch pattern at each patch (random) to fixed patch in image rendering (fix), performance rates increased by {+0.8, +1.6, +1.1, +1.8} on {C10, C100, IN100, P30}.

Filling rate (see Table 2) → 0.10 is better, but there is no significant change with {0.05, 0.10, 0.15}. The top scores for each dataset and the parameter are 92.0, 80.5 and 75.5 with a filling rate of 0.10 on C10, IN100 and P30, respectively. Based on these results, a filling rate of 0.10 appears to be better.

Weight of intra-category fractals (see Table 3) → Interval 0.4 is the best. A larger variance of intra-category tends to perform better in pre-training. Starting from the basic parameter at intervals of 0.1 with {0.8, 0.9, 1.0, 1.1, 1.2} (see Fig. 3), we varied the intervals as 0.1, 0.2, 0.3, 0.4, and 0.5. For the case in which the interval is 0.5, we set {0.01, 0.5, 1.0, 1.5, 2.0} in order to avoid the weighting value being set as zero. A higher variance of intra-category tends to

Table 1. Patch vs. point.

	C10	C100	IN100	P30
Point	87.4	66.1	73.9	73.0
Patch (random)	**92.1**	**72.0**	**78.9**	**73.2**
Patch (fix)	**92.9**	**73.6**	**80.0**	**75.0**

Table 2. Filling rate.

	C10	C100	IN100	P30
.05	91.8	**72.4**	80.2	74.6
.10	**92.0**	72.3	**80.5**	**75.5**
.15	91.7	71.6	80.2	74.3
.20	91.3	70.8	78.8	74.7
.25	91.1	63.2	72.4	74.1

Table 3. Weights.

	C10	C100	IN100	P30
.1	92.1	72.0	78.9	73.2
.2	92.4	72.7	79.2	73.9
.3	92.4	72.6	79.2	74.3
.4	**92.7**	**73.1**	**79.6**	**74.9**
.5	91.8	72.1	78.9	73.5

Table 4. #Dot.

	C10	C100	IN100	P30
100k	**91.3**	70.8	78.8	74.7
200k	90.9	**71.0**	79.2	**74.8**
400k	90.4	70.3	**80.0**	74.5

Table 5. Image size.

	C10	C100	IN100	P30
256	**92.9**	**73.6**	80.0	75.0
362	92.2	73.2	**80.5**	**75.1**
512	90.9	71.0	79.2	73.0
724	90.8	71.0	79.2	73.0
1024	89.6	68.6	77.5	71.9

provide higher accuracy. We confirm that the accuracies varied as {92.1, 92.4, 92.4, **92.7**, 91.8} on C10, where 0.4 is the highest performance rate (92.7), but 0.5 decreases the recognition rate (91.8). We used the weight value with a 0.4 interval, i.e., {0.2, 0.6, 1.0, 1.4, 1.8}.

#Dot (see Table 4) → We selected 200k by considering the accuracy and rendering time. The best parameters for each configurations 100K on C10 (91.3), 200k on C100/P30 (71.0/74.8) and 400k on IN100 (80.0). Although a larger value is suitable on IN100, a lower value tends to be better on C10, C100, and P30. For the #dot parameter, 200k is the most balanced in terms of rendering speed and accuracy.

Image size (see Table 5) → 256×256 or 362×362 is better. In terms of image size, 256×256 [pixel] and 362×362 [pixel] have similar performances, e.g., 73.6 (256) vs. 73.2 (362) on C100. A larger size, such as $1,024 \times 1,024$, is sparse in the image plane. Therefore, the fractal image projection produces better results in the cases of 256×256 [pixel] and 362×362 [pixel].

Moreover, we have additionally conducted two configurations with grayscale and color FractalDB. However, the effect of the color property appears not to be strong in the pre-training phase.

4.2 Comparison to Other Pre-trained Datasets

We compared **Scratch** from random parameters, **Places-30/365** [2], **ImageNet-100/1k** (ILSVRC'12) [1], and **FractalDB-1k/10k** in Table 6. Since our implementation is not completely the same as a representative learning configuration, we implemented the framework fairly with the same parameters and compared the proposed method (FractalDB-1k/10k) with a baseline (Scratch, DeepCluster-10k, Places-30/365, and ImageNet-100/1k).

Table 6. Classification accuracies of the Ours (FractalDB-1k/10k), Scratch, DeepCluster-10k (DC-10k), ImageNet-100/1k and Places-30/365 pre-trained models on representative pre-training datasets. We show the types of pre-trained image (Pre-train Img; which includes {Natural Image (Natural), Formula-driven Image (Formula)}) and Supervision types (Type; which includes {Self-supervision, Supervision, Formula-supervision}). We employed CIFAR-10 (C10), CIFAR-100 (C100), ImageNet-1k (IN1k), Places-365 (P365), classfication set of Pascal VOC 2012 (VOC12) and Omniglot (OG) datasets. The **bold and underlined** values show the best scores, and **bold** values indicate the second best scores.

Method	Pre-train Img	Type	C10	C100	IN1k	P365	VOC12	OG
Scratch	–	–	87.6	62.7	**76.1**	49.9	58.9	1.1
DC-10k	Natural	Self-supervision	89.9	66.9	66.2	**51.5**	67.5	15.2
Places-30	Natural	Supervision	90.1	67.8	69.1	–	69.5	6.4
Places-365	Natural	Supervision	**94.2**	76.9	71.4	–	**78.6**	10.5
ImageNet-100	Natural	Supervision	91.3	70.6	–	49.7	72.0	12.3
ImageNet-1k	Natural	Supervision	**96.8**	**84.6**	–	50.3	**85.8**	17.5
FractalDB-1k	Formula	Formula-supervision	93.4	75.7	70.3	49.5	58.9	**20.9**
FractalDB-10k	Formula	Formula-supervision	94.1	**77.3**	71.5	50.8	73.6	**29.2**

The proposed FractalDB pre-trained model recorded several good performance rates. We respectively describe them by comparing our Formula-driven Supervised Learning with Scratch, Self-supervised and Supervised Learning.

Comparison to Training from Scratch. The FractalDB-1k/10k pre-trained models recorded much higher accuracies than models trained from scratch on relatively small-scale datasets (C10/100, VOC12 and OG). In case of fine-tuning on large-scale datasets (ImageNet/Places365), the effect of pre-training was relatively small. However, in fine-tuning on Places 365, the FractalDB-10k pre-trained model helped to improve the performance rate which was also higher than ImageNet-1k pre-training (FractalDB-10k 50.8 vs. ImageNet-1k 50.3).

Comparison to Self-supervised Learning. We assigned the DeepCluster-10k [32] to compare the automatically generated image categories. The 10k indicates the pre-training with 10k categories. We believe that the auto-annotation with DeepCluster is the most similar method to our formula-driven image dataset. The DeepCluster-10k also assigns the same category to images that has similar image patterns based on K-means clustering. Our FractalDB-1k/10k pre-trained models outperformed the DeepCluster-10k on five different datasets, e.g., FractalDB-10k 94.1 vs. DeepCluster 89.9 (C10), 77.3 vs. DeepCluster-10k 66.9 (C100). Our method is better than the DeepCluster-10k which is a self-supervised learning method to train a feature representation in image recognition.

Comparison to Supervised Learning. We compared four types of supervised pre-training (e.g., ImageNet-1k and Places-365 datasets and their limited categories ImageNet-100 and Places-30 datasets). ImageNet-100 and Places-30 are

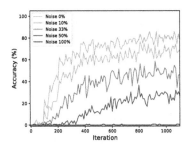

Fig. 5. Noise and accuracy

Table 7. The classification accuracies of the FractalDB-1k/10k (F1k/F10k) and DeepCluster-10k (DC-10k). Mtd/PT Img means Method and Pre-trained images.

Mtd	PT Img	C10	C100	IN1k	P365	VOC12	OG
DC-10k	Natural	89.9	66.9	66.2	51.2	67.5	15.2
DC-10k	Formula	83.1	57.0	65.3	**53.4**	60.4	15.3
F1k	Formula	93.4	75.7	70.3	49.5	58.9	20.9
F10k	Formula	**94.1**	**77.3**	**71.5**	50.8	**73.6**	**29.2**

subsets of ImageNet-1k and Places-365. The numbers correspond to the number of categories. At the beginning, our FractalDB-10k surpassed the ImageNet-100/Places-30 pre-trained models at all fine-tuning datasets. The results show that our framework is more effective than the pre-training with subsets from ImageNet-1k and Places365.

We compare the supervised pre-training methods which are the most promising pre-training approach ever. Although our FractalDB-1k/10k cannot beat them at all settings, our method partially outperformed the ImageNet-1k pre-trained model on Places-365 (FractalDB-10k 50.8 vs. ImageNet-1k 50.3) and Omniglot (FractalDB-10k 29.2 vs. ImageNet-1k 17.5) and Places-365 pre-trained model on CIFAR-100 (FractalDB-10k 77.3 vs. Places-365 76.9) and ImageNet (FractalDB-10k 71.5 vs. Places-365 71.4). The ImageNet-1k pre-trained model is much better than our proposed method on fine-tuning datasets such as C100 and VOC12 since these datasets contain similar categories such as animals and tools.

4.3   Additional Experiments

We also validated the proposed framework in terms of (i) category assignment, (ii) convergence speed, (iii) freezing parameters in fine-tuning, (iv) comparison to other formula-driven image datasets, (v) recognized category analysis and (vi) visualization of first convolutional filters and attention maps.

(i) Category Assignment (see Fig. 5 and Table 7). At the beginning, we validated whether the optimization can be successfully performed using the proposed FractalDB. Figure 5 show the transitioned pre-training accuracies with several rates of label noise. We randomly replaced the category labels. Here, 0% and 100% noise indicate normal training and fully randomized training, respectively. According to the results on FractalDB-1k, a CNN model can successfully classify fractal images, which are defined by iterated functions. Moreover, well-defined categories with a balanced pixel rate allow optimization on FractalDB. When fully randomized labels were assigned in FractalDB training, the architecture could not correct any images and the loss value was static (the accuracies

Table 8. Freezing parameters.

Freezing layer(s)	C10	C100	IN100	P30
Fine-tuning	93.4	75.7	82.7	75.9
Conv1	92.3	72.2	77.9	74.3
Conv1–2	92.0	72.0	77.5	72.9
Conv1–3	89.3	68.0	71.0	68.5
Conv1–4	82.7	56.2	55.0	58.3
Conv1–5	49.4	24.7	21.2	31.4

Table 9. Other formula-driven image datasets with a Bezier curve and Perlin noise.

Pre-training	C10	C100	IN100	P30
Scratch	87.6	60.6	75.3	70.3
Bezier-144	87.6	62.5	72.7	73.5
Bezier-1024	89.7	68.1	73.0	73.6
Perlin-100	90.9	70.2	73.0	73.3
Perlin-1296	90.4	71.1	79.7	74.2
FractalDB-1k	**93.4**	**75.7**	**82.7**	**75.9**

Table 10. Performance rates in which FractalDB was better than the ImageNet pre-trained model on C10/C100/IN100/P30 fine-tuning.

Dataset	Category$^{(classification\%)}$
C10	–
C100	bee[89], chair[92], keyboard[95], maple tree[72], motor cycle[99] orchid[92], pine tree[70]
IN100	Kerry blue terrier[88], marmot[92], giant panda[92], television[80], dough[64], valley[94]
P30	cliff[64], mountain[40], skyscrape[85], tundra[79]

are 0% at almost times). According to the result, we confirmed that the effect of the fractal category is reliable enough to train the image patterns.

Moreover, we used the DeepCluster-10k to automatically assign categories to the FractalDB. Table 7 indicates the comparison between category assignment with DeepCluster-10k (k-means) and FractalDB-1k/10k (IFS). We confirm that the DeepCluster-10k cannot successfully assign a category to fractal images. The gaps between IFS and k-means assignments are {11.0, 20.3, 13.2} on {C10, C100, VOC12}. This obviously indicates that our formula-driven image generation through the principle of IFS and the parameters in equation (2) works well compared to the DeepCluster-10k.

(ii) Convergence Speed (see Fig. 1(b)). The transitioned pre-training accuracies values in FractalDB are similar to those of ImageNet pre-trained model and much faster than scratch from random parameters (Fig. 1(b)). We validated the convergence speed in fine-tuning on C10. As the result of pre-training with FractalDB-1k, we accelerated the convergence speed in fine-tuning which is similar to the ImageNet pre-trained model.

(iii) Freezing Parameters in Fine-Tuning (see Table 8). Although full-parameter fine-tuning is better, conv1 and 2 acquired a highly accurate image

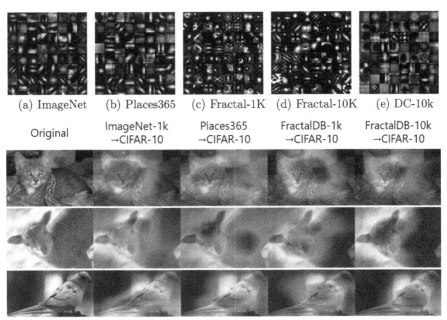

(a) ImageNet	(b) Places365	(c) Fractal-1K	(d) Fractal-10K	(e) DC-10k
Original	ImageNet-1k →CIFAR-10	Places365 →CIFAR-10	FractalDB-1k →CIFAR-10	FractalDB-10k →CIFAR-10

(f) Heatmaps with Grad-CAM. (Left) Input image. (Center-left) Activated heatmaps with ImageNet-1k pre-trained ResNet-50. (Center) Activated heatmaps with Places-365 pre-trained ResNet-50. (Center-Right, Right) Activated heatmaps with FractalDB-1K/10k pre-trained ResNet-50.

Fig. 6. Visualization results: (a)–(e) show the activation of the 1st convolutional layer on ResNet-50, and (f) illustrates attentions with Grad-CAM [50].

representation (Table 8). Freezing the conv1 layer provided only a −1.4 (92.0 vs. 93.4) or −2.8 (72.9 vs. 75.7) decrease from fine-tuning on C10 and C100, respectively. Comparing to other results, such as those for conv1–4/5 freezing, the bottom layer tended to train a better representation.

(iv) Comparison to Other Formula-Driven Image Datasets (see Table 9). At this moment, the proposed FractalDB-1k/10k are better than other formula-driven image datasets. We assigned Perlin noise [46] and Bezier curve [45] to generate image patterns and their categories just as FractalDB made the dataset (see the supplementary material for detailed dataset creation of the Bezier curve and Perlin noise). We confirmed that Perlin noise and the Bezier curve are also beneficial in making a pre-trained model that achieved better rates than scratch training. However, the proposed FractalDB is better than these approaches (Table 9). For a fairer comparison, we cite a similar #category in the formula-driven image datasets, namely FractalDB-1k (total #image: 1M), Bezier-1024 (1.024M) and Perlin-1296 (1.296M). The significantly improved rates are +3.0 (FractalDB-1k 93.4 vs. Perlin-1296 90.4) on C10, +4.6 (FractalDB-10k 75.7 vs. Perlin-1296 71.1) on C100, +3.0 (FractalDB-1k 82.7 vs. Perlin-1296 79.7) on IN100, and +1.7 (FractalDB-1k 75.9 vs. Perlin-1296 74.2) on P30.

(v) Recognized Category Analysis (see Table 10). We investigated Which categories are better recognized by the FractalDB pre-trained model compared to the ImageNet pre-trained model. Table 10 shows the category names and the classification rates. The FractalDB pre-trained model tends to be better when an image contains recursive patterns (e.g., a keyboard, maple trees).

(vi) Visualization of First Convolutional Filters (see Figs. 6(a–e)) and Attention Maps (see Fig. 6f). We visualized first convolutional filters and Grad-CAM [50] with pre-trained ResNet-50. As seen in ImageNet-1k/Places-365/DeepCluster-10k (Figs. 6(a), 6(b) and 6(e)) and FractalDB-1k/10k pre-training (Figs. 6(c) and 6(d)), our pre-trained models obviously generate different feature representations from conventional natural image datasets. Based on the experimental results, we confirmed that the proposed FractalDB successfully pre-trained a CNN model without any natural images even though the convolutional basis filters are different from the natural image pre-training with ImageNet-1k/DeepCluster-10k.

The pre-trained models with Grad-CAM can generate heatmaps fine-tuned on C10 dataset. According to the center-right and right in Fig. 6(f), the FractalDB-1k/10k also look at the objects.

5   Discussion and Conclusion

We achieved the framework of *pre-training without natural images* through formula-driven image projection based on fractals. We successfully pre-trained models on FractalDB and fine-tuned the models on several representative datasets, including CIFAR-10/100, ImageNet, Places and Pascal VOC. The performance rates were higher than those of models trained from scratch and some supervised/self-supervised learning methods. Here, we summarize our observations through exploration as follows.

Towards a Better Pre-trained Dataset. The proposed FractalDB pre-trained model partially outperformed ImageNet-1k/Places365 pre-trained models, e.g., FractalDB-10k 77.3 vs. Places-365 76.9 on CIFAR-100, FractalDB-10k 50.8 vs. ImageNet-1k 50.3 on Places-365. If we could improve the transfer accuracy of the pre-training without natural images, then the ImageNet dataset and the pre-trained model may be replaced so as to protect fairness, preserve privacy, and decrease annotation labor. Recently, for examples, 80M Tiny Images[1] and ImageNet (human-related categories)[2] have been withdrawn the publicly available images.

Are Fractals a Good Rendering Formula? We are looking for better mathematically generated image patterns and their categories. We confirmed that FractalDB is better than datasets based on the Bezier curve and Perlin Noise in the context of pre-trained model (see Table 9). Moreover, the proposed FractalDB can generate a good set of categories, e.g., the fact that the training

---

[1] https://groups.csail.mit.edu/vision/TinyImages/.
[2] http://image-net.org/update-sep-17-2019.

accuracy decreased depending on the label noise (see Figs. 5) and the formula-driven image generation is better than DeepCluster-10k in the most cases, as a method for category assignment (see Table 7) show how the fractal categories worked well.

A Different Image Representation from Human Annotated Datasets. The visual patterns pre-trained by FractalDB acquire a unique feature in a different way from ImageNet-1k (see Fig. 6). In the future, steerable pre-training may be available depending on the fine-tuning task. Through our experiments, we confirm that a pre-trained dataset configuration should be adjusted. We hope that the proposed pre-training framework will suit a broader range of tasks, e.g., object detection and semantic segmentation, and will become a flexibly generated pre-training dataset.

Acknowledgement. – This work was supported by JSPS KAKENHI Grant Number JP19H01134.

– We want to thank Takuma Yagi and Munetaka Minoguchi for their helpful comments during research discussions.

– Computational resource of AI Bridging Cloud Infrastructure (ABCI) provided by National Institute of Advanced Industrial Science and Technology (AIST) was used.

References

1. Deng, J., Dong, W., Socher, R., Li, L.J., Li, K., Fei-Fei, L.: ImageNet: a large-scale hierarchical image database. In: The IEEE International Conference on Computer Vision and Pattern Recognition (CVPR), pp. 248–255 (2009)
2. Zhou, B., Lapedriza, A., Khosla, A., Oliva, A., Torralba, A.: Places: a 10 million image database for scene recognition. IEEE Trans. Pattern Anal. Mach. Intell. (TPAMI) **40**, 1452–1464 (2017)
3. Fellbaum, C.: WordNet: An Electronic Lexical Database. BradfordBooks (1998)
4. Buolamwini, J., Gebru, T.: Gender shades: intersectional accuracy disparities in commercial gender classification. In: Conference on Fairness, Accountability and Transparency (FAT), pp. 77–91 (2018)
5. Yang, K., Qinami, K., Fei-Fei, L., Deng, J., Russakovsky, O.: Towards fairer datasets: filtering and balancing the distribution of the people subtree in the ImageNet hierarchy. In: Conference on Fairness, Accountability and Transparency (FAT) (2020)
6. Varol, G., et al.: Learning from synthetic humans. In: The IEEE International Conference on Computer Vision and Pattern Recognition (CVPR), pp. 109–117 (2017)
7. Mandelbrot, B.: The fractal geometry of nature. Am. J. Phys. **51**, 286 (1983)
8. Everingham, M., Eslami, S.M.A., Van Gool, L., Williams, C.K.I., Winn, J., Zisserman, A.: The pascal visual object classes challenge: a retrospective. Int. J. Comput. Vis. (IJCV) **111**, 98–136 (2015)
9. Lin, T.-Y., et al.: Microsoft COCO: common objects in context. In: Fleet, D., Pajdla, T., Schiele, B., Tuytelaars, T. (eds.) ECCV 2014. LNCS, vol. 8693, pp. 740–755. Springer, Cham (2014). https://doi.org/10.1007/978-3-319-10602-1_48
10. Krasin, I., et al.: OpenImages: a public dataset for large-scale multi-label and multi-class image classification (2017)

11. Kay, W., et al.: The Kinetics Human Action Video Dataset. arXiv pre-print arXiv:1705.06950 (2017)
12. Monfort, M., et al.: Moments in time dataset: one million videos for event understanding. IEEE Trans. Pattern Anal. Mach. Intell. (TPAMI) **42**(2), 502–508 (2019)
13. Donahue, J., Jia, Y., Hoffman, J., Zhang, N., Tzeng, E., Darrell, T.: DeCAF: a deep convolutional activation feature for generic visual recognition. In: International Conference on Machine Learning (ICML), pp. 647–655 (2014)
14. Huh, M., Agrawal, P., Efros, A.A.: What makes ImageNet good for transfer learning? In: Advances in Neural Information Processing Systems NIPS 2016 Workshop (2016)
15. Kornblith, S., Shlens, J., Le, Q.V.: Do better imagenet models transfer better? In: The IEEE International Conference on Computer Vision and Pattern Recognition (CVPR), pp. 2661–2671 (2019)
16. Sun, C., Shrivastava, A., Singh, S., Gupta, A.: Revisiting unreasonable effectiveness of data in deep learning era. In: The IEEE International Conference on Computer Vision (ICCV), pp. 843–852 (2017)
17. Mahajan, D., et al.: Exploring the limits of weakly supervised pretraining. In: European Conference on Computer Vision (ECCV), pp. 181–196 (2018)
18. Krizhevsky, A., Sutskever, I., Hinton, G.E.: ImageNet classification with deep convolutional neural networks. In Pereira, F., Burges, C.J.C., Bottou, L., Weinberger, K.Q. (eds.) Advances in Neural Information Processing Systems (NIPS) 25, pp. 1097–1105 (2012)
19. Simonyan, K., Zisserman, A.: Very deep convolutional networks for large-scale image recognition. In: International Conference on Learning Representations (ICLR) (2015)
20. Szegedy, C., et al.: Going deeper with convolutions. In: The IEEE International Conference on Computer Vision and Pattern Recognition (CVPR), pp. 1–9 (2015)
21. He, K., Zhang, X., Ren, S., Sun, J.: Deep residual learning for image recognition. In: The IEEE International Conference on Computer Vision and Pattern Recognition (CVPR), pp. 770–778 (2016)
22. Xie, S., Girshick, R., Dollár, P., Tu, Z., He, K.: Aggregated residual transformations for deep neural networks. In: The IEEE International Conference on Computer Vision and Pattern Recognition (CVPR), pp. 1492–1500 (2017)
23. Howard, A.G., et al.: MobileNets: Efficient Convolutional Neural Networks for Mobile Vision Applications. arXiv pre-print arXiv:1704.04861 (2017)
24. Sandler, M., Howard, A.G., Zhu, M., Zhmoginov, A., Chen, L.C.: MobileNetv2: Inverted Residuals and Linear Bottlenecks. Mobile Networks for Classification, Detection and Segmentation. arXiv pre-print arXiv:1801.04381 (2018)
25. Howard, A.G., et al.: Searching for MobileNetV3. In: The IEEE International Conference on Computer Vision (ICCV), pp. 1314–1324 (2019)
26. Doersch, C., Gupta, A., Efros, A.: Unsupervised visual representation learning by context prediction. In: The IEEE International Conference on Computer Vision (ICCV), pp. 1422–1430 (2015)
27. Noroozi, M., Favaro, P.: Unsupervised learning of visual representations by solving jigsaw puzzles. In: Leibe, B., Matas, J., Sebe, N., Welling, M. (eds.) ECCV 2016. LNCS, vol. 9910, pp. 69–84. Springer, Cham (2016). https://doi.org/10.1007/978-3-319-46466-4_5
28. Noroozi, M., Vinjimoor, A., Favaro, P., Pirsiavash, H.: Boosting self-supervised learning via knowledge transfer. In: The IEEE International Conference on Computer Vision and Pattern Recognition (CVPR), pp. 9359–9367 (2018)

29. Zhang, R., Isola, P., Efros, A.A.: Colorful image colorization. In: Leibe, B., Matas, J., Sebe, N., Welling, M. (eds.) ECCV 2016. LNCS, vol. 9907, pp. 649–666. Springer, Cham (2016). https://doi.org/10.1007/978-3-319-46487-9_40

30. Noroozi, M., Pirsiavash, H., Favaro, P.: Representation learning by learning to count. In: The IEEE International Conference on Computer Vision (ICCV), pp. 5898–5906 (2017)

31. Gidaris, S., Singh, P., Komodakis, N.: Unsupervised representation learning by predicting image rotations. In: International Conference on Learning Representation (ICLR) (2018)

32. Caron, M., Bojanowski, P., Joulin, A., Douze, M.: Deep clustering for unsupervised learning of visual features. In: European Conference on Computer Vision (ECCV), pp. 132–149 (2018)

33. He, K., Fan, H., Wu, Y., Xie, S., Girshick, R.: Momentum contrast for unsupervised visual representation learning. In: The IEEE International Conference on Computer Vision and Pattern Recognition (CVPR) (2020)

34. Chen, T., Kornblith, S., Norouzi, M., Hinton, G.: A simple framework for contrastive learning of visual representations. In: International Conference on Machine Learning (ICML) (2020)

35. Landini, G., Murry, P.I., Misson, G.P.: Local connected fractal dimensions and lacunarity analyses of 60 degree fluorescein angiograms. Invest. Ophthalmol. Vis. Sci. **36**, 2749–2755 (1995)

36. Smith Jr., T.G., Lange, G.D., Marks, W.B.: Fractal methods and results in cellular morphology - dimentions, lacunarity and multifractals. J. Neurosci. Methods **69**, 123–136 (1996)

37. Barnsley, M.F.: Fractals Everywhere. Academic Press, New York (1988)

38. Monro, D.M., Budbridge, F.: Rendering algorithms for deteministic fractals. In: IEEE Computer Graphics and Its Applications, pp. 32–41 (1995)

39. Chen, Y.Q., Bi, G.: 3-D IFS fractals as real-time graphics model. Comput. Graph. **21**, 367–370 (1997)

40. Pentland, A.P.: Fractal-based description of natural scenes. IEEE Trans. Pattern Anal. Mach. Intell. (TPAMI) **6**, 661–674 (1984)

41. Varma, M., Garg, R.: Locally invariant fractal features for statistical texture classification. In: The IEEE International Conference on Computer Vision (ICCV), pp. 1–8 (2007)

42. Xu, Y., Ji, H., Fermuller, C.: Viewpoint invariant texture description using fractal analysis. Int. J. Comput. Vis. (IJCV) **83**, 85–100 (2009)

43. Larsson, G., Maire, M., Shakhnarovich, G.: FractalNet: ultra-deep neural networks without residuals. In: International Conference on Learning Representation (ICLR) (2017)

44. Falconer, K.: Fractal Geometry: Mathematical Foundations and Applications. Wiley, Hoboken (2004)

45. Farin, G.: Curves and Surfaces for Computer Aided Geometric Design: A Practical Guide. Academic Press, Cambridge (1993)

46. Perlin, K.: Improving noise. ACM Trans. Graph. (TOG) **21**, 681–682 (2002)

47. Krizhevsky, A.: Learning Multiple Layers of Features from Tiny Images (2009)

48. Lake, B.M., Salakhutdinov, R., Tenenbaum, J.B.: Human-level concept learning through probabilistic program induction. Science **350**, 1332–1338 (2015)

49. Bottou, L.: Large-scale machine learning with stochastic gradient descent. In: 19th International Conference on Computational Statistics (COMPSTAT), pp. 177–187 (2010)
50. Selvaraju, R.R., Cogswell, M., Das, A., Vedantam, R., Parikh, D., Batra, D.: Grad-CAM: visual explanations from deep networks via gradient-based localization. In: The IEEE International Conference on Computer Vision (ICCV), pp. 618–626 (2017)

TTPLA: An Aerial-Image Dataset for Detection and Segmentation of Transmission Towers and Power Lines

Rabab Abdelfattah[1]($\boxtimes$), Xiaofeng Wang[1], and Song Wang[2]

[1] Department of Electrical Engineering,
University of South Carolina, Columbia, USA
rabab@email.sc.edu, wangxi@cec.sc.edu
[2] Department of Computer Science and Engineering,
University of South Carolina, Columbia, USA
songwang@cec.sc.edu

Abstract. Accurate detection and segmentation of transmission towers (TTs) and power lines (PLs) from aerial images plays a key role in protecting power-grid security and low-altitude UAV safety. Meanwhile, aerial images of TTs and PLs pose a number of new challenges to the computer vision researchers who work on object detection and segmentation – PLs are long and thin, and may show similar color as the background; TTs can be of various shapes and most likely made up of line structures of various sparsity; The background scene, lighting, and object sizes can vary significantly from one image to another. In this paper we collect and release a new TT/PL Aerial-image (TTPLA) dataset, consisting of 1,100 images with the resolution of $3,840 \times 2,160$ pixels, as well as manually labeled 8,987 instances of TTs and PLs. We develop novel policies for collecting, annotating, and labeling the images in TTPLA. Different from other relevant datasets, TTPLA supports evaluation of instance segmentation, besides detection and semantic segmentation. To build a baseline for detection and segmentation tasks on TTPLA, we report the performance of several state-of-the-art deep learning models on our dataset. TTPLA dataset is publicly available at https://github.com/r3ab/ttpla_dataset.

1 Introduction

Power grid monitoring and inspection is extremely important to prevent power failures and potential blackouts. Traditional methods to inspect transmission towers (TTs) and power lines (PLs) include visual surveys by human inspectors, helicopter-assisted inspection [1], and crawling robots [1], to name a few. However, these methods always suffer from their high costs in time, labor, and finance, as well as inspection accuracy. As an alternative, inspection based on small-scale unmanned aerial vehicles (UAVs) becomes popular and gradually plays an essential role, thanks to its low costs, high mobility and flexibility, and the potential to obtain high-quality images.

© Springer Nature Switzerland AG 2021
H. Ishikawa et al. (Eds.): ACCV 2020, LNCS 12627, pp. 601–618, 2021.
https://doi.org/10.1007/978-3-030-69544-6_36

Autonomous UAV-based power grid inspection requires precise scene under-standing in real-time to enable UAV localization, scene recognition, tracking, aerial monitoring, inspection, and flight safety. The main challenge in fulfilling this requirement, however, points to *background complexity* and *object complex-ity*. Background complexity mainly comes from the similarity between the color of the PLs and their backgrounds. Object complexity can be interpreted from four aspects: (i) Scale imbalance – As discussed in [2], combining strongly corre-lated objects, such as TTs and PLs, together can potentially enhance recognition accuracy, compared with recognizing them separately. However, the scales of TTs and PLs are obviously imbalanced in an image; (ii) Class imbalance – In most cases, each TT is linked to least between 3–4 and up to 10 PLs, which will result in significant imbalance among the number of TTs and PLs [3,4]; (iii) Crowded objects – PLs are very close to each other and sometimes even overlapped in images [5]; and (iv) Complicated structures and/or shapes.

PLs are long and thin which makes the distribution of the related pixels in an image completely different from regular objects in some well-known datasets [6–8]. Meanwhile, TTs may be of various shapes and most likely made up of line structures of various sparsity, as shown in Fig. 1.

Existing datasets on TTs and PLs only support two types of annotation: image-level and seman-tic segmentation [9–12]. As a result, most related computer vision research only classifies and localizes objects in an image without distinguish-ing different objects of the same class [13] (e.g., it can recog-nize and/or localize PLs as one class, but cannot distinguish dif-ferent PLs in the image). To over-come such a limitation, this paper presents a unique dataset on TTs and PLs, TTPLA (TT/PL Aerial-image), focusing on a different type of annotation, instance segmenta-tion, which is a combination of object detection and mask segmentation. Instance segmentation can distinguish instances (or "objects") that belong to the same class and provide a solid under-standing for each individual instance. This is especially useful in power grid inspection, where PLs can be close to each other, occluded, and overlapped.

Fig. 1. Different TTs in TTPLA.

TTPLA dataset places unique challenges to computer vision research on instance segmentation [14–17]. To evaluate TTPLA dataset, we build a baseline on our dataset using Yolact as the instance segmentation model. The results are collected based on different backbones (Resnet-50 and Resnet-101) and different image resolutions 640×360 (preserve aspect ratio), 550×550 and 700×700. The

(a)   (b)   (c)   (d)

Fig. 2. Sample images from public datasets as compared to our dataset TTPLA where (a) dataset [20] with **low resolution 128 × 128 based on PLs images only**, (b) dataset [21] based on **manually cropping PLs images only**, (c) **most of images are not aerial images** [22], and (d) our dataset (TTPLA) on TTs and PLs images without manually cropping.

best average scores for bounding box and mask are 22.96% and 15.72%, respectively (more detailed can be found in Table 3), which are low in general. Another observation is that all of the previously mentioned models use the NMS method to sharply filter the large number of false positives near the ground truth [18,19], while single NMS may not be practical on our dataset since TTPLA considers a crowded scenario. Therefore, using lower NMS threshold leads to missing highly overlapped objects while using higher NMS threshold leads to increased false positives [5]. Overall, the state-of-the-art approaches may not perform well on TTPLA, which actually motivates the development of novel instance segmentation models.

The main contributions of this paper are described as follows.

– We present a public dataset, TTPLA, which is a collection of aerial images on TTs and PLs. The images are taken from different view angles and collected at different time, locations, and backgrounds with different tower structures.
– Novel policies are introduced for collecting and labeling images.
– Pixel-wise annotation level is chosen to label instances in TTPLA. This annotations are provided in the COCO format [6] which can be easily integrated to other datasets to enrich future research in scene understanding field. To the best of our knowledge, TTPLA is the first public image dataset on TTs and PLs, focusing on instance segmentation, while all the related datasets focus on semantic segmentation.
– We provide a baseline on TTPLA by evaluating it using the state-of-the-art deep learning models.

The paper is organized as follows. Prior work is discussed in Sect. 2. The properties of the TTPLA dataset are presented in Sect. 3. Evaluation of TTPLA is demonstrated in Sect. 4. Finally, conclusions are summarized in Sect. 5.

2   Related Work

There have been several research papers released recently based on their published or unpublished datasets on TTs, PLs, and insulators. In this section we will review these datasets, reported in Table 1, with the understanding that there is still a lack of training datasets for TTs and PLs in general, as mentioned in [23–25], due to the difficulty in image collection, especially when UAVs fly close to power grids.

2.1   Datasets Based on TTs Images only

The dataset, introduced in [23], is employed to detect TTs from the aerial images. The dataset consists of 3,200 images in which only 1,600 images contain towers while the rest contains background only. The images size is 64×128 pixels which is scaled down from the original frame sizes (550×480 and 720×576). Objects are labeled by bounding boxes. In [24], four datasets are presented. Only one dataset with 28,674 images is annotated with bounding boxes with image size $6,048 \times 4,032$ pixels. The other three datasets are binary labeled and built on cropped images with image size 256×256. These datasets are exploited to detect and classify TT damage such as missing top caps, cracks in poles and cross arms, woodpecker damage on poles, and rot damage on cross arms. The dataset in [26] includes 600 aerial images for training and testing with resolution $1,280 \times 720$ pixels. Unfortunately, all of these datasets are not available to the public.

Table 1. Related datasets.

Target	Dataset	Public	Image#(Pos.)	Image size	Annotation type	Syn.	Manual
TTs	[23]	No	3,200(1,600)	64×128	bounding box	No	No
TTs	[24]	No	28,674	$6,048 \times 4,032$	bounding box	No	No
TTs	[26]	No	600	$1,280 \times 720$	Binary Mask	No	No
PLs	[20]	Yes	4,000(2,000)	128×128	Binary Classif	No	No
PLs	[21]	Yes	573	540×360	Binary Mask	No	Yes
PLs	[21]	Yes	287	540×360	Binary Mask	No	Yes
PLs	[27]	No	3,568	$5,12 \times 512$	Binary Mask	No	Yes
PLs	[28]	No	718,000	–	Binary Mask	Yes	No
PLs	[29]	No	67,000	480×640	Binary Mask	Yes	No
Both	[22]	Yes	1,290	Various	Class Label	No	No
Both	**TTPLA**	**Yes**	**1,100**	**$3,840 \times 2,160$**	**Instance Seg.**	**No**	**No**

2.2   Datasets Based on PLs Images only

Two datasets are presented in [20] on PL images with video resolutions 576×325 pixels for infrared and $1,920 \times 1,080$ pixels for visible light, respectively. The first dataset is built on image-level class labels while the second dataset consists of binary labels at the pixel-level. Only 2,000 images among the 4,000 images under visible light in the datasets include PLs while the rest does not. The image size is scaled down to 128×128 pixels from the original video sizes as shown in Fig. 2 (a). The image-level class labels are exploited for binary classification training. In the work [30], the dataset in [20] is employed by two CNN-based PL recognition methods to identify whether the images contain PLs without the consideration of localization. The work in [31] also relies on the datasets in [20] by resizing the images to 224×224 pixels. A CNN model is used as a binary classifier to identify whether PLs are present in images. Ground truth of the PL dataset consists of 400 infrared and 400 visible light images with the resolution of 512×512 pixels.

Datasets with Manual Cropping. Two public datasets on PL images are presented in [21], including urban scene and mountain scene captured by UAVs. The Urban scene dataset consists of 453 images for training and 120 images for testing, while the mountain scene dataset consists of 237 and 50 images for training and testing, respectively. The original image size is $3,000 \times 4,000$. However, the images are manually cropped to meaningful regions of 540×360 pixels to get close scenes for PLs as shown in Fig. 2 (b). Pixel-level annotation is used to label the cropped images in both datasets. VGG16 architecture [32] is modified based on richer convolutional features [33] to evaluate both datasets. The dataset in [27] includes 530 PL images captured by UAV with the resolution of $5,472 \times 3,078$ pixels. These images are manually cropped and divided into non-overlapped patches with the size of 512×512 pixels. Then all patches that do not contain any PLs are removed. The total number of images is 3,568 with the size of 512×512 pixels. Nested U-Net architectures are evaluated on this dataset.

In general, manually cropping images may not be practical for real-time UAV operations. UAVs can fly from any directions, which means that TTs and PLs can appear in any region of the images. Manually manipulated images cannot reflect the noisy backgrounds that UAVs may face in real life. Alternatively, automatic image cropping and zooming can be applied in lane detection problems to get the region of interest, because of bird-view imaging [34].

Synthetic Datasets. There are two datasets using synthetic PLs. In the first dataset [28], synthetic images of power lines are rendered using the physically based rendering approach to generate the training dataset. Synthetic PLs are randomly superimposed on 718k high dynamic range images collected from the internet. In addition, data augmentation techniques are used to increase the amount of training data. In the second dataset [29], the synthetic wires from a raytracing engine are superimposed on 67k images. These images are extracted from 154 flight videos available on the internet with image resolution 480×640 [29]. Both datasets are not publicly available.

2.3   Datasets Based on both TTs and PLs Images

ImageNet [22] is regarded as one of the largest datasets for object detection, which includes 1,290 annotated images with labels on TTs and PLs. Most of them are not aerial images as shown in Fig. 2 (c) and there is no top and side view for TTs and PLs. Imaging from the ground provides most of images simple backgrounds such as sky and white clouds, which may be impractical in our scenario since we focus on UAV applications.

3   TTPLA Dataset Properties

Building large-scale aerial datasets is a complicated task, including recording data, extracting and selecting images, and establishing the required annotation policy. In the following subsections we will introduce the procedures in our dataset preparation as well as the properties of the TTPLA dataset.

3.1   Aerial Videos Collection and Images Preparation

Recorded videos are collected by a UAV, Parrot-ANAFI, in two different states in USA to guarantee the varieties of the scenes. The locations are randomly selected without any intentions and treatments to avoid noisy background. The UAV contains 4k HDR camera and up to 2.8× lossless zoom. Zooming is exploited when collecting the video data, in order to guarantee high-resolution of the objects, such as PLs, without manual cropping. The TTPLA dataset is extracted from a set of totally 80 videos. All aerial videos have the resolution of $3,840 \times 2,160$ with 30 fps.

3.2   TTPLA Dataset Policy

Creating a dataset of TTs and PLs needs policies to deal with the diversity of objects during aerial imaging. For instance, towers are built by different materials (e.g., tubular steel, wood, and concrete) with different structures (e.g., single pole, H-frame, horizontal structure, delta structure and guyed structure) and different insulators [35]. Meanwhile, given the shape characteristics of PLs (thin and long), different backgrounds and illumination levels play important roles in PL detection. With these considerations, we introduce the following policy in data collection and annotation.

Recording Characteristics. The aerial images in TTPLA dataset are extracted from videos taken by UAVs. The following discussions focus on four important aspects when recording these videos.

– *View angles* are essential in data collection, specially when the shape of the object varies a lot from different view angles. In TTPLA, all TTs are photographed from different angles such as front view, top view, and side view. This policy, designed specifically for TTs, guarantees that the deep learning models can detect TTs from any angles. It provides the freedom to UAVs to fly along any directions without worrying about the detection accuracy. Various views for different TTs are demonstrated in Fig. 3.

- The images are taken by randomly varying the *zooming level* together with the motion of the camera. Different zooming levels are explored in TTPLA to capture accurate features of PLs, especially with noisy backgrounds as shown in Fig. 4.
- The videos are recorded at different time during a day under different weather conditions.
- *Backgrounds* are important to accurately detect PLs. From the UAV's viewpoint, the backgrounds of most PLs in images are noisy. TTPLA consists of plentiful PLs images with noisy backgrounds, which make extracting PLs a challenging task due to "thin and long" features of PLs [36]. Moreover, the color of PLs can be very close to that of the background (e.g., building, plants, road, lane line) and sometimes PLs may be hidden behind the trees. We include all these cases in TTPLA.

Preparing Images. It is not an easy task to select appropriate frames into TTPLA from a large set of videos. We consider the following aspects to avoid duplicate images. To ensure that the images are not duplicated, the videos are renamed with unique IDs and each video is separately archived. The lengths of the recorded videos are between 1 min to 5 min, which imply 1,800 to 9,000 images per video, given 30 fps. These images are then sampled once every 15 frames before manual inspection, which means 2 images per second. If necessary, we can extract 3 images per second to augment the dataset [34]. The next step is manual inspection of the selected images, given the possibility that sometimes PLs are not clear in images due to day light or complex backgrounds. Another reason of having manual inspection is to make sure that the whole views of TTs are included to keep our recording policy consistent. In addition, manual inspection removes all redundant images from the dataset. Finally, the selected images are renamed by the related video ID, followed by the related frame number.

Segmentation Annotation. There are two types of segmentation: semantic segmentation and instance segmentation. Semantic segmentation assigns only one category label to all pixels that belong to the same class in a single image, while instance segmentation provides a mask at the pixel level to each individual instance in the image. Because we must distinguish each individual PL and TT in UAV inspection, instance segmentation at the pixel level is desired for our dataset. To precisely label TTs and PLs, we use LabelME [37]. Each instance is surrounded carefully by a polygon. Three expert annotators are recruited and in average, each person takes about 45 min to annotate one image. Each image is assigned to only one annotator to construct its full annotations. The annotation consistency between different annotators is actually not a serious issue in this work since 1) our images are mainly taken from a top view and therefore, we have very rare occlusions, 2) the instances in our datasets are well

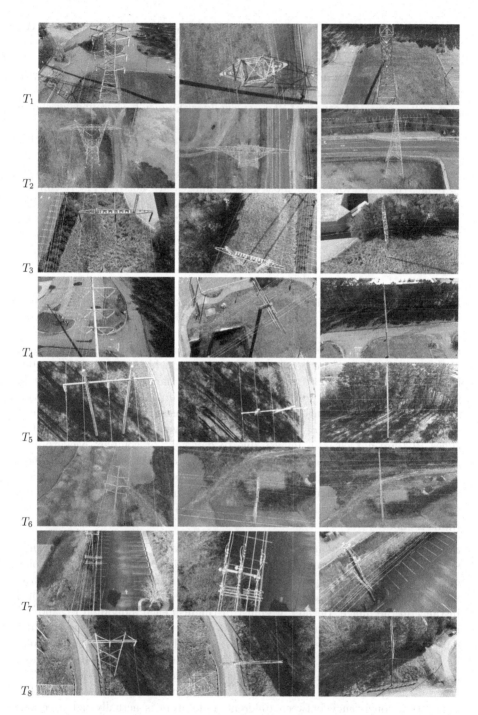

Fig. 3. Different types of TTs in TTPLA. Front view, top view and side view are ordered from the left to the right for each TT shape.

Fig. 4. PLs in the TTPLA dataset.

defined without much ambiguity based on our labeling policy, and 3) the three expert annotators label each assigned image with their highest possible scrutiny. Samples of annotated images in TTPLA dataset are shown in Fig. 5.

Labeling Instances. A new labeling policy is presented to categorize TTs based on lattice types and pole types (tubular steel, concrete, and wooden) [35].

- Lattice TTs are composed of steel angle sections. TTPLA contains different shapes of lattice TTs $(T_1 - T_3)$ in Fig. 3 which are labeled by *"tower-lattice"*.
- Tubular steel, spun concrete, and steel/concrete hybrid poles belong to the same class. These three types of poles have similar appearance. Our dataset contains three different shapes from this class $(T_4 - T_6)$ in Fig. 3. To generate the label for this class, we take the first two letters from each type of poles and label such TTs as *"tower-tucohy"*.
- Wooden TTs have the poles made of wood. TTPLA considers this type of poles because wooden poles are distributed almost everywhere around residential places. So TTPLA contains a lot of different shapes of wooden poles such as T_7 and T_8 in Fig. 3, which are labeled by *"tower-wooden"*.

Fig. 5. Samples of annotated images in TTPLA.

The reason of labeling TTs in this way is to ensure that such a labeling policy is friendly to deep learning models. In general, each lattice tower can be divided into three parts: basic body (upper partition), body extension (middle partition), and leg extension (lower partition). Most lattice towers have similar shape in body extension and leg extension, which means that, if only body and/or leg extensions of two TTs appear in the image, it will be very hard for deep learning models to distinguish these two TTs. This is also true for the TTs under "*tower-tucohy*". Therefore, categorizing TTs based on their shapes (e.g., H-Frame, Lattice and monopole) may not be practical in UAV applications, since we cannot guarantee that UAVs always capture the basic body in the image. To overcome this issue, TTs are categorized based on their structures and materials instead of their shapes in TTPLA dataset. Therefore, our labeling policy presents a good step toward the balance of the dataset. Besides the labels related to TTs, two additional labels are presented:

– The label "*cable*" is used for all PLs in TTPLA.
– The label "*void*" is used for any instance (TT or PL) which is difficult to recognize into image. For example, a PL or even a TT may be labeled by "*void*" if it is almost invisible in the image. Any instances labeled by "*void*" are ignored from evaluation [8].

3.3   Dataset Statistics

Figure 6 describes the relationship between the number of instances per image and the number of images. The left top corner figure demonstrates that there are 659 images that contain 1–6 instances per image and 241 images contains 11–56 instances per image. The others four figures describe the number of each specific object per image versus the number of images such as *cable*, *tower-lattice*, *tower-tucohy*, and *tower-wooden*.

Table 2. Dataset statistics

Category	Classes	Labels	Instances #	Instances/image	Pixels
PLs	Cable	*cable*	8,083	7.3	154M
TTs	Lattice	*tower-lattic*	330	0.3	164M
	Concrete/Steel/Hybrid	*tower-tucohy*	168	0.15	30M
	Wooden	*tower-wooden*	283	0.26	61M
	Void	*void*	173	0.15	0.8M

Statistics on the instances in TTPLA are reported in Table 2. Notice that the number of instances in the cable class is much larger than those of the other classes on TTs. This is because a TT is always connected to at least 2 and up to 10 PLs. Accordingly, TT classes have less training data. As a result, the numbers of instances on TTs and PLs will always be unbalanced in such a dataset focusing on individual instances. Although it is suggested in the Cityscapes dataset [7] that the rare classes can be excluded from the evaluation, it should not be the case for our dataset since we are interested in a combination of both TTs and PLs. In fact, to increase the number of TT instances in the dataset, we include images containing multiple TTs (see the figure at bottom-left in Fig. 5), which are not often seen in other datasets. An interesting observation is that the pixels that PLs and TTs occupied in the images are comparable, as reported in Table 2. It suggests that the dataset actually achieves a balance at the pixel level. It would be interesting to investigate whether such a balance can benefit detection.

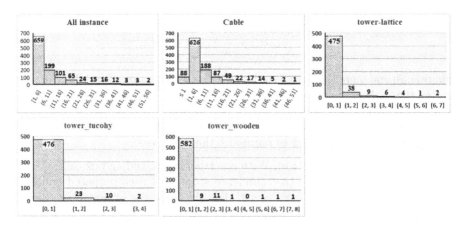

Fig. 6. Number of Instances per Image (x-axis) v.s. Number of Images (y-axis), (a) All instances, (b) *cable*, (c) *tower-lattice*, (d) *tower-tucohy*, and (e) *tower-wooden*.

4   Evaluation

This section presents metrics and loss functions that are used for training and evaluation. The baseline results are provided based on bounding boxes and instance masks.

4.1   Metrics

Instance segmentation on TTPLA is evaluated based on the standard metric of average precision (AP) [8]. The intersection over union (IoU) measures the overlap between a pair of the matched prediction and the ground truth. Consequently, AP is accounted when the IoU is greater than 50% [38]. In the baseline, average precision is calculated for both bounding boxes, denoted by AP_b, and instance mask, denoted by AP_m [17]. Three precision scores are evaluated: $AP_b^{50\%}$, $AP_b^{75\%}$, AP_b^{avg} for bounding box, and $AP_m^{50\%}$, $AP_m^{75\%}$, AP_m^{avg} for masks [14,17], as listed in Table 3. $AP^{50\%}$ means the AP with the overlap value of 50%, $AP^{75\%}$ means the AP with the overlap value of 75%, and AP^{avg} is the average AP value at different IoU thresholds ranging from 50% to 95% with step 5% [7].

4.2   Loss Function

Multi-loss functions are often used for multiple output networks [14,17,39–41] to measure the quality of prediction of each model's outputs by comparing them to the ground truth during the training process. In the baseline model, the multi-loss function L_{loss} is a sum of localization loss L_{loc}, classification loss L_{class}, and mask loss L_{mask}, i.e.,

$$L_{loss} = \frac{\alpha}{N} L_{class} + \frac{\beta}{N} L_{loc} + \frac{\gamma}{A_{gb}} L_{mask} \qquad (1)$$

where α, β, and γ are the weights to balance the contribution of each loss function during the back-propagation. In the configurations, α, β, and γ are set to 1, 1.5, and 6.125, respectively, similar to [17]. In additions, N is the number of boxes that matches the ground truth boxes. Moreover, the area of the ground truth bounding boxes A_{gb} are used to normalize the mask loss.

Classification Loss Function. With one label per bounding box, softmax loss function is used to estimate the confidence score c_i^p of each proposed bounding box i per category p, where $x_{ij}^p = \{0, 1\}$ is the indicator of matching the i-th proposed box to the j-th ground truth box of category p, given $\hat{c}_i^p = \frac{\exp(c_i^p)}{\sum_q \exp(c_i^q)}$

$$L_{class}(x, c) = - \sum_{i \in Pos}^{N} \sum_j x_{ij}^p \log(\hat{c}_i^p) - \sum_{i \in Neg} \log(\hat{c}_i^p). \qquad (2)$$

Localization Loss Function. Each bounding box has its center coordinate (c_x, c_y), width w, and height h. Smooth L_1 loss [40] is used to parameterize the bounding box offsets between the ground truth box g and prediction box l.

$$L_{loc}(x, l, g) = - \sum_{i \in Pos}^{N} \sum_j \sum_{m \in c_x, c_y, w, h} x_{ij}^k \text{smooth}_{L1}(l_i^m - \hat{g}_j^m). \qquad (3)$$

Mask Loss Function. Mask loss function is Binary Cross Entropy (BCE) loss between the predicted mask M_{pr} and the ground truth mask M_{gt} at the pixel level [17]. Using BCE loss can maximize the accuracy of the estimated mask, where $L_{mask} = BCE(M_{gt}, M_{pr})$.

4.3   Baseline Experiment Results

The images in TTPLA are split randomly into subsets of 70%, 10%, and 20% images for training, validation, and testing, respectively. Yolact with different

Table 3. Average precision for different deep learning models on TTPLA.

Backbone	Image size	$AP_b^{50\%}$	$AP_m^{50\%}$	$AP_b^{75\%}$	$AP_m^{75\%}$	AP_b^{avg}	AP_m^{avg}
Resnet-50	Yolact-640 × 360	46.72	34.28	4.99	11.20	16.50	14.52
	Yolact-550 × 550	43.37	28.36	18.36	12.22	20.76	14.70
	Yolact-700 × 700	42.62	30.07	20.36	13.64	21.90	15.72
Resnet-101	Yolact-640 × 360	44.99	32.58	10.00	10.06	18.42	14.05
	Yolact-550 × 550	45.30	28.85	19.80	12.33	22.61	14.68
	Yolact-700 × 700	43.19	28.18	21.27	13.46	22.96	14.88

backbones are evaluated based on the proposed dataset. Yolact produces bounding box, confidence score for a true object, and mask for each predicted object instance. Yolact is trained based on our dataset using two GeFoce GTX-1070 GPU with 8G memory/each. We train the model using different image sizes 640 × 360 (preserve aspect ratio), 550 × 550 and 700 × 700. In addition, different backbones are used in our training such as resnet-101 and resnet-50. All the results on average precision are reported in Table 3. The best average scores for bounding box and mask are 22.96% and 15.72%, respectively, as listed in Table 3. Overall, the average precision for instance mask level is less than that of bounding box.

A brief case study is presented as follows based on the TTPLA dataset. Average precision is evaluated based on true positives and false positives. False positive is considered for any object with IoU less than 50%. In addition, there is an inversely proportional relation between average precision and the number of false positives. Therefore, false positive increases as a result of three types of falseness on classification, detection and segmentation.

Firstly, classification falseness appears as a result of confusion on class labels. Although there is no shape similarity between the classes of PLs and TTs, there is still a small

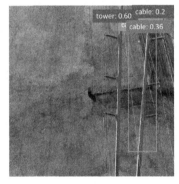

Fig. 7. Classification falseness.

proportion of this type of falseness which is up to 1.3% from the test-set images. Further examination of the results show that the classifier may not be able to distinguish one type of TTs (*tower-tucohy*) and PLs as shown in Fig. 7. One possibility of this confusion is that the color and shape of small-size *tower-tucohy* have high similarity as those of PLs. This type of falseness is considered as a challenge and leaves much scope for improvement.

Secondly, detection falseness is produced due to one of the following two reasons. On one hand, the object is not detected. On the other hand, an object may be detected in a region where there is actually no object. As shown in Fig. 8, there is a wrong detection

Fig. 8. Detection falseness.

of PL in regions of lane line and sidewalk, respectively. Based on what is mentioned in [8], the probability of detection falseness is high similar because PLs do not have predictable visual properties and all PLs have the same features without much distinction. On the other hand, significant shape variation of TTs affects directly the precision of detection. To reflect this point in our dataset, as mentioned in Subsect. 3.2, we collect images for TTs from different views.

Thirdly, segmentation falseness appears when the segmentation mask is not covering the whole object. As mentioned in [8], there is a strong relationship between precision and the object size. In other words, precision can be improved when the number of object pixels increases. This is due to the difficulty of extracting the feature of small objects specially with noisy background. This problem often appears in detecting PLs, because of their long-thin shape and simple appearance. In TTPLA, most PLs have very small width between 1 to 3 pixels. In addition, PLs are so long as compared to the size of images,

Fig. 9. Segmentation falseness.

when compared to the instance objects included in COCO and PASCAL VOC. Consequently, according to Yolact, PLs are detected by only one bounding box and only one mask which in most cases is not covering the whole PL and leads to reduced mask average precision for PLs. Moreover, in most cases the single power line is split up to multiple detecting instances which also increases the falseness for segmentation [42]. This falseness also appears with TTs detection as shown in Fig. 9.

Fourthly, NMS is exploited by instance segmentation detectors [14,17], that produce large numbers of false positives near the ground truth, to suppress the overlapped bounding boxes based on lower confidence score and the overlap threshold [5]. In the crowded scenario, the objects are quite close, overlapped and their predicted bounding boxes can overlap with each other. Therefore, some bounding boxes are suppressed based on overlap threshold of NMS although its nearby bounding boxes are actually for different objects, which reduces the average precision. Changing the overlap threshold may be one solution, however in the crowded scenario it is not a perfect solution since higher NMS threshold leads to increased false positives while lower NMS threshold may increase the miss-rate and remove more true positives [5]. The number of the overlapped bounding boxes per object is reported in Table 4. The overlap is calculated based on threshold 30%, 50%, 75% and 95%, respectively. For example, we have 4,251 overlapped bounding boxes of PLs with threshold 30%. As reported in Table 4, in TTPLA dataset, the total percentage of the overlap between the bounding boxes of different instances is up to 48.9%, 36.8%, 17.9%, 2.5% for threshold 0.3, 0.5, 0.75, 0.95, respectively.

Finally, the analysis results highlight the difficulties to process these real-time images collected by autonomous UAV and reflect the challenges included in our dataset which pose opportunities for further enhancements.

Table 4. Total percentage of overlap on TTPLA.

Category	Overlap (30%)	Overlap (50%)	Overlap (75%)	Overlap (95%)
cable	4,251	3,224	1,570	224
tower-lattice	15	3	0	0
tower-tucohy	20	4	2	0
tower-wooden	22	10	2	0
Total(%)	48.9	36.8	17.9	2.5

5 Conclusion

TTPLA is the first public image dataset with a focus on combined TTs and PLs instance segmentation. TTPLA dataset consists of 1,100 aerial images with resolution of $3,840 \times 2,160$ and contains up to 8,987 instances. Data collection and labeling for TTPLA dataset are highly challenging to ensure the variety in terms of view angles, scales, backgrounds, lighting conditions and zooming levels. Therefore, novel policies are proposed for collecting, annotating, and labeling the aerial images. TTPLA dataset is annotated accurately at the pixel-wise level to be employed by the instance segmentation using deep learning models. Based on TTPLA, a baseline is created using the state-of-the-art learning model, different backbones, and various images sizes. Finally, TTPLA dataset can provide a new challenge to computer vision community and lead to new advancement in detection, classification and instance segmentation.

Acknowledgments. The authors gratefully acknowledge the partial financial support of the National Science Foundation (1830512).

References

1. Luque-Vega, L.F., Castillo-Toledo, B., Loukianov, A., Gonzalez-Jimenez, L.E.: Power line inspection via an unmanned aerial system based on the quadrotor helicopter. In: Proceedings of the IEEE Mediterranean Electrotechnical Conference (MELECON), pp. 393–397 (2014)
2. Hu, H., Gu, J., Zhang, Z., Dai, J., Wei, Y.: Relation networks for object detection. In: Proceedings of the IEEE Conference on Computer Vision and Pattern Recognition (CVPR), pp. 3588–3597 (2018)
3. Ouyang, W., Wang, X., Zhang, C., Yang, X.: Factors in finetuning deep model for object detection with long-tail distribution. In: Proceedings of the IEEE Conference on Computer Vision and Pattern Recognition (CVPR), pp. 864–873 (2016)
4. Pang, J., Chen, K., Shi, J., Feng, H., Ouyang, W., Lin, D.: Libra R-CNN: towards balanced learning for object detection. In: Proceedings of the IEEE Conference on Computer Vision and Pattern Recognition (CVPR), pp. 821–830 (2019)
5. Liu, S., Huang, D., Wang, Y.: Adaptive NMS: refining pedestrian detection in a crowd. In: Proceedings of the IEEE Conference on Computer Vision and Pattern Recognition (CVPR), pp. 6459–6468 (2019)
6. Lin, T.-Y., et al.: Microsoft COCO: common objects in context. In: Fleet, D., Pajdla, T., Schiele, B., Tuytelaars, T. (eds.) ECCV 2014. LNCS, vol. 8693, pp. 740–755. Springer, Cham (2014). https://doi.org/10.1007/978-3-319-10602-1_48
7. Cordts, M., et al.: The cityscapes dataset for semantic urban scene understanding. In: Proceedings of the IEEE Conference on Computer Vision and Pattern Recognition (CVPR), pp. 3213–3223 (2016)
8. Everingham, M., Van Gool, L., Williams, C.K., Winn, J., Zisserman, A.: The pascal visual object classes (VOC) challenge. Int. J. Comput. Vision **88**, 303–338 (2010)
9. Lin, G., Shen, C., Van Den Hengel, A., Reid, I.: Efficient piecewise training of deep structured models for semantic segmentation. In: Proceedings of the IEEE Conference on Computer Vision and Pattern Recognition (CVPR), pp. 3194–3203 (2016)
10. Li, X., Liu, Z., Luo, P., Change Loy, C., Tang, X.: Not all pixels are equal: difficulty-aware semantic segmentation via deep layer cascade. In: Proceedings of the IEEE Conference on Computer Vision and Pattern Recognition (CVPR), pp. 3193–3202 (2017)
11. Papandreou, G., Chen, L.C., Murphy, K.P., Yuille, A.L.: Weakly-and semi-supervised learning of a deep convolutional network for semantic image segmentation. In: Proceedings of the IEEE International Conference on Computer Vision (ICCV), pp. 1742–1750 (2015)
12. Luo, P., Wang, G., Lin, L., Wang, X.: Deep dual learning for semantic image segmentation. In: Proceedings of the IEEE International Conference on Computer Vision (ICCV), pp. 2718–2726 (2017)
13. Ren, M., Zemel, R.S.: End-to-end instance segmentation with recurrent attention. In: Proceedings of the IEEE Conference on Computer Vision and Pattern Recognition (CVPR), pp. 6656–6664 (2017)
14. He, K., Gkioxari, G., Dollár, P., Girshick, R.: Mask R-CNN. In: Proceedings of the IEEE International Conference on Computer Vision (ICCV), pp. 2961–2969 (2017)
15. Xie, E., et al.: PolarMask: single shot instance segmentation with polar representation. In: Proceedings of the IEEE/CVF Conference on Computer Vision and Pattern Recognition, pp. 12193–12202 (2020)

16. Huang, Z., Huang, L., Gong, Y., Huang, C., Wang, X.: Mask scoring R-CNN. In: Proceedings of the IEEE Conference on Computer Vision and Pattern Recognition (CVPR), pp. 6409–6418 (2019)

17. Bolya, D., Zhou, C., Xiao, F., Lee, Y.J.: YOLACT: real-time instance segmentation. In: Proceedings of the IEEE International Conference on Computer Vision (ICCV), pp. 9157–9166 (2019)

18. Bodla, N., Singh, B., Chellappa, R., Davis, L.S.: Soft-NMS-improving object detection with one line of code. In: Proceedings of the IEEE International Conference on Computer Vision (ICCV), pp. 5561–5569 (2017)

19. Hosang, J., Benenson, R., Schiele, B.: Learning non-maximum suppression. In: Proceedings of the IEEE Conference on Computer Vision and Pattern Recognition (CVPR), pp. 4507–4515 (2017)

20. Emre, Y.Ö., Nezih, G.Ö., et al.: Power line image dataset (infrared-IR and visible light-VL). Mendeley Data (2017)

21. Zhang, H., Yang, W., Yu, H., Zhang, H., Xia, G.S.: Detecting power lines in UAV images with convolutional features and structured constraints. Remote Sens. **11**, 1342 (2019)

22. Russakovsky, O., et al.: Imagenet large scale visual recognition challenge. Int. J. Comput. Vision **115**, 211–252 (2015)

23. Sampedro, C., Martinez, C., Chauhan, A., Campoy, P.: A supervised approach to electric tower detection and classification for power line inspection. In: Proceedings of the International Joint Conference on Neural Networks (IJCNN), pp. 1970–1977 (2014)

24. Nguyen, V.N., Jenssen, R., Roverso, D.: Intelligent monitoring and inspection of power line components powered by UAVs and deep learning. IEEE Power Energy Technol. Syst. J. **6**, 11–21 (2019)

25. Candamo, J., Goldgof, D.: Wire detection in low-altitude, urban, and low-quality video frames. In: Proceedings of the International Conference on Pattern Recognition, pp. 1–4 (2008)

26. Hui, X., Bian, J., Zhao, X., Tan, M.: Vision-based autonomous navigation approach for unmanned aerial vehicle transmission-line inspection. Int. J. Adv. Rob. Syst. **15**, 1729881417752821 (2018)

27. Saurav, S., Gidde, P., Singh, S., Saini, R.: Power line segmentation in aerial images using convolutional neural networks. In: Proceedings of the International Conference on Pattern Recognition and Machine Intelligence, pp. 623–632 (2019)

28. Nguyen, V.N., Jenssen, R., Roverso, D.: LS-NET: fast single-shot line-segment detector. arXiv preprint arXiv:1912.09532 (2019)

29. Madaan, R., Maturana, D., Scherer, S.: Wire detection using synthetic data and dilated convolutional networks for unmanned aerial vehicles. In: Proceedings of the IEEE/RSJ International Conference on Intelligent Robots and Systems (IROS), pp. 3487–3494 (2017)

30. Yetgin, O.E., Benligiray, B., Gerek, O.N.: Power line recognition from aerial images with deep learning. IEEE Trans. Aerosp. Electron. Syst. **55**(5), 2241–2252 (2018)

31. Zhang, X., Xiao, G., Gong, K., Zhao, J., Bavirisetti, D.P.: Automatic power line detection for low-altitude aircraft safety based on deep learning. In: Proceedings of the International Conference on Aerospace System Science and Engineering, pp. 169–183 (2018)

32. Simonyan, K., Zisserman, A.: Very deep convolutional networks for large-scale image recognition. arXiv preprint arXiv:1409.1556 (2014)

33. Liu, Y., Cheng, M.M., Hu, X., Wang, K., Bai, X.: Richer convolutional features for edge detection. In: Proceedings of the IEEE Conference on Computer Vision and Pattern Recognition (CVPR), pp. 3000–3009 (2017)
34. Zou, Q., Jiang, H., Dai, Q., Yue, Y., Chen, L., Wang, Q.: Robust lane detection from continuous driving scenes using deep neural networks. IEEE Trans. Veh. Technol. **69**, 41–54 (2019)
35. Fang, S.j., Roy, S., Kramer, J.: Transmission structures. In: Structural Engineering Handbook (1999)
36. Li, D., Wang, X.: The future application of transmission line automatic monitoring and deep learning technology based on vision. In: Proceedings of the IEEE International Conference on Cloud Computing and Big Data Analysis (ICCCBDA), pp. 131–137 (2019)
37. Russell, B.C., Torralba, A., Murphy, K.P., Freeman, W.T.: LabelMe: a database and web-based tool for image annotation. Int. J. Comput. Vision **77**, 157–173 (2008)
38. Hariharan, B., Arbeláez, P., Girshick, R., Malik, J.: Simultaneous detection and segmentation. In: Fleet, D., Pajdla, T., Schiele, B., Tuytelaars, T. (eds.) ECCV 2014. LNCS, vol. 8695, pp. 297–312. Springer, Cham (2014). https://doi.org/10.1007/978-3-319-10584-0_20
39. Liu, W., et al.: SSD: single shot MultiBox detector. In: Leibe, B., Matas, J., Sebe, N., Welling, M. (eds.) ECCV 2016. LNCS, vol. 9905, pp. 21–37. Springer, Cham (2016). https://doi.org/10.1007/978-3-319-46448-0_2
40. Girshick, R.: Fast R-CNN. In: Proceedings of the IEEE International Conference on Computer Vision (ICCV), pp. 1440–1448 (2015)
41. Redmon, J., Divvala, S., Girshick, R., Farhadi, A.: You only look once: unified, real-time object detection. In: Proceedings of the IEEE Conference on Computer Vision and Pattern Recognition (CVPR), pp. 779–788 (2016)
42. De Brabandere, B., Neven, D., Van Gool, L.: Semantic instance segmentation with a discriminative loss function. arXiv preprint arXiv:1708.02551 (2017)

A Day on Campus - An Anomaly Detection Dataset for Events in a Single Camera

Pranav Mantini[✉], Zhenggang Li, and K. Shishir Shah

University of Houston, Houston, TX 77004, USA
{pmantini,zli36}@uh.edu, shah@cs.uh.edu

Abstract. Detecting anomalies in videos is a complex problem with a myriad of applications in video surveillance. However, large and complex datasets that are representative of real-world deployment of surveillance cameras are unavailable. Anomalies in surveillance videos are not well defined and the standard and existing metrics for evaluation do not quantify the performance of algorithms accurately. We provide a large scale dataset, A Day on Campus (ADOC (Dataset available at qil.uh.edu/datasets)), with 25 event types, spanning over 721 instances and occurring over a period of 24 h. This is the largest dataset with localized bounding box annotations that is available to perform anomaly detection. We design a novel metric to evaluate the performance of methods and we perform an evaluation of the state-of-the-art methods to ascertain their readiness to transition into real-world surveillance scenarios.

1 Introduction

Surveillance cameras have become an integral part of public and private infrastructures. They provide a mechanism to actively monitor spaces for events and consequently enhance security. The advancement of sensor technology and the availability of affordable sensors has led to frequent deployment of large camera surveillance networks. Today, a university can have up to a thousand cameras, cities and casinos can have up to tens of thousands of cameras. These networks produce large quantities of video data and it is not possible to manually monitor and identify events. Computer vision algorithms that analyze videos find a natural place in these scenarios.

Given all events that may occur in the view of a surveillance camera, one would like to analyze the video to identify a subset of events that require attention. If the subset of events were known, the problem reduces to that of event detection [1,2], where the goal is to model the events and identify them in videos. However, the events that may occur in a camera view are conditioned on a multitude of contextual factors, like view-point, geo-spatial factors, and etc. These factors are typically unknown and vary from camera to camera as well as events of interest.

© Springer Nature Switzerland AG 2021
H. Ishikawa et al. (Eds.): ACCV 2020, LNCS 12627, pp. 619–635, 2021.
https://doi.org/10.1007/978-3-030-69544-6_37

To address this challenge researchers have resorted to the idea of identifying discordant observations. Edgeworth [3] described discordant observations "as those which present the appearance of differing in respect of their law of frequency from other observations with which they are combined" [3]. Most methods have defined anomaly as a deviation from the normal [4]. Given all observations that may occur and their frequency of occurrences, normal events can be defined as those that have a higher frequency of occurrence, and conversely **anomalous events** are defined as the complementary set of normal events (those that have lower frequency of occurrence). We will extrapolate and argue that the less probable an event is, the more anomalous it is. While we acknowledge that extremely less probable events do not necessarily imply that they are of greater significance from a video surveillance stand point.

1.1   Challenges in Anomaly Detection

Datasets for Anomaly Detection: Today vision algorithms are heavily data driven. One can see the difficulty in gathering a dataset of anomalous events. Such events are not well defined and are defined with respect to normal events, which again are not well defined. Furthermore, anomalous events have a low probability of occurrence and add to this difficulty. Figure 1 shows an example of an image acquired from a surveillance camera deployed at a university campus. An event can be anything happening in the scene including global events such as a weather anomaly to localized events such as a person falling down. We concern ourselves with events that are performed by humans, are affecting humans, and are consequences of human actions. The set of such events may not be independent of other events. For example, a person running can be conditioned on the fact that it is raining. However, we assume that the set of events concerning humans is independent.

Fig. 1. Anomalous events. (Color figure online)

With this assumption, we define events as holistic actions realized over time, and not their realization at individual time instants. For example, in the scenario shown in Fig. 1 (left), the most common action is humans walking across. The blue bounding box shows a person distributing information (in the form of fliers) and their corresponding trajectory (shown in red). While the action of this person at any time instant can be looked as either standing or walking. The holistic action of distributing information is less probable compared to the action of a person walking, and is arguably more anomalous. Another example in the image is the red bounding box that shows a crowd gathered around another person holding a sign. While the individual realization of the people in the crowd is the action of standing, the holistic action of crowd gathering as a consequence of a person holding a sign is unique. Most existing datasets do not contain such complex events, and label simple actions as anomalies. We distinguish them as separate events, where a person walking and standing could have a high frequency of occurrence, and a crowd gathering and a person distributing information are events of low frequency. It is in this respect that we distinguish our definition of anomalous events, and provide a dataset in pursuit of solutions for anomaly detection.

Anomaly Detection in Surveillance Cameras: Surveillance cameras are deployed in a variety of scenarios and are expected to function through varying global conditions like natural illumination changes such as day, night, dawn, etc. and weather changes such as rain, snow, and fog. They are deployed in a variety of scenarios such as indoor, outdoor, crowded areas, etc. Such events also result in a deviation from normal and often tend to produce false positives. A dataset for anomaly detection in surveillance videos should include sufficient variety of global changes, and low and high frequency events to test the effectiveness of algorithms.

Evaluation Criteria: Existing evaluation metrics evaluate anomaly detection as a binary class (normal and anomaly) problem. The current evaluation schemes evaluate how well a method is capable of detecting anomalies while producing the least false positives. They tend to ignore the probability of occurrence of the event. Anomalies are not well defined, and the algorithms can encounter novel anomalies. We argue that it is advantageous to quantify the ability of the algorithm to detect anomalous events based on their probability of occurrence. For example, in the scenario shown in Fig. 1, while it is not as probable as the action of a person walking, it is common to notice a person riding a bicycle. It is much less probable to notice a person walking a dog than a person riding a bicycle. We argue that an algorithm that detects the event that a person is walking a dog, and misses a few detections of a person riding a bicycle is more efficient than one that efficiently detects a person riding a bicycle and misses the less probable events. Most current evaluations weigh the detection of the person riding an bicycle and a person walking a dog equally. We propose an evaluation criteria to account for the probability of occurrence of anomalous events. In this paper we aim to address the above challenges. Our contributions are:

- We introduce a large surveillance dataset consisting 24 h of video from a single camera for anomaly detection with event annotations.
- We introduce an new evaluation criteria for anomaly detection algorithms.
- We perform benchmarking using state-of-the-art algorithms.

Table 1. Comparison of existing dataset.

Datasets	# Abnormal	# Abnormal events	# Scenes	Annotations	Hours
UMN [5]	1,222	3	3	1222 Frame level	~0.07
SubwayExit [6]	720	9	1	720 Frame level	~0.72
SubwayEntrance [6]	2,400	21	1	2400 Frame level	1.6
Avenue [7]	3,820	47	1	3820 Bounding boxes	~0.5
Ped1 [4]	4,005	40	1	2000 Pixel masks	1.5
Ped2 [4]	1,636	20	1	2100 Pixel masks	0.4
ShanghaiTech [8]	17,090	130	13	40791 Pixel masks	3.6
Streetscene [9]	19585	205	3	19585 Bounding boxes	4
ADOC	**97030**	**721**	1	**284125** Bounding boxes	**24**

2 Existing Datasets

Anomaly detection in videos has been a widely researched problem in vision for decades. Traditional approaches were aimed at modeling local [7,10,11] and holistic [12,13] features to perform classification. More recently, various deep learning architectures have been used for anomaly detection viz. Convolutional Neural Networks (CNNs) [14], Long Short Term Memory Networks [15], Auto-encoders (AE), and Generative Adversarial networks (GANs) [16]. For a detailed review of the approaches for anomaly detection we direct readers to existing surveys [17–19].

Anomaly detection is used interchangeably to address two problems. First, a video classification problem, where given numerous videos, the task is to identify if a video contains anomaly or not. The latter is a temporal analysis problem, where, given continuous video from a camera, the task is to decide if each frame is either normal or anomalous. Anomaly detection is challenging because there is no consensus on what the exact definition is. Known activity labels including those to describe criminal or malicious activities is one definition. The other is one that represents rare events, or events that have a lower probability of occurrence. We use the latter in this paper, and hence, we refrain from using the term anomalous events in the paper and rather define them as low-frequency events. Sultani *et al.* [20] proposed a dataset for anomaly detection called UCF-Crime dataset that captures criminal activity well, while we focus on capturing the natural frequency of all human-related events in the scene of a surveillance video. Simple events such as "riding a bike" may not be a meaningful event under the first definition, but if we can construct algorithms that can understand the frequency of this event remains as an open problem. The UCF crime dataset has 128 h from 1900 videos. The average video length is 4 min (70% of videos are ≤ 3 mins long), making it a valuable dataset for the task of video classification. However, this dataset is unsuitable for the task of temporal analysis. Furthermore, major reason vision algorithms fail to transition to real-world is that they produce too many false alarms. There is no comprehensive way of assessing the number of false positives an algorithm produces over a persisted amount of time (eg. a day) when deployed on a single camera. The proposed dataset is the only dataset that provides data for illumination and weather changes for a complex scene throughout an entire day. The proposed dataset is more in alignment with UMN [5], Subway [6], Avenue [7], etc.

Since our objective is to introduce a benchmark dataset that will spur research in anomaly detection as a comprehensive, multi-faceted problem. We briefly review existing datasets and compare their size, scene, complexity and diversity. Table 1 shows the list of existing datasets.

In comparison, we introduce the largest dataset for anomaly detection in video surveillance cameras, consisting of 721 anomalous events localized using 284125 bounding box annotations. The dataset consists of 259123 frames captured over 24 contiguous hours and encapsulates the complexities of a typical surveillance camera.

3   A Day on Campus

The data is acquired from a surveillance camera deployed on a large university campus. It overlooks a walkway leading to various buildings and captures the events performed by students, faculty, and staff on a busy day. The camera captures video at a resolution of 1080p and a frame-rate of 3 frames per second. The video is compressed using H.264 format, which is a lossy compression method and is standard of the surveillance industry. We create a dataset from video captured over a period of 24 contiguous hours. The video encapsulates varying illumination conditions, crowded scenarios with background clutter. The data is annotated with a number of events ranging from low to high frequency.

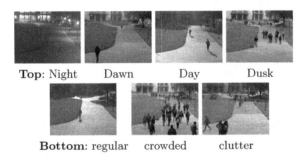

Top: Night   Dawn   Day   Dusk

Bottom: regular   crowded   clutter

Fig. 2. Natural illumination changes occurring in camera view.

Data Variability: Outdoor surveillance cameras undergo regular variations in the scene throughout the day due to illumination changes. Figure 2 (Top) shows example images from the camera, representative of the captured changes in illumination through the day. The camera switches to infrared (IR) mode

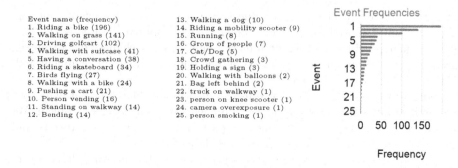

Event name (frequency)
1. Riding a bike (196)
2. Walking on grass (141)
3. Driving golfcart (102)
4. Walking with suitcase (41)
5. Having a conversation (38)
6. Riding a skateboard (34)
7. Birds flying (27)
8. Walking with a bike (24)
9. Pushing a cart (21)
10. Person vending (16)
11. Standing on walkway (14)
12. Bending (14)

13. Walking a dog (10)
14. Riding a mobility scooter (9)
15. Running (8)
16. Group of people (7)
17. Cat/Dog (5)
18. Crowd gathering (3)
19. Holding a sign (3)
20. Walking with balloons (2)
21. Bag left behind (2)
22. truck on walkway (1)
23. person on knee scooter (1)
24. camera overexposure (1)
25. person smoking (1)

Fig. 3. Events and their frequency of occurrence.

in extremely low illumination conditions which is typical of surveillance cameras, this produces a large shift in global image features. Currently, there are no existing datasets for anomaly detection that captures such variations in surveillance cameras. Furthermore, crowded scenarios, background clutter, and occlusion affect the performance of computer vision algorithms. Figure 2 (Bottom) shows example of the regular view of the camera (left), crowded (middle), and view with cluttered background (right: top right corner has a walkway and driveway with various people and cars moving by).

Events and Their Frequencies: There are a wide variety of events that occur in the scene from students walking, riding a bicycle or skateboard, staff driving golf carts to an occasional student walking a dog or carrying balloons. Figure 3 shows a list of the events and their distribution of occurrence rate. There are a total of 721 events in the scene that are considered as low frequency events. The most common activity in the scene is persons walking from one end to the other along the walkway. We estimate a total of 31675 people walking. This is considered as a high frequency event. If we consider the low frequency events as abnormal and the high frequency events as normal. Then the probability of an abnormal event is 0.022.

Event Annotations: The data is annotated using a combination of manual and automatic techniques.

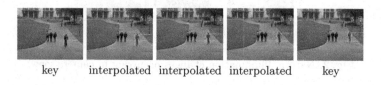

key   interpolated interpolated interpolated   key

Fig. 4. Manual annotations.

Annotating Low Frequency Events: We manually annotate each low frequency event in the dataset. The annotations are performed using Computer

Vision Annotation Tool (CVAT). We annotate key frames for each event and the annotation for the frames between are obtained through interpolation. Each event is annotated and then reviewed for accuracy by two annotators with computer vision background. Figure 4 shows the annotation for an event (riding a bicycle). The annotations are provided in the Multiple Object Tracking (MOT) format. Every event is localized using a tight bounding box, a frame id and contains a unique association ID to form trajectories.

Annotating High Frequency Events: We annotate the high frequency event of walking using automated technique. Given the set of all events occurred on the day, we assume that all the events excluding walking are low frequency and have already been annotated manually. We perform object detection and refine the results to automatically annotate walking. The results of the object detector are refined as shown in Fig. 5 to generate automatic annotations. In step 1, any object that is not a person (car, bicycle, etc) is considered a low frequency event and has been manually annotated. The output from the object detector is filtered and the bounding boxes labeled as person are retained and other are removed. In Fig. 5, the unrefined images show all the detections from the object detector in blue. The green bounding box shows the manual annotation of the person riding a bike. The object detector detects the person on the bicycle, and the bicycle (among other detections). In the first step, all the bounding boxes that are not humans are removed. The resulting annotations are shown in the center image. The set of bounding boxes represents all events that involve humans including low and high frequency events. In the second step, we compute a disjoint set of bounding boxes from the manual annotations by removing all bounding boxes that have and Intersections Over Union (IOU) greater than a threshold value (0.2). The resulting set is assumed to be people walking. This is shown in Fig. 5, the detection from object detector for the person on the bicycle is removed ($IOU \geq 0.2$). The deleted detections are shown in the red bounding box.

Unrefined   step 1: Refined step 2:Refined

Fig. 5. Automatic Annotations. Blue BB: Automatic annotations, Green: Manual annotations, and Red: Deleted detections (Color figure online)

We rely on the accuracy of the object detector for these annotations. Anomaly detection algorithms designed for this scene would consider walking as normal events and is not aimed at detecting and localizing such occurrences, the accuracy of the detection are irrelevant. The annotations provide a way to estimate the comprehensive counts of each event, and subsequently estimate their probability of occurrences. Furthermore, unlike other datasets, they can enable the

Fig. 6. Estimating frequency of people walking, yellow: bounding box is crossing the line, red: bounding box is not crossing the line (Color figure online)

estimation of the false positives produced as a result of humans walking. The automatic annotations are provided in the YOLO format [21] and they do not contain any association across frames to form trajectories of walking. Figure 5 shows an example of automatically generated and filtered annotations.

Estimating the Count of People Walking: We estimate the total frequency of people walking to infer the probability of each event, and subsequently perform a more accurate evaluation of the performance of the algorithm. Most people that are annotated and that are detected are within this area of interest marked by the red box in Fig. 6 (left). To count the total number of people walking across this area. We first perform a perspective projection using the parallel lines in the scene to obtain a birds eye view as shown in Fig. 6 (right) we project the area marked by the red box. Then, we estimate the count of total people walking over the entire video by counting, all the bounding boxes that cross the green line. Given the average pace of a pedestrian, we manually estimate the count of average number of frames over which a pedestrian crosses the line. We divide the total count by the number of bounding boxes detected crossing the line by this number to estimate the total number of walking events.

Numbers: Table 2 lists the count of frames, annotations, and events in the dataset. The dataset is made of 259123 frames, of which 97030 have low frequency events, and 142962 have either low, high or both frequency events. There are a total of 721 events annotated in the dataset. The 721 events are annotated using 13290 manually annotated bounding boxes, and 270835 interpolated bounding boxes. There are total of 284125 annotations representing low frequency events in the dataset. There are a total of 5082993 annotations that capture 31675 human walking over a period of 24 h.

4   A Revised Evaluation Metric

Anomaly detection algorithms are evaluated as a binary class problem, where anomalous events are considered as the positive class and the normal as negative. By our definition, anomalous events occur with a low probability. In general one can assume that the distribution is biased towards the negative class. For example, in the ADOC dataset, there are 31675 samples that belong to negative class and 721 samples that belong to positive class. Currently accuracy and precision are the common metrics to evaluate the performance of the algorithms. Accuracy is defined as $\frac{TP+TN}{TP+FP+TN+FN}$, where TP are true positives, FP are

Table 2. Count of frames, annotations, and events in the dataset.

Description	Count
Low frequency events	
Trajectories	721
Manually annotated bounding boxes	13290
Interpolated bounding boxes	270835
Total bounding boxes	284125
High frequency events	
Automatically annotated bounding boxes	5082993
Estimated number of persons walking	31675
Frame count	
Frames with low frequency events	97030
Frames with events (low and high)	142962
Total frames	259123

false positives, TN are true negatives, and FN are false negatives. An algorithms that detects all events as belonging to the negative class and fails to detect any anomalous event has an accuracy of 0.97 $((0 + 31675)/32396)$. Precision is defined as $\frac{TP}{TP+FP}$, While this metric can quantify the ability of the system to detect anomalies, it does not capture the ability of the system to identify negative samples. It is necessary to quantify the overall capability of the system by aggregating the algorithms capability to detect individual types of events.

Let there be n events that may occur in a surveillance scenario, denoted by $\{e_1, e_2, ..., e_n\}$ with probabilities $\{p_1, p_2, ..., p_n\}$ such that $\Sigma_i p_i = 1$. Now given various algorithms, according to Expected Utility Theory, the decision of which algorithm to choose is dictated by maximizing the expected utility [22].

$$Eu(A) = \Sigma_i p_i U(e_i), \tag{1}$$

where $Eu(A)$ is the expected utility for the algorithm, and $U(e_i)$ is an assigned numerical utility.

For example, if $\{a_1, a_2, ..., a_n\}$ be the accuracy with which the algorithm A detects events $\{e_1, e_2, ..., e_n\}$, respectively. If $U(e_i) = a_i$, then the expected utility reduces to that of computing the expected accuracy $E_a = \Sigma_i p_i a_i$.

Note that similar to computing the accuracy under a binary class assumption, the expected accuracy is high when the system is capable of detecting the high probability events, and the effect of detecting low probability events with a high accuracy is insignificant.

Our motivation to quantify the ability of an algorithm to perform anomalous event detection has roots in prospect theory [23], where we depart from the expected utility theory by overweighting the small probabilities and underweighting the large [24]. The decision of one algorithm over the other is defined by the prospect value $\pi_A = \Sigma_i w_\gamma(p_i) a_i$, where $w_\gamma(p)$ is the probability weighting

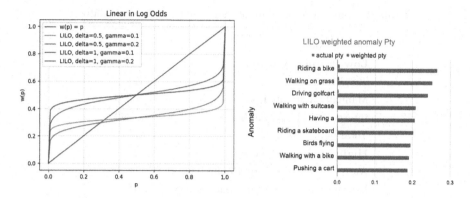

Fig. 7. (left) Linear in Log Odds function, (right), few event probabilities in ADOC dataset weighted by lilo (blue: original probability values, red: lilo weighted probability values) (Color figure online)

function. A simple weighting function is to assume that all events occur with equal probability, i.e. $w_\gamma(p_i) = 1/n$, where the prospect value reduces to the average of the accuracy of the algorithms ability to detect each event. However, considering that the normal class can have a large number of samples, and such probability weighting can undermine the effect of the algorithms inability to detect these events. This can translate to choosing algorithms that produce too many false positives.

Linear in Log Odds (lilo): We adopt the two parameter probability weighting function defined as [25]:

$$w_\gamma(p) = \frac{\delta p^\gamma}{(\delta p^\gamma + (1-p)^\gamma)}, \tag{2}$$

where the γ controls the curvature and δ controls the elevation independently. Note when $\delta = 1$, and $\gamma = 1$ the function reduces to $w_\gamma(p) = p$. Figure 7 show the weighting function for $\delta = 1$, and $\gamma = 0.2$. We compute the expected accuracy value using lilo weighted probabilities (liloAcc) as a metric to quantify the performance of anomaly detection methods. Figure 7 (right) shows the transformed probabilities using the lilo function for each event in the dataset.

Note that the liloAcc metric is bounded, as the accuracy and the probability values are bounded. The maximum value occurs when the accuracy of detecting each event is 1. The maximum value is $\Sigma_i w_\gamma(p_i)$, sum of the lilo weighted probabilities. We use this value to obtain a normalized metric (nliloAcc):

$$nliloAcc = \frac{\Sigma_i w_\gamma(p_i)a_i}{\Sigma_i w_\gamma(p_i)} \tag{3}$$

5   Experimental Design

The goal of the experiments is to ascertain the performance of existing state-of-the-art video anomaly detection algorithms on ADOC dataset. The dataset includes a variety of complex events that are novel, and numerous illumination changes. The experiments provide insight into the readiness of the existing algorithms to transition to real time analysis for anomaly detection.

The dataset consists of 259123 frames captured over 24 h of video. We divide the dataset into two 12 h parts and use them as training and testing patterns. Both partitions contain a combination of day time and night time images. To account for this complexity, we separate the dataset into two partitions, first containing exclusively day images and the latter night. We quantify the capability of algorithms to perform in day time, night time, and overall. We perform the following experiments:

- Experiment **1**: Training: **Day**, Testing: **Day** images
- Experiment **2**: Training: **Night**, Testing: **Night** images
- Experiment **3**: Training: **Day+Night**, Testing: **Day+Night** images

5.1   State of the Art Methods

We choose popular methods from the recent literature and evaluate their performance on the ADOC dataset. We choose methods that have been largely cited and ascertain their readiness to transition into real world analysis of surveillance videos. Anomaly detection methods can be designed to capture a variety of features. Some methods can exclusively encode spatial information or they can encode a combination of spatial and temporal information. Some methods perform analysis on image patches and accumulate information to make decisions while others make an inference on the entire frame. We choose one method that performs analysis on patches by encoding only spatial information, and two other methods that make frame level decisions and encode temporal patterns for anomaly detection. We evaluate the following methods:

- Abnormal Event Detection in Videos using Spatiotemporal Autoencoder (SPAE) (ISNN 2017): The method consists of a spatial feature extractor and a temporal encoder-decoder, which together learn the temporal patterns in videos. This method processes images as a whole and captures temporal patterns among them. We use an input frame size of 227×227 for training and testing.
- Adversarially Learned One-Class Classifier for Novelty Detection [26] (ALOCC) (CVPR 2018): This work proposes a method for novelty detection by training a one class classifier. The framework consists of two modules. The former acts as a pre-processing step for representation learning. The latter performs discrimination to detect novel classes. The paper uses two methods to perform anomaly detection, where a test image is input to the discriminator and the likelihood value is used to detect anomalies. In the second

method, the likelihood value for the reconstructed method is used to detect anomaly. Results from the experiments performed in this paper demonstrate that the latter outperforms the first. If D represents the discriminator and R the encoder-decoder. In the first, the value $D(X)$ is compared against a threshold to infer if X is an anomalies. In the second the value $D(R(X))$ is thresholded to make a decision. We evaluate both methods. The input to the network are patches of images. We use an input frame size of 256×354 for training and testing. We set the patch size to 64×64.

- Future Frame Prediction for Anomaly Detection – A New Baseline [8] (FFP) (CVPR 2018): This method proposes to predict frames into the future, and exploit the inability to predict anomalous events to detect them. A good prediction would imply that it is normal, and vice versa. A UNET is trained by minimizing a loss function that encodes both spatial intensity features and temporal features (optical flow). This method performs analysis at a temporal level and encode both temporal and spatial information for anomaly detection. We use an input frame size of 256×256 for training and testing.

- Memorizing Normality to Detect Anomaly [27] (MemAE) (ICCV 2019): The overall approach involves augmenting an autoencoder with a memory module that is records the prototypical elements of the encoded normal data. This method consist of an encoder, a decoder, and a memory module. The input image is encoded, which is used to retrieve the relevant items from the memory module, which is then reconstructed by the encoder. A larger reconstruction error implies an anomaly. We use the the pre-trained weights on the Ped2 [4] dataset available from the authors for this evaluation.

- Learning Memory-guided Normality for Anomaly Detection [28] (Mnad) (CVPR 2020): This method is similar to the MemAE [27]. It improves the memory module by recording diverse and discriminative normal patterns, by separating memory items explicitly using feature compactness and separateness losses, and enabling using a small number of items compared to MemAE (10 vs 2,000 for MemAE). We use the the pre-trained weights on the Ped2 [4] dataset available from the authors for this evaluation.

5.2   Benchmarks

We compare and quantify the performance of the algorithms under a two class assumption, and then compare them using the proposed lilo weighted expected accuracy metric. The decision of normal and abnormal is made at each level or for a series of frames. Assuming the normal frames to be the negative class, and abnormal as the positive, we quantify the overall accuracy by plotting the Receiver Operating Characteristic (ROC) curves along with their corresponding area under the curve (AUC) as shown in Fig. 8. Then we quantify the capability of each method at the optimal threshold. We define optimal threshold as the point on the ROC curve where the difference between TPR and FPR is maximum. The threshold at which the method detects maximum anomalies while reducing false positives. The results are shown in Table 3.

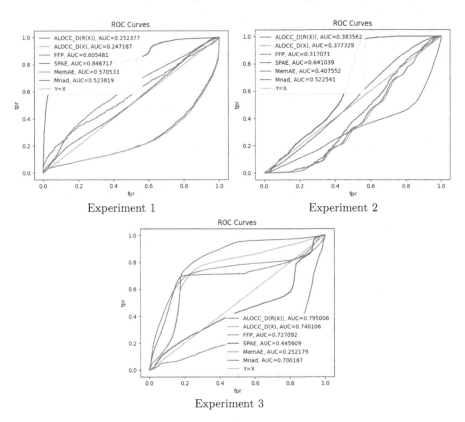

Fig. 8. ROC curve

Experiment 1: Three models are trained and tested on exclusively day time images from the dataset. ALOCC produces a large number of false negatives. FFP does better at prediction than ALOCC, but produces too many false positives. SPAE captures the largest number of true positives, compared to other methods. SPAE has an AUC score of 0.846, with an accuracy of 0.735 and outperforms the other models. Figure 9 shows a bar plot where the x-axis consists of various events ordered by their occurrence rate in ascending order. The plot shows the accuracy of each method in detecting a particular event. SPAE shows an ability to detect events of varying frequency and this is reflected in the nlilo Accuracy score. SPAE and FFP perform temporal analysis while ALOCC performs only spatial analysis. This suggests that temporal analysis is essential when detecting anomalous events.

Experiment 2: Three models are trained and tested on exclusively night images. ALOCC and SPAE tend to produce a large number of false positives. FFP labels most of all frames as negative, and fails to detect abnormal events. SPAE produces a significantly lower false positives than ALOCC. The AUC score suggests that SPAE performs best in this scenario. Despite the fact that FFP fails to detect abnormal events, the accuracy score suggests that it performs best followed by SPAE. Figure 9 shows that SPAE captures abnormal events across varying frequencies best, followed by ALOCC and the FPP. The nlilo Accuracy suggests that SPAE is the best performing algorithm with its relatively high true positives and significantly low false positives. This demonstrates the need for probability distorted metric to evaluate anomaly detection methods.

Table 3. Comparison of performance the state-of-the-art methods at optimal threshold, Acc - accuracy, liloAcc - lilo weighted expected accuracy.

Experiment	Method	Year/conf	TN	FN	TP	FP	AUC	Acc	nliloAcc
1	$ALOCC_{D(R(X))}$	CVPR 18'	10432	53072	1083	113	0.257	0.178	0.299
	$ALOCC_{D(X)}$	CVPR 18'	10427	52970	1185	118	0.247	0.179	0.307
	FFP	CVPR 18'	7477	29166	24989	3068	0.605	0.501	0.583
	$SPAE$	ISNN 17'	9831	16429	37726	714	0.846	0.735	0.698
	$MemAE$	ICCV 19'	8381	35283	18872	2164	0.570	0.421	0.598
	$Mnad$	CVPR 20'	9082	43607	10548	1463	0.523	0.303	0.588
2	$ALOCC_{D(R(X))}$	CVPR 18'	1187	191	20581	48441	0.383	0.309	0.627
	$ALOCC_{D(X)}$	CVPR 18'	1352	202	20570	48276	0.377	0.311	0.656
	FFP	CVPR 18'	49625	20766	6	3	0.346	0.704	0.583
	$SPAE$	ISNN 17'	22226	514	20258	27402	0.641	0.603	0.819
	$MemAE$	ICCV 19'	3080	608	20164	46548	0.407	0.330	0.596
	$Mnad$	CVPR 20'	12041	3239	17533	37587	0.522	0.420	0.651
3	$ALOCC_{D(R(X))}$	CVPR 18'	45071	14845	60082	15102	0.795	0.778	0.824
	$ALOCC_{D(X)}$	CVPR 18'	44415	19042	55885	15758	0.740	0.742	0.795
	FFP	CVPR 18'	47733	22835	52092	12440	0.727	0.738	0.824
	$SPAE$	ISNN 17'	53374	63426	11501	6799	0.445	0.480	0.309
	$MemAE$	ICCV 19'	60173	74911	16	0	0.252	0.445	0.192
	$Mnad$	CVPR 20'	49589	23294	51633	10584	0.700	0.749	0.881

Experiment 3: In this experiment three models are trained and tested on a combination of day time and night time images together. All methods produce higher false positives compared to Experiment 1. MemAE labels most of all frames as negative, and fails to detect abnormal events. AUC and Accuracy scores suggests ALOCC perform better than other methods. Interestingly, Unlike the first two experiments ALOCC outperforms SPAE in Experiment 3. Our inference is that the method generalizes better on exposing to varied illumination. Figure 9 shows that it is able to capture events across frequencies better than SPAE and is comparable to ALOCC. nlilo Accuracy aggregates a similar score for ALOCC and FPP. SPAE underperforms in Experiment 3. This suggests that the model is inefficient at learning features and performing abnormality detection across illuminations. Furthermore, performing patch level analysis seems to be beneficial when learning representation across illuminations. It is able to capture local

features better compared to other methods. We conclude that there is need to perform both temporal analysis and a patch level analysis to build robust algorithms for anomaly detection. Overall Mnad outperfroms the other methods in this experiment.

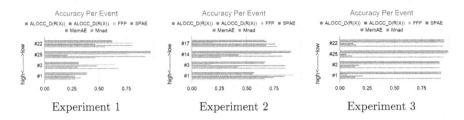

Experiment 1   Experiment 2   Experiment 3

Fig. 9. Bar plot showing the accuracy of detecting example individual events for each method in experiment 1, 2, and 3, x-axis shows event numbers as used in Fig. 3

Discussion: MemAE and Mnad use pretrained weights and are not trained on the adoc dataset (due to the lack of training code and optimal hyper-parameters) unlike the former four methods. Specifically training them on the adoc dataset can improve the detection accuracy. Experiment 1 demonstrates that the state-of-the-art methods fail at detection anomalies and tend to generate too many false negatives. Experiment 2 suggests that the methods tend to produce large numbers of false positives at night time. Experiment 3 suggests that there is much work needed towards designing algorithms that can adapt to varying illuminations. These improvements and the pursuit of robust methods designed with the goal of detecting holistic anomalous events is necessary to realize anomaly detection in surveillance cameras. Experiments also showcase the inconsistencies in adopting generic sensitivity and specificity metrics that are used for binary classification. Given the biased nature of anomaly detection datasets, we advocate the need for probability distorted metrics.

6   Conclusion

We have introduced a complex and a large scale dataset with video from a surveillance camera to enable development of robust algorithms for anomaly detection. We have defined events that are relevant to surveillance cameras in pedestrian environments, and provided a dataset with numerous event annotations. We have defined metrics to account for the biased nature of anomaly detection datasets. We have evaluated the state-of-the-art methods available for anomaly detection on the ADOC dataset. We have accumulated the results and established the required research direction to enable robust anomaly detection in surveillance videos.

References

1. Wang, F., Jiang, Y.G., Ngo, C.W.: Video event detection using motion relativity and visual relatedness. In: Proceedings of the 16th ACM International Conference on Multimedia, pp. 239–248 (2008)
2. Zhang, D., Chang, S.F.: Event detection in baseball video using superimposed caption recognition. In: Proceedings of the Tenth ACM International Conference on Multimedia, pp. 315–318 (2002)
3. Edgeworth, F.Y.: Xli. on discordant observations. London Edinburgh Dublin Philos. Mag. J. Sci. **23**, 364–375 (1887)
4. Mahadevan, V., Li, W., Bhalodia, V., Vasconcelos, N.: Anomaly detection in crowded scenes. In: 2010 IEEE Computer Society Conference on Computer Vision and Pattern Recognition, pp. 1975–1981. IEEE (2010)
5. Mehran, R., Oyama, A., Shah, M.: Abnormal crowd behavior detection using social force model. In: 2009 IEEE Conference on Computer Vision and Pattern Recognition, pp. 935–942. IEEE (2009)
6. Adam, A., Rivlin, E., Shimshoni, I., Reinitz, D.: Robust real-time unusual event detection using multiple fixed-location monitors. IEEE Trans. Pattern Anal. Mach. Intell. **30**, 555–560 (2008)
7. Lu, C., Shi, J., Jia, J.: Abnormal event detection at 150 fps in matlab. In: Proceedings of the IEEE International Conference on Computer Vision, pp. 2720–2727 (2013)
8. Liu, W., Luo, W., Lian, D., Gao, S.: Future frame prediction for anomaly detection-a new baseline. In: Proceedings of the IEEE Conference on Computer Vision and Pattern Recognition, pp. 6536–6545 (2018)
9. Ramachandra, B., Jones, M.: Street scene: a new dataset and evaluation protocol for video anomaly detection. In: The IEEE Winter Conference on Applications of Computer Vision, pp. 2569–2578 (2020)
10. Saligrama, V., Konrad, J., Jodoin, P.M.: Video anomaly identification. IEEE Signal Process. Mag. **27**, 18–33 (2010)
11. Bertini, M., Del Bimbo, A., Seidenari, L.: Multi-scale and real-time non-parametric approach for anomaly detection and localization. Comput. Vis. Image Underst. **116**, 320–329 (2012)
12. Marsden, M., McGuinness, K., Little, S., O'Connor, N.E.: Holistic features for real-time crowd behaviour anomaly detection. In: 2016 IEEE International Conference on Image Processing (ICIP), pp. 918–922. IEEE (2016)
13. Xie, S., Guan, Y.: Motion instability based unsupervised online abnormal behaviors detection. Multimedia Tools Appl. **75**, 7423–7444 (2016)
14. Krizhevsky, A., Sutskever, I., Hinton, G.E.: Imagenet classification with deep convolutional neural networks. In: Advances in Neural Information Processing Systems, pp. 1097–1105 (2012)
15. Hochreiter, S., Schmidhuber, J.: Long short-term memory. Neural Comput. **9**, 1735–1780 (1997)
16. Goodfellow, I., et al.: Generative adversarial nets. In: Advances in Neural Information Processing Systems, pp. 2672–2680 (2014)
17. Pawar, K., Attar, V.: Deep learning approaches for video-based anomalous activity detection. World Wide Web **22**, 571–601 (2019)
18. Chalapathy, R., Chawla, S.: Deep learning for anomaly detection: a survey. arXiv preprint arXiv:1901.03407 (2019)

19. Kumaran, S.K., Dogra, D.P., Roy, P.P.: Anomaly detection in road traffic using visual surveillance: a survey. arXiv preprint arXiv:1901.08292 (2019)
20. Sultani, W., Chen, C., Shah, M.: Real-world anomaly detection in surveillance videos. In: Proceedings of the IEEE Conference on Computer Vision and Pattern Recognition, pp. 6479–6488 (2018)
21. Redmon, J., Farhadi, A.: YOLOv3: an incremental improvement. arXiv (2018)
22. Bernoulli, D.: Exposition of a new theory on the measurement of risk. In: The Kelly Capital Growth Investment Criterion: Theory and Practice, pp. 11–24. World Scientific (2011)
23. Kahneman, D., Tversky, A.: Prospect theory: an analysis of decision under risk. In: Handbook of the Fundamentals of Financial Decision Making: Part I, pp. 99–127. World Scientific (2013)
24. Glaser, C., Trommershäuser, J., Mamassian, P., Maloney, L.T.: Comparison of the distortion of probability information in decision under risk and an equivalent visual task. Psychol. Sci. **23**, 419–426 (2012)
25. Gonzalez, R., Wu, G.: On the shape of the probability weighting function. Cogn. Psychol. **38**, 129–166 (1999)
26. Sabokrou, M., Khalooei, M., Fathy, M., Adeli, E.: Adversarially learned one-class classifier for novelty detection. In: Proceedings of the IEEE Conference on Computer Vision and Pattern Recognition, pp. 3379–3388 (2018)
27. Gong, D., et al.: Memorizing normality to detect anomaly: memory-augmented deep autoencoder for unsupervised anomaly detection. In: Proceedings of the IEEE International Conference on Computer Vision, pp. 1705–1714 (2019)
28. Park, H., Noh, J., Ham, B.: Learning memory-guided normality for anomaly detection. In: Proceedings of the IEEE/CVF Conference on Computer Vision and Pattern Recognition, pp. 14372–14381 (2020)

A Benchmark and Baseline
for Language-Driven Image Editing

Jing Shi[1]([✉]), Ning Xu[2], Trung Bui[2], Franck Dernoncourt[2], Zheng Wen[2], and Chenliang Xu[1]

[1] University of Rochester, Rochester, USA
{j.shi,chenliang.xu}@rochester.edu
[2] Adobe Research, San Jose, USA
{nxu,bui,dernonco}@adobe.com, zhengwen@alumni.stanford.edu

Abstract. Language-driven image editing can significantly save the laborious image editing work and be friendly to the photography novice. However, most similar work can only deal with a specific image domain or can only do global retouching. To solve this new task, we first present a new language-driven image editing dataset that supports both local and global editing with editing operation and mask annotations. Besides, we also propose a baseline method that fully utilizes the annotation to solve this problem. Our new method treats each editing operation as a sub-module and can automatically predict operation parameters. Not only performing well on challenging user data, but such an approach is also highly interpretable. We believe our work, including both the benchmark and the baseline, will advance the image editing area towards a more general and free-form level.

1 Introduction

There are numerous reasons that people want to edit their photos, *e.g.*, remove tourists from wedding photos, improve saturation and contrast to make photos more beautiful, or replace background simply for fun. Therefore, image editing is very useful and important in people's everyday life. However, it is not a simple task for most people. One reason is that current mainstream photo editing softwares (*e.g.* Photoshop) could work only if users understand the concept of various editing operations such as hue, saturation, selection *etc..*, and know how to use them step by step. However, most novice users do not have such knowledge. Another reason is that most editing operations require some manual work, some of which could be very time-consuming. It is even more challenging when editing photos on mobile devices because people have to use their fingers while screen sizes are small (Fig. 1).

In this paper, we propose *language-driven image editing* (LDIE) to make image editing easier for everybody. Specifically, to edit an image, a user only

Electronic supplementary material The online version of this chapter (https://doi.org/10.1007/978-3-030-69544-6_38) contains supplementary material, which is available to authorized users.

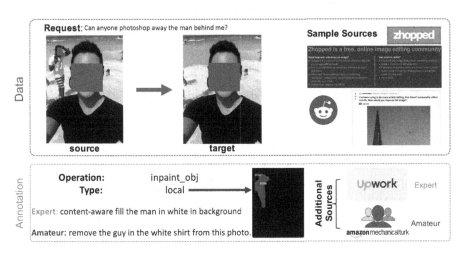

Fig. 1. One example in our newly collected Grounded Image Editing Request (GIER) dataset. Each sample is a triplet. We collected all samples from image-editing-request websites, *e.g.*, Zhopped and Reddit, and we augment language request data from both experts (Upwork) and the crowd-sourcing website (AMT).

needs to provide a natural language request. Our new algorithm will automatically perform all the editing operations to produce the desired image without any manual intervention. The language request can be very detailed, including stepwise instructions such as "increase the brightness and reduce the contrast." But, it could also contain a certain level of vagueness (*e.g.* "make the sky bluer") or even very vague descriptions like "make the image more beautiful," which is particularly useful for novice users. One considerable advantage of the new task is that users no longer need to be involved in the tedious editing process (*e.g.*, determine editing operations and sequences, manual adjustment of parameters, masking *etc.*.), which can be all accomplished by algorithms automatically.

There are a few previous studies that work on similar problems, but none of them can solve our new task. Many works [4–7] explore language-based manipulation for simple image contents such as birds, faces, or shoes. [8,9] only handle the image retouching operation and do not take any language inputs. Although being language-based, [10,11] only solve a single task in image editing (*e.g.*, retouching [10] or recoloring [11]), which are not extendable to other operations. PixelTone [12] solves the problem most similar to ours. However, it requires users to select editing regions manually and can only work for very detailed instructions.

Since no previous works directly solve our new task, we tackle it in two steps. We first collect a dataset named Grounded Image Editing Request (GIER) with 30k samples and 6k unique images, where each sample is a triplet, including one source image, one language request to edit the source image, and one target image which matches the editing request. Table 1 illustrates the comparison of our datasets against the previous one and reflects the advantages of ours. All

Table 1. Comparison between GIER dataset and related existing datasets. *Size* is the number for unique images or image pairs (if paired). *User photo* and *user request* mean the image and request are general and are from real user. *Other annotation* is the annotation of editing mask or editing operation.

Dataset	Size	User photo	User request	Paired image	Other annotations
CUB [1]	11788	✗	✗	✗	✗
Oxford-102 [2]	8189	✗	✗	✗	✗
DeepFashion-Seq [3]	4820	✗	✗	✓	✗
CoDraw [4]	9993	✗	✗	✓	✗
i-CLEVER [4]	10000	✗	✗	✓	✗
IGER (Ours)	6179	✓	✓	✓	✓

our image samples are real data collected from image-editing-request websites Zhopped.com and Reddit.com. We also augment language request data from both the crowd-sourcing website (AMT) and contracted experts (Upwork). We believe our dataset will become an important benchmark in this domain, given its scale and high-quality annotation.

Next, we propose a baseline algorithm for the new task. Given a source image and a language request, our algorithm first predicts desired editing operations and image regions associated with each operation. Then, a modular network that comprises submodules of the predicted operations is automatically constructed to perform the actual editing work and produce the output image. The parameters of each operation are also automatically determined by the modular network. One advantage of our algorithm is its interpretability. At every step, it will produce some human-understandable outputs such as operations and parameters, which can be easily modified by users to improve the editing results. Besides, our method fully leverages all the dataset annotation, and each of its components helps check the quality of the dataset annotation.

We train our algorithm on our newly collected GIER dataset and evaluate it with ablation studies. Experimental results demonstrate the effectiveness of each component of our method. Thus, our method also sets a strong baseline result for this new task.

In summary, the contributions of this paper include:

- We propose a new LDIE task that handles both detailed and vague requests on natural images as well as both global and local editing operations.
- We collect the first large-scale dataset, which comprises all real user requests and images with high-quality annotations.
- We propose a baseline algorithm that is highly interpretable and works well on challenging user data.

The rest of the paper is organized as follows. In Sect. 2, we briefly introduce related work. Sect. 3 describes our dataset and Sect. 4 describes the proposed algorithm in detail. Experimental results are given in Sect. 5, and finally, we conclude the paper in Sect. 6.

2   Related Work

Language-Based Image Manipulation/Generation. Many methods have been proposed recently for language-based image generation [13–15] and manipulation [4–7,11]. In this paper, we propose a new task, LDIE, which automatically performs a series of image editing operations given natural language requests. Methods for image manipulation/generation are dominated by variants of generative adversarial networks (GAN), and they change specific attributes of simple images, which usually only contain one primary object, e.g., faces, birds, or flowers. In contrast, our new task works on everyday image editing operations (*e.g.*, contrast, hue, inpainting *etc.*.) applied to more complex user images from open-domain. A recent work [10] was proposed to edit images with language descriptions globally, and it collected a dataset that contains only global image retouching operations. In contrast, our new task handles both global and local editings, and our dataset comprises all real user requests, which cover diverse editing operations.

Image Editing. The task of image editing involves many subtasks such as object selection, denoising, shadow removal *etc.*. Although many methods have been proposed for each subtask, how to combine the different methods of different subtasks to handle the more general image editing problem was seldom studied before. Laput *et al.* [12] proposed a rule-based approach which maps user phrases to specific image editing operations, and thus does not require any learning. However, this method is quite limited in that it requires each request sentence to describe exactly one editing operation. Besides, it cannot automatically determine operation parameters. There are several works [8–10] proposed for image retouching, which consider multiple global editing operations such as brightness, contrast, and hue. In [8,9], reinforcement learning is applied to learn the optimal parameters for each predefined operation. [10] leverages GANs to learn each operator as a convolutional kernel. Different from these two types of methods, we employ a modular network that was previously proposed for VQA [16–18], and learn optimal parameters for each predefined operator in a fully supervised manner.

Visual Grounding. Our algorithm needs to decide whether an operator is applied locally or globally and where the local area is if it is a local operator. Therefore, visual grounding is an essential component of our algorithm. However, previous visual grounding methods [10,19–22] are not directly applicable to our task due to the complexity of our language requests. For example, an expression for traditional visual grounding only contains the description of a single object. In contrast, our request contains not only object expression but also other information such as editing operators. Besides, each request may include multiple operators, and each could be a local one. Furthermore, each local region is not necessarily a single object. It could also be a group of objects or stuff (*e.g.*, "remove the five people on the grass"). Therefore the visual grounding problem is more challenging in our task.

3 The Grounded Image Editing Request (GIER) Dataset

In this section, we present how we collect a large-scale dataset called *Grounded Image Editing Request* (GIER) to support our new task.

3.1 Dataset Collection

Step 1: Preparation. First, we crawl user data from two image editing websites: Zhopped[1] and Reddit[2]. On the websites, amateur photographers post their images with editing requests, which are answered by Photoshop experts with edited images. Our crawled web data spans from the beginning of the two websites until 4/30/2019, resulting in 38k image pairs. Then, we construct a list of editing operations that cover the majority of the editing operations of the crawled data, which is shown in Table 2.

Step 2: Filtering and Operation Annotation. Although the crawled dataset is large, many samples are too challenging to include. There are mainly two challenges. First, some images contain local editing areas, which are hard to be grounded by the existing segmentation models due to the lack of training labels or other reasons. Second, some editing requests involve adding new objects or background into the original images, which cannot be easily handled by automatic methods.

Table 2. Statistics of all candidate operations. Each column represents the operation, the number of occurrence for each operation, the ratio of each operation over all operations , the ratio of images containing the operation over all images, and the ratio of local operation for each operation.

Operation	#occur	opr%	img%	local%
brightness	3176	16.00	51.40	7.53
contrast	3118	15.70	50.46	4.84
saturation	2812	14.16	45.51	7.15
lightness	2164	10.90	35.02	6.93
hue	2059	10.37	33.32	11.56
remove object	1937	9.76	31.35	99.59
tint	1832	9.23	29.65	7.59
sharpen	842	4.24	13.63	6.18
remove bg	495	2.49	8.01	95.35
crop	405	2.04	6.55	23.95
deform object	227	1.14	3.67	17.18
de-noise	155	0.78	2.51	9.68
dehaze	133	0.67	2.15	11.28
gaussain blur	124	0.62	2.01	73.39
exposure	85	0.43	1.38	5.88
rotate	84	0.42	1.36	1.19
black& white	72	0.36	1.17	16.67
radial blur	65	0.33	1.05	83.08
flip image	23	0.12	0.37	0.00
facet filter	19	0.10	0.31	5.26
rotate object	12	0.06	0.19	41.67
find edges filter	10	0.05	0.16	0.00
flip object	7	0.04	0.11	85.71

To make our dataset more practical, we ask annotators to filter crawled samples belonging to the two challenging cases. To decide whether a local editing operation can be grounded or not, we preprocess each original image by applying the off-the-shelf panoptic segmentation model UPSNet [23] and let annotators check whether the edited areas belong to any pre-segmented regions.

---

[1] http://zhopped.com.
[2] https://www.reddit.com/r/photoshoprequest.

After the filtering work, annotators are further asked to annotate the qualified samples with all possible operations from the operation list in Table 2 as well as the edited region of each operator. To get better-quality annotation, we hire Photoshop experts from Upwork to do the tasks. After the first-round annotation, we do another round of quality control to clean the low-quality annotations.

Step 3: Language Request Annotation. The crawled web data already contains one language request per sample. However, sometimes the original requests do not match the edited images well, which could cause problems for model training. Besides, we are interested in collecting diverse requests from different levels of photographers. Therefore we collect language requests from both the AMT and Upwork. AMT annotators usually have less knowledge about image editing, and Upwork annotators are Photoshop experts.

We present pairs of an original image and an edited image to AMT annotators without showing anything else. This is different from what we give to Upwork annotators, which contains additional information, including the original request as well as the annotation in step 2. To balance the data distribution, we collect three requests from AMT and two requests from Upwork. We also do another round of quality control to clean the bad annotations.

3.2   Data Statistics

The GIER dataset contains 6,179 unique image pairs. Each pair is annotated with five language requests, all possible editing operations, as well as their masks. The average number of operations per image pair is 3.21, and the maximum is 10. The distribution of each operation is show in Table 2. For language requests, the average word length is 8.61; the vocabulary size is 2,275 (after post-processing).

Our newly-collected GIER dataset is highly valuable for LDIE task. First, all data are from real users' editing requests so that they genuinely reflect a large portion of the needs for image editing. Second, we collect language requests from diverse users, which are helpful in making methods trained on our dataset practical for real applications. Third, our dataset is annotated with many different types of ground truth, which makes learning different types of methods possible.

4   A Baseline for Language-Driven Image Editing

We define the task of LDIE as follows. Given an original image and a user request, a method needs to produce an output image that matches the editing request. The closer the output image is to the target image, the better the method is. Contrast from the prevalent GAN-based methods, we propose the baseline model that can edit by sequentially applying interpretable editing operations, requiring the comprehension of both language request and visual context. Since most operations are resolution-independent, our model can also keep the image resolution same as the input. The main body of our model is an operation modular network (Sect. 4.3) shown in our model pipeline (Fig. 2). It stacks multiple editing operations in order and predicts best parameters. Since the layout of operations

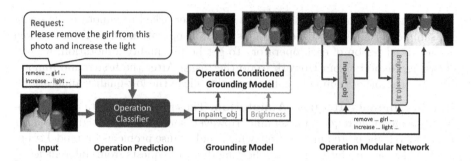

Fig. 2. An overview of the model's pipeline. The input image and request are sent to a multi-label classifier to predict operations. Then, the operation conditioned grounding model takes in the image, the request, and operations and outputs the grounding mask for each operation. Finally, the operation modules are cascaded to form the operation modular network, and each step outputs an interpretable intermediate result.

is discrete variable which is hard to optimize only given the target image, we resort to a supervisely trained operation classifier (Sect. 4.1) to predict needed editing operations and arrange them in a fixed order. Moreover, every editing operation requires a mask to specify where to edit, which is obtained by the operation conditioned grounding model (Sect. 4.2). Although our model is not completely end-to-end trained, it is a valuable initial attempt to address such task in such a compositional and interpretable way.

4.1 Operation Prediction

Since samples in GIER are annotated with ground truth operations, we train a multi-label classification network to predict operations. In Table 2, there are 23 operations, while some of them have too few training examples. Therefore, we pick the top nine operations (brightness and lightness are merged as one operation due to their similarity) as our final classification labels. They cover 90.36% of total operations and are representative of users' editing habits. Both input image and language request are input to the classifier, owning to many unspecific requests which require the perception of the input image. The image is embedded by ResNet18 [24], and the language request is embedded by a bi-directional LSTM [25]. The two features are then concatenated and passed into several fully connected layers to get the final prediction. This model is trained with the multi-label cross-entropy loss.

4.2 Operation Conditioned Grounding Model

In our task, the language of request may contain multiple types of operation-based groundings (*e.g.*, "please remove the girl from this photo and increase the light" in Fig. 2) and each grounding may contain multiple, even disconnected regions (*e.g.*, "remove all pedestrians from the image"). Given such uniqueness

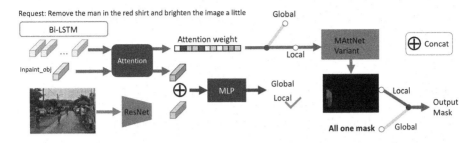

Fig. 3. Network structure of the operation-conditioned grounding model. The operation attends to its related part in the request. And the MLP binary classifier can judge if the operation is local or global. If local, the MAttNet variant will ground the operation related description into mask, otherwise output the all one mask.

of our task, the previous visual grounding methods are not directly applicable. However, they certainly serve as a good starting point. In this section, we will first review a state-of-the-art visual grounding model, MattNet [26], and then show step-by-step how to turn it into a proper grounding model for its use in our task taking into consideration of the operation input and multi-region output.

The Grounding Problem and MattNet. Given a request Q, an operation O, and an image I, the goal is to localize the area of the image to be edited by the operator. We formulate it as a retrieving problem by extracting the region proposals $R = \{R_i\}$ from the image and choosing one or more of the region proposals to make up the target area.

The basic MattNet comprises a language attention network and three visual modules—subject, location, and relationship. The language attention network takes the query Q as input and outputs the modular phrase embeddings for each module $[q^{subj}, q^{loc}, q^{rel}]$ and their attention weights $\{w_{subj}, w_{loc}, w_{rel}\}$. Each module individually calculates the matching score between its query embedding and the corresponding visual feature. Then the matching scores from three modules are weighted averaged by $\{w_{subj}, w_{loc}, w_{rel}\}$. Finally, the ranking loss for positive query-region pair (Q_i, R_i) and negative pair (Q_i, R_j) is:

$$L_{rank} = \Sigma_i(\max(0, \Delta + s(Q_i, R_j) - s(Q_i, R_i)) \\ + \max(0, \Delta + s(Q_j, R_i) - s(Q_i, R_i))), \tag{1}$$

where $s(x, y)$ denotes the matching score between query x and region y, and Δ denotes the positive margin.

Operation Conditioned Language Attention. We extend the language attention network of MattNet. The reason for choosing MattNet is that the editing request frequently describes the objects in the subject-location-relationship format. The request Q of length T represented by word vectors $\{e_t\}_{t=1}^T$ is encoded by a Bi-LSTM and yields the hidden vectors $\{h_t\}_{t=1}^T$. The operation word embedding is o. The operation finds its corresponding noun phrase in the request by using attention. Therefore, the attention weights from the operation to all the request tokens are:

$$\alpha_t^{(o)} = \frac{\exp(\langle o, h_t \rangle)}{\sum_{k=1}^{T} \exp(\langle o, h_k \rangle)}, \tag{2}$$

where $\langle \cdot, \cdot \rangle$ denotes inner product, and the superscript (o) indicates the specific attention for operation o. We keep trainable vectors f_m, where $m \in$ {subj, loc, rel}, from MattNet to compute the attention weights for each of three visual modules:

$$a_{m,t} = \frac{\exp(\langle f_m, h_t \rangle)}{\sum_{k=1}^{T} \exp(\langle f_m, h_k \rangle)}. \tag{3}$$

Then, we can compute an operation conditioned attention and thus, obtain operation conditioned modular phrase embedding:

$$\hat{a}_{m,t} = \frac{\alpha_t a_{m,t}}{\sum_{k=1}^{T} \alpha_k a_{m,k}}, \qquad q_m^{(o)} = \sum_{t=1}^{T} \hat{a}_{m,t}^{(o)} e_t. \tag{4}$$

The other parts of the language attention network remain the same. For the visual modules, we keep the location and relationship modules unchanged. For the subject module, we remove the attribute prediction branch because the template parser [19] is not suitable for our editing request.

Multiple Object Grounding. Since we formulate the task as a retrieving problem, we set a threshold for the matching score to determine multiple grounding objects. If all objects are under the threshold, the top-1 object will be selected. However, an operation might be grounded to the whole image, which requires the model to retrieve all the candidates. To remedy such a problem, we add an extra binary classifier to tell if the operation is local or global, given the context of image and request. The structure is presented in Fig. 3.

Since GIER dataset provides ground truth instance masks, the operation-conditioned grounding model is trained with the ranking loss as Eq. 1.

4.3 Operation Modular Network

After the set of possible operations, along with their masks, are predicted, our method constructs a Operation Modular Network (OMN) to perform the actual editing work. The OMN is composed of submodules, each of which represents a predefined editing operation. Each submodule takes as an input image or the previously edited image, the language request and the mask, and produces an output image. See Fig. 4 for an illustration. The training objective for OMN is learning to predict the best parameter for each operation from the supervised of the target image. Next, we first describe the implementation of each submodule, then the way how we create the modular network, and finally, the loss functions.

Submodule Implementation. We create one submodule for each chosen operation. Among them, six are implemented by differentiable filters which are also

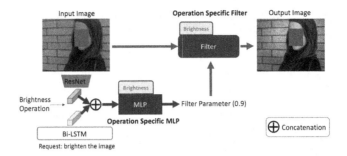

Fig. 4. The structure of a submodule network for the `brightness` operation.

resolution independent. Specifically, `brightness` and `saturation` are implemented by scaling the HSV channels. `sharpness` is achieved by adding the image spatial gradient. `contrast`, `hue`, and `tint` are implemented the same as [8]. For `remove_bg` we simply implement `remove_bg` as changing the masked area to white given our sample distribution, which is non-differentiable. And `inpaint_obj` is implemented by a differentiable neural inpainting model EdgeConnect [27]. Refer to Supplement C for more implementation details.

Except `remove_bg` and `inpaint_obj`, the other operations also require some input parameters, which are automatically predicted by their submodules. Specifically, the request and image features are concatenated and sent to an MLP to predict the parameter. The filter takes in the parameter and mask and yields the output image. Each operation has its individual MLP parameters.

Modular Network Creation. The modular network is created by linking together all predicted operations. However, `remove_bg` is non-differentiable thus would blocked the gradient backpropagation. And `inpaint_obj` is a large network that is computational expensive for gradient. Luckily, these two submodules do not have any parameters to learn. Therefore, we always put them in front of the chain if they exist.

Loss Function. The L1 loss is applied between the final output image I_K and the target image I_{gt} to drive the output image to be similar to the target image:

$$\text{Loss}_{l1} = |I_K - I_{gt}|, \tag{5}$$

where K denotes the number of predicted operations, *i.e.* the length of the submodule chain.

However, only using the supervision at the final step might not guarantee that the intermediate images are adequately learned. Hence, we also propose to use a step-wise triplet loss to enforce the intermediate image to be more similar to the target image than its previous step:

$$\text{Loss}_{tri} = \frac{1}{K} \sum_{k=0}^{K-1} \max(|I_{k+1} - I_{gt}| - |I_k - I_{gt}| + \Delta, 0), \tag{6}$$

Table 3. The F1 score and ROC-AUC score for operation prediction.

	F1					ROC
threshold	0.3	0.4	0.5	0.6	0.7	
val	.7658	.7699	.7620	.7402	.7026	.9111
test	.7686	.7841	7759	.7535	.7172	.9153

Table 4. The operation type classification accuracy

	Accuracy					ROC
Threshold	0.1	0.3	0.5	0.7	0.9	
val	.9328	.9328	.9328	.9328	.9328	.8915
test	.9377	.9387	.9397	.9397	.9397	.8969

Table 5. The grounding results

	F1					IoU					ROC
Threshold	0.15	0.20	0.25	0.30	0.35	0.15	0.20	0.25	0.30	0.35	
val	.6950	.7286	7412	.7280	.6700	.5788	.6328	.6519	.6254	.5439	.8857
test	.6953	.7432	.7626	.7350	.6380	.5682	.6296	.6578	.6203	.5161	.9186

where Δ is a positive margin. It resembles triplet loss by regarding I_{gt} as anchor, I_k as negative sample and I_{k+1} as positive. Note that we should block the gradient of the term $|I_k - I_{gt}|$ to prevent from enlarging the distance between I_{gt} and I_k. Hence final loss is $\text{Loss} = \text{Loss}_{l1} + \lambda\text{Loss}_{tri}$, with balanced weight λ.

5 Experiment

5.1 Experiment Setup

Dataset. We train and evaluate our model in our GIER dataset. The dataset is split into training, validation and testing subset with ratio 8:1:1, resulting in 4934/618/618 image pairs, respectively.

Metrics. For operation prediction, it is a multi-label classification task, hence we evaluate it using F1 score and ROC-AUC. For the operation conditioned grounding, we evaluate two sub-tasks: operation binary classification (local or global) evaluated by accuracy, and the local operation grounding evaluated by F1 score, ROC-AUC and IoU. Since the local operation grounding is formulated as a multi-object retrieving task, F1 score and ROC-AUC are reasonably set as the metrics. Moreover, the selected multiple objects can make up a whole image-level mask, so we also evaluated the mask quality using IoU score computed between the grounded mask and the ground truth mask. To evaluate the final output image, we adopt L1 distance between the predicted image and the target image, where the pixel are normalized from 0 to 1. However, since the request could have many suitable editing, we further conduct human study to get more comprehensive evaluation. The implementation detail is in Supplement D.

5.2 Results: Operation Prediction

The result for operation prediction is shown in Table 3. We evaluate F1 score under different confidence thresholds and observe that the validation and test

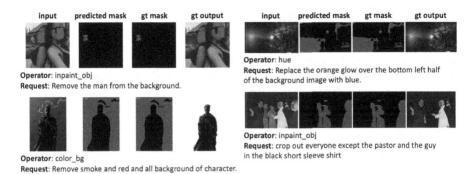

input   predicted mask   gt mask   gt output   input   predicted mask   gt mask   gt output

Operator: inpaint_obj
Request: Remove the man from the background.

Operator: hue
Request: Replace the orange glow over the bottom left half of the background image with blue.

Operator: color_bg
Request: Remove smoke and red and all background of character.

Operator: inpaint_obj
Request: crop out everyone except the pastor and the guy in the black short sleeve shirt

Fig. 5. Visualization for the operation conditioned grounding

Table 6. The comparison between a GAN-based method with our method. The arrow indicates the trend for better performance.

	L1↓	User Rating ↑	User Interact ↑
Target	-	3.60	-
Random Edit	0.1639	-	-
Pix2pixAug [10]	**0.1033**	2.68	13.5%
Our method (UB)	0.0893	-	-
Our method	0.1071	**3.20**	**86.5%**

Table 7. Ablation study 1 and 2 with V and L representing vision and language

Study	Metric	L	V+L
1	ROC	0.9182	0.9153
2	ROC	0.9804	0.8969
	Acc@0.5	0.9508	0.9397

set has the similar trend and achieve best performance at threshold 0.4. And the ROC score also indicate a good performance on operation prediction and can support the later task well. Its visualization can be found in Supplement B.1.

5.3   Results: Operation Conditioned Grounding

For operation type classification, the accuracy is listed in Table 4. For local operation grounding, the quantitative result is in Table 5. F1 score and IoU are evaluated under various confidence thresholds with the same trend, and both attain peak value at threshold 0.25. The ROC score is 0.8857 and 0.9186 for validation and test set, respectively. The evaluation result indicating a good start for the operation modular network. Figure 5 shows the qualitative grounding results for local operations. In many cases the request is to remove distraction persons in the background, such as the first and last row in Fig. 5, requiring the grounding model to distinguish the high-level semantic of foreground and background. Also, the cartoon figures images make the grounding even more challenging. The visualization of the operation attention is in Supplement B.2.

5.4 Results: Language Driven Image Editing

The main quantitative results are shown in Table 6 with L1 and two user evaluation metrics. The comparison methods are described as follows. *Pix2pixAug* is a GAN-based model following the language-augmented pix2pix model in [10]. *Random Edit* is sequentially apply random editing operations with random parameters in random number of steps. *Our method UB* is the performance upper bound for OMN where the ground truth operations and masks are given as input. *Our method* is our full model where operations and masks are predicted. Experiments show that Pix2pixAug has slightly better L1 score, but the user rating and user interactive ratio (detailed in Supplement A.1) strongly indicates that our method is more perceptually appealing to humans, and of more advantageous for human-interactive editing. Also, the performance gap between our method and its upper bound indicates that better operation and mask prediction can bring a large performance gain. Figure 6 demonstrates that our method has better awareness for local editing and more salient editing effect than Pix2pixAug. More visualization of our edited images is in Supplement A.2.

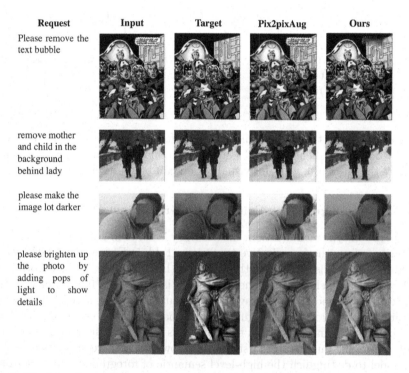

Fig. 6. The visual comparison between our method and a GAN-based method. The first two rows are local editing, our method can correctly remove the designated object, even for text, while pix2pixAug cannot do such local editing. And for the last two rows, our method has more salient editing than pix2pixAug.

Table 8. The comparison between OMN with triplet loss and without triplet loss.

	w/ Triplet	w/o Triplet
L1	0.0893	0.0925

Table 9. The comparison between OMN with fixed and random operation order.

	Fixed order	Random order
L1	0.0893	0.0875

5.5   Ablation Study

Study 1: To investigate the importance of the visual information, we compare the operation prediction performance by using 1) only language feature (L) and 2) concatenation of vision and language feature (V+L). The result is listed in Table 7. We find that pure language feature is comparable with both vision and language feature, indicating that the language information itself usually already contains rich context for operation selection.

Study 2: Also for the grounding task, we compare the global or local classification with or without visual information provided. The comparison is drawn in Table 7. It reveals that purely using language feature is a better way to decide if an operation is local or global. We suspect the reason is that if the operation is described with a location or object phrase, then such operation is of high possibility to be a local operation, so the visual information may not be so helpful compared with language.

Study 3: We explore the effectiveness of the triplet loss applied on each generation step in upper bound setting. Table 8 shows that with the triplet loss the OMN achieves better performance, demonstrating its positive effect.

Study 4: The effect of the operation order is evaluated in Table 9 in upper bound setting. We compare the models trained and test in fixed order and random order, and the result is slightly better for random order than fixed order.

6   Conclusion and Future Direction

In this paper, we propose the LDIE task along with a new GIER dataset which supports both local and global editing and provides object masks and operation annotations. We design a baseline modular network to parse the whole request and execute the operation step-by-step, leading to an interpretable editing process. To handle the unique challenges of visual grounding in this new task, we propose the operation conditioned grounding model extending the MattNet to consider operation input and multi-region output.

Currently our model uses the intermediate operation and mask as supervision to facilitate the modeling and in turn evaluate the annotation quality. However such intermediate operation annotation might contain human bias and how to learn the model that only supervised by target image can be further explored. For evaluation metrics, LDIE task should also evaluate whether the edit is applied to the correct region specified by language. We evaluated this according to the grounding performance, which rely on the intermediate mask ground truth. However, a more general evaluation only depending on target image can be proposed. Finally, more editing operations can be added to the model.

Acknowledgement. This work was partly supported by Adobe Research, NSF 1741472 and 1813709. The article solely reflects the opinions and conclusions of its authors but not the funding agents.

References

1. Wah, C., Branson, S., Welinder, P., Perona, P., Belongie, S.: The caltech-ucsd birds-200-2011 dataset (2011)
2. Nilsback, M.E., Zisserman, A.: Automated flower classification over a large number of classes. In: 2008 Sixth Indian Conference on Computer Vision, Graphics & Image Processing, pp. 722–729. IEEE (2008)
3. Zhu, S., Urtasun, R., Fidler, S., Lin, D., Change Loy, C.: Be your own prada: fashion synthesis with structural coherence. In: ICCV (2017)
4. El-Nouby, A., et al.: Tell, draw, and repeat: generating and modifying images based on continual linguistic instruction. In: ICCV (2019)
5. Nam, S., Kim, Y., Kim, S.J.: Text-adaptive generative adversarial networks: manipulating images with natural language. In: NeurIPS (2018)
6. Cheng, Y., Gan, Z., Li, Y., Liu, J., Gao, J.: Sequential attention GAN for interactive image editing via dialogue. arXiv preprint arXiv:1812.08352 (2018)
7. Shinagawa, S., Yoshino, K., Sakti, S., Suzuki, Y., Nakamura, S.: Interactive image manipulation with natural language instruction commands. arXiv preprint arXiv:1802.08645 (2018)
8. Hu, Y., He, H., Xu, C., Wang, B., Lin, S.: Exposure: a white-box photo post-processing framework. ACM Trans. Graphics (TOG) **37**, 26 (2018)
9. Park, J., Lee, J.Y., Yoo, D., So Kweon, I.: Distort-and-recover: color enhancement using deep reinforcement learning. In: CVPR (2018)
10. Wang, H., Williams, J.D., Kang, S.: Learning to globally edit images with textual description. arXiv preprint arXiv:1810.05786 (2018)
11. Chen, J., Shen, Y., Gao, J., Liu, J., Liu, X.: Language-based image editing with recurrent attentive models. In: CVPR (2018)
12. Laput, G.P., et al.: Pixeltone: a multimodal interface for image editing. In: Proceedings of the SIGCHI Conference on Human Factors in Computing Systems. ACM (2013)
13. Reed, S., Akata, Z., Yan, X., Logeswaran, L., Schiele, B., Lee, H.: Generative adversarial text to image synthesis. arXiv preprint arXiv:1605.05396 (2016)
14. Xu, T., et al.: AttnGAN: fine-grained text to image generation with attentional generative adversarial networks. In: CVPR (2018)
15. Zhang, H., et al.: StackGAN: text to photo-realistic image synthesis with stacked generative adversarial networks. In: ICCV (2017)
16. Andreas, J., Rohrbach, M., Darrell, T., Klein, D.: Neural module networks. In: CVPR (2016)
17. Hu, R., Andreas, J., Rohrbach, M., Darrell, T., Saenko, K.: Learning to reason: end-to-end module networks for visual question answering. In: ICCV (2017)

18. Mao, J., Gan, C., Kohli, P., Tenenbaum, J.B., Wu, J.: The neuro-symbolic concept learner: interpreting scenes, words, and sentences from natural supervision. In: ICLR (2019)
19. Kazemzadeh, S., Ordonez, V., Matten, M., Berg, T.: Referitgame: referring to objects in photographs of natural scenes. In: EMNLP (2014)
20. Hu, R., Xu, H., Rohrbach, M., Feng, J., Saenko, K., Darrell, T.: Natural language object retrieval. In: CVPR (2016)
21. Yang, Z., Gong, B., Wang, L., Huang, W., Yu, D., Luo, J.: A fast and accurate one-stage approach to visual grounding. In: ICCV (2019)
22. Liu, X., Wang, Z., Shao, J., Wang, X., Li, H.: Improving referring expression grounding with cross-modal attention-guided erasing. In: CVPR (2019)
23. Kirillov, A., He, K., Girshick, R., Rother, C., Dollár, P.: Panoptic segmentation. In: CVPR (2019)
24. He, K., Zhang, X., Ren, S., Sun, J.: Deep residual learning for image recognition. In: CVPR (2016)
25. Schuster, M., Paliwal, K.K.: Bidirectional recurrent neural networks. IEEE Trans. Signal Process. **45**, 2673–2681 (1997)
26. Yu, L., et al.: MattNet: Modular attention network for referring expression comprehension. In: CVPR (2018)
27. Nazeri, K., Ng, E., Joseph, T., Qureshi, F., Ebrahimi, M.: Edgeconnect: generative image inpainting with adversarial edge learning. arXiv preprint arXiv:1901.00212 (2019)

Self-supervised Learning of Orc-Bert Augmentor for Recognizing Few-Shot Oracle Characters

Wenhui Han, Xinlin Ren, Hangyu Lin, Yanwei Fu[✉],
and Xiangyang Xue

School of Data Science, Computer Science, and MOE Frontiers Center for Brain Science, Shanghai Key Lab of Intelligent Information Processing, Fudan University, Shanghai, China
{19210980110,20110240015,18210980008,yanweifu,xyxue}@fudan.edu.cn

Abstract. This paper studies the recognition of oracle character, the earliest known hieroglyphs in China. Essentially, oracle character recognition suffers from the problem of data limitation and imbalance. Recognizing the oracle characters of extremely limited samples, naturally, should be taken as the few-shot learning task. Different from the standard few-shot learning setting, our model has only access to large-scale *unlabeled* source Chinese characters and few labeled oracle characters. In such a setting, meta-based or metric-based few-shot methods are failed to be efficiently trained on source unlabeled data; and thus the only possible methodologies are self-supervised learning and data augmentation. Unfortunately, the conventional geometric augmentation always performs the same global transformations to all samples in pixel format, without considering the diversity of each part within a sample. Moreover, to the best of our knowledge, there is no effective self-supervised learning method for few-shot learning. To this end, this paper integrates the idea of self-supervised learning in data augmentation. And we propose a novel data augmentation approach, named Orc-Bert Augmentor pre-trained by self-supervised learning, for few-shot oracle character recognition. Specifically, Orc-Bert Augmentor leverages a self-supervised BERT model pre-trained on large unlabeled Chinese characters datasets to generate sample-wise augmented samples. Given a masked input in vector format, Orc-Bert Augmentor can recover it and then output a pixel format image as augmented data. Different mask proportion brings diverse reconstructed output. Concatenated with Gaussian noise, the model further performs point-wise displacement to improve diversity. Experimentally, we collect two large-scale datasets of oracle characters and other Chinese ancient characters for few-shot oracle character recognition and Orc-Bert Augmentor pre-training. Extensive experiments on few-shot learning demonstrate the effectiveness of our Orc-Bert Augmentor on improving the performance of various networks in the few-shot oracle character recognition.

© Springer Nature Switzerland AG 2021
H. Ishikawa et al. (Eds.): ACCV 2020, LNCS 12627, pp. 652–668, 2021.
https://doi.org/10.1007/978-3-030-69544-6_39

1   Introduction

Oracle characters are the earliest known hieroglyphs in China, which were carved on animal bones or turtle plastrons in purpose of pyromantic divination in the Shang dynasty [15]. Due to the scarcity of oracle bones and the long-tail problem in the usage of characters as shown in Fig. 1, oracle character recognition suffers from the problem of data limitation and imbalance. Recognizing the oracle characters of extremely limited samples, naturally, should be taken as the few-shot learning task, which is topical in computer vision and machine learning communities, recently. Previous researches on oracle character recognition tend to discard characters of extremely limited samples or perform simple geometric augmentation to them [8, 21]. To the best of our knowledge, there is no research focused on few-shot oracle character recognition, which, however, is shown to be a real archaeological scene. Different from standard few-shot learning setting, our task does not assume the existence of large-scale labeled source oracle characters. Formally, we study under a more practical setting, where our model only has access to large-scale *unlabeled* source Chinese characters and few labeled target oracle characters.

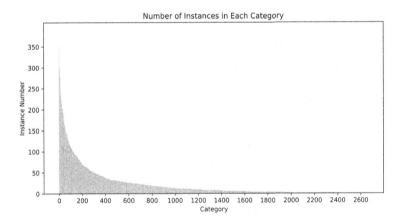

Fig. 1. The distribution of oracle character instances in Oracle-50K. Categories are ordered by number of instances.

In such a setting, meta-based or metric-based few-shot methods are failed to be efficiently trained on source unlabeled data, thus the only possible methodologies are data augmentation and self-supervised learning. Many previous works of few-shot learning [1, 9, 13, 37] utilized data augmentation and synthetic data to break the data limitation. One of the most popular strategies is geometric augmentation which includes scaling, rotation, and perspective transformation. Such methodologies, unfortunately, have to be carefully designed in order to efficiently train a robust classifier.

Simple geometric transformations apply the same fixed augmentation process to all input samples. However, in few-shot scenario, original training samples are so limited that geometric transformations are inefficient to generate numerous and diverse samples specific to an individual sample. What's more, for handwritten text or character recognition, conventional augmentation methods usually perform transformation in image level and fail to take into account the diversity of components of character or text, such as strokes of an oracle character and characters of an English word. Consequently, they can hardly imitate various writing styles to cover diversity at different levels [22].

The stroke orders of Chinese characters contain a lot of information, for which people can usually recognize a character correctly even if it is unfinished or incomplete. In another way, vector format or sequential format character images allow more diverse augmentation than pixel format data, because we can manipulate strokes and points to realize more complicated, stroke-wise, and point-wise data augmentation. However, existing geometric transformation methods are designed for pixel format images and only perform a global transformation, thus it is powerless to conduct effective augmentation to vector format images. A more powerful and complicated augmentation method is needed.

Although the stroke orders of oracle characters have been lost in history, there are two fundamental facts: 1) oracle writing or Shang writing is ancestral to modern Chinese script; 2) the modern Chinese writing system is in a left-to-right then top-to-bottom writing order. We can simply assume oracle character writing is in the same order and generate pesudo online data. To utilize stroke orders of oracle characters, sequence modeling is necessary. BERT [5] or more general transformer structure [29] presents great performances in modeling language; Sketch-BERT [19] extends BERT with sketch embedding and learns sketch representation from vector format data by self-supervised learning of Sketch Gestalt. Moreover, self-supervised pre-training task of both allows utilization of large-scale *unlabeled* data, suitable for our hard and practical setting.

In this paper, we integrate the ideas of self-supervised learning in data augmentation and propose a new data augmentation method, named Orc-Bert Augmentor, for few-shot oracle character recognition and release two characters datasets: one for Orc-Bert Augmentor pre-training and the other for few-shot oracle recognition. Like online approximation in [24], we convert offline character images in pixel format to online data in 5-element vector format, with 2-dimension continuous value for the position, and 3-dimension one-hot value for the state. Then we pre-train BERT by self-supervised learning on vector format large-scale *unlabeled* character datasets and utilize it as augmentor for augmentation of few-shot labeled oracle characters. Typically, we randomly mask points in vector format oracle with different mask probability (the higher mask probability, the harder reconstruction) and then recover the masked input using our Orc-Bert Augmentor. The pre-trained reconstruction model tends to generate a similar specific sample to the original sample, while various mask probability brings diversity. In addition, we perform random point-wise displacement by adding recovered input with Gaussian noise, i.e., a random moving state, to show that Orc-Bert Augmentor is amenable to such a naive strategy. Finally we can easily re-convert it to pixel format image. Extensive experiments on few-shot learning demonstrate the effectiveness of our Orc-Bert Augmentor on improving the performance of various networks in the few-shot oracle character recognition.

To summarize, we boost the few-shot recognition performance of existing networks by proposing a novel data augmentation method. In particular, we make the following contributions:

1. We conceptually formulate the few-shot oracle recognition problem, similar to a real-world archaeology scenario in which we does not assume the existence of large-scale labeled source oracle characters.
2. We propose a novel data augmentation approach named Orc-Bert Augmentor pre-trained by self-supervised learning. Additionally, we would also highlight the novelty of vectorization for oracle characters.
3. We collect 59,081 oracle character images and 221,947 other ancient Chinese character images, based on which we create two datasets named Oracle-FS and Oracle-50K for oracle character recognition. To the best of our knowledge, Oracle-50K is the largest public oracle character dataset until now.

2 Related Work

Oracle Character Recognition. Oracle character, the oldest hieroglyphs in China, is important for modern archaeology, history, Chinese etymologies and calligraphy study [8,38], which has attracted much research interest [8,14,25,32,38]. Different from general Chinese character recognition [35,36,39], oracle character recognition suffers from data insufficiency and data imbalance. To tackle this problem, [8] discards minority categories, [38] proposes the nearest neighbor rule with metric learning, and [21] conducts simple geometric augmentation to characters with too few samples. Unlike all the prior works, we aim to address few-shot oracle character recognition under a more practical setting.

Few-Shot Learning (FSL). Few-shot learning refers to the practice of model training with extremely limited labeled samples for each category. Basically, a few-shot learning model is trained on source/base data with a large number of labeled training samples and then generalized, usually by fine-tuning [33], to relevant but disjoint target/novel data with extremely limited training samples. Recent substantial progress is based on the meta-learning paradigm [7,18,26,27,30] and data augmentation [3]. In our practical setting, meta-based or metric-based few-shot methods are failed to be efficiently trained on source unlabeled data, thus the only possible methodologies are data augmentation and self-supervised learning. However, [3] is designed for few-shot natural image classification, not suitable for characters. In this paper, we propose a novel and powerful augmentation method for vector format characters. Besides, different from few-shot learning with labeled source data or semi-supervised few-shot learning [1,31], we use unlabeled data to pre-train the augmentor.

Data Augmentation. The state-of-art deep neural networks need numerous training data with an unambiguous label. However, compared to our real world, training data usually are limited in quantity and quality, so data augmentation is an effective approach to enlarge training data and boost the overall ability of models. Random geometric augmentation [4], such as rotation, scaling, and perspective transformation, is a popular way and commonly used in classification models trained on natural images [16,34]. But for text or character images, it regards multiple characters in a word or multiple strokes in a character as one entity to perform a global augmentation [22], without considering the diversity of each character or stroke. Different from geometric augmentation, our augmentation method converts pixel format images to points sequence and achieve more complicated augmentation both at the global and local level, satisfying local diversity. Besides, instead of randomly transformation, some works propose to generate samples by using image interpolation [6,20] or combination [17] and generative adversarial network (GAN) [2,23,28], which suffers from producing augmented images very different from original images. As for Orc-Bert Augmentor, the procedure of completing or reconstructing the masked part guarantees the similarity between augmented data and original data. Note that some efficient augmentation algorithms cannot be applied to our setting (without large scale labeled data), like AutoAugment [4] or any semi-supervised learning work.

3   Datasets

The oracle characters, from Bronze Age China, are carved on animal bones or turtle shells for pyromantic divination. So far, more than 150,000 bones and turtle shells had been excavated, including approximately 4,500 unique oracle characters. Only about 2,000 of them have been successfully deciphered [12].

Oracle-20k [8] and OBC306 [12] are two currently known datasets but unfortunately un-public. Oracle-20k consists of 20,039 character-level samples covering 261 glyph classes, in which the largest category contains 291 samples and the smallest contains 25. OBC306 is composed of 300,000 instances cropped from oracle-bone rubbings or images belonging to 306 categories, which is also imbalanced. Due to limited categories in the both above datasets, we collect and publish an oracle dataset, Oracle-50K, with 2,668 unique characters. Figure 2 shows that there is a high degree of intra-class variance in the shapes of oracle characters, resulting from the fact that oracle bones were carved by different ancient people in various regions over tens of hundreds of years. As a result, oracle character recognition or classification is a challenging task.

Oracle-50K.[1] Oracle character instances are collected from three data sources using different strategies, shown in Table 1. Instances from Xiaoxuetang Oracle[2] is collected by our developed crawling tool, wherein there are 24,701 instances

---

[1] https://github.com/wenhui-han/Oracle-50K.git.
[2] http://xiaoxue.iis.sinica.edu.tw/jiaguwen.

Table 1. Statistics of Oracle-50K and other ancient Chinese character datasets, including data source, number of instances, and number of classes.

	Data source	Num. of instances	Num. of classes
Oracle-50K	Xiaoxuetang	13255	1096
	Koukotsu	18671	1850
	Chinese Etymology	27155	1120
	Total	**59081**	**2668**
Other ancient Chinese characters	Font rendering	221947	/

of 2,548 individual characters. However, some instances are not provided a corresponding label represented by one single modern Chinese character, thus we only remain the deciphered instances with 13,255 instances of 1096 categories in Oracle-50K. Koukotsu[3] is a digital oracle character and text database. We utilize the TrueType font file obtained from Koukotsu to generate 18,671 annotated oracle character images belonging to 1850 classes. Chinese Etymology[4] provides 27,155 instances of 1,120 unique characters. It contains not only oracle characters but also bronze, seal, and Liushutong characters, which are also collected for augmentor training.

As we can see from Fig. 1, there exists a long-tail distribution of oracle character instances in Oracle-50K, so recognition or classification of oracle characters, especially for the categories at the distributions' tail, is a natural few-shot learning problem.

Oracle-FS. Based on Oracle-50K, we create a few-shot oracle character recognition dataset under three different few-shot settings (see Table 2). Under the k-shot setting, there are k instances for each category in the training set and 20 instances in the test set. In this paper, we set k = 1, 3, 5.

Table 2. Statistics of Oracle-FS, including number of instances and number of classes.

	k-shot	Num. of instances per class		Num. of classes
		Train	Test	
Oracle-FS	1	1	20	200
	3	3	20	
	5	5	20	

---

[3] http://koukotsu.sakura.ne.jp/top.html.
[4] https://hanziyuan.net/.

The Datasets for Orc-Bert Augmentor Pre-training. To pre-train BERT as our augmentor, we collect a large unlabeled ancient Chinese character dataset, including undeciphered instances of Xiaoxuetang Oracle, bronze, seal, and Liushutong characters of Chinese Etymology, and images generated from various TrueType fonts file of ancient Chinese script.

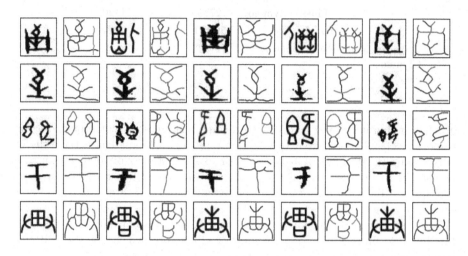

Fig. 2. Examples of oracle character images and corresponding stroke data.

4 Methodology

4.1 Problem Formulation

In this paper, we intend to address the problem of oracle character recognition under few-shot settings. More specifically, we intend to train a more human-like oracle character classifier, capable of learning from one or a few samples. Different from the conventional formulation of few-shot learning, we do not use labeled base/source data. Our classifier would have only access to k annotated training instances for each category and then be tested on 20 instances per class, namely, Oracle-FS, $\mathscr{D} = \{(\mathbf{O}_i, y_i), y_i \in \mathscr{C}\}$. In addition, we have a large amount of unlabeled data to pre-train Orc-Bert under self-supervision. Our proposed framework is illustrated in Fig. 3.

4.2 Overview of Framework

As shown in Fig. 3, our proposed framework consists of the following parts.

First, we utilize the online approximation algorithm in [24] to convert offline oracle character images with annotations and other Chinese ancient characters images without annotations, both in pixel format, to online data in 5-element

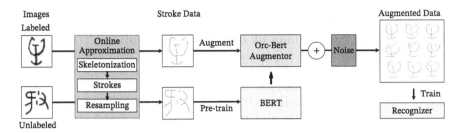

Fig. 3. Schematic illustration of our proposed framework.

vector format (see Fig. 2), including 2-dimension continuous value for the position, and 3 dimensions one-hot value for the state. Thus, a character would be represented as a sequence of points, where each point consists of 5 attributes:

$$\mathbf{O}_i = (\Delta x, \Delta y, p_1, p_2, p_3)$$

where Δx, Δy is the position offsets between two adjacent points, and (p_1, p_2, p_3) is a 3-dimension one-hot vector ($\sum_{i=1}^{3} p_i = 1$). $p_2 = 1, p_3 = 1, p_1 = 1$ indicate the points at the ending of a stroke, the points at the ending of the whole character, and all the rest points, respectively.

Second, after getting stroke data of large-scale unlabeled data, we pre-train Orc-Bert in a self-supervised setting by predicting the masked from the visible.

Then, we utilize our pre-trained Orc-Bert as our augmentor. We randomly mask points at different mask probability and then recover masked input using our pre-trained Orc-Bert. The higher the mask probability, the harder reconstruction. To further improve the diversity of augmented data, we perform random point-wise displacement by adding completed masked input with Gaussian noise or a random moving state and re-convert it to pixel format image.

After augmentation, we train CNN-based classifiers over augmented data.

4.3 Online Approximation

Following the online approximation algorithm in [24], there are 3 steps in this stage. The first step is skeletonization, in which we convert a character image to its corresponding skeleton. The next step is the conversion of the bitmap representation to strokes that is realized by converting the bitmap to graph and then removing cycles and intersections. Finally, we conduct temporal resampling and ordering to get a more sparse points sequence. Different from simple constant time resampling, maximum acceleration resampling is proposed to imitate the dynamic speed of real writing (see [24] for more details).

4.4 Orc-Bert Augmentor

Self-supervised Pre-training of BERT and SketchBERT. BERT [5], a language representation model, is designed to pre-train bidirectional representations from unlabeled data by exploiting the mask-language model and next sequence prediction as pre-training tasks. Expanding BERT to process stroke data in computer vision, SketchBERT [19] proposes a self-supervised learning process that aims at reconstructing the masked part in a sketch. It is common practice in NLP to fine-tune the pre-trained BERT with just one additional task-specific output layer for different downstream tasks. Similarly, pre-trained SktechBERT also aims to be fine-tuned for different downstream tasks, such as sketch recognition and sketch retrieval.

Contrast to SketchBERT. We creatively propose to utilize the reconstruction procedure to generate new samples. The general structure, output layers, and input embedding of Orc-Bert are all slightly different from SketchBERT. Specifically, We adopt a smaller network architecture suitable for our data volume(see implementation details in Sect. 5.1); we add a module after the output layer to convert point sequence to pixel format image; we corrupt input for diverse augmentation (see Sect. 4.4).

Algorithm 1. Orc-Bert Augmentor+PA

---

1. Given an oracle image I from training set $\mathscr{D}_{train}$ and convert I into stroke data $O = (\Delta x, \Delta y, p_1, p_2, p_3)$ using online approximation module;
2. Initialize range $[a, b]$ and step n;
3. Set initial mask probability $m = a$;

repeat

    1) Generate mask M according to mask probability m with the same shape of O and randomly mask O to get $O_{mask} = O \odot M$;

    2) Reconstruct O_{mask} by predicting the masked states p_1, p_2, p_3 and positions $\Delta x, \Delta y$ using pre-trained Orc-Bert Augmentor and get O_{comp};

    3) Sample noise ϵ from Gaussian distribution $N(\mu, \sigma^2)$ in which μ, σ^2 are mean and variance of $(\Delta x, \Delta y)$ of all training samples;

    4) $O_{comp+pa} = O_{comp} + 0.1 * \epsilon$;

    5) Increasing mask probability $m = m + n$;

    6) Convert O_{comp} or $O_{comp+pa}$ back to pixel image I' and save it.

until $m > b$

Pre-training. Pre-training tasks over unlabeled data significantly facilitate the performance of BERT [5] as well as SktechBERT [19]. This auxiliary task is generally as follows: under our oracle character recognition setting, given an input data O in vector format, we perform a mask transformation and get masked input $O_{mask} = O \odot M$, where M is the mask with the same shape of input. In pre-training, Orc-Bert aims to predict the masked positions and states in O_{mask}, and generate O_{comp} as more similar to O as possible. During pre-training, we set default mask probability as 15%.

Augmentation. In augmentation, we adopt dynamic mask probability respectively for each original example to generate numerous augmented data. We discretize the range of magnitudes $[0.1, 0.5]$ into 80 values (uniform spacing) so that we get 80 different mask probability to mask the oracle sequence, respectively. With various degrees of masked input, Orc-Bert Augmentor can generate diverse augmented data. Finally, point-wise displacement is accomplished by simply adding Gaussian noise to positions or offsets of each point.

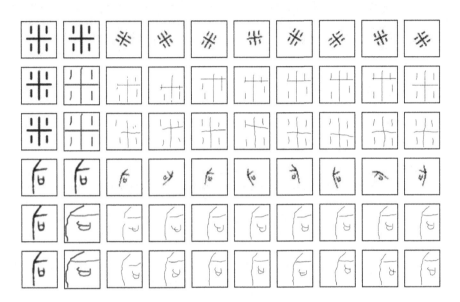

Fig. 4. Examples of augmented data generated by Conventional DA (row1 & 4), Orc-Bert Augmentor (row2 & 5), and Orc-Bert Augmentor+PA (row3 & 6).

5 Experiments

We conduct extensive experiments and show that Orc-Bert Augmentor achieves better performance under three few-shot settings employing different classification networks. Then we confirm this result on ablation studies about the volume of augmented and pre-training data and mask probability.

5.1 Experimental Settings

Datasets. As illustrated in Sect. 3, we mainly employed Oracle-FS in our evaluations. Table 2 presents statistics and train-test split about the dataset. Besides, we employed Oracle-50K(removing Oracle-FS) and all other ancient Chinese characters shown in Table 1 for self-supervised learning of Orc-Bert Augmentor.

Classifiers. Our augmentor is generic, and we can employ different networks as classifier. In this paper, we adopt 4 representative CNN models with various depth and width, including ResNet18, ResNet50, ResNet152 [10], and DenseNet161 [11], to show the effectiveness of our augmentor in boosting the classification performance of conventional networks.

Competitors. From now on, DA denotes Data Augmentation and PA denotes Point-wise Augmentation or Point-wise Displacement in this paper. For comparison, we train classifiers without augmentation (No DA) and with conventional augmentation (Conventional DA) that augment the training samples by random horizontal flipping, cropping with a ratio in $[0.8, 1]$, and rotation with a degree in $[-60°, 60°]$. Besides, we compose PA and Orc-Bert Augmentor for further exploration.

Implementation Details. We implement Orc-Bert Augmentor using PyTorch. In detail, the number of training epochs is 200 with a batch size of 10. We adopt Adam as the optimizer with a learning rate of 0.001 and 0.0001 for classifier training and augmentor pre-training, respectively. All images are resized to 50×50 before online approximation. Augmented images generated by Orc-Bert Augmentor are also 50×50, which would be resized to 224×224 for CNN training. Different from SketchBERT, the number of weight-sharing Transformer layers, hidden size, and the number of self-attention heads in Orc-Bert Augmentor are respectively 8, 128, and 8. The embedding network is a fully-connected network with a structure of 64-128-128 and the corresponding reconstruction network is 4 fully-connected networks with a structure of 128-128-64-5. The max lengths of input oracle stroke data are set as 300.

5.2 Orc-Bert Augmentor Evaluation

In this part, we evaluate our Orc-Bert Augmentor on Oracle-FS using classifiers listed in Sect. 5.1. For Orc-Bert Augmentor, we, by default, leverage our largest pre-training dataset, set mask probability in a range of $[0.1, 0.5]$ with a sampling interval of 0.005, and generate 80 augmented instances for each sample.

Table 3 summarizes the classification accuracy (%) of each neural network classifier employing different augmentation strategies under 3 different few-shot settings. We can find that: 1) Compared with Conventional DA, almost all classifiers employing Orc-Bert Augmentor have achieved higher classification accuracy. Particularly, under the 3-shot setting, the classification accuracy achieved by ResNet50+Orc-Bert Augmentor is 52.9%, about 17% higher than the counterpart of No DA. 2) Compared with 1- and 5-shot settings, classifiers with Orc-Bert Augmentor under 3-shot scenario have improved most significantly. Extremely limited data makes data augmentation less effective because augmentation only based on one original sample is hardly practical. When data volume reaches a specific threshold, marginal effects from data augmentation is diminishing, that's what happens under the 5-shot scenario. 3) Orc-Bert Augmentor brings more significant improvement to classifiers with poorer original performance. 4) Orc-Bert Augmentor+PA achieves the best classification accuracy for almost all networks under all scenarios, showing that simple point-wise displacement is efficacious for stroke data augmentation. Both Orc-Bert Augmentor and PA are generic, which could be composed and applied to various classification networks.

Table 3. Recognition accuracy (%) on Oracle-FS under all three few-shot settings for various classifiers equipped with No DA, Conventional DA, our Orc-Bert Augmentor, and Orc-Bert Augmentor+PA. Here, DA denotes Data Augmentation and PA denotes Point-wise Augmentation or Point-wise Displacement. Specifically, DA augments each input sample by random horizontal flipping, random cropping with a ratio in [0.8,1], and random rotation with a degree in $[-60°, 60°]$. As for Orc-Bert augmentor, we leverage our largest pre-training dataset, systematically sample mask probability in a range of [0.1, 0.5] with a sampling interval of 0.005, and generate 80 augmented instances for each sample. PA indicates point-wise displacement based on Gaussian distribution.

Setting	Model	No DA	Conventional DA	Orc-Bert Augmentor	Orc-Bert Augmentor + PA
1 shot	ResNet-18	18.6	20.9	29.5	**31.9**
	ResNet-50	16.8	23.3	26.2	**29.9**
	ResNet-152	14.0	18.2	26.7	**27.3**
	DenseNet	22.4	24.6	26.4	**28.2**
3 shot	ResNet-18	45.2	46.6	56.2	**57.2**
	ResNet-50	35.8	45.6	52.9	**57.7**
	ResNet-152	38.9	40.9	54.3	**57.1**
	DenseNet	48.6	52.3	56.4	**58.3**
5 shot	ResNet-18	60.8	62.7	65.1	**68.2**
	ResNet-50	55.6	60.8	62.8	**67.9**
	ResNet-152	58.6	61.4	66.1	**67.8**
	DenseNet	**69.3**	65.8	66.6	69.0

5.3   Orc-Bert Augmentor Analysis

In this part, we conduct more experiments to evaluate various aspects of Orc-Bert Augmentor, including pre-training dataset volume, size of augmented data, and mask probability. Note that, in these experiments, we employ ResNet18 as the classifier and perform experiments only under the 1-shot scenario.

Pre-trainging Dataset Volume. We construct 3 *unlabeled* datasets of different volumes for Orc-Bert Augmentor pre-training. Here, Oracle denotes Oracle-50K from which removes Oracle-FS; we add bronze and seal character images collected from Chinese Etymology[5] to Oracle and get Oracle+Bronze+Seal, all characters of which are similar to oracle in shape; Oracle+Bronze+Seal+All Other Ancient Characters is the biggest one, containing some Chinese characters different from oracle. As shown in Table 4, we can see that Orc-Bert Augmentor pre-trained on our largest pre-training dataset boosts the performance

---

[5] https://hanziyuan.net/.

of ResNet18 the most. It indicates that Orc-Bert, like BERT [5], is also beneficial from large-scale pre-training and can be transferred to another domain after being trained on one specific domain of data.

Table 4. Classification accuracy (%) under 1-shot setting for ResNet18 equipped with Orc-Bert Augmentor pre-trained on 3 datasets with various volumes, respectively. From top to bottom, pre-training data volume increases. Other hyperparameters remain the same as Table 3.

Pre-training dataset	Num. of instances	Test acc.
Oracle	64,743	27.2
Oracle+Bronze+Seal	132,788	27.8
Oracle+Bronze+Seal+ All Other Ancient Characters	276,028	**29.5**
No DA	/	18.6

Quantity, Quality, and Diversity of Augmented Data. We discretize the range of magnitudes [0.1, 0.5] into 40/80/400 values as mask probabilities. Each mask probability corresponds to an augmented image. Note that, we employ ResNet18 as the classifier and perform experiments only under the 1-shot setting. From Table 5, it is easy to see that the classifier performance is most improved when the original data is augmented by 80 times, and when we generate too many augmented samples based on extremely limited data, the classifier's performance may be poorer. In addition to the impact of the quantity of augmented data, we can visualize the augmented samples to measure quality and diversity. As shown in Fig. 4, it is obvious that geometric augmentation only performs the image-level transformation, and our Orc-Bert Augmentor can generate more diverse samples. PA further improved the quality and diversity of augmented data.

Table 5. Classification accuracy (%) under 1-shot setting for ResNet18 trained with augmented data of different quantity generated by Orc-Bert Augmentor. Other hyperparameters remain the same as Table 3.

Num. of augmented samples	Test acc.
40	29.2
80	**29.5**
400	28.4
No DA	18.6

Mask Probability. Mask probability is essential to similarity and diversity trade-off. A larger mask probability enhances reconstruction difficulty, generating augmented images very different from original images, while a smaller one brings the opposite results. We conduct a series of experiments with different range of mask probabilities and the results are shown in Table 6. We find that the set of mask probabilities in intermediate-range, $[0.1, 0.5]$, helps augmentor generate the highest-quality images.

Table 6. Classification accuracy (%) under 1-shot setting for ResNet18 trained with augmented data generated by Orc-Bert Augmentor with different range of mask probabilities. Other hyperparameters remain the same as Table 3.

Range of mask prob.	Test acc.
$[0.1, 0.4] \cup [0.6, 0.7]$	26.3
$[0.1, 0.4] \cup [0.5, 0.6]$	29.4
$[0.1, 0.5]$	**29.5**
No DA	18.6

6   Conclusion

In this paper, we intend to address a novel few-shot setting: training few-shot model by only large-scale unlabeled source data, and few labeled target training examples. We propose a novel data augmentation method, named Orc-Bert Augmentor, for few-shot oracle character recognition. It may be the first augmentation method that converts pixel format character images into vector format stroke data and then manipulates strokes and points to generate augmented images. It leverages Orc-Bert pre-trained on large-scale *unlabeled* Chinese characters to recover masked images as augmented data for CNN classifiers training. Besides, we incorporate point-wise displacement with Orc-Bert Augmentor, which presents better performance. Orc-Bert Augmentor is simple yet effective. Extensive experiments under three few-shot settings confirm the effectiveness of our Orc-Bert Augmentor to improve the performance of various networks on few-shot oracle character recognition. Moreover, we collect and publish two datasets: Oracle-50K and Oracle-FS. In the future, we will explore to generate more diverse and higher-quality augmented samples by modifying the loss function or jointly optimizing the augmentor and the classifier. We dedicated to applying our method to more general sketch and handwritten character recognition.

Acknowledgement. This work was supported in part by NSFC Projects (U62 076067), Science and Technology Commission of Shanghai Municipality Projects (19511120700, 19ZR1471800).

References

1. Antoniou, A., Storkey, A.: Assume, augment and learn: unsupervised few-shot meta-learning via random labels and data augmentation. arXiv preprint arXiv:1902.09884 (2019)
2. Bhunia, A.K., Das, A., Bhunia, A.K., Kishore, P.S.R., Roy, P.P.: Handwriting recognition in low-resource scripts using adversarial learning. In: Proceedings of the IEEE/CVF Conference on Computer Vision and Pattern Recognition (CVPR), June 2019
3. Chen, Z., Fu, Y., Wang, Y.-X., Ma, L., Liu, W., Hebert, M.: Image deformation meta-networks for one-shot learning. In: Proceedings of the IEEE Conference on Computer Vision and Pattern Recognition, pp. 8680–8689 (2019)
4. Cubuk, E.D., Zoph, B., Mane, D., Vasudevan, V., Le, Q.V.: Autoaugment: learning augmentation strategies from data. In: Proceedings of the IEEE Conference on Computer Vision and Pattern Recognition, pp. 113–123 (2019)
5. Devlin, J., Chang, M.-W., Lee, K., Toutanova, K.: Bert: pre-training of deep bidirectional transformers for language understanding. arXiv preprint arXiv:1810.04805 (2018)
6. DeVries, T., Taylor, G.W.: Dataset augmentation in feature space. arXiv preprint arXiv:1702.05538, 2017
7. Finn, C., Abbeel, P., Levine, S.: Model-agnostic meta-learning for fast adaptation of deep networks. ArXiv, abs/1703.03400 (2017)
8. Guo, J., Wang, C., Roman-Rangel, E., Chao, H., Rui, Y.: Building hierarchical representations for oracle character and sketch recognition. IEEE Trans. Image Process. **25**(1), 104–118 (2015)
9. Gupta, A., Vedaldi, A., Zisserman, A.: Synthetic data for text localisation in natural images. In: Proceedings of the IEEE Conference on Computer Vision and Pattern Recognition, pp. 2315–2324 (2016)
10. He, K., Zhang, X., Ren, S., Sun, J.: Deep residual learning for image recognition. In: 2016 IEEE Conference on Computer Vision and Pattern Recognition (CVPR), pp. 770–778 (2016)
11. Huang, G., Liu, Z., Weinberger, K.Q.: Densely connected convolutional networks. In: 2017 IEEE Conference on Computer Vision and Pattern Recognition (CVPR), pp. 2261–2269 (2017)
12. Huang, S., Wang, H., Liu, Y., Shi, X., Jin, L.: Obc306: a large-scale oracle bone character recognition dataset. In: 2019 International Conference on Document Analysis and Recognition (ICDAR), pp. 681–688 (2019)
13. Jaderberg, M., Simonyan, K., Vedaldi, A., Zisserman, A.: Reading text in the wild with convolutional neural networks. Int. J. Comput. Vis. **116**(1), 1–20 (2016)
14. Meng, L., Lyu, B., Zhang, Z., Aravinda, C.V., Kamitoku, N., Yamazaki, K.: Oracle bone inscription detector based on SSD. In: Cristani, M., Prati, A., Lanz, O., Messelodi, S., Sebe, N. (eds.) ICIAP 2019. LNCS, vol. 11808, pp. 126–136. Springer, Cham (2019). https://doi.org/10.1007/978-3-030-30754-7_13
15. Keightley. D.N.: Graphs, words, and meanings: three reference works for shang oracle-bone studies, with an excursus on the religious role of the day or sun (1997)
16. Krizhevsky, A., Sutskever, I., Hinton, G.E.: ImageNet classification with deep convolutional neural networks. In: Advances in Neural Information Processing Systems, pp. 1097–1105 (2012)
17. Lemley, J., Bazrafkan, S., Corcoran, P.: Smart augmentation learning an optimal data augmentation strategy. IEEE Access **5**, 5858–5869 (2017)

18. Li, Z., Zhou, F., Chen, F., Li, H.: Meta-SGD: learning to learn quickly for few shot learning. ArXiv, abs/1707.09835 (2017)
19. Lin, H., Fu, Y., Xue, X., Jiang, Y.-G.: Sketch-bert: learning sketch bidirectional encoder representation from transformers by self-supervised learning of sketch gestalt. In: The IEEE/CVF Conference on Computer Vision and Pattern Recognition (CVPR), June 2020
20. Liu, B., Wang, X., Dixit, M., Kwitt, R., Vasconcelos, N.: Feature space transfer for data augmentation. In: Proceedings of the IEEE Conference on Computer Vision and Pattern Recognition, pp. 9090–9098 (2018)
21. Liu, G., Gao, F.: Oracle-bone inscription recognition based on deep convolutional neural network. JCP **13**(12), 1442–1450 (2018)
22. Luo, C., Zhu, Y., Jin, L., Wang, Y.: Learn to augment: joint data augmentation and network optimization for text recognition. In: Proceedings of the IEEE/CVF Conference on Computer Vision and Pattern Recognition, pp. 13746–13755 (2020)
23. Mariani, G., Scheidegger, F., Istrate, R., Bekas, C., Malossi, C.: Bagan: data augmentation with balancing GAN. arXiv preprint arXiv:1803.09655 (2018)
24. Mayr, M., Stumpf, M., Nikolaou, A., Seuret, M., Maier, A., Christlein, V.: Spatio-temporal handwriting imitation. arXiv preprint arXiv:2003.10593 (2020)
25. Meng, L.: Recognition of oracle bone inscriptions by extracting line features on image processing. In: ICPRAM, pp. 606–611 (2017)
26. Ravi, S., Larochelle, H.: Optimization as a model for few-shot learning (2016)
27. Ren, M., et al.: Meta-learning for semi-supervised few-shot classification. arXiv preprint arXiv:1803.00676 (2018)
28. Shrivastava, A., Pfister, T., Tuzel, O., Susskind, J., Wang, W., Webb, R.: Learning from simulated and unsupervised images through adversarial training. In: Proceedings of the IEEE Conference on Computer Vision and Pattern Recognition, pp. 2107–2116 (2017)
29. Vaswani, A., et al.: Attention is all you need. In: Advances in Neural Information Processing Systems, pp. 5998–6008 (2017)
30. Vinyals, O., Blundell, C., Lillicrap, T., Wierstra, D., et al.: Matching networks for one shot learning. In: Advances in Neural Information Processing Systems, pp. 3630–3638 (2016)
31. Wang, Y., Xu, C., Liu, C., Zhang, L., Fu, Y.: Instance credibility inference for few-shot learning. In: Proceedings of the IEEE/CVF Conference on Computer Vision and Pattern Recognition, pp. 12836–12845 (2020)
32. Xing, J., Liu, G., Xiong, J.: Oracle bone inscription detection: a survey of oracle bone inscription detection based on deep learning algorithm. In: Proceedings of the International Conference on Artificial Intelligence, Information Processing and Cloud Computing, pp. 1–8 (2019)
33. Yosinski, J., Clune, J., Bengio, Y., Lipson, H.: How transferable are features in deep neural networks? In: Advances in Neural Information Processing Systems, pp. 3320–3328 (2014)
34. Zagoruyko, S., Komodakis, N.: Wide residual networks. arXiv preprint arXiv:1605.07146, 2016
35. Zhang, X.-Y., Bengio, Y., Liu, C.-L.: Online and offline handwritten Chinese character recognition: a comprehensive study and new benchmark. Pattern Recogn. **61**, 348–360 (2017)
36. Zhang, Y., Liang, S., Nie, S., Liu, W., Peng, S.: Robust offline handwritten character recognition through exploring writer-independent features under the guidance of printed data. Pattern Recogn. Lett. **106**, 20–26 (2018)

37. Zhang, Y., Nie, S., Liu, W., Xu, X., Zhang, D., Shen, H.T.: Sequence-to-sequence domain adaptation network for robust text image recognition. In: Proceedings of the IEEE Conference on Computer Vision and Pattern Recognition, pp. 2740–2749 (2019)
38. Zhang, Y.-K., Zhang, H., Liu, Y.-G., Yang, Q., Liu, C.-Li.: Oracle character recognition by nearest neighbor classification with deep metric learning. In: 2019 International Conference on Document Analysis and Recognition (ICDAR), pp. 309–314. IEEE (2019)
39. Zhong, Z., Zhang, X.-Y., Yin, F., Liu, C.-L.: Handwritten Chinese character recognition with spatial transformer and deep residual networks. In: 2016 23rd International Conference on Pattern Recognition (ICPR), pp. 3440–3445. IEEE (2016)

Understanding Motion in Sign Language:
A New Structured Translation Dataset

Jefferson Rodríguez[1,2] , Juan Chacón[1,2], Edgar Rangel[1,2], Luis Guayacán[1,2],
Claudia Hernández[1], Luisa Hernández[1], and Fabio Martínez[1,2(✉)]

[1] Universidad Industrial de Santander (UIS), Bucaramanga, Colombia
{edgar.rangel,claudia2198723,lfherval}@correo.uis.edu.co
[2] Biomedical Imaging, Vision and Learning Laboratory (BivL2ab),
Bucaramanga, Colombia
{jefferson.rodriguez2,juan.chacon1,luis.guayacan,
famarcar}@saber.uis.edu.co

Abstract. Sign languages are the main mechanism of communication
and interaction in the Deaf community. These languages are highly variable in communication with divergences between gloss representation,
sign configuration, and multiple variants, among others, due to cultural
and regional aspects. Current methods for automatic and continuous
sign translation include robust and deep-learning models that encode
the visual signs representation. Despite the significant progress, the convergence of such models requires huge amounts of data to exploit sign
representation, resulting in very complex models. This fact is associated
to the highest variability but also to the shortage exploration of many
language components that support communication. For instance, gesture
motion and grammatical structure are fundamental components in communication, which can deal with visual and geometrical sign misinter-
pretations during video analysis. This work introduces a new Colombian
sign language translation dataset (CoL-SLTD), that focuses on motion
and structural information, and could be a significant resource to determine the contribution of several language components. Additionally, an
encoder-decoder deep strategy is herein introduced to support automatic
translation, including attention modules that capture short, long, and
structural kinematic dependencies and their respective relationships with
sign recognition. The evaluation in CoL-SLTD proves the relevance of the
motion representation, allowing compact deep architectures to represent
the translation. Also, the proposed strategy shows promising results in
translation, achieving Bleu-4 scores of 35.81 and 4.65 in signer independent and unseen sentences tasks.

1 Introduction

Over 5% of the world's population ($\sim$466 million people) have some form of dis-
abling hearing loss. From this group, today, only the 17% use some hearing aid
to facilitate communication [1]. Thus, Sign language (SL), a spatial, temporal,

© Springer Nature Switzerland AG 2021
H. Ishikawa et al. (Eds.): ACCV 2020, LNCS 12627, pp. 669–684, 2021.
https://doi.org/10.1007/978-3-030-69544-6_40

and motion structured set of gestures, constitutes the main channel for interaction and communication of the Deaf community. Like any language, SL around the world reports many variants due to cultural and regional changes, with more than 300 official languages [2]. Even considering methods that focus on a specific regional SL, like any natural language, the problem remains quite challenging due to marked variability of gestures, the richness of glosses, and the multiple modifications that could have any expression during the communication. This fact introduces a huge challenge to the development of assistive devices that allows automatic translation among sign languages and w.r.t spoken languages.

Regarding the automatic SL recognition (SLR), recent advances in computer vision using deep learning strategies have allowed moving from a naive classification of isolated gestures (ISLR) [3,4] to robust frameworks that allow the continuous recognition (CSLR) and translation of sign languages (SLT) [5,6]. However, the effectiveness of these strategies depends strongly on large labelled datasets and very complex deep models that must deal with sign variations. Moreover, such approaches only exploit, at least at the first levels, the geometric and spatial relationships with glosses captured from appearance information of video sequences. This would make the models, faced with real scenarios, more complex in order to obtain an adequate sign representation. Therefore, it is necessary to review the main components of SL and try to understand how the interaction of signs is produced and focus on modelling the main components of language. For instance, motion is a fundamental primitive in the development of SL gestures that define much of the relationship among glosses and may even redefine the meaning of many communication segments. In terms of automatic processing, this motion SL component could be the key to deal with variance in gestures, reducing complexity in representation models. However, this motion component is still under-explored in the SL domain, and its use is only implicitly included in semantic and relational processing.

In the literature, both new deep models for SLR and datasets that support these tasks have been proposed, which together have allowed a progression in modelling such challenging tasks. Regarding the SL representation models, nowadays, 2D and 3D convolutional networks are used to extract sign descriptors in images and videos, being the main tool in ISLR [3,4]. On the other hand, for CSLR and SLT it is common to find, additionally, recurrent neural networks for temporal modeling of signs. Especially for SLT, the sequence to sequence approach with temporal attention models is used to translate the sign sequence into text [6,7]. Furthermore, some approaches have recently included two-stream approaches to focus on other SL components. For instance, in [8], RGB sequences were modelled together with skeletons to achieve a better representation of the sign communication. In terms of available datasets, there exist different open dataset proposals that record signs from non-intrusive RGB cameras, capturing a significant amount of signs in natural SL communications. These datasets support ISLR [4,9,10], CSLR [5,11] and SLT [12] tasks. Particularly, there are few SLT datasets and those available have long sentences, huge variability of sentences, and words which limit the analysis of additional components of language. Hence, proposing new datasets that allow the analysis of others components, such as movement or structure, could be fundamental to understanding how approaches perform sign translation to improve current performance.

This work presents a new structured SLT dataset dedicated to exploring the complementary SL components such as motion and structure and their roles in communication. Despite the importance of pose and geometry in signs, they are visually affected by multiple variations in automatic video analysis. For example, the capture of such language components based on appearance can dramatically affect the representation of signs. As an additional contribution, this paper introduces a novel encoder-decoder SLT strategy that pays attention to temporal structure and motion to demonstrate the ability of these components to support translation. Three main contributions of this work are:

- A new Colombian SLT dataset dedicated to exploring temporal structure and motion information. The set of phrases and glosses were selected to analyze the structure and motion dependencies in the sentences, therefore, signers naturally describe the motion using different articulators during communication. The dataset is open to the scientific community.
- A structured encoder-decoder deep strategy that fully exploits motion information and structural relations in sentences. For doing so, two kinematic attention models are herein introduced to recover short and long kinematic sign correspondences.
- A full validation with a state-of-the-art strategy, based on the deep encoder-decoder architecture. The evaluation is entirely dedicated to exploring the advantages and limitations of motion analysis. Also, how this SL component can reduce complexity in the translation process.

The paper is organized as follows: Sect. 2 describes the available datasets and the main related approaches focused on SLT, Sect. 3 introduces the proposed SLT dataset, Sect. 4, presents the baseline strategy and the proposed method and Sect. 5 presents a quantitative motion evaluation and the results of our proposed approach.

2   Related Work

Currently, SLT has advanced dramatically due to new gestural representations, translation architectures, and the availability of some datasets that allow more complex and realistic scenarios to be explored. These efforts have allowed the introduction of more difficult problems that require new perspectives and include the analysis of additional linguistic components. The following subsections summarize the state-of-the-art strategies and datasets used today to address SLT.

2.1   SLT Approaches

SLT has been addressed from different approaches, based on strategies that combined convolutional and recurrent networks to try to match an SL with direct

Table 1. Summary of sign language translation datasets.

Dataset	Videos	Sentences	Signers	Lexicon
BOSTON-104	201	113	3	104
RVL-SLLL	140	10	14	104
SIGNUM	780	780	25	450
RWTH-PHOENIX-T	8257	–	9	1066
USTC-ConSents	25000	100	50	178
CoL-SLTD (ours)	1020	39	13	~ 90

correspondence to written languages [6,7]. These architectures were generally integrated into an encoder-decoder framework forming the approach known as sequence to sequence (seq2seq [13]). These models also include attention modules that perform a weak alignment between the grammatical structures of both languages. In [14,15] hierarchical attention components were proposed, to encode SL units in video clips. However, clip-level processing limits complex sign recognition and verbal agreements related to the sentence structure, which depends on the entire context. To cover such limitations, in [16] dense temporal convolutions were used to extract short-term relationships and long-term dependencies. Also, in [17] local and global dependencies were learned from a Bidirectional LSTM and temporal correlation modules. These methods, nevertheless, fail in structural modelling due to the use of the CTC (Connectionist Temporal Classification) loss function, typically used for aligned and independent word sequences. A more detailed sign grammatical structure was explored from a multi-classification task that recognizes isolated words in sentences, while a n-gram module classifies sub-sentences [18]. This approach mitigates the error sentence propagation but the architecture remains limited by the vocabulary size. In a more recent approach, Guo et al. [8] proposed a hierarchical scheme of two streams to describe signs, capture directional and positional verbs, and capture the relationship of motion to the spatial position of articulators in sentences. This approach proves the importance of incorporating a complementary source of sign information by adding skeletons in the decoder module. This hierarchical model merges appearance and positional information reports deficiencies due to misalignment of both information.

2.2 Continuous Sign Language Datasets

Regarding the complexity and diversity of sign languages, there are few datasets that allow exploring SLT tasks. Among these, RVL-SLLL [19] is an American Sign Language (ASL) dataset that allows modelling recognition of connected linguistic contexts on short discourses (10 long sentences), performed under a lexical vocabulary of 104 signs. This dataset has some limitations mainly related to the small number of sentences that difficult the analysis of diverse language components, such as motion information. Similarly, the RWTH-BOSTON-104

Fig. 1. Proposed Col-SLTD: Video sequences were recorded under controlled lighting conditions, on a green background, different clothes and signers with a wide age range. The first two signers (top left) are CODAs (children of deaf adults) and interpreters, the rest of the signers are deaf.

Database [20] has 201 sentences with a vocabulary of 104 signs. Despite the wide range of sentences and structures, this dataset reports a reduced number of videos and signers, which could bias the analysis. In a more linguistically controlled environment, Von et al. [11] proposed a private SIGNUM dataset with 780 pre-defined sentences from German Sign Language, under a lexical vocabulary of 450 signs. The RWTH-PHOENIX-Weather 2014 dataset translation version [6] represents a first large public dataset for SLT with approximately 8000 videos and a vocabulary of 1066 signs and 2887 words. This dataset was built in an uncontrolled scenario but its complexity prevents a detailed linguistic analysis and the language components during communication. Recently, USTC-ConSents is a Chinese language dataset with 5000 videos (wit repetition has 25000 samples) of 100 pre-defined sentences and a lexicon of 178 signs [14]. These datasets represent a huge effort to model sign language but many components of languages remain unexplored because this data limit their analysis. For instance, the analysis and evaluation of kinematic patterns could be associated with verbal agreement and directional and motion verbs. Consequently, capturing data that carefully pays attention in this component could lead to the use of kinematic primitives to help in continuous translation tasks. Table: 1 presents a summary of the above-mentioned datasets.

3   Proposed CoL-SLT Dataset

Sign language, in general, preserves the structural communication Subject-Verb-Object, expressed as a visual combination of hand shapes, articulator locations and movements [21]. The motion shape information is considered the core of the SL, allowing, among others, to differentiate signs related to the pose and also to define the verbal agreement in the sentences [22]. For instance, in American SL, the expression of "I give You" has a similar geometrical description as "You give her", the biggest difference is given by motion direction. Also, while the

Fig. 2. *Top:* Col-SLTD sign example sequence. *Bottom:* The corresponding optical flow representation. This optical flow allows the accurate tracking and large movements codification, typical of sign language.

hand shapes represent noun classes, the combination with motion patterns could represent associated verbs and complete utterances [23].

This work presents a SLT dataset that focuses efforts on capturing well-formed utterances with structural kinematic dependencies, allowing further analysis of this fundamental linguistic component. To the best of our knowledge, this is the first dataset dedicated to quantify and exploit motion patterns to analyze their correspondence with the sentence structures. The proposed dataset incorporates interrogative, affirmative and negative sentences from Colombian Sign Language. Furthermore, this dataset includes different sentence complexities such as verbal and time signs that define subject and object relationships, such as the phrase: "Mary **tells** John that she will buy a house in the **future**". In this dataset, the videos were pre-processed and interpreted first into written Spanish, as the regional equivalence and then also translated to English equivalence. This dataset al.so includes signers of different ages to avoid bias in the analysis and to capture a large variability of the same language. This dataset has been approved by an ethics committee of the educational institution. This approval includes informed consent and participant authorization to use this information for the research community.

The proposed SLT dataset, named CoL-SLTD (Colombian Sign Language Translation Dataset), obtains sign expressions using a conventional RGB camera, which facilitates the naturalness of each sign. Each video sequence was recorded under controlled studio conditions using a green chroma key background with lighting conditions, the position of the participants in front of the camera, and the use of clothing of a different color than the background. In CoL-SLTD, there are 39 sentences, divided into 24 affirmative, 4 negative, and 11 interrogative sentences. Each of the sentences has 3 different repetitions, for a total of 1020 sentences, which allows capturing sign motion variability related to specific expressions. Also, the phrases were performed by 13 participants (between 21 to 80 years old), with sentence length between two to nine signs. Figure 1 illustrates the signers of the proposed dataset. All recorded videos were resized to spatial

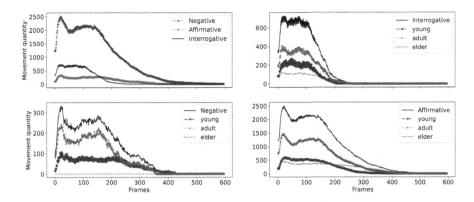

Fig. 3. Motion analysis from optical flow magnitude at frame level: The top left chart compares the quantity of movement present in each frame for the different sentence categories. The remaining three figures analyze the amount of movement performed by signers grouped by age in each sentence type.

resolution of 448×448 with temporal resolutions of 30 and 60 FPS. Also, the whole set was centered on the signer removing a lot of background. Videos have an average length of 3.8 ± 1.5 s and an average number of frames of 233 ± 90.

To support the analysis of the motion component, a kinematic vector field descriptor was calculated for each video sign. For this purpose, an optical flow approach with the capability to recover large displacements and relative sharp motions was selected to capture motion signs descriptions at low or high temporal resolutions [24]. Such cases are almost present in any sign, which reports different velocity and acceleration profiles but are especially observed in the exclamation marks. The resultant velocity field $\mathbf{u}_k := (u_{x_1}, u_{x_2})^T$, for a particular frame t is obtained from a variational Euler-Lagrange minimization, that includes local and non-local restrictions between two consecutive frames: $I(\mathbf{x})_t$, $I(\mathbf{x})_{t+1}$. To capture large displacements, a non-local assumption is introduced by matching key-points with similar velocity field patterns. This final assumption could be formalized as: $E_p(\mathbf{u}) = |g_{t+1}(\mathbf{x}+\mathbf{u}(x)) - g_t(\mathbf{x})|^2$ where p is the descriptor vector and $(g_{(t)}, g_{(t+1)})$ are the computed velocity patterns in matched non-local regions. The captured flow field volume result is highly described, keeping spatial coherence and aggregating motion information patterns as a low-level representation. In Fig. 2 an optical flow sequence computed on the RGB images is illustrated. Also, it is interesting to note in Fig. 3 how important sentence patterns are discovered from the optical flow quantification (motion vector norm in each pixel). For example, two big kinematic moments allow identification of affirmative sentences (bottom right). While in interrogative sentences (top right) the movement peaks are not so marked and conversely, they tend to be constant which means that there is more expressiveness.

Table 2. Statistics of each split proposed for evaluation

	SPLIT 1		SPLIT 2	
	Train	Test	Train	Test
Number of videos	807	213	922	98
Number of signers	10	3	13	13
Number of sentences	24/10/5	24/10/5	22/9/4	2/1/1
Number of signs	∼ 90	∼ 90	∼ 90	∼ 90
Number of words	110	110	110	16

3.1   Evaluation Scheme on CoL-SLTD

Two different evaluations are proposed over Col-SLTD. In a first evaluation, a signer independence split aims to evaluate the capability to translate sequences of signers not seen during training. In this split, a total of 10 signers were selected for training and 3 signers with different ages for testing. In a second evaluation, the task should report the capability to generate sentences not seen during training. In this task, a total of 35 sentences were selected in training and 4 sentences in testing. The words in test sentences have the highest occurrence in training and the sentences involve affirmations, negations, and interrogations. Table 2 summarizes the statistics per split.

A total of three metrics are suggested to evaluate model performance, namely: BLEU score [25], ROUGE-L score (F1-score value) [26] and WER error. The BLEU score measures precision to recover a set of consecutive n-grams. The last two calculate sentence level score and error. The ROUGE-L takes into account similarity regarding sentence structure and identifies longest co-occurrence in compared n-grams sequences and WER error provides complementary information to the scoring metrics.

4   Seq2seq Architecture for SLT

Today, most of the common translation approaches use encoder-decoder architectures, transforming one sequence into another (seq2seq), to translate sign language into a particular written or spoken language. These strategies have shown promising results and therefore these networks are used as a baseline to validate and analyze CoL-SLTD. This section introduces the general principles that follow seq2seq architectures, and how the encoder-decoder model allows for sign translation. Additionally, as a second contribution, a new encoder-decoder scheme is presented here to deal with and address the sign structure and motion component.

4.1   Encoder - Decoder Model

In translation, commonly, the encoder-decoder is composed of two synchronized recurrent neural networks that estimate the conditional probability

$p(y_{\{1:m\}}|x_{\{1:t\}})$, where $(x_1, \ldots, x_t)$ is the sequence of t frames and $(y_1, \ldots, y_m)$ is the corresponding target sequence of m words [13]. On one hand, the encoder codes the inputs in a latent feature space to obtain the state vector h_t at time t. On the other hand, the decoder receives as input the vector h_t to decode and relate with target sequence. The decoder decomposes the conditional probability $p(y_{\{1:m\}}|x_{\{1:t\}})$ into ordered conditional probabilities:

$$p(y_{\{1:m\}}|x_{(1:t)}) = \prod_{m=1}^{M} p(\hat{y}_m|\hat{y}_{\{m-1:1\}}, h_t), \qquad (1)$$

where $p(\hat{y}_m|\hat{y}_{\{m-1:1\}}, h_t)$ is the predicted distribution over all m words in the vocabulary. From recurrent methodology, the decoder learns to predict the next most likely word $\hat{y}_m$, conditioned by sign language encoder representation in h_t and previous predicted words $\hat{y}_{\{m-1:1\}}$. These conditional probabilities are solved from stacked RNN (LSTM and GRU) modules that compute the hidden states through the sequence [6,7,15]. The error in such models is calculated using word-level cross entropy, described as:

$$\ell = 1 - \prod_{m=1}^{M} \sum_{d=1}^{D} p(y_m^d) p(\hat{y}_m^d), \qquad (2)$$

where $p(y_m^d)$ represents the ground truth probability of word y^d at decoding step m and D is the target language vocabulary size.

Baseline Architecture: Herein the NSLT approach was selected to analyze translation on CoL-SLTD [6]. This model uses a pretrained AlexNet 2D-CNN to capture spatial features in each frame x_t. The encoder and the decoder are composed of 4 recurrent layers with GRU units and 1000 neurons in each layer, respectively. This model includes a temporal attention module that provides additional information to the decoding phase by reinforcing the long-term dependencies. Furthermore, this module avoids the vanishing gradients, during the training, as well as the bottleneck caused by the fixed representation of the whole video (very large information) in a fixed embedding vector. The attention module computes a context vector at each decoding step m, as:

$$c_m = \sum_{t=1}^{T} \gamma_t^m h_t, \qquad (3)$$

where γ_t^m represents the relevance weight of an encoder input x_t to generate the word y_m. These weights are calculated by comparing the decoder hidden state $\hbar$ at step m, with all encoder hidden states h_t, through a scoring function, as:

$$\gamma_t^m = \frac{exp(\hbar_m^\top W h_t)}{\sum_{t'=1}^{T} exp(\hbar_m^\top W h_{t'})}, \qquad (4)$$

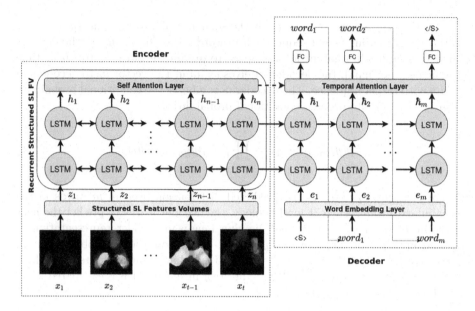

Fig. 4. Proposed structured SLT architecture: Optical flow video is the input to the network. The encoder extracts, at low level, structured kinematic descriptors. Then, at a higher level, the Encoder sequentially processes the descriptors. Finally, they are passed to the Decoder to generate the translation.

where W is a learned parameter. In such sense, the Eq. 4.1 can be rewritten as follows:

$$p(y_{\{1:m\}}|x_{(1:t)}) = \prod_{m=1}^{M} p(\hat{y}_m|\hat{y}_{\{m-1:1\}}, c_{m-1}, h_t).$$ (5)

4.2   Focus on SL Structure

We introduce a new encoder-decoder architecture to robustly include motion modeling and structure in SLT to obtain a very compact representation of the language. At a low level, we use a 3D-CNN network that recovers multiple spatio-temporal features volumes, with relevant short-term kinematic information. Hence, long-term dependencies are captured from an attention module that includes structural and temporal relationships. Also, in the encoder, kinematic descriptors are processed from a stack of bi-directional LSTM modules. These hidden states are refined with a self-attention layer that complements the structural information [27]. Figure 4 illustrates the proposed architecture.

Structured SL Features Volumes Extractor (SFV): Short-term modeling is achieved here by processing optical flow sequences with successive 3D convolutions. This hierarchical scheme obtains multiple non-linear kinematic responses, which describe the motion information, at low levels. Long-term dependencies are modelled on each kinematic response that fully captures the context of the sign. Hence, we apply self-attention [27], along the time axis t' for the complete feature volume $V_r \in \mathbb{N}^{t' \times h' \times w' \times f'}$ for each f' filter responses, in an independent and parallel way. As result, we obtain the square matrix $M'_j \in \mathbb{N}^{t' \times t'}$ which codes the correlation among frames in the same feature filter f'_j. The self-attention computes the weights matrix through the independent projections K (keys) and Q (queries) of the volume Vr in a latent space of dimension p as follows:

$$M'_j = softmax(\frac{Q_{V_r} K_{V_r}^\top}{\sqrt{p}}).$$ (6)

The scaling factor $\frac{1}{\sqrt{p}} = 8$ for $p = 64$ avoids small gradients in softmax [27] and the projections are parameter matrices $W^{Q_{V_r}}$ and $W^{K_{V_r}} \in \mathbb{N}^{hw \times p}$.

To include this structural information we apply the frame feature context, defined for each step t'_i of the filter f'_j as:

$$f'_{jt'_i} = \sum_{l=1}^{t'} f'_{jt'_i} M'^{li}_j$$ (7)

This frame feature context weights each slice $f'_{jt'_i} \in \mathbb{N}^{h' \times w'}$ to include its structural relationship with other slices in the filter. Figure 5 shows the module in detail with some common normalisation, reduction and fully connected layers.

Recurrent Structured SL Features Vectors (RSFV): High-level sequential dependencies are captured here by using a stack of recurrent bi-directional LSTM layers that receive as a input the computed kinematic volume transformed into a matrix Z with n motion descriptors through the last dense layer. Thus, the final hidden state for each Z_k descriptor, where $k = 1 : n$, is the concatenation of each hidden state from both directions: $h_k = [\overrightarrow{h}_k; \overleftarrow{h}_k]$. To update the hidden states h_k, we propose to include a self-attention layer to refine the relationships between these resulting recurrent vectors. Therefore, the new hidden states are calculated by the following matrix way operation:

$$h_{1:n} = softmax(\frac{Q_h K_h^\top}{\sqrt{p_k}})V_h,$$ (8)

where the dimension of the latent space p_k is the same as the hidden vectors $h_k \in R^{512}$ and the projections are parameter matrices W^{Q_h}, W^{K_h} and $W^{V_h} \in \mathbb{N}^{p_k \times p_k}$. For this self-attention the V_h (values) matrix is the result of a third projection of the hidden vectors.

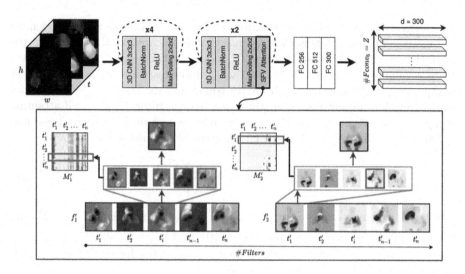

Fig. 5. Structured SL Features Volumes extractor: This proposed module extracts low-level spatio-temporal features volumes through successive 3D-CNN. The SFV attention module takes each resulting convolution and applies self-attention on the whole volume by calculating an attention matrix for each filter in an independent and parallel way. Each feature frame is then related in different proportions to the other frames according to the temporal relationship between them.

5   Experimental Results

The evaluation was designed to determine sign kinematic relevance in CoL-SLTD sentences. Firstly, we analyzed performance with NSLT, trained with 20 epochs, in both RGB and optical flow sequences. This architecture has around 65 Million training parameters (without the AlexNet backbone parameters). Table 3 shows the results obtained for both defined tasks in CoL-SLTD. For Signer Independence evaluation (split 1), the translations generated using the optical flow report around 43% less word error than sentences from the RGB model. The Bleu-4, obtained from flow sequences, also highlights the consistency of the translation with a 46% margin over RGB. These results prove the relevance of the motion in sign recognition and translation.

Regarding the second CoL-SLTD task, to generate unseen sentences (split 2), the Table 3 summarizes the obtained results by using the NSLT approach. This task is much more challenging, which could be associated with a poor local representation of the gesture and a language model bias. Nevertheless, even in this case, the motion shape information shows remarkable results w.r.t RGB sequences.

Taking advantage of the resulting motion representation made it possible to address the problem of the complexity. In this sense, a second experiment was designed to compact the network complexity by reducing the recurrent layers and units. In a first experiment, the NSLT was reduced to approximately 25%

Table 3. Translation results for RGB and Flow images in both splits. *Top* of table: results for split 1, *Bottom:* split 2. The experiments were performed with the complete base architecture and then reduced in different proportions.

SPLIT 1	Data	WER	Rouge-l	Bleu-1	Bleu-2	Bleu-3	Bleu-4
Baseline	RGB	77.41	31.83	30.56	19.78	16.24	14.50
	Flow	34.94	69.91	68.53	63.73	61.42	60.24
Reduction to 75%	Flow	**30.87**	**72.95**	**71.58**	**67.27**	**65.23**	**64.23**
Reduction to 50%	Flow	44.00	62.82	57.09	50.34	47.45	46.07
Reduction to 25%	Flow	62.67	43.92	37.89	26.21	19.67	15.56
SPLIT 2	**Data**	**WER**	**Rouge-l**	**Bleu-1**	**Bleu-2**	**Bleu-3**	**Bleu-4**
Baseline	RGB	77.55	23.43	21.68	7.01	2.91	1.74
	Flow	78.33	**36.96**	**39.67**	**18.94**	**12.17**	**8.69**
Reduction to 75%	Flow	78.96	36.17	38.28	15.94	9.28	6.34
Reduction to 50%	Flow	**77.08**	33.73	32.91	11.41	7.18	5.17
Reduction to 25%	Flow	80.06	24.90	26.61	8.05	0.0	0.0

(around 50M parameters less), using only one recurrent layer with 250 neurons. Surprisingly, this compact network achieves even better results than the original RGB representation. Secondly, the best results obtained were when the architecture was reduced to 75%, using 3 layers of 750 neurons (approximately 25 M parameters less), demonstrating again the potential use of motion components of language to support sign representation.

From CoL-SLTD, the motion component takes on a relevant role in translation, which could be further utilized in specialized architectures that focus on the attention and model kinematic patterns for a better structural language understanding. In this work, a new seq2seq network was also introduced that exploits mainly motion patterns, the main advantage being the robustness on sign representation (around 10 M parameters). This architecture is composed by the feature extractor module (see Fig. 5) and a RNN stack with a total of 256 LSTM units in the first layer and 512 in the second layer for encoder and decoder modules[1]. Table 4 summarizes the achieved result in both CoL-SLTD tasks. In the first task, split 1, the architecture with the RSFV self-service module achieves the best results due to the effectiveness to complement the temporal structure initially learned by the LSTM. Interestingly enough, the combination of RSFV y SFV modules improves the Bleu-1 and rouge-l scores, incorporating relevant short-term dependencies captured in SFV. Similarly, for the second task (using split 2), the proposed network achieves similar performance highlighting the relevance of coding, short and structural motion dependencies and

---

[1] For training, Adam optimizer was selected with a learning rate of 0.0001 and decay of 0.1 every 10 epochs. Also, batches of 1 sample and a dropout of 0.2 in dense and recurrent layers were herein configured. The convolutional weight decay was set to 0.0005 and gradient clipping with a threshold of 5 was also used.

Table 4. Obtained results using the proposed modules in both splits.

SPLIT 1	WER	Rouge-l	Bleu-1	Bleu-2	Bleu-3	Bleu-4
Vanilla approach	64.12	44.39	42.16	33.43	29.91	27.96
SFV module	63.88	45.01	45.90	36.65	32.85	31.02
RSFV module	**58.33**	48.39	47.80	**40.44**	**37.39**	**35.81**
SFV+RSFV modules	59.33	**49.45**	**48.98**	39.98	35.88	33.81
SPLIT 2	**WER**	**Rouge-l**	**Bleu-1**	**Bleu-2**	**Bleu-3**	**Bleu-4**
Vanilla approach	90.42	25.59	26.12	10.89	5.21	2.77
SFV module	**88.85**	**30.59**	**30.05**	**12.86**	**7.09**	**4.65**
RSFV module	89.95	24.63	26.08	9.15	4.07	2.41
SFV+RSFV modules	88.85	26.56	27.45	8.94	3.20	1.70

their relationships with sign recognition. These relevant kinematic and structural relationships are principal attributed to SVF (short-term dependencies) allowing the achievement of the best performance over the vanilla approach in this task.

6   Conclusions

This work introduced a new sign language translation dataset (CoL-SLTD) that allows the exploration and analysis of motion shape, being one of the fundamental components of language. Through taking advantage of such information, a very compact seq2seq approach was also proposed here to address structure in sign language translation tasks, with remarkable results. The results obtained on the CoL-SLTD prove the relevance of kinematic information to complement sign structure and representation, allowing the design of more compact architectures that could be efficient in real-life conditions. Future works include the continuous growth of this motion dedicated dataset and structural approach, bringing to the scientific community an invaluable source of information to explore new components of sign language.

Acknowledgments. This work was partially funded by the Universidad Industrial de Santander. The authors acknowledge the Vicerrectoriá de Investigación y Extensión (VIE) of the Universidad Industrial de Santander for supporting this research registered by the project: *Reconocimiento continuo de expresiones cortas del lenguaje de señas*, with SIVIE code 1293. Also, we gratefully acknowledge the support of NVIDIA Corporation with the donation of the Titan V GPU used for this research.

References

1. WM Centre: Deafness and hearing loss (2020) Visited 28 April 2020
2. WM Centre: Our work (2020) Visited 28 April 2020

3. Joze, H.R.V., Koller, O.: Ms-asl: A large-scale data set and benchmark for understanding american sign language. arXiv preprint arXiv:1812.01053 (2018)
4. Li, D., Rodriguez, C., Yu, X., Li, H.: Word-level deep sign language recognition from video: a new large-scale dataset and methods comparison. In: The IEEE Winter Conference on Applications of Computer Vision, pp. 1459–1469 (2020)
5. Koller, O., Forster, J., Ney, H.: Continuous sign language recognition: towards large vocabulary statistical recognition systems handling multiple signers. Comput. Vis. Image Underst. **141**, 108–125 (2015)
6. Cihan Camgoz, N., Hadfield, S., Koller, O., Ney, H., Bowden, R.: Neural sign language translation. In: Proceedings of the IEEE Conference on Computer Vision and Pattern Recognition, pp. 7784–7793 (2018)
7. Ko, S.K., Kim, C.J., Jung, H., Cho, C.: Neural sign language translation based on human keypoint estimation. arXiv preprint arXiv:1811.11436 (2018)
8. Guo, D., Zhou, W., Li, A., Li, H., Wang, M.: Hierarchical recurrent deep fusion using adaptive clip summarization for sign language translation. IEEE Trans. Image Process. **29**, 1575–1590 (2019)
9. Athitsos, V., Neidle, C., Sclaroff, S., Nash, J., Stefan, A., Yuan, Q., Thangali, A.: The american sign language lexicon video dataset. In: 2008 IEEE Computer Society Conference on Computer Vision and Pattern Recognition Workshops, IEEE, pp. 1–8 (2008)
10. Ronchetti, F., Quiroga, F., Estrebou, C., Lanzarini, L., Rosete, A.: Lsa64: a dataset of argentinian sign language. In: XX II Congreso Argentino de Ciencias de la Computación (CACIC) (2016)
11. Von Agris, U., Kraiss, K.F.: Towards a video corpus for signer-independent continuous sign language recognition. In: Gesture in Human-Computer Interaction and Simulation, Lisbon, May 2007
12. Forster, J., Schmidt, C., Hoyoux, T., Koller, O., Zelle, U., Piater, J.H., Ney, H.: Rwth-phoenix-weather: a large vocabulary sign language recognition and translation corpus. LREC **9**, 3785–3789 (2012)
13. Sutskever, I., Vinyals, O., Le, Q.V.: Sequence to sequence learning with neural networks. In: Advances in neural information processing systems, pp. 3104–3112 (2014)
14. Huang, J., Zhou, W., Zhang, Q., Li, H., Li, W.: Video-based sign language recognition without temporal segmentation. In: Thirty-Second AAAI Conference on Artificial Intelligence (2018)
15. Guo, D., Zhou, W., Li, H., Wang, M.: Hierarchical lstm for sign language translation. In: Thirty-Second AAAI Conference on Artificial Intelligence (2018)
16. Guo, D., Wang, S., Tian, Q., Wang, M.: Dense temporal convolution network for sign language translation. In: Proceedings of the 28th International Joint Conference on Artificial Intelligence, AAAI Press, pp. 744–750 (2019)
17. Song, P., Guo, D., Xin, H., Wang, M.: Parallel temporal encoder for sign language translation. In: 2019 IEEE International Conference on Image Processing (ICIP), IEEE, pp. 1915–1919 (2019)
18. Wei, C., Zhou, W., Pu, J., Li, H.: Deep grammatical multi-classifier for continuous sign language recognition. In: 2019 IEEE Fifth International Conference on Multimedia Big Data (BigMM), IEEE, pp. 435–442 (2019)
19. Martínez, A.M., Wilbur, R.B., Shay, R., Kak, A.C.: Purdue rvl-slll asl database for automatic recognition of american sign language. In: Proceedings. Fourth IEEE International Conference on Multimodal Interfaces, IEEE, pp. 167–172 (2002)

20. Dreuw, P., Rybach, D., Deselaers, T., Zahedi, M., Ney, H.: Speech recognition techniques for a sign language recognition system. In: Interspeech, Antwerp, Belgium, pp. 2513–2516 (2007). ISCA best student paper award Interspeech 2007
21. Stokoe, W.C.: Sign language structure. Annu. Rev. Anthropol. **9**, 365–390 (1980)
22. Sandler, W.: The phonological organization of sign languages. Lang. Linguist. compass **6**, 162–182 (2012)
23. Supalla, T.: The classifier system in american sign language. Noun Classes Categorization **7**, 181–214 (1986)
24. Brox, T., Malik, J.: Large displacement optical flow: descriptor matching in variational motion estimation. IEEE Trans. Pattern Anal. Mach. Intell. **33**, 500–513 (2010)
25. Papineni, K., Roukos, S., Ward, T., Zhu, W.J.: Bleu: a method for automatic evaluation of machine translation. In: Proceedings of the 40th Annual Meeting on Association for computational linguistics, Association for Computational Linguistics, pp. 311–318 (2002)
26. Lin, C.Y.: ROUGE: A package for automatic evaluation of summaries. In: Out, T.S.B. (ed.) Barcelona, pp. 74–81. Association for Computational Linguistics, Spain (2004)
27. Vaswani, A., et al.: Attention is all you need. In: Advances in neural information processing systems, pp. 5998–6008 (2017)

FreezeNet: Full Performance by Reduced Storage Costs

Paul Wimmer[1,2]($\boxtimes$)(iD), Jens Mehnert[1](iD), and Alexandru Condurache[1,2]

[1] Robert Bosch GmbH, Daimlerstrasse 6, 71229 Leonberg, Germany
{Paul.Wimmer,JensEricMarkus.Mehnert,
AlexandruPaul.Condurache}@de.bosch.com
[2] University of Luebeck, Ratzeburger Allee 160, 23562 Luebeck, Germany

Abstract. Pruning generates sparse networks by setting parameters to zero. In this work we improve one-shot pruning methods, applied before training, without adding any additional storage costs while preserving the sparse gradient computations. The main difference to pruning is that we do not sparsify the network's weights but learn just a few key parameters and keep the other ones fixed at their random initialized value. This mechanism is called *freezing the parameters*. Those frozen weights can be stored efficiently with a single 32bit random seed number. The parameters to be frozen are determined one-shot by a single for- and backward pass applied before training starts. We call the introduced method *FreezeNet*. In our experiments we show that FreezeNets achieve good results, especially for extreme freezing rates. Freezing weights preserves the gradient flow throughout the network and consequently, FreezeNets train better and have an increased capacity compared to their pruned counterparts. On the classification tasks MNIST and CIFAR-10/100 we outperform SNIP, in this setting the best reported one-shot pruning method, applied before training. On MNIST, FreezeNet achieves 99.2% performance of the baseline LeNet-5-Caffe architecture, while compressing the number of trained and stored parameters by a factor of ×157.

Keywords: Network pruning · Random weights · Sparse gradients · Preserved gradient flow · Backpropagation

1 Introduction

Between 2012 and 2018, computations required for deep learning research have been increased by estimated $300,000$ times which corresponds to doubling the amount of computations every few months [36]. This rate outruns by far the

---

P. Wimmer, J. Mehnert—Equal contribution.

Electronic supplementary material The online version of this chapter (https:// doi.org/10.1007/978-3-030-69544-6_41) contains supplementary material, which is available to authorized users.

predicted one by Moore's Law [18]. Thus, it is important to reduce computational costs and memory requirements for deep learning while preserving or even improving the status quo regarding performance [36].

Model compression lowers storage costs, speeds up inference after training by reducing the number of computations, or accelerates the training which uses less energy. A method combining these factors is *network pruning*. To follow the call for more sustainability and efficiency in deep learning we improve the best reported pruning method applied before training, SNIP ([29] Single-shot Network Pruning based on Connection Sensitivity), by freezing the parameters instead of setting them to zero.

SNIP finds the most dominant weights in a neural network with a single for- and backward pass, performed once before training starts and immediately prunes the other, less important weights. Hence it is a one-shot pruning method, applied before training. By one-shot pruning we mean pruning in a single step, not iteratively. This leads to sparse gradient computations during training. But if too many parameters are pruned, SNIP networks are not able to train well due to a weak flow of the gradient through the network [39]. In this work we use a SNIP related method for finding the most influential weights in a deep neural network (DNN). We do not follow the common pruning procedure of setting weights to zero, but keep the remaining parameters fixed as initialized which we call *freezing*, schematically shown in Fig. 1. A proper gradient flow throughout the network can be ensured with help of the frozen parameters, even for a small number of trained parameters. The frozen weights also increase the network's expressiveness, without adding any gradient computations—compared to pruned networks. All frozen weights can be stored with a single random seed number. We call these partly frozen DNNs *FreezeNets*.

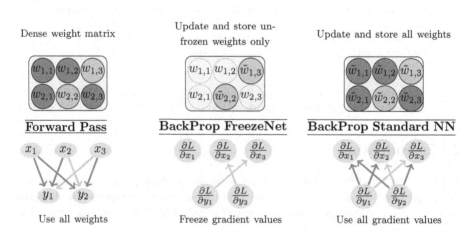

Fig. 1. Graphical illustration of FreezeNet and comparison with a standard neural network (NN) for a fully connected NN with neurons x_1, x_2, x_3 and y_1, y_2, and corresponding weights and gradient values. Best viewed in colour. (Color figure online)

1.1   Contributions of This Paper and Applications

In this work we introduce FreezeNets, which can be applied to any baseline neural network. The key contributions of FreezeNets are:

- Smaller trainable parameter count than one-shot pruning (SNIP), but better results.
- Preservation of gradient flow, even for a small number of trained parameters.
- Efficient way to store frozen weights with a single random seed number.
- More efficient training than the baseline architecture since the same number of gradients as for pruned networks has to be computed.

Theoretically and empirically, we show that a faithful gradient flow, even for a few trainable parameters, can be preserved by using frozen weights. Whereas pruning weights eventually leads to vanishing gradients. By applying weight decay also on the frozen parameters, we modify FreezeNets to generate sparse networks at the end of training. For freezing rates on which SNIP performs well, this modified training generates networks with the same number of non-zero weights as SNIP while reaching better performances.

Due to their sparse gradient computations, FreezeNets are perfectly suitable for applications with a train-inference ratio biased towards training. Especially for research, where networks are trained for a long time and often validated exactly once, FreezeNets provide a good trade-off between reducing training resources and keeping performance. Other applications for FreezeNets are networks that have to be retrained many times due to changing data, as online learning or transfer learning. Since FreezeNets can reduce the number of stored parameters drastically, they are networks cheap to transfer. This could be of interest for autonomous vehicle fleets or internet services. For a given hardware, FreezeNets can be used to increase the size of the largest trainable network since less storage and computations are needed for applying gradient descent.

2   Related Work

2.1   Network Pruning

Pruning methods are used to reduce the amount of parameters in a network [19,28,31]. At the same time, the pruned network should perform equally well, or even better, than the reference network. Speeding up training can be achieved by pruning the network at the beginning of training [29] or at early training steps [12,13]. There are several approaches to prune neural networks. One is penalizing non-zero weights [3,4,20] and thus achieving sparse networks. Nowadays, a more common way is given by using magnitude based pruning [12,13,17,19], leading to pruning early on in training [12,13], on-the-fly during training [17] or at the end of it [19]. These pruned networks have to be fine-tuned afterwards. For high pruning rates, magnitude based pruning works better if this procedure is done iteratively [12,13], therefore leading to many *train-prune(-retrain)* cycles. Pruning can also be achieved by using *neural architecture search* [10,22] or adding computationally cheap branches to predict sparse locations in feature maps [9]. The final pruning strategy we want to present is saliency based pruning. In saliency based pruning, the significance of weights is measured with the Hessian of the loss [28], or the sensitivity of the loss with respect to inclusion/exclusion of each weight [25]. This idea of measuring the effect of inclusion/exclusion of weights was resumed in [29], where a differentiable approximation of this criterion was introduced, the SNIP method. Since SNIP's pruning step is applicable with a single for- and backward pass one-shot before training, its computational overload is negligible. The GraSP (Gradient Signal Preservation) [39] method is also a pruning mechanism, applied one-shot before training. Contrarily to SNIP, they keep the weights possessing the best gradient flow at initialization. For high pruning rates, they achieve better results than SNIP but are outperformed by SNIP for moderate ones.

Dynamic sparse training is a strategy to train pruned networks, but give the sparse architecture a chance to change dynamically during training. Therefore, pruning- and regrowing steps have to be done during the whole training process. The weights to be regrown are determined by random processes [2,30,41], their magnitude [40] or saliency [7,8]. An example of the latter strategy is *Sparse Momentum* [7], measuring saliencies via exponentially smoothed gradients. *Global Sparse Momentum* [8] uses a related idea to FreezeNet by not pruning the untrained weights. But the set of trainable weights can change and the untrained weights are not updated via gradient descent, but with a momentum parameter based on earlier updates. Whereas FreezeNet freezes weights and uses a fixed architecture, thus needs to gauge the best sparse network for all phases of training.

In pruning, the untrained parameters are set to 0 which is not done for FreezeNets, where these parameters are frozen and used to increase the descriptive power of the network. This clearly separates our freezing approach from pruning methods.

2.2   CNNs with Random Weights

The idea of fixing randomly initialized weights in Convolutional Neural Networks (CNNs) was researched in [24], where the authors showed that randomly initialized convolutional filters act orientation selective. In [35] it was shown that randomly initialized CNNs with pooling layers can act inherently frequency selective. Ramanujan et al. [33] showed that in a large randomly initialized base network ResNet50 [21] a smaller, untrained subnetwork is hidden that matches the performance of a ResNet34 [21] trained on ImageNet [6]. Recently, Frankle et al. [14] published an investigation of CNNs with only Batch Normalization [23] parameters trainable. In contrast to their work, we also train biases and chosen weight parameters and reach competitive results with FreezeNets.

A follow-up work of the *Lottery Ticket Hypothesis* [12] deals with the question of why iterative magnitude based pruning works so well [42]. Among others, they also investigate resetting pruned weights to their initial values and keeping them fix. The unpruned parameters are reset to their initial values as well and trained again. This train-prune-retrain cycle is continued until the target rate of fixed parameters is reached. In their experiments they show that this procedure mostly leads to worse results than standard iterative pruning and just outperforms it for extremely high pruning rates.

3   FreezeNets

General Setup. Let $f_\Theta : \mathbb{R}^{d_0} \to [0,1]^c$ be a DNN with parameters $\Theta \subset \mathbb{R}$, used for an image classification task with c classes. We assume a train set (X, Z) with images $X = \{x_1, \ldots, x_N\} \subset \mathbb{R}^{d_0}$ and corresponding labels $Z = \{z_1, \ldots, z_N\} \subset \{0, 1, \ldots, c-1\}$, a test set (X_0, Z_0) and a smooth loss function L to be given. As common for DNNs, the test error is minimized by training the network with help of the training data via stochastic gradient based (SGD) optimization [34] while preventing the network to overfit on the training data.

We define the rate $q := 1 - p$ as the networks *freezing rate*, where p is the rate of trainable weights. A high freezing rate corresponds to few trainable parameters and therefore sparse gradients, whereas a low freezing rate corresponds to many trainable parameters. Freezing is compared to pruning in Sect. 4. For simplicity, a freezing rate q for pruning a network means exactly that $q \cdot 100\%$ of its weights are set to zero. In this work we split the model's parameters into weights W and biases B, only freeze parts of the weights W and keep all biases trainable.

3.1   SNIP

Since pruned networks are constraint on using only parts of their weights, those weights should be chosen as the most influential ones for the given task. Let $\Theta = W \cup B^1$ be the network's parameters and $m \in \{0,1\}^{|W|}$ be a mask that shows if a weight is activated or not. Therefore, the weights that actually contribute to the network's performance are given by $m \odot W$. Here $\odot$ denotes the Hadamard product [5]. The trick used in [29] is to look at the *saliency score*

$$g := \left. \frac{\partial L(m \odot W; B, X, Z)}{\partial m} \right|_{m=1} = \frac{\partial L(W; B, X, Z)}{\partial W} \odot W, \qquad (1)$$

which calculates componentwise the influence of the loss function's change by a small variation of the associated weight's activation.[2] If those changes are big, keeping the corresponding weight is likely to have a greater effect in minimizing the loss function than keeping a weight with a small score. The gradient g can be approximated with just a single forward and backward pass of one training batch before the beginning of training.

---

[1] By an abuse of notation, we also use W and B as the vectors containing all elements of the set of all weights and biases, respectively.

[2] To obtain differentiability in equation (1), the mask is assumed to be continuous, i.e. $m \in \mathbb{R}^{|W|}$.

3.2   Backpropagation in Neural Networks

To simplify the backpropagation formulas, we will deal with a feed-forward, fully connected neural network. Similar equations hold for convolutional layers [21]. Let the input of the network be given by $x^{(0)} \in \mathbb{R}^{d_0}$, the weight matrices are given by $W^{(k)} \in \mathbb{R}^{d_k \times d_{k-1}}$, $k \in \{1, \dots, K\}$ and the forward propagation rules are inductively defined as

- $y^{(k)} := W^{(k)} x^{(k-1)} + b^{(k)}$ for the layers bias $b^{(k)} \in \mathbb{R}^{d_k}$,
- $x^{(k)} := \Phi_{(k)}(y^{(k)})$ for the layers non-linearity $\Phi_{(k)} : \mathbb{R} \to \mathbb{R}$, applied component-wise.

This leads to the partial derivatives used for the backward pass, written compactly in vector or matrix form:

$$\frac{\partial L}{\partial y^{(k)}} = \Phi'_{(k)}\left(y^{(k)}\right) \odot \frac{\partial L}{\partial x^{(k)}} , \quad \frac{\partial L}{\partial x^{(k)}} = \left(W^{(k+1)}\right)^T \cdot \frac{\partial L}{\partial y^{(k+1)}} ,$$
$$\frac{\partial L}{\partial W^{(k)}} = \frac{\partial L}{\partial y^{(k)}} \cdot \left(x^{(k-1)}\right)^T , \quad \frac{\partial L}{\partial b^{(k)}} = \frac{\partial L}{\partial y^{(k)}} \qquad (2)$$

Here, we define $W^{(K+1)} := \mathrm{id} \in \mathbb{R}^{d_K \times d_K}$ and $\frac{\partial L}{\partial y^{(K+1)}} := \frac{\partial L}{\partial x^{(K)}}$. For sparse weight matrices $W^{(k+1)}$, Eqs. (2) can lead to small $\frac{\partial L}{\partial x^{(k)}}$ and consequently small weight gradients $\frac{\partial L}{\partial W^{(k)}}$. In the extreme case of $\frac{\partial L}{\partial y^{(k)}} = 0$ for a layer k, all overlying layers will have $\frac{\partial L}{\partial W^{(l)}} = 0, l \leq k$. Overcoming the gradient's drying up for sparse weight matrices in the backward pass motivated us to freeze weights instead of pruning them.

3.3   FreezeNet

In Algorithm 1 the FreezeNet method is introduced. First, the saliency score g is calculated according to Eq. (1). Then, the freezing threshold ε is defined as the $\lfloor (1-q) \cdot |W_0| \rfloor$-highest magnitude of g. If a saliency score is smaller than the freezing threshold, the corresponding entry in the freezing mask $m \in \mathbb{R}^{|W_0|}$ is set to 0. Otherwise, the entry in m is set to 1. However, we do not delete the non-chosen parameters as done for SNIP pruning, but leave them as initialized. This

---

Algorithm 1. FreezeNet

Require: Freezing rate q, initial parametrization $\Theta_0 = W_0 \cup B_0$, corresponding network f_{Θ_0}, loss function L
1: Compute saliency score $g \in \mathbb{R}^{|W_0|}$ for one training batch, according to equation (1)
2: Define freezing mask $m \in \mathbb{R}^{|W_0|}$
3: Use freezing threshold ε as the $\lfloor (1-q) \cdot |W_0| \rfloor$-highest magnitude of g
4: Set $m_k = 0$ if $|g_k| < \varepsilon$ else $m_k = 1$
5: Start training with forward propagation as usual but backpropagate gradient $m \odot \frac{\partial L}{\partial W_0}$ for weights and $\frac{\partial L}{\partial B_0}$ for biases

---

is achieved with the masked gradient. For computational and storage capacity reasons, it is more efficient to not calculate the partial derivative for the weights with mask value 0, than masking the gradient after its computation.

The amount of memory needed to store a FreezeNet is the same as for standard pruning. With the help of pseudo random number generators, as provided by PyTorch [32] or TensorFlow [1], just the seed used for generating the initial parametrization has to be stored, which is usually an integer and therefore its memory requirement is neglectable. The used pruning/freezing mask together with the trained weights have to be saved for both, pruning and FreezeNets. The masks can be stored efficiently via entropy encoding [11].

In this work, we only freeze weights and keep all biases learnable, as done in the pruning literature [12,13,29,39]. Therefore, we compute the freezing rate as $q = 1 - \frac{\|m\|_0}{|W|}$, where m is the freezing mask calculated for the network's weights W. Here, the pseudo norm $\|\cdot\|_0$ computes the number of non-zero elements in m. Since we deal with extremely high freezing rates, $q > 0.99$, the bias parameters have an effect on the percentage of all trained parameters. Thus, we define the real freezing rate $q_\beta = 1 - \frac{\|m\|_0+|B|}{|W|+|B|}$ and label the x-axes in our plots with both rates.

Pruned networks use masked weight tensors $m \odot W$ in the for- and backward pass. In theory, the number of computations needed for a pruned network can approximately be reduced by a factor of q_β in the forward pass. The frozen networks do not decrease the number of calculations in the forward pass. But without the usage of specialized soft- and hardware, the number of computations performed by a pruned network is not reduced, thus frozen and pruned networks have the same speed in this setting.

In the backward pass, the weight tensor needed to compute $\frac{\partial L}{\partial x^{(k-1)}}$ is given by $m^{(k)} \odot W^{(k)}$ for a pruned network, according to the backpropagation Eqs. (2). Frozen networks compute $\frac{\partial L}{\partial x^{(k-1)}}$ with a dense matrix $W^{(k)}$. On the other hand, not all weight gradients are needed, as only $m^{(k)} \odot \frac{\partial L}{\partial W^{(k)}}$ is required for updating the network's unfrozen weights. Therefore, the computation time in the backward pass is not reduced drastically by FreezeNets, although the number of gradients to be stored. Again, the reduction in memory is approximately given by the rate q_β. The calculation of $\frac{\partial L}{\partial x^{(k-1)}}$ with a dense matrix $W^{(k)}$ helps to preserve a faithful gradient throughout the whole network, even for extremely high freezing rates, as shown in Sect. 4.3. The comparison of training a pruned and a frozen network is summarized in Table 1.

Table 1. Comparison of standard training, pruning before training and a FreezeNet.

Method	# Total weights	# Weights to store	Sparse gradients	Sparse tensor computations	Faithful gradient flow
Standard	D	D	✗	✗	✓
Pruned	$D \cdot (1-q)$	$D \cdot (1-q)$	✓	✓	✗
FreezeNet	D	$D \cdot (1-q)$	✓	✗	✓

692   P. Wimmer et al.

4   Experiments and Discussions

In the following, we present results on the MNIST [27] and CIFAR-10/100 [26]
classification tasks achieved by FreezeNet. Freezing networks is compared with
training sparse networks, exemplified through SNIP [29]. We further analyse how
freezing weights retains the trainability of networks with sparse gradient updates
by preserving a faithful gradient. We use three different network architectures,
the fully connected LeNet-300-100 [27] along with the CNN's LeNet-5-Caffe [27]
and VGG16-D [37]. A more detailed description of the used network architectures can be found in the Supplementary Material. Additionally, we show in the
Supplementary Material that FreezeNets based on a ResNet34 perform well on
Tiny ImageNet.

For our experiments we used PyTorch 1.4.0 [32] and a single Nvidia GeForce
1080ti GPU. In order to achieve a fair comparison regarding hard- and software
settings we recreated SNIP.[3] To prevent a complete loss of information flow
we randomly flag one weight trainable per layer if all weights of this layer are
frozen or pruned for both, SNIP and FreezeNet. This adds at most 3 trainable
parameters for LeNet-300-100, 4 for LeNet-5-Caffe and 16 for VGG16-D. If not
mentioned otherwise, we use Xavier-normal initializations [16] for SNIP and
FreezeNets and apply weight decay on the trainable parameters only. Except
where indicated, the experiments were run five times with different random seeds,
resulting in different network initializations, data orders and additionally for
CIFAR experiments in different data augmentations. In our plots we show the
mean test accuracy together with one standard deviation. A split of 9/1 between
training examples and validation examples is used for early stopping in training.
All other hyperparameters applied in training are listed in the Supplementary
Material.

SGD with momentum [38] is used as optimizer, thus we provide a learning
rate search for FreezeNets in the Supplementary Material. Because $\lambda = 0.1$ works
best for almost all freezing rates, we did not include it in the main body of the
text and use $\lambda = 0.1$ with momentum 0.9 for all presented results. Altogether,
we use the same setup as SNIP in [29] for both, FreezeNets and SNIP pruned
networks.

4.1   MNIST

LeNet-300-100. A common baseline to examine pruning mechanisms on fully
connected networks is given by testing the LeNet-300-100 [27] network on the
MNIST classification task [27], left part of Fig. 2. The trained baseline architecture yields a mean test accuracy of 98.57%. If the freezing rate is lower than
0.95, both methods perform equally well and also match the performance of
the baseline. For higher freezing rates, the advantage of using free, additional
parameters can be seen. FreezeNets also suffer from the loss of trainable weights,
but they are able to compensate it better than SNIP pruned networks do.

---

[3] Based on the official implementation https://github.com/namhoonlee/snip-public.

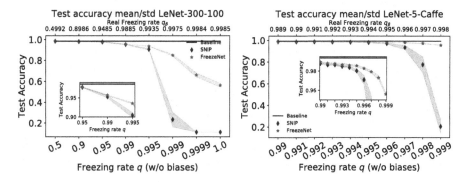

Fig. 2. Left: Test accuracy for SNIP, FreezeNet and the baseline LeNet-300-100. Right: Test accuracy for SNIP and FreezeNet for a LeNet-5-Caffe baseline. The small inserted plots are zoomed in versions for both plots.

Table 2. Comparison of FreezeNet, SNIP and the LeNet-5-Caffe baseline. Results for different *freezing rates* q with corresponding *real freezing rates* q_β are displayed. The *network's size* is calculated without compression. Thus, all weights are stored as 32bit floats. *Compress. Factor FN* is the compression factor gained by FreezeNet for the corresponding freezing rate, calculated via the ratio of the *network sizes* of the baseline and the frozen network.

q	q_β	Network size	Compress. factor FN	Test Acc. SNIP	Test Acc. FreezeNet	$\frac{\text{FreezeNet Acc.}}{\text{Baseline Acc.}}$
0 (Baseline)	1,683.9kB	1	99.36%			1.000
0.9	0.899	170.7kB	9.9	99.24%	99.37%	1.000
0.99	0.989	19.1kB	88.2	98.80%	98.94%	0.996
0.995	0.994	10.7kB	157.4	98.02%	98.55%	0.992
0.999	0.998	3.9kB	431.8	20.57%	95.61%	0.962

LeNet-5-Caffe. For moderate freezing rates $q \in [0.5, 0.95]$, again FreezeNet and SNIP reach equal results and match the baseline's performance as shown in the Supplementary Material. In the right part of Fig. 2, we show the progression of SNIP and FreezeNet for more extreme freezing rates $q \in \{0.99, 0.991, \ldots, 0.999\}$. Until $q = 0.994$ SNIP and FreezeNet perform almost equally, however FreezeNet reaches slightly better results. For higher freezing rates, SNIP's performance drops steeply whereas FreezeNet is able to slow this drop. As Table 2 and Fig. 2 show, a FreezeNet saves parameters with respect to both, the baseline architecture and a SNIP pruned network.

In order to overfit the training data maximally, we change the training setup by training the networks without the usage of weight decay and early stopping. In the left part of Fig. 3, the training accuracies of FreezeNet and SNIP are reported for the last training epoch. Unsurprisingly, too many frozen parameters reduce the model's capacity, as the model is not able to perfectly memorize the training data for rates higher than $q_* = 0.992$. On the other hand, FreezeNets increase the networks capacity compared to SNIP if the same, high freezing rate is used.

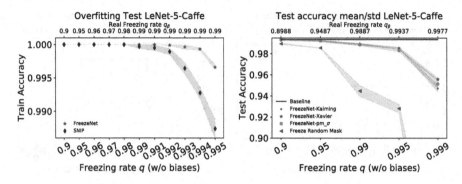

Fig. 3. Left: Final training accuracies for FreezeNet and SNIP, both trained without weight decay. Right: Different initializations for FreezeNets together with a Xavier-normal initialized FreezeNet with randomly generated freezing mask. Both plots are reported for the MNIST classification task with a LeNet-5-Caffe baseline architecture.

4.2 Testing FreezeNets for CIFAR-10/100 on VGG16-D

To test FreezeNets on bigger architectures, we use the VGG16-D architecture [37] and the CIFAR-10/100 datasets. Now, weight decay is applied to all parameters, including the frozen ones, denoted with FreezeNet-WD. As before, weight decay is also used on the unfrozen parameters only, which we again call FreezeNet. We follow the settings in [29] and exchange Dropout layers with Batch Normalization [23] layers. Including the Batch Normalization parameters, the VGG16-D network consists of 15.3 million parameters in total. We train all Batch Normalization parameters and omit them in the freezing rate q. Additionally, we augment the training data by random horizontal flipping and translations up to 4 pixels. For CIFAR-100 we report results for networks initialized with a Kaiming-uniform initialization [21]. The results are summarized in Table 3.

CIFAR-10. If more parameters are trainable, $q \leq 0.95$, SNIP performs slightly worse than the baseline but better than FreezeNet. However, using frozen weights can achieve similar results as the baseline architecture while outperforming SNIP if weight decay is applied to them as well, as shown with FreezeNet-WD. Applying weight decay also on the frozen parameters solely shrinks them to zero. For all occasions where FreezeNet-WD reaches the best results, the frozen weights can safely be pruned at the early stopping time, as they are all shrunk to zero at this point in training. For these freezing rates, FreezeNet-WD can be considered as a pruning mechanism outperforming SNIP without adding any gradient computations For higher freezing rates $q \geq 0.99$, FreezeNet still reaches reasonable results whereas FreezeNet-WD massively drops performance and SNIP even results in random guessing.

Table 3. Comparison of results for the CIFAR-10/100 tasks with a VGG16-D baseline.

			CIFAR-10	CIFAR-100
Method	Freezing rate	Trained parameters	Mean ± Std	Mean ± Std
Baseline	0	15.3mio	**93.0 ± 0.1%**	**71.6 ± 0.6%**
SNIP	0.9	1.5mio	92.9 ± 0.1%	53.9 ± 1.7%
	0.95	780k	92.5 ± 0.1%	48.6 ± 6.6%
	0.99	169k	10.0 ± 0.0%	1.0 ± 0.0%
	0.995	92k	10.0 ± 0.0%	1.0 ± 0.0%
FreezeNet	0.9	1.5mio	92.2 ± 0.1%	**70.7 ± 0.3%**
	0.95	780k	91.7 ± 0.1%	**69.0 ± 0.2%**
	0.99	169k	**88.6 ± 0.1%**	**59.8 ± 0.3%**
	0.995	92k	**86.0 ± 0.1%**	**53.4 ± 0.1%**
FreezeNet-WD	0.9	1.5mio	**93.2 ± 0.2%**	53.1 ± 1.8%
	0.95	780k	**92.8 ± 0.2%**	44.5 ± 5.4%
	0.99	169k	76.1 ± 1.0%	13.1 ± 1.8%
	0.995	92k	74.6 ± 1.1%	11.9 ± 1.4%

CIFAR-100. CIFAR-100 is more complex to solve than CIFAR-10. As the right part of Table 3 shows, SNIP is outperformed by FreezeNet for all freezing rates. Frozen parameters seem to be even more helpful for a sophisticated task. For CIFAR-100, more complex information flows backwards during training, compared to CIFAR-10. Thus, using dense weight matrices in the backward pass helps to provide enough information for the gradients to train successfully. Additionally we hypothesize, that random features generated by frozen parameters can help to improve the network's performance, as more and often closely related classes have to be distinguished. Using small, randomly generated differences between data samples of different, but consimilar classes may help to separate them.

Discussion. Deleting the frozen weights reduces the network's capacity—as shown for the MNIST task, Fig. 3 left. But for small freezing rates, the pruned network still has enough capacity in the forward- and backward propagation. In these cases, the pruned network has a higher generalization capability than the FreezeNet, according to the bias-variance trade-off [15]. Continuously decreasing the network's capacity during training, instead of one-shot, seems to improve the generalization capacity even more, as done with FreezeNet-WD. But for higher freezing rates, unshrunken and frozen parameters improve the performance significantly. For these rates, FreezeNet is still able to learn throughout the whole training process. Whereas FreezeNet-WD reaches a point in training, where the frozen weights are almost zero. Therefore, the gradient does not flow properly through the network, since the pruned SNIP network has zero gradient flow for

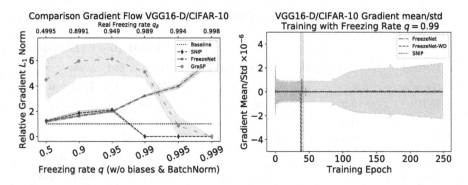

Fig. 4. Left: Shows the relative gradient norm for FreezeNet, SNIP and GraSP networks with respect to the VGG16-D baseline network on the CIFAR-10 dataset. Right: Gradient mean and std, computed over the training data, recorded for one training run with a VGG16-D architecture on the CIFAR-10 task for a freezing rate $q = 0.99$.

these rates, Fig. 4 left. This change of FreezeNet-WD's gradient's behaviour is shown in Fig. 4 right for $q = 0.99$. It should be mentioned that in these cases, FreezeNet-WD will have an early stopping time before all frozen weights are shrunk to zero and FreezeNet-WD can not be pruned without loss in performance.

4.3 Gradient Flow

As theoretically discussed in Sect. 3.2, FreezeNets help to preserve a strong gradient, even for high freezing rates. To check this, we also pruned networks with the GraSP criterion [39] to compare FreezeNets with pruned networks generated to preserve the gradient flow. A detailed description of the GraSP criterion can be found in the Supplementary Material. For this test, 10 different networks were initialized for every freezing rate and three copies of each network were frozen (FreezeNet) or pruned (SNIP and GraSP), respectively. The L_1 norm of the gradient, accumulated over the whole training set, is divided by the number of trainable parameters. As reference, the mean norm of the baseline VGG16-D's gradient is measured as well. These gradient norms, computed for CIFAR-10, are compared in the left part of Fig. 4. For smaller freezing rates, all three methods have bigger gradient values than the baseline, on average. For rates $q \geq 0.95$, decreasing the number of trainable parameters leads to a reduced gradient flow for the pruned networks. Even if the pruning mask is chosen to guarantee the highest possible gradient flow, as approximately done by GraSP. Finally, the gradient vanishes, since the weight tensors become sparse for high pruning rates, as already discussed in Sect. 3.2. FreezeNet's gradient on the other hand is not hindered since its weight tensors are dense. The saliency score (1) is biased towards choosing weights with a high partial derivative. Therefore, FreezeNet's non-zero gradient values even become larger as the number of trainable parameters decreases. For high freezing rates, FreezeNet's gradient is able to flow through the network during the whole training process, whereas SNIP's gradient remains zero all the time—right part of Fig. 4. The right part of Fig. 4 also shows the mutation of FreezeNet-WD's gradient flow during training. First, FreezeNet-WD has similar gradients as FreezeNet since the frozen weights are still big enough. The red peak indicates the point where too many frozen weights are shrunken close to zero, leading to temporarily chaotic gradients and resulting in zero gradient flow.

4.4   Comparison to Pruning Methods

Especially for extreme freezing rates, we see that FreezeNets perform remarkably better than SNIP, which often degenerates to random guessing. In Table 4, we compare our result for LeNet-5-Caffe with *Sparse-Momentum* [7], SNIP, GraSP and three other pruning methods *Connection-Learning* [19], *Dynamic-Network-Surgery* [17] and *Learning-Compression* [3]. Up to now, all results are reported without any change in hyperparameters. To compare FreezeNet with other pruning methods, we change the training setup slightly by using a split of 19/1 for train and validation images for FreezeNet, but keep the remaining hyperparameters fixed. We also recreated results for GraSP [39]. The training setup and the probed hyperparameters for GraSP can be found in the Supplementary Material. All other results are reported from the corresponding papers. As shown in Table 4, the highest accuracy of 99.2% is achieved by the methods *Connection-Learning* and *Sparse-Momentum*. With an accuracy of 99.1% our FreezeNet algorithm performs only slightly worse, however Connection-Learning trains 8.3% of its weights—whereas FreezeNet achieves 99.37% accuracy with 10% trained weights, see Table 2. Sparse-Momentum trains with sparse weights, but updates the gradients of all weights during training and redistributes the learnable weights after each epoch. Thus, their training procedure does neither provide sparse gradient computations nor one-shot pruning and is hence more expensive than FreezeNet. Apart from that, FreezeNet achieves similar results to *Dynamic-Network-Surgery* and better results than *Learning-Compression*, GraSP and SNIP, while not adding any training costs over GraSP and SNIP and even reducing them for *Dynamic-Network-Surgery* and *Learning-Compression*.

4.5   Further Investigations

The right part of Fig. 3 shows on the one hand, that FreezeNet reaches better and more stable results than freezing networks with a randomly generated freezing mask. This accentuates the importance of choosing the freezing mask consciously, for FreezeNets done with the saliency score (1).

On the other hand, different variance scaling initialization schemes are compared for FreezeNets in the right part of Fig. 3. Those initializations help to obtain a satisfying gradient flow at the beginning of the training [16,21]. Results for the Xavier-normal initialization [16], the Kaiming-uniform [21] and the pm_σ-initialization are shown. All of these initializations lead to approximately the same results. Considering all freezing rates, the Xavier-initialization yields the

Table 4. Comparison of different pruning methods with FreezeNet on LeNet-5-Caffe.

Method	Sparse gradients in training	Additional hyperparameters	Percent of trainable parameters	Test accuracy
Baseline [27]	–	–	100%	99.4%
SNIP [29]	✓	✗	1.0%	98.9%
GraSP [39]	✓	✗	1.0%	98.9%
Connection-Learning [19]	✗	✗	8.3%	99.2%
Dynamic-Network-Surgery [17]	✗	✗	0.9%	99.1%
Learning-Compression [3]	✗	✓	1.0%	98.9%
Sparse-Momentum [7]	✗	✓	1.0%	99.2%
FreezeNet (ours)	✓	✗	1.0%	99.1%

best results. The pm_σ-initialization is a variance scaling initialization, using zero mean and a variance of $\sigma^2 = \frac{2}{fan_{in}+fan_{out}}$, layerwise. All weights are set to $+\sigma$ with probability $\frac{1}{2}$ and $-\sigma$ otherwise. Using the pm_σ-initialization shows, that even the simplest variance scaling method leads to good results for FreezeNets.

In the Supplementary Material we exhibit that FreezeNets are robust against reinitializations of their weights after the freezing mask is computed and before the actual training starts. The probability distribution can even be changed between initialization and reinitialization while still leading to the same performance.

5   Conclusions

With FreezeNet we have introduced a pruning related mechanism that is able to reduce the number of trained parameters in a neural network significantly while preserving a high performance. FreezeNets match state-of-the-art pruning algorithms without using their sophisticated and costly training methods, as Table 4 demonstrates. We showed that frozen parameters help to overcome the vanishing gradient occurring in the training of sparse neural networks by preserving a strong gradient signal. They also enhance the expressiveness of a network with few trainable parameters, especially for more complex tasks. With the help of frozen weights, the number of trained parameters can be reduced compared to the related pruning method SNIP. This saves storage space and thus reduces transfer costs for trained networks. For smaller freezing rates, it might be better to weaken the frozen parameters' influence, for example by applying weight decay to them. Advantageously, using weight decay on frozen weights contracts them to zero, leading to sparse neural networks. But for high freezing rates, weight decay in its basic form might not be the best regularization mechanism to apply to FreezeNets, since only shrinking the frozen parameters robs them of a big part of their expressiveness in the forward and backward pass.

References

1. Abadi, M., et al.: Tensorflow: large-scale machine learning on heterogeneous distributed systems. CoRR abs/1603.04467 (2016)
2. Bellec, G., Kappel, D., Maass, W., Legenstein, R.: Deep rewiring: training very sparse deep networks. In: International Conference on Learning Representations. OpenReview.net (2018)
3. Carreira-Perpinan, M.A., Idelbayev, Y.: "Learning-compression" algorithms for neural net pruning. In: 2018 IEEE/CVF Conference on Computer Vision and Pattern Recognition, pp. 8532–8541. IEEE Computer Society (2018)
4. Chauvin, Y.: A back-propagation algorithm with optimal use of hidden units. In: Touretzky, D.S. (ed.) Advances in Neural Information Processing Systems 1. Morgan-Kaufmann, Burlington (1989)
5. Davis, C.: The norm of the schur product operation. Numer. Math. **4**(1), 343–344 (1962)
6. Deng, J., Dong, W., Socher, R., Li, L., Li, K., Fei-Fei, L.: Imagenet: a large-scale hierarchical image database. In: 2009 IEEE Conference on Computer Vision and Pattern Recognition, pp. 248–255. IEEE Computer Society (2009)
7. Dettmers, T., Zettlemoyer, L.: Sparse networks from scratch: faster training without losing performance. CoRR abs/1907.04840 (2019)
8. Ding, X., Ding, G., Zhou, X., Guo, Y., Han, J., Liu, J.: Global sparse momentum SGD for pruning very deep neural networks. In: Wallach, H., Larochelle, H., Beygelzimer, A., d' Alché-Buc, F., Fox, E., Garnett, R. (eds.) Advances in Neural Information Processing Systems 32, pp. 6382–6394. Curran Associates, Inc. (2019)
9. Dong, X., Huang, J., Yang, Y., Yan, S.: More is less: a more complicated network with less inference complexity. In: 2017 IEEE Conference on Computer Vision and Pattern Recognition (CVPR) (2017)
10. Dong, X., Yang, Y.: Network pruning via transformable architecture search. In: Wallach, H., Larochelle, H., Beygelzimer, A., d' Alché-Buc, F., Fox, E., Garnett, R. (eds.) Advances in Neural Information Processing Systems 32, pp. 760–771. Curran Associates, Inc. (2019)
11. Duda, J., Tahboub, K., Gadgil, N.J., Delp, E.J.: The use of asymmetric numeral systems as an accurate replacement for huffman coding. In: Picture Coding Symposium, pp. 65–69 (2015)
12. Frankle, J., Carbin, M.: The lottery ticket hypothesis: finding sparse, trainable neural networks. In: International Conference on Learning Representations (2018)
13. Frankle, J., Dziugaite, G.K., Roy, D.M., Carbin, M.: Stabilizing the lottery ticket hypothesis. CoRR abs/1903.01611 (2019)
14. Frankle, J., Schwab, D.J., Morcos, A.S.: Training batchnorm and only batchnorm: on the expressive power of random features in cnns. CoRR abs/2003.00152 (2020)
15. Geman, S., Bienenstock, E., Doursat, R.: Neural networks and the bias/variance dilemma. Neural Comput. **4**(1), 1–58 (1992)
16. Glorot, X., Bengio, Y.: Understanding the difficulty of training deep feedforward neural networks. In: Teh, Y.W., Titterington, M. (eds.) Proceedings of the Thirteenth International Conference on Artificial Intelligence and Statistics, pp. 249–256. PMLR (2010)
17. Guo, Y., Yao, A., Chen, Y.: Dynamic network surgery for efficient dnns. In: Lee, D.D., Sugiyama, M., Luxburg, U.V., Guyon, I., Garnett, R. (eds.) Advances in Neural Information Processing Systems 29, pp. 1379–1387. Curran Associates, Inc. (2016)

18. Gustafson, J.L.: Moore's law. In: Padua, D. (ed.) Encyclopedia of Parallel Computing, pp. 1177–1184. Springer, US (2011). https://doi.org/10.1007/978-0-387-09766-4

19. Han, S., Pool, J., Tran, J., Dally, W.: Learning both weights and connections for efficient neural network. In: Cortes, C., Lawrence, N.D., Lee, D.D., Sugiyama, M., Garnett, R. (eds.) Advances in Neural Information Processing Systems 28. Curran Associates, Inc. (2015)

20. Hanson, S.J., Pratt, L.Y.: Comparing biases for minimal network construction with back-propagation. In: Touretzky, D.S. (ed.) Advances in Neural Information Processing Systems 1. Morgan-Kaufmann, Burlington (1989)

21. He, K., Zhang, X., Ren, S., Sun, J.: Delving deep into rectifiers: surpassing human-level performance on imagenet classification. CoRR abs/1502.01852 (2015)

22. He, Y., Lin, J., Liu, Z., Wang, H., Li, L.-J., Han, S.: AMC: AutoML for model compression and acceleration on mobile devices. In: Ferrari, V., Hebert, M., Sminchisescu, C., Weiss, Y. (eds.) ECCV 2018. LNCS, vol. 11211, pp. 815–832. Springer, Cham (2018). https://doi.org/10.1007/978-3-030-01234-2_48

23. Ioffe, S., Szegedy, C.: Batch normalization: accelerating deep network training by reducing internal covariate shift. In: Bach, F., Blei, D. (eds.) Proceedings of the 32nd International Conference on Machine Learning, pp. 448–456. PMLR (2015)

24. Jarrett, K., Kavukcuoglu, K., Ranzato, M., LeCun, Y.: What is the best multi-stage architecture for object recognition? In: ICCV, pp. 2146–2153. IEEE (2009)

25. Karnin, E.D.: A simple procedure for pruning back-propagation trained neural networks. IEEE Trans. Neural Networks $1(2)$, 239–242 (1990)

26. Krizhevsky, A.: Learning multiple layers of features from tiny images. University of Toronto (2012). http://www.cs.toronto.edu/~kriz/cifar.html

27. LeCun, Y., Bottou, L., Bengio, Y., Haffner, P.: Gradient-based learning applied to document recognition. Proc. IEEE $86(11)$, 2278–2324 (1998)

28. LeCun, Y., Denker, J.S., Solla, S.A.: Optimal brain damage. In: Touretzky, D.S. (ed.) Advances in Neural Information Processing Systems 2. Morgan-Kaufmann, Burlington (1990)

29. Lee, N., Ajanthan, T., Torr, P.: SNIP: Single-shot network pruning based on connection sensitivity. In: International Conference on Learning Representations. OpenReview.net (2019)

30. Mocanu, D., Mocanu, E., Stone, P., Nguyen, P., Gibescu, M., Liotta, A.: Scalable training of artificial neural networks with adaptive sparse connectivity inspired by network science. Nat. Commun. 9, 1–12 (2018)

31. Mozer, M.C., Smolensky, P.: Skeletonization: a technique for trimming the fat from a network via relevance assessment. In: Touretzky, D.S. (ed.) Advances in Neural Information Processing Systems 1. Morgan-Kaufmann (1989)

32. Paszke, A., Gross, S., Massa, F., Lerer, A., Bradbury, J., Chanan, G., et al.: Pytorch: An imperative style, high-performance deep learning library. Adv. Neural Inf. Process. Syst. 32, 8024–8035 (2019)

33. Ramanujan, V., Wortsman, M., Kembhavi, A., Farhadi, A., Rastegari, M.: What's hidden in a randomly weighted neural network? In: IEEE/CVF Conference on Computer Vision and Pattern Recognition (CVPR). IEEE Computer Society (2020)

34. Robbins, H., Monro, S.: A stochastic approximation method. Ann. Math. Stat. $22(3)$, 400–407 (1951)

35. Saxe, A., Koh, P.W., Chen, Z., Bhand, M., Suresh, B., Ng, A.: On random weights and unsupervised feature learning. In: Getoor, L., Scheffer, T. (eds.) Proceedings of the 28th International Conference on Machine Learning, pp. 1089–1096. ACM (2011)
36. Schwartz, R., Dodge, J., Smith, N.A., Etzioni, O.: Green AI. CoRR abs/1907.10597 (2019)
37. Simonyan, K., Zisserman, A.: Very deep convolutional networks for large-scale image recognition. In: Bengio, Y., LeCun, Y. (eds.) International Conference on Learning Representations. OpenReview.net (2015)
38. Sutskever, I., Martens, J., Dahl, G., Hinton, G.: On the importance of initialization and momentum in deep learning. In: Proceedings of the 30th International Conference on Machine Learning, pp. 1139–1147. PMLR (2013)
39. Wang, C., Zhang, G., Grosse, R.: Picking winning tickets before training by preserving gradient flow. In: International Conference on Learning Representations. OpenReview.net (2020)
40. Wortsman, M., Farhadi, A., Rastegari, M.: Discovering neural wirings. In: Wallach, H., Larochelle, H., Beygelzimer, A., d' Alché-Buc, F., Fox, E., Garnett, R. (eds.) Advances in Neural Information Processing Systems 32, pp. 2684–2694. Curran Associates, Inc. (2019)
41. Xie, S., Kirillov, A., Girshick, R., He, K.: Exploring randomly wired neural networks for image recognition. In: 2019 IEEE/CVF International Conference on Computer Vision (ICCV) (2019)
42. Zhou, H., Lan, J., Liu, R., Yosinski, J.: Deconstructing lottery tickets: zeros, signs, and the supermask. In: Wallach, H., Larochelle, H., Beygelzimer, A., d' Alché-Buc, F., Fox, E., Garnett, R. (eds.) Advances in Neural Information Processing Systems 32, pp. 3597–3607. Curran Associates, Inc. (2019)

Author Index

Printed in the United States
By Bookmasters